For Reference

Not to be taken from this room

GREAT
AMERICAN
COURT CASES

GREAT AMERICAN COURT CASES

Volume III:
Equal Protection
and Family Law

FIRST EDITION

Mark Mikula and
L. Mpho Mabunda,
Editors

Allison McClintic Marion,
Associate Editor

The Gale Group

DETROIT • SAN FRANCISCO • LONDON • BOSTON • WOODBRIDGE, CT

Staff

Mark F. Mikula, L. Mpho Mabunda, Editors

Allison McClintic Marion, Dawn R. Barry, Rebecca Parks, Dave Oblender, Associate Editors
Elizabeth Shaw, Brian J. Koski, Gloria Lam, Catherine Donaldson, Assistant Editors
Linda S. Hubbard, Managing Editor, Multicultural Team

Susan Trosky, Permissions Manager
Margaret A. Chamberlain, Permissions Specialist

Victoria B. Cariappa, Research Manager
Barbara McNeil, Research Specialist

Evi Seoud, Assistant Production Manager

Cynthia Baldwin, Product Design Manager
Eric Johnson, Art Director

Barbara Yarrow, Graphic Services Manager
Randy A. Bassett, Image Database Supervisor
Robert Duncan, Imaging Specialist

Theresa Rocklin, Manager, Technical Support Services
Jeffrey Muhr, Technical Support

Library of Congress Cataloging-in-Publication Data

Great American court cases / Mark F. Mikula and L. Mpho Mabunda, editors;
Allison McClintic Marion, associate editor. -- 1st ed.
  p. cm.
  Includes bibliographical references and index.
  Contents: v. 1. Individual liberties -- v. 2. Criminal justice -- v. 3. Equal protection and family law
-- v. 4. Business and government.
  ISBN 078762947-0 (set).
  1. Law--United States.--Cases. 2. Civil rights--United States-Cases. I. Mikula, Mark F. II. Mabunda,
L. Mpho., 1967-. III. Marion, Allison McClintic.
KF385.A4g68 1999
349.73--dc2
                                                                                       99-11419
                                                                                         CIP

Copyright © 1999
The Gale Group
27500 Drake Road
Farmington Hills, MI 48331-3535
http://www.galegroup.com
800-877-4253
248-699-4253

ISBN 0-7876-2947-2 (set) Vol 1 ISBN 0-7876-2948-0; Vol 2 ISBN 0-7876-2949-9;
Vol 3 ISBN 0-7876-2950-2; Vol 4 ISBN 0-7876-2951-0

10 9 8 7 6 5 4 3 2 1

CONTENTS

Volume III

Equal Protection and Family Law

CONTENTS

Volume I, II, IV

This abbreviated view shows just the issues covered in the other volumes. Consult the Cumulative Index that appears in each volume for all the cases, people, events, and subjects in all four volumes.

Volume I: Individual Liberties

Volume II: Criminal Justice

Volume IV: Business and Government

PREFACE

U.S. citizens take comfort and pride in living under the rule of law. Our elected representatives write and enforce the laws that govern everything from familial relationships to the dealings of multi-billion-dollar corporations, from the quality of the air to the content of the programs broadcast through it. But it is the judicial system that interprets the meaning of the law and makes it tangible to the average citizen through the drama of trials and the force of court orders and judicial opinions.

The four volumes of *Great American Court Cases* profile nearly 800 judicial proceedings. The editors consulted textbooks, curriculum guides, and authoritative Internet sites to identify cases studied for their influence on the development of key aspects of law in the United States. Although the majority of the cases resulted in decisions by the U.S. Supreme Court, nearly 60 cases from state courts or lower-level federal jurisdictions are included because of their impact or their role in an emerging point of law. Comprehensiveness requires that fundamental cases from the nineteenth century and earlier, such as *Marbury v. Madison* (1803) and *Swift v. Tyson* (1842), are included. This is especially true in Volume IV, which covers how laws have shaped the government. Nevertheless, to serve the information needs of today's users, most of the cases are from the twentieth century, with emphasis on the last three decades.

Scope and Arrangement

The case profiles are grouped according to the legal principle on which they reflect, with each volume covering one or two broad areas of the law as follows:

- *Volume I: Individual Liberties* includes cases that have influenced such First and Second Amendment issues as freedom of the press, privacy, the right to bear arms, and the legal concerns emerging from the growth of the Internet. Libel, the Establishment Clause, and other important facets of freedom of speech and freedom of religion are treated in separate essays with their own cases.

- *Volume II: Criminal Justice* covers cases that establish the rights of the accused before, during, and after trial, or address criminal law and procedure, search and seizure, drug laws, the jury, damages, and capital punishment.

- *Volume III: Equal Protection and Family Law* includes cases related to two broad areas of law. Equal protection issues covered in this volume include the broad range of civil rights related issues, from affirmative action, segregation, and voting rights to the special concerns of immigrants, juveniles, the disabled, and gay and lesbian citizens. Family issues covered include child support and custody and reproductive rights. Sexual harassment and the right to die are also represented in this volume.

- *Volume IV: Business and Government* also encompasses two major spheres of the law. Consumer protection, antitrust, and labor-related cases supplement the business fundamentals of contracts and corporate law. The government cases document the legal evolution of the branches of the federal government as well as the federal government's relation to state power. Separate topics address environmental law, military issues, national security, taxation, and the legal history of Native American issues. Appendixes in this volume also present the full text of the U.S. Constitution and its amendments and a chronological table of Supreme Court justices.

Coverage

Issue overviews, averaging 2,000 words in length, provide the context for the case profiles that follow. Case discussions range from 750 to 2,000 words according to their complexity and importance. Each provides the background of the case and issues involved, the main arguments presented by each side, and an explanation of the court's decision, as well as the legal, political, and social impact of the decision. Excerpts from the majority, concurring, and dissenting opinions are often included. Cross-references lead the user to related cases, while suggestions for further reading launch in-depth

---

Deciphering Legal Citations

Great American Court Cases includes citations for the cases covered in the profiles. Three sources, *United States Reports* (U.S.), the *Supreme Court Reporter* (S.Ct.), and the *Lawyers' Edition* (L.Ed.), all cite Supreme Court cases in separate series, resulting in three distinct citation numbers for each case. The citations for *Great American Court Cases*, in most cases, are drawn from *United States Reports*. On rare occasions, because there is a lag between the time that a case is heard and the time that its companion volume is published, the citation has been drawn from another reporter, usually the *Supreme Court Reporter*. In all cases, the structure of the citation is as follows: the volume number precedes the abbreviation for the reporter and is followed by the page number. For instance, *Davis v. Bandemer*, 478 U.S. 109, is included in volume 478 of *United States Reports*, beginning on page 109. Citations for cases tried below the level of the Supreme Court follow a similar structure with an abbreviation for the reporter associated with the lower court falling between the volume and page number. The case *In re Quinlan*, 355 A.2d 647, is covered in volume 355 of the *Atlantic Reporter*, second series (cases for states in the East), beginning on page 355.

---

research. Within each issue section, the cases are arranged from earliest to most recent to indicate the evolution of precedent.

The editors have had to make hard choices when a single case has bearing on more than one issue, as often occurs. The landmark reproductive rights decision in *Roe v. Wade*, for example, is based upon an assertion of privacy rights, so the case could have been placed with either issue. Also, the case of *Marbury v. Madison*, while establishing the concept of judicial review, dealt foremost with a separation of powers issue at the time that it was decided, meriting its inclusion in the separation of powers section of Volume IV. Users should consult the cumulative index that appears in each volume to find cases throughout the set that apply to a particular topic.

A small percentage (under 10 percent) of cases were previously covered in *Women's Rights on Trial* or *Great American Trials*, both Gale products. Selection criteria for each publication were different, but the *Great American Court Cases* editors preferred this slight overlap to omission of landmark cases. Entry elements particular to *Great American Court Cases*, such as the Supreme Court justices' votes, have been added to the material, along with updating as appropriate.

The editors determined that with the focus on constitutional law, sensationalistic cases, such as the O. J. Simpson trial and the trial of Ted Kaczynski, were more appropriately covered in the sidebars that complement the main text rather than receiving full treatment in the main body of the text. Also, at the time of publication, the impeachment trial of Bill Clinton had not reached its conclusion. It, therefore, does not receive coverage in this series.

Additional Features

Great American Court Cases has several features to enhance its usefulness to students and non-professional researchers:

The **legal citation** appears at the head of each case profile, enabling researchers to access the authoritative records of the court action. The "Deciphering Legal Citations" sidebar that is part of this preface explains the elements that make up the citations and remarks on the abbreviations for the various series, called "reporters," where records are published.

Each case opens with a **factbox** so the user can quickly scan (when available): the names of litigants; the initiating litigant's claim; the names of chief lawyers on each side; the name of the judge or justice who wrote the majority opinion or decision, as well as names of those who concurred or dissented; the date and location of the decision; the summary of the decision and comments on the decision's significance.

Sidebars in the case profiles highlight interesting aspects of the legal process or arguments, key participants, or related facts and incidents. Some outline the arguments for and against a particular issue or line of reasoning, which will promote critical thinking as well as fuel debates or mock-trials. Some also discuss related cases that did not warrant their inclusion as a main case in the text.

Approximately **300 photographs and graphics** depict individuals and events related to the cases.

A broad overview of the court system and the disciplines of law is presented in a general essay regarding the structure of the legal system.

Contributors have tried to present the issues and proceedings in language accessible to high school, college, and public library users. Legal terms must sometimes be used for precision, however, so a **glossary** of more than 600 words and phrases appears in each volume.

Users interested in a particular case can locate it by name (e.g., *Brown v. Board of Education*) in the **Alphabetical Listing of Cases** in the back of each volume. Those who wish to trace the changing focus of legal interest and opinion over time will find the **Chronological Listing of Cases** in the back of each volume helpful.

A **Cumulative Index** to cases, people, events, and subjects appears in each volume. The Cumulative Index is repeated in each volume to ensure that multiple users of the set have simultaneous access to its complete contents.

Audience for Great American Court Cases

The four volumes of *Great American Court Cases* cover more U.S. Supreme Court and state or lower federal court cases in greater depth than other works for a non-professional user. The selection of issues and cases, the consistent treatment, and the minimal use of legal jargon were designed with the student user in mind. Court cases bring important issues into focus in a dramatic way. They are increasingly used in curricula for studies of U.S. government, civics, history, and journalism. Law magnet school and pre-law courses can use *Great American Court Cases* to introduce important content in an accessible manner, while mock court programs will find a wide range of source material here. Students with interdisciplinary writing assignments and exercises in critical thinking will also find inspiration. Beyond the classroom, a broad range of people from activists to his-tory buffs and Court TV watchers, will find the set compelling and useful.

Acknowledgments

Leah Knight, Meggin Condino, and Linda Irvin conceptualized *Great American Court Cases* and solicited feedback from potential users. A number of public and school librarians as well as teachers contributed to the development of the set. While several provided early input, Hilda Weisburg of Morristown High School in New Jersey continued to answer questions to help shape the product through its development. Kathy Nemeh and Diane Carter reviewed selected material for legal accuracy.

Two websites, which are freely available to the public, proved indispensible as resources for fact gathering and checking. These websites are the Findlaw site located at http://www.findlaw.com and the Oyez Oyez Oyez site located at http://court.it-services.nwu.edu.oyez.

Suggestions Are Welcome

The editors welcome suggestions on any aspect of this work. Please send comments to: Editors, *Great American Court Cases,* Gale Group, 27500 Drake Rd., Farmington Hills, MI 48331.

THE AMERICAN LEGAL SYSTEM

The most basic function of the American legal system is to maintain peace by resolving disputes. Federal and state courts, tribunals, and administrative bodies do this by applying laws to cases between specific individuals or organizations.

The primary sources of applicable law are federal and state constitutions, statutes, and administrative regulations. Constitutions establish the structure of government, define and limit its power, and seek to protect individuals from unreasonable or unlawful exercises of that power. Legislatures enact statutes—criminal laws, for example—that govern a wide variety of conduct. Administrative bodies promulgate regulations to govern specific areas of business, such as telecommunications and securities.

In theory, courts apply these existing laws rather than creating new law. The legislatures and administrative bodies, however, cannot always anticipate every possible set of circumstances, and the laws do not clearly dictate a result in every case. Frequently, too, the law is intentionally vague to give the courts flexibility to interpret it in ways which serve general public policies rather than to accomplish specific results. There are, however, constitutional limits on how vague a law may be. In general, it must fairly apprise individuals of behavior that it prohibits or compels.

In practice, then, American courts often make law when they decide cases. Under the doctrine of *stare decisis,* courts at the same or lower level in the judicial hierarchy must follow the first court's interpretation of the law in subsequent cases with similar facts. Higher courts in the judicial hierarchy may either accept the lower court's interpretation or reverse it by interpreting the law differently. Courts in other states may rely on the first court's interpretation as persuasive authority concerning the application of similar laws in their states. This tradition of binding and persuasive authority is a by-product of the American judicial system's origins in the common law system of England.

Origins of the American Judicial System: State Judicial Systems

When America declared its independence in 1776, the 13 original colonies had largely informal judicial systems based loosely on the English system of common law. Common law is the body of law that developed in English courts on a case-by-case basis. Under the common law, judges placed great reliance on decisions in prior cases with similar facts. Although state courts today apply laws enacted by legislatures and administrative bodies, they continue the common law tradition of case-by-case interpretation of these laws and reliance on prior judicial decisions.

As the United States expanded southward and westward, it acquired Mexican, Spanish, and French territories, which had legal systems based on the European civil law tradition. Under that tradition, courts in Europe applied detailed civil codes that the legislatures had designed to resolve all potential disputes. Civil codes reflected the natural law concept that there are unchanging, God-made laws that govern human behavior. Unlike in common law systems, civil law courts were not supposed to interpret the law beyond what was provided in the civil codes—they simply resolved disputes by applying the appropriate portion of the code. While the English common law tradition dominated the formation of American state legal systems, remnants of the civil law tradition exist even today, most notably in Louisiana, which based its legal system on the civil law of France.

Origins of the American Judicial System: Federal Judiciary

The federal judiciary was born in 1789 upon adoption of the U.S. Constitution, which vested the judicial power of the United States in "one supreme Court, and in such inferior Courts as the Congress may from time to time ordain and establish." The Constitution created a judicial system that contains elements of both the common and civil law traditions. The latter is evident in one of the purposes expressed in the Constitution's preamble—to "secure the Blessings of Liberty." The

Constitution, however, is subject to case-by-case interpretation by the U.S. Supreme Court, which usually limits itself by the principle of *stare decisis*.

Origins of the American Judicial System: Federalism

The existence of separate federal and state judicial systems in the United States is a hallmark of federalism, which means these systems share authority to resolve legal disputes in their geographic boundaries. Federal and state courts sometimes have concurrent jurisdiction to resolve disputes arising from the same set of circumstances. For instance, federal and state authorities both took judicial action following the bombing of the Alfred P. Murrah Federal Building in Oklahoma City in 1995. Federal and state courts occasionally have exclusive jurisdiction over certain areas of the law. State courts, for instance, typically have exclusive jurisdiction to handle child custody disputes, while federal courts exclusively handle bankruptcy cases. The U.S. Constitution determines whether state and federal courts have concurrent or exclusive jurisdiction over a particular issue.

Structure and Operation of the Courts: Judicial Hierarchy

American state court systems are hierarchical. Most states have trial courts of general jurisdiction where the judges preside over all types of cases, both civil and criminal. Most states also have special courts of limited jurisdiction that hear only certain kinds of cases— domestic relations and family court, juvenile court, and courts for the administration of wills are typical examples. There also are state courts of inferior jurisdiction, such as justices of the peace, small claims court, and traffic court, that handle petty matters. Appeals from all lower courts usually go first to an intermediate appellate court, often called the court of appeals, and then to the state's highest court, often called the supreme court. When a case involves application of the U.S. Constitution or federal law, the parties sometimes may appeal from the state's highest court to the U.S. Supreme Court.

The federal judiciary is similarly hierarchical. Federal district courts handle trials in civil and criminal cases, and appeals from some federal administrative agencies. The federal judiciary also has special courts of limited jurisdiction, such as the Court of Federal Claims, the Court of International Trade, and the Tax Court. Appeals from federal district courts go to one of 11 numbered circuit courts of appeals covering different geographical regions, or to the District of Columbia Court of Appeals. Appeals from the Court of Federal Claims and the Court of International Trade go to the Federal Court of Appeals. Parties may appeal a case from the appellate courts to the U.S. Supreme Court.

Structure and Operation of the Courts: Criminal and Civil Procedure

The progress of a case through the court system is governed by rules of procedure. There are separate rules of civil and criminal procedure because criminal cases require special constitutional safeguards for the accused. The following illustration explains the procedure in a civil case, which generally is a dispute between private individuals. Some of the notable differences between civil and criminal procedures are noted in this discussion.

Rules of civil procedure define and limit the roles of the various persons in a case. The party who brings a case is called the plaintiff, and the person being sued is the defendant. (In criminal cases there is a prosecutor instead of a plaintiff.) As the American legal system is adversarial, the parties are represented by lawyers who must zealously protect their clients' interests. A jury typically hears the evidence and determines the outcome under the substantive law as instructed by the judge. The judge acts as a referee to enforce the rules and explain the applicable law.

While the federal and state courts each have their own rules of civil procedure, the federal process is fairly representative. A federal case begins when a plaintiff files a complaint and summons in a federal district court. The complaint explains the nature of the plaintiff's claim against the defendant. The summons notifies the defendant to appear and to answer the complaint by either admitting or denying the plaintiff's allegations. If the defendant fails to appear and answer, the court may enter a default judgment against the defendant and order the relief sought by the plaintiff. If the defendant appears, he typically files an answer that denies the plaintiff's allegations. The plaintiff's complaint, the defendant's answer, and any reply by the plaintiff are called the pleadings.

The defendant next may file a motion to dismiss, which argues that even if the plaintiff proves everything in his pleadings, the law does not provide any relief. If the judge grants this motion, she dismisses the case. If not, the parties proceed to the discovery phase.

The purpose of discovery is to help the parties identify and narrow the issues for trial, and to require the parties to disclose all of their evidence. The parties begin discovery by making mandatory disclosures containing basic information, such as the identity of persons and documents with evidence related to the pleadings. The parties then answer interrogatories and take depositions. Interrogatories are written questions that a party must answer in writing under an oath that acknowledges a penalty for perjury. Depositions are oral, transcribed proceedings by which a prospective witness, who also is under oath, answers verbal questions posed by the lawyers. Interrogatory answers and deposition transcripts may be used at trial as evidence or to impeach a witness's testimony if she contradicts what she said during discovery.

After discovery, the defendant may make a motion for summary judgment, which argues that even with everything that discovery has revealed, the plaintiff is unable to prove a violation of law warranting relief. If the judge grants this motion, she dismisses the case. Otherwise the case proceeds to trial.

The trial begins when the judge and parties pick a jury. (In civil cases for which there was no right to a jury trial upon adoption of the U.S. Constitution, or when the parties do not want a jury trial, the parties have a bench trial before a judge without a jury.) In some cases a grand jury, consisting usually of 23 members, is called to determine whether grounds exist for a criminal proceeding to be initiated by the state. To pick the jury, the judge or lawyers pose questions to prospective jurors. After hearing the answers, the parties may dismiss a set number of prospective jurors for any reason, although they may not discriminate unlawfully. The parties further may dismiss an unlimited number of jurors for good cause, such as bias in the prospective juror's responses.

Once they have selected 12 jurors, the lawyers present opening statements, which give the jury a roadmap of what the evidence will prove. The plaintiff then presents his case by the testimony of witnesses and the admission of documents into the record of evidence. The presentation is governed by rules of evidence, which the judge enforces to determine what the jury can and cannot hear. The rules of evidence are supposed to give the jury only the most reliable evidence. The defendant is allowed to cross-examine the plaintiff's witnesses to challenge their accuracy, truthfulness, and bias. The defendant presents his evidence after the plaintiff, who then may cross-examine the defendant's witnesses.

At the close of the evidence, each party may ask the judge to enter judgment in his favor on the ground that a reasonable jury could only reach one verdict under the evidence presented. If the judge denies this motion, she instructs the jury about the applicable substantive law, the lawyers make closing arguments to explain the result their clients seek, and the jury retires to deliberate and reach a verdict. After the jury (or the judge in a bench trial) delivers its verdict, each party may ask the judge to reverse the verdict or order a new trial based upon errors the judge made applying the rules of procedure, rules of evidence, or substantive law. If these motions are denied, the parties may file a notice of appeal to the proper circuit court of appeals. Notably, if a person is found not guilty in a criminal proceeding that is not declared a mistrial, that person cannot be tried again for the same crime. This concept of dou-

ble jeopardy has its origin in the Fifth Amendment, which prevents people from being placed at risk of conviction more than once for a single offense.

Cases in the courts of appeals are heard by a panel of three judges. The parties file briefs that explain the errors they think the trial judge made under the rules of procedure, rules of evidence, or substantive law. The court of appeals does not hear the evidence anew, but relies on the record—the trial testimony and documents entered into evidence before the district court. The court also might hear oral argument, during which the parties' lawyers may respond to questions posed by the judges on the panel. The judges then study the record, briefs, and oral argument, discuss the case among themselves, vote on the result, and issue a decision based on the majority vote.

Dissatisfied parties may appeal to the U.S. Supreme Court, which is composed of nine justices. The procedure is similar to that in the courts of appeal, with one major exception: a party first must file a petition for a writ of *certiorari* to convince the Supreme Court that the case is important enough to warrant consideration. The Supreme Court grants the writ—by a vote of four or more justices—for only approximately five percent of the thousands of petitions it receives each year. These lucky few file briefs and engage in oral argument as they did before the court of appeals. After the justices vote, one of the justices voting in the majority writes an opinion explaining the Court's decision. Dissatisfied parties have no further avenue of appeal from this court of last resort.

Structure and Operation of the Courts: Alternative Dispute Resolution

The procedure for pursuing a case, especially a civil case, from trial through appeal is time-consuming. It can take one or more years to get a verdict in the trial court, and five or more years for an appeal to the court of appeals and the Supreme Court. The legal fees and other costs can amount to hundreds of thousands or millions of dollars. The vast majority of civil cases thus settle before going to trial, which means the parties resolve their dispute by agreement. Most criminal cases also settle, a process called plea-bargaining.

Efforts to reduce costs in civil cases have popularized an area of legal procedure called alternative dispute resolution, or ADR. Arbitration, the best known form of ADR, is an informal, abbreviated trial where one or more neutral arbitrators hears and decides the case like a judge and jury. Conciliation, a less common form of ADR, involves submission of the dispute to a neutral third party for her investigation and recommendation. With mediation the parties try to negotiate a resolution with the assistance and guidance of a neutral mediator.

Today many contracts include a clause that requires parties to use ADR to resolve their disagreements. Whether or not they have a contract, many parties voluntarily pursue ADR before going to court. State courts increasingly require parties in certain types of cases to try arbitration or mediation before proceeding to trial. The American Arbitration Association and other organizations support these efforts by designing ADR systems and procedures.

Types of Law

In the United States, where most courts hear cases concerning all areas of law, categorizing the laws is largely arbitrary. In *An Introduction to the Legal System of the United States,* Professor E. Allan Farnsworth suggested a useful distinction between public and private law. Public law generally concerns disputes between the government and individuals. Private law concerns disputes between private individuals.

Types of Law: Public Law

Public law, as described by Professor Farnsworth, includes constitutional, criminal, trade regulation, labor, and tax law. Constitutional law is embodied in the decisions of the U.S. Supreme Court that interpret the federal Constitution. Many of these cases concern whether conduct by the legislative or executive branches of the federal government violate constitutional definitions or limitations on their powers. Under the "political question" doctrine, however, the Supreme Court will decline to decide such a case if the Constitution reserves the issue for the legislative or executive branch without judicial interference.

A large majority of constitutional law cases concern the protection of individual rights from unlawful federal conduct. The Bill of Rights, which comprises the first ten amendments to the Constitution, is the primary source of these rights. For example, the First Amendment protects the freedom of speech, while the Fourth Amendment protects the right to be free from unreasonable search and seizure. The Constitution also protects individual rights from unlawful state conduct. The most important source of this protection is the Fourteenth Amendment, which contains the Due Process and Equal Protection Clauses. By interpretation of these clauses, the U.S. Supreme Court has applied the rights and protections found in the Bill of Rights to state conduct.

Criminal law mostly appears in state penal codes. These codes, while largely based on the common law of England, reflect an effort to arrive at uniform, reliable definitions of crimes. The codes define everything from felonies, such as murder and rape, to misdemeanors and petty offenses. There also are federal sources of criminal law, most notably relating to interstate conduct, such as drug trafficking and fraudulent

use of the mails. Another important source of federal criminal law is the statute that protects civil rights, such as the right to be free from discrimination on the basis of race, color, or creed. Criminal law cases also can involve issues of constitutional law, such as the rights of the accused to remain silent and to be represented by an attorney.

Trade regulation includes antitrust law, which seeks to prevent monopolies and other restraints of trade under America's system of free enterprise. It also includes laws designed to prevent unfair competition among businesses. Labor law protects the well-being of employees and the rights and duties of labor unions. Tax law primarily concerns the federal income tax.

Types of Law: Private Law

Private law, often referred to as civil law, includes tort, contract, family, commercial, and property law. States are the primary source of private law. Tort law is a system of providing compensation between individuals for private wrongs, such as battery and defamation. The enforcement of promises or obligations between individuals is the subject of contract law. Family law deals with the relationships between husband and wife or parent and child: marriage and divorce; spousal abuse and support; and child custody, abuse, support, and adoption. Commercial law, derived primarily from the Uniform Commercial Code, governs the sale and lease of goods. Property law governs transactions in real estate.

The Appointment of Judges

The process for appointing state judges varies from state to state. Most state trial judges are elected by popular vote or by the state legislature. The supreme court judges in most states are appointed for a fixed term by the governor, and then periodically stand unopposed for reelection based on their records. In some states the judges of the highest court are elected by popular vote. State judges usually serve for a fixed term of years or for life, and can be removed only for gross misconduct by formal proceedings.

Federal judges are appointed by the president with the advice and consent of the Senate. This process typically results in the appointment of judges who are members of the president's political party. If the Senate judiciary committee is controlled by the president's opposition party, the confirmation process can be hotly contested. Federal judges are appointed for life, and can be removed only by impeachment and conviction by Congress.

The Role of Judges

State and federal judges perform various important roles in the American legal system. Trial judges referee cases under the rules of procedure and evidence. The trial judge also instructs the jury concerning the substantive law that is applicable to the case. In bench trials, the judge determines the facts, law, and result without a jury. The role of appellate judges is to review the record of evidence before the trial court, decide the applicable substantive law, and either affirm or reverse the result below. In doing so, the appellate judge may announce principles of law for application by trial judges in future cases.

Limitations on Judicial Power

In *Marbury v. Madison* (1803), the Supreme Court said "[i]t is emphatically the province and duty of the judicial department to say what the law is." Judicial power, however, is not unlimited. The U.S. Constitution is the primary source for limitations on federal judicial power. The Constitution constrains federal courts to hear only "cases and controversies," which means actual cases rather than hypothetical situations or stale disputes. Under the political question doctrine, federal courts will not address issues reserved to the legislative or executive branches of the federal government. Congressional authority under the Constitution also limits judicial power. Congress may impeach and convict federal judges for "Treason, Bribery, or other high Crimes and Misdemeanors." If Congress is dissatisfied with a court's interpretation of a statute, it may pass legislation to correct the interpretation, as long as it acts within the constitutional limitations on its own power.

Similarly, state judicial power is restricted by state constitutions, the process for selection and removal of state judges, and the ultimate supremacy of the U.S. Constitution over both state and federal statutes and case law.

Bibliography and Further Reading

Calvi, James V., and Susan Coleman. *American Law and Legal Systems,* 3d ed. Upper Saddle River: Prentice Hall, 1997.

Farnsworth, E. Allan. *An Introduction to the Legal System of the United States,* 3d ed. New York: Oceana Publications, Inc., 1996.

Fowler, Michael Ross. *With Justice for All? The Nature of the American Legal System.* Upper Saddle River: Prentice Hall, 1998.

Van Dervort, Thomas R. *Equal Justice Under the Law.* Minneapolis/Saint Paul: West Publishing Company, 1994.

CONTRIBUTORS

Shannon Armitage

Beth Babini

Holly Barton

Daniel Brannen

Carol Brennan

Michael Broyles

ByLine Communications

Holly Caldwell

Jo-Ann Canning

Diane Carter

Richard Chapman

Chapterhouse

Linda Clemmons

Amy Cooper

Richard Cretan

Julie Davis

Michael Eggert

Grant Eldridge

Robert Gluck

Joel Golden

Carrie Golus

Nancy Gordon

Connor Gorry

Bridget Hall

Richard Clay Hanes

Lauri Harding

James Heiberg

Karl Heil

Robert Jacobson

Constance Johnson

Lois Kallunki

John Kane

Christine Kelley

Edward Knappman

Judson Knight

Paul Kobel

Jacqueline Maurice

Olivia Miller

Nancy Moore

Melynda Neal

New England Publishing Associates

Helene Northway

Carol Page

Akomea Poku-Kankam

Debra Reilly

Mary Scarbrough

Robert Schnakenberg

Bryan Schneider

Maria Sheler-Edwards

Elizabeth Shostak

Ginger Strand

Karen Troshynski-Thomas

Katherine Wagner

Linda Walton

Michael Watkins

Daniel Wisher

Susan Wood

Lisa Wroble

AFFIRMATIVE ACTION

Historic Prejudices

Although affirmative action programs and civil rights legislation both share a common history and address the question of how to end societal discrimination, they provide quite different approaches on how to accomplish that objective. Civil rights legislation forbids individuals or institutions, such as employers or university admissions offices, from considering factors such as color or gender in decision-making processes. Many affirmative action programs, however, do just the opposite. These programs require that color and gender be taken into account when making decisions about who will be hired or admitted to a school and that preference be given to people of color and/or women.

There are no affirmative action laws, per se. Most affirmative action mandates are a result of a series of presidential executive orders and government programs. Affirmative action initiatives were not intended to be permanent measures; rather, they were designed to be temporary actions. The goal of affirmative action is to help support the economic development of minorities and women, who have historically suffered prejudice in employment and educational opportunities in the United States. For affirmative action purposes, it is assumed that these groups are at a disadvantage in our society and need programs to give them a level playing field. The most visible affirmative programs, and the most controversial, are those that involve affirmative preference, such as government set-asides. Set-aside programs have a stated goal that five percent of all government contracts should be awarded to minority- and women-owned businesses. In order to achieve this, it becomes necessary to take race and gender into consideration when making a contract award.

While preference programs have received a great deal of public scrutiny they are not the only affirmative action initiatives. Other measures include affirmative recruitment and affirmative fairness. Affirmative recruitment occurs when an employer or educational institution takes proactive steps to encourage women and minorities to apply for jobs or school admissions. An example of affirmative recruitment is when a corporation participates in a job fair that is targeted to minorities. While the goal of affirmative recruitment is

to make women and minorities aware of opportunities, it does not guarantee that they will be hired by a company or gain admission to a school.

Affirmative fairness assesses the capability of a candidate for a job or promotion or school admissions on an individual basis. The purpose of affirmative fairness is to make the selection process a fair one for minorities and women. For instance, even though an applicant lacks the usual university admission requirements, that does not mean that the person might not have the ability to be a successful student. If that is the case, the admissions office would take into account other factors, such as obstacles this person had to overcome in order to graduate from high school, that would indicate a potential to do well in college. With affirmative fairness, standard measures, such as test scores, would be only one element to determine a candidate's merit. Unfortunately, because affirmative fairness requires weighing many subjective factors, it often is quite impractical to use when qualified applicants far outnumber the available spaces.

Affirmative Action v. Civil Rights

Affirmative action programs are an outgrowth of civil rights laws. Civil rights legislation was created to eliminate the differences in opportunities caused by racial divisions and lines. Although slavery was a prevalent practice in the South in 1787, the authors of the original Constitution chose not to deal with the issue, even though it clearly went against the notion of a free society that was the cornerstone of the country's founding. It would take the ratification of the Thirteenth Amendment in 1865 to outlaw slavery. Three years later, the Fourteenth Amendment guaranteed that the states could not make or enforce any law that would "abridge the privileges or immunities of citizens" or "deprive any person of life, liberty, or property, without the due process of law." It also provided that a state could not deny any citizen "the equal protection of the laws." The Fifteenth Amendment, ratified in 1870, stated that a citizen's right to vote could not be denied or abridged "on account of race, color, or previous condition of servitude."

Following the Civil War Congress passed numerous civil rights laws to ensure the rights of former slaves.

The Civil Rights Act of 1875 guaranteed that everyone, regardless of race or color, should be able to enjoy "inns, public conveyances on land or water, theaters, and other places of public amusement." This piece of legislation would effectively be overturned, however in an 8-1 decision in 1883 by the Supreme Court. In the *Civil Rights Cases,* the Court ruled that the Thirteenth and Fourteenth Amendments applied only to states and that the federal government did not have the authority to outlaw discrimination by private individuals. In his dissenting opinion, Justice John Marshall Harlan I stated that he believed that Congress did have such a right. However, in response to the Court's majority opinion, Southern states began passing laws, commonly called Jim Crow laws, that required separate accommodations for blacks and whites in most public places.

In 1896 the concept of "separate but equal" was upheld by the Supreme Court in *Plessy v. Ferguson.* Mr. Plessy challenged a Louisiana law that required racially separate seating accommodation on trains, after he was arrested for violating this law by trying to sit in a whites-only section. Although the Louisiana law appeared to be in violation of the Fourteenth Amendment's Equal Protection Clause, the Court ruled otherwise, thus allowing for continued segregation of the two races in the South. However, Justice Harlan was once again the sole dissenting voice and wrote that he believed that the Constitution should be "color blind." It would take over 50 years for Justice Harlan's vision of a "color-blind" Constitution to be affirmed. In *Brown v. Board of Education,* the Supreme Court unanimously ruled in 1954 that "separate" public schools were not "equal" for black students. This landmark case would have longlasting repercussions as school districts across the country have spent decades trying to determine the best way to integrate schools.

Affirmative Action in Practice

In 1961 President John Kennedy first used the term "affirmative action" in Executive Order 10925, which required federal contractors to hire more minority employees. The policy, as Kennedy envisioned it, was meant to provide minorities an opportunity to demonstrate their skills. The Civil Rights Act of 1964, passed during the Johnson Administration, guaranteed equality to blacks and effectively ended Jim Crow laws. However, President Johnson believed that the scars caused by years of legal discrimination in the South could not be quickly erased. In a commencement speech that he delivered at Howard University on 4 June 1965, President Johnson said: "You do not take a person who, for years, has been hobbled by chains and liberate him, bring him up to the starting line of a race and then say, You're free to compete with all the others,' and justly believe that you have been completely fair." The pres-

ident then went on to say that freedom alone was not the solution, that there needed to be opportunity and "not just equality as a right and a theory, but equality as a fact." That same year, the president signed Executive Order 11246, which provided a means to implement affirmative action policies. The order required federal contractors to file written affirmative action plans with the Office of Federal Contract Compliance Programs (OFCCP) under the Department of Labor.

It was during the administration of President Richard Nixon that affirmative action programs began requiring specific target goals, or quotas, and timetables for hiring minorities and females. In the late 1960s, the federal government began pushing for the inclusion of more minorities into high-paying, trade-union jobs and in 1969 authorized what would become known as the Philadelphia Plan. The program required construction companies in Philadelphia that received federal contracts to increase the number of racial minorities in that city's construction industry from one percent to 12 percent. The Civil Rights Act of 1972 was passed under the Nixon Administration. The act allowed the department of the Equal Employment Opportunity Commission to file lawsuits and regulate both state and local governments. Further presidential mandates regarding affirmative action appeared over the years, including the Public Works Employment Act, signed by President Jimmy Carter in 1977. This act required state and local government to spend 10 percent of federal funds for public works on Minority Business Enterprises.

Early on, federally mandated set-asides began being challenged in the courts. In 1974, the Supreme Court almost ruled on the constitutionality of university affirmative-action programs in the case of *DeFunis v. Odegaard.* DeFunis, a white male, sued the University of Washington Law School when he was denied admission while minority students with lower test scores were accepted into the program. The case had worked its way up through the appeals courts and during that time, the university had been ordered to admit DeFunis while the case was being reviewed. When DeFunis was only weeks away from graduation, the case came up for review by the U.S. Supreme Court. Instead of ruling on the legality of the admissions process, the Court decided that the case was moot since DeFunis had already finished his law school studies.

Reverse Discrimination

Four years later, the Court finally made a ruling on affirmative-action admissions in *University of California v. Bakke,* a case that raised the issue of "reverse discrimination." Bakke challenged the medical school admissions process at the University of Califonia-Davis Medical School that set aside 16 slots, out of 100, for minority applicants only. In this case, Bakke had not gained admission into the program despite the fact that he had scored higher on medical aptitude tests than minority applicants who were enrolled by the university. The Court ruled that Bakke had been discriminated against and ordered the medical school to admit him. But the Court also upheld affirmative-action procedures, to some degree, by stating that race could be a factor involved in the admissions process. In ruling in cases such as *Bakke,* which centered on equal protection issues, the Court adopted a "strict scrutiny" test. This test was used to determine if the government should be allowed to treat citizens unequally. In order to do so, the Court held that the reasons must be compelling and narrowly defined. In the view of the Court, the university's arguments for affirmative-action admissions did not pass the strict scrutiny test. For example, making up for past instances of specific discrimination would be allowable under strict scrutiny. However, the university's medical school was less than 20 years old and therefore did not have a history of past discrimination.

In 1995 the Supreme Court again used the strict scrutiny test in *Adarand Constructors, Inc. v. Pena,* a case that challenged the 10 percent set-asides for minorities for public works contracts. Adarand sued for race discrimination when his firm had lost a job to a Hispanic-owned construction company, despite the fact that Adarand had been the lowest bidder. The Court ruled that the federal government's arbitrary set-aside goal of 10 percent did not meet the strict scrutiny test. In writing the majority opinion, Justice Sandra Day O'Connor said that the plan failed to meet the test because it did not have a "compelling purpose" and it had not been "narrowly defined." While many people viewed the *Adarand* decision as a death knell for most preference affirmative-action programs, the Court did leave the door open for the constitutionality of programs that were enacted to remedy specific instances of past discrimination, had measurable goals, and a timeframe to achieve the goals.

See also: Civil Rights and Equal Protection, Segregation and Desegregation, Employment Discrimination, Gender Discrimination

Bibliography and Further Reading

Curry, George, ed. *The Affirmative Action Debate.* Reading, MA: Addison-Wesley Publishing Company, Inc. 1996.

Lawrence, Charles R., III, and Matsuda, Mari J. *We Won't Go Back: Making the Case for Affirmative Action.* Boston: Houghton Mifflin Company. 1997.

McWhirter, Darien A. *The End of Affirmative Action: Where Do We Go from Here?* New York: Birch Lane Press. 1996.

MORTON V. MANCARI

Legal Citation: 417 U.S. 535 (1974)

Appellant
Rogers Clark Morton, U.S. Secretary of Interior

Appellee
Mancari, et al.

Appellant's Claim
That the federal government's use of Native American preferences in personnel decisions did not violate equal protection under the Due Process Clause of the Fifth Amendment.

Chief Lawyer for Appellant
Harry R. Sachse

Chief Lawyer for Appellee
Gene E. Franchini

Justices for the Court
Harry A. Blackmun (writing for the Court), William J. Brennan, Jr., Warren E. Burger, William O. Douglas, Thurgood Marshall, Lewis F. Powell, Jr., William H. Rehnquist, Potter Stewart, Byron R. White

Justices Dissenting
None

Place
Washington, D.C.

Date of Decision
17 June 1974

Decision
Upheld the United States' claim and overturned a lower court's decision prohibiting use of Native American preferences in governmental personnel hiring and job promotion practices.

Significance
The ruling established that Native American Indians can be treated differently from other U.S. citizens by the federal government despite antidiscrimination laws. Members of tribes may be considered political rather than racial groups on occasions when the U.S. government bases its actions on long-standing legal responsibilities to protect Native American interests and promote tribal self-government. The Court ruled equal protection under the Fifth Amendment's Due Process Clause does not apply in such cases. The unique status of Native Americans as a separate people became increasingly unpopular with many Americans raised with the beliefs that all citizens should be treated equally under the law.

Since passage of the 1834 Indian Intercourse and Trade Act, Congress promoted Native American hiring preferences in certain governmental Native American services through a number of additional laws. However, until the 1930s the predominantly non-Indian staff of the U.S. Bureau of Indian Affairs (BIA) still held substantial control over the lives and destinies of the many tribes it serviced. Congress finally sought to change that situation. To increase Native American participation in BIA operations, Congress recognized that some forms of preferences and exemptions from normal civil service requirements were needed. In sponsoring a bill, one congressman eloquently expressed the need for an Native American preference by stating,

> The Indians have not only been thus deprived of civil rights and powers, but they have been largely deprived of the opportunity to enter the more important positions in the service of the very bureau which manages their affairs . . . It should be possible for Indians with the requisite vocational and professional training to enter the service of their own people without the necessity of competing with white applicants for these positions.

In response, Congress passed the Indian Reorganization Act (IRA) of 1934, a century after the Indian Trade Act. The IRA strengthened tribal governments while continuing the active role of the BIA in a way more responsive to tribal interests. Among other things, the law extended employment preference to qualified Native Americans for BIA jobs. The purpose of the preference, as outlined by Congress was: (1) to give Native Americans a greater participation in their own government; (2) to further the U.S. government's obligation in protecting tribal interests; and (3) to minimize the conflicts of having non-Native Americans administer matters affecting Native American tribal life. Congress was well aware the preference would result in employment disadvantages for non-Native Americans within the bureau. However, this unavoidable effect was considered necessary to allow the gradual replacement of non-Native Americans with Native Americans to further the goal of Native American self-government.

Soon questions of the government's role in protecting Native Americans interests arose. The Court reaffirmed the federal government's responsibility in assisting tribes toward self-government in *Board of County Commissioners v. Seber* (1943).

In 1964 Congress passed the Civil Rights Act, the first major federal law prohibiting discrimination in private employment on the basis of "race, color, religion, sex, or national origin." Since the act primarily targeted private employment discrimination and not the federal government, Congress passed the 1972 Equal Employment Opportunity (EEO) Act to prohibit discrimination in most areas of federal employment.

Meanwhile, following passage of the IRA, the BIA had implemented the preference with some success. By 1972, the percentage of Native Americans employed in the bureau rose from 34 percent in 1934 to 57 percent. However, success was mostly felt at lower paying positions. To correct this imbalance, the BIA extended the preference in 1972 to promotions within the agency designed to bring more Native Americans into positions of responsibility. This policy was considered a logical extension of the congressional intent of IRA.

Preferences and the Fifth Amendment

Shortly after introduction of the new BIA promotion policy and passage of the EEO Act, several non-Native American employees of the BIA office in Albuquerque, New Mexico, including Mancari, filed a class action suit in the U.S. District Court for the District of New Mexico on behalf of themselves and other non-Native employees. The suit named as defendants the secretary of the interior, the commissioner of Indian affairs, and the BIA directors for the Albuquerque and Navajo area offices. Mancari and the others raised two issues. First, they argued, the 1972 EEO Act repealed the various Native American preference laws passed since 1834. Secondly, they claimed the preference policies under the 1934 IRA directly violated equal protection under the Fifth Amendment by depriving them of their right to opportunities for job promotions and should, therefore, be declared unconstitutional. Mancari argued that implementation and enforcement of the 1972 BIA preference policy affecting job promotions "placed and will continue to place [non-Native employees] at a distinct disadvantage in competing for promotion and training programs with Indian employees, all of which has and will continue to subject the [non-Native employees] to discrimination and deny them equal employment opportunity."

In assessing how the BIA implemented the preference policy, the district court concluded that the repeal of Native American preference laws could indeed be implied from the 1972 EEO Act. However, if Congress repealed the preference laws, then their constitutionality need not be determined. In its decision, the dis-

trict court prohibited "any policy in the [BIA] which would hire, promote, or reassign any person in preference to another solely for the reason that such a person is an Indian." Secretary of Interior Rogers Clark Morton immediately appealed to the Supreme Court which was out of session. In August of 1973, Justice Marshall temporarily blocked the district court's decision from taking effect until the full Court could hear the case in its next regular session combined with a similar case.

Native Americans Not Ethnic

Justice Blackmun, writing for a unanimous Court, found the lower court erred on both issues regarding the implications of the EEO Act and Fifth Amendment application. First, the Court determined that Congress did not intend to repeal Native American preference with the 1972 EEO Act. Blackmun highlighted two specific sections of Title VII of the 1964 Civil Rights Act explicitly exempting from its coverage the preferential employment of "Indians by Indian tribes or by industries located on or near Indian reservations." As a senator stated on the floor of Congress during the passage of the Civil Rights Act, "this exemption is consistent with the Federal Government's policy of encouraging Indian employment and with the special legal position of Indians." In contrast, nowhere did the 1972 EEO Act mention Native American preference. Therefore, Blackmun wrote that merely by extending general racial discrimination prohibitions to federal employment in 1972 without explicitly repealing the Native American preferences, one could not conclude that the protections of Native American preferences in the Civil Rights Act were changed in any way. Therefore, the Court would be mistaken to conclude that Congress intended to consider the long-standing Native American preferences in BIA employment as racially discriminatory without a direct mention. Moreover, Blackmun added that in 1972 shortly after passage of the EEO Act, Congress passed new Native American preferences. These preferences were part of an education bill establishing government programs for training teachers of Native American children. In light of this obvious continued support of Native American preference, it seemed improbable that the same Congress, shortly before, would have condemned BIA preferences as racially discriminatory.

Secondly, the Court found that Native American preference for BIA promotions was reasonable. Morton had argued the preference policy had a rational basis designed to further Native American self-government. Native American preference was a long-standing, important part of the U.S. government's Native American program and traditionally considered an exception to government antidiscrimination policies. Therefore, Blackmun concluded that such preference was not racial discrimination in violation of the Due Process

Clause of the Fifth Amendment. The Supreme Court unanimously reversed the district court's judgement and returned both cases to that court for further consideration.

Impact

Mancari was the first time the Supreme Court considered the question of how Native Americans, who commonly are treated as ethnic groups in many circumstances in U.S. society, could receive special treatment by the government without that treatment being considered racial discrimination. In applying a newly created "rational basis" test to Native American preference, the Court unanimously found that Native American preference in hiring and promotion was not racial discrimination. In order to withstand this test, a law being challenged must be rationally related to a legitimate government interest. In this case, the fostering of Native American self-government and making the BIA more responsive to the needs of Native Americans were found to be legitimate government interests. The preferences also were not violations of the Due Process Clause. As long as the special treatment of Native Americans could be rationally tied to the fulfillment of Congress' unique legal obligations toward Native Americans, the Court gave Congress the benefit of any doubt and did not rule against such laws. If the Native American preference laws were only designed to help Native Americans as individuals, then they could be determined to be racial discrimination.

The primary distinction drawn by the Court in preference policies between Native Americans and non-Natives was political, not racial, since only members of tribes recognized by the U.S. government would benefit. However, the promise *Mancari* held to advance the rights of Indians was not fully realized. Ironically, *Mancari*'s creation of political distinctions exempted persons from equal protection violations which made Native Americans quite vulnerable to adverse treatment. In *United States v. Antelope* (1977) the Court held that in some cases tribal members could be subjected to harsher penalties under the law than non-Native Americans since constitutional equal protection did not apply.

Americans are taught from childhood that "all Americans are equal." Many viewed the unique right of tribes to govern their reservations and enjoy certain government preferences as clear evidence that Native Americans have "more rights" than regular U.S. citizens. The special status of Native Americans continued to raise outcries of "reverse discrimination" even though the Court held such preference was not racial at all, but a federal-tribal relationship, "governmental" in nature. Despite this distinction, opposition grew in the 1990s to eliminate the special status of Native American tribes. In defense, Native Americans viewed their ability to make and enforce laws of a certain territory as essential to preserving a geographic and cultural identity. Having Native Americans in positions of authority in the BIA was a necessary part of enhancing self-government. The Supreme Court showed its willingness to continue supporting this right in *County of Oneida v. Oneida Indian Nation* (1985). The Court further emphasized Congress' unique legal obligations toward Indians. By the 1990s about 80 percent of BIA employees were tribal members and most high level Native American policymaking positions within both the Department of Interior and the BIA were held by Native Americans.

Aside from Native American issues, another very important result of the *Mancari* case was that the Court expressed its unwillingness to support arguments that laws had been repealed merely by implication of later laws being passed. As emphasized in *Traynor v. Turnage* (1988), the Court again asserted that Congress must clearly express such an intent for repeal to exist.

Related Cases

Board of County Commissioners v. Seber, 318 U.S. 705 (1943).
United States v. Antelope, 430 U.S. 641 (1977).
County of Oneida v. Oneida Indian Nation, 470 U.S. 226 (1985).
Traynor v. Turnage, 485 U.S. 535 (1988).

Bibliography and Further Reading

Getches, David H., Charles F. Wilkinson, and Robert A. Williams, Jr. *Cases and Materials on Federal Indian Law*, 3rd ed. St. Paul, MN: West Publishing Co., 1993.

Williams, David C. "The Borders of the Equal Protection Clause: Indians as Peoples." *U.C.L.A. Law Review*, Vol. 38, 1991, pp. 759-870.

UNIVERSITY OF CALIFORNIA V. BAKKE

Legal Citation: 438 U.S. 265 (1978)

Petitioner
The Medical School of the University of California

Respondent
Allan Bakke

Petitioner's Claim
That the California Supreme Court erred in ruling that the school's special-admissions program for minorities violated Bakke's civil rights as a white male when he was denied admission.

Chief Lawyers for Petitioner
Archibald Cox, Paul J. Mishkin, Jack B. Owens, Donald L. Reidhaar

Chief Lawyer for Respondent
Reynold H. Colvin

Justices for the Court
Harry A. Blackmun, William J. Brennan, Jr., Thurgood Marshall, Lewis F. Powell, Jr. (writing for the Court), Byron R. White

Justices Dissenting
Warren E. Burger, William H. Rehnquist, John Paul Stevens, Potter Stewart

Place
Washington, D.C.

Date of Decision
28 June 1978

Decision
That the school's special-admissions program was unconstitutional.

Significance
For the first time, the Supreme Court said there could be such a thing as reverse discrimination.

The University of California operates several campuses throughout the state, and it is one of the largest state-sponsored higher education systems. At the university's campus in Davis, California, a medical school was established in 1968 with an entering class of 50 students. Three years later, the entering class size was doubled to 100 students. Originally, there was no preferential admissions policy for minorities. From 1968 to 1970, the school implemented a special-admissions program to increase minority representation in each entering class.

The special admissions program worked separately from the regular admissions program. Sixteen percent of the entering class was reserved for minorities, and minority applicants were processed and interviewed separately from regular applicants. The grade point averages and standardized test score averages for special-admissions entrants were significantly lower than for regular-admissions entrants.

In 1973, a Caucasian male named Allan Bakke applied to the Davis Medical School. Although Bakke got a combined score of 468 out of a possible 500 from his interviewers, his application was rejected. There were 2,464 applications for the 100 positions in the 1973 entering class, and by the time Bakke's application came up for consideration the school was only taking applicants with scores of 470 or better. Four special-admissions seats were left unfilled, however, and Bakke wrote a bitter letter to Dr. George H. Lowrey, associate dean and chairman of the admissions committee, complaining about the injustice of the special-admissions process.

Bakke applied again in 1974. That year there was even more competition for the 100 entering class positions: the school received 3,737 applications. Lowrey was one of Bakke's interviewers and gave him a low score, which contributed to Bakke's being rejected once again. Furious, Bakke sued the University of California in the Superior Court of California.

Bakke alleged that the medical school's special admissions program acted to exclude him on the basis of his race and violated his rights under the Equal Protection Clause of the Fourteenth Amendment to the

Protestors march against the Bakke decision. © Photograph by Bettye Lane.

U.S. Constitution, the California Constitution, and civil rights legislation. The trial court agreed but refused to order the school to admit Bakke as a student. Bakke appealed to the California Supreme Court, which confirmed the trial court's decision that the school's admissions programs were unconstitutional and ordered the school to admit Bakke.

Reverse Discrimination Claimed

The school appealed to the U.S. Supreme Court and argued their case on 12 October 1977. Bakke's attorney, Colvin, was making his first Supreme Court appearance, and he faced several experienced attorneys. For example, Cox was a former Harvard Law School professor and had served as Watergate Special Prosecutor. Colvin found himself immersed in an argument with Justice Thurgood Marshall, the only African American on the court, over whether minorities should be accorded any preference in the school's admissions process:

> Marshall: You are arguing about keeping somebody out and the other side is arguing about getting somebody in.
>
> Colvin: That's right.
>
> Marshall: So it depends on which way you look at it doesn't it? . . .
>
> Colvin: If I may finish . . .
>
> Marshall: You are talking about your client's rights. Don't these underprivileged people have some rights?
>
> Colvin: They certainly have the right to . . .
>
> Marshall: To eat cake.

On 28 June 1978 Justice Powell announced the decision of the majority in the 5-4 decision. It held that the school's special-admissions policy constituted reverse discrimination and was thus illegal. The court upheld the decision of the California Supreme Court, and affirmed the California court's order that Bakke be admitted to the school. Further, the Court upheld the California court's determination that the school's special-admissions program had to be scrapped. However, the Court held that schools could continue to give preference to minorities, so long as they did not exclude whites from a specific portion of the entering class, like the school had. The Court cited Harvard University's program as a model for an acceptable admissions policy that gave consideration to racial status without violating the civil rights of whites such as Bakke:

> The experience of other university admissions programs, which take race into account in achieving the educational diversity valued by the First Amendment, demonstrates that the assignment of a fixed number of places to a minority group is not a necessary means toward that end. An illuminating example is found in the Harvard College program . . . When the [Harvard] Committee on Admissions reviews the large middle group of applicants who are admissible and deemed capable of doing good work in their courses, the race of an applicant may tip the balance in his favor just as geographic origin or a life spent on a farm may tip the balance in other candidates' cases. A farm boy from Idaho can bring something to Harvard College that a Bostonian can-

not offer. Similarly, a black student can usually bring something that a white person cannot offer.

In Harvard college admissions the committee has not set target quotas for the number of blacks, or of musicians, football players, physicists or Californians to be admitted in a given year.

In a nutshell, the Court had ruled that while schools could give minority applicants some extra preference and consideration, they could not set aside a quota of positions for minority students that excluded whites. Such a program, like that at the Davis Medical School, constituted reverse discrimination. Bakke had won his case and would be admitted as a student. It was the first time that the Supreme Court applied civil rights protection to white students seeking admission to a university.

Related Cases

United Steelworkers of America v. Weber, 443 U.S. 193 (1979).
Hopwood v. Texas, 78 F.3d 932 (5th Cir. 1996).

Bibliography and Further Reading

Caplan, Lincoln. "The Hopwood Effect Kicks in on Campus." *U.S. News & World Report,* December 23, 1996, p. 26.

Cohen, Carl. "Race, Lies, and 'Hopwood.'" *Commentary,* June 1996, p. 39.

Coyle, Marcia. "Court Ducks Affirmative Action Case." *The National Law Journal,* July 15, 1996, p. A10.

Dovidio, John F., and Samuel L. Gaertner. "Affirmative Action, Unintentional Racial Biases, and Intergroup Relations." *Journal of Social Issues,* winter 1996, p. 51.

"Five Cases That Changed American Society." *Scholastic Update,* November 30, 1984, pp. 19-20.

Johnson, John W., ed. *Historic U.S. Court Cases, 1690–1990: An Encyclopedia.* New York: Garland Publishing, 1992.

"Minorities Down at Davis Univ. Since Bakke Case." *Jet,* June 7, 1982, p. 8.

Mooney, Christopher F. *Inequality and the American Conscience: Justice through the Judicial System.* New York: Paulist Press, 1982.

Nacoste, Rupert W. "How Affirmative Action Can Pass Constitutional and Social Psychological Muster." *Journal of Social Issues,* winter 1996, p. 133.

O'Neill, Timothy J. *Bakke & the Politics of Equality: Friends and Foes in the Classroom of Litigation.* Middletown, CT: Wesleyan University Press, 1985.

Pincus, Fred L. "Chilling Admissions: The Affirmative Action Crisis and the Search for Alternatives." *The Nation,* December 14, 1998, p. 39.

Schrag, Peter. "Backing off Bakke: The New Assault on Affirmative Action." *The Nation,* April 22, 1996, p. 11.

Schwartz, Bernard. *Behind Bakke: Affirmative Action and the Supreme Court.* New York: New York University Press, 1988.

Shenk, Joshua Wolf. "Grappling with Diversity." *U.S. News & World Report,* September 1, 1997, p. 93.

"Thumbs Down: Affirmative Action." *The Economist,* March 30, 1996, p. 30.

FULLILOVE V. KLUTZNICK

Legal Citation: 448 U.S. 448 (1980)

Petitioners
H. Earl Fullilove, et al.

Respondent
Philip M. Klutznick, U.S. Secretary of Commerce

Petitioners' Claim
That a provision in the law requiring that ten percent of all federal funds for local public works projects go to minority-owned businesses violates the U.S. Constitution.

Chief Lawyers for Petitioners
Robert G. Benisch, Robert J. Hickey

Chief Lawyer for Respondent
Drew S. Days III

Justices for the Court
Harry A. Blackmun, William J. Brennan, Jr., Warren E. Burger (writing for the Court), Thurgood Marshall, Lewis F. Powell, Jr., Byron R. White

Justices Dissenting
William H. Rehnquist, John Paul Stevens, Potter Stewart

Place
Washington, D.C.

Date of Decision
2 July 1980

Decision
Affirmed lower court rulings rejecting the petitioners' claim that minority "set-asides" were unconstitutional.

Significance
The decision in *Fullilove v. Klutznick* clarified the U.S. Supreme Court's position on the constitutionality of minority set-aside programs. This directly impacted Congress' ability to craft future laws designed to address discrimination in a variety of industries.

The Facts of the Case

Congress had long struggled with the problem of discrimination within the construction industry. Although they made up over ten percent of the population, minority business owners often found themselves shut out of the building trades sector in favor of their white counterparts. In 1977, Congress enacted the Public Works Employment Act to address these grievances. The law provided for a "set-aside" of ten percent of all federal monies for construction to go to minority-owned businesses. This provision was challenged in court by H. Earl Fullilove and a group of non-minority contractors. They claimed that they had sustained economic injury due to the enforcement of the 10 percent set-aside provision. In their view, the program violated their rights under the Equal Protection Clause of the Fifth Amendment to the U.S. Constitution, as well as their right not to be discriminated against under Title VI of the Civil Rights Act of 1964. Named as the respondent in their suit was Philip M. Klutznick, U.S. Secretary of Commerce.

Fullilove and the other contractors first took their case to the U.S. district court. They sought to have the Public Works Employment Act declared unconstitutional and an injunction invoked to prohibit dispersal of more federal money to minority contractors. The district court dismissed these claims, decreeing the set-aside program valid under the Constitution. The case then proceeded to the U.S. Court of Appeals for the Second Circuit. The court of appeals affirmed the district court's judgment on all counts. Fullilove and his co-petitioners had one last avenue of recourse: the U.S. Supreme Court.

The Supreme Court Decides

On 2 July 1980, the Supreme Court issued its decision. A 6-3 plurality of justices affirmed the rulings of the lower courts and rejected Fullilove's claims. While it differed in its reasoning, the six-justice plurality did agree that the set-aside program did not violate either the Equal Protection Clause or the Civil Rights Act.

In his majority opinion, Chief Justice Burger invoked Congress' authority under the Spending Power provi-

Public Works Employment Act

In May of 1977, Congress passed the Public Works Employment Act, which allocated an additional $4 billion for federal grants to be made by the Secretary of Commerce through the Economic Development Administration, to state and local governments for public works programs.

The Public Works Employment Act in a section designated "minority business enterprises" or "MBE" stipulated that no money would be granted to state and local governments, unless at least 10 percent of the projects were awarded to minority businesses. Under the act, minority groups were defined as "Negroes, Spanish-speaking, Orientals, Indians, Eskimos, and Aleuts."

To qualify as a minority business enterprise, at least 50 percent of the business had to be minority owned, and for publicly held businesses, at least 51percent of the stock had to be minority owned.

Under the act, MBE's could be awarded contracts even if they were not the lowest bidders, if their bids resulted from attempts to overcome a prior disadvantage or discrimination.

Source(s): *Constitutional Law*, 13th ed. New York: The Foundation Press Inc., 1997.

---

sion of Article I of the Constitution to justify the set-aside initiative. "Congress has frequently employed the Spending Power to further broaden policy objectives by conditioning receipt of federal moneys upon compliance by the recipient with federal statutory and administrative directives," Burger wrote. He went on to find justification for the law under the clause allowing Congress to regulate commerce as well.

But the crux of Burger's ruling lay in his conclusion that Congress could use racial and ethnic criteria in crafting federal laws designed to remedy discrimination. "[W]e reject the contention that in the remedial context the Congress must act in a wholly 'color-blind' fashion," Burger wrote. He went on to observe:

> It is fundamental that in no organ of government, state or federal, does there repose a more comprehensive remedial power than in the Congress, expressly charged by the Constitution with competence and authority to enforce equal protection guarantees. Congress not only may induce voluntary action to assure compliance with existing federal statutory or constitutional antidiscrimination provisions, but also, where Congress has authority to declare certain conduct unlawful, it may, as here, authorize and induce state action to avoid such conduct.

Justices Powell and Marshall, joined by Brennan and Blackmun, wrote separate concurring opinions in which they stated their own reasons for declaring the set-aside provision constitutional.

The Dissenting Opinion

Dissent in the case came from Justice Stewart, joined in his opinion by Justice Rehnquist. They expressed the view that the set-aside provision was unconstitutional

on its face because it elevated one class of citizens above another, in violation of equal protection requirements. Stewart wrote:

> The Fourteenth Amendment was adopted to ensure that every person must be treated equally by each State regardless of the color of his skin. The Amendment promised to carry to its necessary conclusion a fundamental principle upon which this Nation had been founded—that the law would honor no preference based on lineage . . . Today, the Court derails this achievement and places its imprimatur on the creation once again by government of privileges based on birth.

In a separate dissent, Justice John Paul Stevens decried the absence of hearings to determine where the discrimination was taking place within the construction industry, and which minority groups actually deserved government help.

Impact

In the wake of the *Fullilove v. Klutznick* decision, Congress enacted a number of new minority set-aside programs. State and local governments followed suit, although a number of those laws were later struck down in court.

Related Cases

South Dakota v. Dole, 483 U.S. 203 (1987).
Richmond v. J. A. Croson Co., 488 U.S. 469 (1989).
Adarand Constructors, Inc. v. Pena, 512 U.S. 200 (1995).

Bibliography and Further Reading

Biskupic, Joan, and Elder Witt, eds. *Congressional Quarterly's Guide to the U.S. Supreme Court*, 3rd ed. Washington, DC: Congressional Quarterly, Inc., 1996.

Cushman, Robert F. *Leading Constitutional Decisions.* Englewood Cliffs, NJ: Prentice-Hall, Inc., 1982.

Hall, Kermit L., ed. *The Oxford Companion to the Supreme Court of the United States.* New York: Oxford University Press, 1992.

Koenig, Paul. "Does Congress Abuse Its Spending Clause Power by Attaching Conditions on the Receipt of Federal Law Enforcement Funds to a State's Compliance with 'Megan's Law?'" *Journal of Criminal Law and Criminology,* winter 1998, p. 721.

Rice, Mitchell F., and Maurice Mongkuo. "Did Adarand Kill Minority Set-Asides?" *Public Administration Review,* January-February 1998, p. 82.

BUILDING TRADES COUNCIL V. CITY OF CAMDEN, N.J.

Legal Citation: 465 U.S. 208 (1984)

Appellant
Building & Construction Trades Council of New Jersey

Appellee
City and Council of the City of Camden, New Jersey

Appellant's Claim
A municipal ordinance adopted under a statewide affirmative action program requiring bidders on city projects to reserve 40 percent of all jobs for local residents violated the Equal Protection Clause of the Constitution.

Chief Lawyer for Appellant
Steven K. Kudatsky

Chief Lawyer for Appellee
N. Thomas Foster

Justices for the Court
William J. Brennan, Jr., Warren E. Burger, Thurgood Marshall, Sandra Day O'Connor, Lewis F. Powell, Jr., William H. Rehnquist (writing for the Court), John Paul Stevens, Byron R. White

Justices Dissenting
Harry A. Blackmun

Place
Washington, D.C.

Date of Decision
21 February 1984

Decision
The Court, reversing the New Jersey Supreme Court, agreed with the builders that the municipal ordinance violated the privileges and immunities clause designed to "place the citizens of each state" on "the same footing."

Significance
Municipal programs, designed to encourage minority hiring as well as discourage "middle-class flight" from decaying cities, had to be "carefully tailored" and based on "substantial reason."

In the late 1970s and early 1980s, many cities whose economic woes were offset by federal grants for construction tried to multiply the grants' benefits by reserving jobs for local residents. This "protectionism" had mixed results.

The practices echoed commonplace and largely unchallenged Depression and post World War II-era residence requirements for teachers, police officers, and firefighters. But there was one highly significant difference. In the 1930s and 1940s, almost all municipal funds came out of municipal coffers. However, 25 years later much of the money came from the federal government—with federal strings attached. Moreover, suburbs had grown enormously and many of the federal grants given to cities came out of taxes paid by suburban residents.

Nonetheless, Camden imposed a 40 percent residence requirement for employees of contractors working on city construction projects, and also mandated one-year of residence to qualify for that preference. The Commerce Clause, the Privileges and Immunities Clause, and the Fourteenth Amendment's Equal Protection Clause were all invoked in the suit brought against the Camden plan by the Building and Construction Trades Council.

The city's own action, however, mooted the challenge under the Equal Protection Clause. The one-year qualification for preference was deleted and the simple fact of residence substituted. In addition, the 40 percent resident-hiring "quota" was dropped in place of a "goal." The Supreme Court's decision in *White v. Massachusetts Council of Contruction Employers, Inc.* (1983) mooted the challenge under the Commerce Clause. The Court held that the mayor of Boston had been acting as a market participant rather than a government regulator in issuing an executive order requiring 50 percent of jobs on city-funded construction jobs be reserved for city residents.

But the Supreme Court refused to accept the logic which the New Jersey Supreme Court used to reject the builders' challenge under the Privileges and Immunities Clause. The New Jersey Court argued that a municipal ordinance cannot give rise to the concerns addressed by the clause, because it was designed to place citizens of different states—not municipalities—on "the same footing." Nonetheless, Justice Renhquist argued basic fairness issues were involved. Out-of-state residents do not have "a chance to remedy at the polls any discrimination against them," the justice wrote in the majority decision. Consequently, state and municipal authorities were obliged to establish the necessity of such programs.

As precedent, Justice Rehnquist cited *Mullancy v. Anderson* (1952) which invalidated an "Alaska-Hire" preference on oil and case reserves owned by the state. In striking down Alaska's claim that "ownership in itself" was sufficient justification for discrimination, the court held the state's interest was "not absolute." Therefore, Rehnquist wrote:

> Much the same analysis is appropriate to a city's efforts to bias private employment decisions in favor of its residents on construction projects funded with public monies.

Rehnquist found it:

> . . . impossible to evaluate Camden's justification on the record as it now stands. No trial has ever been held in this case. No findings of fact have been made . . . It would not be appropriate for this court either to make factual determinations as an initial matter or take judicial notice of Camden's decay.

Therefore, Rehnquist ordered the case remanded back to the state supreme court "on the best method for making the necessary findings."

In dissenting, Justice Blackmun cited the historic importance of the Privileges and Immunities Clause. He observed that Andrew Hamilton described the clause as the basis of the Union. Even before the Constitution was adopted the colonies "had shown themselves willing and able . . . to override local protectionist ordinances," Justice Blackmun added. He cited a 1982 Supreme Court decision, also involving Alaska, to argue that the majority had improperly applied the Privileges and Immunities Clause. In that case, the Court struck down a statute allocating state treasury refunds based on length of residence under the equal protection, but not the Privileges and Immunities Clause.

Both the Alaska and Camden statutes discriminated primarily among state residents in a way that disadvantaged nonresidents as well but did not thereby implicate the underlying concerns of the Privileges and Immunities Clause, Justice Blackmun argued. While agreeing out-of-state residents can not seek a "remedy at the polls," Blackmun nevertheless contended the majority's reasoning ignored the fact that "disadvantaged state residents who turn to the legislature . . . further the interests of nonresidents as well as their own," citing cases in Georgia and California as examples.

The majority was overreaching in its distaste at "the unedifying sight of localities fighting for parochial gain at one another's expense," Justice Blackmun asserted. He also pointed out the majority had "conceded that its interpretation of the clause does not attach readily to a constitutional provision." Consequently, the dissenter argued, "the issue before us is not the desirability of the ordinance but its constitutionality—more particularly its constitutionality under the Privileges and Immunities Clause. Because I believe that the clause does not apply to discrimination based on municipal residence, I dissent."

Related Cases

Mullancy v. Anderson, 342 U.S. 415 (1952).
Baldwin v. Montana Fish and Game Commission, 436 U.S. 371 (1978).
Hicklin v. Orbeck, 437 U.S. 518 (1978).
White v. Massachusetts Council of Construction Employers, Inc., 460 U.S. 204 (1983).
Supreme Court of New Hampshire v. Piper, 470 U.S. 274 (1985).
Supreme Court of Virginia v. Friedman, 487 U.S. 59 (1988).

Bibliography and Further Reading

Day, Thomas H. "Hiring Preference Acts; Has the Supreme Court Rendered Them Violations of Privileges and Immunities Clause." *Fordham Law Review,* November, 1985.

Hirsch, Werner Z. and David Floyd "The Substantial Reason Requirement under the Privileges and Immunities Clause." *Southwestern University Law Review,* 1985.

Roberti, Stephen R. "Municipal-based Discrimination and the Privileges and Immunities Clause." *Washington University Journal of Urban and Contemporary Law,* spring, 1986.

"Supreme Court Rules Jobs Set Aside Unconstitutional." *Wall Street Journal,* 22 February 1984.

FIREFIGHTERS LOCAL UNION NO. 1784 V. STOTTS

Legal Citation: 467 U.S. 561 (1984)

Petitioner
Firefighters Local Union No. 1784

Respondents
Carl W. Stotts, et al.

Petitioner's Claim
That a court-ordered injunction resulting in a layoff plan which protected African American employees from layoffs and took precedence over a previous policy of "first hired, last fired" was inappropriate.

Chief Lawyer for Petitioner
Richard B. Fields

Chief Lawyer for Respondents
Allen S. Blair

Justices for the Court
Warren E. Burger, Sandra Day O'Connor, Lewis F. Powell, Jr., William H. Rehnquist, John Paul Stevens, Byron R. White (writing for the Court)

Justices Dissenting
Harry A. Blackmun, William J. Brennan, Jr., Thurgood Marshall

Place
Washington, D.C.

Date of Decision
6 December 1983

Decision
That a court-ordered injunction against a policy which laid off those firefighters with least seniority before those with most seniority, in order to save the jobs of African American firefighters, was inappropriate.

Significance
The Supreme Court refused to allow a program to remedy discrimination by discriminating against a group with seniority.

Affirmative action in the United States has been a political issue since the Civil War. The concept originated with the provision of clothing, land, and education for newly freed slaves. The actual term "affirmative action," however, did not appear until the presidency of John F. Kennedy. The Committee on Equal Employment Opportunity was established by Kennedy's executive order to ensure African Americans could compete for government contracts and employment. President Lyndon Johnson signed the Civil Rights Act of 1964 which was established to end discrimination by private employers, whether or not they were government contractors. Under President Richard Nixon, specific requirements for enforcing contract compliance for affirmative action were developed. These requirements include analyzing the employment of minorities and women in job categories and developing goals and timetables for each category in which minorities and women are underrepresented. Affirmative action, according to the Civil Rights Commission, refers to any action or program which allows the consideration of race, national origin, sex, or disability, along with other criteria. It is used to provide opportunities to a class of qualified persons who have been historically denied those opportunities.

Titles VI and VII of the Civil Rights Act of 1964 form the legislative basis for equal employment opportunity laws and affirmative action programs. Under Title VII, federal courts were given the authority to order employers to implement race- or gender-conscious affirmative action programs. *Firefighters v. Stotts* was one of the first of these court-ordered cases. A group of African American firefighters sued the fire department of Memphis, Tennessee for racial discrimination in hiring and promotion. The outcome was that the Memphis Fire Department and the firefighters group agreed to a court-approved settlement called a "consent decree" which was an affirmative action plan aimed at remedying the discrimination. The firefighters union, however, had previously negotiated a policy of "last hired, first fired" meaning that in the case of a layoff, firefighters with less seniority would be let go first.

Later, the minority firefighters group appealed to the U.S. District Court for the Western District of Tennessee to prevent Memphis from using this system since it would impact the gains they had made in the consent decree. The district court agreed with the firefighters and ordered that layoffs should be made in a way that would not impact the affirmative action plan, but as a result would violate the established seniority system. The firefighters union appealed to the U.S. Court of Appeals but lost when the court agreed with the district court's actions.

The union then asked the Supreme Court to review the case, also known as taking the case on *certiorari.* On 12 June 1984, the Court reversed the lower courts' decisions. Justice White wrote the opinion, supported by Justices Burger, Powell, Rehnquist, and O'Connor. The court stated that because Title VII specifically protects seniority systems (such as the one negotiated by the union) and because the union was not involved in the affirmative action consent decree, the district court had overstepped its boundaries in ordering the injunction. They also interpreted Title VII to state that a court could only give competitive seniority to employees who had actually suffered intentional discrimination. Since the minority firefighters case did not include mention of intentional discrimination, the Court interpreted that any discrimination was unintentional.

Justices Blackmun, Brennan, and Marshall disagreed, arguing that the action was moot since, a month after the layoffs, all laid-off non-minority employees were restored to duty and demoted non-minority employees were offered their previous positions. As a result, the Supreme Court would lack jurisdiction over the case.

Following the Supreme Court's ruling, the Justice Department, under President Ronald Reagan, asked states and cities to get rid of numerical goals in hiring or promoting women and minorities. Since the court had interpreted the intention of the Civil Rights Act of 1964 to be remedying past discrimination against individuals as opposed to entire classes of people, the department felt numerical goals were inappropriate. This was seen widely as a blow to the goals of affirmative action.

Related Cases

Local 28 of Sheet Metal Workers International Association v. Equal Employment Opportunity Commission, 478 U.S. 421 (1986).
Local Number 93, International Association of Firefighters v. City of Cleveland, 478 U.S. 501 (1986).
Johnson v. Transportation Agency of Santa Clara County, 480 U.S. 616 (1987).
Richmond v. J. A. Croson Co., 488 U.S. 469 (1989).

Bibliography and Further Reading

Brody, Carl E., Jr. "A Historical Review of Affirmative Action and the Interpretation of its Legislative Intent by the Supreme Court." *Akron Law Review,* winter, 1996.

Cohen, William, and John Kaplan. *Constitutional Law: Civil Liberty and Individual Rights.* Mineola, NY: The Foundation Press, 1982.

Curry, George, E. *The Affirmative Action Debate.* Reading, MA: Addison Wesley Publishing Co., Inc., 1996.

"Cutback on Quotas." *Time,* 11 March 1985.

Kahlenberg, Richard D. *The Remedy: Class, Race, and Affirmative Action.* New York: Basic Books, 1996.

WYGANT V. JACKSON BOARD OF EDUCATION

Legal Citation: 476 U.S. 267 (1986)

Petitioner
Wendy Wygant, on behalf of a group of laid-off non-minority teachers

Respondent
Jackson Board of Education

Petitioner's Claim
That the Equal Protection Clause of the Fourteenth Amendment was violated by the school district's labor contract under an affirmative action plan, which resulted in minority teachers with less seniority being retained and non-minority teachers with greater seniority being laid off.

Chief Lawyer for Petitioner
K. Preston Dade, Jr.

Chief Lawyer for Respondent
Jerome A. Susskind

Justices for the Court
Warren E. Burger, Sandra Day O'Connor, Lewis F. Powell, Jr. (writing for the Court), William H. Rehnquist, Byron R. White

Justices Dissenting
Harry A. Blackmun, William J. Brennan, Jr., Thurgood Marshall, John Paul Stevens

Place
Washington, D.C.

Date of Decision
6 November 1985

Decision
That the Equal Protection Clause of the Fourteenth Amendment was violated by the school district's labor contract under an affirmative action plan which resulted in minority teachers with less seniority being retained and non-minority teachers with greater seniority being laid off.

Significance
Despite the fact that a labor contract citing specific minority hiring goals and preservation was reached through collective bargaining with affirmative action goals that were to remedy societal discrimination, it was found to violate the Equal Protection Clause as non-minority teachers were harmed in the process of preserving minority percentages in staffing.

In 1973, the Jackson, Michigan, school board and teachers' union evaluated their labor agreement in light of affirmative action goals. Based on a review of student/teacher ratios in 1969 which showed that 15.2 percent of the students and only 3.9 percent of the teachers were African American, the school board revised the contract in order to maintain or improve this ratio. The revision stated that if teacher layoffs were required, teachers with less service or seniority would be laid off first; however, at no time would the percentage of minority teachers laid off exceed the percentage of minority teachers at the time of the layoff.

In 1982 and 1983, teacher layoffs became necessary in the district. As a result of the labor agreement, some minority teachers with less seniority were retained while non-minority teachers with more service were laid off. A group of the non-minority teachers who were laid off sued the Jackson School Board, alleging that the layoff had violated their rights to equal protection under the Fourteenth Amendment. This clause states:

> No State shall make or enforce any law which shall abridge the privileges or immunities of citizens of the United States; nor shall any State deprive any person of life, liberty, or property, without due process of law; nor deny to any person within its jurisdiction the equal protection of the laws.

The U.S. District Court for the Eastern District of Michigan found for the school district, noting that the policy was an attempt to cure discrimination in society by providing minority role models for minority students. The U.S. Court of Appeals for the Sixth Circuit affirmed the lower court's decision.

The teachers' group asked the Supreme Court to review the case, also known as taking the case on *certiorari*. On 19 May 1986, the court reversed the lower courts' decision, but were unable to agree on an opinion between themselves. Five of the justices agreed that the layoffs did violate the Equal Protection Clause, although four filed separate opinions. Justice Powell, joined in his opinion by Justices Burger, Rehnquist, O'Connor, and White, noted that societal discrimination was not enough to provide a compelling state interest to justify the layoff provision in the contract. The school district also needed to show direct discrimination within the district in order for the affirmative action plan to be legitimate. This review of government actions in order to ensure a compelling interest on the part of the state in which the means of implementing the actions are "least restrictive" is also known as "strict scrutiny." Powell also stated that the school board should have based its minority hiring goals on the number of minority teachers as a percentage of the available teaching pool, rather than relative to the racial makeup of the student body.

Justices Marshall, Brennan, and Blackmun dissented. Their opinion was that the layoff provision was arrived at through the collective bargaining process and was therefore a valid method for preserving a hiring policy whose goal was to achieve diversity and stability for all students. In his separate dissent, Justice Stevens stated that the decision to include more minority teachers in the district was valid, regardless of whether the district had proved previous discrimination.

While the Court supported the petitioner's claim that the Equal Protection Clause had been violated, it was clear, given the closely divided opinions of the Court, that the practice of establishing minority hiring and composition goals as a part of employers' affirmative action plans was still under review in 1986. Given the conservative bent of the Supreme Court, it was apparent that affirmative action policies in the United States would be reviewed on a regular basis.

Related Cases

Firefighters v. Cleveland, 478 U.S. 501 (1986).
Martin v. Wilks, 490 U.S. 755 (1989).
Board of Education of the Township of Piscataway v. Taxman, 91 F3d. 1547 (3d Cir. 1996).

Bibliography and Further Reading

Brody, Carl E., Jr. "A Historical Review of Affirmative Action and the Interpretation of Its Legislative Intent by the Supreme Court." *Akron Law Review,* winter 1996.

Curry, George, E. *The Affirmative Action Debate.* Reading, MA: Addison Wesley Publishing Co., Inc., 1996.

"High Court Backs Laid-Off White Teachers (Supreme Court Reverse Discrimination Case)." *Monthly Labor Review,* July 1986.

Kahlenberg, Richard D. *The Remedy: Class, Race, and Affirmative Action.* New York: BasicBooks, 1996.

Lichtenberg, Judith, and David Luban. "The Merits of Merit." *Business and Society Review,* winter 1998, p. 85.

Trippett, Frank. "A Solid Yes to Affirmative Action (Supreme Court Decides for Affirmative Action)." *Time,* July 14, 1986.

LOCAL NUMBER 93, INTERNATIONAL ASSOC. OF FIREFIGHTERS, AFL-CIO C.L.C. V. CITY OF CLEVELAND

Legal Citation: 478 U.S. 501 (1986)

Petitioner
Local Number 93, International Association of Firefighters, AFL-CIO, C.L.C., et al.

Respondent
City of Cleveland, on behalf of local officials

Petitioenrs' Claim
That the city of Cleveland and various local officials discriminated on the basis of race and national origin in the hiring, assignment, and promotion of firefighters within the Cleveland Fire Department.

Chief Lawyer for Petitioners
Edward R. Stege, Jr.

Chief Lawyer for Respondent
John D. Maddox

Justices for the Court
Harry A. Blackmun, William J. Brennan, Jr. (writing for the Court), Thurgood Marshall, Sandra Day O'Connor, Lewis F. Powell, Jr., John Paul Stevens

Justices Dissenting
Warren E. Burger, William H. Rehnquist, Byron R. White

Place
Washington, D.C.

Date of Decision
25 February 1986

Decision
A court-approved settlement between the city of Cleveland and a group of minority firefighters which required a specific number of promotions for minority firefighters was declared as fair and reasonable to non-minority firefighters, even if it benefited individuals who had not been actual victims of the city's race discrimination.

Significance
The court-approved affirmative action settlement was found to be fair and reasonable since the agreement was a voluntary one between the minority firefighters and the city and because the promotions did not harm the non-minority firefighters.

During the 1980s, after the city of Cleveland had been sued for racial discrimination several times and had lost, an organization of African American and Hispanic firefighters, called the Vanguards, brought suit against the city in the federal district court. They alleged that the city had violated Title VII of the Civil Rights Act through racial discrimination in the hiring, assigning, and promoting of firefighters. Titles VI and VII of the Civil Rights Act form the legislative basis for equal employment opportunity laws and affirmative action programs. In a court-approved settlement called a "consent decree," the city agreed to give half of all promotions to minority firefighters. The majority-dominated union, Local 93 of the International Association of Firefighters, appealed to the U.S. Court of Appeals for the Sixth Circuit. The appeals court agreed with the decision, finding that the decree was "fair and reasonable to non-minority firefighters."

The union asked the Supreme Court to review the case, also known as taking the case on *certiorari*. The court did so, and on 2 July 1986, also agreed with the lower court's ruling. Justice Brennan was joined in his opinion by Justices Marshall, Blackmun, Powell, Stevens, and O'Connor. Brennan wrote that, due to the voluntary nature of a consent decree in which both parties agree to the remedy proposed, Title VII did not apply in this case. In addition, although the union did not agree to the consent degree, it was not harmed by it. Justices William Rehnquist and Warren Burger disagreed, stating that the consent decree did fall under Title VII since it was court-ordered, whether or not it was voluntary. In addition, they felt that people benefiting from the decree needed to prove that they were victims of discrimination. Justice White's dissent also stated a need for individuals benefiting from the decree to prove past discrimination.

In an interview with *Nation's Business,* a lawyer with the Mountain States Legal Foundation of Denver which had entered the case on the side of the union, stated: "The Court seems to be setting up a sort of continuum, distinguishing between [affirmative action] programs that involve hiring, promotions or layoffs." In this case, the Court seemed to feel more comfortable with an employer's affirmative action program which dealt with promotions because non-minority employees were not necessarily harmed by the program.

Related Cases

Firefighters Local Union No. 1794 v. Stotts, 467 U.S. 561 (1984).

Local 28 of Sheet Metal Workers International Association v. Equal Employment Opportunity Commission, 478 U.S. 421 (1986).

Wygant v. Jackson Board of Education, 476 U.S. 267 (1986).

Johnson v. Transportation Agency of Santa Clara County, 480 U.S. 616 (1987).

United States v. Paradise, 480 U.S. 149 (1987).

Bibliography and Further Reading

Brody, Carl E., Jr. "A Historical Review of Affirmative Action and the Interpretation of Its Legislative Intent by the Supreme Court." *Akron Law Review,* winter, 1996.

Curry, George, E. *The Affirmative Action Debate.* Reading, MA: Addison Wesley Publishing Co., Inc., 1996.

Mauro, Tony. "The High Court: What It's Up To (Impact of Supreme Court Cases on Business)." *Nation's Business,* September, 1986.

Trippett, Frank. "A Solid Yes to Affirmative Action (Supreme Court Decides for Affirmative Action)." *Time,* 14 July 1986.

RICHMOND V. J. A. CROSON CO.

Legal Citation: 488 U.S. 469 (1989)

Appellant
City of Richmond

Appellee
J. A. Croson Co.

Appellant's Claim
That the Richmond City ordinance that non-minority owned primary contractors on city construction contracts must pledge at least 30 percent "set-aside" (assign that portion of the job) to minority subcontractors, did not violate the Constitution.

Chief Lawyer for Appellant
John Payton

Chief Lawyer for Appellee
Walter H. Ryland

Justices for the Court
Anthony M. Kennedy, Sandra Day O'Connor (writing for the Court), William H. Rehnquist, Antonin Scalia, John Paul Stevens, Byron R. White

Justices Dissenting
Thurgood Marshall, Harry A. Blackmun, William J. Brennan, Jr.

Place
Washington, D.C.

Date of Decision
5 October 1988

Decision
That Richmond's ordinance of requiring non-minority contractors to pledge 30 percent of city construction contracts to minority subcontractors was invalid under the Fourteenth Amendment's Equal Protection Clause.

Significance
In finding that Richmond had not established specific past discrimination to support their minority firm goal in the awarding of municipal construction contracts, the courts established the constitutional standard of "strict scrutiny" for state and local affirmative action contracting programs.

President Lyndon Johnson signed the Civil Rights Act of 1964 which was established to end discrimination by private employers, whether or not they were government contractors. Under President Richard Nixon, specific requirements for enforcing contract compliance for affirmative action were developed. These requirements include analyzing the employment of minorities and women in job categories and developing goals and timetables for each category where minorities and women are under represented. Affirmative action, according to the Civil Rights Commission, refers to any action or program which allows the consideration of race, national origin, sex, or disability, along with other criteria. It is used to provide opportunities to a class of qualified persons who have either been historically or actually denied those opportunities.

In support of such national goals, many local and state governments developed affirmative action programs which used "set-asides" or the practice of "setting aside" a portion of municipal business to support the development of under-utilized businesses owned by minorities and women. In 1983, the city of Richmond, Virginia, in pursuit of the ideals of affirmative action, established a local ordinance requiring non-minority-owned contractors receiving city construction contracts to "set-aside" 30 percent of the subcontracting work for minority contractors. This was based on the fact that, for five years prior to the "set-aside" program, less than 1 percent of city construction contracts were awarded to minority contractors, despite a 50 percent minority population in the city, along with other factors.

Following the adoption of the ordinance, a non-minority-owned contracting firm, J. A. Croson Co., bid on a plumbing contract for the city of Richmond. No other companies placed a bid on the contract. While it did contract with minority subcontractors, Croson was unable to meet the ordinance's requirement of 30 percent in its bid for the job, and so requested a waiver from Richmond. The city denied the waiver and informed them that the contract would be placed up for bid again. Croson sued the city in the U.S. District Court for the Eastern District of Virginia challenging Richmond's ordinance under the equal protection clause of the Fourteenth Amendment. This clause states:

No State shall make or enforce any law which shall abridge the privileges or immunities of citizens of the United States; nor shall any State deprive any person of life, liberty, or property, without due process of law; nor deny to any person within its jurisdiction the equal protection of the laws.

The district court upheld the ordinance, however, in all respects. When Croson appealed to the Fourth District Circuit Court, the court first affirmed the lower court's decision. Then when the decision was sent to the state's supreme court for further review, the court found in favor of Croson. The city of Richmond appealed to the U.S. Supreme Court, which, on 23 January 1989, affirmed the decision in favor of Croson.

In her opinion for the 6-3 majority, Justice O'Connor noted that the city had not documented specific local instances of previous discrimination to support its goal of 30 percent. O'Connor applied the constitutional standard of "strict scrutiny" (the most difficult standard to meet) to racial classifications, which she felt was appropriate given the large minority population in the city and on the city council. This review of government actions in order to ensure a compelling interest on the part of the state, and that the actions are "least restrictive" in its means is also known as "strict scrutiny." In support of its case, Richmond had cited factors demonstrating the need for such a program including a lack of capital, training, and experience on the part of minority contractors, but, according to O'Connor, these were too vague. In addition, despite the fact that Congress had found evidence of discrimination in the construction industry nationally and that, within the city itself, discrimination existed in other industries, Richmond needed to document specific instances within the Richmond construction industry in order to prove a compelling interest on its part.

Justice Marshall, along with Justices Brennan and Blackmun, disagreed. In his dissent, Marshall noted that the decision was a step backward in the Court's affirmative action jurisprudence. He found the evidence of discrimination in the construction industry on a national level supported Richmond's claim and that the ordinance met the standard for applying the Equal Protection Clause to an affirmative action program.

As a result of this ruling, municipalities across the country needed to review and revise their affirmative action programs in order to ensure that they had documented specific instances of discrimination. While it would seem to be a heavy burden for them to bear, according to Linda Faye Williams in *The Affirmative Action Debate*, 60 cities spent more than $30 million in order to establish this documentation following the decision in 1989.

Related Cases

Korematsu v. United States, 323 U.S. 214 (1944).
Shelley v. Kraemer, 334 U.S. 1 (1948).
South Carolina v. Katzenbach, 383 U.S. 301 (1966).
Katzenbach v. Morgan, 384 U.S. 641 (1966).
San Antonio Independent School District v. Demetrio P. Rodriguez, 411 U.S. 1 (1973).
Fullilove v. Klutznick, 448 U.S. 448 (1980).
Wygant v. Jackson Board of Education, 476 U.S. 267 (1986).
Johnson v. Transportation Agency, 480 U.S. 616 (1987).

Bibliography and Further Reading

Aleinikoff, T. Alexander, and Samuel Issacharoff. "Race and Redistricting: Drawing Constitutional Lines After Shaw v. Reno." *Michigan Law Review*, December 1993, p. 588.

Brody, Carl E., Jr. "A Historical Review of Affirmative Action and the Interpretation of Its Legislative Intent by the Supreme Court." *Akron Law Review*, winter, 1996.

Curry, George, E. *The Affirmative Action Debate*. Reading, MA: Addison Wesley Publishing Co., Inc., 1996.

Darden, Joe T. "Impacts of Racism on White Americans, 2d ed." *Urban Studies*, November 1998, p. 2159.

Fein, Bruce. "A Court That Obeys the Law (Recent Supreme Court Decisions)." *National Review*, September 29, 1989.

Hellman, Deborah. "Two Types of Discrimination: The Familiar and the Forgotten." *California Law Review*, March 1998, p. 315.

Kahlenberg, Richard D. *The Remedy: Class, Race, and Affirmative Action*. New York: BasicBooks, 1996.

Lunn, John, and Huey L. Perry. "Justifying Affirmative Action: Highway Construction in Louisiana." *Industrial and Labor Relations Review*, April 1993, p. 464.

Nacoste, Rupert W. "How Affirmative Action Can Pass Constitutional and Social Psychological Muster." *Journal of Social Issues*, winter 1996, p. 133.

Sachs, Andrea. "A Blow To Affirmative Action: The Court Strikes Down a Plan to Aid Minority Businesses." *Time*, February 6, 1989.

"Supreme Court to Review Set-Asides." *Set-Aside Alert*, October 15, 1994.

Ward, James D. "Response to Croson." *Public Administration Review*, September-October 1994, p. 483.

MARTIN V. WILKS

Legal Citation: 490 U.S. 755 (1989)

Petitioner
Robert K. Wilks, et al.

Respondent
John W. Martin, et al.

Petitioner's Claim
That less qualified African Americans were being promoted instead of more qualified caucasians.

Chief Lawyer for Petitioner
Raymond P. Fitzpatrick, Jr.

Chief Lawyers for Respondent
Robert D. Joffe, James P. Alexander

Justices for the Court
Anthony M. Kennedy, Sandra Day O'Connor, William H. Rehnquist (writing for the Court), Antonin Scalia, Byron R. White

Justices Dissenting
Harry A. Blackmun, William J. Brennan, Jr., Thurgood Marshall, John Paul Stevens

Place
Washington, D.C.

Date of Decision
12 June 1989

Decision
Caucasian firefighters not involved in previous civil rights litigation were allowed to claim that promotion decisions after the previous consent decrees were racially discriminatory.

Significance
This was one of the first of many cases involving the issue of reverse discrimination and allowed whites to claim prejudices against minorities.

Beginning in the late 1950s, a growing national awareness triggered one of the greatest periods of federal antidiscrimination legislation. Out of this period came the Civil Rights Act of 1964. In trying to provide a balance for previous discriminatory injustices, it created its own set of problems.

The long circuitous story of *Martin v. Wilks* actually began in 1974. The Ensley Branch of the National Association for the Advancement of Colored People (NAACP) and seven African Americans filed separate class-action complaints against Birmingham, Alabama, and the Jefferson County Personnel Board. They claimed that the city and the board had both hired and promoted firefighters in a racially discriminatory fashion and that these practices violated Title VII of the Civil Rights Act of 1964 and various other federal laws.

Before the case culminated in a judgment, both sides reached a "consent decree." That is, the defendants in the case agreed to cease the discriminatory activities and so the charges were dropped. The city and board devised a sweeping plan that included long-term solutions as well as immediate yearly goals to hire African American firefighters. The decree also included goals for promoting African Americans within the fire department. The district court provisionally approved the decrees and ordered that a notice be published about the upcoming fairness hearings. These notices were published in two local newspapers.

The Birmingham Firefighters Association (BFA) appeared at the hearing and filed objections. Before the decrees were actually approved, the BFA and two members tried to intervene, saying that these decrees would infringe on *their* civil rights. However, the district court ruled that the BFA motion was "untimely," and approved the consent decrees.

At this point, seven caucasian firefighters—all BFA members—filed their own complaint against the city and the board to prevent the decrees from being enforced. The firefighters claimed that the decree would be illegal discrimination against them. The district court ruled against them. The seven firefighters took their case to the U.S. Court of Appeals for the Eleventh Circuit. The appeals court affirmed the district court's previous decision and denied a rehearing.

Reverse Discrimination

"Benign" or "reverse" discrimination stems from problems with affirmation action or preferential treatment programs, which are adopted to specifically aid minorities, but may infringe upon the rights of the majority.

Charges of reverse discrimination have resulted in heated debates and litigation, in the past decade, as majority groups complain about being punished for policies and past discriminatory practices that they did not commit.

While the debate about reverse discrimination is frequently limited to race and ethnic groups, men have complained about discrimination against them as women are promoted and climb the corporate leader.

Source(s): *Constitutional Law*, thirteenth edition. New York: The Foundation Press Inc., 1997.

Later, another group of caucasian firefighters—the Wilks plaintiffs—brought their own suit against Birmingham and the County Personnel Board. They claimed that African Americans were being promoted, not because they were more qualified, but because they were African Americans, in violation the U.S. Constitution and federal laws, including Title VII of the Civil Rights Act of 1964.

Both the city and the board agreed that employment and promotion decisions had been made in favor of African Americans, but the decisions stood because they were made in light of the earlier consent decree. The court allowed several African Americans to defend the decrees—including Martin.

Eventually, the district court dismissed the caucasian firefighters' cases, saying that if the city had hired and promoted African Americans, it was because of the consent decree and therefore there was no case of illegal racial discrimination. In fact, the defendants had demonstrated that the promotion of African Americans was required by one of the consent decrees.

When appealed, the Eleventh Circuit reversed the district court's decision, saying essentially that because Wilks and the others had not been part of the consent decrees, they could claim unlawful reverse discrimination. The court of appeals applauded the worth of sound, voluntary affirmative action plans, but also said that such policies "must yield to the policy against requiring third parties to submit to bargains in which their interests were either ignored or sacrificed." At this point, the case then went to the U.S. Supreme Court.

In a 5-4 decision, the Supreme Court agreed with the appeals court, saying that it was a general principle that

people cannot be deprived of their legal rights when they were not part of a preceding agreement. Specifically, since these firefighters were not participants in the original consent decree, they were free to claim—in a separate district court case—that the promotion decisions made according to the consent decree were racially biased, violating the Constitution and Title VII of the Civil Rights Act of 1964.

In dissent, Justice Stevens said, in part, that just as caucasian employees benefited innocently from illegal racial discrimination, it was inevitable that the same caucasian employees would suffer innocently in sharing some of the load in repairing past damages.

Related Cases
Firefighters v. Cleveland, 478 U.S. 501 (1986).
Wygant v. Jackson Board of Education, 476 U.S. 267 (1986).
Board of Education of the Township of Piscataway v. Taxman, 91 F.3d. 1547 (1996).

Bibliography and Further Reading
Biskupic, Joan, and Elder Witt. *Congressional Quarterly's Guide to the U.S. Supreme Court*, 3rd ed. Washington, DC: Congressional Quarterly, Inc., 1996.

Franke, Janice R. "Retroactivity of the Civil Rights Act of 1991." *American Business Law Journal*, November 1993, p. 483.

Seidman, Louis M., Gerald R. Stone, Cass R. Sunstein, and Mark V. Tushnet. *Constitutional Law*. Boston, MA: Little, Brown and Company, 1986.

Lieberman, Jethro K. *The Evolving Constitution*. New York: Random House, 1992.

METRO BROADCASTING, INC. V. FEDERAL COMMUNICATIONS COMMISSION

Legal Citation: 497 U.S. 547 (1990)

Petitioner
Metro Broadcasting, Inc.

Respondent
Federal Communications Commission

Petitioner's Claim
That federal programs designed to increase minority ownership of broadcast licenses violate the principle of equal protection.

Chief Lawyer for Petitioner
Gregory H. Guillot

Chief Lawyer for Respondent
Daniel M. Armstrong

Justices for the Court
Harry A. Blackmun, William J. Brennan, Jr. (writing for the Court), Thurgood Marshall, John Paul Stevens, Byron R. White

Justices Dissenting
Anthony M. Kennedy, Sandra Day O'Connor, William H. Rehnquist, Antonin Scalia

Place
Washington, D.C.

Date of Decision
27 June 1990

Decision
The Supreme Court upheld Congress's power to enact legislation promoting affirmative action.

Significance
In *Metro Broadcasting*, the Supreme Court for the first time endorsed a federal program intended to promote future minority diversification, rather than merely remedy past racial discrimination.

In 1978, the Federal Communications Commission (FCC) adopted its *Statement of Policy on Minority Ownership of Broadcasting Facilities.* The statement outlined two FCC policies intended to expand minority ownership of broadcast licenses. First, in judging competing license applications, the FCC gave special considerations to those radio or television stations owned or managed by members of minority groups. Second, the FCC permitted a broadcaster who was in danger of losing its license to transfer that license through a so-called "distress sale," but only to a radio or television broadcast organization controlled by members of minority groups. Otherwise, the distressed license holder was obliged to allow the courts to decide who could have the license.

Metro Broadcasting was one of several applicants for a license to operate a new television station in Orlando, Florida. An administrative law judge approved Metro's application. When the FCC reviewed this award, however, it determined that the license should go to one of Metro's competitors, a firm that was 90 percent Hispanic owned. (Metro had only one minority partner who owned 19.8 percent of the company.) Metro appealed this decision to the U.S. Court of Appeals for the District of Columbia. When the court upheld the FCC's decision, Metro took its case to the U.S. Supreme Court.

Supreme Court Upholds Affirmative Action in Broadcasting

In the Supreme Court, Metro challenged the notion that FCC programs aimed at increasing minority ownership would further the national goal of promoting programming diversification. Writing for the Court, Justice Brennan declared that it did. In approving the FCC's policies:

> Congress found that "the effects of past inequities stemming from racial and ethnic discrimination have resulted in a severe underrepresentation of minorities in the media of mass communications." . . . Congress and the Commission do not justify the minority ownership policies strictly as remedies for victims of this discrimination, however. Rather, Con-

gress and the FCC have selected the minority ownership policies primarily to promote programming diversity, and they urge that such diversity is an important governmental objective that can serve as a constitutional basis for the preference policies. We agree.

The FCC adopted the programs at issue specifically in response to a federal law requiring it to promote diversification in programming. Then Congress approved the programs as a valid method of achieving what it considered an important national goal. Whereas in other situations the Court looked with disfavor on statutes that created suspect categories of individuals based on race, here it was prepared to waive the strict scrutiny test. This test required that government use the least disruptive method of advancing a compelling state interest. But in *Metro Broadcasting,* there was a substantial relationship between goals and methods, and that was enough to satisfy five members of the Court.

In an important earlier case concerning affirmative action, *Fullilove v. Klutznick* (1980), the majority gave great weight to the fact that the programs at issue in *Metro Broadcasting* originated with federal legislation. In 1989, the Court had applied strict scrutiny in *Richmond v. J. A. Croson Co.* to defeat a state affirmative action plan on equal protection grounds. A majority of the *Croson* Court distinguished its decision from the decision in *Fullilove* by granting the federal government greater latitude than state governments in enforcing the equal protection mandate of the Fourteenth Amendment. *Metro Broadcasting,* with its emphasis on change rather than compensation, marked a turning point in American social history. With this decision, the Court was, for the first time, giving the federal government more authority than the states had to fashion specific policies for addressing the inequities born of America's racist past.

Related Cases

Fullilove v. Klutznick, 448 U.S. 448 (1980).
Wygant v. Jackson Board of Education, 476 U.S. 267 (1986).
Johnson v. Transportation Agency, 480 U.S. 646 (1987).
Richmond v. J. A. Croson Co., 488 U.S. 469 (1989).

Bibliography and Further Reading

Crenshaw, Kimberle, ed. *Critical Race Theory: The Key Writings that Formed the Movement.* New York, NY: New Press, 1995.

Davis, Abraham L., and Barbara Luck Graham. *The Supreme Court, Race, and Civil Rights.* Thousand Oaks, CA: Sage Publications, 1995.

Gates, E. Nathaniel, ed. *The Judicial Isolation of the "Racially" Oppressed.* New York, NY: Garland, 1997.

Hellman, Deborah. "Two Types of Discrimination: The Familiar and the Forgotten." *California Law Review,* March 1998, p. 315.

ADARAND CONSTRUCTORS, INC. V. PENA

Legal Citation: 512 U.S. 200 (1995)

Petitioner
Adarand Constructors, Inc.

Respondent
Federico Pena, Secretary of Transportation

Petitioner's Claim
That race-based presumptions in federal subcontractor programs violate equal protection under the law.

Chief Lawyer for Petitioner
William Perry Pendley

Chief Lawyer for Respondent
Drew S. Days III, Solicitor General

Justices for the Court
Anthony M. Kennedy, Sandra Day O'Connor (writing for the Court), William H. Rehnquist, Antonin Scalia, Clarence Thomas

Justices Dissenting
Stephen Breyer, Ruth Bader Ginsburg, David H. Souter, John Paul Stevens

Place
Washington, D.C.

Date of Decision
12 June 1995

Decision
Declared that classifications based explicitly on race must be narrowly tailored. The Court furthered compelling government interest by overturning the lower court's ruling against Adarand by a vote of 5-4.

Significance
Although this decision did not prohibit the federal government from involving itself in affirmative action programs, it marked a retreat from the U.S. Supreme Court's earlier endorsement of minority set-aside programs as a remedy for past racial discrimination.

As an element of its affirmative action policy, in the 1960s the federal government adopted Title VII of the Civil Rights Act of 1964 and Executive Orders 10925 and 11246, regulating federal contractors. Such measures were meant to remedy past employment discrimination against minorities. As a result, most federal agency contracts contained a clause giving the primary private contractor a financial incentive to hire subcontractors which have been certified as small businesses controlled by socially and economically disadvantaged individuals. Adarand, a noncertified construction company managed by a white person, submitted the lowest bid on a federal highway project. When it lost out to a certified competitor who had submitted a higher bid, Adarand alleged that this happened only because the "subcontractor compensation clause" in federal agency contracts favored contractors who were members of racial minorities. Such preferences, Adarand alleged, violated the equal protection component of the Fifth Amendment's Due Process Clause.

Adarand lost its suit in the U.S. District Court for the District of Colorado, as well as a subsequent appeal to the U.S. Court of Appeals for the Tenth Circuit. Because the applicable law was unclear, Adarand asked that their case be reviewed by the U.S. Supreme Court. The Supreme Court reversed the lower court's ruling by a vote of 5-4. In the opinion of a majority of the justices, classifications based solely on race are constitutional only if they are narrowly tailored measures that further a compelling government interest. Those in the "subcontractor compensation clause" were not.

Affirmative Action Standards Clarified

In 1980, the U.S. Supreme Court ruled in *Fullilove v. Klutznick* that a 10 percent minority set-aside of federally-funded public works contracts did not violate the equal protection component of the Due Process Clause of the Fifth Amendment. But in 1989, the Court held in *Richmond v. J. A. Croson Company* that state government classifications by race, regardless of whether they were proposed for "remedial" or "benign" purposes, had to be subjected to strict scrutiny in order to pass constitutional muster under the Equal Protection Clause of the Fourteenth Amendment. That is, they must be necessary to achieve a vital governmental interest, and they must be the least intrusive method of achieving that interest. In this case, the Court deemed that the 30 percent of contracts set aside for minority contractors was unconstitutional. When it comes to affirmative action, the Court concluded, states are subject to a different constitutional standard than that which applies to the federal government. Then in 1990, in *Metro Broadcasting, Inc. v. Federal Communications Commission,* the Court indicated what the federal level would be—at least in part. Federal racial categorization for "benign" purposes was to be subjected only to an intermediate level of scrutiny by courts required to rule on their constitutionality.

Metro Broadcasting thus extended *Fullilove,* but *Adarand* marked a significant retreat from the Court's earlier endorsement of so-called minority set-asides as remedial measures. From that point on, federal programs employing racial classifications must, according to the Court's 1995 decision in *Adarand,* meet standards of strict scrutiny. Justice O'Connor, writing for the Court, provided the following justification for partially overruling the more lenient standard the Court had endorsed in *Metro Broadcasting*

> *Metro Broadcasting* undermined important principles of this Court's equal protection jurisprudence, established in a line of cases stretching back over fifty years . . . Those principles together stood for an "embracing" and "intrinsically soun[d]" understanding of equal protection "verified by experience," namely that the Constitution imposes on federal, state, and local governmental actors the same obligation to respect the personal right to equal protection of the laws . . . we cannot adhere to our most recent decision without colliding with an accepted and established doctrine. We also note that *Metro Broadcasting*'s application of different standards of review to federal and state racial classifications has been consistently criticized by commentators.

As this last comment makes clear, the Supreme Court has itself contributed to the confusion surrounding the affirmative action issue. And *Adarand* did not resolve all of this confusion: while the federal government is still permitted to pursue remedial policies, by essentially outlawing race-based preferences, the Court has left the future course of affirmative action in employment in doubt.

Related Cases

Fullilove v. Klutznick, 448 U.S. 448 (1980).
Richmond v. J. A. Croson Co., 488 U.S. 469 (1989).
Metro Broadcasting, Inc. v. Federal Communications Commission, 497 U.S. 547 (1990).

Bibliography and Further Reading

"Adarand Won't Affect DBE Program, DOT Says." *Set-Aside Alert,* July 4, 1997.

"Changes to Affirmative Action Programs Are Inevitable." *Set-Aside Alert,* October 24, 1997.

"Court Decreases Opportunity for Minority Firm." *Planning,* August 1995, p. 20.

Coyle, Marcia. "Supreme Court Ponders Racial Set-Aside Case." *The National Law Journal,* January 23, 1995, p. A1.

Gest, Ted. "Back to the Politicians: Supreme Court Ruling in Adarand Constructors v. Pena Affirmative Action Case." *U.S. News & World Report,* June 26, 1995, pp. 38-39.

Greenhouse, Linda. "Affirmative Action Challenge Seems to Perplex Court: Minority Set-Aside Case." *New York Times,* January 18, 1995, p. D20.

Hair, Penda D. "Color-Blind—or Just Blind? In Affirmative Action Cases, 'Race' is Becoming a Four-Letter Word." *The Nation,* October 14, 1996, p. 12.

"In the Year Since Adarand: What the Courts Have Said So Far." *Set-Aside Alert,* September 9, 1996.

Kaveny, M. Cathleen. "Discrimination and Affirmative Action." *Theological Studies,* June 1996, pp. 286-301.

Lacovara, Philip Allen. "The Supreme Court Ruling That Curtailed Race-Based Federal Affirmative-Action Programs Has Left the Private Sector Wondering If Its Programs May Be Next." *The National Law Journal,* 17 July 1995, p. B5.

"Legislative Background: Recent Action on Affirmative Action." *Congressional Digest,* June-July 1996, p. 171.

Lorber, Lawrence, and J. Robert Kirk. "Supreme Court Didn't Kill Affirmative Action." *The National Law Journal,* July 3, 1995, p. A21.

Mishkind, Charles S. "Reverse Discrimination/Affirmative Action Litigation Update: Where Is It Going?" *Employee Relations Law Journal,* winter 1996, p. 107.

Murrell, Audrey J., and Ray Jones. "Assessing Affirmative Action: Past, Present, and Future." *Journal of Social Issues,* winter 1996, p. 77.

Reade, Steven G., and Rosemary Maxwell. "Federal Affirmative Action Programs, Following Adarand, are Being Revamped to Promote Diversity Through Measures That Don't Use Racial or Gender Preferences." *The National Law Journal,* February 19, 1996, p. B6.

Rice, Mitchell F., and Maurice Mongkuo. "Did Adarand Kill Minority Set-Asides?" *Public Administration Review,* January-February 1998, p. 82.

Robinson, Anthony W. "The Affirmative Action Debate." *Emerge,* November 1996, p. 66.

Rubenfeld, Jed. "Affirmative Action." *Yale Law Journal,* November 1997, p. 427.

"Supreme Court Strikes Blow to Preferences." *Set-Aside Alert,* June 19, 1995.

PISCATAWAY TOWNSHIP BOARD OF EDUCATION V. TAXMAN

Legal Citation: 91 F.3d 1547 (3rd Cir. 1996)

Petitioner
Picataway Township Board of Education

Respondent
Sharon Taxman

Petitioner's Claim
That the Piscataway Board of Education's decision to dismiss a white teacher in order to keep a comparably qualified African American teacher on staff was valid under Title VII of the Civil Rights Act of 1964.

Chief Lawyer for Petitioner
David B. Rubin

Chief Lawyer for Respondent
Stephen E. Klausner

Justices for the Court
Samuel A. Alito, Jr., Edward R. Becker, Robert E. Cowen, Morton I. Greenberg, Carol Los Mansmann (writing for the Court), Richard Lowell Nygaard, Jane R. Roth, H. Lee Sarokin, Walter K. Stapleton

Justices Dissenting
Timothy K. Lewis, Theodore Alexander McKee, Anthony J. Scirica, Dolores K. Sloviter

Place
Washington, D.C.

Date of Decision
14 May 1996

Decision
Piscataway Board of Education's action in dismissing Taxman was held to be a violation of her civil rights.

Significance
The case of *Board of Education of Picataway v. Sharon Taxman* was on its way to the U.S. Supreme Court when a coalition of civil rights groups raised the money to settle the case. The civil rights leaders and the board of education agreed that defeat in the High Court—which seemed likely—would represent a major blow to the cause of affirmative action. Citing the legal dictum that "bad cases make bad law," they preferred to fight the battle over racial preferences in hiring at another time, over a different set of circumstances.

Taxman Fights Dismissal on Racial Grounds

In 1989, the Board of Education of Piscataway, New Jersey received instructions from the school's superintendent to lay off one of the teachers in its business department. At the time, two teachers with equal seniority—having started work on the same day nine years earlier—were on the staff: Sharon Taxman, who was white, and Debra Williams, who was African American. Williams was the only minority teacher in the business department staff. The board conducted a thorough review of the job performance of each teacher and concluded that they were of equal ability and with equal qualifications. In previous cases where seniority or job performance could not be used to determine which staff member to dismiss, the board had simply drawn lots or numbers out of a container. In this case, however, the superintendent of schools decided that affirmative action should be used to "break the tie" between the instructors. Accordingly, he instructed the board to retain Williams and dismiss Taxman. In his view, keeping the only African American teacher on the business faculty would send a message to Piscataway's racially mixed student body that the school board was committed to tolerance and diversity.

Sharon Taxman did not see the issue that way. She filed a complaint with the Equal Employment Opportunity Commission (EEOC), contending that she had been laid off solely on the basis of her race, in violation of Title VII of the Civil Rights Act of 1964. After attempts to resolve the dispute proved unsuccessful, she filed a lawsuit on those same grounds, gaining the support of the U.S. Justice Department. In her lawsuit, Taxman asked for back pay and reinstatement to her old position. In 1992, the board of education rehired Taxman. Nevertheless, she continued to pursue her suit to retrieve lost wages.

Taxman's case first came before a U.S. district court. The judge there ruled in her favor, holding the board liable for discrimination on the basis of race and awarding her $144,000 in damages. The court also ordered the board to give Taxman full seniority reflecting continuous employment from 1980. The board of education then appealed this decision to the U.S. Court of Appeals for the Third Circuit. That court affirmed the district court's decision on 14 May 1996.

Court of Appeals Ruling

The court of appeals defined the issue in simple terms: to decide "whether Title VII permits an employer with a racially balanced work force to grant a non-remedial racial preference in order to promote racial diversity." In other words, they asked whether the Piscataway Board of Education could employ racial hiring preferences even in a case where it was not addressing a past wrong, i.e. discrimination against African Americans in hiring. In boiling down the issue to that question, the court first had to establish that the dismissal of Taxman did not have any remedial basis. It did so in short order, declaring upon a review of the evidence that "black teachers were neither underrepresented nor underutilized in the Piscataway School District work force." In fact, statistics cited by the court showed that the percentage of African American teachers exceeded the percentage of African Americans in the available work force. Thus "the Board's sole purpose in applying its affirmative action policy in this case was to obtain an educational benefit which it believed would result from a racially diverse faculty," Judge Mansmann wrote in his majority opinion.

While lauding this goal in theory, Mansmann found that the board's policy, "devoid of goals and standards, is governed entirely by the Board's whim, leaving the Board free, if it so chooses, to grant racial preferences that do not promote even the policy's claimed purpose. Indeed, under the terms of this policy, the board, in pursuit of a racially diverse work force, could use affirmative action to discriminate against those whom Title VII was enacted to protect. Such a policy unnecessarily trammels the interests of nonminority employees." Accordingly, the court of appeals affirmed the judgment of the district court and awarded back pay to Taxman. It did not, however, grant her claim to punitive damages, because in the court's view, the board had not acted "willfully, wantonly, or outrageously" in this matter.

Dissent and Aftermath

A number of impassioned dissents occurred in the case. Citing the belief "that students derive educational benefit by having a black faculty member in an otherwise all-white department," Chief Judge Sloviter would have left it up to the discretion of the school board which teacher to dismiss. Judge Scirica echoed these sentiments, adding: "I do not believe Title VII prevents a school district, in the exercise of its professional judgment, from preferring one equally qualified teacher over another for a valid educational purpose"— namely, racial diversity. Judge Lewis thought the majority's decision "eviscerates the purpose and the goals of Title VII" and set a horrific precedent for future cases.

The Board of Education of Piscataway did not accept the court of appeals ruling and appealed its case to the U.S. Supreme Court. The case seemed destined to

Sharon Taxman, 1997. © AP/Wide World Photos.

become a major litmus test of the High Court's thinking on affirmative action. But as the day of decision neared, civil rights leaders and other supporters of affirmative action began to fear that the board's case was not morally clear and therefore ill-suited to be a testing ground for the legality of affirmative action in general. Accordingly, in November of 1997, a coalition of civic leaders and civil rights groups decided to raise enough money to settle the case with Sharon Taxman. The school board agreed to pay her more than $400,000, 70 percent of which came from outside sources. The decision of the court of appeals was allowed to stand, and the Supreme Court never heard the case.

Impact

The case of *Piscataway Township Board of Education v. Taxman* required the court of appeals to carefully reexamine Title VII of the Civil Rights Act. Title VII was enacted to further two primary goals: to end discrimination on the basis of race, color, religion, sex or national origin, thereby guaranteeing equal opportunity in the workplace, and to remedy the segregation and underrepresentation of minorities in the work force. A coalition of civil rights groups believed that a successful challenge by Sharon Taxman in the Supreme

Court could have undermined affirmative action through the invocation of Title VII by aggrieved whites in similar circumstances.

Related Cases

Albemarle Paper Co. v. Moody, 422 U.S. 405 (1975).
McDonald v. Santa Fe Trail Transportation Co., 427 U.S. 273 (1976).
United Steelworkers v. Weber, 443 U.S. 193 (1979).
Johnson v. Transportation Agency, Santa Clara County, 480 U.S. 616 (1987).

Bibliography and Further Reading

"Affirmative Action-Settlement Avoids Supreme Court Ruling." *Jet,* December 8, 1997, p. 56.

Barnes, Julian E. "Rights Groups Choose to Settle." *U.S. News & World Report,* December 1, 1997, p. 41.

"The Battle of Piscataway." *The Economist,* August 30, 1997, p. 17.

Hayes, Susan, and Rex Roberts. "A Case of Black and White." *Scholastic Update,* November 3, 1997, p. 2.

Kurtzamn, Daniel. "Legal Experts Welcome Settlement of Schools Case." *Jewish News of Greater Phoenix,* November 28, 1997.

"Piscataway Amicus Project." *Americans United for Affirmative Action,* February 16, 1999, http://www.auaa.org/piscat/index.html.

Reibstein, Larry. "A Tactical Retreat in a Race Case; Civil Rights Leaders Buy Themselves Out of a Bind." *Newsweek,* December 1, 1997, p. 40.

Simpson, Michael D. "What Role Does Race Play?" *NEA Today,* January 1998, p. 25.

Teubner, Gary. "Settlement Avoids Legal Defeat for Affirmative Action." *Seattle Times,* November 22, 1997.

Zirkel, Perry A. "Affirmative Action? It's a Tossup." *Phi Delta Kappan,* December 1996, p. 332.

HOPWOOD V. TEXAS

Legal Citation: 78 F.3d 932 (5th Cir. 1996), 84 F.3d 720 (5th Cir.).

Plaintiff
Cheryl J. Hopwood, et al.

Defendant
State of Texas, et al.

Plaintiff's Claim
That the admissions policy at the University of Texas Law School gave unfair advantage to minority applicants over whites.

Chief Lawyer for Plaintiff
Steven Wayne Smith, Michael Rosman

Chief Defense Lawyer
Members of the firm Vinson & Elkins.

Judges for the Court
Harold R. DeMoss, Jacques L. Wiener, Jr., Jerry E. Smith (writing for the court)

Judges Dissenting
None

Place
New Orleans, Louisiana

Date of Decision
18 March 1996

Decision
That the University of Texas Law School's admissions policy violated the civil rights of four non-minority applicants by using race as a criterion in granting admittance.

Significance
The Fifth U.S. Circuit Court of Appeals decision was both heralded and decried as the end of affirmative action. Hopwood and three others had sued the University of Texas because they had been denied admission to its law school in 1992. They charged the institution with "reverse discrimination"—passing them over for admission in favor of minorities with lower test scores and grades. Although critics of affirmative action had often campaigned for an end to all "race-based preference systems," the *Hopwood* decision was, on paper, an assertion that the particular policy used by the University of Texas Law School violated a 1978 Supreme Court landmark ruling on affirmative action.

Denied Admission

Cheryl Hopwood was one of several non-minority students rejected when she applied for admission to the University of Texas Law School in 1992. Hopwood was about 30 at the time, and had once successfully applied to an Ivy League school for undergraduate study, but was forced to decline because she could not afford it. Instead she attended community colleges in Indiana and California, where she earned a 3.8 grade-point average (GPA) while working 20 to 30 hours a week and doing volunteer work. Hopwood eventually became a certified public accountant, and married. Her first daughter was born with severe health problems, which required her to spend a great deal of time caring for her.

Hopwood's coplaintiffs in the suit against the University of Texas had less distressing circumstances. They were David Rogers, Douglas Wade Carvell, and Kenneth Elliott. All had been rejected by the admissions committee because of either poor test scores or poor academic performance in their undergraduate studies. All four had each received letters from an Austin lawyer, who had obtained the names of those passed over by the admissions committee.

Millions in Damages

With the help of the Washington, D.C.-based Center for Individual Rights, a libertarian-focused, public-interest law firm, their suit was filed on 29 September 1992 against the state of Texas, the Board of Regents of the Texas State University System, the University of Texas Law School, and several individual university officials. Hopwood requested injunctive relief—admittance to the University of Texas Law School—plus $1.3 million in damages, which reflected the projected career earnings had she, in fact, graduated from law school, passed the bar exam, and practiced law. Her petition also asked for an additional $1.5 million for emotional distress. The other plaintiffs also requested compensation from the University of Texas.

The *Hopwood* case first went to trial in the U.S. District Court for the Western District of Texas, Austin Division, in May of 1994. That court found for the University of Texas, and denied injunctive relief and dam-

University Race Quotas

Using race quotas assures that students receive not only a good education, but are exposed to different races and ethnic backgrounds that will prove invaluable in years to come as they enter the work force. Additionally, race quotas help ensure that individuals who have faced discrimination in the past will now be given opportunities previously denied to them. Finally, they can help to correct a racial imbalance in the student body.

However racial quotas are a violation of the Fourteenth Amendment's Equal Protection Clause and thus they should not be used. Discrimination regardless of the motivation is wrong in any form. "Racial preferences appear to 'even the score' . . . only if one embraces the proposition that our society is appropriately viewed as divided into races, making it right than an injustice rendered in the past to a black man should be compensated for by discrimination against a white," wrote Justice Antonin Scalia in *Richmond v. J. A. Croson Co.*

Source(s): *Constitutional Law,* 13th ed. NY: The Foundation Press Inc., 1997.

ages, though it did note that the admissions policy was in violation of the Fourteenth Amendment giving all U.S. citizens equal protection under the law. The decision was appealed and landed on the docket of the next highest court, the Fifth U.S. Circuit Court of Appeals in New Orleans.

The Terms of the Complaint

In their case, the plaintiffs asserted that the University of Texas admissions policy violated their civil rights under Title VI of the Civil Rights Act of 1964. The provision states that:

> No person in the United States shall, on the ground of race, color, or national origin, be excluded from participation in, be denied the benefits of, or be subjected to discrimination under any program or activity reserving Federal financial assistance.

During the court proceedings, officials at the University of Texas revealed that they admitted students under a policy that dealt with non-minorities and "protected" minorities (Hispanic and African American) separately, which is called "dual admissions" and is, under the terms of a 1978 U.S. Supreme Court ruling, unconstitutional. In *University of California v. Bakke* (1978) the Court declared that race was an acceptable factor in a school's admissions policy, provided it was used to correct past discrimination, and to achieve a more diverse student body. It gave approval to using race as a determining factor on an individual basis in considering applicants, but did not allow for a separate system of consideration with lower admissions standards for minorities. The Court also noted that "quotas," or reserving a certain number of places in a school for minorities, was unlawful.

The Former Policy

Some legal analysts found *Hopwood* a poor test case for affirmative action, since the University of Texas Law School so clearly violated the *Bakke* ruling with its policy. Yet that policy had been in place at the University of Texas since 1983, and had been designed to help Hispanic and African American students overcome biases in standardized tests. Arguments questioning the fairness of standardized tests had been supported by data from several studies over the years which had detected such biases. Education specialists also noted that such tests were not always a good predictor of overall academic performance.

The University of Texas Law School had revised its admissions policy by the time *Hopwood* was decided in 1996. However the particulars of the former policy were explained in court. First, applicants were classed according to a "Texas Index" number (TI). This was the score yielded by combining an applicant's GPA with the standardized Law School Admissions Test (LSAT). This landed the applicants into three slots: either presumptive admit, presumptive deny, or discretionary zone. Hopwood first achieved a TI number of 199, which placed her in the presumptive admit category. These same applications were then reviewed to determine whether their high GPA was simply the result of attending a noncompetitive college. Hopwood's was placed in the discretionary zone pile for this reason.

The University of Texas admissions committee then reviewed those applicants in the presumptive deny category to determine whether any mitigating factors were in place. This caused some of the applicants who had been initially rejected to be placed in the discretionary zone category. The committee then set two presumptive admit and denial lines, with lower requirements for minorities. Finally, the discretionary zone candidates were divided into minority and non-minority piles, and reviewed independently. A subcommittee then evaluated the minority applications and made recommendations for admittance. A random three-member panel of the admissions committee reviewed the nonminority applications in the discretionary zone in batches of 30 and made recommendations for admittance. If an applicant received two or three votes from a committee member, their application would be upgraded and they would be offered a spot on the waiting list.

When Hopwood's file was screened as part of the discretionary zone procedure, she received one vote for admission. The same determination was made for Carvell. Both were placed on the waiting list, but were denied admittance when no slots became available as other candidates accepted their offers of enrollment.

The Arguments For and Against Hopwood

Hopwood's particular circumstances and rejection of her application were cited as proof that in some instances, affirmative action policies might work in "reverse." She had survived a difficult background, and excelled in school despite economic and personal hardships. Indeed, Hopwood did have slightly better grades and higher LSAT scores than some of the minority students who were admitted to University of Texas, but admissions committee members explained that several other factors were taken into consideration. Her degree from a noncompetitive school was one determinant. A second determinant was the fact that it had taken her six years to earn an associate's (two-year) degree.

Furthermore, most of Hopwood's high marks had been earned in technical courses, not the kind of analytical ones that law-school professors consider necessary training ground for a legal career. Lawyers for the University of Texas also pointed out that Hopwood's application, as well as those of her coplaintiffs, was lacking. She did not write a personal statement, and included no letters of recommendation, both of which are taken into consideration by committee members.

One of Hopwood's coplaintiffs had included a letter of recommendation from a former professor that was anything but positive. Another plaintiff had been denied admission to several other graduate schools, and upon his University of Texas rejection, his father penned a letter to the dean that complained about "mandatory minority and women quotas." This particular candidate's application was then reconsidered, and one University of Texas official said he was then offered admittance. Both the plaintiff and school officials denied this.

To present their argument, the University of Texas defense team was supported by an expert on causation, Olin Guy Wellborn. This University of Texas law professor and member of the admissions committee, investigated whether the four would have been admitted under a more "constitutional" system that did not have dual standards. Wellborn concluded that there would have been little change in the final selection. The plaintiffs whose application had landed in the "discretionary zone" category—where they were then reviewed individually—would not have received the "yes" votes that would have placed them on the acceptance list or even the waiting list.

The Decision

A three-judge panel of the Fifth U. S. Circuit Court of Appeals declared the University of Texas Law School admission policy unconstitutional. Later, it awarded Hopwood $6,000 in emotional damages. The appeals court theorized that the severe hardships she underwent since the rejection of her University of Texas application—she gave birth to a second daughter in 1993, who died a day later, was separated from her husband in 1995, and her first daughter died later that year—would have made it quite difficult for her to complete the demanding requirements for a law degree.

The Fifth Circuit's decision, technically, barred Texas universities from using race as a basis for admission or financial aid. The University of Texas appealed the decision to the Supreme Court. However, the Supreme Court denied the writ of *certiorari*, or request to review the case.

An End to Affirmative Action?

There remained a great deal of confusion over the terms of the *Hopwood* ruling. Was it specific to just the Uni-

David Rogers, a plaintiff in Hopwood v. Texas, *meets with reporters, 1998.© AP/Wide World Photos.*

*Attorney Steve Smith,
for the plaintiff in
Hopwood v. Texas,
speaks to the House
Committee on Higher
Education, 1997.
© AP/Wide World
Photos.*

versity of Texas and its admission policy, which had since been revised, or did it apply to all state universities inside the jurisdiction of the Fifth Circuit—which included Mississippi and Louisiana as well? Conservatives, who favored the dismantling of affirmative action programs, asserted that the *Hopwood* decision applied across the board.

Just over three months after the *Hopwood* ruling, Texas State Attorney General Dan Morales said that the court's decision should be applied to all Texas schools, not just the University of Texas Law School. In response, Norma Cantu, Assistant Secretary for Civil Rights in the U.S. Department of Education, issued a letter to lawmakers that disagreed with Morales. Cantu declared that the case only applied to the University of Texas Law School's admissions policy, and that the University of Texas system could lose up to $500 million in federal funding if it revoked its affirmative action practices in undergraduate admissions and financial aid.

Senator Phil Gramm drafted a letter to U.S. Secretary of Education Richard Riley stating that the Department of Education needed to revise its position, and that Cantu should retract her statement. The problem was eventually resolved when Cantu's warning was attributed to her "misinterpretation" of two separate government policy statements on the matter. The "compromise" seemed to reflect the Clinton Administration's stance on the matter: "Mend it, but don't end it," which the president proposed in a 1995 speech on affirmative action.

The *Hopwood* decision initiated a great deal of discussion in higher education circles, and there were numerous conferences and debates on the case over the

next year. Supporters of affirmative action say that forced diversity in higher education benefits everybody—it brings more opinions and more viewpoints to classroom discussion. A year after the *Hopwood* ruling, statistics showed a decrease in minority applications at Texas state schools. The University of Texas Law School alone saw a 40 percent decline in minority applications. Qualified minority candidates simply applied elsewhere. Opponents of affirmative action noted that a new requirement for a written essay may have had some effect on the decrease in applications.

Affirmative action remains a divisive political issue inside for public officials. However, a *U.S. News & World Report* article suggests that the American public is not preoccupied with the issue. It cited a poll that showed a greater number of respondents would rather see the Internal Revenue Service abolished than affirmative action programs. In May of 1997, the Texas Senate passed a bill designed to replace affirmative action, which allowed the 35 state universities to grant automatic admission to high school graduates who finished in the top ten percent of their class. The universities would then be allowed to take into account other admission factors such as language proficiency, family educational history, and community service.

Other institutions' schemes to eliminate race as a factor in admissions have resulted in a marked change in diversity. The University of California at Berkeley reformed its admissions guidelines beginning in 1989, and witnessed a drop by 1994 in the number of Hispanics enrolled (from 21 to 17 percent) and blacks (11 to 7 percent), while the number Asian students climbed from 24 to 36 percent.

In other related developments, California voters approved Proposition 209 in late 1996. It called for an end to all of the state's affirmative action programs which had faced a series of court challenges before implementation. The law firm in the *Hopwood* case also challenged admission policies at the University of Michigan, taking on the case of several non-minority students who had been denied admission.

Related Cases

University of California v. Bakke, 438 U.S. 265 (1978).
Hunter by Brandt v. Regent of the University of California, 971 F.Supp. 1316 (1997).
Wessmann by Wessmann v. Boston School Committee, 996 F.Supp. 120 (1998).

Bibliography and Further Reading

"After *Hopwood.*" *Change,* September/October 1996, p. 4.

Edley, Christopher Jr. "Affirmative Action Angst." *Change,* September/October 1996, pp. 13-15.

Elliott, Janet. " *Hopwood* Goes Back to Court." *Legal Times,* April 28, 1997.

Fernandez, Cristina D. "Unmasking *Hopwood.*" *Hispanic,* November 1996.

Hansen, Mark. "The Great Admissions Debate." *ABA Journal,* June 1997, p. 28.

Hentoff, Nat. "Cheryl Hopwood vs. State of Texas." *Village Voice,* November 25, 1997, p. 22.

Hoover, Rusty. "White U-M Hopefuls Get a Break." *Detroit News,* June 14, 1998.

Lum, Lydia. "Difference of Opinion About *Hopwood.*" *Houston Chronicle,* March 25, 1997.

———. "University Applications by Minorities Down." *Houston Chronicle,* April 7, 1997.

Ratcliffe, R. G. "Senate Approves Bill Designed to Boost Minority Enrollments." *Houston Chronicle,* May 8, 1997.

"The *Hopwood* Effect Kicks in On Campus." *U.S. News & World Report,* December 23, 1996, pp. 26-28.

Verhovek, Sam Howe. "For 4 Whites Who Sued University, Race Is the Common Thread." *New York Times,* March 23, 1996, sec. I, p. 6.

ASSISTED SUICIDE AND THE RIGHT TO DIE

History

Although the issues of assisted suicide and the right to die have made headlines for over 20 years, these ideas are not new. In the ancient civilization of Rome, suicide was not punishable if "it was caused by impatience of pain or sickness, or by weariness of life . . . lunacy, or fear of dishonor." Irrational suicide was punishable by the emperor's seizure of all of the victim's property, disinheriting the heirs. The Romans' philosophy was "To live nobly also means to die nobly and at the right time." By the mid-twentieth century, technological advances kept terminally ill and vegetative patients alive longer than ever before. These patients previously would have died quickly from an inability to eat and drink and other complications. But advances in medical science brought right to die issues into the lives of many dying patients and their families. Doctors, patients and families were forced to make decisions about when life should end.

An Ethical Dilemma

The 1975 case of Karen Ann Quinlan was publicized nationwide, illustrating the ethical dilemma that exists because of the use of modern medical equipment such as mechanical respirators and feeding tubes. Quinlan had suffered a respiratory arrest, leaving her in a permanent vegetative state. Her family, in a long legal battle, argued that their daughter would not want to be kept alive in this way, with no hope for recovery. The court eventually granted the Quinlans the right to remove Karen from life support. This case helped define this gray but growing area of ethical and legal controversy. Court cases, such as the U.S. Supreme Court case of *Cruzan v. Director, Missouri Department of Health* (1990), have helped define policy on these issues. Society has become more accepting of policies that honor a terminally ill patient's request to withhold or withdraw medical interventions. However, the issue of assisted suicide, the act of hastening death, has not achieved the same level of comfort for many people.

In June of 1997, the U.S. Supreme Court reaffirmed the right to die in its decisions in the *Washington v. Glucksberg* and *Vacco v. Quill* cases, but emphasized the difference between these types of end-of-life decisions,

"pulling the plug," and physician-assisted suicide. In these cases the Court found that assisted suicide was not a constitutional right and left it to the states to decide whether or not to legalize assisted suicide. An individual's right to refuse treatment is still valid when he or she becomes incompetent. All 50 states and the District of Columbia authorize the use of a written advance medical directive to help honor the decisions of those who are not able to speak for themselves but who have recorded their wishes in a living will or medical power of attorney. Oregon was the first state authorizing physician-assisted suicide in specific circumstances. While Oregon voters had approved the Oregon Death With Dignity Act in November of 1994, the act was challenged in court and enactment was delayed. In February of 1997, the U.S. Supreme Court refused to hear the appeal after the Ninth Circuit Court of Appeals held that the plaintiffs did not have cause to challenge the act. In a repeat voter referendum in November of 1997, Oregon voters refused to repeal the act. Assisted suicide proponents view the issue as an extension of an individual's right to decide on his or her final care. Opponents argue that if assisted suicide is legalized on a national basis, many elderly and dependent individuals will feel guilty for being alive and for not making a substantial contribution to society and will feel obligated to commit suicide.

One supporter of the cause, Dr. Jack Kevorkian of Michigan, otherwise known as "Dr. Death," deserves mention since he has assisted over 120 individuals with their own suicide. Dr. Kevorkian has been jailed, gone on hunger strikes, lost his medical license, dropped the bodies of his patients at the hospital after their deaths, and appeared in court countless times in such attire as a sackcloth and in seventeenth century costumes. His outlandish behavior has attracted attention to the right to die/assisted suicide cause, but some supporters say his behavior has done more harm than good. Recently, he was convicted of second-degree murder in a trial expected to be appealed.

Eight Representative Cases

Recent court cases which played roles in the overall development of policy were:

Sneider v. Abeliuk (California, 1997): The plaintiff sought to recover medical expenses incurred for undesired treatment rendered after a valid decision was made to withhold life support. The action was based on battery, invasion of privacy, interference with personal relationships and violation of constitutional rights. A jury trial was held and the jurors ruled unanimously that the medical center was not at fault. However, the claims of battery for nonconsensual medical care have been well established in a variety of medical situations.

McIver v. Krischer (Florida, 1997): The court maintained that a terminally ill, competent adult, acting under no undue influence, has a constitutional right to choose to accelerate his own death by requesting from his physician a fatal dose of prescription drugs and then thereafter administering them to himself. The court ruled that a state ban on assisted suicide violated both the Florida Privacy Amendment and the Equal Protection Clause of the Fourteenth Amendment to the United States Constitution. The state appealed and the Florida Supreme Court heard oral arguments on 9 May 1997. In *Krischer v. McIver* the Court, in a 5-1 ruling, reversed the decision of the trial court, asserting that Florida's ban on physician-assisted suicide did not violate the Privacy Amendment to Florida's state constitution. Also, the Court, in conformance with the U.S. Supreme Court's recent decisions, held that the ban did not violate the Equal Protection Clause or the Due Process Clause of the U.S. Constitution.

In re Fetus Brown (Illinois, 1997): This case was brought to the appellate court to determine whether a competent, pregnant woman's right to refuse medical treatment can be overridden by the state's interest in the survival of a viable fetus. In this particular case, the pregnant woman was a Jehovah's Witness who refused blood transfusions after a surgery which would save both her life and the life of the fetus. Upon a decision of the circuit court, the woman was restrained, sedated and received a blood transfusion. Several days later she delivered a healthy baby. The woman appealed the circuit court's decision to the appellate court. The appellate court held that "the State may not override a pregnant woman's competent treatment decision, including refusal of recommended invasive medical procedures, to save the life of a viable fetus."

Osgood v. Genesys Regional Medical Center (Michigan, 1997): A Michigan circuit court asserted that Genesys Regional Medical Center was guilty of battery when it misrepresented the nature of the medical procedures it performed as the procedures were in direct opposition to the patient advocate's directions and the directions of the durable power of attorney for health care. A jury awarded damages of approximately $16 million for mental anguish and for incurred and anticipated expenses for medical care and treatment. However, the court reduced the damage award. After further settlement negotiations, neither party appealed the decision.

Anderson v. St. Frances-St. George Hospital (Ohio, 1996): The Ohio Supreme Court specifically recognized that nonconsensual medical treatment is considered battery and may entitle a plaintiff to some relief. The plaintiff was resuscitated despite the existence of a properly issued do-not-resuscitate order and then suffered a disabling stroke several days later. The court, by refusing to recognize a cause of action for "wrongful life" leaves a person with an assault and battery cause of action. However, by using standard and restrictive "causation" analysis, the court ensured that not even battery damages would be recoverable, unless the battery caused subsequent medical injury which caused damage to the patient.

Lee v. Oregon (Oregon, 1997): The U.S. district court held that Oregon's Death with Dignity Act (Measure 16), the first law in the nation to legally authorize physician-assisted suicide, violated the Equal Protection Clause because the safeguards were not sufficient to protect the rights of terminally ill patients who may seek assisted suicide. The Ninth Circuit Court of Appeals, in a 3-0 vote, found that the plaintiffs had no legal standing to challenge Measure 16 because they failed to show any threat of immediate harm and their claim rested upon a "chain of speculative contingencies." The court did not decide the constitutional merits of physician-assisted suicide. The U.S. Supreme Court refused to hear the appeal and in November of 1997 the Oregon voters, in a repeat voter referendum on the issue, refused to repeal the act.

In re Fiori (Pennsylvania, 1996): The court ruled that where there is insufficient evidence of a patient's wishes as to the withdrawal of life-sustaining treatment and the patient is in a permanent vegetative state, then close family members may substitute their own judgment and, with the concurrence of two qualified physicians, order the withdrawal of life-sustaining treatment without seeking court approval. The court was careful to note that the ruling addressed only the narrow issue of whether life support may be terminated for a person in a persistent vegetative state who, when competent, never expressed desires as to specific medical treatment or withdrawal of such.

Compassion In Dying v. Washington (Washington, 1996): The Ninth Circuit Court, after an *en banc* hearing, ruled that the Washington State statute that prohibits assisted suicide is unconstitutional because it implicates the liberty interest of the Fourteenth Amendment. The court specifically ruled that the U.S. Constitution protects the right of competent, terminally ill patients to receive, and the right of physicians to prescribe, medications for the purpose of committing suicide.

Refusal of Treatment

An individual has a constitutional right to request the withdrawal or withholding of medical treatment, even if doing so will result in the person's death. Honoring a person's right to refuse medical treatment, especially at the end of life, is the most widely practiced and accepted right to die procedure in our society. Recent debates over the futility of certain medical treatments, rationing of treatment and the growth of managed care have caused patients' rights advocates to examine the other side of patient autonomy—the right to request or demand treatment. Some ethicists and health care professionals believe that patient autonomy has already gone too far and should be subject to limitations, and that a patient or a patient's family does not have the right to request treatment that is inappropriate or futile. However, a consensus has not been reached about what constitutes inappropriate or futile treatment. As a result, no explicit blueprints exist for circumstances in which patients and their families disagree with their doctor's advice to abandon treatment. The assumption has been that most health care providers, assured that the law permits them to do so, will respect their patient's decisions, or that of their patient's appointed representative. Because of that erroneous assumption, most advance directive laws have imposed no adverse consequences on providers who do not follow the instructions of an advance directive, and may have advanced the belief among some that noncompliance is legally acceptable. In recent years, the outcomes of medical battery cases in which a health care provider imposes medical treatment contrary to the instructions left in an advance directive may change that climate. Claims of battery against physicians for medical care not requested or agreed-upon have been recognized despite the fact that the medical procedure may have been harmless, beneficial, or life-sustaining. If it was performed without the consent of the patient, or the patient's agent, it can be considered a battery.

One case involving medical futility was the 1992 case of "Baby K," an infant born with anencephaly in a Virginia hospital. Anencephalic babies, who are born missing most of their brain, are treated with comfort measures only. However, "Baby K's" mother insisted on aggressive treatment. The physicians treating her believed that it was inappropriate to pursue aggressive treatment for an anencephalic baby and asked a federal court in Virginia to rule on the case. The court ruled that the hospital cannot deny emergency care to any patient, including "Baby K." Ethicists remain divided on this and other such decisions. Some insist that such painful decisions should be made by those closest to the patient. Others contend that the court's ruling to continue futile treatment threatens the medical profession's integrity. As rising health care costs increasingly become a societal focus, difficult decisions must be faced regarding whether or not patient autonomy should be limited and how. The courts are becoming more and more willing to find that battery has occurred in cases in which a health care provider refused to honor the directions left in an advance directive or given by an appointed agent. This trend may serve to make health care providers more aware of the legal responsibility to honor their patients' right to self-determination.

Bibliography and Further Reading

American Civil Liberties Union, American Civil Liberties Union Freedom Network, New York, NY, http://www.aclu.org, 1998.

Cornell Law School, Legal Information Institute, Ithaca, NY, http://www.law.cornell.edu. 1998.

Euthanasia World Directory, Junction City, OR, http://www.efn.org/~ergo, 1998.

Findlaw Internet Legal Resources, Palo Alto, CA, http://www.findlaw.com, 1994-1998.

InfoSynthesis, Inc., Home of the "USSC+" database of Supreme Court Opinions, St. Paul, MN, http://www.usscplus.com, 1998.

McDiarmid, Hugh. "Kevorkian's Theatrics Worry Supporters of Assisted Suicide." *Detroit Free Press*, 17 March 1998.

IN THE MATTER OF QUINLAN

Legal Citation: 355 A.2d 647 (1975)

Plaintiff
Joseph T. Quinlan

Defendant
St. Clare's Hospital

Plaintiff's Claim
That doctors at St. Clare's Hospital should obey Mr. Quinlan's instructions to disconnect his comatose daughter from her respirator and allow her to die.

Chief Lawyers for Plaintiff
Paul W. Armstrong, James Crowley

Chief Defense Lawyers
Ralph Porzio (for Karen Quinlan's physicians), Theodore Einhorn (for the hospital), New Jersey State Attorney General William F. Hyland, Morris County Prosecutor Donald G. Collester, Jr.

Judge
Robert Muir, Jr.

Place
Morristown, New Jersey

Date of Decision
10 November 1975

Decision
Denied Mr. Quinlan the right to authorize termination of "life-assisting apparatus" and granted Karen Quinlan's physicians the right to continue medical treatment over the objections of the Quinlan family. Overturned by the New Jersey Supreme Court, which, on 31 March 1976, ruled that Karen's "right of privacy" included a right to refuse medical treatment and that her father, under the circumstances, could assume this right in her stead.

Significance
This case prompted the adoption of "brain death" as the legal definition of death in some states and the adoption of laws recognizing "living wills" and the "right to die" in other states, as well as the formation of "bioethics" committees in many hospitals. In 1985, the New Jersey Supreme Court ruled that all life-sustaining medical treatment, including artificial feeding, could be withheld from incompetent, terminally ill patients, provided such action was shown to be consistent with the afflicted person's past wishes.

On 15 April 1975, 21-year-old Karen Ann Quinlan passed out and lapsed into a coma after sustaining bruises which were never satisfactorily explained and ingesting tranquilizers "in the therapeutic range" and alcohol. Unable to breathe on her own, she was placed on a respirator.

By the following autumn, Quinlan's family and doctors had given up hope of recovery. Her parents, Julia and Joseph Quinlan, were devout Roman Catholics. The Quinlans consulted their parish priest, Father Thomas Trapasso, and were told that they could, in good conscience, request that Karen be removed from the respirator. The request was made, but Karen's primary physician, Dr. Robert Morse, refused to end the artificial support. In the absence of any other means with which to execute what he believed to be his daughter's wishes, Joseph Quinlan went to court.

By the time of the trial, 20 October 1975, Daniel R. Coburn, an attorney, had become the court-appointed guardian for Karen Quinlan. Morris County Prosecutor Donald G. Collester, Jr., and state Attorney General William F. Hyland joined the case, in an attempt to uphold New Jersey's homicide statutes. During pretrial interviews, Attorney General Hyland described the case as a challenge to New Jersey's long-standing definition of death as the "cessation of vital signs" and one which could result in a new definition based on "cerebral" or "brain death."

However, one week before the trial it was disclosed that Karen Quinlan did not have a "flat" electroencephalograph—a medical test which would have been evidence of a complete absence of brain-wave activity. She also was capable of breathing on her own for short, irregular periods, and had occasionally shown muscle activity which some doctors had described as voluntary. It immediately became clear that the trial would not center on New Jersey's definition of death; rather it would address the more complicated question of whether Karen Quinlan had a "right to die."

Accepted Standards vs. Right to Die

Karen Quinlan's neurologist, Dr. Robert Morse, was the first person to testify. He acknowledged that there

---

Do States That Allow Assisted Suicide Find an Increase in Intentional Suicide Rates?

Oregon is the first, and the only, state in which physician-assisted suicides are legal. Oregon has seen a modest increase in the number of intentional suicides since physician-assisted suicides was approved by a 51% majority in 1994. In November of 1997, voters overwhelming rejected a ballot measure that would have repealed the law. The law requires that a physician wait 15-days before assisting a suicide.

- There were 525 suicides in Oregon in 1994.
- There were 526 suicides in Oregon in 1995.
- There were 533 suicides in Oregon in 1996.

Source(s): Oregon Center for Health Statistics (State Department of Health).

---

was virtually no chance that Quinlan would resume a "cognitive, functional existence." However, he said he saw no medical precedent for disconnecting Quinlan from her respirator and refused to obey a court order to do so. Dr. Arshad Jarved, Quinlan's pulmonary internist, also had refused to act on Joseph Quinlan's request and testified that accepted standards of medical practice did not permit the removal of an individual from a respirator.

The Quinlans' attorney, Paul Armstrong, argued that the right to privacy and religious freedom implied a right to die. He explained his clients' religious view that the respirator was keeping their daughter from God and heaven: "The earthly phase of Karen Quinlan's life has drawn to a close and she should not be held back from enjoyment of a better, more perfect life." Karen Quinlan's court-appointed guardian, Daniel Coburn, saw the matter differently: "This isn't a terminal cancer case where someone is going to die. Where there is hope, you cannot just extinguish a life because it becomes an eyesore."

The following day, Armstrong called as an expert witness Dr. Julius Korein, a neurologist at Bellevue hospital and New York University Medical School. He described Karen Quinlan—by now weighing only 75 pounds—as having signs of severe higher brain disfunction. He testified that she had only "stereotyped" responses, such as blinking or rolling her eyes to stimuli. "This pattern of reactions," he said, "could, in no way, in my opinion, be related to conscious activity." Dr. Korein also described "an accepted but not spoken-of law," according to which physicians withheld aggressive, invasive treatment from patients who were, for example, "riddled with cancer and in pain." He added: "That is the unwritten law and one of the purposes of this trial is to make it the written law." Shortly thereafter, an emotional Joseph Quinlan took the stand and pleading that the court release his daughter from the machines and deliver her to "the hands of the lord."

On the third day, Karen's mother, Julia Ann Quinlan, testified that Karen had made her wishes known on three occasions saying, "Mommy, please don't ever let them keep me alive by extraordinary means." The statements were made, Mrs. Quinlan said, when two of Karen's friends and an aunt finally died after long battles with cancer. "Karen loved life, and if there was any way that she could not live life to the fullest she wanted to be able to die in her own surroundings, instead of being kept alive for months or years." Mrs. Quinlan continued: "I visit her every day and as I see her in her present condition I know in my heart as a mother she would not want to be there. We discussed this many times." Although the defense lawyers objected to such hearsay evidence, Judge Robert Muir, Jr. permitted Karen's sister and one of her friends to give similar testimony. Judge Muir declined, however, to permit a Roman Catholic priest to give expert testimony regarding the church's view of extraordinary medical intervention. "It is not my role to weigh the merits of what a person believes," he explained.

On 23 October 1975, three neurologists—Dr. Fred Plum of the American Association of Neurologists, Dr. Sidney Diamond of Mount Sinai Hospital, and Dr. Stuart Cook of the New Jersey College of Medicine and Dentistry—gave expert medical testimony. The three concurred that Karen Quinlan's lack of higher brain function was "irreversible" and "irreparable." However, all three agreed that Quinlan was alive by both legal and medical definitions and that it would be improper to remove her from the respirator.

Decision is Appealed

On 10 November 1975, Judge Muir, rendered his decision. He refused permission for the removal of the respirator and appointed Daniel R. Coburn to continue acting as the guardian of Karen's "person." Joseph Quinlan was appointed guardian of his daughter's property. Rejecting the Quinlans' plea that their daughter be allowed to pass into life after death, Muir wrote that disconnecting the respirator "is not something in her best interest, in a temporal sense, and it is in a temporal sense that I must operate, whether I believe in life after death or not. The single most important temporal quality that Karen Ann Quinlan has is life. This

Joseph and Julia Quinlan discuss legal matters with attorney Paul Armstrong (center). © AP/Wide World Photos.

Court will not authorize that life to be taken away from her."

On 17 November 1975, the Quinlans filed an appeal, which the New Jersey Supreme Court agreed to hear on an "accelerated schedule." On 26 January 1976, during a three-hour session, the case was argued before the seven justices of New Jersey's highest court. Their unanimous decision named Joseph Quinlan guardian and authorized him to order the removal of the respirator on 31 March 1976. Chief Justice Richard J. Hughes wrote the opinion for the court. He specifically stated that the ruling was not based on the freedom of religion argument favored by the Quinlans. "[S]imply stated, the right to religious beliefs is absolute but conduct in pursuance therefore is not wholly immune from governmental restraint."

Instead, Chief Justice Hughes cited the Supreme Court's decision in the *Griswold v. Connecticut* birth-control case and based the decision on the "right to privacy." It was a right, he continued, that could "be exercised by her guardian under the present circumstances."

Lastly, Justice Hughes dismissed the attorney general's and the Morris County prosecutor's contention that the person removing Quinlan's respirator should be charged with homicide upon her death:

> [T]he exercise of a constitutional right, such as we here find, is protected from criminal prosecution. We do not question the state's undoubted power to punish the taking of human life, but that power does not encompass individuals terminating medical treatment pursuant to their right of privacy.

Neither the hospital, Karen Quinlan's physicians, nor the state of New Jersey chose to appeal the decision to the Supreme Court. Quinlan's respirator was removed in May of 1976. She managed to breathe on her own and remained in a coma for ten years. She died on 11 June 1985.

Related Cases
Garger v. New Jersey, 429 U.S. 922 (1976).
Matter of Conroy, 486 A.2d 1209 (1985).

Bibliography and Further Reading
Colen, B. D. *Karen Ann Quinlan.* New York: Nash, 1976.

Quinlan, Joseph. Karen Ann: *The Quinlans Tell Their Story.* Garden City, NY: Doubleday & Co., 1977.

New York Times: 14, 16, 17, 20, 22–26, 28 September 1975; 1, 3, 8, 10–15, 18–28 October 1975; 2, 5, 8, 9, 11, 12, 16, 18, 21, 23, 25, 26, 28, 29 November 1975; 7, 12, 17–19, 22 December 1975; 19, 26, 27 January 1976; 25 February 1976; 9 March 1976; 1, 2, 7–10, 12, 13 April 1976; 2, 6, 7, 22, 24–30 May 1976; 12 June 1985.

CRUZAN V. DIRECTOR, MISSOURI DEPARTMENT OF HEALTH

Legal Citation: 497 U.S. 261 (1990)

Petitioner
Nancy Beth Cruzan, by her parents and co-guardians, Lester L. Cruzan, et ux.

Respondent
Director, Missouri Department of Health, et al.

Petitioner's Claim
That the state of Missouri had no authority to interfere with the parents' wish to remove the tube that supplied food and water to Nancy Cruzan.

Chief Lawyer for Petitioner
William H. Colby

Chief Lawyer for Respondent
Robert L. Presson, Attorney General of Missouri

Justices for the Court
Anthony M. Kennedy, Sandra Day O'Connor, William H. Rehnquist (writing for the Court), Antonin Scalia, Byron R. White

Justices Dissenting
Harry A. Blackmun, William J. Brennan, Jr., Thurgood Marshall, John Paul Stevens

Place
Washington, D.C.

Date of Decision
25 June 1990

Decision
The Court upheld the Missouri State Supreme Court's decision rejecting the Cruzans' petition to withdraw food and water from their daughter.

Significance
In a first for the U.S. Supreme Court, it entered into the debate surrounding the right-to-die argument, and concluded that the state, in the interests of safeguarding human life at all costs, may overrule relatives and medical professionals on specific human life issues. Some analysts tied the *Cruzan* case—and its appearance at the High Court—to the abortion question, pointing out that it paved the way for increasing judicial intrusions into citizens' privacy.

The Accident

Nancy Beth Cruzan was 25 years old when her car slid out of control on an icy Missouri road and rolled over one January night in 1983. Ejected from the car, she landed in a ditch, and by the time an ambulance arrived and restored vital signs, her brain had been without necessary oxygen for an estimated 12 to 14 minutes; brain damage occurs after six minutes without oxygen. This left her in what doctors defined as a "permanent vegetative state"—she was awake, but unaware; she had some motor reflexes but showed no evidence of cognitive abilities. She could not move, speak, or communicate in any way, though nurses at the Missouri Rehabilitation Center did report that Cruzan was able to turn her body toward someone who spoke to her, and cried on one occasion when a valentine card was read aloud to her. The rest of her body survived the accident relatively intact and, to ease care, doctors surgically implanted a tube in her stomach that provided food and water. Cruzan's life expectancy in this condition was estimated at another 30 years.

By 1988, Cruzan's family had lost hope that their daughter might emerge from her vegetative state. Her parents, Lester and Joyce Cruzan, asked doctors at the center to disconnect the feeding tube, on the grounds that their daughter had, as an adult, made definite statements that if she were to become chronically ill or seriously injured she would not want to live, unless she could get by at least somewhat normally. A local probate court granted authorization to remove the tube, but the state's attorney general, William L. Webster, filed an appeal on the grounds that the parents and a court-appointed legal guardian had not sufficiently proved that Cruzan had once made such statements about refusing medical treatment. The Missouri State Supreme Court reversed the lower court's decision, and the Cruzans appealed to the U.S. Supreme Court.

Who Decides?

It was the first time the High Court had entered into the right-to-die question, treading waters customarily the domain of theologians and philosophers. (The question had arisen in the courts before, most notably with *In the Matter of Quinlan* (1976), but the High Court

Discontinuance of Life-support v. Assisted Suicide

The right to refuse medical treatment is a constitutionally protected liberty interest. Unlike assisted suicide, it lacks the potential element of abuse because patients can establish future previsions to discontinue life support systems such as a living will. Additionally, if the patient is unable to articulate his views or has not signed a living will, family members can express the patient's desire to discontinue life support. Family members can recall conversations during which the patient expressed a desire not to continue with life support. Furthermore, if there is a disagreement among family members about the patient's desire it is easier to determine which side of the family is correctly expressing the patient's wishes.

Yet some argue there is little difference between ending life support and intervening to promote death. Others assert that a patient's physician can more accurately reflect and act on the patient's desire without the emotional entanglements that could hinder the family's judgement. Just as the family member can discuss the patients' wishes, the doctor based on his relationship with the patient prior to the illness, would have the same information.

Source(s): *Constitutional Law: Thirteenth Edition* New York City, NY: The Foundation Press Inc., 1997.

had declined to review the New Jersey State Supreme Court decision.) Conservatives and the spiritually devout offered the argument that life is precious, and must be preserved at all costs. The state arugued that it is required to protect all life, which negates any wishes of Cruzan or her parents. The *Cruzan* case was often twinned in discussions with another significant case pending before the court regarding abortion. In each issue, the justices discussed the constitutional right to privacy and which person or party could carry out such decisions on behalf of another.

The family's lawyer, William H. Colby, presented the argument that Cruzan had said on several occasions that in the case of illness or accident, she would prefer not to live her remaining days on a life-support system, as many people often remark when the issue arises in conversation. Arguing the issue for the Missouri Department of Health, Assistant State Attorney General Robert L. Presson contended that Cruzan's utterances were not specific enough, and were inadmissible as reliable statements in a court of law. Presson asserted that Missouri was acting in Cruzan's best interest in keeping her alive and nourished, and furthermore, that her parents, even as guardians, did not possess any constitutional right to end her life. The Court's role was to determine whether the secondhand oral testimony was indeed sufficient evidence, and ultimately, since Cruzan was unable to communicate her wishes, whether her family or the state had jurisdiction over her life.

Defining Life

Another side of the *Cruzan* question concerned advances in medical technology late in the twentieth century. Medical advances created machines that could perform essential respiratory and cardiac functions. In such situations, some argue, a clearer definition of "life" should be put forward—is the person a thinking, viable

being, capable of surviving with no outside assistance? Countering that argument against the "quality" versus the mere "presence" of life are deeper religious beliefs; many argue that a supreme being is the giver of life, and as such should be the only one able to end it. In this case, however, Cruzan was assisted by a surgically

Lester Cruzan. © Photograph by John Duricka. AP/Wide World Photos.

implanted feeding tube. This measure, according to the American Medical Association, is classified as "medical treatment," and thus may be refused.

On the other hand, some medical ethicists argue that food and water comprise "basic care" and thus fall under the standard extension of kindness that humans must give one another. The Justice Department prepared a brief on the issue prior to the arguments presented for the *Cruzan* case, and conceded that current government policy allowed family members, in consultation with staff physicians, to decide whether or not to continue life-support measures for permanently incapacitated patients in veterans and army hospitals.

The *Cruzan* case also tackled the issue of "informed consent," or a person's ability to understand issues related to their medical care, and with that the granting of permission to doctors to carry them out. Yet this does not address the person who is unable to make decisions. One legal precedent in this area came with a decision made by the New York State Supreme Court in 1980, in which presiding Judge Sol Wachtler ruled that medical treatment could be withdrawn at the request of a patient's legal guardian, if the incapacitated person had made clear statements that s/he did not wish to be kept alive by heroic measures.

Court Rejects Parents' Appeal

Cruzan v. Director, Missouri Department of Health was argued in December of 1989 and seven months later, Chief Justice Rehnquist delivered a majority opinion supporting the 5-4 decision of the Missouri Supreme Court, declaring that the state did indeed have the right to preserve life at all costs. Rehnquist noted in his opinion that the oral evidence presented to the Court by Cruzan's roommate, relating remarks Cruzan had made about not wishing to live life in a hospital bed, did not

offer convincing proof of her wishes, and that her parents, as legal guardians, could not overrule. Rejecting the precedent set by the New York case, the Rehnquist opinion asserted that statements made by a healthy person could not constitute what that same person may have wished under other circumstances—in other words, that a competent person would not decide to starve.

A few months after the Supreme Court ruling in June of 1990, the Cruzan family again went before the original local court in Missouri to present more concrete testimony from witnesses regarding statements their daughter had made, and this time the court granted permission to remove the feeding tube. Nurses at the Missouri Rehabilitation Center opposed the decision, and spoke out publicly, noting that it was illegal to withhold food from a dog, and that they did not wish to have Cruzan's death occur willfully while under their care. Cruzan passed away 12 days later with her parents at her bedside.

Related Cases
In the Matter of Quinlan, 355 A.2d 647 (1976).
Compassion In Dying v. State of Washington, 49 F.3d 586 (1995).

Bibliography and Further Reading

Kinsley, Michael. "To Be Or Not to Be." *New Republic*, 27 November 1989, p. 6.

"Right-to-Die Case Argued." *Congressional Quarterly Weekly Report*, 9 December 1989, p. 3370.

Sanders, Alain L. "Whose Right to Die?" *Time*, 11 December 1990, p. 80.

Urofsky, Melvin I. *Letting Go: Death, Dying, and the Law.* New York: Charles Scribner's Sons, 1993.

WASHINGTON V. GLUCKSBERG

Legal Citation: 512 U.S. 702 (1997)

Petitioner
State of Washington

Respondent
Harold Glucksberg

Petitioner's Claim
That Washington's ban on assisting or aiding a suicide does not violate the Due Process Clause of the Constitution.

Chief Lawyer for Petitioner
William L. Williams, Senior Assistant Attorney General of Washington

Chief Lawyer for Respondent
Kathryn L. Tucker

Justices for the Court
Stephen Breyer, Ruth Bader Ginsburg, Anthony M. Kennedy, Sandra Day O'Connor, William H. Rehnquist (writing for the Court), Antonin Scalia, David H. Souter, John Paul Stevens, Clarence Thomas

Justices Dissenting
None

Place
Washington, D.C.

Date of Decision
26 June 1997

Decision
That Washington's ban on assisted suicide does not violate the constitutional rights of terminally ill patients.

Significance
The Court's decision made it clear that the Constitution does not protect a person's right to commit suicide, thus upholding the laws of a majority of states which prohibit a person from assisting another in committing suicide.

Since the founding of the United States, a vast majority of states have upheld laws which prohibit a person from assisting another in committing suicide. Although not often enforced over much of the nation's history, these laws became the focus of an intense debate over issues of death and dying in the 1990s. Primarily, this debate focused on the right of terminally ill patients to receive assistance from doctors or others in committing suicide. In light of this debate and an apparent increase in the number of physician-assisted suicides, a number of states began to enforce their already existing, but rarely applied, assisted suicide laws. A number of other states passed new laws dealing with the issue, either banning assisted suicide altogether or severely limiting the circumstances in which it could be performed. Finally, bills to legalize physician-assisted suicide were proposed in a number of state legislatures.

Washington Law Challenged

Since its establishment as a U.S. territory in 1854, Washington had a law making it a crime to assist another in committing or attempting to commit suicide. In 1994, a group of doctors and terminally ill patients filed a suit against the state in the U.S. District Court for the Western District of Washington challenging the constitutionality of the law. The district court found that terminally ill patients have a liberty interest protected by the Constitution to commit physician-assisted suicide, and that the Washington law therefore violated the Constitution. The U.S. Court of Appeals for the Ninth Circuit agreed, and affirmed the district court decision. Washington then appealed the decision to the U.S. Supreme Court, which reversed the decision of the district court and court of appeals.

The Fourteenth Amendment to the Constitution provides that a state may not deprive a person of life, liberty, or property without due process of law. Although the Due Process Clause literally reads in terms of the fairness of a procedure used to deprive a person of life, liberty, or property, the Supreme Court has held that the Due Process Clause also protects certain substantive fundamental rights and liberty interests regardless of the fairness of the procedure used to deprive a person of that liberty. This is known as "substantive

Jack Kevorkian

Dr. Jack Kevorkian, also known as the "suicide doctor," says "when your conscience says law is immoral, don't follow it."

Kevorkian, a retired pathologist, claims to observe rigorous standards before conducting an assisted-physician suicide. However, others contend that he does not always follow his own procedures.

Before assisting in a suicide, Kevorkian mandates that candidates receive extensive counseling. Additionally, a psychiatrist examines every candidate. A doctor who specializes in pain control examines patients who complain of constant pain. Kevorkian reviews patients' medical records before assisting with a suicide. Another requirement, before Kevorkian will assist with a suicide, is that the patient suffer from an illness that cannot be cured or treated without unbearable side effects. Kevorkian will not perform an assisted-suicide until at least 24-hours have passed once the patient makes the final request.

Kevorkian was recently convicted of second-degree murder in a trial in Michigan.

Source(s): Cheyfitz, Kirk. "He Breaks His Own Rules: Kevorkian Rushes to Fulfill His Clients' Desire to Die." *Detroit Free Press,* 3 March 1997.

due process." Thus, the Court has held that the Due Process Clause protects a person's right to: marry; have children; raise children and direct his or her education; marital privacy; use contraception; bodily integrity; and abortion. Also, in the 1990 case *Cruzan v. Director, Missouri Department of Health,* the Supreme Court recognized that a person has a right to refuse lifesaving medical treatment. However, the Court concluded that the Due Process Clause does not protect a person's right to commit physician-assisted suicide.

In determining whether a liberty interest is "fundamental," and thus protected by the Due Process Clause, the Court applies a two-part test. First, the asserted right must have historically been regarded as fundamental, that is, it must be "deeply rooted in [the] Nation's history and tradition." (Quoting *Moore v. East Cleveland* [1977]) Second, the asserted right must be carefully described and defined. The Court concluded that the asserted right to physician assisted suicide did not meet either of these requirements. With respect to this second requirement, the Court concluded that the right at issue was not the right to die or to determine the time and manner of one's death, as the court of appeals had defined the issue. Rather, the Court looked at the more narrow issue of whether there was a right to commit suicide with another's assistance.

The Court then analyzed whether this right had a historical basis. With respect to the historical question, the Court reasoned that the right to assisted suicide was not rooted in history because almost every state and most democratic nations have laws banning assisted suicide. Further, "for over 700 years, the Anglo-American common-law tradition has punished and otherwise disapproved of both suicide and assisting suicide." Thus, the Court concluded:

> The history of the law's treatment of assisted suicide in this country has been and continues to be one of rejection of nearly all efforts to permit it. That being the case, the asserted 'right' to assistance in committing suicide is not a fundamental liberty interest protected by the Due Process Clause.

The Court also rejected the argument that its earlier decision in the *Cruzan* case established a right to assisted suicide. The Court reasoned that its decision in *Cruzan* simply affirmed that a person has a right to refuse unwanted medical treatment. However, that issue is far different from whether a person has the right to assistance in committing suicide. Further, the Court noted that the right to refuse medical treatment differs from the right to assistance in committing suicide because historically a person has had the right to refuse medical treatment. Finally, in *Cruzan* the Court noted that most states outlawed assisted suicide but the Court did not suggest that such laws were unconstitutional.

Although the justices did not entirely agree on the reasoning, all nine justices agreed that there is no fundamental right to assisted suicide. Thus, the Court's decision left it up to each individual state to determine in what circumstances physician-assisted suicide would or would not be permitted. As the Court concluded its opinion: "Throughout the Nation, Americans are engaged in an earnest and profound debate about the morality, legality, and practicality of physician-assisted suicide. Our holding permits this debate to continue, as it should in a democratic society."

Related Cases

Moore v. East Cleveland, 431 U.S. 494 (1977).

Cruzan v. Director, Missouri Department of Health, 497 U.S. 261 (1990).

Senior Assistant Attorney General William Williams shakes hands with attorney Kathryn Tucker. © Photograph by Susan Ragan. AP/Wide World Photos.

Bibliography and Further Reading

Annas, George J. *The Rights of Patients: The Basic ACLU Guide to Patient Rights.* Totowa, NJ: Humana Press, 1992.

Beck, Joan. "Backing Away from a Very Slippery Slope." *Chicago Tribune,* June 29, 1997, p. 17.

Berger, Arthur S. *When Life Ends: Legal Overviews, Medicolegal Forms, and Hospital Policies.* Westport, CT: Praeger, 1995.

Gostin, Lawrence O. "Deciding Life and Death in the Courtroom." *JAMA, The Journal of the American Medical Association,* November 12, 1997, p. 1523.

Kemp, Evan J., Jr. "Could You Please Die Now? Disabled People Like Me Have Good Reason to Fear the Push for Assisted Suicide." *Washington Post,* January 5, 1997, p. C1.

Meisel, Alan. *The Right to Die.* New York: John Wiley & Sons, Inc., 1995.

VACCO V. QUILL

Legal Citation: 521 U.S. 793 (1997)

Petitioners
Dennis C. Vacco, Attorney General of New York, et al.

Respondents
Timothy E. Quill, Samuel C. Klagsbrun, Howard A. Grossman

Petitioners' Claim
That a ruling by the U.S. Court of Appeals for the Second Circuit invalidating a New York State statute banning physician-assisted suicide was incorrect.

Chief Lawyer for Petitioners
Barbara Gott Billet, Solicitor General; Daniel Smirlock, assistant Attorney General; Michael S. Popkin, Assistant Attorney General

Chief Lawyer for Respondents
Laurence H. Tribe, David J Burman, Carla A. Kerr, Peter J. Rubin, Kari Anne Smith, Kathryn L. Tucker

Justices for the Court
Stephen Breyer, Ruth Bader Ginsburg, Anthony M. Kennedy, Sandra Day O'Connor, William H. Rehnquist (writing for the Court), Antonin Scalia, David H. Souter, John Paul Stevens, Clarence Thomas

Justices Dissenting
None

Place
Washington, D.C.

Date of Decision
26 June 1997

Decision
Reversed the court of appeals to rule that New York State's ban on physician-assisted suicide did not violate the Equal Protection Clause of the Fourteenth Amendment.

Significance
The ruling provided constitutional sanction to state laws banning physician-assisted suicide. By determining that there was a qualitative legal difference between denying life-prolonging treatment to terminally ill patients and assisting in their death, the Court validated existing statutes in many states, and confirmed that states could draft laws banning assisted suicide that were able to withstand constitutional scrutiny.

A Two-Edged Sword

Advances in medicine have extended human life expectancy dramatically in the 1980s and 1990s. While this was generally viewed as a desirable development, medical science prolonged the lives of terminally ill people, even in cases where their quality of life was poor. As more people with terminal illness lived longer, many who suffered great pain or debilitation expressed a desire to end their suffering through death. Many individuals have sympathized with this outlook, including numerous members of the medical profession. As such, the possibility and reality of physician-assisted suicide has become a regular part of popular debate and a focus of legislative activities.

In the early 1990s, New York State law forbade physicians from assisting terminally ill patients wishing to end their lives. Physicians were allowed, however, to deny life-prolonging treatment to those terminally ill patients who did not wish to receive it. Perceiving a logical incongruity in these statutes three physicians, Timothy E. Quill, Samuel C. Klagsbrun, and Howard A. Grosman brought suit against the New York State Attorney General in U.S. District Court to invalidate the state's ban on assisted suicide.

Equal Protection?

The three physicians claimed that New York State law violated the Equal Protection Clause of the Fourteenth Amendment, since terminally ill patients receiving life-prolonging treatment could choose to die by ending said treatment, while others, who desired to end their lives but were not receiving life-prolonging treatment, could not choose to end their lives with medical assistance. The district court denied the physicians' claim, and the case proceeded to the court of appeals.

The court of appeals reversed the decision of the district court, stating that "New York law does not treat equally all competent persons who are in the final stages of fatal illness and wish to hasten their death." In the court's view, this unequal treatment resulted because "those in the final stages of a terminal illness who are on life support systems are allowed to hasten their deaths by directing the removal of such systems;

States That Allow Assisted Suicide

- Oregon is the only state in which physician assisted suicide is legal.

- In 1994, Oregon became the first state to make it legal for physicians to prescribe lethal doses of drugs to terminally ill patients.

- In October of 1997, the Supreme Court refused to hear a challenge to Oregon's physician-assisted suicide law.

- Oregon's law only allows physicians to administer life-ending drugs after a 15-day waiting period has elapsed.

- Attempts by other states such as New York and Washington to legalize physician-assisted suicides have not withstood legal challenges.

Source(s): Pertman, Adam. "Bills Aim to Disarm Oregon Law on Suicide." *Boston Globe,* 7 October 1998.

but those who are similarly situated, except for the previous attachment of life sustaining equipment, are not allowed to hasten death by self administering prescribed drugs." In other words, the court ruled that the removal of life support and suicide were nearly exactly equivalent. Following this setback the state of New York asked the U.S. Supreme Court to accept the case on *certiorari,* and the Court heard arguments on 8 January 1997.

Omission and Commission

The Supreme Court ruled that New York state's ban on assisted suicide did not violate the Equal Protection Clause of the Fourteenth Amendment. Justice Rehnquist, writing for the Court, rejected the court of appeals' conclusion that removal of life support and assistance with suicide were equivalent acts: "Unlike the Court of Appeals, we think the distinction between assisting suicide and withdrawing life sustaining treatment, a distinction widely recognized and endorsed in the medical profession and our legal traditions, is both important and logical; it is certainly rational." This language was significant in that it allows states to differentiate their treatment of classes of people regardless of Fourteenth Amendment restrictions if they are able to show a reasonable and compelling reason for doing so. The Court went on to enumerate the state's rationale for forbidding assisted suicide: "prohibiting intentional killing and preserving life; preventing suicide; maintaining physicians' role as their patients' healers; protecting vulnerable people from indifference, prejudice, and psychological and financial pressure to end their lives; and avoiding a possible slide toward euthanasia."

Impact

Vacco v. Quill established the interest of the state in prohibiting physicians from assisting in the suicide of terminally ill patients. By identifying a reasonable and compelling state interest in preventing assisted suicide,

the Court removed any argument that terminally ill patients who are not on life support might have had under the Equal Protection Clause of the Fourteenth Amendment. The ruling also provided a precedent for states struggling to develop acceptable statutes outlawing assisted suicide. Despite this precedent, it has been extremely difficult for states in which assisted suicide has been practiced to prevent further occurrences, due

Dennis Vacco, New York Attorney General. © Photograph by Adam Nadel. AP/Wide World Photos.

in some measure to general public support for the right of the dying to control their own demise.

Related Cases

Morissette v. United States, 342 U.S. 246 (1952).
United States v. Bailey, 444 U.S. 394 (1980).
Cruzan v. Missouri Department of Health, 497 U.S. 261 (1990).
Romer v. Evans, 517 U.S. 620 (1996).

Bibliography and Further Reading

Breshnahan, James F. "Palliative Care or Assisted Suicide?" *America,* March 14, 1998, p. 16.

Feinberg, Brett. "The Court Upholds a State Law Prohibiting Physician-Assisted Suicide." *Journal of Criminal Law and Criminology,* spring 1998, p. 847.

Gianelli, Diane M. "Assisted-Suicide Case Consensus: We Need Better End-Of-Life Care." *American Medical News,* April 28, 1997, p. 1.

Gostin, Lawrence O. "Deciding Life and Death in the Courtroom" *JAMA, The Journal of the American Medical Association,* November 12, 1997, p. 1523.

Jewish Law—Legal Briefs ("*Vacco v. Quill*"). http://www.jlaw.com/Briefs/vacco_quill2.html

CIVIL LAW

Civil Law Versus Criminal Law

Civil law refers to a wide array of rules that govern legal matters among private citizens such as injuries, broken contracts, trademark infringement, and fraud. Civil law cases involve either a breach of duty or contract. In addition, civil law actions—suits in civil court—are brought about by private citizens, whereas criminal prosecutions are brought about by the government. Furthermore, civil law remedies for wrongful acts include monetary damages or reimbursements, and injuctions or court orders requiring or banning certain kinds of conduct. In contrast to criminal cases, the defendant—the party accused of being liable for wrongful acts—is not subject to fines or imprisonment.

Overview and Background

The most common kind of civil court cases in the United States are tort cases, which include cases of intentional wrongs, negligence and liability such as fraud, defamation, trespassing, and false imprisonment. *Tort* is the Middle English word meaning "wrong." The plaintiff—the party that suffered the wrongful act and seeks relief in court—is entitled to be restored to the position he or she was in before the tort, whether through economic compensation, medical care, or any other means. This right makes up a fundamental principle of U.S. tort law. Unlike contracts, torts do not involve the violation of any agreed upon course of action. Instead, torts involve the failure to act in a manner generally expected for any given situation. In the 1990s, the majority of tort actions stemmed from automobile injuries and more than 50 percent of all tort cases took at least a year to process.

Every tort case must establish three things. One, the plaintiff must demonstrate that the defendant was bound by a legal duty to act in a certain way. Two, the plaintiff must show that the defendant violated his or her legal duty by failing to act in a certain way. Three, the plaintiff must establish that he or she suffered damages—injuries or losses—as a direct consequence of the defendant's failure to act in the expected way.

Civil law has four main goals. First, it provides an avenue to compensate victims for injuries suffered as a result of the negligent action of others. Second, it holds

the party that caused any injuries or damages responsible for the cost of them. Third, civil law seeks to prevent the future occurrence of negligent, careless, and risky behavior that leads to civil law actions. Fourth, it upholds the rights of people who have suffered injuries or damages as a result of the negligent party.

Civil law cases involve broken agreements and contracts, negligence, strict liability, and intentional wrongful acts—each of which will be explained briefly below. Broken agreements include breaches of written and verbal contracts between two or more parties, which one of the parties finds necessary to resolve through a civil action. Negligence refers to conduct that deviates from what is generally expected in any given situation and covers acts such as careless and reckless driving. Many injury civil actions result from negligence, careless behavior that increases the chances of injuries to people or damage to property.

Intentional wrongs include acts that the perpetrator carries out knowing that they are harmful to people or property, such as assault, battery, fraud, and defamation. When civil law cases hold defendants liable who are not negligent or guilty of intentionally committing wrongful acts, they impose strict liability, which covers beneficial and necessary activities that create high levels of risk to society. Such activities include those involving hazardous materials and substances.

During the latter half of the twentieth century, the number of civil cases rose with the adoption of new liability and negligence policies, which made it easier to sue manufacturers and service providers. The growth stemmed partially from efforts by legal theorists to reduce injuries suffered by consumers, who, these theorists assumed, paid little attention to risks and bought very little accident insurance. To lessen the burden on consumers, these theorists strove to shift more responsibility to producers of goods and providers of services.

Prior to the new tort policies, consumers bore the burden of determining whether products or services they purchased were safe. Afterwards, employers, doctors, and manufacturers among others held a greater share of the responsibility for damages suffered by consumers from defective products and negligent services.

A key case that ushered in the new tort policies was *Vandermark v. Maywood Bell Ford.* In 1958, Chester Vandermark purchased a new car from the Maywood Bell Ford dealership in California. Six weeks later, the car began to malfunction while Chester and his sister Mary were driving in it. Because the brakes failed, the car crashed into a pole, seriously injuring both Vandermarks. They sued the dealer, which denied all responsibility. However, the California Supreme court decided that Maywood Bell Ford was responsible because it acted as "an integral part of the overall producing and marketing enterprise that should bear the cost of injuries resulting from defective products." Other cases such as *MacPherson v. Buick Motor Co.* created a precedent for holding manufacturers responsible for hazardous products later sold to customers who sustain injuries from them. These cases extended the responsibility for dangerous and defective products from retailers back to the manufacturers of the products in order to protect consumers.

Some Like It Hot: Civil Lawsuit Controversy

Of the cases occurring after *Vandermark* and the shift in liability, *Liebeck v. McDonald's* stands out as the one case most often quoted, especially in a discussion of tort reform. In 1994, a jury awarded Stella Liebeck $2.9 million in punitive damages for injuries suffered from spilling McDonald's coffee on her lap. The coffee—kept at 180 degrees—caused third-degree burns and Liebeck spent seven days in the hospital and received multiple skin grafts. A judge reduced the award to $480,000 and the two parties ultimately settled for an undisclosed amount. Critics of the liability shift often refer to this case as a "frivolous lawsuit" with an outrageous award. However, supporters of the court's current view of liability point out that Liebeck initially only sought reimbursement for her medical costs, but the fast food chain refused to negotiate. Liebeck then hired an attorney who had settled another coffee case with McDonald's. During the trial, the attorney exposed company documents that showed about 700 reports of coffee burns, including other complaints of third degree burns. Nevertheless, the company failed to implement safer packaging or warn customers until after *Liebeck.*

Punitive Damage Awards Supply Government with Tax Revenues

The U.S. Supreme Court ruled in December of 1996 that punitive damages awarded in personal injury cases were taxable (*O'glivie v. United States*). In this case, the family of a woman who died of toxic shock syndrome was awarded $1.5 million in actual damages and $10 million in punitive damages from International Playtex Inc. The family paid federal income tax on the punitive damage award, but requested a refund, arguing that the Internal Revenue Service's definition of gross income

does not include damages received from personal injuries or sickness awards. However, the Court held that the family's damages were not received "on account of personal injuries; hence, the gross-income exclusion provision does not apply and the damages are taxable." The Court reasoned that punitive damages are not awarded to compensate for injuries but "to punish reprehensible conduct and to deter its future occurrence."

Double Jeopardy: Civil Suits after Criminal Trials

The civil suit by the families of Nicole Brown Simpson and Ronald Goldman against O.J. Simpson brought national and international attention to an ongoing trend in the U.S. legal system where families seek retribution in civil courts for defendants that are found guilty or even acquitted in criminal courts. Instead of being charged with murder as in the criminal trial, Simpson was sued for wrongful death by the families of victims in the civil trial. Though Simpson was acquitted in the criminal case, he was found negligent in the civil action against him and ordered to pay about $33 million in damages. Legal experts contend that crime victims prefer civil trials to criminal trials because of their "lighter" burden of proof, where the plaintiffs need not prove beyond a reasonable doubt that the defendant committed a wrongful act in order to be compensated. Furthermore, jury decisions do not have to be unanimous in civil cases as in criminal cases. Instead, a jury majority is all that is necessary. Although someone acquitted in a criminal trial cannot be prosecuted for the same crime again, he or she can be tried in civil court for the same wrongful act.

Call for Tort Reform

Because of litigation perceived as frivolous and because of the rising costs of insurance to protect producers and providers of goods and services from lawsuits, manufacturers, critics of tort law and politicians have called for sweeping tort reform that would limit liability and place caps on punitive damage awards. However, even bills for much more modest reforms have failed to become law. In 1996, a Republican-sponsored bill curbing product liability passed through Congress, but President Clinton vetoed it. In mid-1998, Congress debated a similar bill with compromises that Clinton would accept. The bill would limit punitive damage awards to $250,000 in cases against small businesses.

See also: **Criminal Law, Damages**

Bibliography and Further Reading

Bell, Peter A. *Accidental Justice: The Dilemmas of Tort Law.* New Haven: Yale University Press, 1997.

Fein, Bruce. "Clinton Wrong to Stand Behind Punitive Awards." *Insight on the News,* 29 April 1996, 30.

Gest, Ted. "When One Court Case Just Isn't Enough: More Crime Victims Now Seek Civil Remedies." *U.S. News & World Report.* February 24 1997, 28.

Huber, Peter W. *Liability.* New York: Basic Books, Inc., 1988.

"Lawsuit Brawl in the Capital." *U.S. News & World Report,* 13 July 1998, 30.

Nelson, Kristen L. "Does Tort Reform Make Sense?" *Best's Review,* May 1995, 30.

Rosenberg, David. *The Hidden Holmes: His Theory of Torts in History.* Cambridge, Massachusetts: Harvard University Press, 1995.

West's Encyclopedia of American Law. St. Paul, Minnesota: West Publishing, 1998.

SHIMP V. NEW JERSEY BELL TELEPHONE COMPANY

Legal Citation: 368 A. 2d 408 (1976)

Plaintiff
Donna M. Shimp

Defendant
New Jersey Bell Telephone Company

Plaintiff's Claim
An injunction should be issued requiring her employer, New Jersey Bell Telephone Company, to enact a ban on smoking in the workplace.

Chief Lawyer for Plaintiff
Charles A. Sweeney

Chief Defense Lawyer
Stuart B. Finifter

Judge
Philip A. Gruccio (writing for the court)

Place
Superior Court of New Jersey, Chancery Division

Date of Decision
20 December 1976

Decision
An injunction can be issued requiring New Jersey Bell Telephone Company to ban workplace smoking.

Significance
The ruling found that a worker's common law right to a safe working environment is threatened by the presence of second-hand or environmental tobacco smoke (ETS), and that an employee with a medical sensitivity to ETS has the common law right to require an employer to ban smoking in the workplace.

A Major Public Health Concern

Tobacco smoke has been established as a carcinogen and is also associated with emphysema, heart disease, stroke, and other conditions. The health risks incurred by smokers could also affect those who are exposed to tobacco smoke involuntarily. The Environmental Protection Agency estimated that second-hand smoke causes approximately 3,000 lung cancer deaths per year in nonsmokers, and the U.S. Labor Department reported that environmental tobacco smoke (ETS) has killed many more workers than have workplace homicides. Despite concrete evidence on the dangers of ETS, workers exposed to this substance have not had a single clear means through which to pursue remedies for injuries.

Both state and federal courts have grappled with the issue of how best to address the problem of ETS related health problems in the workplace. Plaintiffs have tried several different causes of action under either statutory or regulatory provisions. These include claims under the Americans with Disabilities Act and claims under workers' compensation laws, in which parties sought monetary awards from employers after becoming ill or injured on the job. The decision in *Shimp v. New Jersey Bell Telephone Company,* in which the plaintiff sought injunctive relief instead of damages, is notable in that it was not based on statutory law but on principles of common law. Common law is a body of law, inherited from England, in which courts resolve disputes between parties without regard to any particular statute, or written law. Decisions are based upon precedent (prior decisions) and essentially balance the rights of the parties before the court on the basis of fundamental concepts of equity and common sense.

A Common Law Right

Donna M. Shimp, a secretary at New Jersey Bell Telephone Company, successfully sought injunctive relief against her employer through the common law argument. Shimp was employed in an area in which other employees were permitted to smoke at their desks. She contended that inhalation of the resulting ETS was harmful to her health, and therefore her employer, by condoning the presence of ETS, allowed an unsafe working condition to exist. She brought an action in

Smoking Banned In Public Places

Cigarette smoking can be hazardous to one's health, but breathing the smoke of others can also be dangerous. At least two percent of lung cancer deaths are believed to be caused by passive smoking. Additionally, exposure to second-hand smoke can result in an increase in heart rate and blood pressure, and perilous levels of carbon monoxide in the blood.

Second-hand smoke is even more harmful to babies and children. Babies with parents that smoke are treated at hospitals twice as often for illnesses such as bronchitis and pneumonia.

Opponents of public smoking bans claim the health hazards to non-smokers are not nearly as conclusive as believed. For example, nearly 80% of the studies of lung cancer among non-smokers married to smokers do not demonstrate, through statistically significant information, that they are at greater risk. The arguments for banning smoking in the work place usually rely on the health risk to non-smokers. Yet in research of environmental tobacco smoke in the workplace, more than 85% do not show a statistically significant increase in the danger of lung cancer to non-smokers.

Source(s): Environmental Tobacco Smoke (ETS) and Smoking In Public Places, http:/www.thetma.org.uk/ETS.htm

---

New Jersey Superior Court, Chancery Division, seeking an injunction, or court order, that would require New Jersey Bell Telephone to ban workplace smoking.

Shimp presented affidavits from attending physicians documenting that she was allergic to cigarette smoke and suffered such symptoms as severe throat irritation, nasal irritation, nosebleeds, eye irritation which resulted in corneal abrasion and corneal erosion, headaches, nausea, and vomiting. Shimp was forced to leave the workplace on numerous occasions because of these symptoms. These symptoms abated, however, whenever Shimp remained in an area free of smoke. Shimp attempted to resolve the problem of workplace ETS through her union's collective bargaining grievance procedures, by which it was agreed that the employer would install an exhaust fan in the work area. But because other workers complained of the resulting draft, the fan was often turned off and did not solve the problem. Thus Shimp brought her action in New Jersey Superior Court.

Justice Gruccio decided the issue based on the briefs submitted by the lawyers representing the plaintiff and the defendant. Because the case was a matter of first impression—it involved a legal issue not yet ruled upon in that jurisdiction—Justice Gruccio relied on principles of common law. He considered three issues: whether the Occupation Safety and Health Act (OSHA) and workers' compensation regulations on workplace safety allowed a worker to seek injunctive relief through the courts; whether the plaintiff's complaint was based on a legitimate medical condition; and whether the complaint was causally related to the presence of environmental tobacco smoke in the workplace.

Citing rulings from *McDonald v. Standard Oil Co., Burns v. Delaware and Atlantic Tel. And Tel. Co., Clayton*

v. Ainsworth, Davis v. N.J. Zinc Co., and *Canonica v. Celanese Corp. of America,* Justice Gruccio found that "It is clearly the law in this state that an employee has a right to work in a safe environment." The court stressed that this is a duty imposed both by common law and by the OSHA of 1970. Justice Gruccio emphasized that OSHA's general duty clause imposes on the employer "a duty to eliminate all foreseeable and preventable hazards" and that this clause "recognizes concurrent state power to act either legislatively or judicially under the common law with regard to occupational safety." In addition, the court wrote that nothing in the Workmen's Compensation Act, which regulated procedures for seeking monetary damages after an injury, prohibited workers from pursuing injunctive relief against occupational hazards. Therefore, Justice Gruccio determined that the plaintiff's suit against her employer was a proper cause of action and that the court had authority to resolve the matter.

Clear and Overwhelming Evidence

The court found that the affidavits from the plaintiff's attending physicians confirmed her medical sensitivity to tobacco smoke. Furthermore, Justice Gruccio cited evidence from the 1970 Public Health Cigarette Smoking Act and from the 1975 HEW report, *The Health Consequences of Smoking*, documenting the toxic nature of cigarette smoke. He further noted that the surgeon general's 1972 report of the same title demonstrated that the presence of cigarette smoke increased the carbon monoxide level and added tar, nicotine, and the oxides of nitrogen to the air. Affidavits from several other health professionals, including researchers and specialists in the fields of cancer, cardiovascular disease, allergies, and industrial and occupational medicine, further documented the adverse effects of ETS. "The evidence is clear and overwhelming," wrote Justice Gruccio. "Cigarette smoke . . . [creates] a health hazard not merely to the smoker but to all those around her who must rely on the same air supply." Taking judicial notice of the toxic nature of cigarette smoke, he ordered New Jersey Bell Telephone Company "to provide safe working conditions for plaintiff by restricting the smoking of employees to the non-work area presently used as a lunchroom."

In his analysis, Justice Gruccio stressed two important distinctions between Shimp's claim and that brought in *Canonico v. Celanese Corp. of America* (1951). In that case, the plaintiff sought damages after contracting an illness allegedly resulting from the inhalation of cellulose acetate dust in the workplace. The trial judge dismissed the case, and this decision was upheld on appeal. The dust inhaled by the plaintiff, the courts found, was the necessary by-product of the manufacturing process in which he was employed—in other words, the product could not be produced without creating the dust. The courts therefore ruled that breathing these particles should be considered a risk assumed knowingly by the employee as an "ordinary incident to his employment." Furthermore, the trial judge found no convincing evidence that the cellulose acetate dust was toxic or that the plaintiff's illness was caused by breathing this substance. In *Shimp,* however, the court found that cigarette smoke was not related in any way to the work done at New Jersey Bell Telephone Company and "cannot be regarded as an occupational hazard which plaintiff has voluntarily assumed in pursuing a career as a secretary." Second, the health hazards of secondary smoke have been well documented. Thus, the court determined that "employees' right to a safe working environment makes it clear that smoking must be forbidden in the work area."

Balancing Rights and Legislative Response

In ordering the injunction against New Jersey Bell Telephone, the court acknowledged that the rights of non-smokers in the workplace must be balanced against the rights of smokers, but stated firmly that "The right of an individual to risk his or her own health does not include the right to jeopardize the health of those who must remain around him or her in order to properly perform the duties of their jobs." Justice Gruccio noted that employees who wished to smoke during their own time "should have a reasonably accessible area in which to smoke." He reasoned that limiting smoking to non-work areas would impose no unreasonable hardship upon the employer.

Shimp established the toxic effect of ETS on non-smokers and ruled that the substance should be included among those that an employer should reasonably foresee as a preventable work hazard. This set the stage for workers to bring claims against employ-ers. Responding to employee complaints, and anticipating possible liability, many private employers began to regulate on-the-job smoking. But smokers also asserted their rights, making statutory regulation of workplace smoking a passionately contested issue. As of 1993, according to a *Valparaiso University Law Review* article by Melissa A. Vallone, only 14 states had enacted legislation against ETS, and none of these banned on-the-job smoking entirely. In *Your Rights in the Workplace,* Barbara Kate Repa noted that by 1996 a majority of states had imposed some regulations protecting workers from ETS, but that no federal law directly prohibited workplace smoking. A small handful of cities prohibit workplace smoking outright. On the other hand, about half of the states have laws making it illegal to discriminate against employees who smoke during their free time. "So the ongoing legal battle in most workplaces," Repa concluded, "boils down to a question of what is more important: one person's right to preserve health by avoiding co-workers' tobacco smoke, or another's unfettered right to smoke."

The federal government's first major action against ETS came in 1988, when it banned smoking aboard domestic airline flights of less than two hours' duration. The Environmental Protection Agency (EPA) recommended "that every company have a smoking policy that effectively protects nonsmokers from involuntary exposure to tobacco smoke" but as of the late 1990s, this had not been made into law. New OSHA regulations proposed in 1994 would require all non-industrial businesses to devise and implement plans to protect workers from indoor air pollution, including tobacco smoke. But strong opposition erupted when those proposals were made public. In 1997, President Clinton issued an executive order banning smoking in federal workplaces, but the issue of smoking in private workplaces had not yet been resolved by federal law.

The Path Ahead

Though the *Shimp* case established an employer's common law duty to protect employees from ETS, analysts have found that the cause of action in this case may be questionable. According to Vallone, as of 1993, *Shimp* was the only case to grant injunctive relief to a plaintiff under the common law theory. In a Washington Supreme Court case, *McCarthy v. Department of Social & Health Services* (1988), only four justices—a minority of the court—agreed that plaintiff could claim a common law right to protection from ETS. In a subsequent New Jersey case, *Smith v. Blue Cross & Blue Shield of New Jersey* (1983), the same court that had ruled on *Shimp* suggested that the *Shimp* decision required an employer to enact "Draconian measures" against smoking employees and that it imposed prohibitions that "are too sweeping and go well beyond what is necessary to ensure a safe working environment." Thus, Vallone concluded, "the only court that granted relief to an ETS victim under this [common law] theory later questioned the validity of the decision."

Other workers, though, later won damages (i.e., money settlements) against employers because of the harm resulting from ETS. And liability was broadened to include tobacco companies themselves as well as employers. In a 1991 class action suit, for example, airline flight attendants in the United States won a $300 million settlement against the tobacco industry for injuries caused by breathing ETS on planes. These suits, however, have been time consuming, costly to pursue, and difficult to prove. Because no other case has acknowledged a common law right to protection from ETS as of the late 1990s, and because of the uncertainties involved in statutory or regulatory claims, Vallone argued that workers' compensation laws may, if amended, provide a more efficient remedy for ETS complaints. Yet *Shimp* had not been overruled as of that time; its precedent establishing a common law right to protection from ETS, therefore, remained.

Impact

Shimp v. New Jersey Bell Telephone Company recognized the harm done to workers exposed to ETS and established the common law right of employees to be protected from this substance while on the job. Since then, workers have also sought damages against employers through a variety of means. In addition, states and municipalities as well as private employers are increasingly taking action to protect workers from this type of pollution and to protect themselves from possible lia-

bility. Though no federal legislation as of the late 1990s banned ETS in private workplaces, federal recommendations strongly urged employers to ban on-the-job smoking, and ETS had been prohibited in federal workplaces. *Shimp*, therefore, set an important precedent for employees' rights to be protected from secondhand smoke.

Related Cases

Canonico v. Celanese Corp. of America, 11 N.J. Super. 445 App. Div. (1951).

Smith v. Blue Cross & Blue Shield of New Jersey, No. 6-3617-81E N.J. Super. Ct. Ch. Div. (1983).

McCarthy v. Department of Social & Health Services, 759 P.2d 351 Wash. (1988).

Bibliography and Further Reading

CAW Health, Safety and Environment Newsletter, http://www.caw.ca/hse//newsletter/5.11.html#5.

Executive Order Bans Smoking in Federal Workplace, http://www.usis.it/wireless/wf970811/97081109.html.

Repa, Barbara Kane. *Your Rights in the Workplace, 3rd ed.* Nolo Press, 1996.

Smokers More Deadly Than Robbers, http://www.ash.org/pr/pr950803.html

U.S. Environmental Protection Agency. http://www.epa.gov/iaq/pub/etsbro.html

Vallone, Melissa A. "Employer Liability for Workplace Environmental Tobacco Smoke: Get out of the Fog." *Valparaiso University Law Review,* Vol. 30, 1996.

BUTZ V. ECONOMOU

Legal Citation: 438 U.S. 478 (1978)

Petitioner
Earl L. Butz

Respondent
Arthur N. Economou

Petitioner's Claim
That federal officials acting within the scope of their authority have absolute immunity for allegedly unconstitutional acts.

Chief Lawyer for Petitioner
Daniel M. Friedman

Chief Lawyer for Respondent
David C. Buxbaum

Justices for the Court
Harry A. Blackmun, William J. Brennan, Jr., Thurgood Marshall, Lewis F. Powell, Jr., Byron R. White (writing for the Court)

Justices Dissenting
Warren E. Burger, William H. Rehnquist, John Paul Stevens, Potter Stewart

Place
Washington, D.C.

Date of Decision
29 June 1978

Decision
Federal executive officials are entitled only to qualified immunity in suits brought against them for unconstitutional acts.

Significance
While the decision in *Butz v. Economou* limited the immunity entitled to federal executive officials for constitutional violations, it also extended absolute immunity to various judicial and administrative officials within federal agencies.

Arthur N. Economou was the head of a commodity futures commission company. On 19 February 1970, following an audit, the United States Department of Agriculture issued an administrative complaint alleging that Economou had willfully failed to maintain the minimum financial requirements set down by the department. The Department of Agriculture then tried, unsuccessfully, to revoke the company's registration in an administrative proceeding. Afterwards, Economou filed for damages in district court against several U.S.D.A. officials, including the secretary and assistant secretary of agriculture, the judicial officer, the chief hearing examiner who had recommended sustaining the administrative complaint, and the department attorney who had prosecuted the enforcement proceeding. He claimed that by initiating unauthorized proceedings against him they had violated his constitutional rights.

The Lower Court Rulings

The U.S. District Court for the Southern District of New York was the first to rule. It dismissed Economou's complaint against the individual defendants. The court held that federal officials were entitled to absolute immunity for all discretionary acts within the scope of their authority. Economou then appealed to the U.S. Court of Appeals, which reversed the lower court's ruling. The court of appeals held that federal officials were entitled only to the qualified immunity granted to state government officials. Earl Butz, the U.S. Secretary of Agriculture, appealed this ruling to the U.S. Supreme Court.

The Supreme Court Ruling

On 29 June 1978 the Supreme Court issued its decision. By a narrow vote of 5-4, it ruled in favor of Economou and against Earl Butz. Justice White wrote the majority opinion, in which he was joined by Justices Marshall, Powell, Brennan, and Blackmun. The majority opinion ruled on three points of contention in the case.

Officials Entitled to Qualified Immunity

When a suit is brought against a federal executive official for damages resulting from unconstitutional action, the official is entitled only to qualified, rather than absolute, immunity. Exceptions are to be made in cases where the official can show that absolute immunity is required for the performance of official public duties. Thus federal officials were to be accorded the same level of immunity granted to state officials:

> We agree with the perception of [the lower] courts that, in the absence of congressional direction to the contrary, there is no basis for according to federal officials a higher degree of immunity from liability when sued for a constitutional infringement . . . than is accorded state officials when sued for the identical violation . . . The pressures and uncertainties facing decision makers in state government are little if at all different from those affecting federal officials. We see no merit in holding a state governor liable but immunizing the head of a federal department; in holding the administrator of a federal hospital immune where the superintendent of a state hospital would be liable; in protecting the warden of a federal prison where the warden of a state prison would be vulnerable; or in distinguishing between state and federal police participating in the same investigation. Surely, federal officials should enjoy no greater zone of protection when they violate federal constitutional rules than do state officers.

Officials Not Liable for Mistakes in Judgment

The second principle the Supreme Court established in the *Butz* decision was that federal officials would only be held liable for overt constitutional violations, not mere errors of judgment. In making this holding, the Court relied on the reasoning of the U.S. court of appeals:

> While federal officials will not be liable for mere mistakes in judgment, whether the mistake is one of fact or one of law, there is no substantial basis for holding that executive officers generally may with impunity discharge

their duties in a way that is known to them to violate the Constitution or in a manner that they should know transgresses a clearly established constitutional rule.

Agency Officials Held Absolutely Immune

Finally, the Court ruled that federal hearing examiners, administrative law judges, and other agency officials charged with initiating or sustaining proceedings such as the one brought against Economou were to be afforded absolute immunity from lawsuits. It based this holding on the importance of keeping these officials free from outside influences:

> The discretion which executive officials exercise with respect to the initiation of administrative proceedings might be distorted if their immunity from damages arising from that decision was less than complete . . . We believe that agency officials must make the decision to move forward with an administrative proceeding free from intimidation or harassment. Because the legal remedies already available to the defendant in such a proceeding provide sufficient checks on agency zeal, we hold that those officials who are responsible for the decision to initiate or continue a proceeding subject to agency adjudication are entitled to absolute immunity from damages liability for their parts in that decision.

Related Cases
Monroe v. Pape, 365 U.S. 167 (1960).
Harlow v. Fitzgerald, 457 U.S. 800 (1982).

Bibliography and Further Reading
Biskupic, Joan, and Elder Witt, eds. *Congressional Quarterly's Guide to the U.S. Supreme Court,* 3rd ed. Washington, DC: Congressional Quarterly, Inc., 1996.

Encyclopedia of the American Constitution. New York, NY: Macmillan Publishing Company, 1986.

Hall, Kermit L., ed. *The Oxford Companion to the Supreme Court* . New York: Oxford University Press, 1992.

COUNTY OF SACRAMENTO V. LEWIS

Legal Citation: 118 S.Ct. 1708 (1998)

Petitioners
County of Sacramento, et al.

Respondents
Teri Lewis and Thomas Lewis, representing the estate of Philip Lewis

Petitioners' Claim
Motorcycle passenger Philip Lewis' due process rights were violated when a police officer, in an attempt to apprehend the driver of the motorcycle, chased the motorcycle at high speeds and eventually struck Lewis.

Chief Lawyer for Petitioners
Terence J. Cassidy

Chief Lawyer for Respondents
Paul J. Hedlund

Justices for the Court
Stephen Breyer, Ruth Bader Ginsburg, Anthony M. Kennedy, Sandra Day O'Connor, William H. Rehnquist, Antonin Scalia, David H. Souter (writing for the Court), John Paul Stevens, Clarence Thomas

Justices Dissenting
None

Place
Washington, D.C.

Date of Decision
26 May 1998

Decision
Philip Lewis' substantive due process rights under the U.S. Constitution were not violated during the high-speed police chase; such governmental action gives rise to liability only if the police officer acts in a way that "shocks the conscience" and violates "the decencies of civilized conduct."

Significance
The *Lewis* case required the U.S. Supreme Court to wrestle with the issue of police chases. The Court had to choose between two standards of liability for police officers in the context of due process claims arising out of high speed chases. In holding for the police officer, the Court decided to adopt the standard that gave police officers more freedom to pursue fleeing criminal suspects without fear of legal reprisal.

On the evening of 22 May 1990, Sacramento County sheriff's deputy James Everett Smith and officer Murray Stapp were breaking up a fight when a motorcycle began to approach them at high speed. Stapp yelled at the driver to stop, climbed into his patrol car, moved his car closer to Smith's to hem in the driver, and turned on his patrol car's warning lights. The motorcyclist, 18 year-old Brian Willard, driving with 16 year-old Philip Lewis on the back seat, slipped past the patrol cars and continued to drive at a high rate of speed. Smith turned on his lights and his siren and followed the motorcycle over the next 1.3 miles, reaching speeds of 100 miles per hour.

As Willard attempted to make a hard left turn, the bike spun out of control and Smith's car spun into Lewis at a speed of approximately 40 miles per hour. Lewis was hurtled 70 feet in the air, and he died at the scene. Lewis' parents filed state and federal civil rights claims in federal court against Sacramento County, the Sacramento County Sheriff's Department, and Smith personally, claiming that Smith had violated Lewis' Fourteenth Amendment Due Process Clause right to life by continuing the high-speed chase.

The defendants moved for summary judgment, arguing that no trial was necessary because there was no factual dispute and they were entitled to judgment as a matter of law. The district court granted the motion for all the parties, ruling that the plaintiffs had not established that their son had a due process right in the context of high-speed police chases at the time of the incident. According to the district court, the Lewises could not prevail because the state of the law on due process in federal court was not clearly defined in May of 1990. The Lewises appealed to the Court of Appeals for the Ninth Circuit, which affirmed the ruling on municipal liability but reversed the summary judgment for Smith. According to the appeals court, Lewis did have a substantive due process right in the context of high-speed police pursuits, and there was a question as to whether that right had been violated. Furthermore, the appeals court held that the appropriate standard to be applied by the trial court at trial was "deliberate indifference to, or reckless disregard for, a person's right to life and personal security." Smith asked the

U.S. Supreme Court to hear the case, and the Court consented.

Although there were differences between the justices in their reasoning, a unanimous Court reversed. In the majority opinion, written by Justice Souter, the Court resolved a split between the lower courts on the issue of the proper legal standard for high-speed police chases. Some courts had been asking in similar cases whether the police officer's conduct constituted "deliberate indifference" to human life, while other courts had been asking whether the police officer's conduct was "shocking to the conscience." The Court opted for the latter, higher standard, holding that a police officer engaged in a high-speed chase cannot be held responsible for resulting injuries under the Due Process Clause of the Fourteenth Amendment unless the officer's actions shocked the conscience of a reasonable person.

The Lewises had brought a claim under the Due Process Clause of the Fourteenth Amendment. This particular clause had been described by the Court as encompassing the right to fairness in governmental procedures, but it also had been described as enforcing "more than fair process." (quoting *Washington v. Glucksberg* [1997]) The right to due process, noted the Court, also guaranteed "substantive" due process, or the right to be free from certain governmental actions "regardless of the fairness of the procedures used to imlement them." (quoting *Daniels v. Williams* [1986]) The Court observed that there were two hurdles facing the Lewises: first, that the claim should have been made under some other constitutional provision; and second, that the allegations were "insufficient to state a substantive due process violation." Although the Court determined that the Lewises had properly based claims on the Due Process Clause, it concluded that the alleged actions of Smith did not constitute a violation of their son's substantive due process rights.

The "core concept" of due process, explained the Court, was "protection against arbitrary action." When the allegation involved "executive" action (as in the Lewises' case) as opposed to legislative action, "only the most egregious official conduct" could be called arbitrary if it shocked the conscience by violating "the decencies of civilized conduct." The Court had used the "shock the conscience" standard for about 50 years; it was the highest standard of proof for finding a person liable, and it remained unique to due process analysis to reinforce the notion that only the most egregious type of conduct on the part of government officials can give rise to a claim of executive abuse of power under the Due Process Clause. The guarantees under the Due Process Clause, lectured the Court, did not "entail a body of constitutional law imposing liability whenever someone cloaked with state authority causes harm."

In applying these principles, it was necessary for the Court to examine the context from which the claims arose. In some instances, the "deliberate indifference" standard was appropriate for finding liability on the part of a government actor. In other situations, though, the higher "shock the conscience" standard was appropriate. In claims arising from legislative action, for example, the denial of the right to an attorney or the right to humane prison conditions, the proper standard was "deliberate indifference" because such procedures arose from a deliberate governmental process. In contrast, a high-speed police chase was a situation in which the government actor, i.e. the police officer, had no chance to deliberate. The term "deliberate indifference" suggested that the standard was "sensibly employed only when actual deliberation [was] practical." When an officer had to make a snap decision, "even precipitate recklessness fail[ed] to inch close enough to harmful purpose to spark the shock" that could create liability.

Officer Smith had to make just such a split-second judgment in the motorcycle chase. Furthermore, stated the Court, Smith was not the only person responsible for Lewis' death. The police, in fact, "had done nothing to cause Willard's high-speed driving in the first place," nothing to inspire Willard's disregard for the law, "and nothing (beyond a refusal to call off the chase) to encourage [Willard] to race through traffic at breakneck speed forcing other drivers out of their travel lanes." Considering all the circumstances, the Court concluded that Smith could not be held liable to the Lewises under the Due Process Clause of the Fourteenth Amendment to the U.S Constitution.

Several justices concurred in the judgment. Justice Rehnquist filed a short opinion that restated the holding and his approval of it. Justice Kennedy also wrote a concurring opinion in which Justice O'Connor joined. Justice Kennedy, like Justice Scalia, did not care for the term "shock the conscience" because it was such a subjective standard. However, Justice Kennedy maintained that Justice Souter had clearly explained the application of the term. Furthermore, the standard was not completely subjective because it contained objective considerations, such as history, tradition, and case precedents.

Justices Breyer and Stevens wrote separate concurring opinions. In its opinion, the majority had reached the constitutional issue of due process, and not the question of whether Smith enjoyed immunity from suit as a government official. Justice Stevens believed that the Court should have refrained from answering the constitutional question because the issue was "difficult and unresolved," and because the Court could have affirmed the judgment for Smith on the grounds that, as a government-employed police officer, he was immune from suit.

Justice Thomas joined a fifth concurring opinion, this one written by Justice Scalia. Scalia bluntly offered that the "changes in this Court's jurisprudence are attributable to changes in the Court's membership." Just one year earlier, in *Washington v. Glucksberg,* Justice Scalia reminded the majority, the Court had rejected the "shock the conscience" test. Justice Scalia would have used the standard formulated in *Glucksberg,* which was "whether our Nation has traditionally protected the rights [the Lewises] assert." Nothing in the Court's precedents suggested that "all government conduct deliberately indifferent to life, liberty, or property, violates the Due Process Clause," Scalia noted, so the Lewises could not base their claim on that constitutional provision. Scalia maintained that the Fourteenth Amendment should not be used to eclipse the systems of redress already in place on the state level. Moreover, added Scalia, it was "not fair to say that it was the police officer alone who 'deprived' Lewis of his life." Scalia would have reversed the appeals court's decision, but he would have done so because the Lewises had offered "no textual or historical support for their alleged due process right," not because they had "failed to shock [his] still, soft voice within."

Impact

The *Lewis* holding established that a police officer, sued under the Due Process Clause of the U.S. Constitution over a high-speed chase, will not be held responsible for injury or death resulting from the chase unless the officer's conduct is shocking to the conscience. This rule necessarily applies only in federal court. For claims related to high-speed police chases that are based on state law, states are free to devise their own standard of liability.

Related Cases

Daniels v. Williams, 474 U.S. 327 (1986).
Zinernon v. Burch, 494 U.S. 113 (1990).
Washington v. Glucksberg, 512 U.S. 702 (1997).

Bibliography and Further Reading

Barrett, Edward L., Jr., William Cohen, Jonathan D. Varat. "The Rise and Fall of Due Process." *Constitutional Law: Cases and Materials.* Westbury, NY: The Foundation Press, Inc., 1989.

Dority, Barbara. "More Power, Less Responsibility." *The Humanist,* September-October 1998, p. 3.

Rinkle, Ralf. "Due Process." *The 'Lectric Law Library.* http://www.lectlaw.com

"Supreme Court Limits Liability in Police Chases." *Liability Week,* June 1, 1998.

Tabin, Barrie. "NLC Brings Local Viewpoint to Court in Advocacy Efforts." *Nation's Cities Weekly,* March 2, 1998, p. 4.

Tabin, Barrie. "Supreme Court Affirms Limits on Local Liability for High Speed Chases." *Nation's Cities Weekly,* June 1, 1998, p. 1.

Urbonya, Kathryn R. "Pleading the Fourth; Plaintiffs May Be Able to Sue Under Seizure Law in High-Speed Chases." *ABA Journal,* September 1998, p. 36.

CIVIL RIGHTS AND EQUAL PROTECTION

The Notion of Equality

The term equal in constitutional law is most commonly associated with the notion of human equality. To most, equality refers to the natural and political rights of essentially all persons living in the United States, especially the nation's citizens. For example, the Pledge of Allegiance ends with reference to "liberty and justice for all." However, in the late eighteenth and early nineteenth centuries, the concept of equality with full protected rights did not apply to all persons, only a select group. The concept of equality was, and is, dynamic with different interpretations always evolving regarding questions of race, gender, nationality, and other aspects of life. Though equality in U.S. constitutional law does not mean that all groups must be treated the same, it does protect groups from arbitrary or hostile discrimination. Some clear government purpose or objective must be evident when a group is distinguished in any law.

The Mirage of Equality

The notion of equality was so restricted in the late eighteenth century that the term or even the concept of equality did not appear anywhere in the Constitution or Bill of Rights. Still, the limited idea of equality held by the framers of the Constitution was actually considered bold at the time. Equality was primarily extended only to white adult males with property, not to African Americans, women, or the poor. Not until 1868, following the Civil War, was the concept of equality written into constitutional law. Even then, when the Fourteenth Amendment defining citizenship was drafted, the Equal Protection Clause quietly appeared in a draft with little debate or discussion. The amendment forbade states from "deny[ing] any person within its jurisdiction the equal protection of the laws." As written, the clause only applied to state governments, not federal. The primary intent of the amendment at the time was to provide citizenship to persons of color and assure African Americans they would enjoy the same constitutional civil rights protections as whites. The concept of sex discrimination was nowhere in sight.

Shortly after adoption of the amendment, the Supreme Court began a lengthy period of very narrow interpretations. In *Slaughterhouse Cases* (1873), the Court held that the only national rights protected from state infringement were the rights to petition the federal government and vote in federal elections. Any other state restrictions were beyond the scope of federal protection. That same year in *Bradwell v. Illinois*, the Court upheld a state law banning women from the practice of law. Reflecting social attitudes of the day, the Court found women generally unfit for the rigors of law practice and more suitable to domestic activities. Furthermore, the Court ruled in 1875 that the federal government could not require states to allow women to vote. As a result, until adoption of the Nineteenth Amendment in 1920, women held less of a voting right than African Americans.

Following the *Slaughterhouse* decision, Congress passed the Civil Rights Act of 1875, protecting African Americans from discrimination in public transportation, inns, theaters, and other types of public places. The Court in *Civil Rights Cases* (1883) struck down the law by holding the Fourteenth Amendment only applied to state government discrimination, not actions by private persons. In addition, the Court ruled that Congress could only address discrimination after it occurred and could not prohibit discriminatory state actions in advance. The next major decision came in 1896 when the Court sanctioned the "separate but equal" doctrine in *Plessy v. Ferguson*. The doctrine meant that the Equal Protection Clause would not be violated if facilities provided for African Americans were equal to those provided for whites. As a result, state-imposed racial segregation became pervasive, particularly in the South, which had separate public water fountains and toilets. States also imposed poll taxes and property and literacy tests to limit African Americans from voting. Consequently, over 70 years would pass after adoption of the Fourteenth Amendment before African Americans would begin to benefit from it.

Ironically, aliens, citizens of foreign countries in the United States, fared better than African Americans during this period under the Equal Protection Clause. In *Yick Wo v. Hopkins* (1886), the Court found that San Francisco's policy for renewing business permits was differently applied to Asians and whites with no justifiable governmental reason. Such arbitrariness violated the Asians' right to earn a living, essential for an individual's enjoyment of life. Importantly, the Court ruled that the Fourteenth Amendment protects all individuals from discrimination, not just U.S. citizens. Congress may hold the constitutional power to regulate immigration into the country, but once an individual is allowed entrance, they enjoy the same constitutional protections as citizens.

Through this early time, the Supreme Court focused almost solely on equality of opportunity in the economic marketplace including state taxation issues and economic regulation. The Court established its first standard review test for equal protection cases in *Lindsley v. Natural Carbonic Gas Co.* (1911), a fairly weak test requiring states to show only that a reasonable basis existed for group restrictions. The Court recognized a broad right of government to distinguish between different groups in regulating economic activities as long as the distinctions were not arbitrary. The Equal Protection Clause remained a very weak form of constitutional protection for over half a century after its adoption, unresponsive to claims of individual rights.

A Switch to Individual Rights

In the 1930s and 1940s, a fundamental shift to individual rights protection began. The Equal Protection Clause actually began to protect those for which it was originally designed. In *Missouri ex rel. Gaines v. Canada* (1938), the Court ruled admissions to a state law school based strictly on race violated the clause. In a prisoner sterilization case, *Skinner v. Oklahoma* (1942), the Court again expanded equal protection by declaring a fundamental right to marriage and procreation. The declining tolerance for laws restricting the rights of specific racial groups was further demonstrated in 1944 in *Korematsu v. United States*. Although the Court upheld the government's detention of U.S. citizens of Japanese descent in relocation camps based on wartime emergency, it recognized race issues required tougher court standards.

Following World War II, the "separate but equal" doctrine came under greater criticism led by the National Association for the Advancement of Colored People (NAACP). The ruling of *Brown v. Board of Education* in 1954 essentially began a civil rights revolution in the United States. By striking down the "separate but equal" doctrine, the Court held unconstitutional public school segregation. In the same year, the Court in *Bolling v. Sharpe* applied the Equal Protection Clause to federal laws and actions for the first time. The Fifth Amendment's Due Process Clause served as the key avenue of authority. The Court found the two concepts, equal protection and due process, closely intertwined with equal protection more directly addressing fairness under the law.

The slow progress of integration that followed led to violence in the streets of many cities along with numerous acts of civil disobedience. In response, Congress took action to bring the court-recognized equal protection standards into law. After passing the 1963 Equal Pay Act requiring comparable pay for comparable work for both men and women, Congress took action on racial civil rights issues by passing the landmark Civil Rights Act of 1964. The Civil Rights Act prohibited discrimination based on race, color, national origin, or religion in most privately-owned businesses serving the public. It also promoted equal opportunity in employment on the basis of race, religion, and sex. The act was immediately challenged but quickly and unanimously upheld by the Supreme Court. Also in 1964, equal protection was extended to voters rights in *Reynolds v. Sims*. State electoral districts must have roughly the same number of voters. This decision affirmed the "one person, one vote" doctrine which Congress put into law with the Voting Rights Act of 1965. The Court also struck down residency requirements, poll taxes, and candidate filing fees to provide equal protection to all voters and political candidates. Cases challenging voter district boundaries continued through the nineties.

Building on the earlier *Korematsu* decision while overturning a state law banning interracial marriages, the Court created a second, much tougher test for racial discrimination challenges in *Loving v. Commonwealth of Virginia* (1967). The government must meet the "compelling interest" test. Not only must the government show a compelling interest in justifying a restriction, it must also show that the restriction is narrowly tailored to meet the objective. The following year, in 1968, Congress passed the Fair Housing Act prohibiting discrimination in housing. Making alien status comparable to race, the compelling interest test was extended in 1971 by the Court to aliens in *Graham v. Richardson*.

The civil rights movement of the 1950s and 1960s also raised public consciousness regarding sex discrimination. The protective paternalistic perspective toward women began to change. In 1971 in *Reed v. Reed,* the Court for the first time struck down a state law for arbitrarily discriminating against women. In 1972, Congress passed the Equal Rights Amendment (ERA) guaranteeing women and men the same constitutional protections. However, the Court upheld many gender-based state laws through the seventies, and the ERA died in 1982 due to the lack of state ratification.

In 1972, the Court also began to strike down laws discriminating against illegitimate children and unwed fathers in certain circumstances. In *Weber v. Aetna Casualty & Surety Co.,* the Court found that laws restricting the rights of illegitimate children are contrary to the basic concepts of fairness. Illegitimate children should receive the same protections as other children and not be penalized for their parents' conduct.

For sex discrimination cases, the Court in *Craig v. Boren* (1976) created a third equal protection test more rigorous than "reasonable basis" but weaker than "compelling interest." The government must show an "important governmental objective," or a distinction based on sex would violate the Equal Protection Clause.

The Ongoing Expansion of Equality

Into the 1990s, the Equal Protection Clause continued to take on considerably more and unexpected importance, becoming the focus of extensive legal action as the role of the federal government changed. Newer issues included sexual harassment, gay rights, affirmative action, and assisted suicide. Originally, the role of government was primarily to resolve conflicts and protect individual behavior unless it was extreme. However, government's role shifted in the late twentieth century to promoter of the welfare of the community, even if it meant restricting individual rights. To many, the shift was one from liberty to equality. Social programs placed an increasing burden on the nation to ensure at least the minimum needs for a decent human life for all of its citizens. The constitutional basis for assigning this new role to government was the Equal Protection Clause of the Fourteenth Amendment. Interpretation of the clause expanded, making it the primary constitutional shield safeguarding the civil rights of many distinct groups of people. A truly fundamental change in U.S. law and society had occurred.

Regarding sexual harassment, the Court in *Meritor Savings Bank v. Vinson* (1986) ruled that such claims fell within civil rights law. Such discrimination was considered a violation of equal protection if it unreasonably interfered with an individual's work performance or created a pervasive hostile environment. The issue greatly rose in visibility with Justice Clarence Thomas' confirmation hearings of 1991. In *J. E. B. v Alabama* (1994), the Court ruled women could not be excluded by lawyers from serving on juries based purely on their gender. In 1996, the Court ruled in *United States v. Virginia* that government must demonstrate an "exceedingly persuasive justification" to defend gender-based discrimination. The Court struck down the publicly-funded Virginia Military Institute's tradition of excluding women as a violation of equal protection. Many contended that Paula Jones' initial harassment claim against President Bill Clinton, alleging a constitutional violation of equal protection, underscored an increasingly obscure perception of equal protection through the 1990s. To many, the increasing confusion of plain violations of common decency with constitutional protections diluted constitutional integrity.

Also, in 1996, a circuit court ruled in *Nabozny v. Podlesny* that public school officials may be held liable for failing to stop the harassment of gay students, thus violating their right to equal protection under the law. Thus, sexual orientation fell under the Equal Protection Clause. The more publicized case involving gay rights law occurred when the Supreme Court in *Romer v. Evans* (1996) struck down a Colorado law, passed as a referendum in 1992, prohibiting state or local governments from granting homosexuality a legal minority status. The law did not pass the "rational basis" test according to the Court. Referendum supporters claimed the decision highlighted the Court's confusion of preferential treatment with equal protection. They asserted that the law sought to prevent preferential treatment, not deny equal protection. This ruling, they asserted, presented yet another instance of "social legislation" by the Court.

Governmental affirmative action programs also came under attack in equal protection disputes. The Court ruled in *Adarand Constructors, Inc. v. Pena* (1995) that racial entitlements of any kind were unacceptable and offended moral perceptions of fairness. The following year California voters passed a referendum, entitled the Civil Rights Initiative, striking down affirmative action programs and claiming to establish racial, ethnic, and gender equality under state law in education, employment, and contracting. Ironically, a federal district judge immediately issued an injunction, finding that the proposition violated the Equal Protection Clause. A Court of Appeals later reversed the decision in 1997.

During the late 1990s, physician-assisted suicide entered the equal protection arena. A federal appeals court in New York in 1996 ruled that patients who commit suicide with prescribed drugs should have the same options as those who choose to have their life support equipment turned off. The manner of ending a life was not relevant. A federal appeals court went even further that year finding assisted suicide a fundamental right by striking down a Washington state law.

By the close of the twentieth century three separate tests were used by the courts to judge the constitutionality of challenged laws under the Equal Protection Clause. The toughest "compelling interest" test applied to race and aliens cases, the intermediate "important governmental objective" test applied to gender and legitimacy issues, and the least stringent "rational basis" applied to most other cases. The original intent of the Equal Protection Clause was to give the humblest and poorest the same civil rights as the most powerful and wealthy. As notions of equality continued to expand, some argued that equality of "result" was gradually replacing equality of "opportunity."

See also: **Affirmative Action, Assisted Suicide and the Right to Die, Employment Discrimination, Gender Discrimination, The Rights of Gays and Lesbians, Segregation and Desegregation, Sexual Harrassment**

Bibliography and Further Reading

Devins, Neal, and Davison M. Douglas, eds. *Redefining Equality.* New York: Oxford University Press, 1998.

Forer, Lois G. *Unequal Protection: Women, Children, and the Elderly in Court.* New York: Norton, 1991.

Galloway, Russell W. *Justice for All?: The Rich and Poor in Supreme Court History, 1790-1990.* Durham, NC: Carolina Academic Press, 1991.

Jackson, Donald W. *Even the Children of Strangers: Equality Under the U.S. Constitution.* Lawrence, KS: University Press of Kansas, 1992.

Minow, Martha. *Not Only for Myself: Identity, Politics, and the Law.* New York: New Press, 1997.

Sarat, Austin, and Thomas R. Kearns, eds. *Identities, Politics, and Rights.* Ann Arbor: University of Michigan Press, 1995.

West, Robin. *Progressive Constitutionalism: Reconstructing the Fourteenth Amendment.* Durham, NC: Duke University Press, 1994.

THE AMISTAD

Legal Citation: 40 U.S. 518 (1841)

Appellant
United States

Appellees
Joseph Cinque, et al.

Appellant's Claim
That the slaves aboard the *Amistad* should be convicted of mutiny.

Chief Lawyer for Appellant
Harry D. Gilpin, U.S. Attorney General

Chief Lawyers for Appellees
John Quincy Adams, Roger S. Baldwin

Justices for the Court
Philip P. Barbour, John Catron, John McKinley, John McLean, Joseph Story (writing for the Court), Smith Thompson, Roger Brooke Taney, James M. Wayne

Justices Dissenting
Henry Baldwin

Place
Washington, D.C.

Date of Decision
January 1841

Decision
The Court would not convict the participants in the *Amistad* mutiny.

Significance
When the courts refused to convict slaves from the schooner *Amistad* after they killed their captors in order to free themselves, the decision was widely hailed as a victory for the cause of abolition.

By the 1830s, many countries were beginning to take steps to limit the age-old institution of slavery. Although slavery was still legal in the U.S., it was illegal to bring new slaves into the country. Further, the abolitionist movement, which sought to do away with slavery altogether, was gaining more and more support. Great Britain was strongly in favor of abolition, and had used its naval power to pressure Spain, whose colonies were dominated by slaveowners, to also make it illegal to bring new slaves into any Spanish possessions.

Spanish power in the New World was declining, however, and the government in Madrid lacked the power to enforce its will. The wealthy landowners in Cuba and elsewhere throughout the Spanish New World needed slaves to work their estates, but obeying the import restriction meant waiting for the children of existing slaves to mature. To meet the growing demand for slaves, an illegal slave trade soon emerged. Slavers went to the west coast of Africa, captured healthy young black men and women, and brought them back to Cuba for sale. The colonial authorities did nothing to stop this trade. In 1839, slavers brought back a cargo of slaves from what is now Sierra Leone. Among the slaves was a young man they named Joseph Cinque.

In June of 1839, Jose Ruiz and Pedro Montes purchased 49 captured Africans, including Cinque, in Havana for their estates in the Cuban town of Puerto Principe. Ruiz and Montes put the slaves aboard the schooner *Amistad*, intending to sail from Havana up the Cuban coast to Puerto Principe. The Spanish crew taunted the ignorant slaves, telling them wild stories, such as that their new owners intended to kill and eat them when they arrived. On the night of 1 July, Cinque led the blacks in a successful rebellion and seized control of the ship. Several members of the crew were killed during the struggle, but Ruiz and Montes survived. Cinque ordered Ruiz and Montes to take the ship back to Africa.

The Spaniards sailed east for Africa by day, but secretly reversed course by night. For nearly two months the *Amistad* meandered back and forth, but eventually winds and currents drove it north to the coast of the United States. On 26 August, the *U.S.S.*

JOSEPH CINQUEZ.

The brave Congolese Chief, who prefers death to Slavery, and who now lies in Jail in Irons at New Haven Conn. awaiting his Trial for daring for freedom.

SPEECH TO HIS COMRADE SLAVES AFTER MURDERING THE CAPTAIN &C. AND GETTING POSSESSION OF THE VESSEL AND CARGO

"Brothers we have done that which we purposed, our hands are now clean for we have Striven to regain the precious heritage we received from our fathers We have only to persevere. Where the Sun rises there is our home, our brethren, our fathers Do not seek to defeat my orders, if so I shall sacrifice any one who would endanger the rest, when at home we will kill the Old Man, the young one shall be saved he is kind and gave you bread we must not kill those who give us water. Brothers, I am resolved that it is better to die than be a white mans slave and I will not complain if by dying I save you. Let us be careful what we eat that we may not be sick. The deed is done and I need say no more."

The U.S. Supreme Court upheld the ruling of the U.S. District Court for Connecticut, making Cinque and his followers free. © The Library of Congress.

Washington spotted the *Amistad* off the coast of New York, seized the ship, and brought it into New London, Connecticut.

Cinque on Trial

In New London, Ruiz and Montes described the slave rebellion to the American authorities, and pressed their claim for the return of the *Amistad* with its cargo of slaves. Despite the illegal capture of the slaves, the Spanish government backed Ruiz's and Montes' claim. With the blessing of President Martin Van Buren's administration, District Attorney William S. Holabird charged Cinque and the other blacks with committing murder and piracy aboard the *Amistad*.

The trial was held in the U.S. District Court for Connecticut. The judge was district court judge Andrew T. Judson, assisted by Supreme Court Justice Smith Thompson. The abolitionists hired a team of defense lawyers to represent the blacks, comprised of Roger S. Baldwin, Joshua Leavitt, Seth Staples and the ex-president of the United States, John Quincy Adams.

The trial began on 19 November 1839. The defense lawyers asserted that the blacks had the right to free themselves from the horrible conditions of slavery. In support of their position, they introduced Dr. Richard R. Madden, who had travelled extensively in Cuba and was an expert on slave conditions:

> . . . so terrible were these atrocities, so murderous the system of slavery, so transcendent the evils I witnessed, over all I have ever heard or seen of the rigour of slavery elsewhere, that at first I could hardly believe the evidence of my senses.

Further, as the testimony of Madden and various witnesses made clear, returning Cinque and the others to Cuba meant certain death at the hands of the pro-slavery colonial authorities. In addition, since the blacks had originally been captured in Africa in violation of Spanish law, the abolitionists argued that the blacks were not legally slaves and therefore were not "property" belonging to Ruiz and Montes.

Despite pressure from the Van Buren administration, which wanted to avoid diplomatic tension with Spain, on 13 January 1840 Judge Judson ruled in favor of the Africans. Although the *Amistad* with its goods would be returned to Ruiz and Montes, subject to salvage costs, Cinque and the others:

> . . . were born free, and ever since have been and still of right are free and not slaves.

Further, because they had been illegally enslaved, the Africans were ruled to be innocent of murder and piracy since they had only acted to free themselves. The prosecution appealed Judson's decision to the Supreme Court. The abolitionists had anticipated this move, since five Supreme Court justices, including Chief Justice Roger B. Taney, were Southerners and had owned slaves. The defense relied on John Quincy Adams to present their case, banking on his prestige as much as on his legal ability.

On 22 February 1840 the Supreme Court heard both sides of the argument, and on 9 March issued its opinion. The Court upheld Judson's decision, and so the blacks were finally free. Cinque and the others were returned to Africa.

Technically, the *Amistad* decision did not condemn slavery. It only held that Africans who were not legally slaves could not be considered property. Still, the courts could have easily turned Cinque over to Spanish authorities or returned them to Cuba. Therefore, the case was seen as a victory for the abolitionist cause, and was a milestone in the movement's quest for the total elimination of slavery.

Bibliography and Further Reading

Adams, John Quincy. *Argument in the Case of U.S. v. Cinque.* New York: Arno Press, 1969.

Cable, Mary. *Black Odyssey: the Case of the Slave Ship Amistad.* New York: Penguin Books, 1977 .

"Cinque." *Jet,* March 1984, p. 21.

Jones, Howard. *Mutiny on the Amistad: the Saga of a Slave Revolt and its Impact on American Abolition, Law,* *and Diplomacy.* New York: Oxford University Press, 1987.

Owens, William A. *Slave Mutiny: the Revolt on the Schooner Amistad.* New York: J. Day Co., 1953.

UNITED STATES V. ANTHONY

Legal Citation: 24 F.Cas. 829 (1873)

Plaintiff
United States

Defendant
Susan B. Anthony

Plaintiff's Claim
That Anthony had voted illegally.

Chief Prosecutor
Richard Crowley, U.S. District Attorney

Chief Defense Lawyers
Henry R. Selden, John Van Voorhis

Judge
Supreme Court Justice Ward Hunt

Place
Canandaigua, New York

Date of Decision
18 June 1873

Decision
Anthony was convicted of voting illegally.

Significance
Was one of the first in a series of decisions—including two rendered by the full Supreme Court—which found that Section 1 of the Fourteenth Amendment to the U.S. Constitution did not expand or protect women's rights, an interpretation which remained unchanged for almost 100 years.

United States v. Anthony and several related cases in the 1870s grew out of women's attempts to gain full rights of citizenship through the judicial system. Had this strategy worked, women would have been spared what followed: a 60-year-long, state-by-state legislative campaign for suffrage and 100 years in which the Fourteenth Amendment's Equal Protection Clause was not applied to sex discrimination cases.

In July of 1868, exactly 20 years after the Seneca Falls Convention and American women's first public demand for suffrage, the Fourteenth Amendment was adopted. Section 2, intended to encourage states to grant suffrage to African American men, angered women's rights leaders because it introduced the word "male" into the Constitution and, some thought, called into question the citizenship of females. Francis Minor, an attorney and husband of the Woman Suffrage Association of Missouri's president, Virginia Minor, thought women were looking at the wrong clause. Section 1, he pointed out in 1869, declared

> All persons born or naturalized in the United States, and subject to the jurisdiction thereof, are citizens of the United States and of the State wherein they reside. No State shall make or enforce any law which shall abridge the privileges or immunities of citizens of the United States . . .

Minor wrote that this clause confirmed the citizenship of women and concluded ". . . provisions of the several State Constitutions that exclude women from the franchise on account of sex, are violative alike of the spirit and letter of the Federal Constitution."

Susan B. Anthony and Elizabeth Cady Stanton published Minor's analysis in their newspaper, the *Revolution,* and urged women to go to the polls. In 1871 and 1872, in at least ten states, women did so. Most were turned away, but a few actually managed to vote.

The Almighty Vote

One of those who voted in 1872 was Susan B. Anthony. Before registering in Rochester, New York, she had consulted Judge Henry R. Selden, who agreed that Section 1 of the Fourteenth Amendment should entitle women

Suffrage

Though considered fundamental to political equality and representative government, suffrage, the right to vote, has been difficult to achieve by many in the United States. Originally, only free white men with property held the right.

The first women's rights convention, convened in 1848 in Seneca Falls, New York, made suffrage their primary goal. In 1869 two national advocacy organizations formed. The National Woman Suffrage Association, led by Elizabeth Cady Stanton and Susan B. Anthony, proposed a woman's suffrage amendment to the U.S. Constitution. The American Woman Suffrage Association, led by Lucy Stone, worked to influence individual states. By the end of the nineteenth century only four states had granted full suffrage to women. In 1890 the two groups merged into the National American Women's

Suffrage Association led by Carry Chapman Catt. By 1919 with 27 states granting full or limited suffrage and women having manned the home front during World War I, Congress felt increased pressure to act. Suffragists participated in marches, picketing, vigils, and hunger strikes. Finally, in 1920 the Nineteenth Amendment granted women suffrage.

Not until 1965, a century after the Civil War and in the midst of the civil rights movement did Congress pass the landmark Voters' Rights Act guaranteeing blacks the right to vote as well.

Source(s): Guinier, Lani. *The Tyranny of the Majority: Fundamental Fairness in Representative Democracy.* New York: Free Press, 1994.

---

to suffrage; she carried his written opinion with her and threatened to sue the registrars if they failed to take her oath. They complied. Anthony and 14 female companions were registered and, on 5 November, they voted. On 28 November, Susan B. Anthony, the other 14 women, and the inspectors who had registered them, were arrested.

All parties were offered release upon payment of $500 bail; Anthony alone refused to pay. Henry Selden, acting as her attorney, applied for a writ of *habeas corpus,* and Anthony was temporarily released. A U.S. district judge denied the writ and reset her bail at $1000 on 21 January 1873. Anthony refused to pay, but Selden—who would later explain that he "could not see a lady I respected put in jail"—paid the bail. Anthony was released and immediately lost her right to appeal to the Supreme Court on the basis of the writ of *habeas corpus.*

Preparation for Trial

Since women were not allowed to testify in their own defense in the mid-nineteenth century, Anthony tried to present her side of the story to prospective jurors before the trial, scheduled for 13 May, began. She gave the same speech in all 29 postal districts of her county:

"Friends and Fellow-Citizens, I stand before you under indictment for the alleged crime of having voted at the last presidential election, without having a lawful right to vote . . . We no longer petition legislature or Congress to give of the right to vote, but appeal to women everywhere to exercise their too long neglected 'citizen's right' . . . we throw to the wind the old dogma that governments can give rights.

The Declaration of Independence, the United States Constitution, the constitutions of the several states . . . propose to protect the people in the exercise of their God-given rights. Not one of them pretends to bestow rights . . . One half of the people of this Nation to-day are utterly powerless to blot from the statute books an unjust law, or to write a new and just one. The women, dissatisfied as they are with this form of government, that enforces taxation without representation—that compels them to obey laws to which they have never given their consent—that imprisons and hangs them without a trial by a jury of their peers— that robs them, in marriage of the custody of their own persons, wages, and children—are this half of the people left wholly at the mercy of the other half . . ."

Because Anthony had "prejudiced any possible jury," her trial was moved out of her own Monroe County to Canandaigua, a town in Ontario County, New York, and rescheduled for 17 June. By 16 June, Anthony had spoken in every Ontario village.

The Trial

The trial opened before Judge Ward Hunt on 17 June 1873.

U.S. District Attorney Richard Crowley presented the government's case: "Miss Susan B. Anthony . . . upon the 5th day of November, 1872, . . . voted . . . At that time she was a woman."

Beverly W. Jones, one of the inspectors under indictment for registering Anthony, testified that he had

Susan B. Anthony.
© The Library of
Congress.

indeed registered her and that he had received ballots from her on 5 November.

Crowley introduced the poll list bearing the name of Susan B. Anthony as proof that the woman had voted, and the government rested its case.

Henry Selden then tried to call Anthony to the stand. Crowley objected: "She is not competent as a witness in her own behalf."

The Judge "so held" that Anthony could not testify.

Selden then took the stand and testified that he concurred with Anthony's reading of the Fourteenth Amendment and that he had advised her to cast her ballot. Selden argued: "The only alleged ground of illegality of the defendant's vote is that she is a woman. If the same act has been done by her brother under the same circumstances, the act would have been not only innocent, but honorable and laudable; but having been done by a woman it is said to be a crime. The crime, therefore, consists not in the act done, but in the simple fact that the person doing it was a woman and not a man."

At the conclusion of argument, Judge Hunt read a statement—prepared before he had heard testimony—to the "Gentlemen of the Jury":

. . . The right of voting, or the privilege of voting, is a right or privilege arising under the Constitution of the State, and not of the United States . . . If the State of New York should provide that no person should vote until he had reached the age of thirty-one years, or after he had reached the age of fifty, or that no person having gray hair, or who had not the use of all his limbs, should be entitled to vote, I do not see how it could be held to be a violation of any right derived or held under the Constitution of the United States.

Judge Hunt directed the jury to deliver a verdict of "guilty."

Selden objected, saying, ". . . it is for the jury [to decide]."

Hunt addressed the jury again: ". . . I have decided as a question of law . . . that under the Fourteenth Amendment, which Miss Anthony claims protects her, she was not protected in a right to vote . . . I therefore direct you to find a verdict of guilty."

Hunt then asked the clerk to take the jury's verdict. Selden asked the jurors be polled individually, and

Judge Hunt discharged the jury without asking for its verdict.

The next day, Selden presented a motion and arguments for a new trial, which Hunt denied. Hunt then asked Anthony to stand. "The sentence of the Court is that you pay a fine of $100.00 and the costs of prosecution."

Anthony replied: "May it please your honor, I will never pay a dollar of your unjust penalty . . . 'Resistance to tyranny is obedience to God.'"

Hunt released her, saying, "Madam, the Court will not order to stand committed until the fine is paid."

Anthony never paid the fine.

The Supreme Court Looks at Women and the Fourteenth Amendment

In 1873, the Supreme Court heard the case of Myra Bradwell, who claimed that her Fourteenth Amendment rights were abridged by Illinois' law prohibiting women from the practice of law. The Court found that her rights had not been violated since ". . . the right of females to pursue any lawful employment for a livelihood (the practice of law included)" was not "one of the privileges and immunities of women as citizens." Justice Samuel F. Miller, writing for the majority, explained: "The paramount destiny and mission of woman are to fulfill the noble and benign offices of wife and mother. This is the law of the Creator. And the rules of civil society must be adapted to the general constitution of things . . ."

In its decision on *Minor v. Happersett,* the Supreme Court's unanimous opinion was that the right of suffrage was not one of the privileges and immunities of citizenship and women, although citizens of the United States, could be denied the vote by their respective states.

The first successful Fourteenth Amendment challenge to a sex-biased law was brought by Sally Reed in 1971. Reed's son died intestate and the Idaho court automatically appointed Reed's estranged husband Cecil as administrator of the estate, because of his sex, and denied Reed's own petition, because of hers. More than one hundred years after the adoption of the Fourteenth Amendment, Chief Justice Warren E. Burger delivered the following opinion of the Court: ". . . We have concluded that the arbitrary preference established in favor of males by the Idaho Code cannot stand in the face of the Fourteenth Amendment's command that no State deny the equal protection of the laws to any person within its jurisdiction."

Related Cases

Bradwell v. Illinois, 83 U.S. 130 (1873).
Minor v. Happersett, 88 U.S. 162 (1875).
Reed v. Reed, 404 U.S. 71 (1971).

Bibliography and Further Reading

Barry, Kathleen. *Susan B. Anthony: A Biography.* New York: New York University Press, 1988.

Flexner, Eleanor. *Century of Struggle.* Cambridge, MA: The Belknap Press of Harvard University Press, 1959, revised 1975.

Frost, Elizabeth and Kathryn Cullen-DuPont. *Women's Suffrage in America: An Eyewitness History.* New York: Facts On File, 1992.

Harper, Ida Husted. *Life and Work of Susan B. Anthony.* 1898, rpt. Salem, NH: Ayer Company, 1983.

Stanton, Elizabeth Cady, Susan B. Anthony, and Matilda Joslyn Gage. *History of Woman Suffrage,* Vol. II. 1882, rpt. Salem, NH: Ayer Company, 1985.

UNITED STATES V. CRUIKSHANK

Legal Citation: 92 U.S 542 (1876)

Plaintiff
United States

Defendants
William J. Cruikshank, et al.

Plaintiff's Claim
That the defendants should be convicted of violations of 16 federal laws, including involvement in the lynching of two black men and the violation of the victims' "right and privilege peaceably to assemble together."

Chief Lawyers for Plaintiff
Edwards Pierrepont, Attorney General; Samuel F. Phillips, Solicitor General

Chief Defense Lawyers
David Dudley Field, Reverdy Johnson, R. H. Marr, Philip Phillips

Justices for the Court
Joseph P. Bradley, Nathan Clifford, David Davis, Stephen J. Field, Ward Hunt, Samuel F. Miller, William Strong, Noah H. Swayne, Morrison R. Waite (writing for the court)

Justices Dissenting
None

Place
Washington, D.C.

Date of Decision
March 27, 1876

Decision
Guilty verdicts were overturned.

Significance
The Supreme Court in *Cruikshank* severely limited the ability of the federal government to protect the civil rights of newly-freed African Americans. The federal government would not achieve the power to effectively protect civil rights until well into the twentieth century.

In many ways, the Civil War began as a simple struggle between North and South over whether the Union would survive. Abolishing slavery became its primary purpose only after nearly two years of combat. President Abraham Lincoln was initially hesitant about freeing the slaves, and many leading Northerners such as General George McClellan were openly against abolition. However, after Lincoln finally decided to side with the abolitionists and issued the Emancipation Proclamation, the Civil War became almost a crusade against slavery for the people of the North. Renewed popular enthusiasm for the war, plus the addition of black regiments to Union forces, led to victory for the North in 1865.

African Americans were finally freed, but their hold on liberty was precarious. The former slaves were uneducated, poor, and dependent on white landowners for their living. Many left the land for the industrial cities of the North, but most stayed in the South because they had no skills other than as agricultural laborers. During the early years of Reconstruction, the South was under military occupation and ex-slaves in the states of the former Confederacy were protected from their former masters. Further, it seemed as if the abolitionists had succeeded in obtaining permanent and meaningful legal recognition of African Americans' civil rights through a series of amendments to the Constitution.

The Thirteenth Amendment, forbidding slavery, was ratified in 1865. The Fourteenth Amendment, providing for equal protection and due process under the law, was ratified in 1868. The Fifteenth Amendment, protecting the right to vote, was ratified in 1870. The Fourteenth Amendment is the most extensive of these three amendments, and based upon it, Congress enacted legislation on 31 May 1870 that made it a felony if two or more people conspired to deprive anyone of his or her federal civil rights.

Southern Racism Makes a Comeback

Despite the new legal protections for ex-slaves, as Southern states were re-admitted to the Union and the occupation forces went home, the old ways returned in new guises. Landowners no longer owned slaves, but the practice of sharecropping effectively kept blacks tied to the land and subservient to whites. Southern states

Hate Crimes

A hate, or bias, crime is a verbal or physical assault against a person who is intentionally selected on the basis of their race, color, religion, gender, sexual orientation, ethnic origin, national origin, or disability. Examples include defacing a Jewish synagogue with anti-Semitic symbols, attacking persons who are believed to be gay, or breaking the windows of a Chinese restaurant. Offenses involving such bias-inspired conduct is thought to inflict greater individual and societal harm than other offenses.

Spurred by the rise of hate incidents during the 1980s, approximately 30 states passed laws defining hate crimes. One type of law treats hate crime as distinct offenses with stiff penalties. Another form applies enhanced penalties, such as higher fines and longer jail terms, to existing laws for transgressions specifically motivated by prejudice. At the national level, the Hate Crime Statistics Act of 1990 requires the Federal Bureau of Investigation to collect hate crime statistics.

To avoid infringing on First Amendment protections, hate crime laws may not be so sweeping that they criminalize expressive conduct which cause only hurt feelings or resentment. Laws also may not target a specific subject of speech or restrict a person's thoughts or beliefs. They can take racial bias or other prejudice into account, however, when it motivates illegal action.

Source(s): Jacobs, James B., and Kimberly Potter. *Hate Crimes: Criminal Law & Identity Politics.* New York: Oxford University Press, 1998.

---

passed "Jim Crow" laws enforcing the separation of blacks from whites in public accommodations. What states could not do in public, Southern whites did in private: the Ku Klux Klan (KKK) developed as an instrument of terror to enforce white supremacy. Hard-won black liberties began to slip away.

As Congress' act of 1870 demonstrated, however, the North would not give up without a fight. Three years later, matters came to a head. On 13 April 1873, a Southern mob in Grant Parish, Louisiana numbering nearly 100 people lynched two African American men, Levi Nelson and Alexander Tillman. Apparently Nelson and Tillman had tried to vote in a local election against the wishes of white residents. Approximately 80 people in the lynch mob were indicted for violations of federal law and seventeen were eventually brought to trial, including one William J. Cruikshank. The U.S. attorney in charge, J. R. Beckwith, charged each of them with sixteen violations of the 1870 law. The most important charge was violating the victims' "right and privilege peaceably to assemble together."

Cruikshank and the others, however, were not charged with murder. Nelson and Tillman's murder was a Louisiana state offense, not a violation of the federal law, and the Louisiana authorities did not prosecute. The defendants were brought to trial in New Orleans before a judge of the federal Circuit Court for the District of Louisiana.

Little is known about the actual trial, as the real action was yet to come. Cruikshank and the others were found guilty. The defense lawyers promptly appealed for a stay to Joseph P. Bradley, an associate justice of the U.S. Supreme Court. In that day and age, individual justices of the Supreme Court were charged with hearing appeals in various parts of the country before the appeals went to the full Court in Washington, D.C. The District of Louisiana had been assigned to Bradley.

Justice Bradley granted the defense's motion to stay the guilty verdicts, and Cruikshank's case was sent to the Supreme Court for a final decision. David Dudley Field, Reverdy Johnson, and Philip Phillips joined the defense team, while Attorney General Edwards Pierrepont and Solicitor General Samuel F. Phillips personally assisted the prosecution as both sides prepared for their arguments before the Court.

At the Court's 1874 October term, the prosecution argued that the 1870 act and the Fourteenth Amendment gave the government the power to try and convict offenders like Cruikshank. The defense argued that the Fourteenth Amendment gave the federal government authority to act only against state government violations of civil rights, but not against one citizen's violation of another's civil rights, like Cruikshank's violation of Nelson and Tillman's rights. The defense's argument, that Congress could legislate against only "state action," would have the effect of leaving the federal government powerless to prosecute lynch mobs and groups such as the KKK. African Americans would be protected only by their state courts against white violence, which in the South meant no protection at all.

The Supreme Court Delivers a Crushing Blow

After hearing both sides' arguments, the Court took a year to render its decision. Chief Justice Morrison R. Waite wrote the Court's ruling, which was issued in the

Court's 1875 October Term. Waite's opinion would stymie the federal government's ability to protect African American civil rights for 90 years.

Waite began by reiterating the dual nature of American government:

> We have in our political system a government of the United States and a government of each of the several States. Each one of these governments is distinct from the others, and each has citizens of its own who owe it allegiance, and whose rights, within its jurisdiction, it must protect. The same person may be at the same time a citizen of the United States and a citizen of a State, but his rights of citizenship under one of these governments will be different from those he has under the other.

Waite then stated that the 16 violations of the 1870 act charged against Cruikshank and the others were really simple state conspiracy charges. The federal prosecution was thus unconstitutional. Even the most important charge, violating the victims' "right and privilege peaceably to assemble together," was really a violation of state rights. If the victims had assembled to "petition for a redress of grievances," or some other right specifically granted by the Constitution, then perhaps a federal prosecution would be permissible. Waite refused, however, to give the federal government jurisdiction over any civil rights violation not specifically covered by the Constitution:

> This [case] is nothing else than [an allegation of] a conspiracy to falsely imprison or murder citizens of the United States, being within the territorial jurisdiction of the State of Louisiana . . . Sovereignty, for this purpose, rests alone with the State. It is no more the duty or within the power of the United States to punish for a conspiracy to falsely imprison or murder within a State, than it would be to punish for false imprisonment or murder itself.

Cruikshank and the others would thus go free. Through Waite, the Supreme Court had firmly endorsed the defendants' "state action" argument:

> The Fourteenth Amendment prohibits a State from depriving any person of life, liberty, or property, without due process of law; but this adds nothing to the rights of one citizen as against another.

Because the Court had essentially told people to go to their state governments and courts for protection, African American civil liberties underwent a long eclipse, particularly in the South, from which they would not recover until the 1960s. The Court had turned a blind eye to the fact that in the South, state governments were *de facto* supporters of "private" racism such as that espoused by the the Ku Klux Klan and the lynch mobs.

In the 1960s, the federal government enacted new civil rights laws and moved aggressively to enforce them. This time, in dozens of cases the Court consistently upheld the constitutionality of federal measures. The Court's change in attitude was due to the political upheavals of the time and the new majority of liberal justices. Obstacles such as the "state action" requirement of the Fourteenth Amendment were substantially reduced. Further, the Court allowed the federal government broad civil rights enforcement powers under other sections of the Constitution, such as the federal authority to regulate any conduct that even remotely affects interstate commerce. Cases like *Cruikshank,* however, had prevented the federal government from protecting civil rights 90 years earlier.

Related Cases

United States v. Reese, 92 U.S. 214 (1876).
DeJonge v. Oregon, 299 U.S. 353 (1937).
Hague v. CIO, 307 U.S. 496 (1939).

Bibliography and Further Reading

Burns, James MacGregor. *A People's Charter: The Pursuit of Rights in America.* New York: Knopf, 1991.

Emerson, Thomas Irwin. *Political and Civil Rights in the United States: a Collection of Legal and Related Materials.* Boston: Little, Brown, 1967.

Foner, Eric. "The New View of Reconstruction." *American Heritage,* October 1983, pp. 10-16

Franklin, John Hope. "Mirror for Americans: a Century of Reconstruction History." *American Historical Review,* February 1980, pp. 1-14

Johnson, John W., ed. *Historic U.S. Court Cases, 1690–1990: An Encyclopedia.* New York: Garland Publishing, 1992.

Neely, Mark E. *The Fate of Liberty: Abraham Lincoln and Civil Liberties,* New York: Oxford University Press, 1991.

Nieman, Donald G. *Promises to Keep: African Americans and the Constitutional Order, 1776 to the Present.* New York: Oxford University Press, 1991.

UNITED STATES V. HARRIS

Legal Citation: 106 U.S. 629 (1883)

Plaintiff
United States

Defendant
R. G. Harris, et al.

Plaintiff's Claim
A federal civil rights statute making it a crime for two or more persons to conspire to deprive another person of the equal protection of the laws or of equal privileges or immunities under the laws is constitutional.

Chief Lawyer for Plaintiff
Samuel F. Phillips, U.S. Solicitor General

Chief Defense Lawyer
None

Justices for the Court
Samuel Blatchford, Joseph P. Bradley, Stephen Johnson Field, Horace Gray, John Marshall Harlan I, Stanley Matthews, Samuel Freeman Miller, Morrison Remick Waite, William Burnham Woods (writing for the Court)

Justices Dissenting
None

Place
Washington, D.C.

Date of Decision
22 January 1883

Decision
That the federal statute was unconstitutional. Therefore, the criminal indictment against the defendants was dismissed.

Significance
The ruling invalidated a provision of the federal Civil Rights Act of 1871, also known as the Ku Klux Klan Act, that made it a crime for two or more persons to conspire to deprive another person of the equal protection of the laws or of equal privileges or immunities under the laws. The Supreme Court invalidated the provision because the U.S. Constitution did not authorize Congress to punish private persons for interfering with the exercise of Fourteenth Amendment rights. The Constitution only gave Congress power to regulate state action. The Court's decision gave rise to what is commonly called the "state action" doctrine in civil rights cases.

On 1 January 1863, President Abraham Lincoln issued a proclamation of emancipation for African Americans held in slavery in Confederate states. Between 1865 and 1870, the states ratified to the U.S. Constitution the Thirteenth Amendment which abolished slavery, the Fourteenth Amendment which guaranteed equal protection of the laws, and the Fifteenth Amendment which guaranteed the right to vote. In the late 1860s, a secret white organization called the Ku Klux Klan was founded with the purpose of preventing African Americans from gaining equal access to political power. The Ku Klux Klan beat and murdered African Americans and their white sympathizers to keep them from exercising their rights.

To counter the activities of the organization, the Reconstruction Congress enacted the Civil Rights Act of 1871, also known as the Ku Klux Klan Act. The act extended the protection of federal courts to those who effectively were prevented from exercising their civil rights by the threat of mob violence. The act authorized both criminal and civil actions against those who "conspire or go in disguise upon the highway or on the premises of another for the purpose of depriving" any person of the equal protection of the laws or of equal privileges or immunities under the laws. Although the immediate purpose of the act was to combat animosity against African Americans and their supporters, the language of the act, like that of many Reconstruction statutes, was applicable to incidents beyond the scope of events during the Reconstruction.

In 1876, a grand jury returned an indictment in a federal circuit court in Tennessee charging several persons with criminal violations of the Civil Rights Act following the beating of three African American men and the killing of a fourth, all of whom were, at the time of the incident, under arrest and in the custody of a deputy sheriff. The defendants were charged with conspiring to deprive the victims of the equal protection of the laws and of the right to be protected from violence while under arrest and in custody of the sheriff. The defendants were also charged with conspiring to prevent or hinder the deputy sheriff from keeping the arrested men safe and from providing them the equal protection of the law.

The defendants demurred to the indictment, challenging its validity and seeking its dismissal. The defendants questioned the power of Congress to pass the law on which the indictment was based. Specifically, the defendants claimed that only the states, not the federal government, had the power to enact and enforce legislation prohibiting conspiracies to deprive persons of equal protection of the laws when the conspiracies did not involve state action.

The demurrer was heard in the federal circuit court by a panel of two judges. After oral argument, the circuit court was divided in its opinion on the constitutionality of the act's criminal provisions. Consequently, the circuit court certified the question to the U.S. Supreme Court, pursuant to a federal statute authorizing reconciliation of the division of opinion.

Congress Lacked Power to Pass Law

In a unanimous decision, the Supreme Court ruled that the provision punishing private conspiracies was unconstitutional. The Court began by stating the rules applicable to its analysis. First, the Court had to presume that Congress had constitutional power to pass the statute unless the lack of constitutional authority was clearly demonstrated. Next, the Court stated, "every valid act of Congress must find in the Constitution some warrant for its passage." To summarize the analytical process, the Court quoted Justice Joseph Story's *Commentaries on the Constitution* saying, "Whenever, therefore, a question arises concerning the constitutionality of a particular power, the first question is whether the power be expressed in the Constitution. If it be, the question is decided. If it be not expressed, the next inquiry must be whether it is properly an incident to an express power and necessary to its execution. If it be, then it may be exercised by Congress. If not, Congress cannot exercise it."

Searching the Constitution, the Court found only four paragraphs that could have any reference to the question at hand. Those paragraphs were Section 2 of Article 4 of the original Constitution and the Thirteenth, Fourteenth, and Fifteenth amendments. The Court considered each of these constitutional provisions, in turn, to determine if any of them gave Congress the power to enact the Civil Rights Act provisions criminalizing private conspiracies.

The Court first concluded that the Fifteenth Amendment, guaranteeing the right to vote, did not give Congress that power. The Civil Rights Act criminalized the conduct of private persons who invaded the equal privileges or immunities of others or deprived others of equal protection of the law. It made no reference to conduct of the state or the United States or to voting rights. According to the Court, such a law could not be founded on the Fifteenth Amendment, the sole object of which was to prevent the United States or the states from denying or abridging voting rights based on race, color, or previous condition of servitude.

The Court also found no support for the act's criminal provisions in the Fourteenth Amendment, again because the provisions were directed at the actions of private persons, without reference to the laws of the states, or the administration of those laws by state officials. The Fourteenth Amendment, in the Court's opinion, prohibited states, not private persons, from making or enforcing any law abridging the privileges or immunities of U.S. citizens, depriving any person of life, liberty or property without due process, or denying any person equal protection of the laws. The Court concluded that the Fourteenth Amendment, like the Fifteenth, could not be read to authorize the federal government to regulate private conduct.

Elaborating on its position, the Supreme Court quoted Justice Bradley in *United States v. Cruikshank*, stating that the Fourteenth Amendment "is a guaranty against the exertion of arbitrary and tyrannical power on the part of the government and legislature of the state, not a guaranty against the commission of individual offenses; and the power of congress, whether express or implied, to legislate for the enforcement of such a guaranty, does not extend to the passage of laws for the suppression of crime within the states." To emphasize its point, the Court said, "When the state has been guilty of no violation of [the amendment's] provisions, . . . when, on the contrary, the laws of the state, as enacted by its legislative, and construed by its judicial, and administered by its executive departments, recognize and protect the rights of all persons, (then) the amendment imposes no duty and confers no power upon Congress." The Court held that because the Civil Rights Act applied no matter how well the state may have performed its duty, the act could find no warrant in the Fourteenth Amendment.

The Thirteenth Amendment, abolishing slavery and involuntary servitude, also did not warrant the enactment of the criminal provisions of the act. Although the amendment gave Congress the power to enact enforcing legislation, the Court determined that the civil rights provisions under review were broader than what the Thirteenth Amendment would justify. According to the Court, the provisions could apply even to a conspiracy between two free white men against another free white man to deprive the latter of a right accorded him by the laws of the state or of the United States. The Court concluded by saying, such a law "clearly cannot be authorized by the amendment which simply prohibits slavery and involuntary servitude."

The final constitutional provision considered by the Court was Article 4, Section 2, declaring that the citizens of each state shall be entitled to all the privileges and immunities of citizens of the several states. The object of this provision is to inhibit a state from passing legislation discriminating against citizens of other states. The Court concluded that the criminal provisions of the Civil Rights Act could not find support in this article, again because the article was directed against state action, rather than the actions of private citizens who invade the rights of fellow citizens.

Impact

The Court's ruling that Congress did not have the power under the Constitution to regulate private conduct came during the aftermath of the Civil War when re-establishing political harmony with Southern states was crucial. The decision reflected the federal government's concern that the Fourteenth Amendment not be used to centralize power so as to upset the federal system. This restrictive view of Congress' power rendered ineffective much of the civil rights legislation passed during Reconstruction. This view prevailed until 1966 when six Supreme Court justices expressly stated in *United States v. Guest* (1966), that the specific language of Section 5 of the Fourteenth Amendment empowers Congress to enact laws punishing all conspiracies—with or without state action—that interfere with Fourteenth Amendment rights. In *Guest,* the Court was interpreting a statute passed in 1909 criminalizing precisely the same conduct covered by the 1871 act. Four years later, in *Adickes v. Kress* (1970), the Supreme Court finally declared that *Harris* had been overruled.

Although the *Harris* decision invalidated only the criminal provision of the 1871 act, state action also became an issue in civil damages actions. More than a century after their passage, the Civil Rights Acts of the Reconstruction Era continued to be used to assert a variety of civil constitutional claims and continued to present difficult questions of statutory interpretation.

Related Cases

United States v. Cruikshank, 92 U.S. 542 (1876).
Civil Rights Cases, 109 U.S. 3 (1883).
United States v. Guest, 383 U.S. 745 (1966).
Adickes v. Kress & Co., 398 U.S. 144 (1970).
Griffin v. Breckenridge, 403 U.S. 88 (1971).
Great American Fed. S. & L. Assn. v. Novotny, 442 U.S. 366 (1979).
Carpenters v. Scott, 463 U.S. 825 (1983).
Bray v. Alexandria Clinic, 506 U.S. 263 (1993).

Bibliography and Further Reading

Dubois, W. E. B. *The Souls of Black Folk.* Oregon: Blackstone Audio Books, 1994.

———. *Black Reconstruction in America.* New York: Atheneum, 1995.

Kares, Lauren. "The Unlucky Thirteenth: A Constitutional Amendment in Search of a Doctrine." *Cornell Law Review,* January 1995. http://www.law.cornell.edu/clr/kar.htm.

National Civil Rights Museum. http://www.mecca.org/~crights.

National Association for the Advancement of Colored People. http://www.naacp.org.

Southern Poverty Law Center. http://www.splcenter.org.

Williams, Juan. *Eyes on the Prize: America's Civil Rights Years 1954–1965.* New York: Penguin Books, 1987.

CIVIL RIGHTS CASES

Legal Citation: 109 U.S. 3 (1883)

Appellants
United States in four cases, Mr. and Mrs. Richard A. Robinson in one case.

Appellees
Stanley, Ryan, Nichols, Singleton, Memphis & Charleston RR

Appellants' Claim
That their civil rights had been violated under the Civil Rights Act of 1 March 1875 when various individuals and companies had denied them access to accommodations and privileges of an inn, hotel, theater, and railroad on the grounds of race.

Chief Lawyers for Appellants
Samuel F. Phillips, U.S. Solicitor General Phillips; William M. Randolph for the Robinsons

Chief Lawyers for Appellees
(None for first four cases); William Y. C. Humes, David Postern for Memphis & Charleston RR.

Justices for the Court
Joseph P. Bradley (writing for the Court), Samuel Blatchford, Stephen Johnson Field, Horace Gray, Stanley Matthews, Samuel Freeman Miller, Morrison Remick Waite, William Burnham Woods

Justices Dissenting
John Marshall Harlan I

Place
Washington, D.C.

Date of Decision
15 October 1883

Decision
Overturned the constitutionality of the 1875 Civil Rights Act.

Significance
The Court ruled 8-1 that Congress did not have the constitutional power, under either the original Constitution, nor under the Thirteenth and Fourteenth Amendments, to punish racial discrimination by individuals. With this decision the Court nearly completed the process of nullifying legislation passed during the Reconstruction era designed to grant equal rights to African Americans.

A Challenge to Civil Rights

The five cases which were combined in the Civil Rights Cases were actions against private individuals who had denied rights to African Americans. The first four cases were filed by the solicitor general on 7 November 1882; the fifth case was brought by Richard A. Robinson on 29 March 1883. In setting aside the lower court convictions of the accused, the Court ruled that the provisions of the Civil Rights Act of 1875 went beyond the power of Congress under both the Thirteenth and Fourteenth Amendments.

Two of the cases, against Stanley and Nichols, were indictments for denying accommodations. Two other cases involved theater admission. The case against Ryan was for refusing a seat in the dress circle of Maguire's Theater in San Francisco. The case against Singleton was for denying admission to the Grand Opera House in New York. The fifth case involved Mr. and Mrs. Richard A. Robinson who had brought action against the Memphis and Charleston Railroad Company in Tennessee. A conductor on the line had refused to allow Mrs. Robinson access to the ladies' car because she was of African descent, and traveling with a party the conductor assumed was white. As a consequence, he assumed she was of loose morals and denied her access to the ladies' car.

Justice Bradley delivered the majority opinion, ruling that the U.S. Constitution contained no language dealing with discrimination. When Congress had passed the Civil Rights Act of 1 March 1875, it had based the law upon the Thirteenth and Fourteenth Amendments to the Constitution. Bradley argued that the Thirteenth Amendment related only to slavery, and that discrimination or denial of equal accommodation did not constitute a badge of slavery on the victim of the discrimination. Since the amendment dealt only with slavery, it could not be the basis of the law. The Fourteenth Amendment dealt only with the states. Therefore, under the Fourteenth Amendment, Congress could prohibit discrimination by the states, but not by private citizens. The amendment gave Congress the power to prohibit state laws and state acts, but it did not authorize Congress to create a code for the regulation of private rights. The Court found the assumption that Congress could legislate generally on the subject of rights based on flawed logic. The Tenth Amendment to the Constitution, the ruling pointed out, had reserved to the states, powers not specifically delegated by the Constitution to the federal government. Thus, the individuals who had been discriminated against could only bring civil actions in state courts against those who had injured them, under the laws of the states.

Former slaves, the argument ran, once they became citizens, were not entitled to any special protection of the law, but only the protection by the ordinary modes by which other citizens' rights were protected. Since no other grounds but the Thirteenth and Fourteenth Amendments were put forward to justify the law, the Court ruled that the law was null.

Justice Harlan, a former slave owner, as the sole dissenter, argued that both the substance and the spirit of the Thirteenth and Fourteenth Amendments were being overthrown by the majority opinion. He believed the intent of the amendments had been to guarantee equal rights to African Americans and he believed the Civil Rights Act of 1875 had been enacted with that intent in mind. Looking closely at the language of the Fourteenth Amendment, Harlan argued that while its

intent had been to prohibit the states from all discrimination against citizens on the grounds of race, color, or previous condition of servitude, that language was not intended to prohibit the Congress from enforcing laws against discrimination. Harlan warned that if the Court allowed racial discrimination to persist, in the future, other forms of class discrimination and class tyranny would emerge. In Harlan's opinion, Congress had the power to stop such class tyranny and for that reason he withheld his assent to the Court opinion.

Related Cases

Plessy v. Ferguson, 163 U.S. 537 (1896).

Heart of Atlanta Motel v. United States, 379 U.S. 241 (1964).

Jones v. Alfred H. Mayer Co., 392 U.S. 409 (1968).

Bibliography and Further Reading

Blaustein, Albert, and Robert Zangrando. *Civil Rights and African Americans.* Evanston, IL: Northwestern University Press, 1968.

Johnson, John W. *Historic U.S. Court Cases, 1690–1990: An Encyclopedia.* New York: Garland Publishing, 1992.

Logan, Rayford. *The Negro in American Life and Thought: The Nadir, 1877-1901.* New York: Dial Press, 1954.

YICK WO V. HOPKINS

Legal Citation: 118 U.S. 356 (1886)

Petitioner
Yick Wo

Respondent
Peter Hopkins, San Francisco Sheriff

Petitioner's Claim
That San Francisco was enforcing an ordinance in an unlawfully discriminatory manner against the defendant and other Chinese persons.

Chief Lawyers for Petitioner
Hall McAllister, D. L. Smoot, L. H. Van Schaick

Chief Lawyers for Respondent
Alfred Clarke, H. G. Sieberst

Justices for the Court
Samuel Blatchford, Joseph P. Bradley, Stephen Johnson Field, Horace Gray, John Marshall Harlan I, Stanley Matthews (writing for the Court), Samuel Freeman Miller, Morrison Remick Waite, William Burnham Woods

Justices Dissenting
None

Place
Washington, D.C.

Date of Decision
10 May 1886

Decision
Yick Wo's conviction for violating the ordinance was unconstitutional.

Significance
In *Yick Wo*, the Supreme Court proclaimed that even if a law was non-discriminatory, enforcing the law in a discriminatory manner was unconstitutional.

On 26 May 1880 the city of San Francisco enacted an ordinance requiring all commercial laundries to be in brick or stone buildings. Wooden buildings were permissible, but only with the board of supervisors' approval. The ordinance made no distinction between laundries run by Chinese immigrants and those run by whites. However, the ordinance was enforced in a blatantly racist manner. The board rubber-stamped its approval of white petitions to run laundries in wooden buildings, but denied every one of the nearly 200 Chinese petitions.

Sheriff Peter Hopkins enforced the ordinance, arresting Yick Wo and over 150 other Chinese persons who continued to run laundries in wooden buildings without board approval. Yick Wo was convicted, and ordered to pay a fine of $10 or spend ten days in jail. The California Supreme Court upheld his conviction, and he appealed to the U.S. Supreme Court for an order preventing San Francisco in the person of Sheriff Hopkins from carrying out the sentence.

The Court reversed Yick Wo's conviction, holding that the ordinance was being unfairly administered:

> Though the law itself be fair on its face and impartial in appearance, yet, if it is applied and administered by public authority with an evil eye and an unequal hand, so as practically to make unjust and illegal discriminations between persons in similar circumstances, material to their rights, the denial of equal justice is still within the prohibition of the Constitution . . .

> And while this consent of the supervisors is withheld from [Yick Wo] and from two hundred others who have also petitioned, all of whom happen to be Chinese subjects, eighty others, not Chinese subjects, are permitted to carry on the same business under similar conditions. The fact of this discrimination is admitted. No reason for it is shown, and the conclusion cannot be resisted, that no reason for it exists except hostility to the race and nationality to which the petitioners belong . . .

An anti-Chinese political cartoon from 1880. © Corbis-Bettmann.

The significance of the *Yick Wo* decision is that, even if a law is non-discriminatory, enforcing the law in a discriminatory manner is unconstitutional.

Related Cases
Truax v. Raich, 239 U.S. 33 (1915).
Missouri ex rel Gaines v. Canada, 305 U.S. 337 (1938).
Ambach v. Norwick, 441 U.S. 68 (1979).

Bibliography and Further Reading
Johnson, John W., ed. *Historic U.S. Court Cases, 1690–1990: An Encyclopedia.* New York: Garland Publishing, 1992.

Nelson, William Edward. *The Fourteenth Amendment: From Political Principle to Judicial Doctrine.* Cambridge: Harvard University Press, 1988.

Pole, J. R. *The Pursuit of Equality in American History.* Berkeley: University of California Press, 1978.

UNITED STATES V. WONG KIM ARK

Legal Citation: 169 U.S. 649 (1898)

Appellant
United States

Appellee
Wong Kim Ark

Appellant's Claim
That the U.S. district court's affirmation of Wong's citizenship was in error.

Chief Lawyers for Appellant
Solicitor General Holmes Conrad, George D. Collins

Chief Lawyer for Appellee
Thomas D. Riordan

Justices for the Court
David Josiah Brewer, Henry Billings Brown, Horace Gray (writing for the Court), Rufus Wheeler Peckham, George Shiras, Jr., Edward Douglass White

Justices Dissenting
Melville Weston Fuller, John Marshall Harlan I (Joseph McKenna did not participate)

Place
Washington, D.C.

Date of Decision
28 March 1898

Decision
In favor of appellee Wong.

Significance
This was the first case in which the Court interpreted Section I of the Fourteenth Amendment, in which all persons born in the United States are defined as citizens.

The Locked Golden Gate

In August of 1895, Wong Kim Ark returned to his native San Francisco from China aboard the steamship *Coptic*. When the ship docked, Wong was detained by customs officials who refused to accept his claim that he was an American citizen.

Anti-Chinese laws became a reality a decade before Wong's detention. Railroad owners, mining companies, and other industrial interests in western American states had once welcomed the Chinese as a source of cheap labor. By the 1870s, the backlash from labor unions and non-Chinese workers unwilling to work for low wages pressured the U.S. government to restrict immigration from Asia. The United States and Chinese governments signed a treaty in 1880 agreeing that the United States could regulate but not prohibit the migration of Chinese to America. The signers of the Angell's Treaty did not foresee the energy with which anti-Chinese forces in the U.S. Congress would try to "regulate" Asians out of American life.

In 1880 and 1882, Congress passed a series of laws collectively known as the Chinese Exclusion Acts. These laws suspended the entry of any Chinese laborers into the United States for 10 years and threatened heavy fines for any shipmaster convicted of landing Chinese illegally. Ten classes of Chinese were exempted from the law, including teachers, ministers, diplomats, students, and others who were considered likely to return to their homeland. Significantly, Chinese born in the United States and their children were included among the ten exempt classes.

In 1888, Congress contravened Angell's Treaty by passing The Scott Act, prohibiting Chinese laborers from entering the United States. The 1892 Geary Act forbade the use of writs of *habeas corpus* by any Chinese arrested while in the United States, thus denying aliens the right to challenge deportation proceedings. The constitutionality of this law was upheld by the Supreme Court on 15 May 1893 in *Fong Yue Teng v. United States*.

A Successful Writ

Wong Kim Ark's demand for a writ of *habeas corpus*, however, was granted because of his contention that he was a United States citizen. He charged that the Collector of Customs of the Port of San Francisco and the manager of the steamship company had deprived him of his liberty without due process. The U.S. District Court for Northern California agreed that Wong's Fourteenth Amendment rights had been violated. His detention was ruled illegal and he was released.

The U.S. government appealed the writ, implicitly challenging Wong's citizenship before the Supreme Court on 5 and 8 March 1897. Ironically, both sides accepted most of the basic facts of Wong's life. It was agreed that he had been born in San Francisco in 1873, while his Chinese parents were considered permanent residents of the city. He had visited China temporarily in 1890 and had returned to San Francisco with no difficulty in passing through customs. It was further agreed that since his birth, Wong had never had any other place of residence except California nor had he ever claimed to be anything other than a United States citizen. Although his parents had returned to China in 1890, Wong worked in San Francisco, paid his taxes, and had never participated in any criminal acts. Most significantly, the government's appeal conceded that the Chinese Exclusion Acts under which Wong had been detained should not apply to him if he was indeed a U.S. citizen.

A Question Of Birthright

The government claimed that Wong's parentage should determine his citizenship. Wong's parents were subjects of the Emperor of China at the time of his birth. Therefore, Wong was likewise a foreign subject. According to the appeal, Wong was also Chinese by reason of his "race, language, color and dress." Because he did not belong to any of the classes of Chinese allowed entry under immigration rules, he was technically considered to be a laborer and liable to the terms of the Chinese Exclusion Act.

These arguments were no more successful in Washington D.C. than they had been in San Francisco. The Court rejected the appeal on 28 March 1898, over a year after hearing the case. Writing for the majority, Justice Gray noted the Constitution's deep roots in English common law. By this tradition, all persons born within England's domain could expect protection from the King, to whom they were expected to owe their allegiance. Gray traced the lineage of this concept of determining citizenship by birthplace from its English origins to standard practice in the American states.

The Court found its strongest reason for affirming Wong's citizenship in the Fourteenth Amendment. Ratified by Congress in 1868, the amendment was designed to grant the rights of citizenship to persons of African descent who had been slaves prior to the Civil War. To the majority, Section I of the amendment was unequivocal:

> All persons born or naturalized in the United States, and subject to the jurisdiction thereof, are citizens of the United States and of the State in which they reside.

The Court recognized Congress's right to deny citizenship by passing naturalization laws. In cases where birth was the source of citizenship, however, the Court ruled that Congress had no power to remove a right granted by the Constitution.

Chief Justice Fuller and Justice Harlan dissented. Fuller considered citizenship to be a political concept, not a right defined by the Constitution. By treaty, both China and the United States had agreed that Chinese subjects could not become naturalized American citizens. Fuller cited both Chinese law—by which any Chinese rejecting status as an Imperial subject could be executed—and U.S. Supreme Court decisions upholding restrictive immigration policies. If foreign and U.S. laws prevented alien parents from becoming American citizens, Fuller reasoned, the Fourteenth Amendment could not arbitrarily impose citizenship on their children.

Wong Kim Arks' victory was of great importance to millions of children born in the United States to immigrant parents. However, it was a minor victory for Asian Americans. The Chinese Exclusion Act was renewed indefinitely in 1904 and was not repealed until 17 December 1943.

Related Cases
Yick Wo v. Hopkins, 118 U.S. 356 (1886).
Strauder v. West Virginia, 100 U.S. 303 (1979).

Bibliography and Further Reading
Chan, Sucheng. *Entry Denied: Exclusion and the Chinese Community In America 1882-1943.* Philadelphia: Temple University Press, 1991.

Hoexter, Corinne. *From Canton To California.* New York: Four Winds Press, 1976.

Keller, Morton. *Affairs of State: Public Life In Late Nineteenth Century America.* Cambridge: Belknap Press, 1977.

Kurland, Phillip B. and Gerhard Casper, eds. *Landmark Briefs and Arguments of the Supreme Court of the United States.* Arlington: University Publications of America, 1975.

Tsai, Shih-Shan Henry. *The Chinese Experience In America.* Bloomington: Indiana University Press, 1986.

SKINNER V. OKLAHOMA

Legal Citation: 316 U.S. 535 (1942)

Petitioner
Arthur Skinner

Respondent
State of Oklahoma

Petitioner's Claim
That a state law authorizing sterilization of selected felons held in the Oklahoma penitentiary violates the Fourteenth Amendment's due process of law guarantee.

Chief Lawyers for Petitioner
W. J. Hulsey, H. I. Aston, Guy L. Andrews

Chief Lawyer for Respondent
Mac Q. Williamson, Attorney General of Oklahoma

Justices for the Court
Hugo Lafayette Black, James Francis Byrnes, William O. Douglas (writing for the Court), Felix Frankfurter, Robert H. Jackson, Frank Murphy, Stanley Forman Reed, Owen Josephus Roberts, Harlan Fiske Stone

Justices Dissenting
None

Place
Washington, D.C.

Date of Decision
6 May 1942

Decision
Unanimously upheld Skinner's claim and overturned two lower courts' decisions holding that he was a suitable vasectomy candidate.

Significance
The ruling, the first modern fundamental rights decision by the Court, recognized marriage and procreation (to have children) as basic civil liberties protected by the Fourteenth Amendment's Equal Protection Clause. In addition, the Court applied the "substantive due process" doctrine, previously reserved only for issues involving economic rights, to personal rights and liberties. Other rights similarly recognized over the next 30 years were voting, privacy, interstate travel, and access to justice. Because none of these rights are clearly provided in the Constitution, much public debate grew concerning their legal validity, including within the Court itself.

Following the Civil War, three amendments were added to the Constitution, including the Fourteenth Amendment in 1868. Section 1 of the amendment reads, "nor shall any State deprive any person of life, liberty, or property, without due process of law; nor deny to any person within its jurisdiction the equal protection of the laws." For many years courts applied the Due Process Clause to questions of procedure when states treated classifications of people differently. By the late nineteenth century, the Court added a "substantive" element to due process deliberations by asserting the courts' role was to assess the character of the activity being regulated, not just the manner of the regulation process.

Until the 1920s, the Court applied substantive due process review procedures only to state laws regulating economic and property rights, such as wage and hour laws and price regulation. Then, in 1923 for the first time the Court recognized a noneconomic fundamental right, the right to acquire knowledge through education. The Court held in *Meyer v. Nebraska* certain personal rights not described in the Constitution exist that enable individuals "to enjoy those privileges long recognized at common law as essential to the orderly pursuit of happiness by free men."

Early in the twentieth century, a number of laws were passed across the nation establishing sterilization programs to rid the nation of "undesirables." Shortly after passage of a 1924 Virginia law the first question concerning application of state sterilization came to the Supreme Court in *Buck v. Bell* (1927). The Court upheld the Virginia law and approved the sterilization of Carrie Buck, an 18-year old "feeble-minded" woman held in a state institution. Buck's mental condition was clearly evident in three generations of her family, indicating it was genetically transmittable. The Court held that the sterilization of Buck was best for society and due process had been adequately served.

The protection of personal rights was yet to gain prominence. However, the era of the Court reviewing economic regulation law did come to an end during the 1930s under pressures stemming from the Great Depression and New Deal policies. The Court, as customary, relied on the best judgement of legislators in restricting individual behavior and applied relatively weak tests in assessing fairness.

Oklahoma Prisoner Sterilization

Arthur Skinner, a citizen of the State of Oklahoma, was habitually in trouble with the law. In 1926 Skinner was convicted of stealing three chickens and sentenced to the State Reformatory. In 1929 he was convicted of armed robbery and returned to the Reformatory. In 1934, he was again convicted of armed robbery but this time sent to the Oklahoma state penitentiary. The following year, in 1935, the Oklahoma state legislature passed the Habitual Criminal Sterilization Act. The law defined a "habitual criminal" as one who is convicted of two or more felony convictions in Oklahoma or any other state for crimes of "moral turpitude" and then convicted of a third felony and imprisoned in the State of Oklahoma. The Oklahoma attorney general had authority to initiate actions to sexually sterilize such a felon. If male, sterilization would be by vasectomy. The law provided a right to a jury trial for the felon, but limited the grounds for challenge to whether he fit the definition of a habitual criminal and did not have a health condition precluding sterilization. The law excluded certain crimes, such as embezzlement, as constituting a conviction for sterilization purposes. In 1936 the attorney general selected Skinner for sterilization. Skinner challenged the action and the case went to trial, where he lost. The Oklahoma Supreme Court soon affirmed the decision.

Skinner then appealed to the U.S. Supreme Court arguing the Oklahoma law violated the Fourteenth Amendment's due process guarantee. He was given no opportunity to challenge the notion that he might parent socially undesirable children. He also contended sterilization was cruel and unusual punishment. Because of the fundamental constitutional questions raised by the case, the Court granted the petition for *certiorari*.

Marriage and Procreation Rights

The Court ruled unanimously in favor of Skinner. Justice Douglas, writing for the Court, found the "case touches a sensitive and important area of human rights." Douglas wrote, "Marriage and procreation are fundamental to the very existence and survival of the race." Therefore, any classification a state makes in sterilization law should be subject to the closest judicial scrutiny to guard against "invidious discrimination." Douglas found certain aspects of the Oklahoma law so clearly violated the Equal Protection Clause it was unnecessary to consider arguments raised by Skinner. He found no basis for distinguishing which crimes allow sterilization and which do not since punishments for both embezzlement and larceny were nearly identical in Oklahoma law. Douglas wrote, "Sterilization of

those who have thrice committed grand larceny with immunity for those who are embezzlers is a clear, pointed, unmistakable discrimination." Douglas further noted no scientific evidence was known to suggest that inheritability of criminal traits was associated with one form of violation and not the other. Therefore, the distinction was "conspicuously artificial." Douglas concluded that "Oklahoma deprives certain individuals of a right which is basic to the perpetuation of a race—the right to have off-spring." The Court reversed the decision of the two lower courts.

In concurring, Chief Justice Stone disagreed with Douglas' application of the Equal Protection Clause, choosing to respond instead to Skinner's due process argument. Stone wrote that the "real question" was whether a whole class of citizens could be subjected to "such an invasion of personal liberty" without opportunity to question "whether his criminal tendencies are of an inheritable type." Stone wrote, "A law which condemns, without hearing, all the individuals of a class to so harsh a measure as the present because some or even many merit condemnation, is lacking in the first principles of due process."

Impact

With *Skinner*, the Court charted a new course determining what rights are so fundamental to personal liberty that any laws restricting those rights violate the due process guarantee simply because of the activity they affect. Such issues invoke the Fourteenth Amendment's guarantee of "liberty." As a result, laws affecting such fundamental rights as marriage and procreation were subjected to closer scrutiny by the courts and could only be justified by a governmental compelling interest. The decision thus created the "fundamental interest" test for equal protection cases. The scope of constitutional liberties would soon expand to include a list of newly recognized noneconomic fundamental rights. A line of rulings followed over the next half century considering the substance of state laws under the equal protection guarantee by applying the substantive due process doctrine.

In 1964 voting rights were recognized in *Reynolds v. Sims*. The right to vote, the Court found, bears on the preservation of "other basic civil and political rights." The Court in *Griswold v. Connecticut* (1965) held that the decision to use contraception was a family right and a right of privacy. Any state prohibitions against contraception deprived married couples of that liberty without due process of law. Justice Douglas noted the "right to privacy" surrounding the marital relationship is "older than the Bill of Rights." Two years later, the Court recognized the constitutional right to a choice in marriage in *Loving v. Commonwealth of Virginia* (1967) by striking down a state law prohibiting interracial marriages. In finding the law violated equal protection and denied due process, the Court held, "The freedom to marry (is) . . . one of the vital personal rights essential to the orderly pursuit of happiness by free men." As expressed in the *Griswold* decision, there exists a "realm of family life which the state cannot enter without substantial justification." Through these series of rulings, the Court interpreted the Constitution as placing limits on states' rights to interfere in a person's fundamental decisions concerning family and parenthood. Other fundamental rights identified in the 1960s were an indigent's right to equal access to justice and the right of unhindered interstate travel.

The right to privacy established in *Griswold* rose to greater prominence in *Roe v. Wade* (1973) in recognizing the right of a woman to choose abortion. In *Roe,* the Court found the Fourteenth Amendment's implicit guarantee of personal privacy extended to "activities relating to marriage, procreation, contraception, family relationship, and child rearing and education." The Court further stated only those personal rights determined "fundamental" or "implicit in the concept of ordered liberty" can be included in the guarantee of personal privacy under the Fourteenth Amendment.

Some justices responded they found no right to these liberties expressed or implied anywhere in the Constitution. Justice William Rehnquist in 1972 described such interests "as a judicial superstructure, awkwardly engrafted upon the Constitution itself." Consequently, no further fundamental rights have been identified after the 1960s. The Court denied fundamental rights protection to food, housing, education, and, in the mid-1990s, to sexual orientation in *Romer v. Evans* (1996).

The *Skinner* finding continued to be cited in numerous Court decisions for over a half century after it was issued. The "right to control one's person" was reaffirmed in *Planned Parenthood of Southeastern Pennsylvania v. Casey* (1992). The Court held that,

> personal decisions relating to marriage, procreation, contraception, family relationships, child rearing, and education . . . (were) the

most intimate and personal choices a person may make in a lifetime, choices central to personal dignity and autonomy, . . . (and) central to the liberty protected by the Fourteenth Amendment . . . the right to define one's own concept of existence, of meaning, of the universe, and of the mystery of human life.

The procreation right became much more complex in the 1980s as artificial reproduction technologies expanded. Procreation issues grew beyond the family to include sperm and egg donors and surrogate mothers, and the rights to frozen sperm and embryos after divorce, or even after the death of a spouse. As highlighted in *Kass v. Kass* (1998), courts initially resorted to contract law to resolve such disputes. Many believed these issues would ultimately have to be resolved in the realm of human rights.

Related Cases
Buck v. Bell, 274 U.S. 200 (1927).
Griswold v. Connecticut, 381 U.S. 479 (1965).
Loving v. Commonwealth of Virginia, 388 U.S. 1 (1967).
Roe v. Wade, 410 U.S. 113 (1973).
Planned Parenthood of Southeastern Pennsylvania v. Casey, 505 U.S. 833 (1992).
Romer v. Evans, 116 S. Ct. 1620 (1996).
Kass v. Kass, 91 NY 2nd 554 (1998).

Bibliography and Further Reading
Abernathy, M. Glenn, and Barbara A. Perry. *Civil Liberties under the Constitution.* 6th ed. Columbia, SC: University of South Carolina Press, 1993.

Abraham, Henry J., and Barbara A. Perry. *Freedom & The Court: Civil Rights & Liberties in the United States.* New York: Oxford University Press, 1998.

Blank, Robert, and Janna C. Merrick. *Human Reproduction, Emerging Technologies, and Conflicting Rights.* Washington, DC: Congressional Quarterly Press, 1995.

Moore, Wayne D. *Constitutional Rights and Powers of the People.* Princeton, NJ: Princeton University Press, 1996.

HIRABAYASHI V. UNITED STATES

Legal Citation: 320 U.S. 81 (1943)

Petitioner
Gordon Kiyoshi Hirabayashi

Respondent
United States

Petitioner's Claim
That following Japan's 1941 attack on Pearl Harbor, Congress unconstitutionally delegated its power to a military commander by authorizing him to impose regulations set out by President Roosevelt's executive orders. And that the regulations set through the order unlawfully discriminated against Japanese Americans in violation of the Fifth Amendment.

Chief Lawyers for Petitioner
Frank L. Walters, Harold Evans

Chief Lawyer for Respondent
Charles Fahy

Justices for the Court
Hugo Lafayette Black, William O. Douglas, Felix Frankfurter, Robert H. Jackson, Frank Murphy, Stanley Forman Reed, Owen Josephus Roberts, Wiley Blount Rutledge, Harlan Fiske Stone (writing for the Court)

Justices Dissenting
None

Place
Washington, D.C.

Date of Decision
21 June 1943

Decision
Affirmed the district court's conviction of Hirabayashi for knowingly disregarding military restrictions by finding those restrictions lawfully delegated by Congress and not in violation of the Fifth Amendment.

Significance
In this decision, the Court reasoned that although racial discrimination was usually irrelevant and illegal, "in time of war residents having ethnic affiliations with an invading enemy" might pose a greater threat to national security than other citizens. It also found that the urgency of war sometimes forced government to depend on military authorities to make quick decisions and take action. Based on this reasoning, the president's orders and the implementation of a curfew on Japanese Americans in wartime were deemed constitutional. In 1987 the conviction was successfully challenged and Hirabayashi was vindicated.

An Atmosphere of Suspicion

The roots of the social and legal conditions which surrounded the conviction of Gordon Hirabayashi during World War II can be recognized as early as the late nineteenth century. In 1880 and 1882 the U.S. Congress passed the Chinese Exclusion Acts which blocked Chinese immigration for the next 60 years. In 1908 the Gentlemen's Agreement was adopted, preventing male Japanese workers from entering the United States. In 1922 the U.S. Supreme Court ruled on the *Ozawa* case, prohibiting Japanese immigrants from becoming naturalized citizens, and in 1924 a new immigration law effectively ended Japanese immigration to the United States.

Tatiana Klimova, in *Internment of Japanese Americans: Military Necessity or Racial Prejudice?*, asserted that these official actions were prompted by long-standing white majority hostility toward Asian Americans on the West Coast. She contended that Asian immigrants of the time often willingly took poorly-paid jobs and through hard work, many later became financially successful. This approach, she stated, was seen by the white populace as unfair competition. Accustomed to a different culture and visibly racially different, Asian immigrants also tended to remain within their own communities, she said, which intensified majority feelings that Asian immigrants did not really want to blend into the American way of life. This was the unsteady social relationship between Asian Americans and the dominant society in Pacific Coast states when the Second World War erupted.

On 7 December 1941 the Empire of Japan executed a surprising and devastating attack on an American naval base at Pearl Harbor in Hawaii. The next day the U.S. Congress declared war against Japan, and over the next two months Japan followed with successful attacks on Hong Kong, Manila, Thailand, Singapore, Midway, Wake, and Guam. Predictions of bombing and even the invasion of the U.S. West Coast spread quickly, and with them came rumors of conspiracy by Japanese people living in America. On 19 February 1942 President Franklin D. Roosevelt issued Executive Order No. 9066, which stated that "successful prosecution of war requires every possible protection against espionage

Gordon Hirabayashi testifies before the Commission on Wartime Relocation of the Internment of Civilians on Capitol Hill. © AP/Wide World Photos.

and . . . sabotage." By this order, military commanders were given the authority and discretion to establish military areas and within those areas restrict the movement of anyone they deemed potentially threatening to the national defense.

By the first two weeks of March of 1942, Lt. General J. L. DeWitt, Military Commander of the Western Defense Command, had issued proclamations establishing military areas and zones that included the coastal regions of Oregon and Washington, the state of California, and the southern half of Arizona. The proclamations said further that "certain persons or classes of persons" could be excluded from those areas, or restricted if they stayed within them. On 21 March 1942 Congress made it illegal to defy any restrictions ordered by the military under Executive Order No. 9066 knowingly. Three days later General DeWitt issued another Proclamation confining "all alien Japanese, . . . Germans, . . . Italians, and all persons of Japanese ancestry residing within . . . Military Area No. 1" to their homes between 8:00 PM and 6:00 AM. The same day he also issued several Civil Exclusion Orders requiring that all persons of Japanese ancestry be evacuated from military areas and resettled elsewhere.

A Waiver Of Rights?

Gordon Kiyoshi Hirabayashi was an American citizen born in Seattle, Washington in 1918. His parents had come to the United States from Japan, but Gordon Hirabayashi himself had never been there. In May of 1942 he was a senior attending the University of Washington in Seattle, and so was living within Military Area No. 1. On 9 May 1942 he broke the military curfew by being away from his home after 8:00 p.m. On 11 and 12 May he defied the exclusion orders when he failed to report to a Civil Control Station to register for evacuation. He took these actions purposefully, maintaining that if he had complied he would be waiving his rights as an American citizen. Hirabayashi later turned himself in and was charged.

At his trial in district court he sought dismissal of the charges because he was an American citizen "who had never been a subject of and had never borne allegiance to the Empire of Japan." In a one-day trial in Seattle, the court overruled this, however, and he was convicted of violating the 21 March Act of Congress. Hirabayashi appealed the conviction, and his case went before the Court of Appeals for the Ninth Circuit. That court certified to the U.S. Supreme Court questions of law, and the Supreme Court directed that the entire record be certified so that the case could be heard there as if it had been brought there by appeal.

Equal Protection Versus Winning a War

Before the Supreme Court, Hirabayashi denied neither that he disobeyed the curfew, nor that it was authorized by the President's Executive Order and was punishable under the act of Congress. He even agreed that the exclusion order was a prudent defense measure, if applied to all citizens. What he challenged was that Congress had unconstitutionally delegated powers to the military, and even if those powers had been lawfully delegated, the curfew and exclusion orders discriminated against citizens of Japanese descent.

In its decision, the Court focused on the importance of the conditions under which the disputed regulations were imposed. Writing for the unanimous Court, Chief Justice Stone began with the principle that "the war power of the national government is the power to wage war successfully," which he said included protection of war materials and personnel against harm. Consequently, he reasoned, when conditions required, as the Court believed they did in the weeks and months following the Pearl Harbor attack, it was appropriate for the president and Congress to defer to the judgment and discretion of the military in defending against espionage and sabotage. This deference was obvious throughout the decision—"it is not for any court to sit in review of the wisdom of [military] action or substitute its judgment for theirs."

Justice Stone went on to outline the justifications that the military commander had given for imposing the challenged regulations on Japanese Americans. He made it clear that the Court accepted the military's findings that there was not enough time for individual hearings to determine who were the loyal and disloyal among the Japanese Americans living in restricted areas. It is interesting to note that the Court accepted prevailing cultural factors as support for military belief in the necessity of restricting and relocating Japanese Americans. It said, "social, economic, and political conditions which have prevailed since the close of the last century, when the Japanese began to come to this country . . ., have intensified their solidarity and prevented their assimilation [into] the white population."

The Court was careful to note that racial classifications were under most circumstances irrelevant and unlawful. In one of the most echoed remarks of the decision, the Court said that "distinctions between citizens solely because of their ancestry are by their very nature odious to a free people whose institutions are founded upon the doctrine of equality." The Court further reasoned though, that it did not necessarily follow that during wartime, government could not take ancestry into account when doing what it deemed necessary to successfully wage war and defend national interests. Largely because it deferred to military intelligence, and despite as has been argued, to racist suspicion, the Court found nothing unconstitutional in the curfew and upheld Hirabayashi's conviction. He was imprisoned at an Arizona federal road camp. From the question of internment, the Court distanced itself, saying, "we need not now attempt to define the ultimate boundaries of the war power."

Impact

In the years following this decision, the Supreme Court often defined the constitutionality of racial classifications using this important case and two similar others of the time. Yet since then, as Reggie Oh and Frank Wu stated in *The Evolution of Race in the Law*, the three cases

have also been roundly criticized for "being emphatically based upon acquiescence to racism."

These three cases made history again 40 years after they were first decided. In 1983 lawyers for Gordon Hirabayashi and the two other men, Fred Korematsu and Minoru Yasui, filed petitions asking federal judges to vacate, meaning to rescind or set aside, their wartime convictions. Never before had convictions which had been decided by the U.S. Supreme Court been challenged in such a manner. The petitions were grounded on an obscure federal procedure called a writ of error *coram nobis*, meaning they were asking the original trial court to correct a fundamental error and injustice which occurred at the original trial.

According to Peter Irons in *Justice Delayed: The Record of the Japanese Internment Cases*, this error was the government's in that in 1943 it did not acknowledge a lack of evidence. It had since been discovered that General DeWitt was in fact informed that there was no proof of "acts of sabotage and espionage by Japanese Americans [which] required curfew and evacuation, and no evidence that Japanese Americans were disloyal." Since this evidence had been withheld, the Court's convictions were based on error. During Hirabayashi's hearing in June of 1985, witnesses testified to the suppression of a report which said the military's contention that there was insufficient time to conduct individual loyalty hearings was untrue because *there was no way* to determine loyalty.

This suppression of evidence was found to have limited the arguments that Hirabayashi's lawyers could have made in 1943 to counter the government's claims of "military necessity." Thus the Court concluded that the original conviction was based on "an error of the most fundamental character," and one of Hirabayashi's convictions was vacated. In September of 1987 the U.S. Court of Appeals for the Ninth Circuit also vacated the other conviction against Hirabayashi.

Related Cases

Takao Ozawa v. United States, 260 U.S. 178 (1922).
Toyosaburo Korematsu v. United States, 319 U.S. 432 (1943).
Minoru Yasui v. United States, 320 U.S. 115 (1943).
Adarand Constructors, Inc. v. Pena, 500 U.S. 200 (1995).

Bibliography and Further Reading

Compton's Interactive Encyclopedia. Compton's NewMedia, Inc., 1996.

Crystal, David, ed. *The Cambridge Factfinder,* rev. ed., Cambridge; New York, NY: Cambridge University Press, 1994.

Irons, Peter. *Justice Delayed: The Record of the Japanese American Internment Cases.* Middletown, Connecticut: Wesleyan University Press, 1989.

Japanese American National Museum. "Chronology of World War II Incarceration." *Japanese American National Museum Quarterly,* Vol. 9, no. 3, 1994.

Johnson, John W., ed. *Historic U.S. Court Cases, 1690–1990: An Encyclopedia.* New York: Garland Publishing, 1992.

Klimova, Tatiana A. "Internment of Japanese Americans: Military Necessity or Racial Prejudice?" *The Old Dominion University Quarterly Historical Review,* Vol. 1, no. 1, 1994.

Oh, Reggie, and Frank Wu. "The Evolution of Race in the Law: The Supreme Court Moves from Approving Internment of Japanese Americans to Disapproving Affirmative Action for African Americans." *Michigan Journal of Race & Law,* Vol. 1, no. 1, 1996.

KOREMATSU V. UNITED STATES

Legal Citation: 323 U.S. 214 (1944)

Petitioner
Toyosaburo Korematsu

Respondent
United States

Petitioner's Claim
That the military orders which sent Japanese Americans to internment camps during World War II were not justified by military necessity.

Chief Lawyer for Petitioner
Wayne M. Collins

Chief Lawyer for Respondent
Charles Fahy, U.S. Solicitor General

Justices for the Court
Hugo Lafayette Black (writing for the Court), William O. Douglas, Felix Frankfurter, Stanley Forman Reed, Wiley Blount Rutledge, Harlan Fiske Stone

Justices Dissenting
Robert H. Jackson, Frank Murphy, Owen Josephus Roberts

Place
Washington, D.C.

Date of Decision
18 December 1944

Decision
The orders were upheld as a valid exercise of the war powers the Constitution grants to Congress.

Significance
Korematsu is the only case in Supreme Court history in which the Court, using a strict test for possible racial discrimination, upheld a restriction on civil liberties. The case has since been severely criticized for sanctioning racism.

On 7 December 1941, the Japanese Empire brought the United States into the Second World War by attacking the American Pacific fleet at Pearl Harbor, Hawaii, killing 2,043 Americans and destroying both aircraft and warships. The next day, Congress declared war on Japan, which in effect brought the United States into conflict with the other members of the tripartite alliance, Germany and Italy.

On 27 March 1942, pursuant to an act of Congress, the U.S. military issued an order prohibiting persons of Japanese descent from leaving the West Coast region. On 3 May 1942, this order was modified by another, directing that such persons be excluded from the area. The effect of these orders was the forced internment of Japanese Americans living on the West Coast. They were first obliged to report to assembly centers, from which they were shipped to inland government camps.

Toyosaburo Korematsu, who went by the name Fred, was an American-born descendant of Japanese immigrants who grew up in the San Francisco Bay area. He was rejected for military service for health reasons, but at the time the internment began, he had a good job in the defense industry and a non-Japanese girlfriend. Instead of obeying the military orders, he moved inland from the Bay area, underwent some minor facial surgery, changed his name, and attempted to pass as Mexican American. Eventually, he was arrested, convicted, paroled, and sent to a relocation camp in Utah. After his efforts to challenge his conviction in the lower federal courts proved fruitless, he took his case to the U.S. Supreme Court.

Justice Black's opinion, which was joined by five other justices, is often cited for its proposition that "all legal restrictions which curtail the civil rights of a single racial group are immediately suspect . . . Courts must subject them to the most rigid scrutiny." Although the "strict scrutiny" test would become the standard for judging laws based on racial categories, in this case Justice Black did not find that Fred Korematsu had been discriminated against because of his ethnicity. Instead, Black and a majority of his fellow justices found that Korematsu had disobeyed orders that were justified by military necessity. The Court majority did

Japanese American Internment Camps

In the hysteria following the bombing of Pearl Harbor in December of 1941, federal authorities directed resident Japanese Americans to ten prisons, called internment camps, operated by the U.S. Justice Department. By July of 1942 more than 112,000 people of Japanese ancestry, approximately 70,000 of them American citizens, had been relocated to the camps where they lived for over two years. Camps were mostly located in bleak desert areas such as Poston and Gila River in Arizona, Manzanar and Tule Lake in California, Amache in Colorado, Minidoka in Idaho, Topaz in the salt flats of Utah, and Heart Mountain in Wyoming. Jerome and Rohwer, however, sat in the swampy Mississippi River delta of Arkansas.

The camps were divided into blocks of hastily erected barracks, flimsily partitioned into 20 by 25 foot cubicles to hold on average eight people. Privacy was nonexistent. Furnishings included iron cots, straw mattresses, and a stove. Other barracks served as the mess hall, communal kitchen, recreation hall, and bathhouse. There were also laundry rooms and latrines. Winters were very cold, summers hot and dusty.

Although treated as prisoners, surrounded by barbed wire and watchtowers, in time the camps became town-like. Each camp had offices, schools, a hospital, social activities, and a post office.

Source(s): Okihiro, Gary Y. *Whispered Silences: Japanese Americans and World War II.* Seattle: University of Washington Press, 1996.

---

not question the military's claim that the large number of Japanese Americans living on the West Coast threatened national security, and that the only means of reducing this threat was temporarily to exclude the entire group. The orders, which were issued pursuant to an act of Congress, were a valid exercise of constitutional war powers, the Court reasoned. Korematsu had clearly disobeyed these orders.

Korematsu Dissenters Question Constitutionality of Detentions

Justice Black declined to consider the question of legality or morality of the internment camps. The three dissenters—Justices Roberts, Murphy, and Jackson—vigorously attacked this refusal to confront what they regarded as the real issue in the case. Justice Roberts observed that, faced with "the dilemma that he dare not remain in his home, or voluntarily leave the area, without incurring criminal penalties . . . [Korematsu] did nothing." Justice Jackson added that "Korematsu . . . has been convicted of an act not commonly a crime. It consists merely of being present in the state whereof he is a citizen, near the place where he was born, and where all his life he has lived." Justice Murphy confronted head on the racism inherent in the internment order:

> No adequate reason is given for the failure to treat these Japanese Americans on an individual basis by holding investigations and hearings to separate the loyal from the disloyal, as was done in the case of persons of German and Italian ancestry.

Citing the fact that there had been no imposition of martial law and that four months had elapsed after Pearl Harbor before the first exclusion order had been issued, Murphy questioned the claim of military necessity and dissented from what he called "this legalization of racism."

Jackson did not question the military's authority in making mass arrests, but he feared the ramifications of a Supreme Court endorsement of the internment orders:

> [O]nce a judicial opinion rationalizes such an order to show that it conforms to the Constitution, or rather rationalizes the Constitution to show that the Constitution sanctions such an order, the Court for all time has validated the principle of racial discrimination in criminal procedure and of transplanting American citizens. The principle then lies about like a loaded weapon ready for the hand of any authority that can bring forward a plausible claim of an urgent need.

Korematsu was to provide the standard for judging legislation which is based on race or which violates fundamental constitutional rights. Black's "rigid scrutiny" became the Court's "strict scrutiny" standard. *Korematsu* has never been overruled, although in 1980 Congress authorized payments of $20,000 each to survivors of the internment camps.

Related Cases

Hirabayashi v. United States, 320 U.S. 81 (1943).
Ex parte Mitsuye Endo, 323 U.S. 283 (1944).

Justice Frank Murphy. © The Library of Congress.

Bibliography and Further Reading

Daniels, Roger. *Prisoners Without Trial: Japanese Americans in World War II.* New York, NY: Hill and Wang, 1993.

Johnson, John W., ed. *Historic U.S. Court Cases, 1690–1990: An Encyclopedia.* New York: Garland Publishing, 1992.

McClain, Charles, ed. *The Mass Internment of Japanese Americans and the Quest for Legal Redress.* New York, NY: Garland, 1994.

Smith, Page. *Democracy on Trial: The Japanese American Evacuation and Relocation in World War II.* New York, NY: Simon & Schuster, 1995.

EX PARTE ENDO

Legal Citation: 323 U.S. 283 (1944)

Appellant
Mitsuye Endo

Appellee
United States

Appellant's Claim
That she was unlawfully held at an interment camp.

Chief Lawyer for Appellant
James C. Purcell

Chief Lawyer for Appellee
Charles Fahey, U.S. Solicitor General

Justices for the Court
Hugo Lafayette Black, William O. Douglas (writing for the Court), Felix Frankfurter, Robert H. Jackson, Frank Murphy, Stanley Forman Reed, Owen Josephus Roberts, Wiley Blount Rutledge, Harlan Fiske Stone

Justices Dissenting
None

Place
Washington, D.C.

Date of Decision
18 December 1944

Decision
Reversed the judgment and remanded the cause district court.

Significance
This Supreme Court decision ended what the American Civil Liberties Union later called "the worst single wholesale violation of civil rights of American citizens in our history."

In February of 1942, soon after the Japanese bombed Pearl Harbor in the surprise attack that committed the United States to World War II, President Franklin D. Roosevelt authorized the War Relocation Authority to detain persons of Japanese ancestry living on the West Coast, many of whom were not only American citizens but native-born.

Military commanders were authorized to designate areas from which such persons could be excluded; if they lived within those areas, the military could move them. Lt. General J. L. De Witt, of the Western Defense Command, proclaimed that the entire Pacific Coast of the United States:

> [B]y its geographical location is particularly subject to attack, to attempted invasion by the armed forces of nations with which the United States is now at war, and, in connection therewith, is subject to espionage and acts of sabotage, thereby requiring the adoption of military measures necessary to establish safeguards against such enemy operations.

On those orders, more than 112,000 Japanese Americans, 70,000 of whom were U. S. citizens, were removed from their homes. Meantime, Congress enacted legislation that ratified the president's order.

Mitsuye Endo, a native-born American whose ancestors were Japanese, was taken from her home in Sacramento, California, to the Tule Lake War Relocation Center at Newell, California. Endo was 22. A Methodist who had never visited Japan and neither spoke nor read Japanese, she worked in the California Department of Motor Vehicles. At Tule, she and the others found they could not leave the center without written permission issued by the War Relocation Authority.

Petition and Appeal Stretch Over 21 Months

In July of 1942, through lawyer James Purcell, who had worked with Japanese American lawyers in Sacramento and who was appalled at the treatment the U.S. citizens received, Endo filed a petition for a writ of *habeas corpus* (relief from unlawful confinement) in the U.S. District Court for the Northern District of California.

She asked for her liberty to be restored. One year passed. The petition was denied in July of 1943. In August, Endo appealed to the U.S. Circuit Court of Appeals.

Next, Mitsuye Endo was moved to the Central Utah Relocation Center at Topaz, Utah. It took the Circuit Court of Appeals until 22 April 1944, to decide that it needed to apply to the U.S. Supreme Court for instructions on some questions of law. The Supreme Court promptly demanded the entire record of the Endo case, so that it could "proceed to a decision as if the case had been brought to the Supreme Court by appeal." Thus the case became identified as *Ex parte Endo* (ex parte being a legal way of saying that the case came from one side only).

Confined Under Armed Guard

The Supreme Court soon learned that Mitsuye Endo:

> is a loyal and law-abiding citizen of the United States, that no charge has been made against her, that she is being unlawfully detained, and that she is confined in the Relocation Center under armed guard and held there against her will.

The Court also learned, from one of General De Witt's reports, that:

> Essentially, military necessity required only that the Japanese population be removed from the coastal area and dispersed in the interior . . . That the evacuation program necessarily and ultimately developed into one of complete Federal supervision was due primarily to the fact that the interior states would not accept an uncontrolled Japanese migration.

The military's argument, noted Justice Douglas in the opinion handed down 18 December 1944, was that "but for such supervision there might have been dangerously disorderly migration of unwanted people to unprepared communities" and that "although community hostility towards the evacuees has diminished, it has not disappeared and the continuing control of the Authority over the relocation process is essential to the success of the evacuation program."

Justice Douglas wrote:

> We are of the view that Mitsuye Endo should be given her liberty. We conclude that, whatever power the War Relocation Authority may have to detain other classes of citizens, it has

no authority to subject citizens who are concededly loyal to its leave procedure.

Loyalty is a matter of the heart and mind, not of race, creed, or color. He who is loyal is by definition not a spy or a saboteur. When the power to detain is derived from the power to protect the war effort against espionage and sabotage, detention which has no relationship to that objective is unauthorized.

If we assume (as we do) that the original evacuation was justified, its lawful character was derived from the fact that it was an espionage and sabotage measure, not that there was community hostility to this group of American citizens.

"Mitsuye Endo," concluded the justice, "is entitled to unconditional release by the War Relocation Authority."

By this time, the War Relocation Authority, aware that no military need existed for barring Japanese Americans from the West Coast, had quietly began permitting selected evacuees to return home. The Supreme Court decision effectively ended the detention program, as the Western Defense Command announced that "those persons of Japanese ancestry whose records have stood the test of Army scrutiny during the past two years" would be released from internment after 2 January 1945.

Related Cases
Ex parte Quirin, 317 U.S. 1 (1942).
Hirabayashi v. United States, 320 U.S. 81 (1943).
Korematsu v. United States, 323 U.S. 214 (1944).

Bibliography and Further Reading
Armor, John and Peter Wright. *Manzanar*. New York: Random House, 1988.

Burns, James MacGregor. *Roosevelt: The Soldier of Freedom*. New York: Harcourt Brace Jovanovich, Inc., 1970.

Irons, Peter. *Justice at War*. New York: Oxford University Press, 1983.

Johnson, John W. *Historic U.S. Court Cases, 1690–1990: An Encyclopedia*. New York: Garland Publishing, 1992.

Melendy, H. Brett. *The Oriental Americans*. New York: Twayne Publishers, 1972.

Wilson, Robert A. and Bill Hosokawa. *East to America*. New York: William Morrow and Co., 1980.

WILLIAMSON V. LEE OPTICAL

Legal Citation: 348 U.S. 483 (1955)

Appellant
Mac Q. Williamson, Attorney General of Oklahoma

Appellee
Lee Optical of Oklahoma

Appellant's Claim
That an Oklahoma law, which prohibited persons other than licensed optometrists and ophthalmologists from fitting lenses for eyeglasses, did not constitute a violation of the Due Process Clause in the Fourteenth Amendment to the Constitution.

Chief Lawyer for Appellant
James C. Harkin, Assistant Attorney General of Oklahoma

Chief Lawyer for Appellee
Dick H. Woods

Justices for the Court
Hugo Lafayette Black, Harold Burton, Tom C. Clark, William O. Douglas (writing for the Court), Felix Frankfurter, Sherman Minton, Stanley Forman Reed, Earl Warren

Justices Dissenting
None (John Marshall Harlan II did not participate)

Place
Washington, D.C.

Date of Decision
28 March 1955

Decision
Upheld the power of the legislatures to make state laws regulating business, and declared that "The day is gone when this Court uses the Due Process Clause of the Fourteenth Amendment to strike down state laws . . ."

Significance
Williamson v. Lee Optical was one of several cases marking the death knell of "substantive due process." Starting with the New Deal under President Franklin D. Roosevelt in the 1930s, the implementation of national economic policies had threatened the concept. In 1955, with *Williamson v. Lee Optical,* the Court was in the midst of a paradigm shift in its views on that concept: gone were the days, as Justice Douglas said, when the Court would use substantive due process on behalf of businesspeople such as the appellee in this case; but a day was just dawning when the concept would be applied in favor of other constituencies.

A Vision Problem in Oklahoma

Although it would ultimately involve lofty constitutional ideas, *Williamson v. Lee Optical* arose from a simple and practical set of needs concerning the sale of eyeglasses. Foremost among these, from the perspective of consumers, was the desire to have the fastest, easiest, and cheapest service in fitting a pair of glasses. Such service would likely come from an optician, which the Court would later define as "an artisan qualified to grind lenses, fill prescription, and fit frames." The services of such a practitioner would undoubtedly be cheaper than those of an ophthalmologist, "a duly licensed physician who specializes in the care of eyes"; or of an optometrist, a doctor who "examines eyes for refractive error, recognizes (but does not treat) diseases of the eye, and fills prescriptions for eyeglasses." Whereas an optician would have only the training necessary to carry out his or her fairly limited tasks, the optometrist or ophthalmologist would have the education of a medical doctor, making him or her more than qualified to fit a pair of glasses for a patient—and s/he would most likely charge accordingly.

The question revolved around the right of the state of Oklahoma to prohibit the sale of lenses fitted by an optician. The answer lay in Title 59 of the Oklahoma state laws, Section 2 of which stated in part:

> It shall be unlawful for any person, firm, corporation, company, or partnership not licensed under the provisions of Chapter 11 or Chapter 13 of Title 59, Oklahoma Statutes 1951, to fit, adjust, adapt, or to in any manner apply lenses, frames, prisms, or any other optical appliances to the face of a person . . .

These were only the opening words, but the point was clearly established: since Chapter 11 provided for the licensing of ophthalmologists, and Chapter 13 of optometrists, opticians were effectively kept out of the lens-fitting business in Oklahoma. To opticians, this exclusion seemed particularly unfair, given the existence of retail establishments selling ready-to-wear glasses. Similarly questionable, from the view of the opticians, were provisions making it illegal for them to advertise, or for anyone to rent retail space to any person "purporting to do eye examination or visual care."

Substantive Due Process

Due process of law, guaranteed by the Fifth and Fourteenth amendments to the U.S. Constitution, demands fairness for individuals in legal procedures applied by federal and state governments, respectively. Due process judicial deliberations involve both substantive and procedural dimensions. Whereas procedural due process looks at the manner in which individual rights are protected from governmental arbitrary actions such as right to an attorney or freedom from unreasonable search and seizure, substantive due process addresses the actual subject matter being regulated in a law or regulation, particularly personal rights or liberties.

By the 1990s, substantive due process court decisions had addressed most fundamental liberties expressly found in the first ten amendments as well as liberties not specifically described. Such unspoken liberties include the right to privacy in matters of personal choice—marriage, sexual concerns, parenthood, abortion, or "right to die" issues. The Supreme Court found the guarantee of these liberties embedded in various aspects of U.S. legal history including common law, moral philosophy, equal protection, and court precedents. The Court would sustain state or federal regulation restricting fundamental liberties only if the government could demonstrate a compelling reason in the public interest.

Source(s): Keynes, Edward. *Liberty, Property, and Privacy: Toward a Jurisprudence of Substantive Due Process.* University Park, PA: Pennsylvania State University Press, 1996.

Lee Optical filed a suit in district court, charging that these laws were unconstitutional. The three judges of the district court agreed on most counts. Specifically, under the Due Process Clause of the Fourteenth Amendment, they declared unconstitutional the provision in the Oklahoma statute making it unlawful for anyone who was not a licensed optometrist or ophthalmologist to fit lenses, or to duplicate or replace lenses, except under the written authority of an ophthalmologist or optometrist licensed in Oklahoma. While it was within the power of a state to regulate something as vital as eye examination, the district court held, the requirement in question was not "reasonably and rationally related to the health and welfare of the people." The district court similarly declared unconstitutional most other provisions in the Oklahoma statute, including the prohibition against advertising, with the exception of a portion of Section 3 which made it unlawful to "solicit the sale of spectacles, eye glasses, lenses, frames," etc.

The state of Oklahoma, in the person of Attorney General Mac Q. Williamson, appealed. By the time it came before the Supreme Court, the case had been split into two parts: *Williamson v. Lee Optical,* designated as No. 184 by the Court, in which Oklahoma challenged the lower court's ruling of its laws as unconstitutional; and the case of *Lee Optical v. Williamson* (No. 185), a subordinate legal action challenging the lower court's declaration that the prohibition against soliciting the sale of eyeglasses was indeed constitutional. Along the way to the Supreme Court, both sides attracted national attention from professional associations relating to eye care, and from states. While Dick H. Woods argued for Lee Optical in both 184 and 185, by special leave of the Court, Herbert A. Bergson argued for the Guild of Prescription Opticians as *amici curiae* in 184. Similarly,

whereas Oklahoma's assistant attorney general, James C. Harkin, represented his state as appellant in 184 and appellee in 185, Philip Perlman argued for the American Optometric Association as *amicus curiae*. Joining Oklahoma and the Optometric Association in urging reversal in 184 and affirmation in 185 were the states of Arkansas, California, and Mississippi.

Substantive Due Process: From Slaughterhouse to Optician's Shop

At issue in *Williamson* was the principle of Substantive Due Process, a concept which made its first appearance in the famous *Slaughterhouse Cases* (1873). The latter cases challenged a state monopoly on slaughterhouses in Louisiana, and were brought by a group of butchers who argued that the policy prevented them from practicing their trade. At that time, Justice Joseph P. Bradley stated that "a law which prohibits a large class of citizens from adopting . . . or from following a lawful employment . . . does deprive them of liberty as well as property, without due process of law." The case of *Munn v. Illinois* (1877) was another commerce-related legal action which touched on the question of due process. Had the grain storage facilities at issue in the case not been "affected with a public interest," the Court suggested, it might have given the case closer scrutiny in light of due process.

Such scrutiny finally came, through a long series of steps, with the Court's landmark ruling in *Chicago, Milwaukee and St. Paul Railway Company v. the State of Minnesota* (1890). This time the Court declared a state economic law unconstitutional, and identified the courts of the land, not the state legislatures, as the bodies which should have final say in matters involving business rates. The ruling centered around the question of Due Process, which is guaranteed in Section 1 of the Fourteenth Amendment:

> All persons born or naturalized in the United States, and subject to the jurisdiction thereof, are citizens of the United States and of the State wherein they reside. No State shall make or enforce any law which shall abridge the privileges or immunities of citizens of the United States; nor shall any state deprive any person of life, liberty, or property, without due process of law; nor deny to any person within its jurisdiction the equal protection of the laws.

The ruling in this case found that as a corporate "person," the Chicago, Milwaukee and Saint Paul Railroad was entitled to protection of its rights under the Due Process clause.

Hence in a great irony, the Fourteenth Amendment, passed by Congress following the Civil War with the aim of protecting the rights of freed slaves, instead saw its primary application in service to corporations. In a series of rulings throughout the latter part of the nineteenth century and the early part of the twentieth, the Court upheld corporations' "freedom of contract," and ruled against laws setting minimum wages or maximum daily working hours. The tide of substantive due process in favor of corporations continued for more than a generation, until it was stopped by the Depression and the New Deal programs initiated in the 1930s.

In its 1934 ruling in *Nebbia v. New York*, the Court began to distance itself from its earlier stance, declaring that a state could regulate milk prices whether or not the milk industry could be judged as one "affected with public interest." As for its role of protecting business from the encroachments of state government, the Court declared that it was no longer a "super-legislature." With the liberal President Franklin D. Roosevelt ascendant, the Court began going back on its earlier pro-business activism, and in 1941 Justice Douglas wrote for the unanimous Court in *Olsen v. Nebraska* that "We are not concerned . . . with the wisdom, need, or appropriateness" of a state law regulating employment agency fees. Such questions, Douglas wrote, "suggest a choice which should be left where . . . it was left by the Constitution—to the states and to Congress."

"The Day Is Gone . . ."

Fourteen years later, in *Williamson v. Lee Optical*, Douglas delivered the opinion for a once again unanimous Court of eight judges. (Justice John Marshall Harlan II, recently sworn in, took no part in the proceedings.) The Court reversed in part and affirmed in part, but none of its rulings favored Lee Optical or the Guild of Prescription Opticians: rather, the Court's ruling reversed those parts of the district court judgment which over-

turned Oklahoma law, and affirmed the lower court's ruling that the law prohibiting solicitation of the sale of lenses was constitutional. As he had earlier done in *Olsen,* Douglas made it clear that the Court was not interested in evaluating the state law from the standpoint of logic, reason, or common sense: "The Oklahoma law," he wrote, "may exact a needless, wasteful requirement in many cases." Regardless of this distinct possibility, however, "it is for the legislature, not the courts, to balance the advantages and disadvantages of the new requirement." Furthermore, "the present law does not require a new examination of the eyes every time the frames are changed or the lenses duplicated. For if the old prescription is on file with the opticians, he can go ahead and make the new fitting or duplicate the lenses." But again, "the law need not be in every respect logically consistent with its aims to be constitutional. It is enough that there is an evil at hand for correction, and that it might be thought that the particular legislative measure was a rational way to correct it."

What was at question, instead, was due process, and here too Justice Douglas made quick work of the opticians' case: in perhaps the most famous sentence of his ruling in this case, Douglas announced that

> The day is gone when this Court uses the Due Process Clause of the Fourteenth Amendment to strike down state laws, regulatory of business or industrial conditions, because they may be unwise, improvident, or out of harmony with a particular school of thought.

As for the specific due process questions at issue in *Williamson*, Douglas wrote that these were "answered in principle" by *Roschen v. Ward* (1929), in which the Court upheld a New York law preventing the sale of eyeglasses at a retail outlet without the supervision of a licensed physician or optometrist. The Court at that time had placed its confidence in professionals to uphold the intent of the law: ". . . wherever the requirements of the Act stop, there can be no doubt that the presence and superintendence of the specialist tend to diminish an evil."

Thus the Court dealt with the first portion of the Oklahoma law in question, the part of Section 2 that prevented persons other than licensed optometrists or ophthalmologists from fitting, duplicating, or replacing lenses. Douglas then proceeded to examine the various other claims at issue. With regard to the apparent inequity in the state's exempting retailers of ready-to-wear glasses from its regulations, the Court left that decision up to the state: "The legislature may select one phase of one field and apply a remedy there, neglecting the others . . ." Besides, "The prohibition of the Equal Protection Clause goes no further than the invidious discrimination. We cannot say that that point has been reached here. For all this record shows, the ready-to-wear branch of this business may not loom large in Oklahoma . . ."

As for the prohibition against renting retail space for the purposes of doing eye examination, this was "on the same constitutional footing as the denial to corporations of the right to practice general dentistry." In both situations, the aim was "an attempt to free the profession . . . from all taints of commercialism." The Oklahoma law prohibiting business from soliciting the sale of frames, mountings, and "other optical appliances," the Court held, was likewise constitutional: "An eyeglass frame, considered in isolation, is only a piece of merchandise. But an eyeglass frame is not used in isolation . . . it is used with lenses, and lenses, pertaining as they do to the human eye, enter the field of health." Therefore "we see no constitutional reason why a State may not treat all who deal with the human eye as members of a profession who should use no merchandising methods for obtaining customers." Given this statement, the ruling in 185, regarding the prohibition of soliciting sale of lenses, etc., was obvious. Affirming in part and reversing in part, the Court upheld the constitutionality of all aspects of the Oklahoma law.

Impact

It is interesting to note that both *Griswold v. Connecticut* (1965) and *Roe v. Wade* (1973) make mention of *Williamson* in several places. These two cases, the former involving birth control and the latter abortion, were landmarks not only with regard to personal freedom in sexual matters, but in their "new" application of due process. *Williamson,* while seemingly striking the final blow against due process in its business application, came at a time when the concept was finding new life in relation to privacy and personal freedom. Starting with *Skinner v. Oklahoma* (1942), the Court had begun to apply due process to individual rights, and by

the time of *Griswold,* a decade after *Williamson,* that concept was established. But conservatives were just as wary of the application of due process to personal issues as liberals had been of its uses in favor of business: Justice Black in *Griswold* warned that due process was "no less dangerous when used to enforce this Court's views about personal rights than those about economic rights." Justice William H. Rehnquist, in his dissent from the *Roe v. Wade* decision, made a similar point. In the end, *Williamson* can be seen as a milestone marking the end of one era with regard to due process, and the beginnings of another.

Related Cases
The Slaughterhouse Cases, 83 U.S. 36 (1873).
Munn v. Illinois, 94 U.S. 113, 134 (1877).
Chicago, Milwaukee and St. Paul Railway Company v. the State of Minnesota, 134 U.S. 418 (1890).
Roschen v. Ward, 279 U.S. 337 (1929).
Nebbia v. New York, 291 U.S. 502 (1934).
Olsen v. Nebraska, 313 U.S. 236 (1941).
Skinner v. Oklahoma, 316 U.S. 535 (1942).
Griswold v. Connecticut, 381 U.S. 479 (1965).
Roe v. Wade, 410 U.S. 113 (1973).

Bibliography and Further Reading
Biskupic, Joan, and Elder Witt. *Guide to the U.S. Supreme Court,* third edition. Washington, DC: Congressional Quarterly Inc., 1997.

Hall, Kermit L., ed. *Oxford Companion to the Supreme Court of the United States.* New York: Oxford University Press, 1992.

Levy, Leonard W., ed. *Encyclopedia of the American Constitution.* New York: Macmillan, 1986.

Witt, Elder. *Congressional Quarterly's Guide to the Supreme Court,* 2nd ed. Washington, DC: Congressional Quarterly Inc., 1990.

BOYNTON V. VIRGINIA

Legal Citation: 364 U.S. 454 (1960)

Petitioner
Bruce Boynton

Respondent
Commonwealth of Virginia

Petitioner's Claim
That his arrest for refusing to leave a whites only section in a bus station restaurant violated the Interstate Commerce Act, and the Equal Protection, Due Process, and Commerce Clauses of the U.S. Constitution.

Chief Lawyer for Petitioner
Thurgood Marshall

Chief Lawyer for Respondent
Walter E. Rogers

Justices for the Court
Hugo Lafayette Black (writing for the Court), William J. Brennan, Jr., William O. Douglas, Felix Frankfurter, John Marshall Harlan II, Potter Stewart, Earl Warren

Justices Dissenting
Tom C. Clark, Charles Evans Whittaker

Place
Washington, D.C.

Date of Decision
5 December 1960

Decision
Boynton's conviction was unconstitutional.

Significance
In the often acrimonious battle between the federal government and individual states over racial segregation, Bruce Boynton's suit marked a major breakthrough. For the first time, the federal government sent a clear message that interstate facilities were for the use of all citizens, irrespective of color.

In 1958, Bruce Boynton, a black student at Howard University Law School in Washington, D.C., took a Trailways bus from Washington to his home in Montgomery, Alabama. On a 40-minute layover at the Trailways Bus Terminal in Richmond, Virginia, the passengers went inside to eat. Boynton entered the segregated restaurant, sat in the white section and ordered a sandwich and tea. When asked to move to the colored section, he refused, saying that as an interstate passenger he was protected by federal antisegregation laws. Declining to leave, he was arrested by local police, charged with trespass, and fined $10.

The Commonwealth of Virginia conceded that the conviction could not stand if anything in federal law or the Constitution gave Boynton a right to service in the restaurant. But it found no such right. Lawyers for the National Association for the Advancement of Colored People (NAACP) petitioned the Supreme Court on grounds that Boynton was entitled to such protection under the Constitution.

Pleading that case before the Supreme Court on 12 October 1960 was Thurgood Marshall, who later became the first African American Supreme Court justice. He maintained that Boynton's arrest placed an unreasonable burden on commerce and denied him the equal protection of the law, both points having far-reaching implications. However, the Supreme Court chose not to address this petition from a constitutional standpoint after the Justice Department, intervening as a friend of the court, raised the issue of the Interstate Commerce Act, which expressly forbade "unjust discrimination."

For the act to apply, the relationship between restaurant and terminal had to be clarified. When Trailways built the terminal in 1953, it contracted with Bus Terminal Restaurant of Richmond, Inc., for the latter to provide dining facilities for passengers on Trailways buses. The only interest that Trailways had in the restaurant came in the form of the annual rental, $30,000, plus a percentage of the gross profits. So the question became whether the restaurant was subject to the same federal provisions as Trailways.

Not so, argued Walter E. Rogers, attorney for Virginia. He contended that the restaurant, as private property, fell outside the scope of the Interstate Commerce Act. Boynton, he said, had been justly convicted.

Court Splits, but for Boynton

On 5 December 1960, the Supreme Court decided 7-2 in favor of Boynton, the first time since 1946 it had divided on a matter of racial segregation. A strong factor in the Court's decision had been the earlier testimony of the restaurant manager who conceded that, although the restaurant received "quite a bit of business" from local people, it was primarily for the service of Trailways passengers. Describing this as "much of an understatement," Justice Black, in writing the majority verdict, added:

> Interstate passengers have to eat, and they have a right to expect that this essential transportation food service . . . would be rendered without discrimination prohibited by the Interstate Commerce Act. We are not holding that every time a bus stops at a wholly independent roadside restaurant the act applies . . . [but] where circumstances show that the terminal and restaurant operate as an integral part of the bus carrier's transportation service . . . an interstate passenger need not inquire into documents of title or contractual agreements in order to determine whether he has a right to be served without discrimination.

Anticipating the Supreme Court's decision, Bus Terminal Restaurants, Inc., of Raleigh, North Carolina, announced that, as of August of 1960, none of its establishments would be racially segregated.

The impact of this case was immense. For the first time, a bridge was built between the federal government and the civil rights movement. While many obstacles remained to be conquered in the fight for racial equality, henceforth it would be a struggle fought together.

Related Cases

Curtis v. Roxxo & Mastracco, Inc., 413 F.Supp. 804 (1976).

Bibliography and Further Reading

The Negro History Bulletin. Vol. 26, no. 15, 1972.

Wasby, Stephen L., Anthony A. D'Amato, and Rosemary Metrailer. *Desegregation from Brown to Alexander.* Carbondale, IL.: South Illinois University Press, 1977.

Witt, Elder. *Guide to the Supreme Court.* Washington, DC: Congressional Quarterly, 1990, p. 605.

MONROE V. PAPE

Legal Citation: 365 U.S. 167 (1961)

Petitioners
Monroe, et al.

Respondents
Pape, et al.

Petitioners' Claim
That a warrantless search of their home by police, which included demeaning treatment of the entire family, gave the Monroe family cause to bring suit for civil damages against the city of Chicago and the police officers involved in the search.

Chief Lawyer for Petitioners
Donald Page Moore

Chief Lawyer for Respondents
Sydney R. Drebin

Justices for the Court
Hugo Lafayette Black, William J. Brennan, Jr., Tom C. Clark, John Marshall Harlan II, William O. Douglas (writing for the Court), Felix Frankfurter, Potter Stewart, Earl Warren, Charles Evans Whittaker

Justices Dissenting
None

Place
Washington, D.C.

Date of Decision
20 February 1961

Decision
Upheld the petitioners' claim and overturned two lower court rulings dismissing their right to pursue civil damages against police authorities, while affirming the lower courts' dismissal of petitioners' claims against the city of Chicago.

Significance
The ruling revitalized R.S. 1979 of the U.S. Code, derived from article 1 of the so-called Ku Klux Klan Act of 1871, which was passed to protect individuals against abuse of their human rights by state authorities. By affirming the ability of citizens to bring civil suit for damages against authorities who violate their constitutional rights, the Court struck a blow for the rights of the individual and curtailed certain capricious police activities. However, by also affirming the immunity of municipalities from civil suit by their citizens, the Court established a legal precedent that was not displaced until *Monell v. Department of Social Services*, (1977).

A Turbulent Time

In the years immediately following the Civil War, the southern United States suffered great social and political upheaval. Many white citizens resented the political power wielded by newly freed slaves, and took action to curb their participation in the electoral process through terror and other means. As attacks against African Americans continued into the 1870s, many of which were conducted with the approval and even the participation of local law enforcement authorities, President Ulysses S. Grant asked for congressional action to address the problem.

The Ku Klux Klan Act was passed in 1871 in response to Grant's appeal. When added to the U.S. Code as R.S. 1979, it provided in Section 1 that

> every person who, under color of any statute, ordinance, custom, or usage, of any State or Territory, subjects, or causes to be subjected, any citizen of the United States or other person within the jurisdiction thereof to the deprivation of any rights, privileges, or immunities secured by the Constitution and laws, shall be liable to the party injured in an action at law, suit in equity, or other proper proceeding for redress.

This language allowed individuals whose rights had been violated by authorities to seek redress in civil court, in addition to their constitutional protection from the use of evidence obtained through unreasonable searches and seizures. The act also provided jurisdiction for the federal judiciary in cases involving abridgment of an individual's constitutional rights being tried in state courts.

An Energetic Mistake

While investigating a murder, the Chicago police conducted a warrantless search of the Monroe home. Their search techniques were unorthodox. Thirteen police officers broke into the Monroe house in the early morning hours, made every family member get out of bed and stand naked in the center of the living room, and ransacked the house looking for evidence of Mr. Monroe's involvement in the murder. The search included such actions as emptying drawers onto the floor and the ripping open of mattresses. Mr. Monroe was then taken to the police station and detained for ten hours without specific charges being brought against him. He was not brought before a magistrate at the onset of his ordeal, as was legally required, despite the fact that one was available at the station where he was detained. He was also not allowed to contact his attorney during his detention. Despite all this activity, the police were unable to uncover any evidence linking Mr. Monroe to the murder they were investigating, and were forced to release him without bringing any criminal charges against him.

The Monroe family was unwilling to let matters rest at this stage. They decided to pursue civil suits against the city of Chicago and the police officers under R.S. 1979. The city of Chicago and the individual defendants moved for and received a dismissal of the Monroes' claims in the district court. The case then proceeded to the court of appeals, which upheld the ruling of the district court. The U.S. Supreme Court then agreed to hear the case on a writ of *certiorari*, as the lower court rulings were seen as contradictory to earlier Supreme Court decisions in similar cases. The Court heard arguments in the matter on 8 November 1961.

Equal Protection and the States

The Court ruled unanimously in favor of the petitioners, deciding that they had legal grounds to pursue redress through civil litigation against the police officers responsible for their ordeal. The ruling did not extend to the city of Chicago, however, as the Court interpreted R.S. 1979's second clause as exempting municipalities from liability for the actions of their officers. Justice Douglas, writing for the Court, observed that federal jurisdiction certainly was present in the case, since Fourth Amendment prohibitions against unreasonable searches and seizures are made applicable to the states through the Due Process Clause of the Fourteenth Amendment. Furthermore, although R.S. 1979 was originally created to protect African Americans from the Ku Klux Klan, it was also designed to ensure that the states enforced their own laws equally with regard to all their citizens. In the present case,

the actions of police officers were judged to be so egregious that the exclusion of evidence obtained through their searches (of which there was none in any case) could not possibly recompense the Monroe family for its trouble. Finally, since the state courts were unable to provide any compensatory action to the Monroe family, a federal remedy had to be forthcoming.

Significantly, despite the appearance of a clear victory for the petitioners, the Court's refusal to allow the city of Chicago to be sued would continue to pose a legal barrier to individuals seeking redress for misdeeds of municipalities that could not be compensated for through mere exclusion of evidence.

Impact

The ruling affirmed the right of citizens to seek compensation beyond exclusion of evidence for actions taken "under color of law" by state officials. *Monroe v. Pape* also confirmed the jurisdiction of the federal judiciary in cases where state courts failed to provide sufficient recompense to victims of civil rights infringements by state authorities. By stopping short of making municipalities liable for the actions of their officers, however, the Court failed to fully protect the rights of the individual. This was remedied in *Monell v. Department of Social Services* (1978), in which the Court went beyond *Monroe* to rule that individuals whose civil rights had been violated could seek redress from municipalities as well as from their officers.

Related Cases
United States v. Classic, 313 U.S. 299 (1941).
Screws v. United States, 325 U.S. 91 (1945).
Williams v. United States, 341 U.S. 97 (1951).
Monell v. Department of Social Services, 436 U.S. 658 (1978).

Bibliography and Further Reading
Biskupic, Joan and Elder Witt, eds. *Guide to the U.S. Supreme Court*, 3rd ed. Washington: Congressional Quarterly Inc., 1990.

Hall, Kermit L., ed. *Oxford Companion to the Supreme Court of the United States*, New York: Oxford University Press, 1992.

HEART OF ATLANTA MOTEL V. UNITED STATES

Legal Citation: 379 U.S. 241 (1964)

Appellant
Heart of Atlanta Motel, Inc.

Appellee
United States

Appellant's Claim
That provisions of the Civil Rights Act of 1964, requiring hotel and motel owners to provide accommodations to African Americans, cannot be enforced against privately owned public accommodations.

Chief Lawyer for Appellant
Moreton Rolleston, Jr.

Chief Lawyer for Appellee
Archibald Cox, U.S. Solicitor General

Justices for the Court
Hugo Lafayette Black, William J. Brennan, Jr., Tom C. Clark (writing for the Court), William O. Douglas, Arthur Goldberg, John Marshall Harlan II, Potter Stewart, Earl Warren, Byron R. White

Justices Dissenting
None

Place
Washington, D.C.

Date of Decision
14 December 1964

Decision
By a unanimous decision, the Supreme Court upheld the public accommodations provisions of the Civil Rights Act of 1964.

Significance
Heart of Atlanta Motel marked a turning point in Congress' efforts to promote civil rights through use of its power to regulate interstate commerce.

The Heart of Atlanta Motel was a 216-room establishment located in downtown Atlanta, Georgia, close to several interstate highways. The motel advertised in national magazines and on billboards within Georgia. Approximately 75 percent of the motel's registered guests came from out of state.

In 1964, Congress passed a civil rights act intended to eliminate racial discrimination. Some of the act's most important provisions appeared in a section known as Title II, which insured full access to places of public accommodation to racial minorities. Prior to passage of the act, the Heart of Atlanta Motel had consistently refused to supply African Americans with rooms. Claiming that it was the motel's right as a private business to continue this practice, the motel operator filed suit in the U.S. District Court for the Northern District of Georgia, seeking a judicial declaration that Title II was unconstitutional, as well as an injunction preventing the enforcement of the public accommodations provisions.

The federal government countersued, seeking enforcement of the act against the hotel. The government prevailed in district court, and the hotel operators appealed this judgment to the U.S. Supreme Court.

Supreme Court Affirms Congressional Authority to Regulate Private Business under the Commerce Clause

Justice Clark, writing for a unanimous Court, upheld the power of Congress under the Commerce Clause of Article I of the Constitution to regulate both interstate and intrastate businesses, public as well as private, that affect the nation's commerce:

> [T]he determinative test of the exercise of power by the Congress under the Commerce Clause is simply whether the activity sought to be regulated is "commerce which concerns more States than one" and has a real and substantial relation to the national interest.

The national interest that Congress sought to promote in Title II was undoing racial discrimination. Racial discrimination, in turn, is a moral wrong that

Justice Tom C. Clark.
© Photograph by Peter
Ehrenhaft. Collection of
the Supreme Court of
the United States.

the Constitution authorizes Congress to regulate under the national police power, which is the authority to pass legislation that may restrict individual liberties in the interest of promoting the general welfare.

In 1881, the Supreme Court decided a set of cases collectively called the *Civil Rights Cases,* in which various provisions of the Civil Rights Act of 1875 outlawing discrimination in public accommodations were declared unconstitutional. In the *Civil Rights Cases,* the Court held that the Fourteenth Amendment, which granted citizenship rights to freed slaves and which was the basis for the Civil Rights Act of 1875, could not be enforced against private businesses. So when Congress next addressed the issue of racial discrimination, in 1964, it used its power under the Commerce Clause as the primary authority for the legislation.

The Commerce Clause proved to be a powerful tool for combatting racism. Although the appellant in *Heart of Atlanta Motel* claimed that its operation was local, the Court found that the effects of its policies and practices reached far beyond Atlanta and even beyond the state border. In particular, by refusing to provide rooms for African American travelers, many of whom came from out of state on business, the motel was affecting

interstate commerce. In *Katzenbach v. McClung,* decided the same day, the Court used similar logic in applying the Civil Rights Act of 1964 to a small restaurant that purchased its supplies locally and served mostly local customers. Because some of the restaurant's supplies originally came from out of state, its activities had an impact on interstate commerce. Taken together, *Heart of Atlanta Motel* and *Katzenbach v. McClung* amply demonstrated that Congress had the means to combat racism in America.

Related Cases
Hall v. DeCuir, 95 U.S. 485 (1878).
Civil Rights Cases, 100 U.S. 3 (1887).
Hoke v. United States, 227 U.S. 308 (1913).
Caminetti v. United States, 242 U.S. 470 (1917).
Katzenbach v. McClung, 379 U.S. 294 (1964).
Griffin v. Maryland, 378 U.S. 130 (1971).

Bibliography and Further Reading
Bell, Derrick A. *Race, Racism, and American Law,* 2nd ed. Boston, MA: Little, Brown, 1980.

A protestor opposing the civil rights programs of the Johnson administration. © UPI/Corbis-Bettmann.

Wood, L. Ingleby. *The Drive to Desegregate Places of Public Accommodation.* New York: Garland, 1991.

Nieman, Donald G., ed. *Black Southerners and the Law, 1865-1900.* New York, NY: Garland, 1994.

KATZENBACH V. MCCLUNG

Legal Citation: 379 U.S. 294 (1964)

Appellants
Nicholas Katzenbach, Acting Attorney General, et al.

Appellee
Ollie McClung, Sr.

Appellants' Claim
That a restaurant cannot refuse service to African Americans under the Commerce Clause.

Chief Lawyer for Appellants
Archibald Cox, U.S. Solicitor General

Chief Lawyer for Appellee
Robert McDavid Smith

Justices for the Court
Hugo Lafayette Black, William J. Brennan, Jr., Tom C. Clark (writing for the Court), William O. Douglas, Arthur Goldberg, John Marshall Harlan II, Potter Stewart, Earl Warren, Byron R. White

Justices Dissenting
None

Place
Washington, D.C.

Date of Decision
14 December 1964

Decision
The Supreme Court held that because some of the food served in the appellant's restaurant originated out of state, Congress could, under the Commerce Clause, outlaw racial segregation in this privately-owned business.

Significance
Katzenbach v. McClung was the Court's most expansive reading of Congress's commerce power, which thereafter needed only a "rational basis" for connecting interstate commerce and local economic activity in order to justify federal regulation.

Ollie's Barbeque was a small, family-owned restaurant which operated in Birmingham, Alabama, and which seated 220 customers. It was located on a state highway and was 11 blocks from an interstate highway. In a typical year, approximately half of the food it purchased from a local supplier originated out of state. It catered to local families and white collar workers and provided take-out service to African American customers.

In 1964, Congress passed a Civil Rights Act which was intended to eliminate discrimination against African Americans. One section of the act, Title II, was specifically intended to grant African Americans full access to public facilities such as hotels, restaurants, and public recreation areas. On the same day, the Supreme Court heard challenges to Title II from a motel owner, in *Heart of Atlanta Motel v. United States,* and from Ollie McClung. Both claimed that the federal government had no right to impose any regulations on small, private businesses. Both ultimately lost. Ollie McClung won an initial round when he obtained an injunction in federal district court preventing the government from enforcing Title II against his restaurant. But then the attorney general appealed this decision to the U.S. Supreme Court.

Supreme Court Authorizes Use of Commerce Power to Enforce Civil Rights

Writing for a unanimous Court, Justice Clark observed that Congress could exercise its commerce power to enforce the public accommodations provision of the Civil Rights Act against a restaurant that served food which had passed through interstate commerce. While the impact of the restaurant's segregationist policies was by itself negligible, when all such local activity was added together, the economic effect could be substantial. What is more, Clark wrote, racial discrimination at Ollie's and other restaurants like it could act as a deterrent to individuals and industries who might wish to relocate to Alabama from other states. In order to bring the commerce power to bear on discriminatory practices, Congress need only demonstrate that there was a "rational basis" for doing so:

> Here . . . Congress has determined for itself that refusals of service to Negroes have im-

posed burdens both upon the interstate flow of food and upon the movement of products generally. Of course, the mere fact that Congress has said when particular activity shall be deemed to affect commerce does not preclude further examination by this Court. But where we find that the legislators, in light of the facts and testimony before them, have a rational basis for finding a chosen regulatory scheme necessary to the protection of commerce, our investigation is at an end.

As the Court noted in the *McClung* case, the power of Congress in the field of interstate commerce is "broad and sweeping." It proved to be an effective tool for combatting racism, which the Court, led by Earl Warren, saw not as a local problem, but a national one requiring a nationwide solution. Nothing in *McClung,* though, limits the extensive reach of the commerce power to matters involving racial discrimination. In 1976, the Court struck down legislation based on the Commerce Clause for the first time in 40 years. The issue in *National League of Cities v. Usery* was the legitimacy of the minimum wage and maximum hour provisions of the Fair Labor Standards Act of 1938. But while in *Usery* the Court found these provisions an unconstitutional intrusion of the federal government into affairs properly governed by the state, this opinion was overruled less than a decade later in *Garcia v. San Antonio Metropolitan Transit Authority* (1985). The

conflict between federal authority and states' rights, again fought on Commerce Clause grounds, resurfaced in 1995. In *United States v. Lopez* the Court, by a one-vote majority, struck down the federal Gun-Free School Zone Act of 1990 on grounds that the act exceeded Congress' authority under the Commerce Clause to regulate activities bearing some relation to interstate commerce—in this case the transportation of arms across state lines.

Related Cases
Heart of Atlanta Motel v. United States, 379 U.S. 241 (1964).
National League of Cites v. Usery, 426 U.S. 833 (1976).
Garcia v. San Antonio Metropolitan Transit Authority, 469 U.S. 528 (1985).
United States v. Lopez, 514 U.S. 549 (1995).

Bibliography and Further Reading
Bell, Derrick A., Jr. *Race, Racism, and American Law*, 2nd ed. Boston, MA: Little, Brown, 1980.

Wood, L. Ingleby. *The Drive to Desegregate Places of Public Accommodation.* New York, NY: Garland, 1991.

Johnson, John W., ed. *Historic U.S. Court Cases, 1690–1990: An Encyclopedia.* New York: Garland Publishing, 1992.

Nieman, Donald G., ed. *Black Southerners and the Law, 1865-1900.* New York: Garland, 1994.

UNITED STATES V. GUEST

Legal Citation: 383 U.S. 745 (1966)

Petitioner
United States

Respondent
Herbert Guest, et al.

Petitioner's Claim
That the respondent conspired to deprive black citizens of their rights guaranteed by the Civil Rights Act of 1964.

Chief Lawyer for Petitioner
Thurgood Marshall, U.S. Solicitor General

Chief Lawyers for Respondent
James E. Hudson, Charles J. Bloch

Justices for the Court
Hugo Lafayette Black, William J. Brennan, Jr., Tom C. Clark, Abe Fortas, Potter Stewart (writing for the Court), Byron R. White

Justices Dissenting
William O. Douglas, John Marshall Harlan II, Earl Warren

Place
Washington, D.C.

Date of Decision
28 March 1966

Decision
Reversed the judgment of the district court and held that the allegation of state involvement in conspiracy was sufficient to charge a violation of rights protected by the Fourteenth Amendment. The allegation of false arrest of black citizens was broad enough to cover a charge of active connivance by state agents, constituting a denial of rights protected by the Equal Protection Clause. Thus the district court should not have dismissed that part of the indictment.

Significance
The Supreme Court clarified when the federal law against conspiracy can be used in a case involving interference in the right to travel freely between states. The purpose of the conspiracy must be to impede or prevent interstate travel or to oppress a person exercising that right. Then, whether or not racial discrimination is the motivation, the conspiracy falls under the federal conspiracy law.

Lyndon B. Johnson became president of the United States in November 1963, upon the assassination of President John F. Kennedy. As a memorial to the slain president, Johnson proposed to Congress that it act on a civil rights bill. The Civil Rights Act of 1964 increased federal powers to give access to all races to public facilities, to protect voting rights, and to desegregate schools. Title II of this act made it a federal offense to discriminate against any customer in a place of public accommodation. Six months later, the U.S. Supreme Court decided that the Commerce Clause could be used to bar private discrimination. The Commerce Clause is part of the Constitution that grants to Congress the power to regulate commerce. Freedom marches and riots marked the era when blacks fought for their civil rights. *United States v. Guest* took place against the backdrop of the burgeoning Civil Rights Movement.

Six men were accused of conspiring to injure, oppress, threaten, and intimidate black citizens in Athens, Georgia, beginning in 1964. The men were indicted by a U.S. grand jury in the Middle District of Georgia. They were indicted under 18 U.S.C. Sec. 241, a federal law dealing with conspiracy, for conspiring to deprive black citizens of the free exercise and enjoyment of rights secured by the Constitution and laws of the United States. In particular, the indictment noted the right to use state facilities without discrimination by race, the right freely to engage in interstate travel, and the right to equal enjoyment of privately owned places of public accommodation. These rights had recently been guaranteed by Title II of the Civil Rights Act of 1964. The indictment listed how the accused had conspired to deprive blacks of their rights: shooting, beating, killing, damaging or destroying property, pursuing and threatening with guns, making threatening phone calls, wearing disguises on the highway and premises of others, causing the arrest of blacks by making false reports, and burning crosses at night in public view.

The district court dismissed the indictment against the men on the grounds that it did not involve rights which are attributes of national citizenship. The district court, regarding the right to equal use of public facilities that are owned or operated by the state of Georgia, ruled that 18 U.S.C. 241 did not encompass any Four-

---

Burden of Proof

Burden of proof is the duty of a party to prove an asserted fact. Two concepts embody the burden of proof: the burden of persuasion and the burden of going forward. The latter is also called production burden or burden of evidence.

The burden of persuasion requires the plaintiff or prosecutor to convince the jury, or the judge in non-jury trials, of all the pertinent facts in the case. The degree of proof varies depending on whether the case is a civil or criminal proceeding. In civil cases, the burden must be met by a preponderance of the evidence. Preponderance means the facts are merely more convincing or more probable to the judge or jury than the opposing evidence. Criminal cases require the persuasion

burden to be proof beyond a reasonable doubt. The evidence must be so conclusive that it erases all reasonable doubts. The burden of persuasion is always the responsibility of the prosecution.

The burden of going forward requires either party to prove wrong any evidence that damages their position. To avoid early dismissal by the judge, the prosecution's proof of evidence must prevail. The burden of going forward shifts back and forth from prosecution to defense during the course of a trial.

Source(s): *West's Encyclopedia of American Law.* Minneapolis/St. Paul, MN: West Publishing, 1998.

---

teenth Amendment rights. The Fourteenth Amendment guarantees equal protection. The court also decided that any broader interpretation of sec. 241 would "render it void for indefiniteness." The district court further held that the Equal Protection Clause does not apply to private action, but only to state action. The court claimed that the public-accommodation allegation was inadequate because it did not show that discrimination was the motivation.

Intent to Interfere

The United States appealed directly to the Supreme Court under the Criminal Appeals Act. The Court ruled that it did not have jurisdiction to decide the issue of interference with the right to use public accommodations because of a defect in pleading.

Regarding the district court's claim of "indefiniteness," Justice Stewart noted in his opinion that "inclusion of Fourteenth Amendment rights within the compass of 18 U.S.C. sec. 241 does not render the statute unconstitutionally vague." Because the charge is one of conspiracy, the requirement that the offender must have had the intent to interfere with federal rights is satisfied.

Contrary to the argument of the litigants, the indictment contained an allegation of state involvement. This related to the charge of "causing the arrest of Negroes by means of false reports." This allegation was sufficient to prevent this part of the indictment from being dismissed.

The fourth part of the indictment dealt with conspiracy to prevent free travel from and to Georgia and to prevent the use of highway facilities and other instrumentalities of interstate commerce within Georgia. The Supreme Court ruled that the district court should not

have dismissed this part of the indictment because the right of interstate travel is protected by 18 U.S.C. sec. 241. However, a specific intent to interfere with this federal right must be proved.

Justice Clark noted in his concurrence that the specific language of sec. 5 of the Fourteenth Amendment "empowers the Congress to enact laws punishing all conspiracies—with or without state action—that interfere with Fourteenth Amendment rights." In other words, Congress has the power to outlaw private conspiracies that violate civil rights.

The Right To Travel

Justice Harlan concurred in part and dissented in part. Harlan noted that the majority's decision to hold that the right to travel is protected against private interference is questionable. Harlan felt it "either unwise or impermissible so to read the Constitution." He noted that nothing in the Constitution guarantees the right to travel, but that the right to travel is an aspect of the liberty guaranteed by the Due Process Clause. That clause refers only to governmental action, so it would not apply to *United States v. Guest*.

Harlan added that it is arguable whether conspiracy to discriminate in public accommodations, thus impeding interstate commerce, is dealt with under sec. 241, unaided by Title II of the Civil Rights Act of 1964. Because Congress can legislate in this area, "it seems unnecessary . . . to strain to find a dubious constitutional right."

Impact

United States v. Guest has been cited in many cases dealing with the right of interstate travel. It has been used to show that the constitutional right of interstate travel is a fundamental right. In a 1993 case, *Jayne Bray, et al., Petitioners v. Alexandria Women's Health Clinic et al.*, involving a woman's right to travel interstate to reach an abortion clinic, the opinion cited *United States v. Guest.* The respondents in the abortion clinic case relied upon the right to interstate travel, which in at least some contexts, is a right constitutionally protected against private interference. But all that the clinic noted with respect to that particular right was the district court's finding that many women seeking the services of the clinics in the Washington Metropolitan area travel on the interstate to get there. "That is not enough," noted the opinion. Quoting *United States v. Guest:* Only "if the predominant purpose of the conspiracy is to impede or prevent the exercise of the right of interstate travel, or to oppress a person because of his exercise of that right, then . . . the conspiracy becomes a proper object of the federal conspiracy law."

Related Cases

United States v. Wheeler, 254 U.S. 281 (1920).
Edwards v. California, 314 U.S. 160 (1941).
United States v. Swift & Co., 318 U.S. 442 (1943).
Screws v. United States, 325 U.S. 91 (1945).
United States v. Williams, 341 U.S. 70 (1951).
Aptheker v. Secretary of State, 378 U.S. 500 (1964).
Atlanta Motel v. United States, 379 U.S. 241 (1964).
Jayne Bray, et al., Petitioners v. Alexandria Women's Health Clinic et al., 506 U.S. 263 (1993).

Bibliography and Further Reading

Burns, James MacGregor. *Government by the People.* Englewood Cliffs, NJ: Prentice Hall, 1990.

Congressional Quarterly's Guide to the U.S. Supreme Court. Washington, DC: Congressional Quarterly, Inc., 1979.

FedWorld/FLITE. http://www.fedworld.gov.

Litwack, Leon. *The United States: Becoming a World Power,* Vol. 2. Englewood Cliffs, NJ: Prentice Hall, 1987.

LEVY V. LOUISIANA

Legal Citation: 391 U.S. 68 (1968)

Appellant
Adolph J. Levy

Appellee
State of Louisiana

Appellant's Claim
That a Louisiana law denying illegitimate children the right to recover damages for their mother's wrongful death violates the constitutional guarantee of Due Process and Equal Protection Clauses under the Fourteenth Amendment.

Chief Lawyer for Appellant
Norman Dorsen

Chief Lawyer for Appellee
William A. Porteous III

Justices for the Court
William J. Brennan, Jr., William O. Douglas (writing for the Court), Abe Fortas, Thurgood Marshall, Earl Warren, Byron R. White

Justices Dissenting
Hugo Lafayette Black, John Marshall Harlan II, Potter Stewart

Place
Washington D.C.

Date of Decision
20 May 1968

Decision
The Court ruled in favor of Levy and overturned two lower court decisions by finding that he has the right to claim for wrongful death damages.

Significance
This decision recognized the rights of illegitimate children as similar to the rights of others. The Court recognized illegitimate children as "persons" under Section 1 of the Fourteenth Amendment. The decision held that a state can not create a common legal right for children for certain issues and exclude illegitimate children from the benefit of such a right. The ruling together with later court decisions began defining children's rights more thoroughly.

The Fourteenth Amendment, passed in the wake of the Civil War, stated in part that no state could "deny any person within its jurisdiction the equal protection of the laws." This portion of the amendment became known as the Equal Protection Clause.

In regard to expected social behavior in the United States, illegitimacy has long been considered a "sin" by many. Social perceptions of adultery and illegitimacy were the subject of Nathaniel Hawthorne's classic 1850 novel, *The Scarlet Letter,* which depicts Hester Prynne, a woman who was punished when it was found that she was guilty of adultery and refused to name the father of her illegitimate child. Many moral issues and stigmas of seventeenth century Puritan society, including unwed motherhood and illegitimate children, were still apparent in American society as the twentieth century drew to a close. Prynne was ostracized by her community, but still able to contribute to it.

In American law, children born out of wedlock were often distinguished from those born in marriage. States assigned a special, more limited legal status to illegitimate children. Typically, the various laws were often inconsistent leading to confusion over the actual legal status of illegitimate children in specific situations. For instance, according to Louisiana law, illegitimate children acknowledged by their father were considered natural children. Children with unknown fathers were identified by the title of bastard.

As with many states, Louisiana followed a distinctive course in its restrictions related to common law marriages and illegitimacy. For example, a common-law wife was able to sue under the Louisiana wrongful death statute in the event of the death of her husband. Also, an illegitimate child born to a married woman was normally presumed legitimate. Louisiana made no distinction of legitimacy where incest was a factor. A mother economically dependent on an illegitimate child would be eligible for monetary awards under the Louisiana Workmen's Compensation Act if the child was killed in a work-related accident.

The Levy Family
Louise Levy gave birth to five illegitimate children. They all lived with her and she raised them as any par-

Common Law Marriage

Common law marriage is based on an agreement between two legally competent persons to marry followed by a significant period of living together as husband and wife. The marriage does not rely on ceremony or the completion of specific legal procedures.

Common law marriage is rooted in ancient Roman and early English custom before the mid-1700s. Marriage, then, merely required an agreement to be married and cohabitate. In early America, courts found this form of marriage valid under common law. Marriage law in the United States was left to the states, and by the 1800s many states began requiring marriage ceremonies and other legal formalities including licenses. By the 1990s, only 14 states still recognized common-law marriage.

Legal standards have been established for couples to prove common-law marriages. These standards require consent and mutual agreement to be married, long and consistent cohabitation, and intentional public representation as a married couple. A legally recognized marriage is vital since it affects property rights, insurance and pension benefits, taxation, parenthood issues, and divorce. Establishing whether a marriage is legal or not is essential when a common-law marriage is challenged in any of these areas.

Source(s): *West's Encyclopedia of American Law,* Vol. 3. Minneapolis/St. Paul, MN: West Publishing, 1998.

---

ent would. For an income, Levy worked as a domestic servant. They routinely attended church every Sunday and were enrolled at a parochial school at the family expense. Upon her death, one son, Adolph J. Levy, filed a wrongful death suit under a Louisiana law on behalf of all five children. The suit was against the doctor who treated the mother and the insurance company. Levy claimed two types of damages, the loss of their mother and their pain and suffering.

The Louisiana District Court dismissed the case because of their birth circumstance. The appeals court, in affirming the district court's decision, held that an illegitimate child was not a surviving "child" under state law. Intent of the law was to maintain acceptable "morals and general welfare" by discouraging child birth out of wedlock. After the state supreme court denied the case, Levy appealed to the U.S. Supreme Court.

An Important Reversal: Illegitimate Children as Persons

By vote of 6-3, the Court reversed the two lower court rulings that illegitimate children could not make wrongful death claims under Louisiana law. Justice Douglas, writing a very brief opinion for the majority, first assessed whether illegitimate children were "persons" under the Constitution. Douglas quickly came to the conclusion that they clearly are "persons" within the meaning of the Equal Protection Clause.

The courts had long recognized that states held broad power in making classifications among their citizens. However, Justice Douglas ruled that states may not discriminate against a particular class. Under the Equal Protection Clause, a state's decisions in making classifications must be rational. In this regard, Douglas

could not comprehend how an illegitimate child could not have the same rights as others under the clause. Douglas wrote,

> The rights asserted here involve the intimate, familial relationship between a child and his own mother. When the child's claim of damage for loss of his mother is in issue, why, in terms of "equal protection," should the tortfeasors go free merely because the child is illegitimate? Why should the illegitimate child be denied rights merely because of his birth out of wedlock? He certainly is subject to all the responsibilities of a citizen, including the payment of taxes and conscription under the Selective Service Act.

How could legitimacy of birth have any bearing on the "wrong allegedly inflicted on the mother"?, Douglas pondered. The Levy children were dependent on her biologically and spiritually as much as any other well-cared for children, and upon her death they suffered no less pain by being illegitimate.

In dissent, joined by Justice Black and Justice Stewart, Justice Harlan expressed strong concerns. He could not understand why a state must consider biological relations when recognizing legal relationships. He wrote, "It is, frankly, preposterous to suggest that the State has made illegitimates into nonpersons" as Douglas assumed in reaching his determination.

Harlan argued the state was free to recognize family relationship only between married couples for certain legal purposes. Harlan wrote,

> It is logical to enforce these requirements by declaring that the general class of rights that are dependent upon family relationships shall

be accorded only when the formalities as well as the biology of those relationships are present . . . I could not understand why a State which bases the right to recover for wrongful death strictly on family relationships could not demand that those relationships be formalized.

An Important Reversal

In addressing the rights of illegitimate children, *Levy* was the first Supreme Court case recognizing that illegitimate children may have the same rights as legitimate children under the Equal Protection Clause. The ruling provided a basis for later rulings concerning legitimacy related to workers' compensation survivors benefits in *Weber v. Aetna Casualty & Surety Co.* (1972), and social security benefits in *Mathews v. Lucas* (1976). The Court found in *Weber* that penalizing individuals for something they had no responsibility for, the conduct of their parents before they were born, was highly unjust under the law. The Court also supported a mother recovering wrongful death damages for the death of an illegitimate son in *Glona v. American Guarantee and Liability Insurance Co.* (1968).

Regarding inheritance issues, the Court was less consistent in recognizing the rights of illegitimate children. The Court ruled in *Labine v. Vincent* (1971) that a state could prohibit illegitimate children from claiming inheritance from a father who left no will. The decision actually followed the same line of reasoning as Harlan's dissenting comments in *Levy*. The Court should not be so quick to override the state's authority to regulate its citizens. The Court later wavered in close votes on other inheritance rulings. In family law, *Levy* was one of several crucial rulings that began defining children's rights.

Related Cases

Glona v. American Guarantee and Liability Insurance Co., 391 U.S. 68 (1968).

Labine v. Vincent, 401 U.S. 532 (1971).

Weber v. Aetna Casualty & Surety Co., 406 U.S. 164 (1972).

Mathews v. Lucas, 427 U.S. 495 (1976).

Bibliography and Further Reading

Alston, Philip, ed. *The Best Interests of the Child: Reconciling Culture and Human Rights.* New York: Oxford University Press, 1994.

Gregory, John De Witt, Peter N. Swisher, and Sheryl L. Scheible. *Understanding Family Law.* New York: Matthew Bender, 1993.

Kramer, Donald T. *Legal Rights of Children.* Colorado Springs, CO: Shepard's/McGraw-Hill, 1994.

Mayoue, John C. *Competing Interests in Family Law: Legal Rights and Duties of Third Parties, Spouses, and Significant Others.* Chicago: American Bar Association, Section of Family Law, 1998.

KING V. SMITH

Legal Citation: 392 U.S. 309 (1968)

Petitioner
Robert K King, Commissioner, Department of Pensions and Security, et al.

Respondent
Mrs. Sylvester Smith, et al.

Petitioner's Claim
That Alabama's regulation denying Aid to Families with Dependent Children (AFDC) payments to children based on the presence of a "substitute father" did not violate the Social Security Act and the Equal Protection Clause of the Fourteenth Amendment.

Chief Lawyer for Petitioner
Mary Lee Strapp

Chief Lawyer for Respondent
Martin Garbus

Justices for the Court
Hugo Lafayette Black, William J. Brennan, Jr., William O. Douglas, Abe Fortas, John Marshall Harlan II, Thurgood Marshall, Potter Stewart, Earl Warren (writing for the Court), Byron R. White

Justices Dissenting
None

Place
Washington, D.C.

Date of Decision
17 June 1968

Decision
The Court held that on statutory grounds the state of Alabama's restrictions excluding some children from receiving Aid to Families with Dependent Children (AFDC) exceeded the federal guidelines and wrongfully denied needy children the aid they were due. One concurring justice also found that the statutes violated the Equal Protection Clause of the Fourteenth Amendment.

Significance
The ruling affirmed that the focus of Aid to Families with Dependent Children (AFDC) should be the needs of the child, and that the federal regulations which established AFDC were clear on who could be considered a "parent." While the Court ruled based on the regulations themselves, and not on constitutional grounds, the decision did not reject the argument that welfare payments may have been protected by the Equal Protection Clause of the Fourteenth Amendment.

The Aid to Families with Dependent Children program (AFDC) was established under the Social Security Act of 1935. Its goal was to protect the welfare of dependent children who were deprived of the breadwinning parent, and was a direct result of the hardships experienced during the Great Depression. The Court explained in this case that, "The Act defines a dependent child as one who has been deprived of parental support or care by reason of death, continued absence, or incapacity of a parent, and insofar as relevant in this case aid can be granted under the provision only if a parent of the needy child is continually absent from the home." The Court recognized in this case that states have some say in how the program will be carried out: "There is no question that States have considerable latitude in allocating their AFDC resources, since each State is free to set its own standard of need and to determine the level of benefits by the amount of funds it devotes to the program." But the question of denying otherwise eligible children based on the behavior of the mother was raised, and answered, in the suit brought against the state of Alabama.

In 1964, Alabama enacted regulations that excluded otherwise eligible needy children from receiving AFDC benefits if there was a "substitute father" involved. In this case, the regulations explained, an

> able-bodied man, married or single, is considered a substitute father of all the children of the applicant . . . mother . . . [if] he lives in the home with the child's natural or adoptive mother for the purpose of cohabitation . . . he visits frequently for the purpose of cohabiting with the child's natural or adoptive mother . . . [or] he does not frequent the home but cohabits with the child's natural or adoptive mother elsewhere.

Cohabitation was not directly defined within the regulations, but the Court heard testimony which indicated that it meant "essentially that the man and woman have 'frequent' or 'continuing' sexual relations," although there was no agreement on just how frequent or continuing this contact had to be. Alabama argued that the regulation was "a legitimate way of allocating its limited resources available for AFDC assistance, discourage illicit sexual relationships and illegitimate births, and treat informal married couple[s] like ordinary married couples who are ineligible for AFDC aid so long as their father is in the home."

Mrs. Sylvester Smith and her four children were removed from AFDC rolls in October of 1966 because of the substitute father regulation. Three of the children, whose father had died in 1955, and the fourth child, whose father had left the family in 1963, were all eligible for AFDC except for the substitute father regulation. The "substitute father" in this case was a Mr. Williams, who came to the family's home on weekends and had sexual relations with Mrs. Smith. Mr. Williams was not in any way legally required to provide support for the children, and in fact did not. He lived with his own wife and nine children. After the family stopped receiving aid, a class action suit was heard by a three-judge panel in district court. This court found that the regulations were inconsistent both with the original Social Security Act and with the Fourteenth Amendment's Equal Protection Clause.

In considering the case, the U.S. Supreme Court turned first to the Flemming Ruling, passed by Congress in 1961. The ruling acknowledged the concerns of states regarding illegitimacy and immorality, but made clear that children could not be denied aid based on the questionable morality of the mother. The ruling stated,

> A State plan . . . may not impose an eligibility condition that would deny assistance with respect to a needy child on the basis that the home conditions in which the child lives are unsuitable, while the child continues to reside in the home. Assistance will therefore be continued during the time efforts are being made either to improve the home conditions or to make arrangements for the child elsewhere.

By flatly denying the Smith children aid based on Mrs. Smith's behavior, Alabama violated the Flemming Ruling and the nature of the Social Security Act, which allows only for rehabilitative measures in response to concerns about immorality.

The Court also found that Alabama's regulations did not conform to the definition of a parent, as described in the Social Security Act. Because Alabama's substitute father had no legal obligation to provide for the mother's children, the Court found this irreconcilable with the notion of a parent who would provide economic security for a child. Based on these statutory grounds, the Court held that Alabama's regulations were invalid; the Court did not need to address the constitutional question, that of the Equal Protection Clause of the Fourteenth Amendment.

Justice Douglas, though, wrote a concurring opinion which addressed that clause. Douglas understood Alabama's regulations as "aimed at punishing mothers who have nonmarital sexual relations," without regard for "the economic need of the children, their age, their other means of support." Based on the related *Levy v. Louisiana* (1968) which barred discrimination against illegitimate children under the Fourteenth Amendment, Douglas found that the discrimination in this case, too, fell under the Equal Protection Clause.

Impact

The outcome of this case reinforced the original Social Security Act's definition of a parent, and the appropriate focus on the needs of children, rather than the morality of their mother. Justice Douglas's concurring opinion also stressed the idea that moral judgments have no protection under the Fourteenth Amendment, but should be addressed in other ways.

Related Cases

Levy v. Louisiana, 391 U.S. 68 (1968).
Allen v. Hettleman, 494 F.Supp. 854 (1980).
Sobky v. Smoley, 855 F.Supp. 1123 (1994).

Bibliography and Further Reading

Gordon, Linda. *Brutal Need: Lawyers and the Welfare Rights Movement, 1960–1973*. New Haven, CT: Yale University, 1994.

Isaac, Rael Jean. "War on the Poor." *National Review*, May 15, 1995, pp. 32.

Lurie, Irene. "Temporary Assistance for Needy Families: A Green Light for the States." *Plubius*, March 22, 1997.

Mink, Gwendolyn. "Welfare Reform in Historical Perspective." *Social Justice*, spring 1994, p. 114.

Wilcox, Brian L., Jennifer K. Robbenmolt, Janet E. O'Keeffe, and Marisa E. Pynchon. "Teen Nonmartital Childbearing and Welfare: The Gap Between Research and Political Discourse." *Journal of Social Issues*, September 22, 1996.

JONES V. ALFRED H. MAYER CO.

Legal Citation: 392 U.S. 409 (1968)

Petitioner
Joseph Lee Jones

Respondent
Alfred H. Mayer Co., a housing development company

Petitioner's Claim
That the respondent's refusal to sell him a home strictly because he was black was in violation of the Civil Rights Act of 1866.

Chief Lawyer for Petitioner
Samuel H. Liberman

Chief Lawyer for Respondent
Israel Treiman

Justices for the Court
Hugo Lafayette Black, William J. Brennan, Jr., William O. Douglas, Abe Fortas, Thurgood Marshall, Potter Stewart (writing for the Court), Earl Warren

Justices Dissenting
John Marshall Harlan II, Byron R. White

Place
Washington, D.C.

Date of Decision
17 June 1968

Decision
That the petitioner was entitled to redress under the civil rights law in question.

Significance
That the Civil Rights Act of 1866, which protected black citizens from several different forms of discrimination, applied not only to actions taken by the government or sanctioned by the government, but to actions taken by private individuals as well.

The Alfred H. Mayer Company was developing a subdivision called Paddock Woods in the suburbs of St. Louis, Missouri. The plaintiffs went to look at a house, and some time later contacted the developers again and inquired about the price and the possibility of buying. At that time they were informed that the company had a general policy of not selling to blacks, which Joseph Lee Jones, one of the potential buyers, was. On 2 September 1965 the plaintiffs filed suit in the District Court for the Eastern District of Missouri, seeking injunctive and declarative relief. A large part of their case relied upon Section 1982 of the 1866 Civil Rights Act, which purported to protect for blacks many of the rights enjoyed by white men, including the right to buy and sell property. The district court dismissed the claim on the grounds that Supreme Court decisions had held that Section 1982 only applied to state actions and not to private actions, and the Eighth Circuit Court of Appeals upheld that decision. The Supreme Court granted a writ of *certiorari* to hear the case, and it was argued on the first two days of April, 1968.

The debate before the Supreme Court centered around both the language and the congressional debate preceding the passage of Section 1982. The issue was quite simple: If that section applied to private action, the decisions of the lower courts must be overturned and the plaintiff, now petitioner, would be allowed to sue. If it applied only to state action, the motion would be denied and the case would be null and void. The Court decided that the section did apply to private action, setting a new precedent, striking a blow for civil rights in housing laws, and sparking a spirited and lengthy dissent from Justice Harlan.

The majority opinion, written by Justice Stewart, was in five parts. The first part simply stated that the ruling did not amount to a comprehensive housing law, and was limited in scope to cases fairly identical to the *Jones* case. It also stated that the Civil Rights Act of 1968, just recently passed, did not directly address the precise situation involved in the case and did not render the case irrelevant.

The second part of the opinion concerned precedent, the most directly applicable being that of the *Hurd v. Hodge* case in 1948, which concerned a very similar situation. In that case, however, a federal district court had enforced the restrictive covenants in question. The High Court in that case had overruled the lower court decision, ruling that the district court's enforcement of the racial covenants amounted to state action concerning the covenant, thus bringing 1982 into effect. In that case, however, the black purchasers already had deeds and the court had declared them void; in *Jones* the lower courts had declined to take action, so a new precedent would need to be set.

The Same Right as White Citizens

The third part dealt with the language of Section 1982, which stated that citizens of any race would enjoy "the same right" to purchase and lease property "as is enjoyed by white citizens." It was a very brief section which held that Section 1982 was unambiguous and clear-cut in its intention that all discrimination against blacks was forbidden, and no other interpretation was reasonable.

The fourth section was the lengthiest and triggered much of the disagreement. It studied the debates surrounding the passage of the Civil Rights Act of 1866, and whether or not the Congress at that time believed or intended that the bill would affect private conduct as well as public. This section included information concerning the state of black America in the 1860s, as well as elaborate studies and interpretations of comments and questions uttered by senators and congressmen on the floor during the debates. It concluded that the supporters of the bill understood that the bill would affect all discrimination against blacks, not just that which was sanctioned by state governments.

The fifth section of the decision concerned the question of Congress' power to pass a law such as the Civil Rights Act of 1866 and Section 1982. The answer to this question the Court found in a previous interpretation of the Thirteenth Amendment, which prohibited slavery and gave Congress the power to enforce this prohibition. A subsequent Court ruling determined that the amendment imbued "Congress with power to pass all laws necessary and proper for abolishing all badges and incidents of slavery in the United States." Civil rights issues such as free housing had already been established to fall under the heading of "incidents of slavery," since certain civil rights were so essential to

freedom that a citizen could be held in *de facto* slavery if these were denied.

Justice Douglas wrote a brief but stirring concurrence, pointing out that Jim Crow laws and other widespread customs of the time held black citizens in a condition not resembling freedom, and urged that much more be done to equalize treatment of the races at several levels of society.

Justice Harlan weighed in with a lengthy and contentious dissent, speaking for himself and Justice White. He claimed that precedent was clearly contrary to the majority opinion, that there was ample reason to believe the statute only was meant to apply to state or state-sponsored action, that debate in Congress at the time supported this opinion, and that popular opinion after the Civil War made it impossible to believe that Congress would pass a bill which would prohibit private discrimination in such a manner. He then concluded that the Court should not have heard the case in the first place because the Civil Rights Act of 1968 made its application so narrow as to be nearly irrelevant.

Jones v. Mayer was the focus of some debate within the legal profession. While some hailed the decision as a brave and correct interpretation supporting civil rights, others questioned the soundness of the Court's logic and called the ruling a case of judicial activism. Nevertheless, the ruling found historical significance, marking the first time the Supreme Court ruled that black homebuyers could not be denied by anyone the right to live where they wished because of their race.

Related Cases

Virginia v. Rives, 100 U.S. 313 (1879).
Civil Rights Cases, 109 U.S. 3 (1883).
Hodges v. United States, 203 U.S. 1 (1906).
Buchanon v. Warley, 245 U.S. 60 (1917).
Corrigan v. Buckley, 271 U.S. 323 (1926).
Hurd v. Hodge, 334 U.S. 24 (1948).

Bibliography and Further Reading

American Bar Association Journal, November 1968, p. 1115.

Arkansas Law Review, winter 1969, p. 773.

Virginia Law Review, February 1969, p. 272.

Washburn Law Journal, Volume 8, p. 268.

SHAPIRO V. THOMPSON

Legal Citation: 394 U.S. 618 (1969)

Appellant
Vivian Marie Thompson

Appellee
Shapiro, Commissioner of Welfare of Connecticut

Appellant's Claim
That the denial of state and the District of Columbia welfare benefits to residents of less than one year is discriminatory and violates the Equal Protection Clause of the Fourteenth Amendment.

Chief Lawyer for Appellant
Francis J. MacGregor

Chief Lawyer for Appellee
Archibald Cox

Justices for the Court
William J. Brennan, Jr. (writing for the Court), William O. Douglas, Abe Fortas, Thurgood Marshall, Potter Stewart, Byron R. White

Justices Dissenting
Hugo Lafayette Black, John Marshall Harlan II, Earl Warren

Place
Washington, D.C.

Date of Decision
21 April 1969

Decision
Affirmed the decisions of three district courts which found various state and District of Columbia welfare residency requirements unconstitutional.

Significance
This decision was a landmark in judicial right-to-travel interpretation. The first case to analyze the right to travel in the context of the Equal Protection Clause, it was also the first to apply "strict scrutiny" to the protection of that right and to confirm that government statutes could not even indirectly restrict it. The U.S. Supreme Court had long before established travel as a valid right, but before this case it had never addressed how that right might conflict with a modern government's needs and abilities to withhold benefits. By this ruling the Court gave unprecedented weight to the right.

The Right to Interstate Travel

Vivian Marie Thompson was a 19-year old single mother who was pregnant with her second child when she moved from Massachusetts to Hartford, Connecticut. She first lived with her mother, a Hartford resident, then later moved into her own apartment. Unable to work or attend job training programs because of her pregnancy, she applied for assistance under Connecticut's Aid to Families with Dependent Children (AFDC) program. In accordance with their regulations, the state denied her aid because she had not yet resided in Connecticut for one full year. Thompson brought action against the state in the District Court for the District of Connecticut. That court found that because the waiting period requirement had "a chilling effect on the right to travel" it was unconstitutional. It also held that the same requirements violated the Equal Protection Clause of the Fourteenth Amendment because it was intended, as Connecticut acknowledged, to discourage people who need aid from moving into Connecticut.

On appeal, the case moved on to the U.S. Supreme Court. It was considered together with two similar cases, *Washington v. Legrant,* and *Reynolds v. Smith.* In the *Washington* case, three people had been denied AFDC aid because they had not met a District of Columbia one-year residency requirement. In *Reynolds,* two people had been denied aid in Pennsylvania for the same reason.

Writing for the majority, Justice Brennan first established that the one-year residency requirement created two classes of needy resident families. These two classes, he said, were different only in that one group had resided in the particular area for over one year, and one group for less than a year. That distinction, he stated, was not reason enough for a government to deny one group the necessities of life.

The appellants had argued that the residency requirements were intended to keep public assistance programs functional by preventing a rush of destitute newcomers from draining state welfare resources. They maintained that people who entered welfare programs during their first year of residence in a new state were likely to stay on those programs. This would eventually impair the state's ability to assist its needy long-

Temporary Assistance for Needy Families

Millions of children have benefitted from the Aid to Families with Dependent Children (AFDC) welfare program since its creation in 1935. With the intent to help needy children through a family environment, states were given latitude to determine the level of assistance available to indigent parents and their children for basic necessities. AFDC provided cash assistance to poor single-parent families with children, or to poor families with two parents where the main wage earner was physically or mentally incapacitated.

With the sweeping federal welfare reform legislation of 1996, Temporary Assistance for Needy Families (TANF) replaced AFDC. The new Welfare-to-Work program provides set sums of federal money, "block grants," to states to administer welfare programs with almost complete local control over determining eligi-

bility and benefits. With charges that AFDC made welfare a way of life, TANF requires parents to be working within two years of first receiving aid and limits aid to a maximum of five years in the lifetime of a family, even less in some states. State and local governments also assumed greater responsibility to generate more jobs and provide job training, career counseling, and job placement services.

TANF ended a six decade guarantee of federal welfare checks to all eligible low-income mothers and children, and removed many federal legal protections.

Source(s): Grigsby III, J. Eugene. "Welfare Reform Means Business as Usual." *Journal of the American Planning Association*, winter 1998.

time residents, they said. Justice Brennan centered his response to this on every U.S. citizen's right to travel freely throughout the country. This right was not expressly named in the Constitution, he said, but was a product of both that document and the "nature of our Federal Union." Thus, he reasoned, if a classification of residents was created solely for the purpose of deterring the poor from moving between states, then it was unconstitutional.

The appellants further argued that even if it was unconstitutional for a state to try to prevent an influx of poor into its population, then the requirement could still be justified as a way to keep out those who were moving in simply to try to obtain larger benefits. Justice Brennan responded by noting that the state's requirements did not attempt to find out if that was the applicant's reason for moving, but simply presumed that it was the reason in all cases. Regardless, he wrote, the state could not discriminate against such a motive, no more than they could against an individual who changed residence to take advantage of a better educational system. The appellants presented yet another justification of the requirement: that in differentiating old from new residents, it identified who was making a greater economic contribution to the state through tax payments. Justice Brennan quickly dispensed with an analysis of facts in the case, instead contending that the appellants' reasoning would allow a state to distribute public benefits and services based on a citizen's past tax payments. This, he said, would be forbidden by the Equal Protection Clause.

Justice Brennan then challenged the argument that the waiting period requirement was justified by several administrative purposes. Although he acknowledged

that the state had a valid interest in each purpose, those interests, he concluded, did not outweigh the constitutional right to interstate travel. Finally, the appellants contended that the constitutionality of the waiting period requirement could not be challenged because Congress had approved the requirement. As part of the joint federal-state AFDC program, they argued, Congress had authorized the states and the District of Columbia to impose the waiting period requirement. Justice Brennan disagreed. The relevant provision of the Social Security Act, he wrote, only prevented the Secretary of Health, Education, and Welfare from *rejecting* state AFDC plans simply because they included such a requirement. He suggested that perhaps the provision itself was unconstitutional, in that "Congress may not authorize the States to violate the Equal Protection Clause."

Legitimate Government Objectives?

In his dissenting opinion, Chief Justice Warren disagreed with the majority regarding Congress' powers over and intentions for the waiting period requirement. He believed that Congress did have the power to authorize states to impose minimal residence requirements, and that it had "constitutionally exercised" that power for over 30 years. He wrote also that any restrictions on an individual's right to travel created by the requirement were not substantial enough to outweigh the governmental justifications for the requirement. Finally, he noted that the majority opinion addressed only the "top of the iceberg." There were many other areas where states apply residency requirements, he said, such as voting eligibility and attendance at state-supported universities. He felt the majority decision ignored its implications for these areas.

Justice Harlan also strongly dissented. He disagreed with the majority's reasoning mainly because it was based on an "unwise" expansion of an

> equal protection doctrine of relatively recent vintage: the rule that statutory classifications which either are based upon certain "suspect" criteria or affect "fundamental rights" will be held to deny equal protection unless justified by a "compelling" government interest.

The majority, he wrote, had reached a wrong conclusion using this reasoning because they had simply deemed the appellants' list of governmental objectives either unlawful or not "compelling." Secondly, he was concerned with the "fundamental right" branch of this doctrine.

> Virtually every state statute affects important rights . . . [and] . . . I know of nothing which entitles this Court to pick out particular human activities, characterize them as "fundamental," and give them added protection under an unusually stringent equal protection test.

He proceeded with an analysis in which he weighed the two competing interests: the individual's right to travel against the governmental interests served by the waiting period. He concluded that the residence requirements placed only "indirect and . . . insubstantial" restrictions on travel and the governmental purposes they served were "legitimate and real." Thus, he reasoned, the requirements were constitutional.

Impact

A test was created in *Shapiro* for determining when state waiting period requirements hindered the right to travel and thus prompted "strict scrutiny," and when they did not. This test was criticized for being vague, but the Court did more finely define it in subsequent cases. Over the next 20 years, the question of the constitutionality of such requirements seemed settled. The Court in the 1989 *Eddleman v. Center Township* case referred to "the old and well-established" standard set by *Shapiro*. Meanwhile, state waiting period requirements for welfare aid quickly began to evaporate after *Shapiro*, according to Clark Peterson in "The Resurgence of Durational Residence Requirements." Some were invalidated by the courts and others disappeared due to lack of enforcement. With residency requirements gone, asserted Todd Zubler in "The Right to Migrate and Welfare Reform," people on welfare began to move from state to state in greater numbers. This increased migration, he contended, caused individual states to keep lowering their welfare benefits to avoid becoming a "welfare magnet" state. So *Shapiro*, he concluded, created a dangerous "race to the bottom" among states. In the early 1990s a trend toward reactivating old requirements or enacting new ones began in some

Archibald Cox. © The Library of Congress/Corbis.

states, sometimes in open resistance to *Shapiro*, sometimes carefully worded to avoid its "strict scrutiny." Opinion is divided over whether these new requirements will fail for the reasons set out by *Shapiro*, or whether *Shapiro* will fail to survive future struggles over welfare reform.

Related Cases

The Passenger Cases, 7 How. 283, 492 (1849).
Dunn v. Blumstein, 405 U.S. 330 (1972).
Memorial Hospital v. Maricopa County, 415 U.S. 250 (1974).
Sosna v. Iowa, 419 U.S. 393 (1975).
Zobel v. Williams, 457 U.S. 55 (1982).
Attorney General v. Soto-Lopez, 476 U.S. 898 (1986).

Bibliography and Further Reading

Biskupic, Joan, and Elder Witt. *Congressional Quarterly's Guide to the U.S. Supreme Court*, 3rd ed. Washington, DC: Congressional Quarterly, Inc., 1996.

Cushman, Robert F. *Leading Constitutional Decisions*. Englewood Cliffs, NJ: Prentice-Hall, Inc., 1982.

Hall, Kermit L., ed. *The Oxford Companion to the Supreme Court of the United States*. New York: Oxford University Press, 1992.

Konvitz, Milton R., ed. *Bill of Rights Reader,* 5th ed. Ithaca, NY: Cornell University Press, 1973.

Peterson, Clark A. "The Resurgence of Durational Residence Requirements for the Receipt of Welfare Funds." *Loyola of Los Angeles Law Review.* Vol. 27, no. 1, 1993.

Zubler, Todd. "The Right to Migrate and Welfare Reform: Time for *Shapiro v. Thompson* to Take a Hike." *Valparaiso University Law Review.* Vol. 31, no. 3, 1997.

DANDRIDGE V. WILLIAMS

Legal Citation: 397 U.S. 471 (1970)

Appellant
Edmund P. Dandridge, Jr., et al.

Appellee
Linda Williams et al.

Appellant's Claim
That the Maryland maximum grant regulation was in conflict with the Federal Social Security Act and with equal protection under the Fourteenth Amendment.

Chief Lawyer for Appellant
George W. Liebmann

Chief Lawyer for Appellee
Joseph A. Matera

Justices for the Court
Hugo Lafayette Black, Warren E. Burger, John Marshall Harlan II, Potter Stewart (writing for the Court), Byron R. White

Justices Dissenting
William J. Brennan, Jr., William O. Douglas, Thurgood Marshall (Harry A. Blackmun had not yet been appointed to the Court)

Place
Washington, D.C.

Date of Decision
6 April 1970

Decision
The Supreme Court held that the regulation does not violate the Equal Protection Clause and reversed the lower court's decision.

Significance
The states have the right to regulate the absolute amount of aid received by a family regardless of size or determined need and the regulation was not inconsistent with the Social Security Act nor violative of the Equal Protection Clause.

In connection with its participation in the Federal Aid to Families with Dependent Children program, the state of Maryland imposed, through administrative regulation, a maximum limit on the total amount of aid which any one family unit could receive. The appellants, who had large families, and whose standards of need as computed by the state substantially exceeded the maximum amount of aid which they received under the regulation, brought suit in the U.S. District Court for the District of Maryland. They argued that Maryland's maximum grant regulation was in conflict with the Federal Social Security Act. The appellants also argued that the regulation violated their equal protection rights under the Fourteenth Amendment.

A three-judge District Court was convened and held that the regulation violated the Equal Protection Clause of the Fourteenth Amendment. The case then went to the Supreme Court.

The Supreme Court reversed the decision of the lower court. In an opinion written by Justice Stewart, expressing the views of five members of the court, it was held that the maximum-grant regulation was not inconsistent with the Social Security Act and did not violate the Equal Protection Clause of the Fourteenth Amendment.

Justices Black and Burger concurred with the decision. They relied upon the Secretary of Health, Education, and Welfare's determination that the regulation was consistent with the Social Security Act.

In a dissenting opinion, Justice Douglas said that the maximum-grant regulation was inconsistent with the terms and purposes of the Social Security Act. Douglas added that he would not find it necessary to decide upon the equal protection issue. Justices Marshall and Brennan also held that the maximum-grant regulation was inconsistent with the Social Security Act, but added that such regulation was invalid under the Equal Protection Clause of the Fourteenth Amendment.

Related Cases
Graham v. Richardson, 403 U.S. 365 (1971).
San Antonio Independent School District, et al. v. Demetrio P. Rodriguez, et al., 411 U.S. 1 (1973).

Welfare Regulation

Public welfare assistance programs for the nation's poor have been controversial since before the 1930s Great Depression era, when they were largely operated by state and local governments. Guided by ideals of individualism and self-reliance, welfare benefits are commonly viewed as a privilege, not a right. With rapid expansion of the federal welfare system following passage of the Social Security Act in 1935, many grew to consider welfare benefits to be entitlements.

Under extensive federal oversight, states attempted to locally regulate welfare programs in the 1950s and 1960s through residency requirements, illegitimate children restrictions, and other means. Such efforts were routinely deemed in violation of federal equal protection guarantees. By the 1970s, states were required to provide food stamp and Medicaid programs but were free to determine recipients' eligibility. Similarly, fed-

eral public housing programs consistently relied on local administration. In the 1980s, states began to assume greater freedom to enforce work requirements on welfare recipients.

The 1996 Personal Responsibility and Work Opportunity Reconciliation Act, better known as the Welfare Reform Act, more fully returned regulation of welfare programs to state and local governments. With limited financial resources, states developed new welfare plans under substantially less federal oversight to meet the demands of their needy citizens.

Source(s): Wolch, Jennifer R. "America's New Urban Policy: Welfare Reform and the Fate of American Cities," *Journal of the American Planning Association.* Winter 1998.

Gurley v. Wohlgemuth, 421 F.Supp. 1337 (1976).
Joyner v. Dumpson, 533 F.Supp. 233 (1982).
Daugherty v. Wallace, 621 N.E. 2d 1374 (1993).

Bibliography and Further Reading
Biskupic, Joan, and Elder Witt, eds. *Congressional Quarterly's Guide to the U.S. Supreme Court,* 3rd ed. Washington, DC: Congressional Quarterly, Inc., 1996.

HARRISBURG COALITION AGAINST RUINING THE ENVIRONMENT V. VOLPE

Legal Citation: 330 F. Supp. 918 (M.D. Pa. 1971)

Plaintiff
Harrisburg Coalition Against Ruining the Environment, et al.

Defendant
John A. Volpe, Secretary of the U.S. Department of Transportation, et al.

Plaintiff's Claim
That the construction of two highways through a city park would deny equal housing and recreational opportunities to African American residents in violation of the Equal Protection Clause of the Constitution, and that the Department of Transportation's decision to locate the highways in this area did not comply with the requirements of federal statutes.

Chief Lawyer for Plaintiff
Robert J. Sugarman

Chief Defense Lawyer
Thomas McKevitt

Judge
William J. Nealon

Place
Harrisburg, Pennsylvania

Date of Decision
12 May 1971

Decision
That the plaintiffs failed to show that the construction of the highways would deny equal housing and recreational opportunities to African American residents, but that the secretary of transportation had to reconsider its determination regarding the location of the highways under the appropriate federal statutes.

Significance
The case illustrates how difficult it is to establish an intent to discriminate, which is a violation of the Fourteenth Amendment's Equal Protection Clause.

In the late 1960s and early 1970s, the U.S. Department of Transportation, the State of Pennsylvania, and the City of Harrisburg began discussions concerning the construction of Interstate Route 81 and the Harrisburg River Relief Route through the city of Harrisburg, Pennsylvania. These discussions eventually lead to the decision to construct the highways through a city park in Harrisburg. In 1971, following the decision, a group of citizens and an environmental group filed a lawsuit against the secretary of transportation, the state of Pennsylvania, and the city of Harrisburg in U.S. District Court for the Middle District of Pennsylvania. The plaintiffs sought an injunction prohibiting the construction of the highways through Wildwood Park, a city park located in Harrisburg. The plaintiffs claimed that the proposed construction violated the Equal Protection Clause of the Fourteenth Amendment to the Constitution. They asserted that by closing down the park, the construction would deny African American citizens the same right to participate in recreational activities as afforded white citizens in other parts of the city. They also alleged that the defendants' decision to locate the construction through Wildwood Park did not meet the requirements of several federal statutes. Statutes cited included the Department of Transportation Act, the Federal Aid Highway Act, and the National Environmental Policy Act. After holding hearings on the issues, Judge William Nealon rejected the plaintiffs' claim that the proposed construction discriminated against African American citizens. However, he also concluded that the secretary of transportation had failed to comply with the Department of Transportation Act and the National Environmental Policy Act.

No Evidence of Discriminatory Effect

Judge Nealon first held that the plaintiffs had failed to produce sufficient evidence to support their claim that the proposed construction had a discriminatory effect on African American citizens of Harrisburg. The plaintiffs argued that the city agreed to give portions of Wildwood Park to Pennsylvania for construction of the highways partly because African American citizens were the predominant users of the park. The plaintiffs claimed that this violated their right to equal protection of the laws under the Fourteenth Amendment to the U.S. Constitution. The Equal Protection Clause of the Fourteenth Amendment provides that no state shall "deny to any person within its jurisdiction the equal protection of the laws." The Equal Protection Clause prohibits a state or local government from discriminating against groups of people based on so-called "suspect classifications," such as race or national origin. In order to prove discrimination in violation of the Equal Protection Clause, a plaintiff must establish that the governmental officers acted with a discriminatory intent and that the action of those officers had a discriminatory impact on a particular race.

Judge Nealon rejected this argument, noting that there was no evidence that the city officials were motivated by racial prejudice in agreeing to the construction. He also noted that the evidence presented by the parties showed that the park was used equally by both African American and white citizens. Thus, he concluded that there was insufficient evidence to support a racial discrimination intent, and rejected the plaintiffs' equal protection claim.

However, Judge Nealon agreed with the plaintiffs that the secretary of transportation, in deciding to construct the highways through Wildwood Park, had failed to comply with the requirements of the Department of Transportation Act and the National Environmental Policy Act. The secretary of transportation failed because he did not document findings regarding the impact of the highways on recreational opportunities and on the environment, as required by these two statutes. Because the secretary's decision did not comply with the procedural requirements of these acts, the court remanded the case to the secretary of transportation to issue a decision regarding the con-

struction of the project in accordance with the proper procedures.

Impact

Judge Nealon's decision had little long-term impact for citizens in the vicinity of Wildwood Park. After the court's decision, the secretary documented the findings required by the Department of Transportation Act and the National Environmental Policy Act. Thus, the plaintiffs' victory was short-lived. With respect to the court's decision regarding the plaintiffs' discrimination claim, the Supreme Court later clarified the standard for evaluating equal protection claims based on racial discrimination in the 1977 case *Arlington Heights v. Metropolitan Housing Corp.*

Related Cases

Evans v. Abney, 396 U.S. 435 (1970).
Citizens to Preserve Overton Park, Inc. v. Volpe, 401 U.S. 402 (1971).
Palmer v. Thompson, 403 U.S. 217 (1971).
Arlington Heights v. Metropolitan Housing Corp., 429 U.S. 252 (1977).

Bibliography and Further Reading

Bradley, David, and Shelley Fisher, eds. *The Encyclopedia of Civil Rights in America.* New York: M. E. Sharpe, 1998.

Davis, Kenneth C. *Administrative Law Treatise,* 3rd ed. Boston: Little Brown & Co., 1994.

Franklin, John H., and Genna R. McNeil. *African Americans and the Living Constitution.* Washington, DC: Smithsonian Institution Press, 1995.

McDonald, Laughlin. *The Rights of Racial Minorities: The Basic ACLU Guide to Racial Minority Rights.* Carbondale, IL: Southern Illinois University Press, 1993.

GRAHAM V. RICHARDSON

Legal Citation: 403 U.S. 365 (1971)

Appellant
Carmen Richardson, et al.

Appellee
John O. Graham, Commissioner, Department of Public Welfare, State of Arizona

Appellant's Claim
Arizona's alien residency requirements violated the Equal Protection Clause and the constitutional right to travel; they conflicted with the Social Security Act, as the Supremacy Clause took precedence; Congress had regulatory powers over aliens, not individual states.

Chief Lawyer for Appellant
Anthony B. Ching

Chief Lawyer for Appellee
Michael S. Flam

Justices for the Court
Hugo Lafayette Black, Harry A. Blackmun (writing for the Court), William J. Brennan, Jr., Warren E. Burger, William O. Douglas, John Marshall Harlan II, Thurgood Marshall, Potter Stewart, Byron R. White

Justices Dissenting
None

Place
Washington, D.C.

Date of Decision
14 June 1971

Decision
Provisions of state welfare laws that placed conditions on welfare benefits due to citizenship and imposed durational residency requirements on aliens violated the U.S. Constitution's Equal Protection Clause.

Significance
Until 1971, the Supreme Court upheld the majority of statutes that limited the opportunities of resident aliens to engage in many activities. However, *Graham v. Richardson* was the first in a series of decisions that struck down many other restrictive state laws, restoring to resident aliens the rights guaranteed to them in the Fourteenth Amendment.

When Carmen Richardson became a lawfully admitted resident alien, she had every reason to expect the same treatment as any U.S. citizen under the Equal Protection Clause of the Constitution's Fourteenth Amendment. In July of 1969, 64-year-old Carmen Richardson, an Arizona resident since 1956, became permanently and totally disabled. She met all the requirements for state-administered federal assistance benefits. However, Arizona law included a statute that said to receive welfare benefits, a person had to either be a citizen of the United States or to have lived in the country for 15 years. Of course, this statute applied to aliens only. The case of *Graham v. Richardson* soon became a measure of applying the Fourteenth Amendment's Equal Protection Clause to statutes that restricted the rights of resident aliens, based solely on their being aliens.

Richardson began a class action suit in the district of Arizona on behalf of herself and all other resident aliens of Arizona who could not receive welfare benefits even though they met all the eligibility requirements except for the residency statute. Richardson's suit sought declaratory relief from the state's Department of Public Welfare, the removal of the residency rules, and the benefits she believed were due to her.

Her case's claim was that Arizona's alien residency requirement violated the Equal Protection Clause of the Fourteenth Amendment and the right to travel, as stated in the Constitution. Furthermore, Arizona's alien residency requirement conflicted with the Social Security Act, so the Supremacy Clause took precedence. The suit finally argued that Congress regulated aliens—not the individual states.

A three-judge district court upheld Richardson's motion for summary judgment on the basis that Arizona's law violated the Equal Protection Clause. That the court upheld the motion for a summary judgment basically meant that they believed that the Arizona law was of no relevance due to the Equal Protection Clause and that Richardson was due her benefits as any citizen would be. John O. Graham, Commissioner of the Arizona Department of Public Welfare appealed the decision. Arguments began in front of the Supreme Court on 22 March 1971. The case was decided on 14 June 1971.

The appellant, Graham, argued that when states favored United States citizens over aliens when distributing welfare benefits, it was in agreement with the Fourteenth Amendment's Equal Protection Clause. His case argued that this differentiation involved no "invidious discrimination," because the state of Arizona was not discriminating due to race or nationality. In general, Arizona's point was that the state could justify its alien eligibility restrictions regarding public assistance because a state has "special public interest" favoring its own citizens rather than aliens when apportioning limited resources like welfare benefits.

However, the Supreme Court still decided that a state statute which denied welfare benefits to aliens who had not resided in the United States for an arbitrary number of years violated the Equal Protection Clause. There were further reasons why this particular state statute did not hold up under constitutional scrutiny, relating to the relationship between the federal government and the individual states.

Congress had established a detailed plan to regulate immigration and naturalization. One purpose was to exclude from admission to the United States, those who were "paupers, professional beggars, or vagrants," and who would be likely to depend on public assistance. In fact, part of this congressional plan ruled that if aliens became public charges within five years after entering the country "from causes not affirmatively shown to have arisen after entry" they would be deported. While Congress had provided specific wording for potential immigrants, they had made no direct ruling for those who became needy after entering the country. Congress declared that: "All persons within the jurisdiction of the United States shall have the same right in every State and Territory—to the full and equal benefit of all laws and proceedings for the security of persons and property as is enjoyed by white citizens."

On appeal, the U.S. Supreme Court upheld the district court's ruling. Justice Blackmun's opinion—also held by all of the eight other justices—was that a state statute was unconstitutional under the Fourteenth Amendment's Equal Protection Clause if it withheld welfare benefits from resident aliens or aliens who had not lived in the U.S. for the required number of years. According to Blackmun, the clause included aliens as well as citizens.

The Court also unanimously held that a state statute which discriminated on the basis of "alienness," would interfere with that alien's "right to enter and abide in any state on an equality of equal privileges with all citizens." Poverty-stricken aliens or those who were disabled would be unable to live where they wanted, if individual states could deny them their welfare rights.

Additionally, the Court held that since the U.S. Constitution dictated that the federal government held sway in matters of immigration and naturalization, the state statute was unconstitutional because it interfered with national policies. Finally, the Court held unanimously that section 1402(b) of the Social Security Act of 1935 did not authorize Arizona to withhold welfare benefits from resident aliens who had not lived in the U.S. for a total of 15 years.

Related Cases

Shapiro v. Thompson, 394 U.S. 618 (1969).
Plyler v. Doe, 457 U.S. 202 (1982).
Martinez v. Bynum, 461 U.S. 321 (1983).

Bibliography and Further Reading

Dorsen, N., O. K., and T. Viles Fraenkel. *Civil Liberties in the United States,* Vol. 6, P.F. Collier, 1996.

Hull, Elisabeth. "Resident Aliens and the Equal Protection Clause: The Burger Court's Retreat from Graham v. Richardson." *Brooklyn Law Review,* Vol. 47, no. 1, p. 1.

McWhirter, Darien A. "Urban Residence and Poverty." *Exploring the Constitution,* Vol. 1. The Oryx Press, 1995.

REED V. REED

Legal Citation: 404 U.S. 71 (1971)

Appellant
Sally Reed

Appellee
Cecil Reed

Appellant's Claim
That Sally Reed's constitutional rights were violated by Idaho's law favoring the appointment of a man over a similarly situated woman to act as administrator of an estate.

Chief Lawyers for Appellant
Allen R. Derr, Ruth Bader Ginsburg

Chief Lawyers for Appellee
Charles S. Stout, Myron E. Anderson

Justices for the Court
Hugo Lafayette Black, Harry A. Blackmun, William J. Brennan, Jr., Warren E. Burger (writing for the Court), William O. Douglas, John Marshall Harlan II, Thurgood Marshall, Potter Stewart, Byron R. White

Justices Dissenting
None

Place
Washington, D.C.

Date of Decision
22 November 1971

Decision
That Idaho's law was "based solely on a discrimination prohibited by and therefore violative of the Equal Protection Clause of the Fourteenth Amendment."

Significance
This was the first time in the Fourteenth Amendment's 103-year history that the Supreme Court ruled that its Equal Protection Clause protected women's rights.

Although Section 1 of the Fourteenth Amendment, adopted in 1868, stated that "No State shall make or enforce any law which shall abridge the privileges or immunities of citizens of the United States . . . nor deny to any person within its jurisdiction the equal protection of the laws," the U.S. Supreme Court refused for a century to apply this guarantee to women.

Reed v. Reed was the first case in which the Supreme Court applied the Fourteenth Amendment to women's rights. This "turning point case," as Ruth Bader Ginsburg termed it, began with the suicide of a teenager, Richard Lynn Reed. Richard's adoptive parents, Sally and Cecil Reed, had earlier separated. The boy spent his "tender years" in the custody of his mother but was transferred into the custody of his father once he reached his teens. At 19, using his father's rifle, Richard killed himself. As Ginsburg remembers, Sally Reed had deeply opposed her loss of Richard's custody and had felt that her estranged husband bore some responsibility for their son's death.

Since Richard had died without a will, Sally Reed filed an application to act as administrator of Richard's estate. When Cecil Reed filed a similar petition, the Probate Court of Ada County ordered that he be appointed administrator upon his taking the required oath and filing the required bond.

The court reached this decision without considering the parents' relative merits, but strictly in accordance with Idaho's mandatory probate code. Section 15-312 provided:

> Administration of the estate of a person dying interstate must be granted to some one . . . in the following order:
> 1. The surviving husband or wife or some competent person whom he or she may request to have appointed.
> 2. The children.
> 3. The father or mother . . .

and 15-314:

> [o]f several persons claiming and equally entitled to administer, males must be preferred to females, and relatives of whole to those of the half blood.

Win Some, Lose Some

Sally Reed appealed the probate court's order to the District Court of the Fourth Judicial District of Idaho. She was represented by Allen R. Derr, who maintained that the Idaho law violated Sally Reed's constitutional rights under the Equal Protection Clause of the Fourteenth Amendment. The district court agreed. It held that the two sections of law should be considered void, and directed the probate court to choose between Richard's parents based upon their relative qualifications, regardless of sex.

Cecil Reed quickly appealed to the Idaho Supreme Court. This court rejected the district court's ruling. Finding that Idaho's legislature had "evidently concluded that in general men are better qualified to act as an administrator than women," and that this was "neither an illogical nor arbitrary method devised by the legislature to resolve an issue that would otherwise require a hearing as to the relative merits . . . of the two or more petitioning relatives," Idaho's Supreme Court reinstated Cecil Reed as administrator of his son's estate, since he was male.

Equal Protection

Sally Reed appealed to the U.S. Supreme Court. Ginsburg and others associated with the Women's Rights Project of the American Civil Liberties Union joined Derr to represent her. The Court also received *amicus curiae,* or "friend of the court," briefs from many other organizations. Derr argued Sally Reed's case on 19 October 1971, continuing to insist—as rights advocates had since the 1870s—that women's rights were protected under the Fourteenth Amendment. In contrast, Cecil Reed's lawyers defended Idaho's law as providing a reasonable means of streamlining the probate court's workload.

This time, the Supreme Court unanimously agreed that women's rights were within the province of the Fourteenth Amendment. In the Court's opinion, Chief Justice Burger wrote, "We have concluded that the arbitrary preference established in favor of males . . . cannot stand in the face of the Fourteenth Amendment's command that no State deny the equal protection of the laws to any person within its jurisdiction . . . This Court has consistently recognized that the Fourteenth Amendment does not deny to States the power to treat different classes of persons in different ways . . . [It] does, however, deny to States the power to legislate that different treatment be accorded to persons placed by a statute into different classes on the basis of criteria wholly unrelated to the objective of that statute. A classification 'must be reasonable, not arbitrary . . . '"

Sally Reed and her lawyers thus won for women what Susan B. Anthony, Myra Bradwell, and Virginia Minor had begun to seek in the courts nearly one century before: Fourteenth Amendment protection of women's constitutional rights.

Related Cases

United States v. Anthony, 24 F.Cas. 829 (1873).
Minor v. Happersett, 88 U.S. 162 (1875).

Bibliography and Further Reading

Carey, Eve, and Kathleen Willert Peratis. *Woman and the Law.* Skokie, IL: National Textbook Company in conjunction with the American Civil Liberties Union, 1977.

Davis, Flora. *Moving the Mountain: The Women's Movement in America Since 1960.* New York: Simon & Schuster, 1991.

Goldstein, Leslie Freidman. *The Constitutional Rights of Women.* Madison: The University of Wisconsin Press, rev. ed. 1989.

Johnson, John W., ed. *Historic U.S. Court Cases, 1690–1990: An Encyclopedia.* New York: Garland Publishing, 1992.

New York Times, 28 November 1971, p. 23.

O'Connor, Sandra Day. "Women and the Constitution: A Bicentennial Perspective." *Women, Politics and the Constitution.* Naomi B. Lynn, ed. Binghamton, NY: The Harrington Park Press, 1990.

MOOSE LODGE NO. 107 V. IRVIS

Legal Citation: 407 U.S. 163 (1972)

Appellant
Moose Lodge No. 107

Appellee
Leroy Irvis

Appellant's Claim
That discrimination against an African American man by a private lodge is not "state action" because the state granted the lodge a liquor license.

Chief Lawyer for Appellant
Frederick Bernays Wiener

Chief Lawyer for Appellee
Harry J. Rubin

Justices for the Court
Harry A. Blackmun, Warren E. Burger, Lewis F. Powell, Jr., William H. Rehnquist (writing for the Court), Potter Stewart, Byron R. White

Justices Dissenting
William J. Brennan, Jr., William O. Douglas, Thurgood Marshall

Place
Washington, D.C.

Date of Decision
12 June 1972

Decision
The Moose Lodge is a private club in which the state takes no controlling interest. Therefore, discrimination by the club cannot be outlawed under federal law.

Significance
Moose Lodge No. 107 v. Irvis helped clarify the term "state action" with reference to federal civil rights protections.

Leroy Irvis, an African American man, appeared on the steps of Moose Lodge No. 107 in Harrisburg, Pennsylvania. Though he was at the private club as the guest of a member, he was refused service on the basis of his race. Irvis sued under federal civil rights law to have the lodge's state-issued liquor license revoked until it stopped discriminating. He won his case in district court, where it was ruled that the lodge's discriminatory practice was "state action" because it was licensed by the state of Pennsylvania. Moose Lodge No. 107 appealed the decision to the U.S. Supreme Court, which heard the case argued on 28 February 1972.

The Issues at Stake

The case hinged on the definition of "state action." "State action" means action taken by the state or one of its officers. If state action is taken that discriminates against someone on the basis of race, it violates the Fourteenth Amendment of the U.S. Constitution. However, a discriminatory action taken by a private official is not covered by constitutional protection. Certainly the Moose Lodge was a private club in the everyday sense of the term. It received no federal or state money and restricted access to members and their guests. In some earlier cases, however, the Court had found that a strong enough relationship existed between a state and a private institution to warrant disallowing the institution's discrimination on the grounds that it violated federal law. This was Irvis' contention. Also, there was a question as to whether the state's policy of restricting the distribution of liquor licenses meant that it had turned the lodge into a state-supported monopoly—and thus subjected it to federal civil rights law.

The Supreme Court Decides

On 12 June 1972 the Supreme Court issued its decision in favor of Moose Lodge No. 107 and against Leroy Irvis. Justice Rehnquist wrote the majority opinion, in which he was joined by Chief Justice Burger, Justice Stewart, Justice White, Justice Powell, and Justice Blackmun. The majority dismissed the lower court's ruling that the Moose Lodge's discrimination constituted "state action" because the state had issued its liquor license. In his majority opinion, Rehnquist wrote:

The Court has never held, of course, that discrimination by an otherwise private entity would be violative of the Equal Protection Clause if the private entity receives any sort of benefit or service at all from the State, or if it is subject to state regulation in any degree whatever. Since state-furnished services include such necessities of life as electricity, water, and police and fire protection, such a holding would utterly emasculate the distinction between private as distinguished from State set forth in The Civil Rights Cases and adhered to in subsequent decisions. Our holdings indicate that where the impetus for the discrimination is private, the State must have "significantly involved itself with invidious discriminations . . . in order for the discriminatory action to fall within the ambit of the constitutional prohibition."

On the question of whether the state-licensed lodge represented a state-sponsored monopoly, Rehnquist also sided with the lodge:

> However detailed this type of regulation may be in some particulars, it cannot be aid to in any way foster or encourage racial discrimination. Nor can it be said to make the State in any realistic sense a partner or even a joint venturer in the club's enterprise.

Three justices—Justice Marshall, Justice Brennan, and Justice Douglas—disagreed with the majority view. Douglas and Brennan each wrote separate dissenting opinions, both joined by Marshall. Brennan's took a much different view of the state's relationship to Moose Lodge No. 107:

> When Moose Lodge obtained its liquor license, the State of Pennsylvania became an active participant in the operation of the Lodge bar. Liquor licensing laws are only incidentally revenue measures; they are primarily pervasive regulatory schemes under which the State dictates and continually supervises virtually every detail of the operation of the licensee's business. Very few, if any, other licensed businesses experience such complete state involvement.

In Brennan's view, a strong enough relationship existed between the state of Pennsylvania and the Moose Lodge to have its actions classified as "state action." The lodge's discriminatory policies were thus subject to federal civil rights laws.

Following the Supreme Court decision in *Moose Lodge v. Irvis*, the Pennsylvania Civil Rights Commission took the lodge to court, claiming that its actions violated state law. The Supreme Court refused to hear the case upon appeal, choosing to let the Pennsylvania law stand.

Related Cases
The Civil Rights Cases, 109 U.S. 3 (1883).
Shelley v. Kraemer, 334 U.S. 1 (1948).
Burton v. Wilmington Parking Authority, 365 U.S. 715 (1961).
Reitman v. Mulkey, 387 U.S. 369 (1967).

Bibliography and Further Reading
Bartholomew, Paul Charles. *Summaries of Leading Cases on the Constitution*. Totowa, NJ: Rowan & Allanheld, 1983.

Ducat, Craig R., and Harold W. Chase. *Constitutional Interpretation*. St. Paul, MN: West Publishing Company, 1988.

Encyclopedia of the American Constitution. New York, NY: Macmillan Publishing Company, 1986.

SALYER V. TULARE

Legal Citation: 410 U.S. 719 (1973)

In general, the Equal Protection Clause of the Fourteenth Amendment protects an individual's right to vote. Sometimes, when certain segments of the population have been denied the right to vote, the U.S. Supreme Court has deemed these restrictions or exclusions unconstitutional under the Equal Protection Clause.

However, the Equal Protection Clause does not mean that just because a state law seems to differentiate between different segments of society, there has been a constitutional violation. Rigorous, strict standards have been established to resolve whether the underlying motives behind a statute are prejudicial or helpful in nature. Each case must stand on its own merits. The courts must examine each case's facts and particular circumstances to balance a state's claims of protecting a certain group's interests with the actual interests of the excluded group.

In California, as in other western U.S. areas, different seasons of the year can mean major differences in water availability. Early spring can swell rivers and streams with runoff from melting snow in high mountains. Later in the year, the water can literally dry up. This is why there are so many water storage facilities and dams in these areas. The larger and more populated areas require larger and more expensive projects funded by state and federal resources.

However, many projects are smaller. They may affect a smaller area of land or a more sparsely populated area. In California, the legislature created a number of ways to respond locally to water-related issues. One such measure was the creation of water storage districts. These districts have the power to plan and execute approved water-related projects having to do with acquiring, conserving and distributing water. They can apply tolls and water-use charges, collecting them from everybody who benefits from their water or related services, in proportion to the received services. A board of directors governs each district. Each division within the district elects one director. The elections are in odd-numbered years. These elections are at the heart of *Salyer v. Tulare*.

At the time, 77 people lived in the Tulare Lake Basin Water Storage District. Most of these people worked for

Appellant
Salyer Land Company et al.

Appellee
Tulare Lake Basin Water Storage District

Appellant's Claim
Sections of the California Water Code are unconstitutional and in violation of the Fourteenth Amendment's Equal Protection Clause.

Chief Lawyer for Appellant
Thomas Keister Greer

Chief Lawyer for Appellee
Robert M. Newell

Justices for the Court
Harry A. Blackmun, Warren E. Burger, William H. Rehnquist (writing for the Court), Potter Stewart, Byron R. White

Justices Dissenting
William J. Brennan, Jr., William O. Douglas, Thurgood Marshall

Place
Washington, D.C.

Date of Decision
20 March 1973

Decision
California Water Code is not unconstitutional in allowing only landowners their votes in water district elections, or in allocating votes in proportion to land assessment values.

Significance
This case helped to establish the precedent that on certain occasions, it is constitutionally correct for states to set laws regarding environment, even if it restricts the right for all people to vote.

one of the four corporations that farmed about 85 percent of Tulare's 193,000 acres. The case was instituted by Tulare Lake District landowners, a land-owner lessee and non-land owning district residents. They alleged that two sections of the California Water Code—41000 and 41001—denied voting rights to them guaranteed through the Fourteenth Amendment's Equal Protection Clause.

Section 41000 says that only titled landowners can vote in general elections. Section 41001 states that qualified voters can vote in any precinct in which they own land and they can cast one vote for every $100.00 "or fraction thereof, worth of his land, exclusive of improvements, minerals, and mineral rights therein, in the precinct." So, to vote one had to own land and the allotment of votes depended on how much land was owned. Residents who were not landowners felt they had been disenfranchised by not being allowed to vote and the smaller landowners felt that the votes were too heavily weighted for the larger landowners.

The plaintiffs submitted their case to the three-judge district court which ruled, by majority, that both of the California Water statutes fell within the limits of the Equal Protection Clause. At this point, the Salyer Land Company appealed to the U.S. Supreme Court. The Supreme Court heard the case and in a 6-3 decision, affirmed the district court's ruling.

Based on the circumstances of this particular case, Justice Rehnquist's majority opinion took into account such considerations as the district's limited function and the disproportionate effect of actions on the large landowners.

In his dissenting opinion, Justice Douglas quoted the Supreme Court in the matter of *Reynolds v. Sims*:

> Legislators represent people, not trees or acres. Legislators are elected by voters, not farms or cities or economic interests. As long as ours is a representative form of government, and our legislatures are those instruments of government elected directly by and directly representative of the people, the right to elect legislators in a free and unimpaired fashion is a bedrock of our political system.

Furthermore, said Justice Douglas:

> One corporation can outvote 77 individuals in this district. Four corporations can exercise these governmental power as they choose, leaving every individual inhabitant with a weak, ineffectual voice. The result is a corporate political kingdom undreamed of by those who wrote our constitution.

Related Cases
Reynolds v. Sims, 377 U.S. 533 (1964).

Bibliography and Further Reading
Biskupic, Joan, and Elder Witt, eds. *Congressional Quarterly's Guide to the U.S. Supreme Court,* 3rd ed. Washington, DC: Congressional Quarterly, Inc., 1996.

Seidman, Louis M., Gerald R. Stone, Cass R. Sunstein, Mark V. Tushnet. *Constitutional Law.* Boston: Little, Brown and Company, 1986.

SAN ANTONIO SCHOOL DISTRICT, ET AL. V. RODRIGUEZ, ET AL.

Legal Citation: 411 U.S. 1 (1973)

Since the Fourteenth Amendment was added to the Constitution in 1868, the Supreme Court has used it to help ensure the same rights to all people regardless of race. However, the issues are not always clear cut, as demonstrated in the case of *San Antonio School District, et al. v. Rodriguez, et al.*

Background

When Texas became a state in 1845, its first state constitution established free public schools. Soon, the state enacted a two-way method of financing schools. The state and the local school district would both contribute. By 1883, the Texas legislature amended its constitution to provide local school districts with the power to levy *ad valorem* taxes, to build new school buildings and to maintain existing school buildings. An *ad valorem* tax means the tax is calculated on a property's value—in this case, essentially a property tax.

The state's Permanent School Fund and Available School Fund supplemented whatever funding was provided locally. Public land was set aside to provide this fund with the income necessary to support the state's public schools. The Permanent School Fund, a state *ad valorem* tax, and certain other taxes, provided money to the Available School Fund which actually disbursed most of the state educational funds through the rest of the nineteenth century and into the first half of the twentieth. In 1918, state property taxes were increased to help provide free textbooks to all the schools.

In its earlier history, Texas was mostly rural, helping to distribute population and property wealth throughout the state in a generally even fashion. That changed as the state became more industrialized and population shifted from rural to urban settings.

Soon, the growing differences in population and property wealth in different school districts resulted in larger differences in the amounts being spent locally for education. It also began to become apparent that the Available School Fund could not fill-in the growing chasm between richer and poorer districts.

As the difference grew between the tax base of different school districts, the state designed complex

Appellant
San Antonio Independent School District, et al.

Appellee
Demetrio P. Rodriguez, et al.

Appellant's Claim
The state of Texas financed public education in such a way as to discriminate against children living in poor school districts.

Chief Lawyer for Appellant
Charles Alan Wright

Chief Lawyer for Appellee
Arthur Gochman

Justices for the Court
Harry A. Blackmun, Warren E. Burger, Lewis F. Powell, Jr. (writing for the Court), William H. Rehnquist, Potter Stewart

Justices Dissenting
William J. Brennan, Jr., William O. Douglas, Thurgood Marshall, Byron R. White

Place
Washington, D.C.

Date of Decision
21 March 1973

Decision
That Texas statutes which regulated the financing of public schools based on property taxes in each school district and resulting in per-student funding disparities between the districts did not violate the Fourteenth Amendment's Equal Protection Clause.

Significance
By refusing to overturn the Texas statutes, it also refused to contest the way most states financed public schools even though it led to discrimination against people living in poor school districts.

formulae, such as the Gilmer-Aikin bill, that established the Texas Minimum Foundation School Program. At the time of *San Antonio v. Rodriguez,* this program accounted for about half of the money spent on education in Texas. This program had two goals: to place a heavier financial burden on the wealthier districts, and to make all school districts contribute to its children's education without exhausting the resources of any one district. In practice, wealthier districts had more resources to supplement state and program funding.

Edgewood v. Alamo Heights

In *San Antonio v. Rodriguez,* plaintiffs lived in the Edgewood Independent School District, one of seven in the metropolitan area. It was a residential area where the student body was about 90 percent Mexican American. More than six percent were African Americans. At the time, the average assessed property value was the lowest in the metropolitan area—a mere $5,960.

This area was compared to the Alamo Heights Independent School District, the wealthiest San Antonio school district, with a primarily Caucasian population—only about 18 percent Mexican Americans and less than one percent African Americans. Its average assessed property value was $49,000.

Due to the state's formula for funding public education, with a combination of federal, state and local funding, the Edgewood School District provided $356 per student in the 1967-1968 school year while Alamo Heights provided $594 per student during the same period.

What Happened

Edgewood parents brought suit against the state of Texas in the U.S. District Court for the Western District of Texas. They alleged that the Texas method of funding public education discriminated against those children who happened to live in poorer school districts.

The district court ruled that Texas was financing school systems in a discriminatory fashion, based on wealth. Therefore, under the Equal Protection Clause, it was an unconstitutional system. They found that wealth was a suspect classification, a factor used to determine whether a law denies a class of individuals equal protection. Suspect classifications are those based on race, alienage, national origin, and sex. Also, it was decided that education was a "fundamental right." This meant that the state had to prove that there was a

"compelling state interest" which dictated its policies. In fact, according to the district court, Texas didn't show that there was even a reasonable basis for its school funding policies.

When appealed, the U.S. Supreme Court reversed the district court's decision. Justice Powell, expressing the views of five justices, denied both of the district court's findings. He pointed out that wealth, in and of itself, had never been a suspect classification nor had education ever been a fundamental right. He stated that these children were not being discriminated against because they were poor people, but because of where they lived.

In fact, the opinion went, nobody had shown that any group of children were being discriminated against. No children were absolutely deprived of a public education. The public school funding method did not take away any fundamental rights because education was not a constitutional right. There was no evidence that the school system provided an adequate education for all children.

Justice Powell also found that the Texas method for financing schools did not violate the Equal Protection Clause because there was a sound, rational basis for its existence. It was shown to be helping the state solve the problem of underwriting a public education system in much the same way as virtually every other state.

Related Cases

Meyer v. Nebraska, 262 U.S. 390 (1923).
Pierce v. Society of Sisters, 268 U.S. 510 (1925).
McCollum v. Board of Education, 333 U.S. 203 (1948).
Brown v. Board of Education, 347 U.S. 483 (1954).
Abington School District v. Schempp, 374 U.S. 203 (1963).
Shapiro v. Thompson, 394 U.S. 618 (1969).
Graham v. Richardson, 403 U.S. 365 (1971).

Bibliography and Further Reading

Biskupic, Joan, and Elder Witt, eds. *Congressional Quarterly's Guide to the U.S. Supreme Court,* 3rd ed. Washington, DC: Congressional Quarterly, Inc., 1996.

Cushman, Robert F. *Leading Constitutional Decisions.* Englewood Cliffs, NJ: Prentice-Hall, Inc., 1982.

Hall, Kermit L., ed. *The Oxford Companion to the Supreme Court of the United States.* New York: Oxford University Press, 1992.

McWhirter, Darien A. "Urban Residence and Poverty." in *Exploring the Constitution,* Vol. 1, *Equal Protection.* Phoenix: Oryx Press, 1995.

GEDULDIG V. AIELLO

Legal Citation: 417 U.S. 484 (1974)

In the 1940s, California created an Unemployment Compensation Disability Fund to provide benefits to workers temporarily disabled by injuries or illnesses not covered by workers' compensation. California employees contributed one percent of their salaries to the fund, up to an annual maximum of 85 dollars. In the 1970s, four women who had contributed the required percentages of their salaries to the fund, sued when they found that the fund excluded pregnancy-related disabilities from coverage.

Four Women, Different Pregnancies

Three of the women had a wide range of pregnancy-related disabilities: Carolyn Aiello suffered an ectopic pregnancy that required surgical termination; Elizabeth Johnson endured a tubal pregnancy, also necessitating surgical termination; and Augustina Armendariz miscarried. Jacqueline Jaramillo, however, had a normal pregnancy and delivery. All were excluded according to Section 2626 of the Unemployment Insurance Code, which read:

> "Disability" or "disabled" includes both mental or physical illness and mental or physical injury. An individual shall be deemed disabled in any day in which, because of his [or her] physical or mental condition, he [she] is unable to perform his [her] regular or customary work. In no case shall the term "disability" or "disabled" include any injury or illness caused by or arising in connection with pregnancy up to the termination of such pregnancy and for a period of 28 days thereafter.

A three-judge panel of the federal district court ruled that the fund's pregnancy exclusion violated the Fourteenth Amendment of the U.S. Constitution. Dwight Geduldig, the director of California's Department of Human Resources Development, appealed to the U.S. Supreme Court, which agreed to hear the case.

Another Court Heard

Ten days before the district court ruled in *Geduldig*, the California Court of Appeals ruled in a case brought by another woman who had been denied benefits follow-

Appellant
Dwight Geduldig, director of the California Department of Human Resources Development

Appellees
Carolyn Aiello, Augustina Armendariz, Elizabeth Johnson, Jacqueline Jaramillo

Appellant's Claim
That the district court erred when it ruled that California was required to pay disability benefits to private employees temporarily disabled by their pregnancies.

Chief Lawyer for Appellant
Joanne Condas

Chief Lawyer for Appellees
Wendy W. Williams

Justices for the Court
William J. Brennan, Jr., Warren E. Burger, William H. Rehnquist, Potter Stewart (writing for the Court), Byron R. White

Justices Dissenting
Harry A. Blackmun, William O. Douglas, Thurgood Marshall

Place
Washington, D.C.

Date of Decision
17 June 1974

Significance
This decision, excluding "normal pregnancy" from medical coverage, left women *without* pregnancy problems in an intolerable financial bind. In 1978, Congress finally passed an act to cover problem-free pregnancies and deliveries for women who were otherwise covered for medical disabilities.

Workers' Compensation

Worker's compensation provides lost wages and funds for medical costs to workers injured on the job. All 50 states have workers compensation laws. Injuries covered are commonly associated with specific accidents on the job such as falling on stairs or off a ladder. Occupational-related diseases, such as miner's "black lung" disease, are also covered. The injury must arise from employment. That is, a causal connection between work and the injury must be demonstrated. Also, the injury must occur in the course of employment, during working hours, at a work location, and while performing work duties. Employers must purchase worker's compensation insurance for their employees or provide a self-insured program. Employers often pass along the cost of insurance to their customers.

Worker's compensation laws are no-fault laws meaning benefits are paid without regard to the fault or negligence of either the employer or employee. Benefits include medical and indemnity (compensation) payments. Hospital and other medical payments are made with the goal of returning the employee to the job. Indemnity benefits compensate a worker for loss of income. Should the injury result in death, the worker's spouse and any children up to age 18 may receive payments.

Source(s): Hardy, Benjamin A. Jr., Jack B. Hood, and Harold S. Lewis, Jr. *Workers' Compensation and Employee Protection Laws in a Nutshell.* Minneapolis/St. Paul, MN: West Publishing, 1990.

---

ing an ectopic pregnancy. The court of appeals ruled in this case, *Rentzer v. Unemployment Insurance Appeals Board* (1973), that Section 2626 did not prohibit women from receiving benefits if they suffered medical complications of their pregnancies. The regulations were subsequently rewritten to exclude only "maternity benefits" for normal pregnancies and deliveries, and so Aiello, Armendariz, and Johnson—who had suffered ectopic and tubal pregnancies and a miscarriage, respectively—had their claims approved.

Jaramillo, whose disability claim was denied following a normal pregnancy and delivery, did not benefit from the amendment of the fund's requirements. The new regulations, contained in Section 2626.2, provided that:

> Benefits relating to pregnancy shall be paid under this part only in accordance with the following: (a) Disability benefits shall be paid upon a doctor's certification that the claimant is disabled because of an abnormal and involuntary complication of pregnancy, including but not limited to: puerperal infection, eclampsia, caesarian section delivery, ectopic pregnancy, and toxemia. (b) Disability benefits shall be paid upon a doctor's certification that a condition possibly arising out of pregnancy would disable the claimant without regard to the pregnancy, including but not limited to: anemia, diabetes, embolism, heart disease, hypertension, phlebitis, phlebothrombosis, pyelonephritis, thrombophlebitis, vaginitis, varicse veins, and venous thrombosis.

On 26 March 1974, the attorneys for Geduldig and Jaramillo presented oral arguments before the Supreme Court. Jaramillo's attorney, Wendy W. Williams, remarked that the continued exclusion of pregnancy-related disability claims arising from normal pregnancy and delivery violated the Fourteenth Amendment. Geduldig's attorney, Joanne Condas, insisted that the exclusion served the important governmental objectives of making the insurance program both self-supporting and affordable to all of the state's employees.

Is Normal Pregnancy a Disability?

In his 17 June 1974, opinion for the majority of the Court, Justice Stewart wrote that the Court had evaluated a number of "variables," including "the benefit level deemed appropriate to compensate employee disability, the risks selected to be insured . . . and the contribution rate chosen to maintain the solvency of the program and at the same time to permit low-income employees to participate . . ." Stewart said the Court found that the "essential issue in this case is whether the Equal Protection Clause requires such policies to be sacrificed or compromised in order to finance the payment of benefits to those whose disability is attributable to normal pregnancy and delivery."

The Court found that California, in designing its program, had addressed its legitimate governmental interests without engaging in "invidious discrimination under the Equal Protection Clause." Noting that "there is nothing in the Constitution . . . that requires the State to subordinate or compromise its legitimate interests solely to create a more comprehensive social program than it already has," Stewart wrote that the plan included "no risk from which men are protected and women are not. Likewise, there is no risk from which women are protected and men are not." The court reversed the judgment of the district court, and permitted California to retain the exclusion for disability claims arising from normal pregnancy and delivery.

Creating a Double Standard

Justice Blackmun wrote a spirited dissent, joined by Justices Douglas and Marshall:

> The economic effects caused by pregnancy-related disabilities are functionally indistinguishable from the effects caused by any other disability: wages are lost due to a physical inability to work, and medical expenses are incurred for the delivery of the child and for postpartum care. In my view, by singling out for less favorable treatment a gender-linked disability peculiar to women, the State has created a double standard for disability compensation: a limitation is imposed upon the disabilities for which women workers may recover, while men receive full compensation for all disabilities suffered, including those that affect only or primarily their sex, such as prostatectomies, circumcision, hemophilia, and gout.

Congress to the Rescue

In 1976, the female employees of General Electric sued, claiming that the pregnancy exclusions contained in their company's insurance plan violated Title VII of the Civil Rights Act of 1964. Relying on its decision in *Geduldig*, the Supreme Court ruled that private employers did not violate federal law when they chose to deny medical disability payments to workers with maternity-related absences.

In 1978, Congress amended Title VII to include the Pregnancy Discrimination Act. The act specifically provided that "women affected by pregnancy, childbirth, or related medical conditions shall be treated the same for all employment-related purposes . . . as other persons not so affected but similar in their ability or inability to work . . ."

Related Cases

Cleveland Board of Education v. LaFleur, 414 U.S. 632 (1974).
Cohen v. Chesterfield County School Board, 414 U.S. 632 (1974).
General Electric v. Gilbert, 429 U.S. 125 (1976).
Nashville Gas Co. v. Satty, 434 U.S. 136 (1977).

Bibliography and Further Reading

Edwards, Mark Evan. "Pregnancy Discrimination Litigation: Legal Erosion of Capitalist Ideology Under Equal Employment Opportunity Law," *Social Forces,* September 1996, p. 247.

Gans, David H. "Stereotyping and Difference: The Future of Sex Discrimination Law," *Yale Law Journal,* May 1995, p. 1875.

Goldstein, Leslie Friedman. *The Constitutional Rights of Women: Cases in Law and Social Change,* rev. ed. Madison: University of Wisconsin Press, 1989.

Hoff, Joan. *Law, Gender and Injustice: A Legal History of U.S. Women.* New York: New York University Press, 1991.

Ross, Susan Deller, et al. *The Rights of Women: The Basic ACLU Guide to Women's Rights.* Carbondale: Southern Illinois University Press, 1993.

Trzcinski, Eileen, and William T. Alpert. "Pregnancy and Parental Leave Benefits in the United States and Canada," *Journal of Human Resources,* Spring 1994, p. 535.

WASHINGTON V. DAVIS

Legal Citation: 426 U.S. 229 (1976)

Appellant
Walter E. Washington

Appellee
Alfred E. Davis

Appellant's Claim
That job qualification tests which minorities fail in disproportionate numbers do not violate the Equal Protection Clause.

Chief Lawyer for Appellant
David P. Sutton

Chief Lawyer for Appellee
Richard B. Sobol

Justices for the Court
Harry A. Blackmun, Warren E. Burger, Lewis F. Powell, Jr., William H. Rehnquist, John Paul Stevens, Potter Stewart, Byron R. White (writing for the Court)

Justices Dissenting
William J. Brennan, Jr., Thurgood Marshall

Place
Washington, D.C.

Date of Decision
7 June 1976

Decision
The Supreme Court held that the job tests were not unconstitutional.

Significance
In *Washington,* the Court clearly states that some evidence of discriminatory intent is necessary to demonstrate that employment tests are unconstitutional. What that evidence consists of, however, was not made clear.

On 10 April 1970, two African American police officers filed suit against officials of the police department in Washington, D.C. Their initial claim was that the department's promotions policy was racially discriminatory. Their suit was joined by others who alleged that their applications to become police officers had been rejected, at least in part, because of a written personnel test which African Americans failed in disproportionate numbers. The plaintiffs claimed that police department policies in the District of Columbia—which is governed by federal laws—violated the Due Process Clause of the Fifth Amendment, which reads: "No person shall be . . . deprived of life, liberty, or property, without due process of law."

The federal district court ruled in favor of the police department. On appeal, however, Davis and the other complainants prevailed. The U.S. Court of Appeals for the District of Columbia applied the standard set by the U.S. Supreme Court in the seminal employment discrimination case, *Griggs v. Duke Power Company* (1971), which held that tests which operate to exclude minority groups are unconstitutional. According to *Griggs,* this presumption can only be mitigated if the employer can demonstrate that the tests are substantially related to job performance. Holding that lack of discriminatory intent in administering hiring and promotion exams was irrelevant, the appellate court reversed the decision of the district court. The police officials then petitioned the Supreme Court for review of this decision.

Supreme Court Holds that Evidence of Discriminatory Intent Is Necessary to Prove Racial Discrimination

By a vote of 7-2, the Supreme Court reversed the court of appeals. Writing for the Court, Justice White clearly indicated that the so-called "disproportionate impact" test developed in *Griggs* did not apply here. While *Griggs* interpreted Title VII of the 1964 Civil Rights Act, the same standards did not apply to the applicable law in this case—the Due Process Clause of the Fifth Amendment:

> We have never held that the constitutional standard for adjudicating claims of invidious racial discrimination is identical to the stan-

dards applicable under Title VII, and we decline to do so today. The central purpose of the Equal Protection Clause of the Fourteenth Amendment is the prevention of official conduct discriminating on the basis of race. It is also true that the Due Process Clause of the Fifth Amendment contains an equal protection component prohibiting the United States from invidiously discriminating between individuals or groups . . . But our cases have not embraced the proposition that a law or other official act, without regard to whether it reflects a racially discriminatory purpose, is unconstitutional *solely* because it has a racially discriminatory disproportionate impact.

Although the Court stated that a showing of discriminatory intent was necessary to make out a claim under the Constitution, it was less clear about what sort of showing might pass the test. Justice White indicated that a discriminatory purpose might be inferred from all the facts—including the disproportionate impact of tests or other factors on racial minorities—relevant to a particular case of alleged employment discrimination. But as Justice Brennan pointed out in his dissenting opinion, discriminatory purpose cannot always be distinguished from discriminatory impact.

When the Court revisited the issue in *Personnel Administrator v. Feeney* (1979), this test was clarified: if the potential discriminatory effects of an employment practice were foreseeable and the employer carried them out anyway, this action constitutes discriminatory intent. The burden of proof—and it is a heavy one—was now shifted to the employee, who must show that the employer should have known that a certain practice would negatively impact minority employees.

Related Cases
Strauder v. West Virginia, 100 U.S. 303 (1880).
Yick Wo v. Hopkins, 118 U.S. 356 (1886).
Bolling v. Sharpe, 347 U.S. 497 (1954).
Gomillion v. Lightfoot, 364 U.S. 339 (1960).
Griggs v. Duke Power Company, 401 U.S. 424 (1971).
Personnel Administrator v. Feeney, 442 U.S. 256 (1979).

Justice Byron R. White. © The Library of Congress.

Bibliography and Further Reading

Bloch, Farrell E. *Antidiscrimination Law and Minority Employment: Recruitment Practices and Regulatory Constraints.* Chicago, IL: University of Chicago Press, 1994.

Burstein, Paul. *Discrimination, Jobs, and Politics: The Struggle for Equal Employment Opportunity in the United States Since the New Deal.* Chicago, IL: University of Chicago Press, 1985.

Moreno, Paul D. *From Direct Action to Affirmative Action: Fair Employment Law and Policy in America, 1933-1972.* Baton Rouge: Louisiana State University Press, 1997.

MASSACHUSETTS BOARD OF RETIREMENT V. MURGIA

Legal Citation: 427 U.S. 307 (1976)

Appellant
Massachusetts Board of Retirement, et al.

Appellee
Robert D. Murgia

Appellant's Claim
The state of Massachusetts Board of Retirement believed their provision for mandatory retirement of police officers at age 50 was rationally related to the interest of protecting the public and therefore did not violate the Equal Protection Clause of the Fourteenth Amendment.

Chief Lawyer for Appellant
Terence P. O'Malley

Chief Lawyer for Appellee
Robert D. City

Justices for the Court
Harry A. Blackmun, William J. Brennan, Jr., Warren E. Burger, Lewis F. Powell, Jr., William H. Rehnquist, Potter Stewart, Byron R. White (unsigned)

Justices Dissenting
Thurgood Marshall (John Paul Stevens did not participate)

Place
Washington, D.C.

Date of Decision
25 June 1976

Decision
There was no violation of the Equal Protection Clause: the state of Massachusetts' mandatory retirement provision rationally furthered its purpose of protecting the public by assuring physical fitness of the state police officers.

Significance
Although not the best means available for the purpose of protecting the public, the U.S. Supreme Court found that mandatory retirement of police officers at age 50 was a rational course of action for the state of Massachusetts. The Court also found that old workers were not a discrete and insular group and that the right of governmental employment was, by itself, not fundamental. Therefore, if the reason for a retirement provision was justified by a legitimate state interest, such as public safety, age discrimination was justified.

Old people are subject to age discrimination in every society, especially when employers sometimes believe that age is a viable criteria to measure an ability to work. Employers often perceive older workers as being less productive than younger ones, and discriminate against them when hiring new workers or retiring old workers. To protect the rights of elder workers, Congress enacted the Age Discrimination in Employment Act in 1967. This act was aimed at shielding senior workers from discrimination in hiring, discharging, compensation, and conditions of employment. Moreover, one of its more salient purposes was to prohibit arbitrary age discrimination in employment. One clause of this act allowed age discrimination in hiring or discharging if the employer could prove that youth was an occupational qualification reasonably necessary to the normal operations of the particular business. This clause was applicable when a position involved physically burdensome activity or public safety. Though *Massachusetts Board of Retirement v. Murgia* did not invoke the Age Discrimination in Employment Act, it involved a position of employment, police officer, which required strenuous physical activity and demanded consideration be given to public safety. In this case the U.S. Supreme Court in fact found that age discrimination should receive less judicial scrutiny than discrimination based on race or sex because aging objectively involved a decrease of physical and mental abilities.

Rationality of Mandatory Retirement

The state of Massachusetts' statute required retirement of a uniformed state police officer upon attaining the age of 50. Adhering to this rule, the Massachusetts Board of Retirement retired Robert Murgia, an officer in the uniformed branch of the Massachusetts State Police. Believing he was in excellent health and deprived from his right to work, Murgia filed suit in the U.S. District Court for the District of Massachusetts alleging that he was denied equal protection under the Age Discrimination in Employment Act and the Fourteenth Amendment. His complaint was dismissed, however, because a federal district judge believed that the complaint did not allege a substantial constitutional question. Murgia appealed to the U.S. Court of Appeals

Forced Retirement and Public-Safety Officers

Congress passed the Age Discrimination in Employment Act of 1967 (ADEA) to combat what is sometimes caused "ageism." Among the law's provisions is a prohibition against age discrimination with regard to employees between the ages of 40 and 70 years old. Only if age can be demonstrated to be a "bona fide occupational qualification reasonably necessary to the normal operation of the particular business" is it permissible to fire someone on the basis of their age.

An ordinance in the Baltimore city code required firefighters to retire at the age of 55, and in the mid-1980s six Baltimore firefighters brought an age discrimination suit against the city. The case went before the Supreme Court, which on 17 June 1985 struck down the Baltimore ordinance. According to Justice Thurgood Marshall, who delivered the opinion for a unanimous Court, the legislative history of the ADEA, which was amended

in 1974 and 1977, suggests that Congress did not consider 55 a bona fide occupational limit for public-safety officers; rather, the designation may have been made "arbitrarily" or "for myriad political purposes."

According to an article in *Criminal Justice Newsletter* published soon after the ruling, however, legislators such as Senator Bill Bradley (D-NJ) and others continued to favor different retirement standards for public-safety officers than for other Americans: "I am a strong proponent of the Age Discrimination in Employment Act," Bradley said. "But older Americans have as much reason as anyone to insure that those who must perform emergency services are physically able to do so."

Source(s): "Supreme Court Raises Barrier to Forced Retirement Rules." *Criminal Justice Newsletter,* July 15, 1985, pp. 1-2.

for the First Circuit but the appellate court sent the case back to the lower court with directions to convene a three-judge panel for review of the case. The three-judge court convened and, after looking at a record consisting of allegations and testimonies submitted by the parties, ruled that the provision of the Massachusetts statute was unconstitutional because it lacked rational basis in furthering any substantial state interest.

In their review of the case, the court found that service in the uniformed branch of the Massachusetts State Police was arduous and that high versatility was required from officers. The police officers had been required to pass an extensive physical examination every two years until age 40, and after that a more rigorous annual examination was required until an officer reached the age of 50. Murgia's record included the testimony of three physicians concerning the physiological and psychological demands of the uniformed police profession, the relationship between aging and the ability to work under stress, and aging and the ability to safely perform police functions.

Looking at all of these arguments the district court found that it was not necessary to apply a strict-scrutiny test, because the age classification established by the Massachusetts statutory scheme did not interfere with the exercise of a fundamental right nor did it operate against a suspect class (senior police officers). The court reasoned that a test of rationality should be applied; the test that evaluated constitutionality of classifications by examining whether they rationally furthered an identified state interest. In this case, the state interest was the protection of the public by assuring the physical preparedness of the state's uniformed police.

Ultimately, the court ruled that compulsory retirement at age 50 was irrational (and therefore unconstitutional), because police officers' fitness to perform uniformed police duties was tested individually by annual examination and it was a fact that an officer, in this case Murgia, could pass those examinations after having attained the age of 50.

Dissatisfied with this decision, the Massachusetts Board of Retirement appealed directly to the U.S. Supreme Court, and, in a *per curiam* opinion (an opinion given jointly by all the justices trying a case, with no signatory author), the Supreme Court reversed the decision of the district court.

Not the Best Means . . . But Rational Means

Seven justices of the Supreme Court agreed that the retirement provision of the Massachusetts statute was constitutional. The justices, however, also reasoned that, as written, the act was "imperfect" because it sought to further the state interest of protecting the public by imposing a chronological limitation rather than one based on individualized testing. Justice Stevens did not take part in the consideration or the decision of the case, and Justice Marshall dissented, supporting the district court's decision.

The Supreme Court first decided which test for equal protection analysis should be used in assessing the constitutionality of the mandatory retirement provision. Agreeing with the district court, the justices found that strict scrutiny was not a proper test. It was used only when the exercise of a fundamental right was restricted or when a suspect group was treated unfairly. The Court found that a right of governmental employment was not by itself fundamental, and that a class of uniformed state police officers over 50 did not constitute a suspect class for purposes of equal protection analysis. Instead, the Court held that a suspect class was one "saddled" with disabilities, unequally treated with a specific purpose, or reduced to political powerlessness. In the case of over-50 police officers, the Court found that old age did not even define a discrete and insular group. It merely marked a stage that everyone would reach if they lived out their normal life span. Therefore, justices used the rational-basis standard to examine the age classification of the retirement provision.

The Court found that the retirement provision of the Massachusetts statute satisfied the rationality test because it was realistically related to the identified purpose of protecting the public by assuring physical preparedness of the Massachusetts uniformed police. Mandatory retirement at age 50 served to remove from police service those whose fitness for uniformed work preemptively had decreased with age. The Court reasoned that although the provision could have been tailored to determine fitness more precisely through individualized testing after age 50, a maximum-age limitation rationally satisfied the objective of assuring physical fitness. The Court concluded that the state perhaps had not chosen the best means to accomplish its purpose, but where rationality was the test a state did not violate the Equal Protection Clause merely because the classifications made by its laws were imperfect.

In his dissenting opinion, Justice Marshall agreed with the decision of the district court and reemphasized what he believed was the problem created by not adhering to the results of annual individualized examinations as a means of determining competence. He saw no reason why uniformed police officers could not be able to continue service after attaining the age of 50. The medical examinations would still have the predictive ability concerning a police officer's fitness and they would be sufficient means to protect the state's interest. He concluded that there was no reason for automatically terminating those officers who reached the age of 50, and that such action seemed to him the "height of irrationality."

Impact

In the United States, as throughout the world, older people have often been victims of age discrimination.

They experience problems with being hired for work and are often discharged because employers believe that advancing age objectively reduces their ability to work effectively. Such treatment not only affects the financial status of older people, but also their health. That is why Congress enacted the Age Discrimination in Employment Act in 1967. Nevertheless, under certain circumscribed instances, the U.S. Supreme Court held that age discrimination is sometimes justified because certain professions require excellent physical fitness.

In *Massachusetts Board of Retirement v. Murgia,* the U.S. Supreme Court found that age discrimination in the employment of "over-aged" police officers should be subject to less judicial scrutiny than discrimination by sex or race. The Court also affirmed that the practice of using a "rational basis test" (competence determined by fixed criteria) rather than a strict-scrutiny test in cases where a state's legislation sometimes restricted the availability of employment opportunities by age requirements. The majority opinion reasoned that people grouped by age were not like suspect classes who were discriminated because they were "saddled" with disabilities, unequally treated with a specific purpose, or politically powerless. Thus, according to the Court, some over-aged classes of people did not necessarily constitute a discrete and insular group of people whose constitutional rights could be violated. They were simply a fluid group of which everyone would become a member one day. Therefore, if a position (such as that of police officer) required demanding physical activity from an employee, and if government could rationalize a discrete issue wherein there existed an overriding issue regarding public safety (as in this case), age discrimination was held to be justified.

Related Cases

Shapiro v. Thompson, 394 U.S. 618 (1969).
Dandridge v. Williams, 397 U.S. 471 (1970).
San Antonio School District v. Rodriguez, 411 U.S. 1 (1973).
McIlvaine v. Pennsylvania, 415 U.S. 986 (1974).
Cannon v. Guste, 423 U.S. 918 (1975).
Weisbrod v. Lynn, 420 U.S. 940 (1975).

Bibliography and Further Reading

Jackson, Vicki C. "*Coeur d'Alene*, Federal Courts and the Supremacy of Federal Law." *Constitutional Commentary,* summer 1998, p. 301.

Tushnet, Mark V. "Justice Lewis F. Powell, Jr.: A Biography." *Michigan Law Review,* May 1995, p. 1854.

ARLINGTON HEIGHTS V. METROPOLITAN HOUSING CORP.

Legal Citation: 429 U.S. 252 (1977)

Petitioner
The Village of Arlington Heights, Illinois

Respondent
Metropolitan Housing Development Corporation and several individual residents

Petitioner's Claim
That a decision to deny rezoning on land owned by Metropolitan Housing Development Corporation was not racially motivated in violation of the Equal Protection Clause of the Fourteenth Amendment and conformed to the 1968 Fair Housing Act.

Chief Lawyer for Petitioner
F. Willis Caruso

Chief Lawyer for Respondent
Jack M. Siegel

Justices for the Court
Harry A. Blackmun, Warren E. Burger, Lewis F. Powell, Jr. (writing for the Court), William H. Rehnquist, Potter Stewart

Justices Dissenting
William J. Brennan, Jr., Thurgood Marshall, Byron R. White (John Paul Stevens did not participate)

Place
Washington, D.C.

Date of Decision
11 January 1977

Decision
Ruled in favor of Arlington Heights by reversing a lower court decision and refusing to issue an injunction against a rezoning decision, but sent the case back to the lower courts for further deliberation.

Significance
The case established a key standard for determining when the Equal Protection Clause of the Fourteenth Amendment was violated due to racial discrimination in housing. The simple fact that a decision may result in unequal effects on different racial groups was not sufficient evidence to prove racial discrimination. Those contesting an action on such grounds must also prove an intent to discriminate in the decision-making process. Fair housing proponents claimed the decision perpetuated deceptive segregation decisions made through the process of urban zoning.

Urban zoning gained substantial acceptance in the United States shortly after the beginning of the twentieth century. Zoning is a form of police power provided by the states to their local municipal governments. By limiting certain personal freedoms, communities can better provide for the health, safety, and welfare of their residents. Importantly, zoning regulations must be reasonable and conform with constitutional guarantees of equal protection and due process of the law. Despite being born from good ideals, zoning was frequently used as a means to keep people of lower social status out of certain areas to maintain market values of property. This form of zoning was labeled exclusionary zoning and was condemned by many. In 1968 Congress passed the Fair Housing Act, the first open housing act of the twentieth century. The act supported the notion that citizens should be free to live wherever they choose and can afford. The law prohibited discrimination in the sale and renting of certain types of housing on the basis of race and religion. The Supreme Court, also in 1968, ruled that federal law against housing discrimination applied to all housing. Despite the 1968 law and Court ruling, cases of housing discrimination against African American citizens pervasively continued.

Residential Zoning in Arlington Heights

Arlington Heights, a suburb of Chicago, is located approximately 25 miles northwest of the city's downtown area. Most land in the community was zoned for detached single family homes. During the 1960s, the community saw substantial growth while the population of racial minorities remained low, similar to other communities in northwest Cook County. Near the center of Arlington Heights, a religious order owned an 80-acre parcel. In 1970, the order of St. Viator decided to allocate some of its land for low and moderate income housing. St. Viator chose Metropolitan Housing Development Corporation, a nonprofit developer experienced in using federal housing assistance programs, to organize the project and develop 190 clustered town house units. Metropolitan was also close to completing another project near Arlington Heights at the time.

Metropolitan and St. Viator signed a 99-year lease agreement for a 15-acre parcel in the southeast corner of the order's property. The agreement was dependent upon Metropolitan obtaining a zoning clearance from Arlington Heights and federal housing assistance. The proposed high density residential development clearly did not conform to Arlington Heights' low density zoning ordinance. Therefore, the project could not be built unless the community rezoned the parcel for multiple family housing. If Metropolitan was unsuccessful in securing either the clearance or the funding, the lease would terminate.

Metropolitan filed a petition for rezoning with the community's planning commission. It became the subject of a series of three public meetings in the spring of 1971. Though a number of community groups supported the rezoning, a majority opposed the project. Opponents stressed that many neighboring residents had built or purchased property there relying on the single-family zone classification. Such a rezoning could potentially cause property values for neighboring homes to substantially decline. By the close of the third meeting, the planning commission adopted a motion to recommend denial of the rezoning request to Arlington Heights' board of trustees.

In June of 1972, Metropolitan and three African American Illinois citizens filed a lawsuit in the U.S. District Court for the Northern District of Illinois against Arlington Heights to block the rezoning denial. They claimed the denial violated the Fair Housing Act and the Fourteenth Amendment's equal protection of the law guarantee. The district court ruled in favor of the community by finding they were not motivated by racial discrimination or discrimination against low income groups when they denied rezoning. Their primary concern was to protect existing property values. Metropolitan appealed the decision to the Court of Appeals for the Seventh Circuit. The appeals court reversed the ruling by finding that the "ultimate effect" of the rezoning denial was a racial bias.

Intent Versus Effect

Arlington Heights then appealed to the Supreme Court which accepted the case. Justice Powell, writing for the 5-3 majority, could find no evidence the denial was racially motivated. Instead, Powell, agreeing with the district court's decision, found substantial evidence indicating the zoning decision was primarily prompted by a desire to protect property values and to preserve the zoning plan's integrity.

Arlington Heights argued before the Court that Metropolitan lacked legal standing to pursue their claim because it suffered no economic injury. The city argued that Metropolitan was not the actual property owner of the parcel since its agreement with St. Viator was contingent upon the rezoning. Powell, therefore, first examined the issue of standing. Powell observed that Arlington Heights' action effectively blocked the hous-

ing construction. He wrote that if Metropolitan was able to block the denial, which they could only accomplish through this petition, the barrier to low cost housing would be fully removed.

After consideration, Powell rejected Arlington Heights' argument. It seemed likely that Metropolitan would suffer some economic injury from its denial to rezone. Metropolitan, after all, had already invested thousands of dollars in developing plans for the proposed Lincoln Green community and for studies submitted to Arlington Heights supporting the rezoning request. Powell observed that the plans and studies would be worthless without the rezoning. Despite these factors, Powell wrote that Arlington Heights misunderstood the standing requirement. Sustaining an economic injury was not necessary. Metropolitan, a nonprofit corporation committed to providing low cost housing in areas where it was scarce, held a general interest. Therefore, Metropolitan readily satisfied the standing requirement of the Court.

In support of their petition for rezoning, Metropolitan argued that, as established in *Euclid v Ambler Realty Co.* (1926), it had the right to be free of arbitrary or illogical zoning actions. Metropolitan claimed Arlington Heights' refusal to rezone discriminated against racial minorities and was in violation of the Fourteenth Amendment. Powell found, however, that Metropolitan, being a corporation, had no racial identity and thus could not be discriminated against.

However, a Mr. Ransom, named in the lawsuit along with Metropolitan, was an African American Illinois resident. Working in an Arlington Heights' factory, Ransom lived approximately 20 miles away in a five room Evanston house with his mother and son. Ransom sought and qualified for the housing Metropolitan was to build. He claimed racial discrimination because the housing was blocked.

Powell responded that to prove a violation of the Equal Protection Clause based on racial discrimination, a proof of intent or purpose was necessary. Intent could be determined by examining both circumstantial and direct evidence available. Factors to consider when evaluating racial discrimination included the decision's potential impact, the historical trends and decisions, the sequence of events leading to the decision, and any deviation from normal procedures in making the decision.

In examining Arlington Heights' decision to not rezone, Powell concluded the community had consistently applied its zoning laws following its usual procedures. A buffer zone policy to protect property values existed well before Metropolitan's petition appeared. Powell then applied a recent job discrimination case ruling of the Court in *Washington v. Davis* (1976). He wrote that, with no convincing evidence offered of discriminatory intent, the mere fact that the denial for rezoning happened to have a racially discriminatory effect was "without independent constitutional significance." The Court upheld the Arlington Heights' denial to rezone by reversing the appeals court's decision, but also sent the case back to the appeals court to consider the alleged violation of the Fair Housing Act.

Justice White, joined by Justice Marshall and Justice Brennan, dissented. White contended that the majority should have adhered to traditional Court principles to not apply a precedent that was set after the appeals court had made its decision. The case should have been sent back to the appeals court for them to apply the precedent set in *Davis*. The *Davis* decision had been delivered by the Court after the appeals court had heard the *Arlington Heights* case.

Impact

Ruling in favor of Metropolitan, the appeals court in July of 1977 ruled that the refusal to rezone violated the Fair Housing Act because the effect was discriminatory even though there may have been no intent. The court held that actions predictably perpetuating racial discrimination were as harmful as intentional discrimination. Besides, the goal of the Fair Housing Act was to racially integrate housing throughout the nation.

The *Arlington Heights* decision established the standard for determining racial discrimination in housing by applying the standard established in *Davis*. Governmental actions should not be considered discriminatory solely on the basis of unequal effects. Proof of the intent to discriminate was also necessary. The evidence to be considered included the effect of the official action. Did it weigh more heavily on one minority group than another? Secondly, the historical background of the decision was to be reviewed to determine if the series of official actions were intentionally malicious. Thirdly, did the decision-makers deviate from the normal process? Lastly, any deviations would be assessed to determine if any important facts to the specific case could strongly favor a different resulting decision quite different than the one reached. Proof of such a racially discriminatory intent was required to establish a violation of the Equal Protection Clause.

Fair housing advocates criticized the decision. They believed the Court perpetuated the abuse of zoning powers by maintaining *status quo* segregation and social class distinctions. Such exclusionary zoning hardly served the general welfare of the communities or the nation, they contended. However, the *Arlington Heights* decision perpetuated the Court's reluctance to rule against local zoning decisions.

Related Cases

Euclid v. Ambler Realty Co., 272 U.S. 365 (1926).
Washington v. Davis, 426 U.S. 229 (1976).

Bibliography and Further Reading

Fischler, Raphael. "Health, Safety, and the General Welfare: Markets, Politics, and Social Science in Early Land-Use Regulations and Community Design." *Journal of Urban History,* September 1998.

Juergensmeyer, Julian C., and Thomas E. Roberts. *Land Use Planning and Control Law.* St. Paul, MN: West Group, 1998.

Koebel, C. Theodore, ed. *Shelter and Society: Theory, Research, and Policy for Nonprofit Housing.* Albany: State University of New York Press, 1998.

Tucker, William. *Zoning, Rent Control, and Affordable Housing.* Washington, DC: Cato Institute, 1991.

Young, Kenneth H. *Anderson's American Law of Zoning,* 4th Ed. Deerfield, IL: Clark Boardman Callaghan, 1996.

INGRAHAM ET AL. V. WRIGHT ET AL.

Legal Citation: 430 U.S. 651 (1977)

In October of 1970, James Ingraham was attending eighth grade at Charles R. Drew Junior High in Dade County, Florida. Roosevelt Andrews was enrolled in the ninth grade in the same school. Corporal punishment, allowed throughout the 237 schools in Dade County (as well as in most of Florida), was especially severe at Charles Drew.

Technically, corporal punishment was supposed to be limited to one particular authorized punishment:

> . . . paddling a student on the buttocks with a flat wooden paddle measuring less than two feet long, three to four inches wide, and about one-half inch thick . . . limited to one to five "licks" or blows with the paddle and [resulting] in no apparent physical injury to the student.

Ingraham and Andrews received punishments far more severe than that, as did many of their classmates. For example, Ingraham, who had been slow to respond to his teacher's instructions, was given more than 20 licks with a paddle while being held over a table in the principal's office—a beating so severe that he suffered a hematoma and had to stay out of school for several days. Andrews had been paddled several times for minor misbehavioral problems. Twice he was struck on his arms, once so hard that he lost the full use of his arm for a week.

Cruel and Unusual Punishment?

Ingraham and Andrews filed suit against their principal, the others in the principal's office who had helped punish them, and the superintendent of Dade County schools. They were filing not just for themselves, but also as a class action on behalf of all Dade County students. They claimed that the type of corporal punishment common at their school deprived them of their rights under the Eighth and Fourteenth Amendments of the Constitution.

The Eighth Amendment forbids "cruel and unusual punishment." The Fourteenth Amendment guarantees everyone "due process" before being deprived of life, liberty, or property. In this case, the students claimed that since their punishment had deprived them of their liberty, they had been entitled to a hearing or some other procedure before they were punished.

The case eventually made it to the Supreme Court, which was sharply divided on this issue. A majority of five denied the boys' suit, finding that corporal punishment, even of the severe type that the boys had suffered, does not constitute "cruel and unusual punishment." Nor did the majority believe that students were entitled to a hearing before corporal punishment was administered. A minority of four strongly dissented.

"The Openness of the School Environment"

Justice Powell, writing for the majority, laid out three major arguments. First, Powell declared that the Cruel and Unusual Punishments Clause of the Eighth Amendment does not apply to public schools. In almost all cases, Powell wrote, the clause applies only to criminals. The clause is particularly inappropriate to schools, he argued, "in light of the openness of the school environment, [which] affords significant protection against unjustified corporal punishment of schoolchildren." Because children are free to leave school at the end of the day and because there are witnesses around to virtually everything that occurs, the student is in a very different position from the criminal who is hidden away in a jail where he or she must remain for months or even years.

Second, Powell said, reasonable corporal punishment is acceptable in principle as a means of maintaining order and discipline in the schools. The mere fact of corporal punishment cannot be defined as "cruel and unusual punishment." Severe and unusual corporal punishment—such as that received by Ingraham and Andrews—can be remedied by having parents sue teachers and school districts for civil or even criminal penalties. In effect, Powell was transferring this issue from a federal court down to a state court level.

Finally, Powell held that administering corporal punishment without giving the student a hearing did not violate the student's Fourteenth Amendment rights to "due process." Powell said that in this case, the interest of the school in using corporal punishment had to be balanced against the interest of the child's personal liberty. Powell feared that if schools had to offer hearings every time they administered corporal punishment, they might stop using corporal punishment altogether, and a valuable disciplinary tool would be lost. If society did wish to abolish corporal punishment, Powell said, the way to do so was through the legislature, not through the courts.

"Punishments So Barbaric and Inhumane"

Justice White, joined by Justices Brennan, Marshall, and Stevens, strongly disagreed with virtually every part of the majority argument. First, he said, there was no evidence that the Eighth Amendment was meant to apply only to criminals. Second, even though schools were more open places than prisons, that did not guarantee that no violations of the Eighth Amendment would ever occur there. Third, he did not see why schools could not offer an "informal give-and-take between student and disciplinarian," which would give students "an opportunity to explain [their] version of the facts" before corporal punishment was administered. In fact, this type of school hearing had already been called for in another Supreme Court case.

White did not see how applying the Eighth and the Fourteenth Amendments in this way could possibly discourage teachers from continuing to exercise reasonable corporal punishment, whereas it might very well prevent them from exercising unreasonable punishments—punishments "so barbaric and inhumane that we will not permit them to be imposed on anyone, no matter how opprobrious the offense." White added, somewhat sarcastically, ". . . if it is constitutionally impermissible to cut off someone's ear for the commission of murder, it must be unconstitutional to cut off a child's ear for being late to class."

Corporal Punishment Continues

Ingraham v. Wright has made it much more difficult for parents and students to oppose corporal punishments in the federal courts. Because the decision in *Ingraham* suggested that severe and unjustified punishments be pursued as civil or criminal cases in state court, victims of corporal punishment have no national standard for which to appeal. Instead, they must rely on each state's definition of what type of punishment is unreasonable and what type of relief should be offered.

Since *Ingraham,* a number of federal courts have either refused to hear or have ruled against students who suffered extreme corporal punishment, such as a girl whose teacher pricked her upper arm with a straight pin and a boy whose coach struck him eight times in the kidney area.

Although the Court found that procedural due process did not apply to corporal punishment, it did reserve the possibility that substantive due process might apply. Whereas procedural due process concerns the procedures that are needed before depriving someone of life, liberty, or property, substantive due process refers to the fact of someone having been deprived. In other words, a person who had suffered from a severe and unreasonable application of corporal punishment could not complain that he or she had not received a fair hearing. But that person could complain about what actually happened.

Thus, in the wake of *Ingraham,* one girl complained of being beaten with a five-inch wide rubber paddle, being shoved against a desk, and being "stricken repeatedly and violently," so that she had to go to the emergency room and to remain at the hospital for ten days. A federal court considered this treatment to have violated the girl's right to substantive due process under the Fourteenth Amendment. Yet because there were no clear federal guidelines as to the kind of punishment that warranted this ruling, other courts were reluctant to make similar decisions.

Ingraham v. Wright went a long way toward establishing the legitimacy of corporal punishment without any type of hearing or procedural constraint. Those who are opposed to either the use or the abuse of corporal punishment must now seek their remedies in state legislatures and courts.

Related Cases

Goss v. Lopez, 419 U.S. 565 (1975).
Frost v. City and County of Honolulu, 584 F.Supp. 356 (1984).
Gelber By and Through Gelber v. Rozas, 584 F.Supp. 902 (1984).
Sweaney v. Ada County, Idaho, 119 F.3d 1385 (1997)
Township of West Orange v. Whitman, 8 F.Supp.2d 408 (1998).

Bibliography and Further Reading

"Due Process, Due Politics and Due Respect: Three Models of Legitimate School Governance." *Harvard Law Review.* March, 1981, Vol. 84, no. 5, pp. 1106-1126.

Henderson, Donald H. "Constitutional Implications Involving the Use of Corporal Punishment in the Public Schools: A Comprehensive Review." *The Journal of Law and Education,* summer, 1986, Vol. 15, no. 3, pp. 255-269.

Kerper, Hazel B. *Introduction to the Criminal Justice System,* 2nd ed. Minneapolis: West Publishing Co., 1979.

FOLEY V. CONNELIE

Legal Citation: 435 U.S. 291 (1978)

Appellant
Edmund Foley

Appellee
William G. Connelie, S. A. Smith

Appellant's Claim
Edmund Foley, an alien with legal permanent residence in the United States, claimed that his rights under the Fourteenth Amendment were violated because he was excluded by New York State statute from taking a preliminary state police examination.

Chief Lawyer for Appellant
Jonathan A. Weiss

Chief Lawyer for Appellee
Judith A. Gordon

Justices for the Court
Harry A. Blackmun, Warren E. Burger (writing for the Court), Lewis F. Powell, Jr., William H. Rehnquist, Potter Stewart, Byron R. White

Justices Dissenting
William J. Brennan, Jr., Thurgood Marshall, John Paul Stevens

Place
Washington, D.C.

Date of Decision
22 March 1978

Decision
The U.S. Supreme Court affirmed the decision of the U.S. District Court for the Southern District of New York by ruling that excluding aliens from working in the state police was constitutional. The Court held that the New York State statute did not violate the Equal Protection Clause of the Fourteenth Amendment. According to that statute, no person could participate in activities or proceedings conducted by police officers unless s/he was a citizen of the United States.

Significance
In finding it constitutionally permissible to exclude aliens from service on state police forces, the Court sought to further define which kinds of government positions and offices necessitated citizenship. The Court further defined the limitations of such exclusion by stipulating that states must evidence a link between their interests and the requirement of citizenship for specific state positions. Thus, privileges accorded to immigrants under the U.S. Constitution were further defined as to not only distinguish the limitations of alien status, but also the nature of what it meant to possess citizenship in the United States.

The Rights of Immigrants

As a legal alien, Edmund Foley was a legitimate, permanent resident of United States. He was also eligible, having completed all of the other prerequisites, to become a naturalized citizen after he had resided in the United States for five years. In 1977, Foley applied to take a competitive examination necessary to gain an appointment in the New York State Police. Police authorities, however, applied a New York statute, which precluded persons who were not citizens of the United States from being tested for an appointment to the New York State Police. Foley's application was refused.

Foley appealed to the U.S. District Court for the Southern District of New York, claiming that the state's exclusion of aliens from the New York State Police violated the Equal Protection Clause of the Fourteenth Amendment. After considering the value of the claim, a three-judge assembly of the district court held that the statute was constitutional.

The case was brought to the U.S. Supreme Court. Justices for the majority opinion held that refusing acceptance of aliens into the state's police force did not violate the Fourteenth Amendment. Nonetheless, the opinion submitted by the remaining three, dissenting justices was strong and significant. In presenting their opinion, they cited a decision taken in one of the Court's prior rulings regarding public employment as state police officer. An earlier decree in *Sugarman v. Dougall* (1973), held that "elective and important non-elective positions" that include wide "policymaking responsibilities" were the only state jobs from which aliens could be excluded from participation. Justice Marshall concluded that state troopers participate in the "execution of public policy" by arresting persons who commit a crime or a felony in New York. But, he posited that the conduct of police officers, in principal, was no different than firefighters or sanitation workers whose work in the "execution" of the public policy entailed no more policymaking than the acts of extinguishing a fire or keeping streets clean. In such a sense, troopers participating in "execution of policy," did not constitute a performance of work that could be described as placing them in "executive, policy making positions" of the sort which was clearly excluded in the

Sugarman decision. Pointing out the difference between "execution of policy" and "application of policy," Justice Marshall held that Federal and State Constitutions, statutes, and regulations provide for the *application,* rather than the execution of policy that dictates police conduct. Moreover, since the Court previously recognized the difference between the responsibilities of high officials, and the more limited responsibilities of police officers, Justice Marshall emphasized that the police officer is only applying pre-established rules, not making policy. The dissenting opinion went on to point out that because New York statute authorizes "a New York person" to arrest another who commits a felony or offense in New York (New York Criminal Process Law), the state, in essence, gave authority to all private persons, including aliens, to arrest another person. Thus, because New York Criminal Process Law literally permitted anyone arresting authority, Marshall had serious reservations concerning the majority opinion which claimed that a state trooper's search and arrest authority justified exclusion of aliens from the police force.

Justices Stevens and Brennan, in their dissenting opinion, fully agreed with Justice Marshall. Justice Stevens however, appended the minority opinion and further amplified Marshall's misgivings. He questioned the wisdom of allowing aliens to practice law, but not to be police officers. He cited, as precedent, the case of *In re Griffiths* (1973), wherein the Supreme Court held that a state could not limit the practice of law only to U.S. citizens. Stevens could not understand how the Court could conclude that an alien's legal practice was less involved with public policy making, and therefore more tolerable than an alien serving as a police officer. Neither could he see an appreciable difference between the requisite allegiance and trustworthiness needed by both a lawyer and a police officer. To address such disparity he felt, "the Court should draw the line between policy making and non-policy making positions," and that the Court should identify the group of characteristics that justify the discrimination of aliens. He concluded that the participation of aliens in the so-called making of policy might be refuted, and that the state might not forbid aliens access to employment possibilities without justified reason.

Nonetheless, while the minority opinion presented a viable argument, the Supreme Court's majority opinion prevailed, holding that excluding aliens from the New York State police force was not a constitutional violation. In a 6-3 decision, the Court agreed that because a trooper in New York was a part of the law enforcement body, troopers thus applied public policy. In citing criteria for such judgment, the Court described troopers as officers whose mandate charged them with prevention and detection of crime. They had the power of search, seizure, and arrest without a formal warrant. They could use a weapon to enforce the law. The Court held that the New York statute did not violate the Fourteenth Amendment because police officers were part of the "category of important nonelective officers, who participate directly in the execution of broad public policy." Thus, the majority opinion went on to maintain that by reason of such authority, citizenship might be a relevant factor in fulfilling particular law enforcement positions. The justices conceded that aliens had a right to education, welfare, and the ability to earn and be involved in licensed professions; however, they felt the right to administer government authority and statutes was a privilege reserved for citizens. The majority opinion further reasoned that just as aliens are not permitted to be a member of a jury, it would be also abnormal for citizens to be "subjected to the broad discretionary powers of noncitizen police officers." Neither would it be appropriate for the removal of every statutory exclusion of aliens from all constitutional privileges, because that would erase all differences between citizens and noncitizens, and "depreciate historic values of citizenship." In acknowledging such historical precedent, the justices underscored the notion that becoming a citizen made a person "part of people distinct from others." And with that distinction, a person became "entitled to participate in the process of democratic decision making," such as was involved in the work of police officers. Thus, the Court concluded that the states had a historical power to exclude aliens from participation in a state's official institutions.

Impact

The Supreme Court's majority decision upheld the tacit notion contained in the New York State statute that the position of aliens was different than the position of citizens. However, with that decision, the Court was careful to stipulate that their ruling in no way was intended to encourage exclusion of aliens from practicing their professions. Their only intent was to make clear that only citizens were allowed to be a member of police forces. Moreover, the Court's decision gave New York, hence all states, the freedom to exclude aliens from participating in official state occupations and/or institutions.

An issue that the dissenting opinion embraced, but was largely avoided by the majority decision, was precedence set in the *Sugarman* case. (Even Justice Stewart, who ultimately concurred with the majority decision, expressed doubt about the validity of some of the Court's former decisions.) Minority justices held that the Court's decision only took cursory and superficial account of previous legal interpretations and stipulations forwarded by the Court's decision in the *Sugarman* case. While *Sugarman* specifically delineated between work that involved "policymaking decisions" and positions that merely entailed the execution of policy and despite Marshall's assertion that police duties involved application rather than determination of public policy, the majority decision prevailed.

In determining that the Equal Protection Clause of the Fourteenth Amendment was not violated by a state's citizenship requirement for police officers, the majority opinion held that states must merely show a relationship between their exclusionary policy and a state's interest in that policy. While application of that policy must be examined to determine if a given state position warrants exclusion of aliens, the Court steadfastly maintained that the state police, by virtue of "an almost infinite variety of discretionary powers," justified a state's insistence that police officers also be U.S. citizens. Thus, while being careful to strictly address the exclusion of aliens from the police force, the Court did not address similarly discretionary discrimination in other professions that might be licensed by states. Thus, during the latter decades of the twentieth century amidst a climate of increasing public questioning of constitutional limits on the rights of immigrants, immigrant and alien rights were specifically limited only with regard to positions which touched on making public policy.

Related Cases

Graham v. Richardson, 403 U.S. 365 (1971).
Sugarman v. Dougall, 413 U.S. 634 (1973).
In re Griffiths, 413 U.S. 717 (1973).
Examining Board v. Flores de Otero, 426 U.S. 527 (1976).
Elrod v. Burns, 427 U.S. 347 (1976).
Nyquist v. Mauclet, 432 U.S. 1 (1977).

Bibliography and Further Reading

Biskupic, Joan, and Elder Witt, eds. *Congressional Quarterly's Guide to the U.S. Supreme Court,* 3rd ed. Washington, DC: Congressional Quarterly, Inc., 1996.

HUTTO V. FINNEY

Legal Citation: 437 U.S. 678 (1978)

Petitioners
Terrell Don Hutto, et al.

Respondents
Robert Finney, et al.

Petitioners' Claim
That confining prisoners to isolation cells for more than 30 days is not a violation of the Eighth and Fourteenth Amendments and that the Department of Corrections is exempt from paying the attorney fees of the defendant under the Eleventh Amendment.

Chief Lawyer for Petitioners
Garner L. Taylor, Jr.

Chief Lawyer for Respondents
Philip E. Kaplan

Justices for the Court
Harry A. Blackmun, William J. Brennan, Jr., Thurgood Marshall, John Paul Stevens (writing for the Court), Potter Stewart

Justices Dissenting
Warren E. Burger, Lewis F. Powell, Jr., William H. Rehnquist, Byron R. White

Place
Washington, D.C.

Date of Decision
23 June 1978

Decision
Found that conditions in the Arkansas penal system violated the Eight and Fourteenth Amendments and therefore constituted cruel and unusual punishment.

Significance
The ruling distinguished between acceptable and unacceptable punitive measures in prison and was one of the first successful prisoner lawsuits against a correctional system. The Court determined that isolation for a duration less than 30 days may be constitutional. However, solitary confinement coupled with the prison's living conditions did constitute cruel and unusual punishment, because it jeopardized the health and safety of the inmates.

Background

Prisoners' rights litigation grew out of the Fourteenth Amendment, which applied the Eighth Amendment ban on cruel and unusual punishment to the state level, empowering the accused to challenge their sentences and to seek more humane treatment in prison through lawsuits. Prison riots in the 1950s drew attention to the living conditions and the disciplinary measures used in penitentiaries. The U.S. Supreme Court began reviewing state prison policies and activities during the 1950s, which sparked concern for the well-being of prisoners throughout the country. Prisoner lawsuits against the conditions and practices of the Arkansas correctional system began around 1969.

In 1970, *Holt v. Sarver* ushered in the era of legal battles between Arkansas and its prisoners. As result, the courts became aware of the treatment of prisoners in the Arkansas penal system as well as aware of the indifference to the problems by medical staff. This case helped eliminate the torturing of prisoners and the use of prisoners as guards. Here the courts, for the first time, found a whole prison system faulty and in violation of human rights granted by the Constitution. Judge Henley, who heard the case, characterized the Arkansas prison system as a "dark and evil world completely alien to the free world." *Holt v. Sarver* successfully cleared the way for further litigation by prisoners not only in Arkansas, but also around the country.

The Violations Continue

Hutto v. Finney was a sequel to *Holt v. Sarver* and within this context, inmates objected again to the prison living conditions and disciplinary methods used by the Arkansas prison system. The state correctional system would confine as many as 11 people to isolation cells "eight-by-ten foot rooms without windows" for indefinite periods of time. These isolation cells provided only a sink and a toilet that could only be flushed from outside. Furthermore, inmates confined to the isolation cells received mattresses at night, which were collected in the morning, and although some prisoners had infectious diseases, the mattresses were randomly distributed the next night—a practice that could easily spread diseases around the prison. Prisoners considered

Holt v. Sarver

The Cummins Farm of the Arkansas State Penitentiary was 15,000 acres in size and held approximately 1,000 male inmates. The unit produced cotton, rice, and various other produce. Rather than prison cells, the inmates were housed in open barracks with rows of beds. As most armed guards were inmates serving as "trustees," violent attacks and sexual assaults were common. No rehabilitative or training programs existed.

In 1965, Lawrence J. Holt and several other inmates filed suit against Robert Sarver, Arkansas commissioner of corrections. They claimed their often extended isolation cell confinement, inadequate medical care, and lack of protection from assaults constituted cruel and unusual punishment prohibited by the Eighth Amendment. In an unprecedented response, Federal District Judge J. Smith Henley found that the entire Arkansas system violated the Constitution. The isolation cells were overcrowded and filthy, and the guard trustee system bred hatred and violence. In sum, the overall conditions were "alien to the free world." The court assumed temporary supervision of prison operations.

Until *Holt*, federal court decisions simply identified the unconstitutional character of specific prison practices. The 1969 decision became a watershed ruling for judicial involvement in prison reform by prescribing detailed remedies. An avalanche of court cases followed across the nation in which prisons and county jails were found unconstitutional.

Source(s): Jackson, Bruce. *Killing Time: Life in the Arkansas Penitentiary.* Ithaca, NY: Cornell University Press, 1977.

these conditions a violation of their constitutional rights, a view the district court already shared.

Hearing the trial first, the U.S. District Court for the Eastern District of Arkansas determined that the prison conditions did constitute cruel and unusual punishment. In addition, the court ordered that the Arkansas Department of Correction limit the number of inmates confined in each isolation cell, place a bunk in each cell, stop the low-calorie diet in isolation cells, and confine prisoners to isolation cells for no more than 30 days. Furthermore, the court argued that prison officials acted in bad faith by not improving prison conditions as ordered by previous court decisions and consequently awarded the respondents' attorney's fees paid by the Department of Correction. The Department of Correction appealed the award of attorney's fees as well as the 30 day maximum limit. The U.S. Court of Appeals for the Eighth District agreed with the district court's decision and charged the Department another attorney's fee for the appeal services.

Hutto and the Arkansas Department of Correction then took their dispute to the Supreme Court, maintaining that a isolated confinement period of more than 30 days did not violate prisoner's constitutional rights and that the Department of Correction, as a branch of the state government, was immune to the lower courts' award of attorney's fees under the Eleventh Amendment.

In June of 1978, the U.S. Supreme Court finished reviewing the Federal District Court's decision and upheld its 30-day limit on confinement in isolation cells because the lower court had given the Arkansas correctional system repeated opportunities to improve the cruel and unusual conditions in the isolation cells. The Court reasoned that the 30-day limit would pre-vent overcrowding and hostility resulting from long periods of confinement, and that this limit would not interfere with prison operations and administration. Moreover, the Supreme Court majority agreed with the

Justice John Paul Stevens. © The Library of Congress.

district court's awarding of fee to be paid out of the state's Department of Correction's budget, supporting its finding that prison officials acted negligently in not correcting the system's violations of the Eighth and Fourteenth Amendments. The majority concluded that the Civil Rights Attorney Fees Awards Act of 1976 supported the Court of Appeals decision, since the other party prevailed.

Some Justices Back Petitioner

On the other hand, Justices Powell, Burger, White, and Rehnquist disagreed with awarding of the attorney's fees and contended that the Civil Rights Attorney Fees Awards Act did not authorize the court of appeals to override the Department of Correction's Eleventh Amendment immunity. The Eleventh Amendment prohibits individuals and companies from suing states, granting this privilege only to other states. Justice Rehnquist further argued that the Constitution did not prohibit isolation for a period longer than 30 days in any straightforward way and that the court of appeals should not penalize the Arkansas treasury for the negligence of the prison officials.

Supreme Court Upholds Decision

Nonetheless, the majority agreed with Justice Stevens's opinion and the Court decided to impose the 30-day maximum limit on solitary confinement and to charge the Arkansas Department of Correction attorney's fees in an effort to rid the system of its human rights violations once and for all. Stevens argued that he found "no error in the court's conclusion that, taken as a whole, conditions in the isolation cells continued to violate the prohibition against cruel and unusual punishment" and that "the 30-day limit [would] help to correct these conditions." Consequently, *Hutto v. Finney,* like *Holt v. Sarver* and other related cases, stands as a landmark case concerning prisoner rights trials and legislation. This case is one of the successful challenges to prison conditions where the Supreme Court upheld the lower court's decision and ordered improved living conditions for the entire state correctional system.

Related Cases

Weems v. United States, 217 U.S. 349 (1910).
Holt v. Sarver, (1970).
Estelle v. Gamble, 429 U.S. 97 (1976).

Bibliography and Further Reading

Biskupic, Joan and Elder Witt. *Congressional Quarterly's Guide to the U.S. Supreme Court,* 3rd ed. Washington, DC: Congressional Quarterly, Inc., 1996.

Call, Jack E. "The Supreme Court and Prisoners' Rights." *Federal Probation,* March 1995, p. 36.

Jackson, Bruce. *Killing Time.* Ithaca, NY: Cornell University Press, 1977.

UNITED STATES V. THE PROGRESSIVE

Legal Citation: 467 F. Supp. 990 (1979)

Plaintiff
United States

Defendant
The Progressive, Inc.

Plaintiff's Claim
That *The Progressive* magazine should be prevented from publishing an article concerning how a hydrogen bomb works.

Chief Lawyers for Plaintiff
Thomas S. Martin, Frank M. Tuerkheimer

Chief Defense Lawyer
Earl Munson, Jr.

Judge
Robert W. Warren

Place
Milwaukee, Wisconsin

Date of Decision
26 March 1979

Decision
The Progressive was kept from publishing the article.

Significance
The court's injunction, constituting prior restraint on publication, was the first of its kind in American history.

In 1909, Robert LaFollette, the famous Progressive leader from Wisconsin, founded a monthly news magazine in Madison, Wisconsin called *The Progressive*. The Progressive movement enjoyed some success as a third-party movement in American politics into the 1920s, and the magazine enjoyed a wide circulation. After LaFollette's 1924 bid for the presidency, which won 16 percent of the popular vote, third parties such as the Progressives largely disappeared as a force in American politics until the 1992 campaign of H. Ross Perot. Today, the magazine has a small but loyal audience of approximately 50,000 subscribers.

In 1978, the magazine commissioned freelance writer Howard Morland to write an article concerning government secrecy in the area of energy and nuclear weapons. Energy and nuclear issues were Morland's specialty, and after months of extensive background research Morland wrote "The H-Bomb Secret: How We Got It, Why We're Telling It." On 27 February 1979 Samuel H. Day, Jr., the magazine's managing editor, sent a copy of Morland's draft to the Department of Energy's offices in Germantown, Maryland. Day asked the DOE to verify the technical accuracy of Morland's draft before the magazine published it.

John A. Griffin, DOE's director of classification, and Duane C. Sewell, assistant secretary of energy for defense programs, read the article with alarm. They determined that it contained sensitive material, material that constituted "restricted data" under the Atomic Energy Act. On 1 March 1979 Lynn R. Coleman, DOE's general counsel, phoned Day and Erwin Knoll, another editor involved in the Morland article. Coleman asked that the magazine not publish the article, stating that in addition to DOE, the State Department and the Arms Control and Disarmament Agency believed that publication would damage U.S. efforts to control the worldwide spread of nuclear weapons. The next day, Sewell met with Day, Knoll, and Ronald Carbon, the magazine's publisher.

Despite the government's efforts, on 7 March 1979 the magazine informed Coleman that it would publish the Morland article. The next day, the government sued the magazine in the U.S. District Court for the Western District of Wisconsin, and asked the court to stop publication.

Government Wins Battle, Loses War

The magazine's attorney was Earl Munson, Jr., and the government was represented by Thomas S. Martin and Frank M. Tuerkheimer. On 9 March, the day after the suit was filed, Judge Robert W. Warren in Milwaukee, Wisconsin issued a temporary restraining order against the magazine until a preliminary injunction hearing could be held on 16 March 1979. The hearing was delayed for 10 days, however, and took place on 26 March 1979.

At the hearing, Knoll testified that, despite the government's concerns, the article would actually benefit the United States by promoting public debate free of secrecy:

> [I am] totally convinced that publication of the article will be of substantial benefit to the United States because it will demonstrate that this country's security does not lie in an oppressive and ineffective system of secrecy and classification but in open, honest, and informed public debate about issues which the people must decide.

Judge Warren was in a bind. Under the First Amendment, the injunction that the government wanted constituted a prior restraint on publication, which is difficult to justify legally because of the principle that the law is not broken until an illegal act is actually committed, not before. However, the government had presented very strong evidence that the Morland article would contribute to the spread of nuclear know-how. Warren balanced the two considerations, and came down on the government's side:

> A mistake in ruling against *The Progressive* will seriously infringe cherished First Amendment rights. If a preliminary injunction is issued, it will constitute the first instance of prior restraint against a publication in this fashion in the history of this country, to this Court's knowledge. Such notoriety is not to be sought . . .

> [But] a mistake in ruling against the United States could pave the way for thermonuclear annihilation for us all. In that event, our right to life is extinguished and the right to publish becomes moot.

Therefore, Warren signed a preliminary injunction restraining the magazine, its editors, and Morland from "publishing or otherwise communicating, transmitting, or disclosing in any manner any information designated by the Secretary of Energy as Restricted Data contained in the Morland article." The injunction would last until a full trial could be held.

Having won the first litigation battle, the government ultimately lost the legal war. Inspired by the publicity surrounding the case, other publications such as *Scientific American* began to run articles related to the H-bomb and nuclear power. Neither the Morland article nor any other article, however, contained much more than a general description of how nuclear weapons work and were devoid of the many intricate technical details necessary to design an actual weapon, much less build one. Rather than begin a massive and probably unpopular litigation against the press, the government dropped its proceedings against *The Progressive* before the trial and the Morland article was published. Nevertheless, Warren's injunction, imposing a prior restraint on the article's publication, was the first of its kind in American history.

Related Cases

Trotman v. Board of Trustees of Lincoln University, 635 F.2d 216 (3rd Cir. 1980).
Pepsico, Inc. v. Redmond, 46 F.3d 29 (7th Cir. 1995).

Bibliography and Further Reading

Born Secret: the H-Bomb, The Progressive Case and National Security. New York: Pergamon Press, 1981.

Knoll, Erwin. "The Good it Did." *The Progressive*, February 1991, p. 4.

Morland, Howard. "The Secret Sharer." *The Progressive*, July 1984, pp. 20-21.

Paul, Joel R. "The Geopolitical Constitution: Executive Expediency and Executive Agreements." *California Law Review*, July 1998, p. 671.

Swan, Peter. "A Road Map to Understanding Export Controls: National Security in a Changing Global Environment." *American Business Law Journal*, February 1993, p. 607.

"Through the Looking Glass." *The Progressive*, February 1985, p. 4.

The Secret That Exploded. New York: Random House, 1981.

BELL V. WOLFISH

Legal Citation: 441 U.S. 520 (1979)

Petitioner
Griffin B. Bell

Respondent
Louis Wolfish

Petitioner's Claim
Regulations imposed on pretrial confinees by the New York City Metropolitan Correctional Center did not impinge upon pretrial detainees' constitutional rights (who, as temporary inmates awaiting trial, had the constitutional right to be regarded as detainees who were presumed innocent).

Chief Lawyer for Petitioner
Andrew L. Frey

Chief Lawyer for Respondent
Phylis Skloot Bamberger

Justices for the Court
Harry A. Blackmun, Warren E. Burger, William H. Rehnquist (writing for the Court), Potter Stewart, Byron R. White

Justices Dissenting
William J. Brennan, Jr., Thurgood Marshall, Lewis F. Powell, Jr., John Paul Stevens

Place
Washington, D.C.

Date of Decision
14 May 1979

Decision
Respondents' constitutional right to be treated as unconvicted detainees (despite being incarcerated in a municipal jail) were not violated by New York City Metropolitan Correctional Center regulations and restrictions.

Significance
Due to a lack of adequate facilities, a New York custodial facility placed two pretrial detainees in rooms planned for single occupancy. Because convicted inmates were sharing common areas, pretrial detainees were expected to abide by the same restrictions as those of the prisoners. The justices ruled that pretrial detainees, regardless of where they were housed, were not entitled to receive less restrictive treatment if the institution of confinement had justifiable reasons that mandated sharing common areas with convicted inmates.

The respondent, Louis Wolfish, a detainee in the City of New York Metropolitan Correctional Center (MCC), on behalf of other detainees, demanded abrogation of rules they felt were inappropriately restrictive. The respondents brought a class action lawsuit on behalf of all incarcerated persons (pretrial detainees and sentenced inmates). Incarcerated to ensure their appearance at trial, pretrial detainees were imprisoned with other convicts and, therefore, subject to the same restrictions established by prison management. Unfortunately, because of overcrowding at the facility, administrators had to resort to double-bunking confinees in rooms intended for single occupancy. The detainees, believing that their privacy and personal autonomy were jeopardized, filed a suit in the district court challenging prison conditions and complaining about MCC procedures. Objectionable conditions and procedures cited were "double bunking" (the replacement of single bunks in individual dormitories with double bunks), a "publisher only" rule (inmates could only receive books directly from publishers), the practice of body-cavity searches after visits, a prohibition on packages received (except at Christmas), and the eviction of inmates during room searches. The detainees alleged such practices were unjustified and an infringement on their constitutional rights under the First, Fourth, Fifth, and Fourteenth Amendments.

The U.S. District Court for the Southern District of New York accepted the *Wolfish* case as a class action suit. The court decided that established MCC procedures and restrictions were inordinately restrictive and reasoned that pretrial detainees should not be treated in same manner as sentenced inmates. The district court opined "pretrial detainees (are) presumed to be innocent and held only to ensure their presence at trial"; thus, deprivation of their rights must be justified with "compelling necessity." The court ruled that the MCC should discontinue their restrictive practices, with the proviso that detainees must stay outside their rooms during routine searches.

The court of appeals endorsed the district court and further ordered that conditions of confinement in MCC be evaluated to determine "adequateness" or "inadequateness" of pretrial conditions. The appellate court could not find "compelling necessity" to justify placement of two persons in single occupancy rooms nor (through treatment that presumed guilt) deprivation of due process under the Fifth Amendment. The procedures followed by the New York custodial facility were judged restrictive and unjustified. The U.S. Supreme Court, however, reversed the rulings of the two lower courts.

The court of appeals had found MCC's treatment of pretrial confinees inappropriate according to the "rudiments of due process" and noted that their practices did not meet the burdens of "compelling necessity." But the U.S. Supreme Court found no violation of the Constitution with respect to restrictions and conditions at the detention center. The Court acknowledged that under the Due Process Clause pretrial detainees must not be punished before being proven guilty and that detention was only meant to ensure their presence at trial so detainees should not be treated like convicted inmates. The Supreme Court also reasoned that no matter where inmates were incarcerated or what kind of inmates were accommodated, the purpose of detention excludes a right to live comfortably with no restraints during confinement. Indeed, regulatory restraints could be imposed if "legitimate governmental purpose" existed.

The detainees believed they were burdened by the punishing purpose of MCC regulations. Conversely, petitioners pointed out that holding the detainees was necessary to ensure the appearance of a suspect at trial. Moreover, if incarceration was needed until a defendant was found guilty or innocent, it followed that restrictions during confinement with convicted inmates had to be the same. The majority of justices

agreed. The regulations contributed to safety, maintained order, prevented illegal activities and served a legitimate governmental interest. Contrary to the detainees' claim, the Court did not believe MCC restrictions were intended to unreasonably "torture" inmates.

Although Justice Powell agreed with the findings of the majority opinion of the Court, he nonetheless agreed with dissenting justices that body cavity searches were highly objectionable if administered to pretrial detainees. He opined that anal and genital searches were intrusive and inarguable. Similarly, three other (dissenting) justices found flaws in the majority opinion. They disagreed that the treatment of detainees at MCC was acceptable and instead felt procedures were "arbitrary or purposeless" and represented an unjustifiable burden on the constitutional rights of detainees. The justices pointed out that many detainees were only imprisoned because they could not afford bail; thus, it was not necessary for the petitioner to imply that the state's interest in pretrial detention went beyond a need to ensure a detainee's appearance at trial. The minority justices considered the findings of the Court improper because there did not appear to be any particular, important reason to inflict extraordinary restrictions on pretrial detainees. In writing his own dissenting opinion, Justice Marshall further opined that if there indeed existed a significant, increased need to confine pretrial detainees (especially with convicted inmates), the rationale supporting a governmental interest had to be more extensively justified.

The dissenting justices also disagreed with the Court's rationale in support of the restrictive measures imposed on pretrial detainees at MCC. Justices felt

U.S. Attorney General Griffin Bell holds a jar containing snail darters, 1978. © Photograph by Nick Pergola. Corbis-Bettmann.

"double bunking" was not a proper way to solve the problems of overcrowding in prisons because it was irregular and, especially in the case being considered, intruded on the rights of confinees. They pointed out that MCC administrators might choose less oppressive alternatives to address security concerns. The minority justices could not appreciate a rationale which justified a prohibition on receiving personal packages from outside and a bar to receiving hardback books if they were not sent by the publisher. While prison officials had a reasonable interest in preserving safety, such measures seemed inappropriate given the presumption of innocence which should be granted pretrial detainees. Similarly, the justices felt that evicting detainees from their personal areas during routine searches seemed inappropriate; if inmates were not present during searches, MCC might face an additional, unexpected problem of ensuring the security of personal items or preventing planted contraband by detention officers. However, the minority opinion reserved its most determined objections to comment on the MCC practice of imposing body cavity searches after visits of pretrial detainees. They considered it one of the "most grievous offenses against personal dignity and common decency." Visits were conducted in glass-enclosed rooms and guarded by correction officers, thus it was unlikely that illicit drugs could be passed and smuggled into the facility during visits. (Justice Marshall wryly observed that since inserting objects into the rectum is likely to be a very painful and unpleasant performance, it was difficult to believe that guards would not notice.) Moreover, the justices pointed out that other, more effective options could have been used (e.g., metal detectors, fluoroscope searches of visitor's parcels and handbags) before imposing such a heavy intrusion into a detainee's personal autonomy. Justice Marshall summarized that "only by blinding itself to the facts presented on this record can the Court accept the Government's security rationale."

Justices Brennan and Stevens, in joining with the other two dissenting justices, observed that because a "detainee may not be punished prior to an adjudication of guilt in accordance with due process of law," the Due Process Clause was depreciated and ignored by the Court's ruling. Both men cautioned that the Court should have remained mindful that pretrial detainees were not convicted for any crimes and therefore "their detention may serve only a more limited, regulatory purpose." They cited objective criteria presented in *Kennedy v. Mendoza-Martinez* (1963) that stipulated applicable restrictions for detainees and which, they felt, entitled pretrial detainees at MCC not to be exposed to compulsory constraints nor subjected to treatment beyond the limits of personal rights to which they were constitutionally entitled. Finally, Brennan and Stevens maintained there were no necessary reasons that the New York City Metropolitan Correctional Center's security interests had to be protected with such inordinately severe regulations or procedures.

Impact

Pretrial detainees were deprived of their constitutional rights after the Supreme Court reasoned that institutional needs in this issue justified regulations and administrative procedures at New York City's Metropolitan Correctional Center. The Court found no intention to inordinately punish pretrial detainees nor were restrictive measures a violation of due process of law. The U.S. Supreme Court recognized that sometimes, logical arguments existed for maintaining order and avoiding possible disruptions that might be caused by inmates' unrestrained conduct. In order to achieve its essential aim to provide and preserve discipline and internal order, a detention facility was entitled to impose limitations on certain constitutional rights—such actions were appropriate, legitimate, and permissible. In rendering their decision, the Court definitively held there existed no difference between pretrial confinees and convicted inmates when detained in common facilities. Moreover, the Court ultimately deferred to the expertise of penal officials when determining appropriate practices regarding management and administration of detention facilities.

Related Cases

Kennedy v. Mendoza-Martinez, 372 U.S. 144 (1963).
Wolff v. McDonell, 418 U.S. 539 (1974).
Rhem v. Malcom, 507 F.2d 333, CA2 (1974).
United States ex rel. Wolfish v. Levi, 439 F.Supp. 114 (1977).
Jones v. North Carolina Prisoners' Union, 433 U.S. 119 (1977).

Bibliography and Further Reading

Bennett, Katherine. "Constitutional Issues in Cross-Gender Searches and Visual Observation of Nude Inmates by Opposite-Sex Officers." *Prison Journal,* March 1995, p. 90.

Call, Jack E. "The Supreme Court and Prisoners' Rights." *Federal Probation,* March 1995, p. 36.

Hall, Kermit L., ed. *The Oxford Companion to the Supreme Court of the United States.* New York: Oxford University Press, 1992.

Solove, Daniel J. "Faith Profaned: The Religious Freedom Restoration Act and Religion in the Prisons." *Yale Law Journal,* November 1996, p. 459.

AMBACH V. NORWICK

Legal Citation: 441 U.S. 68 (1979)

Appellants
Gordon M. Ambach, New York Commissioner of Education, and other state officials

Appellees
Susan Norwick, Tarja Dachinger

Appellants' Claim
Norwick and Dachinger should not receive permanent certification as public school teachers because they are not citizens and do not wish to become citizens.

Chief Lawyer for Appellants
Judith A. Gordon, Assistant Attorney General of New York

Chief Lawyer for Appellees
Bruce Ennis, Jr.

Justices for the Court
Warren E. Burger, Lewis F. Powell, Jr. (writing for the Court), William H. Rehnquist, Potter Stewart, Byron R. White

Justices Dissenting
Harry A. Blackmun, William J. Brennan, Jr., Thurgood Marshall, John Paul Stevens

Place
Washington, D.C.

Date of Decision
17 April 1979

Decision
New York may deny public school teaching positions to those aliens that refuse to apply for citizenship.

Significance
A state may bar aliens from government positions with a high degree of responsibility and discretion.

New York law normally denied certification as a public school teacher to noncitizens, unless they declared their intention to acquire citizenship. Susan Norwick was a British subject who moved to the United States in 1965 and married a U.S. citizen. Tara Dachinger, a Finnish subject, came to America in 1966 and also married a U.S. citizen. Although both met the educational requirements for certification, they consistently refused to apply for citizenship. Norwick and Dachinger each applied for a teaching certificate covering nursery school through sixth grade. When their applications were denied, they sued in the district court.

The Fifth and Fourteenth Amendments guarantee all "persons" due process of law and equal protection. The Supreme Court thus has ruled that residents enjoy these rights, whether they be citizens or aliens. However, the Court has tended to grant some leeway to the federal government, which has paramount authority over aliens. Aliens are entitled to the procedural protections of the Fifth Amendment, but the federal government has the authority to deny welfare benefits to aliens and to exclude them from civil service jobs.

The Court has upheld stricter standards against the states. In *Graham v. Richardson* (1971), the Court declared that state laws discriminating against aliens would be subject to its "strict scrutiny." Aliens form a discrete and politically powerless minority. Laws applying exclusively to aliens must be confined within narrow boundaries.

The *Norwick* case reached the district court in 1976. Applying the "close juridical scrutiny" standard of *Graham v. Richardson,* the district court declared that New York had violated the Equal Protection Clause. The New York law, it stated, was too broadly written, since it excluded all aliens from all public school teaching jobs.

New York appealed this decision to the U.S. Supreme Court. In a 5-4 decision, it reversed the district court and declared the New York law constitutional. Justice Powell wrote the majority decision, joined by Justices Burger, Stewart, Rehnquist, and White. Justice Blackmun wrote the dissenting opinion, joined by Brennan, Marshall, and Stevens.

Only Citizens Can Perform the Basic Tasks of Government

Justice Powell began by reviewing previous cases involving aliens. He noted that the Court had permitted states to bar aliens from state employment under certain circumstances. States may practice forms of discrimination that are forbidden to individuals. "The distinction between citizens and aliens, though ordinarily irrelevant to private activity, is fundamental to the definition and government of a state."

In particular, aliens might be forbidden those jobs that require a high degree of responsibility and discretion in the fulfillment of a basic governmental obligation. For example, a state might bar aliens from the police force, a group charged with performing the most fundamental task of government. In all such cases, the state needed only to show "some rational relationship" between the discrimination and a valid state interest.

Like policemen, teachers exercise great discretion in performing a basic task of government. Teachers have direct, often unsupervised, day-to-day contact with students. They act as role models for students, "exerting a subtle but important influence over their perceptions and values." They influence attitudes toward "government, the political process, and a citizen's social responsibility."

They Want to Teach, but They Don't Want to Be Americans

New York's ban on aliens, Justice Powell continued, bears a rational relationship to the state's interest in educating future citizens. The law bars only those aliens who have refused to apply for United States citizenship. Such persons have deliberately chosen to focus their "primary duty and loyalty" on a foreign country and not on the United States.

In dissenting, Justice Blackmun argued that the New York law did not meet the majority's own test. New York, Blackmun stated, had not demonstrated a "rational relationship" between the law and the state's interest in education. For example, New York did not care whether teachers in private schools were citizens. The state even permitted aliens to sit on certain local school boards.

The New York restriction, Blackmun declared, "sweeps indiscriminately" and without precision. It irrationally implies that it is better "to employ a poor citizen teacher than an excellent resident alien teacher." Take, said Blackmun, the example of Spanish language teachers. Why deny this job to a resident alien "who may have lived for 20 years in the culture of Spain or Latin America?"

Justice Lewis F. Powell, Jr., c. 1972. © Archive Photos.

The majority had argued that—in addition to teaching facts—teachers molded a student's values. This emphasis on values also was inconsistent with earlier decisions, Blackmun concluded. For example, the Court allowed aliens to become attorneys, and lawyers are officers of every court in which they practice.

Related Cases
Yick Wo v. Hopkins, 118 U.S. 356 (1886).
Truax v. Raich, 239 U.S. 33 (1915).
Foley v. Connelie, 435 U.S. 291 (1978).

Bibliography and Further Reading
Ancheta, Angelo N. "Protecting Immigrants Against Discrimination." *Trial,* February 1996, p. 46.

Goldfarb, Carl E. "Allocating the Local Apportionment Pie: What Portion for Resident Aliens?" *Yale Law Journal,* April 1995, p. 1441.

The Rights of Aliens and Refugees: The Basic ACLU Guide to Alien and Refugee Rights, 2nd ed. Carbondale: Southern Illinois University Press, 1990.

UNITED STEELWORKERS OF AMERICA V. WEBER

Legal Citation: 443 U.S. 193 (1979)

Petitioner
United Steelworkers of America

Respondent
Brian Weber

Petitioner's Claim
That an affirmative action program implemented by Kaiser Aluminum, in voluntary agreement with the United Steelworkers, did not violate Title VII of the Civil Rights Act of 1964.

Chief Lawyer for Petitioner
Michael E. Gottesman

Chief Lawyer for Respondent
Michael R. Fontham

Justices for the Court
Harry A. Blackmun, William J. Brennan, Jr. (writing for the Court), Thurgood Marshall, Potter Stewart, Byron R. White

Justices Dissenting
Warren E. Burger, William H. Rehnquist (Lewis F. Powell, Jr. and John Paul Stevens did not participate)

Place
Washington, D.C.

Date of Decision
27 June 1979

Decision
Maintained the legality of the affirmative action plan, and reversed the ruling of two lower courts, which had held that the plan violated Title VII.

Significance
Fifteen years after the Civil Rights Act of 1964 and seven years after the implementation of affirmative action programs by the federal government, *United Steelworkers of America v. Weber* was the first Supreme Court case to address the issue of affirmative action in employment. Thus by definition it set a precedent, and the Court's ruling—that affirmative action programs were not in violation of Title VII of the Civil Rights Act as long as private parties entered into such programs voluntarily—seemed to offer a satisfactory litmus test for the legality of affirmative action programs in the workplace. For a few years, Court rulings would follow the pattern set in *Weber*. Eventually, however, it would appear in hindsight that the case had ultimately raised as many questions as it had settled.

Congress passed the Civil Rights Act of 1964, together with the Voting Rights Act of 1965 and other key items of legislation, in an effort to redress severe and long-standing inequities between African Americans and whites in America. As their names suggested, these laws were concerned primarily with securing for all citizens—regardless of color—the basic rights guaranteed in the U.S. Constitution. But the historic civil rights legislation of the mid-1960s had a secondary purpose, an economic one that was embodied in a statement made by President John F. Kennedy when he first introduced the Civil Rights Act in 1963: "There is little value in a Negro's obtaining the right to be admitted to hotels and restaurants if he has no cash in his pocket and no job." In other words, elimination of "separate but equal" facilities such as "White" and "Colored" counters at eating establishments, or removal of the laws which forced African American people to ride in the back of a bus, were not enough in themselves. If the economic plight of African Americans remained such that they could not afford to eat at restaurants, or could not aspire to own their own cars (and thus were no longer forced to ride the bus, front seat or back), that meant that they had not yet begun to enjoy the same degree of economic freedom as whites.

Consequently, during Senate discussion of the Civil Rights Act in 1963, Senator Hubert Humphrey (D-MN) sounded a note very much like that of the president: "What good does it do a Negro to be able to eat in a fine restaurant if he cannot afford to pay the bill? . . . Without a job, one cannot afford public convenience and accommodations." Out of this concern arose the idea of eliminating discrimination in the workplace, for which Humphrey made the case:

> No bill can or should lay claim to eliminating all of the causes and consequences of racial and other types of discrimination . . . [but t]here is reason to believe . . . that national leadership provided by the enactment of Federal legislation dealing with the most troublesome problems will create an atmosphere conducive to voluntary or local resolution of other forms of discrimination.

Civil Rights Act of 1964

The Civil Rights Act of 1964 is the most comprehensive civil rights legislation in U.S. history. Proposed by President John F. Kennedy in 1963, the spirit of the act was to breakdown old patterns of racial segregation and social hierarchy.

Title VII of the act, an extensive source of employment rights, forbids discrimination based on an employee's color, race, national origin, religion, or sex. After 1972, the act applied to all employers or labor unions with 15 or more employees or members, to state and local governments, and to educational institutions. The act created the Equal Employment Opportunity Commission (EEOC) to investigate and prosecute discrimination violations. Its provisions did not apply to federal employees or American Indian tribes.

Additional wide ranging provisions prohibited discrimination in the use of public accommodations or facilities such as hotels, parks, restaurants, theaters, and gas stations. The act also protected an individual's voting rights and directed the Department of Education to oversee school desegregation programs. Title VI authorized the government to cut-off federal funds to any public or private program that did not end discriminatory practices. The act empowered each state attorney general to bring suit against any owner of a public accommodation who discriminated, and against any school system violating desegregation programs.

Source(s): Abraham, Henry J. and Barbara A. Perry. *Freedom & The Court: Civil Rights & Liberties in the United States.* New York: Oxford University Press, 1998.

Hence the language of subsection 703(a) of Title VII of the Civil Rights Act:

> . . . It shall be an unlawful employment practice for an employer (1) to fail or refuse to hire or to discharge any individual . . . because of such individual's race . . . or (2) to limit, segregate, or classify his employees or applicants for employment in any way which would deprive or tend to deprive any individual of equal opportunities . . . because of such individual's race . . .

This was further reinforced in 703(d), which forbade employers, labor organizations, or any combination of the two controlling an apprenticeship or on-the-job training program to discriminate against any individual on the basis of race, color, religion, sex, or national origin.

In spite of its unambiguous language, however, within a short time it became apparent that Title VII was not enough to combat deeply ingrained patterns of discrimination in the workplace. This was the Supreme Court's attitude in *Griggs v. Duke Power Company* (1971), in which it found that a company practice could be discriminatory even if the company did not intend to perpetuate racial imbalance by that policy. For instance, if a company had an open position for a skilled electrician, and freely accepted applications from both African American and white candidates, but African Americans had historically been prohibited from obtaining instruction in the work performed by electricians, then discrimination would be perpetuated, whether or not company policy had been made with that intention in mind. For this reason, in 1972 the federal government, under President Richard Nixon,

enacted Executive Order 11246, which mandated a nationwide policy of affirmative action. Under the guidelines of this program, employers were encouraged to develop a racially balanced workforce, with African Americans and other minorities represented in proportion to their numbers in the population as a whole.

The affirmative action plan challenged in *Weber* came into being two years after Executive Order 11246. In 1974, the United Steelworkers of America union (USWA) entered into a collective bargaining agreement with Kaiser Aluminum Chemical Corporation. The nationwide agreement covered some 15 Kaiser plants, and among its provisions was an affirmative action plan. According to the plan, the company would set aside 50 percent of all openings in its in-plant craft training (i.e., apprenticeship) programs, until the percentage of African American craft workers was equivalent to the percentage of African Americans in the local labor population. At Kaiser's Gramercy, Louisiana plant, only 1.83 percent of all skilled workers were African American, despite the fact that the local labor force was 39 percent African American; hence the company's goal was to have African Americans in approximately 39 percent of its skilled positions. Therefore, in the plant's first year of operation, the company selected seven black and six white trainees for its craft program. The most senior of the African Americans selected had less seniority than several whites—among them Brian Weber—who were rejected for the training program.

Weber instituted a class action suit in the U.S. District Court for the Eastern District of Louisiana. He charged that he and other white employees who were rejected in favor of African American applicants with less seniority had been discriminated against in violation of 703(a) and (d) of Title VII. The district court agreed, and the steelworkers union appealed the case. The Court of Appeals of the Fifth Circuit, in a divided ruling, affirmed the judgment of the lower court. The court held that race-based employment preferences—even those established for the purposes of redressing past imbalances—were discriminatory in violation of Title VII.

The Court Reverses

The case went before the Supreme Court along with two related cases, *Kaiser Aluminum & Chemical Corp. v. Weber et al.* and *United States et al. v. Weber et al.* These were attended by a flurry of *amici curiae* (friend of the court) briefs on both sides. Weighing in for the petitioners, the USWA, were groups such as the American Civil Liberties Union (ACLU), the National Association for the Advancement of Colored People (NAACP), and a number of other unions. Clearly the case had generated a great deal of attention in the legal community, and among the attorneys filing briefs on the side of the petitioners were at least two who would become well-known in later decades: Vernon Jordan for the NAACP, and Gloria Allred for the Women's Equal Rights Legal Defense and Education Fund. A much smaller group filed briefs on the side of the respondent, Weber, among them the California Correctional Officers Association, the Southeastern Legal Foundation, and the United States Justice Foundation.

After hearing arguments on 28 March 1979, the Supreme Court on 27 June reversed the ruling of the lower courts by a vote of 5-2. Writing for a majority that included Justices Stewart, White, Marshall, Blackmun, and himself, Justice Brennan held that neither 703(a) or (d) prohibited race-based affirmative action programs entered into on a voluntary basis by private parties such as the USWA and Kaiser Aluminum.

Weber's case had relied on a literal interpretation of the Court's earlier ruling in *McDonald v. Santa Fe Trail Transp. Co.* (1976), a reliance which the Court found was "misplaced." In *McDonald,* a case which did not involve affirmative action, the Court had ruled that Title VII did indeed protect whites as well as African Americans from certain forms of racial discrimination. But the situation in *Weber* was different, Brennan argued, because Kaiser and USWA had entered into their agreement on a voluntary basis.

Furthermore, the Court held, a closer look at 703(a) and (d) revealed that any interpretation of Title VII which completely eliminated race-based preferences would produce a result "completely at variance with the purpose of the statute." Given the fact that Congress's interest in enacting Title VII had resulted from concern over "the plight of the Negro in our economy," it should be clear that the language in it "was primarily addressed to the problem of opening opportunities for Negroes in occupations which have been traditionally closed to

them." Brennan reinforced his finding on 703(a) and (d) by citing 703(j), which stated that Title VII "shall not be interpreted to require any employer . . . to grant preferential treatment . . . to any group because of . . . race." Race-based preference programs, then, were not to be *required*—but they could be *permitted*.

Justice Blackmun filed a concurring opinion. In it he stated that "additional considerations . . . support the conclusion reached by the Court today." He cited the dissent of Judge Wisdom on the court of appeals, who held that past imbalances in its workforce indicated an "arguable violation" of Title VII on the part of Kaiser Aluminum; hence the affirmative action plan was a "reasonable response." Blackmun favored this more narrow approach, and in spite of agreement with some of the misgivings stated by the dissenters, concurred with the opinion of the majority.

Is It 1984 Yet?

Chief Justice Burger and Justice Rehnquist dissented. Burger, in his opinion, agreed with the Court's judgment—"were I a Member of Congress considering a proposed amendment of Title VII." However, given the fact that they were not making legislation, but were members of the judicial branch of government interpreting a law originating in the legislative branch, he believed that their interpretation of Title VII overstepped the bounds established under the doctrine of the separation of powers. The Court was rewriting Title VII, he said, "to achieve what it regards as a desirable result." And this was unjustifiable, Burger stated, particularly because Title VII was unambiguous in its prohibition of all race-based discrimination. Burger acknowledged the "gross discriminations against minorities" as "one of the dark chapters in the otherwise great history of the American labor movement," and he agreed with all efforts toward voluntary compliance with Title VII. But he quoted Justice Benjamin Cardozo, who in 1921 warned against a "good result" achieved at the expense of judicial honesty.

Rehnquist wrote his own dissenting opinion, in which Burger joined. He began by making reference to *1984,* George Orwell's novel depicting a futuristic police state which manipulates truth and language for its own purposes. The Court's ruling in *Weber,* Rehnquist argued, represented a similar disregard for truth, and he quipped that perhaps they should make it five years later, when it would truly be 1984. Title VII clearly stated that all forms of discrimination in the workplace were prohibited, a view that the Court had affirmed in *Griggs v. Duke Power Company.* Now the Court, like the all-powerful state in *1984,* had suddenly reversed itself, and held that some forms of discrimination were appropriate. Rehnquist followed this with a lengthy discussion of the steps by which Title VII had been passed into law, thereby demonstrating the unambiguous quality of both the language and the intent of that statute.

Impact

The question addressed in *Weber*, Justice Brennan stated, was a narrow one. For more than a century, a large portion of civil rights cases had involved questions of the Fourteenth Amendment; but since in this case no state was involved, the amendment did not apply. Rather, *Weber* was one of a growing list of civil rights cases testing an act of Congress rather than a constitutional amendment. With *University of California v. Bakke* the year before and *Fullilove v. Klutznick* the year after, *Weber* was part of a series of cases that tested the problem of "reverse discrimination"—discrimination against the majority group in favor of the minority. With these three cases, the Court's pattern of protecting affirmative action, even at the expense of apparent injustice to equally qualified white workers, students, or contractors, seemed to be established.

Yet in *Firefighters Local Union No. 1784 v. Carl W. Stotts, et al.* (1984), the Court struck down a lower court's ruling that a fire department laying off workers had to get rid of whites with relatively more seniority, instead of lay off African Americans who had been hired later through an affirmative action program. Title VII, the Court ruled, upheld seniority. In 1986, with *Wygant v. Jackson Board of Education,* the Court reinforced its position in striking down a voluntary affirmative action program that would similarly have laid off more senior whites before less senior African Americans.

On the heels of *Wygant,* however, the Court upheld affirmative action in two other 1986 cases, *Local Number 28 of the Sheet Metal Workers' International v. Equal Employment Opportunity Commission* and *Local Number 93, International Association of Firefighters, AFL-CIO C.L.C. v. City of Cleveland, et al.* It reinforced its position in those cases, which had involved affirmative action for minorities, by its similar ruling in *Johnson v. Transportation Agency* (1987), a case which tested an affirmative action program for women.

Questions revolving around affirmative action and reverse discrimination, however, have remained controversial. In 1996, California voters passed the California Civil Rights Initiative, which forbade any forms of discrimination on the basis of race, sex, color, ethnicity, or national origin. The heated debates that followed, which resulted in a federal court's injunction postponing implementation of the initiative until opponents had an opportunity to challenge it, promise another Supreme Court battle to come.

Related Cases

Griggs v. Duke Power Company, 401 U.S. 424 (1971).
McDonald v. Santa Fe Trail Transp. Co., 427 U.S. 273 (1976).
Regents of University of California v. Bakke, 438 U.S. 265 (1978).
Fullilove v. Klutznick, 448 U.S. 448 (1980).
Firefighters Local Union No. 1784 v. Stotts, 467 U.S. 561 (1984).
Local Number 28 of the Sheet Metal Workers' International v. Equal Employment Opportunity Commission, 478 U.S. 421 (1986).
Wygant v. Jackson Board of Education, 476 U.S. 267 (1986).
Local Number 93, International Association of Firefighters, AFL-CIO C.L.C. v. City of Cleveland, et al., 478 U.S. 501 (1986).
Johnson v. Transportation Agency, 480 U.S. 616 (1987).

Bibliography and Further Reading

Chandler, Ralph C. et al. "Individual Rights: Supplement 2." *The Constitutional Law Dictionary,* Volume 1. Santa Barbara, CA: ABC-Clio, 1991.

Civil Rights and Racial Preferences: A Legal History of Affirmative Action. http://www.puaf.umd.edu.

Hall, Kermit L., ed. *The Oxford Companion to the Supreme Court of the United States.* New York: Oxford University Press, 1992.

Leiser, Burton M., compiler. *Values in Conflict: Life, Liberty, and the Rule of Law.* New York: Macmillan, 1981.

Levy, Leonard W., ed. *Encyclopedia of the American Constitution.* New York: Macmillan, 1986.

U.S. Supreme Court. *United Steelworkers of America v. Weber: Voluntary Affirmative Action Programs.* Chicago: CCH, 1979.

Walker, Richard K. *The Exorbitant Cost of Redistributing Injustice: A Critical View of United Steelworkers of America v. Weber and the Misguided Policy of Numerical Employment.* Newton Centre, MA: Boston College Law School, 1979.

Witt, Elder, advisory editor. *The Supreme Court A to Z. CQ's Encyclopedia of American Government.* Washington, DC: Congressional Quarterly, Inc., 1994.

BEAN V. SOUTHWESTERN WASTE MANAGEMENT CORP.

Legal Citation: 482 F.Supp. 673 (1979)

Plaintiff
Margaret Bean and other Houston residents

Defendant
Southwestern Waste Management Corp.

Plaintiff's Claim
That a decision to issue a permit for a solid waste facility constituted racial discrimination in violation of the Equal Protection Clause of the Fourteenth Amendment.

Chief Lawyer for Plaintiff
Linda McKeever Bullard

Chief Defense Lawyer
Sim Lake

Judge
McDonald

Place
Houston, Texas

Date of Decision
21 December 1979

Decision
Found in favor of Southwestern and denied a preliminary injunction against the facility siting decision.

Significance
The decision established various factors that must be met by an individual in successfully charging that a land use decision is discriminatory. An intent to discriminate must be demonstrated. Decisions that may appear poorly based to some people are not necessarily unconstitutional or illegal. The requirement to establish intent was much more difficult than simply showing that the effects of a governmental decision was unequal on different racial groups.

Following the rise of the civil rights movement in the 1950s and 1960s, a series of cases reached the Supreme Court in the 1970s in which individuals challenged government actions due to the disproportionate impacts on ethnic minorities. In *Washington v. Davis* (1976) and *Arlington Heights v. Metropolitan Housing Corp.* (1977), the Court established tough standards for citizens to prove discrimination. In *Davis,* African American police officer candidates challenged the constitutionality of written tests as being racially discriminatory and in *Arlington Heights* African American Illinois residents challenged the denial of a zoning change by a city blocking a low-income housing development.

In both cases, the Court held that proving a discriminatory racial impact was not enough. The alleged victim must prove an intent to discriminate motivated the decision-makers. Many considered the decisions a blow to the civil rights movement. The Court asserted that a person pressing such a case must not only describe the actual effect of the official action, but also explore the historical background of the decision, the specific sequence of events leading to the challenged decision, how the action may have been a departure from normal procedures, if normal factors were weighed in the decision, and what was the administrative history of the decision. This standard was viewed as almost insurmountable by many.

An earlier case, *Yick Wo v. Hopkins* (1886), involved refusal of a license by the City of San Francisco to a Chinese laundry operator. The Court established a stringent statistical process for examining the disproportionate effect of government actions on minority populations.

Waste Management in Houston

In 1979 the Texas Department of Health (TDH) granted a permit to Southwestern Waste Management Corporation for the construction and operation of a new solid waste facility in East Houston. In reaction, Margaret Bean and several other local residents filed a complaint in October of 1979, challenging the decision. Bean and the other plaintiffs contended the decision was at least partly motivated by racial discrimination in violation of federal law and requested a court order to revoke the permit.

Southwestern denied the allegations and moved to dismiss the case asserting that the state of Texas was the more responsible party for issuing the permit. Southwestern also argued that the district court should not hear the case since Bean had failed to previously request that the TDH conduct a rehearing on the permit.

Laches and State Action

The district court first addressed Southwestern's motion to dismiss the lawsuit and arguments concerning procedural matters. Then the court would consider Bean's request for a preliminary injunction. Judge McDonald, writing for the court, ruled against Southwestern's procedural argument. He pointed out that the Solid Waste Disposal Act allowed revoking a permit through rehearings only in regard to the issues "pertaining to public health, air or water pollution, land use, or violation of this Act or of any other applicable laws or regulations controlling the disposal of solid waste." Bean and the other plaintiffs, instead, sought revocation for none of these reasons, but for an alleged violation of federal law.

Southwestern's request for dismissal of the case was based on the equitable doctrine of laches. Three separate criteria must be established before applying laches. In the *Bean* case, Southwestern must show that a delay occurred in Bean asserting a right or a claim, that no valid reason for Bean's delay existed, and that Bean displayed unreasonable bias against Southwestern. McDonald determined that, based on the evidence, laches was not relevant in the case. Although the site was near completion, and a well attended public hearing had been held on the permit application, McDonald concluded Bean did not know of the site placement until late in the process. Because Bean and the other plaintiffs were not able to exercise their rights, the request for delay was justified.

Southwestern also argued that the lack of state involvement meant the case was not valid and should be dismissed. McDonald found that state action did exist. The permit granted by the TDH was the state action. Therefore, the key question was whether the TDH itself discriminated or supported discrimination in any way. If so, then Bean would be entitled to an injunction to stop operation of the facility.

Next, turning to Bean's request for an injunction, McDonald considered four factors. Bean must demonstrate that: (1) the case had a substantial likelihood of success on the merits; (2) a substantial threat of irreversible injury existed; (3) the threat of injury to Bean was greater than the potential harm of an injunction against Southwestern; and, (4) a preliminary injunction would not harm the public interest.

McDonald found that Bean demonstrated a substantial threat of irreparable injury by arguing they were denied their constitutional rights. McDonald wrote that opening the facility could affect the entire community including "its land values, its tax base, its aesthetics, the health and safety of its inhabitants, and the operation of Smiley High School, located" nearby. McDonald found that "public interest would not be disserved by granting the plaintiffs an injunction."

McDonald noted that a key issue was that Bean had not established a substantial likelihood of a successful lawsuit based on the facts of the case. Bean would have to prove that the decision to issue the permit was based on an intent to discriminate on the basis of race. Statistical evidence was used to establish discriminatory intent in some earlier cases. McDonald also applied the other standards of proof established in *Arlington Heights*.

One avenue for demonstrating racial discrimination was to show how the permit approval by the TDH was part of a geographic pattern of discriminating in the solid waste site placement. However, the available statistical data, both city-wide and in the immediate area, failed to establish such a pattern. For example, city data for 17 sites operating with permits since July of 1978 showed over half of the sites granted permits were actually located in areas with 25 percent or less minority population at the time of their opening. Eighty-two percent of the sites were located in areas with 50 percent or less minority population at the time of their opening. McDonald found that no pattern of discrimination was clearly evident. In addition, no evidence existed as outlined in the *Arlington Heights* case to establish a pattern of discrimination by the TDH.

Next, Bean attempted to prove that the TDH's approval of the permit, in a historical context, constituted discrimination. Three data sets were used to support this argument. However, each set failed to approach standards established in *Yick Wo* and *Gomillion v. Lightfoot* (1960). One set of data focused on two solid waste sites used by the City of Houston. McDonald responded that just two sites were not considered a statistically significant number. However, for those two sites census information revealed that though the proposed site was within an area of 58 percent minority population, the other site was in an area of only 18 percent minority. McDonald concluded that, obviously, no inference of discrimination could be made from this data.

Bean also argued that East Houston contained 15 percent of Houston's solid waste sites, but only seven percent of its population. In addition, only 32 percent of the sites were located in the western half of the city where 73 percent of the white population lived. Since the proposed site location had a 70 percent minority population, Bean argued the statistical disparity indicated racial discrimination. McDonald wrote, "Even considering the 70 percent minority population of the target area, when one looks at where in the target area these particular sites are located, the inference of racial discrimination dissolves." Actually, city-wide data indicated that half of the solid waste sites in Houston were in areas with over 70 percent white population.

However, McDonald noted that in fact a large number of the sites in East Houston were located around the ship channel which contained Houston's industry and not its population. McDonald noted that Houston's population was 39 percent minority, yet only 42 percent of the solid waste sites in the city of Houston were located in tracts with population greater than 39 percent minority. To McDonald this was not a statistically significant difference.

Lastly, Bean asserted that 1975 census data revealed 11 solid waste sites were located in areas with 100 percent minority population, but none were located in census tracts with 100 percent white population. McDonald discounted the 1975 data as not reliable compared to both 1970 and 1979 census data, with the 1975 data appearing to overcount minority population.

Judge McDonald wrote,

> If this Court were TDH, it might very well have denied this permit. It simply does not make sense to put a solid waste site so close to a high school, particularly with no air conditioning . . . It is not my responsibility to decide whether to grant this site a permit. It is my responsibility to decide whether to grant the plaintiffs a preliminary injunction. From the evidence before me, I can say that the plaintiffs have established that the decision to grant a permit was both unfortunate and insensitive. I cannot say that the plaintiffs have established a substantial likelihood of proving that the decision to grant the permit was motivated by purposeful racial discrimination . . .

McDonald ruled that Bean failed to establish a substantial likelihood that the TDH's decision to issue the permit was motivated by purposeful discrimination.

Impact

Bean represented a classic example of citizens fighting the placement of public facilities in their community or neighborhood based on constitutional allegations.

Such facilities were often placed in low-income, inner-city, ethnic neighborhoods. However, the *Bean* decision highlighted that what may be considered poor governmental decisions in some situations were not necessarily unlawful. *Bean* also reinforced tough standards that citizens must meet in legally challenging the placement of public service facilities.

Later known as the "Not in My Back Yard" syndrome, strategies for citizens combating siting decisions of public service facilities grew more sophisticated in the 1990s. Such grass-roots efforts were driven by fears over health risks, lowering property values, higher traffic volume, and noise and air pollution introduced by the developments. As population growth continued in many areas, community planners and governmental decision-makers found it increasingly difficult to place new public service facilities, such as waste disposal sites, without organized opposition from local residents.

To combat the disproportionate effects of more frequently placing non-desirable public facilities in poor and ethnic areas, President Bill Clinton in the 1990s signed an executive order on "environmental justice." The order stressed greater sensitivity of such communities in project planning processes where federal funds were involved.

Related Cases
Yick Wo v. Hopkins, 118 U.S. 356 (1886).
Gomillion v. Lightfoot, 364 U.S. 339 (1960).
Washington v. Davis, 426 U.S. 229 (1976).
Arlington Heights v. Metropolitan Housing Corp., 429 U.S. 252 (1977).

Bibliography and Further Reading
Juergensmeyer, Julian C., and Thomas E. Roberts. *Land Use Planning and Control Law.* St. Paul, MN: West Group, 1998.

Luton, Larry S. *The Politics of Garbage: A Community Perspective on Solid Waste Policy Making.* Pittsburgh: University of Pittsburgh Press, 1996.

Morris, Jane Anne. *Not In My Back Yard: The Handbook.* San Diego: Silvercat Publications, 1994.

Thomas, June M., and Marsha Ritzdorf, eds. *Urban Planning and the African American Community: In the Shadows.* Thousand Oaks, CA: Sage Publications, 1997.

PLYLER V. DOE

Legal Citation: 457 U.S. 202 (1982)

Appellants
J. and R. Doe; certain named and unnamed undocumented alien children, et al.

Appellees
James L. Plyler, et al.

Appellants' Claim
That schools admitting children who could not establish that they had come into the United States legally should still receive state funding.

Chief Lawyer for Appellants
Peter D. Roos for J. and R. Doe et al., Peter A. Schey for certain named and unnamed undocumented alien children et al.

Chief Lawyer for Appellees
John C. Hardy for James L. Plyler et al.; Richard L. Arnett for State of Texas, et al.

Justices for the Court
Harry A. Blackmun, William J. Brennan, Jr. (writing for the Court), Thurgood Marshall, Lewis F. Powell, Jr., John Paul Stevens

Justices Dissenting
Warren E. Burger, Sandra Day O'Connor, William H. Rehnquist, Byron R. White

Place
Washington, D.C.

Date of Decision
15 June 1982

Decision
That the Texas law which withheld funds from local school districts for educating children not legally admitted into the United States and the authorization of these districts to deny these children enrollment, violated the Equal Protection Clause of the Fourteenth Amendment to the Constitution.

Significance
With this decision, states could no longer withhold public education from children simply because they were illegal aliens.

Although it may seem to be a contradiction, the Constitution's Equal Protection Clause provides certain rights to illegal aliens the same as any legal alien or U.S. citizen. The case of *Plyler v. Doe* helped the U.S. Supreme Court guarantee those rights through application of the Equal Protection Clause.

Toward the end of the nineteenth century, the flood of people into the United States made it necessary to begin limiting immigration. That it is illegal to enter the country without permission has not prevented uncountable masses from taking up illegal residence. Border states like California, Arizona, New Mexico, and Texas are especially susceptible to immigrants looking for a better way of life.

In May of 1975, members of the Texas legislature decided that illegal immigration was a problem, and it was necessary to change its existing education statutes. Now, the state would withhold funding from local school districts for educating students who were not legal residents of the United States. The same ruling also allowed local school districts to decide that they could deny admission to students who were illegal residents.

In spite of the ruling, at least one school system—the Tyler Independent School District—allowed children of dubious legal residence to continue enrollment and attendance. This changed in July of 1977 when it announced that in order for these children to enroll, they would be charged a "full tuition fee."

In September of 1977, a class action was filed in the U.S. District Court for the Eastern District of Texas for those Mexican-born, school-age children, who lived in Smith County, and could not prove legal residence in the United States. The action argued that these children were excluded from the Tyler Independent School District public schools.

The suit named as defendants both the school district's superintendent and members of the district's board of trustees. The state of Texas tried to intervene by becoming a *party defendant;* that is, the state wanted the right to provide defense, cross examine witnesses and appeal from judgment.

First, the district court established that there was a class that consisted of all Mexican-born school-age

Right to a Public Education

The American people have always regarded education and the acquisition of knowledge as matters of utmost importance. Yet, the U.S. Constitution makes no mention of education and education has never been acknowledged as a protected fundamental right.

Under the Tenth Amendment, powers not expressly claimed for the federal government became reserved for the states including creation of educational systems. By the early 1900s all states had established free public schools. However, children who were different because of race, disability, culture, language, or gender have often been denied full and fair access to educational opportunities. The tide began to turn in the landmark case of *Brown v. Board of Education* (1954). The Court ruled public education must be made equally available to all children. States uniformly considered education essential to the well-being of society and any child denied the opportunity of an education is denied the chance to succeed in life. In 1975 Congress passed the Education of All Handicapped Children Act providing a free appropriate education in the least restricted environment for all children with disabilities. During the same period, the Court required access to public education for children of aliens, ruled that schools must provide bilingual education, and extended new educational opportunities to girls.

Source(s): Heward, William L. *Exceptional Children: An Introduction to Special Education.* Englewood Cliffs, NJ: Merrill, 1996.

children who lived in the school district. Next, the district court ruled that the defendants had to provide a free education to all members of the plaintiff class, the same as any legal United States resident. This was a *preliminary* ruling, not a permanent decision.

In December of 1977, the plaintiffs moved for *permanent injunctive relief*—assistance from the court to invalidate the statute and correct an injustice. In its case, the state argued that the statutes were merely ways to help avoid financial drains. The district court noted that while these laws may indeed save money, they would not improve the quality of the education. The court also noted that it was only this one small segment of the population which had to bear the responsibilities for the school district's financial burdens. The court pointed out that although these families had immigrated to the United States illegally, they were here to stay and, in fact, may well be future legal residents.

Following this line of reasoning, the court said that these children were poor, lacked crucial English language skills, and were victims of widespread racial prejudice. Preventing them from attending school would only ensure that they remained at the bottom of the socioeconomic ladder. The district court found that the statutes violated the Fourteenth Amendment's Equal Protection Clause which protects all illegal aliens. The district court also ruled that the Supremacy Clause had been violated, that the state law was superseded by the Immigration and Nationality Act as well as federal laws that concerned funding and educational discrimination. The court of appeals decided that the district court had misinterpreted the Supremacy Clause precedents, but agreed that the Texas laws were basically unconstitutional.

This was not the only action against Texas, however. The Judicial Panel on Multidistrict Litigation consolidated other Texas federal district court actions into one case that the U.S. District Court for the Southern District of Texas would hear. This district also confirmed that the Texas law violated the Equal Protection Clause.

Finally, the case was appealed to the U.S. Supreme Court which held the findings of the lower courts in regard to violating the Fourteenth Amendment's Equal Protection Clause. Justice Brennan wrote an opinion that was concurred by Justices Marshall, Blackmun, Powell, and Stevens. It stated that neither the immigrant children's illegal status, nor the state's contention that its resources were limited, established a "sufficient rational basis" for the statute's discriminatory aspects. Brennan's opinion also held that the Equal Protection Clause had been violated. Justice Marshall concurred, saying he believed that to deny public education based on class is "utterly incompatible" with the Equal Protection Clause. Justice Blackmun also concurred, saying that when a state allows some to have a public education and denies it to others, a distinction between classes is inevitable—a fundamental inconsistency with the purpose of the Equal Protection Clause. Finally, Justice Powell agreed, stating that in his opinion, denying education to these children didn't help the state of Texas substantially.

However, Chief Justice Burger was joined by Justice White, Justice Rehnquist, and Justice O'Connor in dissenting, saying that while it was regrettable that Congress had been lax in its enforcement of the country's immigration laws, it was not the Court's responsibility to make up for that laxity.

Related Cases

Yick Wo v. Hopkins, 118 U.S. 356 (1886).

Meyer v. Nebraska, 262 U.S. 390 (1923).

Brown v. Board of Education, 347 U.S. 483 (1954).

Abington School District v. Schempp, 374 U.S. 203 (1963).

Shapiro v. Thompson, 394 U.S. 618 (1969).

Wisconsin v. Yoder, 406 U.S. 205 (1972).

San Antonio Independent School District v. Rodriguez, 411 U.S. 1 (1973).

Ambach v. Norwick, 441 U.S. 68 (1979).

Bibliography and Further Reading

Ancheta, Angelo N. "Protecting Immigrants Against Discrimination." *Trial,* February 1996, p. 46.

Dorsen, N., O. K. Fraenkel, and T. Viles. *Collier's Encyclopedia CD-ROM,* Volume 6. *Civil Liberties In The United States.* P. F. Collier, a Division of Newfield Publications, Inc., 1996.

Goldfarb, Carl E. "Allocating the Local Apportionment Pie: What Portion for Resident Aliens?" *Yale Law Journal,* April 1995, p. 1441.

Gonzalez, Maria Luisa, and Ana Huerta-Macias. "Mi Casa es Su Casa." *Educational Leadership,* October 1997, p. 52.

Hall, Kermit L., ed. *The Oxford Companion to the Supreme Court of the United States.* New York: Oxford University Press, 1992.

"Heading North: After Proposition 187." *The Economist,* November 19, 1994, p. A29.

McWhirter, Darien A. "Urban Residence and Poverty." Chapter 7 *Exploring the Constitution,* Volume 1, *Equal Protection.* Phoenix: Oryx Press, 1995.

Miller, Berna. "Educating Immigrant Children: It's Got to be Done." *Current,* January 1998, p. 3.

Rosen, Jeffrey. "The War on Immigrants: Why the Courts Can't Save Us." *The New Republic,* January 30, 1995, p. 22.

Schwartz, Herman. "No: The Law is Clear, Only the Court has Changed." *ABA Journal,* February 1995, p. 43.

Simpson, Michael D. "Immigrant Backlash Puts Kids at Risk." *NEA Today,* February 1995, p. 17.

Stein, Dan. "Yes: The Supreme Court Must Re-evaluate Existing Law." *ABA Journal,* February 1995, p. 42.

The U.S. Supreme Court, 1982. © UPI/Corbis-Bettmann.

MARTINEZ V. BYNUM

Legal Citation: 461 U.S. 321 (1983)

Petitioner
Oralia Martinez

Respondent
Raymond L. Bynum

Petitioner's Claim
The Texas Education Code 21.031(d) violated the Equal Protection Clause of the Fourteenth Amendment because it denied tuition-free public schooling to minors who were living away from a "parent, guardian, or other person having lawful control of him" for the sole purpose of attending "public, free schools" in the state of Texas.

Chief Lawyer for Petitioner
Edward J. Tuddenham

Chief Lawyer for Respondent
Richard L. Arnett

Justices for the Court
Harry A. Blackmun, William J. Brennan, Jr., Warren E. Burger, Sandra Day O'Connor, Lewis F. Powell, Jr., (writing for the Court), William H. Rehnquist, John Paul Stevens, Byron R. White

Justices Dissenting
Thurgood Marshall

Place
Washington D.C.

Date of Decision
2 May 1983

Decision
The Supreme Court held that Texas Education Code did not violate the Equal Protection Clause of the Fourteenth Amendment. States were permitted by the Constitution to extend the availability of tuition-free education only to *bona fide* residents.

Significance
In affirming the decisions of lower courts, the Court upheld the notion of a state's right to administer internal affairs which affected all U.S. citizens living within a state's jurisdiction. Opponents of this ruling maintained that the ethnic background of their students was the "hidden" criteria by which Texas statute determined access to free education. Nonetheless, the Court's opinion made it possible for states to embark on legislative change which would not always recognize the problems of non-citizens if a state could demonstrate that legislation served a justifiable state interest.

Even though his parents were Mexican citizens who resided in Reynosa, Mexico, Roberto Morales was born in McAllen, Texas, and therefore a United States citizen by birth. At the age of seven, he left Reynosa in 1977 to live with his sister who was married and lived in McAllen. The sole purpose for his return was to gain access to tuition-free education by attending school in the McAllen Independent School District. Although his sister, Oralia Martinez, was his custodian, she was not and did not ever intend to be his legal guardian. Because, according to the Sections 21.031(b) and (c) of the Texas Education Code [hereafter referred to as Section 21.031(d)] a child was entitled to a tuition-free education only if "his parent, guardian, or person having lawful control of him" resided in the school district, Mrs. Martinez did not qualify as a person who had "lawful control" of Roberto. The McAllen Independent School District denied Morales's application for admission in the fall of 1977.

In December of 1977, Oralia Martinez and four other adult custodians of school-age children filed suit in the District Court for the Southern District of Texas against the Texas Commissioner of Education, the Texas Education Agency, four local school districts, and local school officials in each adult's respective school districts. Petitioners claimed that Section 21.031(d) violated the Constitution, including the Equal Protection Clause, the Due Process Clause, and the Privileges and Immunities Clause. Their main claims were that the traditional definition of *bona fide* residency was not applicable, and that statutory provisions were violative. Granting educational benefits only to children of Texas residents and children whose custodial guardians had official, legal guardianship was inconsistent with the Equal Protection Clause of the Fourteenth Amendment.

Petitioners asked for preliminary and permanent injunctive relief. In 1978, a preliminary injunction was denied by the district court. That court's findings characterized the admissions policy of the (sued) school boards as being more than liberal in accepting children into their schools. Even if their parents or legal guardians did not live in the school district children were granted admission if the reason for living apart from birth/legal parents was not strictly for the purpose of attending a particular school. In response to the court's decision, petitioners narrowed the scope of their petition to claim that Section 21.031(d) was unconstitutional on its face. Again, the district court adjudicated in favor of the respondents. On appeal, the U.S. Court of Appeals for the Fifth Circuit affirmed. Considering of the importance of the issues presented by this case, the U.S. Supreme Court agreed to consider the case on *certiorari*.

An 8-1 Decision

A majority of eight justices affirmed the decision of the lower courts and ruled that Section 21.031(d) contained *bona fide* residence requirements which satisfied constitutional standards. The justices characterized the Texas Education Code residence requirement as narrowly defined, uniformly applicable, and appropriately designed to assure that only state residents enjoyed services provided by the state of Texas. Such a requirement did not violate the Equal Protection Clause of the Fourteenth Amendment. The Court emphasized that the uniform admissions policy enforced by Texas school districts (respondents) specifically defined *bona fide* residence requirements for the purpose of determining eligibility of access to free public education.

In explaining their ruling, the written majority opinion cited *Vladis v. Kline* (1973), a case wherein the state statute contained unconstitutional enrollment criteria which created an unappealable assumption of nonresidency for state university students. Unlike Section 21.031(d) which stipulated criteria to which a parent or guardian had to adhere, the state of Connecticut denied residence status to all students who, before they applied for admission, had legal addresses outside of the state regardless of reason. Conversely, the Court concluded that because new or transient residents to Texas were not automatically rendered ineligible, the Texas Education code, did not affect the right of interstate travel. The code simply required that a person should establish residence before asking for the services that were limited to residents.

The justices for the majority believed school districts were justified in requiring that parents of school-aged children must live in the school district where a child would attend school, with intention to stay there, in order to satisfy the basic residence criteria. The Court accepted the respondents' argument that without resident requirements, the proper planning and operation of primary and secondary schools would significantly suffer. An important constitutional criteria was served—the state had authored reasonable legislation because it supported a justifiable interest to preserve state educational financial funds for Texas residents. Indeed, the justices felt that Section 21.031(d) was far more "generous" in granting benefits not only for residents, but for all children whose reason for living in a

district was not exclusively limited to attending a school. A child such as Roberto Morales could attend public school in Texas without paying tuition, if his parents or legal guardians had a *bona fide* intention of remaining in the school district indefinitely. But moreover, the statute also granted free education to children who parents did not intend to remain in the school district indefinitely if the child was not living in the district only to attend a school (e.g., proximity to needed medical care).

Marshall Dissents

As the sole member of the Supreme Court in dissent, Justice Marshall believed that Section 21.031(d) denied some children primary education arbitrarily and was, therefore, unconstitutional on its face under the Equal Protection Clause. Marshall maintained that Texas Education Code subjectively interpreted the motive for school-aged children in the care of the petitioner residing in Texas. A justifiable state interest was, thus, not served. Marshall's dissent turned on a point the majority opinion upheld: Texas statute "employed a traditional residence requirement in a uniform fashion" that was even more "generous" because it permitted some nonresidents to receive free education. Justice Marshall concluded that the Court incorrectly equated the Texas statute with a residence requirement. Although the state might reserve its educational resources for its residents, there was no reasonable support for the rationale that the state might close its schools for those who were not residents who domiciled in the state of Texas. There was a decided difference between the concept of "residence" and "domicile." Under the Texas law, "residence may be temporary or permanent," but generally, residence required conditions more than simple "accommodation." According to the Texas Supreme Court ruling in *Snyder v. Pitts* (1951), "the element of intent to make it a permanent home is not necessary to the establishment of a second residence away from the domicile." Further, Justice Marshall argued the point that the state did not apply that test uniformly. Section 21.031(d) denied free public education to any child who intended to leave the district some time in the future. However, the statute also allowed tuition-free education to children who would stay in the district only for six months or less (whether or not parents were residents of Texas) if they were in the district seeking temporary medical care. On the other hand, the state excluded from free public education a child like Morales who was born in Texas, a legal U.S. citizen, entering the district at the age of seven with the intent of remaining in his school district for at least ten years, until the end of his education. Thus, Marshall reasoned, the Texas statute was not sufficiently, narrowly tailored to achieve the state's claimed interest in preserving educational and financial resources for only state residents.

Impact

In rendering their decision, the U.S. Supreme Court chose to consider the residence of a child's parents or legal guardians as justifiable criteria for determining eligibility and, therefore, access to free public education. The justices did not accept the broader claim of the petitioner that the child was eligible to free public education, regardless of residence of parents, because the student was a legal U.S. citizen who intended to indefinitely reside in the respective school district. Neither did the Court consider that if public school funding/appropriations were commonly funded through property tax receipts within individual school districts, then the rationale of domicile may have been (as Justice Marshall contended) a more dubious criteria than considering "residence" as defined in the Texas Supreme Court ruling in *Snyder v. Pitts*. As such, the majority justices returned to a tradition of jurisprudence (more common in the nineteenth century) which tended to privilege and recognize the sovereignty of individual states with respect to internal matters such as the education of its residents.

The district court, the court of appeals, and the U.S. Supreme Court held that the Texas statute did not violate the Fourteenth Amendment, as petitioner Oralia Martinez claimed. They found that the statute was narrowly tailored, carefully designed, and justified by the state's interest to preserve financial funds for residents closely related to the state. But the dissenting opinion of Justice Marshall challenged the constitutionality of the statute and justification of the *bona fide* residence requirements. His opinion could support the changes that were necessary regarding the rights of the school-age children in the field of the tuition-free public primary education.

Related Cases

Inhabitants of Warren v. Inhabitants of Thomaston, 43 Me. 406 (1857).

Dwyer v. Matson, 163 F.2d 299 (CA10 1947).

Snyder v. Pitts, 150 Tex.407 (1951).

Whitney v. State, 472 S. W. 2d 524 (Tex. Crim. App. 1971).

Dunn v. Blumstein, 405 U.S. 330 (1972).

Brownsville Independent School District v. Gamboa, 498 S. W. 2d 448 (Tex. Civ. App. 1973).

San Antonio Independent School District, et al. Appellants v. Demetrio P. Rodriguez, et al. 411 U.S. 1 (1973).

Vladis v. Kline, 412 U.S. 441 (1973).

Memorial Hospital v. Maricopa County, 415 U.S. 250 (1974).

Milliken v. Bradley, 418 U.S. 717 (1974).

Arredondo v. Brockette, 482 F. Supp. 212 (1979).

Plyler v. Doe, 457 U.S. 202 (1982).

BOB JONES UNIVERSITY V. UNITED STATES

Legal Citation: 461 U.S. 574 (1983)

Petitioner
Bob Jones University

Respondent
Internal Revenue Service (IRS)

Petitioner's Claim
That as a non-profit educational institution, it was entitled to tax-exempt status under Section 501(c)(3) of the Internal Revenue Code of 1954 (IRC), and that the revocation of that status by the IRS—because of the school's policy of racial discrimination in admissions—constituted an abridgement of rights under the freedom of religion clauses of the First Amendment.

Chief Lawyer for Petitioner
William G. McNairy

Chief Lawyer for Respondent
Reynolds, U.S. Assistant Attorney General

Justices for the Court
Harry A. Blackmun, William J. Brennan, Jr., Warren E. Burger (writing for the Court), Thurgood Marshall, Sandra Day O'Connor, John Paul Stevens, Byron R. White

Justices Dissenting
Lewis F. Powell, Jr., William H. Rehnquist

Place
Washington, D.C.

Date of Decision
24 May 1983

Decision
That the petitioner did not qualify as a tax exempt organization under Section 501(c)(3), because its policy of racial discrimination was a goal clearly in opposition to common law standards of charity, and the government's interest in eradicating racial discrimination outweighed whatever burden denial of tax exemption would place on the petitioner.

Significance
Bob Jones University v. United States, along with the companion case of *Goldsboro Christian Schools v. United States*, established the higher importance of the federal interest in ending racial discrimination over that of preserving the tax-exempt status of religious institutions.

Bob Jones University, located in Greenville, South Carolina, was a nondenominational and fundamentalist Christian educational institution. In line with its founders' segregationist beliefs, allegedly based on an interpretation of the Bible, the school practiced racial discrimination in admissions and prohibited African Americans from enrolling. At the same time, the school enjoyed tax-exempt status as a charitable institution under 501(c)(3) of the Internal Revenue Code (IRC) of 1954.

Then in 1970, in the case of *Green v. Connally*, a special three-judge district court ordered the Internal Revenue Service (IRS) to withhold tax exemption from private schools in Mississippi that continued to practice racial discrimination in their admissions policy. The Supreme Court upheld the decision on appeal, in *Coit v. Green* (1971). Therefore the IRS issued Revenue Bulletin 71-447, which revoked tax exemption for any private school that discriminated against applicants on the basis of race. Not only did the new rule require such schools to pay federal taxes, it also removed the tax deduction for individuals who made donations to the school. In 1970, Bob Jones University was informed that it would lose its tax-exempt status, but the school continued to maintain that it was entitled to such status.

In 1975, the Court of Appeals of the Fourth Circuit outlawed racial discrimination by all private schools, a decision upheld by the Supreme Court in *Runyon v. McCrary* (1976). Therefore Bob Jones University was required to open its doors to non-white applicants, and it did allow unmarried black applicants to enroll—but the school maintained a policy of punishing interracial dating with expulsion. In 1976, the university filed tax returns for the period from 1 December 1970 to 31 December 1975, and paid a tax of $21 on one employee for the calendar year of 1975. The IRS responded by informing the school that it owed $489,675.59 in taxes, plus interest.

The U.S. District Court for the District of South Carolina held that by revoking the school's tax exemption, the IRS had overstepped its delegated powers and ordered the IRS to pay back Bob Jones' $21. The Fourth Circuit Court of Appeals, however, reversed the deci-

Private Institutions and Segregation

Private institutions have played an important role in American education. Private schools and universities were dominate in the United States until growth of state-sponsored school systems in the late nineteenth century. As public school desegregation policies came to the forefront in the mid-1950s, local efforts grew to preserve segregation or a least to delay racial integration, particularly in the South. Various states used different tactics, including partially funding the quickly growing number of private segregated schools. One Virginia county completely closed its public school system. The prevailing argument was racial discrimination in private institutions did not violate the Fourteenth Amendment. Segregation proponents claimed they were promoting public health and morals, and preserving the peace.

Federal policy soon became established that private schools with racially-biased policies could not receive public subsidies. Additionally, sectarian private schools could not even discriminate in their admissions based on the Civil Rights Act of 1866. However, "white flight" to private institutions substantially undermined desegregation in public schools as the American education system essentially became racially separate and unequal. Proposals for tuition tax credits, or vouchers, to support private schools in the 1990s propelled debate over the impact of private institutions on community-based racial desegregation goals.

Source(s): Devins, Neal E. *Public Values, Private Schools.* New York: The Falmer Press, 1989.

sion in a divided opinion. Citing *Green v. Connally,* it held that Bob Jones did not meet the commonly understood requirements for a charity, since it practiced racial discrimination.

Defining a Charity

Chief Justice Burger gave the opinion for the Court. He addressed the petitioner's close reading of 501(c)(3): in their interpretation, the rule guaranteed charitable status to corporations organized and operated exclusively for religious or educational purposes, and since their purposes were both, they fell well within the exemption. The chief justice, however, said that it was the duty of the Court to "go beyond the literal language of a statute if reliance on that language would defeat the plain purpose of the statute." Citing a host of earlier Court decisions, as well as speeches in Congress and other official pronouncements of the U.S. government, Burger established a definition of charity. In *Perin v. Carey* (1861), for instance, it was stated that courts should "protect . . . a gift . . . to public charitable uses, provided the same is consistent with local laws and public policies." In a 1917 speech to Congress during a debate on charitable exemptions, a senator had opined that "For every dollar that a man contributes to these public charities, educational, scientific, or otherwise, the public gets 100 percent."

Taxes and Religious Freedom

Under such a definition of charity—as benefiting the common good—it was clear that Bob Jones University did not meet the requirements due to its policy of racial discrimination. The Court had long held that discrimination in public education was contrary to federal pol-

icy, and thus the university was not pursuing an aim that would benefit the public. As for the petitioners' claim that only Congress was able to alter the tax laws, not the IRS, Burger cited the legislative body's tendency to accord the IRS broad powers in making and carrying out tax policy.

The petitioner also addressed the argument that to censure an institution for its sincerely held religious beliefs was a violation of religious freedom under the First Amendment. Burger again cited a host of cases showing that, where the exercise of religious belief is contrary to "an overriding governmental interest," the government had authority to justify limits on religious freedom. An example was the case of *Prince v. Massachusetts* (1944), in which the Jehovah's Witnesses' policy of putting children to work distributing literature came into conflict with child labor laws. As Burger quoted, "The Court found no constitutional infirmity in 'excluding [Jehovah's Witness children] from doing . . . what no other children may do'." And in any case, as the chief justice pointed out, the case revolved not around the abridgement of freedom, but rather the abridgement of tax exemption. (This is rather akin to the arguments in the late 1980s over public funding of controversial artwork. The pro-funding side portrayed it as a question of censorship when in fact the debate revolved around giving or withholding funds.)

Given these considerations, therefore, the Court found that the IRS had acted correctly in its interpretation of 501(c)(3), and it affirmed the judgments of the court of appeals. In his opinion, Chief Justice Burger was joined by the entire Court except for Justices Powell and Rehnquist. Justice Powell concurred with all parts of the decision except certain aspects of the government's right to abridge religious freedom in view of an overriding interest. As for Justice Rehnquist, he agreed with the Court's observation that "there is a strong national policy in this country opposed to racial discrimination." His problem with the decision was that, in his view, it was the job of Congress—and not the IRS or the courts—to decide that organizations which practice racial discrimination are not eligible for 501(c)(3) exemption.

Related Cases

Perin v. Carey, 65 U.S. 465 (1861).

Prince v. Massachusetts, 321 U.S. 296 (1944).

Green v. Connally, 330 F. Supp. 1150 (1970).

Coit v. Green, 404 U.S. 997 (1971).

Runyon v. McCrary, 427 U.S. 160 (1976).

Goldsboro Christian Schools v. United States, 461 U.S. 574 (1983).

Bibliography and Further Reading

Biskupic, Joan, and Elder Witt, eds. *Congressional Quarterly's Guide to the U.S. Supreme Court,* 3rd ed. Washington, DC: Congressional Quarterly, Inc., 1996.

Boyarin, Jonathan. "Circumscribing Constitutional Identities." *Yale Law Journal,* March 1997, p. 1537.

Eskridge, William N., Jr. "A Jurisprudence of 'Coming Out': Religion, Homosexuality, and Collisions of Liberty and Equality in American Public Law." *Yale Law Journal,* June 1997, p. 2411.

Hacker, Jonathan D. "Bargaining with the State." *Michigan Law Review,* May 1994, p. 1855.

Hall, Kermit L., ed. *The Oxford Companion to the Supreme Court of the United States.* New York: Oxford University Press, 1992.

Murphy, Walter F. et al. *American Constitutional Interpretation,* 2nd ed. Westbury, NY: Foundation Press, 1995.

PALMORE V. SIDOTI

Legal Citation: 466 U.S. 429 (1984)

Petitioner
Linda Sidoti Palmore

Respondent
Anthony J. Sidoti

Petitioner's Claim
Depriving a parent of custody because the parent is involved with someone of another race violates the Fourteenth Amendment's Equal Protection Clause.

Chief Lawyer for Petitioner
Robert J. Shapiro

Chief Lawyer for Respondent
John E. Hawtrey

Justices for the Court
Harry A. Blackmun, William J. Brennan, Jr., Warren E. Burger (writing for the Court), Thurgood Marshall, Sandra Day O'Connor, Lewis F. Powell, Jr., William H. Rehnquist, John Paul Stevens, Byron R. White

Justices Dissenting
None

Place
Washington, D.C.

Date of Decision
25 April 1984

Decision
Using race as a factor in awarding child custody violates the Fourteenth Amendment.

Significance
The Court recognized the existence of racial biases in society but held that the law cannot govern in deference to those biases.

The Supreme Court rarely hears child custody cases, but it issued a ruling in *Palmore v. Sidoti* because a constitutional issue was at stake: whether awarding custody based on anticipated racial prejudices violated the Fourteenth Amendment's Equal Protection Clause. Reversing the judgments of the lower courts, the Supreme Court ruled that a parent may not be deprived of child custody solely because he or she is involved in an interracial relationship that might cause the child to face harassment from a disapproving society.

When Linda Sidoti Palmore and Anthony J. Sidoti, both white, were divorced in May of 1980, custody of their three-year old daughter Melanie was awarded to the mother. In September of 1981, the father filed a petition to change the custody status because the living environment at the mother's house had changed. The father said that on several occasions the mother had not properly looked after their daughter, and he protested that the mother was living with a black man, Clarence Palmore, Jr., whom the mother married in November of 1981.

While noting the father's allegations about the mother's treatment of Melanie, the Florida trial court found that both parents were unquestionably devoted to their child and able to provide adequate housing for her. The trial court also said the new spouses of both parents were respectable people. In marrying a black man, however, the mother had created a home environment that both the father and many people in society found unacceptable, the trial court said.

> This Court feels that despite the strides that have been made in bettering relations between the races in this country, it is inevitable that Melanie will, if allowed to remain in her present situation . . ., suffer from the social stigmatization that is sure to come.

The trial court awarded custody to the father, and Florida's Second District Court of Appeals affirmed the ruling without issuing a written opinion. A unanimous Supreme Court then reversed the rulings of the lower courts. The heart of the Fourteenth Amendment, Chief Justice Burger argued, was to eliminate all forms of racial discrimination imposed by the government. In order to be allowed under the Constitution, racial clas-

Interracial Adoption

Interracial, or transracial, adoption involves children whose race or ethnicity differs from that of their adopting parents.

Interracial adoptions within the United States are predominately African American/white adoptions. In 1995, 100,000 children, of which 45 percent were black and 35 percent white, needed adoptive homes. Yet, approximately 67 percent of all families waiting to adopt are white, with some eager to receive a black child. However, due to societal taboos against race mixing, agencies commonly block adoption of black children by white families. Black children are three times less likely than white children to be adopted. As of 1997, federal law prohibited states from denying adoption on the basis of race, color, or national origin. In 1998, Tran-

sracial Adoption Group of Los Angeles estimated 175,000 black or biracial children had been adopted by white parents since 1968, but fewer than 1,000 such adoptions occurred nationwide in 1997. Numbers have vacillated due to changing attitudes and laws.

American families frequently turned to international adoption. In 1997, 3,816 adoptions were from Russia, up from 1,896 in 1995; 3,597 from China, up from 2,130 in 1995; 1,654 from South Korea; 1,228 from North America, excluding the United States; 548 from South America; and, only 186 from Africa.

Source(s): Lewin, Tamar. "New Families Redraw Racial Boundaries." *The New York Times.* 27 October 1998.

---

sifications must serve a "compelling governmental interest" and be absolutely necessary for meeting that purpose. The state's duty to protect children from being harassed by racially intolerant people is a compelling interest, Burger wrote, but it is unconstitutional to protect the children by codifying social prejudices into law.

> The Constitution cannot control such prejudices but neither can it tolerate them. Private biases may be outside the reach of the law, but the law cannot, directly or indirectly, give them effect.

Burger cited the Supreme Court's ruling in a similar case, *Buchanan v. Warley* (1917), in which the Court overturned a Kentucky law prohibiting blacks from buying houses in white residential areas. Although the ordinance aimed to preserve the public peace by making racial confrontations less likely, it did so by taking away constitutionally protected rights.

Recognizing the reality of racial prejudices in American society, Burger said a child living with a racially mixed couple might face problems that a child living with homogenous parents would not. Still, the Court had "little difficulty" concluding that anticipated racial prejudice in society was not sufficient justification for overriding the constitutional right to equal protection under the law.

Related Cases
Buchanan v. Warley, 245 U.S. 60 (1917).
Loving v. Commonwealth of Virginia, 388 U.S. 1 (1967).

Bibliography and Further Reading
Barbash, Fred. "Supreme Court, 9-0, Bars Race from Rulings on Child Custody." *The Washington Post*, April 26, 1984, p. A3.

Forde-Mazrui, Kim. "Black Identity and Child Placement: The Best Interests of Black Biracial Children." *Michigan Law Review*, February 1994, p. 925.

Goldstein, Joseph, et al. *The Best Interests of the Child.* New York: The Free Press, 1996.

Robert Shapiro, 1996. © Photograph by Laurence Agron. Archive Photos.

ALLEN V. WRIGHT, AND DONALD T. REGAN V. INEZ WRIGHT

Legal Citation: 468 U.S. 737 (1984)

Petitioners
W. Wayne Allen, Donald T. Regan

Respondents
Inez Wright, et al.

Petitioners' Claim
Petitioners claimed that although the suit sought declaratory and injunctive relief, the respondents did not have sufficient standing to bring suit since their children never applied for admission to any private school.

Chief Lawyer for Petitioners
Rex E. Lee, U.S. Solicitor General in case No. 81-970, and William J. Landers II, in case No. 81-757

Chief Lawyer for Respondents
Robert H. Kapp

Justices for the Court
Warren E. Burger, Sandra Day O'Connor (writing for the Court), Lewis F. Powell, Jr., William H. Rehnquist, Byron R. White

Justices Dissenting
Harry A. Blackmun, William J. Brennan, Jr., John Paul Stevens (Thurgood Marshall did not participate)

Place
Washington, D.C.

Date of Decision
3 July 1984

Decision
The U.S. Supreme Court held that the respondents (parents of African American public school students in seven states undergoing desegregation) lacked standing to bring suit alleging that the IRS had not fulfilled its obligations regarding the denial of tax-exempt status to private schools that practiced racial discrimination with respect to student enrollment.

Significance
Parents of African American public school children filed a nationwide class action suit alleging that, by permitting tax exemptions for racially discriminatory schools, the IRS did not fulfill its obligation according to provisions of IRS Code. Although the importance of the respondents' claim seemed to be its focus on a government (IRS) practice that seemed to foster expansion of segregated private schools, the Court cited determining criteria as requiring proof of "injury in fact" that was "fairly traceable" to government action.

In 1976, the parents of African American children attending public schools that were undergoing desegregation brought a nationwide suit to the U.S. District Court for the District of Columbia Circuit. Their claim maintained that the Internal Revenue Service (IRS) was not acting in accordance with U.S. Code, which mandated denial of tax-exempt status to racially discriminatory private schools. (At the time, U.S. Code and IRS policy required that a school not be segregated and admit "students of any race in order to be granted tax-exempt status.")

Parents who brought suit had listed 32 segregated private schools with tax-exempt status in their respective domicile areas. In response, W. Wayne Allen, headmaster for one of the private schools named in the suit, initiated a motion to dismiss the complaint based on the parents' lack of standing to bring suit. The district court accepted Allen as a defendant, which led to the stalling of the judicial process for several years. During this period, the IRS proposed a new set of revenue procedures to further define the requirements a private school had to meet in order to obtain tax-exempt status. Although legislation strengthening IRS guidelines was blocked in the U.S. Congress until the end of 1980, the district court granted Allen's motion to dismiss the lawsuit. That decision was subsequently reversed by the U.S. Court of Appeals for the District of Columbia Circuit, which held that parents had standing to bring suit because, as their suit claimed, their children suffered from what amounted to government sanctioning of segregated institutions through tax exemptions. Accordingly, the court of appeals ordered that any educational institution that discriminated racially should not qualify for tax-free status. The case was also remanded to the lower court for final adjudication.

Questions of Standing

The U.S. government and Wayne Allen filed separate petitions to the U.S. Supreme Court. The Court heard arguments for both cases concurrently and decided to reverse the decision of the U.S. Court of Appeals. The majority opinion, shared by five justices, held that the respondents (parents of the African American public school children) did not have legal standing to maintain the lawsuit against the IRS.

Class Action Lawsuits

Class action lawsuits are suits allowing a large number of people with common complaints to sue together. Until 1938, monetary awards were not allowed. Class action suits have involved significant social issues such as public school desegregation and housing issues, as well as product liability and personal injury cases (torts).

In 1997, 1,475 class action suits were filed in federal courts. In the mid-1970s over 3,000 suits were being filed per year. By 1984, this number had declined to under one thousand per year by 1984. The number of suits increased during the 1990s. Class action suits comprised only 0.7 percent of total federal civil suits in the 1997, in contrast to 3.5 percent in 1975.

Between 1973 and 1997, over 39,000 class action suits were filed. Over 41 percent concerned civil rights issues, 8 percent with torts, 13 percent with securities (stocks and bonds), 9 percent with prisoner civil rights, and 6 percent or less with various other issues. However, there was a substantial decrease in the percentages of civil rights cases filed, from almost 56 percent of the class action suits in 1978 to 16 percent in 1997. Securities fell from 34 percent of the class action caseload in 1993 to 21 percent in 1997. Tort cases, however, rose from less than 4 percent in 1978 to over 21 percent in 1997.

Source(s): Hooper, Laural L., Robert J. Niemic, and Thomas E. Willging. *Empirical Study of Class Actions in Four Federal District Courts.* Washington, DC: Federal Judicial Center, 1996.

In this case "standing," as specified under Article III of the U.S. Constitution, pertained to both the jurisdictional propriety and the appropriateness of the claims of litigants. The majority opinion pointed out that, under the principle of "separation of powers," for any court to exercise judicial authority (according to the decision in *Valley Forge College v. Americans United* [1982]), especially with respect to alleged wrongdoing by another branch of government, there had to exist a "case or controversy." Moreover, as stipulated in *Warth v. Seldin* (1975), a court had to ensure the "litigant is entitled to have the court decide the merits or dispute of a legal issue." In the absence of appropriateness in a litigant's "standing," the Court explained that any judicial action would be improper. Specifically, in cases involving alleged governmental injury to a private individual or group, a plaintiff had to allege that some kind of personal injury was sustained that could be traced to (the government's) unlawful conduct and which might be corrected only through judicial intervention. Thus, the Court held the respondents had no viable legal standing to bring suit. Respondents did not allege that their children were victims of the segregationist policy of private schools receiving tax exemptions. Neither did they allege that their children ever applied or would ever apply for any of the mentioned private schools. Either allegation could have allowed the court to recognize a "judicially cognizable injury," which would have been appropriate for judicial redress.

In an earlier decision in *Moose Lodge No. 107 v. Irvis* (1972), the Supreme Court held that the plaintiff had no standing to challenge a club's policy to discriminate racially because Irvis never applied for membership. Similarly, in *Rizzo v. Goode* (1976) and *O'Shea v. Littleton* (1974), plaintiffs did not possess appropriate standing because discrimination was not personally directed at the plaintiffs. Similarly, the claim in the class action suit brought by parents of African American students against Allen (and the IRS) did not evidence judicially cognizable injury. Hence, the Court felt they had no choice but to decide that the respondents held no standing, which made complaint or adjudication appropriate. Further, the justices had difficulty understanding how the allegation that tax-exempt status given to segregated private schools harmed the ability to have all schools (public and private) desegregated. The reduced ability of African American children to receive a desegregated education would only have been "fairly traceable" if the respondents could have demonstrated that a sufficient number of segregated private schools in the area existed *as a direct result* of the IRS extending tax-exempt privileges to them. Moreover, respondents would have had to present convincing evidence that removing tax exemptions would make an obvious difference in public school integration. Justices for the majority, therefore, held that the alleged injury was not "fairly traceable to the asserted unlawful conduct of the IRS."

The majority opinion went on to point out that, considering the arguments presented to the Court, they found difficulty in determining exactly how many racially discriminatory private schools might have had tax-exempt status. They also found questionable whether a change in policy regarding the tax status of private schools would make public school integration more effective. Finally, the Court concluded that even if there existed a viable element of "case or controversy," respondents' arguments presented in Court did not show cause and effect and their case was, at best, weak.

More than voicing opposition to the majority opinion, Justice Brennan provided another perspective in his written decision on behalf of the minority justices. He believed that the Court had used the issues of "standing" and "separation of powers" to avoid consideration of a very important claim. IRS practice was not satisfactory in identifying racially discriminatory schools; thus, their lack of proper protocol resulted in permitting tax-exempt status to schools that practiced racial discrimination. Moreover, the respondents' brief was amply meritorious because it correctly argued that IRS guidelines, as written, inappropriately permitted schools to receive tax-exemptions based on *adopting and certifying* a desegregation policy rather than basing tax-exemptions on *implementation* of desegregation policy.

In direct opposition to the majority decision, the minority believed the "case or controversy" requirement for the respondents' standing was satisfied. In their opinion, the respondents' claim alleged at least one type of injury: in granting tax-exemptions to racially discriminatory private schools, the IRS essentially encouraged expansion that could impede efforts of federal courts and local schools to operate under the dual school system. (Brennan's written opinion observed that the Court had previously recognized that such injury was sufficient to satisfy constitutional standards.) Furthermore, the minority firmly believed that distraction of a child's right to receive an education in a desegregated school, whether public or private, was surely injury in fact. Analogous to the case of *Gladstone Realtors v. Metropolitan Life Ins. Co.* (1976), such injury was also sufficient to satisfy the constitutional requirements of standing. Such injury was also "fairly traceable" to the governmental conduct challenged in the respondents' suit. Accordingly, failure of the IRS to deny tax-exempt status resulted in continued racial discrimination—there existed a direct relationship between government action and injury suffered.

The minority found inappropriate the majority's argument that injury would be "fairly traceable" only if parents listed enough segregated private schools in areas where they lived. In fact, parents had specifically named at least 32 racially discriminatory schools that continued to benefit from tax exemptions. In concluding (and, in a rare moment of adversarial objection), the minority sharply criticized their colleagues, charging that it was only because the respondents' "injury in fact" was "fairly traceable" that the Court was forced to inappropriately and incorrectly introduce the concept of "separation of powers."

Impact

In rendering a decision, the Court wanted to address the issue of standing as an essential matter in suits alleging injury from governmental actions. In rendering its decision, the Court clarified previous rulings by explaining that "injury in fact" was "fairly traceable" only if a plaintiff had suffered personal harm that was both visible and perceptible. Specifically, with regard to cases involving alleged injury sustained through governmental action (or inaction), the injury had to clearly, directly affect a litigant to establish standing and thus support a claim.

The Court did not seek to question the legality of IRS policy with regard to granting tax-exempt status to racially discriminatory schools. (In likely response to this suit, however, the IRS revised and adopted more stringently defined criteria for determining ineligibility for tax-exempt status of schools engaging in racial discrimination of any sort.) Justices chose to focus, instead, on whether respondents had standing to bring suit. The Court conformed to a prior decision, *Simon v. Eastern Kentucky Welfare Rights Organization* (1976), which held "that litigation concerning tax liability is a matter between taxpayer and IRS, with the door barely ajar for third party challenges." By that decision, the Court also reiterated previous guidance in cases that involved third-party challenges in tax liability suits. Moreover, the highest court in the U.S. tacitly warned that, in the period that followed this decision, they would only entertain lawsuits related to racial discrimination if a litigant personally alleged "fairly traceable" and recognizable injury.

Related Cases

Moose Lodge No. 107 v. Irvis, 407 U.S. 163 (1972).
O'Shea v. Littleton, 414 U.S. 488 (1974).
Warth v. Seldin, 422 U.S. 490 (1975).
Rizzo v. Goode, 423 U.S. 362 (1976).
Simon v. Eastern Kentucky Welfare Rights Organization, 426 U.S. 26 (1976).
Gladstone, Realtors v. Metropolitan Life Ins. Co., 441 U.S. 91 (1976).
Valley Forge College v. Americans United, 454 U.S. 464 (1982).

Bibliography and Further Reading

Biskupic, Joan, and Elder Witt, eds. *Congressional Quarterly's Guide to the U.S. Supreme Court,* 3rd ed. Washington, DC: Congressional Quarterly, Inc., 1996.

Mello, Michael. "Defunding Death." *American Criminal Law Review,* summer 1995, p. 933.

UNITED STATES V. PARADISE

Legal Citation: 480 U.S. 149 (1987)

Petitioner
United States

Respondent
Phillip Paradise, Jr.

Petitioner's Claim
The United States claimed that the anti-race discrimination remedy ordered by the district court violated the Equal Protection Clause under the Fourteenth Amendment. (The court order required a "one-for-one" promotion scheme of one black police officer for every white police officer advanced to the rank of corporal.)

Chief Lawyer for Petitioner
Charles Fried, U.S. Solicitor General

Chief Lawyer for Respondent
J. Richard Cohen

Justices for the Court
Harry A. Blackmun, William J. Brennan, Jr. (writing for the Court), Thurgood Marshall, Lewis F. Powell, Jr., John Paul Stevens

Justices Dissenting
Sandra Day O'Connor, William H. Rehnquist, Antonin Scalia, Byron R. White

Place
Washington D.C.

Date of Decision
25 February 1987

Decision
The Supreme Court affirmed prior decisions of the lower courts, that race-conscious relief ordered by the district court did not violate the Fourteenth Amendment. They held that principle of hiring and promoting one black for one white police officer was appropriate and did not violate the constitutional rights of due process or equal protection.

Significance
The Court upheld the district court's order for a "one-for-one" promotion plan to address deliberate discriminatory promotion and hiring practices by the Alabama Department of Public Safety (ADPS). Thus, the Supreme Court ruling did not react to the administration's challenge of the concept of racial quotas. Because the Court's support of this kind of affirmative action was situational, their equivocated support of the concept of racial quotas would later enable that kind of anti-discrimination remedy to be successfully challenged less than a decade after this decision.

In 1972, the Alabama Department of Public Safety (ADPS) was challenged in court by the National Association for the Advancement of Colored People (NAACP) for practices that excluded blacks from equal employment opportunities. The United States, together with Phillip Paradise, joined the suit as party plaintiffs. When the suit was brought to court, the U.S. District Court for the Middle District of Alabama agreed with the plaintiffs that the ADPS systematically excluded blacks from employment and thus violated the Equal Protection Clause under the Fourteenth Amendment. Accordingly, the court ordered an end to discriminatory practices and charged the ADPS with rectifying the effects of past discrimination. The district court (in its 1972 order) directed ADPS to hire one black police officer for each white officer until blacks composed approximately 25 percent of the state police force. The respondent (Paradise, et al.) appealed claiming that white applicants who had higher eligibility rankings than blacks were denied due process or equal protection under the law because of the one-for-one hiring order.

The Court of Appeals for the Fifth Circuit affirmed the decision of the district court. Shortly after that 1974 decision, however, petitioners asked for further relief from the district court. Petitioners claimed that the ADPS artificially restricted the size of the police force (and therefore, the number of new-hire police officers) in order to circumvent the court injunction mandating anti-discrimination measures. The district court agreed and characterized the actions of the ADPS as being solely for the purpose of frustrating or delaying full relief to the petitioners.

Petitioners again returned to the district court in September of 1977 and requested supplemental relief (additional aid or compensation for harm done) for discriminatory promotion practices by the ADPS. The litigants—petitioners and respondents—were not in complete agreement as to how the ADPS would go about mitigating discrimination in the workplace; however, litigants were bound by a "partial consent decree" (ordered in 1979) which was approved by the district court. As a condition of that decree, the ADPS agreed to develop, within one year, a promotion procedure that would be fair to all potential promotees. The ADPS also agreed that they would conform to promotion procedures that met the 1978 Uniform Guidelines on Employment Selection Procedures. (ADPS would develop similar procedures, initially for rank of corporal, and then extend that practice incrementally to upper ranks—sergeant, lieutenant, captain, and major.) Finally, the court's decree explicitly provided that the petitioners could apply for enforcement of its terms or for other appropriate remedy.

More than a year after the deadline set by the 1979 decree, the Alabama Department of Public Safety proposed a selection procedure for promotion and asked for approval from the district court. The petitioners, however, objected to implementation of those procedures, arguing that it had an adverse impact on blacks. As a resolution to that dispute, the district court approved a second consent decree in 1981. In that decree, ADPS proposed a promotion procedure in which position advancement within the department was based on a test administered by the ADPS. Of 262 applicants who tested, 60 were black (23 percent). Of those 60 blacks, only five (8.3 percent) were listed in the top half of the promotion register and the highest-ranked black candidate was ranked eightieth. The U.S. (at that time, in its role as equal party plaintiff) objected to that list, maintaining that it had an adverse impact on blacks. Again, litigants attempted to negotiate their differences over how to implement corrective measures; however, they could not agree. In response, the ADPS made no promotions for the next nine months.

White Officers Intervene

Petitioners returned to the court again in April, 1983, to seek an order enforcing the terms of both the 1979 and 1981 decrees. They also requested that criteria for promotions should be the same as hiring, one-for-one. Soon thereafter, four white officers who had been waiting for promotion sought to intervene, claiming that the two decrees were "unreasonable, illegal, unconstitutional or against public policy." In review, the district court ignored assertions of the white claimants noting that even if the ADPS promoted 79 officers to corporal, none would be black. Thus, ADPS was ordered to submit another promotion schema which consisted of at least 15 qualified persons and did not result in deleterious affect on black officers. The ADPS submitted numerous motions for reconsideration of the court's order but the district court held fast to its ruling. Finally, in February 1984, the ADPS promoted eight white and eight black police officers. Interestingly, the U.S. Justice Department (of the Reagan administration) challenged the court's order, holding that it violated the Fourteenth Amendment; however, the Court of Appeals for the Eleventh Circuit affirmed the district court's decision that the one-for-one promotion scheme did not violate the Constitution of the United States.

"Narrowly Tailored" Requirement Found Acceptable

When the case came before the U.S. Supreme Court the decision of the court of appeals was upheld. A majority of five justices held that the district court's race-conscious relief order was justified by an absolute governmental interest in eliminating the ADPS's exclusion of the blacks from its police force. Further, justices held that because of the ADPS's consistent resistance to the court's orders, the district court's decision was supported by the public interest. The Court ruled the one-for-one promotional requirement was "narrowly tailored," made to serve the purpose of eliminating race discrimination, and was necessary for elimination of the effects of the ADPS's long-standing policy of exclusion of blacks in the upper ranks.

In determining whether the district court's anti-race discrimination remedy was appropriate, the Supreme Court examined and reviewed several aspects of that remedy. It was important to determine if there was a necessity for the remedy, whether it was adequate. Further, the Court needed to determine if the prescribed remedy was flexible in application and how long the remedy had to remain in effect.

The ADPS had initially proposed to promote four blacks and eleven whites. That option, the justices felt, would not have served the district court's purpose because it completely failed to provide quick remedy. Moreover, the ADPS delayed implementation of the court's order for several years. Accordingly, the justices held that the district court had no other alternative than the one-for-one remedy. Further, that remedy was flexible in application at all ranks. If there were no qualified candidates among blacks, the ADPS would also be permitted to promote only white applicants (but only if/when the ADPS had need to promote). Moreover, the district court's order continued in force only until the ADPS could come up with a solution which did not have a discriminatory impact on blacks.

In considering the relationship between the court-ordered numerical relief and the percentage of white and black ADPS personnel, the Supreme Court believed that they should not second-guess the lower court's carefully considered decision. That decision was designed to prevent any unfair impact that could occur from inflexible application. The original decrees dealing with discriminatory hiring practices, and also the decree regarding promotions, required the ADPS to hire/promote 50 percent of all black applicants until 25 percent of the police force was composed of the blacks, or 25 percent of each rank was populated by black officers. The "one-for-one" solution, the Court noted, did not impose an unacceptable burden on innocent third parties through layoffs or discharge of white employees. Simply, white candidates had to compete with qualified black candidates. Finally, finding the district court's order was "narrowly tailored," the Court chose to privilege judicial precedence which established the authority of federal courts to effect speedy redress. The justices noted that according to *Louisiana v. United States* (1965), the Court was obliged to provide a decree which would eliminate the effects of discrimination as soon as possible. Similarly, the majority opined that the Court's decision in *Swann v. Charlotte-Mecklenburg Board of Education* (1971) stipulated that when a violation was proven and existed for a lengthy period, a district court's powers were broad of necessity. In contrast, Justice O'Connor (writing for the minority) expressed concern that the district court ordered the promotion quota without considering any other available alternative that would have a lesser effect on the rights of non-minority police officers.

Impact

When litigation was first initiated in 1972 for *United States v. Paradise* (during the Nixon administration), the government acted as an equal party plaintiff in the lower courts as part of a concerted effort to eliminate the effects of gross racial discrimination in the workplace. However, in the fifteen years that intervened between the beginning of litigation and the Supreme Court's decision, a change of political administrations saw the initial action as an example of unbridled, overzealous enforcement of anti-discrimination remedies. Thus, the case arrived at the highest federal court with the U.S. government directly opposed to court-ordered enforcement of racial quotas to eliminate effects of past discrimination.

Although Supreme Court justices ruled against the United States, their decision was rendered with a slim, 5-4 majority. Moreover, because the ruling specifically addressed circumstances and history which pertained only to the recalcitrance of the Alabama Department of Public Safety, the decision was not entirely applicable in a broader context which might provide lower courts with guidance when considering the constitutionality of legislative measures intended to mitigate institutionalized racial discrimination. Indeed, and perhaps because of the specificity of purpose of their ruling, justices did not seek to define what constituted an appropriate, legal legislative redress for racial discrimination. Thus, by choosing not to confront the executive branch, the Court left an opening for later, successful litigation which sought to eliminate racial quotas and privileging of ethnic minorities as a means of securing equal opportunity based on racial criteria.

Related Cases

Louisiana v. United States, 380 U.S. 145 (1965).
Green v. New Kent County School Board, 391 U.S. 430 (1968).
Swann v. Charlotte-Mecklenburg Board of Education, 402 U.S. 1 (1971).
Sheet Metal Workers v. EEOC, 478 U.S. 421 (1986).

Bibliography and Further Reading

Biskupic, Joan, and Elder Witt. *Congressional Quarterly's Guide to the U.S. Supreme Court,* 3rd ed. Washington, DC: Congressional Quarterly, Inc., 1996.

JOHNSON V. TRANSPORTATION AGENCY

Legal Citation: 480 U.S. 616 (1987)

Petitioner
Paul E. Johnson

Respondent
Transportation Agency of Santa Clara County, California

Petitioner's Claim
That the agency's affirmative action program violated Title VII of the 1964 Civil Rights Act by promoting some and withholding promotion from others on the basis of gender.

Chief Lawyer for Petitioner
Paul J. Larkin, Jr.

Chief Lawyer for Respondent
Penelope M. Cooper

Justices for the Court
Harry A. Blackmun, William J. Brennan, Jr. (writing for the Court), Thurgood Marshall, Sandra Day O'Connor, Lewis F. Powell, Jr., John Paul Stevens

Justices Dissenting
William H. Rehnquist, Antonin Scalia, Byron R. White

Place
Washington, D.C.

Date of Decision
24 March 1987

Decision
The agency's affirmative action program did not violate Title VII provisions.

Significance
The court extended legal protection to a greater range of affirmative action programs: those that are gender-based, those that are used by public employers, and those designed to remedy an uneven distribution of women in the work force even when that employer has not discriminated in the past.

The Santa Clara County Transportation Agency adopted its affirmative action plan in December of 1978, after noticing that the agency's higher positions were disproportionately filled by white males. Women were 36.4 percent of the available labor in the area, but only 22.4 percent of the agency's employees were women. The women were overwhelmingly present in traditionally female fields, accounting for 76 percent of the office and clerical workers, but they made up only 22 percent of the service/maintenance workers, 9.7 percent of the technicians, 8.6 percent of the professionals, and 7.1 percent of the officials and administrators.

The agency's long-term goal was to attain a work force in which women and minorities were present in the same proportions that they were available in the qualified labor pool. This goal was to be achieved by considering race and gender as relevant factors—but not the only factors—in evaluating each case for hiring or promotion. No quotas were established, and no positions were set aside exclusively for women or minorities.

The agency posted a vacancy for a promotional road dispatch position on 12 December 1979. The duties included assigning road crews, allocating resources and keeping records related to road maintenance work. Applicants needed to have at least four years of experience as a dispatch or road maintenance worker for the county. The position was classified as a "skilled craft" job; at that time, none of the agency's 238 skilled craft workers were women.

Diane Joyce and Paul Johnson were among the 12 employees who applied for the promotion. After an evaluation of each applicant's record and an interview process, seven applicants, including Joyce and Johnson, were considered qualified for the job. The applicants were ranked according to their score from the interview. Johnson and another man were tied for second with a score of 75, while Joyce was in third with a score of 73. The three agency supervisors who conducted the interviews recommended that Johnson receive the promotion, but the affirmative action coordinator recommended Joyce. James Graebner, the agency's director, gave the promotion to Joyce. Graebner later testified that his decision was based on several factors:

. . . the combination of [Joyce's] qualifications and Mr. Johnson's qualifications, their test scores, their expertise, their background, affirmative action matters, things like that . . .

Johnson sued the agency, arguing that he had been denied the promotion because of gender, a violation of Title VII of the 1964 Civil Rights Act. Title VII stipulates that an employer cannot withhold a job or promotion from an applicant because of that person's race, color, ethnicity, gender, or religion. The U.S. District Court for the Northern District of California found in Johnson's favor, ruling that Johnson was more qualified than Joyce but that Joyce had received the promotion by reason of her gender.

The Ninth Circuit Court of Appeals reversed this ruling, finding that the agency's affirmative action program met the standards outlined in the Supreme Court's earlier ruling in *Steelworkers v. Weber* (1979). In *Weber,* the Supreme Court allowed for temporary, race-based affirmative action programs as long as such programs did not call for the removal of white workers or absolutely prevent the advancement of any white employees. As long as the measure was designed to "eliminate a manifest racial imbalance" without "unnecessarily trammel[ing] the interests of the white employees," the Supreme Court said such a program would be consistent with the spirit of Title VII. The Ninth Circuit Court found that Santa Clara Transportation Agency's program was a temporary one that did not make it impossible for males to advance. Therefore, the circuit court ruled, the program was consistent with Title VII's intent of "break[ing] down old patterns of racial segregation and hierarchy."

The Supreme Court upheld the circuit court's ruling, 6-3. In his majority opinion, Justice Brennan defended the agency's program.

[The program] requires women to compete with all other qualified applicants. No persons are automatically excluded from consideration; *all* are able to have their qualifications weighed against those of other applicants.

The program allowed for gender to be one factor in evaluating an applicant, but female applicants still needed to meet the same experience and skill requirements as men to be competitive candidates, Brennan said. The majority praised the agency's program for being flexible and allowing for a case-by-case application of the program without setting rigid quotas.

Justice Stevens filed a concurring opinion, in which he recognized that affirmative action programs contradicted the literal reading of Title VII's provision that bars any consideration of race or gender, but he said such programs embody the *spirit* of Title VII. Quoting part of the *Weber* ruling, Stevens said:

Diane Joyce, 1979. © Reproduced by permission of Diane Joyce.

It would be ironic indeed if a law triggered by a Nation's concern over centuries of racial injustice and intended to improve the lot of those who had "been excluded from the American dream for so long" constituted the first legislative prohibition of all voluntary, private, race-conscious efforts to abolish traditional patters of racial segregation and hierarchy.

In her concurring opinion, Justice O'Connor reiterated the consistency of the majority's ruling with the court's precedents, especially *Weber,* but she emphasized the constitutional limits on affirmative action. Affirmative action programs challenge the Fourteenth Amendment's equal protection clause, she said, but such programs can pass constitutional muster if the employer can point to the presence of an unusually low number of women or minorities in the work force. Such a disparity in the composition of the labor pool is considered *prima facia* evidence—evidence accepted on its face as fact unless otherwise proved—of the effects of discrimination, even if the employer had not intentionally discriminated in the past. The presence of discriminatory effects gives the state a compelling interest that allows it to temporarily suspend equal protection considerations, O'Connor said. Under these circumstances, the state and other employers may use affirmative action programs to remedy the lingering effects of past discrimination, she said.

In a thundering dissent, Justice Scalia, joined by Chief Justice Rehnquist and in part by Justice White, criticized the majority's ruling for blatantly contradicting the language of Title VII.

> The Court today completes the process of converting [Title VII] from a guarantee that race or sex will *not* be the basis for employment determinations, to a guarantee that it often *will*.

Scalia called for a literal interpretation of Title VII and scolded the Court for breathing new meaning into the "unambiguous" language of the statute.

Supporters of affirmative action, such as Emily Spitzer, a lawyer with the National Organization of Women's Legal Defense and Education Fund, hailed the ruling. Spitzer told the Chicago Tribune:

> [The ruling will] encourage employers to adopt voluntary affirmative action and promote women, particularly in areas where they have been excluded in the past.

Affirmative action critics argued that the ruling allowed for "reverse discrimination" against white males,

signaling a step backwards from Title VII's goal of attaining a color-blind and gender-blind society.

Related Cases

United Steelworkers of America v. Weber, 443 U.S. 193 (1979).

Fullilove v. Klutznick, 448 U.S. 448 (1980).

Firefighters Local Union #1784 v. Stotts, 467 U.S. 561 (1984).

Wygant v. Jackson Board of Education, 476 U.S. 267 (1986).

Local #28 of the Sheet Metal Workers International v. Equal Employment Opportunity Commission, 478 U.S. 421 (1986).

Local #93 International Association of Firefighters v. City of Cleveland, 478 U.S. 501 (1986).

Bibliography and Further Reading

Elsasser, Glen. "Job Ruling Supports Women." *Chicago Tribune.* March 26, 1987, p. A1.

Hall, Kermit L. *The Oxford Companion to the Supreme Court of the United States.* New York: Oxford University Press, 1992.

Roberts, Paul Craig, and Lawrence M. Stratton, Jr. "Color Code." *National Review,* March 20, 1995, p. 36.

Urofsky, Melvin I. *Affirmative Action on Trial: sex discrimination in Johnson v. Santa Clara.* Lawrence, Kansas: University Press of Kansas, 1997.

SAINT FRANCIS COLLEGE V. AL-KHAZRAJI

Legal Citation: 481 U.S. 604 (1987)

The Facts of the Case

Professor Majid Ghaidan Al-Khazraji, a U.S. citizen born in Iraq, served on the faculty of St. Francis College in Pennsylvania. In January of 1978, he applied for academic tenure, but the college's board of trustees denied his request. Al-Khazraji later left the school's employ and filed complaints with the Pennsylvania Human Relations Commission and the Equal Employment Opportunities Commission (EEOC). Upon advice from the EEOC, Al-Khazraji filed suit in U.S. District Court in 1980, claiming his tenure had been denied on the basis of race, in violation of the U.S. Code.

The Lower Courts Rule

The U.S. District Court first had to determine whether the statute of limitations had expired on Al-Khazraji's right to sue. It held that six-year limitation applied to this case and that Al-Khazraji, therefore, had a right to bring his action in court. The district court then proceeded to the question of Al-Khazraji's right to sue based on racial discrimination. The issue was whether an Arab, classified as a Caucasian under commonly accepted racial criteria, could charge racial discrimination under the U.S. Code. At first, the court sided with Al-Khazraji and ruled that he could, but when St. Francis College moved for summary judgement before a different judge, the court ruled in its favor. The second judge interpreted Al-Khazraji's complaint asserting only discrimination on the basis of national origin and religion, not race. Al-Khazraji then appealed this decision to the U.S. Court of Appeals for the Third Circuit.

The court of appeals reversed the district court's ruling on the merits of the case. It also applied the statute of limitations and ruled that Al-Khazraji had filed his suit in a timely manner. It reasoned that while under current racial classifications Arabs are Caucasians, Al-Khazraji could file a discrimination complaint because Congress had intended to protect all members of any group "that is ethnically and physiognomically distinctive." St. Francis College then appealed this decision to the U.S. Supreme Court.

Petitioners
Saint Francis College et al.

Respondent
Majid Ghaidan Al-Khazraji, etc.

Petitioners' Claim
That a section of the U.S. Code barring racial discrimination did not apply to persons of Arab ancestry.

Chief Lawyer for Petitioners
Nick S. Fisfis

Chief Lawyer for Respondent
Caroline Mitchell

Justices for the Court
Harry A. Blackmun, William J. Brennan, Jr., Thurgood Marshall, Sandra Day O'Connor, Lewis F. Powell, Jr., William H. Rehnquist, Antonin Scalia, John Paul Stevens, Byron R. White (writing for the Court)

Justices Dissenting
None

Place
Washington, D.C.

Date of Decision
18 May 1987

Decision
Affirmed the decision of the U.S. Court of Appeals and granted the respondent the right to state his claim of racial discrimination against St. Francis College.

Significance
The Supreme Court's decision in *Saint Francis College v. Al-Khazraji* clarified the criteria for making a racial discrimination claim under section 1981 of the U.S. Code.

The Supreme Court Affirms

On 18 May 1987, the Supreme Court ruled on the case. In a unanimous decision, the Court affirmed the ruling of the court of appeals and allowed Al-Khazraji to proceed with his complaint. As had two previous courts before it, the Supreme Court first established that there was no "time bar" to Al-Khazraji's complaint, since the six-year statute of limitations applied in this instance. It then moved on to the merits of the case.

In his majority opinion, Justice White made three key determinations. First, he concurred with the ruling of the court of appeals that held that Congress had intended for its anti-discrimination legislation to encompass even those citizens who would be considered Caucasian under commonly accepted racial classification guidelines. After outlining the history and usage of the term "race" in Western culture, White concluded: "We have little trouble in concluding that Congress intended to protect from discrimination identifiable classes of persons who are subjected to intentional discrimination solely because of their ancestry or ethnic characteristics."

Next, White addressed the question of whether persons attempting to claim racial discrimination under Section 1981 must exhibit physical characteristics that single them out for identification—and by extension prejudice. To White, such visible differences were not necessary. "[A] distinctive physiognomy is not essential to qualify for 1981 protection," he wrote.

Finally, White established the criteria for filing a discrimination complaint under Section 1981 of the U.S. Code. "If respondent on remand can prove that he was subjected to intentional discrimination based on the fact that he was born an Arab, rather than solely on the place or nation of his origin, or his religion, he will have made out a case under 1981," White wrote.

Impact

The decision issued by the Supreme Court in *Saint Francis College v. Al-Khazraji* established clear guidelines for future discrimination claims under Section 1981 of the U.S. Code. It reaffirmed the Court's long-standing opinion that, as Justice Brennan observed in his concurring opinion, "pernicious distinctions among individuals based solely on their ancestry are antithetical to the doctrine of equality upon which this nation is founded."

Related Cases

McNally v. United States, 483 U.S. 350 (1987).
Patterson v. McLean Credit Union, 485 U.S. 617 (1988).
Jett v. Dallas Independent School District, 491 U.S. 701 (1989).
Lampf v. Gilbertson, 501 U.S. 350 (1991).

SUPREME COURT OF VIRGINIA V. FRIEDMAN

Legal Citation: 487 U.S 59 (1988)

Appellant
Supreme Court of Virginia, et al.

Appellee
Myrna E. Friedman, et al.

Appellant's Claim
The Virginia Supreme Court Rule 1A:1 required an applicant to be a resident of Virginia for admission to the Virginia Bar. Appellants claimed that this residency requirement did not violate the Privileges and Immunities Clause of the Constitution.

Chief Lawyer for Appellant
Gregory E. Lucyk

Chief Lawyer for Appellee
Cornish F. Hitchcock

Justices for the Court
Harry A. Blackmun, William J. Brennan, Jr., Anthony M. Kennedy (writing for the Court), Thurgood Marshall, Sandra Day O'Connor, John Paul Stevens, Byron R. White

Justices Dissenting
William H. Rehnquist, Antonin Scalia

Place
Washington, D.C.

Date of Decision
20 June 1988

Decision
The Supreme Court affirmed the court of appeals decision that the residency requirement of the Virginia Rule violated the Privileges and Immunities Clause.

Significance
The Supreme Court of Virginia failed to prove that its residency requirement as a prerequisite for admission to the Virginia State Bar Association did not discriminate against nonresidents. The Court found that the right to practice law was an essential activity protected by conditional criteria stipulated under the Privileges and Immunities Clause. This decision reaffirmed a standard of implementation of the Privileges and Immunities Clause set in previous precedents, which could be applied to other professions regarded as vital to national interests.

Myrna E. Friedman, a resident of Virginia from 1977 to 1986, was employed as a civilian attorney by the Department of the Navy in Arlington, Virginia, from 1977 to 1981, and as an attorney in private practice in Washington, D.C., from 1982 to 1986. In January of 1986 she started working as associate general counsel for ERC International, Inc., a Delaware corporation, and she was practicing and maintaining her offices at the company's place of business in Vienna, Virginia. In February of 1986 she married and moved to Maryland. Four months later, in June of 1986, she applied for admission to the Virginia bar "on motion." Because she had experience practicing law, she requested admission to the Virginia bar without taking Virginia's bar examination.

The Virginia Supreme Court Rule 1A:1 permits admission on motion of qualified lawyers who had been admitted to practice in another state. This rule was designed as an ameliorative provision for those lawyers who had previously practiced in another jurisdiction and who wanted to become new residents of Virginia. The rule required, among other things, reciprocity between states; the other jurisdiction must admit Virginia's attorneys without examination. As a part of the procedure, the Virginia Supreme Court stipulated that the applicant:

> (a) Is a proper person to practice law, (b) Has made such progress in the practice of law that it would be unreasonable to require him to take an examination, (c) Has become a permanent resident of the Commonwealth, (d) Intends to practice full-time as a member of the Virginia bar.

Friedman offered her arguments in a letter accompanying her application saying that she would practice full-time as a member of the Virginia bar and that she would keep informed of changes in the local law. Stating that her petition as a nonresident for admission to the bar, on motion, was under the protection of the Privileges and Immunities Clause of Article IV, 2, of the Federal Constitution, she also referred to the U.S. Supreme Court's decision in *Supreme Court of New Hampshire v. Piper* (1985). However, Friedman's request

---

Privileges and Immunities Clause: Residency Requirements

Residency is the length of time a person must stay in a particular area to enjoy certain legal protections or benefits. States have frequently sought to limit the amount of benefits or protections a person new to the state, or not a resident, might receive. For some rights, such as to file suit in state courts, a person must simply prove they have sufficient interests in a state, such as through business. However, durational residency requirements may actually demand a person actually live in the state for a specified period of time.

When residency requirements are applied to fundamental constitutional rights, such as welfare and public housing benefits, basic medical care, and voting, the state must demonstrate a strong compelling interest.

Often such requirements violate the Equal Protection Clause by restricting the fundamental constitutional right for the poor to travel between states as others do. For other rights or privileges, including to run for public office, practice a profession, government employment, attend certain public schools, and initiate a lawsuit, the state must only demonstrate a reasonable basis for the restriction. By the 1990s most states had dropped durational requirements for voting and enacted motor-voter laws, meaning a person can vote when they apply for a drivers license.

Source(s): *West's Encyclopedia of American Law.* Minneapolis/St. Paul, MN: West Publishing, 1998.

---

was denied on the grounds that she was no longer a resident of Virginia. The rationale for denial by the clerk of the Supreme Court of Virginia stated that the court had concluded that the U.S. Supreme Court's decision in *Piper* was not applicable to the "discretionary" residence requirement of the Virginia rule. (Virginia had "discretionary" freedom to choose to apply the residency requirement as a condition of admission by reciprocity.)

The case of *Supreme Court of New Hampshire v. Piper* (1985) invalidated a state residency requirement for admission to practice, holding that it violated the Privileges and Immunities Clause. The clause forbade any discrimination against residents of other states in favor of its own and was intended to create a national economic union, but it also protected other interests relating to the union (e.g., in *Doe v. Bolton* [1973], the right to seek medical care). The clause is self-executory: its enforcement is dependent upon the judicial process. In deciding the *Piper* case, the U.S. Supreme Court used a previously established, two-pronged test which was intended for residency restrictions that may have limited privileges and immunities protections. The test examined if the activity in question was essential for the interest of the nation and whether restrictions bore a substantial relationship to the objectives of a state. In the *Piper* case, the Court also recognized the right to practice law as an essential activity.

Higher Courts' Decisions

In the U.S. District Court for the Eastern District of Virginia, Friedman filed suit against the Supreme Court of Virginia and the clerk of the court. She claimed that Virginia's residency requirement violated the Privileges and Immunities Clause. The district court ruled in

Friedman's favor, and the Court of Appeals for the Fourth Circuit affirmed.

In the trial before the district court, the attorney for the Supreme Court of Virginia and its clerk reasoned that the Privileges and Immunities Clause was not violated by the residency requirement of the Virginia rule as long as all applicants were allowed to gain admission to the bar by passing the bar examination. The appellant's next argument was that the residency requirement, together with the full-time practice requirement, was designed to guarantee that a lawyer admitted on motion would be as committed to service and as familiar with Virginia law as an attorney who entered the Virginia bar by examination.

The district court disagreed with the appellant's argument because the Privileges and Immunities Clause was implicated whenever a state did not permit qualified nonresidents to practice law within its borders on terms of substantial equality with its own residents. Moreover, the court reasoned that it was mere speculation that residents would respect their commitments to practice full time in Virginia more than nonresidents. The state, without violating constitutional protections, could also further its interest in having lawyers well-acquainted with legal developments by using other equally effective means, such as the requirement that applicants maintain an office in Virginia. Referring to the two-pronged test used in *Supreme Court of New Hampshire v. Piper*, the Court concluded that there was not substantial reason for discrimination, nor did the discrimination bear a substantial relationship to the objectives of the state. Subsequently, the lower court's decision was unanimously affirmed by the court of appeals. Dissatisfied with that decision, the Supreme Court of Virginia and its clerk appealed again and the U.S. Supreme Court agreed to hear their case.

Higher Courts' Decisions Affirmed

After considering previous court decisions and reviewing arguments, the U.S. Supreme Court, on a 7-2 vote, affirmed the decision of the district court and the court of appeals, holding that Virginia's residency requirement for admission on motion to the state's bar violated the Privileges and Immunities Clause. Since this clause of the Constitution is enforced only through the judicial process, the Court employed a two-pronged test to resolve the case. All appellant's arguments were carefully considered to determine if they satisfied the two inquiries of the test. The action in question was considered of national and state interests.

Appellants contended that the residency requirement of the Virginia rule offended neither part of the two-pronged test; neither was discretionary admission provided by this rule a privilege protected by the Privileges and Immunities Clause. First, admission on motion was not the only means of entering the Virginia Bar since an applicant, without regard to residence, could gain admission by passing the bar examination. Second, the privilege of admission on motion was not protected by the clause because the state could, without constitutional violation, require all applicants to pass an examination.

Writing for the majority, Justice Kennedy decided that neither argument was persuasive. Kennedy wrote that after considering Supreme Court precedents, the practice of law was sufficiently basic to the national economy, and therefore, with regard to the first question of the two-pronged test, it was protected by the clause. Kennedy pointed out that Supreme Court of Virginia's argument contradicted precedence, notably, *Supreme Court of New Hampshire v. Piper*. In that case, the rule was struck down even though it had not resulted in the total exclusion of nonresidents from the practice of law in the state. The appellant's second argument was equally irrelevant since "a state's abstract authority to require from . . . resident and nonresident alike that which it has chosen to demand from the nonresident alone has never been held to shield the discriminatory distinction from the reach of the Privileges and Immunities Clause." While Justice Kennedy conceded that the Privileges and Immunities Clause was not an absolute where substantial reasons for discrimination existed, he felt the degree of discrimination enforced by the Supreme Court of Virginia bore a close relation to such reasons.

The majority opinion ruled that the Supreme Court of Virginia's two main justifications for the residence requirement did not sufficiently satisfy the two-pronged test. The Court held that the ability or willingness of a nonresident attorney to respect the bar and further its interests to the same degree as a resident lawyer did not depend on whether s/he entered the bar on motion or on examination. Kennedy wrote that it was indisputable that Friedman had a substantial stake in the practice of law in Virginia and there appeared to be no reason why she would not "remain abreast of changes in the law." As to Virginia's justified concern to have its attorneys abreast of legal developments, the Court noted that there were alternative means to achieve this end without infringing constitutional protections. For example, Kennedy affirmed the court of appeals explanation that the requirement for applicants to maintain an office in Virginia was equally effective as the residency restriction and therefore rendered the residency restriction largely redundant.

Chief Justice Rehnquist and Justice Scalia felt that, with respect to earlier precedents, the Privileges and Immunities Clause did not "require States to ignore residency when admitting lawyers to practice in the way that they must ignore residency when licensing traders in foreign goods . . ." (*Ward v. Maryland* [1871]). In addition, Rehnquist wrote that Virginia's rule allowing admission on motion was intended to help lawyers who would become new residents of Virginia. This rule enabled them to gain admission to the Virginia bar on the basis of their previous practice. In Rehnquist's opinion, the Court's decision penalized Virginia for that, and he expressed his concern that Virginia might decide to eliminate admission on motion altogether.

Impact

The U.S. Supreme Court's ruling affirmed a new standard of implementation of the Privileges and Immunities Clause of Article IV, 2, of the Constitution. More importantly, the decision reestablished precedence set in *Supreme Court of New Hampshire v. Piper*. The right to practice law was recognized as an activity essential for the interest of the nation and therefore protected by the Privileges and Immunities Clause. In turn, by holding to the two-pronged test for the right to pursue a licensed profession, this case firmly established a standard that may be applied to other licensed professions, such as medicine, if it is estimated to be essential to national interests.

Related Cases

Ward v. Maryland, 12 Wall 418 (1871).
Doe v. Bolton, 410 U.S. 179 (1973).
Baldwin v. Montana Fish & Game Comm., 436 U.S. 371 (1978).
Hicklin v. Orbeck, 437 U.S. 518 (1978).
Supreme Court of New Hampshire v. Piper, 470 U.S. 274 (1985).

Bibliography and Further Reading

Illinois State Bar Association. "ISBA Advisory Opinion on Professional Conduct." *Courts Bulletin and Opinions.* 1997. http://www.illinoisbar.org/CourtsBull/EthicsOpinions/92-06.html.

PATTERSON V. MCLEAN CREDIT UNION

Legal Citation: 491 U.S. 164 (1989)

Petitioner
Brenda Patterson

Respondent
McLean Credit Union

Petitioner's Claim
That the Civil Rights Act of 1866, which prohibits racial discrimination in the "making and enforcing" of contracts, covers problems arising from conditions of employment, such as harassment and failure to promote.

Chief Lawyers for Petitioner
Julius LeVonne Chambers, Penda D. Hair

Chief Lawyers for Respondent
Roger S. Kaplan, H. Lee Davis, Jr.

Justices for the Court
Harry A. Blackmun, William J. Brennan, Jr., Anthony M. Kennedy (writing for the Court), Thurgood Marshall, Sandra Day O'Connor, William H. Rehnquist, Antonin Scalia, John Paul Stevens, Byron R. White

Justices Dissenting
None

Place
Washington, D.C.

Date of Decision
15 June 1989

Decision
That the Civil Right Act of 1866 does not prohibit racial discrimination in conditions of employment beyond the formation of the employment contract.

Significance
By taking a narrow reading of the Civil Rights Act, the Court left many minority employees with no redress for harassment and other forms of discrimination in employment. The public and political response to the decision helped lead to the passage of the Civil Rights Act of 1991, which reversed this decision.

Immediately following the Civil War, Congress passed a number of laws and constitutional amendments designed to guarantee the newly-freed slaves the same rights and privileges enjoyed by white Americans. Although discrimination by the states was prevented by the Thirteenth, Fourteenth, and Fifteenth Amendments, there was still widespread discrimination against African Americans by private citizens. For example, whites would not sell land to African Americans, and African Americans were beaten or killed for refusing to work for their former white slave-owners or for showing "insubordination" to whites. Among the laws passed by Congress was the Civil Rights Act of 1866. One provision of this act, commonly referred to as "section 1981," provided that all citizens, regardless of race, "shall have the same right . . . to make and enforce contracts . . . as is enjoyed by white citizens." Lyman Trumball, who was chairman of the Senate Judiciary Committee at the time, expressed the sentiment of a large part of the population when he described the act as "the most important measure . . . since the adoption of the constitutional amendment abolishing slavery." Although initially limiting the law by implying that section 1981 only prohibits discrimination by the government, the Supreme Court later explicitly held that section 1981 covers discrimination by private persons. In the case *Runyon v. McCrary,* decided in 1976, the Court concluded that section 1981 prohibits purely private discrimination.

Brenda Patterson's case against the McLean Credit Union began as a fairly typical civil rights suit, but went on the become a rallying point for civil rights advocates. Patterson, an African American bank teller employed by the McLean Credit Union, filed a suit against the credit union in 1985. Alleging that she was subjected to a pattern of harassment during her ten years of employment, mostly by her supervisor, Patterson sought to recover under section 1981. The trial court directed a verdict in favor of the credit union, concluding that because on the job harassment does not relate to the "making" or "enforcing" of a contract, it does not fall under section 1981. Patterson appealed her case to the court of appeals, which agreed with the trial court. Patterson then sought to appeal her case to

Civil Rights Act of 1991

The Civil Rights Act of 1991 amended a number of existing civil rights laws concerned with employment discrimination claims by including provisions for recovery of damages, jury trials, and obtaining relief from on-the-job violations. Previously, only traditional awards of back pay, job reinstatement, and attorney's fees were allowed. Amending Title VII of the Civil Rights Act of 1964 and the American With Disabilities Act of 1990, the 1991 act provides the potential to also award compensatory (future monetary loss, emotional pain and suffering) and punitive (awards in excess of actual damages as punishment) damages. In addition, a person alleging intentional discrimination may request a jury trial to determine liability. Previously, a judge could decide key issues.

The act allows employees to sue for damages experienced through discrimination in hiring, promotion, dismissal, and other terms of employment. In order to protect from expensive lawsuits, employers were encouraged to carefully review their existing policies and practices, and to train supervisors so that hiring, daily management, and termination decisions are nondiscriminatory. Also, the burden of proof shifted from the aggrieved worker to the employer. The employer must justify the challenged employment practice by proving its consistency with a business necessity.

Source(s): Naidoff, Caren E.I. "Understanding the Civil Rights Act of 1991," *Management Review,* April 1992.

---

the U.S. Supreme Court through a procedure known as a petition for a writ of *certiorari*. The Court granted the petition, and the parties argued the case before the Court on 29 February 1988.

Court Reconsiders Whether Section 1981 Prohibits Any Private Discrimination

After hearing oral arguments on the issue of whether section 1981 prohibits on the job harassment, however, Justices Rehnquist, White, O'Connor, Scalia, and Kennedy concluded that the Court should reconsider its earlier decision that section 1981 covers private discrimination. As Charles Fried, U.S. solicitor general at the time, recalled in his book *Order and Law:* "In the spring of 1988 the civil-rights community was shocked when, instead of deciding the *Patterson* case, the Court ordered reargument on whether *Runyon v. McCrary,* the 1976 case that proclaimed the extension of Section 1981 to discrimination in private contracting, should be overruled." The four other justices strongly criticized this decision, including Justice Stevens, who had himself questioned whether *Runyon* was correctly decided. The decision to reconsider *Runyon* galvanized the civil-rights community. By the time the Court heard reargument in the case, the NAACP had entered the case on behalf of Patterson, and briefs supporting Patterson's case had been filed by the American Bar Association, 47 state attorney generals, 66 U.S. Senators, and Solicitor General Fried on behalf of the Reagan administration.

Civil-rights advocates received a partial victory when the Court issued its decision on 15 June 1989. All nine justices agreed that the *Runyon* decision should not be overturned. Even those justices who thought that *Runyon* had been incorrectly decided concluded that the

decision must be allowed to stand under the doctrine known as "*stare decisis*." This doctrine provides that previous decisions should not be overturned frequently because to do so would cause uncertainty in the law and would not be fair to other litigants. The Court, in an opinion written by Justice Kennedy, "reaffirm[ed] that [section] 1981 prohibits racial discrimination in the making and enforcement of private contracts."

As tremendous as the victory was for civil rights advocates, however, their defeat was equally as devastating. Addressing the initial issue presented in the case, a majority of the justices held that section 1981 does not prohibit racial harassment suffered by employees. The justices reasoned that section 1981 prohibits only discrimination in the making and enforcement of contracts, and that discrimination which occurs after a person has been hired does not relate to either the "making" or "enforcement" of a contract. Recognizing, however, the limitation that its decision would place on civil rights claims, the Court reminded Congress that it could amend the law to cover the type of harassment suffered by Patterson:

> The law now reflects society's consensus that discrimination based on the color of one's skin is a profound wrong of tragic dimension. Neither our words nor our decisions should be interpreted as signaling one inch of retreat from Congress' policy to forbid discrimination in the private, as well as in the public, sphere. Nevertheless, in the area of private discrimination . . . our role is limited to interpreting what Congress may do and has done. The statute before us, which is only a part of Congress' extensive civil rights legislation, does not cover the acts of harassment alleged here.

Patterson Overturned

The effect of the Court's decision was profound. Although another civil rights law known as Title VII of the Civil Rights Act of 1964 does prohibit racial harassment by employers, that law applies only to companies with 15 or more employees, leaving over 11 million employees unprotected from racial harassment at the time of the *Patterson* decision. Following the decision, hundreds of claims of racial harassment were dismissed by courts. In 1991, Congress dealt with the problem by passing the Civil Rights Act of 1991. One section of this act explicitly overturned the *Patterson* decision by adding a new provision to section 1981. This new provision clearly provides that section 1981 prohibits all aspects of discrimination in contractual relationships, including harassment. Although Brenda Patterson lost her case, the civil rights advocates fighting for her cause were able to assure, through passage of the Civil Rights Act of 1991, that the harassment she suffered is now prohibited by section 1981.

Related Cases

Plessy v. Ferguson, 163 U.S. 537 (1896).
Brown v. Board of Education of Topeka, 347 U.S. 483 (1954).
Jones v. Alfred H. Mayer Co., 392 U.S. 409 (1968).
Bob Jones University v. United States, 461 U.S. 574 (1983).

Bibliography and Further Reading

Cathcart, David A., et al. *The Civil Rights Act of 1991.* Philadelphia: American Law Institute, 1993.

Franke, Janice R. "Retroactivity of the Civil Rights Act of 1991." *American Business Law Journal,* November 1993, p. 483.

Fried, Charles. *Order & Law: Arguing the Reagan Revolution—A Firsthand Account.* New York: Simon & Schuster, 1991.

Hukill, Craig. "Labor and the Supreme Court: Significant Issues of 1992–1996." *Monthly Labor Review,* January 1997, p. 3.

Knee, Jonathan A. "The Administration Plays Politics with Rights and Lives." *Baltimore Evening Sun,* October 21, 1991, p. A21.

Marshall, Lawrence C. "In One Case, a Positive Development the Critics Shouldn't Ignore." *Chicago Tribune,* June 21, 1989, p. 19.

McDonnell, Brett. "Dynamic Statutory Interpretations and Sluggish Social Movements." *California Law Review,* July 1997, p. 919.

Reams, Bernard D., and Fay Couture, eds. *The Civil Rights Act of 1991: A Legislative History of Public Law.* Buffalo: William S. Hein & Co., 1994.

Savage, David G. *Turning Right: The Making of the Rehnquist Supreme Court.* New York: John Wiley & Sons, Inc., 1992.

Tokaji, Daniel Patrick. "The Persistence of Prejudice." *Yale Law Review,* November 1993, p. 567.

EAST BIBB TWIGGS NEIGHBORHOOD ASSOC. V. MACON-BIBB COUNTY PLANNING AND ZONING COMMISSION

Legal Citation: 706 F. Supp. 880 (M.D. Ga. 1989)

Plaintiff
East Bibb Twiggs Neighborhood Association, et al.

Defendant
Macon-Bibb County Planning and Zoning Commission, et al.

Plaintiff's Claim
That the county planning and zoning commission's decision to allow the creation of a private landfill in an area in which most of the residents were black was motivated by racial discrimination, and thus unconstitutional

Chief Lawyer for Plaintiff
Lonzy F. Edwards

Chief Defense Lawyer
O. Hale Almand

Judge
Wilbur D. Owens

Place
Macon, Georgia

Date of Decision
16 February 1989

Decision
That the plaintiff failed to present sufficient evidence that the planning and zoning commission's decision was impermissibly motivated by racial discrimination.

Significance
The court's decision exemplifies the difficult task facing citizens bringing claims that government officials took certain actions for racially discriminatory reasons. The court's decision makes clear that these hurdles to establishing discrimination apply equally to claims of environmental discrimination as they do to other claims of discrimination.

In the 1980s, both the government and the public became increasingly aware of environmental problems such as waste disposal and the need for better ways of protecting the environment. At the same time, the courts continued to recognize the problems of racism and prohibit discrimination on the part of state and local government officials. This led to the rise during this time of claims of environmental racism in the federal courts. *East Bibb Twiggs Neighborhood Association v. Macon-Bibb County Planning and Zoning Commission* represents a typical environmental discrimination case.

In 1986, Robert Mullis applied to the joint planning commission of the City of Macon and Bibb County, Georgia, for a permit to operate a waste landfill in Bibb County. The proposed landfill was to occupy an area populated predominantly by black citizens. On 30 June 1986, the commission denied the application concluding that the landfill was unacceptable because it would be located in a predominantly residential area and would involve increased noise and truck traffic through the area. However, Mullis sought and was granted a rehearing on his application. At the second hearing, Mullis addressed the concerns raised by the commission when it initially denied his application. In opposition to the application, a number of citizens expressed concern over the proposed landfill, specifically arguing that it would lower property values, increase noise and traffic, present health risks associated with vermin and insect infestation, and effect the water supply. Apparently satisfied with Mullis's resolution of the commission's concerns, the commission approved the application to operate a landfill at the proposed site.

Following the commission's approval of Mullis's application, the East Bibb Neighborhood Association and a number of individual residents in the area filed a lawsuit in the U.S. District Court for the Middle District of Georgia against the commission, the commission's members, and Mullis. The plaintiffs alleged that the commission's decision to locate the landfill in a predominantly black area was based on racial discrimination, and thus violated the Equal Protection Clause of the United States Constitution. The case was tried before District Judge Wilbur Owens, who concluded that there was no evidence that the commission's decision was racially motivated.

"Not In My Back Yard"

A common aspect of life in American society late in the twentieth century was community opposition to the siting of public facilities. Known as the "Not In My Back Yard" (NIMBY) syndrome, community planners faced increasing difficulty in locating various public service facilities. The facilities included landfills, prisons, power plants, homes for the elderly and mentally-retarded, substance-abuse facilities, group homes for HIV-AIDS infected persons, child daycare centers, outpatient medical facilities, and schools. NIMBY became quite effective at killing much-needed projects for the population at-large.

Neighborhood-based opposition originally grew from fear of decreased property value in addition to anticipated introduction of unwanted persons, noise, pollution, traffic, and odors, among other things seen as threats to the residents' quality of life. Earlier on, such facilities were routinely placed in lower income, inner-city neighborhoods less able to raise resistance. Facility saturation of some areas resulted. Eventually, these communities became increasingly mobilized to correct the past inequities. The NIMBY syndrome became relevant across all class, socioeconomic, and racial boundaries.

In reaction to the NIMBY trend, planners attempted education strategies, cooperative planning, fair-share policies, forced siting, community compensation, and conflict resolution techniques to varying degrees of success. Fair-share policies involved coercing neighborhoods to accept responsibility for their share of larger community and regional needs.

Source(s): Morris, Jane Anne. *Not In My Back Yard: The Handbook.* San Diego, CA: Silvercat Publications, 1994.

Commission's Decision Not Racially Motivated

The Equal Protection Clause of the Fourteenth Amendment to the Constitution provides that no state shall "deny to any person within its jurisdiction the equal protection of the laws." This provision prohibits a state or local government from discriminating against groups of people based on so-called "suspect classifications," such as race or national origin. In order to prove discrimination in violation of the Equal Protection Clause, a plaintiff must establish that the governmental officers acted with a discriminatory intent and that the action of those officers had a discriminatory impact. In the 1977 case *Arlington Heights v. Metropolitan Housing Corp.* the U.S. Supreme Court recognized five factors as relevant in determining whether the government officials acted with a discriminatory purpose. First, the court must look at whether the challenged action affects one racial group more heavily than another. Second, the court looks at the historical background of the decision to see if it exhibits any indications that the governmental action was based on a discriminatory purpose. Third, the court should look at the specific events leading up to the governmental action. Fourth, the court must examine whether the decision making process was different in the challenged case than in other similar cases. Finally, the court should look to the legislative or administrative history of the challenged decision.

Applying these factors to the commission's decision, Judge Owens concluded that "the Commission's decision to approve [the landfill] was not motivated by the intent to discriminate against black persons." With respect to the first *Arlington Heights* factor, Judge Owens concluded that the commission's decision did not disproportionately affect black citizens. He noted that although the approved landfill was located in a predominantly black neighborhood, the only other privately operated landfill in the county was located in a predominately white neighborhood. Judge Owens also rejected the plaintiff's argument that the historical background showed that the commission had a history of locating undesirable land uses in predominantly black areas. He reasoned that this argument was rebutted by the fact that the only other privately operated landfill was located in a white area, and by the fact that the commission cannot choose to place landfills anywhere on its own. Rather, the commission only considers applications by private parties, and considers each such application separately.

With respect to the third *Arlington Heights* factor, Judge Owens concluded that the specific sequence of events leading up to the commission's decision to grant Mullis's application did not evidence any discriminatory purpose. He noted that the plaintiffs had failed to offer any evidence of specific events showing that the commission acted with a discriminatory purpose. Rather, Judge Owens concluded, "[t]he statements of the various commissioners during their deliberations indicates a real concern about both the desires of the opposing citizens and the needs of the community in general. Similarly, with respect to the fourth *Arlington Heights* factor, Judge Owens found no evidence that the commission had deviated from its normal practice in a discriminatory manner. He noted that although the commission requested input from both the city of Macon and Bibb County, the commission's seeking of this input was based on its desire to come up with a comprehensive plan for addressing the community's waste management problems, rather than for any improper, racially motivated purpose.

Finally, with respect to the fifth *Arlington Heights* factor, Judge Owens found nothing in the legislative history of the commission's decision to indicate that racial considerations played a role in the commission's approval of the landfill. The plaintiffs argued that because the commission originally denied the application, but later approved it, the commission's reconsideration of its position must have been motivated by some racial purpose. He noted that the three commissioners who changed their votes had expressed reservations concerning the impact of the landfill on the citizens of the area at the first hearing on Mullis's application. However, they stated at the second hearing that they changed their votes because they were satisfied that their reservations were unfounded based on a report by the Georgia Department of Natural Resources approving the site and on their own personal inspections of the site. Having found that none of the *Arlington Heights* factors supported a finding of racial discrimination, Judge Owens concluded:

> The voluminous transcript of the hearings before and the deliberations by the Commission portray the Commissioners as concerned citizens and effective public servants. At no time does it appear to this court that the Commission abdicated its responsibility either to the public at large, to the particular concerned citizens, or to [Mullis]. Rather, it appears to this court that the Commission carefully and thoughtfully addressed a serious problem and that it made a decision based upon the merits and not upon any improper racial animus.

Accordingly, Judge Owens rejected the plaintiff's equal protection challenge and entered judgment in favor of the defendants.

Impact

The plaintiffs appealed the district court's decision to the U.S. Court of Appeals for the Eleventh Circuit. That court affirmed Judge Owens's decision, for the reasons reflected in his opinion. *East Bibb* represents a fairly typical equal protection case alleging that government officials took a particular action based on impermissible racial discrimination. The court's decision demonstrates the difficulty plaintiffs have in establishing such racial discrimination under the Fourteenth Amendment.

Related Cases

Arlington Heights v. Metropolitan Housing Corp., 429 U.S. 252 (1977).

R.I.S.E., Inc. v. Kay, 768 F.Supp. 1144 (1991).

Rozar v. Mullis, 85 F.3d 556 (1996).

Bibliography and Further Reading

Bradley, David, and Shelley Fisher, eds. *The Encyclopedia of Civil Rights in America.* New York: M. E. Sharpe, 1998.

Bullard, Robert D. *Confronting Environmental Racism: Voices from the Grass Roots.* Boston: South End Press, 1993.

———. *Dumping in Dixie: Race, Class, and Environmental Quality,* 2nd ed. Boulder, CO: Westview Press, 1994.

———. *Unequal Protection: Environmental Justice and Communities of Color.* San Francisco: Sierra Club Books, 1994.

Franklin, John H., and Genna R. McNeil. *African Americans and the Living Constitution.* Washington, DC: Smithsonian Institution Press, 1995.

McDonald, Laughlin. *The Rights of Racial Minorities: The Basic ACLU Guide to Racial Minority Rights.* Carbondale, IL: Southern Illinois University Press, 1993.

GREGORY V. ASHCROFT

Legal Citation: 501 U.S. 452 (1991)

Petitioners
Ellis Gregory, Jr., Anthony P. Nugent, Jr.

Respondent
John D. Ashcroft, Governor of Missouri

Petitioners' Claim
The Missouri Constitution's mandatory retirement provision required retirement of state judges over age 70. Petitioners claimed it violated the Age Discrimination in Employment Act (ADEA), and the Equal Protection Clause of the Fourteenth Amendment because it irrationally distinguished between old and younger judges, and between state judges and other state officials not subject to the mandatory retirement provision.

Chief Lawyer for Petitioners
Jim J. Shoemaker

Chief Lawyer for Respondent
James B. Deutsch

Justices for the Court
Anthony M. Kennedy, Sandra Day O'Connor (writing for the Court), William H. Rehnquist, Antonin Scalia, David H. Souter, John Paul Stevens, Byron R. White

Justices Dissenting
Harry A. Blackmun, Thurgood Marshall

Place
Washington, D.C.

Date of Decision
20 June 1991

Decision
The Missouri mandatory retirement provision did not violate the ADEA because its language did not explicitly protect state judges. Neither was the Equal Protection Clause violated because the Court ruled the ADEA rationally furthered the state interest of providing fully functioning judiciaries.

Significance
Missouri's Constitution was challenged as being in violation of federal statute and the U.S. Constitution; however, the Supreme Court rejected petitioners' arguments. The Court held that a state's constitutional provision concerning such an important issue as the right to define the qualifications of a state's highest officials could not be overridden if it did not explicitly oppose federal statutes.

Judges Challenge Mandatory Retirement

An article of the state of Missouri Constitution dictated that all judges other than municipal judges should retire at age 70. Because increasing age often involves deterioration of mental and physical abilities, this provision was enacted to ensure state judges were fully capable of performing their duties. Subject to this provision were two Missouri state judges: Ellis Gregory, Jr., a judge for the Twenty-First Judicial Circuit, and Anthony P. Nugent, Jr., a judge for the Missouri Court of Appeals, Western District. Both had been appointed to their positions by respondent, Governor John D. Ashcroft of Missouri, and had been retained in office through infrequent retention elections. They ran unopposed and were subject only to a "yes or no" vote. Before dismissal, petitioners sued Ashcroft, the governor of Missouri, in U.S. District Court for the Eastern District of Missouri, challenging the mandatory retirement provision of the Missouri Constitution. They stated that it violated the Age Discrimination in Employment Act (ADEA) and the Equal Protection Clause of the Fourteenth Amendment, "No State shall . . . deny to any person within its jurisdiction the equal protection of the laws."

The ADEA, enacted by Congress in 1967, protected senior workers from discrimination in hiring, firing, and in conditions of employment. This act was amended in 1974 also naming states as employers. The term "employees" was also redefined to exclude from the ADEA protection any person elected to public office, or any person chosen by such officer to be on his/her personal staff, or an appointee on the policymaking level, or an immediate adviser on legal questions.

The district court held that mandatory retirement did not violate the ADEA. Because the two judges were appointed by an elected official (the governor), and their judicial duties included making policy by establishing rules of practice on local and state level, judges were "appointees on a policymaking level." They were, therefore, excluded from the protection of the ADEA. The court also applied the "rational basis standard" of the Equal Protection analysis and found it was satisfied because Missouri had a justifiable rationale for distinguishing between judges and other state officials not subject to the provision. Other officials, unable to perform their duties because of age, could be removed from office considerably easier than judges who ran unopposed in retention elections and whose deterioration in abilities the voters could less easily perceive. The two judges' claims were rejected and the governor of Missouri dismissed them.

Petitioners appealed to the U.S. Court of Appeals for the Eighth Circuit, but this court affirmed the dismissal. The appellate court agreed with the district court's finding that judges were appointees on the policymaking level and consequently not protected by the ADEA. It also held that the state rationally distinguished between judges over and judges under 70. Following this decision, the U.S. Supreme Court granted *certiorari* (a written order to a lower court to forward the proceedings of a case for review).

Both Claims Overturned Again

In a 7-2 opinion, the Supreme Court affirmed the decision of the court of appeals. Justice O'Connor, who delivered the opinion of the Court, first resolved how to apply ambiguous text contained in the ADEA. She maintained the lower court's decision wrongly interpreted that the federal statute (the ADEA) could upset the constitutional balance between states and the federal government. (Congress enacted the ADEA and extended it to the states.)

O'Connor explained that the U.S. Constitution established a system of dual, concurrent sovereignty between the states and the federal government (the only exception was the Supremacy Clause which gave advantage to the federal government). Since Missouri's right to define the qualifications of its highest state officials was protected by the Tenth Amendment—"the powers not delegated to the United States by the Constitution, nor prohibited by it to the States, are reserved to the States respectively, or to the people"—O'Connor held it obligatory for the Court to be certain of Congress's intent before finding that a federal law overrode the balance. The Court had already previously ruled that Congress had made its intent "unmistakably clear in the language of the statute" (embodied in the ADEA provisions) not to override Missouri's right to dismiss high state officials (*Will v. Michigan Dept. of State Police* [1989]). Knowing that the Congress did not readily interfere with a state's sovereign powers, the Court gave clear guidance regarding interpretation of the ADEA using the "plain statement rule."

The ADEA stated that the term "employee" (as a person protected by ADEA provisions) should not include "any person elected to public office in any State by the qualified voters thereof, or any person chosen by such officer to be on such officer's personal staff, or an appointee on the policymaking level or an immediate adviser with respect to the exercise of the constitutional

or legal powers of the office." Governor Ashcroft, respondent, claimed that the ADEA's exclusion from its protection of certain public officials pertained to the two petitioners, because they were appointed by an elected official (the governor himself), and because they were appointees on the policymaking level. His lawyer argued that state judges did make policy because they fashioned and applied common law adopted in Missouri. Moreover, the two judges' courts made policy by establishing rules of practice on a local and state level.

Petitioners Assert Portions of Act Not Applicable

The petitioners' counter-argument was that judges merely resolved factual disputes and decided questions of law and did not make policy. In addition, the two judges claimed that the phrase "appointees on the policymaking level" was closely related to other parts of the provision which referred to those in close, working relationships with the elected official who appointed them. Thus, because it was illegal for the judges to work closely with such an elected official as governor, that provision of the ADEA did not apply to judges.

The Court found that the governor's arguments were more persuasive because he relied on "the plain lan-

John D. Ashcroft, Governor of Missouri. © Photograph by Arnold Sachs. Archive Photos.

guage" of the statute. The ADEA nowhere explicitly stated that judges were protected by it, and O'Connor wrote the Court would not read the ADEA to cover state judges unless Congress had made it clear that judges were protected by it. Moreover, by such interpretation, judges were not only "policymakers," but also persons "on policymaking level."

Turning to the petitioners' equal protection violation claim, the Court applied the rational basis standard of its equal protection analysis (which was satisfied if a state rationally furthered a legitimate state interest). The two judges argued that the state did not have rational basis to make two distinctions: between judges who had reached age 70 and younger judges, and between judges 70 and over and other state officials who were not subject to mandatory retirement. The Court again found respondent's arguments more reasonable. The attorney for the governor reasoned that the mandatory retirement provision helped a state uphold the public need for fully functioning judiciaries. Moreover, the mandatory retirement provision avoided tedious and perplexing determinations about which judge, at a certain age, was not physically and mentally qualified, and it increased the opportunity for young qualified persons to share in the judiciary. The Court found all these interests compelling for Missouri. It was rational to conclude that the threat of deterioration at age 70 was sufficiently great and the alternatives for removal from office (infrequent retention elections in which judges ran unopposed, voluntary retirement, or even impeachment) were sufficiently inadequate. Thus, Missouri's mandatory retirement provision did not violate the Equal Protection Clause.

Four Justices Differ in Opinions

Justice White, joined by Justice Stevens (concurring and dissenting in part), agreed with the majority opinion that neither the ADEA nor the Equal Protection Clause prohibited Missouri's mandatory retirement provision. On the other hand, White could not agree with the majority's use of the "plain statement" requirement for application of federal statute (the ADEA) to state activities (the mandatory retirement provision of the Missouri Constitution). Congress's intent to regulate age discrimination by states through enacting the ADEA was "unmistakably clear in the language of the statute." Therefore, the ADEA could have been imposed over Missouri's constitutional provision for mandatory retirement for its state judges without fear of violating the balance of federal and state sovereignties.

Dissenting Justices Blackmun and Marshall were of the opinion that parts of cited ADEA text should be viewed as related to one another (that was the argument of the two Missouri judges), and thus concluded that the intention of Congress was not to exclude state judges from the ADEA protection. State judges were not

"on [a] policymaking level" because they were not accountable to the official who appointed them and were precluded from working closely with that official once they had been appointed. In addition, Justice Blackmun stated that when a statutory term was ambiguous or undefined, the Court should defer to a reasonable interpretation of that term proffered by the agency entrusted with administering the statute. Blackmun referred to *Chevron USA Inc. v. Natural Resources Defense Council, Inc.* (1984). The Equal Employment Opportunity Commission (EEOC), the agency which was entitled to administer the ADEA, had a position that an appointed judge was not an "appointee on the policymaking level." Nonetheless, the dissenting argument was countered by Justice White's opinion that the EEOC was entitled to little if any deference by the Supreme Court and that its position was inconsistent with "the plain language" of the ADEA.

Impact

Every state is entitled to a certain level of sovereignty. In turn, state sovereignty is carefully balanced with the sovereignty of the federal government. In spite of this balance, Congress has power to impose a federal statute on a state statute or constitution, but does not usually exercise that power lightly. Fearing that Congress's intentions could be misread, the Supreme Court applied "the plain statement" requirement in this case, where the state statute was challenged as being in violation of federal statute and the Constitution. Reading the federal statute enacted by Congress in search of a plain statement, the Court found that the ADEA nowhere made it clear that state judges were protected by it. Therefore, Missouri's mandatory retirement provision for its state judges did not violate the ADEA. Neither did it violate the Equal Protection Clause of the Fourteenth Amendment because it rationally furthered a legitimate state interest to uphold the public demand for fully functioning judiciaries. As a final outcome, this decision established that a state's right to define the qualifications of its highest state officials could not be overridden by the ADEA's prohibition of age discrimination. Nor would a state violate the Fourteenth Amendment's Equal Protection Clause as long as its requirements reasonably served a legitimate state interest.

Related Cases

Massachusetts Board of Retirement v. Murgia, 427 U.S. 307 (1976).
Penhurst State School and Hospital v. Halderman, 451 U.S. 1 (1981).
EEOC v. Wyoming, 460 U.S. 226 (1983).
Chevron USA v. Natural Resources Defense Council, Inc., 467 U.S. 837 (1984).
Atascadero State Hospital v. Scanlon, 473 U.S. 234 (1985).
Will v. Michigan Dept. of State Police, 191 U.S. 58 (1989).

Bibliography and Further Reading

Carvajal, Alejandr. "State and Local 'Free Burma' Laws: The Case for Sub-National Trade Sanctions." *Law and Policy in International Business,* winter 1998, p. 257.

Farber, Daniel A. "The Constitution's Forgotten Cover Letter: An Essay on the New Federalism and the Original Understanding." *Michigan Law Review,* December 1995, p. 615.

Rosenbloom, David H., and Bernard H. Ross. "Toward a New Jurisprudence of Constitutional Federalism: The Supreme Court in the 1990s and Public Administration." *American Review of Public Administration,* June 1998, p. 107.

Wise, Charles. "Judicial Federalism: The Resurgence of the Supreme Court's Role in the Protection of State Sovereignty." *Public Administration Review,* March-April 1998, p. 95.

R.I.S.E., Inc. v. Kay

Legal Citation: 768 F. Supp 1144 (1993)

Plaintiff
Residents Involved in Saving the Environment, Inc., and others

Defendant
King and Queen County Board of Supervisors consisting of five members: R. A. Kay, Jr., R. H. Bourne, J. R. Walton, R. F. Alsop, and W. L. Hickman

Plaintiff's Claim
That placing a landfill in a predominantly African American area results in a racially disproportionate impact and violates the Fourteenth Amendment's Equal Protection Clause.

Chief Lawyer for Plaintiff
Sa'ad El-Amin

Chief Defense Lawyer
John Granville Douglass

Judge
Richard L. Williams (writing for the court)

Place
Richmond, Virginia

Date of Decision
21 June 1991

Decision
Ruled in favor of the Virginia county and allowed the project to proceed by finding that the racially disproportionate impact was not intentional.

Significance
The district court established distinct standards for individuals and organizations legally challenging sanitary landfill siting decisions by local governments. To challenge such decisions on constitutional grounds such as racial discrimination the petitioner must establish that placement of a landfill in a predominately African American area resulted from intentional discrimination in violation of the Equal Protection Clause. The ruling provided a useful guideline for local and state governments across the nation in making difficult decisions under public scrutiny.

Concerns over the placement of public facilities in neighborhoods and communities grew dramatically through the 1970s and 1980s following emergence of the U.S. environmental movement in the 1960s. Siting decisions by state and local governments were often challenged on constitutional grounds. Normally, opponents to the facilities claimed violations of the equal protection and Due Process Clauses of the Fourteenth Amendment. In a challenge against proposed low income housing in a Chicago suburb, the U.S. Supreme Court in *Arlington Heights v. Metropolitan Housing Corp.* (1977) identified a number of factors to be considered in determining whether an action was truly unconstitutionally discriminatory. Building on a previous ruling in *Washington v. Davis* (1976), the first question was: what actual effect does the official action pose? Second, what was the historical background of the decision? Third, what was the specific sequence of events leading up to the challenged decision? Fourth, was the action a departure from normal procedures? Fifth, was the action a departure from normal criteria? And lastly, what was the administrative history of the decision? The *Davis* and *Arlington Heights* decisions dismayed civil rights groups throughout the nation. The requirement to prove discriminatory intent behind decisions was considerably tougher than simply demonstrating the disproportionate effects of government actions on minority populations.

The King and Queen Landfill Dilemma

In 1986, King Land Corporation established a private landfill on a 120-acre site in King and Queen County, Virginia. With no existing county zoning ordinance at that time regarding landfill placement, King Land did not need to obtain county approval. The King Land landfill became an environmental disaster from the beginning as dumping began without the necessary geotechnical tests performed beforehand. Later, tests showed that incinerator ash had been buried in ground water areas and no clay soil was present to prohibit ground water pollution.

An attorney hired by the county board of supervisors to legally challenge the King Land operation advised the board to devise a zoning ordinance. The county soon implemented an ordinance in August of 1986 and then obtained a court injunction preventing King Land from operating its landfill under its state-issued permit. King Land applied for a variance to the ordinance to resume use of the landfill but the county denied its application. Racial composition of the residential area surrounding the King Land landfill was predominantly white.

In 1987, Virginia issued new state regulations for solid waste disposal in landfills. The new regulations posed a significant financial problem for King and Queen County. Three existing county landfills had to be closed for not meeting the new environmental standards at a cost of almost two million dollars. The county could not afford to close the existing landfills and develop a new landfill that would comply with the new state regulations.

In an effort to solve its waste disposal problems, the county began negotiations with the Chesapeake Corporation to develop a shared landfill. As envisioned, Chesapeake would build the landfill, the county would operate it, and both could use it for waste disposal. Chesapeake soon found a 420 acre potential landfill site in what was known as the Piedmont Tract. The company hired an engineering company from Charlotte, North Carolina to conduct soil studies. Tests determined the site was suitable for landfill development.

In the summer of 1988 Chesapeake changed its mind and decided to expand an existing landfill to satisfy its own waste disposal needs. Several months later, in January of 1989, county supervisors met with Chesapeake to once again jointly pursue a property for a landfill site. Chesapeake identified at least two sites for possible landfill development: the Piedmont Tract again and one other. At a regular county board of supervisors meeting in October of 1989, board members in a public session appointed a citizen's "liaison committee" to explore alternatives for the county's future waste disposal needs. At another public hearing the following month, the county planning commission proposed amendments to the zoning ordinance regarding landfills which were accepted by the board. A few days later, still in November, Supervisor Robert Kay publicly announced the 420-acre Piedmont site was officially under consideration and recommended the county acquire an option to purchase it.

In December of 1989, in another public hearing, the county, with the assistance of its liaison committee, reaffirmed it could not afford to operate its own landfill. As a result, the county board adopted Kay's resolution to execute a purchase option agreement with Chesapeake for the Piedmont site. The agreement was promptly signed. With those decisions made, the board published public notices in local newspapers for public hearings on the landfill issue. Letters and petitions in opposition to the Piedmont landfill option soon began arriving.

Community Mobilization

In January of 1990, citizens concerned about the proposed landfill met in the Second Mt. Olive Baptist Church with three county supervisors and a city administrator. The citizens expressed concerns that the proposed landfill would reduce the quality of life of area residents by increasing noise, dust and odor. They were also worried the landfill would result in a decrease in the area's property values. Even Reverend Taylor of the church argued that it would interfere with worship and social activities. Many believed major improvements in access roads would be necessary.

In February, the board held a public hearing and invited Browning-Ferris Industries to make a presentation about operation of regional landfills. Present at the meeting were 225 citizens. Fifteen spoke in opposition to the proposal. In addition, the board was presented with a petition signed by 947 individuals opposing the regional landfill. After considering these comments, the board voted unanimously to authorize development of a landfill. In response, a Concerned Citizen's Steering Committee sent a letter to the county board of supervisors requesting that the board establish a Regional Landfill Citizen's Advisory Committee to assess other siting possibilities before signing any actual purchase contracts. Soon, a list of alternative sites to the Piedmont site was narrowed to one, the Mantapike Tract. The minority population of the area surrounding the Mantapike Tract was 85 percent African American.

Upon inspection of the Mantapike site, Browning-Ferris Industries reported to the board that the site was environmentally unsuitable because of the slope of the land and a stream running through it. With the site selection narrowed to the Piedmont tract, local citizens formed Residents Involved in Saving the Environment, Inc. (RISE), in May of 1990. RISE was a biracial group concerned over environmental protection issues. Race discrimination was not initially identified as a significant public issue by the group.

In July of 1990, the county approved a planning commission's recommendation that the Piedmont Tract be rezoned from agricultural production to an industrial area. In an August public hearing, the board passed a resolution to finally sign a lease for the Piedmont site with Browning-Ferris Industries who would operate the landfill. Though the population of King and Queen County was approximately 50 percent African American, 64 percent of those living within a half-mile radius of the proposed regional landfill site were African American. RISE filed a lawsuit in federal district court claiming the proposed siting of the landfill was racially discriminatory violating the Equal Protection Clause of the Fourteenth Amendment.

In hearing the case, Judge Richard L. Williams applied the standard established in *Arlington Heights* to determine if the county's decision violated the Constitution. In order to assess the intent of the county in its decisions, Williams first evaluated the effect of the government action in this case. After weighing the statistics concerning landfills in King and Queen County, Williams concluded the historical placement of landfills in predominantly black communities provided "an important starting point" for determining whether official action was motivated by discriminatory intent. Williams found, indeed, that landfill placement in the county since 1969 posed a disproportionate impact on black residents. But what of the other factors, such as sequence of events leading to the county decision and deviation from existing procedures for making zoning changes? Williams found that "the plaintiffs have not provided any evidence that satisfies the remainder of the discriminatory purpose equation set forth in *Arlington Heights*. Careful examination of the administrative steps taken by the board of supervisors to negotiate the purchase of the Piedmont Tract and authorize its use as a landfill site reveals nothing unusual or suspicious." The frequent public hearings provided ample opportunity for citizen involvement. The record demonstrated to Williams that the county board's opposition to the King Land landfill and its approval of the newly proposed Piedmont landfill was not based on the racial composition of the respective neighborhoods in which the landfills were located. The key issue weighed by the county was the relative environmental suitability of the sites.

The record clearly indicated the board of supervisors had preferred the Piedmont tract because tests had found it environmentally suitable for landfill development. Establishment of a citizens advisory group and evaluating the suitability of the alternative site, recommended by the Concerned Citizens' Steering Committee, indicated that public comment was considered. The discussion with landfill contractor, Browning-Ferris Industries, to minimize the impact of the landfill on the Second Mt. Olive Church, and improving access roads showed that the board of supervisors had followed normal procedures.

Williams asserted that the Equal Protection Clause did not impose an affirmative duty to equalize the impact of official decisions on different racial groups.

RISE had not provided sufficient evidence to meet the *Arlington Heights'* legal standard. Williams wrote, "official action will not be held unconstitutional solely because it results in a racially disproportionate impact. Such action violates the Fourteenth Amendment's Equal Protection Clause only if it is intentionally discriminatory." The county could proceed with its plans.

Impact

Increasingly typical for the late twentieth century, a community organization had formed specifically to oppose a local governmental decision. The legal challenge against the proposed regional landfill failed to prove the placement in a predominately African American area was intentionally discriminatory in violation of Equal Protection Clause of the Fourteenth Amendment. The ruling highlighted to other municipalities across the nation what they must do to withstand organized challenges to their decisions. Appropriate actions included open meetings and documenting how public input was considered in reaching decisions. Most importantly, a well defined process for decision making must be established and then strictly followed.

Related Cases

Euclid v. Ambler Realty Co., 272 U.S. 365 (1926).
Washington v. Davis, 426 U.S. 229 (1976).
Arlington Heights v. Metropolitan Housing Corp., 429 U.S. 252 (1977).

Bibliography and Further Reading

Alexander, Judd H. *In Defense of Garbage*. Westport, CN: Praeger, 1993.

Luton, Larry S. *The Politics of Garbage: A Community Perspective on Solid Waste Policy Making*. Pittsburgh: University of Pittsburgh Press, 1996.

Noble, George. *Siting Landfills and Other LULUs*. Lancaster, PA: Technomic Publishing Co., 1992.

Thomas, June M., and Marsha Ritzdorf, eds. *Urban Planning and the African American Community: In the Shadows*. Thousand Oaks, CA: Sage Publications, 1997.

Wright, Robert R. *Land Use In a Nutshell*, 3rd ed. St. Paul, MN: West Publishing, 1994.

J. E. B. v. Alabama ex rel T. B.

Legal Citation: 511 U.S. 127 (1994)

Petitioner
J. E. B.

Respondent
Alabama ex rel T. B.

Petitioner's Claim
Because *Batson v. Kentucky* (1986) prohibited peremptory challenges based on racial discrimination, intentional discrimination on the basis of gender was also violative of the Equal Protection Clause of the Fourteenth Amendment.

Chief Lawyer for Petitioner
John F. Porter III

Chief Lawyer for Respondent
Lois B. Brasfield

Justices for the Court
Harry A. Blackmun (writing for the Court), Ruth Bader Ginsburg, Anthony M. Kennedy, Sandra Day O'Connor, David H. Souter, John Paul Stevens

Justices Dissenting
William H. Rehnquist, Antonin Scalia, Clarence Thomas

Place
Washington, D.C.

Date of Decision
19 April 1994

Decision
Peremptory challenges on the basis of gender were inconsistent with the Equal Protection Clause. Respondent's biased exercise of peremptory challenges was unconstitutional.

Significance
The U.S. Supreme Court had to determine whether its 1986 decision in *Batson v. Kentucky* (prohibiting exercise of peremptory challenges on the basis of race) could be similarly applied to a case where peremptory challenges were exercised on the basis of gender. Although respondent's rational that exclusion of jurors on the basis of sex could be justified because of expectations that male jurors might be predisposed to the arguments of the father, the Court reasoned that such stereotypical considerations could not validly exclude jurors. Intentional sex-based peremptory strikes were prohibited just as peremptory strikes based on racial discrimination.

The Peremptory Challenge

In order to determine paternity and get support for her minor child, respondent T. B. (mother), represented by the state of Alabama, filed a paternity suit against J. E. B. (alleged father). The trial court called 36 potential jurors (24 female, 12 male) for the panel. Three jurors were excluded by the court, so only 10 male jurors remained when the state exercised its nine of ten peremptory strikes to eliminate male jurors from the panel. Objecting to the peremptory challenges of the respondent, the petitioner invoked *Batson v. Kentucky* (1986) wherein peremptory strikes directed just to exclude jurors on the basis of race were held unacceptable and inconsistent with Equal Protection Clause of the Fourteenth Amendment. He contended that a similar nondiscriminatory standard was applicable to the respondent's intention to impanel a jury which could diminish his possibility of an impartial trial. Despite the petitioner's objections, an all-female jury was seated and found the petitioner to be the father of the child in question; the court ordered him to pay child support. On appeal, the Alabama Court of Civil Appeals upheld the findings of the lower court.

Respondent (Alabama ex rel T. B.) contended that pretrial selection of a jury on the basis of gender should not be constrained as in *Batson v. Kentucky*. Instead, the respondent's attorney argued that discrimination on the basis of sex was never so delicate and critical as racial discrimination. Moreover, peremptory strikes of potential male jurors were justified because, historically, data suggested men could have a tendency to be more favorably inclined to arguments of males; conversely, women could be predisposed to arguments on behalf of the respondent. Finally, counsel for the respondent suggested that the Supreme Court might be more interested in determining paternity than disposition of peremptory actions.

Six U.S. Supreme Court justices held that exclusion of jurors solely because of their sex was inconsistent with the Fourteenth Amendment's Equal Protection Clause. At the outset, they emphasized that regardless of whether the trial was civil or criminal, all participants in the trial must enjoy adequate, equal protection with respect to jury selection. Historical prejudices

Peremptory Challenges

During the final phase of jury selection, attorneys on both sides question prospective jurors to determine their suitability to sit on the jury. Their goal is to dismiss jurors who might be biased against the interests of their clients. This process is called *voir dire*. During *voir dire* attorneys use two means to eliminate potential jurors: challenge for cause and peremptory challenge. When an attorney has reason to believe a juror will show partiality or be unfit to perform the duties of a juror, she may explain to the judge her reasoning and have the juror dismissed *for cause*. The number of challenges for cause dismissals is not unlimited, however. Attorneys may also reject potential jurors by peremptory challenge, excusing a juror without stating specific reason or cause. Peremptory challenge allows an attorney to exclude persons who cannot be successfully challenged for cause. The number of these challenges is also limited and set by law or court rules. The objective of peremptory challenge is to further ensure a fair, impartial jury.

Race or gender may not be the basis of a peremptory challenge. However, in the 1990s controversy raged over whether true elimination of race and gender bias had been achieved.

Source(s): Epstein, Lee, and Thomas G. Walker. *Constitutional Law for a Changing America: Rights, Liberties, and Justice.* Washington, DC: Congressional Quarterly Press, 1995.

and stereotypes that could jeopardize an equitable and fair trial had to be avoided, thus the practice of peremptory challenges had to be guided by equal protection principles. Justices recognized that peremptory challenges based on gender were resurgent and recalled discriminatory exclusion of women as a significant fact in history; it was an irregular practice of the judicial system for many years. Nonetheless, since women were endowed with the same right as men to participate in trials and became trusted members of jury panels, no questions about appropriateness of sex should exist. Justices posited that the only concern should be fairness in court rooms and that discrimination did not promote that fundamental feature of the judicial system. Thus, no relevance existed in supposing that men or women in the court room would act or have a tendency to act as a group. Further, discrimination among members of a jury pool was contrary to quality jurisprudence. No grounds existed to support conventionalized ideas that men and women had dissimilar perspectives which could incline toward one litigant.

Different Discrimination?

The Court did not find that certain cases might justify suppositions that men and women could have different standpoints which would substantiate distinctions and exclusions on the basis of gender. Justices found that similar prejudicial attitudes had (historically) befallen African Americans and women, therefore, gender based classifications were equally unacceptable. In explaining the majority rationale, Justice Blackmun pointed out that the history of sex and racial discrimination influenced the Court's judgement that only "an exceedingly persuasive justification" would ever justify sex-based classifications. Specifically, such classifications were dependent on "whether discrimination on the basis of gender in jury selection substantially furthers the state's legitimate interest in achieving a fair and impartial trial."

In the interest of securing unprejudiced trials, the majority disapproved of peremptory challenges based on gender stereotypes. They rejected the respondent's argument that gender simply could be viewed as an issue apart from race discrimination and that exclusions on the basis of gender could not cause harm to participants in the judicial process. They also pointed out that discrimination in court rooms, regardless of how well-intended, harmfully affected fairness of proceedings. They allowed, however, that some circumstances (such as rape or sexual harassment trials), might merit peremptory challenges based on gender. But the Court explained that prejudicial approaches about competence and abilities of male and female members of the jury could not be confirmed as an admissible and lawful means of reaching justice. Majority justices found as inappropriate the respondent's argument "that men deserve no protection from gender discrimination in jury selection because they are not victims of historical discrimination." To the contrary, the justices felt "all persons, when granted the opportunity to serve on a jury, have the right not to be excluded summarily because of discriminatory and stereotypical presumptions that reflect and reinforce patterns of historical discrimination."

The Court majority stressed that their opinion did not abolish use of all peremptory strikes. Peremptory challenges were acceptable if used to remove jurors from the panel if litigants felt that somebody could be "less acceptable" or if they found other attributes or reasons to exclude other than by gender or race. Justices hinted that peremptory strikes (when justification is required) had to be founded in some other rational excuse or juror's characteristic except gender. They did not devalue the legitimate and practical usefulness of peremptory challenges, but they stressed that they were not rights protected by the Constitution and that their purpose was to impanel an impartial jury. The justices found that "gender simply may not serve as a proxy for bias."

Need for Limited Use

Justice O'Connor filed a concurring opinion. She also felt that the Equal Protection Clause prohibited elimination of jurors by gender but she felt that the Court's conclusion should have been "limited to the government's use of gender-based peremptory strikes." Justice O'Connor recognized that the substance of peremptory challenges was to empower litigants to choose members of a jury without offering particular reasons or being exposed to the court's control or inquiry for such movement. O'Connor further believed that the opportunity to create an impartial jury pool might be reduced by the ruling of the Court; she believed that sometimes gender-based presumptions could be correct. She thus maintained that the Court should have limited gender-based peremptory challenges only to the government's use but should have allowed their unlimited use by private civil contestants and criminal defendants.

Justice Kennedy also supported the posture of the majority and he emphasized that the exclusion of male or female jurors as a consequence of peremptory strikes was not less intrusive than prohibition to serve as a juror just because of gender. Further, he said: "it is important to recognize that a juror sits not as a representative of a racial group, but as an individual citizen."

The Dissent

Three justices joined Justice Scalia's dissenting opinion. (Chief Justice Rehnquist, separately, also mentioned that he could not find so many similarities between sex and race discrimination. Accordingly, he would not accept the ruling in *Batson v. Kentucky* as reference for such holdings of the majority.) Scalia thought that this decision of the majority could damage administration of justice by reducing the strength of peremptory challenges. He said that peremptory challenges had the purpose of achieving the goal in impartial and fair trials and that the use of peremptory strikes on the basis of sex could not cause the same harm as peremptories directed to African American jurors. The minority opinion criticized the Court's reliance on historical discrimination against woman to find use of peremptory challenges unconstitutional. Justice Scalia found it irrelevant and argued that no indicators existed which would show that the petitioner suffered some impairment because, like the respondent, he also had a chance to exercise his peremptory strikes. Scalia pointed out

that the Court actually supported the petitioner's claim although harm was not done to him but to stricken jurors. Dissenting justices maintained that the coexistence of peremptory challenges with the Equal Protection Clause should have not been questioned because the main purpose of peremptories was to provide litigants with the opportunity to seat an impartial jury. The Court's decision thus appeared to diminish the purpose of peremptories especially when the primary feature of peremptories was that reasons for strikes did not have to be given. Consequently, the minority justices believed the judicial system could be adversely affected because the Court seemed to be promoting a practice that could end up with "quests for reasoned peremptories."

Impact

The judgement of the U.S. Supreme Court resolved the question of whether peremptory challenges, exercised because of gender prejudices, could survive "the heightened equal protection scrutiny." Majority justices held that equal protection principles applied when intentional peremptory challenges were exercised solely on the basis of gender. Discrimination and exclusion of jurors from the jury pool solely because of gender was, therefore, an intrusive exercise of peremptory challenges which was inconsistent with the integrity of the judicial system. The majority of the justices found that sex stereotypes were inappropriate and that gender bias could not justify exclusion of male/female jurors. Impartial juries had to be regarded as a competent collective not a matter of gender-based groups. In his separate concurring opinion, Justice Kennedy aptly summarized the Court's rationale: "the Constitution guarantees a right only to an impartial jury, not to a jury composed of members of a particular race or gender."

Related Cases

Batson v. Kentucky, 476 U.S. 79 (1986).
Wiley v. Com., 978 S.W.2d 333 (1998).

Bibliography and Further Reading

Chemerinsky, Erwin. "The End of Gender-Based Peremptory Challenges." *Trial*, August 1994, p. 69.

Cipriani, Karen L. "The Numbers Don't Add Up: Challenging the Premise of J. E. B. v. Alabama ex rel. T. B." *American Criminal Law Review*, summer 1994, p. 1253.

Deverman, Beth A. "Fourteenth Amendment—Equal Protection: The Supreme Court's Prohibition of Gender-Based Peremptory Challenges." *Journal of Criminal Law and Criminology*, spring 1995, p. 1028.

Hall, Kermit L. *The Oxford Companion to the Supreme Court of the United States*. New York: Oxford University Press, 1992.

Ogletree, Charles J. "Just Say No! A Proposal to Eliminate Racially Discriminatory Uses of Peremptory Challenges." *American Criminal Law Review,* summer 1994, p. 1099.

Salman, Robert R. "Gender Bias Examined in Jury Selection Process." *The National Law Journal,* June 6, 1994, p. C8.

Skaggs, Jason M. "Justifying Gender-Based Affirmative Action Under United States v. Virginia's 'Exceedingly Persuasive Justification' Standard." *California Law Review,* October 1998, p. 1169.

UNITED STATES V. ARMSTRONG

Legal Citation: 517 U.S. 456 (1996)

Petitioner
United States

Respondent
Christopher Lee Armstrong, et al.

Petitioner's Claim
That the government need not provide discovery (relevant documents) in a case of alleged selective prosecution unless the respondent provides a plausible basis for believing that others in similar situations have not been prosecuted.

Chief Lawyer for Petitioner
Drew S. Days III

Chief Lawyer for Respondent
Barbara E. O'Connor

Justices for the Court
Stephen Breyer, Ruth Bader Ginsburg, Anthony M. Kennedy, Sandra Day O'Connor, William H. Rehnquist (writing for the Court), Antonin Scalia, David H. Souter, Clarence Thomas,

Justices Dissenting
John Paul Stevens

Place
Washington, D.C.

Date of Decision
13 May 1996

Decision
Upheld the government's claim that African Americans prosecuted for drug offenses failed to provide enough evidence to obtain discovery supporting their claim of selective prosecution. They failed to show that the government chose not to prosecute those in similar situations.

Significance
The Supreme Court's reversal of a circuit court's decision meant that the government did not have to open its files in response to the charge that African Americans were being selectively targeted for federal prosecution of crack cocaine offenses.

For three months in 1992, three informants infiltrated an alleged crack distribution ring at the behest of agents from the Federal Bureau of Alcohol, Tobacco, and Firearms and police officers from Inglewood, California. During this time, the informants purchased a total of 124.3 grams of crack from the suspects. When agents arrested Christopher Lee Armstrong and an accomplice, they discovered more crack and a loaded firearm. Two other members of the crack ring were arrested later. Armstrong was indicted in April of 1992 in the U.S. District Court for the Central District of California on charges of conspiring to possess with intent to distribute more than 50 grams of cocaine base (crack) and federal firearms offenses.

Those arrested filed a motion for discovery or dismissal on the grounds that they were chosen for federal prosecution because they were African Americans. Discovery refers to turning over for examination documents relevant to a person's defense. To support their motion, the defendants offered an affidavit from a paralegal specialist stating that of the 24 similar cases closed by the federal public defender in the previous year, all the defendants had been black.

Although the government opposed the discovery motion, the district court granted it. The court ordered that the government supply a list of all cases from the last three years that involved both cocaine and firearms offenses, identifying the race of the defendants and the levels of law enforcement involved in the investigations. The government was also asked to explain how it decided to prosecute those defendants for federal cocaine offenses.

The government asked the court to reconsider its discovery order, with federal and local agents explaining that race played no role in their investigation. A government attorney noted that they decided to prosecute because the case involved over 100 grams of cocaine base, multiple sales took place with multiple defendants, many federal firearms offenses occurred combined with drug dealing, and audio and video tapes of the activity existed. Also, several of the defendants had criminal histories that included narcotics and firearms violations. All this led the agents to believe that the defendants were a fairly substantial crack cocaine ring.

Federal Bureau of Alcohol, Tobacco and Firearms

The Bureau of Alcohol, Tobacco and Firearms (ATF), chartered in 1971, is an agency of the U.S. Department of Treasury headquartered in Washington, D.C. The ATF has wide ranging responsibilities in the areas of regulating alcohol and tobacco, collecting alcohol and tobacco taxes, regulating firearms and explosives, and law enforcement.

By regulating the production and distribution of alcohol and tobacco, the ATF controls advertising and labeling, and directs the relationships between producers, wholesalers, and retailers. The agency inspects factories and businesses, issues licenses, and tests products. The ATF collects billions of dollars in taxes from alcohol and tobacco manufacturers every year.

Likewise, the ATF oversees laws regulating the manufacturers, dealers, and importers of firearms, ammuni-

tion, and explosives. In addition, ATF special agents, working closely with other law enforcement agencies, investigate illegal possession and use of firearms and explosives, smugglers, bombers, arsonists, gangs, and criminal organizations.

The agency lost its relative anonymity with its controversial involvement in the siege of the Branch Davidians of Waco, Texas in 1993. Believing weapons and explosives were stockpiled, ATF blockaded and finally took the compound by force. Eighty-five members of the cult perished. Throughout the 1990s, the visibility of ATF in combating violent anti-government groups substantially increased.

Source(s): Vizzard, William J. *In the Cross Fire: A Political History of the Bureau of Alcohol, Tobacco and Firearms.* Boulder, CO: Lynne Rienner, 1997.

The government also provided a report which noted that Jamaicans, Haitians, and black street gangs controlled the making and selling of crack.

The defendants' attorneys responded by submitting an affidavit from an intake coordinator at a drug treatment center who noted that an equal number of Caucasians and minorities were drug dealers and users. A "study" noted that of all 24 similar cases closed by the federal public defenders office in 1991, all the defendants were black. A criminal defense attorney, David R. Reed, stated that in his experience, he had never handled nor heard of a crack cocaine case involving non-black defendants in federal court and that many non-blacks are prosecuted in state, rather than federal, court for crack offenses. A newspaper article noted that federal crack defendants receive a harsher punishment than if they had been arrested for having powder cocaine and that most of them are black.

The district court would not reconsider its request that the government provide the documents. The government refused to comply with the discovery order, so the court dismissed the case against the defendants.

A three-judge panel of the Court of Appeals for the Ninth Circuit reversed the decision. They stated that to get the requested documents in a selective-prosecution claim, the defendants would need to show a strong reason to believe that others in similar situations had not been prosecuted. Selective prosecution refers to prosecuting only people belonging to a certain group for a specific offense.

However, when all the judges of the court of appeals reheard the case, they affirmed the earlier dismissal,

stating that the defendants were not required to show that the government failed to prosecute others in similar situations. The court also noted that the district court judge did have the power to order the discovery.

The U.S. Supreme Court heard arguments in the case on 26 February 1996 to determine the appropriate standard for discovery for a selective-prosecution claim. In an 8-1 decision, the Court reversed the court of appeals' ruling. Chief Justice Rehnquist delivered the Court's opinion.

Selective Prosecution Claims

Armstrong's attorney, Barbara E. O'Connor, felt that the Federal Rule of Criminal Procedure 16, which dealt with discovery in criminal cases, supported the result reached in the court of appeals. The rule stated that the government would provide to the defendant documents which are relevant to the defendant's defense, or which will be used by the government as evidence, or were obtained from the defendant. O'Connor argued that government documents that discussed prosecution strategy in cocaine cases were relevant to the selective-prosecution claim. Rehnquist interpreted the rule to mean that documents need only be provided for the defendant's response to the case-in-chief, not for the preparation of selective-prosecution claims.

Rehnquist noted that a selective-prosecution claim asks a court to exercise judicial power over the executive branch's responsibility to prosecute. Rehnquist expressed concern that the performance of a prosecutor's duties not be impaired. If the basis of a prosecution is examined, it delays the criminal proceedings, chills law enforcement, and might undermine the effectiveness of prosecutors by making known the government's enforcement policy.

A selective-prosecution claim requires that the claimant demonstrate that the federal prosecutorial policy "had a discriminatory effect and that it was motivated by a discriminatory purpose." To show the effect was discriminatory in a race case, "the claimant must show that similarly situated individuals of a different race were not prosecuted." Because discovery imposes many costs on the government, diverts prosecutors' resources, and may disclose strategy, the standard for discovery must be as rigorous as the standard for proving a selective-prosecution claim.

The court of appeals made its decision based on the concept that people of all races commit all types of crimes, but statistics do not support this. In fact, statistics show that 90 percent of the people sentenced in 1994 for crack cocaine trafficking were black; 93.4 percent of convicted LSD dealers were white; 91 percent of those convicted for pornography or prostitution were white.

The materials that Armstrong presented failed to show the existence of the essential elements of a selective-prosecution claim. The "study" did not identify individuals who were not black and could have been prosecuted for the same offenses, but who were not prosecuted. The newspaper article was not relevant to discrimination in decisions to prosecute. The affidavits recounted hearsay, personal conclusions, and anecdotal evidence. Rehnquist noted, "We think the required threshold—a credible showing of different treatment of similarly situated persons—adequately balances the Government's interest in vigorous prosecution and the defendant's interest in avoiding selective prosecution." The judgment of the court of appeals was reversed and the case was remanded.

Justice Breyer concurred but noted that the Federal Rule of Criminal Procedure 16 should not limit the defendant's discovery rights to the government's case-in-chief. Breyer held that the rule should provide a broad authorization for discovery.

Judicial Vigilance Necessary in Drug Prosecutions

Justice Stevens dissented in this case. He agreed that the facts presented to the district court showing that the defendants had been singled out because of race were not sufficient. However, he felt that the district judge did not abuse her discretion when she concluded that the facts were sufficiently disturbing to require some response from the government. Breyer pointed out that three circumstances underscore the need for judicial vigilance in certain types of drug prosecutions. First, the Anti-Drug Abuse Act of 1986 established high penalties for the possession and selling of crack cocaine. One gram of crack is treated as the equivalent of 100 grams of powder cocaine, resulting in sentences for crack offenders that average three to eight times longer than for powder offenders. The prison terms for those convicted in state systems in crack cases are much shorter than in the federal system. "Finally, it is undisputed that the brunt of the elevated federal penalties falls heavily on blacks. While 65 percent of the persons who have used crack are white, in 1993 they represented only 4 percent of the federal offenders convicted of trafficking in crack. Eighty-eight percent of such offenders were black."

These troubling racial patterns of enforcement call for concern about the fairness of how people are charged with crack offenses. The federal judges in the Central District of California need to scrutinize the evidence that black defendants are prosecuted in federal court, but other races are prosecuted in state court. Breyer noted that the district judge was within her discretion to ask for information that would show what standards governed the choice between a prosecution in federal versus state court.

Breyer disagreed with the majority that the affidavits submitted by Armstrong were hearsay and anecdotal. He felt that evidence based on a drug counselor's personal observations or an attorney's practice in state and federal court can tend to show the existence of a selective prosecution. Breyer summed up his dissent by stating, "In this case, the evidence was sufficiently disturbing to persuade the District Judge to order discovery that might help explain the conspicuous racial pattern of cases before her Court."

Impact

As a result of the Court's decision, the Federal Public Defender's office in Los Angeles said it will look for comparable crack cocaine cases of non-African Americans that were prosecuted in state court, as opposed to federal court. Although *United States v. Armstrong* was seen as a setback for defense attorneys, they continue to find creative ways to attack crack penalties.

Related Cases
Ah Sin v. Wittman, 198 U.S. 500 (1905).
Oyler v. Boles, 368 U.S. 448 (1962).
Wayte v. United States, 470 U.S. 598 (1985).
Hunter v. Underwood, 471 U.S. 222 (1985).
Batson v. Kentucky, 476 U.S. 79 (1986).
Wade v. United States, 504 U.S. 181 (1992).

Bibliography and Further Reading
Gastwirth, Joseph L., and Tapan K. Nayak. "Statistical Aspects of Cases Concerning Racial Discrimination in Drug Sentencing." *Journal of Criminal Law and Criminology,* winter 1997, p. 583.

Harris, David A. "'Driving While Black' and All Other Traffic Offenses." *Journal of Criminal Law and Criminolgy*, winter 1997, p. 544.

Jampol, Melissa L. "Goodbye to the Defense of Selective Prosecution." *Journal of Criminal Law and Criminology,* spring 1997, p. 932.

Johnson, Sheri Lynn. "Race, Crime, and the Law." *Yale Law Journal,* June 1998, p. 2619.

Karlan, Pamela S. "Race, Rights, and Remedies in Criminal Adjudication." *Michigan Law Review,* June 1998, p. 2001.

Poulin, Anne Bowen. "Prosecutorial Discretion and Selective Prosecution." *American Criminal Law Review,* Spring 1997, p. 1071.

POTTINGER V. CITY OF MIAMI

Legal Citation: No. 91-5316, No. 92-5145, No. 95-4555 (1997)

Plaintiffs
Michael Pottinger, Peter Carter, Berry Young

Defendant
City of Miami

Plaintiffs' Claim
That the city of Miami had a policy of harassing homeless people and routinely seized and destroyed their property in violation of their constitutional rights.

Chief Lawyer for Plaintiffs
Benjamin S. Waxman

Chief Defense Lawyer
Quinn Jones III

Justices for the Court
Joseph W. Hatchett (writing for the court), R. Lanier Anderson, Peter T. Fay

Justices Dissenting
None

Place
Atlanta, Georgia

Date of Decision
2 February 1996

Decision
That a settlement agreement between the homeless of Miami and the City of Miami would provide for police training, law enforcement contracts with the homeless, record keeping, an advisory committee, and $600,000 compensation for the homeless.

Significance
Pottinger v. City of Miami is a landmark class action case brought on behalf of the homeless. The case is a model of how these types of cases can be resolved.

The homeless of Miami, Florida, filed a class action lawsuit in the U.S. District Court for the Southern District of Florida against the city of Miami in December of 1988. The homeless charged that the Miami police had a policy of harassing homeless people for sleeping, eating, and performing life sustaining activities in public places with the purpose of driving them out of the city or rendering them invisible. In addition, the class asserted that the city routinely seized and destroyed its members' property and failed to follow its inventory procedures when confiscating personal property. The class asserted that the city's activities constituted cruel and unusual punishment, malicious abuse of process, and unlawful searches and seizures, in violation of due process, the right to privacy, and the Equal Protection Clause. The class asked for declaratory judgment, compensatory damages, and reasonable attorney's fees. Additionally, the class sought to stop the city from arresting homeless people for conducting necessary life sustaining activities and from destroying their personal property.

City's Treatment of Homeless Violated Their Constitutional Rights

The district court ruled that the city's practice of arresting homeless individuals for harmless life sustaining activities that they are forced to perform in public is unconstitutional because the arrests constituted cruel and unusual punishment in violation of the Eighth Amendment, restricted innocent conduct in violation of the Due Process Clause of the Fourteenth Amendment, and burdened the fundamental right to travel in violation of the Equal Protection Clause. The court also determined that the city's practice of seizing and destroying the property of homeless people without following its written procedures for found or seized property violated the class's Fourth Amendment rights.

On 16 November 1992, the district court entered its findings of fact and conclusions and order on the plaintiffs' request for declaratory and injunctive relief. The district court ordered the following: (1) the parties must meet and establish two safe zones where homeless people may remain without being arrested for harmless activities; (2) the city's police department may not

Homeless Rights

Homelessness in America significantly escalated through the 1980s with estimates of possibly as many as three million people living on the streets or in temporary facilities by the late 1990s. As the numbers increased, the occurrence of homeless families with children became more prevalent. Also, with increased visibility came reactions from society to suppress the visibility and intrusion of homelessness on communities. Nationally, Congress lacked a clear response to the increasing problem. Consequently, states and local governments began taking action citing health problems and increasing crime in locations where street people congregate. New laws restricted panhandling on streets, loitering, camping in public spaces, and sleeping in the public. Advocates for homeless rights claimed the laws constituted homeless harassment. Police tearing down shacks and tents and destroying personal property constituted illegal search and seizure, anti-panhandling ordinances unconstitutionally restricted free speech, and loitering ordinances violated peoples' right to travel.

Advocates pressed for recognition of right to shelter and emergency assistance, child welfare, mental health care, voting rights, and right to education. The New York Coalition for the Homeless successfully gained state and city support for housing for the homeless mentally ill. However, communities generally only provided minimal assistance in response to court orders or to avoid expensive lawsuits.

Source(s): Stoner, Madeleine R. *The Civil Rights of Homeless People: Law, Social Policy, and Social Work Practice.* New York: Aldine de Gruyler, 1995.

arrest homeless people for performing harmless life sustaining acts in the two designated safe zones; (3) the city may not arrest homeless people for sleeping or eating in two primary locales until the parties agree upon the location of the new safe zones; (4) the city's police department may not destroy homeless persons' property; (5) the city must follow its written procedures governing the handling of personal property; and (6) the city must provide the public with five days notice before cleaning parks to enable homeless people to move their property to a nearby place the city may designate. The city appealed, challenging the basis and scope of the district court's injunction.

C. Clyde Atkins, judge for the U.S. Court of Appeals, Eleventh Circuit, heard the city's appeal on 2 December 1994. He noted that since the district court's 1992 order, the city and private entities had constructed homeless shelters to address the problems on which the district court had ruled. Certain provisions of the injunction were unclear. For example, it was unclear whether the city may arrest homeless people for engaging in lawful conduct when they are outside the safe zones, or whether the city must transport homeless people to the safe zones. Finally, the parties did not comply with the district court's order directing them to establish safe zones through negotiation. Atkins remanded (sent back) the case for the district court to address these concerns. He stated that the district court should issue appropriate clarifying language to guide the city in its determination of the scope of its duties under the injunction, and the district court should consider whether its injunction should be modified in light of recent events. The district court should address these concerns within a reasonable time.

On 7 April 1995, following an evidentiary hearing, the district court entered its findings on order of the Eleventh Circuit Court of Appeals. The district court ultimately concluded that "though improvement in the overall situation is occurring via the Dade County Homeless Assistance Trust, the salient facts of this case have not changed substantially . . ." Thus, the district court determined that its original injunction should remain in effect with few modifications.

On 7 February 1996, following further briefing and oral argument, the Eleventh Circuit Court of Appeals entered an interim order referring this matter to a mediator for settlement discussions. The parties engaged in extensive settlement negotiations and agreed to resolve each and every remaining issue in this case.

Negotiations Lead To Settlement Agreement

As a result of the lawsuit, Miami participated in a countywide effort to provide services and assistance to homeless people. In keeping with its past and ongoing efforts, Miami committed itself to ensuring that the legal and constitutional rights of all homeless people be fully respected by all city policies, rules, regulations, practices, officials, and personnel. On 18 December 1997, Miami Mayor Xavier Suarez signed a resolution approving a settlement with the American Civil Liberties Union of Florida to end the nine-year lawsuit filed on behalf of the homeless people of Miami. The settlement agreement resulted from the collective efforts of American Civil Liberties Union (ACLU) attorneys on behalf of the homeless, the city attorney's office, and many other community leaders, homeless activists, and homeless people over the last two years. The agreement provided for police training regarding the circumstances and rights of homeless people. Miami agreed to implement various forms of training for its law enforcement officers to sensitize them to the unique struggle and circumstances of homeless persons and to ensure that their legal rights shall be fully respected.

The agreement set up a protocol for law enforcement contacts with homeless persons to prevent arrests, harassment, and the destruction of their property. The Miami Police Department adopted a departmental order regarding the treatment of the homeless within the city which reflected the city's commitment to respect the constitutional rights of homeless people and implemented the protocol which law enforcement officers must follow when they encounter homeless persons. Records regarding police contacts were mandated. An advisory committee was set up to monitor compliance with the agreement. The committee has monitored all police contacts with homeless people by interviewing them on the streets, by patrolling with police officers, by accompanying city outreach workers in areas with high concentrations of the homeless, by overseeing police training, by reviewing the training curriculum, and by reviewing information on file with the appropriate unit within the Miami Police Department. The advisory committee has also received and has investigated complaints by homeless people. A $600,000 compensation fund was set up for the homeless who have been injured by the unconstitutional conduct that was condemned by the federal courts. Each successful claimant was awarded a debit card in the amount of $1,500.00. Attorney fees for the plaintiffs' lawyers were also included in the settlement.

Impact

Cooperating ACLU attorney Benjamin S. Waxman noted that this was a landmark settlement recognizing that the homeless cannot be denied fundamental constitutional rights simply because they are homeless. Waxman felt that the settlement showed the best of what can be achieved when two sides of a dispute work together to find common ground to accomplish a mutual goal. The settlement may serve as a model for how other cities treat the homeless.

On 1 April 1998, the ACLU expanded *Torres v. Metropolitan Dade County and City of Miami,* a case involving Hispanic men arrested for "loitering for purposes of temporary employment." The ACLU was concerned that police enforcement was directed exclusively at one ethnic group. Andy Kayton, Legal Director of the ACLU of Florida, stated that the *Pottinger* case is a good model for how these types of cases can be resolved. He hoped that the county and city could discuss the problems involving the Hispanic day laborers in the same way that the problem with the homeless of Miami was discussed and resolved.

Related Cases

Newell v. Prudential Ins. Co. of America, 904 F. 2d 644 (1990).

Alabama-Tombigbee Rivers Coalition v. Dept. of Interior, 26 F. 3d 1103 (1994).

Bibliography and Further Reading

ACLU of Florida. http://www.aclufl.org.

Ellickson, Robert C. "Controlling Chronic Misconduct in City Spaces." *Yale Law Journal,* March 1996, p. 1165.

CUSTODY AND CHILD SUPPORT

Introduction

Of all issues facing partners following dissolution of their marriage, by far the most emotional, stressful and controversial one is that which addresses the future care and custody of children born of the marriage. All states require natural or adoptive parents to support their children until the children reach the age of majority (with some exceptions) or go on active military duty. All states consider the best interests of the children in awarding custody to one or both parents. Most states have visitation statutes addressing the rights of grandparents, other relatives, and non-custodial parents to spend time with the children. A majority of states have adopted uniform laws to prevent "forum-shopping" and the abduction or relocation of children to states with laws more advantageous to the relocating parent. Domestic issues such as child support and custody tend to clog state court systems and tax court resources, often causing a delay in other civil matters on the docket. As a result, many states are creating separate family law or domestic law divisions within their court systems, to expedite the handling of these claims as well as promote judicial economy.

Child Custody

Upon dissolution of a marriage, states require that the courts address child custody as part of the divorce judgment. This involves issues of both legal and physical custody, sole or joint. Legal custody involves the right to make major decisions affecting the child, whereas physical custody addresses the day-to-day care and living arrangements for the child. Many courts will rule separately on legal and physical custody, and for each, whether such custody is vested in one parent or both. All rulings are subject to modification upon petition of either party to the court, as a result of an alleged significant change in circumstances.

Historically, early common law gave custody of the children to the father, as children were considered "property" in the eyes of the law. This was followed by the Talfourd Act, which instructed the courts to award custody of children "of tender years" to their mother. Many states then created a legal presumption that the mother should be granted custody. The presumption

corresponded appropriately with social mores and attitudes of the time that endorsed the perception of female parents as nurturing, domestically-oriented care-providers. Finally, in the latter half of the twentieth century, courts have modified statutes to remove any presumption of gender fitness for custody, for the most part relegating it to the role of a tie-breaker factor, if all else was equal. Courts now rely on judicial discretion and determination of "the best interests of the child." The Uniform Marriage and Divorce Act (UMDA), which, among other things, standardizes the criteria used to determine custody, has been adopted in many states. However, the UMDA criteria are ultimately weighted and factored in conjunction with the considerable latitude and discretion afforded the courts. In any event, a consideration of the child's best interests would theoretically include such factors as the wishes of the child's parents toward custody; the wishes of the child as to his preference for custodian; the child's adjustment to his home, school and community; the interaction and interrelationship of the child with his parents, siblings or others; and the mental, physical and financial health of all individuals involved. In contested battles for custody, most courts will not consider conduct or fault in the marriage on the part of a potential custodian that does not affect his or her relationship with the child. Unless a court has convincing evidence before it that harm may come to the child or a parent, most states prefer shared (joint) custody and parental decision-making. In fact, some courts have now created statutory presumptions of joint custody, to be ordered absent any convincing evidence that it would not be in the best interests of the child.

Variations abound. Some courts disfavor "split custody" which awards custody of one or more children to one parent, and the remaining children to the other parent. Other courts favor split custody as it has the appearance of fairness. Split custody has been criticized as disruptive of the emotional bond and support gained between siblings, and often leads to polarized feelings. Often when this determination is employed, it is usually to address a temporary circumstance. Another variation is referred to as "bird's nest" custody. The children remain in one home and the parents alternately move in and out. This provides environmental stability to children, instead of being "shipped off" from parent to parent, and often contributes toward more consistent parenting. Still other courts will order alternating or "serial" custody wherein children will live with one parent for a long time (typically a year), then switch to the other. This is to be distinguished from joint custody in that the custodial parent has sole, not joint, custody during the time the child is with him/her. Finally, a court may deem both parents unfit for custody, or the parents have voluntarily relinquished their right to custody. In these circumstances, third parties may be granted custody, including grandparents, godparents, stepparents, and family friends. However, in most jurisdictions, there is a presumption that the biological parent has a "natural" right to the child superior to the claims of third parties.

Custody principles have been taxed to address arguments over frozen embryo, domestic pets, and children born outside of the marriage. Conversely, in the absence of fit biological parents, courts have applied "best interest" criteria in granting custody to adoptive parents, "psychological parents" (those who have established a significant emotional bond with a child) and (at least in Michigan and Wisconsin) to "equitable parents" (typically, a spouse who is neither a biological nor adoptive parent to the child).

In addition to the common "best interests of the child" criteria, courts vary in their consideration of other factors in awarding custody. Additional criteria frequently weighed are the parent's ability to meet the needs of the child, the moral fitness and conduct of the parent, a history of any child abuse, the geographic distance between the parents' homes, the hostility of one parent toward the other, and the sexual orientation of the parent. In the 1984 case of *Palmore v. Sidoti,* the U.S. Supreme Court ruled that it was unconstitutional for a court to consider race when a noncustodial parent petitions a court for a change in custody. The court held that societal stigma, especially a racial one, cannot serve as a sole or determinative basis for a custody decision. In many state courts, this argument has been raised in defense of granting custody to homosexual parents, but often fails for its distinguishing facts.

Most custody decisions are made by a judge or magistrate within the state's court system. In a handful of states, a jury may hear arguments and decide. Many states also provide for the appointment of an independent guardian *ad litem* to represent the child's interests so that the child is shielded from being a party to the dispute, or actually having to testify or respond to the court's inquiry. In such cases, the guardian may be a court-assigned stranger, or a nominated family relative or attorney. Many courts also provide for mediation or arbitration of custody disputes. Often the medi-

ations are confidential by statutory provision, and serve merely to provide a forum for extra-judicial resolution or recommendation. In many states, the court may order a custody investigation and/or solicit recommendations by independent or court-appointed evaluators (mediators, "Friend of the Court" appointees, etc.). Additionally, statutes often provide courts with the power to compel parents to participate in mediation to resolve custody disputes before bringing the matter before the court. A court's power to adjudicate custody matters is generally terminated when the child either reaches the age of majority, or is "emancipated" by getting married, joining the military, or is adopted by other parents. This must be determined judicially, not by the parents or child. There is continuing jurisdiction of the courts in some circumstances, as when the child is legally incompetent.

Visitation

The correlative rights of noncustodial parents are those of visitation. Visitation rights may also be judicially granted to others affected by the custody award, such as grandparents, relatives, siblings, and persons having a significant interest in the welfare of the child, such as a non-biological, foster or adoptive parent. This is true even where the parents object to the visitation as interfering with their right to raise their children as they see fit. Moreover, many states have expressly created language granting visitation rights to otherwise fit, biological fathers (but unwed parents) of children, whether or not the biological mother has since seen the father. The implication of the U.S. Supreme Court case of *Vanderlaan v. Vanderlaan* is that in any circumstance where the father, mother and child have lived in a *de facto* (actual, if not officially recognized) family setting, the father has potential visitation rights. Many states go beyond that in granting visitation to estranged or recently-ascertained biological fathers.

There are several classifications of visitation which may be awarded. "Reasonable visitation" allows the parents to create their own visitation schedule, most applicable in non-adversarial divorce cases. The noncustodial parent is allowed to see the child upon "reasonable notice" to the custodial parent. A "fixed-schedule" visitation, or court-scheduled visitation is imposed when there is parental conflict over visitation rights. It must be emphasized that many courts have held that custodial parents have more than a duty to simply let visitation happen according to the court's order. In cases where noncustodial parents assign low priority to meeting fixed-schedule visitations, courts may order that the custodial parent actually deliver the child to the noncustodial parent for purposes of visitation. Such courts reason that until a child is old enough to make his own decisions not to visit with the noncustodial parent, frequent exposure to that parent will facilitate independent development of the child's perception of that parent, as well as insure that the child has had the benefit of emotional and physical development under both parents. However, when a noncustodial parent has a history of violent or destructive behavior, especially toward the child, courts will order "supervised visitation." Such visitation requires that an adult other than the custodial parent be present at all times during the visitation. The adult may be someone agreed upon by the parties, or an independent person appointed by the court, but in all circumstances, the court must approve the particular person chosen. Restricted or supervised visitation may also be ordered when a noncustodial parent has not seen the child for a long time (until he or she can demonstrate ability to care for the child). The same is often ordered where the parent may not impose any direct harm upon the child, but may engage in harmful conduct in the presence of the child, such as with substance abuse, cruelty to animals, or a history of reckless vehicle driving. Again, the operative language in visitation disputes focuses on the "best interests of the child." As with custody decisions, visitation awards and decisions are subject to modification upon petition of a party or other interested person, whenever new evidence or changes in circumstance warrant such review or modification. Again, the court's authority is terminated upon the child reaching the age of majority, or being judicially declared as "emancipated" following marriage of the child, joining the military, etc., but may continue in the presence of a legally-incompetent child.

Child Support

Inextricably bound to the states' powers to adjudicate custody and visitation rights are the states' powers to impose and order the payment of financial support to the custodial parent. While both parents are responsible for their children, the custodial parent generally meets that obligation through the act of custody. The noncustodial parent meets that obligation by paying for the child's care. Court-imposed support orders are most often the result of divorced parents, but can arise from other circumstances such as legal separation, annulment and paternity actions involving "presumed" or "acknowledged" fathers. Child support payments are distinct awards not related to alimony or other "rehabilitative support" payments.

States now require that child support awards be computed by a mandated formula which weighs certain factors or criteria such as the needs of the child, the relative income and assets of the parents, and the standard of living to which the child was formerly accustomed. Many statutes permit a court to depart from the presumed correct formula, and modify the award where it is unjust or inappropriate by reason of facts peculiar to that case. A court may also overrule the private parties'

non-judicial agreement. Also included in most support orders are provisions dictating to whom the payments should be made (the custodial parent, an officer of the court, etc.). A child support order may also contain provisions mandating that the paying party maintain health and life insurance policies to protect against interruption or loss of support. Security deposits may be required, along with the payment of late fees and COLA (Cost of Living Adjustments).

Child support ends upon the child's reaching the age of majority, or upon a judicially-determined emancipation of the child through marriage, adoption, military service, etc. Conversely, state provisions often mandate continued support until the child completes a certain level of education or attains a certain age past majority, whichever comes first. Most states mandate continued coverage for disabled or legally-incompetent children. As with orders for custody and visitation, support orders are subject to modification upon petition to the court for good cause (change in circumstances).

Enforcement

Various state and federal laws protect rights of visitation, custody and support secured by court order. Federal laws include the Family Support Act of 1988, which emphasized enforcement of child support orders against delinquent parents. The act mandated that all new or modified support orders contain automatic wage attachment provisions, along with automatic tracking and monitoring systems for parents defaulting in payments. The Revised Uniform Reciprocal Enforcement of Support Act (RURESA) (or its predecessor) has been enacted in all states, or replaced/supplemented by the Uniform Interstate Family Support Act of 1992 (UIFSA). This law provides the process for enforcing child support orders against persons living in another state. In conjunction with this law, many states have developed parent locator services to aid enforcement.

The Uniform Child Custody Jurisdiction Act (UCCJA) statutorily enhances the constitutional "full faith and credit" clause by facilitating enforcement of other states' custody orders, thus avoiding relitigation of custody decisions in the prior state. It requires that litigation concerning custody take place in the forum state with which the child and his family have the closest connection and where significant evidence is most readily available. Several provisions thus serve to deter abductions and unilateral removals of children for the purpose of "forum-shopping." The Parental Kidnapping Prevention Act also parallels several provisions in the UCCJA by requiring courts to enforce judgments of other states. International kidnapping is addressed in the International Child Abduction Remedies Act.

See also: **Family Law**

Bibliography and Further Reading

Haas, Carol and the editors of Consumer Reports Books. *The Consumer Reports Law Book.* New York: Consumers Union of United States, Inc., 1994.

Jost, Kenneth. *The Supreme Court Yearbook.* Washington, D.C., 1996

Leonard, Robin, and Richard Elias. *Nolo's Pocket Guide to Family Law.* Berkeley: Nolo Press, 1994.

Lyster, Mimi E. *Child Custody.* Berkeley: Nolo Press, 1995.

Watnik, Webster. *Child Custody Made Simple.* Claremont: Single Parent Press, 1997.

SANTOSKY V. KRAMER

Legal Citation: 455 U.S. 745 (1982)

Petitioners
John and Annie Santosky

Respondent
Kramer, Commissioner of Dept. Social Services, Ulster County

Petitioners' Claim
Fair preponderance of evidence is unconstitutional when used to terminate parental rights.

Chief Lawyer for Petitioners
Martin Guggenheim

Chief Lawyer for Respondent
Steven D. Scavuzzo

Justices for the Court
Harry A. Blackmun (writing for the Court), William J. Brennan, Jr., Thurgood Marshall, Lewis F. Powell, Jr., John Paul Stevens

Justices Dissenting
Warren E. Burger, Sandra Day O'Connor, William H. Rehnquist, Byron R. White

Place
Washington, D.C.

Date of Decision
24 March 1982

Decision
Fair preponderance violates due process guaranteed by the Fourteenth Amendment.

Significance
The Court's decision regarding parental rights was that they may only be terminated by showing "clear and convincing" evidence. This changed the standard, which was, in some states "fair preponderance."

The right to raise one's own children was at stake in the landmark case *Santosky v. Kramer*. In 1982 this case caught the attention of parents, especially in the state of New York. In 1973 Commissioner Kramer of the Ulster County Department of Social Services had three children removed from the Santosky home. Kramer insisted that if the children remained in the home they would be subjected to parental neglect. John and Annie Santosky challenged this decision in New York Family Court. Their challenge's premise was that New York state's process of deciding whether or not children should be permanently removed from the care of their parents was unconstitutional. At that time, the state of New York was in the minority of states that required only a "fair preponderance of the evidence" as the standard to support parental neglect.

A majority of states did not use the "fair preponderance of the evidence" standard. They used the "clear and convincing evidence" standard. What this means is most states, in deciding what was a fair procedure to define permanent parental neglect believed that a stricter process should be used since dissolving a family was a serious issue. The Santoskys said that New York's standard of "fair preponderance of the evidence" violated their rights to due process under the Fourteenth Amendment to the U.S. Constitution.

Both the New York Family Court and the Appellate Division of the New York Supreme Court decided the current standard, "fair preponderance of the evidence" was valid and they upheld Commissioner Kramer's decision to permanently deny custody to the Santoskys. However, after the New York Court of Appeals would not hear the Santosky's appeal, the U.S. Supreme Court, in a 5-4 ruling, overturned the lower court rulings.

According to the *New York Times*, Justice Blackmun said "before a State may sever completely and irrevocably the rights of parents in their natural child, due process requires that the State support its allegations by at least clear and convincing evidence." Justices Marshall, Brennan, Powell and Stevens agreed with Blackmun, but Justices Rehnquist, O'Connor, White and Chief Justice Burger dissented.

The dissenters said that the five justices who voted to overturn the lower court rulings did not focus on what they thought to be the correct thing—the protection of the children. In the same *New York Times* article Justice Rehnquist was quoted as saying this about the case: "When the interests of the child and the State in a stable, nurturing homelife are balanced against the interests of the parents in the rearing of the child, it cannot be said that either set of interests is so clearly paramount as to require that the risk of error be allocated to one side or the other." Justice Rehnquist made the argument that New York state spent over $15,000 to try and rehabilitate the Santoskys. This did not work, so the state then decided to press for permanent removal of their parental rights.

Also making statements during the Supreme Court hearings were Mr. and Mrs. John Balogh. The Baloghs were the foster parents of one of the Santosky children beginning five days after the child was born in 1974. According to the *New York Times* article, the Baloghs said that raising the standard of proof in custody cases "will only serve to increase the risk that neglected children will remain in the limbo of foster care."

Although Justice Blackmun and the majority of the justices on the Supreme Court voted in this case to upgrade the standard of proof in parental custody cases, they did not make any statements regarding the merits of the Santoskys. In other words, even though they voted to change the standard of proof, the courts were allowed to proceed but they had to meet the new standards if they were to permanently remove custody from the Santoskys.

Santosky v. Kramer, therefore, erased the less strict standard used by some states regarding parental custody rights—"preponderance of the evidence"—and imposed a new, more stringent standard—"clear and convincing evidence." The U.S. Supreme Court did this because the majority of justices felt the existing standard was not sufficient in protecting parents' rights to the care, management, and custody of their own children.

Related Cases

Meyer v. Nebraska, 262 U.S. 390 (1923).

Pierce v. Society of Sisters, 268 U.S. 510 (1925).

In re Winship, 397 U.S. 358 (1970).

Moore v. East Cleveland, 431 U.S. 494 (1977).

Bibliography and Further Reading

"Court Overturns Child Abuse Law." *New York Times,* March 25, 1982, p. A28-1.

Hall, Kermit L., ed. *The Oxford Companion to the Supreme Court of the United States.* New York: Oxford University Press, 1992.

Klicka, Christopher J., and Douglas W. Phillips. "Why Parental Rights Laws Are Necessary." *Educational Leadership,* November 1997, p. 80.

Meyers, Alaya B. "Rejecting the Clear and Convincing Evidence Standard for Proof of Incompetence." *Journal of Criminal Law and Criminology,* spring 1997, p. 1016.

Phillips, Michael R. "The Constitutionality of Employer-Accessible Child Abuse Registries." *Michigan Law Review,* October 1993, p. 139.

CLARK V. JETER

Legal Citation: 486 U.S. 456 (1988)

Petitioner
Cherlyn Clark

Respondent
Gene Jeter

Petitioner's Claim
That Pennsylvania's six-year statute of limitations for paternity actions violates the Equal Protection Clause of the Fourteenth Amendment.

Chief Lawyer for Petitioner
Evalynn Welling

Chief Lawyer for Respondent
Craig A. McLean

Justices for the Court
Harry A. Blackmun, William J. Brennan, Jr., Anthony M. Kennedy, Thurgood Marshall, Sandra Day O'Connor (writing for the Court), William H. Rehnquist, Antonin Scalia, John Paul Stevens, Byron R. White

Justices Dissenting
None

Place
Washington, D.C.

Date of Decision
6 June 1988

Decision
Held that Pennsylvania's six-year statute of limitations for paternity actions violates the Equal Protection Clause of the Fourteenth Amendment.

Significance
The ruling acknowledged the constitutional right of children born out of wedlock to seek support from their fathers without the restriction of a time limit. The Supreme Court ruled that the Pennsylvania law prohibiting paternity claims after six years did not "provide a reasonable opportunity" for an illegitimate child to obtain parental support. The Court also ruled that the six-year limit, which the state had adopted to prevent the litigation of "stale or fraudulent claims," was not necessary to deter such actions.

New Directions in Family Law

In the second half of the twentieth century, changes in American society challenged traditional notions of family. Substantial increases in divorce rates, illegitimate births, and single-parent families created problems relating to the financial support of children. The welfare system struggled to cope with increased demands, while taxpayers complained about the burden of supporting children born out of wedlock. Welfare reforms encouraged mothers to identify fathers of illegitimate children to obtain financial support from them. But because putative fathers had a right to protect themselves from the risk of fraudulent claims, existing state statutes imposed time limits after which illegitimate children could no longer bring paternity actions.

On 11 June 1973, Cherlyn Clark gave birth to a daughter out of wedlock. Ten years later, Clark filed a support complaint on the child's behalf against Gene Jeter, the alleged father, in the Court of Common Pleas of Allegheny County, Pennsylvania. Blood tests showed a 99.3 percent probability that Jeter was the child's father, but the court entered judgment for Jeter because Pennsylvania law required paternity claims to be brought within six years of the birth of an illegitimate child. The mother argued that this law violated the Equal Protection and Due Process Clauses of the Fourteenth Amendment to the U.S. Constitution, but the court rejected this argument. The mother appealed to the Superior Court of Pennsylvania.

While the appeal was pending, the Pennsylvania legislature, to comply with the federal Child Support Enforcement Amendments of 1984, changed the law that had established the six-year statute of limitations. The new law, passed on 30 October 1985, allowed paternity claims to be brought within 18 years of a child's birth. In Clark's appeal, however, the Superior Court ruled that the new law was not retroactive and that the six-year statute of limitations did not violate the Constitution.

The U.S. Supreme Court issued a writ of *certiorari*, directing the lower court to forward the case proceedings for review, and decided to take the case to consider issues of constitutionality. The Court did not address the argument that Pennsylvania's new 18-year statute of limitation was retroactive. Though it is usual

---

Pro and Con: DNA Testing

DNA testing is one tool used in courts to determine biological relations to children. It has also become a powerful weapon in the fight against crime. DNA evidence has significant advantages over traditional forensic techniques. The DNA evidence at a crime scene is usually more plentiful and may be gathered from a number of sources. It does not decay: samples may be analyzed even years after the fact; dramatically, this longevity has in fact resulted in the release from prison of people who were wrongly convicted of crimes.

The basic science underlying DNA "fingerprinting" is accepted by critics of DNA evidence in court cases. They maintain, however, that mistakes are often made during laboratory work. Another contention is that the accuracy of probability estimates—the likelihood of making such a match by chance—are overstated.

Remedies proposed to allay these concerns include "sample splitting," wherein each sample is divided in half and tested at two separate laboratories, and testing of laboratories to determine the quality of their work.

Source(s): "DNA Evidence: Boon or Boondoggle for Criminal Justice?" *West's Encyclopedia of American Law.* Minneapolis, MN: West, 1998.

---

for the Court to consider an issue of statutory interpretation before considering constitutional claims, in this case the Court determined that Clark had not presented an adequate federal pre-emption argument to the lower courts. Writing for the unanimous Court, Justice O'Connor noted that the "question of how to interpret the Pennsylvania statute ultimately is a matter of state law." Therefore, the Court went on to consider the equal protection claim.

Important Precedents

Citing *Weber v. Aetna Casualty & Surety Co.* (1972), Justice O'Connor noted that the Court had ruled restrictions that "burden illegitimate children for the sake of punishing the illicit relations of their parents" are unconstitutional. In three previous cases concerning paternity claims by illegitimate children, Justice O'Connor wrote, restrictions on the child's right to obtain paternal support were found to violate the Equal Protection Clause to the Fourteenth Amendment. In *Gomez v. Perez* (1973), the Court struck down a Texas law that denied illegitimate children the right to sue for paternal support while granting that right to legitimate children. The Court ruled that "once a state posits a judicially enforceable right on behalf of children to needed support from their natural fathers there is no constitutionally sufficient justification for denying such an essential right to a child simply because its natural father has not married its mother." In *Mills v. Hableutzel* (1982), the Court struck down a Texas one-year statute of limitations for paternity claims, ruling that this period of time was insufficient to give an illegitimate child "reasonable opportunity" to bring a paternity claim. And in *Pickett v. Brown* (1983), the Court struck down a Tennessee law imposing a two-year limit on paternity claims. In these cases, the Court identified two criteria by which to evaluate statutes of limitations

on paternity claims. First, the period during which an illegitimate child could bring a claim must be of reasonable length to protect the child's interests. Second, any time restriction must be necessary to prevent the litigation of "stale or fraudulent" claims against a putative father, who might have difficulty establishing evidence in his defense after the passage of time.

Justice O'Connor indicated that in *Mills v. Hableutzel*, the Court reasoned that the mother of an illegitimate child would be likely to experience emotional and financial complexities during the child's first year and might find it difficult to bring a paternity claim during that brief time. Furthermore, the Court rejected the argument that this time limit was necessary to avoid fraud because it would be unlikely that evidence a putative father could use in his defense would be lost during the course of one year. Extending this reasoning to *Pickett v. Brown*, the Court ruled that Tennessee's two-year statute of limitations was also too short, and that the time limit was not necessary to prevent problems of proof or fraudulent claims, since new blood testing procedures could establish proof of paternity with good reliability.

In *Clark v. Jeter*, the Court found that Pennsylvania's six-year statute of limitations violated the Equal Protection Clause of the Fourteenth Amendment. Justice O'Connor wrote, "Even six years does not necessarily provide a reasonable opportunity to assert a claim on behalf of an illegitimate child" and noted that psychological and social issues might prevent a mother of a child born out of wedlock from pressing a claim within this time period. Justice O'Connor also reasoned that financial difficulties would be likely to increase as a child grew older. "Thus is it questionable whether a State acts reasonably when it requires most paternity and support actions to be brought within six years of an illegitimate child's birth."

The Court also rejected the argument that Pennsylvania's six-year statute of limitation was necessary to prevent fraud in paternity claims. Pennsylvania allowed paternity suits to be brought more than six years after the illegitimate child's birth if the suit was brought within two years of a support payment by the father, and imposed no time limits on some other types of paternity litigation. Pennsylvania's inheritance laws permitted an illegitimate child to bring a paternity suit as long as there was "clear and convincing evidence" that the alleged father was the child's father. And Pennsylvania imposed no statute of limitations on a father's right to establish paternity. Furthermore, the Court reasoned, Pennsylvania's new law establishing an 18-year statute of limitations "is a tacit concession that proof problems are not overwhelming."

Moreover, the Court noted that advances in biotechnology have changed the ways in which proof of paternity is established. In previous years, evidence of paternity was not scientifically accurate and paternity claims were difficult to prove or defend after the passage of time. Sophisticated DNA testing, however, can eliminate over 99 percent of those falsely accused of fathering a child and can be administered at any time. The availability of this reliable testing, wrote Justice O'Connor, "is an additional reason to doubt that Pennsylvania had a substantial reason for limiting the time within which paternity and support actions could be brought." In a unanimous decision, the Supreme Court ruled that Pennsylvania's six-year statute of limitations violated the Equal Protection Clause of the Fourteenth Amendment and remanded the case for further proceedings.

Impact

Clark v. Jeter continued a consistent trend in twentieth century family law to extend constitutionally protected rights to children. Through the end of the nineteenth century, the Supreme Court had traditionally avoided adjudicating family conflicts, preferring to leave such matters to the individual states. But rapid social changes in the twentieth century created conflicts that necessitated federal judicial involvement. Divorce rates, women entering the workforce, abortion and contraception, and nontraditional family structures created controversies that were brought to the nation's courts. As Kermit L. Hall pointed out in *The Oxford Companion to the Supreme Court,* "the family became a battleground for contests spawned by social change [and] the federal government, and especially the Supreme Court, became one of the primary arenas of that struggle."

The basis of the Court's intervention in family law was the Fourteenth Amendment, which guarantees due process of law and equal protection to all persons within its jurisdiction. Passed in 1868, the Fourteenth Amendment had been adopted to rectify discriminatory race laws after the Civil War and was central to the Civil Rights movement of the 1960s. The heightened attention to individual rights resulting from the Civil Rights movement, wrote Hall, "sparked new concerns about national family policies and a new sense of rights consciousness among family members." The Supreme Court began to give new rights to children born out of wedlock, departing from the tradition of Anglo-Saxon law that had privileged marriage by denying family rights to illegitimate children. Starting with *Levy v. Louisiana* (1968), in which the Court ruled that illegitimate children had the same right as legitimate children to sue for damages after their mother's death, the Court began to develop a new set of standards pertaining to cases of illegitimacy. In the years since, the Court has consistently struck down obstacles to illegitimate children seeking parental support, but sought to balance children's rights with the rights of putative fathers to defend themselves against false paternity claims.

With new genetic testing that can determine paternity to a greater than 99 percent certainty, the Court found that statutes of limitation on paternity claims, instituted to protect the alleged father's right to establish a defense against a fraudulent claim, are no longer necessary. *Clark v. Jeter* continues the trend to extend equal protection guarantees to children born out of wedlock.

Related Cases

Levy v. Louisiana, 391 U.S. 68 (1968).
Weber v. Aetna Casualty Surety Co., 406 U.S. 164 (1972).
Gomez v. Perez, 409 U.S. 535 (1973).
Mills v. Hableutzel, 456 U.S. 91 (1982).
Pickett v. Brown, 462 U.S. 1 (1983).

Bibliography and Further Reading

Brienza, Julie. "Paternity Settlements Ruled Unconstitutional by Michigan Court." *Trial,* August 1995, p. 80.

Hall, Kermit L., ed. *The Oxford Companion to the Supreme Court of the United States.* New York: Oxford University Press, 1992.

Lieberman, Jethro K. *The Enduring Constitution: An Exploration of the First Two Hundred Years.* New York: Harper & Row, 1987.

IN RE BABY GIRL CLAUSEN

Legal Citation: 502 N. W. 2d 649 (1993)

Appellants
Jan and Roberta DeBoer

Appellees
Daniel Schmidt and Cara Clausen

Appellants' Claim
That Michigan courts could modify Iowa custody orders under authority of the Uniform Child Custody Jurisdiction Act.

Chief Lawyer for Appellants
Suellyn Scarecchia

Chief Lawyers for Appellees
Richard S. Victor, Scott Bassett, Marian L. Faupel

Justices for the Court
Patricia J. Boyle, James Brickley, Michael F. Cavanagh (writing for the court), Richard A. Griffin, Conrad L. Mallatt, Jr., Dorothy Comstock Riley

Justice Dissenting
Charles Levin

Place
Lansing, Michigan

Date of Decision
2 July 1993

Decision
Found in favor of the Clausens by upholding a Michigan court of appeals ruling that denied the DeBoers legal standing to challenge for custody of baby girl Clausen.

Significance
The ruling asserted legal precedence of the Parental Kidnapping Prevention Act over previous federal law by compelling states to honor custody requests from other states. Issues focused on the "best interest of the child" proved not significant for court custody determinations. Though issues of inconsistent interstate child custody processes had been the subject of much debate and reform efforts, inconsistency in court rulings and treatment of children as property still remained as chief concerns of child protection advocates.

Enforcement of interstate child custody orders long presented vexing problems. In early child custody cases, courts traditionally resolved jurisdiction (the power to hear and determine a case) disputes on one or more of the following factors: the father's permanent home, the child's place of residence at the beginning of the dispute, or the child's physical presence in a state other than the child's permanent residence. Uncertainty concerning jurisdiction was further complicated by the Full Faith and Credit Clause in Article IV of the U.S. Constitution under which courts could freely modify the custody orders of sister states. The clause only demands that a state court give the same respect to another state's judgement that it affords its own. Courts historically did not view custody orders as final, even in the state of issue.

In an attempt to reduce jurisdictional disputes, the Supreme Court in *May v. Anderson* (1953) limited the exercise of jurisdiction to courts possessing jurisdiction over the subject of the custody request. With confusion persisting due to inconsistent rulings and enforcement of child custody orders, the National Conference of Commissioners on Uniform State Laws lobbied for the Uniform Child Custody Jurisdiction Act (UCCJA) of 1968. The UCCJA established a formal set of jurisdictional criteria to guide courts in making more consistent claims of jurisdiction over such disputes by largely deferring to states where the child had their most significant contacts. Despite widespread acceptance of the UCCJA by the states, variations in state laws implementing the federal law and differing interpretations resulted in continuing uncertainty about the enforceability of child custody decisions. In 1980, Congress responded again by passing the Parental Kidnapping Prevention Act (PKPA) requiring states to enforce child custody decisions by courts of other states when in the best interest of the child. The act also defined the "home state" as "the State in which, immediately preceding the time involved, the child lived with his parents, a parent, or a person acting as parent, for at least six consecutive months, and in the case of a child less than six months old, the State in which the child lived from birth with any of such persons."

Concerning child custody orders in general, the U.S. legal system traditionally regarded children as the property of their parents, commonly resolving custody

Parental Kidnapping Prevention Act

In 1980, Congress recognized and addressed a growing problem in the United States and its territories. Child custody and visitation disputes between parents were sometimes becoming kidnapping cases. In a dispute, the child could be removed from one parent and taken out of state. Then the other parent would appeal to the court in the new state for a custody or visitation ruling, thereby circumventing the original court's ruling or jurisdiction.

The Parental Kidnapping Prevention Act of 1980, passed by Congress and signed into law by the president on 28 December 1980, was designed to stop this practice. This legislation established a national standard in custody battles involving more than one state court jurisdiction. The act prohibits one state court from changing a child custody order made by another state. The only exceptions are if the original court clearly no longer has jurisdiction over the matter, or has not accepted jurisdiction in order to change the original decree.

Source(s): http://www.brandeslaw.com/uccja.htm.
28 USC Sec. 1738A
http://www.divorcenet.com:80/28uscode.html.

---

matters with a bias toward keeping children with their biological parents. As a result, the "best interests of a child" were overshadowed by the rights of the biological family. In the 1990s, the courts still tended to focus on the capabilities of the parents rather than on the children's needs.

A Change of Heart

On 8 February 1991, Cara Clausen, age 28 and single, gave birth to a baby girl in Cedar Rapids, Iowa. Cara decided she was unable to raise the child on her own and arranged, through an attorney, to have Jan and Roberta DeBoer, who had been desperately trying to adopt for several years, adopt the baby. On 25 February at a routine court hearing, Cara gave the judge a signed release of parental rights. The judge also received a signed release from Cara's boyfriend at the time, Scott Seefeldt, whom Cara named as the baby's father. With all the appropriate steps taken, the judge severed Cara and Scott's parental rights. The DeBoers and the baby returned home to Michigan.

Days later in a sudden change of heart, Cara announced she wanted the baby after all. More significantly, Cara had lied about the identity of the child's father. The actual biological father was Dan Schmidt with whom she had broken up with months before. This revelation meant that while Cara's parental rights had been severed, Dan's had not. With Dan and Cara planning marriage, Cara filed a motion on 6 March to have her daughter returned. Dan did the same a week later. The DeBoers, finally finding a healthy newborn to adopt, maintained they should not be penalized for Cara's erratic behavior. The DeBoers were unable to finalize the adoption as a result of the dispute and legally fought back.

In November of 1991, a district court in Iowa upon hearing the case facts found that Dan Schmidt was the biological father and had not abandoned the child. As a result, the court ruled the adoption void and ordered the child returned by the DeBoers. The DeBoers were granted a legal stay allowing them to keep the child while they appealed the district court's decision. An appellate court affirmed the district court's decision as did the Iowa Supreme Court. In addition, the supreme court maintained that a natural parent's right to custody could not to be disrupted without a showing of parental unfitness which was not established by the DeBoers. With the case returned for trial from the Iowa Supreme Court, the district court in early December of 1992 terminated the DeBoers' right as temporary guardians of the girl.

On the same day their rights were terminated in Iowa, the DeBoers filed a petition in a Michigan circuit court asking the court to assume jurisdiction under the UCCJA. The DeBoers requested the court to find the Iowa custody order not enforceable and return custody back to the them. In response, the Michigan circuit court asserted jurisdiction to determine the best interests of the child. Upon appeal by the Schmidts, the Michigan court of appeals reversed the Michigan circuit court's decision in March of 1993, concluding the Michigan circuit court lacked jurisdiction under UCCJA. The court of appeals also found that, due to the termination of their guardianship, the DeBoers lacked legal standing to challenge the Iowa court order. The DeBoers appealed the case to the Supreme Court of Michigan.

Iowa Is Judged Home

In a 6-1 decision, the Michigan Supreme Court found Iowa had jurisdiction over the adoption proceeding under the PKPA's home state jurisdiction requirement. Chief Justice Michael F. Cavanaugh, in writing for the court, rejected the DeBoers' argument that Michigan

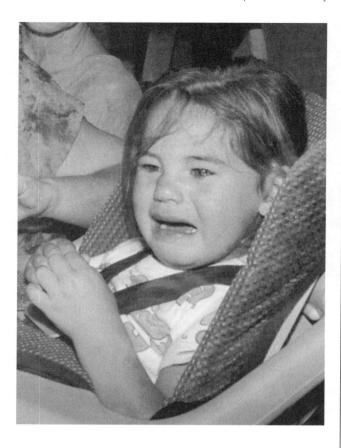

Baby Jessica cries as she is taken away from her adoptive parents, August 1993. © Photograph by Lennox Mclendon. AP/Wide World Photos.

courts could modify the Iowa custody ruling. Cavanaugh found that the Iowa courts consistently followed the guidelines of the PKPA and established Iowa as the home state for baby Clausen. The Iowa custody was thus awarded due to the full faith and credit afforded to decrees from sister states under the PKPA in conformity with the U.S. Constitution. Therefore, Michigan courts could not exercise jurisdiction over the interstate custody dispute. Cavanaugh also rejected the DeBoers' argument that PKPA and UCCJA required an analysis concerning the best interests of the girl since neither act contained a test to measure the child's best interests.

Because an Iowa district court terminated the DeBoers' rights as temporary guardians under the PKPA, the Michigan Supreme Court determined that the DeBoers had no legal authority in seeking custody in Michigan courts. Thus, when the temporary custody order was terminated, the DeBoers became third parties to the girl and no longer had a legal basis to claim custody.

In the lone dissenting opinion, Justice Levin insisted PKPA actually provided Michigan with jurisdiction to modify the Iowa court order. Levine argued Michigan had both home site status and a sufficient connection to the case for establishing jurisdiction. The girl lived with the DeBoers in Michigan from February of 1991 until July of 1993. She only resided in Iowa for less than three weeks, during which time she was never in custody of either biological parent. According to the facts, Levin contended Michigan indeed had proper jurisdiction under PKPA. Levin argued the majority's finding directly contradicted congressional intent and, if widely accepted, freed courts to manipulate the PKPA in order to justify their own decisions in future child custody cases. Levin wrote that the PKPA actually seeks to avoid courts "blindly ignoring the consideration of the child's best interests."

Impact

The U.S. Supreme Court refused to grant a further stay to the DeBoers in July of 1993. The parental rights doctrine and "best interests of the child" standards continue to be inconsistently applied in child custody cases. The parental rights doctrine maintains that a biological parent is presumed to be the best parent until they are affirmatively shown as unfit. Through the 1990s, a trend toward considering the best interest of the child grew as promoted in *Clausen*'s dissenting opinion. Despite this trend, Iowa courts in *Clausen* declared they could not, and should not, consider the interests of the child, maintaining throughout that only if Dan Schmidt was determined to be unfit as a parent could the courts consider the interests of the child. By deferring to Iowa, the Michigan Supreme Court decision refused to consider evidence of a psychological relationship between the child and third parties. Critics argued the child was treated merely as property rather than as a person with fundamental rights.

Three other child custody decisions were handed down in the month following the *Clausen* ruling, further contributing to the confusion surrounding custody cases. In *Twigg v. Mays*, a Florida circuit court determined that a 14-year-old girl, accidentally switched at birth with another baby in the hospital, could not be forced to visit her biological parents. The court ruled that "mere" biological ties were not sufficient to determine the legal parents, and that the only father she has ever known was not just her "psychological" father, but her legal father as well. A few days later, a Florida appellate court allowed a 12-year-old boy to sever ties with his birth-mother under advisement of several adults and a court-appointed guardian. A Vermont court order exemplified the confusion surrounding custody cases. A judge ordered a birth certificate of a nine-month-old boy changed to reflect the names of the adoptive mother and the biological father, although the father was not aware of the adoption until six weeks after the birth.

The ability of biological parents to win custody varies from state to state. Some states allow parents up to two years to return and claim either fraud or duress in order to win back a child. In Iowa, where the Schmidts lived, court rulings allow fathers to "come back at any point in the child's life."

Conflicting local rulings and legislation prompted many adoption agencies and children's rights advocates to press the *Clausen* case to the U.S. Supreme Court. They argued that only clear guidance set forth by the Court could produce predictable and consistent lower court rulings. As the twentieth century closed, the uncertainty surrounding the rights of biological parents and the best interests of the child continued to complicate the complex and emotional custody cases.

Related Cases

May v. Anderson, 345 U.S. 528 (1953).
In re Brandon L.E., 183 W.Va. 113 (S.E.2d 515 1990).
In re Gregory Kingsley, 1992 WO 551484 (Fla. Ct. App. 1992).

Twigg v. Mays, 1993 WL 330624 (Fla. Cir. Ct. Aug. 18, 1993).

Bibliography and Further Reading

Guralnick, Mark S. *Interstate Child Custody Litigation: Tools, Techniques, and Strategies.* Chicago: American Bar Association, Section of Family Law, 1993.

Hardin, Mark. *Early Termination of Parental Rights: Developing Appropriate Statutory Grounds.* Chicago: American Bar Association, Center on Children and Law, 1996.

Ingrassia, Michele, and Karen Springen. "She's Not Baby Jessica Anymore." *Newsweek,* March 21, 1994, pp. 60-64.

Mayoue, John C. *Competing Interests in Family Law: Legal Rights and Duties of Third Parties, Spouses, and Significant Others.* Chicago: American Bar Association, Section of Family Law, 1998.

Waldman, Steven, and Lincoln Caplan. "The Politics of Adoption." *Newsweek,* March 22, 1994, pp. 64–65.

TIERCE V. ELLIS

Legal Citation: 624 So.2d 553 (Ala 1993)

Appellant
Dennis Ray Tierce

Appellee
Sheila Ellis

Appellant's Claim
That the circuit court ruling that appellant was not the biological son of his father be reversed.

Chief Lawyer for Appellant
Borden M. Ray, Jr.

Chief Lawyer for Appellee
Dan M. Gibson

Justices for the Court
Oscar W. Adams, Jr., Sonny Hornsby, Gorman Houston (writing for the court), Mark Kennedy, Janie L. Shores

Justices Dissenting
Kenneth I. Ingram, Alva Hugh Maddox

Place
Montgomery, Alabama

Date of Decision
10 September 1993

Decision
That the rule of repose, which dictates that claims must be initiated within 20 years, applies to a illegitimacy claim, and that the lower court ruling therefore be reversed.

Significance
This decision upheld Alabama's rule of repose as absolute. This rule exists to prevent antiquated or outdated claims from being brought before the courts. Even if the facts of a case are undisputed and evidence shows justification for a claim, the rule of repose disallows any claim that has not been initiated within the specified time.

The state of Alabama's rule of repose does not permit legal actions to be brought to the courts if they have not been initiated within 20 years from the time when they could have begun. This ensures that the courts do not become clogged with "antiquated" claims many years after the matter in question has passed. The facts of the case and the merits of the argument do not matter if the issue has not been initiated within 20 years, the claim cannot be brought to the courts.

The rule of repose is not the same thing as a statute of limitations. Different types of claims are governed by different statutes of limitations—in some states, for example, the statute of limitations for paternity claims is 18 years. Other types of claims are regulated by varying statutes of limitations. But the rule of repose sets a limit of 20 years for all claims.

A Matter of Inheritance

In November of 1942, William Copeland Tierce and Irene Elizabeth Batchelder were married. From February of 1944 to December of 1945, William Tierce was posted overseas for military service. When he returned to the United States in 1945, he discovered that his wife was six months pregnant. He filed for divorce on 2 February 1946 on grounds of adultery, and the divorce was finalized on 4 February 1946. The unborn child, Dennis Ray Tierce, was not made a party to the divorce proceedings and the question of his paternity was not adjudicated. When Dennis Ray was born on 4 April 1946, his father was listed on the birth certificate as William Tierce.

William Tierce married again and had five children with his second wife. He died in December 1972, and his father, John C. Tierce, died in December 1989. In the list of heirs filed by John C. Tierce's executors, Dennis Ray Tierce was listed as William's son and an heir to John Tierce's estate. Sheila Ellis, one of William Tierce's daughters, then filed a declaratory action asking the court to find Dennis Ray Tierce not the son of William Tierce and therefore not a legitimate heir. The trial court ruled that Dennis Ray was not William's biological son and therefore not an heir to the estate. Dennis Ray appealed the decision to the Supreme Court of Alabama, which reversed the lower court's decision.

Statute of Limitations

Laws that stipulate a time limit under which a legal matter may be filed with a court are referred to as Statute of Limitation laws. These laws may be at the state or federal level, depending upon the issue. The intent is to eliminate legal proceedings in civil and criminal matters where the evidence may have been destroyed, the facts of the case may have become muddied with the passage of time, or some of the parties to the case may be deceased.

Child custody issues usually are determined in a family court at the state level. Custody of children may be addressed until the individual reaches the "age of majority." This varies depending on state law. A child may also be considered emancipated, another term meaning a person is a legally an adult, when he or she can effectively support him/herself financially. The marriage of a person also indicates emancipation. A court no longer has authority in custody issues after a person is considered emancipated.

Source(s): *West's Encyclopedia of American Law*, Vol. 2. Minneapolis, MN: West Publishing, 1998.

Presumption of Paternity

In its deliberations, the court stressed that Alabama statute 26-17-5(a)(1) states that a child born within 300 days after the termination of a marriage is presumed to be the child of the husband in that marriage. Dennis Ray Tierce was born two months after the termination of the marriage. "[T]he presumption that the husband of the mother of a child born [or conceived] during marriage is the father of that child is often said to be one of the strongest presumptions know to the law," quoted Justice Houston in his opinion for the majority. The court further noted that the Alabama law required either clear and convincing evidence, or a judgment that established paternity by another man, before the presumption of paternity could be rebutted. Since the question of Dennis Ray Tierce's paternity had not been brought before the divorce court, the divorce did not destroy the usual presumption of paternity.

Because William Tierce had never brought the paternity matter to court and more than 20 years had elapsed, the court found that the rule of repose barred Sheila Ellis's claim. "The rule of repose does not depend on evidence of prejudice, nor does it depend on any statute of limitations," the court determined. The court stressed that the rule of repose "'operates as an absolute bar to claims that are unasserted for 20 years.'" William Tierce—had he been alive—would not have been permitted to bring a claim to bastardize Dennis Ray after this time, and the rule of repose similarly prevented his daughter from bringing such a claim.

Dissent Urges Justices to Decide by Facts

Though five justices agreed in the decision to reverse the lower court's finding, Justices Maddox and Ingram dissented. Justice Maddox, in his dissenting opinion, argued that "the evidence clearly and convincingly shows that it is naturally, physically, or scientifically impossible for the husband to be the father." He argued that the legal issues in this case should be decided based on the facts, without the application of statutory or common law presumptions that he believed had been "exploded."

Impact

The *Tierce* decision confirmed that Alabama's rule of repose is absolute—claims that have not been initiated within 20 years may not be brought to the courts. Because the rule of repose barred Sheila Ellis's claim refuting her father's paternity of Dennis Ray Tierce, Dennis Ray's status as the presumed son of William was unchanged. But the decision did not settle whether Dennis Ray Tierce was an heir to the estate. In a subsequent proceeding, the executors of William Tierce's estate filed for a declaratory judgment to determine whether the result in *Tierce* required that Dennis Ray be designated an heir under the terms of William's will. The trial court found that because William had never recognized Dennis Ray as his son and had specifically noted that his heirs should be his lineal, or biological, descendants, Dennis Ray should not be considered an heir. Dennis Ray then appealed to the Alabama Supreme Court, which upheld the trial court's judgment. In this case, *Tierce v. Gilliam* (1994), the court noted that "Although the rule of repose prevents a direct challenge to Dennis Ray's paternity, his resulting legal status as a 'lineal descendant' cannot be asserted to thwart the testator's intent."

Though the ruling in *Tierce v. Ellis* cited the presumption of paternity as one of the "strongest presumptions known to law," it did not establish this presumption as absolute. In an earlier case in the Alabama Court of Appeals, *Ingram v. State of Alabama* (1978), the court had been presented with facts similar to those in *Tierce*—a child was born while its parents were still married, but the husband claimed he was not the father. In this case, the court noted that the presumption of paternity is not conclusive and can be overcome by proof of impotence or other conditions that would show paternity to have been impossible.

Related Cases

Jackson v. Jackson, 259 Ala 267, 268, 66 So.2d 745, 746 (1953).

Ingram v. State of Alabama, 364 So. 2d 329 (1978).

Leonard v. Leonard, 360 So.2d 710 (Ala. 1978).

Tierce v. Gilliam, 652 So.2d 254 (1994).

IN RE MARRIAGE OF BUZZANCA

Legal Citation: 61 Cal.App. 4th 1410 (1998)

Appellant
Luanne H. Buzzanca

Appellee
John A. Buzzanca

Appellant's Claim
That she should receive support for the child born because she and her then-husband initiated medical procedures to create the child.

Chief Lawyer for Appellant
Robert R. Walmsley

Chief Lawyer for Appellee
Thomas P. Stabile

Judges for the Court
Thomas F. Crosby, Jr., David G. Sills (writing for the court), Edward J. Wallin

Judges Dissenting
None

Place
Santa Ana, California

Date of Decision
10 March 1998

Decision
Reversed the decision of the trial court and declared the Buzzancas the lawful parents of Jaycee. Remanded the matter of child support so that an appropriate permanent child support order could be made.

Significance
California has formulated a rule of law that will help avoid the situation of a "parentless" child becoming the state's responsibility. The ruling also extended comprehensive legal protection to couples considering the use of donated gametes. Because of the ruling, it is no longer necessary for an intended mother to pursue a step-parent adoption.

John and Luanne Buzzanca tried unsuccessfully for many years to have a child. In 1994 they had a fertility clinic combine an egg and sperm from anonymous donors. This embryo was implanted in Pamela Snell, a surrogate, whom the Buzzancas engaged to carry the baby to term. On 30 March 1995, one month before the baby was due, John Buzzanca filed for divorce and alleged that there were no children from the marriage. Luanne filed a response on 20 April 1995 stating that the couple was expecting a child by way of surrogate contract. Luanne cared for the baby, Jaycee Louise, since infancy and had actual physical custody since birth. In February of 1997, the court accepted a stipulation that Pamela Snell, the surrogate, and her husband, were not the "biological parents" of Jaycee.

Judge Monarch of the Superior Court of Orange County, at a hearing in March of 1997, ruled that Luanne was not the lawful mother of the child and therefore John could not be the lawful father or owe any child support money. Monarch stated, "One, there's no genetic tie between Luanne and the child. Two, she is not the gestational mother. Three, she has not adopted the child. That . . . is clear and convincing evidence that she's not the legal mother."

A Medical Procedure Was Initiated And Consented To By Intended Parents

Luanne filed an appeal and the court granted a stay, which kept the support order for Jaycee. John argued that the written surrogacy agreement was signed two weeks after the implantation took place. The court found that an oral agreement had been made prior to implantation. John then testified that Luanne had told him she would assume all responsibility for the care of the child. John contended that the surrogate was the legal mother and her husband the legal father. John's lawyer commented at the oral arguments that "if the surrogate and her husband cannot support Jaycee, the burden should fall on the taxpayers."

Justice Sills wrote the opinion for the three judge panel of the California Court of Appeal for the Fourth Appellate District, Division Three. Sills felt that the trial court had reached "an extraordinary conclusion: Jaycee had no lawful parents." He disagreed. "Jaycee never would have been born had not Luanne and John both agreed to have a fertilized egg implanted in a surrogate." The trial judge erred because he assumed that legal motherhood could only be established either by giving birth or by contributing an egg. He failed to note that fatherhood can be established by a man consenting to allow his wife to be artificially inseminated. In such a case, the husband is the "lawful father" because he consented to the procreation of the child. The same rule can be applied in this case. A husband and a wife should be deemed the lawful parents of a child after a surrogate bears a biologically unrelated child on their behalf. A child was procreated because a medical procedure was initiated and consented to by intended parents. Therefore, both John and Luanne are the lawful parents of Jaycee.

The establishment of fatherhood and the consequent duty to support when a husband consents to the artificial insemination of his wife is one of the well-established rules in family law. In *People v. Sorenson* (1968) the court stated, "A reasonable man who . . . actively participated and consents to his wife's artificial insemination in the hope that a child will be produced whom they will treat as their own, knows that such behavior carries with it the legal responsibilities of fatherhood and criminal responsibility for nonsupport." A family court in New York held the lesbian partner of a woman who was artificially inseminated responsible for the support of their two children.

John argued that all forms of artificial reproduction in which the intended parents have no biological relationship to the child result in legal parentlessness. Thus adoption is necessary. Sills noted that public policy and common sense favor the establishment of legal parenthood with the concomitant responsibility. The Family Code section 7570 states that there is a compelling state interest in establishing paternity for all children. "It would be lunatic for the Legislature to declare that establishing paternity is a compelling state interest yet conclude that establishing maternity is not," noted Sills.

Sills held that Luanne and John should have been declared the lawful parents of Jaycee since they both consented to the act that brought the child into being. John alleged that Luanne promised to assume all responsibility for the child. Even if this were the case, "it could make no difference as to John's lawful paternity. It is well established that parents cannot, by agreement, limit or abrogate a child's right to support."

Sills concluded that the Buzzancas are Jaycee's lawful parents "given their initiating role as the intended parents in her conception and birth." Sills noted that in the most famous custody case of all times, described in the Bible in 1 Kings 3: 25-26, where two women

claimed to be the mother of a newborn, intent to parent was the ultimate basis of the decision. Sills noted that King Solomon resolved the issue "by novel evidentiary device designed to ferret out intent to parent." Sills reversed the decision of the trial court and declared the Buzzancas the lawful parents of Jaycee. He also remanded the matter of child support so that an appropriate permanent child support order could be made.

The court called on the legislature to sort out the parental rights and responsibilities of those involved in artificial reproduction. The legislature can impose a broader order, which even though it might not be perfect on a case-by-case basis, would bring some predictability to those who seek to make use of artificial reproductive techniques.

Impact

California has formulated a rule of law that will help avoid the situation of a "parentless" child becoming the state's responsibility. The ruling also extended comprehensive legal protection to couples considering the use of donated gametes. Because of the ruling in *In re Marriage of Buzzanca*, it is no longer necessary for an intended mother to pursue a stepparent adoption. All intended parents can now finalize their parental rights through a judgment of maternity and paternity. This allows the initial birth certificate to be issued in the names of the intended parents. Thus an amended birth certificate does not need to be issued later.

At a symposium called "Changing Conceptions: How Science and Law Are Shaping Future Generations" at Chicago-Kent College of Law, several experts commented on the *Buzzanca* case. Arthur Caplan, director of the Center for Bioethics at the University of Pennsylvania said, "It's unacceptable to have a parentless child." R. Alta Charo, associate professor of law and medical ethics at the University of Wisconsin believes that Jaycee Louise Buzzanca has many parents. "The courts have not recognized that. The definition of legal parenthood is still the question. They should all be considered parents and worry about the custodial issue within that group." Some experts in the field have called for a U.S. regulatory system for new reproductive technologies to protect the welfare of the children created and to clarify the rights and responsibilities of the adults involved.

Related Cases

People v. Sorenson, 68 C.2d 280 (1968).
In the Matter of Baby M, 537 A.2d 1127 (1988).
Johnson v. Calvert, 5 C.4th 84 (1993).
Doe v. Doe, 710 A.2d 1297 (1998).

Bibliography and Further Reading

"ART into Science: Regulation of Fertility Techniques." *Science*, July 31, 1998, p. 651.

Foote, Donna. "And Baby Makes One." *Newsweek,* February 2, 1998, p. 68.

Jaroff, Leon. "Six Parents, One Orphan." *Time,* December 1, 1997, p. 45.

Lopez, Kathryn Jean. "Egg Heads." *National Review,* September 1, 1998, p. 26.

Momjian, Mark. "Surrogacy Agreements Pose Biotech Quandary for Courts." *The National Law Journal,* May 11, 1998, p. B7.

EMPLOYMENT DISCRIMINATION

Overview

Historically, an employer and employee had a strict "at will" relationship. That is, the employer could reject a job applicant or demote or discharge an employee for no reason or for any reason whatsoever, including a motive to discriminate on the basis of age, disability, race, religion, or sex. The employer was even free to implement a discriminatory wage scale. In turn, an employee was entitled to quit at any time for any reason or for no reason. Employees were afforded some relief with the rise of unionism. An employer that was bound by a collective bargaining agreement could discipline or fire an employee only in accordance with the terms of the agreement. However, even the unions were accused of practicing discriminatory representation methods. In 1963, Congress passed the Equal Pay Act, which bans employers from discriminating against employees on the basis of sex as to the payment of wages. With a few exceptions, this law requires employers to pay equal wages for equal work.

Congress subsequently enacted Title VII of the Civil Rights Act of 1964, which had a profound impact on employer-employee relationships. It prohibits employers from discriminating against employees on the grounds of color, national origin, race, religion, or sex. The term "sex" encompasses pregnancy, childbirth, and related medical conditions. More specifically, Title VII forbids employers from engaging in the following practices: (1) failing or refusing to hire or firing or otherwise discriminating against a person with respect to "compensation, terms, conditions, or privileges of employment;" and (2) limiting, segregating, or classifying employees or job applicants "in any way which would deprive or tend to deprive any individual of employment opportunities or adversely affect his status as an employee." Labor unions and employment agencies are also subject to the provisions under Title VII. Pursuant to Executive Order 11246, certain employers, such as those with federal contracts, were required to implement affirmative action plans in furtherance of Title VII. Basically, an affirmative action plan is one which establishes a preferential hiring and promotional plan for minorities and women. Such a plan is intended to redress past discrimination and remedy the underutilization of minorities and women in the workforce. Fearing lawsuits, many employers not covered under Executive Order 11246 voluntarily established affirmative action programs. Non-minorities and males have criticized affirmative action programs as constituting reverse discrimination. Recently, affirmative action plans have been struck down in the context of college admissions programs. Accordingly, the longevity of affirmative action is questionable. Subsequent to Title VII, Congress enacted statutes which protect employees from discrimination on the basis of age. The Age Discrimination in Employment Act of 1967 shields workers over the age of 40. Moreover, the Older Workers Benefit Protection Act of 1990 safeguards the benefits of older workers.

Congress also passed legislation which prohibits discrimination against employees with mental and physical disabilities. Both the Americans with Disabilities Act of 1990 and the Vocational Rehabilitation Act of 1973 protect disabled workers. The latter applies to a narrower pool of employers.

Similar to Title VII, the statutes prohibiting age and disability discrimination apply to all facets of employment. That is, they protect an individual from discrimination in terms of job advertisements, during the initial job application procedure and throughout the employment relationship. Congress created the Equal Employment Opportunity Commission (EEOC) for the purpose of enforcing the federal employment discrimination laws. Among other things, the EEOC has the power to investigate discrimination claims, engage in educational activities, and make technical studies. The EEOC also issues guidelines, which are contained in the Code of Federal Regulations (CFR). Generally, the above federal statutes regulate employers that are federal agencies, are engaged in an industry that has an affect on interstate commerce (trade between states), or have a business or financial relationship with the federal government—i.e., federal contractors or recipients of federal funds. States have passed parallel laws to cover those employers that do no fall within the parameters of the federal enactments. A state law may even prohibit employer practices which are not banned under federal authority, such as discrimination on the basis of height or weight.

Today, "at-will" employment (a job relationship that is not subject to a collective bargaining agreement) is still a reality. However, the above federal statutes and their state counterparts serve to restrict the circumstances under which an employer can hire, compensate, promote, or discharge an employee.

Burdens of Proof

In an employment discrimination suit, the aggrieved job applicant or employee will have the initial burden of establishing that he/she is entitled to protection under the relevant statute and that the employer discriminated against him/her in violation of that statute. For instance, an employee claiming race discrimination would rely on Title VII, while an employee claiming age discrimination would invoke the Age Discrimination in Employment Act. A 50-year-old disabled woman may claim protection under Title VII, the Age Discrimination in Employment Act, and the Americans with Disabilities Act. The burden of proof will then shift to the employer to articulate a legitimate, nondiscriminatory reason for its action. By way of example, an employer may allege that a job applicant lacked the requisite skills or that an employee was discharged for poor performance, insubordination, or habitual tardiness. After the employer has offered a reason for its conduct, the burden of proof will shift back again to the job applicant or employee to show that such reason constitutes a mere pretext for discrimination.

An employee claiming violation under the Equal Pay Act will seek back pay. The amount awarded will be the difference between the aggrieved employee's wages and the wages of the employee of the opposite sex who had been performing the same job as the aggrieved employee. Back pay, reinstatement, and injunctive relief may be granted under Title VII, the Age Discrimination in Employment Act, and the Americans with Disabilities Act. This is a means to remedy the wage discrimination.

Specific Types of Employment Discrimination

In a claim for age discrimination, a person must prove that he/she: (1) is over the age of 40; (2) possesses the requisite qualifications for the position in question; and (3) was the object of a negative employment decision that had been based solely on his/her age. Given the present climate of corporate "downsizing," an employer may very well argue that an employee's lay-off had been motivated by economic necessity. However, the employer will be liable for age discrimination if the employee is able to show that the employer engaged in a pattern of laying-off older workers and maintaining younger employees.

To prevail on a claim for disability-related employment discrimination, a job applicant or employee must establish that he/she: (1) is "disabled"; (2) is qualified with or without reasonable accommodation to perform the essential functions of the job in question; and (3) was discriminated against solely on the basis of his/her "disability." Under the Americans with Disabilities Act, a "disability" is "a physical or mental impairment that substantially limits one or more of the major activities of life." Conditions and diseases such as hearing impairments, cerebral palsy, epilepsy, cancer, and heart disease are covered under the act. In *Bragdon v. Abbott* (1998), the United States Supreme Court held that the HIV infection also constitutes a "disability," even if it is not yet symptomatic.

Generally, an employer is obligated to reasonably accommodate a disabled employee, unless a reasonable accommodation would cause the employer to suffer an undue hardship, in terms of significant difficulty or expense. Therefore, all of a disabled worker's requests for accommodation need not be fulfilled. Given the employer's particular circumstances, it may be reasonable for the employer to modify a disabled employee's work schedule. However, it would not be reasonable for the employer to permanently assign a majority of the disabled worker's duties to other employees.

An employee who wishes to pursue a race discrimination claim under Title VII would allege that an employer had either directly discriminated against him/her or had indirectly discriminated against him/her by enforcing a policy which had the effect of discriminating against his/her race even though the policy was racially neutral on its face. The first type of discrimination is referred to as "disparate treatment," while the second type is called "disparate impact." Under the "disparate treatment" theory, an employee who claims that he/she was denied a promotion on the basis of race must demonstrate that he/she: (1) was qualified for the position in question; (2) had been performing his/her work according to legitimate business expectations; (3) but was denied a promotion despite his/her performance; and (4) similarly situated employees who are not protected under Title VII were given more favorable treatment. Under the "disparate impact" theory, an employee must establish that he/she was denied a promotion because a particular policy had the illegal effect of discriminating against his/her race.

To make out a claim for religious discrimination, an employee must allege that he/she has: (1) a bona fide belief that compliance with a workplace rule or policy is contrary to his/her "religion"; (2) informed his/her employer about the conflict; and (3) suffered an adverse employment consequence solely on the basis of his/her religious belief. Under Title VII, the word "religion" refers to moral and ethical beliefs, as well as to organized religions. Atheists are also afforded protection against religious discrimination. However, mere political beliefs do not fall within the scope of Title VII. Furthermore, religious organizations are not subject to the prohibitions against religious discrimination. For instance, a church is entitled to hire only members of its particular faith to serve as ministers. As in a disability discrimination claim, the employer in a religious discrimination case has a duty of reasonable accommodation. That is, the employer must make a reasonable effort to accommodate an employee's religious beliefs unless an accommodation would result in an undue hardship. The reasonableness of a requested accommodation must be viewed in light of the totality of circumstances. Depending on the situation, it may be reasonable for the employer to relieve an employee from working overtime so that the employee can attend services in connection with a religious holiday.

Similar to an employee who claims racial discrimination, a worker who alleges sex discrimination may proceed under a "disparate treatment" or a "disparate impact" theory. In *UAW v. Johnson Controls, Inc.* (1991), the United States Supreme Court found that an employment policy, which was aimed at protecting fertile women from the dangers of lead exposure, constituted impermissible disparate treatment of female workers.

An employee may also have a claim for sexual harassment, which basically involves unwelcome sexual advances, requests for favors of a sexual nature, and other verbal or physical sexual conduct. Surprisingly, in *Burlington Industries, Inc. v. Ellerth* (1998), the United States Supreme Court found that a worker may pursue a claim for sexual harassment even though she failed to report her supervisor's offensive conduct and even though she received a promotion during the time that the sexual harassment had allegedly occurred. A sexual harassment suit may be brought by a male claiming unwelcome sexual advances by a female, or by a female claiming similar conduct by a male. Additionally, in *Oncale v. Sundowner Offshore Services Incorporated et al* (1998), the U.S. Supreme Court determined that same-sex sexual harassment is actionable under Title VII. This means that a male may claim that he was sexually harassed by another male and a female may claim that she was sexually harassed by another female.

See also: **Affirmative Action, Gender Discrimination, Sexual Harassment**

Bibliography and Further Reading

Filipp, Mark R. *Employment Law Answer Book.* New York, NY: Panel Publishers, 1998

Jasper, Margaret C. *Employee Rights in the Workplace.* Dobbs Ferry, NY: Oceana Publications, Inc., 1997

Petrocelli, William. *Sexual Harassment on the Job,* 3rd Ed. Berkeley, CA: Nolo Press, 1998

HICKLIN V. ORBECK

Legal Citation: 437 U.S. 518 (1978)

Appellants
Tommy Ray Woodruff, Frederick A. Mathers, Emmett Ray, Betty Cloud, Joseph G. O'Brien, et al.

Appellee
Edmund Orbeck, Alaska Commissioner of Labor

Appellants' Claim
That the "Alaska Hire" statute, giving Alaska residents preference in all hiring for jobs created by the state's oil and gas industry was unconstitutional.

Chief Lawyer for Appellants
Robert H. Wagstaff

Chief Lawyer for Appellee
Ronald W. Lorensen, Assistant Attorney General of Alaska

Justices for the Court
Harry A. Blackmun, William J. Brennan, Jr. (writing for the Court), Warren E. Burger, Thurgood Marshall, Lewis F. Powell, Jr., William H. Rehnquist, John Paul Stevens, Potter Stewart, Byron R. White

Justices Dissenting
None

Place
Washington, D.C.

Date of Decision
22 June 1978

Decision
That the "Alaska Hire" statute was unconstitutional and should be struck down.

Significance
The decision limited the kind of preferential treatment that a state can give its own residents when it comes to employment.

The question that was asked in *Hicklin v. Orbeck* concerned whether a state can require that some kinds of jobs go to state residents before people from other states. It was Alaska's intention to do just that which led several people who were not Alaska residents to file suit against the State Department of Labor in search of an equal chance at jobs working on the Trans-Alaska Pipeline.

In 1972, the Alaska Hire statute was passed. The statute basically required that work in Alaska's oil and gas industry go to "qualified Alaska residents" in preference to nonresidents, and that nonresidents be laid off before any resident "working in the same trade or craft" was terminated.

Work for Residents Only

Three years later, construction on the Trans-Alaska Pipeline was at its peak, and Alaska Hire began to be seriously enforced. At the same time, some Alaska residents complained that the law was not being enforced well enough. So on 1 March 1976, Alaska Commissioner of Labor Edmund Orbeck issued an order to all unions supplying pipeline workers, commanding them to send all qualified Alaska residents out to be hired before they sent any nonresidents.

Tommy Ray Woodruff, Frederick A. Mathers, Emmett Ray, Betty Cloud, Joseph G. O'Brien, and a group of other pipeline workers were furious. None of them were Alaska residents. (To be a state resident, you must show that you are committed to living there, by registering to vote in that state, having a permanent home there, and not claiming residency in any other state. Thus, even if Woodruff, Mathers, and the rest had spent several months in Alaska, they were not technically residents.)

All but one of the nonresident group had worked on the pipeline before. On 28 April, they filed a complaint in superior court, objecting to the Alaska Hire statute.

At that time, the law also required eligible workers to have been residents for one year. The group of workers objected to that requirement as well. Eventually, Alaska's supreme court struck down the one-year requirement. However, according to a 3-2 vote of the state supreme court, the law's general preference for Alaska residents was permitted by the Constitution.

Many States, One Nation

When the Supreme Court decided to hear this case, they began by looking at a clause from Article IV, Section 2, of the U.S. Constitution: "The citizens of each state shall be entitled to all privileges and immunities of citizens in the several states." To explain this clause further, Justice Brennan quoted an 1869 Supreme Court case. The purpose of the clause, he wrote, is:

> . . . to place the citizens of each State upon the same footing with citizens of other States . . . It has been justly said that no provision in the constitution has tended so strongly to constitute the citizens of the United States one people as this.

Therefore, Justice Brennan explained, the Supreme Court had unanimously decided to strike down Alaska Hire. Even without the one-year residency requirement, giving this kind of preferential treatment to Alaska residents was unconstitutional.

Brennan went on to explain the Court's reasoning in more detail. He acknowledged that a state might be justified in restricting employment to residents if nonresidents were the reason for the employment problem. Everyone agreed that Alaska had a "uniquely high" unemployment rate. Certainly the state was entitled to address it.

However, Brennan continued, the reason for Alaska's unemployment had nothing to do with nonresidents coming in and taking jobs away from local people. Rather, according to a report by the Federal Field Committee for Development Planning in Alaska, the state's unemployment problem came from very different sources:

> Those who need the jobs the most tend to be undereducated, untrained, or living in areas of the state remote from job opportunities. Unless unemployed residents—most of whom are Eskimos and Indians—have access to job markets and receive the education and training required to fit them into Alaska's increasingly technological economy . . . new jobs will continue to be filled by persons from other states who have the necessary qualifications.

Whose Resources Are They?

Alaska had argued that it owned the oil and gas on its territory, so it had a right to ensure that its own citizens benefited from those resources. The Court did not agree. First, it pointed out, the law was written in such a way as to extend to employers who:

> . . . have no connection whatsoever with the State's oil and gas, perform no work on state

Justice William J. Brennan, Jr. © Photograph by Robert S. Oakes. Collection of the Supreme Court of the United States.

land, have no contractual relationship with the State, and receive no payment from the State . . . The only limit of any consequence on the Act's reach is the requirement that "the activity which generates the employment must take place inside the state."

To refute this way of thinking about state resources, Justice Brennan again quoted from an earlier decision. Citing a 1911 case called *West v. Kansas Natural Gas*, he portrayed the absurd consequences that might result from each state jealously guarding its resources for the sole benefit of its own citizens:

> The Court reasoned that if a State could so prefer its own economic well-being to that of the Nation as a whole, "Pennsylvania might keep its coal, the Northwest its timber, [and] the mining States their minerals," so that "embargo may be retaliated by embargo" with the result that "commerce [would] be halted at state lines."

Finally, although the people suing had not challenged the Alaska law under the Commerce Clause—also from Article IV of the Constitution—the Court held that this clause, too, made the Alaska law invalid:

. . . the Commerce Clause circumscribes a State's ability to prefer its own citizens in the utilization of natural resources found within its borders, but destined for interstate commerce . . . Here, the oil and gas upon which Alaska hinges its discrimination against nonresidents are of profound national importance . . . As Mr. Justice Cardozo observed, the Constitution "was framed upon the theory that the peoples of the several States must sink or swim together, and that in the long run prosperity and salvation are in union and not division."

Related Cases

McCready v. Virginia, 94 U.S. 391 (1877).
West v. Kansas Natural Gas, 221 U.S. 229 (1911).
Pennsylvania v. West Virginia, 262 U.S. 553 (1923).
Foster Packing Co. v. Haydel, 278 U.S. 1 (1928).
Baldwin v. G. A. F. Seelig, Inc., 294 U.S. 511 (1935).
Toomer v. Witsell, 334 U.S. 358 (1948).
Mullaney v. Anderson, 342 U.S. 415 (1952).
Austin v. New Hampshire, 420 U.S. 656 (1975).
Baldwin v. Montana Fish and Game Commission, 436 U.S. 371 (1978).

Bibliography and Further Reading

Biskupic, Joan, and Elder Witt, eds. *Congressional Quarterly's Guide to the U.S. Supreme Court*, 3rd ed. Washington, DC: Congressional Quarterly, Inc., 1996.

"Significant Decisions in Labor Cases." *Monthly Labor Review*. Vol. 101, October 1978, pp. 53-54.

PERSONNEL ADMINISTRATOR V. FEENEY

Legal Citation: 442 U.S. 256 (1979)

Appellant
Personnel Administrator of Massachusetts et al.

Appellee
Helen B. Feeney

Appellant's Claim
Although the intent of the Massachusetts Veteran's Preference Statute was to benefit a social category of veterans (in which women traditionally represented a significantly small percentage), the act was not gender-biased.

Chief Lawyer for Appellant
Thomas R. Kiley, Assistant Attorney General of Massachusetts

Chief Lawyer for Appellee
Richard P. Ward

Justices for the Court
Harry A. Blackmun, Warren E. Burger, Lewis F. Powell, Jr., William H. Rehnquist, John Paul Stevens, Potter Stewart (writing for the Court), Byron R. White

Justices Dissenting
William J. Brennan, Jr., Thurgood Marshall

Place
Washington, D.C.

Date of Decision
5 June 1979

Decision
Lifetime benefits extended to veterans which allowed hiring preference over non-veterans, under Massachusetts statute, did not violate Fourteenth Amendment equal protection standards. Discrimination against women was not at issue because statutory preferences made a distinction only between veterans and non-veterans rather than between men and women.

Significance
Appellee Feeney claimed that the Massachusetts Veteran's Preference Statute violated the equal protection of women in the workplace. The district court reaffirmed a lower court ruling in favor of appellee; thus, the U.S. Supreme Court was presented with the opportunity to determine if veteran-preference statutes did "in granting an absolute lifetime preference to veterans," discriminate "against women in violation of the Equal Protection Clause of the Fourteenth Amendment." While, statistically, such provisions were extended to a significantly low number of female veterans, the Court concluded that no discriminatory intent existed because the preference was extended to a non-gender based class that included applicants of both sexes.

The appellee, Helen B. Feeney, worked for about 12 years as an employee in the Massachusetts state civil service. In 1971, she succeeded in passing competitive examinations for a state government job. Her scores were remarkably good but because she was not a veteran, she was not included in the "eligible list" of applicants. Because of their eligibility for hiring preference, veterans who had scored below her in the civil service exams were place above her in the final, overall ranking of applicants. Two years later, when Feeney retested, she was again eliminated from the eligible list. Concluding that her efforts to get a better job in the state domain were frustrated because of hiring preferences to veterans, she decided to litigate that issue on the basis that the Massachusetts statute promoted gender discrimination against women. Feeney claimed that the preference extended to veterans made it almost impossible for her to get the same chance for appointment to official civil positions and thus, unfairly, decreased her employment opportunities. Its existence discriminated against women under the equal protection provisions of the Fourteenth Amendment and the statute's "absolute-preference formula" was unacceptable because it not only diminished employment opportunities, but also, in effect, excluded women from serving in the best Massachusetts civil jobs.

The district court decided in favor of the appellee. They recognized the essential importance of the veterans' preference statute but held that, nonetheless, the result of such beneficial treatment caused a severe, negative impact on female applicants. The ruling of the district court held that Massachusetts should find a less intrusive way to provide veterans the benefits that they deserved.

The Attorney General of Massachusetts appealed to the U.S. Supreme Court. On the basis of a previous Court ruling in *Washington v. Davis* (1976), the Court vacated the lower court's judgment. In remanding remanded the case back for reconsideration, the district court was reminded that any "disproportionate impact" of a neutral law like that pertaining to veterans-hiring preferences, "must be traced to a purpose to discriminate on the basis of race."

On reconsideration, the district court showed its resolve to seek specific guidance from the higher court with respect to language contained in state statutes which seemed to establish class preferences which, tacitly, discriminated by gender. Again, the court found veterans' hiring preferences to be essentially non-neutral. Women were traditionally excluded from the class (veterans) which typically benefited under the preference statute and, therefore, the outcome of its effect could not be considered "unintended." Again, the Massachusetts Attorney General appealed the lower court's decision to the U.S. Supreme Court.

The majority of Supreme Court justices again elected to reverse the lower court's judgment. They found no violation of equal protection standards and no discriminatory intent under the Massachusetts Veterans' Preference Statute. The majority opinion explained that Massachusetts' hiring preference was open for all people "honorably discharged from the United States Armed Forces" who served actively at least 3 months or at least one day during "wartime." Moreover the statute made possible for citizens of this category, "any person, male or female, including a nurse," to benefit by being placed ahead of non-veteran social categories. Although the appellee scored better than individuals from the category of veterans, her claim that the statute promoted gender-based preference was not a viable argument because statutory preferences advanced "legitimate and worthy purposes." The Court recognized a long-established, legitimate, national practice to reward veterans for their devotion to their country through military service.

The justices conceded that it was not unusual that such benefits were sometimes characterized as male-oriented since women represented a smaller portion of the veteran population. The Court also conceded that there were many laws which have a different impact on particular categories of society. However, the existence of such laws did not mean that their intent was to legislate bias in favor of privileged groups and at the expense of non-favored groups. Constitutional protection was not at issue in cases wherein laws, based on rational principles, resulted in uneven effects on certain groups within a class. If legislation of a law was based upon valid, logical standards, its validity could not be questioned by relying on another legal paradigm, for example race; instead, a litigant needed to offer argument, rationale, and evidence that specific discrimination had occurred. In citing *Washington v. Davis* and *Arlington Heights v. Metropolitan Housing Corp.* (1977), the majority justices stated that "even if a neutral law has a disproportionately adverse effect upon a racial minority, it is unconstitutional under the Equal Protection Clause only if that impact can be traced to a discriminatory purpose." Finding no such discriminatory purpose in the appellee's argument, the Court held that there was no convincing justification to invoke equal protection standards.

By emphasizing that civil employment was not a constitutional right, the Court signaled that alleged differentiation based on sex in selection of employees had to be exceedingly justified to tender a constitutional challenge under the rubric of Fourteenth Amendment equal protection. The plurality of the Court underscored the appellee's admission that the challenged statute was neutral and not gender based, and that the purpose of preferences contained therein did not necessarily represent discrimination against woman but extended hiring preferences to veterans. The Massachusetts' law, in practice, had no other intention than to distinguish between veterans and non-veterans, therefore the statute was based on a neutral classification. The justices reasoned that the appellee's claim of gender-based discrimination could not be validated to the fact that the statute was predominantly inclined to men only because fewer women were veterans. Further, language of the statute was very explicit in defining the category of veterans and was not preclusive for women who served in the military. Regularly, the statute affected a significant number of male non-veterans as well.

In responding to both the findings of the district court and the appellee's claim that preferences provided to veterans discriminate against women, the Supreme Court addressed different arguments. First, they found it improper to challenge the Massachusetts veterans' statute on the grounds that only a handful of women could achieve hiring preferences; the alleged discriminatory intent was non-evident because the statute gave preference only to a well-defined category of veterans. Thus, since preferences had been legislated on a neutral, nondiscriminatory basis, evidence which showed that women were most burdened by provisions of the statute was not relevant to contest sex discrimination. The justices further noted that neither was the "history of discrimination against women in the military . . . on trial in this case." Finally, addressing the appellee's contention that the consequences of the law were obvious, inevitable, and (therefore) intended, the Court explained that purposeful discrimination implied "more than intent as volition or intent as awareness of consequences." According to their ruling in *United Jewish Organizations v. Carey* (1977), it suggested "that the decisionmaker, in this case a state legislature, selected or reaffirmed a particular course of action at least in part 'because of,' not merely 'in spite of,' its adverse effects upon an identifiable group." Justices could see no original legislative intent to legalize gender discrimination by benefiting a category of veterans. Instead, the language of the Massachusetts' statute clearly defined a veteran as "any person . . ." so distinctions remained only between veterans and non-veterans, not between men and women.

Two dissenting justices noted that mere intention to discriminate was rarely clearly evident. They contended that any legislation was discriminatory which gave advantage to one group or class while excluding the possibility of another group or class reaching such an advantage. Because only two percent of the female population in Massachusetts were veterans, the method by which the state chose to benefit veterans was, therefore, not appropriate. They pointed out that even if characterized as a non-neutral statute, its provisions enabled the almost 98 percent male veteran population to be given preference over non-veterans, regardless of scores on the civil service exam. Thus, the legislation of a lifetime preference law favoring veterans "created a gender-based civil service hierarchy, with women occupying low-grade clerical and secretarial jobs and men holding more responsible and remunerative positions." The justices suggested that limiting the duration of absolute preference by reducing the span of time a veteran could claim preference could considerably lessen the negative consequences from the existence of such a law. As written, however, the minority justices concluded that the statute discriminated against a large number of Massachusetts women and was not constitutionally legal.

Impact

The majority of U.S. Supreme Court justices did not underestimate nor ignore the fact that the effect of the Massachusetts Veterans Preference Statute mainly burdened the female population. Their employment opportunities were diminished while competing with a category of veterans who were primarily male. But the Court emphasized that in order for a claim of discrimination to be valid, disproportionate impact did not provide sufficient rationale. A litigant had to show discriminatory purpose. Stressing that "the Fourteenth Amendment guarantees equal laws, not equal results," the justices found no gender-based legislative motive in the statute, the language of which was "neutral" in that the only differentiation made distinguished between veterans and non-veterans. Although admitting that there existed past objections to granting veterans hiring preferences, the majority justices concluded that with respect to statutory preferences, whether authored at the state or federal level, "the constitutional standard required a finding (that) the legislature acted because of them, not merely in spite of them."

Related Cases

Washington v. Davis, 426 U.S. 229 (1976).

Massachusetts Bd. of Retirement v. Murgia, 427 U.S. 307 (1976).

Arlington Heights v. Metropolitan Housing Corp., 429 U.S. 252 (1977).

United Jewish Organizations v. Carey, 430 U.S. 144 (1977).

Bibliography and Further Reading

Brownstein, Alan E. "Constitutional Wish Granting and the Property Rights Genie." *Constitutional Commentary,* spring 1996.

Hall, Kermit L., ed. *The Oxford Companion to the Supreme Court of the United States.* New York: Oxford University Press, 1992.

Hunter, Rosemary C. and Elaine W. Shoben. "Disparate Impact Discrimination: American Oddity or Internationally Accepted Concept?" *Berkeley Journal of Employment and Labor Law,* summer 1998.

FAMILY LAW

Family

The family is one of the most common and oldest human social institutions. It is believed to originate from the child's need for care and the mother's ability to nurse. Family in Western society derived from ancient traditions, such as the Hebrews of the Middle East, where the father was considered the most powerful member. In the United States, family normally refers to a group of kin-related individuals sharing a home. On average, traditional families in America consist of a husband, wife, and one or two children. There is a general conception of families as entities separate from society, in which issues are solved internally. But families and society are integrally intertwined. Consequently, family law evolved as a means to maintain order in society. Family law is a general term traditionally addressing marriage, divorce, domestic disputes, and paternity. It developed from common law and is handled primarily at the state level. The courts and state legislatures have acted throughout time to preserve the institution of marriage due to its moral influence on the population. Though the First Amendment has been interpreted as significantly limiting the extent to which the state can interfere with parents over how they raise their children, certain exceptions are recognized when the health and safety of children are jeopardized.

Origins of Family Law

In Western society, the family has historically served as the key means for passing ownership of land and other wealth down through generations. During the Middle Ages of Europe, inheritance was of primary importance in families, given the uncertainties of life. Formal rules of inheritance provided for family continuity. The rise of feudal lords increased regulation of marriage, such as determining how land could be disposed by widows. The Magna Carta of 1215 addressed various aspects of inheritance. It provided greater protection to widows and children, including the forced sale of inheritance to pay debts. The Magna Carta underscored the crucial connection between early property law and the central place of the family in medieval society. This relationship formed the basis for English common law.

Colonists in America, influenced by Puritan and Protestant beliefs, adopted principles from English law. They believed that the well-being of the commonwealth largely depended on the proper discharge of family responsibilities. Protestants viewed marriage as a contract rather than a sacrament, while Puritans stressed the responsibilities of family members. During the colonial period, fathers held sole legal authority over children of the family. State governments replaced colonial governments after independence from Britain and retained primary governmental powers to regulate family matters. With the progression of the Industrial Revolution into the nineteenth century, husbands increasingly worked away from the home and wives assumed greater responsibilities for raising children. This shift in roles of family members greatly influenced development of family law over the next century. For example, the "tender years" doctrine was adopted, routinely awarding mothers custody of their children in a divorce. By the mid-twentieth century, an emphasis on individual rights and privacy grew in family law including greater freedom to dissolve marriages. In a prisoner sterilization case, *Skinner v. Oklahoma* (1942), the Court expanded equal protection of the law by declaring marriage and procreation fundamental rights. *Griswold v. Connecticut* (1965), the first Court ruling to address privacy rights, upheld a couple's right to use birth control.

Marriage and Divorce

Marriage resides at the intersection of public and private life. Though the home is protected by rights to privacy, marriage is a public legal institution filled with privileges and obligations integrated into the community at large. Vows are declared publicly and the community becomes a stakeholder in the relationship. Consequently, states consider marriage a contractual relationship subject to state regulation in order to protect the general welfare of their citizens. States independently establish the minimum age at which individuals may marry, marriage procedures, the duties and obligations created by the marital relationship, the effect of marriage on property, and grounds for divorce.

Originally under English common law, one spouse could not sue the other. By the late nineteenth century, the Married Women's Property Act allowed wives, and later husbands, to sue for property losses. Cases dealing with personal issues, not property, have been allowed only to a limited extent, such as injury due to vehicle negligence, domestic violence, or sexually transmitted disease. Fewer restrictions apply to suits between children and parents. A child can sue parents for breach of contract, property loss, and even personal injury under certain circumstances. States have established varying levels of protection for parents against lawsuits. Some states invoked a "reasonable parent" standard which focuses on parents' exercise of discretion and authority except when parental action is outrageous. In 1993, a Florida teenager successfully sued for "divorce" from a parent by claiming lack of adequate support.

Divorce between spouses not only alters their legal status, but also introduces issues concerning division of property, continued support of dependent children, and child custody concerns. Through the regulation of grounds for divorce and its procedures, each state has designated specific courts to deliberate divorce proceedings.

Originally, grounds for divorce were few and narrowly defined, with the most common grounds being adultery, cruelty, desertion, and impotence. In the traditional fault-based system of divorce, if one of the grounds was present in a marriage, then an individual could proceed with a divorce suit against the spouse at fault. Often the finding of fault greatly influenced the amount of alimony paid afterwards. However, in the mid-1960s, no-fault divorce was born in California and led to a "divorce revolution." Soon, all states adopted some form of no-fault divorce in which the spouses, together, could cite incompatibility, irreconcilable differences, or some length of separation as reason for divorce. The court could then grant the divorce. Many states retained both forms of divorce.

By the late 1990s, divorce reforms began to spread through the states again as the no-fault system was blamed for a substantial increase in divorce and inadequate protection of the financial security of spouses and children. Reformers claimed that although marriage is more than a legal business partnership, the no-fault system treated it as less with few legally binding commitments. Some believed a spouse should at least have the right of a judicial hearing before a no-fault divorce could be granted. A hearing on fault in a marriage dispute could actually serve to deter some divorces. In essence, an effort has begun to reform the structure of legal incentives under which marital relationships operate and to make divorce expensive for those at fault.

Several states recognize common law marriage after a couple lives together for a certain length of time, and the couple demonstrates that they either intend to marry or are representing themselves to others as married. Until the late 1990s, all states restricted marriage to the union of a man and woman. Same-sex couples could not enjoy the legal benefits of marriage. In contrast to national efforts to maintain the traditional definition of family in federal law, states in the late 1990s began to individually consider proposals recognizing same-sex marriages. Hawaii led the way in adopting such measures. Many believed the nature of marital relations was a private matter that government should not dictate.

Children

When couples have children, those children become stakeholders in the marriage. By the mid-twentieth century, most states assigned both parents equal responsibility for the support and care of their children. When a parent fails to provide adequate food, clothing, medical care, education, supervision, or general guidance, the parent may be found guilty of neglect and local welfare departments can conduct investigations. In neglect cases that persist, children can be placed for adoption. The Uniform Marriage and Divorce Act was passed by Congress in 1970. It provided extensive standards governing marriage, divorce, property, alimony, child support, and custody. In 1989, the United Nations Convention on the Rights of the Child was adopted by the U.N. General Assembly which promoted children's legal rights as individuals. Issues focused on nutrition, health care, and other forms of protection. Numerous organizations sponsoring children's rights were established.

Collecting child support payments from an ex-spouse has long been a major issue in family law. Congress passed the Uniform Reciprocal Enforcement of Support Act to assist parents in collecting unpaid child support from ex-spouses residing in other states. The act proved ineffective due to high work loads and a low priority by local authorities. The ability of divorced parents to collect child support payments from unwilling (deadbeat) ex-spouses greatly increased in the 1990s. The Association for Children Enforcement of Support was formed to help find ex-spouses. Also, the Welfare Reform Act, which passed in 1996 and turned the major federal welfare program over to states, included provisions for a national deadbeat tracking system and required employers to report new hires to the state. Laws expanded to allow wages to be garnished, professional and drivers licenses revoked, retirement and welfare benefits withheld, and tax refunds and even lottery winnings redirected. In addition, liens could be placed on real estate and personal property, and bank accounts.

Children can also terminate legal ties to parental control through a declaration of "emancipation." They may then enter into contracts and purchase assets.

Emancipation is normally considered automatic when serving on active duty in the military or holding a job and living apart from the family home.

Property in the Family

Historically, common law regarded a married couple as a legal entity with the husband as the head of the household. He controlled all marital property, including property brought into marriage by the wife. If the wife outlived the husband, she could recapture her rights over the property she brought into the marriage. During the 1970s, the United States Supreme Court struck down many gender-based laws, holding that the laws violated the Equal Protection Clause of the Fourteenth Amendment. For example, in *Reed v. Reed* (1971) the Supreme Court struck down a state law that preferred men over women as administrators for descendants' estates. Now husbands and wives can manage their own property.

Some states adhere to the English common law "title theory" of property which attaches ownership of an asset during marriage to the spouse who holds the title. Title to a marital asset is held by the spouse who earned the funds to purchase the asset, unless title was shifted by gift, contract, or a court order. The owner of the property can manage, control, and dispose of the property without the consent of, or even giving notice to, the other spouse. If the purchaser of the asset includes the other spouse on the title, it is presumed the spouse intended to present the other spouse with a gift unless evidence demonstrates otherwise.

Other states are known as community property states. This property system, created in Spain and France, is based on a sharing or partnership theory of marriage. It presumes each spouse, whether directly or indirectly, contributes equally to the accumulation of assets during the marriage. The homemaker provides intangible contributions to the marital relationship, and property acquired through the efforts of either spouse is regarded as marital property owned equally between the two. Spouses can also hold separate property including assets acquired through gifts or inheritance prior to marriage.

In a common law property system, traditionally the wife would have nothing to leave at death since the husband already controlled all of the property. However, a husband could choose to leave his estate to someone other than the widow, thus leaving the widow destitute. To prevent this unfairness, over the years states devised methods of granting surviving spouses some rights to marital property. The most common form still implemented today is the "statutory elective share." This method entitles a surviving spouse to a legally prescribed portion, typically one-third to one-half, of the deceased spouse's property owned at the time of death.

In community property jurisdictions, the deceased spouse may dispose of his or her one-half of the estate through a will along with any separate property. The surviving spouse has no right to survivorship in this system unless the property was left to him or her in the will.

By the late 1990s, division of pensions became a major divorce asset issue and the subject of proposed state legislation. State laws and the Retirement Equity Act of 1984 traditionally allowed spouses to obtain rights to the other's pension benefits if divorced. Increasing use of 401(K) pension plans meant that pension funds might be the largest asset of a family besides a home. However, due to the flexibility of such plans which made them attractive, protection of spousal financial interests following divorce were lessened in valuing and dividing the pension benefits. Proposed restrictions for withdrawal of funds were opposed by the pension industry for fear of increased liability and the greater record keeping demands a new system might pose. Inclusion of pension benefit clauses became an increasingly important part of the court order approving a property settlement agreement.

Duties and Rights of Spouses

Under common law, the husband had a duty to support his wife, while the wife had a duty to perform household chores and other services for the husband. Generally, courts, as in *McGuire v. McGuire* (1953), were unwilling to set a specific standard of support to be provided by the husband while the family remained intact. Family living standards were considered a matter of concern for the family, and the courts found no grounds to interfere with such marital matters for the most part. However, courts have the option of intervening by applying the "doctrine of necessities." Under this doctrine, a husband or wife could be held responsible for the purchase of essential goods or services, including food, clothing, shelter, and medical and legal expenses. Similarly, a spouse could be held liable for the other spouse's debts and contracts regardless of her or his consent or knowledge of the purchases.

All states today require husbands to provide necessities for their wives and children, and in many states wives face similar requirements. Debts incurred during marriage, especially for necessities, are normally considered joint debts, even if spouses are living apart but are not divorced. Creditors may therefore sue either spouse to recover such debts. In many states, debts incurred before marriage by one spouse do not become the responsibility of the other spouse. However, marital property may be claimed by creditors if the original debtor cannot pay pre-marriage debts. After divorce, debt is allocated to each ex-spouse in accordance with the state's property laws. Debts are often divided equally, especially when associated with providing necessities. Creditors can sue either ex-spouse regardless of the split.

An individual also holds the right to file personal injury and wrongful death lawsuits on behalf of a spouse or child. Under common law principles, a spouse has the right to receive compensation from the wrongdoer for the love, affection, care, services, companionship, and sexual relations that she or he, as the surviving spouse, is now denied. These aspects of marital relations are collectively known as "consortium" and any person who willfully interferes with this relation is liable for damages. In order to recover such compensation, most courts require proof that the wrongdoer intentionally or negligently harmed the spouse or the child and caused physical injury or death. Loss of consortium is limited to married couples. Unmarried cohabitants may not receive any compensation for such a loss. In wrongful death cases, the surviving spouse and children of the deceased generally also qualify for compensation from the wrongdoer for the amount of future income which would have been provided by the deceased or incapacitated spouse. Regarding misdeeds of a child, parents are not liable under common law for a child's wrongful activities unless the actions were somehow supported by a parent. However, by the 1970s, states began making parents liable in civil suits for damages caused by their children.

Criminal Law

Criminal law involving family issues includes spousal rape, assault, and child abuse and molestation. Most states prohibit prosecution of a husband for the rape of his wife while still living together, although this prohibition is increasingly being challenged. This prohibition stems from the common law concept that once a woman married, she granted consent to intercourse with her husband that cannot be rescinded, and rape was traditionally defined as the unlawful "carnal knowledge" without consent. In *Smith v. State* (1981) and *Commonwealth v. Chretien* (1981) the courts held that a wife could rescind marital consent once she lived apart from her husband. By the mid-1990s, 11 states allowed for prosecution of husbands who rape their wife while living apart.

Assault includes domestic violence, such as when one spouse physically attacks the other. Spouses may obtain temporary restraining orders barring the abuser from the home and prohibiting further violent acts. The assault or violation of an order can result in criminal prosecution. Local authorities were historically reluctant to become involved in domestic disputes, but this has changed during the 1990s with the rising incidence of abuse and increased public awareness.

When a parent without custody removes a child from the custodial parent, he or she may be found guilty of felony kidnapping as addressed in the Parental Kidnapping Prevention Act of 1980. A court upheld the precedence of the law essentially protecting parental

rights over other standards protecting children's rights in *In re Baby Girl Clausen* (1993).

Child abuse escalated throughout the 1990s. Estimates are that 1.5 million children suffered from moderate to severe child abuse each year during this period. Abuse included physical, sexual, and emotional mistreatment, and extreme cases of neglect. Almost 80 percent of the abuse was committed by the parents. Although it is a devastating crime, abuse appeared to be immune from legal prevention and protection. Several states passed laws requiring persons to report suspected child abuse. In some cases, the abused child is removed from the home and placed in care of the state. Financial costs for institutional care correspondingly increased throughout the decade. With poverty identified as a key factor, reformers sought to assure the economic well-being of families. Child abuse reporting laws and monitoring by juvenile courts and social workers proved to be the primary preventative measures available. Abuse is normally an important factor in custody hearings. Incest, which is marriage or sexual relations between close relatives including stepparents, also constitutes a crime, and it is regarded as child abuse when it occurs between a parent and child.

Family Law Reform

As divorce rates and the incidence of illegitimate children escalated, a strong call was made in the 1990s for family law reform. The Clinton administration pushed through the Family and Medical Leave Act of 1993 to encourage greater responsiveness of family members to family needs. The Violence Against Women Act, passed the following year, addressed domestic violence. As the twentieth century came to a close, the perceived "collapse" of the institution of marriage raised fundamental issues. Many believed family law should establish society's expectations about the commitments of family members and more clearly define the boundaries of family. Increased regulation of family life was demanded with increased moral commitments imposed. Proposals were made to increasingly treat the family as a legal entity, rather than just a collection of individuals, subject to social responsibilities. Some claimed that family law became inappropriately "constitutionalized." Individual rights in the Bill of Rights, designed to protect individual liberties from government action, were over expanded to interpersonal disputes.

In 1996, the Commission on Child and Family Welfare submitted a report to Congress entitled, "Parenting Our Children: In the Best Interest of the Nation." The commission found that over one-fourth of children in the United States lived with only one parent and often lacked adequate nurturing and financial support. The report focused on getting both divorced parents actively involved in their children's lives. The commission emphasized that parents' primary concern, regardless of marital status, should be for the well-being of their children. The report identified ways in which courts could reduce the adversarial nature of custody hearings, including mandatory mediation to resolve disputes and development of parenting plans. It also found that courts with family law jurisdiction frequently had the least resources as well as lower legal status than other courts.

The Uniform Parentage Act, adopted by many states, established court procedures and standards for determining paternity of children when paternity is contested. However, the image of the family is radically changing in several ways at the conclusion of the twentieth century. Consequently, family law is being challenged to regulate unprecedented situations. No longer are cases strictly between family members. With artificial reproduction methods, questions arise concerning who the "real" parents are. For instance, does a surrogate mother with no biological relationship to the child she gives birth to have rights to him or her? What are the rights and responsibilities of an ex-husband when his ex-wife wishes to implant the frozen eggs that he fertilized during their marriage? The question arises as to whether these relationships should be addressed through contract and property law as the court resorted to in *Kass v. Kass* (1998). Family law was clearly entering uncharted territory as the twenty-first century approached.

See also: **Privacy, Criminal Law, Custody and Child Support, Reproductive Rights, The Rights of Gays and Lesbians, Contract Law**

Bibliography and Further Reading

Gregory, John De Witt, Peter N. Swisher, and Sheryl L. Scheible. *Understanding Family Law.* New York: Matthew Bender, 1993.

Krause, Harry D., editor. *Family Law.* New York: New York University Press, 1992.

Krause, Harry D., editor. *Child Law: Parent, Child, and State.* New York: New York University Press, 1992.

Olson, Colleen M. *Domestic Relations Law for Paralegals.* Cincinnati: Anderson Publishing Co., 1994.

Russell, Diana E. H. *Rape in Marriage.* Bloomington: Indiana University Press, 1990.

Tingley, John, and Nicholas B. Svalino. *Marital Property Law.* Deerfield, IL: Clark Boardman Callaghan, 1994.

PRINCE V. PRINCE

Legal Citation: 1 Rich, S.C. (1845)

Plaintiff
Sarah Prince

Defendant
George Prince

Plaintiff's Claim
That she should be provided alimony and child support after her husband deserted her, even when he had no property or fixed or permanent income.

Chief Lawyer for Plaintiff
Elliott

Chief Defense Lawyers
Magrath, Yeadon

Judges
Benjamin Faneuil Dunkin, Johnson

Place
Charleston, South Carolina

Date of Decision
March 1845

Decision
A husband, when he has the income, is responsible for alimony and child support.

Significance
South Carolina took a fresh look at the idea of support for a deserted wife, deciding that a husband who had the means of supporting his wife, even though he had no visible property or fixed and permanent income, should be responsible for alimony and the support of the couple's children.

A Step Up

Colonial marriages were easy to make but hard to end. A man and woman could marry by simply agreeing to live together. Even couples who preferred a religious ceremony did not need to follow formal procedures. However, different colonies granted divorce either rarely or not at all. New Englanders were granted divorce for adultery, cruelty, and desertion. However, divorce with the right to remarry was illegal throughout the South. Legal separations took their place—without the right to remarry. South Carolina was particularly rigid, refusing to grant divorces even for a husband's adultery. To allow a woman the right to divorce her husband for his extramarital affairs insulted her husband's honor.

Prince v. Prince was a step forward for wives in the state. It set a precedent for helping wives financially when husbands abandoned them. Earlier law required husbands to support their estranged wives, but only if the men owned property from which to pay.

An Informal Marriage

Sarah and George Prince were married in 1834. The ceremony took place in Portsmouth, England, on 2 March 1835, in the Jewish faith. A simple certificate confirmed the union. Within the year, the couple had a son. Shortly after the baby's birth, George began mistreating Sarah, finally abandoning her for America. There he began living with another woman. As an apothecary, a dealer in botanical medicines, George made from $15 to $20 each day. He lived in comfort, yet he did not contribute any money to his family, and left Sarah to support their son alone.

So Sarah followed him to South Carolina. There she asked the court for alimony, not only for herself, but for her son as well. The case came to trial in Charleston in January of 1841. George's attorney claimed that his client was poor, possessing no property from which to pay alimony. George denied that he had ever married Sarah, claiming the child was not his. He produced witnesses who said that under Hebrew law, the certificate signed by the couple was for a betrothal only. Sarah's

---

Prenuptial Agreements

Popularly known as prenuptial agreements or "pre-nups", in legal circles they are known as premarital agreements. Whatever the name, these are contracts between two people made prior to marriage, with the idea in mind that the union could end in divorce. Prenuptials, which provide for the distribution of property and other interests in the event of a marital breakup, are the only form of contract to address issues such as child custody.

Though the concept of prenuptials may seem modern, they in fact have a long history. Among Jews since the time of Christ, there has been a form of premarital contract called a *ketubah*, whose purpose has been generally to protect the property of the prospective bride.

This was also the case in English common-law prenuptial agreements of the 1500s, which became the model for the modern American version. Because women had an inferior status in society, and were placed at an economic disadvantage with regard to their prospective husbands, a prenuptial was considered essential to protect the rights of a wealthy woman.

Every U.S. state has laws governing prenuptial agreements. Most of these are based on the model Uniform Premarital Agreement Act developed by the Commissioners on Uniform State Laws.

Source(s): *West's Encyclopedia of American Law.* St. Paul, MN: West Group, 1998.

---

side called witnesses who established the couple had lived together in marriage. Some had carried money from George to Sarah for her bed and board during the early days of their separation.

After listening to testimony about whether the Princes had a real marriage or not under Jewish law, the court decided that a ceremony had taken place. The marriage was valid, though informal. George had indeed deserted Sarah.

The only question remaining was whether George had the money to pay support. Since he was self-employed, he appeared to have no permanent or fixed income and no real property. The court commented, "If the condition in life of the parties is such that neither had property, and they were both to labor for subsistence, it is very questionable whether a case for alimony is presented."

The Court Investigates

Chancellors Dunkin and Johnson then appointed a court assistant ("Master") to investigate George's finances. The Master completed his investigation in 1844 and the case came before the court. The report read:

> The Master does not find any proof that the defendant is in possession of any estate, either real or personal; but from the testimony submitted, he finds that he is in the receipt of money; that he lives comfortably and well; and that in the Master's own mind there is little doubt that he is in possession of funds sufficient to meet any decree that may be awarded against him.

Then the court reviewed the evidence showing George lived the good life:

> The evidence reported shows the existence of considerable income . . . It appears that the defendant has been in the habit of taking boarders; that he vends medicines, and occasionally administers them; that he lives in a hired house, for which he regularly pays considerable rent; and that he supports a woman who lives with him.

The court reasoned George's income might be $1,800 a year. As to whether he was bound to contribute to the support of the wife he had deserted, the court wrote:

> By marriage the husband becomes entitled to whatever [property] the wife may possess, and to all her earnings. She is reduced to a state of comparative servitude. She cannot change her situation by another marriage, more agreeable or more beneficial to her. She is deprived of the power of making contracts; and, of course, of the means of accumulating property, or laying by the means of subsistence in sickness or old age. Will it do to say that the husband, entitling himself to all these advantages, and subjecting the wife to all these disabilities, by the marriage, is not bound, by all the means in his power, to sustain her? And if he deserts her, shall his desertion, which is, itself, a wrong, excuse him from the performance of this obligation? Certainly not. It would be a reproach to the law if this were so. God knows, the condition of all women, but especially of married women, is bad enough by the common law of England, and advancing civilization loudly demands its amelioration. But that law, which almost enslaves the wife, makes the

Benjamin Faneuil Dunkin, 1863. © *South Caroliniana Library, University of South Carolina.*

husband liable for her support. It is a duty he has undertaken, with her aid, if he chooses to avail himself of it; and for which he is bound, if he rejects that assistance.

George had to pay Sarah alimony and the court told the Master to hear evidence on whether the child was George's or not and, if so, to order that George pay for his education and support as well. George lost his appeal of the decision.

Before this trial, husbands had paid alimony out of the livings they made from their property. *Prince v. Prince* granted alimony out of the husband's income, protecting more women. The empathy shown by the court eventually led to more liberal divorce laws in America. Even South Carolina developed rules to provide for a wife's support when the marriage was irretrievable. This reflected a broader change ushered in by Jacksonian democracy, which extended to greater numbers of people the same rights that had formerly been enjoyed by a privileged few.

Related Cases

In the Matter of Bolling, 56 A.D.2d 722 (1977).
In re Marriage of Buzzanca, 61 Cal.App. 4th 1410 (1998).

Bibliography and Further Reading

Hoffer, Peter Charles. *Law and People in Colonial America.* Baltimore: The Johns Hopkins University Press, 1992.

Wortman, Marlene Stein. *Women in American Law,* Vol. I. New York: Holmes & Meier Publishers, 1985.

SHAW V. SHAW

Legal Citation: 17 Day Conn. 189 (1845)

Plaintiff
Emeline Shaw

Defendant
Daniel T. Shaw

Plaintiff's Claim
That she be granted a divorce on the ground of intolerable cruelty.

Chief Lawyers for Plaintiff
Sedgwick, Seymour

Chief Defense Lawyers
Church, Hubbard

Justices for the Court
Joel Hinman, Henry Waite, Chief Justice Thomas S. Williams (writing for the court)

Justices Dissenting
Samuel Church (William L. Storrs did not participate)

Place
Litchfield, Connecticut

Date of Decision
June 1845

Decision
The court denied Shaw her divorce.

Significance
This case illustrates why divorces were so rare during most of American history. Patriarchal rights were a given, spousal rape was not considered bodily harm severe enough to constitute cruelty, and jealously was apparently justified in the eyes of the courts.

Divorce, until recently, has been rare in America. During the colonial period, anyone seeking a divorce had to produce written proof of the date of marriage and obtain signed petitions of support. In those days, the most frequent petitioners were abandoned wives. However, after the war for independence, many of the new states reformed their divorce laws, with women successfully suing for divorce as easily as men. In the South, however, courts rarely permitted divorce for any reason. Couples who wanted to separate had three options. The first was divorce *a vinculo matrimonii*, or absolute divorce, which permitted remarriage. Connecticut and Massachusetts granted this type of divorce and only for adultery, cruelty, and desertion. The second option was divorce *a mensa et thoro,* a permanent separation "from bed and board." This arrangement was more common, but did not permit either party to remarry. The third option was a private divorce in which couples simply lived apart.

Connecticut's divorce laws were more liberal than any other state except Massachusetts. In these two states—probably because of the influence of the Puritans who viewed marriage as a civil, not religious, ceremony—marriages were more easily dissolved. Connecticut divorce degrees gave each party the legal status of unmarried persons. Therefore, divorced women could own and control property, sue or be sued, engage in business, and participate in other activities denied to wives.

Sticks and Stones

In Connecticut, if a wife was in physical danger in her home, her husband had to support her somewhere else. Cruelty was a major cause of legal separation and divorce. However, a woman had to fear injury or death to expect a court to free her from the marriage. *Shaw v. Shaw* illustrates how narrowly the courts viewed cruelty even up to the mid-nineteenth century.

Emeline and Daniel Shaw married on 24 October 1841, and lived together until 10 June 1844. On that day, Emeline left Daniel to live with her mother—and went to court for a divorce charging him with cruelty. At a hearing before Justice Joel Hinman at the Febru-

---

Spousal Abuse

According to Daniel E. Koshland in *Science*, 29 percent of American women murdered in 1992 were killed by their husbands, former husbands, or "suitors." Koshland noted, "The type of person who is a batterer tends to become a stalker after the breakup of the relationship, a situation in which the woman frequently concludes (correctly) that her situation can become more perilous if she tries to leave."

Why do more women not take action in such situations? Koshland noted the prevalence of cultural norms which almost seem to mandate domestic violence by placing the wife in a subservient role to her husband. In addition, women who stay with abusers are often motivated by economic dependence and a desire to protect the home and the children—again, attitudes that arise from prevailing societal standards regarding gender roles.

Source(s): Koshland, Daniel E. Jr. "The Spousal Abuse Problem." *Science*, 22 July 1994.

---

ary of 1845 term of the superior court in Litchfield, she claimed her husband often spoke to her in angry, abusive, and obscene language, even in front of her children (by a former husband). He called her names, such as "old hypocrite," and "ugly devil." He implied she was a slut and accused her of going to New York to have intercourse with other men.

Emeline testified that Daniel was unreasonably jealous of her, and would not allow her to visit her friends or family—particularly with her mother or his. On one occasion, when her mother-in-law had come to see the ailing Emeline, Daniel turned her away, forbidding her to come again. At another time, when Emeline wanted to sleep overnight at her mother's house—her health being so poor she could not have intercourse with Daniel—he tried to stop her by locking her door. She escaped out a window. In short, Daniel was intolerably cruel to Emeline.

Patriarchal Power

In February of 1845, after a preliminary hearing, the dispute went to Connecticut's Supreme Court of Errors.

Daniel's lawyers argued that he was not guilty of "intolerable cruelty" because these words meant "personal violence," resulting in extreme suffering or death—or, at least, endangering one's life or health. Daniel's actions were not "cruel" in either sense—certainly not extreme enough to allow for even a divorce *a mensa et thoro*. Finally, words, however abusive, are not legal cruelty. Daniel's violence did not endanger life, injure his wife, or disturb the peace. For such lesser cruelties, the remedy lay with the legislature, not the courts.

Emeline's lawyers argued that the supreme court should permit the Shaws to separate. By endangering his "blameless" wife's health, Daniel had forfeited his right to Emeline's company. Even though Daniel committed no bodily harm to his wife, his behavior defeated "the great ends of marriage." Especially offensive was his insulting and obscene language in front of

the children, the mental "torture" he inflicted upon her by denying her access to her friends and family, and his "barbarous and disgusting abuse of his marital rights" by rape.

For the court, Chief Justice Williams first asked what constituted intolerable cruelty:

What is that "intolerable cruelty" spoken of in the statute? It doubtless speaks of acts done to the wife herself; and we understand it to impart barbarous, savage, inhuman acts. They must be of that character as to be in fact intolerable, *not* to be borne. The legislature must have had in view acts as cruel at least for those for which, under the head of *extreme cruelty*, the ecclesiastical courts in Great Britain divorce *a mensa et thoro;* and those decisions may furnish some assistance upon the subject . . .

The chief justice accepted Daniel's lawyers' argument that words, however abusive, did not amount to legal cruelty. He also agreed that Daniel's violence did not endanger his wife's life, injure her, or disturb the peace. Rationalizing Daniel's abusive language, Williams said:

The first thing to be considered . . . is the language made use of, by this defendant, towards his wife. It is vulgar, obscene, harsh . . . They were, however, accompanied by no act or menace indicating violence to her person . . . but when we look further, and find, that he was jealous of his wife, it is not so much to be wondered at, as we have been told by authority, that "jealousy is the rage of man." The unfortunate victim of this passion is indeed to be pitied; but the law furnishes no remedy for conduct like this.

Refusing to let Emeline visit her own mother and relatives was "harsh, if not cruel," the court agreed. However, it upheld the rule of patriarchy, concluding:

Litchfield County Courthouse. © Litchfield Historical Society.

As the husband must have the right to say who shall be admitted to his house, and in some measure to regulate the intercourse of his wife, the court cannot draw a line by which his authority can be restrained.

Chief Justice Williams added that even unreasonable exercise of a husband's authority was not the kind of cruelty that would warrant a separation. He attributed Daniel's rape of his wife to his ignorance of Emeline's condition. Daniel did not know he was hurting her, and besides, she suffered no "real" harm. In conclusion, nothing the husband had done to the wife, rape included, was unlawful:

Were these acts, such acts of intolerable cruelty as are a cause of separation? No case of this kind is known to have been brought before the court . . . The cases [of violence] found in the books, are cases of violence, where the natural consequence would be injurious or dangerous, and where the act, therefore, was unlawful. Here the act in itself was a lawful act—in ordinary circumstances, not injurious nor dangerous . . . Are we to couple an act of this kind with an act where a violent blow is given, which must greatly injure or endanger, and which was so intended?

Therefore, the court refused to allow Emeline either to divorce or separate from Daniel.

Shaw v. Shaw illustrates how supportive the courts were of the idea that the husband was the head of the house: The "husband must have the right to say who shall be admitted to his house, and in some measure to regulate the intercourse of his wife." His rape of his wife, unlike today, was neither criminal nor cruel.

In 1978, only three states had laws that did not grant married men immunity from the rape of their wives. That year, the trial of *Oregon v. Rideout* led many other states to abolish marital and cohabitation exemptions to rape.

Related Cases
Oregon v. Rideout, 108,866 Circuit Court, County of Marion, Oregon (1978).

Bibliography and Further Reading
Hoff, Joan. *Law, Gender, and Injustice: A Legal History of U.S. Women.* New York: New York University Press, 1991.

Hoffer, Peter Charles. *Law and People in Colonial America.* Baltimore: Johns Hopkins University Press, 1992.

Kerber, Linda K. *Women's America: Refocusing the Past.* New York: Oxford University Press, 1991.

Salmon, Marylynn. *Women and the Law of Property in Early America.* Chapel Hill: University of North Carolina Press, 1986.

Wortman, Marlene Stein. *Women in American Law,* Vol. I. New York: Holmes & Meier Publishers, 1985.

MOORE V. EAST CLEVELAND

Official Legal Citation: 431 U.S. 494 (1977)

Appellant
Inez Moore

Appellee
City of East Cleveland, Ohio

Appellant's Claim
Moore claimed that the city of East Cleveland's housing ordinance, limiting the occupancy of a housing unit to a single family, violated her rights to due process and equal protection under the Fourteenth Amendment of the U.S. Constitution by the ordinance's narrow definition of "family."

Chief Lawyer for Appellant
Edward R. Stege, Jr.

Chief Lawyer for Appellee
Leonard Young

Justices for the Court
Harry A. Blackmun, William J. Brennan, Jr., Thurgood Marshall, Lewis F. Powell, Jr. (writing for the Court), John Paul Stevens

Justices Dissenting
Warren E. Burger, William H. Rehnquist, Potter Stewart, Byron R. White

Place
Washington, D.C.

Date of Decision
31 May 1977

Decision
The Court ruled in favor of Inez Moore, finding that the East Cleveland Housing Ordinance violated her constitutional rights. They determined that the housing ordinance was arbitrary and did not meet the goals of preventing overcrowded housing units, minimizing traffic congestion and parking problems, and reducing the financial burden on the local school system.

Significance
While unable to reach a unified opinion, the Court held that the ordinance arbitrarily regulated the family without justifying or satisfying the goals established by the ordinance. The Court determined that the protection of the "sanctity of the family" guaranteed by the U.S. Constitution extended beyond the nuclear family (consisting of a married couple and dependent children) to the extended family (grandparents, aunts, uncles, and other family members).

Sanctity of the Family

Inez Moore lived with her unmarried son, Dale Moore, and two grandsons, Dale, Jr., and John Moore, Jr. John Moore, Jr. joined her household after the death of his mother, and Moore became the primary caregiver of the child. They resided in a single-family housing unit within the community of East Cleveland, Ohio.

An East Cleveland city housing ordinance restricted the occupancy of housing units to the members of a single family. This ordinance narrowly and definitively limited the categories of family relationships that could make up the housekeeping unit. Legal family members included the head of household; dependent, unmarried children; and parents of the head of household. The ordinance also provided a variance clause allowing non-traditional family units to ask for and be granted an exception to the definition, permitting family members not included in the categorization to legally live within the dwelling.

In 1973 the city of East Cleveland cited Moore with a violation of the city housing ordinance and instructed her to place John in another home. The child was considered an illegal resident of the dwelling. Upon failing to comply with the ordinance, Moore was charged with a misdemeanor criminal offense, which carried a fine of $25 and a sentence of five days in jail. She filed to have her case dismissed, claiming that the ordinance was unconstitutional. Her motion for dismissal was overruled. The Ohio Court of Appeals upheld the criminal charges, and the Ohio Supreme Court denied her a review.

Moore v. East Cleveland came before the U.S. Supreme Court in November of 1976. The claims of this case were that the housing ordinance violated Moore's right to due process and denied her the right to equal protection of the law. The East Cleveland city housing ordinance denied Moore the freedom to make a choice regarding where and with whom her young grandson could live. East Cleveland made a distinct decision about the categories of relatives who may live together, and the city made the personal choice of Moore prosecutable on the grounds that the ordinance was serving the public good and protecting the city's quality of life.

In making their decision, the justices examined the definition of "family." In effect, they had to determine what constitutes a family and if there is a difference in the protection of the nuclear family versus the extended family. Justice Powell, announcing the decision of the Court, relied upon the history and tradition of the family in American society and the protection guaranteed by the Fourteenth Amendment of the U.S. Constitution. Throughout the history of the United States it has been common for the extended family of close relatives and family friends to come together as a single unit, participating in the activities and duties of raising children and caring for the elderly or disabled. As waves of immigrants arrived in the United States, they joined relatives and shared common households. Powell stated in the Court's opinion,

> Ours is by no means a tradition limited to respect for the bonds uniting the members of the nuclear family. The tradition of uncles, aunts, cousins, and especially grandparents sharing a household along with parents and children has roots equally venerable and equally deserving of constitutional recognition.

The Fourteenth Amendment of the U.S. Constitution recognizes the freedom of personal choices in marrying, raising a family, and other matters of private family life. Powell suggested that the sanctity of an extended family that made the choice to support one another is no less than that of the nuclear family. The determination was made by the majority justices that Moore's extended family was entitled to the same and equal protection as other more traditional families under the Constitution. The choice to raise her grandson within her home was a private family matter into which the city and state could not interfere without having a substantial relationship to public health, safety, or general welfare.

It was on these grounds that the Court declared the East Cleveland housing ordinance unconstitutional. The justices found that the ordinance intruded upon Moore's decision to raise her grandson within her household in an arbitrary manner and without serving a public good. By denying her the right to raise the child in the manner that she saw fit and prosecuting her, the city and state intruded upon her basic liberties as granted by the U.S. Constitution. The justices saw this violation of rights as "a taking of property without due process and without just compensation" because Moore would be required to move out of her home and into another neighborhood where she would not be in violation of the East Cleveland ordinance if she chose to keep John Moore, Jr., in her home.

The Dissenting Opinions

Justices Burger, Rehnquist, Stewart, and White entered dissenting opinions on the case; their opinions did not concur. Chief Justice Burger expressed the opinion that Moore, while certainly having a right to examine the constitutionality of the ordinance, should have sought an administrative resolution to her case before having it brought before the Supreme Court. He indicated that Moore deliberately circumvented the variance clause of the housing ordinance, and, instead, chose to seek relief from a higher court. The housing ordinance made provisions for citizens to directly appeal to the city of East Cleveland for exceptions to the definition of legal housing residents. Burger believed that Moore negated her right to higher appeals by not following the appropriate actions to attempt to resolve her problem locally.

Justice Stewart, entering an opinion on behalf of himself and Rehnquist, suggested that the East Cleveland housing ordinance did not violate the rights protected by the Fourteenth Amendment. The city of East Cleveland was making an honest effort to promote public health, safety, and general welfare through limitations on who and what constituted a single family. Both Stewart and Rehnquist agreed that "extended" family did not equate to the fundamental decisions protected by the U.S. Constitution such as the right to marry, the right to bear and raise children, and the right to provide children with a private education. They determined that the housing ordinance did not interfere with these very basic rights.

Finally, Justice White entered an opinion that the East Cleveland housing ordinance did not violate the Due Process Clause. The ordinance served the very real need of East Cleveland to protect its citizens, and the city had a rational justification for the zoning limitations. He stated that the Court could not and should not interfere with a state or local governmental decision because it appears arbitrary or unreasonable unless there is a "deprivation of life, liberty, or property." His argument was that Moore was supporting two families in a single-family dwelling, and by doing so was in direct violation of a city ordinance. She was not deprived of any freedoms by the ordinance; she could move to another part of the Cleveland metropolitan area and raise the children in a single home without being in violation of any housing ordinance.

Impact

The decision by the Supreme Court that the East Cleveland housing ordinance violated the Fourteenth Amendment of the U.S. Constitution called the definition of family under strict scrutiny. The Court was required to examine what elements made up a family and whether an extended family had the same rights of protection afforded to nuclear families. It was determined in *Moore v. East Cleveland* that a family regardless of its categories of relations was protected by the right to privacy, the right to due process, and the right to equal protection. A state or local government did not have the right to arbitrarily define what elements could make up a family unless the definition directly supported the objectives of public health, safety, and general welfare of the community.

Related Cases

Meyer v. Nebraska, 262 U.S. 116 (1923).
Euclid v. Ambler Realty Co., 272 U.S. 365 (1926).
Berman v. Parker, 348 U.S. 26 (1954).

Poe v. Ullman, 367 U.S. 497 (1961).
Eisenstadt v. Baird, 405 U.S. 438 (1972).
Wisconsin v. Yoder, 406 U.S. 205 (1972).

Bibliography and Further Reading

Biskupic, Joan, and Elder Witt, eds. *Congressional Quarterly's Guide to the U.S. Supreme Court,* 3rd ed. Washington, DC: Congressional Quarterly, Inc., 1996.

OREGON V. RIDEOUT

Legal Citation: 108,866 Circuit Court, County of Marion Oregon (1978)

Plaintiff
State of Oregon

Defendant
John J. Rideout

Plaintiff's Claim
That the defendant was guilty of first-degree rape.

Chief Lawyer for Plaintiff
Gary D. Gortmaker

Chief Defense Lawyer
Charles Burt

Judge
Richard Barber

Place
Salem, Oregon

Dates of Decision
27 December 1978

Decision
Not guilty.

Significance
For the first time in modern American history, a man faced trial for raping his wife. A national public discussion of the issue followed questioning whether a man had an absolute sexual right to his spouse's—or cohabitant's—body. Two other states besides Oregon had passed laws that did not grant married (or cohabitating) men immunity from the rape of their wives—and New Jersey was about to come on board. The *Rideout* trial led many other states to abolish marital and cohabitation exemptions to rape.

In 1978, Oregon, Delaware, and Iowa were the only states that did not recognize "marital privilege" as a defense against rape. All other states followed common law, which defined rape as "the forcible penetration of the body of a woman not the wife of the perpetrator."

On 10 October 1978, 23-year-old Greta Rideout telephoned the police for help, saying "My husband just got through beating me." When a police officer arrived at her home, Rideout said her husband had raped her. On 18 October, John Rideout was indicted on a charge of first degree rape.

Does Marriage Mean Consent?

In November, a circuit court judge denied Rideout's request to have the case dismissed on constitutional grounds. When it became clear that the criminal trial would proceed, District Attorney Gortmaker asked Judge Barber to prohibit "common law defenses," that is, a defense of John Rideout's actions based upon the common law presumption that a wife cannot refuse to have intercourse with her husband. Gortmaker argued that Oregon's law, passed in 1977, had replaced English common law within the state. The judge denied the motion.

Charles Burt, Rideout's lawyer, explained the common law "marital privilege" for prospective jurors on 19 December. He said that the issue was not whether the couple had had sex on 11 October, but whether there had been "forcible compulsion" and whether a woman's marriage to a man meant she could not say "no."

Dr. Gilbert Geis, a professor of criminology at the University of California at Irvine and a specialist in the issue of spousal exemption, spoke to Les Ledbetter of the *New York Times* during the trial. He traced husbands' immunity from charges of rape to a seventeenth century English jurist, Judge Matthew Hale. Hale's promulgation, as recorded in the 1736 "Historia Placitorum Coronae, A History of the Pleas to the Crown," explains that "the husband cannot be guilty of a rape committed by himself upon his lawful wife, for by the mutual matrimonial consent and contract the wife hath given up herself in this kind unto the husband which

---

Spousal Rape

Spousal or marital rape occurs when a husband forces a wife to have sex with him when she is unwilling to do so. Most states have some kind of marital-rape statute, though many of these laws tend to be lax, or to apply only in situations of separated couples. There are no marital-rape laws on the books in Alabama, Arkansas, Georgia, Illinois, Kentucky, or West Virginia, and in the case of Alabama and West Virginia, neither a husband or a man who lives in state of "cohabitation" with a woman may be charged with rape.

Cohabitants cannot be charged with rape in Montana, Nevada, Delaware, or Pennsylvania. In these four states, along with 21 others, a husband cannot be charged with marital rape if he and the wife are living together; only

in cases of legal separation is marital rape a punishable offense. Informal separation, as opposed to legal separation, marks a threshold for situations in which marital rape can be charged in six states: Oklahoma, Wyoming, Ohio, Louisiana, Virginia, and Maryland.

Only 12 states have firm marital-rape laws which govern situations of married couples living in the same house. These are mostly states with more liberal traditions, including California, Washington, Oregon, Iowa, Minnesota, Florida, New York, New Jersey, and all of New England except Maine.

Source(s): Fast, Julius, and Timothy Fast. *The Legal Atlas of the United States*. New York: Facts on File, 1997.

---

she cannot retract." (Dr. Geis also pointed out Hale's other claim to fame was the number of witches hung by his order during the 1660s.)

No Help from Friends . . .

The lawyers made their opening arguments before Barber and a jury of eight women and four men on 20 December. The prosecution told the jury to prepare themselves for Greta Rideout's testimony that her husband had struck and raped her within sight of the couple's crying two-year-old daughter. The defense countered by saying that Greta Rideout had a "serious sexual problem" and that his 21-year-old client "honestly believed if you are married to a woman, you have a right to sex."

During the following two days, a number of the couple's friends, neighbors, and relatives testified for the prosecution. While witnesses agreed that John did, indeed, beat his wife, a few gave testimony that raised questions about Greta's motives for accusing him of rape.

David Lowe testified that during an argument prior to 10 October, he had heard Greta warn her husband that she would have him arrested under Oregon's new rape law. The manager of the Rideout's apartment building, Jackie Godfrey, testified that following John's arrest, Greta had mentioned a $50,000 offer from the Warner Brothers film company. Jackie Godfrey's daughter, Eugenia, and her husband, Wayne, also testified as to the conversation.

Testimony given by two other prosecution witnesses, Jenny Reisch and John Rideout's half-brother Jack Hinkle, substantiated that the Rideouts had a troubled marriage, but they also cast doubt on Greta's truthfulness. At the beginning of the trial, Burt had said that Greta Rideout taunted her husband by saying that she, and

her friend Jenny, had once had a lesbian relationship. Jenny testified that there had been no such relationship, and that Greta Rideout's story had been "made up" to "bait" John.

Burt told the court that Greta said she had been raped by Hinkle. However, Hinkle testified that he had never raped his sister-in-law. He also testified that the Rideouts had once lived with him, and that they had been in the habit of "play[ing] games" that involved chasing each other through various rooms before having sex.

Other testimony was less open to interpretation. Dr. Lewis Sayers, the physician who examined Greta after the incident, testified that both her mental and physical condition were "probably from a forced act of intercourse." Officer Deborah Cleveland, who arrested John, said his comment about his wife's battered jaw was, "If I'd done it right she wouldn't be here to complain."

Greta was the prosecution's last witness. She testified that her husband routinely demanded sex two to three times a week and violent sex once a week. She also said that her husband frequently kicked and hit her. On 10 October, she woke at 9:00 a.m. and did housework while her husband, a student, slept until the afternoon. Upon waking, he demanded that she have sex with him. Greta refused, saying she had to get ready for work. He began to chase her, she recalled. "I was afraid of him. He was very angry. I'd never seen him that angry."

She testified that her husband had said, "You are my wife. You should do what I want." There was a physical fight, in front of their two-year-old daughter. When John ordered the child to leave the room, she obeyed, but Greta could hear her daughter crying, "Mommy,

Greta Rideout arrives for court, 1978. © AP/Wide World Photos.

Mommy!" Finally, having been beaten and hit especially hard in her jaw, Greta gave in.

Afterward, Greta continued, her husband dragged her to the bathroom and forced her to look at her bruised face in the mirror. He told her, "This is what you'll get for not cooperating from now on." He also threatened to tell lies about her if she went to the police and said that if he were ever arrested, "I'll find you and that will be the end of you."

During the prosecution's presentation of its case, the jury also heard the tape of Greta's call to the police on October 10, and visited the couple's apartment.

John was the only defense witness. His excuse was, "She hit me first." He admitted to hitting her, but testified that he had apologized, saying "'Greta, I'm sorry. I didn't mean to do that.' She said it was all right," he continued, and then they kissed and had "voluntary" sexual intercourse.

Lose One, Win Some

On 27 December 1978, after three hours of deliberations, the jury found John Rideout not guilty. A member of the jury, Pauline Speerstra, told the press afterward that the validity of Oregon's law had not been an issue in reaching their verdict. Rather, she said, since "we didn't know who to trust," the jury had reached its verdict based upon a finding of reasonable doubt.

Although John was acquitted, the publicity his trial afforded Oregon's law made many feel, as one newspaper editorial put it, that "an end to the common-law notion that rape is permissible in marriage is long overdue. A society that considers it a crime for a man to beat his wife should certainly consider it a crime for him to assault her sexually." By the early 1990s, only four states retained marital exemptions for rape.

Many recall that the couple reconciled two weeks after the trial. What is often forgotten is that the Rideouts separated three months later and finally divorced. Moreover, John Rideout later broke into Greta Rideout's home and received a suspended sentence. Continuing to harass her, he later went to prison.

Related Cases
Shaw v. Shaw, 17 Day Conn. 189 (1845).
Packard v. Packard, 27 FAM LQ 515 (1864).

Michael M. v. Superior Court of Sonoma County, 450 U.S. 464 (1981).

Bibliography and Further Reading

Brownmiller, Susan. *Against Our Will: Men, Women and Rape*. New York: Simon & Schuster, 1975.

Davis, Flora. *Moving the Mountain: The Women's Movement in America Since 1960*. New York: Simon & Schuster, 1991.

New York Times. December 20-24, 26-28, 31 1978.

ORR V. ORR

Legal Citation: 440 U.S. 268 (1979)

Appellant
William Herbert Orr

Appellee
Lillian M. Orr

Appellant's Claim
That Alabama's alimony statutes were unconstitutional.

Chief Lawyer for Appellant
John L. Capell III

Chief Lawyer for Appellee
W. F. Horsley

Justices for the Court
Harry A. Blackmun, William J. Brennan, Jr. (writing for the Court), Thurgood Marshall, John Paul Stevens, Potter Stewart, Byron R. White

Justices Dissenting
Warren E. Burger, Lewis F. Powell, Jr., William H. Rehnquist

Place
Washington, D.C.

Date of Decision
5 March 1979

Decision
Invalidated Alabama's statutes by which husbands, but not wives, might be required to pay alimony upon divorce.

Significance
Rejected the premise that married women are necessarily dependent upon their husbands for financial support.

Lillian and William Orr divorced in Alabama on 26 February 1974. The decree directed William to pay Lillian $1,240 per month in alimony. Soon he either fell behind or stopped paying altogether, and Lillian brought contempt proceedings against him in the Circuit Court of Lee County, Alabama, demanding back payments.

In defense, William claimed that Alabama's alimony statutes violated the Equal Protection Clause of the Fourteenth Amendment, since they required only husbands—never wives—to pay alimony. Lillian believed the law was constitutional. The court agreed with her and ordered William to pay the back alimony plus Lillian's legal fees. William promptly appealed the judgment to the Court of Civil Appeals of Alabama.

On 16 March 1977, the court ruled that alimony laws—"designed" to help "the wife of a broken marriage who needs financial assistance"—were constitutional. The judgment against William must stand. William next petitioned the Supreme Court of Alabama for a writ of *certiorari*—an order that the lower court send the trial records to the superior court for review. In May, the state supreme court granted this writ—only to reverse itself six months later, saying the writ had been "improvidently granted." William then appealed to the U.S. Supreme Court, which agreed to hear the case.

Questions Never Asked

The arguments took place on 27 November 1978. Lillian could have objected to William's standing to sue. She could have claimed that his suit came too late; after all, he had not complained at the time of the divorce. And she could have argued that since they had both agreed and signed on the dotted line, they were bound by state contract law—so it did not matter whether the alimony laws were constitutional or not. William would still have to pay. However, to the surprise of the justices, she offered none of these arguments. Lillian stood by her original contention that the only issue before the Court was the constitutional one.

Therefore, the Court addressed these arguments for her. First, it granted William standing to sue. Justice Brennan said: "There is no question but that Mr. Orr

Alimony

Alimony is a type of payment, secured by court order, whereby one member of a divorcing couple agrees to make regular payments toward the support of the other member. Usually the person making the payment is the former husband, and the person receiving payment is the former wife. This has been so even since the mass entrance of women into the workplace following the gains of the feminist movement in the early 1970s, because males still tend to earn more than females—even for comparable work.

Alimony is a form of support, and is generally awarded in situations where divorcing couples have children. Since men gain sole custody of the children only rarely, it is likely that the former wife will be responsible for raising them.

In alimony settlements, the income of the higher-earning spouse is treated as an asset, and unless he is in his peak earning years, it is most often an asset that has not reached full maturity. Sometimes the judge will award a token sum of alimony, such as $1.00 a year, in order to facilitate further challenges on the part of the wife, given the fact that it is easier to modify an existing award than to establish one after the divorce is final.

Source(s): *West's Encyclopedia of American Law*, Vol. 1. St. Paul, MN: West Group, 1998.

---

bears a burden he would not bear if he were female. This is highlighted, although not altered, by transposing it to the sphere of race. There is no doubt that a state law imposing alimony obligations on blacks but not on whites could be challenged by a black who was required to pay. The burden alone is sufficient to establish standing."

Second, the Court found that the "unexcused tardiness" of William's challenge "might well have constituted a procedural default under state law, and if Alabama had refused to hear Mr. Orr's constitutional objection on that ground, we might have been without jurisdiction to hear it here."

The third question was whether the Supreme Court should refuse jurisdiction because Alabama's contract laws might have furnished a valid basis for a lower court decision in favor of Lillian. In response, Brennan quoted *Anderson v. Brand* (1938): "We cannot refuse jurisdiction because the state court might have based its decision . . . upon an independent and adequate non-federal ground."

A Woman's Place Is . . .

Turning to the merits of the case, Brennan stressed that recent Supreme Court decisions had established that "classifications by gender must serve important governmental objectives and must be substantially related to achievement of those objectives." He then examined what might have been three objectives of the alimony statutes in question.

William had suggested that Alabama preferred wives to play dependent roles within families and reinforced that model by requiring husbands to pay alimony. As Brennan pointed out—citing the 1975 case *Stanton v. Stanton* as one example—a law intending to further that state objective could not stand.

Brennan then turned to the opinion of the Alabama Court of Civil Appeals that said divorced wives needed financial aid. The legislature might have meant to "provide help for needy spouses" and "use[d] sex as a proxy for need." The legislature might also have had "a goal of compensating women for past discrimination dur-

Justice William J. Brennan, Jr. © The Library of Congress.

ing marriage, which assertedly had left them unprepared to fend for themselves in the working world after divorce. Of course, . . . assisting needy spouses is a legitimate and important governmental objective."

Citing the 1979 case *Califano v. Webster,* Brennan remarked that reducing the disparity of incomes between men and women caused by the "long history of discrimination" was an important goal. However, there were other ways to achieve it besides burdening husbands. Alabama required individual hearings before any divorce. These could determine which spouses were "needy" and "which women were in fact discriminated against vis-a-vis their husbands, as well as which family units defied the stereotype and left the husband dependent on the wife."

Brennan concluded his discussion with a few remarks about women's "proper place":

> Legislative classifications which distribute benefits and burdens on the basis of gender carry the inherent risk of reinforcing stereotypes about the "proper place" of women and their need for special protection . . . Thus, even statutes purportedly designed to compensate for and ameliorate the effects of past discrimination must be carefully tailored. Where, as here, the State's compensatory and ameliorative purposes are as well served by a gender-neutral classification as one that gender classifies and therefore carries with it the baggage of sexual stereotypes, the State cannot be permitted to classify on the basis of sex.

A Divorce Decision Changes the Meaning of Marriage

The laws governing marriage are more often evaluated during divorce proceedings than during the life of an intact marriage. Thus, in settling the Orrs' dispute about their divorce decree, the Supreme Court radically changed the legal basis of marriage in America. As editor Leslie Friedman Goldstein points out, Anglo-American law had held that the "legal core" of marriage was a woman's obligation to provide sexual and domestic services and a man's obligation to provide financial support. The Court's ruling in *Orr v. Orr* was a complete rejection of such assumptions and one that, in Goldstein's words, "seismically altered" the marriage institution.

Related Cases
Stanton v. Stanton, 421 U.S. 7 (1975).
Califano v. Webster, 430 U.S. 313 (1977).

Bibliography and Further Reading

Goldstein, Leslie Friedman. *The Constitutional Rights of Women,* rev. ed. Madison: The University of Wisconsin Press, 1989.

New York Times, March 1979, pp. 6, 7, 11.

O'Connor, Sandra Day. "Women and the Constitution: A Bicentennial Perspective." in *Women, Politics and the Constitution.* Naomi B. Lynn, ed. Binghamton, NY: Harrington Park Press, 1990.

DeShaney v. Winnebago County Department of Social Services

Legal Citation: 489 U.S. 189 (1989)

Petitioner
Melody DeShaney for her son, Joshua DeShaney

Respondent
Winnebago County Department of Social Services

Petitioner's Claim
That the social workers and the county had violated Joshua DeShaney's right to due process under the Fourteenth Amendment by its failure to intervene to protect Joshua from his father's violence.

Chief Lawyer for Petitioner
Donald J. Sullivan

Chief Lawyer for Respondent
Mark J. Mingo

Justices for the Court
Anthony M. Kennedy, Sandra Day O'Connor, William H. Rehnquist (writing for the Court), Antonin Scalia, John Paul Stevens, Byron R. White

Justices Dissenting
Harry A. Blackmun, William J. Brennan, Jr., Thurgood Marshall

Place
Washington, D.C.

Date of Decision
22 February 1989

Decision
That Winnebago County Department of Social Services was not responsible for Joshua's severe beating, even though they had ample evidence that abuse was occurring and did nothing to prevent it.

Significance
That the state could not be held liable for child abuse, even if they knew that abuse was occurring and did nothing to prevent it.

"Undeniably tragic"

The facts of *DeShaney v. Winnebago County Department of Social Services* are, as Chief Justice Rehnquist wrote in his majority opinion, "undeniably tragic." Despite the tragic nature of the case, however, the Supreme Court, in a 6-3 ruling, found that states did not have a constitutional duty to protect children from abusive parents.

Young Joshua DeShaney was at the center of the case. Joshua was born in 1979 in Wyoming. In 1980, his parents divorced, and Joshua's father was awarded custody. Joshua and his father left Wyoming and moved to Wisconsin. Soon after arriving in Wisconsin, child welfare agencies were notified that Joshua was being abused by his father. The first indication came in 1982 when DeShaney's second wife reported that her soon to be ex-husband regularly abused her step-son. The Winnebago County Department of Social Services (DSS) interviewed the father, but did not take any action because he denied the charges.

Soon after, in January of 1983, Joshua was brought to the emergency room for his first of many visits. After treating his bruises, the attending physicians notified the DSS that Joshua's injuries were consistent with child abuse. At this time, the DSS brought together a team of child-care workers to discuss the case, and even placed Joshua under the state's care for three days. No charges were brought against the father, however, although the team did recommend that Joshua be enrolled in a head-start program and that his father should attend counseling. In addition, a social worker, Anne Kemmeter, was assigned to take charge of the case.

Over the next year, Kemmeter visited Joshua's home approximately 20 times. She did not see Joshua at every visit, but did note bumps and bruises on his body when she was allowed to see him. At one time, Kemmeter even described a lesion on his chin that looked like a cigarette burn. In addition, Joshua's father had failed to follow through with enrolling Joshua in pre-school and had not attended counseling sessions. At the same time Kemmeter made her numerous house visits, Joshua appeared in the emergency room at least two more times, and again the doctors reported suspicions of child

The Custody Battle

One Friday afternoon during the O. J. Simpson trial, Marcia Clark had to leave the courthouse early in order to pick up her two boys. On the following Monday she faced accusations from the defense that she had used her children as an excuse to stall in her case preparation. Also on that day, Clark's former husband Gordon filed a suit for custody of the boys, charging that she was "never home and never has any time to spend with them."

According to Department of Labor statistics, there are 23 million working mothers in America, and 80 percent of all divorced mothers are among their ranks. Legal practice has tended to favor custody for the woman, with men only gaining custody in 11 percent of cases. In the 1800s, though, husbands usually got custody, and in the 1970s, a number of courts tried the approach of joint, or shared, custody. But as LynNell Hancock and Judith Regan observed in a *Newsweek* article on the Clark case, "It turns out that couples who couldn't live together often can't manage children together, either."

Source(s): Hancock, LynNell and Judith Regan. "Putting Working Moms in Custody." *Newsweek*, 13 March 1995.

abuse to the DSS. Still, the state did not make any move to remove Joshua from the custody of his father, despite the fact, as Kemmeter later admitted, "I just knew the phone would ring one day and Joshua would be dead."

Who was protecting Joshua?

Although Joshua did not die from his father's abuse, on 8 March 1984, Joshua DeShaney was beaten so badly by his father that he fell into a coma. Despite emergency brain surgery—where the doctors found evidence of months of bleeding—when Joshua came out of his coma he was paralyzed and profoundly retarded. Joshua would need to be institutionalized for the rest of his life and could never again function on his own. The final beating occurred only one day after Kemmeter had visited DeShaney's home.

For his crimes, Randy DeShaney was found guilty of child abuse, and sentenced to serve two to four years in prison. He served less than two years before being paroled. Not content with her husband being punished for his crimes, Melody DeShaney, Joshua's mother, sued the Winnebago County Department of Social Services for sitting idly by and writing notes on the case, while not taking any concrete steps to remove her son from danger. DeShaney's lawyers argued that the social workers and the county had violated her son's right to Due Process under the Fourteenth Amendment by its failure to intervene to protect Joshua from his father's violence. According to the Due Process Clause of the Fourteenth Amendment, "[n]o state shall . . . deprive any person of life, liberty, or property, without due process of law." The case charged that Joshua's rights to liberty had been violated by the state's passive handling of the abuse they witnessed.

The Supreme Court ruled against the plaintiff and decided that Joshua's Fourteenth Amendment rights had not been violated. As Chief Justice Rehnquist wrote in his majority opinion, "nothing in the language of

the Due Process Clause itself requires the State to protect the life, liberty, and property of its citizens from invasion by private actors." In other words, Joshua's father hurt Joshua, not Kemmeter, the emergency room doctors, or the police officers. Joshua had been deprived of his liberty, but at the hands of his father, and not the Winnebago County Department of Social Services. The Fourteenth Amendment said that people needed to be protected from the state, but not from each other.

Despite the fact that Randy DeShaney had hurt Joshua, and not the state, the plaintiff charged that Joshua had entered into a "special relationship with the state" that required them to take care of him. Once again, the Court rejected this claim. Rehnquist wrote: "While the state may have been aware of the dangers that Joshua faced . . . it played no part in their creation, nor did it do anything to render him more vulnerable to them." The state "does not become the permanent guarantor of an individual's safety by once having offered him shelter."

Three of the justices dissented, saying that the county had an obligation to protect Joshua from his father's abuse once they learned about it, even if the Fourteenth Amendment did not specifically address this issue. As Justice Blackmun wrote: "Poor Joshua! Victim of repeated attacks . . . and abandoned by respondents [the county] who placed him in a dangerous predicament and who knew or learned what was going on yet did essentially nothing . . ."

Impact

After the ruling, there was an outcry against the case from child welfare advocates, who claimed that children were being denied their constitutional rights. Newspapers across the nation criticized the decision, in commentaries such as "No Comment From Joshua" in the *Washington Post*, and "An 'Undeniably Tragic' Ruling" in *The Boston Globe*. Critics charged that the court based its decision on a cold, detached, and rational reading of the law, without considering the ramifications of their decision on children.

Other critics, looking back on the *DeShaney* decision, have charged that the case set a dangerous precedent for taking away the rights of children. For example, Kathleen Fischer, writing in the *Journal of Juvenile Law*, entitled her article "Where Have all the Heroes Gone? A Study of Juvenile Related Decisions Following *DeShaney*." Fischer argues that following in the wake of the *DeShaney* case, courts have ruled against supporting the rights of children against abusive adults. She writes: "One would conclude that each actor's rights [in cases following *DeShaney*] are being protected except for those of the children, who need the protection most of all."

Related Cases
Estelle v. Gamble, 429 U.S. 97 (1976).
Ingraham v. Wright, 430 U.S. 651 (1977).
Youngberg v. Romeo, 457 U.S. 307 (1982).

Bibliography and Further Reading
Elsasser, Glen. "Court: States Not Liable for Child Abuse." *Chicago Tribune.* 23 February 1989.

Farber, Daniel A. "Government Liability After *DeShaney*." *Trial.* May 1989, 18-20.

Fischer, Kathleen. "Where Have all the Heroes Gone? A Study of Juvenile Related Decisions Following *DeShaney*." *Journal of Juvenile Law,* Vol. 11, no. 1, 1990, pp. 23-32.

Hentoff, Nat. "No Comment from Joshua." *Washington Post.* 18 November 1989.

Kemp, James M. " *DeShaney* and Its Progeny—The Failure to Mandate that Public Schools Protect Our Tender Youth." *Journal of Law and Education,* Vol. 24, no. 4, fall, 1995, pp. 679-688.

Kilpatrick, James. "Court was Right in DeShaney Case." *San Francisco Chronicle.* 2 March 1989.

Oren, Laura. " *DeShaney's* Unfinished Business: The Foster Child's Due Process Right to Safety." *North Carolina Law Review,* Vol. 69, no. 1, November, 1990, pp. 113-158.

Reidinger, Paul. "Why Did No One Protect This Child?" *ABA Journal.* 1 December 1988, pp. 49-51.

"States Don't Have to Protect Kids, High Court Says." *San Francisco Chronicle.* 23 February 1989.

Stern, Lynne Jodi. "Young Lives Betrayed: *DeShaney v. Winnebago County Department of Social Services*." *New England Law Review.* Vol. 25, no. 4, summer, 1991, pp. 1251-1293.

"An 'Undeniably Tragic' Ruling." *The Boston Globe.* 24 February 1989.

KINGSLEY V. KINGSLEY

Legal Citation: 623 So.2d 780 (1993)

Appellant
Rachel Kingsley

Appellees
Gregory Kingsley, Jerri A. Blair, the George Russ family, and the State of Florida

Appellant's Claim
That a minor has no legal right to terminate parental rights solely on his own initiative.

Chief Lawyer for Appellant
Jane E. Carey

Chief Lawyer for Appellees
George H. Russ

Judges for the Court
George N. Diamantis (writing for the court), Jacqueline R. Griffin

Judges Dissenting
Charles M. Harris

Place
Daytona Beach, Florida

Date of Decision
18 August 1993

Decision
Ruled in favor of Gregory Kingsley by finding that clear and convincing evidence of abandonment supported termination.

Significance
The court held that a minor child does not have the capacity to terminate parental rights on his own behalf. However, because a petition for termination was filed on Gregory's behalf by other parties, termination was allowed. In effect, the court allowed Gregory Kingsley to "divorce" his natural mother. The case was part of a trend in courts deciding more frequently in the best interest of the child against parental authority concerning education and health issues. The competency of children to make legal claims on their own increasingly became a subject of intense debate between children's rights advocates and others.

The conflict between children's rights and parental rights has often come to the forefront in American history. During the Industrial Revolution, child labor laws were sought to protect children from parents forcing them to work as adults. A side effect of such debate was the recognition that parental authority was not absolute. Traditionally, courts assumed parents knew what was best by considering children as property and parental rights as paramount. Several court cases in the twentieth century focused on parental rights in choosing how their children would be educated.

By the 1970s, courts began applying "the best interests of the child" principle in ruling against parents. In 1989, the United Nations passed a resolution recognizing the children's rights in freedom from discrimination, health care, education, and freedom of thought. In a political era of emphasizing the promotion of family values by major political parties during election campaigns, the issue of children's legal rights persistently arose along with women's rights, minority rights, and rights of the disabled. In the 1990s, First Lady Hillary Rodham Clinton campaigned for the acceptance that children were competent to exercise legal standing. The Supreme Court seemingly sought a middle ground in its decisions, basically recognizing the dominance of parental rights except in clear-cut cases where children were in need of protection. Physical abuse cases often presented clear needs to favor the child's best interest, but emotional abuse cases presented much more difficult situations to judge. State and local governments remained inconsistent in their recognition of parental and child rights.

A Child as a Person

In 1992, Gregory Kingsley, at 11 years of age, was living in foster care while his poor and unemployed mother, Rachel, had lived for two years in Missouri without trying to contact him. His parents were divorced and his brother, Jeremiah, was in foster care suffering from the neurological disorder, Tourette's syndrome. When the Missouri Department of Human Resource Services recommended that Gregory be reunited with his mother, he filed a petition in the juvenile division of Florida's Orange County circuit court to terminate the parental rights of his natural parents. In a separate action, he also filed for adoption by his foster parents in the civil division of the same circuit court.

The first question to be resolved by the courts was whether Gregory as a minor was a "person" under the law who could initiate lawsuits. In July of 1992, the trial court ruled that Gregory was indeed a natural person under the law, and understood the situation. Therefore, Gregory had legal standing to seek termination of the parental rights even though an unemancipated minor.

George and Elizabeth Russ, a Mormon couple with children of their own, had taken Gregory in as a foster child. They also filed adoption papers in September of 1992. Gregory Kingsley's natural father readily agreed to the adoption petition and soon died while the case was still proceeding through the courts. But repeated petitions for termination of parental rights by the mother, Rachel Kingsley, received no response.

Later in September, the court decided to try the issues of termination and adoption together. After two days of trial, the court terminated Rachel's parental rights, and in a separate order, granted the adoption to the Russ'. Rachel appealed to the district court of appeals.

By a 2-1 majority, the District Court of Appeals of Florida for the Fifth District partially affirmed the district court's ruling and remanded Gregory's case back to the district court for further consideration. In presenting the court's findings, Judge Diamantis, writing for the majority, first examined the legal ability of a minor to file a lawsuit. Rachel Kingsley argued that Gregory could not seek termination of parental rights on his own behalf. She contended courts historically ruled that unemancipated minors did not have legal standing to initiate legal actions on their own. The restriction, in fact, was included in Florida civil law which stated,

> When an infant or incompetent person has a representative, such as a guardian or other like fiduciary, the representative may sue or defend on behalf of the infant or incompetent person. An infant or incompetent person who does not have a duly appointed representative may sue by next friend or by a *guardian ad litem*. The court shall appoint a *guardian ad litem* for an infant or incompetent person not otherwise represented in an action or shall make such other order as it deems proper for the protection of the infant or incompetent person.

A *guardian ad litem* is a person appointed by the court to represent the child in the best interests of the child. An *attorney ad litem* is a person appointed by the court to represent a person as his counsel in the legal pro-

ceeding. Diamantis was concerned that the district court simply appointing one of Gregory's attorneys as his *guardian ad litem* was insufficient.

However, Diamantis wrote,

> Although we conclude that the trial court erred in allowing Gregory to file the petition in his own name because Gregory lacked the requisite legal capacity, this error was rendered harmless by the fact that separate petitions for termination of parental rights were filed on behalf of Gregory by the foster father, the *guardian ad litem*, HRS (Department of Health and Rehabilitative Services), and the foster mother.

Diamantis then turned to the second question, termination of Rachel's parental rights. Gregory contended the level of proof needed should be a "preponderance of the evidence" rather than the more stringent "clear and convincing evidence." Gregory argued that a child's right to be raised free of abuse and neglect should be at least equal to a parent's right to maintain a formal relationship with the child. Diamantis disagreed by holding that Florida law applicable to termination of parental rights cases required clear and convincing evidence.

However, Diamantis did find that clear and convincing evidence existed in Gregory's case concerning abandonment and neglect. The Florida Supreme Court had previously defined "clear and convincing evidence" as believable evidence with facts distinctly remembered, testimony specific, and no confusion over the facts. Florida law also defined abandonment as "a situation in which the parent . . . of a child . . ., while being able, makes no provision for the child's support and makes no effort to communicate with the child, which situation is sufficient to evince a willful rejection of parental obligations." Marginal efforts were normally not sufficient. Judge Diamantis concurred with the appeals court finding of abandonment based on strong supporting evidence.

Improper Parental Comparisons

The third issue involved the adoption order. Rachel Kingsley argued the district court should not have tried the termination and adoption cases simultaneously. Such action by the court violated her rights to procedural due process of the law. Mistakenly, according to Rachel, the court had shifted its focus from the abandonment and neglect issue to comparing her parenting skills with those of the proposed adoptive parents. This comparison ignored her fundamental interest in Gregory on its own merit. Diamantis agreed with Rachel.

He ruled that trying the two petitions separately would avoid this inappropriate comparison of parenting skills. Such comparisons could unnecessarily influence termination decisions. Diamantis wrote that termination cases must focus solely on issues of abandonment, neglect, or abuse. That a child may be better off with the prospective adoptive parents was not legally relevant in deciding termination. Natural parents retain custody unless found unfit. Another could not obtain custody merely because they might provide better care.

Diamantis found that Rachel's appeal regarding termination effectively suspended the adoption case. When Rachel contested termination in district court, the court should have immediately suspended any further consideration of the adoption issue. Diamantis was especially concerned that the adoption order was issued prior to terminating parental rights contrary to Florida law. The law specifically stated that an appeal of an order terminating parental rights automatically suspended any placement of the child for adoption. Diamantis affirmed the order terminating Rachel's parental rights, but reversed the adoption order.

Judge Harris, in dissent, argued the court should have simply judged whether Rachel had really done something so bad that she should lose her child. Although agreeing with the majority that Gregory had no legal standing as a minor, Harris insisted Rachel should have had a new hearing on the abandonment issue. He believed the district court's error in considering abandonment and adoption together was not as "harmless" as the majority ruled. Adoption issues likely tainted the abandonment arguments too severely to be ignored as the majority were doing.

Impact

Gregory became the topic of talk shows and two movies made for television. His story encouraged other children to seek legal help with their problems and raised hopes of foster care parents interested in adopting children with no legal guardians. The increased reporting of child abuse incidences throughout the nation, often in high-profile news stories, greatly supported efforts to recognize children's rights. By the late 1990s estimates projected that 1.5 million children were subjected to moderate or serious abuse across the nation annually. Still, courts across the nation commonly ruled in favor of recognizing parental rights despite prior neglect and abuse. In response, Congress passed the Adoption and Safe Families Act of 1997 requiring courts to consider past histories of abuse in deciding to terminate parental rights for those children already in state foster care sys-

tems. States were threatened with loss of federal child-welfare funds if they did not conform with the act.

Some family advocates were concerned that the concept of children's rights was often discriminatory against poor and single mothers of color. Also, the publicity of such cases could have long-term effects on the children themselves. Advocates for the poor and minorities encouraged family preservation programs in attempting to more assertively help the parents before removing the children from their homes.

Kingsley helped define the limits of children's rights in U.S. law. Unemancipated minor children could not terminate parental rights in their own right, but needed an adult advocate to represent them in addition to a lawyer in legal proceedings. Many still believed *Kingsley* set a dangerous precedent with the child being named as the plaintiff, rather than the anticipated foster parents or public agency. Issues over the government's right to act on behalf of children in opposition to their parents continued concerning denial of medical care for religious purposes, ineffective home schooling, and right to abortion without parental permission. Some feared the government was assuming too much of a decision-making role in family matters. What was traditionally considered parental inherent rights were being diminished. In reaction, children's rights advocates argued the notion children were, in essence, the property of their parents was ill-founded and outdated.

Related Cases

Santosky v. Kramer, 455 U.S. 745 (1982).
Padgett v. Department of Health and Rehabilitative Services, 577 So.2d 565 (1991).
Twigg v. Mays, WL 330624 (Fla. Cir. Cty. 1993).
Smith v. Langford, 255 So.2d 712 (1997).

Bibliography and Further Reading

Alston, Philip, ed. *The Best Interests of the Child: Reconciling Culture and Human Rights.* New York: Oxford University Press, 1994.

Kramer, Donald T. *Legal Rights of Children.* Colorado Springs, CO: Shepard's/McGraw-Hill, 1994.

Mezey, Susan G. *Children in Court: Public Policymaking and Federal Court Decisions.* Albany: State University of New York Press, 1996.

Shapiro, Andrew L. "Children in Court-the New Crusade." *The Nation,* September 27, 1993.

TWIGG V. MAYS

Legal Citation: WL 330624 (Fla.Cir.Cty. 1993)

Plaintiff
Ernest and Regina Twigg

Defendant
Robert Mays

Plaintiff's Claim
That the parental rights held by the Twiggs compelled that they be granted custody of 14-year-old Kimberley Mays who was switched at birth with another newborn.

Chief Lawyer for Plaintiff
John Blakely

Chief Defense Lawyers
George Russ, David Denkin (*guardian ad litem*)

Judge
Stephen Dakan

Place
Sarasota County, Florida

Date of Decision
18 August 1993

Decision
Ruled in favor of Mays, by terminating the Twiggs' legal rights to Kimberly and clearing the way for Robert Mays to adopt her.

Significance
The ruling was one of a series of Florida cases testing children's legal rights. Despite the several decisions made through the 1990s, children's rights remained poorly defined and the subject of much controversy. While this decision supported "the best interest of the child" principle and found in favor of what was considered best for Kimberly Mays, other decisions in the early 1990s were still favoring the rights of biological parents over the best interests of the children where they conflicted. Such contradictory rulings created uncertainty over the rights of biological parents and children's rights.

The emerging legal clout of children, particularly those not in state custody and stuck in abusive situations and with no adult advocates, became increasingly examined in 1980s. Issues included the right of juveniles to hire attorneys and file motions on their own behalf.

Florida, known for its retirement communities, became a stage for a series of cases focused on children's legal rights. In the 1989 case of a pregnant 15-year-old Lake County girl seeking an abortion without parental consent, the Florida Supreme Court ruled a child enjoys the same constitutional right to privacy as an adult. In 1992, Gregory Kingsley, an 11-year-old boy, sued the state and his biological parents seeking permission to be adopted by the family of George Russ. An Orlando judge in 1993 dissolved the rights of Gregory's biological mother after finding her unfit, thus granting Gregory a divorce from his biological parents.

Switched at Birth

Kimberly Mays was born to Ernest and Regina Twigg of Sebring, Florida, in 1978 at Hardee Memorial Hospital in Wauchula, a small rural town in Florida. Somehow her identification tag was switched at the hospital with another girl's and Kimberly went home with the wrong parents. As a result, the Twiggs raised the other girl, Arlena who at ten years of age died during heart surgery in 1988. Shockingly, blood tests taken at the hospital revealed that Arlena was not related to the Twiggs. The Twiggs, from their Langhorne, Pennsylvania home, began a nationwide search for their biological daughter.

Kimberly had gone home with Robert and Barbara Mays. Barbara later died of cancer and a second marriage of Robert's ended in divorce. The Twiggs' search led them to Robert, a roofing salesman, living alone with the girl he thought of as his only child.

For a year the Twiggs, who had seven other children ages 9 to 24, insisted Robert Mays submit to genetic testing. They even moved back to Florida to be near Kimberly. Robert finally relented, but had the Twiggs sign an agreement promising that should Kimberly be their biological daughter, they would only seek visitation rights, not actual custody. The tests indeed proved that Kimberly was the Twiggs' biological daughter. Vis-

---

Child Emancipation

The term "child emancipation" is often used in conjunction with *majority*, or the age at which a young person is old enough to make his or her own decisions—and to experience the consequences of those decisions. This age is usually set at 18, and it marks the point when a child is free to leave home, and likewise when parents are no longer compelled legally to support the child. It is also the age at which a young person who commits a crime will no longer be charged as a juvenile (with all the attendant legal protections), but will be prosecuted as an adult.

Source(s): Fast, Julius, and Timothy Fast. *The Legal Atlas of the United States.* New York: Facts on File, 1997.

---

its by the Twiggs to see Kimberly began in 1990. However, Robert abruptly stopped the visits after only five sessions claiming they were too disruptive to the girl's schoolwork and attitude. For the next several years, the Twiggs fought Robert over Kimberly.

In the meantime, the book *The Baby Swap Conspiracy* was published. The author, Loretta Schwartz-Nobel, suggested the baby switch at the Wauchula hospital had been intentional. Kimberly was greatly disturbed by the books claims about her father and deceased mother. Kimberly, wanting to stay with Robert who had raised her for nearly 15 years, saw a television movie about young Gregory Kingsley who had just successfully sued his mother in Florida for termination of parental rights. Kimberly contacted Gregory's new father and lawyer, George Russ, to represent her against her biological parents. Kimberly cited allegations made against Robert by Ernest and Regina Twigg as the reason she wished to terminate relations with the Twiggs and be adopted by Robert. The Twiggs' questioned Kimberly's legal guidance in pursuing such a case and contended no proper basis for a "divorce" case existed since the Twiggs had no previous custody of Kimberly.

Kimberly filed papers in the Florida circuit court to sever whatever legal ties to her biological parents that Florida law might recognize. The documents were highly critical of the Twiggs in a personal nature. Among the allegations, Kimberly charged that Regina Twigg "had emotional and psychological problems" for which she had failed to seek counseling. She also claimed the Twiggs "neglected and abused" their other children by letting them go unwashed, underfed, and leaving them with strangers. She also claimed the Twiggs were trying to undermine Kimberly's relationship with Robert Mays.

The Rights of a Child

In June of 1993, Circuit Judge Stephen Dakan in a preliminary ruling found that Kimberly, despite being a minor, had the right to sue her biological parents for "divorce" to keep them from legally removing her from Robert Mays. Dakan wrote that "surely a minor child has the right to assert a constitutional privilege to resist an attempt to remove her from the only home she has known and declare her the child of strangers." Nonetheless, the Twiggs responded by suing Robert Mays for visitation rights.

On 2 August 1993 the trial on the Twiggs' claim began. Judge Dakan was to decide whether the Twiggs, the biological parents, would have visitation rights to Kimberly, or whether all legal ties between them would be severed.

Kimberly argued the key question to be answered was, "What constitutes a family?" George Russ, in arguing against visitation by the Twiggs, stated, "Biology alone without more does not create or sustain a fam-

Kimberly Mays Twigg, 1993. © AP/Wide World Photos.

ily." Kimberly, he contended, held a loving, psychological bond with Robert. To legally require her to visit a family she considered strangers would be humiliating to a child.

The Twiggs' countered they at least held a right to visit the child who was their flesh and blood. They stressed that Robert did not live up to the 1978 agreement allowing the Twiggs visitation. This action by Mays had been devastating to the Twiggs. It was as if Kimberly had been taken from them twice.

Despite Mays' assertions that the visitations were upsetting to Kimberly, the Twiggs and their children testified to the contrary that Kimberly appeared "vivacious, bubbly, lovely and sweet." She actually seemed to enjoy her few visits with the family. Kimberly even called Regina "mom" while playing at a miniature golf course. Kimberly even enjoyed a special bedroom set up for her in the Twiggs' seven-bedroom Sebring home, furnished with dolls and a large photograph of Kimberly over the bed.

The Twiggs argued Kimberly's feelings should not be considered. Because of her youth, she likely did not fully appreciate the implications of her decisions. "I really don't think she knows the impact of what she is doing. When she has her own children and looks back, she may really regret the decision she has made now," argued Regina.

Psychologist Dr. Harold Smith testified on behalf of the Twiggs that ninth-graders still tended to think like children, lacking the maturity to decide important matters such as where to live. He further testified that visitation could cause no harm, that children are normally easily adaptable to such arrangements. Court-appointed psychologist Herbert Goldstein contradicted Smith's opinions. He asserted that visits with the Twiggs could prove devastating to Kimberly. Goldstein also contended Regina Twigg had psychological problems causing her to put her needs ahead of others. Kimberly begged Judge Dakan to end her torment and pleaded for refuge from the Twiggs, not wanting to ever see them again.

After two weeks of trial, Judge Dakan ruled Kimberly was free to cease any further contact with her biological parents and affirmed that the man who raised her was her legal father. Dakan wrote that Kimberly's psychological relationship with Robert should be considered more important than her biological link to the Twiggs. Dakan wrote, "The effect of this judgment is that the Twiggs have no legal interest in or right to Kimberly Mays; that Robert Mays' legal status as the father of Kimberly Mays remains unchanged."

It is clear, Dakan wrote, "that the Twiggs are seen by her as a constant source of danger to her father and to her family relationship." He contended the Twiggs' aggressiveness to obtain visitation rights and their attacks on Robert "created a chasm between Kimberly Mays and the Twiggs that may never be bridged."

Impact

As with Gregory Kingsley before her, Kimberly's story inspired a 1991 made-for-television mini-series *Switched at Birth*, a book, and a 1993 interview with Barbara Walters on the television program *20/20*. Though the trial was over, surprising events related to the case continued to unfold. Later Patricia Webb, a dying woman who worked as a nurse's aide at Hardee Memorial Hospital in 1978, proclaimed that two babies had been deliberately switched under doctor's orders. Threats were made to safeguard the secret. Parties to the *Twigg* case expressed doubt over the claim since it also contradicted some aspects of Barbara Mays' medical record concerning the diagnosis of cervical cancer which eventually lead to her death.

In March of 1994, Kimberly Mays moved out of the home she had fought to keep. With her father's signed permission, Kimberly entered a YMCA Youth Shelter in Sarasota, a residential house for runaways and troubled youths. Astonishingly, Kimberly decided to live with the Twiggs.

The *Twigg* case highlighted the controversies in child custody and children's rights cases. Dakan's decision was remarkable in its recognition of the "psychological parent" over biological parental rights. Also in 1993, in the *In re Baby Girl Clausen* case, a court ruling went the opposite direction by ruling in favor of the biological parents claiming custody from adoptive parents. In *Twigg*, the court following "in the best interest of the child" principle, in *Clausen* it recognized the compelling arguments in favor of the rights of the biological family. *Clausen* favored parental rights over children's needs, *Twigg* chose the opposite.

Ironically, several years later another case arose involving children unknowingly switched at birth. In July of 1998, a three-year-old girl survived a Virginia traffic accident that killed her parents. Hospital tests shockingly revealed she was not their biological child. During the following months while the child was being taken care of by her grandparents, the biological parents and another child were identified. Visitation procedures between the two families were agreed upon. However, custody arguments soon arose, and by December of 1998, the possibility of lawsuits against the University of Virginia Medical Center in Charlottesville were threatened. The rights of children in such situations still remain poorly defined.

Related Cases

Padgett v. Department of Health and Rehabilitative Services, 577 So.2d 565 (Fla. 1991).
Kingsley v. Kingsley, 623 So 2d 780 (1993).

In Re Baby Girl Clausen, 442 Mich. 648, 502 N. W. 2d 649 (1993).

Smith v. Langford, 255 So.2d 712 (Fla. 1st DCA 1997).

Bibliography and Further Reading

Gregory, John De Witt, Peter N. Swisher, and Sheryl L. Scheible. *Understanding Family Law.* New York: Matthew Bender, 1993.

Krause, Harry D., ed. *Child Law: Parent, Child, and State.* New York: New York University Press, 1992.

Mayoue, John C. *Competing Interests in Family Law: Legal Rights and Duties of Third Parties, Spouses, and Significant Others.* Chicago: American Bar Association, Section of Family Law, 1998.

GENDER DISCRIMINATION

Definition

Gender discrimination, or sex discrimination, may be characterized as the unequal treatment of a person based solely on that person's sex. While females have historically laid claim to the cry of unequal treatment, modern civil rights laws banning sex discrimination have been construed to protect males as well, especially in the area of employment.

History

During the early years of this country, women were not entitled to the same rights and privileges as men. Women were not allowed to vote and were usually required to surrender control of their property to their husband upon marriage. Moreover, their educational and occupational opportunities were severely limited. It was commonly believed that a woman's place was in the home, raising children and tending to domestic affairs.

The first real efforts to achieve equality for women occurred in the 1800s. During the early part of that century, coeducational studies at the university level were offered for the first time. State laws were passed which allowed women to retain their property after marriage. Also, the first women's rights convention was held. Many who supported women's rights became active in the abolitionist movement during the Civil War era. Some even became well-known public orators, an uncommon occupation for women at the time.

The quest for equality continued after the Civil War. In 1869, the Wyoming Territory passed a law which allowed women to vote and serve on juries. Several other western territories and states subsequently granted women the right to vote. Women's rights advocates were outraged that the Fifteenth Amendment, which was ratified in 1870, prohibited the states from denying voting rights on the ground of race, but not on the basis of sex. In 1878, Congress considered a Constitutional amendment giving women the right to vote. Although the amendment failed, it was revitalized every year for a period of 40 years. The movement for women's suffrage was led, among others, by Susan B. Anthony, who was arrested for voting in a presidential election, and by Lucy Stone, who was one of the first American women to retain her maiden name after marriage. In 1920, women were finally given the constitutional right to vote in the Nineteenth Amendment, which provided that "[t]he right of citizens of the United States to vote shall not be denied or abridged by the United States or by any State on account of sex."

The women's rights movement lost its impetus after the ratification of the Nineteenth Amendment. It was not until the 1960s that it regained its momentum. With more women rejecting the traditional role of housewife and entering the work force, there was an increased demand for equal rights and opportunities. In response, Congress passed the Equal Pay Act of 1963, which prohibits employers from discriminating against employees on the ground of sex with respect to the terms of compensation. The following year, Congress enacted Title VII of the Civil Rights Act of 1964, which bans discrimination in employment on the basis of sex, among other grounds. Males, as well as females, have been granted protection against sex discrimination under both the Equal Pay Act and Title VII.

In 1972, Congress submitted the Equal Rights Amendment (ERA) to the states for ratification. Basically, the ERA barred all discrimination on the ground of sex. However, the ERA suffered defeat after the necessary number of states failed to ratify it within the mandatory ten-year deadline. To date, women are still struggling with the issue of equality in their personal and professional relationships. Thirty-five years after the passage of the Equal Pay Act, women have still not achieved equality in wages.

Discrimination in the Acquisition of Credit

The Equal Credit Opportunity Act of 1968, as amended, prohibits a creditor from discriminating against an individual on the grounds of sex or marital status with respect to the granting of credit. This means that a woman cannot be denied a credit card or personal loan solely on the basis of her gender. Furthermore, a creditor is barred from requiring a married woman to apply for credit in her spouse's name.

Discrimination in Education: Access to Educational Opportunities

Women college students have traditionally been denied access to the educational opportunities offered by all-male, military-oriented institutions of higher learning. (Note that these establishments are not part of any branch of the armed forces). They have been denied admission on the grounds that the physical training would be too rigorous for them, their presence would adversely affect the morale of the male students, and their inclusion would necessarily result in the reduction of standards.

However, the United States Supreme Court discredited such reasons in *United States v Virginia* (1996), when it held as unconstitutional the male-only admission policy practiced by the Virginia Military Institute (VMI). The Supreme Court found that such policy violated the equal protection clause under the Fourteenth Amendment, which provides that no state shall "deny to any person within its jurisdiction the equal protection of the laws." Established in 1839, VMI was the only remaining single-sex public institution of higher learning in Virginia. Its goal was to produce "citizen-soldiers" who were prepared for leadership in civilian life and military service. In furtherance of this goal, VMI used an "adversative method," which included mental stress, absence of privacy with constant surveillance, and minute regulation of behavior.

The Supreme Court determined that sex classifications may not be used to create or perpetuate the legal, social, and economic inferiority of females. Furthermore, the Supreme Court rejected VMI's argument that the establishment of a separate program for women would cure the constitutional violation. In this regard, the Supreme Court pointed out that an all-female college would not afford its students an opportunity to experience the same rigorous military training that was provided by VMI. It would also deprive the female students of the prestige, traditions, and community standing available to their male counterparts at VMI.

Discrimination in Education: Participation in Athletic Programs

Title IX of the Education Amendments of 1972 prohibits sex discrimination in federally funded education programs, including athletic activities. In passing Title IX, Congress intended to prevent the use of federal resources to promote gender discrimination. Title IX does not require a state university to maintain any athletic program at all. However, it does require a state school to provide equal athletic opportunities to both sexes if the school does choose to offer athletics to its students. Title IX has prompted much litigation by female college athletes, who claim that they are not provided with the same benefits, treatment, services, and opportunities as their male counterparts. If a state

university has eliminated a female varsity team, the aggrieved athletes must show that the university failed to provide female students with athletic opportunities that are proportionate to their percentage in the student body.

Discrimination in Employment

The Equal Pay Act of 1963 prohibits employers that are engaged in an industry affecting commerce from discriminating against their employees on the basis of sex, with respect to the payment of wages. In essence, the act mandates equal pay when members of both sexes have jobs which require the comparable execution of skill, effort, and responsibility and which are performed under similar working conditions. Wages established on any of the following methods are exempt from the "equal pay for equal work" rule: (1) a seniority system; (2) a merit system; (3) a system that measures earnings by either quantity or quality of production; or (4) a differential that is based on a consideration other than sex. However, none of the above methods would justify an employer's practice of paying married women less than either men or single women when all three categories of employees have substantially similar positions.

Title VII of the Civil Rights Act of 1964 bars employers from discriminating against individuals on the ground of sex. To fall within the parameters of the act, an employer must be engaged in an industry which affects interstate commerce and must have 15 or more employees. State discrimination laws govern employers that do not come under Title VII. The term "sex" includes pregnancy, childbirth, and related medical conditions. However, Title VII's protections are not limited to females. Both men and women have pursued sex discrimination claims under Title VII. An employer is prohibited from advertising for help in a sexually discriminatory manner, as well as from making a hiring decision that is based on an applicant's sex. Furthermore, an employer is precluded from denying a promotion to an employee or from deciding to discharge an employee on the basis of gender. An employee who has been treated differently than similarly situated employees of the opposite sex, with respect to a term, condition, or privilege of employment, may sue the employer under a "disparate treatment" theory. In defense, the employer will attempt to articulate a legitimate, nondiscriminatory reason for its conduct. By way of example, an employer may contend that the employee had been discharged for poor job performance or failure to comply with company policies. After the employer offers an explanation for its action, the employee will be given an opportunity to show that the reason was merely a pretext for a discriminatory motive.

Alternatively, an employee may commence suit under a "disparate impact" theory if the employer has a policy or rule which has a disproportionate impact on members of that employee's gender. For example, the employer may have a rule which has the effect of promoting or perpetuating discrimination against females even though the rule does not apparently discriminate against women. An employer may restrict a job routine to people who meet a certain height requirement. If a majority of women in the general population do not meet that requirement, then the law can be found to have a disparate impact on female employees.

Sexual harassment is another form of prohibited sex discrimination under Title VII. This typically involves unwelcome sexual advances, requests for favors of a sexual nature, or other offensive verbal or physical conduct of a sexual nature. A female employee may claim sexual harassment by a male employee, and, in turn, a male worker may allege unwanted sexual advances by a female worker. The United States Supreme Court recognized same-sex sexual harassment in *Oncale v Sundowner Offshore Services, Inc.* (1998), which involved a male worker's claim that he had been forcibly subjected to sex-related, humiliating conduct by male co-workers, including a physical assault and the threat of rape.

See also: **Civil Law, Employment Discrimination**

Bibliography and Further Reading

Filipp, Mark R. *Employment Law Answer Book.* New York, NY: Panel Publishers, 1998

Jasper, Margaret C. *Employee Rights in the Workplace.* Dobbs Ferry, NY: Oceana Publications, Inc., 1997

Petrocelli, William. *Sexual Harassment on the Job,* 3rd Ed. Berkeley, CA: Nolo Press, 1998

Rowbotham, Sheila. *A Century of Women.* New York, NY: Viking, 1997

Schneider, Dorothy & Carl J. *American Women in the Progressive Era.* New York, NY: Facts on File, 1993

PACKARD V. PACKARD

Legal Citation: 27 FAM LQ 515 (1864)

Plaintiff
Reverend Theophilus Packard, Jr.

Defendant
Elizabeth Parsons Ware Packard

Plaintiff's Claim
That his wife was insane and that he was therefore entitled to confine her at home.

Chief Lawyer for Plaintiff
No record extant

Chief Defense Lawyers
John W. Orr, Stephen Moore

Judge
Circuit Court Judge Charles R. Starr

Place
Kankakee, Illinois

Date of Decision
18 January 1864

Decision
Elizabeth Packard was declared sane and her liberty was restored.

Significance
In 1864, Illinois law permitted a man to institutionalize his wife "without the evidence of insanity required in other cases." After her own court-ordered release, Elizabeth Packard campaigned to change the law in Illinois and similar laws in 30 other states. During her lifetime, four states revised their laws.

Near the end of 1863, the Reverend Theophilus Packard locked his wife Elizabeth in the nursery of their home and nailed the windows shut. He had earlier had her committed for three years to the Illinois State Hospital for the Insane, based only upon on his own observation that she was "slightly insane," a condition he attributed to "excessive application of body and mind." In many states in the nineteenth century, it was a husband's legal prerogative to so institutionalize his wife, and Elizabeth had no recourse against that earlier confinement. Now, however, she had a valid argument: The law did not permit a husband to "put away" a wife in her own home. Elizabeth Packard dropped a letter of complaint out her window, which was delivered to her friend, Sarah Haslett. Haslett immediately appealed to Judge Charles Starr.

Judge Starr issued a writ of *habeas corpus* and ordered Reverend Packard to bring Elizabeth to his chambers on 12 January 1864. Packard produced Elizabeth and a written statement explaining that she "was discharged from [the Illinois State] Asylum without being cured and is incurably insane . . . [and] the undersigned has allowed her all the liberty compatible with her welfare and safety." Unimpressed, the judge scheduled a jury trial to determine whether or not Elizabeth Packard was insane.

Reverend Packard's Case Against His Wife

Reverend Packard was a Calvinist minister with an austere interpretation of his faith, and he claimed his wife's religious views had convinced him of her insanity. Dr. Christopher Knott, who had spoken with Elizabeth prior to her commitment to Illinois State, testified that "Her mind appeared to be excited on the subject of religion. On all other subjects she was perfectly rational . . . I take her to be a lady of fine mental abilities . . . I would say she was insane," he concluded, "the same as I would say Henry Ward Beecher, Spurgeon, Horace Greeley and like persons are insane."

Dr. J. W. Brown had been falsely introduced to Elizabeth as a sewing machine salesman several weeks before, and had surreptitiously interviewed her during what she thought was a sales pitch. She had described her husband, Dr. Brown testified, as wishing that "the despotism of man may prevail over the wife," but it was during their discussion of religion that he "had not the slightest difficulty in concluding that she was hopelessly insane." Elizabeth Packard, Dr. Brown said, had claimed to be "the personification of the Ghost." Moreover, "She found fault that Mr. Packard would not discuss their points of difference in religion in an open manly way instead of going around and denouncing her as crazy to her friends and to the church. She had a great aversion to being called insane. Before I got through the conversation she exhibited a great dislike to me."

Abijah Dole, the husband of Reverend Packard's sister, Sybil, testified that he knew Elizabeth had become disoriented because she told him that she no longer wished to live with Reverend Packard. Dole also testified that Elizabeth had requested a letter terminating her membership in her husband's church. "Was that an indication of insanity?" Elizabeth's lawyer, John W. Orr, inquired. Dole replied: "She would not leave the church unless she was insane."

Sybil Dole also testified against Elizabeth, stating that "She accused Dr. Packard very strangely of depriving her of her rights of conscience—that he would not allow her to think for herself on religious questions because they differed on these topics."

Sarah Rumsey, a young woman who had briefly served as a mother's helper for the Packards, also gave evidence of what she considered Elizabeth Packard's insanity: "She wanted the flower beds in the front yard cleaned out and tried to get Mr. Packard to do it. He would not. She put on an old dress and went to work and cleaned out the weeds . . . until she was almost melted down with the heat . . . Then she went to her room and took a bath and dressed herself and lay down exhausted . . . She was angry and excited and showed ill-will."

Finally, a certificate concerning Elizabeth's discharge from the Illinois State Hospital, issued by superintendent Dr. Andrew McFarland, was read. It said that Elizabeth Packard was discharged because she could not be cured. Reverend Packard's lawyers rested their case.

Mrs. Packard Defends Her Sanity

Mrs. Packard's lawyers, Stephen Moore and J. W. Orr, asked her to read aloud an essay which she had written for a Bible class. It contained statements such as ". . . the Christian farmer has no more reason to expect success in his farming operations than the impenitent sinner." Then Mr. and Mrs. Blessing, Methodist neighbors of the Packards, testified in turn as to Mrs. Packard's sanity.

Sarah Haslett described Elizabeth's housekeeping efforts upon her release from the Illinois State Hospi-

Elizabeth Parsons Ware Packard, 1864. © Illinois State Historical Society.

tal: "I called to see her a few days after she returned from Jacksonville. She was in the yard cleaning feather beds . . . The house needed cleaning. And when I called again it looked as if the mistress of the house was home." Haslett then testified about her friend's in-home confinement and described the sealed window, "fastened with nails on the inside and two screws passing through the lower part of the upper sash and the upper part of the lower sash from the outside."

The last person to testify on Mrs. Packard's behalf was a Dr. Duncanson, who was both a physician and theologian. He testified that he had conversed with Mrs. Packard for three hours, and he disagreed with Dr. Brown's understanding of Mrs. Packard's thoughts concerning her relationship to the Holy Ghost. Mrs. Packard later wrote, "A spiritual woman is a living temple of the Holy Ghost." At her trial, Dr. Duncanson located this belief in a neglected sixteenth century doctrine expounded by Socinus of Italy. "I did not agree with . . . her on many things," Duncanson testified, "but I do not call people insane because they differ with me . . . You might with as much propriety call Christ insane . . . or Luther, or Robert Fuller . . . I pronounce her a sane woman and wish we had a nation of such women."

The Verdict

On 18 January, the jury reached its verdict in seven minutes. "We, the undersigned, Jurors in the case of Mrs. Elizabeth P. W. Packard, alleged to be insane, having heard the evidence . . . are satisfied that [she] is sane." Judge Starr ordered ". . . that Mrs. Elizabeth P. W. Packard be relieved of all restraints incompatible with her condition as a sane woman." Neither the judge nor jury addressed the question of whether, had Mrs. Packard been found insane, Mr. Packard had the right to confine her at home rather than in an asylum.

Mr. and Mrs. Packard remained married but estranged for the remainder of their lives. Elizabeth Packard wrote, lectured, and lobbied on behalf of the rights of women and those alleged to be insane; she was instrumental in changing the commitment laws in four states and in passing a married women's property law in Illinois.

Related Cases

Shaw v. Shaw, 17 Day Conn. 189 (1845).

Oregon v. Rideout, 108,866 Circuit Court, County of Marion, Oregon (1978).

Bibliography and Further Reading

Burnham, John Chynoweth. "Elizabeth Parsons Ware Packard," in *Notable American Women, 1906-1950.* Edward T. James, Janet Wilson James and Paul S. Boyer, eds. Cambridge, MA: The Belknap Press of Harvard University Press, 1971.

Packard, Elizabeth Parsons Ware. *Great Disclosure of Spiritual Wickedness!! in high places. With an appeal to the government to protect the inalienable rights of married women.* Written under the inspection of Dr. M'Farland, Superintendent of Insane asylum, Jacksonville, IL, 4th ed. Boston, Published by the authoress, 1865.

The house from which Mrs. Packard was kidnapped on 18 June 1860.

———. *Marital Power Exemplified in Mrs. Packard's Trial and self-defense from the charge of insanity, or, Three years imprisonment for religious belief, by the arbitrary will of a husband, with an appeal to the government to so change the laws as to afford legal protection to married women.* Hartford, CT: Case, Lockwood & Co., 1866.

———. *The prisoners' hidden life, or Insane asylums unveiled: as demonstrated by the Report of the Investigating Committee of the Legislature of Illinois, together with Mrs. Packard's coadjutors' testimony.* Chicago: The Author; A. B. Case, Printer, 1868.

———. *The mystic key; or, The asylum secret unlocked.* Hartford, CT: Case, Lockwood & Brainard Co., 1886.

Sapinsley, Barbara. *The Private War of Mrs. Packard.* New York: Paragon House, 1991.

BRADWELL V. ILLINOIS

Legal Citation: 83 U.S. 130 (1873)

Appellant
Myra Bradwell

Appellee
State of Illinois

Appellant's Claim
That Illinois' refusal to admit women to the bar was a violation of Bradwell's constitutional rights.

Chief Lawyer for Appellant
Matthew H. Carpenter

Chief Lawyer for Appellee
None

Justices for the Court
Joseph P. Bradley, Salmon Portland Chase, Nathan Clifford, David Davis, Stephen Johnson Field, Samuel Freeman Miller (writing for the Court), William Strong, Noah Haynes Swayne

Justices Dissenting
None

Place
Washington, D.C.

Date of Decision
15 April 1873

Decision
That Bradwell's constitutional rights had not been violated.

Significance
This case was the first argued before the Supreme Court regarding the Fourteenth Amendment's protection to women's citizenship rights. Still, Bradwell was unsuccessful in gaining the right to become an attorney.

Myra Bradwell, editor of the *Chicago Legal News,* passed the Illinois law exam in August of 1869. When she applied for admission to the Illinois bar in September of 1869, she submitted the required certificate of qualification and also a separate written application addressing the fact that she was a woman. She conceded that the Illinois Revised Statutes described attorneys as males, *"authoriz[ing] him,"* for example, *"to appear in all the courts* [emphasis added]."

She then cited one section of the statutes: "When any party or person is described or referred to by words importing the masculine gender, females as well as males shall be deemed to be included." She pointed out that "Section 3 of our Declaration of Rights says 'that all men have a natural and indefeasible right to worship Almighty God,' etc. It will not be contended, that women are not included within this provision."

The Marriage Disability

The court refused to admit her. The refusal was based ". . . upon the ground that you would not be bound by the obligations necessary to be assumed where the relation of attorney and client shall exist, by reason of the disability imposed by your married condition—it being assumed that you are a married woman . . ."

The disability referred to was a married woman's *feme covert* status, which was nothing less than her civil and legal death upon marriage. For example, married women—in Illinois up until the year of Bradwell's application—could neither make contracts nor own property. Bradwell took no comfort from the fact that "persons under twenty-one" had also been denied admission "upon the same ground . . ."

Bradwell took another view of her married status. She filed an energetically worded brief with the Illinois Supreme Court the next month. She explained, "Your petitioner admits to your honors that she is a married woman (although she believes the fact does not appear in the record), but insists most firmly that under the laws of Illinois it is neither a crime nor a disqualification." She discussed cases in which married female business owners had operated as *feme sole* traders (women entitled to conduct business as if single), her own history as

Front page from the Chicago Legal News, 10 September 1887.

the successful editor and an undisputed stockholder of the *Chicago Legal News*, and the Iowa bar's recent decision to admit Arabella Mansfield. She also discussed the state's Act of 1869, which had removed some of the *feme covert* "disabilit[ies]" referred to by the Court.

Under that act, married women were no longer to be classed with infants since "a married woman may sue in her own name for her earnings, an infant may not." Bradwell claimed that a woman could now be held "liable as an attorney upon any contract made by her in that capacity." The act also protected a married woman's right to any money she earned whether as an attorney or a sewing-women. "Is it for the court to say, in advance, that it will not admit a married woman?" she asked.

Bradwell amended her brief a few weeks later to include the claim that her constitutional rights, especially as protected by the Fourteenth Amendment's guarantee that "no State shall make or enforce any law which shall abridge the privileges and immunities of citizenship," were being abridged by the State of Illinois.

The Female Disability

The court was not persuaded. It ignored her Fourteenth Amendment argument and claimed only that she had too broadly interpreted the impact of the Act of 1869. Those recent changes in Illinois property law, the Chief Justice wrote, affected only a woman's individual and separate holdings. Their "common law . . . disabilities in regard to making contracts" had not been ameliorated to an extent that would have "invited them to enter, equally with men, upon those fields of trade and speculation by which property is acquired though the agency of contracts."

The court also found that a woman, solely on the grounds of gender and even without her common law legal disabilities, was unfit to practice: "[A]fter further consultation . . . we find ourselves constrained to hold

that the sex of the applicant *independent* of coverture, is, as our law stands, a sufficient reason for not granting this license [emphasis added]." Finally, the court disagreed with Bradwell's interpretation of the revised statutes, declaring that females *may* be included in masculine gender words but *not* "where there is anything in the subject or context repugnant to such construction. This is the case in the present instance."

All or Nothing

Bradwell appealed to the U.S. Supreme Court. Matthew H. Carpenter, a U.S. senator from Wisconsin, acted as her attorney. (Illinois did not send an attorney to defend its position.) He argued that Bradwell's Fourteenth Amendment rights had indeed been violated. He asked, "Can this Court say that when the Fourteenth Amendment declared 'the privileges of no citizen shall be abridged,' it meant that the privileges of no male citizen or unmarried female citizen shall be abridged?"

If Bradwell's choice of profession or employment was not protected by this clause, Carpenter said, then neither was anyone else's. If no female could practice law, then neither could a "colored citizen." "If this provision does not open all the professions, all the avocations, all the methods . . . to the colored as well as the white man, then the Legislatures of the State may exclude colored men from all the honorable pursuits of life, and compel them to support their existence in a condition of servitude." Conversely, if the amendment does protect colored people, then "it protects every citizen, black or white, male or female." On the very same basis, Carpenter declared, the State of Illinois had no right to bar Myra Bradwell from the practice of law.

God's Say So

The Supreme Court ruled that Illinois was entitled to restrict the practice of law—and indeed any other profession—to men. Justice Miller, delivering the Court's opinion, said that citizenship was irrelevant to one's admission to the bar and therefore not within the province of Fourteenth Amendment protection.

Justice Bradley, in his concurring opinion, offered particularly biting observations on a woman's place in American society. To agree with Bradwell's claim of Fourteenth Amendment protection, Bradley wrote, would mean ". . . that it is one of the privileges and immunities of women as citizens to engage in any and every profession, occupation or employment in civil life." Explaining his opinion of the impropriety of such a notion, he insisted that the very idea of women having a distinct career from her husband would interfere with "family harmony" not to mention that "the paramount destiny and mission of woman are to fulfill the noble and benign offices of wife and mother. This is the law of the Creator."

He added that "many of the special rules of law flowing from and dependent upon this cardinal principle still exist in full force in most states. One of these is that a married woman is incapable, without her husband's consent, of making contracts which shall be binding on her or him." Therefore, no woman could be an attorney—married or not—because even if there were exceptions to the general rule, society must adapt "to the general constitution of things."

Bradwell was significant in its treatment of women's *feme covert* status, highlighting the fact that unmarried women felt the legal impact of their wedded sisters' *feme covert* status. This High Court's opinion would be maintained until its 1971 decision in *Reed v. Reed.*

Related Cases

Colgate v. Harvey, 296 U.S. 404 (1935).
Reed v. Reed, 404 U.S. 71 (1971).

Bibliography and Further Reading

Cary, Eve, and Kathleen Willert Peratis. *Woman and the Law.* Skokie, IL: National Textbook Co. in conjunction with the American Civil Liberties Union, New York, 1977.

Flexner, Eleanor. *Century of Struggle: The Woman's Rights Movement in the United States.* Cambridge, MA: The Belknap Press of Harvard University Press, 1959, rev. 1975.

Frost, Elizabeth, and Kathryn Cullen-DuPont. *Women's Suffrage in America: An Eyewitness History.* New York: Facts on File, 1992.

Goldstein, Leslie Friedman. *The Constitutional Rights of Women,* rev. ed. Madison: University of Wisconsin Press, 1989.

Johnson, John W. *Historic U.S. Court Cases, 1690–1990: An Encyclopedia.* New York: Garland Publishing, 1992.

Stanton, Elizabeth Cady, Susan B. Anthony, and Matilda Joslyn Gage, eds. *History of Woman Suffrage,* Vol. 2, 1882, reprint, Salem, NH: Ayer Company, Publishers, 1985.

Myra Bradwell. © Illinois State Historical Library.

MINOR V. HAPPERSETT

Legal Citation: 88 U.S. 162 (1875)

Appellant
Virginia Minor (with Francis Minor, her husband, as required by Missouri law, which did not permit married women to bring suit on their own)

Appellee
Reese Happersett

Appellant's Claim
That Virginia Minor's constitutional rights were violated by Happersett's refusal to register her to vote in the election of 1872.

Chief Lawyers for Appellant
Francis Minor, John M. Rum, John B. Henderson

Chief Lawyer for Appellee
No opposing counsel

Justices for the Court
Joseph P. Bradley, Nathan Clifford, David Davis, Stephen Johnson Field, Ward Hunt, Samuel Freeman Miller, William Strong, Noah Haynes Swayne, Morrison Remick Waite (writing for the Court)

Justices Dissenting
None

Place
Washington, D.C.

Date of Decision
29 March 1875

Decision
The Fourteenth Amendment did not guarantee Virginia Minor's right to vote, although she was found to be a citizen of the United States.

Significance
This case marked the second time in two years that the Supreme Court declined to extend Fourteenth Amendment protection to women's rights. Suffrage, the specific "privilege of citizenship" denied in the case, would not be obtained by women nationwide until ratification of the Nineteenth Amendment in 1920.

As Supreme Court justice Sandra Day O'Connor pointed out, the adoption of the Fourteenth Amendment to the U.S. Constitution in 1868 "introduced sex-specific language into the Constitution: Section 2 of the Amendment, which dealt with the legislative representation and voting, said that if the right to vote were 'denied to any of the *male* inhabitants' of a state aged twenty-one or over [emphasis O'Connor's] then the proportional representation in that state would be reduced accordingly."

Prior to the Fourteenth Amendment, the Constitution referred to the president as "he" but to all other Americans as "citizens" and "persons," without reference to their gender. But the Fourteenth Amendment's "sex-specific language" in section 2 excluded women and raised questions about women's citizenship. For this reason, Susan B. Anthony, Elizabeth Cady Stanton, and other nineteenth-century women's rights activists fiercely opposed its adoption. (Lucy Stone and other women suffragists reluctantly supported black male suffrage, regardless of the perceived cost to women.)

The "New Departure"

After the amendment's ratification and adoption, attorney Francis Minor—husband of Virginia Minor, the president of the Woman Suffrage Association of Missouri—argued that its section 1 was actually an advance for women. Section 1 of the Fourteenth Amendment states:

> All persons born or naturalized in the United States, and subject to the jurisdiction thereof, are citizens of the United States and of the State wherein they reside. No state shall make or enforce any law which shall abridge the privileges or immunities of citizens of the United States; nor shall any State deprive any person of life, liberty, or property, without due process of law; nor deny to any person within its jurisdiction the equal protection of the laws.

Minor drafted resolutions explaining his view that the Constitution, as amended by the Fourteenth Amendment, now guaranteed the right of suffrage to women:

The Fourteenth Amendment

The Fourteenth Amendment, ratified in 1868, is the most prominent of the three Aamendments designed to secure the civil rights of the millions of slaves freed during the Civil War. Indeed, the Fourteenth is one of the most important of all constitutional amendments, and has been the case of more legal action—and more discussion by legal scholars—than any other part of the Constitution.

Most of the attention centers on the first of the amendment's five sections. Section 1 extends the rights to due process and equal protection under the law, first applied to the federal government in the Fifth Amendment, to the states. This was a revolutionary step, because it was primarily under state governments that citizens' civil rights were being violated.

The other four sections of the amendment relate chiefly to situations prevailing at the time, and have enjoyed considerably less attention than section 1 in years since. Thus for instance section 3 denies the opportunity of service in Congress or as president or vice president to anyone who "engaged in insurrection or rebellion against" the federal government—i.e. in the Confederacy. Likewise section 4 validates the debt incurred by the federal government during the war, but invalidates that incurred by the Confederate government.

Source(s): *West's Encyclopedia of American Law.* St. Paul, MN: West Group, 1998.

Resolved, 1: That the immunities and privileges of American citizenship, however defined, are National in character and paramount to all State authority.

2: That while the Constitution of the United States leaves the qualifications of electors to the several States, it nowhere gives them the right to deprive any citizen of the elective franchise which is possessed by any other citizen—to regulate, not including the right to prohibit the franchise.

3: That, as the Constitution of the United States expressly declares that no State shall make or enforce any laws that shall abridge the privileges or immunities of citizens of the United States, those provisions of the several State Constitutions that exclude women from the franchise on account of sex, are violative alike of the spirit and letter of the Federal Constitution.

4: That, as the subject of naturalization is expressly withheld from the States, and as the

A delegation of female suffragists presents a statement in favor of women's voting before the Judiciary Committee of the House of Representatives, 1871. © The Library of Congress.

A cartoon satirizing "How it would be if some ladies had their own way." © The Library of Congress.

States clearly have no right to deprive of the franchise naturalized citizens, among whom women are expressly included, still more clearly they have no right to deprive native-born women of this right.

Missouri's Woman Suffrage Association endorsed Francis Minor's resolutions, and by the end of 1869, they had been endorsed by the National Woman Suffrage Association. Stanton and Anthony published them in their newspaper *Revolution,* and at least 150 women in ten states chose to act on them.

They turned out to vote in the 1871 and 1872 elections. Some, including Anthony, were prosecuted for successfully voting; others, like Virginia Minor, sued their states or voting officials for turning them away. The *Minor* case eventually reached the Supreme Court.

A Constitutional Approach

In their petition filed in December of 1872, Virginia Minor's attorneys argued her constitutional rights had been abridged. They cited Article I, section 9, that no bill of attainder shall be passed; Article I, section 10, prohibiting states from passing bills of attainder or "any title of nobility—a status that 'male citizens' seemed to have been awarded; Article IV, section 2, which gave citizens of the states privileges and immunities of citizens in all of the States"; Article IV, section 4, guaranteeing to every state a republican form of government and the Fifth Amendment's guarantee that "no person shall be . . . deprived of life, liberty, or property without due process of law."

They also cited the Ninth Amendment, which reserves to the people any rights not expressly granted to the government. The last amendment cited was the Fourteenth Amendment, section 1, using the same resolutions Minor had thought out back in 1869.

Reese Happersett's attorney maintained that "the defendant was justified in refusing to register the plaintiff on account of her sex." Both the Circuit Court of St. Louis and the Supreme Court of Missouri agreed. Both courts acquitted Happersett and upheld Missouri's denial of suffrage to women.

All or Nothing

Plaintiffs' argument and briefs presented to the Supreme Court repeated points made before the lower courts and also contained a new claim: "There can be no half-way citizenship. Woman, as a citizen of the United States, is entitled to all the benefits of that position, and liable to all its obligations, or to none." They cited several previous Supreme Court decisions, including *Scott v. Sandford,* the infamous judicial reply to the question of whether "the class of persons who had been imported as slaves [or] their descendants . . . *free* or not," were or ever could be citizens. Chief Justice Roger Brooke Taney had written in the majority opinion that they could not (a decision later invalidated by the adoption of the Fourteenth Amendment), but he stressed that a finding of citizenship would have conferred rights no state could abridge:

If persons of the African race are citizens of a State, and of the United States, they would be entitled to all of these privileges and immunities in every State, and the State could not restrict them; for they would hold these privileges and immunities under the paramount authority of the Federal Government, and its courts would be bound to maintain and enforce them, the Constitution [of an individual state] and the laws of the State to the contrary notwithstanding . . .

Pointing out that section 1 of the Fourteenth Amendment granted citizenship to women as well as to black males, the plaintiffs' attorneys argued that both groups, by the standards set in *Dred Scott,* were now guaranteed a citizen's "privileges and immunities." They next cited the Supreme Court's 1873 *Slaughterhouse* decision as evidence that suffrage was one of the rights of citizenship: "The Negro having by the Fourteenth Amendment been declared a citizen of the United States is thus made a voter in every state of the Union." Therefore, they reasoned, a state's abridgment of its female citizen's right of suffrage was a violation of the U.S. Constitution.

Unanimously, however, the Supreme Court found otherwise. Chief Justice Waite wrote in the majority opinion that women born or naturalized in the United States were in fact—and had been even prior to the adoption of the Fourteenth Amendment—citizens of the United States. He found, however, that the right of suffrage was not one of the privileges and immunities of citizenship, and that the states were entitled to exclude women from the polls. It would take nearly a century before the Supreme Court would apply Fourteenth Amendment protection to women's rights.

Related Cases

Scott v. Sanford, 60 U.S. 293 (1857).
Slaughterhouse Cases, 16 U.S. 36 (1873).
U.S. v. Susan B. Anthony 24 F.Cas. 829 (1873).

Bibliography and Further Reading

Cary, Eve, and Kathleen Willert Peratis. *Woman and the Law.* Skokie, IL: National Textbook Co. in conjunction with the American Civil Liberties Union, 1977.

Flexner, Eleanor. *Century of Struggle: The Woman's Rights Movement in the United States.* Cambridge, MA: The Belknap Press of Harvard University Press, 1959, rev. 1975.

Frost, Elizabeth, and Kathryn Cullen-DuPont. *Women's Suffrage in America: An Eyewitness History.* New York: Facts on File, 1992.

Goldstein, Leslie Friedman. *The Constitutional Rights of Women,* rev. ed. Madison: University of Wisconsin Press, 1989.

Stanton, Elizabeth Cady, Susan B. Anthony, and Matilda Joslyn Gage, eds. *History of Woman Suffrage,* Vol. 2, 1998, reprint, Salem, NH: Ayer Company Publishers, 1985.

HOYT V. FLORIDA

Legal Citation: 368 U.S. 57 (1961)

Appellant
Gwendolyn Hoyt

Appellee
State of Florida

Appellant's Claim
That a Florida law providing that women could serve on juries only at their own request deprived criminal defendants in the state from equal protection of the laws.

Chief Lawyer for Appellant
Herbert B. Ehrmann

Chief Lawyer for Appellee
George R. Georgieff

Justices for the Court
Hugo Lafayette Black, William J. Brennan, Jr., Tom C. Clark, William O. Douglas, Felix Frankfurter, John Marshall Harlan II (writing for the Court), Potter Stewart, Earl Warren, Charles Evans Whittaker

Justices Dissenting
None

Place
Washington, D.C.

Date of Decision
20 November 1961

Decision
The Court upheld the Florida statute, as well as Gwendolyn Hoyt's conviction.

Significance
Hoyt v. Florida confirmed the gender bias inherent in the law in the early 1960s, ruling that women could be kept from serving on juries if states felt that their exclusion was warranted.

Gwendolyn Hoyt was convicted of second-degree murder in state court in Hillsborough County, Florida. She had killed her husband with a baseball bat following an argument over his infidelity. The fight resulted when he refused her offer of forgiveness. At her trial, Hoyt pleaded temporary insanity. She was tried before an all-male jury, which resulted from a Florida law that provided that women could serve as jurors only if they specifically requested to be put on the jury rolls (only ten women appeared on the list of ten thousand jurors eligible to serve in Hillsborough County at the time of Hoyt's trial). After she was found guilty, Hoyt appealed to the Florida Supreme Court, declaring that because none of the eligible women served on the jury that convicted her, she had been deprived of her Fourteenth Amendment right to equal protection under the law. Hoyt alleged that female jurors would have better understood her plight and would, therefore, have acted as more reliable determiners of her temporary insanity defense than men.

When the state supreme court upheld her conviction, Hoyt appealed her case to the U.S. Supreme Court. Writing for a unanimous Court, Justice Harlan began by reciting a truism of constitutional law, making it clear that women were not granted additional rights under the Fourteenth Amendment:

> [T]he right to an impartially selected jury assured by the Fourteenth Amendment . . . does not entitle one accused of a crime to a jury tailored to the circumstances of the particular case . . . It requires only that the jury be indiscriminately drawn from among those eligible in the community for jury service . . .

Unfortunately, this truism fell short of explaining why the jury that tried Gwendolyn Hoyt contained no women. As the Supreme Court had itself recognized 15 years earlier, in *Ballard v. United States* (1946), a fair cross section of the community—as represented by a jury—would almost certainly include women.

Court Upholds Double Standard Regarding Jury Service

Instead of following the implications of the Court's ruling in *Ballard*, the nine justices who ruled against Hoyt

First Use of the Temporary Insanity Plea

The first use of the temporary insanity plea occurred in 1859 when Daniel Sickles, leader of the Democratic party, used it as his defense in the murder of Philip Barton Key, who had been having an affair with Sickles's wife, Teresa. Sickles's defense team tried to appeal to the "unwritten law" to make Key's murder look like justifiable homicide.

Sickles found out about the affair between his wife and Key on 24 February 1859. Sickles had Teresa sign a detailed confession and consulted two of his political cronies for advice. Unaware that Sickles knew everything, Key tried to signal Teresa from Lafayette Park, which was across from the Sickles' house, on 27 February. Enraged, Sickles stormed out of the house and gunned Key down amongst the Sunday afternoon strollers in the park.

The high publicity surrounding the event made it difficult to locate jurors who did not sympathize with Sickles. One of Sickles's advisors, former Secretary of the Treasury Robert J. Walker, testified that Sickles was in "an agony of despair, the most terrible thing I ever saw in my life . . . I feared if it continued he would become permanently insane."

The judge instructed the jurors that, in the eyes of the law, any delay between becoming aware of an adultery and the slaying of the adulterer by an enraged husband made the killing deliberate murder, or at the very least manslaughter. On 26 April 1859, the jury returned a not guilty verdict.

Source(s): Knappman, Edward W., ed. *Great American Trials.* Detroit, MI: Visible Ink Press, 1994.

---

fell back on sexual stereotypes in upholding the Florida jury statute:

Despite the enlightened emancipation of women from the restrictions and protections of bygone years . . . [a] woman is still regarded as the center of home and family life. We cannot say that it is constitutionally impermissible for a State . . . to conclude that a woman should be relieved from the civic duty of jury service unless she herself determines that such service is consistent with her own special responsibilities.

It would be another 14 years before the Supreme Court would effectively overrule its holding in *Hoyt* with *Taylor v. Louisiana* (1975), in which a male defendant successfully fought his rape conviction by arguing that the Sixth Amendment right to be tried by a jury of his peers was violated by a state "volunteers only" jury service law that resulted in an all-male jury. Although the Court distinguished *Hoyt* on grounds that it had been decided on the basis of the Fourteenth

Amendment, the *Taylor* Court found that provisions that systematically produce all-male jury panels—provisions like the one at issue in Gwendolyn Hoyt's case—are unconstitutional. This ruling was later extended in *Duren v. Missouri* (1979), in which the Court outlawed a state statute which allowed women to be exempted from jury service and which had resulted in juries that were at least 85 percent male.

Related Cases
Ballard v. United States, 329 U.S. 187 (1946).
Taylor v. Louisiana, 419 U.S. 522 (1975).
Duren v. Missouri, 439 U.S. 357 (1979).

Bibliography and Further Reading
DiPerna, Paula. *Juries on Trial: Faces of American Justice.* New York: Dembner Books, 1984.

Hans, Valerie P., and Neil Vidmar. *Judging the Jury.* New York: Plenum Press, 1986.

Otten, Laura A. *Women's Rights and the Law.* Westport, CT: Praeger, 1993.

BOWE V. COLGATE-PALMOLIVE

Legal Citation: 416 F.2d 711 (1969)

Appellants
Thelma Bowe et al.

Appellees
Colgate-Palmolive Company and International Chemical Workers Union, Local #15

Appellants' Claim
That companies do not have the right to segregate jobs on the basis of gender by limiting women to less strenuous jobs.

Chief Lawyer for Appellants
Marion W. Garnett

Chief Lawyer for Appellees
Herbert L. Segal

Judges
Walter J. Cummings, Otto Kerner, Henry S. Wise

Place
Chicago, Illinois

Date of Decision
26 September 1969

Decision
Companies may not use job classification systems that discriminate on the basis of gender. If a weight-lifting limit is used as a general guideline, it must apply to both men and women—providing employees the opportunity to demonstrate their suitability for physically demanding jobs on an individual basis.

Significance
Many jobs that had been for men only were made available for women—so long as they could meet the physical requirements. The bona fide occupational qualification exception to Title VII—permitting discrimination where it is reasonably necessary to the job—therefore would no longer be used to exclude women from most job opportunities.

The passage of Title VII of the 1964 Civil Rights Act raised the hopes of millions of American women who believed they would now receive fair treatment in the workplace. The law makes it "an unlawful employment practice for any employer . . . to discriminate against any individual with respect to his compensation, terms, conditions, or privileges of employment, because of such individual's race, color, religion, sex, or national origin." It took effect in July of 1965.

However, the legal battles that accompanied the enforcement of this legislation unearthed sexism unchanged by law. This sexism—sometimes remnants of earlier protective legislation for women—was no longer a legal excuse to exclude women from the work place. Still women had to sue to combat sex discrimination and workplace restrictions.

The experiences of Thelma Bowe, an employee of the Colgate-Palmolive plant in Jeffersonville, Indiana, illustrated the challenges that women continued to face in combating sex discrimination that persisted even after the Civil Rights Act.

Protective Legislation

Colgate, like many companies, had placed a weight limit on items female employees might be required to lift. Such restrictions on women could also include maximum hours rules and prohibitions on nighttime work. These regulations were mostly products of the Progressive Era, which lasted from 1900 to World War I. The women's groups and unions who had promoted these laws had benevolent motives. Unfortunately, like most protective laws, this legislation had proven to be a liability to women.

The Colgate company's weight-lifting limit for women originated with World War II and the company's first large-scale influx of women workers as replacements for men away in military service. Jobs were specifically fashioned for these women. The work was less physically demanding and did not require the lifting of more than 25 pounds.

As the servicemen returned, however, the company and the union continued to set aside less strenuous jobs for women—reserving jobs requiring more physical sta-

---

Bona Fide Occupational Qualification

The term bona fide occupation qualification (BFOQ) usually arises in reference to situations involving age discrimination, though it is possible for the notion of a BFOQ to be used in gender-discrimination lawsuits as well. A BFOQ is, as its name suggests, an essential requirement for performing a given job.

To use an extraordinary example, a prospective astronaut would need to be physically fit in all regards, including 20/20 vision, and should possess a great deal of mental and physical poise. These are all BFOQs, and persons with nervous conditions, bad eyesight, poor

sense of balance, a handicap of any kind, or other such challenges need not apply.

But being a male is by no means a BFOQ for the job of astronaut, as Sally Ride proved when she became the first American woman to go into space in 1983. Nor is age a clear BFOQ, as shown by 77-year-old Senator (and former astronaut) John Glenn when he returned to outer space in 1998.

Source(s): *West's Encyclopedia of American Law*, Vol. 2. St. Paul, MN: West Group, 1998.

---

mina for men. But by the second wave of feminism in the 1960s, almost all women's groups were unequivocally opposed to these laws and rules, describing them as paternalistic and instrumental in limiting women's job opportunities—not to mention resulting in lower pay.

Gender Segregation

The Colgate company had also maintained separate seniority systems for men and women. The seniority ranking affected not only an employee's ability to obtain much sought-after assignments, but also layoffs. Women were let go before men with less seniority and called back to work the same way. This segregation continued even after the company had made minor changes and relabeled the practices to appear more gender-neutral.

Bowe was one victim of this discrimination. She, along with other female coworkers, filed charges with the Equal Employment Opportunity Commission (EEOC). However, they could not obtain an agreement from Colgate. Therefore, the women brought a class-action lawsuit against the company, heard by the U.S. District Court for the Southern District of Indiana on 30 June 1967. Colgate eventually made reconciliation attempts and recalled laid-off plaintiffs after a strike, yet the suit continued over the issue of back pay and the sex-segregation system.

The First Round

The district court refused to equate racial and sex-based discrimination, and endorsed the idea that the bona fide occupational qualification exception does not have to be based on what is absolutely necessary, but rather what is "reasonably necessary." By emphasizing the word "reasonably" and choosing to interpret it to mean that some options are left open for employers, the court found in favor of Colgate's establishment of the weight-lifting limit.

Since the genesis of the weight-lifting restriction was the well-being of female employees, the court declared that Colgate had acted reasonably because it had studied various state weight-lifting regulations before arriving at its own precise limit (rather than determining it in an arbitrary fashion). Furthermore, the court said, it would be impractical to determine weight-lifting ability on an individual basis.

The court's decisions were also fueled by the EEOC's own position at the time: Some protective laws could conceivably be reasonable and therefore should not be overturned. Protective laws—and more discretion for the employer—demanded the adoption of a "common sense" approach, allowing a degree of discretion in hiring even under Title VII.

Appeals Court Overrules

Two years later, the U.S. District Court of Appeals for the Seventh Circuit, heard the case in Chicago. On 26 September 1969, the judges reversed most of the lower court's decision. It found that, although a defendant would have to defend himself or herself twice, it was necessary to allow plaintiffs to pursue remedies through both the courts and through arbitration, because each channel might offer different remedies. However, remedies should only be enacted at the end of the entire process so that there was no duplication, which would be unfair to a defendant.

Although the appeals court found the district court's approach to be "carefully reasoned and conscientious," it also concluded that the decision was based on a misunderstanding of the purpose of Title VII. Just because state protective laws could stand as long as they did not conflict with Title VII, the district court could not conclude that those same laws were not affected by Title VII.

The EEOC's position at the time—that Congress did not mean to overturn all protective laws—was taken out of context by the lower court. The EEOC's limited interpretation of the bona fide occupational qualification exception did not allow the labeling of jobs as "male" or "female," since labeling would exclude men or women from many job opportunities.

The appeals court emphasized that the practice of creating seniority systems that segregate "light" and "heavy" jobs may not be used if they merely disguise gender classifications or make it more difficult for men or women to advance into positions for which they normally would be suitable. The court pointed to three cases coming before *Bowe* in which the EEOC had favored individual testing of weight-lifting ability, rather than weight-lifting limits based on sex.

The court also ruled that since there was a lack of agreement about precisely how much weight women can lift from state to state, and since many of those limits were too old to be relevant to the physical condition of contemporary women, weight-lifting ability should be tested individually. The conditions of work and the manner in which weight-lifting should be performed should also be taken into account.

Colgate could maintain its current 35-pound weight-lifting limit only as it applied to both men and women. Colgate was required to give notice to all employees that they would be regularly granted opportunities to prove their suitability for more physically demanding jobs. Employees who have this capacity must be allowed to pursue any position and be paid appropriately for their level of seniority.

Regarding the other issues, on 28 November 1973, the U.S. Court of Appeals for the Seventh Circuit, sent the case back to the district court to create a system in which seniority and other disputes were handled fairly. The court extended the right to get back pay to additional plaintiffs. It granted the right to sue for back pay even to plaintiffs who had not filed a charge with the EEOC and instructed Colgate to notify employees that this opportunity was available. Title VII suits must, by definition, be class-action suits because they were based on a quality shared by a class of people.

Echoing the views of other courts on Title VII suits and on racial discrimination cases, the court found that Title VII suits were meant to advance public policy endorsed by Congress. The intent of Congress was not just to change a defendant's behavior, but for other types of redress (such as back pay), as well. The goal of Title VII was clearly to end discrimination and to compensate its victims. The most efficient way of achieving this result would be through class-action suits.

Impact

The *Bowe* case was an early victory for the feminist movement. Discrimination on the basis of sex was subsequently challenged in the area of inheritance law in *Reed v. Reed* (1971); military regulations in *Frontiero v. Richardson* (1973) and *Rostker v. Goldberg* (1981); and equality in education in *Mississippi University for Women v. Hogan* (1982). Each of these cases challenged gender stereotypes which were codified in legislative statutes such as the one which enabled Colgate to place weight limits on items female employees could be required to carry. Such cases represent considerable progress in the area of sex discrimination, particularly when we consider that in cases such as *Bradwell v. Illinois* (1873), the Supreme Court upheld a state action denying women the right to practice law. Despite the legal progress made with respect to gender discrimination, it is clear that social traditions have precedents on the matter.

Related Cases

Adkins v. Children's Hospital, 261 U.S. 525 (1923).

Bibliography and Further Reading

Case, Mary Anne C. "Desegregating Gender from Sex and Sexual Orientation." *Yale Law Journal,* Oct 1995.

Chafe, William Henry. *The American Woman in the 20th Century.* New York: Oxford University Press, 1991.

De Hart Mathews, Jane, and Linda K. Kerber, eds. *Women's America: Refocusing the Past.* New York: Oxford University Press, 1982.

Lehrer, Susan. *Origins of Protective Labor Legislation for Women.* 1905-1925. Albany: State University of New York Press, 1989.

FRONTIERO V. RICHARDSON

Legal Citation: 411 U.S. 677 (1973)

Petitioners
Sharron A. Frontiero, Joseph Frontiero

Respondents
Elliot L. Richardson, Secretary of Defense, et al.

Petitioners' Claim
That requiring different criteria for male spouses of female military personnel—as opposed to female spouses—to qualify for benefits is a violation of the Fifth Amendment.

Chief Lawyer for Petitioners
Joseph L. Levin, Jr.

Chief Lawyer for Respondents
Samuel Huntington

Justices for the Court
Harry A. Blackmun, William J. Brennan, Jr. (writing for the Court), Warren E. Burger, William O. Douglas, Thurgood Marshall, Lewis F. Powell, Jr., Potter Stewart, Byron R. White

Justices Dissenting
William H. Rehnquist

Place
Washington, D.C.

Date of Decision
14 May 1973

Decision
The federal statutes violated the Fifth Amendment's Due Process Clause and were overturned.

Significance
The assumption that "the husband in our society is generally the 'breadwinner' in the family [while] the wife [is] typically the 'dependent' partner," was shown to be no longer valid. The justices also came within one vote of finding sex an "inherently suspect" category for equal protection purposes.

In this lawsuit, Sharron Frontiero, a married U.S. Air Force lieutenant, and her husband, Joseph, a veteran and full-time college student, challenged a federal statute. The law automatically granted male members of the "uniformed forces" housing and other benefits for their wives. However, it required its female members to demonstrate the "actual dependency" of their husbands before granting the same benefit.

According to the statute, a woman's husband was "actually dependent" if his wife provided more than half of his living expenses. Because Joseph Frontiero received $205 per month in veteran's benefits, Sharron Frontiero paid less than half of his living expenses, which were $354 per month. Denied the increased medical and dental benefits for her husband and the same housing allowance that a married male lieutenant automatically received for his spouse, the Frontieros sued. In 1972, the three-judge U.S. Court for the Middle District of Alabama denied the Frontieros request for relief. Next the Frontieros appealed to the U.S. Supreme Court.

A Federal Problem

The Frontieros claimed the federal government had abridged their rights. They said that the law violated the Due Process Clause of the Fifth Amendment. (While the Fifth Amendment actually contains only "due process" language and no "equal protection" clause, it had long been interpreted by the Supreme Court to require the federal government to grant the same "equal protection" specifically required of the states by the Fourteenth Amendment.)

Ruth Bader Ginsburg had argued another case on behalf of the Women's Rights Project (WRP) of the American Civil Liberties Union, and the WRP now asked the Frontieros' lawyer, Joseph J. Levin, Jr., if the organization might join his Supreme Court appeal. He agreed. The Court granted special leave for the organization to act as *amicus curiae,* and gave Ginsburg 10 of the 30 minutes in which the Frontieros' case was argued.

A Matter of Convenience

The Court heard arguments on 17 January 1973. Samuel Huntington, representing the federal government, argued that, in the uniformed services, men and women were treated differently by the law for "administrative convenience." He said that American wives were usually dependent upon their husbands, but that American husbands were not usually dependent upon their wives.

For this reason, Congress had reasonably decided that it was cost-effective simply to view all wives as financially dependent without requiring all the male members of the uniformed services to document that fact. In contrast, if most men were not dependent upon their wives, it was cost-effective and not administratively burdensome to review each female member's documentation of a husband's actual dependency.

Levin argued that the statute unreasonably discriminated because of sex, which was in violation of the Fifth Amendment. He argued that it was discriminatory "as a procedural matter" to require documentation of spousal dependency from women but not from men. In addition, and as a substantive matter, he also pointed out that it was unfair that a male member who provided less than one-half of a wife's living expenses received spousal benefits, while a "similarly situated" female member obtained none.

Ginsburg focused on the level of judicious scrutiny applied in sex discrimination cases. The Court viewed all laws discriminating because of race, religion, or national origin as "inherently suspect" and subject to "strict judicial scrutiny." To withstand a constitutional challenge, such laws needed to serve a necessary relationship to a compelling state interest. Ginsburg asked the Court to find sex discrimination as inherently suspect as discrimination based on race, religion, or national origin, and to apply strict judicial scrutiny in this and future sex discrimination cases.

Strict Scrutiny

On 14 May 1973, the Court—with only Justice Rehnquist dissenting—overturned the federal statute. Four of the justices—Brennan, Douglas, Marshall, and White—agreed that laws discriminating because of sex were inherently suspect and subject to strict judicial scrutiny. Brennan detailed the historical similarities in race and sex discrimination in America, and the "accident of birth" common to each person's identity insofar as race and national origin:

> Our statute books gradually became laden with gross, stereotyped distinctions between the sexes and, indeed throughout much of the 19th century the position of women in our society was, in many respects, comparable to that of blacks under the pre-Civil War slave codes. Neither slaves nor women would hold office, serve on juries, or bring suit in their own names, and

married women traditionally were denied the legal capacity to hold or convey property or to serve as legal guardians of their own children . . . And although blacks were guaranteed the right to vote in 1870, women were denied even that right . . . until adoption of the Nineteenth Amendment half a century later . . . Nevertheless, . . . women still face pervasive, although at times more subtle, discrimination . . . Moreover, since sex, like race and national origin, is an immutable characteristic determined solely by the accident of birth, the imposition of special disabilities upon the members of a particular sex would seem to violate the basic concept of our system that legal burdens should bear some relationship to individual responsibility . . . statutory distinctions between the sexes often have the effect of relegating the entire class of females to inferior legal status without regard to the actual capabilities of its individual members.

Justice Stewart agreed that the challenged statutes "work an invidious discrimination in violation of the Constitution," but did not address the scrutiny issue. Powell, joined by Burger and Blackmun, also agreed "that the challenged statutes constitute an unconstitutional discrimination against servicewomen in violation of the Due Process Clause of the Fifth Amendment." However, Powell specifically added that he could not agree that classifications based upon sex were "inherently suspect" like those based on race, alienage, and national origin. Therefore, "strict scrutiny" was not to be a standard for the Court. Not until 1976 did the Court employ a midlevel test known as "heightened scrutiny."

Related Cases
Weinberger v. Wiesenfeld, 420 U.S. 636 (1975).
Califano v. Goldfarb, 430 U.S. 199 (1977).

Bibliography and Further Reading
Cary, Eve, and Kathleen Willert Peratis. *Woman and the Law.* Skokie, IL: National Textbook Company in conjunction with the American Civil Liberties Union, 1977.

Goldstein, Leslie Friedman. *The Constitutional Rights of Women: Cases in Law and Social Change,* rev. ed. Madison: The University of Wisconsin Press, 1989.

Hoff, Joan. *Law, Gender, and Injustice: A Legal History of U.S. Women.* New York: New York University Press, 1991.

Johnson, John W. *Historic U.S. Court Cases, 1690-1990: An Encyclopedia.* New York: Garland Publishing, 1992.

Von Drehle, David. "A Trailblazer's Step-by-Step Assault on the Status Quo." *The Washington Post National Weekly Edition,* 26 July-1 August 1993.

CLEVELAND BOARD OF EDUCATION V. LAFLEUR

Legal Citation: 414 U.S. 632 (1974)

Petitioners
Cleveland Board of Education, et al.

Respondents
Jo Carol LaFleur, Ann Elizabeth Nelson

Petitioners' Claim
That a school board policy mandating that pregnant teachers go on an unpaid leave of absence beginning five months before the expected birth of the child and ending the school semester after the child is three months old was constitutional under the Fourteenth Amendment.

Chief Lawyer for Petitioners
Charles F. Clarke

Chief Lawyer for Respondents
Jane M. Picker

Justices for the Court
Harry A. Blackmun, William J. Brennan, Jr., William O. Douglas, Thurgood Marshall, Lewis F. Powell, Jr., Potter Stewart (writing for the Court), Byron R. White

Justices Dissenting
Warren E. Burger, William H. Rehnquist

Place
Washington, D.C.

Date of Decision
21 January 1974

Decision
Denied the petitioners' claim and upheld the ruling of the court of appeals that the school board's policy regarding mandatory unpaid leave for pregnant teachers violated the Due Process Clause of the Fourteenth Amendment and was not legally binding.

Significance
The ruling represented a watershed for cases involving workplace discrimination on the basis of gender. Because different individuals were judged to be capable of working further into their pregnancies than the school board's maternity leave policy would allow, that policy was judged to be overbroad. By using this reasoning in reaching its decision, the Court established that all corporate maternity leave schemes, in order to be constitutional, must be formed so as to allow women to work as long, and to return to their jobs as soon, as they are medically fit to do so. This, in turn, meant the end of mandatory maternity leave policies.

Mandatory Maternity Leave

The second half of the twentieth century witnessed a rapid expansion of the role and status of women outside the home. As women increasingly occupied important positions in business and the professions, they were often faced with archaic rules governing gender-related health issues. Among such rules were those that enabled employers to dismiss or force into unpaid leave of absence those workers who became pregnant. Just such a rule was maintained by the Cleveland, Ohio school board to govern maternity leave. Under the policy, pregnant teachers were required to go on unpaid leave beginning five months before the expected birth date of their child. Furthermore, teachers were not allowed to return to work under the policy until the semester following their child's attaining the age of three months, subject to medical approval.

During the 1970-71 school year Cleveland, Ohio junior high school teachers Jo Carol LaFleur and Mary Elizabeth Nelson informed the school board that they were pregnant, and were forced to go on unpaid leave in March of 1971 in accordance with the policy. Neither LaFleur nor Wilson wished to take their leave at that time, preferring instead to wait until the end of the school year in June. As such, they each brought suit against the school board in the U.S. District Court for the Northern District of Ohio, challenging the constitutionality of the policy. The district court rejected LaFleur and Nelson's contentions, holding that the policy was constitutional. The respondents then appealed the case to the U.S. Court of Appeals for the Sixth Circuit, which reversed the decision of the district court on the grounds that the policy violated the Equal Protection Clause of the Fourteenth Amendment. The school board then appealed the case to the U.S. Supreme Court, which heard arguments on the matter on 15 October 1973.

A Violation of Due Process?

The Court held the policy to be unconstitutional under the Due Process Clause of the Fourteenth Amendment by a 7-2 margin. Writing for the majority, Justice Stewart noted that the Court had long since established that "freedom of personal choice in matters of marriage and

---

Maternity Leave

In December of 1997, the women's magazine *Redbook* ran a long series of articles advising women how to make the most of the maternity-leave opportunities afforded by the Family and Medical Leave Act of 1993. The latter guarantees 12 weeks of unpaid leave for the 2.1 million working American women who give birth or adopt children each year, but according to the article, its provisions do not go far enough.

Yet there was a time when expectations were much lower, a time when Martha Gilbert and other female employees at various General Electric plants in Virginia filed lawsuits against an employer who—like many in the 1970s and before—simply made no provisions whatever for maternity leave. The case came before the Supreme Court as *General Electric Co. v. Gilbert* (1976), and though the company won the appeal, Gilbert and other women ultimately won: in 1978, President Jimmy Carter signed legislation adding provisions regarding pregnancy discrimination to the Civil Rights Act of 1964.

Source(s): Eberlein, Tamara. "Get the Best Maternity Leave for You (and Your Baby)." *Redbook*, December 1997.

Sturgeon, Jeff. "General Electric Workers' Suit Paved Way for Paid Maternity Leave." *Knight-Ridder/Tribune Business News*, 12 October 1998.

---

family life is one of the liberties protected by the Due Process Clause of the Fourteenth Amendment" in numerous cases, including *Prince v. Massachusetts* (1944), *Griswold v. Connecticut* (1965), and *Roe v. Wade* (1973). As such, any policy of an employer regarding employees who decide to become pregnant must not "needlessly, arbitrarily, or capriciously impinge upon this vital area of a [person's] constitutional liberty." In fact, the school board had argued along these lines, advancing the position that the maternity leave policy was essential to maintaining "continuity of classroom instruction" for its students. Sending teachers on their enforced maternity leave so long before their due date, the school board argued, was an administrative imper-

ative given the difficulty of securing a long-term substitute teacher and the necessity of insuring that pregnant teachers did not become debilitated on the job.

In rejecting the school board's arguments, the Court observed that the policy could, in fact, impede the continuity of classroom instruction, depending upon the point in the school year at which the teacher was forced to go on leave. Furthermore, the physical ability to remain on the job while pregnant varied greatly among individual women, rendering any policy mandating that all pregnant women cease work at the same point in their pregnancies arbitrary. The Court maintained that the only way to determine a pregnant

Jo Carol LaFleur speaks with Sidney Picker, the husband of attorney Jane M. Picker. © Jane M. Picker.

woman's fitness to continue in her job was on a strictly medical basis.

The Court also ruled that the policy's provisions for the return to work of women that were on maternity leave were unconstitutional under the Due Process Clause. Once again, given the differing physical capacities of individuals, any policy dictating the time of return for all workers was, by definition, arbitrary. The school board could continue to require teachers wishing to return to work following maternity leave to first secure verification of their fitness from a physician.

Impact

Cleveland Board of Education v. LaFleur marked a milestone in the legal status of women in the workplace. With mandatory maternity leaves, not to mention the arbitrary firing of employees who became pregnant, rendered effectively unconstitutional, employers were forced to devise human resources policies more accommodating to the unique needs of women. Significantly, however, the Court found the policy unconstitutional with regard to the Due Process Clause and not the Equal Protection Cause as the respondents had originally argued. As such, this case was of limited value as a legal precedent for other cases involving the rights of women in the workplace. This legal limitation was soon demon-

strated in *Geduldig v. Aiello* (1974), in which the Court ruled that the state of California did not have to offer medical coverage of pregnancy-related medical expenses for its employees. In the end, it took legislative activity in the form of the Pregnancy Discrimination Act of 1978 to establish that employers must treat pregnancy as any other physical condition.

Related Cases

Prince v. Massachusetts, 321 U.S. 158 (1944).
Griswold v. Connecticut, 381 U.S. 479 (1965).
Roe v. Wade, 410 U.S. 113 (1973).
Geduldig v. Aiello, 417 U.S. 484 (1974).

Bibliography and Further Reading

Biskupic, Joan, and Elder Witt, eds. *Guide to the U.S. Supreme Court,* 3rd ed. Washington: Congressional Quarterly Inc., 1990.

Edwards, Mark Evan. "Pregnancy Discrimination Litigation: Legal Erosion of Capitalist Ideology Under Equal Employment Opportunity Law." *Social Forces,* September 1996, p. 247.

Hall, Kermit L., ed. *The Oxford Companion to the Supreme Court of the United States,* New York: Oxford University Press, 1992.

KAHN V. SHEVIN

Legal Citation: 416 U.S. 351 (1974)

Appellant
Mel Kahn

Appellee
Robert L. Shevin, et al.

Appellant's Claim
That a Florida law granting a tax exemption to widows but not widowers was unconstitutional.

Chief Lawyer for Appellant
Sydney H. McKenzie III

Chief Lawyer for Appellee
Ruth Bader Ginsburg

Justices for the Court
Harry A. Blackmun, Warren E. Burger, William O. Douglas (writing for the Court), Lewis F. Powell, Jr., Potter Stewart, William H. Rehnquist

Justices Dissenting
William J. Brennan, Jr., Thurgood Marshall, Byron R. White

Place
Washington, D.C.

Date of Decision
24 April 1974

Decision
Florida's granting of tax benefits to widows but not widowers was found to be valid under the Constitution.

Significance
The Supreme Court's decision in *Kahn v. Shevin* validated the use of gender classifications in instances where lawmakers are trying to achieve benevolent social goals.

The Facts of the Case

Since 1941, the state of Florida had a law on its books which gave a $500 annual property tax exemption to women whose husbands had died. However, the statute provided no such tax relief to men whose wives had died. When Mel Kahn, a Florida widower, had his application for a tax exemption denied by the Tax Assessor's Office, he filed suit in circuit court. In his complaint, Kahn alleged that the granting of benefits to widows only violated his constitutional right to equal protection under the Fourteenth Amendment. He asked to have the statute declared unconstitutional.

The Lower Courts Rule

The Circuit Court for Dade County found in Kahn's favor. It ruled that the law in question violated the Equal Protection Clause because the classification "widow" was based upon gender. The state then appealed to the Florida State Supreme Court, which reversed the circuit court's judgment. In its view, the "widow" classification was permissible because it related in a "fair and substantial" way to the purpose of the law, which was to reduce "the disparity between the economic capabilities of a man and a woman." "The challenged tax law is reasonably designed to further the state policy of cushioning the financial impact of spousal loss upon the sex for whom that loss imposes a disproportionately heavy burden," the state supreme court determined. Unsatisfied with this reversal, Mel Kahn then appealed to the U.S. Supreme Court, which agreed to hear the case.

The Supreme Court Decides

On 24 April 1974, the Supreme Court issued its decision. In a 6-3 vote, the Court affirmed the judgment of the Florida State Supreme Court and found the statute valid under the Constitution. In doing so, the Court majority relied heavily on its belief that "the financial difficulties confronting the lone woman in Florida or in any other State exceed those facing the man." It noted the male-dominated socialization process, outright discrimination, and an inhospitable job market for women as reasons why some form of redress might be warranted. Florida's differing treatment of widows and widowers, therefore, could be justified because the gender classification served a benevolent social purpose.

Writing for the majority, Justice Douglas observed:

> We deal here with a state tax law reasonably designed to further the state policy of cushioning the financial impact of spousal loss upon the sex for which that loss imposes a disproportionately heavy burden. We have long held that "[w]here taxation is concerned and no specific federal right, apart from equal protection, is imperiled, the States have large leeway in making classifications and drawing lines which in their judgment produce reasonable systems of taxation." A state tax law is not arbitrary although it "discriminate[s] in favor of a certain class . . . if the discrimination is founded upon a reasonable distinction, or difference in state policy," not in conflict with the U.S. Constitution. This principle has weathered nearly a century of Supreme Court adjudication, and it applies here as well. The statute before us is well within those limits.

Dissenting Opinions

Three justices dissented in this case. Justice Brennan, joined by Justice Marshall, objected to the majority decision on the grounds that the same ends could have been better served by less sweeping legislation. A state may enact gender-specific legislation, Brennan wrote, but "only when the State bears the burden of demonstrating that the challenged legislation serves overriding or compelling interests that cannot be achieved either by a more carefully tailored legislative classification or by the use of feasible, less drastic means." In the view of these two justices, Florida would have served its widows equally well by drafting a more narrow law that denied exemptions to financially secure widows.

A separate dissent came from Justice White, who found no compelling reason to confer state benefits upon women rather than men. "[T]here are many rich widows who need no largess from the State . . ." White wrote. "At the same time, there are many widowers who are needy and who are in more desperate financial straits and have less access to the job market than many widows. Yet none of them qualifies for the exemption." White held the Florida statute violative of the Equal Protection Clause. While gender-based classifications had a place in the law, in his view they "require more justification than the State has offered" in this case.

Impact

The Supreme Court's decision in *Kahn v. Shevin* upheld benevolent gender classifications and was a benchmark for many similar cases to follow. Often the Court reaffirmed the opinion set forth here; at other times, it used *Kahn v. Shevin* as an example of the right way to wrote gender classifications into law in order to strike down other, less constitutionally valid attempts to do so.

Related Cases

Schlesinger v. Ballard, 419 U.S. 498 (1975).
Weinberger v. Wiesenfeld, 420 U.S. 636 (1975).
Califano v. Goldfarb, 430 U.S. 199 (1977).
Califano v. Webster, 430 U.S. 313 (1977).

Bibliography and Further Reading

Biskupic, Joan, and Elder Witt. *Congressional Quarterly's Guide to the U.S. Supreme Court,* 3rd ed. Washington, DC: Congressional Quarterly, Inc., 1996.

Chandler, Ralph C. *The Constitutional Law Dictionary.* Santa Barbara, CA: ABC-Clio, Inc., 1987.

Cushman, Robert F. *Leading Constitutional Decisions.* Englewood Cliffs, NJ: Prentice-Hall, Inc., 1982.

Johnson, John W., ed. *Historic U.S. Court Cases, 1690–1990: An Encyclopedia.* New York: Garland Publishing, 1992.

SCHLESINGER V. BALLARD

Legal Citation: 419 U.S. 498 (1975)

Appellant
James R. Schlesinger, U.S. Secretary of Defense

Appellee
Robert C. Ballard

Appellant's Claim
That a rule establishing different guidelines regarding mandatory discharge for male and female officers in the U.S. Navy did not constitute a violation of the Fifth Amendment's Due Process Clause.

Chief Lawyer for Appellant
Harriet S. Shapiro

Chief Lawyer for Appellee
Charles R. Khoury, Jr.

Justices for the Court
Harry A. Blackmun, Warren E. Burger, Lewis F. Powell, Jr., William H. Rehnquist, Potter Stewart (writing for the Court)

Justices Dissenting
William J. Brennan, Jr., William O. Douglas, Thurgood Marshall, Byron R. White

Place
Washington, D.C.

Date of Decision
15 January 1975

Decision
That the differing classifications regarding rules for discharge and promotion of males and females are based in rationality; and that in exercising its broad constitutional mandate in making these classifications, Congress did not violate the Due Process Clause of the Fifth Amendment.

Significance
Schlesinger v. Ballard touched peripherally on the volatile subjects of women in combat and of the principle behind affirmative action—that is, the application of differing sets of rules to different groups of people in order to attain a level playing field. The Court's decision in *Schlesinger*, to uphold statutes which provided different rules of tenure for men and women, signaled a willingness on the Court's part to accept certain types of discrimination inasmuch as the intent was to establish greater fairness. It was difficult, from a feminist perspective, to agree on the ultimate meaning of *Schlesinger*: on the one hand, the ruling helped to ensure greater opportunities for women; on the other, to some it seemed based on an underlying view of women as "the weaker sex."

Lieutenant Ballard Receives a Mandatory Discharge

At the beginning of the events which brought about his legal action, Robert C. Ballard had actively served with the U.S. Navy for nine years. An officer, he had attained the rank of lieutenant, at the pay grade O-3. He had been unsuccessful, however, in his efforts to obtain promotion to lieutenant commander. His second attempt at promotion had failed, and he was therefore subject to mandatory discharge under guidelines established in Title 10 U.S.C. 6382 (a), which states in part:

> Each officer on the active list of the Navy serving in the grade of lieutenant, except an officer in the Nurse Corps . . . shall be honorably discharged on June 30 of the fiscal year in which he is considered as having failed of selection for promotion to the grade of lieutenant commander or major for the second time.

According to the Supreme Court when it later reviewed his case, Ballard would receive a "lump-sum" severance payment of $15,000, guaranteed under section (c) of the same code; but by being forced to leave the service seven years short of the 20 years necessary to be designated as "retired" from the military, he would miss out on substantial retirement benefits.

Ballard brought suit in federal court, citing a different rule governing mandatory discharge for female officers who similarly failed to obtain promotion. Title 10 U.S.C. 6401 (a), the rule governing females in a situation similar to Ballard's, stated that

> Each woman officer on the active list of the Navy, appointed under section 5590 of this title, who holds a permanent appointment in the grade of lieutenant . . . shall be honorably discharged on June 30 of the fiscal year in which—(1) she is not on a promotion list; and (2) she has completed 13 years of active commissioned service in the Navy . . .

Thus, it appeared that women enjoyed an unfair advantage over men, namely that a female officer had three more years to qualify for promotion before the Navy discharged her. This, Ballard charged, was an instance of unconstitutional discrimination in violation of the Fifth Amendment's Due Process Clause. The latter provides that no person shall "be deprived of life, liberty, or property, without due process of law." Cited less often than the due process provision in the Fourteenth Amendment, which carries with it an Equal Protection Clause, the clause in the Fifth Amendment "prohibits the Federal Government from engaging in discrimination that is 'so unjustifiable as to be violative of due process'," according to the Supreme Court's later review of Ballard's case.

The district court judge agreed with Ballard, and issued a temporary restraining order prohibiting the navy from discharging him. A three-judge district court panel was then convened to hear Ballard's claim, whereupon they issued a preliminary injunction against his discharge. Next the same panel reviewed the case to make a decision on its merits. As would the Supreme Court in its later review, the panel used *Frontiero v. Richardson* (1973) as its guide, and found that the mandatory-discharge rules under challenge were put in place solely for reasons of fiscal and administrative policy. In other words, there was no compelling reason to favor women over men in the rules; therefore the court held that 6382 was unconstitutional, and that 6401 discriminated in favor of women without providing sufficient justification for doing so. The court then enjoined the U.S. Navy from discharging Ballard, and the navy appealed in the name James Schlesinger, Defense Secretary under the administration of President Gerald R. Ford. As is often true when a case reaches the nation's highest court, there were well-known personalities involved on both sides. Solicitor General Robert Bork, whose nomination to the Supreme Court would be rejected by Congress following a bitter ideological battle more than a decade later, filed a brief on behalf of the appellants. Noted attorney Charles R. Khoury argued for the appellee, and with him on the brief was Morris S. Dees, Jr., founder of the Southern Poverty Law Center in Montgomery, Alabama, and a famous champion of civil-rights cases.

Frontiero and Reed Offer a Guide— And a Contrast

In its review of the case before it, the Court examined the Navy's rationale behind the differing rules governing men in 6382 and women in 6401. At the root of the system controlling rules of promotion and attrition, explained Justice Stewart for the majority, was the need to limit the number of officers. The higher the pay grade, the greater the limitations. Under those general guidelines, the Navy had in place a variety of systems for selection and promotion. One system, for instance, governed promotion of male line officers—that is, officers with command over a specific body of troops; another system was in place for most male and female

James Schlesinger, c. 1970. © The Library of Congress/Corbis.

staff officers—i.e., officers who lack a command, but rather serve on the staff of a higher-ranking officer. A line-officer position tends to offer better prospects for promotion that a staff position. Underlying all of the Navy's rules of promotion, again, was the principle of limiting the number of officers at higher grades: "Because the Navy has a pyramidal organizational structure," Justice Stewart wrote, "fewer officers are needed at each high rank than are needed in the rank below. In the absence of some mandatory attrition of naval officers, the result would be stagnation of promotion of younger officers and disincentive to naval service." Hence the application of a philosophy informally called "up and out": simply put, an officer should either move up, or move out of the way so that someone else could move up.

But these rules, logical as they may have seemed, failed to explain the differing rationale for promoting women. This Stewart next addressed by reviewing two related cases, *Frontiero v. Richardson* and *Reed v. Reed* (1971). *Frontiero* addressed "the right of a female member of the uniformed services to claim her spouse as a 'dependent' for the purposes of obtaining increased quarters allowances and medical and dental benefits . . . on an equal footing with male members." The governing statutes held that a male member of the armed forces could automatically claim his wife as a dependent, whereas a female in the military could only claim her husband as a dependent if she could show that she provided more than one-half of his support. "The challenged classification," wrote Stewart, "was based exclusively on gender, and the Government conceded that the different treatment of men and women service members was based solely upon considerations of administrative convenience." Accordingly the Court struck down the statute with the words:

> any statutory scheme which draws a sharp line between the sexes, solely for the purpose of

achieving administrative convenience, necessarily commands 'dissimilar treatment for men
and women who are . . . similarly situated' . . .
We therefore conclude that . . . the challenged
statutes violate the Due Process Clause of the
Fifth Amendment insofar as they require a
female member to prove the dependency of
her husband.

The phrase "dissimilar treatment for men and
women who are . . . similarly situated" came from an
earlier case, *Reed*. In that instance, the statute in question was an Idaho probate code provision which gave
a "mandatory" preference for men over women to serve
as the administrator of a deceased person's estate. The
Court judged that the Idaho statute, which allowed no
consideration of the different parties' relative qualifications, was in place simply "to reduce probate
expenses by eliminating contests over the relative qualifications of men and women otherwise similarly situated." The Court found that law in violation of the
Equal Protection Clause in the Fourteenth Amendment.

But what was at issue in *Schlesinger* was not equal
protection or due process under the Fourteenth Amendment; rather, it was a question of due process as guaranteed in the Fifth. Also, in both of the earlier cases,
"the challenged clarifications based on sex were
premised on overbroad generalizations that could not
be tolerated under the Constitution." The code challenged by *Schlesinger,* on the other hand, was based not
on "archaic and overbroad generalizations, but, instead,
[on] the demonstrable fact that male and female line
officers in the navy are not similarly situated with
respect to opportunities for professional service."
Specifically, another section of Title 10, 6015, forbade
women from assignment "to duty in aircraft that are
engaged in combat missions [or] to duty on vessels of
the Navy other than hospital ships and transports."
Generally in the military, combat service is one of the
surest guarantees of promotion, and since women by
definition could not garner such service, Congress had
retained the 13-year clause for them as a means of
ensuring "fair and equitable career advancement programs." And Lt. Ballard, as the Court noted, had "not
challenged the current restrictions on women's officers'
participation in combat and in most sea duty."

The rational basis for the different rules, the Court
observed, was further reinforced by the fact that in situations where males and females were placed on an
equal footing, no distinction was made between them
with regard to promotion and attrition. Hence certain
women staff officers in the medical, dental, judge advocate general's (legal), and medical service corps were
subjected to the same tenure rules as men; similarly
men in the nurse corps—by definition a non-combat-
ant entity— enjoyed the same 13-year provision as their
female counterparts. In conclusion, the Court rein-

forced the constitutional separation of powers: "The
responsibility for determining how best our Armed
Forces shall attend to that business [war] rests with Congress . . . and with the President." Because it could not
be demonstrated that Congress had violated the Due
Process Clause of the Fifth Amendment, the Court
reversed the lower court's ruling.

A Different Reading of the Legislative History

Justice Brennan presented a dissenting opinion in
which he was joined by Justices Douglas and Marshall
and, in part, by Justice White. Observing that in his
view "a legal classification . . . premised solely upon
gender must be subject to close judicial scrutiny," Brennan launched into a close reading of the legislative history behind the various statutes, which had resulted in
the differing periods of tenure. In so doing, he suggested at the outset, the result might be quite different
from that which the Court had obtained in its majority ruling. "I find nothing in the statutory scheme or
the legislative history," he wrote,

to support the supposition that Congress
intended . . . to compensate women for other
forms of disadvantage visited upon them by
the Navy. Thus, the gender-based classification
of which appellee complains is not related,
rationally or otherwise, to any legitimate legislative purpose fairly to be inferred from the
statutory scheme or its history, and cannot be
sustained.

In his review of the statute's history, Brennan went
back almost three decades, to the enacting of the
Women's Armed Services Integration Act, to which
6401 was related. Due to differences in procedure for
promotion between males and females, the provisions
for mandatory separation of women officers had been
made a function of time served, not of opportunities
for promotion. The purpose of the differing separation
provisions, Brennan wrote, sprang from a desire on the
part of Congress to equate the tenure in years for female
lieutenants with that of the average male lieutenant
prior to mandatory separation. When Congress
reviewed aspects of its rules regarding promotion and
career opportunities for women in 1967, it did so "as
the Court notes, to provide women with 'fair and equitable career advancement programs.'" But "contrary to
the Court's assumption, Congress determined to
achieve this goal, not by providing special compensatory treatment for women, but by removing most of
the restrictions upon them and then subjecting them
to the same provisions generally governing men."

Brennan went on to illustrate this assertion by citing various provisions in Congress's 1967 act, and concluded that "to infer a determination purposely to per-

petuate a longer retention period for women line officers is, therefore, entirely to misconceive Congress' perception of the problem and of the proper solution." While he professed to applaud the aim of redressing gender imbalance, Brennan indicated, he did not believe it proper to view the tenure provisions as serving this purpose. Therefore he voted to affirm the lower court's ruling.

Impact

From the standpoint of women's rights, it appeared on one level that *Schlesinger* gave women what amounted to special privileges, at least in the Court's treatment of the tenure statutes, while still demanding and receiving equal rights. But this was only on one level: on another, the case simply served to highlight the fact that differing promotional opportunities between men and women were virtually a fact of life. Likewise the case was at odds with decisions such as *Stanton v. Stanton* (1975) and *Craig v. Boren* (1976), which sought to establish complete parity between males and females with regard to the age of majority. As for its raising of

the issue of women in combat, the case helped pave the way for *Rostker v. Goldberg* (1981), in which the Court rejected inclusion of women in the draft by a vote of 6-3.

Related Cases

Reed v. Reed, 404 U.S. 71 (1971).
Frontiero v. Richardson, 411 U.S. 677 (1973).
Kahn v. Shevin, 416 U.S. 351 (1974).
Weinberger v. Weisenfeld, 420 U.S. 636 (1975).
Craig v. Boren, 429 U.S. 190 (1976).
Rostker v. Goldberg, 448 U.S. 1306 (1980).

Bibliography and Further Reading

Biskupic, Joan and Elder Witt. *Guide to the U.S. Supreme Court,* 3rd ed. Washington, DC: Congressional Quarterly Inc., 1997.

Levy, Leonard W., ed. *Encyclopedia of the American Constitution.* New York: Macmillan, 1986.

Witt, Elder. *Congressional Quarterly's Guide to the Supreme Court,* 2nd ed. Washington, DC: Congressional Quarterly Inc., 1990.

STANTON V. STANTON

Legal Citation: 421 U.S. 7 (1975)

Appellant
Thelma B. Stanton

Appellee
James Lawrence Stanton, Jr.

Appellant's Claim
That a Utah statute was discriminatory and therefore unconstitutional because it set the age of majority for females at 18 and males at 21, thus denying due process and equal protection as guaranteed under the Fourteenth Amendment to the Constitution.

Chief Lawyer for Appellee
J. Dennis Frederick

Chief Lawyer for Appellant
Bryce E. Roe

Justices for the Court
Harry A. Blackmun (writing for the Court), William J. Brennan, Jr., Warren E. Burger, William O. Douglas, Thurgood Marshall, Lewis F. Powell, Jr., Potter Stewart, Byron R. White

Justices Dissenting
William H. Rehnquist

Place
Washington, D.C.

Date of Decision
15 April 1975

Decision
That the basis for the statute's establishment of different ages of majority was not rational, and that it denied women equal protection under the law.

Significance
Stanton v. Stanton followed *Reed v. Reed* (1971) in applying the standard of rationality to questions of preference for males. The latter had been the first case in which the Supreme Court directly challenged the issue of discrimination against females to the extent of declaring a state law invalid; with *Stanton* the Court solidified this stance. Together the cases helped usher in an era of increased attention to equal protection for women under the Fourteenth Amendment.

Thelma B. Stanton, who would become the appellant in *Stanton v. Stanton,* married James Lawrence Stanton, Jr., in Elko, Nevada, in February of 1951. Two years later, in February of 1953, they had a daughter they named Sherri Lyn; and in January of 1955, the Stantons had a son, Rick Arlund. The couple moved to Utah, and in 1960, when Sherri was seven years old and Rick five, the Stantons divorced. As part of the divorce proceedings in the District Court of Salt Lake County, the court awarded custody of the children to their mother and provided for alimony and child support as follows:

> Defendant is ordered to pay to plaintiff the sum of $300.00 per month as child support and alimony, $100.00 per month for each child as child support and $100.00 per month as alimony, to be paid on or before the 1st day of each month through the office of the Salt Lake County Clerk.

When Thelma Stanton remarried, the court changed its decree to relieve her former husband James from continuing to make alimony payments; the stipulations as to child support, however, would remain in effect until the children reached majority. James also remarried, and continued making child-support payments— until some time shortly after 12 February 1971, when Sherri became 18 years old. Two years later, in May of 1973, Thelma asked the divorce court to enter a judgment in her favor and against James for a variety of issues, particularly the support of the children during the period after each had attained the age of 18. The court, however, judged that on 12 February 1971, Sherri had attained her majority in accordance with Section 15-2-1 of Utah Code Annotated 1953. According to the Supreme Court, the latter is like many state statutes in having "little or no [available] legislative history," but seems to be based on an 1852 territorial act. It defines the "period of minority" thus: "The period of minority extends in males to the age of twenty-one years and in females to that of eighteen years; but all minors obtain their majority by marriage." Therefore, the divorce court denied Thelma Stanton's motion, ruling that the "defendant is not obligated to plaintiff for maintenance and support of Sherri Lyn Stanton since that date [12 February 1971]."

Parental Responsibility

When an adult commits a crime, or causes damage to property that belongs to someone else, that adult is held legally liable; but when a child is the responsible party, the question of liability is more involved.

Most states have some sort of law governing the degree of a parent's financial responsibility for damage done by his or her child. Oregon and Louisiana have the most stringent laws, holding parents liable for damage caused by a child in any type of circumstance, whether such damage was willful and malicious or not.

Eight states have particularly liberal laws, at least from the standpoint of parental liability. In Oklahoma, Iowa, West Virginia, and Maryland, parents are liable only if a child commits a crime involving malicious or willful property damage, or personal injury. Florida, Delaware, New Jersey, and New York are even more permissive: in those four states, the standard is malicious or willful criminal activity involving property damage (without the inclusion of incidents involving personal injury).

Source(s): Fast, Julius, and Timothy Fast. *The Legal Atlas of the United States.* New York: Facts on File, 1997.

Thelma Stanton appealed to the Supreme Court of Utah. In her case before the state's highest court, she held that Section 15-2-1 was discriminatory, and denied due process and equal protection in violation of the Fourteenth Amendment. The court responded that the statute did indeed treat males and females differently, but that differences in treatment were to be excused "so long as there is a reasonable basis for the classification, which is related to the purposes of the act, and it applies equally and uniformly to all persons within the class."

One might have assumed that a law which incorporated what the court called "old notions" would have established a lower age of majority for males than for females, not a higher one. But the establishment of a lower age of majority was based on the following ideas, in the court's words: "that generally it is the man's primary responsibility to provide a home and its essentials"; that "it is a salutary thing for [the man] to get a good education and/or training before he undertakes those responsibilities"; and that "girls tend generally to mature physically, emotionally and mentally before boys" and "they generally tend to marry earlier." Thus while a young male—in 1852, at least, if not in 1975—might be continuing his education in preparation for a career in which he would be expected to support a wife and family, a female might already be married and under the care of another male. On the basis of that logic, the Utah high court concluded that "there is no basis upon which we would be justified in concluding that the statute is so beyond a reasonable doubt in conflict with constitutional provisions that it should be stricken down as invalid." Therefore the law stood, and Thelma was entitled to support for Rick until he turned 21; but she was not entitled to support for Sherri after the latter turned 18.

Challenging "Old Notions"

After Thelma Stanton appealed to the U.S. Supreme Court, James Stanton's counsel attempted to show the

Court that she lacked standing for two reasons. In giving the opinion for an 8-1 Court, however, Justice Blackmun rejected both of these arguments. First, James had posited that the support issue was moot because, by the time the case went before the Court, Sherri was 21 years old, having reached her majority by any state's standard in February of 1974. Second, James tried to contend that because Thelma herself did not belong to the age group identified by the Utah statute, she therefore lacked a personal stake in the proceedings; and that furthermore she had agreed to Utah's definition of the age of majority when she signed the papers stipulating support payments back in 1960.

With regard to the first argument, Blackmun wrote that the claim of mootness

> overlooks the fact that what is at issue is support for the daughter during her years between 18 and 21. If appellee, under the divorce decree, is obligated for Sherri's support during that period, it is an obligation that has not been fulfilled, and there is an amount past due and owing from the appellee.

Far from being moot, then, the issue at hand was "a continuing live case or controversy." As for James's claim that Thelma had no direct interest in the case, the Court similarly dismissed this: "We are satisfied that it makes no difference whether the appellant's interest . . . is regarded as an interest personal to appellant or as that of a fiduciary." As the person responsible for a minor child, the custodial parent in this situation (i.e., Thelma) would actually be the one who had a right to support money—not the minor child herself. Furthermore, the Uniform Civil Liability for Support Act, which had been in effect in Utah since 1957, stated that "Every woman shall support her child"; hence, "the appellant herself thus had a legal obligation under Utah law to support her daughter until Sherri became

21 . . . Her interest in the controversy . . . is distinct and significant and . . . assures . . . proper standing on her part."

Turning to the specific merits of the case, Blackmun addressed each side's position. Whereas the appellant contended that the statute denied equal protection, the appellee claimed in turn that it was a test of rationality—i.e., that the difference in ages of majority had a logical basis, and was not a result of discrimination. In evaluating these claims, the Court used *Reed v. Reed* (1971) as its guide. The earlier case had sprung from an equal protection challenge to an Idaho law which gave preference to males over females when it came to a question of who should act as administrator over the estate of a deceased child. In its ruling, which struck down the Idaho statute, the Court had adopted a position first established in *Royster Guano Co. v. Virginia* (1920), stating that "a classification 'must be reasonable, not arbitrary, and must rest upon some ground of difference having a fair and substantial relation to the object of the legislation, so that all persons similarly circumstanced shall be treated alike.'"

Seen under the light of this logic, the Utah statute lacked rationality. This was particularly so with regard to the Utah court's position that females tend to marry earlier than males; since the law in that state indicated that "all minors obtain their majority by marriage," this was a meaningless point. More importantly, the Court held, whether or not one endorsed the "old notions" embodied in the Utah statute, the Utah court had imposed "criteria wholly unrelated to the objectivity of that statute." Not only was a minor a minor, the U.S. Supreme Court stated, whether male or female, but "no longer is the female destined solely for the home and the rearing of the family, and only the male for the marketplace and the world of ideas."

In a further statement of the changing positions of women, the Court continued:

> Women's activities and responsibilities are increasing and expanding. Coeducation is a fact, not a rarity. The presence of women in business, in the professions, in government and, indeed, in all walks of life where education is a desirable, if not always necessary . . . is apparent and a proper subject of judicial notice. If a specified age of minority is required for the boy in order to assure him parental support while he attains his education and training, so, too, is it for the girl. To distinguish between the two on educational grounds is to be self-serving: if the female is not to be supported as long as the male, she hardly can be expected to attend school as long as he does, and bringing her education to an end earlier

Thelma B. Stanton, 1993. © Reproduced by permission of Thelma Stanton.

coincides with the role-typing society has long imposed.

After reviewing a variety of other state statutes regarding the ages of majority—including other statements in Utah's own code—the Court concluded that there was no rational basis for the law. Finally, it was the Court's judgment that Section 15-2-1 "denies the equal protection of the laws, as guaranteed by the Fourteenth Amendment."

Dissent and a Postscript

Justice Rehnquist offered dissent on the basis that the case before the Court was not a proper constitutional question. "This case," he wrote, "arises only because appellant and appellee made no provision in their property settlement agreement fixing the age at which appellee's obligation to support his son or daughter would terminate." The age-of-majority question had arisen because the Utah Supreme Court had simply turned to what seemed the most appropriate state law for establishing a cut-off point. Furthermore, Utah had in place, in its Uniform Civil Liability for Support Act, a provision defining "child" as "a son or daughter under the age of twenty-one years." For these and other reasons, including the Court's "established policy of avoiding unnecessary constitutional adjudication," Rehnquist moved to dismiss the appeal.

A postscript to the case came two years later, with *Stanton v. Stanton* (1977), or "Stanton II." At the conclusion of the first *Stanton* case, the Court noted the fact that it had not fully settled the issues of the appellee's actual monetary obligation to the appellant. This was especially so since James Stanton was asserting that if the ages of majority should be made equal, they should both be set at the age of 18. At the end of the 1975 case, the Court had remanded it to Utah's high court so that the latter could resolve the state-law issues involved. Instead, the Utah Supreme Court used the opportunity to allege the constitutionality of the age-of-majority statute once again.

The Utah Supreme Court then passed the case on to the District Court of Salt Lake County, which in the U.S. Supreme Court's words "correctly recognized . . . that the only issue before it was whether . . . both sexes should be deemed to attain majority either at age 18 or at age 21." That court chose twenty-one as the proper age, and ordered Thelma Stanton a judgment of more than $3,600, consisting of $2,700 past due support money, more than $500 in interest, and the remainder in costs. The Utah Supreme Court, however, reversed this on appeal, and further reinforced its allegiance to Section 15-2-1 with the statement that "regardless of what a judge may think about equality, his thinking cannot change the facts of life . . ." On appeal to the U.S. Supreme Court, the Utah court's judgment was vacated. By this point, even James Stanton was starting to back down, to judge from a footnote in the case: "Even the appellee recognizes the impropriety of the reversal of the costs factor . . ."

Impact

Stanton would bear heavily on *Craig v. Boren* (1976), a case challenging an Oklahoma statute that set the legal drinking age at 21 for males and 18 for females. Once again the Court would rule, this time 7-2, that the statute relied on gender classifications that were unconstitutional under the Equal Protection Clause. *Mississippi University for Women v. Hogan* (1982) also relied on *Stanton* in its attack on gender-based classifications. *Stanton* helped signal a trend throughout the 1970s, one which continued into the 1990s, of attempts to establish equality of males and females before the law.

Related Cases

Royster Guano Co. v. Virginia, 253 U.S. 412, 415 (1920).
Reed v. Reed, 404 U.S. 71 (1971).
Schlesinger v. Ballard, 419 U.S. 498 (1975).
Craig v. Boren, 429 U.S. 190 (1976).
Stanton v. Stanton II, 429 U.S. 501 (1977).
University of California Regents v. Bakke, 438 U.S. 265 (1978).

Bibliography and Further Reading

Biskupic, Joan, and Elder Witt. *Guide to the U.S. Supreme Court,* third edition. Washington, DC: Congressional Quarterly Inc., 1997.

Hall, Kermit L., ed. *The Oxford Companion to the Supreme Court of the United States.* New York: Oxford University Press, 1992.

Levy, Leonard W., ed. *Encyclopedia of the American Constitution.* New York: Macmillan, 1986.

Witt, Elder. *Congressional Quarterly's Guide to the Supreme Court,* second edition. Washington, DC: Congressional Quarterly Inc., 1990.

CRAIG V. BOREN

Legal Citation: 429 U.S. 190 (1976)

Appellants
Curtis Craig, for men between the ages of 18 and 21 wanting to purchase 3.2 percent beer in the state of Oklahoma and Ms. Whitener, a licensed vendor for 3.2 percent beer, for other vendors.

Appellee
David Boren, Governor of Oklahoma

Appellants' Claim
That Oklahoma laws prohibiting the sale of 3.2 percent beer to males under 21 and females under 18 discriminated against males between the ages of 18 and 21.

Chief Lawyer for Appellants
Frederick P. Gilbert

Chief Lawyer for Appellee
James H. Gray

Justices for the Court
Harry A. Blackmun, William J. Brennan, Jr. (writing for the Court), Thurgood Marshall, Lewis F. Powell, Jr., John Paul Stevens, Potter Stewart, Byron R. White

Justices Dissenting
Warren E. Burger, William H. Rehnquist

Place
Washington, D.C.

Date of Decision
5 October 1976

Decision
That the Oklahoma laws restricting the sale of 3.2 percent beer to males over 21 and females over 18 violated the Equal Protection Clause of the Fourteenth Amendment by discriminating on the basis of gender.

Significance
That the gender classification in the laws did not serve "important governmental objectives" in order to be exempt from the Equal Protection Clause, nor did the state's power to regulate alcoholic beverages exempt it from this clause.

In the 1970s, the state of Oklahoma allowed the sale of what is known as 3.2 percent beer to individuals under the age of 21. This was justified in that the beer did not necessarily cause intoxication since the percentage of actual alcohol was relatively low. The Oklahoma statute governing these sales made it legal for males over the age of 21, and females over the age of 18 to purchase this beer.

On 20 December 1972, Curtis Craig, a male between the ages of 18 and 21 and Ms. Whitener, a licensed 3.2 percent beer vendor, brought suit in the District Court for the Western District of Oklahoma. They sought Craig's exemption from Oklahoma against the enforcement of this law on the grounds that it discriminated against men between the ages of 18 and 21 and was therefore unconstitutional. A three-judge court dismissed their case, deciding the law was constitutional.

Craig and Whitener appealed directly to the Supreme Court, since the suit questioned state law. On 20 December 1976, the Court reversed the district court's decision. The opinion was written by Justice Brennan and supported by White, Marshall, Powell, Stevens, and Blackmun. By the time the suit had reached the Supreme Court, Craig had reached the age of 21 and could legally drink per the Oklahoma law. Therefore, the Court found his suit moot or insignificant since the law no longer affected him and he had only sought relief from the law. However, Whitener could seek relief from the law since she was subject to the loss of her vendor license for violating it.

In order for a gender-based classification such as the one in Oklahoma to be exempt from the Equal Protection Clause, the state needed to show that the classification served key government goals such as the protection of its citizens. Oklahoma claimed that their goal in developing the law was to improve traffic safety. This was based on statistics that showed that .18 percent of females and 2 percent of males ages 18-21 were arrested for driving while under the influence of alcohol. The majority of the justices found this to be insignificant, since the statutes affected a much larger number of citizens than had actually been shown to be delinquent.

In addition, 3.2 percent beer was not found to be necessarily intoxicating, so the statistic did not necessarily apply to the statute. Finally, the state's claim to broad power in controlling the sale, purchase, and consumption of alcohol within Oklahoma under the Twenty-first Amendment did not allow it to discriminate in these areas.

Justices Burger and Rehnquist disagreed with the ruling for different reasons. Burger felt the vendor should not be allowed to "assert the constitutional rights of her customers." Rehnquist thought the state had a rational reason for the statute and should therefore be constitutional under the "rational basis" test of equal protection. In any case, the state of Oklahoma, along with other states with similar gender-based alcohol laws, needed to review and revise their statutes.

Related Cases

Michael M. v. Superior Court of Sonoma County, California, 450 U.S. 464 (1981).

Murphy v. Edmonds, 601 A.2d 102 (1992).

Bibliography and Further Reading

Cohen, William, and John Kaplan. *Constitutional Law: Civil Liberty and Individual Rights.* Mineola, NY: The Foundation Press, 1982.

Gans, David H. "Stereotyping and Difference: The Future of Sex Discrimination Law." *Yale Law Journal,* May 1995, p. 1875.

Hellman, Deborah. "Two Types of Discrimination: The Familiar and the Forgotten." *California Law Review,* March 1998, p. 315.

Kauper, Paul G., and Francis X Beytagh. *Constitutional Law: Cases and Materials.* Boston: Little, Brown, 1980.

DOTHARD V. RAWLINSON

Legal Citation: 433 U.S. 321 (1977)

Petitioner
E. C. Dothard, et al.

Respondent
Dianne Rawlinson, et al.

Petitioner's Claim
That an Alabama law establishing height and weight requirements for state prison guards and barring women from serving as guards in male prisons was permissible under federal civil rights law.

Chief Lawyer for Petitioner
C. Daniel Evans

Chief Lawyer for Respondent
Pamela S. Horowitz

Justices for the Court
Harry A. Blackmun, William J. Brennan, Jr., Warren E. Burger, Thurgood Marshall, Lewis F. Powell, Jr., William H. Rehnquist, John Paul Stevens, Potter Stewart (writing for the Court)

Justices Dissenting
Byron R. White

Place
Washington, D.C.

Date of Decision
27 June 1977

Decision
Alabama's ban on women prison guards was permissible under federal civil rights law, but its height and weight requirements were not.

Significance
The Supreme Court's decision in *Dothard v. Rawlinson* clarified the Court's interpretation of Title VII of the Civil Rights Act of 1964.

Case Background

Title VII of the Civil Rights Act of 1964 bars discrimination in hiring based on gender. It has also been interpreted to prohibit other forms of discrimination, which, while not specifically based on gender, serve by indirect means to eliminate women from a pool of job applicants. The case of Dianne Rawlinson tested the Supreme Court's understanding of this law.

Rawlinson, a citizen of the state of Alabama, applied for a job as a state prison guard. Her application was rejected because she failed to meet a state requirement that all prison guards must be at least 5 feet 2 inches tall and weigh a minimum of 120 pounds. A separate regulation prohibited women from serving as guards in maximum security male prisons in positions that involve close contact with inmates. Rawlinson filed a complaint with the Equal Employment Opportunity Commission (EEOC) and brought a class action lawsuit against Alabama corrections officials, challenging the height and weight requirements and the "close contact" regulation. She claimed these rules violated her rights under Title VII of the Civil Rights Act of 1964. The case first went before a three-judge panel of the U.S. District Court for the Middle District of Alabama.

The District Court Rules

The district court ruled in Rawlinson's favor on both counts. It relied on national statistics that outlined the comparative heights and weights of men and women to show that the Alabama prison guard requirements would exclude more than 40 percent of the female population but less than one percent of the male population. The court held that this, on its face, was evidence of sex discrimination against women. On the issue of the "close contact" prohibition, the district court rejected the state of Alabama's contention that being male was a necessary qualification for serving as a guard in a male penitentiary. It decreed that this regulation was impermissible under Title VII as well. E. C. Dothard, the director of Alabama's Department of Public Safety, then appealed the case to the U.S. Supreme Court on the state's behalf.

A Split Decision

On 27 June 1977, the Supreme Court ruled on the case. In a split decision, the Court affirmed part of the district court's ruling and rejected another part. Specifically, the majority affirmed the lower court's ruling that the height and weight requirement was discriminatory on its face, but rejected the claim that the banning of women from close contact positions in male prisons was a violation of civil rights law.

On the first question, the Court held that Rawlinson had indeed shown evidence of employment discrimination by pointing out, through the use of national statistics, the disproportionate impact in hiring the height and weight standards had on women as opposed to men. Furthermore, the Court found that the state of Alabama had done nothing to show that the height and weight requirements had any relationship to job performance on the grounds that size or strength was a necessary condition for employment as a prison guard. The state of Alabama, Justice Stewart wrote in his majority opinion, "produced no evidence correlating the height and weight requirements with the requisite amount of strength thought essential to good job performance. Indeed, they failed to offer evidence of any kind in specific justification of the statutory standards."

But Stewart and the rest of the majority parted company with the district court on the issue of the "close contact" prohibition. The Supreme Court considered this regulation a *"bona fide* occupational qualification" and therefore not grounds for a discrimination complaint under Title VII. In defending this assertion, the Court cited the violent atmosphere of male penitentiaries, the close contact with guards necessitated by dormitory style living arrangements and chronic understaffing, and the presence of sex offenders in the prison population. The Court concluded that the presence of female guards would therefore pose a significant security problem. "A woman's relative ability to maintain order in a male, maximum-security, unclassified penitentiary of the type Alabama now runs could be directly reduced by her womanhood," wrote Justice Stewart. "There would also be a real risk that other inmates, deprived of a normal heterosexual environment, would assault women guards because they were women."

Dissenting Opinions

Only one full dissent occurred in the case. Justice White argued that Rawlinson had not shown a discriminatory hiring pattern due to the height and weight require-

ment because she relied on height and weight statistics about the population at large and not the pool of applicants for prison guard positions in Alabama. In his opinion, therefore, Rawlinson did not meet the weight requirement to serve as a prison guard and should have had no grounds to sue on the issue of the "close contact" provision.

Other dissenting opinions came from Justices Marshall and Brennan, who concurred with the Court's position as to the height and weight requirement, but disagreed with the ruling on "close contact." These two justices argued that no evidence existed to show that women prison guards are at any more risk of attack by inmates than male prison guards. They also asserted that violent behavior among the prison population should not be used as an excuse for denying job opportunities to female applicants

Impact

The Supreme Court's decision in *Dothard v. Rawlinson* was referred to in a number of subsequent sex discrimination cases.

Related Cases

Furnco Construction Corp. v. Waters, 438 U.S. 567 (1978).
Connecticut v. Teal, 457 U.S. 440 (1982).
Wards Cove Packing v. Atonio, 490 U.S. 642 (1989).
Automobile Workers v. Johnson Controls, Inc., 499 U.S. 187 (1991).

Bibliography and Further Reading

Bible, John. "Discrimination in Job Applications and Interviews." *Supervision,* November 1998, p. 9.

Biskupic, Joan, and Elder Witt, eds. *Congressional Quarterly's Guide to the U.S. Supreme Court,* 3rd ed. Washington, DC: Congressional Quarterly, Inc., 1996.

Hunter, Rosemary C., and Elaine W. Shoben. "Disparate Impact Discrimination: American Oddity or Internationally Accepted Concept?" *Berkeley Journal of Employment and Labor Law,* summer 1998, p. 108.

Lye, Linda Cheng Yee. "Title VII's Tangled Tale: The Erosion and Confusion of Disparate Impact and the Business Necessity Defense." *Berkeley Journal of Employment and Labor Law,* winter 1998, p. 315.

Varca, Philip E., and Patricia Pattison. "Evidentiary Standards in Employment Discrimination." *Personnel Psychology,* summer 1993, p. 239.

CALIFANO V. GOLDFARB

Legal Citation: 430 U.S. 199 (1977)

Appellant
Joseph A. Califano, Jr., Secretary of Health, Education, and Welfare on behalf of the Social Security benefits program

Appellee
Leon Goldfarb, on behalf of widowers seeking survivors benefits from the program

Appellant's Claim
That the Social Security Act's gender-based distinction requiring widowers to prove that they were dependent on their spouses for at least half of their support in order to receive survivor benefits, did not discriminate against the deceased females.

Chief Lawyer for Appellant
Keith A. Jones

Chief Lawyer for Appellee
Ruth Bader Ginsburg

Justices for the Court
William J. Brennan, Jr. (writing for the Court), Thurgood Marshall, Lewis F. Powell, Jr., John Paul Stevens, Byron R. White

Justices Dissenting
Harry A. Blackmun, Warren E. Burger, William H. Rehnquist, Potter Stewart

Place
Washington, D.C.

Date of Decision
5 October 1977

Decision
That the Social Security Act's gender-based distinction requiring widowers to prove that they were dependent on their spouses for at least half of their support in order to receive survivor benefits, discriminated against the deceased spouses by violating the Fifth Amendment's pledge of equal protection under the law.

Significance
Widowers would no longer have to prove dependency on their spouses in order to receive survivor benefits from the Social Security employment taxes their spouses had paid throughout their lives.

When a person in the United States begins working, he also begins paying Social Security tax which provides protection for him and his family in the form of Social Security benefits, once he retires or dies. Prior to this case, according to the Social Security Act, when a female who has accrued these benefits dies, her spouse must prove that he was dependent on his wife for at least half of his support, in order to claim survivor benefits. A woman whose husband has died, on the contrary, does not need to prove such dependency upon her husband's income in order to receive the same benefits.

Mrs. Hannah Goldfarb worked as a secretary in the New York City public school system for almost 25 years until she died in 1968. Her husband, Leon, sought survivor's benefits but was turned down as he could not prove the needed dependency. He challenged the constitutionality of the Social Security Act's gender-distinction in the U.S. District Court for the Eastern District of New York. The three judges of the district court agreed with Goldfarb, finding that the burden of proof discriminated against female wage-earners by providing them less protection for their families than men received. Joseph Califano, U.S. Secretary of Health, Education, and Welfare at that time, appealed directly to the Supreme Court on behalf of the Social Security program.

The Court agreed with the lower court's decision, although it could not agree on an opinion among the justices. Justice Brennan was joined in his opinion by Justices White, Marshall, and Powell. It stated that the gender-based distinction violated equal protection under Due Process Clause of the Fifth Amendment since women's employment and contributions to Social Security resulted in less protection for their families than men's contributions did. Justice Stevens, in his own opinion, found that the distinction actually discriminated against men and was the "accidental by-product of a traditional way of thinking about females." This presumption rested on the fact that men were rarely dependent on their wives for half their income. Men were therefore requested to confirm this dependency. Stevens felt it unjust that men needed to prove dependency on their spouses. He continued, noting something more than an "accident" was needed to justify unequal treatment of the surviving spouses.

Justices Burger, Stewart, Blackmun, and Rehnquist disagreed that the classification was discriminatory. Rehnquist's opinion argued that it was justified on the basis of "administrative convenience" given that a widow's dependency on her husband is most often the case. Rehnquist also noted the classification was justified by referencing a previous case involving widows and property tax which relieved widows in order to improve their "characteristically depressed" condition.

As a result of this ruling, the Social Security Act needed to be amended in order to eliminate the burden of proof for widowers, providing equal protection for both female and male workers and their families who would receive benefits from Social Security.

Related Cases

Arizona Governing Committee v. Norris, 463 U.S. 1073 (1983).

Bibliography and Further Reading

Cohen, William, and John Kaplan. *Constitutional Law: Civil Liberty and Individual Rights.* Mineola, NY: The Foundation Press, 1982.

Kauper, Paul G., and Francis X. Beytagh. *Constitutional Law: Cases and Materials.* Boston: Little, Brown, 1980.

ROSTKER V. GOLDBERG

Legal Citation: 453 U.S. 57 (1981)

Petitioner
Dr. Bernard Rostker, Director of the Selective Service System

Respondent
Robert L. Goldberg

Petitioner's Claim
That the exemption of women from the registration requirements of the Selective Service System did not violate the Constitution by discriminating between men and women.

Chief Lawyer for Petitioner
Wade H. McCree, U.S. Solicitor General

Chief Lawyer for Respondent
Donald L. Weinberg

Justices for the Court
Harry A. Blackmun, Warren E. Burger, Sandra Day O'Connor, Lewis F. Powell, Jr., William H. Rehnquist (writing for the Court), John Paul Stevens

Justices Dissenting
William J. Brennan, Jr., Thurgood Marshall, Byron R. White

Place
Washington, D.C.

Date of Decision
25 June 1981

Decision
That the Selective Service System exemption for women does not violate the Constitution.

Significance
The Court's decision reinforced Congress' broad powers to pass laws with respect to raising and maintaining the armed forces of the United States, and validated the male-only draft. The decision has had only limited impact, however, on the Court's resolution of gender discrimination issues outside the military context.

During the height of the Vietnam War, one of the most divisive issues was the drafting of males to serve as soldiers in the nation's armed forces under the Military Selective Service Act, originally enacted in 1948. Since the passage of the act, only males were subject to the draft, although there were a number of proposals in the late 1960s to include women. A number of influential people thought that the draft should include women, including the feminist Margaret Meade and numerous government officials. In 1971, Robert L. Goldberg and several other men brought a suit in the U.S. District Court in Pennsylvania challenging the constitutionality of the male only draft. The suit, which was brought on behalf of all men required to register under the Selective Service Act, argued that the Selective Service Act violated the Fifth Amendment to the Constitution by denying men the equal protection of the laws by treating them differently from women solely on the basis of their gender. However, because the registration requirements were discontinued by President Gerald Ford in 1975, the case remained inactive.

President Carter Reactivates the Selective Service System

In 1979 President Jimmy Carter issued a proclamation to reactivate the registration requirement. President Carter felt that this step was a necessary response to the Soviet Union's invasion of Afghanistan. Although there were numerous proposals in Congress to have the registration requirements include both males and females, Congress refused to amend the Selective Service Act. Thus, beginning on 21 July 1980 all males were once again required to register with the Selective Service System. With this reinstation of the Selective Service Act, Goldberg's original lawsuit challenging the male-only registration requirement was reactivated. Just days before the registration requirement was to go into effect, the district court issued its decision that the male-only registration requirement was unconstitutional because it discriminated against men on the basis of their gender. The government, through Director of the Selective Service System Bernard Rostker, appealed the decision to the U.S. Supreme Court.

Women and the Selective Service Exemption

In 1995, House Speaker Newt Gingrich caused controversy when he discussed the idea of women in combat from a politically incorrect standpoint—that is, he did not believe women had any business going to war. At around the same time, Shannon Faulkner was making headlines as she attempted to become the first female cadet at South Carolina's all-male military academy, The Citadel. Though she waged a long legal battle, Faulkner, weakened by stress, proved physically incapable of keeping up with her classmates and within the first week of school, she had to drop out.

Later, however, other more physically fit young women successfully endured the tough conditions at The Citadel. Women have proven capable of serving in the military, and in positions such as military intelligence or the medical fields, they have served with distinction at the front lines. But the idea of women fighting wars as infantrymen in foxholes remains difficult for most of society to accept—mostly because certain segments of society find it hard to imagine that very many women would want to do so.

In a 6-3 decision, the Court reversed the district court's decision and concluded that the male-only registration requirements of the Selective Service Act did not violate the constitution. The court first noted that Congress has broad powers to pass laws relating to military affairs, and that courts are not qualified to make military decisions. Thus, courts should not lightly disregard the judgment of Congress in this area. More importantly, the Court noted that the purpose of the registration requirement is to be able to draft combat troops in time of war. Because women were, at the time, excluded from combat positions, Congress did not act unreasonably in concluding that registering women for the draft would serve no purpose:

> The exemption of women from registration is not only sufficiently but also closely related to Congress' purpose in authorizing registration . . . The fact that Congress and the Executive have decided that women should not serve in combat fully justifies Congress in not authorizing their registration, since the purpose of registration is to develop a pool of potential combat troops.

Justices Brennan, Marshall, and White disagreed with the Court's decision and dissented. Justice Marshall was particularly critical, accusing the Court of adopting a traditional view of the "proper role" of women and of "categorically exclud[ing] women from a fundamental civic obligation."

Validity of *Rostker* Questioned

In the early 1990s, the restriction on women from serving in combat roles in the military was ended. The *Rostker* decision relied heavily on the facts that women were excluded from combat and that the purpose of the registration requirement was to identify combat troops for time of war. Because women may now serve in combat roles, many have questioned whether the *Rostker* decision is still valid. However, regardless of whether the decision is still valid, it has been of little significance in the Court's resolution of other gender discrimination issues. The case has been considered a case relating to Congress' power to raise and maintain the nation's armed forces. Its reasoning and decision has not been extended by the Court

Wade Hampton McCree, Jr., 1977. © AP/Wide World Photos.

Bernard Rostker (right) and Kenneth Kizer. © Photograph by Dennis Cook. AP/Wide World Photos.

to other gender-discrimination issues outside of military affairs.

Related Cases
Reed v. Reed, 404 U.S. 71 (1971).
Columbia Broadcasting System v. Democratic National Committee, 412 U.S. 94 (1973).
Greer v. Spock, 424 U.S. 828 (1976).
Craig v. Boren, 429 U.S. 190 (1976).

Bibliography and Further Reading
Bobbitt, Philip. "National Service: Unwise or Unconstitutional." *Registration and the Draft.* ed. Martin Anderson. Palo Alto: Hoover Press, 1982.

Chavez, Linda. "The First Generation of Draft Daughters?; If Women Can Fight, Then Can Also Be Conscripted." *Washington Post,* July 11, 1993, p. C3.

Decew, Judith Wagner. "The Combat Exclusion and the Role of Women in the Military." *Hypatia,* winter 1995, p. 56.

Ginsburg, Ruth Bader. "Sex Discrimination." *The Burger Court: The Counter-Revolution That Wasn't.* ed. Vincent Blasi. New Haven: Yale University Press, 1983.

Jaeger, Nicole E. "Maybe Soldiers Have Rights After All!" *Journal of Criminal Law and Criminology,* spring 1997, p. 895.

MacKenzie, Ross. "On the Modern Military Meaning of 'Full Gender Equality.'" *Richmond Times-Dispatch,* March 2, 1995, p. A13.

Marmion, Harry A. *Selective Service: Conflict and Compromise.* New York: John Wiley & Sons, Inc., 1968.

MICHAEL M. v. SUPERIOR COURT OF SONOMA COUNTY

Legal Citation: 450 U.S. 464 (1987)

In June of 1978, three men, including the defendant Michael M., approached a 16 1/2 year old female and her sister. The 16 1/2 year old, Sharon, left the others with Michael M. and they began to kiss. When he made sexual advances and was turned away, Michael M. hit the young woman, and she then submitted to intercourse with him. A charge was filed in the Municipal Court of Sonoma County, California, that Michael M., a 17 1/2 year old male, had unlawful sexual intercourse with a woman under the age of 18, and was in violation of California's "statutory rape" statute. Michael M. sought to have this complaint set aside on both state and federal constitutional grounds, claiming that the statute unlawfully discriminated on the basis of gender since men alone could be charged under the law.

The California Supreme Court's Ruling

Both the trial court and the California Court of Appeals denied this request. The case was then taken to the Supreme Court of California, which upheld the California State statute. The state supreme court recognized that the statute made a distinction on the basis of sex because it provided that only males may violate this law, but held that this distinction was appropriate to the circumstance. The gender specific classification, it argued, was not only supported by social convention, but also by the biological fact that only the woman can become pregnant. Gender was also seen as a means for identifying both the offender and the victim. The state's "compelling interest" in preventing teen pregnancies, the social consequences of teen pregnancies and the risks inherent in teenage childbearing also supported the court's decision.

The U.S. Supreme Court's Ruling

Appeal of this decision was taken to the U.S. Supreme Court. The Court voted 5-4 to uphold the statute, but the majority could not agree on the reasons for doing so (this is called a plurality opinion). The Court stated that California's statutory rape law did not violate the Equal Protection Clause of the Fourteenth Amendment. Justice Rehnquist announced the Court's decision and Justices Brennan, White, Marshall and Stevens dissented.

Petitioner
Michael M.

Respondent
Superior Court of Sonoma County

Petitioner's Claim
That the California "statutory rape" statute unlawfully discriminated on the basis of gender.

Chief Lawyer for Petitioner
Gregory F. Jilka

Chief Lawyer for Respondent
Sandy R. Kriegler

Justices for the Court
Harry A. Blackmun, Sandra Day O'Connor, Lewis F. Powell, Jr., William H. Rehnquist (writing for the Court), Antonin Scalia

Justices Dissenting
William J. Brennan, Jr., Thurgood Marshall, John Paul Stevens, Byron R. White

Place
Washington, D.C.

Date of Decision
23 March 1981

Decision
The Court upheld the statute.

Significance
Allowed for a sex-based bias in a statute regarding sexual offenses.

When the Rapist Isn't a Stranger

In the popular perception, rape is a crime most often between strangers: for instance, a lone woman is walking down a dark alley, where she is accosted by an assailant she has never seen before and will never see again unless he is caught.

This view, however pervasive it may be, is inaccurate, as has become clear through increasing societal awareness of date rape and acquaintance rape—not to mention Department of Justice statistics, which show that the majority of rape victims knew their assailants. One 1994 Justice Department study, for example, showed that of all types of crime studied, rape had the highest percentage of incidents involving non-strangers: 77 percent. By contrast, figures were as low as 18 percent for completed robbery without injury, meaning that in 82 percent of all such crimes reported, the victim did not know the perpetrator.

Another Justice Department study offered some information on relationship of victims to the perpetrator. Though in a third of instances, the data showed only that the rapist was well-known to the victim without specifying relationship. Ten percent of rapes, according to this study, were committed by spouses, ex-spouses, or other relatives.

Source(s): *Bureau of Justice Statistics Sourcebook of Criminal Justice Statistics—1996.* Washington, DC: U.S. Government, 1997.

Justice Rehnquist's opinion made many separate arguments in favor of the statute. First, the opinion stated that gender-based classifications were not "'inherently suspect' so as to be subject to so-called 'strict scrutiny,' but will be upheld if they bear a 'fair and substantial relationship' to legitimate state ends." In other words, the statute had only to prove some legitimate state end in order to be upheld. The purpose of the statute in preventing underage pregnancy was determined to be legitimate because of the potential harm that could be done to young women. They also expressed the opinion that pregnancy poses a health risk to young women, but does not pose such a risk to men.

What is more, the justices determined that the Equal Protection Clause of the Fourteenth Amendment does not necessarily require that any statute apply equally to everyone; nor does it require things which are different, such as the circumstances surrounding gender, to be treated the same. As long as the limitations or rules being selectively applied to one gender are based on realistic sex differences, the law can be seen as constitutional.

The opinion also considered whether the statute was necessary to deter teenage pregnancy. The defendants claimed that a gender neutral statute would serve equally well. Yet the justices claimed that this was not the question at issue; the statute may not have been drawn as precisely as it might have been, but the statute was within constitutional limitations. They also reasoned that a gender-neutral statute would reduce a woman's likelihood to report violations if she herself might be subject to prosecution. The concurring justices raised the possibility that a broad statute applicable to both sexes might, in fact, be unenforceable.

The argument also addressed the presumption that the scope of the statute might be too broad, since it makes it unlawful to have intercourse with young females who cannot become pregnant. Their opinion stated that the U.S. Constitution did not require the statute to limit its scope by excluding young girls; what is more, even if it did, the damage that very young girls can sustain from intercourse is reason enough to include them in the protection of the statute.

Finally, they determined that the statute was not unconstitutional because Michael M. was under 18 at the time of intercourse. The assumption by the state that the male is the aggressor and therefore culpable at the time was seen as legitimate. They held that the state prevented illegitimate pregnancy by providing men a deterrent for such aggressive action. The age of the man was seen as irrelevant, since both young men and old are capable of inflicting damage.

Sandy R. Kriegler.
© Reproduced by permission of Superior Court Judge Sandy R. Kriegler.

Dissenting Opinion

A dissenting opinion by Justice Brennan stated that Rehnquist's opinion placed too much emphasis on California's goal of preventing teenage pregnancy and not enough emphasis on whether the discrimination on the basis of sex was warranted and related to that goal. The dissenters argued that the state did not provide enough evidence to establish the legitimacy of its goal (preventing teenage pregnancy), nor did it prove the relationship between the gender-based discrimination and that objective. They looked for California to provide evidence that there are fewer teenage pregnancies under the statutory rape law than there would be if the law were gender neutral, as well as evidence that because it punishes only males, it more effectively deters underaged women from having sexual intercourse. The state did not provide that kind of evidence, and therefore the dissenting justices were not convinced.

The dissenting opinion also pointed out that at the time, there were 37 states which have gender-neutral statutory rape laws, and that California had revised other sections of the Penal Code to make them gender-neutral. They also stated that common sense dictates that gender-neutral laws are potentially greater deterrents for underage sexual activity, since it makes both men and women subject to criminal punishment, therefore impacting twice as many potential violators. Justice Stevens, in a separate dissent, suggested that there is no reason to exempt a woman from the scope of the law, when the woman is capable of using her own judgment of whether or not to assume the risk of sexual intercourse.

Implications

The Court's opinion is significant because it gives an extraordinary amount of weight to a state's after-the-fact assertion of the original reason it enacted the statute. Additionally, though the statute may not have been carefully drawn at the outset, the Court deter-mined that the resulting legal action was appropriate and legitimate. The overall legitimacy of the goal, and the relationship of the statute to that goal, rendered the sex-based classification of the statute permissible.

This decision may raise questions on other equal-protection issues such as how one is able to determine whether or not men and women are "similarly situated" with respect to the aim of the law. The decision also raised questions regarding in what respect and to what extent, men and women are supposed to be similarly situated for an appropriate gender-based classification to be made. These questions were not answered by the majority opinion and are therefore still open to interpretation. Though in the past the Court has determined that, with regard to the Equal Protection Clause of the Fourteenth Amendment, a legal classification must be reasonable in relation to the objectives of the law, this may be subject to differing opinions on what is "reasonable." The Court must be very careful in how it interprets this clause. The results of such interpretation could be inconsistent at best, and in fact "the Supreme Court has successively imposed different constitutional frameworks for reviewing legislation that draws lines between the sexes."

Related Cases

Kahn v. Shevin, 416 U.S. 351 (1974).
Schlesinger v. Ballard, 419 U.S. 498 (1975).
Craig v. Boren, 429 U.S. 190 (1976).

Bibliography and Further Reading

Baer, Judith. *Equality Under the Constitution: Reclaiming the Fourteenth Amendment.* Ithaca, NY: Cornell University Press, 1983.

Kanowitz, Leo. *Equal Rights: The Male Stake.* Albuquerque, NM: University of New Mexico Press, 1981.

Kirp, David L., Yudof, Mark G., and Strong Franks, Marlene. *Gender Justice.* Chicago: University of Chicago Press, 1986.

MISSISSIPPI UNIVERSITY FOR WOMEN V. HOGAN

Legal Citation: 458 U.S. 718 (1982)

Petitioner
Mississippi University for Women

Respondent
Joe Hogan

Petitioner's Claim
That the state-supported school's nursing program did not violate gender-equity statutes, and it could continue its single-sex admission policy.

Chief Lawyer for Petitioner
Hunter M. Gholson

Chief Lawyer for Respondent
Wilbur O. Colom

Justices for the Court
William J. Brennan, Jr., Thurgood Marshall, Sandra Day O'Connor (writing for the Court), John Paul Stevens, Byron R. White

Justices Dissenting
Harry A. Blackmun, Warren E. Burger, Lewis F. Powell, Jr., William H. Rehnquist

Place
Washington, D.C.

Date of Decision
1 July 1982

Decision
That the Mississippi University for Women had violated Hogan's constitutional right to equal protection of the law by barring him admission to its nursing school.

Significance
Men are entitled to protection under the same anti-bias laws as women.

In 1979 Joe Hogan applied to the nursing school of the Mississippi University for Women. The school, located in his hometown of Columbus, granted four-year baccalaureate degrees. Hogan had worked in a medical center since he was eighteen, and was, at the time, a nursing supervisor and a surgical nurse in Columbus. He sought to further his professional skills and receive the higher wages nurses with degrees earned.

Vestiges of Old South

However, the Mississippi University for Women was a single-sex school, and its nursing program was open only to women, though men were allowed to audit courses. The state-funded institution was founded in 1884 as the Mississippi Industrial Institute and College for the Education of White Girls of the State of Mississippi. It was the first women-only, state-supported school in the country, though private single-sex institutions were quite common. (At the time of the Hogan case, the only other single-sex, state-funded university in the United States was Texas Women's University, which already had a co-educational nursing school.) Mississippi University for Women's school of nursing was founded in 1971, and had been offering Mississippi women a four-year degree in the profession since 1974. The nearest co-educational nursing program was 147 miles away. Hogan's application for admission to the Mississippi University for Women was rejected on the basis of his gender, though he had met the other requirements. School officials suggested he audit courses.

"Minimal Scrutiny"

Instead Hogan filed an action in the U.S. District Court for the Northern District of Mississippi, asserting that the school's policy violated the Fourteenth Amendment, which declared that states cannot make or enforce a law that violates constitutional freedoms, because citizens are entitled to equal protection. His suit requested injunctive relief—a change in the Mississippi University's women-only admissions policy—as well as damages. The district court denied injunctive relief and supported the single-sex admission policy by applying the "minimal scrutiny" test. Up to this point

Callaway Hall on the campus of Mississippi University for Women in Columbus, Mississippi. © Public Affairs Office, Mississippi University For Women.

in time, most discrimination cases were judged using minimal scrutiny, which declared a gender-specific statute to be valid if there was a rational correlation to a sensible legislative goal. In this case, the court conceded that providing women with the option of a female-only nursing education was a valid state objective and thus passed the minimal scrutiny gauge.

"Intermediate Scrutiny"

Hogan took his case further. The Fifth Circuit Court of Appeals in New Orleans reversed the lower court's decision, declaring that "rational relationship" in the minimal scrutiny test of constitutionality was misused. In explanation, the judicial body asserted that there were no inherent biological differences between men and women to rationalize separate educational facilities for nursing. It also pointed out that Mississippi was providing a unique educational opportunity for females, but not for males. Its ruling asserted that "intermediate scrutiny"—rather than minimal—should instead be applied, and that the admission policy to both the nursing school, and the Mississippi University for Women as a whole, was indeed unconstitutional. Hogan should be admitted, the appeals court declared. The Mississippi

University for Women petitioned the U.S. Supreme Court to review that decision.

To feminists, the case's appearance before the High Court was viewed with some unease: if the Court upheld the legality of a policy that discriminated against men, then the language of the decision might be used to uphold statutes or policies that excluded women. The intermediate scrutiny test also came into question. It had been used as a judicial yardstick by the Supreme Court since the early 1970s in several noteworthy sex discrimination cases. However, by the time of the Hogan case, certain signals given by the more conservative justices had caused concern among feminist lawyers that the Court would no longer apply the intermediate scrutiny test. The High Court had recently heard challenges to male-only draft registration and statutory rape laws, and had given signs of this shift in its attitudes toward such cases. Furthermore, there were also signals that the Court might now shift the burden of proof in gender-discrimination cases to plaintiffs; customarily the government entity had to prove in court that its statute or policy decree was justified.

O'Connor Rejects University's Arguments

Arguing its case, lawyers for the Mississippi University for Women asserted that its single-sex nursing school was a form of "affirmative action," or part of a program to rectify past discrimination by providing preferential treatment to women or minorities. The Court upheld the appeals court ruling favoring Hogan in a 5-4 decision. Justice O'Connor, the first female Supreme Court appointee, delivered the written opinion. In it, O'Connor rejected the school's argument that its policy was a form of affirmative action, noting that over 98 percent of all nursing degrees awarded in the United States were earned by women; there did not seem to be any obstacles to women in their pursuit of a nursing education. By restricting its program to women, O'Connor remarked, the Mississippi University for Women perpetuated the stereotype of nursing as "women's work." The school had also argued that allowing men into the program would negatively affect the quality of education for its female students, but this argument was also rejected on the grounds that the school already allowed men to sit in on classes.

Dissenting justices argued that the majority's reasoning was too rigid, and that single-sex educational opportunities were a historic and vital part of the American educational landscape. Hogan, they argued, brought his gender-discrimination case because he would have been inconvenienced to commute to another school. But legal analysts pointed out that it was unfair for the state to present obstacles or inconvenience to a man, just as it would have been for women to have had to face such hurdles.

Related Cases

Katzenbach v. Morgan, 384 U.S. 641 (1966).
Reed v. Reed, 404 U.S. 71 (1971).
Craig v. Boren, 429 U.S. 190 (1976).
Califano v. Goldfarb, 430 U.S. 199 (1977).
Califano v. Webster, 430 U.S. 313 (1977).
Orr v. Orr, 440 U.S. 268 (1979).
Kirchberg v. Feenstra, 450 U.S. 455 (1981).

Bibliography and Further Reading

American Bar Association Journal, Vol. 68, October 1982, pp. 1299-1300.

Gans, David H. "Stereotyping and Difference: The Future of Sex Discrimination Law." *Yale Law Journal,* May 1995, p. 1875.

Greenhouse, Linda. "Court Says School Cannot Bar Men." *New York Times,* July 2, 1982, p. 1.

Harvard Law Review, Vol. 96, November 1982, pp. 110-120.

Skaggs, Jason M. "Justifying Gender-Based Affirmative Action Under United States v. Virginia's 'Exceedingly Persuasive Justification' Standard." *California Law Review,* October 1998, p. 1169.

ARIZONA GOVERNING COMMITTEE V. NORRIS

Legal Citation: 463 U.S. 1073 (1983)

Petitioner
Arizona Governing Committee for Tax Deferred Annuity and Deferred Compensation Plans on behalf of deferred compensation and retirement plans

Respondent
Nathalie Norris, on behalf of employees receiving benefits from employee-sponsored retirement plans

Petitioner's Claim
That the state's retirement plan did not violate the Civil Rights Act in paying lower benefits to women than to men, because of women's longer life expectancy.

Chief Lawyer for Petitioner
James H. Geary

Chief Lawyer for Respondent
Louis J. Caruso

Justices for the Court
William J. Brennan, Jr., Thurgood Marshall (writing for the Court), Sandra Day O'Connor, John Paul Stevens, Byron R. White

Justices Dissenting
Harry A. Blackmun, Warren E. Burger, Lewis F. Powell, Jr., William H. Rehnquist

Place
Washington, D.C.

Date of Decision
28 March 1983

Decision
That a state retirement plan which paid lower benefits to women than to men violated the Civil Rights Act.

Significance
The decision effectively prevented employers from offering annuity plans that offer men and women unequal benefits.

With the erosion of traditional pensions, employers throughout the country began offering their employees the opportunity to enroll in deferred compensation plans. Employees who enrolled in these plans saved a portion of their earnings in tax-deferred accounts, which allowed them to postpone paying federal income tax on these dollars until they retired.

The state of Arizona worked with several investment companies to offer this benefit to its employees. The companies generally offered three different types of payment options upon retirement: a single lump-sum amount on retirement, payments of a certain amount over a certain period of time, or monthly payments of an agreed amount through the end of the person's life known as annuity payments.

Natalie Norris worked as a supervisor in the Arizona Department of Economic Security. In 1975, she began contributing to a deferred compensation plan offered by the state, choosing the annuity or monthly payment option. After contributing for a period of time, she learned that at retirement, she would receive $34 a month less than male state employees who deferred the same amount of compensation and would retire at the same time. All of the companies offering annuity plans to state of Arizona employees used mortality tables which calculated monthly retirement benefits. These tables incorporated the fact that women live longer than men, and would therefore receive less money per month. Norris attempted to address this issue to the state and the retirement companies but was unable to resolve the situation. She then filed a class-action suit in the U.S. District Court for the District of Arizona, alleging that the plan violated Title VII of the Civil Rights Act of 1964 by discriminating on the basis of gender.

The district court agreed that the plan violated Title VII and ordered the state to stop using the gender-based mortality tables and to pay those female employees, who had already retired, benefits equal to those paid to men. The state appealed to the U.S. Court of Appeals for the Ninth District and lost. The state then asked the Supreme Court to review the case, on *certiorari.* In a 5-4 decision, the Court agreed that the plan violated Title VII.

The opinions themselves were split amongst the justices, but in essence, the Court found that under Title VII, gender could not be properly used to predict longevity. In addition, Title VII required employers to treat employees as individuals, not as members of a class such as gender, race, or religion. Although the retirement plan companies had developed the discriminatory mortality tables, the state was legally responsible since it had entered into a contract with the companies on behalf of the employees. While some of the justices felt that previous Court decisions on related issues gave the state and benefit companies fair warning to change their policies, thereby making them liable to pay "back benefits" to already-retired employees, they were in the minority. The Court majority found that, due to the extraordinary financial burden that would be placed on the companies in order to provide these "back-benefits," a revised plan removing the gender discrimination would not be retroactive.

While the Court's ruling effectively prevented employers from offering unequal retirement benefits to men and women, its initial impact would be on men. In an interview with *Time*, Michael Stuntz of the American Council on Life Insurance said, "It looks as if proportionately more men would have their pensions reduced while more women would have their pensions increased."

Related Cases

Califano v. Goldfarb, 430 U.S. 199 (1977).
Spirt v. Teachers Insurance and Annuity Assoc., 735 F.2d 23 (2nd Cir. 1984).

Bibliography and Further Reading

Garcia, Guy D. "Turning the Sexual Tables," *Time,* July 18, 1983.

McCarthy, David D., and John A. Turner. "Risk Classification and Sex Discrimination in Pension Plans," *Journal of Risk and Insurance,* March 1993, p. 85.

HECKLER V. MATHEWS, ET AL.

Legal Citation: 465 U.S. 728 (1984)

Petitioner
Margaret M. Heckler, Secretary of Health and Human Services

Respondent
Robert H. Mathews, et al.

Petitioner's Claim
By permitting a brief, five-year exclusion period which temporarily revived gender-based discrimination in awarding retiree benefits to spouses, the Social Security Act, as amended in 1977, did not violate the Due Process Clause of the Fourteenth Amendment.

Chief Lawyer for Petitioner
Mark L. Levy

Chief Lawyer for Respondent
John R. Benn

Justices for the Court
Harry A. Blackmun, William J. Brennan, Jr. (writing for the Court), Warren E. Burger, Thurgood Marshall, Sandra Day O'Connor, Lewis F. Powell, Jr., William H. Rehnquist, John Paul Stevens, Byron R. White

Justices Dissenting
None

Place
Washington, D.C.

Date of Decision
5 March 1984

Decision
Although 1977 amendments to the Social Security Act permitted unequal awarding of benefits between men and women, the U.S. Supreme Court upheld the lower court ruling that there was no violation of the Due Process Clause; the provisions of a five-year exemption only temporarily revived gender-based discrimination for the justifiable protection of people who planned their retirements based on the old law.

Significance
In *Heckler v. Mathews, et al.* the Court reinforced the collaborative role between legislative and judicial branches of the government. The Court's ruling remained consistent with past decisions which held that gender discrimination was permissible under circumstances in which the government had a rational, overriding justification.

Question of Gender Based Classification

During 1977, the docket of the U.S. Supreme Court contained one case for review which attracted the concern and attention of all three branches of government—judicial, legislative, and executive. By agreeing to hear arguments in *Califano v. Goldfarb* (1977), the Court decided the constitutionality of gender-based distinctions which governed awarding of Social Security benefits to spouses concurrently drawing government pensions. In considering Goldfarb's claim, a widower who had been denied benefits to which widows were entitled, the Court found that the provisions of the Social Security Act imposed a gender-based distinction which unfairly burdened "a widower but not a widow with the task of proving dependency upon the deceased spouse." Specifically, men were required to prove that at least half their support derived from a wife's income at the time of death while women who survived their spouses were entitled to benefits regardless of how much support derived from their deceased spouse. Thus, the Court affirmed the decision of a lower, U.S. district court "that the different treatment of men and women mandated by 402 (f) (1) (D) (a provision of the Social Security Act) constituted invidious discrimination against female wage earners by affording them less protection for their surviving spouses than is provided to male employees." Throughout 1977, the Court also reiterated the *Goldfarb* decision with two follow up cases, *Califano v. Silbowitz* (1977) and *Jablon v. Califano* (1977).

Before the calendar year elapsed, Congress responded with almost unprecedented unanimity and swiftness by amending Social Security legislation. Because of the Court's *Goldfarb* decision, men would receive previously unawarded benefits and also collect them retroactively. Fearing that the system would become overloaded and possibly go bankrupt, Congress authored and passed a revised statute which changed the eligibility criteria by which all beneficiaries were awarded spousal benefits. SSR 79-26 under Title II (Increase in Delayed Retirement Credit, and Delayed Retirement Credit for Widows or Widowers) stipulated that benefits for all spouses, regardless of gender, would be reduced according to a formula that was based on how much money a retiree received from federal or

Gender and Reverse Discrimination

Women have long fought for equal rights in areas of compensation that range from pay to benefits; but cases such as *Heckler* signify a counter-trend, that of reverse-discrimination lawsuits. The most famous of these was *University of California v. Bakke* (1978), which challenged reverse discrimination on the basis of race; but challenges on the basis of gender have been viewed differently by the Supreme Court. This is perhaps because gender, unlike race, was not a factor in the drafting or the passage of the Fourteenth Amendment.

Part of what makes questions about reverse discrimination difficult is the fact that they can be approached on different levels. There is, for instance, the political or legal level, based on the Constitution, statutes, and general beliefs about fairness. But there are also viewpoints based on tradition or on actual practices. Thus for instance alimony laws, which have tended to favor women, are written that way because past experience—at least, prior to the 1970s—showed that women were more likely than men to be financially hurt in a divorce settlement.

Source(s): Branch, Kathryn. "Are Women Really Worth as Much as Men?: Employment Inequities, Gender Roles, and Public Policy (Part 3 or 4)." *Duke Journal of Gender Law and Policy*, 1 January 1994.

state pensions. However, legislators understood that many future retirees had made financial plans based on the way the Social Security Act had been written before being amended in 1977. Thus, so that change of law would not adversely impact people facing impending retirement, provisions of the 1977 amendment allowed for a five-year exemption period for spouses who, prior to 1982, would become eligible to receive spousal benefits. To ensure their intention to keep the Social Security fund from being depleted, Congress also passed a severability clause which stipulated that if any part of SSR 79-26 was declared unconstitutional, that the pension-offset clause would still remain in effect as the new law of the land.

Individual Rights and Congressional Intent

After Robert Mathews retired from the U.S. Postal Service, he applied for Social Security spousal benefits on his wife's account. Unlike non-civil servant retirees, Mathews did not have to offset double benefits against his spouse's account; civil servants could receive full spousal benefits along with their government pensions. However, under the provisions of Social Security Act (as amended by Congress in 1977), Mathews was denied benefits because he did not depend on his wife for one-half support. After being administratively denied benefits, Mathews requested and received a hearing by an Administrative Law Judge (ALJ) who declared valid the decision to withhold benefits. Mathews pursued his claim via the Appeals Counsel of the Department of Health and Human Services (DHHS); that review also affirmed denial of benefits. As a result, the Secretary of DHHS, Margaret Heckler, issued an official decision on behalf of the DHHS to enforce the findings of the ALJ and Appeals Counsel.

Mathews continued to believe he had been unjustly denied benefits to which he was entitled and had exhausted all available administrative avenues available through the DHHS. He then filed suit on behalf of himself and the class of other nondependent men affected by Heckler's decision. In presenting his case before the U.S. District Court for the Northern District of Alabama, Mathews sought a declarative judgment ruling that the pension offset of the 1977 amended Social Security Act was unconstitutional.

The linchpin to Mathews's argument was the Supreme Court's ruling in *Califano v. Goldfarb*. According to the *Goldfarb* ruling, gender discrimination was inherent in the pension offset exemption because it violated due process for nondependent men who were similarly situated as nondependent woman who received benefits. Further, Mathews's attorney claimed the *Goldfarb* decision rendered the severability clause unconstitutional—it perpetuated gender discrimination against nondependent men by enforcing the offset exemption clause even though it was held violative of the U.S. Constitution.

In considering the class action claim, the district court first determined that Mathews indeed had standing to bring suit. The pension offset exemption and severability clause assumed gender-based classification; therefore, withholding benefits from the "excluded class" of nondependent men while extending benefits to the "favored class" constituted unequal treatment. Mathews's "injury" qualified him for legal redress. In examining the issues raised in the suit, the district court pointed out that discrimination could only be upheld if it served "important governmental objectives and [was] substantially related to achievement of those objectives." However, the rationale behind the exclusion exemption of the pension offset was faulty. As the Supreme Court ruled in *Goldfarb*, "Women would have relied upon the practices of the Social Security Administration, yet men would not have relied upon a decision of the Supreme Court." That, the district court believed, violated equal protection provided by the Due Process Clause of the Fifth Amendment.

Finally, in considering the congressional offset provision of the amended Social Security Act, the justices held that even if the person achieved success in challenging the provision's constitutionality, the outcome would still penalize litigants because the pension offset would still remain in effect. The district court viewed such an outcome as merely a means by which Congress made any challenge "fruitless." Further, since the court felt Congress had intended to serve a governmental interest in not penalizing retirees, the severability clause was "an adroit attempt to discourage the bringing of an action by destroying standing." Thus, the district court held the offset exemption and severability clause as unconstitutional and ordered the DHHS to pay benefits without consideration of dependency and without offset of benefits. After the ruling of the district court, the Secretary of DHHS directly appealed to the Supreme Court for a reversal of the decision.

Circumvention of Legislative Intent

In considering the petitioner's claim, the U.S. Supreme Court too, needed to establish the validity of Mathews's (now the respondent) standing to bring suit. The Court considered both petitioner's and respondent's arguments. The petitioner maintained that benefits were awarded according to classifications (that of retirees) and were not tied to a monetary award of benefits; hence, there was no differentiation by gender. By agreeing with this point, the justices held that the respondent (Mathews) could reasonably qualify as representative of a class lawsuit. But, to further ascertain the respondent's validity, the Court needed to apply "case or controversy" criteria established by *Gladstone, Realtors v. Village of Bellwood* (1979) and *Simon v. Eastern Kentucky Welfare Rights Organization* (1976). By not awarding the same benefits to nondependent men and women, the DHHS appeared to be stigmatizing a "disfavored group" in a manner that could cause "serious noneconomic injuries." Hence, according to the legal rubric of *Gladstone*, the respondent had satisfied the need to show injury due to the conduct of DHHS. Further, since the severability clause would result in withdrawal of benefits from which the respondent could gain relief "by a favorable decision," and since the respondent invoked the right to equitable treatment in which "the appropriate remedy is a mandate of equal treatment," the respondent qualified for standing in accordance with the *Simon* decision.

In considering the rationale of the lower district court, the justices agreed that the pension offset applied only to men who could show that half their support derived from their spouse's income (ruled unconstitutionally gender-biased according to the *Goldfarb* decision). However, the Court reasoned that "favoring con-

structions of statutes to avoid constitutional questions" did not "license a court to usurp the policymaking and legislative functions of the duly elected representatives." Hence, after they carefully examined the language of the (1977) amended Social Security Act, the justices held that Congress specifically intended to grant a five-year extension only to address the need of retirees who made plans according to pre-*Goldfarb* legislation. Thus, the Supreme Court reasoned that, "the congressional aim of preventing a fiscal drain on the Social Security trust fund" was circumvented by the district court's requirement that benefits be extended to all retirees.

Ultimately, in a unanimous ruling, the Supreme Court re-confirmed its position regarding discrimination by rendering a decision that was historically and legally consistent with previous rulings. While the pension offset exception did temporarily restore gender-based classifications when awarding retiree benefits, discrimination was "directly and substantially" linked to an important government objective. Congress' only intent was to protect "individuals who planned their retirements in reasonable reliance on the law in effect" prior to the *Goldfarb* decision. Thus, the exception discriminated "not according to archaic generalizations" about gender roles, but on whether people planned their retirement expecting to receive Social Security benefits according to the law. Accordingly, the Supreme Court reversed the decision of the lower court and, tacitly, upheld the constitutionality of Social Security Act as amended by Congress in December of 1977.

Impact

In a series of 1977 rulings including *Goldfarb, Silbowitz*, and *Jablon*, the Supreme Court set into motion a public debate regarding the viability and future of retiree benefits as secured under the Social Security Act. Although the Court's decisions held gender discrimination as improper, its decisions also pushed Americans into making decisions about the priority of certain social values—one which society deemed fair, sexual equality, against the need to provide for retirees without bankrupting the system. Legislators grappled with the potential of a complete breakdown in the fiscal viability of the Social Security fund and the added pressure from retirees as voiced by the extremely strong lobby of the Association of Aged and Retired People. Their solution, a pension offset which would not take effect for five years, became an issue which eventually returned to the source of its instigation, the Supreme Court. The justices voted unanimously to uphold the amended language of the Social Security Act. Their unanimity, however, was not entirely self-motivated. While their decision averted a rift between the judiciary and legislative branches of government, the Court had maintained a consistency in their ruling which reflected historical Supreme Court jurisprudence. More importantly, their decision sought to define a perennial question which confronted and would continue to confront the Court in the years that followed. The issue revolved around the need to protect the rights of the minority and yet continue to sustain the will of the majority.

Related Cases

Simon v. Eastern Kentucky Welfare Rights Organization, 426 U.S. 26 (1976).

Califano v. Goldfarb, 430 U.S. 199 (1977).
Califano v. Silbowitz, 430 U.S. 924 (1977).
Jablon v. Califano, 430 U.S. 924 (1977).
Gladstone, Realtors v. Village of Bellwood, 441 U.S. 91 (1979).

Bibliography and Further Reading

Hall, Kermit L., ed. *The Oxford Companion to the Supreme Court of the United States.* New York: Oxford University Press, 1992.

BOARD OF DIRECTORS, ROTARY INTERNATIONAL V. ROTARY CLUB OF DUARTE

Legal Citation: 481 U.S. 587 (1987)

Petitioner

Board of Directors, Rotary International

Respondent
Rotary Club of Duarte

Petitioner's Claim
That a California law prohibiting gender discrimination in business organizations violates the First Amendment right to freedom of association.

Chief Lawyer for Petitioner
Judith Resnik

Chief Lawyer for Respondent
William P. Sutter

Justices for the Court
William J. Brennan, Jr., Thurgood Marshall, Lewis F. Powell, Jr. (writing for the Court), William H. Rehnquist, Antonin Scalia, John Paul Stevens, Byron R. White

Justices Dissenting
None (Harry A. Blackmun and Sandra Day O'Connor did not participate)

Place
Washington, D.C.

Date of Decision
4 May 1987

Decision
A California law requiring full and equal accommodations to both sexes in business establishments is constitutional and does not violate the First Amendment when applied to a broad-based business and professional organization.

Significance
The Court found that the law did not violate the right of club members to freedom of association. Further, that the organization in question had a broad and potentially large membership with high turnover, was inclusive by nature, frequently included strangers in its activities, and had a broad public purpose. Freedom of association goes to protect more intimate organizations, the Court said. The Court also found that the admission of women did not violate the First Amendment right of expressive association, since it would not affect the purpose of the club.

Local California Rotary Chapter Creates "International" Incident

California adopted a law, popularly called the Unruh Civil Rights Act, that entitled all persons, regardless of sex, to equal accommodations, facilities, privileges, advantages, and services in business establishments. The local Rotary Club of Duarte, California, admitted women members in 1977. Rotary International, its parent organization, revoked its charter because the organization's rules state membership is limited to men.

The Rotary Club of Duarte and two of its women members sued Rotary International under the Unruh Civil Rights Act, seeking an injunction to prevent the parent organization from enforcing the rules against women or revoking its charter. A California trial court found that neither Rotary International nor the Rotary Club of Duarte were business establishments under the law, and ruled for Rotary International. The Duarte club appealed, and the California Court of Appeals reversed, finding substantial business benefits in the Rotary organization. The appeal court also concluded that membership in Rotary clubs was not a "continuous, personal and social" relationship taking place primarily in private and that the admission of women would not interfere with the organization's purposes. It also found that the organization's exclusion of women was not protected by the First Amendment.

The California Supreme Court declined to hear the case. Subsequently Rotary International petitioned the U.S. Supreme Court for review, since the case involved a federal constitutional question. The U.S. Supreme Court affirmed the holding of the California Court of Appeals.

Membership Originally Open to Men Only

Rotary International was formed in 1905 as a worldwide organization of business and professional men who provided community service, promoted high ethical standards, and worked for world peace. Individual members join local Rotary Clubs, and those clubs belong to the international organization. At the time of the hearing before the Supreme Court in 1987, there were 19,788 Rotary Clubs with over 900,000 members in 157 countries.

Rotary Clubs invite members under a classification system listing different businesses and professions. An active member is elected for each category, and that member may propose a second member in the same field, so that each classification can have two active members. Each club may adopt other requirements for membership. Although the rules provide that membership can only be extended to men, the organization does allow female relatives of members to be active in affiliated organizations.

The Supreme Court applied the reasoning of *Roberts v. U.S. Jaycees* (1984), a case in which the Court upheld a Minnesota law requiring the Jaycees to admit women. In *Roberts,* the Court found that the Constitution protects citizens against unjustified government interference with their right to intimate or private relationships, and that it protects their right to associate for expressive association such as religion or protected speech. To determine an individual's right to join a particular organization requires an assessment of where the organization falls on a scale from private relationships to very public ones, the Court said. Factors such as "size, selectivity, and whether others are excluded from critical aspects of the relationship" are used to determine the extent of constitutional protection.

Court Found Female Membership Reduced Discrimination

"The evidence in this case indicates that the relationship among Rotary Club members is not the kind of intimate or private relation that warrants constitutional protection," the Court observed. It noted that local Rotary clubs range in size from 20 to more than 900, and that there is about a ten percent turnover each year. New prospects are regularly reviewed, and the club is supposed to include members so as to be a "true cross-section of the business and professional life of the community." Even though membership is not open to everyone, the Court found that large, inclusive membership was encouraged, and concluded that applying the Unruh Civil Rights Act and opening membership to women would not interfere with Rotary members' right to private association.

The Court also said that the admission of women would not prevent Rotary Clubs from carrying out their purposes. It noted that the organization does not take political stands, though it does engage in community service. The Court found nothing in the Unruh Civil Rights Act that would prevent the groups from continuing such services. And the Court further noted that "[e]ven if the Unruh [Civil Rights] Act does work some slight infringement on Rotary members' right of expressive association, that infringement is justified because it serves the state's compelling interest in eliminating discrimination against women." It went on to observe that in the *Roberts* case, "we recognized that the state's compelling interest in assuring equal access to women extends to the acquisition of leadership skills and business contacts, as well as tangible goods and services."

Related Cases
Roberts v. United States Jaycees, 468 U.S. 609 (1984).
Beynon v. St. George-Dixie Lodge No. 1783, Benev. & Protective Order of Elks, 854 P.2d 513 (1993).
South Boston Allied War Veterans Council v. City of Boston, 875 F.Supp. 891 (1995).

Bibliography and Further Reading
Baldwin, Gordon B. "The Library Bill of Rights—A Critique." *Library Trends,* summer 1996, p. 7.

Biskupic, Joan, and Elder Witt, eds. *Congressional Quarterly's Guide to the U.S. Supreme Court,* 3rd ed. Washington, DC: Congressional Quarterly, Inc., 1996.

AUTOMOBILE WORKERS V. JOHNSON CONTROLS

Legal Citation: 499 U.S. 187 (1991)

Petitioners
International Union, United Automobile, Aerospace, and Agricultural Implement Workers of America, UAW, et al.

Respondent
Johnson Controls, Inc.

Petitioners' Claim
That Johnson Controls' "fetal protection policy" is sex discrimination prohibited by the Pregnancy Discrimination Act (PDA).

Chief Lawyer for Petitioners
Marsha S. Berzon

Chief Lawyer for Respondent
Stanley S. Jaspan

Justices for the Court
Harry A. Blackmun (writing for the Court), Anthony M. Kennedy, Thurgood Marshall, Sandra Day O'Connor, William H. Rehnquist, Antonin Scalia, David H. Souter, John Paul Stevens, Byron R. White

Justices Dissenting
None

Place
Washington, D.C.

Date of Decision
20 March 1991

Decision
Johnson Controls' fetal protection policy was in violation of Title VII of the Civil Rights Act of 1964, as amended by the PDA.

Significance
This decision gave women the opportunity to make their own reasoned decisions about pregnancy and dangerous work.

Johnson Controls, Inc. manufactures batteries—a process that utilizes lead as a primary ingredient. Men's and women's exposure to lead may have a negative impact on health, including birth defects in children. Some studies have suggested lead exposure may affect fertility in both men and women.

Before the passage of Title VII of the Civil Rights Act of 1964, Johnson Controls hired men only. Title VII banned this practice. However, once women began working at the company in 1977, it issued an official policy regarding female exposure to lead:

> Since not all women who can become mothers wish to become mothers (or will become mothers), it would appear to be illegal discrimination to treat all who are capable of pregnancy as though they will become pregnant.

Johnson urged women not to apply for lead-exposed positions if they hoped to bear children. However, it made them eligible for this work provided they signed a statement that they understood the risks, including a higher than normal rate of miscarriage.

During the next five years, eight women with blood levels above 30 micrograms per deciliter—the level considered by the Occupational Safety and Health Administration (OSHA) to be the critical threshold for workers hoping to have children—became pregnant. None of the children born of these pregnancies had any apparent birth defects or abnormalities. Still, Johnson Controls decided to exclude women of childbearing age from lead-exposed jobs or positions from which one would be eligible for promotion to a lead-exposed job. The policy defined "women . . . capable of bearing children" as "all women except those whose inability to bear children is medically documented."

Women and Children First

Various unions filed a class-action lawsuit claiming that Johnson's fetal protection policy was sex discrimination. Some employees joined them: Mary Craig, a young woman who became sterilized rather than lose her job; Elsie Nason, a 50-year-old divorcee, who had to transfer to a lower-paying but lead-free position; and

---

Fetal Protection Policies

Fetal protection policies are workplace rules which prevent women from taking part in specific jobs if those women are of childbearing age and fertile. Long before *Johnson Controls*, the concept of fetal protection policies had become controversial, a fact due in part to the rise of the women's movement during the early 1970s. Because no such restrictions applied to male workers, these policies were thought to be sexual discrimination, and thus a violation of Title VII of the Civil Rights Act of 1964.

Source(s): *West's Encyclopedia of American Law.* St. Paul, MN: West Group, 1998.

Donald Penney, who had been denied leave of absence to lower his lead level before fathering a child.

In its 1985 opinion, the district court stressed there was every likelihood that exposure to lead placed a fetus at risk—as well as affected the reproductive abilities of would-be parents. However, the court thought the same amount of lead exposure would affect the fetus more.

Therefore, since the union and its employees had not offered an acceptable alternative policy to protect the fetus, the court found that the company's policy had been a "business necessity" and decided in favor of Johnson Controls. The defeated groups appealed.

Defining "Business Necessity"

The Court of Appeals for the Seventh Circuit asked three questions about fetal protection policies to determine whether they were business necessities. The questions covered whether there was a substantial health risk to the fetus, if that hazard to the fetus was transferred only through women, and whether there was "a less discriminatory alternative equally capable of preventing the health hazard to the fetus."

In 1989, the court found that there was no dispute about the first question—lead exposure did present a hazard to a fetus. On the question of whether the father transmitted a health risk to the fetus, the court ruled the evidence "at best, speculative and unconvincing." As for a less discriminatory plan, the court found that the union and its employees failed to present an alternative.

Johnson Controls' policy was a business necessity and, therefore, was not illegal discrimination. The court also decided that such policies could exclude women under the *bona fide* occupational qualification standard *(BFOQ)* exemption of Title VII, which allowed discrimination if gender was critical to the job. None of the other courts of appeals had held this, however, so the Supreme Court granted *certiorari* to resolve the conflict.

"Outright and Explicit" Discrimination

The opinion of the Supreme Court, delivered by Justice Blackmun, found Johnson Controls had discriminated against women: "The bias in Johnson Controls' policy is obvious. Fertile men, but not fertile women, are given a choice as to whether they wish to risk their reproductive health for a particular job."

The Court also held that the appeals court's application of the business necessity test was a mistake, because it "is more lenient for the employer" than the test required by Title VII. In an earlier decision, *Wards Cove Packing v. Atonio* (1989), the Supreme Court had ruled that the employee, and not the employer, bore the burden of proving a discriminatory policy was not a "business necessity." However, this "burden" was applicable only in cases where discrimination was a consequence of a neutral policy—never in cases of explicitly gender-based sex discrimination. To make his point clear, Blackmun quoted the Equal Employment Opportunity Commission (EEOC): "For the plaintiff to bear the burden of proof in a case in which there is direct evidence of a facially discriminatory policy is wholly inconsistent with settled Title VII law . . . *bona fide occupational qualification* is the better approach."

The *BFOQ* Considered

Title VII permitted an employer to discriminate on the basis of "religion, sex, or national origin" only when a genuine *BFOQ* existed that was "reasonably necessary to the normal operation of that particular business or enterprise." Johnson Controls argued that its safety concerns were "reasonably related" and that its fetal protection policy discriminated on the basis of a *BFOQ* of female sterility.

Blackmun conceded that *BFOQ*'s had sometimes been upheld due to safety concerns. Citing a decision in which an airline's mandatory retirement policy had withstood an age discrimination charge, he explained that the safety concerns had "involved the possibility that, because of age-connected debility, a flight engineer might not properly assist the pilot, and might thereby cause a safety emergency." He stressed, however, a danger must be related to "third parties . . . indispensable to the particular business at issue" to establish a *BFOQ*. Johnson Controls' policies were not.

None of Your Business

Recalling *Dothard v. Rawlinson* (1977), Blackmun wrote, "danger to a woman herself does not justify discrimination." Similarly, the risks a pregnant woman assumed on behalf of her fetus were not her employer's concern. On this point, Blackmun cited a number of lower court cases that upheld the layoffs of pregnant flight attendants "at different points during the first five months of pregnancy . . . to ensure the safety of passengers." Two of these opinions, he noted, "pointedly indicated that fetal, as opposed to passenger, safety was best left to the mother."

In 1978, the PDA provided that "women affected by pregnancy, childbirth, or related medical conditions shall be treated the same for all employment-related purposes . . ." The legislative history of the act confirmed that Congress intended to amend Title VII to prohibit employers from "requir[ing] a pregnant woman to stop working at any time during her pregnancy unless she is unable to do her work . . . Congress indicated that the employer may take into account only the woman's ability to get her job done."

Any decision regarding work prior to or during pregnancy, Blackmun concluded, "was reserved for each individual woman to make for herself." The Court dismissed Johnson Controls' more general argument that its "moral and ethical concerns about the welfare of the next generation . . . suffice[d] to establish a BFOQ of female sterility." Such decisions, Blackmun said, "must be left to the parents . . . rather than the employers . . . Title VII and the PDA simply do not allow a woman's dismissal because of her failure to submit to sterilization."

It is Up to the Women

A question still remained for Johnson Controls about the company's liability if fertile women were not excluded from hazardous work. Blackmun conceded that more than 40 states permitted lawsuits to recover for prenatal injuries. However, the right to recover in the cases was uniformly based on negligence or on wrongful death. Johnson Controls had the power, to "comply with the lead standard developed by OSHA and warn its female employees about the damaging effects of lead."

Therefore, Blackmun rejected the tort liability claim, saying: "If . . . Title VII bans sex-specific fetal protection policies, the employer fully informs the women of the risk, and the employer has not acted negligently, the basis for holding an employer liable seems remote at best."

Perhaps anticipating a mixed reaction to this decision, Blackmun concluded that "our holding today that Title VII, as so amended . . . is neither remarkable nor unprecedented. Concern for a woman's existing or potential offspring historically has been the excuse for denying women equal employment opportunities . . . It is no more appropriate for the courts than it is for individual employers to decide whether a woman's reproductive role is more important to herself and her family than her economic role. Congress has left this choice to the woman as hers to make."

Related Cases

Ward's Cove Packing v. Atonio, 490 U.S. 642 (1989).
Radovanic v. Centex Real Estate Corporation, 767 F.Supp. 1322 (W.D.N.C. 1991).
Krauel v. Iowa Methodist Medical Center, 95 F.3d 674 (1996).

Bibliography and Further Reading

Faludi, Susan. *Backlash: The Undeclared War Against American Women*. New York: Crown Publishers, 1991.

Hearit, Keith Michael. "On the Use of Transcendence as an Apologia Strategy" *Public Relations Review*, fall 1997, p. 217.

Hoff, Joan. *Law, Gender and Injustice: A Legal History of U.S. Women*. New York: New York University Press, 1991.

Rosen, Ruth. "What Feminist Victory in the Court?" *New York Times*, April 1, 1991.

UNITED STATES V. VIRGINIA

Legal Citation: 518 U.S. 515 (1996)

Petitioner
United States

Respondents
Commonwealth of Virginia, Governor Lawrence Douglas Wilder; Virginia Military Institute, et al.

Petitioner's Claim
That the male-only admissions policy of the state-supported Virginia Military Institute (V.M.I.) violated the Fourteenth Amendment.

Chief Lawyer for Petitioner
Paul Bender, U.S. Deputy Solicitor General

Chief Lawyer for Respondent
Theodore B. Olsen

Justices for the Court
Stephen Breyer, Ruth Bader Ginsburg (writing for the Court), Anthony M. Kennedy, Sandra Day O'Connor, William H. Rehnquist, David H. Souter, John Paul Stevens

Justices Dissenting
Antonin Scalia (Clarence Thomas did not participate)

Place
Washington D.C.

Date of Decision
26 June 1996

Decision
Excluding women from state-supported schools was a violation of the Fourteenth Amendment.

Significance
The last two state-supported all-male colleges were forced to admit women or forego state funding.

The U.S. Supreme Court has long grouped race, national origin, and religion as "inherently suspect" classifications for Fourteenth Amendment purposes—meaning that any legislation targeting these groups must pass a "strict scrutiny" test. This test determines if the proposed law serves a compelling state interest that cannot be served by any other means. Legislation discriminated on the basis of sex, however, has never been found inherently suspect by the Court.

In 1995, it seemed this might change. President Bill Clinton instructed his administration to file a brief asking the U.S. Supreme Court to use *United States v. Commonwealth of Virginia* "as a vehicle for declaring that government actions that discriminate on the basis of sex should be subject to the same strict constitutional scrutiny the Court applies to official distinctions on the basis of race."

Virginia governor L. Douglas Wilder had said that the refusal of the Virginia Military Institute (V.M.I.) to admit women offended his "personal philosophy." He added that "no person should be denied admittance to a state-supported school because of his or her gender." Since he agreed to abide by the court decision, he did not participate in the suit. The state attorney general, also agreeing to abide by the court's ruling, withdrew as well—leaving a *pro bono* counsel to seek a "stay of proceedings" on behalf of Virginia and the governor.

Sex Discrimination at V.M.I.

On 1 March 1990, the U.S. Department of Justice sued V.M.I. after a female high school student complained of the school's all-male admissions policy. In the two years prior to this complaint, approximately 300 young women had had their inquiries rebuffed by the institute.

The United States contended that V.M.I.'s exclusion of women violated the Equal Protection Clause of the Fourteenth Amendment and the precedent established in *Mississippi University for Women v. Hogan* (1982). In that case, the Supreme Court ruled that men could not be excluded from Mississippi's state-supported nursing college.

During a six day trial, the district court examined the 150-year history of the institution, which was founded in 1839 by the Virginia legislature to produce "citizen-soldiers, educated and honorable men who are suited for leadership in civilian life and who can provide military leadership when necessary." The court also looked at the "adversative" method used to produce these "citizen-soldiers." The training "emphasizes physical rigor, mental stress, absolute equality of treatment, absence of privacy, minute regulation of behavior, and indoctrination of values . . . designed to foster in V.M.I. cadets doubts about previous beliefs and experiences and to instill in cadets new values . . . [in] a hostile, spartan environment . . ."

In 1991, the district court ruled that "diversity in education" was a legitimate state interest. Both V.M.I.'s male-only admissions policy and its "distinctive educational methods" were substantially related to this legitimate state. Therefore, V.M.I.'s exclusion of women was upheld. The United States appealed.

History Repeats Itself

Circuit Court judge Paul V. Niemeyer delivered the opinion of the Fourth Circuit Court of Appeals on 5 October 1992. He noted that in May of 1864, during the Civil War, V.M.I. cadets bravely fought Union troops at New Market, Virginia. Now, he said, "the combatants have again confronted each other, but this time the venue is in this court." He pointed out that:

> the outcome of each confrontation finds resolution in the Equal Protection Clause. When the Civil War was over, to assure the abolition of slavery and the federal government's supervision over that policy, *all* states, north and south, yielded substantial sovereignty to the federal government in the ratification of the Fourteenth Amendment, and every state for the first time was expressly directed by federal authority not to deny any *person* within the state's jurisdiction "equal protection of the laws." The [United States] government now relies on this clause to attack V.M.I.'s admissions policy.

A Catch-22

The court ruled that the exclusion of women from the type of education provided at V.M.I. violated the Equal Protection Clause, but it also found that single-gender enrollment formed the basis of "the unique characteristics of V.M.I.'s program." But admitting women would so change V.M.I. that their admission would destroy the "unique characteristics" women sought. Therefore, Virginia's violation of the Fourteenth Amendment did not necessarily lay in its failure to admit women to V.M.I. Rather, the violation lay in its failure to provide

Shannon Faulkner, 1994. © AP/Wide World Photos.

women with an equal opportunity to develop the leadership and other skills developed by men at the school.

Niemeyer wrote that the court would "not order that women be admitted to V.M.I. if alternatives are available" but would instead remand the case to the district court "to give to the commonwealth the responsibility to select a course it chooses, so long as the guarantees of the Fourteenth Amendment are satisfied."

Among the means of bringing V.M.I. into compliance with the Fourteenth Amendment, Niemeyer suggested that Virginia "might properly decide to admit women to V.M.I. and adjust the program to implement that choice, or it might establish parallel institutions or parallel programs, or it might abandon state support of V.M.I., leaving V.M.I. the option to pursue its own policies as a private institution."

V.M.I. requested a hearing *en banc,* or by the full circuit court, which was denied. Virginia and V.M.I. subsequently established a state-funded military-style program for women at Mary Baldwin College, a private women's college in Staunton, Virginia. The program was approved by the federal court and began operation in the summer of 1995. Virginia nonetheless appealed the federal circuit court ruling to the Supreme Court, which agreed to hear the case.

A New Look to the Court

Ruth Bader Ginsburg, a recent appointee to the Supreme Court, shared the president's desire to establish a strict scrutiny standard for sex discrimination. As a civil rights lawyer in the 1970s, Ginsburg had helped to win the first women's rights case by using the Fourteenth Amendment, *Reed v. Reed* (1971). In the 1973 case *Frontiero v. Richardson,* she had come within one vote of persuading the Court to adopt the strict scrutiny standard in sex discrimination cases. She also had helped to win a case in 1976 establishing the alternate "mid-level or *heightened*" scrutiny standard adopted for sex discrimination cases in *Craig v. Boren.*

On 26 June 1996, the Court ruled 7-1 that V.M.I. must either forgo state funding or admit women. The opinion, written by Ginsburg, stopped short of establishing a strict scrutiny standard for sex discrimination. However, it thoroughly reviewed and perhaps strengthened the just-short of strict standard the court demanded. Ginsburg first repeated the Court's ruling in previous cases that sex discrimination must "serve important governmental objectives" and be "substantially related to the achievement of those objectives" Then she added some specifics:

> The justification must be genuine, not hypothesized or invented post hoc in response to litigation. And it must not rely on overboard generalizations about the different talents, capacities, or preferences of males and females . . . "Inherent differences" between men and women, we have come to appreciate, remain cause for celebration, but not for denigration of the members of either sex or for artificial constraints on an individual's opportunity. Sex classifications may be used to compensate women "for particular economic disabilities (they have) suffered," to "promot(e) equal employment opportunity," and to advance full development of the talent and capacities of our nation's people. But such classifications may not be used, as they once were, to create or perpetuate the legal, social and economic inferiority of women.

Weighing the facts in this case "against the review standard just described," the Court agreed with the Fourth Circuit that the all-male admission policy of the state-supported school violated the Fourteenth Amendment. The supposed state goal of offering educational diversity, Ginsburg said, was not served by a plan that provided "a unique educational benefit only to males." Such a plan, she continued, while "liberally" providing for "the State's sons . . . makes no provisions whatever for her daughters. That is not equal protection." She also brushed aside Virginia's argument that V.M.I.'s program would be "destroy(ed)" if women were admitted. This was reminiscent of the same "ancient and familiar fear" that had long kept women out of the legal and other professions, she said—and possibly just as misguided. "Women's successful entry into the Federal military academies," she wrote, "and their participation in the nation's military forces, indicate that Virginia's fears for the future of V.M.I. may not be solidly grounded."

Turning to the Fourth Circuit's approval of a parallel program for females at the Mary Baldwin College, Ginsburg called it a "pale shadow" of V.M.I.'s illustrious and famed schooling. It was not a program most women would choose to join, she acknowledged. But "generalizations about the way women are, estimates of what is appropriate for most women, no longer justify denying opportunity to women whose talent and capacity place them outside the average description." She said V.M.I. was for the select few of either sex by pointing out that Virginia had never tried to claim the program "suited most men."

Ginsburg cited many precedent-setting cases during the reading of her opinion. Many of them, she had argued before the court as a pioneering feminist lawyer. One case in which she was not involved, *Mississippi University for Women v. Hogan* (1982) was the first to prompt a decision that a state could not fund sex-segregated schools. Sandra Day O'Connor, the only other female justice, wrote that decision in 1982. On the morning of 26 June 1996, Ginsburg cited *Hogan,* and than stopped speaking to look toward O'Connor. O'Connor smiled, just a little, and Ginsburg continued reading her opinion: "Women seeking and fit for a V.M.I. quality education cannot be offered anything less under the State's obligation to afford the genuinely equal protection."

Justice Rehnquist issued a concurring opinion. He said he might have been persuaded to let a truly equal parallel program suffice and that he thought the majority decision had needlessly introduced new legal terminology. Justice Antonin Scalia wholeheartedly dissented from the entire decision.

The decision has forced V.M.I. and the Citadel, the last two state-supported, all-male colleges in the country, to admit women or forego public funding. Two days after the ruling, Citadel officials said they would admit women, while V.M.I. officials simply said they "must discourage" speculation that they would be able to keep out women. Four female cadets entered the Citadel in August of 1996—under much calmer circumstances than did Shannon Faulkner one year earlier. Faulkner had been embroiled in a legal fight, had been the only woman on campus, and had been ignored and taunted by male students at the Citadel—she became ill as a result of the stress and dropped out.

Related Cases

Reed v. Reed, 404 U.S. 71 (1971).
Frontiero v. Richardson, 411 U.S. 677 (1973).

Craig v. Boren, 429 U.S. 190 (1976).
Mississippi University for Women v. Hogan, 458 U.S. 718 (1982).

Bibliography and Further Reading
Coyle, Marcia. "Court Asks Why VMI Must Stay Stag." *The National Law Journal,* January 29, 1996, p. A14.

Coyle, Marcia. "High Court Goes for Skeptical Scrutiny on Gender." *The National Law Journal,* July 8, 1996, p. A12.

Elshtain, Jean Bethke. *Women and War.* New York: Basic Books, 1987.

Hellman, Deborah. "Two Types of Discrimination: The Familiar and the Forgotten." *California Law Review,* March 1998, p. 315.

Lovell, Amy. "Other Students Always Used to Say, 'Look at the Dykes': Protecting Students from Peer Sexual Orientation Harassment." *California Law Review,* May 1998, p. 617.

New York Times, April 4, 1991; April 24, 1991; June 18-19, 1991; August 13, 1992; October 6, 1992; October 14, 1992; November 19, 1992; September 26, 1993;

October 13, 1993; June 1, 1995; December 27, 1995; January 18, 1996; June 27-28, 1996.

Sadker, Myra, and David Sadker. *Failing at Fairness: How America's Schools Cheat Girls.* New York: Charles Scribners Sons, 1994.

Salomone, Rosemary C. "The VMI Case: Affirmation of Equal Educational Opportunity for Women." *Trial,* October 1996, p. 67.

Samborn, Hope Viner. "Scrutiny Scrutinized; Case Sparks Debate on Intermediate Standard." *ABA Journal,* September 1996, p. 29.

Skaggs, Jason M. "Justifying Gender-Based Affirmative Action Under United States v. Virginia's 'Exceedingly Persuasive Justification' Standard." *California Law Review,* October 1998, p. 1169.

Smith, Bruce. "No Easy Ride Predicted as Women Enter Citadel." *Detroit News,* August 25, 1996.

Sullivan, Kathleen M. "Decisions Expand Equal Protection Rights." *The National Law Journal,* July 29, 1996, p. C7.

Widiss, Deborah A. "Re-viewing History: The Use of the Past as Negative Precedent in United States v. Virginia." *Yale Law Journal,* October 1998, p. 237.

IMMIGRANTS' RIGHTS

Background and Overview

From the founding of the United States to the late 1990s, some 55 million immigrants have come to the country, according to the American Civil Liberties Union (ACLU). Furthermore, not including Native Americans, everyone in the United States is an immigrant or the descendant of immigrants. The Statue of Liberty bears the inscribed invitation "Give us your tired, your poor, your huddled masses yearning to breathe free" as a testament to the country's commitment to immigration and the role it has played and continues to play in the development of the country. Despite its foundation on immigration, calls for tougher immigration laws and restrictions on immigrants' rights have rung out periodically throughout the country's history, especially in times of economic and social turmoil. For example, mobs used Irish Catholic immigrants as scapegoats during the depression of the 1840s and persecuted them, burning a convent in Boston and starting a riot in Philadelphia. In addition, many immigrants were deported in the 1920s during the communist scare for simply being suspected of holding views akin to communism without any hearing. Also, Japanese immigrants had their homes and property confiscated and were held in camps until the end of World War II.

Each year, the country admits approximately 800,000 legal immigrants wishing to settle in the United States as permanent residents. This number includes 400,000 who join close family members who are already legal immigrants in the United States, 140,000 people who will fill jobs for which the U.S. Bureau of Labor finds a shortage of U.S. workers, and 110,000 refugees who have demonstrated persecution in their homelands. The Immigration and Naturalization Service estimated the number of undocumented immigrants that enter the country each year is about 275,000 or less than 1 percent of the population.

Immigrants generally are entitled to many of the rights native-born citizens enjoy. The Constitution and the Bill of Rights provide alien immigrants with the same rights as U.S. citizens, although they cannot vote or hold federal elective offices unless they become citizens. Through the Equal Protection Clause of the Fourteenth Amendment, immigrants are protected from many state laws and regulations that violate their rights guaranteed by the Constitution. Depending on their status, immigrants may or may not have to pay taxes: resident immigrants must pay taxes, while nonresident immigrants often qualify for tax exemptions.

Although it is a crime to enter the country unlawfully and punishable by deportation, the U.S. Supreme Court has ruled on many occasions that once in the country immigrants have the right to a hearing that satisfies the Due Process Clause of the Fourteenth Amendment. As early as 1903 in *Yamataya v. Fisher,* the Court has upheld this right of immigrants, whether legal or illegal. Because of cases such as *Yamataya v. Fisher,* immigrants generally are entitled to a hearing before an immigration judge and review by a federal judge, representation by a lawyer, reasonable notice of charges, reasonable time to examine evidence, interpretation for non-English speakers, and straightforward and convincing proof that the government has valid reasons for deportation, according to the American Civil Liberties Union (ACLU).

Key Legislation

The Immigration Reform and Control Act (IRCA) of 1986 put in place a series of requirements aimed at reducing the number of undocumented immigrants in the country. The IRCA's primary method of achieving this goal included imposing penalties on employers who willingly hired illegal immigrants. In addition, the IRCA contained specific provisions responding to the dependence of seasonal agriculture on immigrant labor.

The Immigration Act of 1990, on the other hand, mainly dealt with establishing limits on the number of legal immigrants admitted each year and creating provisions for admitting more immigrants from underrepresented countries. As a result, the number of immigrants admitted to fill jobs became limited to 140,000. The act also contained a preference system for determining which immigrants to admit, favoring immigrants seeking to be reunited with their families, those filling jobs, and those contributing to the greater diversity of the country.

The Illegal Immigration Reform and Immigrant Responsibility Act of 1996 (IIRIRA) contained a variety of measures designed to prevent the escalation of illegal immigrants and to expedite the deportation of illegal immigrants. Ultimately, some of these measures provoked intense debate over whether they were constitutional. Some of its key provisions include increasing the size of the Border Patrol by the year 2001, restricting the admission of previously deported illegal immigrants, limiting legal review and appeals for immigrants convicted of crimes, and increasing the size of immigrant detention centers.

Landmark Cases

In many cases, the U.S. Supreme Court has held that only Congress is empowered to enact immigrant law. However, throughout the country's history, various states have tried to limit immigrant rights. The Supreme Court often has ruled against such discriminatory laws over the years. For example, in *Yick Wo v. Hopkins* (1886), the Supreme Court found that the Fourteenth Amendment's guarantee of equal protection applied to citizens as well as to immigrants. In this case, San Francisco relied on an ordinance restricting laundry businesses from operating in certain kinds of buildings to ban Chinese-owned laundries. Yick Wo had run a laundry in the city for 22 years in the same building, but was denied a new license in 1885—along with numerous other laundry operations of Chinese immigrants—because of alleged violations of a safety ordinance prohibiting laundry businesses from occupying wooden buildings. However, the Court discovered that of the city's 320 laundries, 310 were constructed of wood and only the laundries run by Chinese immigrants (240) were denied new licenses, while the remaining laundries stood to benefit from the discriminatory enforcement of the ordinance. Justice Matthews, writing for the majority, found that while the ordinance itself violated no one's rights, the enforcement of it clearly drew "an arbitrary line, on one side of which [were] those who [were] permitted to pursue their industry by the mere will and consent of the supervisors, and on the other those from whom that consent [was] withheld, at their mere will and pleasure."

The U.S. Supreme Court echoed the tenor of this decision in 1971, ruling in *Graham v. Richardson* that legal immigrants could not be refused welfare benefits from the states. This case also signaled that equal protection cases would be subject to the same thorough review that racial discrimination cases receive. Here, the Court found state statutes denying welfare benefits to resident immigrants and to immigrants who had not resided in the country for a certain number of years unconstitutional. The Court determined that such statutes undercut and interfered with the federal government's exclusive power over immigrant affairs. Through a number of following decisions, the Court banned many restrictive state laws that violated the

rights of immigrants, eliminating statutes that prevented immigrants from obtaining competitive civil service employment, engineering licenses, and licenses to practice law.

However, the U.S. Supreme Court's stance softened in the late 1970s and 1980s, as it upheld New York's restrictive policies denying teacher certification to alien immigrants in *Ambach v. Norwick* (1979). The Court found that the state's policy not to grant permanent public school teacher certification to immigrants with an alien status unless they intended to apply for citizenship did not violate the Fourteenth Amendment's Equal Protection Clause. The Court reasoned that since previous decisions had banned alien immigrants from holding public employment or limited their holding of public positions, New York's policy did not violate the Equal Protection Clause. Similarly, the Court upheld California's law preventing alien immigrants from serving as probation officers in *Cabell v. Chavez-Salido* (1982). The Court held that "a citizenship requirement is an appropriate limitation on those who exercise and, therefore, symbolize this power of the political community over those who fall within its jurisdiction."

Nevertheless, the Court shifted its position again in the 1982 case *Plyler v. Doe*, ruling that the children of undocumented immigrants have the right to attend public schools. Texas adopted a policy of prohibiting the children of undocumented immigrants from receiving a public school education. However, the Court found that although illegal immigrants and their children are not citizens, they still are entitled to the Fourteenth Amendment's protections. Because the state law greatly limited the potential of these children by refusing them education and because the state could not demonstrate that the law served a "compelling state interest," the Court declared it unconstitutional.

Current Issues in Immigrants' Rights

Immigration policies and immigrants' rights came under attack in the mid- to late-1990s as California adopted laws that would restrict public services such as public school education and non-emergency health care to illegal aliens and require immigrant students to learn English. California voters passed the controversial Proposition 187 in 1994. The bill's supporters contended that undocumented immigrants cost the state billions of dollars in public services annually.

In addition, several members of Congress, including House Speaker Newt Gingrich, proposed making English the country's national language, which force immigrants to learn and use English. Moreover, Congress passed welfare reform legislation (Personal Responsibility and Work Opportunity Reconciliation Act of 1996) that cut Medicaid, Supplementary Security Income, and federal food stamps to legal immigrants. Although Congress approved an extension of Medicaid and Supplementary Security Income to about 500,000 immigrants who entered the country legally prior to the adoption of the welfare reform policies, it failed to pass any bills for permanently providing minor, elderly, and disabled legal immigrants with Medicaid and Supplementary Security Income by mid-1998. Therefore, the ACLU, the state of Florida, and various organizations took steps to restore such benefits to legal immigrants by suing the Social Security Administration in cases such as *Sutich v. Callahan* (1997) and challenging California's immigrant laws in cases such as *League of United Latin American Citizens v. Pete Wilson* (1997).

Furthermore, members of Congress eyed Proposition 187 as a possible national solution to illegal immigration. In 1996, Congress debated passing the Gallegly amendment, a national law that would deny children of illegal immigrants public education and other public services. Although Congress finally dropped the amendment from an immigrant bill it sent to the president, some members continued to push for such legislation as a separate bill in the late 1990s.

Despite its concessions, the Illegal Immigration Reform and Immigrant Responsibility Act of 1996 still contained a number of controversial measures, including one that made deporting both documented and undocumented immigrants easier and one that deprived federal judges of the power to review deportation cases and grant deportation waivers. However, U.S. District Court Judge Jack B. Weinstein heard a case brought before the court by American Civil Liberties Union that disputed this interpretation of the Immigrant Act and concluded that federal courts still held the power to review deportation cases and grant waivers.

See also: **Civil Rights and Equal Protection**

Bibliography and Further Reading

American Civil Liberties Union. "The Rights of Immigrants." Fall 1997. Available from http://www.aclu.org/library/pbp20htm.

Anderson, George M. "Fortress North America: The New Immigration Law." *America*, 9 May 1998, 3.

"A Time for Congressional Compassion to Immigrants." *National Catholic Reporter*, 10 October 1997, 24.

Conniff, Ruth. "Going Hungry." *The Progressive*, July 1998, 9.

Federation for American Immigration Reform. "U.S. Immigration History." July 1996. Available from http://www.fairus.org.

FindLaw. "FindLaw:Internet Legal Resources." 1998. Available from http://www.findlaw.com.

"No Justice for Immigrants." *The Progressive*, November 1997, 8.

Peart, Karen N. "English Spoken Here: Should Schools and Street Signs Be in English Only?" *Scholastic Update*, 15 November 1996, 7.

West's Encyclopedia of American Law. St. Paul, Minnesota: West Publishing, 1998.

TRUAX V. RAICH

Legal Citation: 239 U.S. 33 (1915)

Appellants
William Truax, Sr., Wiley E. Jones, W. G. Gilmore

Appellee
Mike Raich

Appellants' Claim
That a U.S. district court erred in preventing enforcement of Arizona's Anti-Alien Act.

Chief Lawyers for Appellants
Wiley E. Jones, Leslie C. Hardy, George W. Harben

Chief Lawyers for Appellee
Alexander Britton, Evans Browne, Francis W. Clements

Justices for the Court
Louis D. Brandeis, William Rufus Day, Oliver Wendell Holmes, Charles Evans Hughes (writing for the Court), Joseph McKenna, Mahlon Pitney, Willis Van Devanter, Edward Douglass White

Justices Dissenting
James Clark McReynolds

Place
Washington, D.C.

Date of Decision
1 November 1915

Decision
Against the appellants, affirming the district court's injunction against enforcement of Arizona's law.

Significance
By declaring Arizona's law unconstitutional, the Supreme Court established the right to earn a living as a basic freedom not to be withheld from resident aliens.

The Anti-Alien Law

When Mike Raich was in danger of losing his job at the Bisbee, Arizona restaurant where he worked as a cook, it had nothing to do with his abilities as a chef. The Austrian-born Raich was the victim of a 1914 Arizona law requiring all businesses with five or more employees to hire a work force that was at least 80 percent native-born American.

Arizona's Anti-Alien Employment Act first appeared before voters in a statewide public referendum. When the measure passed, Raich's boss, William Truax warned the cook that keeping him on would mean $100 fines and 30 days in jail for both of them. Truax told Raich that he could expect to be fired as soon as the act became law.

On 15 December 1914, the day after the act was signed into law, Raich filed a suit in Arizona's U.S. district court, charging that the act denied his Fourteenth Amendment right to equal protection under the law. Arizona Attorney General Wiley E. Jones, Cochise County Attorney W. G. Gilmore, and William Truax were named as defendants. Raich was not alone in his anger over the bill. Formal protests were lodged by the English and Italian embassies, whose governments sensed that the terms of the law represented an abrogation of international treaties. The Japanese government, whose citizens were the specific targets of xenophobic American laws, took its concerns to the U.S. State Department.

Raich's suit resulted in a temporary court order preventing Truax from dismissing the cook. When the county attorney's office learned that Truax was forbidden to fire Raich under the restraining order, Gilmore's office had Truax arrested for violating the Anti-Alien Act. The arrest appeared to be a legal formality, for Gilmore, Truax, and Jones joined in asking for a dismissal of Raich's suit against them. On 7 January 1915, however, a federal district court in San Francisco ruled that Arizona's Anti-Alien Law was unconstitutional. The special three-judge tribunal made permanent the temporary restraining order against Raich's dismissal. Thus prevented from enforcing the Arizona law, the defendants appealed to the U.S. Supreme Court.

The Right to Earn a Living

In presenting their case before the Court, the appellants did not bother disputing Raich's allegation that his Fourteenth Amendment rights had been infringed. Instead, they challenged the suit on other grounds. Raich, they claimed, had no right to sue the state of Arizona nor should his suit be allowed to prevent the enforcement of a criminal statute. It was also argued that the facts of the case did not constitute grounds for Raich to bring a civil lawsuit, a "suit in equity," in what was essentially a criminal matter.

When the Court delivered its decision on 1 November 1915, Justice Hughes' written opinion succinctly disposed of the appellants' claims. By naming Truax, Jones, and Gilmore as defendants, Justice Hughes pointed out that Raich had not sued the state of Arizona. Rather, the suit was directed at Jones and Gilmore as officers of a state attempting to interfere with Raich's employment through an unconstitutional law. As for the characterization of Raich's employment as a criminal matter and therefore inappropriate for consideration by "a court of equity," Justice Hughes wrote that civil lawsuits were proper if they sought to prevent prosecutions under unconstitutional laws. Furthermore, the Court defined the right to earn a living as a property right, which was plainly an appropriate issue for consideration in such a suit.

Justice McReynolds dissented, commenting that the Eleventh Amendment prohibition against federal courts meddling in the enforcement of state criminal statutes should apply. To the majority of the Court, however, the Fourteenth Amendment was more applicable to the Raich controversy. Justice Hughes pointed out that the power to regulate immigration and the admittance of aliens to the United States was reserved for the federal government, not the states. In the 1886 *Yick Wo v. Hopkins* decision, the Court had held that the protections of the Fourteenth Amendment extended equal protection of American laws to any foreigner who legally entered the United States. Local statutes could be enacted to protect the health, safety, morals, and welfare of state citizens. Such laws could not, however, interfere with the ordinary right to earn a livelihood.

"It requires no argument to show that the right to work for a living in the common occupations of the community is of the very essence of the personal freedom and opportunity that it was the purpose of the Fourteenth Amendment to secure," wrote Justice Hughes. "If this could be refused solely upon the basis of race or nationality the prohibition of the denial to any person of the equal protection of the laws would be a barren form of words."

Arizona's Anti-Alien Law was finished, but William Truax's problems with his employees were far from over. Only a year after the *Raich* decision, Truax sued his

Justice Charles Evans Hughes. © Archive Photos.

kitchen staff for joining a local Cooks & Waiters Union boycott, claiming they were wrecking his business by picketing his restaurant. The suit wound up before the Supreme Court as the 1921 *Truax v. Corrigan* case.

Related Cases

Yick Wo v. Hopkins, 118 U.S. 356 (1886).
Truax v. Corrigan, 257 U.S. 312 (1921).

Bibliography and Further Reading

"Anti-Alien Law Declared Void." *New York Times,* November 2, 1915, p. 7.

"Arizona Alien Law Void." *New York Times,* January 8, 1915, p. 1.

Hall, Kermit L., ed. *The Oxford Companion to the Supreme Court Of The United States.* New York: Oxford University Press, 1992.

Kurland, Phillip B., and Gerhard Casper, ed. *Landmark Briefs and Arguments of the Supreme Court of the United States,* Vol. 17. Arlington: University Publications of America, 1975.

Witt, Elder. *Congressional Quarterly's Guide to the U.S. Supreme Court,* 2nd ed. Washington, DC: Congressional Quarterly, 1990.

PEREZ V. BROWNELL

Legal Citation: 356 U.S. 44 (1958)

Petitioner
Clemente Martinez Perez

Respondent
Herbert Brownell, Jr.

Petitioner's Claim
That Congress exceeded its authority in enacting certain sections of the Nationality Act of 1940, which were used to deny petitioner his U.S. citizenship.

Chief Lawyer for Petitioner
Charles A. Horsky

Chief Lawyers for Respondent
Oscar H. Davis; J. Lee Rankin, U.S. Solicitor General

Justices for the Court
William J. Brennan, Jr., Harold Burton, Tom C. Clark, Felix Frankfurter (writing for the Court), John Marshall Harlan II

Justices Dissenting
Hugo Lafayette Black, William O. Douglas, Earl Warren, Charles Evans Whittaker

Place
Washington, D.C.

Date of Decision
31 March 1958

Decision
Petitioner's claim denied.

Significance
Citing Congress's implied power to direct foreign affairs, the Court said the legislature could expatriate U.S. citizens who voted in another country's elections. Some voluntary actions that Congress deemed harmful to the country were sufficient grounds for revoking U.S. citizenship.

Until 1868, the U.S. Constitution did not explicitly spell out who was an American citizen. The Fourteenth Amendment, ratified that year, granted U.S. citizenship and its benefits to "all persons born or naturalized in the United States." The Constitution, in Article I, Section 8, also gave Congress the power to regulate the naturalization process, but it did not mention how—or if—Congress could take away the right of citizenship. Congress, however, did recognize that Americans could voluntarily renounce their citizenship, and the Supreme Court found some instances in which certain acts—such as marrying a foreigner and moving to the spouse's homeland—amounted to a voluntary expatriation. But, was voting in a foreign election one of those voluntary acts? That question was at the crux of *Perez v. Brownell.*

Clemente Perez was born in El Paso, Texas, in 1909, making him an American citizen. When Perez was 10 or 11, his parents moved to Mexico; only some years later did they tell him he was an American citizen. Perez lived in Mexico until 1943, when he reentered the United States as an alien worker. Perez did not want to admit he was a U.S. citizen; since World War II was underway, he would have had to register for the draft. As an American, Perez should have returned to register when the war broke out, a provision of the Nationality Act of 1940. Not registering was punishable by loss of citizenship. Instead, Perez shuttled between America and Mexico through 1944, always claiming to be a native-born Mexican.

After the war, Perez tried to enter El Paso as an American citizen. During several immigration hearings, Perez admitted that he had deliberately avoided military service during World War II. He also revealed he had voted in Mexican elections. Under the Nationality Act, this was also grounds for losing citizenship. The government ruled Perez had expatriated himself and ordered him out of the country.

Perez made one more try to reclaim his citizenship. In 1952 he entered America as an immigrant worker. When immigration officials picked him up the next year, his visa was no longer valid. To avoid deportation, Perez again asserted his American citizenship and again he was rebuked. Perez then took the matter to court, but both the U.S. District Court and Ninth Court of Appeals denied Perez's suit to restore his nationality. The U.S. Supreme Court then agreed to hear the case to address its constitutional issues.

Congress Can Seek to Limit "Embarrassing" Actions

The Court voted 5-4 to deny Perez's claim. According to Justice Frankfurter's decision, the first key point was Congress's authority to pass the Nationality Act. Frankfurter said the Constitution does not specifically grant Congress the power to regulate foreign affairs, but through its legislative duties Congress can "deal affirmatively with foreign nations" or "reduce to a minimum the frictions that are unavoidable in a world of sovereigns . . ." Passing the Nationality Act was a valid use of congressional power.

Next, Frankfurter examined whether preventing Americans from voting in foreign elections was a legitimate use of that power. (In its decision, the Court only focused on Perez's voting in Mexico, not his attempt to avoid military service). It was, since:

> . . . the activities of the citizens of one nation when in another country can easily cause serious embarrassments to the government of their own country as well as to their fellow citizens. We cannot deny to Congress the reasonable belief that these difficulties might well become acute, to the point of jeopardizing the successful conduct of international relations, when the citizen of one country chooses to participate in the political or governmental affairs of another country. The citizen may by his action unwittingly promote or encourage a course of conduct contrary to the interests of his own government.

Lastly, the Court found that the punishment of expatriation fit the act committed, even if by voting in a foreign land a citizen did not intend to give up his citizenship. "The termination of citizenship terminates the problem."

Fourteenth Amendment Guarantee in Jeopardy

In a dissent joined by Justices William Douglas and Hugo Black, Chief Justice Earl Warren stressed that the Fourteenth Amendment granted citizenship to everyone born or naturalized in this country. That right was the basis of all others and could not be taken away. While acknowledging a person's right to voluntarily renounce his citizenship, Warren did not consider voting in a foreign country necessarily harmful. Elections occur for many reasons, and Congress was too broadly insistent that by voting in any foreign election, Americans were in effect renouncing their citizenship.

Historically, until 1928, America had allowed aliens to vote in presidential elections. Before that, 22 states had given aliens the right to vote. By allowing this, Warren argued, the nation did not assume aliens had given up allegiance to their homelands. "How then can we attach such significance to any vote of a United States citizen in a foreign election?"

Almost a decade later, the minority's concerns about unfairly denying citizenship arose again. *Afroyim v. Rusk* (1967) involved a naturalized citizen who voted in a foreign election. This time, the Court overturned its ruling in *Perez*, asserting Congress could not under any circumstance take away citizenship without a person's assent. But only four years later, in *Rogers v. Bellei*, the Court made a distinction between a person born or naturalized in the United States versus a citizen born or naturalized abroad. In this instance, the Court upheld a law that required people born outside the country had to have at least one U.S. parent living in the United States for five consecutive years, or lose their citizenship. The defendant, like Clemente Perez, was stripped of his nationality.

Related Cases

United States v. Wong Kim Ark, 169 U.S. 649 (1898).
Bailey v. Alabama, 219 U.S. 219 (1911).

Herbert Brownell, Jr., U.S. Attorney General. © UPI/Corbis-Bettmann.

United States v. Curtiss-Wright Export Corp., 299 U.S. 304 (1936).

Bibliography and Further Reading

Biskupic, Joan, and Elder Witt. *Guide to the U.S. Supreme Court,* 3rd ed. Washington, DC: Congressional Quarterly, Inc., 1997.

Hall, Kermit L., ed. *The Oxford Companion to the Supreme Court of the United States.* New York: Oxford Press, 1992.

Nowak, John E., Ronald D. Rotunda, and J. Nelson Young. *Constitutional Law,* 2nd ed. St. Paul: West Publishing Company, 1984.

Witt, Elder. *The Supreme Court A to Z.* CQ's Encyclopedia of American Government. Washington, DC: Congressional Quarterly, Inc., 1993.

SCHNEIDER V. RUSK

Legal Citation: 377 U.S. 163 (1964)

Appellant
Angelika L. Schneider

Appellee
Dean Rusk, U.S. Secretary of State

Appellant's Claim
That a section of the 1952 Immigration and Naturalization Act, which stripped the citizenship of naturalized Americans who lived abroad for more than three years was unconstitutional.

Chief Lawyer for Appellant
Milton V. Freeman

Chief Lawyer for Appellee
Bruce J. Terris

Justices for the Court
Hugo Lafayette Black, William O. Douglas (writing for the Court), Arthur Goldberg, Potter Stewart, Earl Warren

Justices Dissenting
Tom C. Clark, John Marshall Harlan II, Byron R. White (William J. Brennan, Jr. did not participate)

Place
Washington, D.C.

Date of Decision
18 May 1964

Decision
Upheld appellant's claim.

Significance
The Court continued a trend of limiting when Congress could force naturalized Americans to involuntarily give up their citizenship.

The privileges of American citizenship have enticed millions of immigrants to come to the United States and adopt this country as their homeland. According to the Fourteenth Amendment, "all persons born or naturalized in the United States" are American citizens, and Congress has the power to regulate naturalization, the process by which foreigners become citizens. The Constitution, however, does not spell out when people can be expatriated, or stripped of their citizenship. This issue has been left to the Supreme Court to decide.

For much of its history, the Court ruled that Americans could not voluntarily expatriate themselves, without the government's consent. But in the twentieth century, the Court recognized the right of Americans to freely renounce their citizenship. A thornier constitutional issue has been involuntary expatriation: when Congress declares that, after committing certain acts, people can be stripped of their citizenship. In *Perez v. Brownell* (1958), the Court ruled that by voting in a foreign election, citizens implicitly renounce their citizenship, and Congress can make that action grounds for expatriation.

At the same time, however, the Court ruled that a law expatriating a citizen who deserted the military during wartime was not constitutional (*Trop v. Dulles* [1958]). In *Kennedy v. Mendoza-Martinez* (1963), the Court held that a citizen who lived in a foreign country during wartime to avoid the draft could not be expatriated. A year later, the Court once again examined involuntary expatriation.

No "Second Class Citizenship" Allowed

Schneider v. Rusk dealt with the rights of naturalized Americans. Angelika Schneider, a native of Germany, had come to the United States as a child. She and her parents were naturalized, and Schneider lived in America through her college years. Afterward, she went abroad to continue her studies and married a German citizen. Schneider then settled in Germany and began a family. Twice she returned to America for brief visits. In 1959, when Schneider tried to renew her U.S. passport, the State Department refused her request, saying she was no longer an American citizen.

The government based its decision on a section of the 1952 Immigration and Naturalization Act. The law

Dean Rusk, U.S. Secretary of State. © The Library of Congress/Corbis.

said naturalized citizens who lived in their native lands for three years lost their American citizenship. The government believed returning to one's homeland weakened a naturalized citizen's allegiance to the United States, and sometimes put the American government in conflict with foreign nations. In 1962, almost 1,000 people had been expatriated under this law.

Schneider sued the State Department to regain her citizenship. A district court found for the government, and Schneider appealed to the Supreme Court. In his decision, Justice Douglas noted that the justices' views on expatriation had varied in the past, but in this case, the Court ruled 5-3 that the pertinent provision of the Immigration and Naturalization Act was unconstitutional.

Douglas wrote, "We start from the premise that the rights of citizenship of the native born and of the naturalized person are of the same dignity and are coextensive." He then cited the Court's past disagreements on expatriation, and concluded with the majority's reasoning in the present case:

> This statute proceeds on the impermissible assumption that naturalized citizens as a class are less reliable and bear less allegiance to this country than do the native born. This is an assumption that is impossible for us to make.

Moreover, while the Fifth Amendment contains no equal protection clause, it does forbid discrimination that is "so unjustifiable as to be violative of due process" . . . The discrimination aimed at naturalized citizens drastically limits their right to live and work abroad in way that other citizens may. It creates indeed a second-class citizenship.

The Historical Record for Residency

In the view of the three dissenting justices, Schneider's choice to live in Germany amounted to her renouncing her citizenship. Justice Clark noted that almost 30 other countries expatriated naturalized citizens who lived in their native lands for a number of years. Clark also turned to the earliest days of the Republic to bolster his argument for the importance of requiring naturalized citizens to live in America. Quoting James Madison, Clark wrote, "It may be a question of some nicety, how far we can make our law to admit an alien to the right of citizenship, step by step; but there is no doubt we may, and ought to require residence as an essential."

The dissenters also believed that Schneider's wanting both her German residence and American citizenship was a selfish act. Clark wrote, "She wishes to retain her citizenship on a standby basis of her own benefit in the event of trouble."

The majority's view, however, continued to hold sway on the Court. Three years later, in *Afroyim v. Rusk* (1967) the Court said Congress could not, under any circumstances, expatriate a naturalized American (or a native citizen, for that matter) without a person's consent. Congress does have the right, though, to expatriate if a naturalized person obtained citizenship using fraud or misrepresentation.

The issue of expatriation is not as clear-cut for citizens born or naturalized abroad. In *Rogers v. Bellei* (1971), the Court upheld a law that required people born outside the country, and who have just one U.S. parent, to live in America for at least five consecutive years, or lose their citizenship.

Related Cases
Perez v. Brownell, 356 U.S. 44 (1958).
Trop v. Dulles, 356 U.S. 86 (1958).
Kennedy v. Mendoza-Martinez, 372 U.S. 144 (1963).
Afroyim v. Rusk, 387 U.S. 253 (1967).

Bibliography and Further Reading
Biskupic, Joan, and Elder Witt. *Guide to the U.S. Supreme Court,* 3rd edition. Washington, DC: Congressional Quarterly, Inc., 1997.

New York Times, 19 May 1964.

Nowak, John E., Ronald D. Rotunda, and J. Nelson Young. *Constitutional Law,* 2nd edition. St. Paul: West Publishing Company, 1984.

AFROYIM V. RUSK

Legal Citation: 387 U.S. 253 (1967)

Petitioner
Afroyim

Respondent
Dean Rusk, U.S. Secretary of State

Petitioner's Claim
Section 401(e) of the Nationality Act of 1940, 8 U.S.C. sec. 801 (1946), which provided that American citizens automatically lost their citizenship if they voted in a foreign election, was unconstitutional under the Fourteenth Amendment.

Chief Lawyer for Petitioner
Edward J. Ennis

Chief Lawyer for Respondent
Charles Gordon

Justices for the Court
Hugo Lafayette Black (writing for the Court), William J. Brennan, Jr., William O. Douglas, Abe Fortas, Earl Warren

Justices Dissenting
Tom C. Clark, John Marshall Harlan II, Potter Stewart, Byron R. White

Place
Washington, D.C.

Date of Decision
29 May 1967

Decision
Held that the Fourteenth Amendment prevents Congress from adopting any laws divesting American citizens of their citizenship.

Significance
The ruling overturned the 1958 decision in *Perez v. Brownell*, which found that Congress had the authority to provide for involuntary expatriation of a citizen who voted in a foreign election. The Court concluded that the Fourteenth Amendment provides that once citizenship is granted, it cannot be "shifted, canceled, or diluted at the will of the Federal Government." The Court also said that the language of the Constitution and the legislative history of earlier citizenship laws strongly indicated that Congress never had the power to revoke citizenship.

Afroyim, born in Poland, was naturalized as an American citizen in 1926. He moved to Israel in 1950 and voted in an Israeli election in 1951, but he never renounced his American citizenship. In 1960, the U.S. State Department refused to renew his passport, ruling that he had lost his citizenship by voting in a foreign election. He sued the secretary of state, seeking a declaratory judgment that the law was unconstitutional. Applying *Perez v. Brownell,* the district court and court of appeals both rejected his argument, and he asked the Supreme Court for review.

The Fourteenth Amendment provides that, "All persons born or naturalized in the United States . . . are citizens of the United States . . ." The Court said, "The Amendment can most reasonably be read as defining a citizenship which a citizen keeps unless he voluntarily relinquishes it." Although the Fourteenth Amendment was primarily intended to protect the citizenship rights given to blacks in the Civil Rights Act of 1866, the Court concluded that it clearly applied to all citizens, regardless of how their citizenship was obtained. As the opinion said, "Though the framers of the Amendment were not particularly concerned with the problem of expatriation, it seems undeniable from the language they used that they wanted to put citizenship beyond the power of any governmental unit to destroy."

The Court noted that the *Perez* case "ha[d] been a source of controversy and confusion," and that the Court had "consistently invalidated" other statutes allowing involuntary removal of citizenship. It found that the dissent in *Perez* correctly concluded that the government cannot take away citizenship for voting in a foreign election. "To uphold Congress' power to take away a man's citizenship because he voted in a foreign election in violation of sec. 401(e) would be equivalent to holding that Congress has the power to 'abridge,' 'affect,' 'restrict the effect of,' and 'take away' citizenship" in violation of the Fourteenth Amendment, the Court said.

The Court also noted that even without the Fourteenth Amendment the Constitution gives Congress no express powers to take away citizenship. It commented that "[i]n our country the people are sovereign" and concluded that congressional power over issues of citizenship is correspondingly limited. Looking at legislative history of early congressional wrangles with expatriation issues, the Court concluded that most early efforts to allow cancellation of citizenship were stopped because the members of Congress felt that they had no authority to take away citizenship.

The case was decided by a 5-4 vote, and a strong dissent written by Justice Harlan argued that the *Perez* case should have been upheld. Harlan argued that the citizenship clause of the Fourteenth Amendment simply declared the existing law, and made it clear that rights of the former slaves could not be stripped from them. The dissent concluded that "nothing in the history, purposes, or language of the clause suggests that it forbids Congress in all circumstances to withdraw the citizenship of an unwilling citizen."

Related Cases

Perez v. Brownell, 356 U.S. 44 (1958).
Bellei v. Rusk, 296 F.Supp 1247 (DCDC 1969).
Vance v. Terrazas, 444 U.S. 252 (1980).

Bibliography and Further Reading

Biskupic, Joan, and Elder Witt, eds. *Congressional Quarterly's Guide to the U.S. Supreme Court,* 3rd ed. Washington, DC: Congressional Quarterly, Inc., 1996.

Miller, John J. "Loyalty Duel: Will the Rise of Dual Citizenship Create a World Without Patriotism?" *National Review,* May 18, 1998, p. 32.

SUTICH V. CALLAHAN

Legal Citation: No. 97 Civ. 1027 SI (N.D. Cal. 1997)

Plaintiffs
Ivo Sutich, Saman Muy (by her *guardian ad litem* Eam Tak), Roshanak Partovi, Maria Klein, Wing Yim Chan, on behalf of themselves and all other persons similarly situated

Defendant
John J. Callahan, Acting Commissioner of the Social Security Administration

Plaintiffs' Claim
That Section 402 of the Personal Responsibility and Work Opportunity Reconciliation Act of 1996, which rendered legal resident aliens ineligible for Supplemental Security Income, violates the Due Process Clause of the Fifth Amendment to the Constitution.

Judge
Claudia Wilken

Place
San Francisco, California

Date of Decision
13 January 1998

Decision
Due to congressional restoration of Supplemental Security Income benefits for legal resident aliens as part of the Balanced Budget Act, the plaintiffs' case was dismissed without prejudice.

Significance
At least peripherally, *Sutich* seems to countenance philosophical questions of compassion versus self-reliance, of the benevolent state versus the well-managed one. As the attorneys for the plaintiff made clear in their presentation of the case, the legislation challenged in *Sutich* did not merely fail to achieve any of its purported goals such as fostering self-reliance; it would have achieved very nearly the opposite result, and at a great human cost.

Hearts against Heads

British Prime Minister David Lloyd George once said, "A young man who isn't a Socialist hasn't got a heart; an old man who is a Socialist hasn't got a head." This celebrated European wisdom can be applied to America's political culture by substituting the word "liberal" for "socialist." Indeed, American political life since the 1930s has often been characterized as a battle between big-government liberals who are all heart and no head, and self-reliant conservatives who are all head and no heart. Though this is a gross oversimplification, it would not be recycled in so many campaign speeches if it did not hold some truth. Liberals tend to favor social programs more than conservatives. These opposing views have resulted in questionable policy making decisions: liberal spending has produced a bloated bureaucracy; and the conservative emphasis on fiscal responsibility has spawned reactionary legislation such as that challenged in *Sutich v. Callahan*.

The Social Security Administration was established in the 1930s as part of a larger initiative by President Franklin D. Roosevelt's administration to make government more responsive to the needs of its citizens. Social Security is an extension of the provisions for retirement income established in Title II of the Social Security Act of 1972. However, Title XVI of the Social Security Act provides for a much smaller program of assistance to extremely needy persons—the Supplemental Security Income (SSI) program. This program was established to assist individuals who are either elderly, disabled, incapable of gainful employment in the United States, and who possess resources amounting to $2000 or less.

Clearly those eligible for SSI are an extremely unenviable class of people. The attorneys for the plaintiffs in *Sutich* described them as having "no buffer between them and destitution." The neediness of the recipients, combined with the modesty of SSI grants, would seem to make the system unassailable. But this was not the case highlighted by the Personal Responsibility and Work Opportunity Reconciliation Act of 1996, dubbed "The Welfare Reform Act." Section 402 of the act denied SSI benefits to noncitizens, with only a few

John Callahan, Social Security Administration Commissioner, 1997. © Photograph by Greg Gibson. AP/Wide World Photos.

exceptions, namely for those who could document 40 "qualifying" quarters of employment such as: refugees, asylums, veterans, their spouses, and their dependent children. The remaining group of noncitizen SSI recipients—by far the vast majority—would be left to fend for themselves.

Though liberal commentators describe the Welfare Reform Act immoral, conservatives insist that it grew out of a legitimate and widespread concern over the ever-inflating size of the federal government. Overworked taxpayers were weary of their hard-earned dollars being used "to pay others not to work." For some this concern was surpassed only by the idea of those dollars being used to pay foreigners not to work. Voters in California, for instance, became incensed at the idea of illegal aliens receiving welfare and food stamps, and passed that state's controversial Proposition 187, which denied such benefits to persons living in the United States illegally, during the 1994 elections.

Republicans may have initiated the sweeping cuts in federal spending that followed the 1994 "Republican Revolution," which brought their party to power in both houses of Congress for the first time in 40 years. However, many Democrats supported the change in policy which illustrates the broad-based acceptance for such measures. President Clinton, signed the welfare reform bill into law on 22 August 1996. Among its provisions was Section 402, which cut off SSI payments to noncitizens as of 22 August 1997. The elimination of SSI benefits for resident aliens was politically popular but it came at a high cost for those who relied on the assistance.

The Impact of Welfare Reform

On 27 March 1997, a group of attorneys filed a class-action suit before Judge Susan Illston in the U.S. District Court for the Northern District of California. The plaintiff's legal counsel, led by Judith Z. Gold and others in the San Francisco firm of Heller Ehrman White & McAuliffe, came form the American Civil Liberties Union (ACLU), Protection & Advocacy Inc., and a variety of other groups representing minorities, immigrants, the elderly, and the disabled. The suit named its defendant John J. Callahan, Acting Commissioner of the Social Security Administration, who was being sued in his official capacity. Specifically, the plaintiffs charged that by cutting off their SSI benefits, the Social Security Administration had sought to abridge their Fifth Amendment rights to due process, seeking a declaratory judgment to this effect.

Gold and the other attorneys devoted the majority of their brief to examining a representative group of plaintiffs in order to illustrate the vast human suffering caused by Section 402. The case engendered empathy for those who would suffer from the cuts. However, it was framed in an appeal that questioned the logic of cost-cutting. All five of the named plaintiffs were lawful residents of the United States prior to the 22 August 1996 enactment of the Welfare Reform Act but were unable to obtain citizenship for reasons closely tied to their eligibility for SSI benefits. Each of the plaintiffs had been denied benefits within 65 days of the filing of the lawsuit, or would be denied such benefits on or before 22 August 1997.

At the center of the plaintiffs' brief was a series of five dossiers, portraits of representative persons affected by the SSI cuts. Two came from eastern or central Europe, two from east Asia, and one from central Asia. Two were refugees from communist regimes, two more emigrated from countries on the borders of communist countries, and a fifth came from a nation with a historically anti-American tradition. All had migrated to America seeking a better life in one way or another, and several were allowed into the country due to specific congressional measures regarding political asylum. Each was disabled in some way, and unable to support himself or herself without SSI assistance.

First among the named plaintiffs was 67-year-old Ivo Sutich. He had made what his attorneys called "a daring escape" from Marshal Tito's Communist Yugoslavia in 1954, and had entered the United States through the Department of State's Escapee Program two years later. A decade later, Sutich was diagnosed a with mental illness, and involuntarily institutionalized in a California mental-health facility. Following his discharge, Sutich applied for SSI benefits in December of 1996. In addition to his mental illness and his age, he was also legally blind. Sutich was ineligible for the program because he was not a U.S. citizen. "Naturalization," the attorneys noted, "is not a meaningful solution for Mr. Sutich." Given his mental illness, they argued, it was unlikely he would be accepted for citizenship. Denial of the SSI benefits would likely force him to an existence on the streets, if not a state mental institution.

Saman Muy, another refugee from a communist regime, was a 16-year-old Cambodian girl who was paralyzed from the chest down from the age of three. She and her parents escaped their native Cambodia four years after the Vietnamese ousted the repressive Pol Pot regime. Each day she received nine different medications, and required assistance using the bathroom, entering and leaving the apartment building where her family lived, and undertaking other activities of daily life. With the entire family confined to a one-bedroom apartment, and with the high cost of Saman's upkeep, the elimination of SSI benefits rendered the entire Muy family's future uncertain. Again, naturalization was "not a meaningful solution." As a minor, Saman was dependent on her parents to apply for citizenship, both of whom had been denied citizenship. Her stepfather was denied on the basis of mental disorders stemming from his experiences in war-torn Cambodia and her mother was denied because she could not speak English.

Wing Yim Chan, a 60-year-old who immigrated to the United States from Hong Kong, seemed to represent an immigrant's version of the American dream gone bad. Having worked for seven years as a seamstress in a garment factory, she had begun to suffer vision problems as a result of eye strain associated with the work. Unsuccessful eye surgery had left her blind in 1995, and her employer had fired her. Other named plaintiffs included Roshanak Partovi, who had come from Iran in 1987 and was later diagnosed with breast cancer, and Maria Klein, who had immigrated from Germany in 1957 and had been repeatedly institutionalized for chronic paranoid schizophrenia.

The Results of Counterproductive Laws

At the time their attorneys filed the lawsuit in March of 1997, Sutich and Partovi had already been denied SSI benefits, and Muy, Klein, and Chan would be cut off on or before 22 August. The class-action represented two subclasses of individuals that would, according to their brief, be irreparably damaged by section 402 of the Welfare Reform Act.

In a section regarding Congress's intent in passing the Welfare Reform Act, the plaintiffs' legal counsel noted the law's counterproductive qualities. Specifically, Congress had cited two interests served by Section 402: first, that it would discourage illegal immigrants from the expectation of receiving SSI benefits; and second, it would encourage self-reliance. With regard to the first point, the brief pointed out that "persons not lawfully present in the United States have *never* been eligible for SSI. Therefore it is irrational to suggest that injuring people *already* here *legally* . . . will deter other people from immigrating *illegally* in the future" (all emphasis original). As for the issue of self-reliance, the plaintiffs' counsel noted that Section 402 would actually result in their clients becoming more, not less, dependent on government help—and therefore the alleged cost-cutting measures in Section 402 would end up creating a much greater expense for the public: ". . . denying lawful permanent residents these benefits will render them *less* self-reliant since they will be in danger of becoming homeless, hungry, and unable to care for themselves. Thousands of them, ironically, will end up in state institutions at great public expense."

Although the issue of SSI eligibility, and the larger concern of balancing the budget, had attracted great attention in the media, the *Sutich* case received little attention. On 17 June 1997, the ACLU issued a press release stating that U.S. District Court Judge Claudia Wilken would hear oral arguments in the case two days later. *Sutich* was part of a larger movement to counterbalance some of the more sweeping measures in the Welfare Reform Act. The result was that in late 1997, Congress passed the Balanced Budget Act, which, among other things, restored SSI benefits to most legal residents. In December of that year, the Social Security Administration issued a directive to return otherwise eligible noncitizens to the SSI beneficiary roles, and the *Sutich* case was dismissed without prejudice on 13 January 1998.

Impact

Following the dismissal of *Sutich*, the ACLU's Alan Schlosser said "Congress corrected unjust legislation which would have threatened the lives of full-fledged members of our society. . . ." Earlier, when the case was still pending, he had agreed with the use of the term "death notices" to characterize letters announcing the removal of SSI benefits: "This is not hyperbole," he said. "People who receive the notices cannot reasonably foresee any future for themselves except homelessness and starvation. At least two people—and probably more—have already reacted to their 'death notices' by committing suicide." Schlosser's observations relied heavily on emotional appeal, whereas that part of the plaintiffs' brief that noted the counterproductive results of Section 402 relied heavily on logic. Viewed from either perspective, Section 402 was an ill-advised venture. The impact of other aspects of the Welfare Reform Act was less dramatic, however, the fate of Section 402 illustrated the unwillingness of the American people to compromise social responsibility for fiscal prudence.

Related Cases

Abreu v. Callahan, No. 97 Civ. 2126 (S.D. N.Y. 1997).
Rodriguez v. United States of America, No. 97 Civ. 1182 (S.D. Fla. 1997).

Bibliography and Further Reading

American Civil Liberties Union. http://www.aclu.org

Hing, Bill Ong. "Don't Give Me Your Tired, Your Poor: Conflicted Immigrant Stories and Welfare Reform." *Harvard Civil Rights-Civil Liberties Law Review,* winter 1998, pp. 159–82.

"Supplemental Security Income." *Social Security Bulletin,* Annual 1994, Suppl. pp. 69–72.

Wolchok, Carol Leslie. "Demands and Anxiety: The Effects of the New Immigration Law." *Human Rights,* spring 1997, pp. 12–13.

JUVENILE LAW AND JUSTICE

Juvenile law refers to that body of law dealing with juveniles, or persons who are not yet adults. The definition of a juvenile varies from state to state according to the age at which a person is deemed to reach adulthood. In at least one state (Wyoming), the age of adulthood is 19; for some legal purposes, other states set the age at 16, and still others set the age at 17 or 18.

Juvenile law is a special blend of law created especially for juveniles to account for their immaturity and innocence. There are three basic categories of children over which juvenile courts have jurisdiction: children accused of committing a crime; children who are in need of protection from the state; and children who have committed a status offense. A status offense is conduct that is prohibited only to children, and not to adults. Examples of status offenses include failure to attend school (known as truancy), failure to obey reasonable parental controls, cigarette smoking, drinking of alcohol, possession of pornography, and flight from home.

Before the creation of juvenile law in the late nineteenth century, children in the United States generally were treated under the law as adults. For criminal behavior, only children under the age of seven were immune from criminal prosecution. A child of seven or older, if convicted of a crime warranting incarceration, was sentenced to prison with adults. During the nineteenth century, some states created separate work farms and reform schools to serve as secure facilities for children. That was, however, the extent of the special treatment for children until the Progressive political movement seized on the issue.

In the late nineteenth century, large cities were fast becoming repositories for the country's underclass as massive industrialization forced growing numbers into poverty. Progressive legislators, concerned about the swelling ranks of poor, unsupervised children in urban areas, argued that children were different from adults and proposed that they should be treated differently under the law. Along with mandatory school attendance, the Progressives proposed a new court system for troubled children. Troubled children were not "black-guard" children or inherently bad. Rather, they simply were trapped in bad conditions. In other words,

there were no bad children; there simply were children in bad situations. To keep their communities from being overrun by needy children in bad situations, state governments became like surrogate parents to poor and unsupervised children.

Juvenile Courts

Reform-minded legislators in Illinois created the first separate court for children in the state's Juvenile Court Act of 1899. The juvenile court established in Illinois became the model for juvenile court systems across the country. State legislatures began to create juvenile courts and to give them a tremendous amount of authority to control a wide variety of children. In Illinois, this included

> any child who for any reason is destitute or homeless or abandoned; or dependent on the public for support; or has not proper parental care or guardianship; or who habitually begs or receives alms; or who is found living in any house of ill fame or with any vicious or disreputable person . . . and any child under the age of 8 years who is found peddling or selling any article or singing or playing any musical instrument upon the street or giving any public entertainment.

Juvenile courts could place such children with a foster family or in a reform school for any of these status offenses.

The first juvenile courts were intended to benefit needy juveniles who needed the basic necessities of life and a measure of adult guidance. By requiring that the state care for needy children, the act swept many children into the court system where the state could monitor their maturation. Under the original Illinois model, juveniles found to be within the juvenile court's jurisdiction remained under the court's control until they reached the age of 21.

Juvenile courts also de-criminalized juvenile transgressions. No longer would juvenile crime be prosecuted in adult court, and no longer would the proceeding be called a prosecution. Instead, juvenile criminal proceedings were called "hearings" or "adjudications." Juveniles were not charged in an indictment or information, but instead were brought before the court with a "petition." Juveniles were not tried before juries, but before a juvenile court judge. If a juvenile was found to have committed a crime, he or she was adjudged "delinquent" instead of guilty. Sentences were fashioned according to the best interests of the juvenile instead of inflicting punishment to fit the crime. Juveniles were supposed to be rehabilitated, not punished. The form and substance of juvenile court, from start to finish, was designed to treat juveniles with more tenderness than was afforded in the adult court system.

The "System"

For all the tenderness associated with the age group, the new juvenile courts cast a large net, and many juveniles found themselves involuntarily caught up in a system of courts and state agencies. Foster homes and reform schools, though well intentioned, were unattractive to many juveniles, and many poor parents were forcibly deprived of their children. Despite its shortcomings, the juvenile court system was arguably successful in reigning in a growing problem of youth vagrancy and crime. The power of the juvenile law model grew in popularity throughout the twentieth century, and all states now maintain a separate juvenile code in their statutes. The federal government has a juvenile court system, but it only deals with juveniles under the age of eighteen who are accused of committing a federal crime.

When a juvenile is suspected of committing a crime, he or she may be arrested and brought to jail and then released or detained through the adjudication. The jail may or may not be the same secure facility that houses adults; juveniles should be kept separate from adult populations, but that is not always possible. At the adjudication, juveniles have the right to: notice of the charges; confront and question witnesses; present testimony; be free from self-incrimination; and be represented by an attorney. The prosecution has discretion to charge as much or as little as he or she sees fit. In any case, the prosecutor must prove beyond a reasonable doubt that the juvenile committed the criminal act that is charged; this is the burden of proof that is required to convict adults. Juveniles accused of crimes do not have the right to a free, court-appointed attorney unless they are accused of a serious crime that warrants commitment to a secure facility. In most cases, though, a juvenile court judge will appoint an attorney to represent a juvenile who cannot afford to hire an attorney.

If a juvenile accused of a crime is found to have committed the offense, he or she is adjudged "delinquent." The disposition of the case is then in the discretion of the juvenile court judge. Depending on the crime com-

mitted, a juvenile delinquent may be placed on probation, ordered to perform community service, ordered to pay a fine, ordered to pay restitution, or ordered to perform, or refrain from, any number of specific acts. These measures may be combined in any way by the juvenile court judge.

The most severe disposition of a juvenile adjudication is placement of the juvenile in a secure facility. These facilities are called reformatories, youth development centers, or some other name that connotes rehabilitation. Although the facilities are designed to rehabilitate and educate juvenile delinquents, they are similar to prisons in that they are structured to prevent escape. A juvenile may be committed to such a facility for a length of days or years, depending on the offense committed. In any case, a juvenile may be held in a secure facility for an adjudication of juvenile delinquency only until a prescribed age. This age varies from state to state and ranges anywhere from 18 to 21 years.

Juvenile or Adult?

In a growing number of cases, a juvenile may be prosecuted as an adult. A "waiver" or "transfer" to adult court means that the juvenile may be prosecuted and sentenced under the same rules that govern adult criminal trials. Transfer to adult court is governed by statute and occurs only when the juvenile stands accused of a serious felony or violent crime. A conviction in adult court can result in a sentence equivalent to that received by an adult. For first-degree murder, this can even mean death. Capital punishment cannot, however, be imposed on a juvenile who was less than 16 years old at the time of the offense.

When a juvenile commits a status offense, the law's response is somewhat different than its response to a criminal act. A police officer coming in contact with a juvenile status offender may simply give the juvenile a warning, but repeated offenses may lead to an adjudication of delinquency.

Juvenile courts also exercise authority over children who are in need of social services. This includes juveniles whose parents are unable to care for them and children who are abused or neglected. A number of low-level status offenses may cause a juvenile court to treat the juvenile as a child in need of services, and order the juvenile to live in a foster home or state reformatory.

Most juvenile courts have a building or room of their own. A juvenile court is separate from adult courtrooms and is arranged or conducted in a way that is less intimidating than the arrangements in adult courtrooms. In most states, the proceedings take place in private and the records and identities of juveniles likewise are kept private. Some states, like Wisconsin, are allowing the public increased access to juvenile records and proceedings.

Juvenile Law

The general concept of a juvenile law is widely accepted. Most persons agree that children should not be treated the same as adults under the law. There are, however, differing opinions as to the methods and results of contemporary juvenile law, especially that body of law dealing with juvenile crime. In the 1960s, when juveniles gained many of the same constitutional procedural rights as adults (*In re Gault* [1967]), the trend in juvenile law was rehabilitation and education of juvenile transgressors. Since the late 1980s, public discussion of juvenile law has been dominated by calls for stricter controls and harsher punishments. Juveniles accused of crimes were transferred to adult court in record numbers during the 1990s. In 1995, Professor John J. Dilulio, Jr. wrote an article called "The Coming of the Super-Predators" for *The Weekly Standard*. Dilulio's dramatic treatise, which documented the increasing rate of violent crime and homicides by juveniles, touched a nerve around the country. The term "super-predator" quickly became a commonplace expression for describing juveniles responsible for the perceived increase in violent crime. According to James Q. Wilson, Professor of Public Policy for the University of California at Los Angeles, these were juveniles who, when caught for a crime, "show us the blank, unremorseful stare of a feral, presocial being." U.S. Representative Bill McCollum proposed legislation in 1996 called the Violent Youth Predator Act of 1996. The bill, designed to automatically prosecute repeat violent federal offenders as adults and to increase jail time for certain crimes, was re-named after it received harsh public criticism. The Violent and Repeat Juvenile Offender Act of 1997 was still pending in Congress at the time of this writing.

Critics of the shift toward punishment of juveniles note that the public perception of juvenile crime is skewed by political rhetoric and increased media coverage. Juvenile crime rates, according to many, generally remain constant, and the only shifts are in increased law enforcement, the gathering and interpretation of crime statistics, and public mood. Thomas J. Bernard, a Professor at Pennsylvania State University, argues that juvenile justice policies in the Unites States follow a "cyclical pattern" in which a lenient period is followed by a period of harsh treatment; when stronger punishments do not decrease juvenile crime, another lenient period of reform, rehabilitation and education ensues. For some juvenile law observers, the only answer is increased education and rehabilitation. Charles J. Aron and Michele S.C. Hurley, two juvenile law practitioners writing for the publication *Champion*, submit that "[m]any juvenile offenders live lives more problematic and horrific than most adults can imagine. Such backgrounds call for rehabilitation, not punishment; opportunity, not ostracism. They are, after all, children."

See also: Juvenile Courts

Bibliography and Further Reading

Aron, Charles J., Hurley, Michele S.C., "Juvenile Justice At the Crossroads," *Champion*, Volume 22, p. 10. National Association of Criminal Defense Lawyers, Inc., June, 1998.

Bernard, Thomas J., *The Cycle of Juvenile Justice.* New York: Oxford University Press, 1992.

Dilulio, John J. Jr., "Stop Crime Where It Starts," *The New York Times*, 31 July 1996, Section A, p. 15.

Dilulio, John J. Jr., "The Coming of the Super-Predators," *The Weekly Standard*, 27 November 1995, p. 24.

"Juvenile Law," *West's Encyclopedia of American Law*, Volume 6, p. 313. St. Paul: West Group, 1998.

Lindsey, Michael, "Legislative Super-Predators," *Criminal Justice*, Volume 12, p. 52. American Bar Association, Winter, 1998.

Leiner, Helen, "Juvenile Justice: Act Now!" *Champion*, Volume 22, p. 11. National Association of Criminal Defense Lawyers, Inc., June, 1998.

Schmidt, Paul W., "Dangerous Children and the Regulated Family: the Shifting Focus of Parental Responsibility Laws," *New York University Law Review*, Volume 73, p. 667. New York: New York University Law Review, May, 1998.

GOSS V. LOPEZ

Legal Citation: 419 U.S. 565 (1975)

Appellant
Norval Goss, et al.

Appellee
Eileen Lopez, et al.

Appellant's Claim
That the suspension of a public school student without a hearing does not violate the Due Process Clause of the Fourteenth Amendment.

Chief Lawyer for Appellant
Thomas A. Bustin

Chief Lawyer for Appellee
Peter D. Roos

Justices for the Court
William J. Brennan, Jr., William O. Douglas, Thurgood Marshall, Potter Stewart, Byron R. White (writing for the Court)

Justices Dissenting
Harry A. Blackmun, Warren E. Burger, Lewis F. Powell, Jr., William H. Rehnquist

Place
Washington, D.C.

Date of Decision
22 January 1975

Decision
The Due Process Clause of the Fourteenth Amendment is violated when a student is suspended without notice and hearing.

Significance
In *Goss v. Lopez*, the Supreme Court ruled that students have both a "property interest" and a "liberty interest" in public education.

According to Ohio law, a public school principal could suspend students for up to ten days without a hearing. A group of Columbus, Ohio high school students, who had been suspended from school for misconduct, brought a class action suit against school officials on the grounds that their constitutional rights had been violated. They sought to have Ohio's public school suspension statute declared unconstitutional and to have the suspensions removed from their official records.

The Lower Court Rulings

The U.S. District Court for the Southern District of Ohio ruled in favor of the students. In their ruling, the three-judge panel declared that the students were denied due process of law in violation of the Fourteenth Amendment because they were "suspended without hearing prior to suspension or within a reasonable time thereafter." The Ohio law was struck down, and school officials were enjoined from issuing any more suspensions in this manner. Not pleased with this decision, the Ohio public school system appealed the case to the Supreme Court.

The Majority's Argument

In his majority opinion, Justice White held that students have a "property interest" in attending school since the state guarantees them a free public education. To suspend them from school, therefore, is in effect to deprive them of their property. While this interest must be balanced against the school system's interest in maintaining order and discipline, due process must be respected at all times. As Justice White wrote:

> The authority possessed by the State to prescribe and enforce standards of conduct in its schools, although concededly very broad, must be exercised consistently with constitutional safeguards. Among other things, the State is constrained to recognize a student's legitimate entitlement to a public education as a property interest which is protected by the Due Process Clause and which may not be taken away for misconduct without adherence to the minimum procedures required by that Clause.

Justice White also found that, because a suspension can damage a child's reputation, the child's "liberty interest" may be violated if unsubstantiated charges are brought against him. Accordingly, the child must be given the opportunity to hear the charges and reply:

> If sustained and recorded, those charges could seriously damage the students' standing with their fellow pupils and their teachers as well as interfere with later opportunities for higher education and employment. It is apparent that the claimed right of the State to determine unilaterally and without process whether that misconduct has occurred immediately collides with the requirements of the Constitution.

The Court did not go so far as to command that suspended students be granted the same rights as accused criminals. In doing so, it recognized the impracticality of such a scheme and noted the damaging effect this might have in an educational setting:

> We stop short of construing the Due Process Clause to require, countrywide, that hearings in connection with short suspensions must afford the student the opportunity to secure counsel, to confront and cross-examine witnesses supporting the charge, or to call his own witnesses to verify his version of the incident. Brief disciplinary suspensions are almost countless. To impose in each such case even truncated trial-type procedures might well overwhelm administrative facilities in many places and, by diverting resources, cost more than it would save in educational effectiveness. Moreover, further formalizing the suspension process and escalating its formality and adversary nature may not only make it too costly as a regular disciplinary tool but also destroy its effectiveness as part of the teaching process.

The Dissent

In his dissenting opinion, Justice Powell dismissed the notion that a ten-day suspension represents an infringement of the interests of students serious enough to require constitutional protection. His dissent contended that the Court's decision opened the door for unnecessary meddling by the courts into the day-to-day operations of the public school system:

> The State's interest, broadly put, is in the proper functioning of its public school system for the benefit of all pupils and the public generally. Few rulings would interfere more extensively in the daily functioning of schools than subjecting routine discipline to the formalities and judicial oversight of due process. Suspensions are one of the traditional means—ranging from keeping a student after class to permanent expulsion—used to maintain discipline in the schools. It is common knowledge that maintaining order and reasonable decorum in school buildings and classrooms is a major educational problem, and one which has increased significantly in magnitude in recent years. Often the teacher, in protecting the rights of other children to an education (if not his or their safety), is compelled to rely on the power to suspend.

Goss v. Lopez raised some basic and vital questions in the areas of public education, individual rights, and judicial intervention. The narrow decision in this case reflected the strong arguments on both sides of the issues.

Related Cases

Tinker v. Des Moines Independent Community School District, 393 U.S. 503 (1969).
Goldberg v. Kelly, 397 U.S. 254 (1970).
Connell v. Higgenbotham, 403 U.S. 207 (1971).
Arnett v. Kennedy, 416 U.S. 134 (1974).
Bethel School District No. 403 v. Fraser, 478 U.S. 675 (1986).

Bibliography and Further Reading

Bartholomew, Paul Charles. *Summaries of Leading Cases on the Constitution*. Totowa, NJ: Rowan & Allanheld, 1983.

Encyclopedia of the American Constitution. New York, NY: Macmillan Publishing Company, 1986.

A Reference Guide to the U.S. Supreme Court. New York, NY: Sachem Publishing Associates, Inc., 1986.

Toby, Jackson. "Getting Serious About School Discipline," *The Public Interest*, Fall 1998, p. 68.

PARHAM V. J. R.

Legal Citation: 442 U.S. 584 (1979)

Appellants
Parham, Commissioner, Department of Human Resources, et al.

Appellees
J. R., et al.

Appellants' Claim
That a federal district court had erred in ruling that a minor was allowed a hearing prior to being committed to a mental institution.

Chief Lawyer for Appellants
John L. Cromartie, Jr.

Chief Lawyer for Appellees
R. Douglas Lackey

Justices for the Court
Harry A. Blackmun, Warren E. Burger (writing for the Court), Lewis F. Powell, Jr., William H. Rehnquist, Potter Stewart, Byron R. White

Justices Dissenting
William J. Brennan, Jr., Thurgood Marshall, John Paul Stevens

Place
Washington, D.C.

Date of Decision
20 June 1979

Decision
Overturned a lower court's decision that would have barred the commitment of minors to mental institutions without a prior hearing.

Significance
Halted a trend that had granted minors increasing constitutional protections.

The 1979 Supreme Court ruling in *Parham v. J. R.* reversed a federal court decision that banned minors from being committed to mental health facilities without an adversary hearing; in essence, it ruled that parents did have the right to commit their children.

Georgia law allowed a minor to be admitted for observation to a psychiatric hospital upon request of a parent; the staff would then judge a patient's suitability for treatment and could suggest an indefinite stay. In presenting its case, the state proved that many minors admitted to state-funded mental-health institutions had already undergone outpatient treatment at a community health center. In most cases, a minor would not be admitted to the separate juvenile unit of a psychiatric facility without a referral from a community clinic. One hospital, however, had a higher rate of admitting patients without referrals, and that was Milledgeville's Central State Regional Hospital.

Two Tragic Predicaments

J. L. had been admitted to Central State Hospital in 1970 when he was six years old. He was described as hyperkinetic and aggressive and had been expelled from school. His mother and stepfather admitted him after two months of outpatient treatment had proven unsuccessful. From his admittance in 1970, various home-visit programs were attempted, to re-integrate him with his family and the outside community, but his mother and stepfather maintained they could not control him, and relinquished parental rights in 1974. Hospital employees familiar with J. L.'s course of therapy suggested that he would do better in a foster home with a more sympathetic support structure, but Georgia's Department of Family and Children Services was unable to provide this. In 1975, J. L. filed suit requesting a "less drastic" treatment option than being confined indefinitely to Central State Hospital.

The co-plaintiff in the original suit, J. R., had been removed from his parental home as an infant because of neglect. He lived in a total of seven foster homes, and was eventually termed disruptive and incorrigible. He had also undergone outpatient care, in this case for several months, but made little progress. His final set of foster parents requested him to be removed from their home, and the Department of Family and Children Services stepped in and, having nowhere else to place him, petitioned for his admission to Central State Hospital. Upon admission, doctors and specialists conducted interviews with J. R. and found him to be borderline retarded. His suit also requested placement in a less drastic environment.

The Due Process Argument

The original claim filed by J. R. and J. L. with Georgia's federal district court asserted that confinement to Central State Hospital violated their Fourteenth Amendment rights to due process, which states in part that no state may "deprive any person of life, liberty, or property without due process of law." A panel of three judges agreed, and ordered Georgia's Department of Family and Children Services to come up with a "non-hospital" facility for such minors. A recent National Institute for Mental Health study cited in the case found that most of the elderly patients had been committed as children, supporting the feeling that such "untreatable" minors were "dumped" there because the state, or their family, had no other options—and sadly, might remain there the rest of their natural lives.

Georgia authorities, represented by its commissioner for its Department of Human Resources, appealed, and the case was first argued before the U.S. Supreme Court in December of 1977. It was re-argued in October of 1978, and decided on 20 June 1979. The first minor named in the case, J. L., died before it was heard.

Minors and the Constitution

Since the 1960s, the American judicial system had come to recognize that juveniles and the mentally challenged or mentally ill have many of the same rights as other Americans. In step with other successful legal challenges of the civil-rights era, there came an acknowledgment from the state that certain societal institutions, such as the family, and the medical profession, were indeed fallible. The Court's decision on *Parham v. J. R.* reversed this trend. In its decision written by Chief Justice Burger, the Court ruled that an adversary hearing is not required for parents to commit a child to a mental-health facility (or in the case of wards of the court, by the state agency acting *in loco parentis*).

The Court found that professionals working in the separate units for minors within Georgia's psychiatric hospitals, including Central State Hospital, screened admissions adequately, and reviewed their progress regularly. Furthermore, the Court noted that parents generally act in the best interests of their children, and that juveniles are incapable of making their own decisions regarding relatively weighty or complex issues. Supporting this was the assertion that no adversary hearing is required when a minor needs surgery. It did, however, concur that there was some risk regarding parents' committing their children to psychiatric facilities, and suggested a "neutral factfinder" inquiry be undertaken at the time of admission, which would include an interview with the minor.

Justices Brennan, Marshall, and Stevens concurred with the majority opinion as well as dissented from it. Criticism of the ruling centered on the observation that when a situation arrives at the point where parents request that the child be committed, relations within the household have already arrived at serious deterioration—or, in other words, children who exhibit anti-social behavior usually come from disturbed home environments. Critics also found fault with the Court's comparison of admission into a mental hospital with surgery, contending the two were very different procedures.

Related Cases

Meyer v. Nebraska, 262 U.S. 390 (1923).
Pierce v. Society of Sisters, 268 U.S. 510 (1925).
Wisconsin v. Yoder, 406 U.S. 205 (1972).

Bibliography and Further Reading

Harvard Law Review, Vol. 93, November 1979, pp. 88-89.

Kramer, Donald T. *Legal Rights of Children,* 2nd ed. New York: McGraw-Hill, 1994.

"Mental Health . . . Commitment of Juveniles." *ABA Journal,* Vol. 65, September, 1979, p. 1391.

SCHALL V. MARTIN

Legal Citation: 467 U.S. 253 (1984)

Appellant
Schall, Commissioner of New York City Department of Juvenile Justice

Appellees
Gregory Martin, Luis Rosario, Kenneth Morgan

Appellant's Claim
That pretrial preventive detention of juveniles under New York's Family Court Act does not violate the "fundamental fairness" requirement of the Fourteenth Amendment's Due Process Clause.

Chief Lawyer for Appellant
Judith A. Gordon, Assistant Attorney General of New York

Chief Lawyer for Appellees
Martin Guggenheim

Justices for the Court
Harry A. Blackmun, Warren E. Burger, Sandra Day O'Connor, Lewis F. Powell, Jr., William H. Rehnquist (writing for the Court), Byron R. White

Justices Dissenting
William J. Brennan, Jr., Thurgood Marshall, John Paul Stevens

Place
Washington, D.C.

Date of Decision
4 June 1984

Decision
Upheld the state of New York's claim and overturned two lower courts' decisions banning pretrial detention of juveniles.

Significance
The ruling settled the dispute over whether preventive detention of juveniles, considered likely to engage in further crime prior to their trials, serves a legitimate state objective. The state successfully argued that its system of procedural protections satisfied requirements of the Due Process Clause of the Fourteenth Amendment. As highlighted by the dissenting opinion, the need for substantially reforming the nation's juvenile court systems became widely recognized. Both the proponents of tougher punishment and advocates for a juvenile rehabilitation emphasis sought to reduce the informal arbitrariness of juvenile judicial decisions by providing more structured sentencing guides. The practice of detaining juveniles received increased public support during a period of rising youth violence in the 1990s.

In the late 1970s, the New York Family Court Act allowed short term detention (confinement) of accused juveniles prior to having their cases resolved. Under normal procedures, following arrest of a juvenile, a probation officer would determine if the case should go to juvenile court based on an interview with the juvenile and the arresting officer. If so, an "initial appearance" hearing was held next. There a judge determined if preventive detention was justified based on whether the juvenile was at "serious risk" to commit more offenses prior to a final hearing. A formal consideration of specific facts in the case was not required. If detained, the juvenile was entitled to as many as two more hearings within 14 days after the initial appearance for serious crimes, three days for lesser offenses. The maximum potential detention time for serious offenses was 17 days, for others it was six. Juveniles were kept separate from adult criminals and screened to determine whether non-secure or secure detention facilities were appropriate. Both included educational and recreational programs and counseling by social workers.

Between December of 1977 and March of 1978, police arrested three 14-year old juveniles, Gregory Martin, Luis Rosario, and Kenneth Morgan, in three separate incidents on a variety of charges including robbery, assault, and possession of a loaded gun. Given their ages, they came within jurisdiction of New York's Family Court. Martin, detained for 15 days between arrest and resolution of his case, was found guilty and placed on two years probation. Rosario, who had other assault charges pending, was detained for six days. His case was later dropped. Morgan, who also had charges pending from another incident, was detained for eight days. He was found guilty and placed in custody for 18 months.

While in detention, Martin filed a suit on behalf of all similarly detained juveniles challenging the legality of preventive detention. Joined later by Rosario and Morgan in the suit, Martin claimed pretrial detention violated the Due Process and Equal Protection Clauses of the Fourteenth Amendment. Due process guarantees each individual fairness before the law in legal proceedings. Equal Protection essentially requires that a law be a reasonable means of achieving a government objective. The U.S. District Court accepted the case.

Curfews for Juveniles

The effectiveness and constitutionality of curfew ordinances for juveniles are highly controversial.

Cities with high juvenile crime rates considering a curfew may remain on firm constitutional ground. Dallas, Texas' curfew has become a model for other cities, reporting a 30 percent drop in violent crimes by juveniles since 1994. The Fifth Circuit Court of Appeals allowed the Dallas curfew ordinance. President Clinton has supported curfews, and funds have been appropriated in this regard. Across the United States, the percentage of the 200 largest cities utilizing curfews rose from less than 50 percent in 1990, to almost 75 percent in 1995.

Curfew ordinances have been challenged as unconstitutional by the American Civil Liberties Union (ACLU),

parents, and juveniles. Although the U.S. Supreme Court has not addressed the issue, some state courts have found curfews unconstitutional. Washington and California courts have rejected curfews unless it can be shown that their use will clearly correct a specific problem. While some cities have seen dramatic drops in youth crime, according to a survey of 387 cities by the U.S. Conference of Mayors, only around 30 percent of respondents described the results as "very effective."

Source(s): Court Decisions—Juvenile Curfews, http://www.mrsc.org/legal/curfew/courtcur.htm.
Keeping Our Kids on the Right Track, http://www.usdoj.gov/ag/rttrack.htm.
The Seattle Times, http://www.seattletimes.com/extra/browse/html97/altcurf_040797.html.

During the trial both sides provided case histories of over 30 individuals including general statistics on the relation between pretrial detention and how the cases were ultimately resolved. Testimony also centered on general juvenile court processes. After weighing the evidence, the district court ruled the Family Court Act did not violate the Equal Protection Clause, but did violate due process. The district court ordered the release of all detained juveniles. The state appealed to the U.S. Court of Appeals which affirmed the district court decision. The appeals court found that "the vast majority of juveniles detained" are ultimately released after their cases were heard. Therefore, the detention served more as a punishment for untried juveniles than a prevention of additional crime. The lack of any significant confinement after their trials contradicted any claimed need for pretrial confinement for community protection. Consequently, the court determined the process was unconstitutional toward all juveniles.

Juvenile System of Justice

During the early period of U.S. history, courts treated juveniles accused of crimes as "little" adults. Though reformatories came into existence in the early nineteenth century, a substantially different philosophy in treating juveniles did not evolve until near the end of that century. Concepts that "childhood" was a distinctly different stage of life and that juveniles had greater receptiveness to rehabilitation then gained acceptance. By 1925 almost all states had established juvenile court systems distinctly separate from the adult legal system. The recognized state paternal-like interest in the welfare of children made juvenile proceedings quite different than those for adults. The systems

emphasized rehabilitation, informality, low visibility, and avoidance of criminal-like convictions. Preventive detention became central to the juvenile justice system. However, formal procedural protections provided by the Due Process Clause of the Fourteenth Amendment had fallen by the wayside with the separation from adult courts.

Not until the 1960s did the Supreme Court enter the issue of constitutional rights in juvenile systems. In *In re Gault* (1967), the Court ruled "that certain basic constitutional protections enjoyed by adults accused of crimes also apply to juveniles." These protections included application of the Due Process Clause. In *Bell v. Wolfish* (1979), the Court found due process required that preventive detention not constitute punishment. However, the Court held in *McKeiver v. Pennsylvania* (1971) that juveniles did not have a right to trial. In effect, most of the Bill of Rights was extended to juvenile offenders regarding procedural matters. The detailed interpretation of these rights for juveniles was left for later cases.

Is Teenage Preventive Detention Legal?

In 1984 the Supreme Court granted *certiorari* to the *Schall* case to determine the constitutionality of juvenile preventive detention under the Due Process Clause. The Court split the question concerning detention into two parts. First, does preventive detention serve a legitimate state interest, such as protection of property or citizens' safety? Secondly, are procedural safeguards adequate to ensure fairness? Justice Rehnquist, writing for the majority in a 6-3 vote, found that preventive detention of juveniles "serves the legitimate state objective . . . of protecting both the juvenile and society from the hazards of pretrial crime." Rehnquist wrote "if parental control falters, the state must play its part" and the juvenile's liberty may be outweighed by state's interest in promoting the child's welfare. The Court recognized that juveniles often lack experience and judgement to avoid detrimental situations. Regarding the second question, the system of hearings created by the state to review each case served to satisfy "fundamental fairness" required by due process. This system provided sufficient safeguards against unnecessary court actions since the juvenile had various means of appealing the detention while being held. Rehnquist did not find that pretrial detention was punishment as found by the lower courts and, in fact, noted "some obvious flaws in the statistics and case histories" used by the lower courts. Regarding prediction of future criminal conduct, the Court held that a prediction was reasonably attained through experienced assessments by the New York Family Court judge based on a variety of factors. Rehnquist considered Martin's argument that many juveniles are released immediately following their trial not relevant to the appropriateness of preventative detention. Many released juveniles were, in fact, subject to conditions or probation, similar to the close supervision provided by detention. Rehnquist concluded the detention process authorized by state law is fairly applied and does not violate due process.

Joined in dissent by Justices Brennan and Stevens, Justice Marshall wrote that neither the argument of state interest nor the adequate existence of procedural safeguards justified preventive detention as authorized by the Family Court Act. Regarding state interest in protecting juveniles from wrongdoing, Marshall noted those juveniles assigned to secured facilities were often given institutional clothing and mixed with juveniles already convicted of serious crimes. Given the impressionability of juveniles, the pretrial detention authorized by the New York law likely caused injury equivalent to adult imprisonment. Marshall asserted the state must show much more urgent interest than simply "legitimate" to justify "deprivation of liberty." Secondly, in regard to procedural safeguards, Marshall highlighted that "initial appearance" hearings to determine if detention is justified usually lasted less than 15 minutes. He further noted juvenile court-assigned lawyers usually knew little of the juvenile's background and character, the lack of rules to fairly guide judges' determinations, minimal first hand knowledge of the incident at question, and sketchy initial appearance records the judge had for assisting his consideration. These factors made the process significantly arbitrary, thus not measuring up to the fairness standard of due process.

Impact

After *Gault* recognized substantial rights of juveniles in the justice system, a series of cases including *Schall*

dealt with a juvenile's right to trial, preventive detention, and the possibility of capital punishment. The Court increasingly yielded to states in dealing with juvenile justice matters.

General opinion grew through the 1980s and 1990s that the juvenile justice system, characterized by highly inconsistent procedures and sentencing, was in great disrepair. Nationwide statistics indicated that from 1985 to 1994 teen arrests for violent crimes rose 72 percent, while corresponding adult arrests fell four percent. Meanwhile, government efforts in controlling youth activities were met with charges of racial and social class bias. The public increasingly favored punishment over rehabilitation. Juvenile court judges increasingly assigned juvenile cases to adult courts. Some state legislatures responded by creating stiffer penalties, particularly for serious juvenile crimes. Studies showed teen crime fell significantly in those areas where tougher treatment occurred. As a result, Congress passed the Violent Crime Control and Law Enforcement Act of 1994 offering funding grants to states adopting tougher punishment standards. In reaction, advocates for juveniles pointed to other studies showing rehabilitation measures promoted by juvenile justice systems still worked in many cases.

Due process questions, as in *Schall*, rose again in the late 1990s with other systems of preventive detention. Often without the benefit of a trial, juveniles were sent to "bootcamps" for youths at risk. The camps offered tough treatment characterized as "behavior modification" or "attitude adjustment." The *Schall* decision was also used as a guide for preventive detention of other classes of people in civil law cases including the mentally incompetent and drug and alcohol addicts.

Juvenile preventive detention issues continued to attract considerable debate through the late 1990s. Pretrial detention was criticized on the basis that future criminal behavior by individuals can not be reliably predicted. Many individuals could be wrongly detained. The likelihood of guilt was recommended as a larger factor to be considered in addition to history of violent behavior. Society continued to struggle with balancing an juvenile's right to presumption of innocence before trial with increasing fears of crime.

Related Cases

In re Gault, 387 U.S. 1 (1967).
McKeiver v. Pennsylvania, 403 U.S. 528 (1971).
Bell v. Wolfish, 441 U.S. 520 (1979).
Reno v. Flores, 507 U.S. 292 (1993).

Bibliography and Further Reading

"Federalize State Juvenile Crimes: A Federal Case?" *U.S. News & World Report,* 27 January 1997.

Feld, Barry C. *Justice for Children: The Right to Counsel and the Juvenile Courts.* Boston: Northeastern University Press, 1993.

"Is This Camp or Jail?" *Time,* 26 January 1998.

National Center for Juvenile Justice. http://www.ncjj. org

"Teen Crime: More and More Teens Are Being Tried as Adults—A Good Idea?" *Current Events,* 24 October 1997.

NEW JERSEY V. T.L.O.

Legal Citation: 469 U.S. 325 (1985)

Petitioner
T.L.O.

Respondent
New Jersey

Petitioner's Claim
That her Fourth Amendment rights regarding search and seizure had been violated.

Chief Lawyer for Petitioner
Lois De Julio

Chief Lawyer for Respondent
Allan J. Nodes

Justices for the Court
Harry A. Blackmun, Warren E. Burger, Sandra Day O'Connor, Lewis F. Powell, Jr., William H. Rehnquist, Byron R. White (writing for the Court)

Justices Dissenting
William J. Brennan, Jr., Thurgood Marshall, John Paul Stevens

Place
Washington, D.C.

Date of Decision
15 January 1985

Decision
Her Fourth Amendment rights had not been violated and illegal drugs found in her purse were admissible as evidence in juvenile proceedings.

Significance
In *New Jersey v. T.L.O.*, the U.S. Supreme Court set forth the principles governing searches by public school authorities.

In the 1760s, the British government turned its back on the ancient concept of reasonable search and seizure when it authorized writs of assistance, which allowed a British agent to authorize that any home, shop, or place of business be searched. Writs of assistance were issued so agents could search for smuggled goods on which customs duty had not been paid. Agents were issued these writs without any reasonable grounds to believe that a building held smuggled goods. The writs did not state what was being searched for, did not name the persons involved, and were valid for indefinite periods of time. These writs helped spark the flame of the American Revolution and made it so that at the 1787 and 1788 ratifying conventions, the Fourth Amendment was added to the U.S. Constitution.

The Fourth Amendment states that people can expect to be protected "in their persons, houses, papers and effects" from "unreasonable searches and seizures." Unfortunately the concept of "unreasonable" is unclear and at the heart of many Supreme Court search and seizure cases. However, four elements need to be established in a search and seizure question: what the meaning of probable cause is; what a search or a seizure is; what circumstances dictate the need for a search warrant; and finally, what legal ramifications of a search or seizure makes them unconstitutional. Many of these questions arose in the case of *New Jersey v. T.L.O.*

A New Jersey high school teacher entered a restroom to find a 14-year old freshman smoking a cigarette which violated the school's rules. The teacher took the student to the principal's office. An assistant vice principal questioned the student about her behavior. The freshman denied that she was smoking in the restroom and asserted that she did not smoke cigarettes at all.

The assistant vice principal demanded the student's purse and opened it to find an open pack of cigarettes. When the assistant vice principal took the cigarettes out of the purse, there was a pack of rolling papers, such as one might use with marijuana. The assistant vice principal then searched the purse very thoroughly to find such things as a small quantity of marijuana, a marijuana pipe, a quantity of plastic bags, a large amount of $1 bills, a list of students who owed her

Do Students Have the Same Right to Protection against Unreasonable Search?

The Fourth Amendment provides U.S. citizens with guarantees against unreasonable search and seizure by authorities. Students may assert their protection from unreasonable searches under the same constitutional right. A student suspected of wrongdoing may attempt to use this defense as a means of avoiding being detected and disciplined. Trying to avoid seizure of cigarettes or other contraband not allowed on school premises, juveniles may attempt to deny searches of their personal property. Or if a search does take place, the juvenile may attempt to suppress evidence discovered, if court action ensues.

In a public school setting, however, the school may set and publish the guidelines determining the test for "reasonableness" of a search. This may depend upon the severity of the suspected offense by the student. Issues involving safety to all students may justify searches of students' personal property while on school premises. Some property used by the student, like lockers, are owned by the school. Additionally, because of public funding, greater latitude may be given to school officials attempting to provide a safe and orderly educational environment for all students.

Source(s): Findlaw. http://www.findlaw.com/casecode/supreme.html.
http://www.usdoj.gov.osg/1984/sg840165.txt.

---

money and two letters which left no doubt that she was dealing marijuana.

In delinquency proceedings against the student, a New Jersey juvenile court allowed the evidence to be admitted. The juvenile court ruled that a school official had the right to search a student if the official suspects reasonably that the student has committed a crime, is committing a crime, or is about to commit a crime. Furthermore, a school official can search a student if there is a reasonable cause to believe that the search is crucial to maintain school discipline or to enforce school policy. In this case, said the juvenile court, these standards dictated that this was a reasonable search.

The court ruled that the student was a delinquent, sentencing her to a year's probation. The appellate court affirmed the juvenile court's ruling that the student's Fourth Amendment rights had not been violated, but annulled the delinquency ruling. The appellate court returned the case to determine whether the student had waived her Fifth Amendment rights willingly and voluntarily before she confessed.

The student appealed the Fourth Amendment ruling to the Supreme Court of New Jersey which reversed the appellate division's judgment, and ordered that the evidence in the purse be suppressed because the search was not reasonable.

The U.S. Supreme Court heard the case on *certiorari* and reversed the ruling of the Supreme Court of New Jersey. Justice White wrote an opinion with which Powell, Rehnquist, O'Connor and Burger agreed. Justices Brennan, Marshall and Stevens joined the opinion, but only partially.

The concurring justices all decided that the Fourth Amendment's unreasonable search and seizure prohibition applies to searches made by public school officials. Further rulings were that school officials did not need to get a warrant before searching a student under their authority and that school officials do not need to follow the search requirement of probable cause to presume that a student is violating, has violated, or will violate the law. Whether a student search is legal depends on the reasonableness of the search in accordance with the circumstances surrounding the search. Finally, this particular search was not unreasonable relative to the Fourth Amendment.

Related Cases

West Virginia State Board of Education v. Barnette, 319 U.S. 624 (1943).
Tinker v. Des Moines Independent Community School District, 393 U.S. 503 (1969).
Goss v. Lopez, 419 U.S. 565 (1975).
Ingraham v. Wright, 430 U.S. 651 (1977).

Bibliography and Further Reading

Foldesy, George, and Dan King. "Strip Search in Schools: Beyond the Boundries of the Law?" *The Clearing House,* May-June 1995, p. 275.

Lieberman, Jethro K. *The Evolving Constitution.* New York: Random House, 1992.

Seidman, Louis M., Gerald R. Stone, Cass R. Sunstein, Mark V. Tushnet. *Constitutional Law.* Little, Brown and Company, 1986.

MARYLAND V. CRAIG

Legal Citation: 497 U.S. 836 (1990)

Petitioner
State of Maryland

Respondent
Sandra Ann Craig

Petitioner's Claim
That allowing an alleged victim of child abuse to testify by closed circuit television violates the Sixth Amendment right of criminal defendants to confront their accusers in court.

Chief Lawyer for Petitioner
J. Joseph Curran, Jr.

Chief Lawyer for Respondent
William H. Murphy, Jr.

Justices for the Court
Harry A. Blackmun, Anthony M. Kennedy, Sandra Day O'Connor (writing for the Court), William H. Rehnquist, Byron R. White

Justices Dissenting
William J. Brennan, Jr., Thurgood Marshall, Antonin Scalia, John Paul Stevens

Place
Washington, D.C.

Date of Decision
27 June 1990

Decision
The Supreme Court found that because the closed circuit procedure did not rule out cross-examination, it satisfied the essential purpose of the Sixth Amendment Confrontation Clause.

Significance
Craig was a significantly different interpretation of the Confrontation Clause. The Court justified going outside the clear meaning of the text by citing the special circumstances of victims of child abuse.

Sandra Ann Craig owned and operated a kindergarten and prekindergarten daycare center in Howard County, Maryland. In October of 1986, she was charged by a grand jury with sexually assaulting a six-year-old girl who had been in her care from August of 1984 to June of 1986. Before the case went to trial, the prosecution invoked a state law that allowed victims of child abuse to testify via one-way closed circuit television. The law permitted the child witness, the prosecutor, and the defense lawyer to withdraw to a separate room, where the witness was examined and cross-examined while a video monitor relayed these events to the judge, jury, and defendant in the courtroom. During this time, the child cannot see the defendant, but the defendant remains in electronic communication with defense counsel.

The Maryland statute permitted the procedure to be invoked only in situations where the child witness would suffer emotional distress to the extent of being unable to communicate if obliged to be in contact with his or her alleged attacker. In support of its request to use this procedure in *Craig*, the prosecution named a number of older children who had also allegedly been sexually abused by Sandra Craig and who an expert witness declared would suffer emotional distress if forced to testify in Craig's presence. Craig objected to use of the procedure, but the trial court allowed it, and Craig was convicted on all counts. After her conviction was upheld by two state appellate courts, Craig took her case to the U.S. Supreme Court.

Court Overrides Plain Language of the Sixth Amendment

The section of the Sixth Amendment at issue in Craig's case reads: "In all criminal prosecutions, the accused shall enjoy the right . . . to be confronted with the witnesses against him." By the time the Supreme Court heard *Craig*, it was settled law that the Fourteenth Amendment makes the Confrontation Clause applicable in state courts. Writing for the one-vote majority that upheld the Maryland statute, Justice O'Connor was obliged to ignore the plain meaning of the Constitution:

> [T]hough we reaffirm the importance of face-to-face confrontation with witnesses appearing

at the trial, we cannot say that such confrontation is an indispensable element of the Sixth Amendment's guarantee of the right to confront one's accusers . . . This interpretation of the Confrontation Clause is consistent with our cases holding that other Sixth Amendment rights must also be interpreted in the context of the necessities of trial and the adversary process . . . We see no reason to treat the face-to-face component of the confrontation right any differently, and indeed we think it would be anomalous to do so.

O'Connor went on to explain that the procedure authorized by the Maryland statute violated neither the truth-seeking nor the "symbolic" purposes of the Confrontation Clause. The procedure required the child witness to testify under oath, and permitted both cross-examination and observation of the witness's demeanor.

The four dissenters—Scalia, Brennan, Marshall, and Stevens—did not agree that the purposes of the Confrontation Clause were symbolic. While conceding that the Maryland procedure conformed to "currently favored public policy" and might not be unfair, they did not believe that the Court had any business substituting social policy for the plain meaning of the Constitution. As recently as 1988, the Court had unequivocally stated, in *Coy v. Iowa* that "the Confrontation Clause guarantees the defendant a face-to-face meeting with witnesses appearing before the trier of fact."

In a companion case to *Craig, Idaho v. Wright* (1990), the Court ruled by a vote of 5-4 that a physician's account of a child's statements about his alleged sexual abuse by another adult were inadmissible because they were unreliable. The issue of the proper procedure for trying alleged child molesters remained largely unresolved.

Related Cases
Coy v. Iowa, 487 U.S. 1012 (1988).
Idaho v. Wright, 497 U.S. 805 (1990).

Bibliography and Further Reading

Dziech, Billie Wright, and Charles B. Schudson. *On Trial: America's Courts and Their Treatment of Sexually Abused Children.* Boston, MA: Beacon Press, 1989.

Friedman, Barry. "Dialogue and Judicial Review." *Michigan Law Review,* February 1993, p. 577.

Goodman, Allison C. "Two Critical Evidentiary Issues in Child Sexual Abuse Cases." *American Criminal Law Review,* spring 1995, p. 855.

Goodman, Gail S., and Bette L. Bottoms, eds. *Child Victims, Child Witnesses: Understanding and Improving Testimony.* New York, NY: Guilford Press, 1993.

Murphy, Cornelius M. "Justice Scalia and the Confrontation Clause." *American Criminal Law Review,* spring 1997, p. 1243.

Perry, Nancy Walker, and Lawrence S. Wrightsman. *The Child Witness: Legal Issues and Dilemmas.* Newbury Park, CA: Sage Publications, 1991.

NORTH CAROLINA V. T. D. R.

Legal Citation: 495 S.E.2d 700 (1998)

Appellant
State of North Carolina

Appellee
T. D. R. (an unidentified juvenile)

Appellate's Claim
That denial of a request for a two-week trial extension to gather new evidence did not violate the Due Process Clause of the Fourteenth Amendment.

Chief Lawyer for Appellant
Michael F. Easley

Chief Lawyer for Appelee
Kevin P. Bradley

Justice for the Court
Burley B. Mitchell, Jr. (writing for the court)

Place
Durham, North Carolina

Date of Decision
6 February 1998

Decision
Upheld the state of North Carolina's claim by reversing two lower courts' decisions and returning the case to the lower courts for reinstatement of indictments against T. D. R.

Significance
The ruling recognized flexibility lower state courts have in trying violent juvenile offenders as adults. The case characterized the responsiveness of state governments, including court systems, to public demands for toughening punishment measures of violent and destructive crimes, even when performed by youths.

To many the juvenile justice system had fallen into chaos toward the end of the twentieth century. While violent crime in the United States decreased in general through the 1990s, violent crime by teens rose dramatically. The juvenile court system, originally established to try youths under the age of 18, was increasingly accused of letting violent teen criminals off with nothing more than "a slap on the wrist."

Traditionally, the age of the juvenile and the seriousness of the offense were the key criteria considered when determining whether to try a juvenile as an adult. With respect to age, 21 states had no minimum age requirement for a juvenile to be tried as an adult, and of the remaining 29 states, minimum age requirements ranged from seven to 16 years of age. The primary offenses for which juveniles were tried as adults included the more serious crimes such as murder, offenses involving serious personal injury, property crimes, public order offenses, and drug offenses. Some states tried juveniles as adults if their alleged offense would normally constitute a felony and evidence existed of prior felony convictions. Moreover, some states allowed juveniles to be tried as adults if they were considered unlikely to respond to the treatment available in juvenile detention facilities.

Trying juveniles in the adult court system always sparked heated debate. Fear of random violence committed by young teens became one of the nation's greatest concerns by the late 1990s. Encouraged by the Violent Crime Control and Law Enforcement Act of 1994, many state legislatures enacted "get tough" measures ensuring violent teen offenders would be punished "appropriately" for their crime. Two prominent viewpoints existed in the debate of trying teens as adults. The conservative position maintained that treating teens as adults was an effective way to express public outrage for the offenses of wayward youth by ensuring punishment. The opposing viewpoint contended that trying teens as adults was too harsh. Embracing the motto that "children are the future of this country," juvenile advocates contended that society had a responsibility to rehabilitate youth while plenty of time still existed to lead productive lives. Also, juveniles incarcerated with hardened adult criminals were easy prey for sexual assault and other forms of violence. However, a seeming increase of highly publicized violent crimes committed by the hands of young teens and even pre-teens occurred through the 1990s, including an outbreak of school shootings. The rehabilitation stance gradually lost ground to the more conservative punishment stance to appease the public's outcry for more severe treatment of violent teen offenders.

Teen Assault and Court Jurisdiction

In August of 1996 a 15-year-old juvenile, known as T. D. R., broke into a woman's home. He forced the woman into a bedroom where at knife point he sexually assaulted her. Before leaving, T. D. R. cut off the victim's hair and forced her into a closet. Upon apprehension, the state of North Carolina filed a juvenile petition alleging T. D. R. a delinquent as a result of committing first-degree rape and burglary.

In a district court hearing, T. D. R. waived his right to present evidence and agreed that probable cause did exist, that he in fact committed the crime. T. D. R. also requested a two-week continuance, a request for more time before the trial would begin, in order to undergo psychological evaluations. The evaluations could then be admitted as evidence concerning the issue of whether his case should be transferred to superior court for trial as an adult. The district court denied the continuance, and transferred jurisdiction, the power to hear and determine a case, over T. D. R. to superior court to try him as an adult on both charges in addition to first-degree kidnapping.

In February of 1997 the superior court determined that the district court denied T. D. R. "due process of law and fundamental fairness by its refusal to hear or consider the juvenile's evidence with regard to the appropriateness of retaining jurisdiction in the district court." The court ordered the indictments dismissed and sent the case back to the district court. The state of North Carolina appealed the decision.

In March of 1997, the appeals court overruled the February superior court decision and sent the case back to superior court with the indictments reinstated. The court of appeals ruled that district court orders transferring jurisdiction over a juvenile to superior court were subject to review by the court of appeals only after the final judgement of the superior court. While T. D. R. had not focused on the issue of jurisdiction in his appeal, the juvenile did claim he was denied due process after the district court had not granted the continuance he had originally requested. The Supreme Court of North Carolina agreed to hear the case.

When Juveniles Are Adults

The Supreme Court of North Carolina reversed the court of appeal's ruling. Chief Justice Mitchell, writing for the court, found that the court of appeals had

authority to hear any direct appeal in a juvenile transfer order, not just those with final decisions. Since the juvenile transfer order terminated district court jurisdiction by sending the case to a superior court, the district court action was completed. In addition, Mitchell ruled the superior court did not have legal authority to conduct a review of district court transfer order. Only the court of appeals possessed proper jurisdiction for review of district court orders transferring jurisdiction over juveniles to the superior court.

Mitchell found that the district court had legal authority to transfer T. D. R.'s case to superior court for adult trial since he was (1) older than 13 years-of-age; (2) had allegedly committed an offense constituting a Class A felony if committed by an adult; and, (3) had completed a district court probable cause hearing.

If the district court had found probable cause, but the offense was not a Class A felony, the district court would have had to determine whether the "needs of the juvenile or the best interest of the State will be served by transfer of the case to Superior Court." Mitchell wrote that in order to avoid due process constitutionality challenges as addressed by the U.S. Supreme Court in *Schall v. Martin*, the district court should have allowed T. D. R. a hearing in which the juvenile, represented by counsel, could have testified on his own behalf, calling and examining witnesses, and producing other evidence dealing with the issue of whether the he should be sent to the superior court to be tried as an adult. Mitchell held that juveniles should be afforded the same constitutional guarantees as adults in criminal prosecutions.

Mitchell also concluded that the superior court had authority to review the indictment against T. D. R. and to dismiss charges if T. D. R.'s rights had been "flagrantly violated and there is such irreparable prejudice to the defendant's preparation of his case that there is no remedy but to dismiss the prosecution." Mitchell held this requirement for dismissal was not satisfied since T. D. R. was merely denied more time to gather evidence to respond to the state's expert witness, which T. D. R. argued was available had the additional time been granted. Mitchell wrote that denial of such motions are reviewed on appeal only if the defendant can demonstrate "gross abuse" of discretion. Mitchell asserted T. D. R. had over three months to gather evidence, and at no time offered an explanation why this time was not sufficient. In fact, T. D. R. not only had ample time to gather evidence, but the district court delayed the hearing date more than once, and assisted T. D. R. in gathering evidence when requested. As a result, Mitchell concluded the district court neither abused its discretion nor committed any constitutional error in denying T. D. R.'s motion for continuance.

Consequently, Mitchell continued, the superior court order dismissing the indictments, and returning the case to district court was in error, and should have been reversed by the court of appeals. To set the case record straight again, Mitchell reversed the court of appeals' ruling and the superior court's order. He then returned the case to the court of appeals under orders to return the matter to the superior court for reinstatement of the indictments against T. D. R. Any further proceedings should be in accordance with trying T. D. R. as an adult.

Impact

Criminal punishment became increasingly politicized in the 1990s. Trying children as adults was often justified on grounds that teens who committed violent crimes should receive punishment comparable to their crimes. In addition, it was believed by many that stiff penalties served as deterrents to other teens who might commit murder or other serious crimes. The prospect of serving life with hardened criminals in adult prison might make those teens think twice. The possibility of only being sent to a juvenile detention for several years, it was argued, in no way provided the same deterrent. Legislatures were hesitant to pass any legislation that could be seen as being soft on crime. The public outcry for stiffer penalties became deafening, and the legislators were not about to deny the public what it yearned for. Previously, trying a juvenile as an adult was seen as a last resort after all avenues of the juvenile system had been utilized. By the 1990s, however, juveniles were being initially tried as adults because of public demand in most states. Whether this trend was the best avenue of trial and punishment was basically irrelevant in the politically conservative environment that existed.

Juvenile advocates, on the other hand, maintained that trying juveniles as adults was only a short-sighted, "knee-jerk" solution to a complex social condition.

They argued that in satisfying the public's rage against violent teen perpetrators, the system was merely setting these offenders up for a reappearance into society with a criminal label, and in all likelihood, becoming even more dangerous to society after being locked up with adult criminals. Those supporting this contention believed that rather than locking these teens up, society as a whole needed to devise a community solution, since crime has traditionally been viewed as a community disease.

As youth crime escalated through the 1990s with few plausible alternatives to trying teens as adults who commit violent crimes, submersing teens into adult criminal systems remained society's popular response. Many believed that until the juvenile system experienced a complete overhaul to more effectively deal with violent teens, such as the use of juries in the process, elimination of legal counsel shortcomings, and applying consistently stricter punishment for violent crimes, states would continue to escalate trying juveniles as adults.

Related Cases

In re Gault, 387 U.S. 1 (1967).

Breed v. Jones, 421 U.S. 519 (1975).

In re Arthur, 231 S.E.2d 614 (1977).

Schall v. Martin, 467 U.S. 253 (1984).

Bibliography and Further Reading

Current Events. Teen Crime: More and More Teens Are Being Tried as Adults—A Good Idea? 24 October 1997.

Feld, Barry C. *Justice for Children: The Right to Counsel and the Juvenile Courts.* Boston: Northeastern University Press, 1993.

Krisberg, Barry, and James F. Austin. *Reinventing Juvenile Justice.* Newbury Park: SAGE Publications, 1993.

"Juvenile Offenders: Should They Be Tried in Adult Courts?" *USA Today,* January, 1998.

REPRODUCTIVE RIGHTS

Definition

The term "reproductive rights" is commonly understood to refer to legal developments in the area of abortion. When the term is employed the first thought that often comes to mind is "abortion rights." Abortion issues certainly fall within the general category of reproductive rights and, indeed, have attracted the most attention from the media, the legal community, and the public in general. However, there are a host of other important issues related to "reproductive rights." Contraception, sex education, condom availability programs, involuntary sterilization, surrogacy, and in-vitro fertilization are issues that have been taken up in the courts expanding the range of "reproductive rights" implicit in the Constitution.

History

Until the mid-1800s abortion was not a crime in this country. However, by the beginning of the 1900s, it was banned in every state. In 1930, approximately 800,000 abortions were performed illegally, resulting in an annual death toll of approximately 8,000 to 17,000. *Griswold v. Connecticut* (1965) represented the first major development in reproductive rights. In *Griswold* the Court ruled a Connecticut statute that prohibited both married and unmarried couples from using contraceptives unconstitutional. *Griswold* was important because it marked the first time the Court acknowledged a "right to privacy" in the Constitution. Although the case dealt specifically with "marital privacy," the ruling would have far reaching effects for subsequent right to privacy issue—including reproductive rights. All subsequent reproductive rights defined by the courts owe their origin, directly or indirectly, to *Griswold*, which codified the notion of a right to privacy in America's legal system for the first time. In *Eisenstadt v. Baird* (1972), consistent with *Griswold* the Court extended the right to use contraceptives to single people. These initial reproductive rights victories laid the foundation for a constitutional challenge to the abortion ban in 1973.

In *Roe v. Wade,* (1973) the U.S. Supreme Court found that the fundamental constitutional right to privacy applied to the right to procure an abortion. The Court found the right "broad enough to encompass a woman's decision whether or not to terminate her pregnancy." The Texas statute that was challenged in *Roe* prohibited abortions any time during the first trimester except in cases that threatened the life of the mother. The Court found that statutes that prohibited abortions were in violation of the Equal Protection Clause of the Fourteenth Amendment. In addition, the Court settled the previously undetermined issue of viability; the Court established that a fetus was considered to be a "viable" human at about 24-28 weeks. States were permitted to regulate abortions after viability in order to protect the life of the fetus unless the procedure was necessary to preserve the life or health of the mother.

A Succession of Court Battles

In *Bigelow v. Virginia* (1975) the Court invalidated a Virginia statute that prohibited the use of abortion service advertisements. A year later the landmark case, *Planned Parenthood of Central Missouri v. Danforth* (1976), invalidated a statutory provision requiring unmarried minors to obtain the written consent of one parent before obtaining an abortion. The statute was invalidated because it did not allow for alternatives to parental consent such as a judicial waiver. Similarly, the Court invalidated provisions of a Missouri statute that required a married woman to obtain consent from her husband to obtain an abortion, a physician to preserve the life and health of a fetus at every stage of pregnancy, and prohibited the use of saline amniocentesis as a method of abortion.

Although opponents to abortion lost the battle over the legality of the procedure, they held out hope that access to the procedure could be curtailed by limiting public funds for abortions. In 1976 Congress passed the Hyde Amendment which banned the use of Medicaid and other federal funds for nearly all abortions. Shortly thereafter a series of Supreme Court decisions upheld the principle behind the Hyde Amendment. *Maher v. Roe* (1977), *Beal v. Doe* (1977) and *Poelker v. Doe* (1977), upheld the prohibition of public funds to provide abortions not deemed "medically necessary."

In 1979 the Court reaffirmed its ruling in *Planned Parenthood of Central Missouri v. Danforth* which held that unmarried minors cannot be required to obtain parental consent to have an abortion. In 8-1 vote, the Court invalidated a Massachusetts law requiring parental consent to an abortion for a minor in *Bellotti v. Baird* II. The *Bellotti* ruling was important for several reasons. Initially, the Court objected to states requiring parental consent for abortions because the Missouri statute did not allow for a judicial waiver to stand in lieu of written parental consent. In *Bellotti* the Court decided that states could not require parental consent for minors even if a statute allowed room for a judicial waiver to override the absence of consent. The judicial waiver in question would have allowed a minor to have an abortion in the absence of parental consent if she adequately demonstrated maturity in court. Four justices ruled the judicial waiver process unconstitutional because it would have required prior parental consultation. Four other justices ruled the statute unconstitutional on the grounds that the principle of allowing a third party, a parent or a judge, to determine whether a minor was mature enough to seek an abortion was flawed. However, in their decision, the Court left the door open for states to enforce parental consent for minors without violating the Constitution. In his opinion Justice Blackmun confessed that the Court was not persuaded that forcing parental consent "unconstitutionally burdened a minor's right to seek an abortion."

In *H. L. v. Matheson* (1981) the Court upheld a state statute that required a doctor to "notify, if possible" the parents of a minor before an abortion is performed. However, in 1983, the Court invalidated provisions of an Ohio statute which would have required parental notification and consent, doctors to make sure that minors seeking an abortion were "truly informed," and a 24 hour waiting period for minors in *Akron v. Akron Center for Reproductive Health.* Then, in 1990, the Court resolved the issue of parental consent by offering two opinions consistent with Blackmun's ruling in *Bellotti.* In *Hodgson v. Minnesota* the Court upheld a statute that prohibited minors from seeking an abortion unless both parents have been notified 48 hours prior to the procedure. Similarly, in *Ohio v. Akron Center for Reproductive Health* the Court upheld an Ohio statute that required one parent to be notified prior to administering an abortion to a minor. As a result of these rulings, over 30 states now require either parental notice or consent for a minor seeking an abortion.

In the 25 years since *Roe v. Wade,* abortion opponents have managed to impose legal restrictions designed to limit the frequency of the procedure. Opposition to abortion seems to be gathering momentum. In 1983, the U.S. solicitor general began urging the Supreme Court to overturn *Roe v. Wade.* In addition, the persuasion of the Supreme Court has been slowly drifting toward conservatism. During the Reagan and Bush administrations, both of whom opposed abortion, five Supreme Court justices were appointed (Sandra Day O'Connor, Antonin Scalia, Anthony M. Kennedy, David H. Souter and Clarence Thomas).

The Court showed its conservative leaning in *Webster v. Reproductive Health Services* (1989). Here, the Court expanded the opportunity for states to regulate abortions and fell one vote short of overturning *Roe.* The *Webster* ruling upheld provisions of a Missouri statute that prohibited the use of public facilities or personnel to perform abortions, and required a physician to perform tests to determine the viability of a fetus beyond the 20 week mark. After this ruling, Utah, Louisiana, and the territory of Guam enacted statutes that prohibit virtually all forms of abortions.

When the Supreme Court agreed to review *Planned Parenthood of Southeastern Pennsylvania v. Casey* in 1992, it was essentially faced with the proposition of affirming or overturning its decision in *Roe.* Although the Court did not overturn *Roe,* it granted the states considerable latitude to regulate abortions. Most importantly, the Court's ruling in *Casey* permitted states to regulate abortions prior to "viability," provided that such regulations did not impose an "undue burden" on a mother seeking an abortion. Under the "undue burden test," stringent state regulations can exist within the framework of the Constitution as long as they do not place a "substantial obstacle in the path of a woman seeking an abortion of a nonviable fetus." Although the Court expanded the states regulatory capacity in *Casey,* it did not prohibit abortions. Since 1992, the Court has been less willing to grant full briefings and oral argument in abortion cases. Prior to the *Casey* ruling only three states enforced three or more restrictions on abortions. In 1998, the number of states enforcing three or more restrictions had risen to 17. Moreover, since *Casey,* the number of states enforcing mandatory waiting periods before obtaining an abortion rose from zero to 12 and the enactment of consent or mandatory parental notice laws for minors has increased from 17 to 30. The Court was initially liberal in its application of the right to privacy to abortion practices. However, since *Roe* Supreme Court decisions have generally restricted reproductive rights in the area of abortion.

Abortion-Related Legislation Becomes a Must

In 84 percent of U.S. counties no physicians are willing to perform an abortion. Between 1977 and 1994 more than 2,500 bombings, arsons, blockades and episodes of vandalism were directed at abortion clinics. In response to these acts of violence, Congress passed The Freedom of Access to Clinic Entrances Act of 1994 (FACE). This statute prohibits the use or threats of force, physical obstruction, and property damage directed at people obtaining or providing reproductive care. In 1996, Congress passed a bill prohibiting state medical schools from requiring abortion training and threatened withdrawal of federal and state funding from such programs.

In 1997, Congress passed legislation, the Partial Birth Abortion Ban of 1997, which prohibited physicians from performing certain abortion procedures. President Clinton vetoed the bill on the grounds that it did not contain provisions for performing the procedures to preserve a woman's health—provisions which were established in prior decisions of the Supreme Court.

There is evidence to suggest that opposition to abortion practices is growing. Some anti-abortion groups have even tried to justify terrorism to discourage the practice. In 1997, for example, the National Organization for Women filed a class action lawsuit under the Racketeer Influenced and Corrupt Organizations Act. In *National Organization for Women, Inc. v. Scheidler,* a state court rejected the defendants' claim that their "moral imperative" to stop abortion made terrorism necessary and acceptable. More recently, Congress drafted the Child Custody Protection Act of 1998, which would prohibit the transport of a minor across state lines for an abortion unless the minor had already fulfilled the requirements of her home state's parental involvement law.

A Constant Threat

In May of 1998, in accordance with the 1997 Wisconsin Act 219, doctors in Wisconsin stopped performing abortions and women choosing to terminate their pregnancies were forced to cross state lines to do so. The law defined the beginning of human life at the point of conception and imposes a life sentence for abortion providers in Wisconsin. A federal trial is scheduled to test the law's constitutionality. Requests from abortion providers to have the courts issue temporary restraining orders, which would allow access to abortion services while the law is being challenged, have been denied.

The outcome of the legal challenge to the Wisconsin statute will have a tremendous impact on the extent to which other states restrict abortions and it may well result in the reversal of *Roe v. Wade.* In addition to Wisconsin's challenge to *Roe,* Congress is expected to override President Clinton's veto of the Partial Birth Abortion Ban of 1997 in the fall of 1999.

Contraception Rights

Though far less devisive than abortion, the regulation of contraception use has been the focus of heated legal debate. In 1965, *Griswold v. Connecticut* set the precedent for legal debate over contraception rights. In *Griswold* the Court ruled that states cannot prohibit married couples from using contraceptives. In *Eisenstadt v. Baird* (1972), consistent with the *Griswold* decision, the Court invalidated a law that prohibited the distribution of contraceptives to unmarried individuals. The decision

extended the constitutional right to privacy to unwed individuals. Likewise, in 1977, the Court struck down a New York law that prohibited the sale or distribution of contraceptives to minors in *Carey v. Population Services International.* Each of these cases served to broaden reproductive rights in the area of contraceptive use.

Since *Carey,* changes in the congressional climate have brought about new rulings which challenge old precedents. In July of 1998 the House Appropriations Committee, by a 32-24 vote, gave approval to an amendment requiring teens seeking prescription contraception at Title X family planning clinics to have parental consent or to have clinics notify parents five business days in advance of providing such products. Despite the fact that most health insurance plans provide coverage for prescription drugs, the majority exclude coverage for prescription contraceptives. In addition, while most insurance plans cover routine outpatient surgeries, elective sterilization procedures are usually not covered.

Surrogacy and In-vitro Fertilization

Legal issues related to surrogacy and in-vitro fertilization have been addressed by the courts on a case by case basis. In 1985, William and Dr. Elizabeth Stern contracted with Mary Beth Whitehead to be a "surrogate mother." Under the terms of the contract, Whitehead would be artificially inseminated with Stern's sperm making Whitehead the child's biological mother. Whitehead agreed to give the child to the Sterns after giving birth, relinquishing her parental rights. The Sterns agreed to pay Whitehead $10,000 plus her medical bills.

When the child was born, Whitehead refused to give the child to the Sterns. The Sterns sued for custody. The case, which became known as *In re Baby M,* was publicized nationwide in the mid-1980s. The New Jersey State Supreme Court ruled that the contract was invalid. The court ruled that payment to a "surrogate mother" was illegal because it constituted child selling and granted parental rights to Mr. Stern and Mrs. Whitehead.

Since both William Stern and Mary Beth Whitehead had parental rights to Baby M, the court had to resolve the issue of custody in accordance with the best interests of the child. When a court order gave Stern temporary custody of Baby M, Whitehead and her husband fled with the baby. Because of the Whiteheads' behavior and financial instability, the court awarded custody to Mr. Stern. However, Mrs. Whitehead was granted visitation rights.

Early in 1999, a California appellate court ruled on the highly publicized "parentless child" case. In *In Re Marriage of Buzzanca,* a married couple, John and Luanne Buzzanca, arranged a surrogacy contract in which an anonymous egg and sperm were implanted in a surrogate mother's womb.

One month before the child's expected birth, the Buzzancas separated and petitioned for divorce. When the child (Jaycee) was born, the hospital released the child to Luanne Buzzanca in accordance with the surrogacy contract. She then filed for child support payments from John Buzzanca. He convinced the trial court that support payments could not be ordered because the baby was not the "child of the marriage" pursuant to California Family Code Section 2010. The appellate court disagreed and ordered the family law court to determine an appropriate child support order. After a three year battle, the appellate court ruled that John Buzzanca and Luanne Buzzanca are the legal parents of Jaycee.

The appellate court in *Buzzanca* relied on *Johnson v. Calvert* (1993), in which the California Supreme Court first upheld the legality of a gestational surrogacy contract. The *Johnson* case ruled that, according to the California Uniform Parentage Act, both the intended mother and the gestational mother could establish parentage. The intended father was also ruled a potential parent by the action of entering into the surrogacy agreement. The court explained that: "John admits he signed the surrogacy agreement, which for all practical purposes caused Jaycee's conception every bit as much as if he had caused her birth the old fashioned way."

In *Moschetta v. Moschetta* (1994), a surrogate mother was artificially inseminated with the sperm of the intended father. The surrogate was the biological mother as well as the birth mother, and sought custody after the intended father left her with the child. The court did not recognize the surrogacy contract as an advance waiver of the surrogate's parental rights and looked instead at the parties' intent at the time of the contract to determine parental rights.

Reproductive rights related to surrogacy and in-vitro fertilization often involve legal and ethical issues which the courts cannot address with broad rulings. The particularities of the cases usually dictate the rulings. Other reproductive rights issues such as abortion and the use and dissemination of contraceptives lend themselves to more definitive judgments by the courts. As new medical technologies are developed, the courts will continue to be called upon to resolve complex legal issues related to reproductive rights.

See also: **Civil Rights and Equal Protection**

Bibliography and Further Reading

American Civil Liberties Union, American Civil Liberties Union Freedom Network, New York, NY, http://www.aclu.org, 1998.

California Abortion Rights Action League, Reproductive Health and Rights Center, San Francisco, CA, http://www.caral.org, 1998.

Cornell Law School, Legal Information Institute, Ithaca, NY, http://www.law.cornell.edu. 1998.

Findlaw Internet Legal Resources, Palo Alto, CA, http://www.findlaw.com, 1994-1998.

InfoSynthesis, Inc., Home of the "USSC+" database of Supreme Court Opinions, St. Paul, MN, http://www.usscplus.com, 1998.

National Abortion & Reproductive Rights Action League, Washington, D.C., http://www.naral.org, 1998.

National Organization for Women, "Fight the Radical Right," Washington, D.C., http://www.now.org, 1995-1998.

New York Civil Liberties Union, New York, NY, http://www.nyclu.org, 1998.

MASSACHUSETTS V. BANGS

Legal Citation: 9 Mass. 386 (1812)

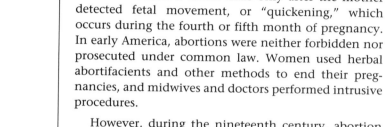

Common law in both England and America held that abortion became a moral issue only after the mother detected fetal movement, or "quickening," which occurs during the fourth or fifth month of pregnancy. In early America, abortions were neither forbidden nor prosecuted under common law. Women used herbal abortifacients and other methods to end their pregnancies, and midwives and doctors performed intrusive procedures.

However, during the nineteenth century, abortion became a crime. *Massachusetts v. Bangs* illustrates how judicial opinion began to change. During the October court term of 1810, Isaiah Bangs was arrested and indicted for the assault and battery of a pregnant woman, Lucy Holman, and for forcing her to swallow a drug causing abortion. The jury found Bangs guilty of assault and battery for the abortion, but not for forcing the woman to take the drug. The jury thought she had done this voluntarily.

The solicitor general had to withdraw the assault and battery charge. Bangs now appealed that the indictment did not describe a criminal offense except those the solicitor general had withdrawn.

Bangs' lawyer, Mr. Fay, claimed:

> No abortion was produced; and if there had been, there is no [proof] that the woman was quick with child; both [of] which circumstances are necessary ingredients in the offense intended to be charged in the indictment.

The solicitor general disagreed, arguing that the woman's consent to take the drug did not make administering it lawful. The court decided it could not pass sentence in the case:

> The assault and battery are out of the case, and no abortion is alleged to have followed the taking of the potion; and if an abortion had been alleged and proved to have ensued, the [proof] that the woman was quick with child at the time is a necessary part of the indictment.

In other words, for an indictment to be valid, it must contain the allegations that the woman was pregnant with a "quickened baby" and that an abortion did take place.

Prosecution
The State of Massachusetts

Defendant
Isaiah Bangs

Crimes Charged
Causing an abortion, committing assault and battery on Lucy Holman and administering a harmful drug to her.

Chief Prosecutor
Solicitor General

Chief Defense Lawyer
Fay

Justices for the Court
Chief Justice Theophilus Parsons, Isaac Parker, Samuel Sewall

Justices Dissenting
None

Place
Cambridge, Massachusetts

Date of Decision
October term, 1812

Decision
Bangs was found not guilty.

Significance
Common law tradition permitted a woman to abort a fetus up until "quickening." This began to change in the nineteenth century, as this case shows.

Impact

Although Bangs got off on a technicality, the severity of the charges showed that public attitudes were becoming more restrictive. During the nineteenth century, a few states began to declare abortion illegal after the fourth month of pregnancy—for example, Connecticut (1821), Missouri (1827), and Illinois (1827). In 1840, 10 of the 26 states had placed restrictions on abortions. In 1965, the laws in all 50 states prohibited abortion, restricting its use to life-threatening situations.

In some states, legislators modified these laws to make exceptions for rape, incest, or fetal deformity. In 1973, the battle to remove all restrictions on abortion resulted in the U.S. Supreme Court's landmark *Roe v. Wade* ruling, invalidating all state laws that prohibited abortion during the first 12 weeks after conception.

Related Cases

Roe v. Wade, 410 U.S. 113 (1973).

Bibliography and Further Reading

Costa, Marie. *Abortion.* Santa Barbara, CA: ABC-CLIO, 1991.

Garrow, David J. *Liberty and Sexuality: The Right to Privacy and the Making of Roe v. Wade.* New York: Macmillan/Lisa Drew Books, 1994.

Hoff, Joan. *Law, Gender, and Injustice: A Legal History of U.S. Women.* New York: New York University Press, 1991.

Hymowitz, Carol, and Michaele Weissman. *A History of Women in America.* New York: Bantam, 1978.

Kerber, Linda K. *Women's America: Refocusing the Past.* New York: Oxford University Press, 1991.

Salmon, Marylynn. *Women and the Law of Property in Early America.* Chapel Hill: University of North Carolina Press, 1986.

Wortman, Marlene Stein. *Women in American Law. Vol. I: From Colonial Times to the New Deal.* New York: Holmes & Meier Publishers, 1985.

NEW YORK V. SANGER

Legal Citation: 118 N.E. 637 (1918)

Appellant
Margaret H. Sanger

Appellee
State of New York

Appellant's Claim
That the Comstock Act of 1873 violated both the federal and state Constitutions; therefore Sanger was not guilty of a criminal act when she opened the first birth control clinic.

Chief Lawyer for Appellant
Jonah J. Goldstein

Chief Lawyer for Appellee
Harry E. Lewis

Justices for the Court
William S. Andrews, Benjamin N. Cardozo, Emory A. Chase, Frederick Collin, Frederick E. Crane (writing for the court), William H. Cuddeback, Frank H. Hiscock, John W. Hogan, Cuthbert W. Pound

Place
New York, New York

Date of Decision
8 January 1918

Decision
The lower court's guilty decision was affirmed.

Significance
This decision allowed doctors to advise their married patients about birth control for health purposes. Sanger later interpreted this ruling as grounds to start legal doctor-staffed birth control clinics in 1923.

Margaret Sanger was born Margaret Louise Higgins in Corning, New York on 14 September 1883, one of 11 surviving children. Believing her mother's 18 pregnancies caused her death at age 50, Sanger founded the American birth control movement—and went to jail at least nine times for her efforts. She lived to see birth control become a legal practice throughout the United States in 1965.

Up from Poverty

After two years of study at Claverack College and Hudson River Institute, the Higgins' finances were exhausted, so their daughter went to work at the White Plains Hospital in New York. There she completed two years of nurse's training, and in 1902, she married William Sanger in a quick wedding that allowed her to report to her 4:30 A.M. shift the next day.

As a home nurse in New York City, Sanger ministered to maternity patients in the slums of the lower east side. However, when a truck driver's wife died painfully from a self-induced abortion, Sanger left nursing forever, turning to birth control education.

During 1910 and 1911, Sanger gave a series of lectures to Socialist Party women on female sexuality. Her popularity resulted in an invitation to become a columnist for the party paper, *The Call*. In one column she explicitly condemned customs that forced women to rely on men for support. In another, she warned about the dangers of syphilis—prompting the U.S. Postal Service's refusal to mail *The Call* under the 40-year-old federal Comstock Act that banned the topic as obscene.

Comstock's Law

After the Civil War, more rigid American attitudes had led to the passage of the Comstock Act in 1873. The law classified contraceptive literature as obscene—illegal to mail through the U.S. Post Office. It stifled the dissemination of birth control information, even in newspaper ads. It also made it a misdemeanor for a person to sell, give away, advertise, or offer for sale, any instrument, article, drug, or medicine that would prevent contraception. It was even unlawful to give someone verbal information on contraception. Until this time, the nation's birthrates had been declining and the sale of contraception devices increasing.

Sanger wanted to flout the Comstock Act, so she launched her own monthly magazine, *The Woman Rebel,* publishing it from her dining room table. Because the words "birth control" appeared, and with it the promise to provide women with contraceptive advice, the U.S. Post Office refused to mail the magazine. Sanger could go to jail if she continued publication.

Still Sanger continued. Predictably, police arrested her in August of 1914. Indicted on four criminal counts carrying a maximum sentence of 45 years, she fled to Europe one day before her trial. The next year, she returned. Soon after her daughter, Peggy, died of pneumonia. In February of 1916, perhaps in response to a public sympathy for Sanger, prosecutor Harold Content dropped the charges.

Civilly Disobedient

Sanger threw herself into promoting birth control. On 16 October 1916, using a $50 donation, she and her sister, Ethel Byrne, opened the country's first birth control clinic—an act of civil disobedience.

The clinic occupied two rooms on the ground floor at 46 Amboy Street, near Pitkin Avenue in the Brownsville section of Brooklyn, New York. Its staff consisted of Sanger, Byrne, Fania Mindell—who spoke Yiddish—and a social worker, Elizabeth Stuyvesant. During the ten days before police closed the clinic, nearly five hundred women came through its doors.

On the ninth day after the clinic's opening, a "Mrs." Whitehurst walked in to buy a ten-cent sex education pamphlet. A member of the vice squad, she returned the next day with three other officers, shouting, "I'm a police officer. You're under arrest."

According to the *Brooklyn Eagle,* the police "half-dragged, half-carried" the sisters to a paddy wagon. The local station freed them after they posted a $500 bail. A few weeks later, Sanger reopened the clinic, but again police shut it down, charging Sanger with creating a public nuisance. They arrested Byrne soon after.

Sanger immediately hired attorney Jonah J. Goldstein to represent them. During Byrne's trial, he argued that New York's Comstock Law—which permitted the distribution of birth control information only in case of medical need—denied the poor their right to chose

Margaret Sanger (left) and Lillian Fassett on their way to court.
© *UPI/Corbis-Bettmann.*

the size of their families. Nonetheless, the court found Byrne guilty of distributing "obscene" birth control information, sentencing her to 32 days in the workhouse on Blackwell's Island.

Byrne announced she would go on a hunger strike, "to die, if need be, for my sex." Four days after she began her fast, New York City's corrections commissioner announced Byrne would be the first inmate in U.S. history to be forcibly fed through a tube inserted in her throat. The *New York Times* daily covered the painful details of her feedings of brandy, milk, and eggs on its front page.

As a result of all the publicity, the National Birth Control League stepped in to defend the sisters. Called the "Committee of 100," they held a rally at Carnegie Hall shortly after Byrne's sentencing. Three thousand people showed up to hear Sanger speak. Several days later, some of the group took Sanger to the office of Governor Charles Whitman to plead for her sister's release. Whitman said he would only pardon Byrne if Sanger promised not to reopen the clinic. At first, Sanger refused, but after visiting her weakened sister, she reluctantly accepted the governor's terms. Against her will, Byrne left the workhouse, carried on a stretcher.

Meanwhile, Sanger and Mindell went to trial on 29 January 1917, at the Court of Special Sessions in Brooklyn. The court fined Mindell $50 for selling copies of Sanger's article *What Every Girl Should Know*. Sanger was tried for trafficking in obscene materials. Policewoman Whitehurst testified she had found a box of suppositories and a rubber pessary (a contraceptive device that works something like a diaphragm) in the back room of the Brownsville clinic. Other witnesses implied Sanger had gone beyond verbal instruction to actually fit clients with the devices.

One of the three-judge panel, Freschi, was the most empathetic. He permitted the defense to call a long list of Brownsville mothers who recounted their problems with venereal disease, poverty, and unwanted pregnancies. Eventually Freschi agreed to suspend Sanger's sentence if she promised not to reopen her clinic. She refused: "I cannot promise to obey a law I do not respect." The court, having found her guilty, allowed her the choice of a $5,000 fine or one month in the workhouse. She chose the workhouse.

However, Sanger vowed to repeat her sister's hunger strike, so the workhouse on Blackwell's Island refused to admit her. Instead, she went to the penitentiary for women in Queens, New York.

The Door Is Opened

After her release, Sanger filed an *ex post facto* appeal. Goldstein argued it before the Court of Appeals of the State of New York, saying: The Comstock Act "violates both the federal and state Constitutions," and by preventing the

dissemination of information to all persons . . . it fails to make provision for cases of women who suffer from certain infirmities . . . endangers their lives and brings about a condition injurious to their health.

However, the court thought the Comstock Act was within the police powers of the legislature, because it benefited "the morals and health of the community." On the other hand, if the law prevented a "duly licensed physician" from taking proper care of his married patients, then the law would be unconstitutional. However, Sanger was not a doctor, and therefore the law did not apply to her. Besides, physicians were "excepted from the provisions of this act."

Nevertheless, warned Judge Frederick E. Crane, the law does not allow even doctors to advertise such matters or to give "promiscuous advice to patients irrespective of their condition." It does protect a doctor who "gives such help or advice to a married person to cure or prevent disease."

With these words, Crane upheld Sanger's conviction under the New York obscenity law—laypeople could not distribute information on birth control without violating the 1873 Comstock Act. However, by claiming that the Comstock Act provided for a medical "exception," Crane established the right of doctors to provide contraceptive advice to married women for "the cure and prevention of disease." (Formerly "disease" meant venereal disease and applied to men only. Crane broadened the interpretation of "disease" to include women's ailments.)

Sanger used Crane's decision to launch a nationwide chain of doctor-staffed birth control clinics, and lobbied for state laws allowing "doctors only" to prescribe contraceptive devices. In 1921, her emboldened American Birth Control League tried to remove all state and federal restrictions on the right of physicians to prescribe birth control devices. Not until *United States v. One Package* (1936), did Sanger achieve her goal of reversing the Comstock Act's classification of birth control literature as obscene. Thirty-five years later Congress rewrote the statute to remove any mention of birth control. Many states banned the use of contraceptives by married couples until *Griswold v. Connecticut* (1965), and not until 1972 could unmarried couples legally use birth control devices (*Eisenstadt v. Baird*).

Related Cases
United States v. One Package, 86 F.2d 737 (1936).
Griswold v. Connecticut, 381 U.S. 479 (1965).
Eisenstadt v. Baird, 405 U.S. 438 (1972).

Bibliography and Further Reading
Chesler, Ellen. *Woman of Valor: Margaret Sanger and the Birth Control Movement in America.* New York: Anchor Books/Doubleday, 1993.

Garrow, David J. *Liberty and Sexuality: The Right to Privacy and the Making of Roe v. Wade.* New York: Lisa Drew Books/Macmillan, 1994.

Planned Parenthood. *A Tradition of Choice: Planned Parenthood at 75.* New York: Planned Parenthood Federation of America, 1991.

BUCK V. BELL

Legal Citation: 274 U.S. 200 (1927)

Appellant
Carrie Buck

Appellee
Dr. J. H. Bell

Appellant's Claim
That Virginia's eugenic sterilization law violated Carrie Buck's constitutional rights.

Chief Lawyer for Appellant
Irving Whitehead

Chief Defense Lawyer
Aubrey E. Strode

Justices for the Court
Louis D. Brandeis, Oliver Wendell Holmes (writing for the Court), James Clark McReynolds, Edward Terry Sanford, Harlan Fiske Stone, George Sutherland, William Howard Taft, Willis Van Devanter

Justices Dissenting
Pierce Butler

Place
Washington, D.C.

Date of Decision
2 May 1927

Decision
Upheld as constitutional Virginia's compulsory sterilization of young women considered "unfit [to] continue their kind".

Significance
Virginia's law served as a model for similar laws in 30 states, under which 50,000 U.S. citizens were sterilized without their consent. During the Nuremberg war trials, Nazi lawyers cited *Buck v. Bell* as acceptable precedent for the sterilization of 2 million people in its "Rassenhygiene" (race hygiene) program.

The Supreme Court's decision in *Buck v. Bell* resulted in only one letter of sympathy to the soon-to-be sterilized Carrie Buck and surprisingly little newspaper coverage. Oliver Wendell Holmes, who wrote the decision, had no second thoughts. As he wrote in a letter later that month, "One decision . . . gave me pleasure, establishing the constitutionality of a law permitting the sterilization of imbeciles." The decision had far-reaching and disastrous consequences, however, not only for Carrie Buck—who was not "feebleminded" or retarded—but for many other similarly sterilized individuals and the peoples involved in World War II.

Emma Buck was the widowed mother of three small children, whom she supported through prostitution and with the help of charity until they were taken from her. On 1 April 1920, she was brought before Charlottesville, Virginia Justice of the Peace Charles D. Shackleford. After a cursory interview, Shackleford committed Emma Buck to the Virginia Colony for Epileptics and Feebleminded, in Lynchburg, Virginia.

At the age of three, Emma Buck's daughter Carrie had joined the family of J. T. and Alice Dobbs. Her school records indicate a normal progression through five years, until she was withdrawn from school by the Dobbs so that she could assume more of the family's housework. The Dobbs were completely satisfied until Carrie turned 17. Then, during what Carrie claimed was a rape by the Dobbs' son, she became pregnant.

The Dobbs brought Carrie before Shackleford and asked him to commit her to the Colony for the Epileptic and Feebleminded, as he had her mother. The Dobbs and their family doctor testified that Carrie was feebleminded; a second doctor agreed. That same day, 24 January 1924, Shackleford signed the order committing the second member of the Buck family to the state colony. The Dobbs institutionalized Carrie as soon as her daughter Vivian was born; they then raised the infant as their own.

Virginia Approaches its Courts with a "Solution"

Dr. Albert Priddy, the first superintendent of the colony, advocated eugenics—the controlled mating of

Eugenics

Eugenics is a social and scientific theory that promotes the improvement of the human race through selective breeding. The idea became popular during the late nineteenth century; Sir Francis Galton is recognized as the "intellectual father of modern eugenics"; Charles Darwin's Theory of Evolution by Natural Selection in 1859 introduced the concepts behind eugenics.

Eugenics concepts have been applied in many different ways. One program may seek to increase the number of individuals with positive genetic traits, such as high intelligence and physical strength. In the United States and Europe, several thousand children are born annually to women artificially inseminated with donor sperm of men possessing these qualities.

A program seeking to reduce the number of members of society with major genetic problems may involve the mandatory sterilization of persons exhibiting such handicaps, thereby preventing reproduction. This is a negative eugenic program. Hitler's program to wipe out the Jewish people during World War II was perhaps the most terrible example of negative eugenics.

Scientific advances in in vitro fertilization, embryo transfer, and other fertility methods may increase the control a society has in determining the characteristics of future generations.

Source(s): Encarta, http://encarta.msn.com/index/conciseindex/22/02247000.htm. Grolier Electronic Publishing, Inc.

---

humans to "improve" the species—as society's best response to the presence of those he called "mental defectives." In the seven years prior to Carrie Buck's arrival, he had sterilized 75 to 100 young women without their consent, claiming that he had operated to cure "pelvic disease." In 1924 the Virginia Assembly adopted an bill permitting the forced sterilization of "feebleminded" or "socially inadequate person[s]." It had been prepared by Aubrey Strode, a state legislator and chief administrator of the Colony for the Epileptic and Feebleminded. Strode had worked from a model sterilization act drafted by American eugenicist Harry H. Laughlin, who considered compulsory sterilization to be "the practical application of those fundamental biological and social principles which determine the racial endowments and the racial health—physical, mental and spiritual—of future generations."

Carrie Buck as a Test Case

On 19 November 1924, *Buck v. Priddy* was argued before Judge Bennett Gordon in the Circuit Court of Amherst County. Aubrey Strode represented Dr. Priddy, who had come to have Buck declared feebleminded and suitable for compulsory sterilization. Irving Whitehead, a lifelong friend to Strode and one of the first board members of the colony, represented Buck in a manner that seems to have been halfhearted. Whitehead's fee was paid by the colony.

Anne Harris, a Charlottesville district nurse, was the first witness. She testified that "Emma Buck, Carrie Buck's mother . . . was living in the worst neighborhoods, and that she was not able to, or would not, work and support her children, and that they were on the streets more or less."

Strode asked, "What about the character of her offspring?"

Harris replied, "Well, I don't know anything very definite about the children, except they don't seem to be able to do any more than their mother."

Strode pounced. "Well, that is the crux of the matter. Are they mentally normal children?"

And Harris responded, "No, sir, they are not."

Harris then admitted during Whitehead's cross examination: "I really know very little about Carrie after she left her mother [at age 3]. Before that time she was most too small."

Three teachers testified about Carrie's sister, brother, and cousin, using descriptions such as "dull in her books."

There was additional testimony about several of Carrie's other relatives, one of whom was described as "right peculiar." The testimony did not relate to Carrie herself until Caroline Wilhelm—a Red Cross social worker contacted by the Dobbs family during Carrie's pregnancy, took the stand.

Strode asked Wilhelm, "From your experience as a social worker, if Carrie were discharged from the Colony still capable of child-bearing, is she likely to become the parent of deficient offspring?"

Wilhelm replied, "I should judge so. I think a girl of her mentality is more or less at the mercy of other people . . . Her mother had three illegitimate children, and I should say that Carrie would be very likely to have illegitimate children."

Strode concluded, "So that the only way that she could likely be kept from increasing her own kind would be by either segregation or something that would stop her power to propagate."

Wilhelm next testified about Carrie's daughter, Vivian "It seems difficult to judge probabilities of child as young as that [eight months], but it seems to me not quite a normal baby."

Whitehead, on cross-examination, raised what should have been a pivotal point: "The question of pregnancy is not evidence of feeblemindedness, is it? The fact that, as we say, she made a miss-step [sic]— went wrong—is that evidence of feeblemindedness?"

Wilhelm replied, "No, but a feebleminded girl is much more likely to go wrong."

Arthur Estabrook of the Carnegie Institute of Washington testified, discussing his 14 years of genetic research and his studies of "groups of mental defectives." Of his conclusions in *The Jukes* in 1915, a study of one family over four years, he said, "The result of the study was to show that certain definite laws of heredity were being shown by the family, in that the feeblemindedness was being inherited . . . and . . . was the basis of the antisocial conduct, showing up in the criminality and the pauperism."

Spode asked, "From what you know of Carrie Buck, would you say that by the laws of heredity she is a feeble-minded person and probably the potential parent of socially inadequate offspring likewise afflicted?"

And Estabrook replied, "I would."

Dr. Priddy testified last. Carrie Buck, he said, "would cease to be a charge on society if sterilized. It would remove one potential source of the incalculable number of descendants who would be feebleminded. She would contribute to the raising of the general mental average and standard [by not reproducing]."

And, finally, Harry H. Laughlin's deposition was read into the court record. Dr. Priddy had written Laughlin, describing Carrie and asking for Laughlin's help in enforcing the sterilization law against her. The information contained in Dr. Priddy's own letter forms the basis of Laughlin's sworn testimony: Carrie, he wrote, has "a mental age of 9 years, . . . a record during her life of immorality, prostitution, and untruthfulness; has never been self-sustaining; has one illegitimate child, now about six months old and supposed to be mentally defective . . . She is . . . a potential parent of socially inadequate or defective offspring." There is no evidence that Carrie Buck was examined by Laughlin.

In February of 1925, Judge Gordon upheld the Virginia sterilization law and ordered the sterilization of Carrie Buck. Irving Whitehead appealed to the Virginia Court of Appeals. (The case was now *Buck v. Bell* because Dr. Priddy had died a few weeks earlier and Dr. J. H. Bell had taken his place at the colony.) The appeals court decision upheld the circuit court decision.

Supreme Court Reviews Case

In the brief he submitted to the Supreme Court, Whitehead claimed Fourteenth Amendment protection of a person's "full bodily integrity." He also predicated the "worst kind of tyranny" if there were no "limits of the power of the state (which, in the end, is nothing more than the faction in control of the government) to rid itself of those citizens deemed undesirable." Strode, in contrast, likened compulsory sterilization to compulsory vaccination.

Justice Holmes delivered the nearly unanimous opinion on 2 May 1927:

> We have seen more than once that the public welfare may call upon the best citizens for their lives. It would be strange if it could not call upon those who already sap the strength of the state for their lesser sacrifices, often felt to be much by those concerned, in order to prevent our being swamped with incompetence. It is better for all the world, if instead of waiting to execute offspring for crime, or to let them starve for their imbecility, society can prevent those who are manifestly unfit from continuing their kind. The principle that sustains com-

Carrie Buck Eagle and her husband William Eagle, 1936.
© *Reproduced by permission of Mrs. A.T. Newberry, Bland, Virginia.*

pulsory vaccination is broad enough to cover cutting the Fallopian tubes.

Only Justice Butler dissented. Carrie Buck was sterilized by Dr. Bell on 19 October 1927. Shortly thereafter, she was paroled from the Virginia colony. She married twice: William Davis Eagle in 1932 and, after his death, Charlie Detamore. The letters she wrote to the Virginia colony seeking custody of her mother, as well as the recollections of her own minister, neighbors and health care providers, belie the notion that Carrie Buck was "feebleminded" or retarded.

Other Applications Result from *Buck v. Bell*

Laws similar to the Virginia statutes were passed in 30 other states, leading to the forcible sterilization of more than 50,000 people, including Carrie Buck's sister Doris.

Harry L. Laughlin, author of the model sterilization act adapted by Aubrey Strode for Virginia, made his draft available to state and foreign governments, and his model became Germany's Hereditary Health Law in 1933. In appreciation, he was awarded an honorary degree from Heidelberg University in 1936. After World War II, defending the forcible sterilization of 2 million people, Nazi lawyers cited this law and pointed out that the U.S. Supreme Court, in *Buck v. Bell*, had declared such laws constitutional.

Buck v. Bell has yet to be reversed by the Supreme Court. In 1973, *Roe v. Wade* guaranteed women the right to make their own decisions concerning abortion during the first two trimesters of pregnancy. The decision, written by Justice Harry Blackmun, balances the interests of the state and the woman and finds in favor of the woman's right of privacy. Nonetheless, citing *Buck v. Bell*, Justice Blackmun specifically denies "the claim . . . that one has an unlimited right to do with one's body as one pleases."

Related Cases

Matter of Romero, 790 P.2d 819 (1990).
Fieger v. Thomas, 74 F.3d 740 (1996).

Bibliography and Further Reading

Cushman, Robert F. *Cases in Constitutional Law*, 6th ed. Englewood Cliffs, NJ: Prentice Hall. 1984.

Smith, J. David, and K. Ray Nelson. *The Sterilization of Carrie Buck: Was She Feebleminded or Society's Pawn.* Far Hills, NJ: New Horizon Press, 1989.

UNITED STATES V. ONE PACKAGE

Legal Citation: 86 F. 2d 737 (1936)

Appellant
United States

Appellee
Dr. Hannah M. Stone, claimant for "one package" (of merchandise)

Appellant's Claim
That Stone did not have the legal right to import one package of contraceptive devices into the United States, according to the 1930 Tariff Act.

Chief Lawyer for Appellant
Morris L. Ernst

Chief Lawyer for Appellee
Lamar Hardy

Judges
Augustus N. Hand, Learned Hand, Thomas Swan

Place
New York, New York

Date of Decision
7 December 1936

Decision
Laws prohibiting Americans from importing contraceptive devices or items causing "unlawful abortion" did not apply to physicians who used the items to protect the health of patients.

Significance
This decision allowed contraceptive devices to be imported into the United States, paving the way for the 1937 decision of the American Medical Association that birth control was a medical service that could be taught in schools of medicine.

Anti-obscenity laws became popular in the states after the Civil War. So censorious was public opinion that in 1869 Harriet Beecher Stowe endured widespread criticism for mentioning Lord Byron's incestuous activities with his sister in the *Atlantic Monthly*. In 1873, Congress passed the federal Comstock Act, which made criminal the mailing or advertising of "obscene" materials—including literature on birth control.

No Fun for Anyone

The act was named after Anthony Comstock of New Canaan, Connecticut. Devotion to his mother—who died when he was ten—compelled him to "protect" women from smut, quack doctors, and other influences he thought harmful to them. In 1872, he joined a YMCA fight against pornographic literature. To persuade Congress to pass the federal obscenity act, Comstock displayed piles of pornography, along with contraceptives, and abortifacients (items that cause abortion), damning them all as equally immoral.

Comstock was a busy man. He founded the New York Society for the Suppression of Vice to arrest "criminal offenders," a term that included writers, poets, painters (those who used nude models), abortionists, and advertisers of birth control devices. He prodded government agents to harass druggists and physicians who sold or distributed birth control devices. As special investigator for the post office in New York City, in 1905, he instituted legal proceedings against George Bernard Shaw's play *Mrs. Warren's Profession*. Shaw retaliated by calling his opponent's puritanical endeavors "Comstockery."

Comstock's Nemesis

"Comstockery" resulted in the jailing of Margaret Sanger at least nine times for campaigning for the right of women to use birth control. Born Margaret Higgins on 14 September 1879, in Corning, New York, the future reformer was one of eleven children. She attributed her mother's early death at age fifty to her frequent pregnancies.

After the death of her mother, the young teacher turned to medicine, enrolling in White Plains Hospi-

Dr. Hannah M. Stone,
1936. © Francis A.
Countway Library of
Medicine, Boston,
Massachusetts.

tal—a drafty 12-bed building with no plumbing or central heating—where she completed two years of nurse's training. She became head nurse in the woman's ward, and in 1912, married William Sanger in a quick ceremony—reporting for her 4:30 a.m. shift the next day.

With $50, Sanger and her sister Ethel Byrne opened the first birth control clinic in America on 16 October 1916—an act of civil disobedience. The clinic occupied two rooms at 46 Amboy Street in the Brownsville section of Brooklyn, New York. In the ten days before police closed the clinic, almost 500 women arrived to get information about birth control and contraceptive devices. Sanger was arrested and sentenced to 30 days in prison. Her appeal to the New York Court of Appeals resulted in a 1918 ruling that allowed doctors to advise their married patients about birth control for health reasons.

Five years after opening her clinic, Sanger founded the American Birth Control League, which lobbied politicians to make contraception legal. The group urged Congress to exempt doctors from laws that banned the prescription and mailing of contraceptive devices.

To achieve that end, Sanger asked the staff of her American Birth Control League to find proof that the Comstock Act did impede the distribution of birth control materials. They found it in the 1930 amendment to the Tariff Act. This law used original 1873 Comstock Act language prohibiting "the importation into the United States, from any foreign country, any article whatever for preventing conception, or induced abortion."

In 1932, at Sanger's request, a Japanese doctor sent her a package of contraceptive supplies. Customs officers stopped the package. Sanger asked the physician to mail the package again, this time addressing it to her part-time employee, Dr. Hannah M. Stone, a qualified, licensed gynecologist. At the arrival of the package of 120 rubber pessaries (devices placed in the vagina to block conception), agents again confiscated it, ordering Dr. Stone to return it. Sanger, the American Birth Control League, Dr. Stone, the National Committee on Maternal Health, and lawyer Morris Ernst immediately went to court, claiming the supplies were medical exemptions under the law. Using Dr. Stone as the claimant, they filed the case in the U.S. District Court for the Southern District in New York City on 10 November 1933.

A Public Sea Change

It took two years before the case came to trial. During this time, contraception was so popular that the government's regulatory agents could not stop birth control items from being bought and sold. Druggists and doctors dispensed them with impunity and even the Sears, Roebuck catalog advertised them as "preventives." In 1935, the *American Medicine* journal noted that mailing contraceptive devices was "as firmly established as the postage stamp."

Polls at this time showed that 70 percent of the American public wanted birth control made legal. One poll, commissioned by *Ladies' Home Journal,* found that 79 percent of readers—51 percent of them Catholic—favored loosening the laws.

Influenced by this change in attitude, the district court agreed to hear *United States v. One Package* in 1935. Dr. Stone testified that she had imported the pessaries for experimental purposes, to test them for reliability in preventing contraception and disease. She said she also prescribed them to women who should not bear children. The United States sought a decision directing the forfeiture and destruction of "one package" of pessaries. On 6 January 1936, Judge Grover Moscowitz ruled that the Tariff Act did not extend to the prevention of contraceptives intended for medical use.

However, the government appealed, and Ernst, relying on donations to cover his fees, defended his client before a three-judge panel of the Second Circuit Court of Appeals in New York. At the trial, a number of doctors spoke on Dr. Stone's behalf. Even a government witness agreed with them, saying that from a medical standpoint, sometimes it was vital to *prescribe* a contraceptive for some patients to prevent or cure disease.

The judges reached their decision on 7 December 1936. They believed that while only the Tariff Act was at issue in this case, all aspects of the Comstock Act were part of a consistent effort to suppress immoral articles and obscene literature. As for the Tariff Act itself, Section 305(a) had coupled the word "unlawful" with the word "abortion," though not with the word "contraception," making the importation of contraceptive items legal. The court also decided contraceptives were necessary for the lawful purposes Dr. Stone had described and allowed them to enter the United States.

Fallout

In 1937, the American Medical Association (AMA) finally reversed its long-held refusal to study contraception and began to support state and federal reforms. As Sanger biographer Ellen Chesler has written, the AMA regarded birth control "as a responsible element of normal sexual hygiene in married life. To this end, it recommended that the subject be taught in medical schools, that scientific investigation of various commercial materials and methods be promoted, and finally that the legal rights of physicians in relation to the use of contraceptives be clarified."

Although the birth control movement claimed victory in *United States v. One Package,* not until 1971 would Congress rewrite the Comstock law to remove the specific mention of birth control material. The use of contraceptive devices—even for married couples—remained illegal until 1965, when the Supreme Court overturned the laws in 1964 with *Griswold v. Connecti-*cut. In 1972, the Court made the use of contraceptive items lawful for single people as well in *Eisenstadt v. Baird.*

Related Cases

New York v. Sanger, 118 N.E. 637 (1918).
Griswold v. Connecticut, 381 U.S. 479 (1964).
Eisenstadt v. Baird, 405 U.S. 438 (1972).

Bibliography and Further Reading

Chesler, Ellen. *Woman of Valor: Margaret Sanger and the Birth Control Movement in America.* New York: Doubleday/Anchor Books, 1992.

Garrow, David J. *Liberty and Sexuality: The Right to Privacy and the Making of Roe v. Wade.* New York: Macmillan Publishing Group, 1994.

Sicherman, Barbara, and Carol Hurd Green. *Notable American Women: The Modern Period.* Cambridge, MA: The Belknap Press, 1980.

POE V. ULLMAN

Legal Citation: 367 U.S. 497 (1961)

Appellant
Paul and Pauline Poe, et al.

Appellee
Ullman, State's Attorney

Appellant's Claim
A statute written in 1879 in the state of Connecticut prohibited the use of contraceptives to prevent pregnancy and also prohibited physicians from prescribing and advising the use of contraceptives. Paul and Pauline Poe, Mrs. Jane Doe, and Doctor C. Lee Buxton challenged the constitutionality of this statute, claiming that it interfered with their right to privacy and violated their liberties protected by due process as guaranteed by the Fourteenth Amendment of the U.S. Constitution.

Chief Lawyer for Appellant
Fowler W. Harper

Chief Lawyer for Appellee
Raymond J. Cannon

Justices for the Court
William J. Brennan, Jr., Tom C. Clark, Felix Frankfurter (writing for the Court), Earl Warren, Charles Evans Whittaker

Justices Dissenting
Hugo Lafayette Black, William O. Douglas, John Marshall Harlan II, Potter Stewart

Place
Washington, D.C.

Date of Decision
19 June 1961

Decision
In a 5-4 decision, the Court dismissed the case with no determination upon the constitutionality of the Connecticut anti-contraceptive statute.

Significance
This case examined the constitutionality of a Connecticut statute which prohibited the dissemination and use of contraceptives and which was prosecutable by the state. The Court was required to determine if this statute violated the right to privacy guaranteed by the Fifth Amendment and the liberty protected by due process of the Fourteenth Amendment of the U.S. Constitution. Ultimately the Supreme Court dismissed the case, finding that it involved only a threatened and not actual application of the state statute, and finding no applicable immediacy or injury which deemed it necessary to make a ruling on constitutionality.

Justiciability of the Claim

An 1879 state of Connecticut statute prohibited advising use of contraceptive devices and the actual use of contraceptives to prevent pregnancy, including use by married couples. Research of the succeeding years indicated that this statute had been enacted once in 1940, charging a physician and two nurses with operating a birth-control clinic (*State v. Nelson*). In 1960 Planned Parenthood Federation of America, Inc., on behalf of the appellants—Paul and Pauline Poe, Jane Doe, and Dr. C. Lee Buxton—prepared a case which challenged the constitutionality of this statute, making the claim that it violated the appellants' right to privacy and violated their liberties protected and guaranteed by the Constitution of the United States.

Both Pauline Poe and Jane Doe experienced pregnancies that resulted in children who did not live past birth due to congenital abnormalities, near-death illness, and felt extreme mental anguish upon the termination of the pregnancies. Their physician, in both cases, Dr. C. Lee Buxton, advised them that further pregnancies would end similarly, and in Mrs. Doe's case her probable death. He advised that the best prevention of further difficulties was some method of contraception. However, the Connecticut law prohibited Dr. Buxton from disseminating prescriptions or advice about contraceptive methods to either of these women on the grounds that it could result in criminal prosecution. The only recourse would be for the married couples to abstain from intimate relations in order to prevent pregnancy.

Poe v. Ullman was first heard in the Supreme Court of Errors of Connecticut where the complaint was dismissed. The appellants then requested a declaratory judgment from the U.S. Supreme Court, which would formally make the statute unconstitutional. The two claims were, first, that by invoking the anti-contraceptive law, the married couples were denied the right to make decisions about the most intimate and private parts of their lives. Secondly it was stated that the threat of prosecution for the private use of contraceptives deprived them of the protection of due process under the law. Buxton also claimed that the Connecticut law prohibiting him from giving sound and safe advice to his patients denied him the right of due process of practicing his profession and earning a living based on his training as a physician.

In a 5-4 decision, Justice Frankfurter, delivering the opinion of the Court, dismissed the case. He wrote that the case before them did not clearly indicate a direct threat of prosecution by the state's attorney if the appellants acquired and used contraceptive devices. In the course of research the Court found that contraceptives were readily available in Connecticut drug stores, and yet there had been no prosecutions in that state for the sale of these items. Frankfurter went on to write that law enforcement officials were more likely to notice the open, public sales of contraceptives than the use of contraceptives in the privacy of the appellants' homes. It was the opinion of the majority that *Poe v. Ullman* had no sense of urgency nor a real and direct injury to the appellants, which are the basis for the justification of a case.

Defining the Right to Privacy

Justices Douglas and Harlan had a dissenting view of *Poe v. Ullman*. They wrote that the opinion of the majority left the appellants open to prosecution by an unconstitutional law. Both justices felt that the constitutionality of the Connecticut anti-contraceptive law should be thoroughly examined by the Court. They cited the Court's inclination to dismiss the case as trivial and lacking in substantive support and precedents as being a grave injustice to the Poes, Mrs. Doe, and Dr. Buxton. In looking at the arguments and evidence brought before the Court, both Douglas and Harlan shared the opinion that this case did involve constitutional decisions.

The heart of the dissenting opinion revolved around the definition of "the right to privacy." Douglas and Harlan questioned the state of Connecticut's authority to invade the bedroom of a married couple and examine the private and intimate relationship between spouses. Harlan wrote in his opinion,

> I consider that this Connecticut legislation, as construed to apply to these appellants, violates the Fourteenth Amendment. I believe that a statute making it a criminal offense for married couples to use contraceptives is an intolerable and unjustifiable invasion of privacy in

the conduct of the most intimate concerns of an individual's personal life.

Douglas and Harlan agreed that the only barrier between the appellants and prosecution was the "whim of the prosecutor." While the state might not physically invade the home, the concept of protection from illegal search and seizure of personal property was much broader in scope, protecting the spiritual nature of privacy as well as the physical.

In 1965 the Supreme Court was faced with another case with the same issue of the constitutionality of anti-contraceptive laws for married couples in *Griswold v. Connecticut*. Unlike the dismissal of *Poe v. Ullman* the Supreme Court concluded in a 7-2 decision that the statute did violate the right to privacy. The right to privacy was viewed as a constitutional principle guaranteed by the Fourth, Fifth and Fourteenth Amendments, and fully protected by the Constitution.

Impact

With the dismissal of *Poe v. Ullman* and the dissenting opinions, the right to privacy came under closer scrutiny by the Supreme Court. The justices began to define this principle in greater detail; instead of right to privacy law only covering only the unlawful invasion of a property, it began to reflect protection needed during the unlawful invasion into the private and personal relationships of the lives of Americans. Future Court decisions would reflect back on *Poe v. Ullman*, and use it as a defining moment and precedent for the guaranteed right of privacy.

Related Cases

Tileston v. Ullman, 318 U.S. 44 (1943).
Griswold v. Connecticut, 381 U.S. 479 (1965).
Roe v. Wade, 410 U.S. 113 (1973).

Bibliography and Further Reading

"Lecture Summaries, Part 2, Politics 115a, Brandeis University. Fall 1997." http://www.brandeis.edu/departments/politics/lecture2.html

Wulf, Melvin L. "On the Origins of Privacy: Constitutional Practice." *The Nation*, Vol. 252, no. 20, May 27, 1991, p. 700.

UNITED STATES V. VUITCH

Legal Citation: 402 U.S. 62 (1971)

Appellant
United States

Appellee
Dr. Milan Vuitch

Appellant's Claim
That the governing standard of the District of Columbia's anti-abortion law, which states that the mother's "life" and "health" must be at risk in order for an abortion to be performed, is not unconstitutionally vague.

Chief Lawyer for Appellant
Samuel Huntington

Chief Lawyers for Appellee
Joseph L. Nellis and Norman Dorsen

Justices for the Court
Hugo Lafayette Black (writing for the Court), Harry A. Blackmun, Warren E. Burger, John Marshall Harlan II, Byron R. White

Justices Dissenting
William O. Douglas, Potter Stewart (William J. Brennan, Jr. and Thurgood Marshall did not participate)

Place
Washington, D.C.

Date of Decision
21 April 1971

Decision
The Supreme Court reversed the judgment of the district court.

Significance
Vuitch was the first decision to rule on the constitutionality of anti-abortion laws. In its aftermath, abortion rights advocates realized that the mere absence of anti-abortion laws was insufficient protection for women. Women would need legislation or court decisions to win their right to end a pregnancy.

In 1971, two years before the historic *Roe v. Wade* legalized a woman's right to end her pregnancy, a U.S. district court heard the case of Dr. Milan Vuitch. Vuitch was a physician charged with the crime of inducing a medical abortion in violation of the District of Columbia Code. This law, unchanged since 1901, made abortion a crime unless "done . . . for the preservation of the mother's life or health" and under the direction of a licensed physician. The statute was typical of anti-abortion laws in many states.

Vuitch was a Serbian youth who had studied medicine in Hungary before immigrating to the United States in the mid-1950s. In 1962, shortly after receiving his medical license, Vuitch started performing abortions in Washington D.C., Maryland, and Virginia. At a time when abortion was illegal in most states, Vuitch was one of few physicians willing to risk his profession and liberty by taking on referrals from the budding abortion rights movement. By 1964, he was performing abortions on a full-time basis, eventually ten to 20 each week.

Over the next five years, police tried repeatedly to shut down Vuitch's practice, arresting him more than 12 times. However, except for one conviction in Montgomery County, Maryland, on appeal in 1971, courts found Vuitch innocent.

On 21 April 1971, a court indicted the 54-year-old physician for violating the District of Columbia Code. In a momentous breakthrough for abortion rights advocates, Federal District Judge Gerhard A. Gesell declared the law unconstitutionally vague, and dismissed the indictments against Vuitch without waiting for a trial. Gesell stated that under this law, "a physician would not know if he was committing a crime when he performed an abortion, because a jury might later disagree with his opinion that the mother's health required it. [Thus] the doctors' problem was particularly acute because the burden was on them to prove that the abortion was justified."

This decision left the district without any law on abortion. The public hospital on which most of the district's poor residents relied, D.C. General, soon stopped giving abortions. Private hospitals were similarly restrictive. The National Abortion Rights Action League (NARAL), in conjunction with the American Civil Liberties Union (ACLU), sued D.C. General Hospital twice, obtaining two court orders that forced the hospital to perform more abortions.

In this atmosphere, the Justice Department appealed to the U.S. Supreme Court. Attorneys argued that Vuitch had "performed abortions for any woman who desired one, without considering [if] the woman's health [was in jeopardy]."

Is the Abortion Law Constitutional?

Gesell had found the D.C. abortion law vague for two reasons. First, once an abortion took place, the physician "is presumed guilty and remains so unless a jury can be persuaded that his acts were necessary for the preservation of the woman's life and health." Second, the judge felt disturbed by the "ambivalent and uncertain word 'health.'"

The trial court had examined *Williams v. United States* (1943) to determine that the D.C. law placed the burden of proof on the defendant once prosecutors had proved an abortion had taken place. In that case, the Court of Appeals for the D.C. Circuit Court had held that the prosecution did not have to prove abortion was unnecessary to preserve life or health to win.

However, Justice Black—on behalf of the Supreme Court majority—stated that "whether or not this is a correct reading of *Williams* . . . it is an erroneous interpretation of the statute." The D.C. law had "expressly authorized" physicians to perform abortions to preserve a woman's life or health. It did not presume the guilt of a doctor for performing the operation.

The Court also agreed that the word "health" carried an "uncertain" and "ambivalent" meaning, which failed to inform a "defendant of the charge against him and therefore . . . offends the Due Process Clause of the Constitution." Gesell had felt the term vague because it did not account for "varying degrees of mental as well as physical health."

The Supreme Court looked to *Doe v. General Hospital of the District of Columbia* (1970) for guidance. Judge Joseph Waddy had permitted abortions there "for mental health reasons whether or not the patient had a previous history of mental defects." Therefore, the Court found "no reason why this interpretation of the statute should not be followed." Black continued: "*Webster's Dictionary* . . . defines health as the 'state of being . . . sound in body [or] mind.' Viewed in this light, the term 'health' presents no problem of vagueness."

The majority decided "the District of Columbia abortion law is not unconstitutionally vague," and "the trial court erred in dismissing the indictment on that ground."

Although Black reversed Gesell's decision, he said that the District law should give "physicians considerable latitude [within the law's restrictions] to perform legal abortions." He added that in future abortion trials, the government must prove that the mother's health was not endangered.

Opinion of the Minority

While agreeing with the Court's opinion regarding jurisdiction over the appeal, Justice Douglas felt that the D.C. abortion law did not meet the requirements of procedural due process. He insisted that a physician's judgment to determine the necessity of a woman's abortion was "highly subjective [and] dependent on the training and insight of the particular physician." He then raised a question regarding the standard of the D.C. anti-abortion law. "Is the statutory standard so easy to manipulate that although physicians can make good-faith decisions based on the standard, juries can nonetheless make felons out of them?" To further his point, Douglas quoted from *Roe v. Wade*, then making its way through the Texas courts: A court "evaluating the statutory standard" dealing with abortion laws in Texas, was convinced that the law was unconstitutionally vague:

> How *likely* must death be? Must death be certain if the abortion is not performed? Is it enough that the woman could not undergo birth without an ascertainably higher possibility of death than would normally be the case? What if the woman threatened suicide if the abortion was not performed? . . . Is it sufficient if having the child will shorten the life of the woman by a number of years?

Douglas reminded the Court that "abortion statutes [are] heavily weighted with religious teachings and ethical concepts . . ." This encouraged prejudice in the jury. He felt "the drafting of [new] abortion laws [should] protect good-faith medical practitioners from the treacheries of the present law."

The People v. Leon P. Belous

Douglas also mentioned *People v. Leon P. Belous* (1969). This case involved California physician Belous, who had practiced medicine for 35 years and had performed abortions during many of those years. A California court convicted Belous in 1967 for violating the state's anti-abortion law (before the passage of a new reform law). The court found him guilty of having accepted a kickback from another doctor to whom he had referred a pregnant student.

Belous appealed to the three-judge panel of the Second District Court of Appeals, but the panel affirmed the lower court's ruling, believing the physician had indeed accepted kickbacks. Belous then hired civil rights attorneys A. L. Wirin and Fred Okrand to appeal his case to the California Supreme Court. California abortion rights activists quickly rallied around him, believing his case would prove to the state's high court that anti-abortion laws were unconstitutional. The attorneys believed that the principles of 1964's *Griswold v. Connecticut* should protect a woman's privacy and personal autonomy in child-bearing. They also felt that states should not interfere with a doctor-patient relationship when it came to the termination of a pregnancy.

Oral arguments took place on 4 March 1969, before the seven-judge California Supreme Court. On 5 September, the court handed down its much anticipated decision. By a vote of 4-3, Raymond A. Peter's majority overturned the conviction of Belous because California's pre-1967 antiabortion law was too vague to be constitutional.

The old law had allowed women to end their pregnancies in only one instance: when necessary to preserve a woman's life. The words "necessary" and "preserve" were unconstitutionally vague. The court explained: "A showing of immediacy or certainty of death is not essential for a lawful abortion."

The majority also ruled that "The fundamental right of women to choose whether to bear children follows from the Supreme Court's and this court's repeated acknowledgment of a 'right to privacy' or 'liberty' in matters related to marriage, family, and sex." The court listed *Griswold v. Connecticut* (1964) among other precedents for its decision.

As an ironic footnote, in the District of Columbia, the Supreme Court's overturning of *United States v. Vuitch* in 1971 and upholding of the original law restricting abortion yielded greater access to abortion than ever before. As Vuitch emphasized, "This is a big step forward. Now the government lawyer will be in the position of challenging my medical decision. What are the jury members going to decide when a lawyer tries to tell them that the doctor is wrong about a medical matter? What the Supreme Court did," he pointed out, "was throw the whole mess on the shoulders of American physicians; and that is the correct position."

Related Cases
Griswold v. Connecticut, 381 U.S. 479 (1964).
Roe v. Wade, 410 U.S. 113 (1973).

Bibliography and Further Reading
"Ambivalence on Abortion." *Time*, 3 May 1971.

Davis, Flora. *Moving the Mountain: The Women's Movement in America Since 1960.* New York: Simon and Schuster/Touchstone, 1992.

Garrow, David J. *Liberty and Sexuality: The Right to Privacy and the Making of Roe v. Wade.* New York: Macmillan, 1994.

Graham, Fred, P. "High Court Upholds D.C. Abortion Law." *New York Times,* 22 April 1971.

MacKenzie, John P., and Stuart Auerback. "D.C. Abortion Law Upheld by Supreme Court, 5 to 2." *The Washington Post,* 22 April 1971.

EISENSTADT V. BAIRD

Legal Citation: 405 U.S. 438 (1972)

Appellant
Thomas Eisenstadt, sheriff of Suffolk County, Massachusetts

Appellee
William R. Baird, Jr.

Appellant's Claim
That the lower courts erred in overturning Baird's conviction on charges of distributing contraceptives without a medical license and to unmarried people.

Chief Lawyer for Appellant
Joseph R. Nolan

Chief Lawyers for Appellee
Joseph Balliro before the lower courts; Joseph D. Tydings before the Supreme Court

Justices for the Court
Harry A. Blackmun, William J. Brennan, Jr. (writing for the Court), William O. Douglas, Thurgood Marshall, Potter Stewart, Byron R. White

Justices Dissenting
Warren E. Burger (Lewis F. Powell, Jr., and William H. Rehnquist joined the Court too late in 1972 to participate)

Place
Washington, D.C.

Date of Decision
22 March 1972

Decision
Upheld lower court reversals of Baird's conviction and invalidated state laws restricting the use of contraceptives to married people.

Significance
In addition to making contraceptives legally available to unmarried people throughout the United States, the decision described the constitutional right of privacy in language that foreshadowed the Court's 1973 finding that the right to privacy protected a woman's right to have an abortion.

Although the Supreme Court struck down state laws prohibiting the use of contraceptives by married couples in 1964's *Griswold v. Connecticut,* furnishing contraceptives to unmarried people in many states continued to be illegal. Massachusetts prohibited the distribution of contraceptives to anyone without a medical prescription and to unmarried people under any circumstances. Violation was punishable by up to five years imprisonment.

In the spring of 1967, birth control activist William R. Baird, Jr., accepted an invitation from Boston University students to lecture and "distribute free lists of abortionists and birth control devices to interested coeds." Prior to Baird's visit, the *B.U. News* published an article in which Baird, a former medical student who had once worked for a pharmaceutical company, explained that he had become a birth control and abortion rights activist after witnessing the death of a young mother of eight who had been admitted to an emergency room after an illegal abortion. Saying that more than ten thousand women had died from illegal abortions in 1966, he condemned laws making contraceptives available only to married women under a doctor's care and declared that he would "test this law in Massachusetts . . . No group, no law, no individual can dictate to a woman what goes on in her own body."

When Baird took the stage in an auditorium at Boston University on 6 April, there were 1,500 to 2,000 people in the audience—and three vice squad officers in the wings. *B.U. News* editor Raymond Mungo introduced Baird, saying, "We are here to test the legal aspects of the birth control and abortion laws in the state of Massachusetts."

When Baird announced his intention to distribute contraceptive foam and a list of places outside the United States where one might secure an abortion, he addressed the vice squad directly, reminding them to "do your duty." Telling the students that "the only way we can change the law is to get the case into a court of law," he urged them to approach and to take the offered information and contraceptive foam. He was arrested as soon as he started handing out the materials.

Among the Lower Courts

Baird was tried before Massachusetts Superior Court Judge Donald B. Macaulay in October of 1967. Represented by attorney Joseph J. Balliro, who took the case without charge, Baird waived his right to a jury trial.

Assistant District Attorney Joseph R. Nolan called police lieutenant Joseph Jordan to the stand. Jordan, who had arrested Baird at Boston University, described Baird's speech and his actions. Balliro argued that the Massachusetts law was unconstitutional. Macaulay found Baird guilty of violating the law, but postponed Baird's sentencing until an appeal was heard.

The Massachusetts Supreme Judicial Court heard the case in November of 1968. Nolan characterized Baird's actions at Boston University as "an invitation to promiscuity and sexual license," and he defended the commonwealth's objective of "preventing the distribution of articles designed to prevent conception which may have undesirable, if not dangerous, physical consequences."

In April of 1969, the court overturned Baird's conviction for displaying contraceptives, on the basis that this had been part of a speech protected by the First Amendment. However, it affirmed Baird's criminal conviction for distributing the contraceptive foam on the basis that Baird was not a physician, nurse, or pharmacist legally entitled in Massachusetts to engage in such conduct. Returning to the Suffolk County Superior Court, Baird was sentenced to three months. Macaulay agreed to postpone Baird's imprisonment pending an appeal to the Supreme Court, but, to the surprise of many, the Court would not hear Baird's appeal.

Balliro filed a *habeas corpus* petition in federal district court. When U.S. District Judge Anthony J. Julian had not ruled by 20 February, Baird went to the Charles Street jail in Boston and surrendered to Suffolk County sheriff Thomas Eisenstadt. Julian heard oral arguments at the end of the month and in March of 1970, denied the *habeas corpus* petition. The denial entitled Baird to appeal to the First Circuit Court of Appeals. This court ordered that Baird be set free until his appeal could be heard. On 6 July, the court ruled that the Massachusetts birth control law was unconstitutional and reversed Baird's remaining conviction.

At the Supreme Court

Eisenstadt appealed to the Supreme Court. This time, the Court announced that it would hear the appeal.

William R. Baird, Jr., 1967.

Oral arguments were presented on 19 and 20 November 1971, before seven justices. Nolan, arguing for Massachusetts, emphasized Baird's lack of a medical license and claimed that "there are some very dangerous side lights and side effects to the use of many contraceptives."

Nolan dismissed any possible comparison to *Griswold*, which had been decided on the basis of a married couple's "right to privacy," since this case involved a very public display of contraceptives. Joseph Tydings, a former U.S. senator from Maryland, who had replaced Balliro as Baird's attorney, said that the Massachusetts law was "inherently unconstitutional because there is no compelling state reason for it."

On 22 March 1972, the Supreme Court agreed and affirmed the judgment of the First Circuit Court of Appeals. The majority opinion, written by Justice Brennan, further defined the Ninth Amendment right of privacy first enunciated in *Griswold*:

> If under *Griswold* the distribution of contraceptives to married persons cannot be prohibited, a ban on distribution to unmarried persons would be equally impermissible. It is true that in *Griswold* the right of privacy in question inhered in the marital relationship. Yet the marital couple is not an independent entity with a mind and heart of its own, but an association of two individuals each with a separate intellectual and emotional make-up. If the right of privacy means anything, it is the right of the *individual,* married or single, to be free from unwarranted governmental intrusion into matters so fundamentally affecting a person as the decision whether to bear or beget a child.

In 1973, the right to privacy was found by the Supreme Court to protect a woman's right to terminate her pregnancy, in *Roe v. Wade.* Four years later, the Supreme Court, citing *Eisenstadt,* ruled that states could not prohibit the distribution of contraceptives to unmarried minors (*Carey v. Population Services International,* 1977).

Related Cases

Griswold v. Connecticut, 381 U.S. 479 (1964).
Roe v. Wade, 410 U.S. 113 (1973).

Bibliography and Further Reading

Carey, Eve, and Kathleen Willert Peratis. *Woman and the Law.* Skokie, IL: National Textbook Co. in conjunction with the American Civil Liberties Union, 1977.

Faux, Marian. *Roe v. Wade.* New York: Macmillan, 1988.

Garrow, David J. *Liberty & Sexuality: The Right to Privacy and the Making of Roe v. Wade.* New York: Macmillan, 1994.

Goldstein, Leslie Friedman. *The Constitutional Rights of Women,* rev. ed. Madison: University of Wisconsin Press, 1989.

New York Times, 3 December 1968; 20 May 1969; 2 June 1969; 12 July 1970; 21 September 1971; and 23, 25 March 1972.

ROE V. WADE

Legal Citation: 410 U.S. 113 (1973)

Plaintiff
Norma McCorvey, using "Jane Roe" as an alias and representing all pregnant women in a class-action suit

Defendant
Henry B. Wade, Texas District Attorney

Plaintiff's Claim
The Texas' abortion laws violated McCorvey's and other women's constitutional rights.

Chief Lawyers for Plaintiff
Sarah Weddington and Linda Coffee

Chief Defense Lawyers
Jay Floyd and Robert Flowers

Justices for the Court
Harry A. Blackmun (writing for the Court), William J. Brennan, Jr., Warren E. Burger, William O. Douglas, Thurgood Marshall, Lewis F. Powell, Jr., Potter Stewart

Justices Dissenting
William H. Rehnquist, Byron R. White

Place
Washington, D.C.

Date of Decision
22 January 1973

Decision
Overturned all state laws restricting women's access to abortions during the first trimester of pregnancy and let stand second-trimester restrictions only insofar as they were designed to protect the health of pregnant women.

Significance
The case was the first to establish that a woman, rather than her physician, might be the party injured by a state's criminalization of abortion. Moreover, the decision was in large measure based on an implied "right to privacy" in the U.S. Constitution, which the majority held was violated by state laws restricting a woman's right to abort a fetus prior to its viability outside her womb.

The Supreme Court's landmark decision legalizing abortion in *Roe v. Wade* aroused more passion than perhaps any other in the Court's history. One segment of the population, energized by Catholic and fundamentalist religious beliefs, held that aborting the unborn was no less than murder. Another segment of the American people was just as convinced and just as adamant that denying a woman's "right to choose" whether or not to bear a child was an intolerable governmental restriction of her freedom and privacy. The decision in 1973 triggered a 20 year battle between its opponents, the self-described "Right to Life" movement who sought to overturn it, and its proponents, the "Pro-Choice" advocates who worked to prevent it from being reversed or being whittled away. Justice Blackmun, who wrote the majority opinion, had his life threatened and his mailbox filled with letters calling him "Butcher of Dachau, murderer, Pontius Pilate, [and] Adolph Hitler." Each of the other justices received thousands of letters of condemnation as well.

Support for abortion rights had been growing steadily in the years prior to the decision and continued to increase afterward. In 1968, for example, less than 15 percent of the participants in a Gallup Poll approved "of liberalizing the abortion laws," while 40 percent of Gallup Poll respondents approved in the following year. By mid-1972, the Gallup Poll reported 73 percent of all participants and 56 of Catholic participants believed "that the decision to undergo an abortion is a matter that should be left solely to the woman and her physician."

Those who object to *Roe v. Wade* do so with a seemingly undying passion; nearly 20 years later, their opposition is well-organized, well-funded and at times, even violent. It also has been partially successful: The basic decision still stands, but the High Court has narrowed it somewhat by permitting states to regulate abortion for minors and abortions performed in tax-supported institutions.

Norma McCorvey Tests the Law

The "Jane Roe" whose name would be attached to this national divide was actually 21-year-old Norma McCorvey. McCorvey's marriage had ended, and her daughter, age 5, was being reared by McCorvey's mother and stepfather. In the summer of 1969, McCorvey was working as a ticket seller for a traveling carnival; by early autumn she had lost her job and had become pregnant. McCorvey wanted to end her pregnancy, but abortion was illegal in Texas except in cases where it was deemed necessary to save a woman's life. McCorvey's search for an illegal abortionist was unsuccessful.

However, it led her to two young attorneys, both women and both interested in challenging the existing laws: Linda Coffee and Sarah Weddington. Although there was virtually no chance that McCorvey herself would be helped if Coffee and Weddington succeeded in overturning the abortion laws (one could count on pregnancy coming to a conclusion well before any lawsuit simultaneously began), McCorvey agreed to become Coffee's and Weddington's plaintiff in a test case.

Texas had passed its anti-abortion law in 1859. Like other such laws in the United States, it punished only the persons performing or "furnishing the means for" an abortion. This posed a problem for Coffee and Weddington: They knew it could be argued that a pregnant woman, presumably not the target of a law restricting medical practice, lacked "standing to sue" regarding that law's supposed unconstitutionality. If they passed this hurdle with McCorvey's case, they knew they would face another: When McCorvey gave birth or at least passed the point where an abortion could be safely performed, her case—having resolved itself—might be declared moot and thrown out of court. Linda Coffee prepared and filed the pleading anyway.

Constitutional Issues

Coffee and Weddington decided to attack the constitutionality of the Texas abortion law on the grounds that it violated the Fourteenth and Ninth Amendments to the U.S. Constitution. The Due Process Clause of the Fourteenth Amendment guaranteed equal protection under the law to all citizens and, in particular, required that laws be clearly written. Physicians accused of performing illegal abortions usually cited the Fourteenth Amendment in their defense, claiming that the law was not specific enough with regard to when a woman's life might be threatened by pregnancy and childbirth. However, since Coffee and Weddington wanted a decision that rested on a pregnant woman's right to decide for herself whether or not an abortion was necessary, they based their argument first and foremost on the Ninth Amendment, which states: "The enumeration in the Constitution, of certain rights, shall not be construed to deny or disparage others retained by the people." Until 1965, this had usually been interpreted to mean that rights not specifically granted to the federal government were retained by the states. In 1965, however *Griswold v. Connecticut* reached the Supreme Court and prompted

a different interpretation of that amendment. Estelle Griswold, Planned Parenthood League of Connecticut's executive director and Dr. Charles Lee Burton had been arrested for providing birth-control information and contraceptives, actions then illegal under Connecticut law. Found guilty in the Connecticut courts, the two appealed to the Supreme Court, which overturned their convictions and ruled the Connecticut law unconstitutional. Of particular note to Coffee and Weddington was Justice Douglas's discussion of the Ninth Amendment in his majority opinion. Rights not specifically listed in the Constitution were retained by the people, Douglas emphasized, and one of these rights was the right to privacy. This right to privacy, Coffee and Weddington would argue, should certainly protect the right of a woman to decide whether or not to become a mother.

John Tolles was the assistant district attorney chosen by District Attorney Henry Wade to defend his enforcement of the Texas abortion law. Attorney General Crawford Martin chose Robert Flowers, head of the enforcement division, to defend the Texas law itself, and Flowers passed this task on to his assistant chief, Jay Floyd. The state prepared its case primarily on the basis that a fetus had legal rights, which ought to be protected.

State Court Favors Plaintiff

The Three-Judge Court Act of 1910 had created courts in which a panel of three judges drawn from a single appellate circuit might resolve interstate commerce disputes between the federal and state governments. Another act, passed in 1937, required that such a panel hear any case questioning the constitutionality of a state law. On 23 May 1970, Coffee, Weddington, Tolles, and Floyd appeared in the Fifth Circuit Court in Dallas, Texas, before Judges Irving S. Goldberg, William McLaughlin Taylor, and Sarah Tigham Hughes, for whom Coffee had once clerked. The courtroom was jammed with concerned women and reporters. Norma McCorvey, or "Jane Roe," who was not required to be present, stayed home.

Coffee and Weddington had amended their case to a class-action suit so that McCorvey would represent not just herself but all pregnant women. They had also been joined in their suit by an "intervenor," Dr. James Hallford, who had been arrested for performing abortions. Hallford's attorneys, Fred Bruner and Roy Merrill, planned to use the traditional physician's defense, the Fourteenth Amendment.

Coffee spoke first. She had to establish that McCorvey did, indeed, have "standing to sue" and that the question was a serious, constitutional one on which the three judges should rule. At one point she said: "I think the [abortion] statute is so bad that the court is just really going to have to strike it all down. I don't think it's worth salvaging."

Sarah Weddington. © AP/Wide World Photos.

Weddington approached the bench next. This was her courtroom debut, and she knew it was an important case. She said she disagreed with the "justification which the state alleges for the state abortion statute, that is, the protection of the life of the child . . . [L]ife is an ongoing process. It is almost impossible," Weddington continued, "to define a point at which life begins or perhaps even at which life ends."

When asked by Judge Goldberg whether the legalization of abortion would promote promiscuity, Weddington said that young women "are already promiscuous when the statute is in effect, and in fact, these are some of the girls who need this right and who have the most socially compelling arguments why they should be allowed abortions—the young still in school, those unable to shoulder the responsibility of a child—these girls should not be put through the pregnancy and should be entitled to an abortion."

Before Weddington stepped down to listen to Fred Bruner's Fourteenth Amendment defense of his physician client, Judge Goldberg asked her if she thought the abortion law was weaker in terms of the Ninth or Fourteenth Amendment. Weddington gave her answer immediately: "I believe it is more vulnerable on the Ninth Amendment basis."

After Bruner addressed the judges, Floyd rose to speak for the state. He claimed that "Roe" must certainly have reached the point in her pregnancy where an abortion would be considered unsafe and therefore had no case. Judge Goldberg flatly disagreed.

Tolles followed for the state, and argued strenuously against a woman's having the right to choose an abortion. "I personally think," he said, "and I think the state's position will be and is, that the right of the child to life is superior to that woman's right to privacy."

The judges did not agree. On 17 June 1970, they issued their opinion: "[T]he Texas abortion laws must be declared unconstitutional because they deprive single women and married couples, of their right, secured by the Ninth Amendment, to choose whether to have children."

Supreme Court Hears the Case

The Fifth Circuit Court had issued declarative relief, that is, it had declared the challenged law unconstitutional. It had not, however, issued injunctive relief, which would have been an order for Texas to end its enforcement of that law. For this reason, Weddington and Coffee were entitled to appeal directly to the U.S. Supreme Court, which agreed to hear their case.

Forty-two *amici curiae,* or "friend of the court" briefs, were filed in support of a woman's right to choose an abortion from organizations as varied as the New York Academy of Medicine, the American College of Gynecologists and Obstetricians, Planned Parenthood, and the California chapter of the National Organization for Women. There was also a "woman's brief," signed by such noteworthy women as anthropologist Margaret Mead; Barnard College President Millicent McIntosh; Oregon's past U.S. Senator, Maurine Nuebuerger; and feminist theologian Mary Daly. This brief stated, as Marian Faux summarized it, "that even if a fetus were found to be a legal person, a woman still could not be compelled to nurture it in her body against her will."

On 13 December 1971, Weddington stood before the Supreme Court and contended the state's ability to compel women to bear children left women without any control over their lives. Then she argued against Tolles' claim that a fetus was entitled to protection. "[T]he Constitution, as I read it . . . attaches protection to the person at the time of birth. Those persons born are citizens."

When Floyd's turn came, he said that "Roe" must surely have given birth by now and thus could not represent pregnant women in a class-action suit. Asked how any pregnant woman could hope to challenge Texas' abortion laws, Floyd replied: "There are situations in which . . . no remedy is provided. Now, I think she makes her choice prior to the time she becomes pregnant. That is the time of the choice . . . Once a child is born, a woman no longer has a choice; and I think pregnancy makes that choice as well."

Floyd was then questioned as to why, if abortion was equivalent to murder, no state had ever punished the women involved. He was also questioned about the fact that doctors who performed abortions were not charged with premeditated murder but "ordinary felony murder," a lesser charge. Finally, he was asked to clarify when life began according to the state of Texas. After several attempts to answer the question, Floyd could only say: "I don't—Mr. Justice—there are unanswerable questions in this field."

Since there had been only seven sitting justices when *Roe v. Wade* was argued, the justices decided that such an important case should be re-argued when two newly appointed justices—William Rehnquist and Lewis Powell—joined the Court, restoring the number of justices to nine. Weddington, Coffee, Tolles, and Floyd did so 10 October 1972, repeating their basic arguments.

Landmark Decision

On 22 January 1973, Justice Blackmun read his majority opinion to a room filled with reporters. Reviewing the history of abortion in the United States, he pointed out that "The restrictive criminal abortion laws in effect in a majority of states today . . . are not of ancient or even common law origin." Instead, he said they seemed to have been passed to protect women from a procedure that was, in the nineteenth century, likely to endanger their health. That rationale no longer existed, Justice Blackmun declared, since medical advances had made abortion as safe or safer than childbirth for women.

Justice Blackmun next discussed the High Court's acknowledgment of a "right of personal privacy" in various decisions, including the recent *Griswold v. Connecticut* birth control case. Then he delivered the crux of his decision:

> This right of privacy, whether it be founded in the Fourteenth Amendment's concept of personal liberty and restrictions on state action . . . or . . . in the Ninth Amendment's reservation of rights to the people, is broad enough to encompass a woman's decision to terminate her pregnancy.

Continuing, Justice Blackmun disagreed with Texas' claim that it had the right to "infringe [on] Roe's rights" to protect "prenatal life." He discussed the use of the word "person" in the U.S. Constitution and found that no such use had "any possible prenatal application," and he specifically found that "the word 'person,' as used in the Fourteenth Amendment, does not include the unborn."

However, Justice Blackmun said, neither the woman's right to privacy nor the fetus' lack of a right to the state's protection was absolute:

Henry Wade, 1965. © AP/Wide World Photos.

> [T]he State does have an important and legitimate interest in preserving and protecting the health of the pregnant woman . . . and . . . it has still *another* important and legitimate interest in protecting the potentiality of human life. These interests are separate and distinct. Each grows in substantiality as the woman approaches term and, at a point during the pregnancy, each becomes "compelling."

Finally, Justice Blackmun's decision in *Roe v. Wade* provided the states with a formula to balance these competing interests. During the first trimester of pregnancy, the abortion decision would be "left to the medical judgment of the pregnant woman's attending physician." During the second trimester, a state might "regulate the abortion procedure in ways that are reasonably related to maternal health." From the end of the second trimester "subsequent to viability," a state might "regulate, and even proscribe, abortion except where it is necessary, in appropriate legal judgment, for the preservation of the life or health of the mother."

Justices Rehnquist and White dissented. Justice Rehnquist, in his brief, said:

> I have difficulty in concluding, as the Court does, that the right of "privacy" is involved in

this case. Texas by the statute here challenged bars the performance of a medical abortion by a licensed physician on a plaintiff such as Roe. A transaction resulting in an operation such as this is not "private" in the ordinary usage of the word.

. . . I agree with the statement . . . that . . . "liberty," embraces more than the rights found in the Bill of Rights. But that liberty is not guaranteed absolutely against deprivation without due process of law.

Justice White wrote in his dissent:

At the heart of the controversy in these cases are those recurring pregnancies that pose no danger whatsoever to the life or health of the mother but are nevertheless unwanted for any one or more of a variety of reasons—convenience, family planning, economics, dislike of children, the embarrassment of illegitimacy, etc.

The common claim before us is that for any one of such reasons, or for no reason at all . . . any woman is entitled to an abortion at her request if she is able to find a medical advisor willing to undertake the procedure.

The Court for the most part sustains this position: . . . during the period prior to the time the fetus becomes viable, the Constitution of the United States values the convenience, whim or caprice of the putative mother more than the life or potential life of the fetus.

Impact

Every state was affected. New York, which had previously permitted abortion until the twenty-fourth week of pregnancy, had to extend that period by several weeks, and the laws of Alaska, Hawaii, and Washington required similar amendments. Fifteen states needed a complete overhaul of their abortion laws, while 31 states—including Texas—had strict anti-abortion laws which became immediately and entirely invalid.

In the spring of 1973, with support from the Catholic Church, the Committee of Ten Million began a petition drive demanding a "human rights amendment," to ban abortion in the United States. Several proposed constitutional amendments were introduced and discussed in Congress, including proposals for amendments that prohibited abortions even when required to save a mother's life. These attempts failed, and Roe's opponents tried to organize the legislatures of 34 states to call for a constitutional convention; in the mid-1980s, this strategy was abandoned as well.

The Republican Party has since adopted the "pro-life" position as part of its party platform, gaining Catholic and fundamentalist members and losing enough support among women to create a 24 percent "gender gap" in the 1988 elections. The Democratic Party—which supports Roe v. Wade—also benefited from the women's vote in the 1992 presidential election, in which Bill Clinton, a supporter of a woman's right to an abortion, was elected president.

Subsequent Developments

Many of the Supreme Court's most liberal members have retired since Roe v. Wade was decided in 1973, and their conservative successors have indicated a willingness to re-examine the decision and its implications. On 30 June 1980, in Harris v. McRae, the High Court ruled that neither the federal nor local government was obligated to pay for abortions for women on welfare, even if their abortions were medically necessary. More recently, Webster v. Reproductive Health Services, 3 July 1989, granted states new authority to restrict abortions in tax-supported institutions, and Rust v. Sullivan, 23 May 1991, upheld federal regulations that denied government financial aid to family planning clinics that provided information about abortion. Yet, for the time being, the effect of the decision remains intact: A state may not prohibit a woman from aborting a fetus during the first three months of pregnancy and may only regulate abortions during the second three months in the interest of the pregnant woman's health.

Related Cases

Griswold v. Connecticut, 381 U.S. 479 (1964).
Harris v. McRae, 448 U.S. 297 (1980).
Webster v. Reproductive Health Services, 492 U.S. 490 (1989).
Rust v. Sullivan, 500 U.S. 173 (1991).

Bibliography and Further Reading

Abraham, Henry J. The Judicial Process, 4th ed. New York: Oxford University Press, 1980.

Cary, Eve, and Kathleen Willert Peratis. Woman and the Law. Skokie, IL: National Textbook Co. in conjunction with the American Civil Liberties Union, New York, 1977.

Cushman, Robert F. Cases in Constitutional Law, 7th ed. Englewood Cliffs, NJ: Prentice Hall, 1989.

———. Leading Constitutional Decisions. Englewood Cliffs, NJ: Prentice-Hall, Inc., 1982.

Davis, Flora. Moving the Mountain: The Women's Movement in America Since 1960. New York: Simon & Schuster, 1991.

Ehrenreich, Barbara, and Deidre English. For Her Own Good: 150 Years of the Expert's Advice to Women. New York: Doubleday, 1979.

Faludi, Susan. *Backlash: The Undeclared War against American Women.* New York: Crown Publishers, 1991.

Faux, Marian. *Roe v. Wade.* New York: Macmillan Co., 1988.

Hall, Kermit L., ed. *The Oxford Companion to the Supreme Court of the United States.* New York: Oxford University Press, 1992.

Johnson, John W., ed. *Historic U.S. Court Cases, 1690-1990: An Encyclopedia.* New York: Garland Publishing, 1992.

Petchesky, Rosalind Pollack. *Abortion and Woman's Choice.* Boston: Northeastern University Press, 1990.

Rosten, Leo. *Religions of America: Ferment and Faith in an Age of Crisis.* New York: Simon & Schuster, 1975.

DOE v. BOLTON

Legal Citation: 410 U.S. 179 (1973)

Appellant
Mary Doe

Appellee
Arthur K. Bolton, Attorney General of Georgia

Appellant's Claim
That a Georgia abortion law was unconstitutional because it invaded the rights of privacy and liberty, denied equal protection and procedural due process, and was vague.

Chief Lawyer for Appellant
Margie Pitts Hames

Chief Lawyer for Appellee
Dorothy T. Beasley

Justices for the Court
Harry A. Blackmun (writing for the Court), William J. Brennan, Jr., Warren E. Burger, William O. Douglas, Thurgood Marshall, Lewis F. Powell, Jr., Potter Stewart

Justices Dissenting
William H. Rehnquist, Byron R. White

Place
Washington, D.C.

Date of Decision
22 January 1973

Decision
Modified and affirmed the district court's ruling and decided that the three procedural conditions of the law violated the Fourteenth Amendment and that the residence requirement violated the Privileges and Immunities Clause of the Constitution.

Significance
Before 1973, the legality of abortion was left to the legislatures of the states. However, in 1973, the Supreme Court made it an issue of federal constitutional law by holding that abortion was a constitutional right. From then on, whether abortion was legal or not depended on the Supreme Court's decisions.

Mary Doe was a 22 year old resident of Georgia, married, and nine weeks pregnant. She already had three children. The two older ones had been placed in a foster home because Doe was poor and unable to care for them. The youngest had been put up for adoption. Doe's husband had recently abandoned her, forcing her to live with her impoverished parents and their eight children. Doe and her husband, a sporadically employed construction worker, eventually reconciled. Doe had been a mental patient at the state hospital. She had been told that an abortion would be less dangerous to her health than giving birth to the child she carried. Moreover, if she gave birth to the child, she would be unable to care for or support it.

On 25 March 1970, Doe applied for an abortion to the Abortion Committee of Grady Memorial Hospital in Atlanta, Georgia. Her application was denied on the ground that her situation was not described in Georgia's abortion law. This law allowed abortions only if a continued pregnancy would endanger a pregnant woman's life or injure her health; the fetus would be born with a serious defect; or the pregnancy resulted from rape.

Mary Doe and nine physicians brought a federal action in the Northern District of Georgia against the state's attorney general, the district attorney of Fulton County, and the chief of police of Atlanta. Doe wanted the court to declare that the Georgia abortion laws were unconstitutional in their entirety. She also wanted an injunction restraining the defendants from enforcing the abortion statutes. Doe alleged in her suit that because her application for an abortion was denied, she was forced either to relinquish "her right to decide when and how many children she will bear" or seek an abortion that was illegal. This invaded her rights of privacy and liberty in matters relating to family, marriage, and sex, and deprived her of the right to choose whether to bear children. This violated the rights guaranteed by the First, Fourth, Fifth, Ninth, and Fourteenth Amendments. The Georgia abortion laws also denied her equal protection and procedural due process and, because they were unconstitutionally vague, deterred hospitals and doctors from performing abortions. The doctors in the suit alleged that the Georgia laws "chilled and deterred" them from practicing their profession and deprived them of the rights guaranteed by the First, Fourth, and Fourteenth Amendments.

The district court ruled that limiting the reasons why an abortion may be sought improperly restricted Doe's right of privacy and of personal liberty, which should include the decision to abort a pregnancy. Thus the court held invalid the part of the law that limited abortions to three situations, but refused to issue an injunction. The court, however, held that Georgia's interest in protection of health and the existence of a "potential of independent human existence" justified state regulation of "the manner of performance as well as the quality of the final decision to abort." The court refused to strike down the provisions of the statute that required a woman wanting an abortion: to be a resident of Georgia; to get two other physicians to approve the procedure; to have the abortion performed in a hospital accredited by the joint Commission of Accreditation of Hospitals; and to have the abortion approved by a hospital committee.

Health Includes Physical, Emotional, and Psychological Well-being

Claiming that they were entitled to an injunction and to broader relief, the plaintiffs appealed directly to the Supreme Court. *Doe v. Bolton* was the companion case to *Roe v. Wade* (1973), the landmark case in which the Court ruled that the Fourteenth Amendment provided a fundamental right for women to obtain abortions. The Court held that the "right to privacy," assured the freedom of a person to abort unless the state had a "compelling interest" in preventing the abortion.

In *Doe v. Bolton*, Doe argued that the Georgia statute, as it stood after the district court's decision, was unconstitutionally vague. The law still stated that it was a crime for a doctor to perform an abortion except when it was "based upon his best clinical judgment that an abortion is necessary." Doe contended that the word "necessary" did not let physicians know what conduct was not allowed and that the statute was subject to many different interpretations. The Court responded that "medical judgment may be exercised in the light of all factors—physical, emotional, psychological, familial, and the woman's age—relevant to the well-being of the patient. All these factors may relate to health."

The Georgia abortion statute required three procedural steps of a woman wanting an abortion: the abortion had to be performed in an accredited hospital; it had to be approved by the hospital staff abortion committee; and two other physicians, besides the woman's own doctor, had to examine her and confirm the decision to abort. Doe argued that these three procedural demands unduly restricted the woman's right to privacy and denied procedural due process and equal protection. Regarding the requirement that abortions be

performed in accredited hospitals, the Court stated that after the end of the first trimester of pregnancy, Georgia may adopt standards for licensing all facilities where abortions may be performed. But because the hospital requirement of the law failed to exclude the first trimester of pregnancy, that requirement was invalid. Regarding committee approval of the abortion, the Court stated, "The woman's right to receive medical care in accordance with her licensed physician's best judgment and the physician's right to administer it are substantially limited by this statutorily imposed overview." Regarding the required two physician concurrence, the Court felt that it had no rational connections with a patient's needs and unduly infringed on the physician's right to practice.

Doe attacked the Georgia residency requirement as violating the right to travel. The Court noted, "Just as the Privileges and Immunities Clause . . . protects persons who enter other states to ply their trade . . . so must it protect persons who enter Georgia seeking the medical services that are available there." Blackmun concluded the opinion by noting that the provisions of the law ruled on in this case all violated the Fourteenth Amendment.

Chief Justice Burger wrote in his concurring opinion, "I agree that, under the Fourteenth Amendment to the Constitution, the abortion statutes of Georgia and Texas impermissibly limit the performance of abortions necessary to protect the health of pregnant women, using the term health in its broadest medical context." Burger would allow a state to require the certification of two physicians to support an abortion. He noted that the Court in this case rejected any claim that the Constitution requires abortions on demand.

Justice Douglas wrote a concurring opinion. He noted that some rights, such as the freedom of choice regarding marriage, divorce, procreation, contraception, and the education of children are subject to some control by the police power. Rights such as the freedom to care for one's health and person are fundamental but are subject to regulation on showing of "compelling state interest." Douglas noted that the Georgia abortion statute went against the idea that a woman is free to make the basic decision of whether or not to bear an unwanted child. Childbirth may deprive a woman of her preferred lifestyle and force upon her a radically different and undesired future. Women denied abortions under the Georgia law may have to abandon educational plans, lose income, forego careers, and bear the stigma of unwed motherhood. But the state also has interests to protect including the woman's health and the life of the fetus after quickening.

Douglas felt that the Georgia law resulted in the "total destruction of the right of privacy between physician and patient and the intimacy of relation which that entails. The right to seek advice on one's health and the right to place reliance on the physician of one's choice are basic to Fourteenth Amendment values."

The Issue Should Be Left To The People

Justice White dissented. He felt that the majority's position was that before "the fetus becomes viable, the Constitution . . . values the convenience, whim, or caprice of the putative mother more than the life or potential life of the fetus; the Constitution, therefore, guarantees the right to an abortion as against any state law or policy seeking to protect the fetus from an abortion . . ." White did not support this view. He felt that the Court was simply fashioning a new constitutional right for pregnant women. He believed that the people and legislatures of the states could not now weigh the relative importance of the continued existence and development of the fetus against the impact on the mother. White felt that this was an "improvident and extravagant exercise of the power of judicial review." He noted that the Court apparently valued the convenience of the pregnant mother more than the continued existence and development of the life she carried. No constitutional warrant existed for imposing this order of priorities on the people and state legislatures. This is an area where "reasonable men may easily and heatedly differ . . ." White felt a constitutional barrier should not prevent states from protecting human life and the Court should not invest mothers and doctors with the constitutionally protected right to exterminate human life. He felt that the issue should be left to the people and to the political processes.

Justice Rehnquist also dissented. He believed that the compelling-state-interest standard was an inappropriate measure of the constitutionality of state abortion laws.

Impact

In *Roe v. Wade* and *Doe v. Bolton* the Court upheld a woman's right to an abortion. Notably the *Doe* case

defined "health" as including a woman's age, and physical, psychological, and familial factors. Through the mid-1980s, the Court adhered to its rulings in those cases, despite state challenges. In 1989 came the first sharp departure from the 1973 rulings. In *Webster v. Reproductive Health Services* (1989), the Court decided to let stand a Missouri law stating that human life began at conception, that barred the use of state property for abortions, and that required viability tests for advanced pregnancies. Some state legislatures began to pass new abortion restrictions after this decision. In *Planned Parenthood of Southeastern Pennsylvania v. Casey* (1992), the Court reached a practical compromise allowing limited state regulation of abortion, yet still preserving general access to abortion. The Court decided that abortion after viability (20-22 weeks) can be banned and pre-viability laws only have to meet the new "undue burden" standard, meaning that a "compelling" state interest is not required as long as the law does not form a "substantial obstacle" to obtaining an abortion. This case has replaced *Roe v. Wade* as the dominant precedent on abortion.

Related Cases

United States v. Vuitch, 402 U.S. 62 (1971).
Roe v. Wade, 410 U.S. 113 (1973).
Webster v. Reproductive Health Services, 492 U.S. 490 (1989).
Planned Parenthood of Southeastern Pennsylvania v. Casey, 505 U.S. 833 (1992).

Bibliography and Further Reading

Abortion Law Homepage. http://member.aol.com/abtrng/

Hall, Kermit L., ed. *The Oxford Companion to the Supreme Court of the United States.* New York: Oxford Press, 1992.

Levy, Leonard W., ed. *Encyclopedia of the American Constitution.* Vol. 4. New York: Macmillan, 1986.

PLANNED PARENTHOOD OF CENTRAL MISSOURI V. DANFORTH

Legal Citation: 428 U.S. 52 (1976)

Appellant
Planned Parenthood of Central Missouri; David Hall, M.D.; Michael Freiman, M.D.

Appellee
John C. Danforth, Attorney General of Missouri

Appellant's Claim
That under the guidelines established by the Court in *Roe v. Wade* and *Doe v. Bolton,* and under the Eighth and Fourteenth Amendments to the Constitution, a Missouri abortion statute is unconstitutional.

Chief Lawyer for Appellee
John C. Danforth

Chief Lawyer for Appellant
Frank Susman

Justices for the Court
Harry A. Blackmun (writing for the Court), William J. Brennan, Jr., Thurgood Marshall, Lewis F. Powell, Jr., Potter Stewart

Justices Dissenting
Warren E. Burger, William H. Rehnquist, John Paul Stevens, Byron R. White

Place
Washington, D.C.

Date of Decision
1 July 1976

Decision
In a complex eight-part ruling, the Court struck down Missouri's requirements that a married woman should receive the consent of her husband, and a minor of her parents, before receiving an abortion. It also invalidated laws proscribing the abortion procedure of saline amniocentesis and requiring physicians to preserve the fetus's life whatever the stage of pregnancy. The Court upheld state provisions regarding viability of a fetus, written consent by the pregnant woman, and the keeping of abortion records; and refused to rule on an eighth provision, for which it held that the appellants lacked standing to challenge.

Significance
In the wake of the Court's monumental ruling in *Roe v. Wade* and *Doe v. Bolton,* which established the legality of abortion, many states had adopted strict statutes designed to place limits on that practice. *Danforth* marked the first significant challenge to these post-*Roe* laws. It expanded the rights established in the earlier cases through its ruling that requirements of spousal and parental consent for abortion are constitutional.

A Question of Viability

Planned Parenthood of Central Missouri v. Danforth was, as the Court announced in its opening comments on the case, a "logical and anticipated corollary to" *Roe v. Wade* (1973) and *Doe v. Bolton* (1973), two cases that had legalized abortion. Not long after those decisions, the Court reviewed a case in which a 1969 Missouri abortion law had come under constitutional challenge. A panel of three federal judges in the Western District of Missouri, in an unreported decision, declared the Missouri statutes unconstitutional. The Supreme Court affirmed this decision. Meanwhile, a number of states, Missouri among them, sought to enact tougher abortion laws in order to curtail the number of situations in which abortion might be permissible. In June of 1974, the Missouri General Assembly passed House Bill 1211 (which the Court designated as "act"), and the state governor signed it into law on 14 June 1974.

The act set a number of stipulations regarding abortion, and three days after its passage, it was challenged in the U.S. Court for the Eastern District of Missouri. Leading the list of plaintiffs was Planned Parenthood of Central Missouri, a non-profit corporation that maintained an abortion clinic in Columbia, Missouri. David Hall and Michael Freiman, both physicians who regularly performed abortions, joined Planned Parenthood in that action, which they brought "on behalf of the entire class consisting of duly licensed physicians and surgeons" involved, or interested in being involved, in performing abortions; and "on behalf of the entire class consisting of their patients desiring the termination of pregnancy, all within the State of Missouri." According to their suit, the Missouri statute deprived themselves and their patients of various constitutional rights, including "the right to privacy in the physician-patient relationship"; the physician's "right to practice medicine according to the highest standards of medical practice"; a woman's right to decide whether or not she should have children; her "right to life due to the inherent risk involved in childbirth"; physicians' right to give medical advice, and patients' right to receive it; the patients' right to be free from cruel and unusual punishment under the Eighth Amendment, in this case such punishment being "coercing them to bear each pregnancy they conceive"; and the physician's right to due process of law under the Fourteenth Amendment.

In all, the case challenged some nine provisions in the Missouri statute, some of which the district court held as unconstitutional. With regard to those parts deemed constitutional, the people bringing suit appealed; likewise the state of Missouri, in a subordinate legal action designated as *Danforth v. Planned Parenthood of Central Missouri,* appealed the lower court's rulings against certain of its state laws. On the side of the appellants, the Center for Constitutional Rights and the Planned Parenthood Federation of America Inc. filed briefs of *amici curiae.* Likewise the United States Catholic Conference, Lawyers for Life Inc., and Missouri Nurses for Life filed briefs on behalf of the appellees.

The Court's ruling in *Danforth* was a complex one, divided into eight parts. A majority agreed on all eight, but four—White, Burger, Rehnquist, and Stevens— dissented on a number of the parts. Beginning its ruling, the Court noted that under *Roe,* it had established the existence of a "right of privacy, whether it be founded in the Fourth Amendment's concept of personal liberty . . . or . . . in the Ninth Amendment's reservation of rights to the people." It had "emphatically rejected," however, the notion that "the woman's right is absolute and that she is entitled to terminate her pregnancy at whatever time, in whatever way, and for whatever reason she alone chooses." Rather, state interests must be taken into consideration as well. The Court tied the permissibility of state regulations to three stages of pregnancy: (1) a period approximating the first trimester or three months, when the state could not interfere at all in the decision to abort; (2) a period in which the state could "reasonably regulate the abortion procedure to preserve and protect maternal health"; and (3) a stage when the fetus is determined to be viable, "a point purposefully left flexible for professional determination," at which time the state could "regulate an abortion to protect the life of the fetus and even . . . proscribe abortion except where it is necessary . . . for the life or health of the mother."

The Court then turned to the various challenged statutes. The first of these was section 7, which declared that if an infant survived an abortion not performed for reasons of health or to save life, that child would be taken from its parents and declared a ward of the state. Given the fact that this particular statute had nothing to do with the physicians or Planned Parenthood, the Court ruled that the appellants lacked standing, and declined to make any judgment whatever on the statute itself.

Next it turned to the challenging question of viability, which Missouri defined in section 2 (2) as "that stage of fetal development when the life of the unborn child may be continued indefinitely outside the womb by natural or artificial life-supportive systems." In *Roe,*

the Court had loosely defined "viable" as the point at which the fetus was "potentially able to live outside the mother's womb, albeit with artificial aid," and had noted that this usually falls around the seventh month or the twenty-eighth week of pregnancy. "In any event," wrote Justice Blackmun for the Court, "we agree with the District Court that it is not the proper function of the legislature or the courts to place viability, which essentially is a medical concept, at a specific point in the gestation period." Therefore the Court concluded that section 2 (2) did not overstep the limits on state regulation established in *Roe.*

Three Issues of Consent

The Court next approached three provisions in the statutes requiring one form of consent or another before an abortion could be performed: section 3 (2), by which a woman had to provide written consent that she had agreed to the abortion before she underwent it; section 3 (3), which required that a married woman's husband give his consent to the abortion in situations where the operation was not necessary to preserve the woman's life; and section 3 (4), which required the consent of parents before a minor could have an abortion.

The Court found section 3 (2), the requirement of written consent, constitutional. The appellants had charged that the statute violated *Roe* by adding an "extra layer and burden of regulation on the abortion decision"; the district court, however, had ruled that the decision to end a pregnancy is "often a stressful one," and that 3 (2) "insures that the pregnant woman retains control over the discretions of her consulting physician." The Court agreed, despite the fact that with rare exceptions, Missouri required no written consent for other types of medical procedures. Abortion, clearly, was a special type of operation; and in any case, "We could not say that a requirement imposed by the State that a prior written consent for any surgery would be unconstitutional."

As for section 3 (3), requiring spousal consent, the Court found this statute unconstitutional. The appellees had argued that marriage was an institution to be respected under Missouri law; therefore, "a change in the family structure set in motion by mutual consent should be terminated only by mutual consent." In the view of the appellants, section 3 (3) made it possible for a husband to demand that his wife not abort, whether or not she felt that was the best decision. The Court held to the logic that "Inasmuch as it is the woman who physically bears the child . . . the balance weighs in her favor" when it comes to final decision-making power. Therefore, it declared section 3 (3) unconstitutional.

The Court similarly found section 3 (4), the requirement of parental consent for minors, unconstitutional. The appellees had pointed out that, due to the desire of the state to protect their best interests, minors already enjoyed fewer rights than adults, and were thus prohibited from purchasing alcohol, firearms, tobacco, and pornography. The appellants, on the other hand, argued that Missouri made no other requirements for adult consent, even in the situation of a minor giving birth to a child. The district court had taken the side of the appellees, finding "a compelling basis" for the state's interest "in safeguarding the authority of the family relationship." The Supreme Court, however, ruled that "constitutional rights do not mature and come into being magically only when one attains the state-defined age of majority." Furthermore, it was not likely that the parental consent law, by "providing the parent with absolute power" would necessarily "serve to strengthen the family unit." That being said, the Court made clear that it "does not suggest that every minor, regardless of age or maturity, may give effective consent for termination of her pregnancy."

Three Other Provisions

Section 9 of the Missouri statute prohibited the use of saline amniocentesis, the injection of "a saline or other fluid" into the amniotic sac in place of amniotic fluid. The Court likewise rejected this provision because it proscribed "the most commonly used abortion procedure in the country and one that is safer, with respect to infant mortality, than even the continuation of pregnancy until normal childbirth." According to the appellants, 70 percent of all abortions after the first trimester were performed according to this procedure, and thus it amounted to a *de facto* prohibition of second-trimester abortions. They also presented evidence that the mortality rate was actually higher in childbirth than in cases where women had received saline amniocentesis; nonetheless, the district court had ruled that the restriction it imposed protected the health of the mother. The Supreme Court did not agree, "particularly in light of the present unavailability" in Missouri of the prostaglandin method, a technique deemed even safer than saline amniocentesis.

Section 10 of the act put in place record keeping requirements whereby clinics would report details of "all abortions performed to assure that they are done only under and in accordance with the provisions of the law." Section 11 required that these records be kept on file for seven years. The appellants challenged these as yet another burden and extra layer of regulation, but the district court had treated them as essential statistical requirements. In spite of "important and sometimes conflicting interests affected by record keeping requirements," the Supreme Court held that these were "reasonably directed to the preservation of maternal health . . ." Therefore, it allowed the two laws to stand.

Finally, the Court approached section 6 (1), which stated that

No person who performs or induces an abortion shall fail to exercise that degree of professional skill, care and diligence to preserve the life and health of the fetus which such person would be required to exercise in order to preserve the life and health of any fetus intended to be born and not aborted. Any physician or person assisting in the abortion who shall fail to take such measures . . . shall be deemed guilty of manslaughter [and] shall be liable in an action for damages.

The district court had judged this as unconstitutionally overbroad, and the Supreme Court agreed.

Concurrence and Dissent

In a concurring opinion, Justice Stewart made mention of certain specific issues addressed in the Court's rulings on viability, parental consent, and the consent of the husband. The last of these, he said, "seems to me a rather more difficult problem than the Court acknowledges." He cited earlier decisions such as *Stanley v. Illinois* (1972), in which the Court had established that a man's right to be a father was a constitutionally protected freedom.

Justice White, joined by Chief Justice Burger and Justice Rehnquist, concurred in part and dissented in part. With regard to spousal consent in section 3 (3), he disagreed with the Court's finding that the state was simply delegating to the husband rights which should belong exclusively to the wife. Citing *Stanley,* he wrote that "A father's interest in having a child—perhaps his only child—may be unmatched by any other interest in his life." As for the requirement of parental consent in section 3 (4), White held that "The purpose of the requirement is to vindicate the very right created in *Roe v. Wade* . . . the right of the pregnant woman to decide 'whether or not to terminate her pregnancy.'" The state of Missouri was simply attempting to "protect the minor unmarried woman from making the decision in a way which is not in her own best interests."

Addressing the prohibition of saline amniocentesis in section 9, Justice White wrote that "Legislative history reveals that the Missouri Legislature viewed saline amniocentesis as a far less safe method of abortion than the so-called prostaglandin method." Furthermore, the fact that the prostaglandin method was not available in Missouri did not by any means indicate that it was unavailable to Missouri women, who could obtain it elsewhere.

As for section 6 (1) and its seemingly contradictory requirement that the physician attempt to preserve the life of the fetus being aborted, Justice White wrote that

If this section is read in any way other than through a microscope, it is plainly intended to require that, where a 'fetus [may have] the capability of meaningful life outside the mother's womb,' . . . the abortion be handled in a way which is designed to preserve that life notwithstanding the mother's desire to terminate it.

Common sense would dictate, then, that

if the pregnancy is to be terminated at a time when there is no chance of life outside the womb, a physician would not be required to exercise any care or skill to preserve the life of the fetus during abortion no matter what the mother's desires.

Therefore, despite the fact that section 6 (1) was "ambiguous," Justice White held that it should not be declared unconstitutional.

Finally, Justice Stevens concurred in part and dissented in part. Like Justice White, he held that the parental consent requirement in section 3 (4) was not inconsistent with the Court's ruling in *Roe*, and for much the same reason. Furthermore, "It is unrealistic, in my judgment, to assume that every parent-child relationship is either (a) so perfect that communication . . . will take place routinely"—i.e., that the law in section 3 (4) would be unnecessary—"or (b) so imperfect that the absence of communication reflects the child's correct prediction that the parent will exercise his or her veto arbitrarily to further a selfish interest," which would mean that section 3 (4) would be harmful without exception.

Impact

Although several elements of *Danforth* had the potential for enormous impact on abortion law, by far the most significant were those parts dealing with consent in one form or another. Five years later, in *H. L. v. Matheson* (1981), the Court sustained a requirement for parental consent, and continued to uphold similar laws in other cases. In the area of written consent by the woman herself, the state of Ohio sought to expand on the authority conceded to Missouri in *Danforth*, and established requirements challenged in *Akron v. Akron*

Center for Reproductive Health (1983). By a vote of 6-3, the Court voted to strike down these more stringent requirements, which it held were designed to dissuade the pregnant woman from having an abortion. In 1986, it also invalidated a less broad Pennsylvania law which required a doctor to counsel a pregnant woman on the risks inherent in an abortion, and to inform her of the options available if she chose to carry the child to term.

Related Cases

Stanley v. Illinois, 405 U.S. 645 (1972).
Roe v. Wade, 410 U.S. 113 (1973).
Doe v. Bolton, 410 U.S. 179 (1973).
Bellotti v. Baird, 428 U.S. 132 (1976).
Beal v. Doe, 432 U.S. 454 (1977).
Maher v. Roe, 432 U.S. 464 (1977).
Harris v. McRae, 448 U.S. 297 (1980).
Akron v. Akron Center for Reproductive Health, 462 U.S. 416 (1983).

Bibliography and Further Reading

Claus, Marcie R. "Abortion: A Minor's Prerogative via *Planned Parenthood of Central Missouri v. Danforth.*" *Illinois Bar Journal,* Vol. 75, August 1987, pp. 674-78.

Hall, Kermit L., ed. *The Oxford Companion to the Supreme Court of the United States.* New York: Oxford University Press, 1992

Leister, Burton M., compiler. *Values in Conflict: Life, Liberty, and the Rule of Law.* New York: Macmillan, 1981.

Levy, Leonard W., ed. *Encyclopedia of the American Constitution.* New York: Macmillan, 1986.

O'Neill, Onora, and William Ruddick, eds. *Having Children: Philosophical and Legal Reflections on Parenthood: Essays.* New York: Oxford University Press, 1979.

"Whose Womb Is It Anyway: Are Paternal Rights Alive and Well Despite *Danforth*?" *Cardozo Law Review,* Vol. 11, February 1990, pp. 685-711.

Witt, Elder, ed. *The Supreme Court A to Z. CQ's Encyclopedia of American Government,* revised ed. Washington, DC: Congressional Quarterly, Inc., 1994

BEAL V. DOE

Legal Citation: 432 U.S. 438 (1977)

Petitioner
Beal, Secretary, Department of Public Welfare of Pennsylvania, et al.

Respondent
"Jane Doe"

Petitioner's Claim
That Title XIX of the Social Security Act, a statute governing the federal Medicaid program, did not require states participating in that program to provide financial assistance for non-therapeutic abortions—i.e., abortions that are not deemed medically necessary.

Chief Lawyer for Petitioner
Norman J. Watkins

Chief Lawyer for Respondent
Judd F. Crosby

Justices for the Court
Warren E. Burger, Lewis F. Powell, Jr. (writing for the Court), William H. Rehnquist, John Paul Stevens, Potter Stewart, Byron R. White

Justices Dissenting
Harry A. Blackmun, William J. Brennan, Jr., Thurgood Marshall

Place
Washington, D.C.

Date of Decision
20 June 1977

Decision
That Title XIX neither required states to fund non-therapeutic abortions nor prevented them from doing so.

Significance
Together with *Maher v. Roe* and *Poelker v. Doe*, all of them decided on 20 June 1977, *Beal v. Doe* addressed the controversial issue of public provisions for abortion. *Beal* and *Maher* involved public funding for abortion in Pennsylvania and Connecticut respectively, *Poelker* involved the use of publicly run hospitals for the purpose of terminating pregnancies in St. Louis. The three cases raised, rather than settled, questions regarding abortion in public facilities and/or with public funds.

Title XIX, Medicaid, and Pennsylvania

In 1965, the federal government established Medicaid as a program providing government-funded medical assistance to the poor, and in 1970, Congress passed Title XIX of the Social Security Act, which regulated Medicaid. States were to administer their Medicaid programs and provide qualified individuals with assistance in five areas: inpatient hospital services, outpatient hospital services, other laboratory and X-ray services, skilled nursing facility/family planning services, and physicians' services furnished by a physician. Title XIX did not require that states provide funding for abortion; it could not have, since that practice would not become legal for another three years, when the Supreme Court made its historic decisions in *Roe v. Wade* and *Doe v. Bolton*. Title XIX did not, in fact, require states to fund all forms of medical treatment within the five categories, but it did impel states to use "reasonable standards . . . for determining . . . the extent of medical assistance under the plan . . . consistent with the objectives of [Title XIX.]"

The respondent in *Beal v. Doe*, "Jane Doe," was eligible for medical assistance under Medicaid, and she requested funding for an abortion. Her home state of Pennsylvania, however, had regulations in place forbidding financial assistance for any but therapeutic (that is, medically necessary) abortions. Following denial of the respondent's application, she and others filed an action with the U.S. District Court for the Western District of Pennsylvania, alleging that the state had violated both Title XIX and the provision of equal protection under the Fourteenth Amendment to the Constitution. In the suit, she sought declaratory and injunctive relief—i.e., a statement of the exact law by the court, and an injunction against the State of Pennsylvania.

As would occur when the case went on to higher courts, the three-judge panel of the district court reviewed the suit from both the statutory and constitutional standpoints, the statutory issue being the alleged violation of Title XIX, and the constitutional one being the question of equal protection. The court ruled against Pennsylvania on both issues, and granted a declaratory judgement that the state's requirement was unconstitutional as applied during the first trimester. Pennsylvania's Secretary of Public Welfare Beal took the case to the U.S. Court of Appeals for the Third Circuit, which reversed on the statutory issue. The court did, however, declare that Title XIX prohibited participating states from requiring a physician's certificate of medical necessity before funding a first- or second-trimester abortion. It did not address the constitutional issue.

A Question of Statutory Construction

When *Beal v. Doe* reached the Supreme Court, the only question before the Court was one of statutory construction. In his opinion for the majority, Justice Powell quoted a statement he had made in *Blue Chip Stamps v. Manor Drug Stores* (1975): "The starting point in every case involving construction of a statute is the language itself." Looking strictly at the language, he found that Title XIX did not require the funding of non-therapeutic abortions; nor did it require participating states to fund every possible medical procedure that fell within the five established categories. "[S]erious statutory questions might be presented," Powell wrote, if a state plan did not include coverage of necessary medical treatment. But that was not the case here, and "it is not inconsistent with the Act's goals to refuse to fund unnecessary (though perhaps desirable) medical services."

The respondents had asserted that exclusion of non-therapeutic abortions from Medicaid coverage was unreasonable both from the standpoint of economics and health. In the case of economics, it would be much cheaper for a state to pay for an abortion than it would be to provide financial assistance to an indigent woman having a baby. As for the health argument, the respondents presented data which showed that a woman was more likely to die in childbirth than from an early abortion. Nonetheless, the Court cited its holding in *Roe v. Wade* to the effect that the state had "a strong interest in encouraging normal childbirth"; furthermore, "nothing in Title XIX suggests that it is unreasonable for a State to further that interest."

Powell noted the fact that at the time of Title XIX's passage, non-therapeutic abortions were against the law in most states. Title XIX was administered by the Department of Health, Education, and Welfare (HEW), later renamed the Department of Health and Human Services, and HEW held that the statute "allows, but does not mandate, funding for such abortions." For these reasons, the Court ruled in favor of the respondents and reversed the lower court's decision.

The Court left one question open, involving the Pennsylvania program's requirement that financial assistance required the written opinion of two physicians—in addition to the attending physician—attesting to the necessity of the operation. "Whether or not," the Court wrote, "that aspect of Pennsylvania's program . . . interferes with the attending physician's judgment in a manner not contemplated by Congress should be considered on remand."

Dissent: Forcing Poor Women to Have Children

The dissenting justices each filed an opinion. Justice Brennan, joined by Justices Marshall and Blackmun in his opinion, began by disagreeing with the Court's position that elective abortions did not belong among the "necessary medical services" for which Pennsylvania was required to provide funding. Pregnancy was "unquestionably a condition requiring medical services," and therefore any treatment associated with it—including the termination of the pregnancy—should be covered as well. That choice should belong not to the states, Brennan held, but to the doctors, a concept reinforced in a statement by the Senate Finance Committee in its 1965 report on the Medicaid bill: the physician, the committee recommended, "is to be the key figure in determining utilization of health services." The Court's previous decisions in *Roe* and *Doe* concurred with this judgment, Brennan held, but its current position did not.

Brennan reasoned that if Pennsylvania was not required to fund non-therapeutic abortions, then it had the authority to refuse funding for therapeutic ones or even for live births because any of these could be judged unnecessary. He further cited a 1972 amendment to the 1970 act which reinforced his argument with its statement that one purpose of Medicaid was to assist recipients in attaining or maintaining their ability to care for themselves. This could be achieved, the amendment said, in part by helping individuals "control family size in order to enhance their capacity and ability to seek employment and better meet family needs."

Brennan treated the majority's observation that abortions were illegal in 1965 as a moot point, because the Medicaid Act "deals with general categories of medical services, not with specific procedures." As for the judgment expressed by HEW, Brennan treated this as irrelevant because "The principle of according weight to agency interpretation is inapplicable when a departmental interpretation . . . is patently inconsistent with the controlling statute." Brennan further rejected Pennsylvania's claim of health and financial reasons behind the statute, using an argument similar to that of the respondents: the cost and health risks of abortion were actually lower than those for live birth.

"The Court's construction," Brennan said near his conclusion, "can only result as a practical matter in forcing penniless pregnant women to have children they would not have borne if the State had not weighted the scales to make their choice to have abortions substantially more onerous." He closed by briefly addressing the unanswered question regarding the requirement that two physicians other than the attending physician must agree to the procedure in writing before it could be performed. Due to the "paramount role played by the attending physician in the abortion decision," Brennan held, he would judge that portion of the statute invalid as well.

Marshall took a similar, though stronger, position in his own dissent. Like Brennan, he asserted that "the enactments challenged here brutally coerce poor women to bear children whom society will scorn for every day of their lives"; but he also held that "the government actions in these cases, ostensibly taken to 'encourage' women to carry pregnancies to term, are in reality intended to impose a moral viewpoint that no state may constitutionally enforce." Laws such as the Pennsylvania statute under discussion, as well as those others examined by the Court in the other two abortion-related cases that day, had been made by people opposed to the Court's decisions in *Roe* and *Doe,* in order "to circumvent the commands of the Constitution and impose their moral choices upon the rest of society."

In Marshall's view, the fact that many of the women seeking abortions under Medicaid were members of minority groups, and that most were poor, meant that the Court's decision would hurt the most vulnerable members of society. Given also the fact that "opposition remains strong against increasing Aid to Families With Dependent Children [welfare] benefits for impoverished mothers and children," the effects would be particularly hurtful. "I am appalled," Marshall wrote, "at the ethical bankruptcy of those who preach a 'right to life' that means, under present social policies, a bare existence in utter misery for so many poor women and their children."

After examining the Court's decisions in *Maher* and *Poelker,* Marshall judged that the statutes questioned in those cases and the current one were all violative of the Fourteenth Amendment's Equal Protection Clause. He commented on the Court's retreat from its position in *Roe* and *Doe,* which he compared to *Brown v. Board of Education* for their controversial qualities. The decision in *Beal,* he wrote, would only help "well-financed and carefully orchestrated lobbying campaigns" persuade public officials to put more restrictions into place. "The effect," he concluded,

> will be to relegate millions of people to lives of poverty and despair. When elected leaders cower before public pressure, this Court, more than ever, must not shirk its duty to enforce the Constitution for the benefit of the poor and powerless.

Blackmun, in an opinion joined by Brennan and Marshall, echoed the theme that withholding public funds for abortion was equal in practice to forcing poor

women to have children they did not want. The Court's ruling, he wrote, implied that even if the government refused to pay for it, a poor woman could come up with the funds for an abortion from some other source. This he compared to the alleged statement of Marie Antoinette when told that the peasants of France had no bread: "Let them eat cake." In concluding words not unlike those of Marshall, Blackmun suggested that the Court was ignoring "another world 'out there' . . ." As a consequence of this, he wrote, "the cancer of poverty will continue to grow. This is a sad day for those who regard the Constitution as a force that would serve justice to all evenhandedly and, in so doing, would better the lot of the poorest among us."

Impact

Beal, along with its two companion cases, left in its wake a growing uncertainty as to laws governing abortion in a public arena. To abortion-rights advocates, the cases were judged as a setback because they failed to extend the practice of abortion (and as some argued, actually prevented poor women from receiving abortions); but opponents of abortion gained little from the cases either. *Beal* and its companions simply helped to establish the fact of abortion's legality as decided four years earlier in *Roe v. Wade* and *Doe v. Bolton,* and left open the question of public funding. The Court affirmed its position in *Harris v. McRae* (1980), in which it upheld the so-called Hyde Amendment to Title XIX, which forbade the use of federal funds for non-therapeutic abortions.

Related Cases
Roe v. Wade, 410 U.S. 113 (1973).
Doe v. Bolton, 410 U.S. 179 (1973).
Bellotti v. Baird, 428 U.S. 132 (1976).
Maher v. Roe, 432 U.S. 464 (1977).
Poelker v. Doe, 432 U.S. 519 (1977).
Harris v. McRae, 448 U.S. 297 (1980).
Akron v. Akron Center for Reproductive Health, 462 U.S. 416 (1983).

Bibliography and Further Reading
Chandler, Ralph C., Richard A. Enslen, and Peter G. Renstrom. *The Constitutional Law Dictionary,* Vol. 1: *Individual Rights: Supplement 2.* Santa Barbara, CA: ABC-Clio, 1991.

Goldstein, Leslie Friedman. *Contemporary Cases in Women's Rights.* Madison, WI: University of Wisconsin Press, 1994.

Harrison, Maureen, and Steve Gilbert, eds. *Abortion Decisions of the U.S. Supreme Court: The 1970s.* Beverly Hills, CA: Excellent Books, 1993.

Levy, Leonard W., ed. *Encyclopedia of the American Constitution.* New York: Macmillan, 1986.

MAHER V. ROE

Legal Citation: 432 U.S. 464 (1977)

Appellant
Maher, Connecticut Commissioner of Social Services

Appellees
Mary Poe, Susan Roe

Appellant's Claim
That the Connecticut Welfare Department regulation that limits state Medicaid benefits for first trimester abortions to those that are "medically necessary" violates the Fourteenth Amendment rights of low-income women to equal protection under the law, since the state did provide Medicaid benefits to cover childbirth expenses.

Chief Lawyer for Appellant
Lucy V. Katz

Chief Lawyer for Appellees
Edmund C. Walsh, Assistant Attorney General of Connecticut

Justices for the Court
Warren E. Burger, Lewis F. Powell, Jr. (writing for the Court), William H. Rehnquist, John Paul Stevens, Potter Stewart, Byron R. White

Justices Dissenting
Harry A. Blackmun, William J. Brennan, Jr., Thurgood Marshall

Place
Washington, D.C.

Date of Decision
20 June 1977

Decision
That states have a right to favor childbirth over abortion by funding one under Medicaid while refusing to fund the other.

Significance
The decision represented a trend to limit the availability of abortion, particularly to poor women, by denying state and federal funds for abortions.

In 1973, the Supreme Court handed down a landmark decision, *Roe v. Wade,* certifying that a woman's constitutional right to privacy also guaranteed her right to choose to have an abortion. State laws against abortion had to be struck down in the wake of this decision, which pro-choice advocates hailed as a victory.

But the decision also created a backlash of anti-abortion sentiment. Although the Supreme Court had made it impossible to outlaw abortion outright, those who believed abortion was wrong tried to stop women from having this procedure in many other ways.

For example, Congress passed the Hyde Amendment to the Social Security Act, which provided that federal funds could not be used to reimburse states for Medicaid-funded abortions unless the life of the mother was threatened by the pregnancy, or unless the pregnancy was due to rape or incest. Medicaid is a federally funded program administered by the states to help low-income people get medical care. Although the Hyde Amendment left states the option of paying for women's abortions out of their own funds, most states felt they could not afford that. Thus, cutting off federal funds made it very unlikely that low-income women would be able to have abortions, even though the Hyde Amendment had not actually made abortions illegal, or even forbidden states to pay for them.

Doctor's Certification Needed

The Connecticut state welfare regulations also mandated that Medicaid funds could not be used to pay for abortions, unless a doctor certified that an abortion was medically necessary to save the life or health of the mother. In 1974, two Connecticut women decided to challenge that rule.

Mary Poe (a pseudonym used to protect the woman's identity) was a 16-year-old high school junior who had already had an abortion at a Connecticut hospital. The hospital believed that Poe was covered under Medicaid. But when Poe could not get a doctor to certify that her abortion was medically necessary, the hospital could not be reimbursed and pressed Poe to pay the hospital bill of $244.

Susan Roe (also a pseudonym) was an unwed mother of three children. When she got pregnant with her fourth child, she wanted to get an abortion, but her doctor refused to say that the procedure was medically necessary. Together, the two women filed a complaint in district court, saying that the Connecticut regulations had violated their rights to equal protection and due process of law under the Fourteenth Amendment.

The women made three key points: (1) It was unfair for Connecticut's Medicaid program to fund childbirth but not abortion. (2) It was unfair for Connecticut's Medicaid program to demand certification that abortion was medically necessary, when such certification was not required for any other medical procedure covered by Medicaid. (3) By denying funding, the Connecticut Medicaid regulation deprived poor women of their constitutional right of privacy to decide for themselves whether they wanted an abortion.

The district court found in favor of the women. The court interpreted the Social Security Act to uphold the claim that each state had to fund abortions for women on Medicaid, even though federal funds had been denied. The Supreme Court, however, did not agree. They ruled that states have the right to fund or not fund abortions as they choose, even if they are also funding childbirth, or if their decisions mean that poor women will not be able to afford abortions.

Not a Protected Class

First, the Court held that the women could not refer to their equal rights as poor people, because "[f]inancial need alone does not identify a . . . class for purposes of equal protection analysis." In other words, for people to argue that they are being discriminated against, they have to show that they belong to a group, and that their discrimination results from their membership in that group. But, said the Court, being poor does not make you a member of a group that is being discriminated against, at least not for the purposes of the law. Second, the Court held that the Connecticut regulation did not violate the women's right to privacy, or the right to choose an abortion as guaranteed by *Roe v. Wade*. A poor woman was perfectly free to have an abortion. The state was simply not going to help her pay for it.

The Court also ruled that states had the right to establish policies that favored childbirth over abortion. Connecticut's Medicaid regulations had the right to require different rules for abortion than for other medical procedures, because "[other] procedures do not involve the termination of a potential human life."

A Distressing Insensitivity

Justices Brennan, Marshall, and Blackmun dissented from the Court's opinion. Justice Brennan wrote an opinion for the three of them, claiming that "a distressing insensitivity to the plight of impoverished pregnant women is inherent in the Court's analysis."

The Connecticut scheme clearly impinges upon . . . [women's] privacy by bringing financial pressures on indigent women that force them to bear children they would not otherwise have . . . We have repeatedly found that infringements of fundamental rights are not limited to outright denials of those rights . . . but also to restraints that make exercise of those rights more difficult.

Indeed, the regulations in Connecticut and in many other states gave welfare mothers with unwanted pregnancies several unpleasant choices. If they went ahead and bore the child, they would receive virtually no more money to take care of it. In 1981, four years after *Maher v. Roe*, the grant for a fourth person in a welfare household ranged from $24.00 per month in Mississippi to $90.00 in California.

Alternately, a woman might try to find a doctor who would perform an abortion for free, but few doctors were willing to perform such a service. A woman might use her welfare money to pay for an abortion rather than for rent or food. But in Texas, for example, an abortion costs about three months of welfare payments, while in Mississippi, the procedure cost four months payments. Finally, a woman might try to borrow the money from a friend or relative, paying it back more gradually out of her welfare payments.

Legal Consequences of *Maher v. Roe*

The *Maher* case helped make it much easier for state governments to deny funding for abortions. For example, *Maher* was cited as a precedent in a 1980 case that eventually upheld the Hyde Amendment.

Besides the immediate consequences for poor women who could not get funding for abortions, *Maher v. Roe* also affected the way the Supreme Court defined "rights" in general. The case, despite the objections of the dissenters, established the precedent that the government is not responsible for helping citizens exercise their rights. Moreover, governments are allowed to set policy that support citizens in exercising some rights (having children) while failing to support them in exercising others (having abortions.)

Thus, in a later case known as *Selective Service System v. Minnesota Pub. Int.* (1984), the Court ruled that college students who were receiving federal educational assistance had to certify that they had registered for the draft as a condition of getting aid. Technically, under the Fifth Amendment, the government cannot require a person to testify against himself or herself. So it would have been unconstitutional to pass a law requiring all students to certify that they had registered for the draft. Students who were dependent on government aid, however, could be required to waive their rights in exchange for receiving the aid. Just as poor women were still theoretically free to have abortions, needy students were still theoretically free to refuse to testify against themselves.

Related Cases

Roe v. Wade, 410 U.S. 113 (1973).

Akron v. Akron Center for Reproductive Health, 462 U.S. 416 (1983).

Planned Parenthood Association of Kansas City v. Ashcroft, 462 U.S. 476 (1983).

Selective Service System v. Minnesota Pub. Int., 468 U.S. 841 (1984).

Thornburgh v. American College of Obstetricians and Gynecologists, 476 U.S. 747 (1986).

Webster v. Reproductive Health Services, 492 U.S. 490 (1989).

Hodgson v. Minnesota, 497 U.S. 417 (1990).

Ohio v. Akron Center for Reproductive Health, 497 U.S. 502 (1990).

Planned Parenthood of Southeastern Pennsylvania v. Casey, 505 U.S. 833 (1992).

Bibliography and Further Reading

Failinger, Marie A. "An Offer She Can't Refuse: When Fundamental Rights and Conditions on Government Benefits Collide." *Villanova Law Review,* Vol. 31 no. 3-4, June 1986, pp. 833-929.

Fein, Bruce E. *Significant Decisions of the Supreme Court, 1976-1977 Term.* Washington, DC: American Enterprise Institute for Public Policy Research, 1978.

Oelsner, Lesley. "Court Rules States May Deny Medicaid for Some Abortions." *New York Times,* 21 June 1977, pp. 1, 20.

Young, Rowland L. "Court Ends Term with Holdings on Abortion, Court Closings." *American Bar Association Journal,* Vol. 66, August 1980, pp. 994-996

POELKER V. DOE

Legal Citation: 432 U.S. 519 (1977)

Petitioners
John H. Poelker, et al.

Respondents
Jane Doe, et al.

Petitioners' Claim
That the city of St. Louis, in electing as a policy choice to provide publicly financed hospital services for childbirth but not for nontherapeutic abortions, did not violate the Equal Protection Clause of the Fourteenth Amendment.

Chief Lawyer for Petitioners
Eugene P. Freeman

Chief Lawyer for Respondents
Frank Susman

Justices for the Court
Warren E. Burger, Lewis F. Powell, Jr., William H. Rehnquist, John Paul Stevens, Potter Stewart, Byron R. White

Justices Dissenting
Harry A. Blackmun, William J. Brennan, Jr., Thurgood Marshall

Place
Washington, D.C.

Date of Decision
20 June 1977

Decision
Upheld that the city of St. Louis did not violate Fourteenth Amendment equal protection, thereby reversing the judgement of the Court of Appeals for the Eighth Circuit.

Significance
The ruling specified that a hospital was allowed to refuse the performance of abortions based on hospital policy that was not influenced by city officials. However, this ruling also brought to light a certain form of discrimination caused by policies of this type that affected indigent mothers who wished to have abortions but could not afford to pay for them at private clinics.

In the *Roe v. Wade* case of 1973 it was decided by the U.S. Supreme Court that the Constitution of the United States embraced a woman's right to terminate her pregnancy by abortion. The Court maintained that this right to abortion fell within the right to privacy, and was protected by the Fourteenth Amendment. This was initially determined through a debate concerning the use of contraceptives in *Griswold v. Connecticut* (1965). The Court's decision in *Roe v. Wade* granted women complete autonomy over pregnancy during the first trimester and interpreted the levels of state interest for the second and third trimesters. This ruling influenced the laws of 46 states and spurred debate nationwide. *Roe v. Wade* acted as the precedent for such Supreme Court cases as *Poe v. Gernstein* (1974), *Whalen v. Roe* (1975), and *Connecticut v. Menill* (1975). The fundamental issue of women's autonomy during pregnancy was at the heart of each of these cases. *Poelker v. Doe* was no exception; however, this case defined the means in which a hospital could legally refuse to perform an abortion without crossing the boundaries of personal freedom.

An indigent woman, known to the court only as Jane Doe, sought to obtain an abortion at Starkloff Hospital, a Jesuit institution run by the University of St. Louis. It is important to note that the abortion requested by Doe was nontherapeutic—her health was not endangered by the pregnancy. The hospital refused to perform the abortion. As a result, Doe brought a civil rights class action suit in the U.S. District Court for the Easter District of Missouri, alleging that her constitutional rights had been violated.

The initial trial ruled against Doe. However, this ruling was reversed by the Court of Appeals for the Eight Circuit. The court of appeals determined that Doe's rights had been violated due to a combination of two elements: a policy directive from Mayor Poelker of St. Louis to the Director of Health and Hospitals and the hospital's staffing practice. The mayor's policy directive backed his own personal belief against abortion, prohibiting their performance in city hospitals unless there was threat of extreme physiological injury or death to the mother. Under the staffing practice, doctors and students at the obstetrics-gynecology clinic of Starkloff

Hospital were members of the faculty and students of the St. Louis University School of Medicine. This came about during the 1950s, when the city of St. Louis was experiencing accreditation problems; St. Louis University and Washington University offered to staff the city-run Starkloff and Homer G. Phillips Hospitals. As a result the doctors and students staffing Starkloff Hospital were considered city employees. However, St. Louis University was a Jesuit institution that expressed strong anti-abortion views. Because of this paradox, the court of appeals stated that the staffing policy of Starkloff Hospital denied the "constitutional rights of indigent pregnant women . . . long after those rights had been clearly enunciated." It is interesting to note that Jane Doe never approached Homer G. Phillips Hospital for the abortion; ironically, this hospital was staffed by Washington University and was non-sectarian.

In essence, the appeals court used these facts to portray the case as an issue of equal protection. Jane Doe, as an indigent woman, could not afford to pay a private clinic for her abortion. Therefore, her only option lay in the use of a public hospital—which refused her this service. This was viewed as discrimination of indigent women, as "no other women similarly situated are so coerced." Other factors taken into consideration by the court of appeals included a previous decision in *Wulff v. Singleton* (1976) that had found a state Medicaid statute unconstitutional because it would not provide benefits to women seeking elective abortions but did provide them for women who carried their pregnancies to term, and the decisions made in *Roe v. Wade* and *Doe v. Bolton*. With this data, the court of appeals reversed with the opinion that Starkloff Hospital's refusal to grant Jane Doe an abortion "constituted invidious discrimination, violative of equal protection under the Fourteenth Amendment."

Another Reversal

While the Supreme Court agreed that the constitutional question concerning discrimination presented in *Poelker v. Doe* was identical in principle to that represented by a state's denial of Medicaid benefits for abortions while providing them for childbirth, they still found grounds to reverse the decision made by the Court of Appeals for the Eighth Circuit. Key to this decision was the manner in which the hospital refused to perform the abortion—as a policy choice. An important aspect of arriving at this conclusion was the determination that there was no direct contact between the doctors and staff of the hospital and Mayor Poelker—and therefore no direct influence concerning the mayor's personal opposition to abortion. Indeed, the Court deemed that the mayor's personal opinions concerning abortion were not relevant to the case and declared that the policy of denying city funds for abortions such as that requested by Doe was a matter of public debate and could be decided at the polls. The Supreme Court determined that the city of St. Louis did not violate the Equal Protection Clause of the Fourteenth Amendment. A city is well within its constitutional rights to provide, as a policy choice, publicly financed hospital services for childbirth while not offering services for nontherapeutic abortions.

Upon arriving at this decision, the Supreme Court also deemed that the court of appeals erred in reversing the decision of the Federal District Court and that

Three generations of women protest Mayor John Poelker's refusal to allow city hospitals to perform abortions, 1977. © UPI/Corbis-Bettmann.

it had wrongly awarded attorneys' fees to the prevailing party.

Complicated Issues

Justices Brennan, Marshall and Blackmun dissented, stating that the city of St. Louis infringed on the constitutional rights of indigent women by providing physicians and medical facilities for maternity care, but not offering the same for indigent women who exercise their constitutionally protected right to abortion. This situation posed what they termed as a "significant, and in some cases insurmountable, obstacle to indigent pregnant women who cannot pay for abortions in . . . private facilities." They pointed out other problems created by the Court's holding. What of doctors working for public hospitals that were willing to perform abortions, but could not do so due to the ruling? What would happen in small communities where a public hospital was the only means of medical care? Another important issue to note was that at the time of this decision only 18 percent of all public hospitals in the United States provided abortion services, with ten states completely lacking public hospitals providing these services.

Drawing primarily from *Roe v. Wade* and the cases following it, Justices Brennan, Blackmun, and Marshall pointed out that the city policy coerced women to bear children that they did not wish to produce and that the state's anti-abortion morality preferred only "normal childbirth." They felt that St. Louis's policy preference was insufficient to justify its transgression on the constitutional right of women to choose abortion.

Related Cases

Griswold v. Connecticut, 381 U.S. 479 (1965).
Roe v. Wade, 410 U.S. 113 (1973).
Doe v. Bolton, 410 U.S. 179 (1973).
Wulff v. Singleton, 428 U.S. 106 (1976).
Maher v. Roe, 432 U.S. 464 (1977).
Bellotti v. Baird, 443 U.S. 622 (1979).

Bibliography and Further Reading

Mahoney, Hildegarde Marie. "National Health Care Legislation and the Funding of Abortion." *America,* October 16, 1993, p. 8.

COLAUTTI V. FRANKLIN

Legal Citation: 439 U.S. 379 (1979)

Appellant
Aldo Colautti

Appellee
John Franklin, M.D.

Appellant's Claim
That a Pennsylvania statute dealing with abortion and the viability of fetuses was not unconstitutionally vague.

Chief Lawyer for Appellant
Carol Los Mansmann

Chief Lawyer for Appellee
Roland Morris

Justices for the Court
Harry A. Blackmun (writing for the Court), William J. Brennan, Jr., Thurgood Marshall, Lewis F. Powell, Jr., John Paul Stevens, Potter Stewart

Justices Dissenting
Warren E. Burger, William H. Rehnquist, Byron R. White

Place
Washington, D.C.

Date of Decision
9 January 1979

Decision
Affirmed the judgment of the district court that the viability-determination requirement of the Pennsylvania Abortion Control Act was void due to vagueness. The law's standard-of-care provision was also found to be impermissibly vague.

Significance
Colautti v. Franklin was one of the many Supreme Court decisions made between 1976 and 1986 that struck down state laws that attempted to discourage abortion.

The Pennsylvania Abortion Control Act was passed by the Pennsylvania legislature, over the governor's veto, in 1974, the year after the Supreme Court's decision in *Roe v. Wade* (1973). The Pennsylvania Abortion Control Act held a physician to potential criminal liability if he or she performed an abortion and failed to use a technique prescribed by law when the fetus is viable or when there is sufficient reason to believe that the fetus may be viable. Section 5(a) of the act stated that if the fetus was or may be viable, the person performing the abortion was required to exercise the same care to preserve the life and health of the fetus as would be required in the case of a fetus intended to be born alive. The person performing the abortion was also required to adopt the abortion technique providing the best opportunity for the fetus to be aborted alive, so long as a different technique was not necessary to preserve the life or health of the mother.

A three-judge panel of the U.S. District Court for the Eastern District of Pennsylvania declared that section 5(a) of the act was unconstitutionally vague, overly broad, and forbade the enforcement of the law. Each side of the case sought a class-action determination and the appellant's motion to this effect was granted. The case went to trial in January of 1975. Expert witnesses testified about all aspects of abortion procedures. The court upheld some of the acts provisions and found others unconstitutional. It invalidated the viability-determination and standard-of-care provisions of section 5(a).

A Specific Definition of Viability

Justice Blackmun, in his opinion for the majority, noted that three previous Supreme Court cases provided essential background for *Colautti v. Franklin*. These cases were *Roe v. Wade* (1973), *Doe v. Bolton* (1973), and *Planned Parenthood of Central Missouri v. Danforth* (1976). In *Roe v. Wade,* the Court held that a fetus is considered viable if it is potentially able to live outside its mother's womb, albeit with artificial aid. The Court also noted that viability is usually placed at about seven months (28 weeks) but may occur earlier, even at 24 weeks. The Court intentionally left this point flexible for anticipated advancements in medicine. *Roe v. Wade* also stressed repeatedly that the physician has the central role in consulting with the woman about an abortion.

In *Doe v. Bolton,* the Court found it critical that a physician's judgment about an abortion may be exercised in the light of all factors—physical, emotional, psychological, familial, and the woman's age—relevant to the well-being of the patient.

In *Planned Parenthood of Central Missouri v. Danforth,* the Court stressed that viability is a matter of medical judgment, skill, and technical ability requiring the meaning of the word to be flexible. The Court refused to specify an exact number of weeks of pregnancy that would be the point of viability.

In *Colautti v. Franklin,* the Court once again refused to give a specific definition of viability, except to state that viability is reached when, in the judgment of the attending physician on the particular facts of the case before him, there is a reasonable likelihood of the fetus sustaining survival outside the womb, with or without artificial support. Because this point may differ with each pregnancy, neither legislature nor the courts may proclaim one of the elements such as weeks of gestation or fetal weight as the determining factor of viability or when the state should take an interest in the life of the fetus.

Dr. Franklin argued that requiring the physician to observe the care standard when he determines the fetus is viable, or when there is sufficient reason to believe that the fetus may be viable, is unconstitutionally vague. The viability-determination requirement is vague because it fails to inform the physician when his duty to the fetus arises. It also does not make the physician's good-faith determination of viability conclusive. It is constitutionally overbroad because it carves out a new time period prior to the stage of viability. This could restrict couples who want an abortion because the fetus is not healthy. The standard of care, particularly the requirement regarding the use of the technique which was most likely to abort the fetus alive, is void due to vagueness and unconstitutionally restrictive because it does not allow the physician enough discretion to determine which abortion technique is appropriate.

Aldo Colautti, the secretary of welfare for Pennsylvania, argued that the Pennsylvania statute deals only with post-viability abortions. The term "may be viable" describes the statistical probability of fetal survival. He felt that the standard of care provision preserves the flexibility required for sound medical practice. He also noted that the provision simply requires that when a physician has a choice of procedures of equal risk to the woman, the doctor must choose the one least likely to be fatal to the fetus.

The majority of the Court agreed with Dr. Franklin that the viability-determination requirement was ambiguous and void because of vagueness. The statute required that a person who performs an abortion make a determination based on his experience, judgment, or professional competence that the fetus is not viable. The statute did not clarify if this decision should be based on a purely subjective standard or on a mixture of the subjective and objective. The term "may be viable" was unclear as to whether it referred to viability as defined in previous cases or if it meant an undefined gray area prior to the stage of viability. In the phrase "sufficient reason to believe that the fetus may be viable," the term "sufficient reason" was ambiguous as to whether it was from the perspective of the attending physician or a cross section of the medical community. Also, the distinction between "is viable" and "may be viable" was elusive. For these reasons, the statute did not give broad discretion to the physician. It conditioned possible criminal liability on confusing and ambiguous criteria. It therefore presented serious problems of notice, discriminatory application, and a "chilling effect" on the exercise of constitutional rights.

The vagueness of the viability-determination requirement was compounded by the fact that the physician was subject to possible criminal liability without regard to fault. The Court felt the act was little more than a trap for those who act in good faith. The dangers of criminal liability were great here because of the ambiguity of the viability determination. A number of imprecise variables must be considered when attempting to determine the probability of meaningful life outside the womb. Thus this can only be determined with great difficulty. The fact that experts will disagree over the determination will have a chilling effect on the willingness of physicians to perform abortions near the point of viability. State regulation that impinges upon this determination, if it is to be constitutional, must let the physician make his or her best medical judgment.

The Court also concluded that the standard-of-care provision of the act was impermissibly vague. Extensive testimony by physicians revealed that in the absence of section 5(a), they would choose a saline amino-infusion for a second trimester abortion. Their method of choice under 5(a) varied widely, but they generally agreed that each method had disadvantages for the woman.

Colautti argued that the only legally relevant consideration was that alternatives exist among abortion methods. He also felt that the physician must make a competent and good faith medical judgment on the feasibility of protecting the fetus's chance of survival, consistent with the life and health of the woman. The Court noted that the statute does not clearly specify that the woman's life and health must always come first. Also, life and health of the mother does not necessarily imply that all factors relevant to the welfare of the woman may be taken into account by the physician. It was unclear whether the physician's duty to the patient or the fetus was more important. Physicians were not certain if the statute required a trade-off between the woman's health and the additional percentage points of fetal survival. The Court concluded that the standard of care provision of the statute was void because of this vagueness.

An Intrusion upon the Police Powers of the States

Justice White, writing the dissent, felt that the Court had now withdrawn from the states a substantial measure of power to protect fetal life. "Only those with unalterable determination to invalidate the Pennsylvania Act can draw any measurable difference insofar as vagueness is concerned between 'viability' defined as the ability to survive and 'viability' defined as that stage at which the fetus may have the ability to survive." White noted that the majority's decision was constitutionally an unwarranted intrusion upon the police powers of the states. Regarding the potential criminal liability of physicians, White commented, "I do not see how it can be seriously argued that a doctor who makes a good-faith mistake about whether a fetus is or is not viable could be successfully prosecuted for criminal homicide." White concluded his dissent by stating that the majority decision in this case issued a "warning to the States, in the name of vagueness, that they should not attempt to forbid or regulate abortions when there is a chance for the survival of the fetus, but it is not sufficiently large that the abortionist considers the fetus to be viable."

Impact

Some states designed laws, not to take away the choice of having an abortion, but to discourage abortions.

Among these statutes were laws that prohibited certain abortion techniques, required patient counseling, established a waiting period, or required that abortions be performed in hospitals rather than clinics. Several Supreme Court decisions between 1976 and 1986 overturned these provisions on the grounds of vagueness or unreasonableness. In 1980, the anti-abortion movement played a pivotal role in the election of Ronald Reagan to the presidency. Reagan had promised to appoint Supreme Court justices who would make abortions illegal. In 1986, Reagan elevated William H. Rehnquist, an abortion foe, to the position of chief justice. In 1989, the case *Webster v. Reproductive Health Services* represented a significant retreat from abortion rights. That decision upheld a Missouri law that required viability testing in abortion cases after 20 weeks. The *Webster* case was only one vote short of overturning *Roe v. Wade*. In the 1990s, constitutional doctrine regarding abortion continued to be unstable and politicized.

Related Cases

Roe v. Wade, 410 U.S. 113 (1973).
Doe v. Bolton, 410 U.S. 179 (1973).
Planned Parenthood of Central Missouri v. Danforth, 428 U.S. 52 (1976).
Webster v. Reproductive Health Services, 492 U.S. 490 (1989).

Bibliography and Further Reading

Gans Epner, Janet E., Harry S. Jonas, and Daniel L. Seckinger. "Late-Term Abortion." *Journal of the American Medical Association*, August 26, 1998, p. 724.

Hall, Kermit L., ed. *The Oxford Companion to the Supreme Court of the United States*. New York: Oxford Press, 1992.

BELLOTTI V. BAIRD

Legal Citation: 443 U.S. 622 (1979)

Appellant
Francis X. Bellotti, Attorney General of Massachusetts

Appellee
William R. Baird, Jr.

Appellant's Claim
Massachusetts' Act to Protect Unborn Children and Maternal Health is constitutional even if minor women are not permitted to have an abortion without parental consent and cannot obtain a court order permitting abortion without notification of parents.

Chief Lawyer for Appellant
Gerrick F. Cole

Chief Lawyers for Appellee
Joseph J. Balliro, John H. Henn

Justices for the Court
Harry A. Blackmun, William J. Brennan, Jr., Warren E. Burger, Thurgood Marshall, Lewis F. Powell, Jr. (writing for the Court), William H. Rehnquist, John Paul Stevens, Potter Stewart

Justices Dissenting
Byron R. White

Place
Washington, D.C.

Date of Decision
2 July 1979

Decision
The U.S Supreme Court affirmed a federal district court's finding that a Massachusetts statute regulating abortions to minors was unconstitutional because it required notification and consultation of parents, even if a court found an adolescent competent and sufficiently mature to make her own decision about receiving an abortion.

Significance
The U.S. Supreme Court's decision did more than reaffirm a woman's constitutionally-protected right to choose to have an abortion. Although a state could restrict access to abortion by requiring parental consent, an alternative for redress had to be available through the courts. Moreover, a state's requirement for parental consent could not be, in application, inconsistent with judicial guidance in *Planned Parenthood of Central Missouri v. Danforth* (1976), which was equivalent to what was an "absolute, and possibly arbitrary, veto."

In the late summer of 1974, the legislature of the state of Massachusetts overrode the governor's veto and adopted an act regulating abortion in that state. The act to Protect Unborn Children and Maternal Health (Unborn Children Act) required parental (or guardian's) consent for an unmarried women under 18 years of age to obtain an abortion. The statute also stipulated that if any parent or guardian refused, consent could be granted by order of a superior court if, after a hearing, the presiding judge believed there was sufficient justification "for good cause."

As soon as the law was passed, public controversy arose between pro- and anti-abortion factions. Thus, although scheduled to become law at the end of October of 1974, a suit filed in the U.S. District Court of Massachusetts prevented enactment of the statute. The thrust of the claim—brought by William R. Baird, Jr. (championed as a key figure for the pro-abortion movement), Parents' Aid Society, four anonymous, pregnant female adolescents, and Dr. Gerald Zupnick (director of a Parents' Aid center)—argued that the Unborn Children Act violated the Due Process and Equal Protection Clauses of the Fourteenth Amendment.

The district court found merit in the appellees' (then plaintiffs') arguments. A preliminary court order was issued enjoining the enactment of the statute. In rendering a decision, the district court held as unconstitutional the provision of the Unborn Children Act requiring parental consent.

One of the main arguments centered on the notion that all adolescents who were pregnant were qualified to decide, independently, whether to terminate a pregnancy. The district court did not accept that premise, but did believe that a "substantial number of females under the age of eighteen are capable of forming a valid consent," and "a significant number of (these) are unwilling to tell their parents." The court also noted, "there can be no doubt that a female's constitutional right to an abortion in the first trimester does not depend upon her calendar age." Hence, justices of the district court believed Massachusetts' statute did not serve the best interests of minor, pregnant women.

The appellants later requested a judicial review by the United States Supreme Court. While the Court

Bill Baird carries a cross while participating in a pro-choice demonstration, 1986. © AP/Wide World Photos.

acknowledged its jurisdiction in the matter, the justices also held the opinion that the case should have been resolved by the Massachusetts Supreme Judicial Court. The case was remanded back to the lower court with instructions that the district court should have refrained from ruling on the statute's constitutionality without first certifying to the state court questions which would clarify the meaning and intent of the law.

In certifying to the state court, the district court posed two critical questions. Did the Unborn Children Act allow adolescents, regardless of maturity, to gain judicial consent for an abortion without consulting parents? And, if a superior court ascertained a minor had already made an informed, reasonable decision to abort a fetus, could a justice refuse consent if s/he felt that the decision of the court or a parent was better? The Supreme Court of Massachusetts answered that without parental consent, it was not possible for a minor to gain judicial approval for a nonemergency abortion unless her parents were not available. Parents also had to be notified of all judicial proceedings. Moreover, a superior court could overrule a minor's decision regardless of the quality of that decision.

After certification from the state court, the district court declared the statute unconstitutional and issued a permanent injunction. The court held that a large majority of minors were capable of making independent and informed decisions. Therefore, parental consent was an unnecessary burden on a minor woman's right to an abortion. The justices (the case impaneled three) also held that the act violated the constitutional guarantees of a pregnant minor because a court or parents could deny consent on any grounds regardless of

whether the minor had made an informed, reasoned decision. The state appealed the decision of the district court to the U.S. Supreme Court.

In arguing its case, the appellant's (Massachusetts) attorney both questioned whether the judgment of the district court provided appropriate remedy and questioned whether the U.S. Supreme Court had jurisdiction to judge the statute's constitutionality. Counsel pointed out that state legislators were motivated to enact the Unborn Children Act in response to the growing rate of teenage pregnancies (one million teen women aged 15 to 19 became pregnant each year). Since, in the opinion of state legislators, adolescents were not equipped to make informed and independent decisions regarding abortion, the statute's intent, counsel argued, was to protect and promote the best interests of minors. The appellants, therefore, felt it was inappropriate to invalidate the act because parental consent was required. The state's legislators believed that abortion was a difficult decision for which only a minor's family could provide the best help and advice. Counsel pointed out that the American Academy of Pediatrics, in 1973, concluded that minors were not equipped to make a rational decision regarding abortion. Thus, by requiring parental consent for an abortion, legislators believed that it would encourage supportive parental counseling which would be in the best interests of minor women. Counsel for the appellants further maintained that the statute seemed rather liberal because it only restricted minor women with regard to sterilization and abortion.

In arguing their case, the chief attorney for the appellees expressed that the clause of the Unborn Children Act requiring parental consent for an abortion imposed an undue burden upon a minor. He pointed out that in *Roe v. Wade* (1973), the Court had ruled that every woman had a constitutional right to decide, in consultation with her physician, whether to bear a child or to terminate a pregnancy. Thus, the statute's provisions seemed to be in violation of a woman's constitutional rights because it demanded judicial consent, which could be denied even if a minor was found mature enough to make an informed decision. Furthermore, in requiring parental consent, the act did not take into account parents who had been separated for years or whether the mother's doctor even approved of abortion. On the surface, the statute's provision that a superior court's consent for an abortion could be based on "good cause," in fact was spurious, since the consent of both parents was still required regardless of a judge's findings.

In adjunct testimony, John H. Henn (a representative from the Parenthood League) voiced concern that the provisions of the Massachusetts statute seemed to impose an unreasonable burden even for a minor mature enough to make informed decision. Having to go to court and fight her parents could only result in disrupting family relations, whether she "beat" her family in court or lost her case. Moreover, the state's interest in safeguarding minor women was already met through existing Massachusetts law because physicians were required to assess the maturity of a woman seeking an abortion.

In expressing the majority opinion of the Court, Justice Powell explained that their decision was mitigated by three principles which had been previously recognized by the Court. First, the Court recognized the unique role of minors in the social and legal system. Because "neither the Fourteenth Amendment nor the Bill of Rights is for adults alone," minors were entitled to constitutional protection. However, Powell pointed out that *Ginsberg v. New York* (1968) found that the state was entitled to limit a minor's freedom of choice if such limitation was in the minor's best interests. Children were not equipped for and did not have the experience or perspective to make mature choices. Moreover, he explained, the Court had recognized that the guiding role of parents was very important in the upbringing of children. In *Pierce v. Society of Sisters* (1925), the Court held that "the child is not the mere creature of the State; those who nurture him and direct his destiny have the right, coupled with the high duty, to recognize and prepare him for additional obligations."

Despite previous decisions with respect to the legal roles of parents and children, the Court found that the Unborn Children Act infringed on the constitutional right of a woman to choose to terminate her pregnancy. Both *Roe v. Wade* and *Doe v. Bolton* (1973) unequivocally established that a woman, even a minor, may, after consultation with a physician, terminate her pregnancy. The justices agreed that the state had an interest in encouraging minors to inform their parents and that together, they should seek a solution whether or not the minor should bear a child. But, the Court noted, a significant number of pregnant minors were not willing to inform their parents. Sometimes justifiable, mitigating factors such as a historical unwillingness to parent, child abuse, or even abandonment by parents rendered the Massachusetts statute's parental consent requirement an ineffective measure, which only served to restrict the constitutional right of a pregnant, minor woman.

A woman who chose to terminate her pregnancy was entitled to constitutional protection. Thus, the justices did not favor granting a "third-party veto" even if by a judge or appointed administrator. Citing *Planned Parenthood of Central Missouri v. Danforth,* Stevens explained that the Court had not only invalidated another statute requiring spousal approval but also one requiring parent consent (for minor unmarried woman) as a prerequisite to gain an abortion. The Court thus found the Massachusetts Unborn Children Act was not within constitutional limits and the justices affirmed the judgment of the district court.

Justice White wrote the dissenting opinion. (Note: Since White also dissented in *Planned Parenthood of Central Missouri v. Danforth,* some comments reflected opinions expressed in that decision.) He felt that there was one critical factor which kept the *Danforth* ruling from being applicable to the Unborn Children Act. Though the Missouri statute was invalidated (because it required spousal or one parent's consent to an abortion), the Massachusetts statute left an alternative means of redress in which a pregnant minor could seek an independent decision by a superior court. In part, echoing his objections in *Danforth,* Justice White summed up the dissenting opinion by noting that he could not "imagine that the U.S. Constitution could forbid any parental consultation or even notice to parents if their minor child has filed proceedings of this sort before the court."

Impact

Amid a major social debate within America regarding the social, legal, and religious issues related to abortion, the Court rendered a verdict that both reinforced *Roe v. Wade* and provided additional judicial guidance. Unequivocally, a woman—even a minor, unmarried woman—had the right to an abortion. Justices rationalized that the Constitution was not designed for adults alone; thus, the Massachusetts Unborn Children Act was adjudicated as unconstitutional because it infringed on the constitutionally-guaranteed right of every woman to seek an abortion. However, the justices pointed out that the rationale for rendering their verdict also depended on the observation that, in application, the statute amounted to nothing more than legislative enforcement of absolute parental consent and/or consultation as a prerequisite for a minor woman's abortion. While such restriction was not inherently in opposition to their decision in *Planned Parenthood of Central Missouri v. Danforth,* a state had to provide a genuine, alternative means by which a minor could gain approval for legal abortion.

Related Cases

Pierce v. Society of Sisters, 268 U.S. 510 (1925).
McKeiver v. Pennsylvania, 403 U.S. 528 (1971).
Roe v. Wade, 410 U.S. 113 (1973).
Doe v. Bolton, 410 U.S. 179 (1973).

Planned Parenthood of Central Missouri v. Danforth, 428 U.S. 52 (1976).

Bibliography and Further Reading

Benshoof, Janet. "Abortion Rights and Wrongs." *The Nation,* October 14, 1996, p. 19.

The Center for Reproductive Law and Policy. http://www.crlp.org

Oberman, Michelle. "Turning Girls into Women: Re-Evaluating Modern Statutory Rape Law." *Journal of Criminal Law and Criminology,* summer 1994, p. 15.

HARRIS V. MCRAE

Legal Citation: 448 U.S. 297 (1980)

Appellants
Secretary of Health and Human Services Patricia R. Harris, joined by Senators James L. Buckley and Jesse A. Helms, and Representative Henry J. Hyde as "intervenor-defendants"

Appellees
Cora McRae, on behalf of herself and all New York state women similarly situated, and the New York City Health and Hospitals Corp.

Appellants' Claim
That the Hyde Amendment was constitutional, and that states did not have to pay the costs of indigent women's abortions, even those found medically necessary.

Chief Lawyer for Appellants
Wade H. McCree, Jr., U.S. Solicitor General

Chief Lawyer for Appellees
Rhonda Copelon

Justices for the Court
Warren E. Burger, Lewis F. Powell, Jr., William H. Rehnquist, Potter Stewart (writing for the Court), Byron R. White

Justices Dissenting
Harry A. Blackmun, William J. Brennan, Jr., Thurgood Marshall, John Paul Stevens

Place
Washington, D.C.

Date of Decision
30 June 1980

Decision
Under the Hyde Amendment, states participating in the Medicaid program could not receive federal reimbursements for even medically necessary abortions and did not have to pay for them.

Significance
This ruling meant that the federal government would not subsidize abortions for poor women—even when a medical necessity.

Following its 1973 decision to make abortion legal in *Roe v. Wade,* the Supreme Court ruled on a number of state attempts to limit women's access to (or state support for) abortions. In careful "pick and choose" decisions, the Court found some restrictions—no saline abortions, attempting to preserve the life of aborted fetuses, and prior written consent of husbands or minors' parents—to be unconstitutional.

Other restrictions—prohibiting the abortion of a "viable" fetus, certain record-keeping regulations on abortion providers, and requiring pregnant women to furnish written consent prior to an abortion—were considered constitutional. Finally, in 1980, the Court ruled on the constitutionality of an even more severe measure: the federal Hyde Amendment, which withheld Medicaid funding even in cases of medically necessary abortions.

The Hyde Amendment

In 1965, Congress created the Medicaid program for the poor and infirm by adding Title XIX to the Social Security Act. Eleven years later, Congress passed the first of the Hyde Amendments to Medicaid—imposing varying degrees of financial restrictions on abortions. In 1980, Congress decided that no money would be provided for abortions unless the mother's health was endangered by a term pregnancy. Victims of rape or incest—if they reported their pregnancy promptly—could also receive the federally-sponsored medical procedures.

The same day that the first Hyde Amendment was enacted, Cora McRae, a pregnant Medicaid recipient seeking an abortion, filed a legal challenge to the amendment in the District Court for the Eastern District of New York. (Like Norma McCorvey, the plaintiff in *Roe v. Wade,* McRae delivered her child before the suit reached its conclusion.) She claimed that "the Hyde Amendment violated the First, Fourth, Fifth, and Ninth Amendments of the Constitution insofar as it limited the funding of abortions to those necessary to save the life of the mother, while permitting the funding of costs associated with childbirth."

The following day, district judge John F. Dooling, Jr., issued a preliminary injunction. His full decision, issued three weeks later, was in full agreement with McRae. The case was also certified as a class action suit on behalf of all Medicaid-eligible New York State women who were pregnant or potentially pregnant and who would seek abortions during the 24 weeks of gestation.

Health and Human Services secretary, Patricia R. Harris, immediately appealed to the Supreme Court. Having just upheld the withdrawal of funding for "unnecessary" abortions in *Beal v. Doe* (1977) and *Maher v. Roe* (1977), the Court vacated the injunction against the enforcement of the Hyde Amendment and sent McRae's case back to Dooling for reevaluation against these recent decisions.

Back at the District Court

Before reconsidering the merits of the case, Dooling gave permission for a number of additional plaintiffs to intervene. In their amended complaint, the plaintiffs asserted that any state participating in the Medicaid program must provide the means for medically necessary abortions, whether or not they would be reimbursed by the federal government. The plaintiffs also challenged the constitutionality of the Hyde Amendment, claiming that it violated both the religion clause of the First Amendment (because its views coincided with the Catholic Church) and the Fifth Amendment. (The Courts have interpreted the Fifth Amendment as containing implied Due Process and Equal Protection Clauses. Thus, the federal government must grant equal protection to its citizens in the same manner as the Fourteenth Amendment requires states to grant equal protection to their citizens.)

Dooling, although dissolving his earlier injunction, held a trial on the merits of McRae's claims. He released a 214-page ruling finding that Title XIX would have required states to make medically necessary abortions available to poor women but that the Hyde Amendment, if constitutional, would remove that responsibility.

The judge ruled that the federal government had not violated the First Amendment's prohibition against a state-sponsored religion. However, the amendment did violate the free exercise clause of the First Amendment by prohibiting an affected woman from seeking a medically necessary abortion in accordance with "her religious beliefs under certain Protestant and Jewish tenants."

Finding that the amendment also violated the Due Process Clause of the Fifth Amendment, Dooling ruled that all versions of the amendment were invalid. He ordered Harris to "authorize the expenditure of federal matching funds" for medically necessary abortions.

Returning to the Supreme Court

Attorney Wade H. McCree, Jr., appealed Dooling's ruling to the Supreme Court. He shifted attention from maternal health to fetal preservation, stating "that the

Hyde Amendment is rationally related to the legitimate governmental interests in preserving potential human life and encouraging childbirth."

One of the justices asked him, "Would you make the same rational basis argument . . . if it was her [McRae's] death rather than adverse impact on her health that was involved?"

McCree answered, "I think I would say that you would make the rational relation . . . It doesn't prevent this woman from obtaining an abortion; it just denies her federal funding . . ."

The Court pressed, "Don't we have to assume for purposes of analysis at least that some women will be denied abortions if they don't receive federal funding?"

McCree agreed: "Oh, I think we have to. I don't think there is any question about that."

The Court responded: "We therefore must also assume that some of these women will suffer serious medical harm."

That was not Congress's concern, McCree implied: "We must assume that . . . just because *Roe* said that the state could not punish a person . . . for obtaining an abortion . . . that still did not obligate the state or the federal government to reimburse her . . ."

Did the Hyde Amendment violate the First Amendment? McCree had "difficulty" with the idea that to "refuse funding for them would somehow deny their First Amendment right to freedom of religion and free exercise of religion." To the contrary, he argued "the Free Exercise Clause prevents interference [with religion] . . . but doesn't obligate the state to finance it." He pointed out that the state is not required to give a citizen religious objects "for example, a Bible or any religious artifacts" so that the religion may be "freely" practiced.

A Matter of Survival

McRae's attorney, Rhonda Copelon, spoke passionately for all poor women affected by the amendment:

> This case . . . involves the survival and the health of potentially millions of poor women . . . and it involves reaffirmation of the simple rule of law . . . this Court recognized in *Roe v. Wade* . . . This case arises in the context of a Medicaid program designed to provide a broad range of medically necessary and essential services for poor people throughout the country . . . but for the Hyde Amendment, it would cover abortions as a mandatory medically necessary service . . . [The Hyde Amendments] preclude the exercise of sound medical judgment about the health of a pregnant woman or indeed even of fetal life. They prefer fetal life

at the expense of maternal health and even maternal life.

Copelon argued that the "strict scrutiny" standard should be applied to the case, rather than the less arduous "rational basis" standard, although she felt even the lesser test could not be met by a law that favored a fetus over a poor woman whose health was endangered by pregnancy. "The . . . Constitution, . . . protects born people, [and] one cannot make that trade-off between people who exist and the potentiality of future life . . . This is a fundamentally irrational trade-off."

One of the justices asked: "Is this an argument that the fetus is not a person for purposes of the Constitution?"

Copelon answered, "It is not a person for the purposes of the Constitution, and I dare say that in our health-care system, even if some whole person's life is at stake, we don't ask another person to involuntarily sacrifice their health and their life for their well-being."

Turning to the First Amendment aspects of the case, Copelon claimed that "the proponents of the Hyde Amendment sought to take a position . . . on the question of when human life begins. That question, this Court held in *Roe v. Wade,* is impermissible, and I submit that it is impermissible under the Fifth Amendment . . . [and] impermissible under the First Amendment, in both the . . . establishment clause and free exercise clause."

The Decision

However, the Supreme Court ruled in favor of the government. After noting that a state does not have to pay for even medically necessary abortions, Justice Stewart turned to the constitutionality of the amendment itself. Referring to *Maher v. Roe,* one of the two 1977 cases in which a state's lack of funding for nontherapeutic abortions had been upheld, he wrote:

> Regardless of whether the freedom of a woman to choose to terminate her pregnancy for health reasons lies at the core or the periphery of the due process liberty recognized in *Wade,* it simply does not follow that a woman's freedom of choice carries with it a constitutional entitlement to the financial resources to avail herself of the full range of protected choices.

> The reason why was explained in *Maher:* although government may not place obstacles in the path of a woman's freedom of choice, it need not remove those not of its own creation. Indigency falls in the later category.

Turning to the religious issues in the case, Stewart dealt first with McRae's claim that the Hyde Amendment violated the "Establishment Clause because it

incorporates into law the doctrines of the Roman Catholic Church . . ." Noting that the government was free to pass laws against larceny, even though "the Judaeo-Christian religions oppose stealing," Stewart wrote that "we are convinced that the fact that the funding restrictions in the Hyde Amendment may coincide with the religious tenants of the Roman Catholic Church does not, without more, contravene the Establishment Clause."

The issue of what level of scrutiny ought to be applied was the last addressed. After finding that the "rational relationship" test was sufficient, Stewart concluded:

> The Hyde Amendment, by encouraging childbirth except in the most urgent circumstances, is rationally related to the legitimate governmental objective of protecting potential life. By subsidizing the medical expenses of indigent women who carry their pregnancies to term while not subsidizing abortions (except those whose lives are threatened), Congress has established incentives that make childbirth a more attractive alternative than abortion for persons eligible for Medicaid . . . Nor is it irrational that Congress has authorized federal reimbursement for medically necessary services generally, but not for certain medically necessary abortions. Abortion is inherently different from other medical procedures, because no other procedure involves the purposeful termination of a potential life.

The Hyde Amendment has been passed, in one version or another, in every subsequent year. The versions passed in 1993, and since, have reinstated funding for abortions requested by victims of incest or rape.

Related Cases
Beal v. Doe, 432 U.S. 438 (1977).
Maher v. Roe, 432 U.S. 464 (1977).

Bibliography and Further Reading
Benshoof, Janet. "Planned Parenthood v. Casey: The Impact of the New Undue Burden Standard on Reproductive Health Care." *JAMA, The Journal of the American Medical Association,* May 5, 1993, p. 2249.

Garrow, David J. *Liberty & Sexuality: The Right to Privacy and the Making of Roe v. Wade.* New York: Macmillan Publishing Company, 1994.

Goldstein, Leslie Friedman. *The Constitutional Rights of Women,* rev. ed. Madison: University of Wisconsin Press, 1989.

Guitton, Stephanie, and Peter Irons, eds. *May It Please the Court: Arguments on Abortion* (live recordings and transcripts). New York: The New Press, 1995.

Hoff, Joan. *Law, Gender & Injustice: A Legal History of U.S. Women*. New York: New York University Press, 1991.

Mahoney, Hildegarde Marie. "National Health Care Legislation and the Funding of Abortion." *America*, October 16, 1993, p. 8.

Rhode, Deborah L. "Adolescent Pregnancy and Public Policy." *Political Science Quarterly*, winter 1993, p. 635.

AKRON V. AKRON CENTER FOR REPRODUCTIVE HEALTH

Legal Citation: 462 U.S. 416 (1983)

Petitioner
City of Akron

Respondent
Akron Center for Reproductive Health, Inc.

Petitioner's Claim
That restrictions of a city ordinance on abortions performed during the second trimester of pregnancy do not violate a woman's right to abortion. The Akron Center for Reproductive Health countersued.

Chief Lawyer for Petitioner
Alan G. Segedy

Chief Lawyer for Respondent
Stephan Landsman

Justices for the Court
Harry A. Blackmun, William J. Brennan, Jr., Warren E. Burger, Thurgood Marshall, Lewis F. Powell, Jr. (writing for the Court), John Paul Stevens

Justices Dissenting
Sandra Day O'Connor, William H. Rehnquist, Byron R. White

Place
Washington D.C.

Date of Decision
15 June 1983

Decision
The restrictions were struck down by a vote of 6-3 as an unconstitutional attempt to hinder access to abortion.

Significance
Akron Center for Reproductive Health, in which Justice O'Connor wrote her first major abortion opinion, a dissent, indicated that the future of abortion rights was in doubt—in part because O'Connor seemed to be emerging as a swing vote in the heated abortion debate. Although she did not indicate a desire to outlaw abortion altogether, she made it clear that she had objections to *Roe v. Wade,* the landmark 1973 decision establishing a woman's right to abortion.

In 1973, in *Roe v. Wade,* the U.S. Supreme Court held that the constitutional right to privacy included a woman's right to abortion. The decision proved to be highly contentious, and many states and municipalities attempted to devise methods of restricting access to abortion—focusing particularly on the second trimester of pregnancy, during which the Supreme Court permitted some regulation of abortion if needed to protect the mother's health.

In 1978, the city of Akron, Ohio, passed an ordinance requiring that all abortions performed in the second trimester of pregnancy be performed in a hospital, rather than a clinic. The regulations also required that parents give consent before abortions could be performed on unmarried minors under the age of 15. They also required that the attending physician insure that the patient give her fully informed consent to the procedure, that there be a 24-hour waiting period between the time a consent form is signed and the time the abortion is performed, and that the fetal remains be disposed of in a humane and sanitary manner.

In 1978, the Akron Center for Reproductive Health, an abortion clinic, sued in U.S. District Court for the Northern District of Ohio, challenging the constitutionality of the Akron provisions. After the district court invalidated some parts of the ordinance while upholding others, the U.S. Court of Appeals for the Sixth Circuit affirmed parts of this decision, while reversing other aspects of the lower court's ruling. This rather chaotic result gave rise to three petitions for *certiorari,* or review, to the Supreme Court, which granted two: Akron's and the abortion clinic's.

Right to Abortion Upheld, But Imperiled

The Supreme Court upheld Akron's hospitalization requirement, while affirming the lower court's ruling that the provisions on parental consent, informed consent, waiting period, and disposal of fetal remains were unconstitutional. The latter provisions, the Court said, only succeeded in making abortions more expensive, not in making them safer for the mother. Justice Powell wrote the opinion for the Court, which voted 6-3 against the main thrust of the Akron ordinance.

Abortion Statistics

In the United States, about 25 percent of pregnancies are terminated by women through abortion. This compares similarly to statistics of Canadian women aborting pregnancies; about 21 percent. Countries where contraceptives are less available, report higher abortion rates. In Russia, about 60 percent, and Romania, 78 percent. The percentage of women terminating pregnancies in the United States has been declining since 1979.

In the United States, the Alan Guttmacher Institute (AGI) has tracked the number of abortions since 1970. These figures are obtained directly from providers. The AGI calculates that considering a four percent under-reporting of abortions, nearly 37 million abortions have been performed in the United States since 1973. In 1995, 1.2 million were reported by AGI; in 1996 and 1997, the Centers for Disease Control estimated 1.4 million and 1.3 million respectively for each year.

In 1992, the United States rate of abortion was 26 out of every 1,000 women between the ages of 15 to 44 years. In the same year, the ratio of abortion in the United States was 27.5 abortions per 100 live births.

Source(s): http://www.religioustolerance.org/abortion.htm
http://www.bfl.org/stats.htm.

The significance of *Akron v. Akron Center for Reproductive Health,* however, grew out of the dissenting opinion written by the Court's newest member, O'Connor, the first female Supreme Court justice. Ever since it was handed down, *Roe v. Wade,* which was decided by a vote of 7-2, had been hotly debated. It now appeared that there was a growing consensus within the Court itself that *Roe* needed to be curtailed, if not overturned. O'Connor's dissent, in which she objected to the trimester approach taken in *Roe,* proved to be highly influential. Such an approach, she argued, was likely to prove unworkable as technological innovation pushed the time of fetal viability further and further back. Restrictions such as those at issue in *Akron* should be permitted to stand so long as they did not place an "undue burden" on a mother's decision about whether or not to terminate her pregnancy. For O'Connor, restrictions such as a waiting period were desirable:

> [T]he decision to abort is "a stressful one," and the waiting period reasonably relates to the State's interest in ensuring that a woman does not make this serious decision in undue haste. The decision also has grave consequences for the fetus, whose life the State has a compelling interest to protect and preserve . . . The waiting period is surely a small cost to impose to ensure that the woman's decision is well considered in light of its certain and irreparable consequences on fetal life, and the possible effects on her own.

Votes on subsequent abortion cases coming before the Court grew ever closer until, in *Webster v. Reproductive Health Services* (1989), the Court did away with the trimester framework altogether. Although O'Con-

nor voted with the 5-4 majority in *Webster,* she declined to join in with the view that *Roe v. Wade* should be reversed outright. In 1992, in the case of *Planned Parenthood of Southeastern Pennsylvania v. Casey,* she joined Justices Kennedy and Souter in drafting a majority opinion reaffirming the fundamentals of *Roe v. Wade.*

Related Cases

Roe v. Wade, 410 U.S. 113 (1973).
Webster v. Reproductive Health Services, 492 U.S. 490 (1989).
Planned Parenthood of Southeastern Pennsylvania v. Casey, 505 U.S. 833 (1992).

Bibliography and Further Reading

Abortion and the States: Political Change and Future Regulation. Chicago: American Bar Association, 1993.

Abortion Decisions of the U.S. Supreme Court. Beverly Hills, CA: Excellent Books, 1993.

Benshoof, Janet. "Abortion Rights and Wrongs: Undue Burdens—The Rhetoric is Pro-'Roe,' But the Reality is Anti-Choice." *The Nation,* October 14, 1996, p. 19.

Benshoof, Janet. "Planned Parenthood v. Casey: The Impact of the New Undue Burden Standard on Reproductive Health Care." *JAMA, The Journal of the American Medical Association,* May 5, 1993, p. 2249.

Ford, John Christopher. "The Casey Standard for Evaluating Facial Attacks on Abortion Statutes." *Michigan Law Review,* March 1997, p. 1443.

Goldstein, Leslie Friedman. *Contemporary Cases in Women's Rights.* Madison, WI: University of Wisconsin Press, 1994.

THORNBURGH V. AMERICAN COLLEGE OF OBSTETRICIANS AND GYNECOLOGISTS

Legal Citation: 476 U.S. 747 (1986)

Appellant
Richard Thornburgh, U.S. Attorney General

Appellee
American College of Obstetricians and Gynecologists

Appellant's Claim
That new regulations imposed by Pennsylvania on abortion do not unconstitutionally restrict a woman's right to have an abortion.

Chief Lawyer for Appellant
Andrew S. Gordon

Chief Lawyer for Appellee
Kathryn Kolbert

Justices for the Court
Harry A. Blackmun (writing for the Court), William J. Brennan, Jr., Thurgood Marshall, Lewis F. Powell, Jr., John Paul Stevens

Justices Dissenting
Warren E. Burger, Sandra Day O'Connor, William H. Rehnquist, Byron R. White

Place
Washington, D.C.

Date of Decision
11 June 1986

Decision
The Supreme Court struck down the regulations.

Significance
Reaffirmed *Roe v. Wade*.

In 1973, the Supreme Court delivered a 7-2 decision in favor of a constitutional right to abortion. Even that landmark decision was not without restrictions, however. Although during the first three months of pregnancy a woman has an essentially unrestricted right to abortion, during months three through six of her pregnancy, the state has a right to regulate abortion to protect her health, and in the final three months of gestation, the Court authorized states to impose severe restrictions on abortion to protect the life of the fetus.

Over the next decade, the Court upheld a number of state legislative attempts to control and even restrict abortion. But in 1983 and again in 1986, two Supreme Court decisions struck down regulations it considered thinly veiled attempts simply to make abortions more difficult to obtain and to circumvent the guidelines of *Roe v. Wade* (1973). In *Akron v. Akron Center for Reproductive Health* (1983), the Court threw out a prohibition on performing second-trimester abortions in clinics rather than hospitals, a requirement that doctors give women detailed information about the procedure before consent forms are signed, and a 24-hour waiting period between the time the consent form was signed and the procedure is performed.

In *Thornburgh*, the American College of Obstetrics and Gynecology challenged the Pennsylvania Abortion Control Act. The act contained a requirement that women seeking abortions be given detailed information about the procedure in advance, that complex records must be kept, that doctors performing abortions use the technique least likely to harm the fetus, and that a second doctor be present during abortion procedures. After the U.S. District Court for the Eastern District of Pennsylvania ruled in favor of the plaintiffs, and the court of appeals upheld this ruling, Richard Thornburgh, the governor of Pennsylvania, appealed to the U.S. Supreme Court.

Supreme Court Upholds the Right to Abortion

Justice Blackmun, author of the majority opinion in *Roe*, also wrote the opinion of the Court here. Blackmun expressed considerable impatience with attempts

Richard Thornburgh, U.S. Attorney General. © UPI/Corbis-Bettmann.

on the part of Pennsylvania and other states to restrict access to abortion:

> In the years since this Court's decision in *Roe*, States and municipalities have adopted a number of measures seemingly designed to prevent a woman, with the advice of her surgeon, from exercising her freedom of choice . . . The States are not free, under the guise of protecting maternal health or potential life, to intimidate women unto continuing pregnancies. Appellants claim that the statutory provisions before us today further legitimate compelling interests of the Commonwealth. Close analysis of those provisions, however, shows that they wholly subordinate constitutional privacy interests and concerns with maternal health in an effort to deter a woman from making a decision that, with her physician, is hers to make.

The Court went on to say that the information requirement was an attempt to intrude on the privileged relationship between doctor and patient. The record keeping requirement, in addition be being cumbersome, posed the risk of violating the woman's privacy. Forcing doctors to choose the technique least harmful to the fetus could put the mother's health in jeopardy, as could an enforced wait for a second doctor to arrive simply to observe the procedure.

Of the four dissenting justices, Chief Justice Burger wrote the most negative appraisal of the majority's opinion. Burger thought that *Roe* had made abortion on demand a constitutional right; he said without qualification that he thought the precedent should be overturned. White conceded that there was a constitutional right to choose abortion, but because he did not consider it a "fundamental" right, he believed that states should be given a great deal of latitude to regulate, and even restrict abortion.

With the retirement of Justice Powell in 1987 and his replacement by Anthony Kennedy the next year, the delicate balance of attitudes favoring abortion tilted in the opposite direction. In *Webster v. Reproductive Health Services* (1987) the Court came very close to overturning *Roe* outright. Four subsequent Court appointments, two by a Republican administration and two by a Democratic administration, have done little to resolve the abortion debate.

Related Cases
Roe v. Wade, 410 U.S. 113 (1973).
Akron v. Akron Center for Reproductive Health, 462 U.S. 416 (1983).
Webster v. Reproductive Health Services, 492 U.S. 490 (1989).

Bibliography and Further Reading
Garrow, David J. *Liberty and Sexuality: The Right to Privacy and the Making of Roe v. Wade.* New York, NY: Macmillan, 1994.

Horan, Dennis J., Edward R. Grant, and Paige C. Cunningham, eds. *Abortion and the Constitution: Reversing Roe v. Wade Through the Courts.* Washington, DC: Georgetown University Press, 1987.

Rubin, Eva R. *Abortion, Politics, and the Courts: Roe v. Wade and its Aftermath,* rev. ed. Westport, CT: Greenwood Press, 1987.

IN THE MATTER OF BABY M

Legal Citation: 537 A.2d 1127 (1988)

Appellant
Mary Beth Whitehead

Appellees
William and Elizabeth Stern

Appellant's Claim
That the surrogacy contract was invalid and conflicted with parental rights and adoption statutes.

Chief Lawyers for Appellant
Harold Cassidy, Randy Wolf

Chief Lawyer for Appellees
Gary Skoloff

Justices for the Court
Robert Clifford, Marie L. Garibaldi, Alan B. Handler, Daniel O'Horn, Stewart G. Pollock, Gary S. Stein, Robert N. Wilentz (writing for the court)

Justices Dissenting
None

Place
Trenton, New Jersey

Date of Decision
3 February 1988

Decision
The New Jersey Supreme Court invalidated the surrogacy contract, finding it contrary to New Jersey law. It restored Whitehead's parental rights and invalidated Elizabeth Stern's adoption, but granted William Stern custody of the infant.

Significance
This was the first widely followed trial to wrestle with the ethical questions raised by "reproductive technology." This case rejected the legality of surrogacy contracts while eliciting a divided response from feminists. Some asserted the primacy of a mother's claim to her child; others argued that any nullification of the contract would constitute a restriction upon a woman's right to control her own body.

Melissa Stern's conception took place under an agreement signed at Noel Keane's Infertility Center of New York on 5 February 1985. There were three parties to the agreement: Richard Whitehead gave his consent to the agreement's "purposes, intents, and provisions" and to the insemination of Mary Beth Whitehead, his wife, and with the sperm of William Stern. In addition, since any child born to Mary Beth Whitehead would legally be the child of her husband, he agreed that he would "surrender immediate custody of the child" and "terminate his parental rights."

Mary Beth Whitehead agreed to be artificially inseminated and to form no "parent-child relationship" with the baby. She agreed that she would, upon delivery of the child, surrender her parental rights to William Stern; and she further agreed that she would, during the term of the pregnancy, relinquish her right to make a decision about an abortion. She was permitted to seek an abortion only if the fetus was "physiologically abnormal" or if the inseminating physician agreed an abortion was required to insure her "physical health." Mary Beth Whitehead then agreed that it was William Stern's right to require amniocentesis testing and that she would "abort the fetus upon demand of WILLIAM STERN should a congenital or genetic abnormality be diagnosed." Despite the limitation of Whitehead's right to seek an abortion, the contract allocated responsibility for the child in the event that Whitehead refused to fulfill this part of her agreement: "If MARY BETH WHITEHEAD refuses to abort the fetus upon demand of WILLIAM STERN, his obligations as stated in this Agreement shall cease forthwith, except as to obligations of paternity imposed by statute." Finally, the Whiteheads "agree[d] to assume all risks, including the risk of death, which are incidental to conception, pregnancy, [and] childbirth."

William Stern agreed to pay ten thousand dollars to Mary Beth Whitehead. Although the ten thousand dollars was described as "compensation for services and expenses" and the contract specifically stated that the fee should "in no way be construed as a fee for termination of parental rights or a payment in exchange for a consent to surrender the child for adoption," it was payable only upon Mary Beth Whitehead's surrender

Surrogate Mothers

In 1978, Louise Brown was born in England, becoming the first baby born through in vitro fertilization (IVF). Since then, over 33,000 babies have been born through surrogacy methods; 7,000 in 1994 alone.

Between 1988 and 1995, the number of women in the United States suffering from infertility problems rose from 4.9 million to 6.1 million; an increase of 25 percent. It is estimated, that of these fertility problems in women, about 35 percent can be attributed to blocked fallopian tubes. In the late 1990s, approximately 315 clinics in the United States offered services to infertile couples and individuals; there are hundreds of additional clinics worldwide.

Success rates for in vitro fertilization vary. The Center for Surrogate Parenting, Inc. (CSP) of Los Angeles, California, reported a 78 percent success rate in 1996 for IVF when using a freshly donated egg; the rate dropped to only 25 percent when a frozen egg was used. CSP reported a 45 percent pregnancy rate in 1997 for a fresh egg; 20 percent for frozen. A 1989 study suggests about 27.5 percent of clients successfully bore a child using embryo transfer.

Source(s): http://cgi.pathfinder.com/time/magazine/
1997/dom/971201/box3.html
www.surroparenting.com/ivf.html
www.surroparenting.com/statspg.html

of a live infant. If Mary Beth Whitehead suffered a miscarriage prior to the fifth month of pregnancy, she would receive no compensation. The contract also noted: if the "child is miscarried, dies or is stillborn subsequent to the fourth month of pregnancy and said child does not survive," William Stern would pay Mary Beth Whitehead one thousand dollars. He also paid ten thousand dollars to Noel Keane, for his services in arranging the surrogacy agreement.

William Stern's wife, Betsy, was not a party to the agreement, nor was she mentioned by name. The contract referred only to William Stern's wife. The first such reference was in the statement that the contract's "sole purpose . . . is to enable WILLIAM STERN and his infertile wife to have a child which is biologically related to WILLIAM STERN." The other reference stated, "In the event of the death of WILLIAM STERN, prior or subsequent to the birth of said child, it is hereby understood and agreed by MARY BETH WHITEHEAD, Surrogate, and RICHARD WHITEHEAD, her husband, that the child will be placed in the custody of WILLIAM STERN'S wife."

Events did not go according to the contractual script. On 27 March 1986, Mary Beth Whitehead gave birth to a daughter. She named the infant "Sara Elizabeth Whitehead," took her home, and turned down the ten thousand dollars. On Easter Sunday, 30 March, the Sterns took the infant to their home. The baby was back at the Whitehead home on 31 March; in the second week of April, Whitehead told the Sterns she would never be able to give up her daughter. The Sterns responded by hiring attorney Gary Skoloff to fight for the contract's enforcement. The police arrived to remove "Melissa Elizabeth Stern" from the Whitehead's custody; shown the birth certificate for "Sara Elizabeth Whitehead," they left. When the police returned, Mary

Beth Whitehead passed her daughter through an open window to her husband and pleaded with him to make a run for it.

The Trial Begins

The trial commenced on 5 January 1987, by which time a *guardian ad litem* had been appointed for the child, known as "Baby M." The Sterns had received temporary custody. Mary Beth Whitehead, who had been ordered by Judge Harvey Sorkow to discontinue breast-feeding the child, had been temporarily awarded two one-hour visits each week, "strictly supervised under constant surveillance . . . in a sequestered, supervised setting to prevent flight or harm."

Skoloff framed the "issue to be decided" as "whether a promise to make the gift of life should be enforced." He stated that "Mary Beth Whitehead agreed to give Bill Stern a child of his own flesh and blood" and emphasized that Betsy Stern's multiple sclerosis "rendered her, as a practical matter, infertile . . . because she could not carry a baby without significant risk to her health."

Harold Cassidy, the attorney for Mary Beth Whitehead, offered an alternative view in his own opening remarks: "The only reason that the Sterns did not attempt to conceive a child was . . . because Mrs. Stern had a career that had to be advanced . . . What Mrs. Stern has is [multiple sclerosis] diagnosed as the mildest form. She was never even diagnosed until after we deposed her in this case . . . We're here," Cassidy summed up, "not because Betsy Stern is infertile but because one woman stood up and said there are some things that money can't buy." A neurologist affiliated with the Mount Sinai School of Medicine testified that Betsy Stern was afflicted with "a very, very, very slight case of MS, if any."

When the issue of custody was brought up, Skoloff stated that contract law and the infant's best interests dictated that exclusive custody should be awarded to the Sterns: "If there is one case in the United States, where joint custody will not work, where visitation rights will not work, where maintaining parental rights will not work, this is it." He addressed Sorkow directly: "Your Honor, under both the contract theory and the best-interest theory, you must terminate the rights of Mary Beth Whitehead and allow Bill Stern and Betsy Stern to be Melissa's mother and father."

Baby M's *guardian ad litem*, Lorraine Abraham, took the stand to make her own recommendation. She told the court that she had relied, in part, upon the opinions of three experts in forming her own conclusion: psychologist Dr. David Brodzinsky; social worker Dr. Judith Brown Greif; and psychiatrist Dr. Marshall Schechter. Abraham stated that the experts "will . . . recommend to this court that custody be awarded to the Sterns and visitation denied at this time." Abraham, required to offer her own opinion as *guardian ad litem*, added that she was "compelled by the overwhelming weight of [the three experts'] investigation to join in their recommendation."

During Betsy Stern's testimony, she was asked by Randy Wolf, one of Whitehead's lawyers, "Were you concerned about what effect taking the baby away from Mary Beth Whitehead would have on the baby?"

Stern responded: "I knew it would be hard on Mary Beth and in Melissa's best interest."

Wolf then said: "Now, I believe you testified that if Mary Beth Whitehead receives custody of the baby, you don't want to visit."

Stern replied, "That is correct. I do not want to visit."

Skoloff next raised questions about Whitehead's fitness as a mother. Whitehead had hidden in Florida with Baby M shortly after the infant's birth, and Skoloff represented this as evidence of instability. He then played for the court a taped telephone conversation between Mary Beth Whitehead and William Stern:

Stern: I want my daughter back.

Whitehead: And I want her, too, so what do we do, cut her in half?

Stern: No, no, we don't cut her in half.

Whitehead: You want me, you want me to kill myself and the baby?

Stern: No, that's why I gave her to you in the first place, because I didn't want you to kill yourself.

Whitehead: I've been breast-feeding her for four months. She's bonded to me, Bill. I sleep in the same bed with her. She won't even sleep by herself. What are you going to do when you get this kid that's screaming and carrying on for her mother?

Stern: I'll be her father. I'll be a father to her. I am her father. You made an agreement. You signed an agreement.

Whitehead: Forget it, Bill. I'll tell you right now I'd rather see me and her dead before you get her.

The following day, it was Mary Beth Whitehead's turn to testify. One of her attorneys asked, "If you don't get custody of Sara, do you want to see her?"

Whitehead replied:

Yes, I'm her mother, and whether this court only lets me see her two minutes a week, two hours a week, or two days, I'm her mother and I want to see her, no matter what.

Expert testimony followed. Dr. Lee Salk, the influential child psychologist, testified for the Sterns. Already termed a "third-party gestator" in court documents, Whitehead would now be called "a surrogate uterus." "The legal term that's been used is 'termination of parental rights,'" Salk began,

and I don't see that there were any parental rights that existed in the first place . . . The

Mary Beth Whitehead, 1989. © Photograph by Faye Ellmann.

agreement involved the provision of an ovum by Mrs. Whitehead for artificial insemination in exchange for ten thousand dollars . . . and so my feeling is that in both structural and functional terms, Mr. and Mrs. Stern's role as parents was achieved by a surrogate uterus and not a surrogate mother.

Dr. Marshall Schechter testified, as predicted by Abraham, that he believed custody should be awarded to the Sterns. He declared that Whitehead suffered from a "borderline personality disorder" and that "handing the baby out of the window to Mr. Whitehead is an unpredictable, impulsive act that falls under this category." Then, citing (among other things) that Whitehead dyed her hair to conceal its premature whiteness, he added the diagnosis of "narcissistic personality disorder."

Boston psychiatric social worker Dr. Phyllis Silverman refuted Schechter's characterization of Whitehead's behavior as "crazy":

> Mrs. Whitehead's reaction is like that of other "birth mothers" who suffer pain, grief, and rage for as long as thirty years after giving up a child. The bond of a nursing mother with her child is very powerful.

"By These Standards, We Are All Unfit Mothers"

Outside the courtroom, 121 prominent women refuted Schechter's contentions and the "expert opinions" of Brodzinsky and Greif. On 12 March 1987, they issued a document entitled "By These Standards, We Are All Unfit Mothers." The document quoted from each of the expert's testimony and included the *New York Times'* summary of what commentators called Dr. Schechter's "Patty Cake" test:

> Dr. Schechter faulted Mrs. Whitehead for saying "Hooray!" when the baby played Patty Cake by clapping her hands together. The more appropriate response for Mrs. Whitehead, he said, was to imitate the child by clapping her hands together and saying "Patty Cake" to reinforce the child's behavior. He also criticized Mrs. Whitehead for having four pandas of various size available for Baby M to play with. Dr. Schechter said pots, pans and spoons would have been more suitable.

Signed by Andrea Dworkin, Nora Ephron, Marilyn French, Betty Friedan, Carly Simon, Susan Sontag, Gloria Steinem, Meryl Streep, Vera B. Williams, and others, the document concluded with the statement that "we strongly urge . . . legislators and jurists . . . to recognize that a mother need not be perfect to 'deserve' her child."

When Cassidy made the closing argument on behalf of Mary Beth Whitehead, he reemphasized that Betsy Stern was not, as Whitehead had been told, infertile. He also stressed that termination of parental rights was permitted by law only in the event "of actual abandonment or abuse of the child." Finally, he warned that a ruling in favor of the contract's enforcement would lead to "one class of Americans . . . exploit[ing] another class. And it will always be the wife of the sanitation worker who must bear the children of the pediatrician."

Sorkow announced his verdict on 31 March 1987: "The parental rights of the defendant, Mary Beth Whitehead, are terminated. Mr. Stern is formally judged the father of Melissa Stern." Betsy Stern was then escorted into Sorkow's chambers, where she adopted Baby M.

New Jersey Supreme Court's Opinion

The Supreme Court of New Jersey overturned the lower court's ruling on 2 February 1988. It invalidated the surrogacy contract, annulled Betsy Stern's adoption of Baby M, and restored the parental rights of Mary Beth Whitehead. Writing for a unanimous court, Chief Justice Wilentz said:

> We do not know of, and cannot conceive of, any other case where a perfectly fit mother was expected to surrender her newly born infant, perhaps forever, and was then told she was a bad mother because she did not.

The justices then dealt with the issue as a difference between "the natural father and the natural mother, [both of whose claims] are entitled to equal weight." Custody was awarded to William Stern and the trial court was instructed to set visitation for Mary Beth Whitehead.

The court awarded Whitehead visitation on Tuesdays and Thursdays from 10:30 a.m. to 4:30 p.m.; every other weekend; and two weeks during the summer. (Holidays were also divided: the Sterns were entitled to Melissa's company on her birthday, Christmas Day, and Mother's Day, among other occasions.) Since Melissa is now in school during the week, and the Sterns live in New Jersey and Whitehead on Long Island, Whitehead reports that these circumstances have made it increasingly difficult for her to comply with the court-imposed schedule for visits with her daughter. In a recent interview, she said she would seek either a revision of the agreement's terms or move the rest of her family closer to Melissa's other home in New Jersey.

The New Jersey Supreme Court decision prohibited additional surrogacy arrangements in that state unless "the surrogate mother volunteers, without any payment, to act as a surrogate and is given the right to change her mind and to assert her parental rights."

Seventeen other states have since adopted similar guidelines.

Bibliography and Further Reading

Chesler, Phyllis. *Sacred Bond: The Legacy of Baby M.* New York: Times Books, 1988.

Fox, Robin. "Babies for Sale." *The Public Interest,* spring 1993, p. 14.

Sack, Kevin, "New York is Urged to Outlaw Surrogate Parenting for Pay." *New York Times,* May 15, 1992.

Squire, Susan. "Whatever Happened to Baby M?" *Redbook,* January 1994.

Whitehead, Mary Beth, with Loretta Schwartz-Nobel. *A Mother's Story: The Truth About the Baby M Case.* New York: St. Martin's Press, 1989.

WEBSTER V. REPRODUCTIVE HEALTH SERVICES

Legal Citation: 492 U.S. 490 (1989)

Appellants
William L. Webster, Attorney General of Missouri, et al.

Appellees
Reproductive Health Services, et al.

Appellants' Claim
That the U.S. Court of Appeals for the Eighth Circuit erred in overturning Missouri's laws restricting access to abortions.

Chief Lawyers for Appellants
William L. Webster, representing himself *pro se* (without counsel)

Chief Lawyer for Appellees
Frank Susman

Justices for the Court
Harry A. Blackmun, William J. Brennan, Jr., Anthony M. Kennedy, Thurgood Marshall, Sandra Day O'Connor, William H. Rehnquist (writing for the Court), Antonin Scalia, John Paul Stevens, Byron R. White

Justices Dissenting
None

Place
Washington, D.C.

Date of Decision
3 July 1989

Decision
Upheld Missouri's restrictions on access to abortion.

Significance
This decision, while not granting the Bush administration's request to overturn *Roe v. Wade,* upheld Missouri's restrictions on abortion and all but invited other states to pass further restrictive legislation.

In September of 1988, Justice Blackmun, author of the 1973 landmark opinion *Roe v. Wade,* stunned an audience at the University of Arkansas and made national headlines when he questioned whether abortions would remain legal in America. "Will *Roe v. Wade* go down the drain?" he asked bluntly. He answered his rhetorical question with equal bluntness: "There's a very distinct possibility that it will, this term. You can count votes."

Earlier in 1986, the Supreme Court overturned a group of restrictive state requirements in its decision in *Thornburgh v. American College of Obstetricians and Gynecologists.* These overturned laws included certain requirements. First, the state had to inform women about the stages of fetal development, the possibility of adoption assistance, and the risks associated with abortion. Second, the state must compile detailed public records of each woman's age, marital status, race, reason for seeking abortion, and number of prior pregnancies. Third, if there was any possibility the fetus could live outside the womb (about 23 weeks), a second doctor must be present to care for the fetus before the abortion begins—regardless of whether the delay endangers the mother's life or not. Fourth, abortions of viable fetuses must be performed using whichever method offers the best chance for live birth unless that method "would present a significantly greater risk to the life or health of the mother."

The vote in *Thornburgh* had been a close 5-4, and Justice Powell—challenged in that case—had since retired. Anthony M. Kennedy was Powell's successor, and his views on abortion were a matter of pessimistic speculation among abortion rights supporters. If he chose to join *Thornburgh's* four minority justices in a future abortion rights case, legalized abortion might disappear.

Missouri, having had a number of restrictive regulations overturned by the Supreme Court and another set upheld, passed a tough law in June of 1986. The statute began with a preamble setting forth the state legislature's "finding" that "the life of each human being begins at conception," and that "unborn children have protectable interests in life, health, and well-being."

As Chief Justice Rehnquist summarized later, the legislation "further requires that all Missouri laws be interpreted to provide unborn children with the same rights enjoyed by other persons, subject to the federal Constitution and [the Supreme] Court's precedents." They also included requirements that a physician make "such medical examinations and tests as are necessary to make a finding of the gestational age, weight, and lung maturity of the unborn child" if the physician thought the woman might be twenty or more weeks pregnant. Further, no public facilities or employees were to assist at or perform abortions nor may public funds be used to "encourag[e] or counsel" a woman to obtain an abortion, unless her pregnancy threatened her life.

Before the end of the month, Reproductive Health Services, Planned Parenthood of Kansas City, and five medical providers employed by Missouri challenged the act in the U.S. District Court for the Western District of Missouri. The district court issued an order restraining enforcement of much of the act, and after a trial in December of 1986, declared the act unconstitutional. The Court of Appeals for the Eighth Circuit upheld the lower court decision two years later, and Missouri appealed to the U.S. Supreme Court.

In March of 1989, the Supreme Court agreed that the administration of President George Bush could take part in the oral argument on behalf of Missouri. The Bush administration quickly made it clear that it planned to ask for nothing less than the complete overturn of *Roe v. Wade*. In angry response, 300,000 demonstrators gathered in Washington, D.C., to demand that abortion remain legal.

Friends of the Court

A record-breaking 78 *amicus curiae* briefs were filed. That was almost double the 42 such briefs filed in *Roe v. Wade*. This was a clear indication that both sides of the abortion debate viewed the forthcoming decision as a crucial one.

William L. Webster was first to address the Court. He outlined the three basic areas of Missouri's statute:

> The first, the constitutional boundaries on the limitations of public funding; the second, the effect of and the facial constitutionality of legislation declaring that life begins at conception; and, third, the ability of a state to require a physician to perform tests and to make and record findings when determining viability.

He contended that legal decisions at all judicial levels since 1973 had "repeatedly interpreted that [*Roe v. Wade*] mandate, frequently strictly against the states. One result is that states have effectively been forbidden . . . to regulate abortion in any significant way."

Webster defended his state's law forbidding the abortion-related employment of any public facility or person on the public payroll. He argued that "the government is certainly not obligated in and of itself to become an advocate for abortion." He characterized the act's preamble—declaring that Missouri believed human life begins at conception—as "an abstract, philosophical statement of the legislature" which "doesn't affect anyone" and states should be entitled to "have a philosophical statement of when they contend life begins."

Finally, he defended Missouri's requirement that physicians perform specific tests in order to verify fetal viability. Every state has a legitimate and compelling interest, he emphasized, in the fetus, most especially when it becomes viable. Therefore, doctors should perform whatever tests are necessary to protect unborn viable babies.

Dumping *Roe*

Charles Fried, arguing for the Bush administration, asked the Court to overturn *Roe v. Wade*. He insisted that such a ruling would not undermine Americans' other privacy rights and that legislatures and communities were entitled to frame laws based on the assumption that a fetus was a person, whether or not the Constitution specifically addressed that question. He insisted that the Court was not being asked to "unravel the fabric of unenumerated and privacy rights which this Court has woven . . . Rather, we are asking the Court to pull this one thread . . . Abortion is different."

Abortion means the deliberate ending of a potential life, Fried pointed out. To many legislators, it is actual life, he added, and "though we do not believe that the Fourteenth Amendment takes any position . . . it is an utter *non sequitur* to say that, therefore, the organized community must also take no position . . . and may not use such a position as a premise for regulation."

Kennedy asked Fried whether he thought *Griswold v. Connecticut* (1964), which legalized the use of contraceptives by married couples and enunciated the right to privacy upon which *Roe* was largely based, should stand. When Fried agreed that *Griswold* should stand, Kennedy asked if there was "a fundamental right involved in that case."

In Fried's opinion, *Griswold* involved a "right which was well established in a whole fabric of quite concrete matters . . . not an abstraction such as the right to control one's body, an abstraction such as the right to be let alone; it involved quite concrete intrusions into the details of marital intimacy."

Roe Must Not Go

Reproductive Health Services attorney Frank Susman went next into the fray. He immediately attacked the very idea of a reversal of *Roe:* "[Fried] suggests that he

Frank Susman, 1989. © Reproduced by permission of Frank Susman.

does not seek to unravel the whole cloth of procreational rights, but merely to pull a thread. It has always been my personal experience that, when I pull a thread, my sleeve falls off." He argued that the contraceptive rights protected by *Griswold* and the abortion rights protected by *Roe* no longer stood apart:

> It is not a thread he is after. It is the full range of procreational choices that constitute the fundamental right that has been recognized by this Court. For better or worse, there no longer exists any bright line between the fundamental right that was established in *Griswold* and the fundamental right of abortion that was established in *Roe*.

Pressed by Kennedy, Susman conceded that *Roe* granted the state a "compelling interest . . . in potential fetal life after the point of viability," and that this was, as Kennedy phrased it, "a line drawing." Susman said that the line between fetal viability and non-viability "was more easily drawn" for "many cogent reasons" than the line between the two landmark decisions.

Susman then discussed the medical safety of legalized abortion, noting that the procedure was "seventeen times safer than childbirth, 100 times safer than appendectomy." He also noted that while 30 percent of all American pregnancies ended in abortion, the "rate has not changed one whit from the time the Constitution was enacted through the 1800s and through the 1900s." He then discussed the legal history of abortion, pointing out that it had not been a common law crime prior to its criminalization in the mid-nineteenth century.

Justice Scalia's questions also went back to *Roe*, and its ruling that a fetus was not a "person" within the meaning of the Constitution. Susman responded with an objection to Missouri's preamble declaring that human life began at conception, arguing that it "is not something that is verifiable as fact. It is a question verifiable only by reliance upon faith."

Activists on both sides of the abortion debate gathered to demonstrate outside the courthouse that morning, and Susman referred to them in answering Scalia:

> The very debate that went on outside this morning, outside this building, and has gone on in various towns and communities across our nation, is the same debate that every woman who becomes pregnant and doesn't wish to be pregnant has with herself.

> Women do not make these decisions lightly. They agonize over them . . . The very fact that it is so contested is one of those things that makes me believe that it must remain as a fundamental right with the individual and that the state legislatures have no business invading this decision.

Both Sides Now

Rehnquist announced the Court's decision. While the nine justices took eight separate positions on some of the questions raised, five agreed that Missouri's prohibition of the use of public facilities and public employees to perform or counsel about abortion, as well as its law requiring doctors to perform tests regarding fetal viability, was constitutional. The Court also permitted Missouri to retain its policy statement that human life begins at conception because the statement had no legal effect.

Roe v. Wade was not overturned, but neither was it wholeheartedly affirmed: Rehnquist, joined by Justices Kennedy and White, noted with sorrow that the facts presented in *Webster* "afford us no occasion to revisit the holding of *Roe* . . . [but] [t]o the extent indicated in our opinion, we would modify and narrow *Roe* and succeeding cases." Justice O'Connor said: "When the constitutional invalidity of a State's abortion statute actually turns on the constitutional validity of *Roe v. Wade*, there will be enough time to examine *Roe*. And to do so carefully . . ." An angry Scalia responded by castigating his colleagues for their failure to use the opportunity to overturn the 1973 decision. In 1992, however, the Court firmly upheld *Roe* in *Planned Parenthood of Southeastern Pennsylvania v. Casey*. This time the justices put respect for earlier Court decisions ahead of ideology and political pressure.

Related Cases

Griswold v. Connecticut, 381 U.S. 479 (1965).
Roe v. Wade, 410 U.S. 113 (1973).
Planned Parenthood of Southeastern Pennsylvania v. Casey, 505 U.S. 883 (1992).

Bibliography and Further Reading

Asma, Stephen T. "Abortion and the Embarrassing Saint." *The Humanist*, May-June 1994, p. 30.

Deflem, Mathieu. "The Boundaries of Abortion Law." *Social Forces*, March 1998, p. 775.

Dillon, Michele. "Argumentative Complexity of Abortion Discourse." *Public Opinion Quarterly*, fall 1993, p. 305.

Garrow, David J. *Liberty and Sexuality: The Right to Privacy and the Making of Roe v. Wade*. New York: Macmillan, 1994.

Guitton, Stephanie, and Peter Irons, eds. *May It Please the Court: Arguments on Abortion* (live recordings and transcripts). New York: The New Press, 1995.

Hoff, Joan. *Law, Gender, and Injustice: A Legal History of U.S. Women*. New York: New York University Press, 1991.

Johnson, John W., ed. *Historic U.S. Court Cases, 1690-1990: An Encyclopedia*. New York: Garland Publishing, 1992.

Kelly, James R. "A Dispatch from the Abortion Wars." *America*, September 17, 1994, p. 8.

Toon, Mari Boor. "Donning Sackcloth and Ashes: Webster v. Reproductive Health Services and Moral Agony in Abortion Rights Rhetoric." *Communication Quarterly*, summer 1996, p. 265.

Wlezien, Christopher. "Abortion Rates in the United States." *Political Science Quarterly*, spring 1997, p. 177.

HODGSON V. MINNESOTA

Legal Citation: 497 U.S. 417 (1990)

Petitioner
Jane Hodgson, et al.

Respondent
State of Minnesota, et al.

Petitioner's Claim
That a Minnesota law requiring minors to notify both their parents before obtaining an abortion was unconstitutional.

Chief Lawyer for Respondent
John Tunheim

Chief Lawyer for Petitioner
Janet Benshoof

Justices for the Court
Harry A. Blackmun, William J. Brennan, Jr., Thurgood Marshall, Sandra Day O'Connor, John Paul Stevens (writing for the Court)

Justices Dissenting
Anthony M. Kennedy, William H. Rehnquist, Antonin Scalia, Byron R. White

Place
Washington, D.C.

Date of Decision
25 June 1990

Decision
Affirmed the decision of the U.S. Court of Appeals holding the two-parent notification policy unconstitutional where there is no provision for judicial bypass.

Significance
The Supreme Court's decision in *Hodgson v. Minnesota* slowed the trend toward restriction of abortion rights begun in *Webster v. Reproductive Health Services*. However, its split judgment reflected the ambivalence of the Court in cases dealing with statutory constraints on the availability of abortion.

Judicial Background

The landmark case of *Roe v. Wade* (1973), in which the petitioner successfully challenged a Texas law prohibiting abortions except to save the woman's life, established the benchmark for all future abortion decisions of the U.S. Supreme Court. The Supreme Court, in that decision, held that the right to privacy extends to the decision of a woman, in consultation with her physician, to terminate her pregnancy. By the time *Hodgson v. Minnesota* was decided in 1990, the U.S. Supreme Court had ruled on abortion rights cases for almost 17 years. For most of that time, attempts by states to place restrictions on the availability of abortions were ruled unconstitutional. However, changes in the makeup and temperament of the Court during the 1980s served to arrest this trend. As a result, observers watched the *Hodgson* decision closely for indications of which way the Court would proceed in the future.

The case revolved around two key issues: the right of a minor to terminate a pregnancy without notifying her parents, and the ability of a state to impose a waiting period on those seeking an abortion. The Supreme Court had dealt with both those issues before. In *Planned Parenthood of Central Missouri v. Danforth* (1976), the Court had held that parental and spousal consent requirements were unconstitutional because they delegate to third parties an absolute veto power that the state does not itself possess. In *Akron v. Akron Center for Reproductive Health* (1983) the Court had held that an Ohio law requiring a woman to wait 24 hours between consenting to and receiving an abortion was unconstitutional. However, the Court soon took a dramatic turn toward the restriction of abortion rights. In *Webster v. Reproductive Health Services* (1989), the Court upheld a Missouri law forbidding the use of public facilities for abortions not necessary to save a woman's life. It ruled that the state may implement a policy favoring childbirth over abortion by allocation of public resources such as hospitals and medical staff. It was in this atmosphere of uncertainty over the Court's intentions that the *Hodgson v. Minnesota* case was heard.

The Case at Hand

In 1981, the state of Minnesota enacted a parental notification law for abortion. The law required women under the age of 18 to inform both of their parents of their desire to terminate a pregnancy. After 48 hours, the woman could then have an abortion performed with or without parental consent. Exceptions to this rule were made in cases of medical emergency, parental abuse, or neglect. A separate provision of the law provided for a "judicial bypass" of parental notification. Through this procedure, a judge could allow a minor to have an abortion if he or she felt the woman was sufficiently mature enough to make the decision, or if notifying the parents did not serve the woman's best interests. A group of Minnesota citizens, comprised of pregnant minors, doctors, and abortion rights advocates, filed suit in the U.S. District Court. They hoped to have the law struck down as unconstitutional.

The Lower Courts Rule

In 1986, the U.S. District Court for the District of Minnesota issued its first decision in the case. It struck down as unconstitutional two of the three key parts of the law: the parental notification requirement and the 48-hour waiting period. Although it did hold that the judicial bypass provision of the law complied with the Constitution, the district court enjoined the state of Minnesota from enforcing the law in its entirety. The state then took its case to the U.S. court of appeals. The court of appeals agreed with the district court that parental notification without the possibility of judicial bypass violated the U.S. Constitution. However, it held that both the 48-hour waiting period and the notification requirement with judicial bypass provision passed constitutional muster. Accordingly, it reversed the district court decision. The original petitioners then appealed to the U.S. Supreme Court.

The Supreme Court Affirms the Court of Appeals Decision

On 25 June 1990, the Supreme Court ruled on the case. A five-justice majority affirmed the decision of the court of appeals, striking down the notification requirement without judicial bypass as unconstitutional. Five justices also agreed that the provision in the Minnesota law requiring notification with judicial bypass was constitutional. However, the justices disagreed on the particulars of this part of the decision and issued separate opinions on the matter.

On the issue of notification without judicial bypass, the Court found that this was not a reasonable way to ensure that parents become involved in a minor's decision to terminate a pregnancy. Writing for the majority, Justice Stevens opined:

> The requirement that both parents be notified, whether or not both wish to be notified or have assumed responsibility for the upbring-

ing of the child, does not reasonably further any legitimate state interest. Any such interest in supporting the authority of a parent, who is presumed to act in the minor's best interest, to assure that the abortion decision is knowing, intelligent, and deliberate, would be fully served by a one-parent notification requirement as to functioning families, where notice to either parent would normally constitute notice to both.

Futhermore, Stevens reasoned, the two-parent notification requirement was unrealistic—potentially even harmful—in a world where functional two-parent households are increasingly rare.

> [A]s the record demonstrates, the two-parent requirement actually disserves the state interest in protecting and assisting the minor with respect to the thousands of dysfunctional families affected by the statute, where the requirement proved positively harmful. There is no merit to the argument that the two-parent requirement is justified because, in the ideal family, the minor should make her decision only after consultation with both parents, who should naturally be concerned with her welfare. The State has no legitimate interest in conforming family life to a state-designed ideal by requiring family members to talk together.

As to the issue of notification with judicial bypass, a different majority coalesced around the view that consultation with a judge was a reasonable safety valve in cases where both the minor's parents could not be located or properly notified. "[A] judicial bypass is an expeditious and efficient means by which to separate the applications of the law which are constitutional from those which are not." Justice Kennedy concluded.

Voices of Dissent

The most passionate voices of dissent in the case were those most closely identified with, and those most profoundly skeptical of, the concept of constitutionally protected abortion rights. On the one hand, Justices Marshall, Brennan, and Blackmun took the view that any requirement that a minor notify parents before terminating a pregnancy was unconstitutional on its face. Writing for the dissenters, Justice Marshall opined:

> The parental notification and 48-hour delay requirements . . . do not satisfy the strict scrutiny applicable to laws restricting a woman's constitutional right to have an abortion. The judicial bypass procedure cannot salvage those requirements because that procedure itself is unconstitutional.

On the other hand, Justice Scalia was equally adamant that the Court had no right to be ruling on such matters in the first place.

> The random and unpredictable results of our . . . unchanneled individual views make it increasingly evident, term after term, that the tools for this job are not to be found in the lawyer's—and hence not in the judge's—workbox. I continue to dissent from this enterprise of devising an Abortion Code, and from the illusion that we have authority to do so.

Impact

The "split decision" issued by the Court in *Hodgson v. Minnesota* did little to clarify the Court's position on the restriction of abortion rights, but provided grist for both sides of the issue in subsequent cases.

Related Cases

Roe v. Wade, 410 U.S. 113 (1973).

Akron v. Akron Center for Reproductive Health, 462 U.S. 416 (1983).

Webster v. Reproductive Health Services, 492 U.S. 490 (1989).

Planned Parenthood of Southeastern Pennsylvania v. Casey, 505 U.S. 833 (1992).

Bibliography and Further Reading

Biskupic, Joan, and Elder Witt. *Congressional Quarterly's Guide to the U.S. Supreme Court,* 3rd ed. Washington, DC: Congressional Quarterly, Inc., 1996.

Hall, Kermit L., ed. *The Oxford Companion to the Supreme Court of the United States.* New York: Oxford University Press, 1992.

Harrison, Maureen, and Steve Gilbert, eds. *Abortion Decisions of the U.S. Supreme Court: The 1990s.* Beverly Hills, CA: Excellent Books, 1993.

Rhode, Deborah L. "Adolescent Pregnancy and Public Policy." *Political Science Quarterly,* winter 1993, p. 635.

RUST V. SULLIVAN

Legal Citation: 500 U.S. 173 (1991)

Petitioners
Irving Rust, et al.

Respondent
Louis W. Sullivan, U.S. Secretary of Health and Human Services

Petitioners' Claim
That federal regulations forbidding family planning clinics from providing their clients with information about abortion violate both the right to freedom of speech and a woman's right to abortion.

Chief Lawyer for Petitioners
Laurence H. Tribe

Chief Lawyer for Respondent
Kenneth W. Starr, U.S. Solicitor General

Justices for the Court
Anthony M. Kennedy, William H. Rehnquist (writing for the Court), Antonin Scalia, David H. Souter, Byron R. White

Justices Dissenting
Harry A. Blackmun, Thurgood Marshall, Sandra Day O'Connor, John Paul Stevens

Place
Washington, D.C.

Date of Decision
23 May 1991

Decision
The Supreme Court upheld the new federal regulations.

Significance
Rust proved to be an indicator of the Court's shifting attitudes toward abortion, as well as a major pronouncement about the doctrine of unconstitutional spending, which holds that federal funds may only be spent on those purposes for which they are allocated.

In 1988, Secretary of Health and Human Services Louis W. Sullivan issued regulations preventing family-planning services which received federal funds under the Public Service Act's Title X from dispensing any information about abortion. Irving Rust was just one of the clinic directors and doctors who filed suit to prevent the regulations from going into effect. These plaintiffs challenged the "gag rule" as both a violation of the First Amendment guarantee of free speech and an unconstitutional attempt to interfere with the right to abortion upheld in *Roe v. Wade* (1973). After these suits failed in the federal district courts and were similarly defeated on appeal, Rust and others petitioned the U.S. Supreme Court for review. The Supreme Court consolidated the cases and decided them as one.

Roe v. Wade has proven to be one of the most controversial decisions ever handed down by the Court. Much of the legal wrangling has centered on control of the federal funds which Congress allocated in 1970 to support family planning clinics. The Public Health Service Act stipulated that none of these funds could be used to support programs where abortion was used as a method of birth control. Between 1971 and 1986, government regulations prevented the clinics from providing abortions. In 1986, new rules strictly divided those clinics receiving federal funds from abortion providers. Then in 1988, towards the end of President Ronald Reagan's second term, his conservative administration imposed the "gag rule."

Supreme Court Rejects Challenges to the "Gag Rule" on Federally Funded Family Planning Clinics

The Supreme Court divided sharply over the issues presented by *Rust.* Writing for the one-vote majority, Chief Justice Rehnquist declared that the 1988 regulation was an acceptable interpretation of the 1970 statute. Because it provided funds for family planning while prohibiting assistance for abortion, the statute was ambiguous. But it was the Department of Health and Human Services' job to administer the law, and

Luis W. Sullivan, U.S. Secretary of Health and Human Services, 1992. © AP/Wide World Photos.

their regulation did not violate Congress' mandate. The courts, wrote Rehnquist, should defer to legislative intent.

Adding to this line of argument, Rehnquist went on to justify the regulation by citing the doctrine of unconstitutional conditions, which holds that government can impose conditions—even seemingly unconstitutional ones—on recipients of federal funds. The goal of such conditions is to insure that the monies are spent solely for the intended purposes:

> The condition that federal funds will be used only to further the purposes of a grant does not violate constitutional rights . . . By requiring that the Title X grantee engage in abortion-related activity separately from activity receiving federal funding, Congress has . . . not denied it the right to engage in abortion-related activities. Congress has merely refused to fund such activities out of the public fisc . . . The same principles apply to petitioners' claim that the regulations abridge the free speech rights of the grantee's staff.

Just as Title X does not prohibit fund recipients from performing abortions elsewhere, the new regulation does not prevent clinic professionals from giving abortion advice in other locations. Rehnquist conceded that it would be simpler for women to decide whether or not to choose abortion if information were available at their family planning clinics. But the constitutionally granted right to abortion did not, he maintained, require the government to change the mandate of its program.

On its face, *Rust* seemed to be another step in the Court's progress towards overturning *Roe v. Wade*. Justice Souter, who was participating in an abortion-related case for the first time, cast his vote with the usual anti-abortion coalition voting to uphold the gag rule. However, the closeness of the vote owed a great deal to the fact that Justice O'Connor, often considered a member of the Court's conservative wing, had dissented. The future of a woman's right to abortion remained in doubt.

Related Cases

Roe v. Wade, 410 U.S. 113 (1973).
Harris v. McRae, 448 U.S. 297 (1980).
Akron v. Akron Center for Reproductive Health, 462 U.S. 416 (1983).
Thornburgh v. American College of Obstetricians and Gynecologists, 476 U.S. 747 (1986).

Justice William H. Rehnquist. © Photograph by Dane Penland, Smithsonian Institution. Collection of the Supreme Court of the United States.

Webster v. Reproductive Health Services, 492 U.S. 490 (1989).

Bibliography and Further Reading

LaMarche, Gara, ed. *Speech & Equality: Do We Really Have to Choose?* New York, NY: New York University Press, 1996.

Reagan. Leslie J. *When Abortion Was a Crime: Women, Medicine, and Law in the United States, 1876-1973.* Berkeley: University of California Press, 1997.

Yarnold, Barbara M. *Abortion Politics in the Federal Courts: Right Versus Right.* Westport, CT: Praeger, 1995.

NATIONAL ORGANIZATION FOR WOMEN, INC. V. SCHEIDLER

Legal Citation: 510 U.S. 249 (1994)

Petitioner
National Organization for Women, Inc. (NOW); Delaware Women's Health Organization, Inc. (DWHO); Summit Women's Health Organization, Inc. (SWHO)

Respondent
Joseph Scheidler, Pro-Life Action Network (PLAN), et al.

Petitioner's Claim
That respondents belonged to a nationwide conspiracy to shut down abortion clinics in violation of the Racketeer Influenced and Corrupt Organizations (RICO) chapter of the Organized Crime Control Act of 1970.

Chief Lawyer for Petitioner
Fay Clayton

Chief Lawyer for Respondent
Robert Blakey

Justices for the Court
Harry A. Blackmun, Ruth Bader Ginsburg, Anthony M. Kennedy, Sandra Day O'Connor, William H. Rehnquist (writing for the Court), Antonin Scalia, David H. Souter, John Paul Stevens, Clarence Thomas

Justices Dissenting
None

Place
Washington, D.C.

Date of Decision
24 January 1994

Decision
That attempts by the anti-abortion groups in question to hinder the business of the abortion clinics constituted racketeering, even though there was no economic purpose behind such activities; therefore the respondents could be charged under the RICO provisions.

Significance
In *National Organization for Women, Inc. v. Scheidler*, pro-choice and pro-life forces fought yet another battle in a war that had been going on since the Supreme Court legalized abortion with *Roe v. Wade* (1973). Like its predecessor and a number of other abortion-related challenges in the Supreme Court, *Scheidler* was decisively in favor of the pro-choice side. But the nature of that victory— involving as it did the reapplication of a crime statute formerly wielded against Mafia bosses and drug lords to prevent abortion protesters from blocking access to clinics—would raise some disturbing First Amendment questions.

Access v. Protest

The long, heated, and bitter battle over the abortion issue can be characterized in any number of ways, depending upon one's views. To feminist groups such as the National Organization for Women (NOW), who helped to initiate the suit that would become *National Organization for Women, Inc. v. Scheidler*, anti-abortion protests were simply an attempt, orchestrated by religious groups and other male-dominated organizations, to prevent women from exercising free choice over their bodies. To groups based around a religious or moral opposition to abortion—groups such as the Pro-Life Action Network (PLAN), who became respondents in *Scheidler*—the abortion industry was seen as a big and profitable business which cloaks itself under the banners of feminism and choice. And—to get to the crux of *Scheidler*—in the eyes of abortion protesters, protesting abortion is a constitutionally protected right of free speech. To the women going to clinics for abortions, however, the exercise of that right (often accompanied by shouting, pushing, or other abusive behavior) infringes on their own right of free access.

The fight over protest and access had been going on for many years when NOW took Joseph Scheidler, PLAN, and other abortion opponents to the U.S. District Court for the Northern District of Illinois. The suit charged them with violations of the Sherman Anti-Trust Act, which forbids any attempt at "restraint of trade"; and—in an innovative use of law—with violations of sections 1962(a), (c), and (d) of the Racketeer Influenced and Corrupt Organizations (RICO) chapter of the Organized Crime Control Act of 1970.

David van Biema of *Time* magazine described the latter, written in an attempt to impede the spread of the Mafia's criminal empire, as "a law with teeth—and a voracious appetite." Written in broad language, van Biema indicated, the law made not just the crime-syndicate bosses, but all their underlings, culpable for unlawful activities committed by a criminal organization. "RICO quickly proved a sterling Mob stopper," van Biema wrote, "as dozens of capos like New York City's John Gotti can testify." The latter, nicknamed "the Dapper Don" for his elegant style of dress, had been perhaps the most powerful Mafia figure in New

York before the FBI captured him on the RICO statute and he entered prison in 1991. "But when lawyers of the mid-1980s realized how broadly written [RICO] was," van Biema continued, "it mutated wildly." Next to come under the scope of RICO were junk-bond magnates such as Michael Milken; then came persons charged with sexual harassment. Though the statute was still being used against illegal activity, with each mutation, it was moving further and further away from the crime bosses for whom it had been written.

In the present case, the use of RICO and the Sherman Act stemmed from charges, which Scheidler and others did not attempt to deny, that their aim was to shut down abortion clinics and convince women not to have abortions. In their suit, which charged the respondents with violations of various state laws, NOW and the other petitioners sought injunctive relief, along with damages, costs, and attorneys' fees. Further pursuing the RICO argument, the petitioners amended their complaint to include a "RICO Case Statement" which offered further details about the enterprise, pattern, and victims of the respondents. According to the amended complaint, Scheidler and others belonged to a nationwide conspiracy to shut down abortion clinics by means of racketeering and extortion in violation of the Hobbs Act, which defines extortion as "the obtaining of property from another, with his consent, induced by wrongful use of actual or threatened force, violence, or fear, or under color of official right." The petitioners charged that the respondents had, in the words of the U.S. Supreme Court, "conspired to use threatened or actual force, violence or fear to induce clinic employees, doctors, and patients to give up their jobs, give up their economic right to practice medicine, and give up their right to obtain medical services at the clinics." That conspiracy, in the petitioners' words, had "injured the business and/or property interests" of the clinics.

The district court dismissed the case, citing *Eastern Railroad Presidents Conference v. Noerr Motor Freight, Inc.* (1961): since the activities in question "involve[d] political opponents, not commercial competitors, and political objectives, not marketplace goals," the Sherman Act was not relevant. Holding that "some profit-generating purpose must be alleged in order to state a RICO claim," the district court held that the petitioners lacked standing to sue. The court of appeals affirmed this judgment. Any income received by the respondents, the court held, had come from voluntary donations of members and supporters, not from extortion against the clinics.

A New Reading of RICO

The U.S. Supreme Court reversed the lower court's ruling by a unanimous vote. Writing for the Court, Chief Justice Rehnquist first held that the clinics had standing to bring their claim. Citing *Hishon v. King* (1984), he noted that because their complaint had been dis-missed at the pleading stage, it would not have to be sustained "if relief could be granted under any set of facts that could be proved consistent with the allegations." Nothing was needed to confer standing, the Chief Justice wrote, other than the extortion and injury allegations in the complaint.

Not only did the petitioners have standing to bring their case before the Court, RICO could be used against the respondents. The statutes contained no provision stating that the racketeering enterprise had to be economically motivated, and though "arguably an enterprise engaged in interstate or foreign commerce would have a profit-seeking motive," RICO's use of the word "affect" suggested an alternative interpretation. Consulting the dictionary, the Chief Justice found that Webster defined "affect" as "to have a detrimental influence on"—something an enterprise could do without making, or seeking to make, a profit.

Nor does "enterprise" necessarily indicate an economic motive. Whereas in (a) and (b), an enterprise is "an entity acquired through illegal activity or the money generated from illegal activity," in (c) it "connotes generally the vehicle through which the unlawful pattern of racketeering activity is committed." An enterprise, the Court held, "need only be an association in fact that engages in a pattern of racketeering activity." For further proof that an economic motive need not be cited, the Court made reference to the congressional statement of findings that precedes the RICO chapter and "refers to activities that drain billions of dollars from America's economy." The activities cited in *Scheidler*, particularly preventing access to clinics, might not benefit the perpetrators; but they unquestionably drained income from the clinics, and hence impeded the flow of commerce. If the congressional findings were not enough, one had only to note the 1984 amendments broadening a set of guidelines on RICO prosecutions issued by the Department of Justice in 1981. Finally, "the statutory language is unambiguous, and there is no clearly expressed intent to the contrary in the legislative history that would warrant a different construction." Accordingly the Court overruled the judgment of the lower court.

A Chilling Effect

Not only was it unanimous, the Court's opinion in *Scheidler* was remarkably short—only eight pages, including footnotes. This belied the complexity of the free-speech issues it raised, issues addressed briefly by Justice Souter in a concurring opinion joined by Justice Kennedy. Quoting from *Lucas v. Alexander* (1929), Souter noted that "a law 'must be construed with an eye to possible constitutional limitations so as to avoid doubts as to its validity." In this particular case, Souter noted, the language of the statute was unambiguous, and therefore it was pointless to challenge RICO on that basis. And even if RICO's meaning were debatable, this would not mean that an economic motive requirement should be written into the statute, "since such a requirement would correspond only poorly to free speech patterns."

Finally, the economic requirement would be unnecessary, Souter suggested, because it would make more sense to challenge RICO on the basis of free speech. In fact, he all but invited future petitioners to do so: "Accordingly," he wrote, "it is important to stress that nothing in the Court's opinion precludes a RICO defendant from raising the First Amendment in its defense in a particular case." In *National Association for the Advancement of Colored People v. Claiborne Hardware Co.* (1982), for instance, the Court had ruled that a state law prohibiting interference with business could not constitutionally be allied to a civil rights boycott of white merchants. Justice Souter concluded by warning that "I think it prudent to notice that RICO actions could deter protected advocacy, and to caution courts applying RICO to bear in mind the First Amendment interests that could be at stake."

Feminists and pro-choice advocates were exultant over the decision, as van Biema noted in *Time* soon

afterward. Judith Lichtman of the Women's Legal Defense Fund called it "a victory for women . . . By this decision, the Court rightly recognized the danger that this national conspiracy of harassment, stalkings, bombings, shootings and chemical attacks poses to women and health care providers." Such a statement, van Biema observed, offered a too-broad interpretation of what was in fact a narrow Court opinion—and, incidentally, a too-broad interpretation of the constituency it benefited. Regarding the characterization of *Scheidler* as "a victory for women," van Biema wrote that this "may depend on whether a woman is for or against abortion rights." The ruling seemed a solution to the tragic situation surrounding abortion clinics, which was symbolized by the shooting of Dr. David Gunn in Alabama in March of 1993 by an anti-abortion zealot. Clearly the extremist fringes of the pro-life movement had created a threat to personal safety and individual liberty, but the *Scheidler* decision offered protection against such incidents with a ruling that introduced the potential for a chilling effect on free speech. Randell Terry, a leader in the Operation Rescue organization, called the decision "A vulgar betrayal of over 200 years of tolerance toward protest." Scheidler, Terry's one-time mentor, viewed with disdain attempts to

Joseph Scheidler, 1998.
© Photograph by Mike
Fisher. AP/Wide World
Photos.

obtain treble damages from him: "You can't get blood from a turnip," he said.

One individual who expressed deep concern about the ruling—and high hopes for the next round of legal battles, the federal civil trial—was G. Robert Blakey. In the present case, he was the lawyer for Scheidler and other respondents; but 23 years before, he had held a role that gave him special insight on RICO. Blakey, it turns out, was the individual who drafted the statute as chief counsel to the Senate Judiciary Subcommittee on Criminal Laws. At the time, he said, Senator Edward Kennedy expressed fears that President Richard M. Nixon would use the statute against anti-war protesters. Therefore Blakey and Kennedy sat down in the Monocle Restaurant in Washington, D.C. one day to alter the bill's language. Later, after the federal civil trial that followed *Scheidler,* Blakey decried the methods used to criminalize forms of free speech and protest: "This ruling," he said, "makes the Boston Tea Party a RICO [violation]."

Impact

Later in *Madsen v. Women's Health Center, Inc.* (1994), the Court ruled 6-3 that judges could establish "buffer zones" to keep protesters away from abortion clinics. Though not potentially as restrictive of free speech as *Scheidler,* the *Madsen* ruling still raised concerns, even on the Court that passed it. Chief Justice Rehnquist, again writing for the majority, warned judges not to "restrict more speech than necessary." Also in 1994, Congress passed the Freedom of Access to Clinics Act, which prevented protesters from blocking access to an abortion clinic. As for the civil trial that followed *Scheidler,* it did not go well for PLAN. Ordinarily a protest group would enjoy the support of the ACLU, the NAACP, and other civil-liberties and -rights organizations; but given PLAN's anti-abortion stance and the political realities that create inflexible and opposing power blocs, such groups did not take up PLAN's cause. Nor did the support of its traditional constituency—religious and conservative groups—prove a powerful force in PLAN's favor. Terry and Operation Rescue set-

tled out of court in February of 1998, and a jury in Chicago in April found the remaining defendants guilty of conspiracy under RICO. The defendants were liable to two clinics for $85,000 in damages, which under the racketeering law would be multiplied by three—to $255,000. More facilities were expected to file claims under the class-action suit.

Related Cases

Eastern Railroad Presidents Conference v. Noerr Motor Freight, Inc., 365 U.S. 127 (1961).
United States v. Turkette, 452 U.S. 576 (1981).
National Association for the Advancement of Colored People v. Claiborne Hardware Co. 458 U.S. 886 (1982).
Hishon v. King, 467 U.S. 69 (1984).
Sedima, S.P.R.L. v. Imrex Co., 473 U.S. 479 (1985).
United States v. Flynn, 488 U.S. 974 (1988).
Northeast Women's Center, Inc. v. McMonagle, 493 U.S. 901 (1989).
Madsen v. Women's Health Center, Inc., 513 U.S. 753 (1994).

Bibliography and Further Reading

Allison, Bridget, Christopher Iorillo, Theodore John Katopis, Susan Lynch, Emily C. Shanahan, and Erin Sokol. "Racketeer Influenced and Corrupt Organizations." *American Criminal Law Review,* spring 1998, p. 1103.

Pasternak, Judy. "Jury Rules Against Abortion Protesters." *Los Angeles Times,* April 21, 1998, p. A28.

Rooney, John Flynn. "Keep Anti-Abortion RICO Suit Moving, Judge Says." *Chicago Daily Law Bulletin,* October 21, 1994, p. 1.

Van Biema, David. "Your Activist, My Mobster: A Ruling by the High Court Enables Foes to Use a Voracious Racketeering Law Against Pro-Lifer Leaders." *Time,* February 7, 1994, p. 32.

Witt, Elder. *Congressional Quarterly's Guide to the Supreme Court,* 2nd ed. Washington, DC: Congressional Quarterly Inc., 1990.

KASS V. KASS

Legal Citation: 673 N.Y.S. 2d 350 (1998)

Appellant
Maureen Kass

Appellee
Steven Kass

Appellant's Claim
That five stored, frozen human embryos be granted to the woman who donated the eggs so she might fulfill her constitutional right to have children.

Chief Lawyers for Appellant
Vincent F. Stempel, Lisa Ann Spero

Chief Lawyer for Appellee
Linda T. Armatti-Epstein

Justices for the Court
Joseph W. Bellacosa, Carmen Beauchamp Ciparick, Judith S. Kaye (writing for the court), Howard Levine, George Bundy Smith, Vito J. Titone, Richard C. Wesley

Justices Dissenting
None

Place
Albany, New York, New York State Court of Appeals

Date of Decision
7 May 1998

Decision
A previous agreement signed by the two parties donating the embryos to an "in vitro fertilization" research program held precedence over other claims.

Significance
The ruling involved one of the first cases to reach the courts concerning new artificial human reproduction technologies. However, in this case the court avoided basing their decision on individual parental rights and, instead, ruled on the validity of a previous agreement between the prospective parents under common contract law. Nonetheless, the case served notice to the legal and political communities that guidance from states and Congress was urgently needed to set standards the courts could follow in the new complex realm of artificial reproduction.

Thousands of children were born into the world in the 1980s and 1990s through a process known as "in vitro fertilization" (IVF). IVF, in fact, became the best known method of assisted reproduction. Every year tens of thousands of frozen embryos were routinely stored in liquid nitrogen canisters, with many remaining in that state for years with no specific instructions for their use or disposal. Consequently, a potential quagmire of legal and ethical questions were left in the wake of such scientific advances.

In 1942 the U.S. Supreme Court found in *Skinner v. Oklahoma* that reproduction was an important basic right in a citizen's "pursuit of happiness." However, not until the late 1980s did cases begin reaching the courts regarding artificial reproduction. In 1989 a federal district court in *York v. Jones* found that individuals contributing sperm and eggs held fundamental property interests in frozen embryos. The Tennessee Supreme Court in a 1992 *Davis v. Davis* ruling attempted to define a framework for resolving disputes between divorcing couples over the future of frozen embryos. The framework recognized the basic right of all persons to have children, and required a balancing of the interest in becoming "a genetic parent," as opposed to an interest in avoiding genetic parenthood. In *Davis,* by applying this balancing test, the court found that the husband's interest in avoiding genetic parenthood was more significant than the woman's desire to donate the embryos to a childless couple.

When Maureen and Steven Kass discovered shortly after their marriage in 1988 that she was biologically unable to become pregnant, the couple began an "in vitro" fertilization treatment. IVF treatment involves surgical removal of eggs from a woman's ovaries, fertilizing them with a man's sperm, and then placing the fertilized eggs in the uterus of the woman or a surrogate mother. Some zygotes, or embryos, are commonly frozen for possible future use. Before initiating their procedure, the Kasses signed a consent form stipulating the embryos could not be used for impregnation without the consent of both Maureen and Steven. Otherwise, if ultimately not used, the embryos would be donated for research purposes. The agreement also required that in the event of a divorce, ownership of the embryos would be decided through either a property settlement or court decision.

After ten failed attempts at achieving pregnancy the couple divorced without reaching further agreement as to the disposition of the five remaining embryos frozen and stored in a Long Island laboratory. A battle over the rights to the embryos began in 1993 when Ms. Kass went to court seeking sole custody of the remaining embryos so she could once again attempt impregnation.

Embryo Custody

In 1995, the New York Supreme Court in Nassau County granted Maureen Kass sole custody of the embryos. The court determined that she had "exclusive decisional authority over a nonviable fetus," and that "a husband's rights and controls of the procreative (reproductive) process end when the sperm and the egg are combined." The court based its decision on the landmark *Roe v. Wade* (1973) ruling. In *Roe* the U.S. Supreme Court held that a woman has a fundamental right to determine the fate of her fetus before it reaches viability, a point at which the baby could survive outside of the womb, with medical assistance if need be. The court reasoned that a woman involved in the IVF process should have the same right to determine her embryo's fate as a pregnant woman would enjoy under *Roe*.

Steven Kass appealed to the New York State Court of Appeals which, in a split decision, reversed the lower court's ruling. The court declared that "a woman's established rights over her body were not relevant until an embryo was gestating (being carried) in her uterus." Moreover, the court also unanimously recognized that when two parties enter into an agreement prior to an "in vitro" procedure the arrangement should be honored. The agreement unambiguously stipulated that if a dispute arose, the Kasses desired to donate the remaining embryos for research purposes. Ms. Kass appealed to the New York Court of Appeals.

Embryos as Property

In a unanimous decision, the New York Court of Appeals ruled in favor of upholding the contract which required both parties' consent before the embryos could be used for impregnation. Ms. Kass could not use the frozen embryos to impregnate herself without the consent of her former husband. Chief Judge Judith S. Kaye, delivering the majority's opinion, stressed the consent agreement, formally agreed upon prior to the dispute, must be honored and enforced. Kaye wrote that the disposition of the embryos did not invade a woman's right to privacy or any physical bodily integrity regarding reproductive choice. Also, Ms. Kass had not argued that the consent agreement violated any public policy, or that it was not enforceable due to their circumstances. In fact, the agreement was developed to protect against the mishandling of the embryos if a dispute arose, and

to prevent the decision being taken out of their hands by a stranger.

Thus, the *Kass* court did find that the one question left to decide was whether the consent agreement was sufficiently written to resolve the specific situation in which the couple found themselves. In making such a determination, Kaye wrote that the court could only look within the "four corners" of the document, meaning that only the parties' intent reflected in the written document would be considered. When conducting such an analysis, the court may also consider the current relation of the individuals to each other and the circumstances surrounding the document's execution. Such a process would guard against any assumptions by the court that may be counter to what the parties originally desired. If the overall intention of the parties is clear in the agreement, the agreement should apply, and be fully enforced. Regarding the Kasses, the court determined through analyzing their document that the agreement "unequivocally manifest[s]" their intentions, and the embryos should be donated to the IVF program for research.

Impact

The outcome of the *Kass* case denied any broadening of the fundamental privacy protection afforded a woman by the Supreme Court in the landmark *Roe v. Wade* decision. The *Kass* court's decision also demonstrated how the law has struggled to keep pace with the rapid advances in biomedical research. Such advances, particularly in the artificial reproduction realm, led to much debate in the 1990s as to the proper role of the courts in settling disputes like that between the Kasses. The debate of how best to regulate the field of artificial reproduction was far from resolution by the close of the twentieth century. In fact, the *Kass* decision appeared to conflict directly with the only previous court ruling concerning the disposition of frozen embryos. The Tennessee case of *Davis v. Davis* ruled that the person seeking to avoid having children should prevail.

The New York court, in relying on the consent agreement, essentially used contract law to settle the dispute. In doing so, the court avoided addressing ethical questions swirling around artificial reproduction. Future courts may not have contracts available to refer to, or some courts may even choose not to honor such a contract. Ideally, legislatures were needed to provide methods by which courts could rule in cases concerning artificial reproduction disputes.

Given the lack of existing legislative guidance, Judge Kaye strongly recommended that couples should carefully draft an agreement addressing every possible situation that could arise before entering an IVF program. Uncertainties are numerous in the IVF program where the cryopreservation, or freezing of the embryos, extends viability indefinitely. Over the course of time, minds and circumstances change; disputes erupt; and divorce, death, disappearance, or incapacity can all occur. Such an agreement should certainly specify how embryos should be used in cases where the two individuals cannot agree on the use. As Kaye noted, decisions surrounding disposition of embryos is a "quintessential personal and private decision in which the court should play no role."

Abortion opponents and religious organizations immediately criticized the decision by the treating of embryos as if they were "merely" property. Such groups believed that the parties who created the embryos had no right to prevent the unborn children from achieving life.

Other organizations, particularly feminist groups, considered the removal of the reproductive process from the woman's body and "commercialization" of the process by contract law as the ultimate exploitation of women. An argument against recognizing a fundamental right to abortion in *Roe v. Wade* was that it could encourage male sexual aggressiveness. If a man impregnated a woman, he could "get off the hook" from unwanted fatherhood by having the woman abort the fetus. Yet, as the argument went, the woman would likely carry the often overpowering burden of having the life of their offspring "torn" from her body. It was argued similar results could follow from artificial means of reproduction. The ability to purchase eggs and reproductive fluids, or the renting out of a womb as a gestating space essentially created a "reproductive marketplace."

The use of women's parts in artificial reproduction was both welcomed and fiercely rejected. Those whom were unable to achieve pregnancy naturally were presented with numerous ways in which they could become parents. As in *Roe*, some argued that the woman's body was merely being used as a provider of "spare parts" and, as a result, cheapened.

The artificial reproduction process also gave rise to another debate. The question of what exactly constitutes "motherhood" were raised. Is the woman who carried and delivered the child considered the mother, or the woman who provided the genetic material? What of the woman who did neither, but provided the child with the love and nurturing during the critical years of the child's development? Legal definitions in the states were changing to keep up with scientific advances, but these changes did not necessarily result in consistency among the states. Many looked to Congress to establish broad standards for states to follow as the technology continued to advance.

The changing times made it clear that legislatures could no longer afford to be left in the wake of science, especially in the area of artificial reproduction. Guidelines were needed that provided clear guidance for courts to follow in deciding disputes, as in *Kass*, concerning the disposition of products of the artificial reproductive process.

Related Cases
Skinner v. Oklahoma, 316 U.S. 535 (1942).
Roe v. Wade, 410 U.S. 113 (1973).
York v. Jones, 717 F. Supp. 421 (E.D. Va.) (1989).
Davis v. Davis, 842 S.W. 2d 588 (1992).

Bibliography and Further Reading
Blank, Robert, and Janna C. Merrick. *Human Reproduction, Emerging Technologies, and Conflicting Rights.* Washington, DC: Congressional Quarterly Inc., 1995.

Brienza, Julie. "Assisted Reproductive Technology Studied by New York Task Force." *Trial,* July 1998, p. 109.

Brienza, Julie. "Fate of Embryo Rests with Wife." *Trial,* April 1995, p. 94.

Brienza, Julie. "Frozen Embryos to Find Home in Research Lab, Court Rules." *Trial,* July 1998, p. 111.

Kunen, James S. "Fertility Rights." *People Weekly,* May 18, 1998, p. 179.

New York Times. "Court Blocks Embryo Use over Ex-Husband's Rights." May 8, 1998.

Van Dyck, Jose. *Manufacturing Babies and Public Consent: Debating the New Reproductive Technologies.* New York: New York University Press, 1995.

Walther, Deborah Kay. "'Ownership' of the Fertilized Ovum in Vitro." *Family Law Quarterly* Vol. 26, 1992, pp. 235-256.

RIGHTS OF GAYS AND LESBIANS

Gay and Lesbian Civil Rights

The average American does not realize that that it is legal to discriminate against another American on the basis of sexual orientation. A Greenberg Research poll in 1996 found that 85 percent of Americans did not know that federal civil rights laws do not prohibit firing a person solely on the basis of sexual orientation. Current laws do not provide a remedy to gay and lesbian citizens who seek legal protection. The Equal Protection Clause of the Fourteenth Amendment guarantees that no state shall "deny to any person within its jurisdiction the equal protection of the laws," meaning that citizens in similar circumstances should be treated alike. Only actions that aim to discriminate violate Equal Rights Protection. To use this as a defense when treated unfairly, one must prove intentional discrimination, not just negligence.

The gay and lesbian civil rights movement presses for fairness in five major areas: employment and the work environment (including the school environment), military service, health care issues, state ballot initiatives prohibiting gay civil-rights ordinances, and custody rights and state laws prohibiting same-sex marriage.

A Gallup poll in late 1996 found that 84 percent of Americans believe that gays should have equal rights in terms of the job opportunities available to them, up from 74 percent in 1992 and 56 percent in 1977. The poll also showed that 90 percent of Americans have no problem with gays as sales people, and two third approve of gays working in the president's cabinet, in the armed forces and as doctors. The Gallup survey also found that 60 percent approved of gays as high school teachers, 55 percent approved of gays as elementary teachers and 53 percent approved of gay clergy.

The gay and lesbian civil rights movement has been guided by the Lambda Legal Defense and Education Fund, Inc., which was founded in 1973. Lambda's court battles have broken ground in issues such as honorable discharge from the military, medical coverage for AIDS patients, domestic benefits for gay couples, adoption and visitation rights for gay parents, and protection for gay and lesbian immigrants.

Employment and School Fairness

Harassment at school and in the work environment due to sexual orientation is not always legally defensible. Massachusetts, Vermont, Wisconsin and the District of Columbia have statutes that address sexual orientation discrimination in schools. Other states do not. Laws prohibiting discrimination based on sex are more common, but the victim of harassment must demonstrate that the school acted or failed to act because of the victim's sexual orientation and made a decision based on that sexual orientation. It is difficult to provide evidence to this effect.

The most prominent federal sex discrimination statutes are Title IX and Title VII. Title IX applies to sex discrimination in education or any activity receiving federal financial assistance. Courts are reluctant to interpret the prohibition against sex discrimination as a prohibition against sexual orientation discrimination, but in a few cases sexual orientation discrimination has been included.

Title VII of the Civil Rights Act of 1964 applies to sex discrimination in employment, and applies to compensation, extension of health care benefits to a spouse, and retirement. Discrimination in employment on the basis of sexual orientation is currently legal in 41 states, meaning individuals may be fired from their jobs solely because of sexual orientation, even when it has no bearing on their job performance.

Sexual harassment claims fall under this statute. Gay and lesbian cases sought to show that sexual orientation discrimination is sex discrimination. Courts rejecting this argument most commonly did so by examining the harasser's motivation. Proof of the employer/harasser's discriminatory motive is crucial to the plaintiff's case. The first lawsuits applying this standard resulted in a variety of decisions and no consistent holdings. The 1969 case of *Norton v. Macy* held that sexual orientation that does not affect performance on the job or the public reputation of the job cannot be the basis for discrimination. But in 1977, the Federal Appellate Court for the Ninth Circuit determined that the Equal Employment Opportunity Commissions could fire an employee for being gay because of his openness about his homosexuality. Then in March of 1998, the Supreme Court ruled in *Oncale v. Sundowner Offshore Services Incorporated et al.* that Title VII's prohibition aganst sex discrimination extends to same-sex sexual harassment.

Many companies and organizations extend benefits to homosexual partners of their employees despite controversy, with the list including such names as The American Red Cross, Federal Express, Barnes & Noble, Walt Disney Company, Levi Strauss, Microsoft, IBM, and Time Warner.

In June of 1998, President Clinton amended Executive Order No. 11,478, which governs equal employment opportunity in the federal government, by adding sexual orientation to the list of prohibited bases for discrimination. Executive Order No. 11,478 was first signed by President Nixon to prohibit discrimination in federal employment on the grounds of race, color, sex, religion or national origin. It was later amended to add disability and age to the list.

Clinton's amendment extends protection under the Civil Service Reform Act of 1978, which specifies that federal civilian employers cannot discriminate for or against any employee or applicant on the basis of conduct which does not adversely affect the performance of the employee or the performance of others. The Office of Personnel Management in 1980 sent a memorandum clarifying that the Reform Act of 1978 protects gay and lesbian federal employees from discrimination. The result is that federal employees have several avenues of appeal when discrimination on the basis of sexual orientation occurs.

But the implementation of policy on an agency-by-agency basis has not been uniform. The Departments of Justice, Agriculture and Transportation developed model policies with clear anti-discrimination statements backed up by clear processes to address grievances. Other agencies failed to adopt any sexual orientation discrimination policy, meaning that a federal worker with a complaint had to go to court. Gay plaintiffs usually lose when courts conclude that the employer's actions result from employee conduct, and that the two are not mutually exclusive.

Legislation proposed by four Senators to remedy the hostile workplace environment narrowly failed to pass when voted on by the 104th Congress. The Employment Non-Discrimination Act was reintroduced in the 105th Congress with 33 co-sponsors.

Serving in the Armed Forces

Historically, homosexuals have been banned from military service. A report by the Government Accounting Office based on Defense Department data from 1980 to 1990 found that the various service branches discharged around 1,500 people each year due to sexual orientation. The GAO also calculated that it cost the

government $27 million to recruit and train replacements for gays discharged in 1990. Between 1980 and 1990, 227 officers and 16,692 enlisted men and women either resigned or were discharged because of their sexual orientation, even though U. S. Department of Defense studies released in 1989 showed that gays and lesbians in the military have the highest performance records on the average of any single subgroup, consistently in the top 5 percent.

In 1993, the Clinton administration created a new policy for homosexuals in the armed services that took effect in October of 1993. The "Don't ask, Don't tell" policy allows gays to serve as long as they are silent about their sexual orientation and do not engage in homosexual acts. Clinton's intention was to make it easier for gays and lesbians to serve in the armed forces. A study done two years later by the Service Members' Legal Defense Network found that the policy did not make life better for gay service persons. Air force discharges for homosexuality were up 30 percent in 1995 over 1994, and discharges for homosexuality for the armed forces overall increased 21 percent.

A navy petty officer, Keith Meinhold, tested the constitutionality of Clinton's redirected policy by declaring his homosexuality on national TV. The navy discharged him immediately. Meinhold sued, won, and was reinstated. The U. S. Court of Appeals for the Fourth Circuit upheld Clinton's policy for gays in the military in a case brought by homosexual service members who challenge the legality of the regulations of Clinton's policy.

Same-Sex Marriage and Custody

While the Supreme Court has long recognized that the right to marry is a fundamental right, the right to a same-sex marriage had been universally rejected by courts until *Baehr v. Miike* in 1996. The Hawaii Circuit Court held that the failure to legalize same-sex marriages violates the Equal Protection Clause of the Hawaii constitution. Anticipating that same-sex marriage would become legal, Congress passed the Defense of Marriage Act (DOMA) in 1996, which defines "marriage" and "spouse" under federal law to include only partners of the opposite sex. This classification excludes same-sex partners from federal benefits. Another provision of DOMA provides is that a state does not have to recognize same-sex marriages performed in other states. This provision will likely be challenged constitutionally on the grounds that it violates the Full Faith and Credit Clause of Article IV, which says that "Full faith and credit shall be given in each state to the public acts, records, and judicial proceedings of every other state." No constitutional challenges to DOMA have been filed in court to date.

Battles for custody and adoption of children follow a similar path. In 1995 a New York Court of Appeals issued a ruling allowing co-parent adoptions.

Then in July, 1998, a New York high court removed two boys from their father's custody because of the father's sexual orientation. The judge ruled the gay household would likely create emotional difficulty for the children.

Health Care

The AIDS epidemic aroused public fear of gay and lesbian citizens. Many insurance companies refused medical coverage to gays. Initially, almost any treatment was exempt from coverage because it was considered experimental. Other insurance company strategies included stretching out the legal process to let the AIDS patient die before a judgment was entered in favor of the patient and a more recent effort to place monetary limits on medical coverage. Lambda filed suit in January of 1998 against Mutual of Omaha to abolish caps on insurance payments with respect to the treatment of HIV and AIDS patients, alleging that the caps violated the federal Americans with Disabilities Act and the Illinois Insurance Code.

Lambda won a case in the New York Court of Appeals that required an insurance company to pay AIDS related disability claims on behalf of a homosexual who had paid premiums for five years. The largest national survey of AIDS policies and education programs in the workplace by the Center for Disease Control revealed in 1996 that nearly half of American worksites had implemented HIV/AIDS workplace policies, and one in six work sites offered their employees education programs that address HIV and AIDS. Nearly all worksites offered group health insurance, although 5 percent limited or excluded HIV from at least one of the policies offered to employees.

City and State Ordinances

In *Romer v. Evans* (1996), one of Lamba's biggest successes, the Supreme Court struck down a Colorado statute that denied certain protections to gays. In 1993, Cincinnati amended its charter to prohibit city government from extending preferential treatment to gays and lesbians. San Francisco's city attorney gathered support from eight other cities to ask the U. S. Supreme Court to invalidate the Cincinnati law and overturn the Sixth Circuit U. S. Court of Appeals decision that upheld the law. In April of 1998, the Fort Collins city council adopted an ordinance that prohibits sexual orientation discrimination in housing, employment and public accommodations.

Opposition

Opposers of the gay and lesbian civil rights movement have accused gays of seeking special treatment and seeking to introduce quotas to employment regulations. Gays serving in the armed forces are typically categorized as representing a security risk. President Clinton's Executive Order was opposed by House representatives who drafted an amendment to the Treasury/Postal Service appropriations bill that would prohibit the expenditure of funds to implement, administer or enforce the order. Other citizen groups such as the Southern Baptist Convention, called on the president to rescind the order.

A key issue argued in courts, in scientific studies and in public debates is whether gay men and women choose to be gay or if it is genetic. In the Supreme Court's first case addressing the constitutional rights of gays and lesbians, *Bowers v. Hardwick* (1986) lawyers supporting gays used choice-affirming arguments and lost.

See also: Civil Rights and Equal Protection

Bibliography and Further Reading
"Americans Growing More Tolerant of Gays." Gallup Organization Press Release, 14 December 1996; Internet, available http://www.gallup.com/poll/news/961214.html.

Carelli, Richard. "Same-Sex Harassment is Illegal High Court Decision Gives First-Ever Remedy To Victims." *The Daily Record* (Baltimore), 5 March, 1998; p. 9.

Hamilton, Heather. "Comment: The Defense of Marriage Act: A Critical Analysis of Its Constitutionality Under the Full Faith and Credit Clause." *DePaul Law Review,* summer 1998.

Kostmayer, Peter H. "Pass the Military Freedom Act of 1992." *Congressional Record,* Daily Ed., 27 July 1992, p.E2265-2266

Lewis, Neil A. "Court Upholds Clinton Policy on Gay Troops." *New York Times,* 6 April 1996; p. 1.

Lovell, Amy. "Other Students Always Used To Say, 'Look at the Dykes': Protecting Students from Peer Sexual Orientation Harassment." *California Law Review,* May 1998.

McGowan, Sharon. "Recent Development: The Fate of ENDA In The Wake of Maine." *Harvard Journal on Legislation,* summer 1998.

Miller, Olivia. "Snapshots of Discrimination." *Workforce Diversity,* spring 1996, pp. 28-31.

Pickhardt, Jonathan. "Note: Choose or Loose: Embracing Theories of Choice in Gay Rights Litigation Strategies." *New York Law Review,* June 1998.

Rosellini, Lynn. "One True Gay Life in the Navy." *U.S. News & World Report,* 6 February 1995; p. 60-1.

Shenon, Philip. "When 'Don't Ask, Don't Tell' Means to Ask and Do Tell All." *New York Times,* 3 March 1996; p. 7.

Varona, Anthony, Kevin Layton, and Christine Clark-Trevino. "Order Offers Equal, Not Special, Protection for Gays." *New Jersey Law Journal,* 6 July 1998; p. 21

BOWERS V. HARDWICK

Legal Citation: 478 U.S. 186 (1986)

Appellant
Michael J. Bowers, Attorney General of Georgia

Appellee
Michael Hardwick

Appellant's Claim
That a state statute making sodomy a criminal offense does not violate the constitutionally protected right to privacy.

Chief Lawyer for Appellant
Michael E. Hobs

Chief Lawyer for Appellee
Laurence Tribe

Justices for the Court
Warren E. Burger, Sandra Day O'Connor, Lewis F. Powell, Jr., William H. Rehnquist, Byron R. White (writing for the Court)

Justices Dissenting
Harry A. Blackmun, William J. Brennan, Jr., Thurgood Marshall, John Paul Stevens

Place
Washington, D.C.

Date of Decision
30 June 1986

Decision
The Supreme Court upheld the Georgia law, reasoning that there is no fundamental right granted to homosexuals to engage in consensual sodomy.

Significance
In *Bowers*, the Supreme Court retreated from its earlier position that consensual sexual activity that is not obscene was protected by a constitutional right to privacy.

Michael Hardwick was a gay Atlanta bartender who was convicted under a Georgia anti-sodomy statute after he was discovered engaging in oral sex with another man. A police officer, who had come to serve Hardwick with a warrant for not having paid a fine for drinking in public, was admitted into Hardwick's home by another tenant who did not know whether Hardwick was there. The police officer then entered Hardwick's bedroom, where he found Hardwick and his partner having sex. Hardwick was arrested and charged with criminal sodomy.

The district attorney decided not to prosecute the case against Hardwick until he had further evidence, but Hardwick brought suit in federal district court challenging the constitutionality of the state law insofar as it made consensual sodomy a criminal offense. After his case was dismissed, he appealed this ruling to the U.S. Court of Appeals for the Eleventh Circuit, which found that the law violated Hardwick's right to privacy and ordered the lower court to try the case. Before the trial could go forward, Michael Bowers, the Georgia attorney general, petitioned the U.S. Supreme Court for a review of the circuit court's ruling.

Justice White wrote the majority opinion for the Court, upholding the Georgia anti-sodomy statute. Although in cases like *Griswold v. Connecticut* (1965; establishing the right of married couples to use contraceptives) and *Roe v. Wade* (1973; establishing a woman's right to abortion) the Court had upheld a constitutional right to privacy where sexual matters were concerned, White now distinguished those precedents from the case before the Court.

> Accepting the decisions in these cases . . . we think it evident that none of the rights announced in those cases bears any resemblance to the claimed constitutional right of homosexuals to engage in acts of sodomy that is asserted in this case. No connection between family, marriage, or procreation on the one hand and homosexual activity on the other has been demonstrated . . . Moreover, any claim that these cases nevertheless stand for the proposition that any kind of private sex-

---

Domestic Partnership Laws

Cities across the United States have established registries allowing couples to gain recognition for their relationships outside of marriage. Registering as a couple is open to heterosexual as well as gay and lesbian partners. Although the formation of these domestic partnerships has yet to be challenged by the courts, registration may provide committed couples with some of the legal benefits previously only given to married couples.

Under a domestic partnership agreement, the terms, definitions, and means of beginning and ending a partnership are spelled out. Many of the requirements for entering into a partnership agreement are very similar to those for marriage.

The partnership provides a recognition of the status of the relationship. In some situations, it may offer a partner new benefits. For example, if the agreement is recognized by one partner's employer, this may allow the other individual a means to obtain health insurance and other benefits previously considered spousal benefits.

Some of the cities offering registration of domestic partnership agreements include Madison, Wisconsin; New York and Ithaca, New York; Ann Arbor, Michigan; Minneapolis, Minnesota; Cambridge, Massachusetts; Atlanta, Georgia; San Francisco, West Hollywood, Sacramento, and Berkeley, California; Hartford, Connecticut; and New Orleans, Louisiana.

Source(s): Model Domestic Partnership, http://www.aclu.org/issues/gay/dpmodel.html.
The National Journal of Sexual Orientation Law, http://sunsite.unc.edu/gaylaw/issue1/becker.html. *New York Times*, 1 August 1993.

---

ual conduct between consenting adults is constitutionally insulated from state proscription is unsupportable.

Powell's Swing Vote Changes the Outcome

Justice Blackmun, dissented bitterly: "The Court's cramped reading of the issue before it makes for a short opinion, but it does little to make for a persuasive one." Blackmun, who was originally to have written the opinion of the Court in *Bowers*, lost that assignment when Justice Powell, who held the swing vote, changed his stance. The opinion was now assigned to White, who favored upholding the anti-sodomy statute.

At first Powell had favored striking down the Georgia statute, but because Hardwick was not to receive any prison time for his offense, Powell could not justify overturning the state law used to convict Hardwick. As Powell saw it, in *Bowers*, the deciding factor was the Eighth Amendment, not the right to privacy. He could not have condoned a prison sentence, which would in this case constitute constitutionally proscribed cruel and unusual punishment. Since there was to be no such punishment, and since he, like White, did not find a constitutional basis for upholding a fundamental right to private consensual homosexual activity, Powell changed his mind. (Powell would later publicly confess that changing his vote in *Bowers* had probably been a mistake.)

Blackmun, who had written the opinion of the Court in the landmark *Roe v. Wade* case, was outraged. Contrary to the majority view, he said, *Bowers* was not about

"a fundamental right to engage in homosexual sodomy . . . Rather, this case is about the most comprehensive of rights and the right most valued by civilized men," namely, "the right to be let alone."

Related Cases

Griswold v. Connecticut, 381 U.S. 479 (1965).
Roe v. Wade, 410 U.S. 113 (1973).

Bibliography and Further Reading

Alderman, Ellen. *The Right to Privacy.* New York: Knopf, 1995.

Amar, Akhil Reed. "Attainder and Amendment 2: Romer's Rightness," *Michigan Law Review*, October 1996, p. 203.

"The Constitutional Status of Sexual Orientation: Homosexuality as a Suspect Classification." *Harvard Law Review*, Vol. 98, 1984, pp. 1285-1309.

De Stefano, George. "The Pleasure Principle: Sex, Backlash, and the Struggle for Gay Freedom." *The Nation*, November 2, 1998, p. 25.

Dripps, Donald A. "A New Era for Gay Rights?" *Trial*, September 1996, p. 18.

Greenawalt, Kent. "Legal Enforcement of Morality." *Journal of Criminal Law and Criminology*, winter 1995, p. 710.

Homosexuality: Debating the Issues. Amherst, NY: Prometheus Books, 1995.

"Impossible to Define?" *The Economist,* May 27, 1995, p. A27.

Koppelman, Andrew. "Sexual Orientation and Human Rights." *Michigan Law Review,* May 1997, p. 1636.

Ponnoru, Ramesh. "Kennedy's Queer Opinion." *National Review,* June 17, 1996, p. 22.

Simon, Norman C. "The Evolution of Lesbian and Gay Rights." *Annual Survey of American Law,* November 1996, p. 105.

"What's Wrong with 'Rights.'" *Harper's Magazine,* June 1996, p. 15.

CAMMERMEYER V. ASPIN

Legal Citation: 850 F.Supp. 910 (1994)

Plaintiff
Margarethe Cammermeyer, Colonel

Defendants
Les Aspin, U.S. Secretary of Defense, et al.

Plaintiff's Claim
That her discharge from service in the National Guard—based solely on her statement that she is a lesbian—was in violation of her constitutional rights.

Chief Lawyers for Plaintiff
Jeffrey I. Tilden, Michael H. Himes, Mary Newcombe

Chief Defense Lawyer
David M. Glass

Judge
Thomas Zilly

Place
Seattle, Washington

Date of Decision
1 June 1994

Decision
Cammermeyer's discharge violated her equal protection and substantive due process rights but not her right to freedom of speech and association.

Significance
As the highest ranking and most highly decorated officer ever to have been discharged for homosexual status from any branch of the U.S. armed forces, Cammermeyer's case represents a milestone for those lesbians and gays who "serve in silence" and for those who support their efforts.

Margarethe Cammermeyer's fitness to serve as a nurse in the U.S. military seemed completely self-evident from her record, which included a Bronze Star for distinguished service in Vietnam. That the government ordered her discharge following her statement that she was a lesbian—and ordered it over the protests of her immediate supervisors and Washington governor Booth Gardner, commander-in-chief of the Washington State National Guard—prompted intense media attention and public debate as to the merits of the military's exclusionary policies.

A Military Discharge

Cammermeyer applied to the Army War College in April of 1989 to receive training to further her career goal of becoming chief nurse of the National Guard Bureau. During a related top secret security check, Cammermeyer—a divorced mother of four who had recently fallen in love with a female artist—was asked to disclose her sexual orientation. She answered that she was a lesbian and afterward initialed a statement explaining, "I am a Lesbian. Lesbianism is an orientation I have, emotional in nature, toward women. It does not imply sexual activity . . ."

The Washington State National Guard decided not to replace Cammermeyer as chief nurse and told her that "unless forced to do so" by the Department of the Army in Washington, D.C., they would not pursue her discharge. The National Guard also gave Cammermeyer the opportunity to resign quietly, which she turned down.

In October, the U.S. Army began proceedings to withdraw Cammermeyer's federal recognition of her state National Guard rank—based on Regulation AR 135-175. The regulation, which had been in effect since 1982, required the discharge from the military of any "member [who] has stated that he/she is a homosexual or bisexual, unless there is a further finding that the member is not a homosexual or bisexual."

Cammermeyer continued to serve as chief nurse, earning superb evaluations, while a military retention board conducted a three-year-long investigation. Although she was given several opportunities to retract her statement, she never did so. Telling the truth, she later explained, "was the very premise of everything I stood for in my entire life and career."

She told the truth again at a two-day hearing before the military retention board in July of 1991. At its conclusion, the board recommended that Cammermeyer's federal recognition be withdrawn. Assuming the recommendation was followed, the state National Guard would soon be forced to discharge Cammermeyer.

Colonel Patsy Thompson, former chief nurse of the National Guard Bureau, was clearly reluctant to make this recommendation. Before reading it, she read another statement on behalf of all its members:

> I truly believe that you are one of the great Americans, Margarethe. And I've admired you for a long time and the work that you've done and all that you've done for the Army National Guard. When I was Chief Nurse, I said many times, I am really glad we have Margarethe Cammermeyer . . . She's doing such an outstanding job. We're really fortunate that she came to us. And I really mean that. And I still do mean that.

Thompson also read statements from "just a few of the people that you've touched in your thirty years of military career," including statements from one nurse who called it "a rare privilege to work under you during your tenure as Chief Nurse" and another who said Cammermeyer's "ability to lead and inspire others was obvious . . ." Nevertheless, she said, it was also her "sad duty" to read the board's official recommendation that Colonel Cammermeyer's federal recognition be withdrawn—an action that would result in her discharge.

Cammermeyer was honorably discharged on 11 June 1992, and she promptly filed a suit against the U.S. Army in the U.S. District Court, Seattle, Washington.

Summary Judgment

Cammermeyer and the U.S. government filed cross-motions for summary judgment in the case and presented oral arguments as to these motions on 20 April 1994. The court granted Cammermeyer's motion for summary judgment regarding her Fifth Amendment equal protection and substantive due process claims.

The court also granted the government's motion for summary judgment regarding all of Cammermeyer's other claims. A motion for summary judgment is granted where there is no factual dispute or where there is a "need to weigh the evidence at issue" and "the party is entitled to a judgment as a matter of law." In such cases, the court bases its ruling on the already accumulated and undisputed record, without hearing further oral argument.

Reviewing the documentation concerning Cammermeyer's service and discharge, as well as the precedent

Margarethe Cammermeyer appears at a news conference in Seattle, 1994. © AP/Wide World Photos.

set by other courts with regard to the military and homosexuals, the court found that homosexuals were not, like members of a race, nationality, or religious group, a suspect class for equal protection purposes. Neither, District Judge Thomas Zilly wrote, were their equal protection claims subject to the heightened security accorded those who face discrimination based on gender. For a law that discriminates against homosexuals to survive an equal protection claim, Zilly wrote, it need only be found rationally related to a legitimate purpose.

Legitimate But Not Rational

The court found that the government's stated purpose, to "maintain the readiness and combat effectiveness of its armed forces," was indeed a legitimate one. It did not, however, agree that discharging Cammermeyer was rationally related to this goal. Dismissing the government's claim that homosexuality is "incompati[ble] with military service and interfere[s] with military mission," Zilly noted that in "Canada, Australia, France, Israel, Spain, Sweden, the Netherlands, Denmark, Finland, Norway, and Japan," homosexuals serve without incident. He also cited several studies commissioned by the U.S. government that found "the presence of homosexuals in the military is not an issue and has not created problems in the functioning of military units."

The court was likewise persuaded by evidence refuting the government's claims that homosexual service would damage discipline, good order, and morale; unit cohesion; heterosexual privacy; and its ability to recruit and retain military personnel. After dismissing these arguments, Zilly turned to polling results indicating that "40 to 79 percent of the public favors allowing homosexuals to serve in the military." However, Zilly wrote, "to the extent public disapproval of homosexual service in the military is based on prejudice, such disapproval would not be a legitimate basis for the government's policy."

Finally, Zilly cited Cammermeyer herself as the strongest argument against the government's contention that homosexuality was not compatible with military service:

> Certainly, the undisputed evidence in this case relating to Colonel Cammermeyer's service strongly supports the conclusion that acknowledged homosexuality is not incompatible with military service. Cammermeyer served in the Army and the Washington State National Guard with distinction. She was a highly trained, decorated and dedicated officer in the military . . . After she disclosed her lesbian status in April 1989, she continued to perform her military duties for over three years until her discharge. Her final evaluation, dated July 31, 1992 . . . described her as having continued to serve the Washington Army National Guard "with dedicated professionalism." It is ironic that after over three years as an acknowledged homosexual servicemember, Cammermeyer was evaluated as having "the potential to assume responsibility at NGB level as Chief Nurse," yet she was discharged because of the alleged incompatibility of her sexual orientation with military service.

The court set aside Cammermeyer's claim that the "Constitution confers a fundamental right of privacy upon a person to be a homosexual," saying that it did not need to decide this question in order to resolve her claim. "The court," Zilly wrote, "has already held that the Army regulation challenged here is based solely on prejudice. As such, it cannot withstand even rational basis review. Regulations based solely on prejudice are irrational as a matter of law and serve no legitimate governmental purpose."

The district court ordered that Cammermeyer be reinstated to her former position with all the rights, honors, and privileges accorded an officer of her rank. That order has been stayed pending the government's appeal, and Cammermeyer currently works in a civilian position at a veterans' hospital.

Impact

Since *Cammermeyer* the military has adopted a "don't ask, don't tell" (DADT) policy toward homosexuals in the military. The policy was instituted as a result of a compromise between those who wanted to lift the ban on gays in the military and those who wanted to preserve it. President Clinton forced the compromise by bringing the issue to the nation's attention when he pledged to lift the ban after his election in 1992. His proposal was met with considerable resistance by conservatives which resulted in the compromise. Specifically, the new policy prohibits the military from inquiring into the sexual orientation of military personnel without specific cause. However, the policy reserves the right to the military to discharge homosexuals if their behavior undermines military capability—specifically, unit cohisiveness. In *Thomasson v. Perry* (1996) the federal courts ruled that the DADT policy did not violate an individual's Fifth Amendment equal protection rights or an individual's First Amendment freedom of speech rights. Both gay activists and military traditionalists seem discontented by the compromise policy. However, for the time being, the courts and policy makers see it as the only amicable solution.

Related Cases
Meinhold v. U.S. Dept. of Defense, 34 F.3d 1469 (1994).
McVeigh v. Cohen, 983 F.Supp. 215 (1997).

Bibliography and Further Reading
Cammermeyer, Margarethe, with Chris Fisher. *Service in Silence*. New York: Viking, 1994.

"Lesbians, Long Overlooked, Are Central to Debate on Military Ban." *New York Times*, 4 May 1993.

Shenon, Philip. "Armed Forces Still Question Homosexuals." *New York Times*, 27 February 1996.

Shilts, Randy. *Conduct Unbecoming*. New York: St. Martin's Press, 1993.

ROMER V. EVANS

Legal Citation: 517 U.S. 620 (1996)

Petitioner
Roy Romer, Governor of Colorado, et al.

Respondent
Richard G. Evans, et al.

Petitioner's Claim
That the lower court erred in striking down a Colorado constitutional amendment that prohibited any government efforts to protect homosexuals from discrimination.

Chief Lawyer for Petitioner
Timothy M. Tymkovich

Chief Lawyer for Respondent
Jean E. Dubofsky

Justices for the Court
Stephen Breyer, Ruth Bader Ginsburg, Anthony M. Kennedy (writing for the Court), Sandra Day O'Connor, David H. Souter, John Paul Stevens

Justices Dissenting
William H. Rehnquist, Antonin Scalia, Clarence Thomas

Place
Washington, D.C.

Date of Decision
20 May 1996

Decision
Denied the petitioner's claim, affirming the unconstitutionality of the state amendment.

Significance
For the first time, the Supreme Court gave homosexuals constitutional protection against government or private discrimination. The issue, however, spurred emotional debate on both sides, promising future legal battles over the rights of gays and lesbians.

For hundreds of years, most homosexuals in America kept their sexuality hidden. Religious teachings condemned their behavior, and state and local laws made homosexual acts illegal. Then came the Stonewall riots. On 27 June 1969, New York police raided the Stonewall Inn, a gay bar in Greenwich Village, just as police across America had raided other gay bars before. But this time, the people inside the Stonewall clashed with the police. For the next three nights, gays rioted in New York, releasing years of pent-up frustration over their legal and social persecution.

From that point on, gays and lesbians grew more outspoken in their quest for tolerance. A year after the Stonewall riots, 5,000 homosexuals marched in New York City to commemorate the event. The movement for equality grew during the 1970s and 1980s, and in 1987, more than half-a-million gays and lesbians rallied in Washington, D.C. to demand fair legal treatment.

At that time, however, the Supreme Court had just dealt the gay rights movement a major setback. In *Bowers v. Hardwick* (1986), the Court refused to grant gays a constitutional right of privacy to engage in homosexual acts. The ruling upheld a Georgia law, and similar laws in more than 20 states, that made sodomy a crime. Homosexuals also faced growing vocal opposition from some religious groups and others concerned about public morality. Colorado became the first legal battleground between gays and their detractors, as state voters approved an amendment denying gays and lesbians protection from discrimination.

Amendment 2—An Effort to End "Special" Rights for Homosexuals

To support gay rights, some Colorado communities, including Denver and Boulder, passed local ordinances that prohibited discrimination because of a person's sexual orientation. The ordinance applied to practices in employment, housing, and education. In 1992, a group called Colorado for Family Values felt they had to take a stand against the increasing legal tolerance of homosexuality. The group led an effort to amend the state constitution so the existing anti-discrimination laws would be repealed. Their proposed amendment

Roy Romer, Governor of Colorado, in 1992. © Photograph by Joseph Sohm. ChromoSohn Inc./Corbis.

would also prohibit any future attempts to protect the legal status of homosexuals based on their sexual orientation. In November, Colorado voters approved the ballot measure, known as Amendment 2.

Soon after the election, Richard Evans, a gay municipal worker in Denver, and other homosexuals, went to court to stop Amendment 2 from going into effect. The trial court issued a preliminary injunction, which the state appealed to the Colorado Supreme Court. The supreme court said the amendment denied gays the right to participate in the political process; the court supported the injunction and ordered the case back to the trial court. After hearing arguments, the trial court ruled that the state could not enforce the amendment, and the state supreme court once again upheld the lower court. The U.S. Supreme Court then agreed to hear the case.

The Court's membership had changed considerably in the ten years since the last major case addressing homosexual rights; only three sitting justices had heard *Bowers v. Hardwick*. In certain ways, some legal experts thought, the Court in 1996 was more conservative than it had been in 1986. But by a clear 6-3 majority, the Court ruled that Amendment 2 was unconstitutional, as it denied homosexuals their right to equal protection as guaranteed in the Fourteenth Amendment.

The state of Colorado had argued that Amendment 2 was merely taking back special rights that the local ordinances granted to homosexuals. Justice Kennedy, who wrote the decision, strongly disagreed:

> We cannot accept the view that Amendment 2's prohibition on specific legal protections

does no more than deprive homosexuals of special rights. To the contrary, the amendment imposes a special disability upon those persons alone. Homosexuals are forbidden the safeguards that others enjoy or may seek without constraint . . . We find nothing special in the protections Amendment 2 withholds. These are protections taken for granted by most people either because they already have them or do not need them; these are protections against exclusion from an almost limitless number of transactions and endeavors that constitute ordinary civic life in a free society.

Kennedy also noted that Amendment 2 failed to meet any "rational relationship to some legitimate end," a standard the Court had previously used in addressing issues of equal protection. Amendment 2, it seemed to him, was "born of animosity toward the class of persons affected."

Skirmish in the "Cultural War"

Kennedy's decision did not mention *Bowers v. Hardwick*, but Justice Scalia relied on that precedent in his dissent, which was joined by Chief Justice Rehnquist and Justice Thomas. "If it is constitutionally permissible," Scalia wrote, "for a State to make homosexual conduct criminal, surely it is constitutionally permissible for a State to enact other laws merely *disfavoring* homosexual conduct."

Scalia, known for his sometimes caustic style, harshly criticized Kennedy's decision. He said the majority's reasoning was ". . . long on emotive utterance and . . . short on legal citation." He also argued that the Court was getting involved in a "cultural war" about toleration for homosexuals that was best left to the voters and the legislatures, not the courts.

To *Washington Post* reporter Joan Biskupic, the strong words in both decisions "went to the core of a passionate social debate playing out in legislatures and living rooms . . ." across America. Homosexual organizations cheered the ruling. "This is the most important victory ever for lesbian and gay rights," said Suzanne Goldberg, one of the lawyers who helped scuttle Amendment 2. Some conservative groups were not as pleased. Gary Bauer of the Family Research Council said, "This is not an ending point . . . this creates a pressure cooker atmosphere."

Related Cases
Shelley v. Kraemer, 334 U.S. 1 (1948).
Sweatt v. Painter, 339 U.S. 629 (1950).
Reynolds v. Sims, 377 U.S. 533 (1964).
Brandenburg v. Ohio, 395 U.S. 444 (1969).
Personnel Administrator of Massachusetts v. Feeney, 442 U.S. 256 (1979).
Bowers v. Hardwick, 478 U.S. 186 (1986).

Bibliography and Further Reading
Amar, Akhil Reed. "Attainder and Amendment 2: Romer's Rightness." *Michigan Law Review,* October 1996, p. 203.

Arkes, Holly. "Odd Couples: The Defense of Marriage Act Will Firm Up the Authority of the States to Reject Gay Marriage." *National Review,* August 12, 1996, p. 48.

Balkin, J.M. "The Constitution of Status." *Yale Law Journal,* June 1997, p. 2313.

Dripps, Donald A. "A New Era for Gay Rights?" *Trial,* September 1996, p. 18.

Foner, Eric, and John Garraty, eds. *The Reader's Companion to American History.* Boston: Houghton Mifflin, 1991.

"Gay Justice." *The Nation,* June 10, 1996, p. 4.

Hall, Kermit L., ed. *The Oxford Companion to the Supreme Court of the United States.* New York: Oxford Press, 1992.

Hellman, Deborah. "Two Types of Discrimination: The Familiar and the Forgotten." *California Law Review,* March 1998, p. 315.

Hills, Roderick M., Jr. "Is Amendment 2 Really a Bill of Attainder? Some Questions About Professor Amar's Analysis of Romer." *Michigan Law Review,* October 1996, p. 236.

Kaplan, David A., and Daniel Klaidman. "A Battle, Not the War." *Newsweek,* June 3, 1996, p. 24.

The New York Times. May 21, 1996; May 26, 1996.

Sullivan, Kathleen M. "Decisions Expand Equal Protections Rights." *The National Law Journal,* July 29, 1996, p. C7.

"A Victory for Rationality: Homosexuals." *The Economist,* May 25, 1996, p. 30.

The Washington Post. May 21, 1996.

BAEHR V. MIIKE

Legal Citation: 950 P.2d 1234 (1996)

Plaintiffs
Ninia Baehr, Genora Dancel, Tammy Rodrigues, Antoinette Pregil, Pat Lagon, and Joseph Melillo

Defendant
Lawrence H. Miike, Director of Hawaii Department of Health

Plaintiffs' Claim
That the use of a Hawaii statute to forbid marriages by partners of the same sex violated the Equal Protection Clause of the Hawaii Constitution.

Chief Lawyer for Plaintiffs
Daniel R. Foley

Chief Defense Lawyer
Rick J. Eichor, Deputy Attorney General of Hawaii

Judge
Kevin S. C. Chang, Judge of the First Circuit Court, State of Hawaii

Place
Honolulu, Hawaii

Date of Decision
3 December 1996

Decision
That the application of Hawaii Revised Statute 572-1 to deny a marriage contract to same-sex partners violated the Equal Protection Clause of the Hawaii Constitution, and was therefore invalid.

Significance
For centuries, societies throughout the world had operated on the assumption that the only valid legal marriage contract could be one between a man and a woman. *Baehr v. Miike* challenged this principle, and became a ruling with the potential to rival the impact of landmark U.S. Supreme Court decisions such as *Brown v. Board of Education* (1954) or *Roe v. Wade* (1973).

Same Sex Marriages

In December of 1990, three couples living in Honolulu, Hawaii applied for marriage licenses. But these were no ordinary couples. Ninia Baehr and Genora Dancel were both women; so too were Tammy Rodrigues and Antoinette Pregil—and the third couple, Pat Lagon and Joseph Melillo, were both men. The state department of health denied their applications, citing Hawaii Revised Statute 572-1, which according to the department implicitly defines a legally binding marriage as one between a man and a woman. The three couples filed suit against the state, naming John Lewin, then director of the department, as defendant. The case thus began its life as *Baehr v. Lewin,* but in the course of its long legal existence Baehr was replaced by Lawrence H. Miike, and the case was accordingly renamed as *Baehr v. Miike* on 23 April 1996. In any event, Miike was no more the target of this suit than had been Dallas County District Attorney Henry Wade in *Roe v. Wade.* In both instances, it was not the men themselves who were under challenge, but the laws which they upheld through their offices.

Under Hawaii law, the case went to a state circuit court. That court dismissed the suit in October of 1991, and the plaintiffs appealed to the Hawaii Supreme Court. The suit charged that the department's application of 572-1 violated the plaintiffs' rights under both the Right to Privacy and the Equal Protection Clauses of the Hawaii Constitution. The high court struck down the first of these challenges, but agreed with the plaintiffs on the second. "[B]y its plain language," the court held, "the Hawaii Constitution prohibits state-sanctioned discrimination against any person in the exercise of his or her civil rights on the basis of sex." The court held that 572-1 presented a sex-based classification—which was prohibited under the Hawaii Equal Protection Clause—rather than a classification with regard to homosexuality, which was not specifically addressed in the clause. Perhaps it was true that society defined marriage as being between a man and a woman, the court suggested, but until the Supreme Court struck it down in *Loving v. Commonwealth of Virginia* (1967), that Southern state had in place a law which held marriage between people of different races to be unnatural. If a race-based classification could be invalidated, so too could a gender-based rule.

The Burden of Proof Is on the State

Following its 1993 ruling, the state supreme court remanded the case to the circuit court. Because the high court had found reason to agree with the plaintiff's contentions regarding the unconstitutionality of 572-1's application in the present case, Hawaii law dictated that now it was incumbent on the defendant to prove its use of the statute constitutional. In other words, the burden of proof was on the director of the Department of Health to demonstrate that his forbidding any marriages other than opposite-sex unions "furthers compelling state interests and is narrowly drawn to avoid unnecessary abridgments of constitutional rights." Originally scheduled for September of 1995, the circuit court trial was postponed due to a vote on same-sex marriage laws in the state legislature. The legislative session, however, failed to produce any changes in the laws, and the case finally came before Judge Kevin S. C. Chang of the First Circuit Court of Hawaii in September of 1996.

By now the case had generated considerable attention, and numerous entities filed *amici curiae* briefs. The lines were sharply drawn: on one side were the Christian Legal Society, the Hawaii Catholic Society, and the Mormon Church, which filed briefs for the defendant along with eleven states; on the other were the American Civil Liberties Union (ACLU), along with Lambda, a legal defense fund for gay rights. Several other groups filed briefs.

As the trial began, Miike held that he would prove five "compelling state interests" behind 572-1:

> protecting the health and welfare of children and other persons . . . fostering procreation within a marital setting . . . securing or assuring recognition of Hawaii marriages in other jurisdictions . . . protecting the State's public fisc [treasury] from the reasonably foreseeable effects of State approval of same-sex marriage in the laws of Hawaii . . . [and] protecting civil liberties, including the reasonably foreseeable effects of State approval of same-sex marriages, on its citizens.

Most significant among these, from the defendant's pre-trial memorandum, was the first. To support his position that legalized same-sex marriages would have an adverse effect on children, he presented testimony from four expert witnesses.

Both Sides Marshal Their Experts

The first of the state's four expert witnesses was Kyle D. Pruett, M.D., a psychiatrist specializing in child

Circuit Court Judge Kevin Chang listens to the opening statement made by Deputy Attorney General Rick Eichor. © Photograph by Tony Stringer. AP/Wide World Photos.

development. Pruett had conducted a ten-year study, beginning in 1981, in which he assessed the development of children raised primarily by their fathers in an intact, two-parent household of the traditional kind. His study produced significant findings to uphold the notion that the best possible environment in which to raise a child was one in which two biological parents remained married. Yet he also stated that same-sex parents can and do raise emotionally healthy children, an observation garnered from his own clinical experience, and he believed that same-sex couples should be able to adopt children. If two parents provided a child with a nurturing environment, he indicated, this was a more important factor in their development than the genders of the two parents in question.

The state next called David Eggebeen, Ph.D., a sociologist whose work focused on demographic issues relating to families and children. Families were changing, Dr. Eggebeen testified: the marriage rate was going down, along with the birth rate; but the median age of marriage for women was rising, as was the divorce rate, the number of young adults living together outside of marriage, the birth rate for unwed mothers, and the

Attorney Dan Foley listens to the opening statement. Joseph Melillo and Pat Lagon listen in the background. © AP/Wide World Photos.

number of women in the labor force. Nonetheless, six out of ten children were still being raised in homes with both biological parents, and Eggebeen testified that children raised in a single-parent home are at a "heightened risk" for problems such as poor grades and teenage pregnancy. Step-parents were no substitute for biological parents, he held, and a same-sex marriage—where obviously at least one of the parents had no biological relation to the child—was equivalent to a step-parent situation. Yet there were exceptions to this proposition, and Eggebeen agreed that same-sex parents ought to be able to adopt children. He also testified that children of same-sex marriages would benefit if their parents received the legal privileges that went with legal union, including income tax advantages, public assistance, enforcement of alimony and child support, inheritance rights, and the right to prosecute wrongful death actions.

Judge Chang found the third witness to be problematic. Richard Williams, Ph.D., was a psychologist specializing in statistical analysis, but he questioned many of the basic precepts governing the discipline of psychology. He held that the majority of studies in the social sciences had inherent flaws of theory and methodology, and therefore Judge Chang did not place much weight on his contentions regarding studies of same-sex parents. "At times," Chang wrote, "Dr. Williams expressed severe views. For instance, Dr. Williams believes that there is no scientific proof that evolution occurred." Moreover, Williams "admitted that his critique of studies regarding gay and lesbian parenting is a minority position."

Finally, the state called Thomas S. Merrill, Ph.D., a psychologist whose areas of expertise included human development, gender development, and relationships relevant to the development of children. Merrill had limited clinical experience with gay and lesbian parents, however, and he offered no opinion as to the development of children in families with parents of the same sex. However, he did testify that the sexual orientation of a parent is not an indicator of that person's fitness as a parent, and that same-sex couples with children do manage to be successful parents.

Given that the burden of proof was on the defendant, the plaintiffs were under no requirement to produce experts of their own. Nonetheless, they called four as well: Pepper Schwartz, Ph.D.; Charlotte Patterson, Ph.D.; David Brodzinsky, Ph.D.; and Robert Bidwell, M.D. The court cited the testimonies of Drs. Schwartz and Brodzinsky as "especially credible." The former, a sociologist with expertise in the areas of gender, sexuality, and the human family, held that the nurturing relationship between parent and child was more important to the child's development than either the parenting structure or biology. Brodzinsky, a psychologist whose focus was on adoption and other forms of non-biological parenting, Judge Chang wrote, "expressed his strong view regarding the issue of whether there is a best family environment [in which] to raise children." Answering a question on his view' regarding the state's position that "we somehow need to identify a best family for children," Brodzinsky replied, "I find that offensive truthfully." He called this idea "a distortion of the research literature."

In his Specific Findings with regard to the case, Judge Chang found that the defendant had failed to provide sufficient evidence to establish any of his claims. From the testimony of his experts—not to mention those of the plaintiffs—it seemed clear that the nurturing relationship was more important than the structure of the marriage; that a parent's sexual orientation was not necessarily an indicator of his or her ability to raise children; and that gay parents could raise children as happy and well-adjusted as those of their heterosexual counterparts. Furthermore, gay and lesbian couples in Hawaii were already allowed to adopt children and provide foster care. Far from proving the defendant's contention that same-sex marriage would adversely effect children, Judge Chang held, the testimony had shown that those children would stand to gain if their parents were accorded the benefits associated with traditional marriages.

A Landmark Ruling—And a Reaction

Judge Chang, as the sole judge and "trier of fact" in this case, had full power to decide its outcome. He held that the state department of health's use of 572-1 did establish a sex-based classification which denied gay and lesbian couples the rights and privileges accorded to heterosexual couples. In *Dean v. District of Columbia*, a 1995 case in which the District of Columbia Court of Appeals supported the District's refusal to issue a marriage license to a gay couple, one judge who dissented in part wrote that

> if the government cannot cite actual prejudice to the public majority from a change in the law to allow same-sex marriages . . . then the public majority will not have a sound basis for claiming a compelling, or even a substantial, state interest in withholding the marriage statute from same-sex couples; a mere feeling of distaste or even revulsion at what someone

is or does . . . cannot justify inherently discriminatory legislation . . .

The defendant, Judge Chang wrote, had failed in the present case to show compelling evidence that such "prejudice or harm" to the majority would result from allowing same-sex marriages. Even if he had established this, however, the defendant had not shown sufficient proof that 572-1 was "narrowly tailored to avoid unnecessary abridgements of constitutional rights."

Hence the circuit court ruled the sex-based classification in 572-1 unconstitutional under the Equal Protection Clause of Article I, section 5 of the Hawaii Constitution. The defendant and his agents were enjoined from denying any marriage applications solely on the basis of the sex of both applicants. Finally, all costs of the trial were, to the extent permitted by law, imposed against the defendant and awarded in favor of the plaintiffs.

The victory for the plaintiffs in *Baehr,* however, was only another step in a long process. Because of the massive upheaval that would undoubtedly ensue from his ruling, Judge Chang stayed enforcement of the judgment pending the state's appeal to the Hawaii Supreme Court. The reason for this was that if the high court reversed the ruling, marriages would be rendered at least temporarily invalid until the case could be decided. The fight continued in the legislature, where various measures both upholding and challenging gay marriages were raised, and in November of 1998, Hawaii voters were presented with a ballot for a proposed constitutional amendment which would allow the legislature to reserve legal marriages to opposite-sex couples. As for the state's appeal in *Baehr v. Miike,* as of mid-1998, all briefs had been submitted to the state supreme court. People in Hawaii, and in the rest of the nation, awaited its ruling.

Impact

In his Conclusions of Law, Judge Chang had noted the possible ramifications of *Baehr* in light of Article IV, section 1 of the U.S. Constitution, which provides in part that states must recognize the "public acts, records and judicial proceedings of every other State." The question of whether other states would recognize or refuse to recognize same-sex marriages made in Hawaii was an important one: if a couple were married in Hawaii, then moved to a state which did not recognize same-sex marriages, they would be denied the rights Hawaii had conferred on them. Such a controversy would undoubtedly require a decision by the Supreme Court. Throughout 1997 and 1998, a number of related issues arose across corners of the nation: *Baker v. Vermont,* a case in that state which became the second legal challenge to different-sex marriage laws; an action in a California federal court regarding a San Francisco domestic partnership ordinance; and an Alaska court's decision to allow a same-sex marriage lawsuit to proceed. In mid-1998, the *Baehr* controversy simmered, with the ever-present potential to ignite into a legal battle in the nation's highest court. Both sides could at least agree on one thing about *Baehr*: it was, to borrow a term from television cliffhangers, "to be continued."

Related Cases
Loving v. Commonwealth of Virginia, 388 U.S. 1 (1967).
Dean v. District of Columbia, 653 A.2d 307 (1995).

Bibliography and Further Reading
Bradley, Gerard V. "Marriage Penalty: The Union of Gay Couples in Hawaii Implies Not an Expansion of Marriage—But Its End." *National Review,* 26 January 1998.

Homer, Steven K. "Against Marriage." *Harvard Civil Rights-Civil Liberties Law Review,* summer, 1994, pp. 505-530.

Koppelman, Andrew. "Why Discrimination Against Lesbians and Gay Men Is Sex Discrimination." *New York University Law Review,* May 1994, pp. 197-287.

Kramer, Larry. "Same-Sex Marriage, Conflict of Laws, and the Unconstitutional Public Policy Exception." *Yale Law Journal,* May 1997, pp. 1965-2008.

Mawyer, Martin. "The Case Against Gay Marriages." *Gannett News Service,* 25 September 1995.

"The Test-Case Countries." *Nation,* 2 August 1997.

Wilson, James Q. "Against Homosexual Marriage." *Commentary,* 1 March 1996.

McVeigh v. Cohen

Legal Citation: 983 F.Supp. 215 (1998)

One of the first issues approached by President Bill Clinton after his inauguration in January of 1993 was the question of gays in the military. For years, of course, homosexual males and females had served in the armed forces without announcing their sexual orientation. After President Clinton was elected, he and various activist groups wanted to gain full recognition for gays in the military. This would include the benefits that would accrue to domestic partners, and would prevent the military services from discharging members on the basis of sexual orientation. After a long and bitter fight between the president, the military, and Congress, the various sides reached a compromise known popularly as "Don't Ask, Don't Tell"; or, as Judge Sporkin characterized it in *McVeigh v. Cohen*, "Don't Ask, Don't Tell, Don't Pursue." This meant that the military would not ask personnel about their sexual orientation, and personnel would not volunteer information—or, presumably, make any overt displays of their sexuality. Neither side would pursue the issue without provocation. Few were entirely happy with this "solution," but it seemed reasonably fair, relying as it did on the good behavior of both parties. At the time, however, some observers considered a conflict inevitable, as one side or another would overstep the boundaries.

"Boysrch"—or, the *Other Timothy McVeigh*

Ever since the Oklahoma City bombing of 19 April 1995, the name "Timothy McVeigh" has been highly recognizable—so much so that the judge in *McVeigh v. Cohen* began his ruling by referring to "Plaintiff Timothy R. McVeigh, who bears no relation to the Oklahoma City bombing defendant . . ." In addition to his name and its unfortunate connotation, U.S. Navy Senior Chief Timothy McVeigh had at least one other problem in his life: he was a highly decorated noncommissioned officer in the navy, but if his superiors had reason to believe he was gay, he could be discharged. If McVeigh continued in the military for another three years, he would be eligible to retire with outstanding benefits; but if he suffered a less than honorable discharge, he would have little to show for his 17 years of service. There was no reason, however, to reveal his sexual orientation, if indeed he was gay: under the "Don't Ask, Don't Tell"

Plaintiff
Timothy R. McVeigh

Defendant
William Cohen, U.S. Secretary of Defense, et al.

Plaintiff's Claim
That by investigating his sexual orientation, the navy violated his rights under the Electronic Communications Privacy Act of 1996, the Administrative Procedure Act, Department of Defense policy, and the Fourth and Fifth Amendments to the U.S. Constitution; therefore, he sought that the Navy be enjoined from its attempts to discharge him.

Chief Lawyer for Plaintiff
Christopher Wolf

Chief Defense Lawyer
David Glass

Judge
U.S. District Judge Stanley Sporkin

Place
Washington, D.C.

Date of Decision
26 January 1998

Decision
That plaintiff's case passed a four-part test for preliminary injunction, and the defendants were preliminarily enjoined from taking any adverse action against the defendant on the basis of his alleged sexual orientation, pending final resolution of the plaintiff's complaint.

Significance
This case attempted to deal with the new policy of "Don't Ask, Don't Tell" and its constitutionality.

*Timothy R. McVeigh,
U.S. Navy Senior Chief
Petty Officer.
© AP/Wide World
Photos.*

policy, McVeigh was under no compunction to make a statement as to his preferences, nor was the navy free to pry into his personal life.

Then on 2 September 1997, McVeigh sent a fateful electronic mail, or e-mail, message through the America Online Service (AOL). The note was a response to a request from Helen Hajne, a civilian coordinating a drive to collect toys for children of U.S.S. *Chicago* crew members. McVeigh, who served on the *Chicago,* a submarine, sent her a note under the alias "boysrch@aol.com," and signed it "Tim." Hajne, also an AOL subscriber, searched the alias on the member directory and discovered that "boysrch" was named Tim; worked for the military; and lived in Honolulu, Hawaii. There was no further information as to his full name, address, or

phone number; however, "Tim" listed his marital status as "gay," and included among his interests "boy watching" and "collecting pics of other young studs."

Hajne's husband, like McVeigh, was a non-commissioned officer aboard the *Chicago,* and after she passed the e-mail message and profile to him, the materials ultimately made their way to the desk of Commander John Mickey. The latter, the equivalent of a general in the army, served as captain of the ship—and McVeigh's commanding officer. He passed the evidence to Lieutenant Karin S. Morean, the principal legal adviser for the ship and a member of the JAG (Judge Advocate General's) Corp. By this point, the navy suspected McVeigh as the "Tim" who had written the note, but just to make sure, Morean asked a Navy paralegal, Legalman First Class Joseph M. Kaiser, to contact AOL. When Kaiser called AOL's toll-free number, he spoke with a technical services representative. Without identifying himself as a member of the navy—let alone of its legal corps— Kaiser told the AOL representative that he had received a fact sheet, and wanted to confirm a member's profile. His intention, as per Morean's orders, was to connect "boysrch" with the user profile which McVeigh had filled out under his own name; and indeed, the AOL representative confirmed that "boysrch" and McVeigh were one and the same.

After receiving this verification, Morean contacted McVeigh to inform him that the navy had obtained an indication that he had made "a statement of homosexuality" in violation of the "Don't Ask, Don't Tell" policy. She advised him of his right to remain silent in relation to the military's prohibition against "sodomy and indecent acts" covered in the Uniform

---

Electronic Communications Privacy Act of 1986

The Electronic Communications Privacy Act (ECPA) began as an "anti-wiretapping" law, and was intended to curtail the government's ability to wiretap telephone conversations without the consent of the parties. The need for this protection from government eavesdropping became clear after the Watergate scandal during President Nixon's administration in the 1960s. The original act demanded a "judicial warrant" be issued before telephone conversations could be intercepted.

In 1986, President Reagan signed the ECPA extending the areas of protection. In addition to previous provisions against government wiretapping of telephones, all types of electronic communications are protected from eavesdropping. No data or voice transmissions may legally be listened in on by any individual or business. In addition to public and private telecommunica-

tions carriers and computer transmittals, also included are communications transmitted on pagers, electronic mail (e-mail), and cell phones. The act also prohibits "unauthorized access" to any stored messages on a server, as well as prohibiting the "interception" of any communications in process.

Some limitations in the act may allow an employer to review an employee's e-mail, or a system operator to turn over information to authorities if an e-mail message suggests illegal activity.

Source(s): http://www.digitalcentury.com/encyclo/
update/ecpa.html
http://www.wsrv.clas.virginia.edu/~klb6q/
infopaper/ECPA.html.

Code of Military Justice (UCMJ). Soon afterward, on 22 September 1997, the navy informed McVeigh that it had commenced an "administrative separation," or discharge proceedings, on the basis of his "homosexual conduct, as evidenced by your statement that you are a homosexual."

Six weeks later, on 7 November 1997, the navy conducted a discharge hearing before a three-member board. McVeigh testified regarding his e-mail message to Hajne, thus implicitly identifying himself as its author, but also presented evidence that he had been involved in several heterosexual relationships—including an engagement to one woman. Nonetheless, the board ruled that the navy had sufficient evidence to charge McVeigh with "homosexual conduct." This being a dischargeable offense, the navy further accelerated its proceedings to make McVeigh's discharge final at 5:00 a.m. Eastern Standard Time on Friday, 16 January 1998.

The day before this was to happen, however, McVeigh commenced his lawsuit in U.S. District Court, naming Defense Secretary William Cohen as defendant. The navy put off his separation until Wednesday, 20 January. On Wednesday morning the court held a hearing at which the navy initially refused to honor the judge's request for more time to consider the case. It rescheduled the discharge to take place on Friday, 23 January. But on 22 January, the navy told the court that it would give it until Tuesday, 27 January, to make a decision on the case. If a decision was not made before that date, McVeigh would be removed from service. The court, in the person of Judge Stanley Sporkin, made its ruling on 26 January.

Judge Sporkin Rules

In order to be granted his request for preliminary injunction—that is, for the court to order the navy to stop its discharge proceedings—McVeigh had to show four things, in Judge Sporkin's words: "1) a substantial likelihood of success on the merits; 2) irreparable harm or injury absent an injunction; 3) less harm or injury to the other parties involved; and 4) the service of the public interest." It was Judge Sporkin's holding that McVeigh met all four conditions, and for that reason the court granted a preliminary injunction barring his discharge.

Of the four criteria, Judge Sporkin devoted the most attention to the first: McVeigh's chances of winning on the merits of his case. "As its core," Judge Sporkin wrote,

the Plaintiff's complaint is with the Navy's compliance, or lack thereof, with its new regulations under the 'Don't Ask, Don't Tell, Don't Pursue' policy. Plaintiff contends that he did not 'tell,' as prescribed by the statute, but

William Cohen, U.S. Secretary of Defense, 1998. © Photograph by David Longstreath. AP/Wide World Photos.

that nonetheless, the navy impermissibly 'asked' and zealously 'pursued.'

The guidelines governing that policy required that a commander receive "credible information" regarding sexual orientation, not "just a belief or suspicion." Credible information would include the testimony of "a reliable person" that he or she had directly observed an act or statement by the person which "a reasonable person would believe was intended to convey the fact that he or she engages in or has a propensity or intent to engage in homosexual acts." In the present case, the navy had nothing more than an e-mail message and a user profile which it merely suspected were authored by the plaintiff.

Still addressing the first of the four criteria, Judge Sporkin made it clear that its lack of "credible information" was not as important as the fact that the navy had "affirmatively [taken] steps to confirm the identity of the e-mail responders" and thus "violated the very essence of 'Don't Ask, Don't Pursue' by launching a search and destroy mission." Not only did this violate the "Don't Pursue" policy, it was in violation of the Electronic Communications Privacy Act (ECPA) of 1996. The latter, passed by Congress in response to fears over privacy on the Internet, gave the government authority to obtain information from an online service provider such as AOL only if it had obtained a warrant, had given the subscriber notice of its intentions, and had issued a subpoena or received a court order authorizing its action.

Judge Sporkin concluded the "Substantial Likelihood of Success on the Merits" section of his four-part test with a stern rebuke of the navy:

> this court . . . cannot understand why the Navy would seek to discharge an officer who has served his country in a distinguished manner just because he might be gay. Plaintiff's case 'vividly underscores the folly of a policy that systematically excludes a whole class of persons . . . ' [T]he Court must note that the defenses mounted against gays in the military have been tried before in our nation's history—against blacks and women . . . Surely, it is time to move beyond this vestige of discrimination and misconception of gay men and women.

Judge Sporkin made short order of the other three criteria: clearly the less than honorable discharge would cause "Irreparable Harm" to McVeigh; the "Harm to Other Parties" was nil if McVeigh won, whereas the navy would actually benefit from his continued service; and finally, the "Public Interest" was clear on the basis of privacy and civil rights.

Judge Sporkin's Ruling and the Continuing Saga

The present case only being concerned with a preliminary injunction, Judge Sporkin offered speculation that "when this case is finally determined . . . [it will be] on the basis of the 'Don't Ask, Don't Tell, Don't Pursue' policy." But in order to make that policy work, both sides would need to exercise some restraint. Up to this point, it was clear who had failed to do so: "So far . . . while Plaintiff complied with the requirements imposed on him . . . the Defendant went further than the policy permits." Judge Sporkin ordered that, on the basis of the plaintiff's show of good cause, the motion for a preliminary injunction was granted. The navy was thus enjoined from taking any action against McVeigh on the basis of his sexual orientation, "pending final resolution of Plaintiff's Complaint." Finally, the two parties were ordered to appear again in court on 29 January 1998 for a status conference, at which time they would together determine a briefing schedule and a date for a hearing on final injunctive relief.

As David Loundy of the *Chicago Daily Law Bulletin* reported, McVeigh had a possible case not only against the navy, but against AOL for providing information that it should not have provided. AOL, as Loundy wrote, "pleaded 'OOPs.' McVeigh is reportedly considering a lawsuit."

With regard to *McVeigh,* the "Gay/Lesbian Issues" online site reported that the navy had "taken a hard line since Sporkin's ruling." It had refused to return McVeigh to his former chief of boat position, an action which David Glass of the Justice Department defended by referring to "the confined conditions aboard the nuclear submarine." The navy had until 30 March 1998 to appeal the decision, and on 27 March Judge Sporkin ordered the military to return McVeigh to his former position. According to attorney Christopher Wolf, McVeigh had been put on "demeaning" jobs such as trash detail, and had been subjected to a $745-a-month reduction in pay. Judge Sporkin scheduled a compliance hearing for 1 June, and ruled that the navy would have to pay McVeigh's legal expenses. It is not likely that this will be the last federal case testing the "Don't Ask, Don't Tell" policy.

Impact

Involving as it did gay rights and the Internet, *McVeigh* dealt with issues that regularly made headlines in the 1990s; but it also involved concerns perennial to Americans, especially the right to privacy. Loundy offered a few conclusions in this regard. The "Bork Bill"—named after Judge Robert Bork, whose movie rental records had been obtained by a journalist during Bork's ultimately unsuccessful Supreme Court nomination hearings in 1986—had been "One of the fastest laws of any kind passed in this country," Loundy noted. "In other words . . . the minimal privacy rights U.S. citizens still enjoy are important." Second, with regard to AOL, "'Oops' is not a recognized defense under the Electronic Communications Privacy Act." Third, "if you are a user of electronic communications, do not be dumb . . ." McVeigh's troubles could have been avoided, Loundy suggested, had he not made the error of writing to Hajne under the "boysrch" profile. This may be true, but the case also raised serious questions about the military's policy with regard to gay members, and the lengths to which service branches will go in researching and prosecuting suspected homosexuality.

Related Cases

Elzie v. Aspin, 897 F.Supp 1 (1995).
Able v. United States, 88 F.3d 1280 (1996).
Bohach v. The City of Reno, 932 F.Supp. 1232 (1996).
Thomasson v. Perry, 80 F.3d 915 (1996).
Richenberg v. Perry, 97 F.3d 256 (1996).
Phillips v. Perry, 106 F.3d 1420 (1997).
United States v. Charbonneau, 979 F.Supp. 1177 (1997).

Bibliography and Further Reading

Bull, Chris. "No More Evasive Actions." *The Advocate,* Dec. 8, 1998, p. 28.

Gallaghar, John. "Don't Ask, Don't Log On." *The Advocate,* March 3, 1998, p. 35.

Loundy, David J. "Navy Goes Overboard in Hunt for Submariner," *Chicago Daily Law Bulletin,* February 12, 1998, p. 5.

Yaukey, John. "Judge Tells Navy to Give Gay Sailor Meaningful Work." Gannett News Service, March 27, 1998.

CURRAN V. MOUNT DIABLO COUNCIL OF THE BOY SCOUTS OF AMERICA

Legal Citation: 147 Cal.App.3d 712 (1998)

Plaintiff
Timothy Curran

Defendant
Mount Diablo Council of the Boy Scouts of America

Plaintiff's Claim
That the Boy Scouts should not reject his application for the position of assistant scoutmaster just because he is a homosexual.

Chief Lawyer for Plaintiff
Jon Davidson

Chief Defense Lawyer
George Davidson

Justices for the Court
Ronald George (writing for the court), Ming W. Chin, Stanley Mosk, Marvin R. Baxter, Kathryn M. Werdegar, Joyce L. Kennard, Janice R. Brown

Justices Dissenting
None

Place
Sacramento, California

Date of Decision
23 March 1998

Decision
That the Boy Scouts is not a business establishment within the scope of the Civil Rights Act and therefore may exclude gays, atheists, and agnostics.

Significance
The California Supreme Court's decision that the Boy Scouts of America was not a business, allows the 5.8 million-member organization to deny admission to homosexuals, agnostics, and atheists in California. The decision clarified some of the legal parameters that separate a business from a private organization.

Timothy Curran, now a television documentary producer in Miami, was a 19-year-old Eagle Scout in 1981 when the Boy Scouts refused to allow him to become an assistant scoutmaster because of his homosexuality. Curran belonged to a Contra Costa County Boy Scout troop from 1976 until 1980. He applied to become an assistant scoutmaster. When an Oakland, California newspaper featured Curran in an article about "growing up gay," the national office of the Boy Scouts sent him a letter stating that he had been banned from the organization.

Curran sued the Boy Scouts of America (BSA) in 1981, seeking an injunction that would prohibit the BSA from rejecting his application. After years of debate and pretrial motions, the first phase of the trial began on 20 September 1990. On 6 November 1990 the Los Angeles Superior Court ruled that the BSA was a business under the state's civil rights law. On 25 July 1991, the same court ruled that the BSA was entitled to exclude homosexuals from its organization under the First Amendment, which includes the right of expressive association. The court also ruled that excluding homosexuals from the BSA was not a violation of the Fourteenth Amendment. On 29 March 1994, the court of appeals ruled that the BSA was not a business and may deny membership to homosexuals in its efforts to form an intimate and expressive association.

Exclusion of Gays, Atheists, And Agnostics

On 5 January 1998, the California Supreme Court heard arguments in the case. Curran's American Civil Liberties Union (ACLU) lawyer, Jon Davidson, argued that the BSA is subject to California's Unruh Civil Rights Act, which bars discrimination on the basis of race, sex, national origin, religion, and sexual orientation. The BSA argued that it had the right to establish its own membership and leadership standards, it was not a business, and it should be allowed to set its own rules, including the exclusion of gay people. The right to exclude gays, it argued, was protected under the First Amendment's freedom of assembly privilege.

On 23 March 1998, the California Supreme Court voted unanimously that the Boy Scouts organization was not a business establishment within the scope of the Unruh Civil Rights Act of 1959 and could therefore exclude gays, atheists, and agnostics. The court held that given the Boy Scouts' overall purpose and function, the organization could not reasonably be found to constitute a business establishment. Chief Justice George wrote the court's lead opinion. In it he stated, "Scouts meet regularly in small groups (often in private homes) that are intended to foster close friendship, trust, and loyalty. The Boy Scouts is an expressive social organization whose primary function is the inculcation of values in its youth members." Boy Scouts participate in many activities designed to teach the moral principles to which the organization subscribes. George noted that "nonmembers cannot purchase entry to pack or troop meetings, overnight hikes, the national jamboree or any portion of the Boy Scouts' extended training and educational process."

Comparing this case to *Isbister v. Boys' Club of Santa Cruz* (1985), the court noted that the Civil Rights Act applied to Boys' Clubs, which are a "place of public accommodation or amusement." But the Boy Scouts is not the functional equivalent of a place of public amusement. Membership into the Boy Scouts is not simply an admission ticket to a recreational facility open to a large segment of the public. Comparing the case to *Warfield v. Peninsula Golf & Country Club* (1995), the court noted that the Boy Scouts is not like a private country club that permits nonmembers to use its facilities. Although the BSA engages in business transactions, its primary function is the inculcation of values in its members. Its small social group structure and activities are not comparable to those of a traditional place of public amusement.

In a parallel case, Michael and William Randall sued the Boy Scouts of Orange County, California, because they were barred from the organization in 1990 after they refused to declare a belief in God. The Randalls charged the Boy Scouts with religious discrimination. In 1991, a temporary restraining order and a preliminary injunction barred the BSA from prohibiting the Randalls from participating in scouting, requiring them to use the word "God," or from requiring their participation in religious events or requirements. On 20 November 1992, the trial began and on 7 May 1992 the Orange County Superior Court ruled that the Boy Scouts is a business and is subject to the state Civil Rights Act. The court of appeals affirmed this decision on 28 February 1994. The California Supreme Court heard the case on 5 January 1998 and rendered its decision on 23 March 1998. The ruling held that because the Boy Scouts is a private organization and not a business, it may exclude homosexuals, agnostics, and atheists.

Boy Scouts in New Jersey

In a related case in New Jersey, James Dale, a Boy Scout since the age of eight, who later became an Eagle Scout and assistant scoutmaster, sued after he was expelled by the Monmouth Council of the Boy Scouts in 1990 for being gay. In 1995 a New Jersey superior court upheld the refusal of the Boy Scouts to admit an avowed homosexual to a Scout leadership position. Dale alleged that his dismissal violated New Jersey laws forbidding discrimination in places of public accommodation. The court held that the Boy Scouts was not a place of public accommodation, but a private entity promoting certain moral concepts and values. The court also noted that not everyone has the right to become a Boy Scout. Those who want to join must conform to the conditions of membership. Judge Patrick J. McGann called the Boy Scouts "a moral organization" and described homosexuality as "a serious moral wrong." The court said that because the group is a private organization, it has a constitutional right to decide who can belong.

The appellate division of the state superior court overruled this decision on 2 March 1998. The court held that the Boy Scouts must follow New Jersey's antidiscrimination law. The decision stated: "There is absolutely no evidence before us, empirical or otherwise, supporting a conclusion that a gay scoutmaster, solely because he is a homosexual, does not posses the strength of character necessary to properly care for, or to impart BSA humanitarian ideals to the young boys in his charge." The BSA planned to file an appeal with the New Jersey Supreme Court.

Impact

In both the *Curran* and *Randall* cases, four justices of the California Supreme Court offered separate, concurring opinions, each of which pointed out the need to further clarify what constitutes a business establishment under the Unruh Civil Rights Act. The ruling in the two California cases will affect the court's decision in a similar case involving a teenager, Katrina Yeaw, of Rocklin, California. She contends that the Boy Scouts discriminated against her when it denied her admission based on gender.

The BSA is appealing the New Jersey case to the state's supreme court. If it loses, it will appeal the decision to the U.S. Supreme Court. A dozen other suits involving similar issues are making their way through the courts. If the New Jersey case reaches the Supreme Court, much of the confusion surrounding the BSA's right to exclude certain individuals from the organization will undoubtedly be cleared up.

Related Cases

Isbister v. Boys' Club of Santa Cruz, 40 C. 3d 72 (1985).
Warfield v. Peninsula Golf & Country Club, 10 C. 4th 594 (1995).
Dale v. Boy Scouts of America, No. Mon-C-330-92 (1998).

Bibliography and Further Reading

"California's Top Court Lets Scouts Bar Agnostics and Homosexuals." *Liability Week,* March 30, 1998.

Donohue, William A. "Culture Wars Against the Boy Scouts." *Society,* May-June 1994, p. 59.

Hills, Roderick M., Jr. "Antidiscrimination Law and Social Equality." *Michigan Law Review,* May 1997, p. 1588.

Shoop, Julie Gannon. "Boy Scouts May Exclude Gays and Atheists, California Court Holds." *Trial,* June 1998, p. 19.

RIGHTS OF THE DISABLED

Background

In 1990, Congress passed the Americans with Disabilities Act (ADA). The purpose of the ADA is to eliminate discrimination against disabled individuals, as well as to provide clear standards to remedy the issues involved in such discrimination. At the time, Congress made several significant findings, including that 43,000,00 Americans possess one or more physical or mental disabilities and that this number will increase as the population ages. Moreover, Congress determined that society has been inclined to isolate and segregate persons with disabilities and that discrimination against such persons remains a serious social problem. Congress further recognized that, unlike individuals who have been discriminated against on the basis of race, color, sex, national origin, religion, or age, persons with disabilities have often lacked legal recourse to redress discrimination against them. Additionally, Congress acknowledged that disabled individuals occupy an inferior status in society due to characteristics which are beyond their control. Finally, Congress stated that this country's proper goal regarding disabled individuals is to assure equal opportunity, full participation, independent living, and self-sufficiency.

Definition of "Disability"

The ADA defines the term "disability" as a physical or mental impairment which substantially limits at least one major life activity of an individual. Generally, a major life activity is any function that an average individual can perform with little or no trouble, such as caring for oneself, hearing, lifting, seeing, speaking, talking, walking, and working. Examples of "disabilities" are: alcoholism, arthritis, cancer, cerebral palsy, cystic fibrosis, hearing impairment, heart disease, high blood pressure, mental retardation, multiple sclerosis, speech impairment, and visual impairment. Additionally, a "disability" may result from a history of, or a perception as having, a physical or mental impairment which substantially limits a major life activity. In *Bragdon v. Abbott,* (1998), the United States Supreme Court held that infection with the HIV virus constitutes a "disability," even if the symptomatic stage has not yet been reached. Absent unusual circumstances, pregnancy and related medical conditions are not regarded as "disabilities." Also excluded are homosexuality, bisexuality, transvestism, compulsive gambling, and kleptomania.

The key is that the condition or disease must limit an individual's major life activity. It is therefore possible that two people with the same condition or disease may be treated differently under the ADA. By way of example, arthritis in a particular individual may result in the limitation of mobility, while arthritis in another individual may manifest itself in only occasional stiffness and soreness. The individual in the first example would be "disabled" since the major life activity of walking had been substantially limited. However, the other individual would not be "disabled" inasmuch as there had not been a substantial limitation on a major life activity.

Employment

Title I of the ADA addresses the issue of equal employment opportunities for the disabled. Basically, the ADA prohibits an employer from discriminating against a disabled person solely on the basis of that person's disability with respect to the terms, conditions, and privileges of employment. The employer's decisions to hire, promote, fire, establish rates of compensation, and provide training are all covered under the ADA. To fall within the scope of the ADA, an employer must be engaged in an industry affecting interstate commerce (commerce between states) and have 15 or more employees. Employers that are not governed by the ADA are subject to parallel state discrimination laws. Also covered under the ADA are employment agencies, labor organizations, and joint labor-management committees.

A person is protected under the ADA if he/she is a "qualified individual with a disability." This phrase does not include a person who is currently engaged in illegal drug use. However, it does refer to a disabled individual who, with or without accommodation, is able to perform the essential functions of the job. For instance, a person with a visual impairment in one eye would be a "qualified individual with a disability" if he/she is still able to handle the requisite work duties.

Conversely, that person would not be a "qualified individual with a disability" if the visual impairment prevents him/her from handling his/her essential job tasks. The person in the first example would fall within the parameters of the ADA while the person in the second example would not.

Prohibited discrimination includes, but is not limited to, the following conduct by an employer: (1) limiting, segregating, or classifying a job applicant or employee in a way which negatively impacts on the opportunities or status of the job applicant or employee; (2) participating in a contractual relationship with another business which subjects the employer's disabled employees to discrimination; (3) using standards which have the effect of either discriminating on the ground of disability or perpetuating such discrimination; (4) failing to reasonably accommodate an individual with a disability; (5) using employment tests that tend to screen out persons with disabilities; and (6) failing to administer employment tests to individuals with impaired manual, sensory, or speaking skills so that the results accurately reflect the skills and aptitude of the job applicant or employee.

The ban against discrimination also applies to medical inquiries and examinations. In this regard, an employer is precluded from asking a job applicant as to whether he/she has a disability and from inquiring into the nature and severity of the disability. However, an employer is permitted to inquire into the job applicant's ability to perform the job functions. While the ADA forbids an employer from requiring a preemployment medical examination, it permits a medical examination after an offer of employment has been made, provided that all new employees are subjected to such an examination and the information obtained is treated confidentially. For the purpose of the ADA, a test to determine the illegal use of drugs is not considered to be a medical examination. Therefore, an employer is not barred from conducting drug testing on job applicants and employees and from making employment decisions on the basis of the test results.

The employer is obligated to make reasonable accommodations with respect to the mental or physical limitations of a "qualified individual with a disability." For example, an employer may provide such a person with a parking space that is in close proximity to the work premises, reassign the person to a vacant position, or modify his/her work schedule. A request for an unreasonable accommodation need not be fulfilled. Moreover, an employer is exempted from the duty of reasonable accommodation if such accommodation would result in an undue hardship, in terms of a significant difficulty or expense. For instance, an employer need not shift the lion's share of the disabled individual's duties to other employees. Additionally, an employer would not be required to grant a disabled individual an indefinite leave of absence, with full compensation and benefits, unless the employer also has a policy of granting such leaves to other employees. The issues of whether a requested accommodation is reasonable and whether the employer would suffer an undue hardship are to be determined by considering the totality of underlying circumstances of each particular situation.

Public Services

Title II of the ADA prohibits governmental entities from discriminating against disabled individuals with respect to their participation in, or receipt of, benefits from public services, programs, or activities. A governmental body is required to make reasonable modifications to its rules, policies, or practices so that all of its services, programs, and activities are accessible to the disabled. Such modifications include the removal of architectural, communication, or transportation barriers or the provision of auxiliary aids and services. For example, wheelchair ramps are typically installed at a public building's points of ingress and egress. The disabled must also have ready access to other parts of a public building, including the bathrooms, drinking fountains, and telephones. All accessible features, such as ramps and elevators, must be kept in good working order. Telecommunication devices (TDDs) should be used to facilitate communication with the hearing impaired. Public transportation systems must be accessible to the disabled, especially those with wheelchairs. However, a governmental entity is not required to supply a disabled individual with a wheelchair, hearing device, or reading glasses. Neither is it obligated to attend to a disabled individual's personal needs, such as providing assistance with eating.

Public Accommodations

Title III of the ADA bars discrimination by private entities that provide public accommodations and services. Such private entities include, but are not limited to, bars, cleaners, concert halls, convention centers, educational sites, gas stations, hotels, lecture halls, libraries, motels, museums, parks, restaurants, stadiums, stores, theaters, and zoos. It is illegal for these entities to deny an individual the full and equal enjoyment of goods, services, facilities, privileges, advantages, or accommodations solely on the basis of that individual's disability. Places of public accommodation are required to remove architectural barriers where the removal can be achieved without undue difficulty or expense. For example, a restaurant might install an entrance ramp and rearrange tables to facilitate the use of wheelchairs. Along the same lines, a lecture hall might provide a reasonable number of wheelchair seating spaces.

Other Statutes

Several other statutes also protect the rights of disabled individuals. Similar to the ADA, the Rehabilitation Act of 1973, prohibits discrimination on the basis of disability. While the Rehabilitation Act governs only programs and activities which receive federal funding, the ADA applies to those entities that do not receive federal assistance. The Fair Housing Act of 1968, bars discrimination against disabled individuals with respect to the sale or rental of a dwelling. Moreover, the Developmentally Disabled Assistance and Bill of Rights Act of 1996, is designed to improve the conditions of those with mental impairments.

See also: Civil Rights and Equal Protection, Employment Discrimination

Bibliography and Further Reading

Filipp, Mark R. *Employment Law Answer Book.* New York, NY: Panel Publishers, 1998

Jasper, Margaret C. *Employee Rights in the Workplace.* Dobbs Ferry, NY: Oceana Publications, Inc., 1997

Johnson, Mary, ed. *People With Disabilities Explain It All For You.* Louisville, KY: Advocado Press, 1992

O'CONNOR V. DONALDSON

Legal Citation: 422 U.S. 563 (1975)

Petitioner
Kenneth Donaldson

Respondent
Dr. J. B. O'Connor

Petitioner's Claim
That O'Connor, as the representative of the Florida State Hospital at Chattahoochee, had violated Donaldson's constitutional rights by keeping him in custody against his will for nearly 15 years for his supposed mental illness.

Chief Lawyer for Petitioner
Raymond W. Gearney

Chief Lawyer for Respondent
Bruce J. Ennis, Jr.

Justices for the Court
Harry A. Blackmun, William J. Brennan, Jr., Warren E. Burger, William O. Douglas, Thurgood Marshall, Lewis F. Powell, Jr., William H. Rehnquist, Potter Stewart (writing for the Court), Byron R. White

Justices Dissenting
None

Place
Washington, D.C.

Date of Decision
26 June 1975

Decision
In a unanimous decision, the Supreme Court ruled that Donaldson possessed certain constitutional rights, and that he could gather damages from individuals who had taken away his rights.

Significance
That mentally ill persons have constitutional rights.

During the turbulent decades of the 1960s and 1970s many minority groups began to fight for their rights. African Americans worked to gain basic civil rights, including the right to vote, order a hamburger at a segregated lunch counter, and sit in the front of a crowded bus. Women tried to achieve equal pay for equal work, universal day care, and have men take responsibility for the home and child care. Gays and lesbians worked to halt the discrimination they faced every day.

Within this context of social activism, mentally ill persons also began to challenge the health system that often warehoused them in mental institutions for years at a time, sometimes without receiving any treatment to help cure their disorder. Nondangerous patients were housed with dangerous patients, and severe overcrowding in many institutions assured that many patients went for years without meeting with a licensed psychiatrist. In addition, many patients were denied their basic civil rights, including the right to a trial by jury. Others were committed to institutions against their will for an indefinite period of time.

Mental health advocates chose to use the court system to try to rectify the abuses found within the mental health system across the nation. In choosing to appeal to the court system to protect the civil rights of persons with a mental illness, mental health advocates followed the lead of other minority groups who had successfully won their own civil rights by appealing to the courts. For example, African Americans won the right to attend formerly segregated schools by court order, while women received the right to abortion in the controversial case of *Roe v. Wade.* Judging from the success of these past cases, lawyers, usually under the aegis of the American Civil Liberties Union (ACLU), sent test cases to court to fight against the involuntary commitment of patients, the warehousing of nondangerous patients for years without cause, and the right to treatment if patients were forced to remain within a hospital. As Bruce Ennis, an early advocate for the rights of the mentally ill commented in *The Legal Rights of the Mentally Handicapped,* mentally ill persons were "our country's most profoundly victimized minorities."

Individuals with Disabilities Education Act

In 1975 an important law was passed guaranteeing "free, appropriate public education" to children with physical, mental, or emotional disabilities—from birth to age 21, or high school graduation. According to the Department of Education, approximately 5.8 million children in the United States were disabled.

Federal funds are provided to public schools who agree to provide "appropriate" instruction to students deemed "eligible." The test for appropriateness depends upon the child's disability. A written evaluation is required to determine each disabled student's needs. The Individuals with Disabilities Education Act (IDEA) mandates an Individual Education Program (IEP) be prepared for each student which addresses his or her specific educational needs, and the means for meeting them.

IDEA was initially named the Education for All Handicapped Children Act. IDEA has been amended several times since 1975. The original intent was to provide public education for disabled children who otherwise would have been educated at home, or in an institutional setting. According to the Department of Education, a 1997 amendment to IDEA ". . . strengthens academic expectations and accountability."

Source(s): Department of Education. Individuals with Disabilities Education Act, http://www. civilrights.com/idea.html, www.edweek. org/context/glossary/idea.htm.

The strategy of appealing to the courts to achieve the rights for the mentally ill led to a flurry of lawsuits instituted on behalf of mental patients. One of the first of these lawsuits to reach the Supreme Court was the case of *O'Connor v. Donaldson*. In a unanimous decision, the Supreme Court ruled that Donaldson possessed certain rights and that he could be awarded damages from individuals who had taken away his rights. *O'Connor v. Donaldson* was one of the first cases to attempt to define the rights of mentally ill individuals.

In 1956, Kenneth Donaldson, a 48–year-old man from Philadelphia, traveled to Florida to visit his elderly parents. While there, Donaldson reported that he believed one of his neighbors in Philadelphia might be poisoning his food. His father, worried that his son suffered from paranoid delusions, petitioned the court for a sanity hearing. Donaldson was evaluated, diagnosed with "paranoid schizophrenia," and civilly committed to the Florida State mental health system. At his commitment trial, Donaldson did not have legal counsel present to represent his case.

Once he entered the Florida hospital, Donaldson was placed with dangerous criminals, even though he had never been proved to be dangerous to himself or others. His ward was also dangerously understaffed, with only one doctor—who happened to be an obstetrician—for over 1,000 male patients. There were no psychiatrists or counselors, and the only nurse on site worked in the infirmary. Because of the severe overcrowding and lack of doctors, Donaldson claimed that he did not receive any treatment during his 14 and a half year stay at the Florida State hospital. During the trial, the hospital administration admitted that the only treatment Donaldson received was "milieu therapy"— which was really a euphemism for confinement in the hospital itself. For most of his years in the hospital, Donaldson was simply kept in a room with 60 other patients, most of whom were criminally committed.

Beginning immediately upon arrival in the hospital, and for the next 14 and a half years, Donaldson fought to speak to a lawyer and have his case heard before a court. Donaldson argued that he should be freed because he was not provided with counsel at his commitment hearing; he was not mentally ill or dangerous to himself or others; and if he was mentally ill, the state had not offered any treatment for his affliction. Later, Donaldson also complained that he had not been released, despite the promise by two different sources to take responsibility for his care. In 1963, for example, a reputable half-way home for mentally ill persons in Minnesota had offered to assume responsibility for Donaldson. In addition, a college friend had sought to have the state release Donaldson to his care. Seemingly with no cause, both of these offers were rejected.

Finally, Donaldson received a hearing for his case and was released from the hospital. He immediately found a job as a hotel clerk and had no difficulty holding his job or living on his own. Despite his release from the hospital, his case eventually worked its way up to the Supreme Court where it was heard in October of 1975.

The Supreme Court ruled unanimously in favor of Donaldson, although its decision was a narrow interpretation of the case. First, the Court ruled on the ability of the state to hospitalize mentally ill persons. The Court ruled that the diagnosis of mental illness does not alone justify confining persons against their will and for an indefinite time. As Justice Stewart wrote in the Supreme Court opinion, "a State cannot constitutionally confine without more a nondangerous indi-

Bruce J. Ennis, Jr. © Photograph by Mpozi Mshale Tolbert. AP/Wide World Photos.

vidual who is capable of surviving safely in freedom by himself or with the help of willing and responsible family members or friends." The ruling, however, only applied to involuntarily civilly committed patients who were not dangerous to themselves or others.

Second, *O'Connor v Donaldson* held that state hospital officials were liable to pay damages if their actions violated the constitutional rights of the patient. In the case of Donaldson, Dr. J. B. O'Connor, the director of the Florida State Hospital where Donaldson resided, could be held liable for his refusal to release Donaldson, provide him with legal counsel, and offer him any viable treatment.

Third, and most important, the Supreme Court decision recognized the necessity of court cases protecting the rights of mentally ill persons, and encouraged other cases of the same nature. Finally, although many have interpreted the *Donaldson* case as supporting a right to treatment, the Court did not go that far in their ruling. Justice Stewart, writing for the majority, explained that

"there is no reason now to decide whether mentally ill persons dangerous to themselves or to others have a right to treatment upon compulsory confinement by the state." The way was open, however, for other cases to address the right of patients to receive treatment if they are hospitalized for mental illness.

The case of *O'Connor v. Donaldson* recognized that civilly committed mental patients have constitutional rights. If these rights were violated, the patient could sue the health care officials for taking away their rights. Although narrowly construed, perhaps the most important legacy of *O'Connor v. Donaldson* was that it encouraged others to challenge the system and protect the rights of America's "most profoundly victimized minorities." Although many of the rights of mental patients were challenged in the 1980s and 1990s, Donaldson's case helped pave the way for the deinstitutionalization of thousands of patients in the 1960s and 1970s.

Related Cases

Minnesota ex rel Pearson v. Probate Court, 309 U.S. 270 (1940).
Shelton v. Tucker, 364 U.S. 479 (1960).
In re Gault, 387 U.S. 1 (1967).
Cohen v. Caligornia, 403 U.S. 15 (1971).
McKeiver v. Pennsylvania, 403 U.S. 528 (1971).

Bibliography and Further Reading

Bradley, Valerie and Gary Clark, eds. *Paper Victories and Hard Realities: The Implementation of the Legal and Constitutional Rights of the Mentally Disabled.* Washington, DC: The Health Policy Center, 1976.

Brakel, Samuel Jan, John Danoy, and Barbara A. Weiner, eds. *The Mentally Disabled and the Law.* Chicago: American Bar Foundation, 1985.

Ennis, Bruce J. and Paul R. Friedman, eds. *Legal Rights of the Mentally Handicaped.* New York: Practicing Law Institute/The Mental Health Law Project, 1974.

Ennis, Bruce J. *Prisoners of Psychiatry: Mental Patients, Psychiatrists, and the Law.* New York: Harcourt Brace Jovanovich, Inc., 1972.

Lundergan, E. Kirsten. "The Right to be Present: Should it Apply to the Involuntary Civil Committment Hearing." *New Mexico Law Review,* 17 (Winter 1987), 165-187.

Sales, Bruce D. and Daniel W. Shuman, eds. *Law, Mental Health, and Mental Disorder.* Pacific Grove, CA: Brooks/Cole Publishing Company, 1996.

YOUNGBERG V. ROMEO

Legal Citation: 457 U.S. 307 (1982)

Petitioners
Duane Youngberg, Superintendent, Penhurst State School and Hospital, et al.

Respondents
Nicholas Romeo, an incompetent, by his mother, Paula Romeo

Petitioners' Claim
That the proper standard of liability is the Eighth Amendment, and that the Pennsylvania State Institution properly adhered to the standards of the law in treating the respondent's son, a severely mentally handicapped individual.

Chief Lawyer for Petitioners
David H. Allshouse

Chief Lawyer for Respondents
Edmond A. Tiryak

Justices for the Court
Harry A. Blackmun, William J. Brennan, Jr., Warren E. Burger, Thurgood Marshall, Sandra Day O'Connor, Lewis F. Powell, Jr. (writing for the Court), William H. Rehnquist, John Paul Stevens, Byron R. White

Justices Dissenting
None

Place
Washington, D.C.

Date of Decision
18 June 1982

Decision
Involuntarily committed retarded persons were held to have due process liberty interests requiring state to provide minimally adequate training to ensure safety and freedom from undue restraint.

Significance
Individuals are constitutionally protected under the Due Process Clause of the Fourteenth Amendment to reasonably safe conditions on confinement. The proper method for determining whether the state has protected those rights is whether professional judgment was exercised, showing deference to the judgment exercised by a qualified professional, whose decision is preemptively valid.

Nicholas Romeo, a mentally retarded person who was involuntarily committed to a Pennsylvania State institution upon his mother's petition, was injured on numerous occasions while a patient at the institution. Paula Romeo, his mother, filed a complaint in the U.S. District Court for the Eastern District of Pennsylvania seeking damages against the institution's officials, alleging that these officials knew, or should have known, that her son was suffering injuries and that they failed to institute appropriate preventive procedures. She claimed that they had thereby violated her son's rights under the Eighth and Fourteenth Amendments. She also filed a second amended complaint, alleging that the officials were restraining her son for prolonged periods on a routine basis and claiming damages for the officials' failure to provide him with appropriate treatment or programs for his mental retardation. At the close of trial, the district court instructed the jury on the assumption that the proper standard of liability was that of the Eighth Amendment, and a verdict was returned for the official. The U.S. Court of Appeals for the Third Circuit reversed and remanded for a new trial, holding that the Eighth Amendment was not an appropriate source for determining the rights of the involuntarily committed, but that the Fourteenth Amendment, and the liberty interest protected therein, provided the proper constitutional basis for these rights.

On *certiorari*, the U.S. Supreme Court vacated and remanded. In an opinion written by Justice Powell, it was held that mentally retarded individuals have liberty interests under the Due Process Clause of the Fourteenth Amendment which required the state to provide him with minimally adequate or reasonable training to ensure safety and freedom from undue restraint. Powell also wrote that the state was under a duty to provide the mentally retarded with such training as an appropriate professional would consider reasonable to ensure the safety of the patient and to facilitate the patient's ability to function free from bodily restraints.

In a concurring decision written by Justice Blackmun and joined by Justices Brennan and O'Connor, Blackmun expressed the view that the Court properly left unresolved, because of the less-than-fully developed record, the issues as to the individual committed under state law for care and treatment. However, Chief Justice Burger, concurring in the judgment but in a separate decision, stated that a mentally retarded person involuntarily committed to a state institution, had no constitutional right to training, or habilitation.

Related Cases

Ingram v. Wright, 430 U.S. 651 (1977).
Hutto v. Finney, 437 U.S. 678 (1978).
Harris v. McRae, 448 U.S. 297 (1980).

Bibliography and Further Reading

"Due Process of Law; Incompetent or Insane Persons; Mental Illness." *AIR Quick Index.*

CLEBURNE V. CLEBURNE LIVING CENTER

Legal Citation: 473 U.S. 432 (1985)

Petitioner
City of Cleburne

Respondent
Cleburne Living Center

Petitioner's Claim
That the decision to deny the Cleburne Living Center a zoning permit was constitutional.

Chief Lawyer for Petitioner
Earl Luna, Robert T. Miller, Jr., Mary Milford

Chief Lawyer for Respondent
Renea Hicks, Diane Shisk, Caryl Oberman

Justices for the Court
Harry A. Blackmun, Warren E. Burger, Sandra Day O'Connor, Lewis F. Powell, Jr., William H. Rehnquist, Byron R. White (writing for the Court)

Justices Dissenting
William J. Brennan, Jr., Thurgood Marshall, John Paul Stevens

Place
Washington, D.C.

Date of Decision
1 July 1985

Decision
The denial of a permit to the Cleburne Living Center was found to be based on prejudice and therefore unconstitutional.

Significance
The case helped improve rights of the mentally retarded.

Handicapped or differently abled persons were at the center of the Supreme Court's decision in *Cleburne v. Cleburne Living Center.* In July of 1985, the High Court ruled that the city of Cleburne, Texas, violated the U.S. Constitution when it denied a zoning permit to the Cleburne Living Center (CLC). The center applied for a zoning permit for a house for the retarded. The house the center wanted to lease for the retarded was a residential group home.

The city of Cleburne classified the group home as a "hospital for the feebleminded" and told CLC they had to apply for a special use permit. CLC applied but the city denied them the special use permit. After the Cleburne City Council denied the center the permit, CLC filed suit. The suit stated that the city had violated the equal protection rights of CLC and its potential residents. CLC cited the Equal Protection Clause of the Fourteenth Amendment to the U.S. Constitution. The Equal Protection Clause states that no state shall "deny to any person within its jurisdiction the equal protection of the laws." What this means is that all people in similar situations should be treated the same.

It is up to the courts to devise standards when dealing with a challenge to the Equal Protection Clause. In this case, different standards were used by different courts. In district court, the city of Cleburne won; the district court upheld its decision not to grant CLC its special use permit. CLC appealed this decision and the court of appeals reversed the district court's decision. Finally, the Supreme Court affirmed the court of appeals decision, but clarified its ruling.

The district court used the "heightened-scrutiny" equal protection test in making its decision. "Heightened-scrutiny" refers to a law singling out members of certain groups for special treatment. If groups such as racial minorities, illegitimate children, women, or aliens are singled out for particular treatment in a law, that law is unconstitutional. It is unconstitutional unless the law serves either an "important" or "compelling" interest to the government.

The court of appeals, in reversing the district court's decision in *Cleburne v. Cleburne Living Center,* stated that the retarded, as a group, were entitled to "heightened

Should Facilities for Mentally Retarded Persons be Allowed in Neighborhoods?

Opening a group home for mentally disabled individuals within family neighborhoods may cause significant controversy between the organization trying to establish housing for its potential residents, and the existing neighbors.

The right to establish group homes within residential areas of a city or town is protected under the federal Fair Housing Act of 1968. This act provides greater access to housing for the disabled, and protects against discriminatory practices. Further, a group home can be viewed no differently than any other person's home. As a result, a city cannot stipulate that a group home not be located in any area deemed "residential."

Residents in neighborhoods where group homes try to locate may become alarmed by the prospect of mentally retarded persons living in their midst. In some cases, neighbors fear that the group home may lack adequate supervision for its residents. Some cite fear for the safety of the children in the neighborhood. Others believe residents suffering from psychiatric problems should be barred from group homes. Even others cite the potential effect these group homes might have on their property value.

Source(s): Findlaw. http://www.findlaw.com/casecode/ supreme.html.

The Record Online, http://www.bergen. com/psouth/boardjc199807093.htm.

---

scrutiny." The reasoning used by the court of appeals was that the retarded lacked political power and also had a history of being discriminated against. Although all nine of the Supreme Court justices agreed that when the city of Cleburne denied the zoning permit it did so in violation of the Constitution, they disagreed on the underlying question involved. They disagreed with the lower court's reasoning but agreed with its end result.

According to the *New York Times,* the Supreme Court said that "mere negative attitudes, vague fear, and irrational prejudice may not form the basis for official action placing the retarded at a disadvantage."

The Supreme Court found these factors at the center of the city of Cleburne's decision—a decision, it must be noted, not to permit a group home for 13 retarded citizens in an area that was already zoned for nursing homes, group homes and apartments. The Supreme Court justices even went as far as to state that not only was the city of Cleburne's decision unconstitutional, it was, the Court said, irrational. However, the Court also said that the retarded as a group do not have the characteristics to receive "heightened scrutiny." Justice White told the *New York Times* that the reasoning used by the court of appeals to come to a decision in *Cleburne v. Cleburne Living Center* was incorrect. White said mental retardation is a broad phrase and decisions about treating the retarded are "very much a task for legislators guided by qualified professionals and not by the perhaps ill-informed opinions of the judiciary."

Justice Marshall criticized the Supreme Court's ruling in this case. Marshall said that the Court "pretends" that its equal protection analysis uses a firm set of categories. He argued that the Court has adjusted the degree of justification it demands based on more sen-

sitive calculations. By voting that the city of Cleburne's ordinance was invalid, the Supreme Court did much for the mentally retarded in general. Although mentally retarded people are different, the Court stated, the difference is irrelevant—inappropriate, unless the proposal in question threatens a city's interests in a way those granted permits would not. However, viewed as a constitutional test case by advocates for the mentally retarded *Cleburne v. Cleburne Living Center,* when looked at in a specific way, only sheds light on the Supreme Court's mixed message.

Related Cases
Schweiker v. Wilson, 450 U.S. 221 (1981).
Plyler v. Doe, 457 U.S. 202 (1982).

Bibliography and Further Reading
Farber, Daniel A., and Suzanna Sherry. "The Pariah Principle." *Constitutional Commentary,* winter 1996, p. 257.

Goldfarb, Carl E. "Allocating the Local Apportionment Pie: What Portion for Resident Aliens?" *Yale Law Journal,* April 1995, p. 1441.

Lauber, Daniel. "Group Think: A Recent Supreme Court Ruling Should Make Local Governments Reconsider Their Community Residence Regulations." *Planning,* October 1995, p. 11.

"Supreme Court Denies Retarded Special Legal Status Under Law." *New York Times,* July 2, 1985.

The Villanova Center for Information and Policy. "*Cleburne v. Cleburne Living Center,* 473 U.S. 432." *Flite Database,* June 23, 1997.

Wolff, Tobias Barrington. "Principled Silence," *Yale Law Journal,* October 1996, p. 247.

SEGREGATION AND DESEGREGATION

Separate but Equal

De jure segregation, or the legal separation of races—in this case African Americans and whites—developed in the late nineteenth century. Prior to this, *de facto* segregation, or the separation of races on the basis of custom, was carried out by the institution of slavery. A series of constitutional amendments helped bring an end to *de facto* segregation. The Emancipation Proclamation of 1863 and the subsequent ratification of the Thirteenth Amendment to the Constitution in 1865, which outlawed the institution of slavery, signfied the beginning of the end of *de facto* segregation. The Fourteenth (1868) and Fifteenth (1870) Amendments extended fundamental civil rights such as due process and the right to vote to African Americans. However, states intent on segregating the races devised ways to circumvent the Constitution. For example, legal codes were enacted in the South designed to restrict the freedom of African Americans such as prohibiting first-class seating on railway cars, and denying African Americans access to public schools. Although the post-Civil War Reconstruction legislation discouraged much of these types of laws, Southern states took measures to re-institute segregation. The body of laws which was instituted with the intent to legally separate African Americans from whites was known as "Jim Crow Laws."

The federal government responded with what would be a long line of civil rights legislation. The first of such measures was the Civil Rights Acts of 1866 and 1870, which guaranteed equal rights under the law for all people living under U.S. jurisdiction. Included under the acts were the rights to sue and be sued, the rights to own real and personal property, and the rights to testify and present evidence in courts of law. In 1875 Congress was forced to enact legislation when many whites refused to make such public facilities as hotels and railroads available to African Americans. The 1875 Civil Rights Act prohibited such discrimination and provided for the "full and equal enjoyment" of such public establishments. Southern states, however, largely ignored these federal laws, or contested their constitutionality in the courts. Southern segregationists, relying on the Tenth Amendment, claimed that the federal government did not have constitutional authority to tell the states how to run their affairs. In many instances, the Supreme Court sided with the states. In *United States v. Reese* (1876) and *United States v. Cruikshank* (1876) the Court limited the federal government's ability to protect the civil rights of African Americans. In these cases the Court declined to uphold an indictment against southerners who prevented qualified African Americans from voting. The decisions limited the power of the federal government to enforce the Fifteenth Amendment. The *Civil Rights Cases* of 1883 found the Civil Rights Act of 1871 unconstitutional because it did not confine statutory provisions to discriminatory practices of the states (i.e. the Civil Rights legislation was too broad). The most influential decision by the Court came in 1896 with *Plessy v. Ferguson*. Here, the Court upheld a Louisiana law which required "separate but equal" railway facilities for African Americans and whites. The Court determined that laws requiring separation of the races do not necessarily imply the inferiority of either race and that the notion of "separate but equal" facilities does not violate the Fourteenth Amendment. The only dissenting voice on the Court was that of Justice John Marshall Harlan, who quite accurately predicted the effect of the ruling: "Our constitution is color-blind, and neither knows nor tolerates classes among citizens . . . In my opinion, the judgment this day rendered will, in time, prove to be quite as pernicious as the decision made by this tribunal in the Dred Scott case . . ." Just before the Civil War, in *Dred Scott v. Sandford* (1857) Justice Taney delivered perhaps the most regrettable opinion ever issued by the Supreme Court. After being enslaved, Dred Scott sued on the grounds that his residency in a territory that banned slavery made him free. Justice Taney not only rejected Scott's argument but went out of his way to suggest that Dred Scott did not even have the right to sue in federal court because, legally, he was not a citizen. He also went on to say that Congress did not have the power to prohibit slavery in any state.

Plessy v. Ferguson (1896) was a landmark decision which sanctioned *de jure* segregation which precipitated a host of Jim Crow laws restricting the rights of African Americans in all spheres of life from education to voting. The 1898 Supreme Court decision in *Williams v.*

Mississippi essentially approved legal disenfranchisement. African Americans were denied the vote by the use of literacy tests, poll taxes and so-called grandfather clauses which denied suffrage to anyone whose grandfather had been ineligible to vote. It would be another half century before the federal government enacted civil rights laws that deterred legal segregation.

The Face of Segregation

The first segregation laws to be passed dealt with separation of the races on trains. A majority of southern states passed laws that designated African American and white seating laws for both trains and railway station waiting rooms by 1910. In time, streetcars, theaters, amusement parks, hospitals, jails, swimming pools, drinking fountains, and schools, were all targeted by state and local segregation laws. The military was also segregated, with African American soldiers usually serving in menial positions. Education was a particular focal point for segregation; it soon became clear that the "separate but equal" clause of *Plessy v. Ferguson* was not being observed. For example, by 1915 South Carolina was spending 12 times as much per capita to educate white children than African American children. Conditions were somewhat better out of the South. By 1900, 18 states of the North and West had passed laws designed to discourage racial discrimination practices. However, *de facto* segregation was still the rule rather than the exception throughout the country.

In 1910, approximately 90 percent of the African American population lived in the South and 30 percent of the total population of the South was African American. By and large, the entire African American population in the South was denied basic civil rights. In the first decade of the twentieth century, over 300,000 African Americans fled such oppressive conditions for northern and western states in what has been called the Great Migration. This demographic change has continued throughout the century. However, the demographic changes brought on new tensions between the races which resulted in race riots in 1917 and 1919 in both border and Northern states. Thirty-eight people were killed in the Chicago race riots of 1919 which was instigated when four African Americans attempted to enter a *de facto* white beach on Lake Michigan.

In response to the discriminatory laws of *de facto* segregation African Americans began to organize, beginning with the formation of the National Urban League in 1909. The NUL concentrated its resources on helping working class African Americans adjust to new urban environments. The extremely influential National Association for the Advancement of Colored People (NAACP) formed shortly thereafter. Founded in 1910, the organization concentrated its resources on the three tenets of education, litigation and legislation. Their first legal success came with the 1915 Supreme

Court decision in *Guinn v. United States,* in which an Oklahoma grandfather clause was stuck down. Then, in *Buchanan v. Warley,* (1917), the Court ruled that a Kentucky statute forcing residential segregation violated the Constitution. Another NAACP legal victory came in 1919 when the Court upheld the right of African American citizens to serve on juries in *State v. Young.* The NAACP also called attention to the need for anti-lynching legislation.

However, African American leaders were not of one mind in determining the best strategy with which to combat segregation. Some influential leaders such as Booker T. Washington, felt that the best approach for improving the condition of African Americans was economic advancement. Civil and political justice, he argued, would follow. Toward this end, he founded the Tuskegee Institute, which was designed to provide African Americans with an industrial education that would enable African Americans to find better jobs. This strategy was supported by many whites just as eager to put an end to racial disharmony. Other African American leaders such as W. E. B. Du Bois and representatives of the NAACP insisted that the best approach to racial equality was to fight for immediate universal political and civil equality. They saw Washington and his policy of "accommodation" as leading African Americans backward into slavery, pointing out that education was difficult to come by for African Americans in the South. The rampant poverty in the South allowed for only a three-month school year for African Americans who were fortunate enough to go to school. In addition, African American teachers made less than convicts. Although county training schools began to emerge in the South, they merely provided an industrial education which served to keep southern African Americans in a subordinate economic position.

Throughout the first half of the twentieth century modest progress was made in the fight against racial discrimination and segregation. Militant white racism, exemplified in organizations such as the Ku Klux Klan, reached its peak in the mid-1920s, with membership reaching an all-time high of five million in 1929. However, many states disapproved of the atrocious intimidation tactics employed by the Klan which helped reduce membership to less than 100,000. The number of lynchings dropped from 83 to 7 in 1929. U.S. involvement in world affairs also served as a vehicle for progress in the area of racial discrimination as many African Americans courageously answered the call of military service during World War I, though in segregated regiments.

Although the political and social climate was progressing, the Supreme Court was still reluctant to address the important issues of racial equality. The Great Depression was particularly hard on African Americans who were already in an economically compromising position. Education for African Americans continued to be problematic. In the 1930s, while the average expenditure per student per year in schools was $80, for African Americans it was only $15. Increasingly, in the North, African Americans began to fight segregation in the schools. In Philadelphia, for example, concerted efforts by the Education Equity League and the NAACP resulted in desegregated schools, the admittance of African American teachers in African American and white schools, and placement of an African American on a school board by 1940. The NAACP also established a strategy to tackle *Plessy v. Ferguson* in the courts, by slowly chipping away at the "separate but equal" doctrine in specific cases. For example, *Murray v. Maryland* (1936) forced Maryland to desegregate its law schools and *McLaurin v. Oklahoma State Regents for Higher Education* (1950) and *Sweatt v. Painter* (1950) addressed graduate school inequalities. Still, the Court did not reverse the position it advanced in *Plessy*. The NAACP legal defense team continued to look for the case that might reverse that decision and open the floodgates of reform. Meanwhile, America was drawn into another world war in which African Americans again took part despite their unequal treatment at home.

Brown v. Board of Education

The NAACP finally got its test case when Oliver Brown, of Topeka, Kansas, a welder for the railroad, decided to challenge segregation laws. Brown refused to send his daughter through the switchyard of a railway, to an all-African American school a mile away, when a school was located merely seven blocks from his home. That school, which happened to be all-white, denied Linda Brown admittance when Mr. Brown tried to enroll her. Brown persisted, and the NAACP Legal Defense Fund, led by Thurgood Marshall, stepped in to help with the defense. Marshall and the NAACP lawyers took the case to the Supreme Court, where the Court was forced to address the issue of segregation. In a landmark decision in 1954, the Court overturned the "separate but equal" provision of *Plessy,* and declared that "separate educational facilities are inherently unequal" and a violation of the Equal Protection Clause of the Fourteenth Amendment. In addition, the Court remanded all other such cases to district courts, with the direction to desegregate schools "with all deliberate speed."

Desegregation, however, was a painfully slow process, taking more than 20 years to institute. Initially, the South refused to comply with desegregation laws; it took legal action and federal troops and marshals to enforce the laws. In 1957 U.S. marshals were used to enforce desegregation laws in a highly publicized incident in Little Rock, Arkansas. Alabama governor George Wallace physically resisted the desegregation of the University of Alabama in 1963. Federal troops were called upon to quell disorder at the University of Mississippi when James Meredith was admitted to the all-white college.

The legacy of *Brown v. Board of Education,* however, went far beyond schools. In effect, the Court had implied that segregation was no longer legal in any domain: educational institutions, transportation facilities, public places, housing complexes, or the voting booth. In 1957, Congress passed its first Civil Rights Act in more than 80 years. Even the military had been desegregated by executive order in 1948, though discrimination persisted. African American organizations were quick to capitalize on the changing political and social climate. The Congress of Racial Equality (CORE), founded in 1942, was highly influential in spreading its confrontational tactics to other groups. In the 1940s CORE employed direct, nonviolent action to end segregation. The organization used sit-ins and stand-ins in Chicago and organized the Freedom Ride in 1947, which tested freedom of transportation in the South in 1947. By 1960 the desegregation movement was taking on national proportions. Desegregation was no longer an issue for the "South," as African Americans continued to migrate to the North and West. New leaders such as Dr. Martin Luther King, Jr., of the Southern Christian Leadership Conference (SCLC), applied the nonviolent strategies espoused by CORE and Mahatma Gandhi's passive resistance which forged a new resistance to racial intolerance. King helped stage a successful boycott of the Montgomery, Alabama bus system in 1955. The boycott protested the arrest of Rosa Parks who refused to move to the African American section of a public bus. Thereafter boycotts and picketing spread to other southern cities as a new weapon in the arsenal against segregation. From 1955 to 1960, such tactics helped to integrate schools, transportation, and public places in the border states. However the Deep South stubbornly resisted the new laws.

The sit-in movement of the 1960s began in Greensboro, North Carolina, in an attempt to desegregate a public lunch counter. The movement spread across the South to restaurants, department stores, theaters, and libraries, as a nonviolent response to racial intolerance. In the summer of 1961 the Freedom Rides resumed. White and African American students from the North and South rode southern transportation units and tested hotels for compliance with desegregation laws. Roughly 70,000 students participated in the desegregation movement that summer, which resulted in 3,600 arrests. White supremacists in the South met these tactics with increased violence and, on one occasion shot down a Mississippi field secretary for the NAACP, Medgar Evers, in 1963. The Klan also killed four African American girls in a church bombing in Birmingham, Alabama and murdered three volunteers of the Congress of Federated Organizations who were teaching African Americans in rural Mississippi how to register to vote. The nation was stunned by news footage from Birmingham, Alabama in 1963 depicting the use of dogs and fire hoses to deter peaceful protesters. The civil rights movement reached its zenith with the 1963 march on Washington, in which 250,000 people participated.

The federal government responded with the Civil Rights Act of 1964, the most comprehensive legislation of its kind. This act prohibited segregation in all privately owned public facilities which were subject in any way to interstate commerce provisions. The Civil Rights Act prohibited discriminatory practices for public accommodations, facilities, education, and federally assisted programs and employment. The constitutionality of the Civil Rights Act of 1964 was challenged in *Heart of Atlanta Motel v. United States* (1964). The Court held that the public accommodations section of the Civil Rights Act of 1964 was constitutional. Title VII of the 1964 act prohibits discrimination based on an employee's race, color, sex, religion, or national origin. Further congressional laws and executive orders were put in place to guarantee voting rights and equal housing. The Voting Rights Act of 1965 was aimed primarily at guaranteeing African American suffrage, while the Civil Rights Act of 1968 focused on discriminatory policies in housing. Such unfair practices as zoning to achieve racial segregation and redlining—in which lending institutions discriminated against minorities—were declared illegal. In *Jones v. Alfred H. Mayer Co.* (1968), the Supreme Court found it illegal to refuse to rent or sell to a person on the basis of race.

These gains were met by fierce resistance from those intent on preserving segregation. Despite legal guarantees, whites still found ways to discriminate against African Americans. Rioting broke out in the Los Angeles ghetto of Watts in 1965, a result of frustration and poverty. In the summer of 1967 more riots broke out in 30 different cities, leaving 100 dead, 2,000 injured, and causing millions of dollars in property damage. The assassination of Martin Luther King, Jr. in 1968 set the desegregation movement back decades. The movement divided into conservative and radical organizations. Newer groups such as the Black Muslims and Black Panthers elected leaders such as H. Rap Brown and Huey Newton who advocated Black Nationalism and revolution.

Meanwhile, school desegregation was encouraged by the 1971 Supreme Court decision in *Swann v. Charlotte-Mecklenburg Board of Education,* which held busing in the service of integrating schools constitutional. Busing has continued to be a hotly contested issue by both African Americans and whites. Throughout the 1970s and 1980s further gains were made with the institution of affirmative action programs designed to promote social and economic justice. However, the constitutionality of such programs has been called into question through such cases as *University of California v. Bakke* (1978) and *United Steel Workers of America v. Weber* (1979). Affirmative action, which has been described as reverse discrimination, was outlawed by California voters in 1996 with the adoption of proposition 209. While the legal foundations of segregation have been dismantled, *de facto* segregation is still practiced. Significant gains have been made in areas such as education, transportation, access to public accommodation, and representation. The Congressional Black Caucus, which began with only six members in 1969, has become a formidable political force over the years. Many African Americans have been elected to public office and appointed to federal courts which is indicative of progress made. However, political, social, and economic disparities between African Americans and whites seem to suggest that racial equality is still a distant ideal.

See also: **Affirmative Action, Civil Rights and Equal Protection, Voting Rights**

Bibliography and Further Reading

Barnes, Catherine A. *Journey from Jim Crow: The Desegregation of Southern Transit.* New York: Columbia University Press, 1983.

Bell, Derrick A., Jr., ed. *Civil Rights: Leading Cases.* Boston: Little, Brown and Company, 1980.

Cashman, Sean Dennis. *African-Americans and the Quest for Civil Rights, 1900-1990.* New York: New York University Press, 1991.

Lively, Donald E. *The Constitution and Race.* New York: Praeger, 1992.

Massey, Douglas S., and Nancy A. Denton. *American Apartheid: Segregation and the Making of the Underclass.* Cambridge: Harvard University Press, 1993.

PLESSY V. FERGUSON

Legal Citation: 163 U.S. 537 (1896)

Petitioner
Homer A. Plessy

Respondent
J. H. Ferguson, New Orleans Criminal District Court Judge

Petitioner's Claim
That Louisiana's law requiring blacks to ride in separate railroad cars violated Plessy's right to equal protection under the law.

Chief Lawyers for Petitioner
F. D. McKenney, S. F. Phillips

Chief Lawyer for Respondent
M. J. Cunningham, Louisiana Attorney General

Justices for the Court
Henry Billings Brown (writing for the Court), Stephen Johnson Field, Melville Weston Fuller, Horace Gray, Rufus Wheeler Peckham, George Shiras, Jr., Edward Douglass White

Justices Dissenting
John Marshall Harlan I (David Josiah Brewer did not participate)

Place
Washington, D.C.

Date of Decision
18 May 1896

Decision
That laws providing for "separate but equal" treatment of blacks and whites were constitutional.

Significance
The Supreme Court's decision effectively sanctioned discriminatory state legislation. *Plessy* was not fully overruled until the 1950s and 1960s, beginning with *Brown v. Board of Education* in 1954.

In the years following the Supreme Court's 1875 decision in *United States v. Cruikshank,* which limited the federal government's ability to protect African Americans' civil rights, many states in the South and elsewhere enacted laws discriminating against African Americans. These laws ranged from restrictions on voting, such as literacy tests and the poll tax, to requirements that blacks and whites attend separate schools and use separate public facilities.

On 7 June 1892, Homer A. Plessy bought a train ticket for travel from New Orleans to Covington, Louisiana. Plessy's ancestry was one-eighth black and the rest white, but under Louisiana law he was considered to be black and was required to ride in the blacks-only railroad car. Plessy sat in the whites-only railroad car, refused to move, and was promptly arrested and thrown into the New Orleans jail.

Judge John H. Ferguson of the District Court of Orleans Parish presided over Plessy's trial for the crime of having refused to leave the whites-only car, and Plessy was found guilty. Plessy's conviction was upheld by the Louisiana Supreme Court, and Plessy appealed to the U.S. Supreme Court for an order forbidding Louisiana in the person of Judge Ferguson from carrying out the conviction.

Ferguson was represented by Louisiana Attorney General M. J. Cunningham and Plessy by F. D. McKenney and S. F. Phillips. On 13 April 1896, Plessy's lawyers argued before the Supreme Court that Louisiana had violated Plessy's Fourteenth Amendment right to equal protection under the law. Attorney General Cunningham argued that the law merely made a distinction between blacks and whites, but did not necessarily treat blacks as inferiors, since theoretically the law provided for "separate but equal" railroad car accommodations.

On 18 May 1896, the Court issued its decision. It upheld the Louisiana law:

> A statute which implies merely a legal distinction between the white and colored races—a distinction which is found in the color of the two races, and which must always exist so long as white men are distinguished from the other race by color—has no tendency to destroy the legal equality of the two races.

A caricature of President Johnson vetoing the Freedman's Act of 1866. © Corbis-Bettmann.

Therefore, the Court affirmed Plessy's sentence, namely a $25 fine or 20 days in jail. Further, the Court endorsed the "separate but equal" doctrine, ignoring the fact that blacks had practically no power to make sure that their "separate" facilities were really "equal" to those of whites. In the years to come, black railroad cars, schools and other facilities were rarely as good as those of whites. Only Justice Harlan dissented from the Court's decision. Harlan's dissent was an uncannily accurate prediction of *Plessy*'s effect:

> Our Constitution is color-blind, and neither knows nor tolerates classes among citizens . . . In my opinion, the judgment this day rendered will, in time, prove to be quite as pernicious as the decision made by this tribunal in the *Dred Scott* case . . . The present decision, it may well be apprehended, will not only stimulate aggressions, more or less brutal and irritating, upon the admitted rights of colored citizens, but will encourage the belief that it is possible, by means of state enactments, to defeat the beneficent purposes by which the people of the United States had in view when they adopted the recent amendments of the Constitution

It was not until the 1950s and the 1960s that the Supreme Court began to reverse *Plessy*. In the landmark 1954 case of *Brown v. Board of Education,* the Court held that separate black and white schools were unconstitutional, and later cases abolished the separate but equal doctrine in other areas affecting civil rights as well.

Related Cases

Strauder v. West Virginia, 100 U.S. 303 (1879).
Civil Rights Cases, 109 U.S. 3 (1883).
Yick Wo v. Hopkins, 118 U.S. 356 (1886).
Missouri ex rel. Gaines v. Canada, 305 U.S. 337 (1938).
Brown v. Board of Education of Topeka, 347 U.S. 483 (1954).

Bibliography and Further Reading

Jackson, Donald W. *Even the Children of Strangers: Equality under the U.S. Constitution.* Lawrence: University Press of Kansas, 1992.

"Separate But Equal"

The "separate but equal" standard established by the Supreme Court in *Plessy* has become more or less synonymous with institutionalized racial segregation. According to the "separate but equal" doctrine, if a state could prove that blacks enjoyed accommodations equal to those for whites, that state could legally sanction segregated schools and other public facilities, as was the case in most of the South.

The very fact that facilities were separate meant that they were inherently unequal, since the whole purpose of the so-called Jim Crow Laws in the South was to keep black people out of the places enjoyed by whites. But beyond this logical fallacy, in practice the facilities were simply unequal: thus for instance most black schools were housed in sub-standard buildings, and African American students used outdated textbooks. With *Sweatt v. Painter* (1950), when a token law school for blacks was ruled unequal to facilities for whites, the Court indicated its willingness to overturn the separate but equal principle, as it would do four years later in *Brown.*

Source(s): Bradley, David and Shelley Fisher, Fishkin, eds. *The Encyclopedia of Civil Rights in America.* Armonk, NY: Sharpe, 1998.

Johnson, John W., ed. *Historic U.S. Court Cases, 1690-1990: An Encyclopedia.* New York: Garland Publishing, 1992.

Kull, Andrew. *The Color-Blind Constitution.* Cambridge, MA: Harvard University Press, 1992.

Olson, Otto H. *The Thin Disguise: Turning Point in Negro History.* New York: Humanities Press, 1967.

BUCHANAN V. WARLEY

Legal Citation: 245 U.S. 60 (1917)

Appellant
William Warley

Appellee
William H. Buchanan

Appellant's Claim
Defendant illegally refused to pay full contracted price for a home lot. He claimed a city ordinance prohibiting blacks from living in white neighborhoods deprived him of property's full value.

Chief Lawyers for Appellant
Moorfield Storey, Clayton B. Blakey

Chief Lawyers for Appellee
Pendleton Beckley, Stuart Chevalier

Justices for the Court
Louis D. Brandeis, John Hessin Clarke, William R. Day (writing for the Court), Oliver Wendell Holmes, Joseph McKenna, James Clark McReynolds, Mahlon Pitney, Willis Van Devanter, Edward Douglass White

Justices Dissenting
None

Place
Washington, D.C.

Date of Decision
5 November 1917

Decision
Outlawed local ordinances preventing blacks from moving into white neighborhoods as unconstitutional interference with private property sales between whites and blacks.

Significance
The unanimous decision, upholding the right of whites and blacks to sell residential property to one another, was the first exception to state segregation laws sanctioned under *Plessy v. Ferguson* (1898). Hailed by the public at the time as upholding personal rights as well as property rights, *Buchanan v. Warley* is now seen by legal commentators as a precursor to *Brown v. Board of Education* (1954).

The 1917 *Buchanan v. Warley* decision broke "the backbone of segregation," sociologist W. E. B. du Bois recalled gratefully 20 years later, even though Jim Crow still ruled public education and transportation.

The test case was brought by a white real estate agent after a black civil rights activist refused to pay full price for a house lot. A Louisville, Kentucky, ordinance prohibiting blacks from moving into white neighborhoods made the lot less valuable, William Warley, the activist, claimed. The result was a "landmark decision in modest dress," stated the late constitutional scholar, Alexander M. Bickel of Yale. The decision "breathed life into Reconstruction principles," Bickel observed, building "a constitutional foundation for the belated principles of racial justice that gathered momentum after World War II."

Buchanan v. Warley was largely forgotten after *Brown v. Board of Education* in 1954. The 56 years between *Plessy v. Ferguson* and *Brown v. Board of Education* had been assumed to be a "slough of despond for the constitutional rights of black people." But, in fact, the 1917 decision was the first great triumph of the National Association for the Advancement of Colored People (NAACP), and was heralded at the time as "A Momentous Decision" by *The Nation:* "[T]he Supreme Court has, once again, proven a true bulwark of the liberties and rights of the colored population of the United States."

Before World War I, starting in Baltimore, border and "upper South" states passed local residential segregation ordinances as blacks from the "deep South" began to migrate north. Coincidentally, local chapters of the newly formed NAACP were being created; and Warley, the president of the Louisville chapter, agreed to buy a house lot from Charles H. Buchanan, a friendly white real estate agent. Warley withheld $100 of the $250 price, however, because the ordinance did not allow him to "occupy said property as a residence."

Buchanan sued and city attorneys, recognizing other laws could also be invalidated, joined the case on Warley's ostensible behalf. Indeed, the North Carolina Appeals Court had struck down "so revolutionary a public policy," citing the history of Celtic pales in Ireland

and Jewish ghettoes in Russia. The Louisville ordinance, nevertheless, was upheld by the Kentucky Court of Appeals. Warley was represented before the Supreme Court by Moorfield Storey, a lawyer from Boston who, as a young abolitionist, participated in the impeachment trial of President Andrew Johnson after the Civil War.

Storey contended that the ordinance deprived African Americans of legal rights and had adverse social consequences for blacks, but not for whites. Storey, who was the first president of the NAACP, argued, "A law which forbids a Negro to rise [does not] forbid a white man to fall," and it is "the common law right of every landowner to occupy his house or to sell or let it to whomever he pleases."

The unanimous decision, written by Justice Day, described the ordinance as a "drastic measure . . . based wholly upon color, that and nothing more." Day was a former secretary of state from Ohio who had negotiated the annexation of the Philippines and Puerto Rico after the Spanish-American War, which Storey had opposed as president of the Anti-Imperialist League. The two men did, however, share common New England abolitionist roots. Justice Day also found the ordinance served no public health or safety purpose, and was not "essential to the maintenance of the purity of the races." The judge observed under the ordinance "colored servants in white families are permitted, and nearby residences of colored persons."

Storey worried that "the prejudice of some judges might lead them to dissent," but the two Southern judges, Chief Justice White of Louisiana, a former Confederate soldier, and Justice McReynolds of Tennessee, concurred. Justice Holmes, often called "the Yankee from Olympus," did draft a dissent, but not so much because of residential segregation concerns. Holmes suspected collusion between Buchanan, Warley and the NAACP with the result that the case, consequently, was not "an honest and actual antagonistic assertion of rights." He later shelved the dissent.

Buchanan v. Warley has been faulted as merely upholding property rights rather than affirming equal protection of personal rights under the law. It did, admittedly, encourage private restrictive covenants, which were not outlawed until the 1950s. Justice Day, in his decision, nevertheless, did cite "certain amendments" adopted after the Civil War "fixing certain fundamental rights which all are bound to respect" as guiding. He referred repeatedly to the Fourteenth Amendment as prohibiting the states from "depriving any person of life, liberty or property without due process of law." *Buchanan v. Warley* clearly sent a signal, according to Bickel, "that in the second decade of

Chief Justice Edward Douglass White. © Archive Photos.

the twentieth century Jim Crow no longer had a casual apologist in the Supreme Court of the United States."

Related Cases
Plessy v. Ferguson, 163 U.S. 537 (1896).
Corrigan v. Buckley, 271 U.S. 323 (1926).
Brown v. Board of Education of Topeka, 347 U.S. 483 (1954).

Bibliography and Further Reading
Bickel, Alexander M., and Benno C. Schmidt. *History of the Supreme Court of the United States.* New York: Macmillan, 1984

Hixson, W. B., Jr. *Moorfield Story and the Abolitionist Tradition.* New York: Oxford University Press, 1972.

McLean, Joseph E. *William Rufus Day: Supreme Court Justice from Ohio.* Baltimore, MD: Johns Hopkins University Press, 1946.

Woodward, Vann C. *The Strange Career of Jim Crow.* New York: Oxford University Press, 1974.

STATE OF MISSOURI EX REL. GAINES V. CANADA

Legal Citation: 305 U.S. 337 (1938)

Appellant
Lloyd L. Gaines

Appellee
S. W. Canada, Registrar of the University of Missouri

Appellant's Claim
That rejection of an African American applicant by the all-white University of Missouri Law School violates equal protection under the law as mandated by the Fourteenth Amendment.

Chief Lawyers for Appellant
Charles F. Houston and S. R. Redmond

Chief Lawyers for Appellee
William S. Hogsett and Fred L. Williams

Justices for the Court
Hugo Lafayette Black, Louis D. Brandeis, Charles Evans Hughes (writing for the Court), Stanley Forman Reed, Owen Josephus Roberts, Harlan Fiske Stone

Justices Dissenting
Pierce Butler, James Clark McReynolds (Benjamin N. Cardozo did not participate)

Place
Washington, D.C.

Date of Decision
12 December 1938

Decision
The Supreme Court ordered the university to admit Gaines.

Significance
Gaines marked a turning point in the reevaluation of the "separate but equal" standard that had been the law of the land since the infamous *Plessy v. Ferguson* decision in 1896.

Lloyd Gaines was an African American resident of Missouri who sought admission to the all-white state university law school. In his quest, Gaines was assisted by the state of Missouri ("ex rel." indicates a case brought by the state on behalf of an individual) and by the National Association for the Advancement of Colored People (NAACP), which looked on his as a test case. The goal of the NAACP was to overturn the "separate but equal" standard for determining what types of segregation were legal.

Gaines had applied to the University of Missouri Law School because there was no law school for blacks in the state. When in due course his application was rejected, Gaines appealed to the state courts for an order compelling the university to admit him. Because the university said it had plans to create an in-state law school for blacks and offered to pay Gaines's tuition at another law school in the meantime, the Missouri courts upheld the decision not to accept Gaines. Gaines's attorney, Charles H. Houston, who played an important role in the NAACP's campaign to overturn *Plessy v. Ferguson* (1896), petitioned the U.S. Supreme Court for review.

Supreme Court Redefines "Separate But Equal"

The NAACP had concentrated its efforts in the field of public education. In 1938, although the Court was still unwilling to overturn "separate but equal," it began to regard with skepticism state claims that all-black state sponsored institutions of higher learning were equivalent to their all-white counterparts. In Gaines's case, the proposal to establish an in-state law school for black students was just that—a proposal. Furthermore, the option of paying for Gaines to attend an out-of-state law school offended the principle of equal protection. As Chief Justice Hughes wrote in the opinion of the Court:

> [T]he obligation of the State to give the protection of equal laws can be performed only where its laws operate . . . it is there that the equality of legal right must be maintained. That obligation is imposed by the Constitution upon the States severally as governmental enti-

ties . . . It is an obligation the burden of which cannot be cast by one State upon another, and no State can be excused from performance by what another State may do or fail to do.

The Supreme Court was not yet ready to throw out "separate but equal," but with *Gaines* the Court began to concede the difficulty—indeed, the near impossibility—of a state maintaining segregated black and white institutions which would be truly equal. In a similar subsequent case, *Sweatt v. Painter* (1950), the Court concluded that an all-black law school could not be the equivalent of an all-white law school precisely because the former excluded those with whom the black graduates would have to contend throughout their professional lives. And in *McLaurin v. Oklahoma State Regents for Higher Education* (1950), the Court ruled against a scheme for educating black and white graduate students in separate classrooms at the same institution. It was but a brief step to the watershed *Brown v. Board of Education* (1954) case, which overturned *Plessy v. Ferguson* once and for all.

The NAACP won Lloyd Gaines's case almost in spite of him. In August of 1937, he informed Houston that while he waited for the University of Missouri Law School to accept him, he intended to work towards an M.A. in economics at the University of Michigan. This was a major blow for the NAACP, as Gaines was proposing to use Missouri's money to fund an out-of-state education—a move that would completely undermine the NAACP's equal protection argument. Houston scrambled to help Gaines find alternative sources of financing. In October of 1939, after the Supreme Court had ruled in his favor and ordered the Missouri Supreme Court to reconsider his case under new guidelines, Gaines simply disappeared. When the University of Missouri subsequently moved the state supreme court for dismissal of the case, the NAACP did not oppose the motion.

Related Cases

Plessy v. Ferguson, 163 U.S. 537 (1896).
McLaurin v. Oklahoma State Regents for Higher Education, 339 U.S. 637 (1950).
Sweatt v. Painter, 339 U.S. 629 (1950).
Brown v. Board of Education of Topeka, 347 U.S. 483 (1954).

Bibliography and Further Reading

Armor, David J. *Forced Justice: School Desegregation and the Law.* New York, NY: Oxford University Press, 1995.

Greenberg, Jack. *Crusaders in the Courts: How a Dedicated Band of Lawyers Fought for the Civil Rights Revolution.* New York, NY: Basic Books, 1994.

Wolters, Raymond. *The Burden of Brown: Thirty Years of School Desegregation.* Knoxville: University of Tennessee Press, 1984.

MORGAN V. COMMONWEALTH OF VIRGINIA

Legal Citation: 328 U.S. 373 (1946)

Appellant
Irene Morgan

Appellee
Commonwealth of Virginia

Appellant's Claim
That forced segregation on buses traveling between states is unconstitutional.

Chief Lawyers for Appellant
William H. Hastie, Thurgood Marshall

Chief Lawyer for Appellee
Abran P. Staples

Justices for the Court
Hugo Lafayette Black, William O. Douglas, Felix Frankfurter, Frank Murphy, Stanley Forman Reed (writing for the Court), Wiley Blount Rutledge

Justices Dissenting
Harold Burton (Robert H. Jackson and Harlan Fiske Stone did not participate)

Place
Washington, D.C.

Date of Decision
3 June 1946

Decision
Forced racial segregation on buses traveling between states is an impermissible burden on interstate commerce.

Significance
Morgan was a significant step on the road to overturning the rule of "separate by equal" that had been the law of the land ever since *Plessy v. Ferguson* (1896).

Irene Morgan, an African American woman, got on a Greyhound bus in Glouster County, Virginia, bound for Baltimore, Maryland. Morgan was asked to sit at the back of the bus, as the laws of Virginia dictated she must. When she refused, she was arrested, convicted, and fined ten dollars. When the Supreme Court of Virginia affirmed her conviction, Morgan appealed to the U.S. Supreme Court.

Morgan was aided in her challenge to Virginia's "Jim Crow" segregation laws by the National Association for the Advancement of Colored People (NAACP), which had in the 1930s begun a campaign to overturn the "separate but equal" doctrine that permitted such laws to exist. The doctrine originated with *Plessy v. Ferguson* an infamous 1896 case in which the Supreme Court upheld a Louisiana statute requiring railroads to provide racially segregated rail cars. Over the next six decades it remained the law of the land. "Separate but equal" gained symbolic significance as a multitude of Jim Crow segregation laws were passed, regulating most aspects of public life in the American South.

Like Homer Plessy, Irene Morgan was an African American involved in a test case (Plessy was acting on behalf of the Citizens' Committee to Test the Constitutionality of the Separate Car Act). And like Plessy, Morgan was arrested for refusing to move to the "colored only" section of a public transportation vehicle that was traveling between states. But whereas Plessy and his lawyers had challenged a Jim Crow law on grounds that it violated Thirteenth and Fourteenth Amendment prohibitions on racial discrimination, Morgan and her NAACP lawyers (one of them the future Supreme Court Justice Thurgood Marshall) based their appeal on the Commerce Clause.

The Commerce Clause appears in Article I, section 8 of the Constitution and grants Congress the power to "regulate Commerce . . . among the several States." The commerce power has proven itself a flexible—and powerful—tool. One of its most effective uses has been in combatting institutionalized racism. It was finally codified into law with passage of the Civil Rights Act of 1964, but by that time it had already been used many times by the Supreme Court as grounds for overturning discriminatory statutes.

Court Finds that Mandatory Segregation on Public Motor Carriers Traveling Between States Violates Commerce Clause

As Hastie and Marshall argued, the Court had, before *Plessy,* used the Commerce Clause to strike down state mandated segregation. In *Hall v. DeCuir* (1878), a Louisiana statute requiring racial segregation on interstate common carriers was struck down as imposing an impermissible burden on interstate commerce. Now, writing for the Court, Justice Reed followed the same logic in overturning the Virginia law:

> This statute is attacked on the ground that it imposes undue burdens on interstate commerce . . . Burdens upon commerce are those actions of a state which directly 'impair the usefulness of its facilities for such traffic.' [Quoting *Illinois Central Railroad v. Illinois* (1896)] That impairment, we think, may arise from other causes than costs or delays. A burden may arise from a state statute which requires interstate passengers to order their movement on the vehicle in accordance with local rather than national requirements.

In other words, forcing passengers to reconfigure themselves every time they crossed state lines was unconstitutional.

Morgan effectively overruled *Louisiana, New Orleans & Texas Railway Co. v. Mississippi* (1890), in which the Court had upheld a state law virtually identical to the one struck down several years earlier on Commerce Clause grounds in *Hall v. DeCuir* (1878). Although segregation on buses traveling in the South still occurred after *Morgan,* this decision made it clear that it was only a matter of time before such practices would be outlawed everywhere.

Related Cases

Hall v. DeCuir, 95 U.S. 485 (1878).
Louisiana, New Orleans & Texas Railway Co. v. Mississippi, 133 U.S. 587 (1890).
Plessy v. Ferguson, 163 U.S. 537 (1896).

Bibliography and Further Reading

Barnes, Catherine A. *Journey from Jim Crow: The Desegregation of Southern Transit.* New York, NY: Columbia University Press, 1983.

Lofgren, Charles A. *The Plessy Case: A Legal-Historical Interpretation.* New York, NY: Oxford University Press, 1987.

Nieman, Donald G., ed. *Black Southerners and the Law, 1865-1900.* New York, NY: Garland, 1994.

SHELLEY V. KRAEMER

Legal Citation: 334 U.S. 1 (1948)

Appellant
J. D. Shelley

Appellee
Louis Kraemer

Appellant's Claim
That restrictive covenants in real estate contracts preventing occupancy by African Americans violates the Fourteenth Amendment guarantee of equal protection of the laws.

Chief Lawyers for Appellant
George L. Vaughn, Herman Willer

Chief Lawyer for Appellee
Gerald L. Seegers

Justices for the Court
Hugo Lafayette Black, Harold Burton, William O. Douglas, Felix Frankfurter, Frank Murphy, Fred Moore Vinson (writing for the Court)

Justices Dissenting
None (Robert H. Jackson, Stanley Forman Reed, Wiley Blount Rutledge did not participate)

Place
Washington, D.C.

Date of Decision
3 May 1948

Decision
The Supreme Court ruled that although such covenants can be created, they cannot be enforced by state or federal courts.

Significance
The impact of *Shelley* on the emerging civil rights struggle was enormous. After this decision, a powerful form of racial discrimination in housing was no longer judicially enforceable.

In February of 1911, 29 of the 30 owners of property in a St. Louis, Missouri, neighborhood signed an agreement not to rent or sell their property to African Americans or Asian Americans. The 29 signatories held 47 of the 57 parcels of land involved. At the time of the signing, five of the parcels were owned by African Americans. One of these African American families had lived on their land since 1882.

In October of 1945, J. D. Shelley and his wife, who were African American, bought a parcel of land in the neighborhood from someone named Fitzgerald. The Shelleys apparently had no knowledge of the restrictive covenant attached to the land. The following October, Louis Kraemer and his wife, who owned other property that was covered by the restrictive covenant, went to the circuit court of the city of St. Louis in an effort to enforce the agreement and take the land deed away from the Shelleys. The trial court ruled against the Kraemers, declaring that the agreement was invalid because it had never been signed by all the affected parties. The Supreme Court of Missouri reversed this decision. The Shelleys then petitioned the U.S. Supreme Court for review of the case.

Supreme Court Declares Racially Discriminatory Restrictive Covenants Unenforceable

Agreements that restrict land use are common and usually legal. The Shelleys argued, however, that a racially biased restrictive covenant violated their right to equal protection under law, guaranteed at the state level by the Fourteenth Amendment. Whereas most such covenants seek to restrict land use, the covenant in question unconstitutionally sought to bar certain races of people.

Segregation in housing was at one time enforced by municipal zoning laws. After the Court declared such laws unconstitutional in *Buchanan v. Warley* (1917), property holders turned to private agreements as a means of enforcing housing segregation. At the time that *Shelley* was brought before the courts, such agreements were being routinely enforced in the North and had begun spreading to the rest of the country.

In reaching its decision, the Court split some fine legal hairs. Writing for the Court, Chief Justice Vinson declared that the St. Louis restrictive covenant was a private agreement, and therefore the Court had no power to prohibit it. What had been ruled out in *Buchanan* were restrictions imposed by the state, and such "state action" was clearly unconstitutional. Judicial enforcement of private restrictive covenants was not state action, but when the covenants were themselves unconstitutional, the courts were prohibited from putting them into effect:

> These are not cases . . . in which the States have merely abstained from action, leaving private individuals free to impose such discrimination as they see fit. Rather, these are cases in which the States have made available to such individuals the full coercive power of government to deny to petitioners, on the grounds of race or color, the enjoyment of property rights in premises which petitioners are willing and financially able to acquire and which the grantors are willing to sell. The difference between judicial enforcement and nonenforcement of the restrictive covenants is the difference to petitioners between being denied rights of property available to other members of the community and being accorded full enjoyment of those rights on an equal footing.

The *Shelley* Court paid scant attention to the sociological data supplied by the parties. It also paid little attention to the fact that there was evidence that the courts that had been enforcing discriminatory restrictive covenants had been themselves adopting segregationist policies. The whole argument of the Court's opinion rather disingenuously failed to note that at a

Justice Frederick Moore Vinson. © Photograph by Harris and Ewing. Collection of the Supreme Court of the United States.

certain point judicial enforcement of private agreements becomes indistinguishable from state action. Still, the impact of *Shelley v. Kraemer* was undeniable. Suddenly, discrimination in housing was a serious issue with constitutional implications. The decision both discouraged future discriminatory restrictive covenants and encouraged those engaged in the civil rights movement to expand their struggle.

Related Cases
Buchanan v. Warley, 245 U.S. 60 (1917).
Jones v. Mayer, 392 U.S. 409 (1968).

Bibliography and Further Reading
Allen, Francis A. "Remembering *Shelley v. Kraemer.*" *Washington University Law Quarterly*, Vol. 67, 1989, pp. 709-735.

Chicago's Restrictive Real Estate Covenants

The term "restrictive real estate covenants" might seem dry, but the term signifies a highly dramatic aspect in the history of segregation. Wendy Plotkin studied covenants designed to keep African Americans out of suburban Chicago neighborhoods, and noted that a number of respected institutions, including local YMCAs and the University of Chicago, upheld the practice.

One of the first significant challenges to the covenants came from a local African American Republican leader, NAACP member, and real-estate developer Carl Hansberry, who in 1937 bought a home in all-white Washington Park. Hansberry's daughter Lorraine, two-years-old at the time, would later grow up and write

Raisin in the Sun (1959), a memoir which recorded the challenges her family faced as it integrated Washington Park.

Raisin in the Sun, which became a film starring Sidney Poitier, was not the only important work inspired by the efforts to integrate Chicago's neighborhoods. Noted African American poet Langston Hughes wrote a poem entitled "Restrictive Covenants," and the subject of Chicago's restrictive covenants figured heavily in *An American Dilemma* by Gunnar Myrdal, a significant work of sociology.

Source(s): Plotkin, Wendy. *"Racial Restrictive Covenants in U.S."* www.iuc.edu.

Kirp, David L., John P. Dwyer, and Larry A. Rosenthal, eds. *Our Town: Race, Housing, and the Soul of Suburbia.* New Brunswick, NJ: Rutgers University Press, 1995.

Tussman, Joseph, ed. *The Supreme Court on Racial Discrimination.* New York: Oxford University Press, 1963.

MCLAURIN V. OKLAHOMA STATE REGENTS FOR HIGHER EDUCATION

Legal Citation: 339 U.S. 637 (1950)

Petitioner
George McLaurin

Respondent
Oklahoma State Regents for Higher Education, et al.

Petitioner's Claim
That an Oklahoma state law mandating racial segregation in postgraduate education violated the Equal Protection Clause of the Fourteenth Amendment.

Chief Lawyers for Petitioner
Robert L. Carter, Amos T. Hall

Chief Lawyer for Respondents
Fred Hansen

Justices for the Court
Hugo Lafayette Black, Harold Burton, Tom C. Clark, William O. Douglas, Felix Frankfurter, Robert H. Jackson, Sherman Minton, Stanley Forman Reed, Fred Moore Vinson (writing for the Court)

Justices Dissenting
None

Place
Washington, D.C.

Date of Decision
5 June 1950

Decision
Upheld the petitioner's claim and reversed a lower court ruling, holding that the segregation practiced by the University of Oklahoma's Graduate School of Education was in violation of the Equal Protection Clause of the Fourteenth Amendment.

Significance
The ruling provided further evidence of the Court's abandonment of the "separate but equal" approach to racial segregation in education as advanced in *Plessy v. Ferguson* (1896). This doctrine was replaced with complete opposition to segregation in education, which the Court established in *Lloyd Gaines v. University of Missouri* (1937) and *Sipuel v. University of Oklahoma* (1948). Eventually, the Court's stand against educational segregation yielded what is arguably its most historic decision in *Brown v. Board of Education* (1954).

Separate but Equal

At the time of its ratification, the Fourteenth Amendment to the Constitution of the United States was interpreted as prohibiting state discrimination on the basis of race. Given the deep divisions between the races, particularly in the years prior to the Civil War, it is not surprising that many states codified racial discrimination with segregationist statutes. Racial tensions did not disappear with the end of the Civil War, and states in both the North and South continued to pass segregationist legislation. In fact, this approach to race relations was sanctioned by the Supreme Court in *Plessy v. Ferguson*. In this case, the Court ruled that a Boston, Massachusetts statute mandating racial segregation in schools and on public transportation was constitutional. The Court stated that "the object of the [Fourteenth] Amendment was undoubtedly to enforce the absolute equality of the two races before the law, but in the nature of things it could not have been intended to abolish distinctions based upon color." Thus, *Plessy v. Ferguson* established the "separate but equal" doctrine, which rendered virtually all segregationist statutes legally binding provided that facilities of equal quality existed for all races. In reality, of course, the facilities available to African Americans were seldom equal to those available to the majority under segregation.

Abandonment of the "Separate but Equal" Doctrine

The nation endured separate but equal educational facilities for nearly half a century. As time passed, however, the doctrine succumbed to its own internal contradictions. Moreover, integration in the armed forces during the Second World War removed some opposition to integration of society as a whole. In *Lloyd Gaines v. University of Missouri* (1937), the Court ruled that the University could not deny Mr. Gaines admission, since no equivalent institution for African Americans existed in the state at the time of his application for admission. The Court continued its movement away from *Plessy v. Ferguson* in *Sipuel v. University of Oklahoma* (1948) when it reversed lower court decisions that interpreted *Gaines* as not requiring states with segregation-

G. E. McLaurin sits apart from other students as he attends the University of Oklahoma.
© UPI/Corbis-Bettmann.

ist laws to admit African American students to white postsecondary educational institutions. Clearly, the days of "separate but equal" were numbered.

Not Separate but Still Unequal

George W. McLaurin, a young man of African descent pursuing his doctorate, secured admission to the Graduate School of Education of the University of Oklahoma shortly after the Court's decision in *Sipuel*. National legal and legislative institutions may have been moving away from segregationism, but many states, including Oklahoma, most certainly were not. The state's university system had grudgingly begun to accept African American students, but segregationism was alive and well on campus.

George McLaurin found his personal situation within the Graduate School of Education unbearable. Although he was allowed to attend the University of Oklahoma and, by his own stipulation, was not placed at a disadvantage in any way, the treatment he received was inhumane. McLaurin was forced to sit at a designated desk in an anteroom attached to the classroom where his fellow students sat, to use only a designated space in the mezzanine of the library, and to eat at a

designated table and at a different time than his fellow students in the university's cafeteria.

Legal Action

McLaurin filed a motion with the district court to compel the university to allow him a more normal campus life. This motion was denied on the grounds that his treatment did not violate the Equal Protection Clause of the Fourteenth Amendment, since it did not affect his ability to receive the same education as his classmates. The university did take voluntary action, however, removing a railing surrounding McLaurin's designated eating place and also taking down a sign over his table that read: "Reserved for Colored Only." McLaurin was also allowed to sit in the same classroom as the other students, although made to occupy a specified section, and to eat at the same time as his classmates. He still found his situation unsatisfactory, however, and his case was appealed to the U.S. Supreme Court, which heard arguments on 3 and 4 April 1950.

Equal Protection or Equal Treatment?

Chief Justice Vinson delivered the opinion for a unanimous Court, which ruled that the University of Oklahoma's treatment of McLaurin, even in its modified form, was unconstitutional and must be stopped. Vinson had a strong personal interest in civil rights cases, and worked tirelessly behind the scenes to insure unanimity in the decision so as not to dilute the message he believed the Court should send to society. The Court was careful to point out that it was only ruling on the narrow question of "whether a state may, after admitting a student to graduate instruction in its state university, afford him different treatment from other students solely because of his race." However, the Court was also willing to face the wider implications of its decision.

> Our society grows increasingly complex, and our need for trained leaders increases correspondingly. Appellant's case represents, perhaps, the epitome of that need, for he is attempting to obtain an advanced degree in education, to become, by definition, a leader and trainer of others.

The Court thus ruled that separate but equal facilities worked against the national interest, and strongly implied that they would no longer be tolerated in the field of education.

Impact

McLaurin v. Oklahoma State Regents for Higher Education represents a watershed for the Civil Rights Movement in the United States. In conjunction with *Sweatt v. Painter* (1950), in which, on the same day that it announced its ruling in *McLaurin*, the Court ruled that the University of Texas Law School had to admit African American students despite the existence of traditionally black law schools within the state, the case marked the beginning of the end of the legal doctrine of separate but equal within higher education in the United States. Despite Chief Justice Vinson's death in 1953, the Court continued its advocacy of racial integration under his successor, Earl Warren. Under Warren, the Court completely disposed of the doctrine of separate but equal and delivered what may be its most famous and influential decision: that states could not bar children of African American descent from attending public primary and secondary schools in *Brown v. Board of Education* (1954).

Related Cases

Plessy v. Ferguson, 163 U.S. 537 (1896).
Lloyd Gaines v. University of Missouri, 305 U.S. 337 (1937).
Sipuel v. University of Oklahoma, 332 U.S. 631 (1948).
Sweatt v. Painter, 339 U.S. 629 (1950).
Brown v. Board of Education, 347 U.S. 483 (1954).

Bibliography and Further Reading

Biskupic, Joan, and Elder Witt, eds. *Guide to the U.S. Supreme Court,* 3rd ed. Washington: Congressional Quarterly Inc., 1990.

Elliott, Stephen P., ed. *A Reference Guide to the U.S. Supreme Court,* New York: Facts on File Publications, 1986.

Hall, Kermit L., ed. *The Oxford Companion to the Supreme Court of the United States,* New York: Oxford University Press, 1992.

SWEATT V. PAINTER

Legal Citation: 339 U.S. 629 (1950)

Appellant
Heman Marion Sweatt

Appellee
Theophilis Shickel Painter

Appellant's Claim
That the refusal of the University of Texas to admit him to its law school violated his Fourteenth Amendment right to equal protection of the laws.

Chief Lawyers for Appellant
W. J. Durham and Thurgood Marshall

Chief Lawyers for Appellee
Price Daniel and Joe R. Greenhill

Justices for the Court
Hugo Lafayette Black, Harold Burton, Tom C. Clark, William O. Douglas, Felix Frankfurter, Robert H. Jackson, Sherman Minton, Stanley Forman Reed, Fred Moore Vinson (writing for the Court)

Justices Dissenting
None

Place
Washington, D.C.

Date of Decision
5 June 1950

Decision
The Supreme Court ordered the university to admit Sweatt.

Significance
While not overruling the segregation imposed by *Plessy v. Ferguson* (1896) outright, the Court went some distance toward outlawing official segregation by stating that the university could not possibly create an all-black law school that was "separate but equal."

Heman Marion Sweatt was an African American mailman living in Houston, Texas, who wanted to go to law school. When he was rejected by the all-white University of Texas School of Law for entrance during the February 1946 term, it was solely because he was black. At that time, no law school in the state admitted black students.

Sweatt then brought suit against Theophilis Painter and other members of the university board of regents, requesting that the court issue an order compelling them to admit him. The court agreed with Sweatt that in denying him the chance to obtain a legal education, the university was denying him his right to equal protection of the laws, guaranteed by the Fourteenth Amendment. But instead of ordering that Sweatt be admitted, the court held his case over for six months to allow Texas to create a separate law school for blacks. When the six months had expired, the court again declined to issue an order for Sweatt's admission, owing to the fact that the university had vowed to open a separate but equal law school for blacks in two months' time.

Sweatt appealed this ruling to the Texas Court of Civil Appeals. While his appeal was pending, the university did open a separate law school for blacks, but Sweatt refused to register. His case was sent back to the trial court, which determined that the new law school offered an education equivalent to that enjoyed by white law students at the University of Texas. With that, the trial court dismissed Sweatt's case. Sweatt, with the backing of the National Association for the Advancement of Colored People (NAACP) and the help of their premier attorney, Thurgood Marshall, petitioned the U.S. Supreme Court for review.

Court Finds that "Separate" Facilities Cannot be "Equal"

Marshall, who would himself later become a Supreme Court justice, realized that Sweatt left the Court with an easy way out. They could hand Heman Sweatt a hollow victory by declaring that Texas's all-black law school was not equal, while at the same time declining to overturn *Plessy v. Ferguson*. *Plessy*, which had been the law of the land since 1896, held that "separate but

Chief Justice Fred Moore Vinson

Robert W. Langran of the Supreme Court Historical Society noted that of eight Supreme Court justices rated as "failures" by authors Albert P. Blaustein and Roy M. Mersky in a 1978 volume entitled *The First One Hundred Justices: Statistical Studies on the Supreme Court of the United States*, only one was a chief justice, Fred Moore Vinson. Vinson (1890-1953), appointed chief in 1946, served just seven years, until his death, making his the shortest tenure of a chief justice during the twentieth century.

According to Langran, the authors' identification of Vinson and others as "failures" reveals an ideological bias. Although he tended to offer conservative opinions in cases involving the political rights of radicals,

his views on race helped pave the way for many important civil rights rulings. Thus, for instance, in Vinson's first major opinion, *Shelley v. Kraemer* (1948), he held that restrictive covenants designed to keep African Americans out of white neighborhoods represented a violation of the Fourteenth Amendment. Likewise in *Sweatt v. Painter* (1950), he led a unanimous Court in refusing to accept an attempt by the University of Texas Law School to justify its "separate but equal" facility for black students.

Source(s): Langran, Robert W. "Why Are Some Supreme Court Justices Rated as 'Failures?'" Supreme Court Historical Society, http://metalab.unc.edu.

equal" treatment of the races was constitutionally permissible. In the 1940s, the NAACP had begun a vigorous campaign to overturn *Plessy*, and although *Sweatt* brought the organization nearer to its goal, Marshall had accurately predicted how the Court would rule. Writing for a unanimous Court, Chief Justice Vinson concluded:

> [Sweatt] may claim his full constitutional right; legal education equivalent to that offered by the State to students of other races. Such education is not available to him in a separate law school as offered by the State. We cannot, therefore, agree with respondents that the doctrine of *Plessy v. Ferguson* . . . requires affirmance of the judgment [of the state court]. Nor need we reach petitioner's contention that *Plessy v. Ferguson* should be reexamined in the light of contemporary knowledge respecting the purposes of the Fourteenth Amendment and the effects of racial segregation.

In another case decided the same day, *McLaurin v. Oklahoma State Regents for Higher Education* (1950), the Court edged somewhat closer to overturning *Plessy*. George McLaurin, an African American citizen of Oklahoma, had been admitted into an all-white graduate school, but he was obliged to remain segregated from

his fellow students. In ruling that this treatment handicapped McLaurin, the Court in effect held that once blacks are admitted to white schools, there can be no racial discrimination within the institution. It would be four more years before the Supreme Court overturned *Plessy* in the watershed case of *Brown v. Board of Education* (1954). After the Court decided *Brown* and the cases that grew out of it, there could be no more officially sanctioned segregation in public education—or in any public institutions.

Related Cases

Plessy v. Ferguson, 163 U.S. 537 (1896).
Shelley v. Kraemer, 334 U.S. 1 (1948).
McLaurin v. Oklahoma State Regents for a Higher Education, 339 U.S. 637 (1950).
Brown v. Board of Education, 347 U.S. 483 (1954).

Bibliography and Further Reading

Davis, Abraham L. *The Supreme Court, Race, and Civil Rights* Thousand Oaks, CA: Sage Publications, 1995.

Desegregation of Public Education. New York, NY: Garland, 1991.

Greenberg, Jack. *Crusaders in the Courts: How a Dedicated Band of Lawyers Fought for the Civil Rights Revolution.* New York: Basic Books, 1994.

BROWN V. BOARD OF EDUCATION

Legal Citation: 347 U.S. 483 (1954)

Appellants
Several parents of African American children of elementary school age in Topeka, Kansas

Appellee
Board of Education of Topeka, Kansas

Appellants' Claim
That the segregation of white and African American children in the public schools of Topeka solely on the basis of race denied the African American children equal protection under the law guaranteed by the Fourteenth Amendment.

Chief Lawyers for Appellants
Robert L. Carter, Thurgood Marshall, Spottswood W. Robinson, Charles S. Scott

Chief Lawyers for Appellees
Harold R. Fatzer, Paul E. Wilson

Justices for the Court
Hugo Lafayette Black, Harold Burton, Tom C. Clark, William O. Douglas, Felix Frankfurter, Robert H. Jackson, Sherman Minton, Stanley Forman Reed, Earl Warren

Justices Dissenting
None

Place
Washington, D.C.

Date of Decision
17 May 1954

Decision
Segregated schools violate the Equal Protection Clause of the Fourteenth Amendment.

Significance
Brown v. Board of Education held that segregated schools were unconstitutional, overturning the "separate but equal" doctrine of *Plessy v. Ferguson* (1896).

Sometimes in history, events of great importance happen unexpectedly to modest men. Such was the case with Oliver Brown, whose desire that his children be able to attend the public school closest to their home resulted in a fundamental transformation of race relations in the United States.

Brown was born in 1919 and lived in Topeka, Kansas, where he worked as a welder for a railroad. Brown's family literally lived on the wrong side of the tracks: their house was close to Brown's place of work, and the neighborhood bordered on a major switchyard. Not only could the Brown family hear the trains day and night, but because the Topeka school system was segregated, the Brown children had to walk through the switchyard to get to the black school a mile away. There was another school only seven blocks away, but it was exclusively for white children.

In September of 1950, when his daughter Linda was to enter the third grade, Brown took her to the whites-only school and tried to enroll her. Brown had no history of racial activism, and outside of work his only major activity was serving as an assistant pastor in the local church. He was simply tired of seeing his daughter being forced to go through the switchyard to go to a school far from home because she was black. The principal of the white school refused to enroll Brown's daughter. Brown sought help from McKinley Burnett, head of the local branch of the National Association for the Advancement of Colored People, or NAACP.

NAACP Takes on Topeka Board of Education

Burnett's organization had wanted to challenge segregation for quite some time, but until Brown came to them they had never had the right plaintiff at the right time. Segregation, in the public schools and elsewhere, was a fact of life in Topeka as in so many other places, and few were willing to challenge it. Now that he had Brown, who was joined by several other black parents in Topeka with children in blacks-only public schools, Burnett and the NAACP decided that the time was ripe for legal action.

On 22 March 1951 Brown's NAACP lawyers filed a lawsuit in the U.S. District Court for the District of Kansas, requesting an injunction forbidding Topeka from continuing to segregate its public schools. The court tried the case 25-26 June, 1951. Brown and the other black parents testified to the fact that their children were denied admission to white schools. One parent, Silas Fleming, explained why he and the other parents wanted to get their children into the white schools:

> It wasn't to cast any insinuations that our teachers are not capable of teaching our children because they are supreme, extremely intelligent and are capable of teaching my kids or white kids or black kids. But my point was that not only I and my children are craving light: the entire colored race is craving light, and the only way to reach the light is to start our children together in their infancy and they come up together.

Next, the court listened to expert witnesses who testified that segregated schools were inherently unequal because separation sent a message to black children that they were inferior. This stigma could never be eliminated from a segregated school system, as Dr. Hugh W. Speer, chairman of the University of Kansas City's department of elementary school education, testified:

> For example, if the colored children are denied the experience in school of associating with white children, who represent 90 percent of our national society in which these colored children must live, then the colored child's curriculum is being greatly curtailed. The Topeka curriculum or any school curriculum cannot be equal under segregation.

The Board of Education's lawyers retorted that since most restaurants, bathrooms, and public facilities in Kansas City also were segregated, segregated schools were only preparing black children for the realities of life as black adults. Segregation pervaded every aspect of life in Topeka as in so many other places, and it was beyond the court's jurisdiction to act on anything in this one lawsuit but the legality of school segregation. The board's argument did not convince the judges. The board was assuming that segregation was a natural and desirable way of life for the races to live.

Next, the board argued that segregated schools did not necessarily result in any detrimental effect. After all, hadn't Frederick Douglass, Booker T. Washington, and George Washington Carver, among other great African Americans, achieved so much in the face of obstacles far worse than segregated educational facilities? The fallacy in this argument was obvious, however. While some exceptional people were capable of rising above any adversity, for the majority of African Americans the discriminatory effect of segregation meant a lessening of opportunities. Dr. Horace B. English, a psychology professor at Ohio State University, testified:

Chief Justice Earl Warren. © The Library of Congess.

> There is a tendency for us to live up to, or perhaps I should say down to, social expectations and to learn what people say we can learn, and legal segregation definitely depresses the Negro's expectancy and is therefore prejudicial to his learning.

On 3 August 1951 the court issued its decision. The three judges noted that the leading Supreme Court opinion on public school segregation was the 1896 case *Plessy v. Ferguson. Plessy* legitimized the doctrine of "separate but equal" school systems for blacks and whites, and *Plessy* had not been overturned by the Supreme Court or even seriously questioned, despite some nibbling away at the doctrine's edges in a few recent cases. Therefore, regardless of the experts' testimony that separate-but-equal schools were inherently impossible, the court felt compelled to deny Brown and the other plaintiffs their request for an injunction. The court made it clear, however, that it did not relish its role in upholding Topeka's segregation:

> Segregation of white and colored children in public schools has a detrimental effect upon the colored children. The impact is greater when it has the sanction of the law; for the policy of separating the races is usually inter-

preted as denoting the inferiority of the Negro group. A sense of inferiority affects the motivation of a child to learn. Segregation with the sanction of law, therefore, has a tendency to [compromise] the educational and mental development of Negro children and to deprive them of some of the benefits they would receive in a racial[ly] integrated school system.

Fight Goes to Supreme Court

On 1 October 1951 the plaintiffs filed a petition for appeal. Under certain special procedural rules, they were able to go directly to the U.S. Supreme Court instead of going through federal court of appeals. On 9 June 1952 the Supreme Court put the case on its docket and consolidated it with several other cases from across the country where school segregation policies were being challenged. The Court scheduled a hearing for 9 December 1952 in Washington, D.C., during which the plaintiffs—now appellants—and the board of education would present their arguments.

The 9 December 1952 hearing ended in a stalemate. After listening to both sides reiterate the arguments they had made before the district court, the Supreme Court ordered another hearing, to take place 8 December 1953. The Court directed the parties to confine their re-argument to certain specific issues that especially concerned the justices, dealing mostly with the ratification of the Fourteenth Amendment by the states in 1868. Since the appellants' lawsuit rested on the Equal Protection Clause of this amendment, the Court wanted to know more about the circumstances surrounding the amendment's adoption. For example, the Court was interested in the debates in Congress and in the state legislatures, the views of the proponents and opponents of the amendment, and existing segregation practices. Although the NAACP, Brown, and the other appellants were disappointed that their case would be on hold for another year, the Court's order for re-argument signaled its willingness to reconsider the separate-but-equal doctrine of *Plessy*.

Court Throws Out *Plessy*; Declares Segregation Illegal

After the 8 December 1953 re-argument, the Court announced its decision on 17 May 1954. According to the published opinion, the re-argument had not revealed anything that shed light on whether the adoption of the Fourteenth Amendment had been specifically intended to preclude segregated schools:

> Even in the North, the conditions of public education did not approximate those existing today. The curriculum was usually rudimentary; ungraded schools were common in rural areas; the school term was but three months a

year in many states; and compulsory school attendance was virtually unknown. As a consequence, it is not surprising that there should be so little in the history of the Fourteenth Amendment relating to its intended effect on public education.

Instead, the Court endorsed the appellants' central thesis that segregation was inherently unequal no matter how much effort the school system made to ensure that black and white schools had equivalent facilities, staffing, books, buses, and so forth. The Court reviewed some recent cases in which it had cautiously made an exception to *Plessy* where certain graduate schools were involved. In those cases, the Court said that segregation was unequal because the blacks' professional careers were hurt by the stigma of having attended schools considered to be inferior, and where they did not have the opportunity to make contacts or have intellectual discourse with their white counterparts. With this support, the Court was ready to declare that all segregation in public schools was unconstitutional:

> We conclude that in the field of public education the doctrine of "separate but equal" has no place. Separate educational facilities are inherently unequal. Therefore, we hold that the [appellants] and others similarly situated for whom the actions have been brought are, by reason of the segregation complained of, deprived of the equal protection of the laws guaranteed by the Fourteenth Amendment.

After nearly 60 years of legalized discrimination, the Court had thrown out *Plessy v. Ferguson.* It would take 20 years for the Court's decision to be fully implemented, however—long after Oliver Brown died in 1961. In 1955, the Court said that all American school systems must desegregate "with all deliberate speed," but most local schools in the South did nothing until they were brought to court one by one. The process dragged on throughout the rest of the 1950s, during the 1960s, and into the early 1970s. Meanwhile, particularly during the civil rights movement of the 1960s, the Court acted to strike down all the other forms of legal segregation in American society, from bus stations and public libraries to restrooms.

The process was painful and often violent, frequently accompanied by federal intervention and mass demonstrations. By the 1970s, however, desegregation was a fact. *Brown v. Board of Education* not only made it possible to demolish segregated public school systems, but it was the landmark that served as a catalyst for further antidiscrimination decisions by the Supreme Court.

Related Cases

Strauder v. West Virginia, 100 U.S. 303 (1880).
Plessy v. Ferguson, 163 U.S. 537 (1898).

Sweatt v. Painter, 339 U.S. 629 (1950).

McLaurin v. Oklahoma State Regents, 339 U.S. 637 (1950).

Swann v. Charlotte-Mecklenburg Board of Education, 402 U.S. 1 (1971).

Milliken v. Bradley, 433 U.S. 267 (1974).

Washington v. Seattle School District No. 1, 458 U.S. 457 (1982).

Bob Jones University v. United States, 461 U.S. 574 (1983).

Bibliography and Further Reading

"The Day Race Relations Changed Forever: U.S. Supreme Court Desegregation Decision of May 17, 1954 Was Hailed by Many as the 'Second Emancipation Proclamation.'" *Ebony,* May 1985, pp. 108-112.

Johnson, John W. *Historic U.S. Court Cases, 1690-1990: An Encyclopedia.* New York: Garland Publishing, 1992.

Kluger, Richard. *Simple Justice: the History of Brown v. Board of Education and Black America's Struggle for Equality.* New York: Alfred A. Knopf, 1976.

Orlich, Donald C. "Brown v. Board of Education: Time for a Reassessment." *Phi Delta Kappan,* April 1991, pp. 631-632.

Sudo, Phil. "Five Little People Who Changed U.S. History." *Scholastic Update,* January 1990, pp. 8-10.

White, Jack E. "The Heirs of Oliver Brown." *Time,* July 6, 1987, pp. 88-89.

BOLLING V. SHARPE

Legal Citation: 347 U.S. 497 (1954)

Petitioners
Bolling and other African American children residents in the District of Columbia

Respondents
The District of Columbia public school system

Petitioners' Claim
Because racial segregation in the public schools is unconstitutional, they should be allowed to attend white schools that had rejected them.

Chief Lawyers for Petitioners
George E. C. Hayes, James M. Nabrit, George M. Johnson, Herbert O. Reid, Charles W. Quick

Chief Lawyers for Respondents
Milton D. Korman, Vernon E. West, Chester H. Gray, Lyman J. Umstead

Justices for the Court
Hugo Lafayette Black, Harold Burton, Tom C. Clark, William O. Douglas, Felix Frankfurter, Robert H. Jackson, Sherman Minton, Stanley Forman Reed, Earl Warren (writing for the Court)

Justices Dissenting
None

Place
Washington, D.C.

Date of Decision
17 May 1954

Decision
Racial segregation among District of Columbia school children was not legal under the Constitution.

Significance
The Court incorporated the Fourteenth Amendment's Equal Protection Clause (which applied only to the states) into the Fifth Amendment's Due Process Clause (which applied to the federal government).

Bolling v. Sharpe was one of several racial segregation cases decided in May of 1954. The National Association for the Advancement of Colored People (NAACP) had brought five cases on appeal to the Supreme Court, all challenging the assignment of black and white children to separate public schools. The more famous decision, *Brown v. Board of Education,* consolidated four cases from Delaware, Kansas, South Carolina, and Virginia. *Bolling v. Sharpe* concerned the District of Columbia.

Separate Can Never Be Equal

In *Brown,* the Court ruled that segregation in the public schools deprived black children of "equal protection of the law." It thus violated one of the guarantees in the Fourteenth Amendment: "No state shall deny to any person within its jurisdiction the equal protection of the laws." Some 60 years earlier in *Plessy v. Ferguson* (1896), the Court allowed states to provide "separate but equal" facilities for different races. Reversing *Plessy,* the Court declared in *Brown* that segregation was inherently unequal.

Writing the majority opinion, Chief Justice Warren maintained that even if the "physical facilities and other 'tangible' factors are equal," segregation is psychologically harmful. It generates in black children a "feeling of inferiority as to their status in the community that may affect their hearts and minds in a way unlikely ever to be undone."

In *Bolling v. Sharpe,* issued the same day as the *Brown* decision, the Court applied the same reasoning to schools in the District of Columbia. Chief Justice Warren, again writing for the unanimous court, was determined to end segregation in the District of Columbia. "In view of our decision that the Constitution prohibits the states from maintaining racially segregated public schools, it would be unthinkable that the same Constitution would impose a lesser duty on the Federal Government."

"Due Process" Requires "Equal Protection"

Chief Justice Warren was well aware of the legal difficulties in extending the principles of the *Brown* decision to the District of Columbia. The Fourteenth

Amendment, with its Equal Protection Clause, had been adopted in 1868 to protect individuals—particularly the former slaves—against injustice at the state and local level. It was never intended to affect the federal government, which has authority over the District of Columbia.

To resolve this difficulty, Chief Justice Warren incorporated the Fourteenth Amendment's Equal Protection Clause into the Fifth Amendment, which does apply to the federal government. Under the Fifth Amendment, no person "shall be deprived of life, liberty, or property, without due process of law." The phrase *due process,* Warren argued, must include "equal protection of the laws."

The Fifth Amendment was adopted 80 years before the Fourteenth Amendment. The two amendments had entirely different legislative histories, and the courts had given differing interpretations to "due process" and "equal protection." As Chief Justice Warren recognized, the two phrases are "not always interchangeable." Nevertheless, Warren maintained that in some sense, due process implies equality. The two concepts "both stemming from our American ideal of fairness, are not mutually exclusive."

Whatever the term means, the Fifth Amendment required due process only when the federal government was acting to take away life, liberty, or property. Warren did not claim that segregation deprived black school children of life or property. However, he declared that segregation did take away their "liberty" if that word was defined in the broadest sense possible.

The Chief Justice declared that "Liberty under law extends to the full range of conduct which the individual is free to pursue." Any legal conduct, such as going to school, is part of this constitutionally protected liberty. Thus the government cannot restrict going to school—or any other personal conduct—without a "proper" objective.

> Segregation in public education is not reasonably related to any proper governmental objective, and thus it imposes on Negro children of

the District of Columbia a burden that constitutes an arbitrary deprivation of their liberty in violation of the Due Process Clause.

In *Bolling v. Sharpe,* the Supreme Court practiced a form of reverse incorporation. For some years, the Court had argued that the Fourteenth Amendment incorporated the Bill of Rights. In *Bolling,* it ruled that the Bill of Rights incorporated part of the Fourteenth Amendment. Subsequent decisions have recognized that due process and equal protection are not always coextensive. Overall, however, the Court has continued to hold that federal as well as state laws must be in accordance with the Fourteenth Amendment's Equal Protection Clause.

Related Cases

Plessy v. Ferguson, 163 U.S. 537 (1896).
Brown v. Board of Education of Topeka, 347 U.S. 483 (1954).

Bibliography and Further Reading

Currie, David P. *The Constitution in the Supreme Court: The Second Century, 1888-1986.* Chicago: University of Chicago Press, 1990.

Ducat, Craig R. *Modes of Constitutional Interpretation.* Saint Paul: West, 1978.

Graglia, L. A. *Disaster by Degree: The Supreme Court Decisions on Race and the Schools.* Ithaca: Cornell University Press, 1976.

Kluger, R. *Simple Justice: The History of Brown v. Board of Education and Black America's Struggle for Equality.* New York: Knopf, 1975.

Wasby, Stephen L., Anthony A. D'Amato, and Rosemary Metrailer. *Desegregation from Brown to Alexander: An Exploration of Supreme Court Strategies.* Carbondale: Southern Illinois University Press, 1977.

Wilkinson, J. H. *From Brown to Bakke: The Supreme Court and School Integration.* New York: Oxford University Press, 1979.

EVANS V. NEWTON

Legal Citation: 382 U.S. 296

Petitioner
Evans, et al.

Respondent
Newton, et al.

Petitioner's Claim
That a Macon, Georgia park that had been left to the city on the condition that it be open to white people be desegregated, even though the park had recently reverted to private control.

Chief Lawyer for Petitioner
Jack Greenberg

Chief Lawyers for Respondent
C. Baxter Jones and Frank C. Jones

Justices for the Court
William J. Brennan, Jr., Tom C. Clark, William O. Douglas (writing for the Court), Abe Fortas, Earl Warren, Byron R. White

Justices Dissenting
Hugo Lafayette Black, John Marshall Harlan II, Potter Stewart

Place
Washington, D.C.

Date of Decision
17 January 1966

Decision
Upheld the petitioners' claim, reversing the decisions of two lower courts and ruling that, due to its history as a public facility, and to the public nature of parks in general, the park must be operated on a desegregated basis.

Significance
The ruling opened a number of seemingly private activities to scrutiny regarding their adherence to the equal protection requirements of the Fourteenth Amendment. Following the Court's decision in this case, the operation of private establishments within public buildings was considered a public activity, and as such was required to adhere to constitutional requirements.

The decade of the 1960s was a time of great social and political upheaval. Popular causes, such as the women's movement and the crusade against American participation in the conflict in Vietnam, emerged and gained nearly unprecedented political momentum. The most significant movement among the political causes of the decade, however, was the Civil Rights movement. The 1960s saw the end of segregation in the southern United States, and a serious attempt to address issues of racial discrimination in the desegregated North. Throughout the decade, the Supreme Court showed its sympathy for the causes of desegregation and racial equity, consistently interpreting the Constitution in such a way as to create a more just society. From a contemporary perspective it is difficult to believe the level of resistance that certain racial equity measures encountered only a short time ago.

A Bequest to the Public

Upon his death in 1911, former United States Senator Augustus O. Bacon left a tract of land within the city of Macon, Georgia, for use as a public park. However, the bequest came with a condition: that the park be maintained for the use of white people only. Senator Bacon, while stating that he had "only the kindest feelings toward Negroes," also believed that "in their social relations the two races should remain forever separated." And so it was, for a time.

Eventually the City of Macon opened the park to use by all its citizens on the grounds that, as a public facility, the segregation of the park would not stand up to a test of constitutionality. When the city made this adjustment in its policy regarding the park, several park trustees took exception and brought suit against the city. The trustees contended that instead of desegregating the park, the city should let it revert to private control, thus exempting it from the need to abide by the equal protection requirements of the Fourteenth Amendment. At this point in the proceedings, a group of African Americans joined the dispute, asking that the city not be allowed to appoint private trustees to operate the park. The City of Macon thereupon resigned as the park's trustee, and the court was forced

De Facto Segregation

De facto segregation is segregation "by the facts." It exists in a situation where no law dictates segregation, but where segregation occurs simply as a matter of practice. It has a different legal meaning than de jure segregation, or segregation by law: the Fourteenth Amendment has long been understood to invalidate de jure segregation, but its use with regard to de facto segregation has been more difficult.

De facto segregation verges into the area of freedom of association, which is generally understood to be protected under the Constitution—though not in the years since the Civil Rights movement of the 1960s, when freedom of association signified discrimination. Many observers have noted that America since the 1960s has been more or less in a state of de facto segregation in some areas. For instance, African American students and white students, who are free to sit with one another at college cafeteria tables around the country, tend to separate into small racial groups. This is voluntary segregation, a more difficult phenomenon to counteract because it is beyond the reach of law.

Source(s): Bradley, David and Shelley Fisher Fishkin, eds. *The Encyclopedia of Civil Rights in America.* Armonk, NY: Sharpe, 1998.

---

to appoint trustees to take over its operation. African American groups then appealed the case to the Georgia Supreme Court, which held that Senator Bacon had the right to leave his property to any subgroup of individuals he desired. The Georgia Supreme Court further held that, in its present guise as a privately operated facility, the park trustees could allow or deny access to whomever they wished. The state supreme court also ruled that the appointment of private trustees to maintain the segregation of the park and insure compliance with the conditions of Senator Bacon's will was a legally acceptable solution to the situation. The case was then appealed to the U.S. Supreme Court, which heard arguments in the matter on 9 and 10 November 1965.

A Public or a Private Facility?

William O. Douglas, writing for the majority, identified two conflicting principles operating in this case: the right of the individual to select the people with whom he or she wishes to associate; and the Equal Protection Clause of the Fourteenth Amendment, which prohibits state preferences for any particular class of person. In the Court's view, the Fourteenth Amendment took precedence in this case, and, by a 5-3 margin, the decision of the Georgia Supreme Court was reversed and the park was ordered to open to the public on a desegregated basis.

In reaching its decision, the Court had to determine the exact status of the park. The park had operated for years as a segregated public facility, for somewhat less time as a desegregated public facility, and for a brief time in the very recent past as a segregated private facility. As the Court noted, "conduct that is formally 'private' may become so entwined with governmental policies or so impregnated with a governmental character as to become subject to the constitutional limi-

tations placed upon state action." The park was judged to fall into this category, given its years of public operation, during which time it was maintained and policed by state authorities. In the Court's view, participation by agents of the state would always be integral to the park's operation, given maintenance of roads and sidewalks leading to the park, for instance, and the use of public utilities such as light and water in the park's operation. As such, regardless of its ownership status, the park qualified as a public facility, and had to adhere to constitutional standards in its admittance policies.

Impact

Evans v. Newton was an important case for supporters of desegregation and racial equity. In its broad definition of a public facility, the Court made a number of previously private facilities subject to the same scrutiny as public places. Businesses operating within public buildings, for example, would now have to maintain constitutional policies regarding the clientele they served. Significantly, following the Court's ruling in this case, the newly appointed private trustees of the park decided to shut it down altogether rather than desegregate it. This led to another case, *Evans v. Abney* (1970), brought by African American groups who claimed that the park's closing violated their constitutional right to equal protection. The Court did not credit their argument, however, ruling that the park's closure affected all races equally, and as such was constitutional.

Related Cases

Pennsylvania v. Board of Directors of the City Trusts of Philadelphia, 357 U.S. 570 (1958).
Evans v. Abney, 396 U.S. 435 (1970).
Palmer v. Thompson, 403 U.S. 217 (1971).

Bibliography and Further Reading

Biskupic, Joan, and Elder Witt, eds. *Guide to the U.S. Supreme Court,* 3rd ed. Washington, DC: Congressional Quarterly Inc., 1990.

Hall, Kermit L., ed. *The Oxford Companion to the Supreme Court of the United States,* New York: Oxford University Press, 1992.

LEE V. WASHINGTON

Legal Citation: 390 U.S. 333 (1968)

Petitioner
Frank Lee, et al.

Respondent
Caliph Washington, et al.

Petitioner's Claim
That an Alabama law segregating blacks from whites in prisons and jails was constitutionally permissible.

Chief Lawyer for Respondent
Nicholas S. Hare, Special Assistant Attorney General of Alabama

Chief Lawyer for Petitioner
Charles Morgan, Jr.

Justices for the Court
Hugo Lafayette Black, William J. Brennan, Jr., William O. Douglas, Abe Fortas, John Marshall Harlan II, Thurgood Marshall, Potter Stewart, Earl Warren, Byron R. White

Justices Dissenting
None

Place
Washington, D.C.

Date of Decision
11 March 1968

Decision
The Alabama law segregating blacks from whites in jails and prisons was held to be unconstitutional under the Fourteenth Amendment.

Significance
The Supreme Court's decision in *Lee v. Washington* reaffirmed the Court's determination to end segregation, not only in schools but in other public institutions. It also confirmed the right of prisoners to file class action lawsuits against the state.

The Facts of the Case

The state of Alabama had a law on its books that mandated racial segregation in the state penal system and in county, city, and town jails. A group of prisoners being incarcerated in Alabama brought a class action suit challenging the statute. They sought an injunction to halt the implementation of the segregation system and to have the statute declared unconstitutional. The prisoners' suit was successful. A three-judge panel of the U.S. District Court for the Middle District of Alabama entered a decree declaring the segregation statutes to be in violation of the prisoners' rights under the Fourteenth Amendment to the Constitution. The district court also set up a timetable for desegregation of Alabama's prisons and jails. However, Frank Lee, the Commissioner of Corrections for the state of Alabama, brought a direct appeal to the U.S. Supreme Court, which agreed to hear the case in November of 1967.

The Supreme Court Rules

On 11 March 1967, the Supreme Court issued its decision. A unanimous majority agreed to affirm the judgement of the district court with regard both to the unconstitutionality of the segregation statute and the advisability of the district court's desegregation schedule. Also, the Court held that prisoners confined in Alabama jails did in fact have standing to bring a class action. As the majority opinion stated: "The State's contentions that Rule 23 of the Federal Rules of Civil Procedure, which relates to class actions, was violated in this case and that the challenged statutes are not unconstitutional are without merit."

On the large issue at hand, the Court held that statutes requiring segregation in prisons and jails are a violation of the Fourteenth Amendment. Orders directing desegregation regardless of the fact that they failed to make an allowance for the necessities of prison security and discipline were nonetheless constitutional. "The . . . contention of the State is that the specific orders directing desegregation of prisons and jails make no allowance for the necessities of prison security and discipline," the opinion continued. "But we do not so read the 'Order, Judgment and Decree'

Prisoner Lawsuits

In 1996, Congress passed the Prison Litigation Reform Act (PLRA), which discouraged frivolous lawsuits by inmates. "When asked whether the . . . PLRA has helped corrections," wrote Susan B. Vandenbraak in *Corrections Today*, "I inevitably think about one of the inmates serving consecutive life sentences in Pennsylvania . . . To amuse himself, this offender files lawsuits." Vandenbraak went on to say that although this inmate was just one of 35,000 in a single institution, his litigation constituted three percent of the caseload emerging from the prisons. One case by another inmate involved a complaint because that individual had received crunchy peanut butter rather than smooth.

Clearly such cases are frivolous, and they impose an enormous burden on taxpayers, particularly through costly "consent decrees." But there is another side to the issue, as made plain by a 1997 National Public Radio (NPR) story about inmates who filed a lawsuit against a Georgia prison over what they charged was an unprovoked beating. If true, the incident could constitute a violation of civil rights, and many citizens would agree that prisoners ought to have a right to file such suits. The PLRA, according to Vandenbraak, "carefully protect[s] legitimate claims and preserve[s] the full power of the federal court to remedy constitutional violations."

Source(s): Levs, Joshua, et al. "Georgia Prison Beatings." *All Things Considered,* 23 July 1997.

Vandenbraak, Susan B. "PLRA: A Step in the Right Direction." *Corrections Today,* August 1998.

---

of the District Court, which when read as a whole we find unexceptionable."

Concurring Opinion

While joining the opinion of the Court, Justices Black, Harlan, and Stewart fashioned a concurrence that emphasized a point they felt was left muted in the majority opinion. They wrote: "[W]e wish to make explicit something that is left to be gathered only by implication from the Court's opinion. This is that prison authorities have the right, acting in good faith and in particularized circumstances, to take into account racial tensions in maintaining security, discipline, and good order in prisons and jails. We are unwilling to assume that state or local prison authorities might mistakenly regard such an explicit pronouncement as evincing any dilution of this Court's firm commitment to the Fourteenth Amendment's prohibition of racial discrimination."

Impact

The Supreme Court's decision in *Lee v. Washington* emboldened other prisoners to file class action suits without fear of having them thrown out of court for lack of standing. It also brought desegregation litigation out of the schools and into the new arena of prisons and jails.

Related Cases

Turner v. Safley, 482 U.S. 78 (1971).

Cruz v. Beto, 405 U.S. 319 (1972).

Goosby v. Osser, 409 U.S. 512 (1973).

Jones v. North Carolina Prisoners' Union, 433 U.S. 119 (1977).

Bibliography and Further Reading

Belbot, Barbara A., and James W. Marquart. "The Political Community Model and Prisoner Litigation." *Prison Journal,* September 1998, p. 299.

Biskupic, Joan, and Elder Witt, eds. *Congressional Quarterly's Guide to the U.S. Supreme Court,* 3rd ed. Washington, DC: Congressional Quarterly, Inc., 1996.

Call, Jack E. "The Supreme Court and Prisoners' Rights." *Federal Probation,* March 1995, p. 36.

Ross, Lee E., and Darnell F. Hawkins. "Legal and Historical Views on Racial Biases in Prison." *Corrections Today,* April 1995, p. 192.

GREEN V. COUNTY SCHOOL BOARD

Legal Citation: 391 U.S. 430 (1968)

Petitioners
Charles C. Green, et al.

Respondents
County School Board of New Kent County, Virginia, et al.

Petitioners' Claim
That the New Kent County School Board's "freedom of choice" plan allowing students to choose their own public schools is not an acceptable method for reversing segregation.

Chief Lawyer for Petitioners
Samuel W. Tucker, Jack Greenberg

Chief Lawyer for Respondents
Frederick T. Gray

Justices for the Court
Hugo Lafayette Black, William J. Brennan, Jr. (writing for the Court), William O. Douglas, Abe Fortas, John Marshall Harlan II, Thurgood Marshall, Potter Stewart, Earl Warren, Byron R. White

Justices Dissenting
None

Place
Washington, D.C.

Date of Decision
27 May 1968

Decision
The New Kent County School Board's "freedom of choice" plan was deemed an unacceptable means of undoing segregation.

Significance
The Supreme Court's decision in *Green v. County School Board* restated the Court's resolve to end segregated schooling and established more specific parameters for allowable and effective means to that end.

Historical Background

Segregated schooling at all levels was a fact of American life. The Supreme Court decision in *Plessy v. Ferguson* (1896) paved the way for a half century of racial segregation by establishing the "separate but equal doctrine" allowing states and school boards to provide separate accommodations provided they were equal in all other respects. Beginning in the 1930s, the National Association for the Advancement of Colored People (NAACP) embarked on a legal strategy designed to challenge this doctrine. They began by bringing cases against segregated universities, hoping to establish precedents in higher education that they could then use to challenge the separate but equal doctrine in primary and secondary schools. These initial measures were largely successful.

The NAACP's legal strategy came to fruition in the landmark *Brown v. Board of Education* (1954) decision. In that case, the Supreme Court reversed *Plessy v. Ferguson* and declared that classifications based solely on race violate the Fourteenth Amendment to the U.S. Constitution. The decision promised a swift and sweeping end to segregation in the South and elsewhere, but this momentum was slowed by a second *Brown* decision, known as *Brown II*, the following year. That decision blunted the impact of the first by allowing states the opportunity to delay implementation of desegregation. It was in this environment of implementation that the case of *Green v. County School Board* played out.

The Facts at Hand

New Kent County in Virginia was divided nearly equally between black and white citizens. However, the County School Board of New Kent County had long maintained a segregated public school system. A school on one side of the county served only white students, while a school on the other side of the county was composed entirely of black students. In order to comply with a desegregation order, the board adopted a plan that allowed students every year to choose which school they wanted to attend. A number of black pupils chose to attend the district's all-white school. However, no white pupils chose to attend the district's all-black school. A group of students and their parents challenged the plan, claiming it was not an acceptable means of achieving a single non-racial school system.

The case first went before the U.S. Court of Appeals for the Fourth Circuit. The district court approved the freedom of choice plan once the school board agreed to hear teachers on a non-discriminatory basis. Green and the other petitioners then took their case to the U.S. court of appeals. The court of appeals affirmed the district court's ruling on the issue of freedom of choice, leaving the petitioners one last recourse, the U.S. Supreme Court.

The Supreme Court Reverses

On 27 May 1968, the Supreme Court issued its decision. All nine justices agreed to overturn the judgement of the court of appeals with regard to the freedom of choice plan. In rendering its decision, the Court held the plan to the standard mandated in *Brown v. Board of Education* that school boards must "effectuate a transition to a racially nondiscriminatory school system." The justices placed the burden on the school board to provide a desegregation plan that has a realistic chance to produce immediate results. While it did not rule out the possible use of a freedom of choice scheme to achieve desegregation, it did rule it out where better, faster, and more effective means of achieving that end exist.

Writing for the unanimous majority, Justice Brennan was unequivocal:

> The New Kent School Board's "freedom-of-choice" plan cannot be accepted as a sufficient step to "effectuate a transition" to a unitary system. In three years of operation not a single white child has chosen to attend Watkins school and although 115 Negro children enrolled in New Kent school in 1967 . . . 85 percent of the Negro children in the system

still attend the all-Negro Watkins school. In other words, the school system remains a dual system. Rather than further the dismantling of the dual system, the plan has operated simply to burden children and their parents with a responsibility which *Brown II* placed squarely on the School Board. The Board must be required to formulate a new plan and, in light of other courses which appear open to the Board, such as zoning, fashion steps which promise realistically to convert promptly to a system without a "white" school and a "Negro" school, but just schools.

Impact

The Supreme Court's decision *Green v. County School Board* retained flexibility for states and local school boards to craft their own desegregation plans, but reaffirmed the Court's willingness to intervene if those plans did not provide substantial and swift progress in complying with the edicts of *Brown v. Board of Education.*

Related Cases

Alexander v. Board of Education, 396 U.S. 19 (1969).
Dowell v. Board of Education, 396 U.S. 269 (1969).
Board of Education v. Swann, 402 U.S. 43 (1971).
United States v. Edgar, 404 U.S. 1206 (1971).

Bibliography and Further Reading

Biskupic, Joan, and Elder Witt, eds. *Congressional Quarterly's Guide to the U.S. Supreme Court,* 3rd ed. Washington, DC: Congressional Quarterly, Inc., 1996.

Hall, Kermit L., ed. *The Oxford Companion to the Supreme Court of the United States.* New York: Oxford University Press, 1992.

SWANN V. CHARLOTTE-MECKLENBURG BOARD OF EDUCATION

Legal Citation: 402 U.S. 1 (1971)

Appellant
James E. Swann

Appellee
Charlotte-Mecklenburg Board of Education

Appellant's Claim
That the local public schools were not doing enough to integrate their student bodies.

Chief Lawyers for Appellant
Julius LeVonne Chambers and James M. Nabritt III

Chief Lawyers for Appellee
William J. Waggoner and Benjamin S. Horack

Justices for the Court
Hugo Lafayette Black, Harry A. Blackmun, William J. Brennan, Jr., Warren E. Burger (writing for the Court), William O. Douglas, John Marshall Harlan II, Thurgood Marshall, Potter Stewart, Byron R. White

Justices Dissenting
None

Place
Washington, D.C.

Date of Decision
20 April 1971

Decision
The Supreme Court upheld the desegregation plan developed by the federal court overseeing public school integration in the district.

Significance
Swann is important for its endorsement of school busing as a means of achieving racial integration.

In 1955, the U.S. Supreme Court ordered school districts to pursue integration "with all deliberate speed." That order was handed down in *Brown v. Board of Education II,* the case in which the High Court gave lower federal courts the task of developing plans to implement desegregation following the first *Brown v. Board of Education* case, which had been decided a year earlier. Dual school systems—one white, one black—had previously been written into the law, and a public that had grown accustomed to official segregation now resisted court efforts to impose change. Resistance was most pronounced in the South. Local officials there sometimes devised plans which appeared to be neutral but which actually slowed the process of school integration. In *Griffin v. County School Board* (1964), for example, the Supreme Court was faced with a Virginia school board that closed down all of its public schools and handed out tuition grants to private schools as a means of avoiding court-ordered desegregation. Declaring that there had been too much deliberation and not enough speed, the Supreme Court ordered the public schools reopened.

In *Green v. County School Board* (1968), the Court struck down a "freedom of choice" plan, which ostensibly permitted students to attend either a white school or a black school, because of its failure to bring about the changes required by *Brown II*. It was not enough for school boards simply to remove the legal restraints keeping the races apart. Allowing students to "choose" which school they wanted to attend was not realistic. What was needed was a system that would quickly reconstitute schools, so that the student body of each would come to resemble the larger population mix. As more and more white families fled the cities, busing black children out to suburban schools seemed the only way to achieve the racial balance required by *Brown II*.

The Charlotte-Mecklenburg school district included not only the city of Charlotte, North Carolina, but also largely rural Mecklenburg County. Twenty-nine percent of school-age children were black, most of them concentrated in one area of Charlotte. Despite implementation of a desegregation plan in 1965, this situation remained largely unchanged. In the wake of *Green,* James Swann and others challenged the efficacy of this plan. Then, in 1968, the federal district court overseeing desegregation in Charlotte-Mecklenburg adopted an ambitious—and very expensive—busing program.

Supreme Court Upholds School Busing

The district court's plan proved to be highly controversial. So did the Supreme Court opinion upholding this plan. Writing for a unanimous Court, Chief Justice Burger gave qualified endorsement to the 71-29 white-to-black ratio required by the district court plan:

> If we were to read the holding of the District Court to require, as a matter of substantive constitutional right, any particular degree of racial balance or mixing, that approach would be disapproved and we would be obliged to reverse. The constitutional command to desegregate schools does not mean that every school in every community must always reflect the racial composition of the school system as a whole . . . We see [however] that the use made of mathematical ratios was no more than a starting point in the process of shaping a remedy, rather than an inflexible requirement.

The district court found that the only way to approach the ideal was to bus students, and the Supreme Court agreed—again in a less than straightforward fashion: "In these circumstances, we find no basis for holding that the local school authorities may not be required to employ bus transportation as one tool of school desegregation. Desegregation plans cannot be limited to the walk-in school."

At the time the Court handed down the *Swann* decision, school segregation had long been a stubborn problem. It would continue to be so, in part because of the less than ringing endorsement the High Court gave court-supervised plans in *Swann*. Court-imposed busing proved to be highly unpopular, especially in the North. In the 1970s, the Court did little to promote desegregation remedies, and in *Milliken v. Bradley* (1974), it actually overruled a district court order that would have merged three school districts to eliminate segregation in one. Two years later, the Court's reluctance to enforce desegregation plans was made even clearer in *Pasadena Board of Education v. Spangler* (1976). Because racial imbalances in the Pasadena public school systems were not the result of intentionally segregationist policies, the Court reasoned, there was no obligation to remedy the situation.

Related Cases

Brown v. Board of Education, 347 U.S. 483 (1954).
Brown v. Board of Education II, 349 U.S. 294 (1955).
Griffin v. County Schoolboard, 377 U.S. 218 (1964).
Green v. County School Board, 391 U.S. 430 (1968).
Pasadena Board of Education v. Spangler, 427 U.S. 424 (1976).
Milliken v. Bradley, 433 U.S. 267 (1977).

Bibliography and Further Reading

Desegregation of Public Education. New York, NY: Garland Press, 1991.

Dimond, Paul R. *Beyond Busing: Inside the Challenge to Urban Segregation.* Ann Arbor: University of Michigan Press, 1985.

Johnson, John W., ed. *Historic U.S. Court Cases, 1690–1990: An Encyclopedia.* New York: Garland Publishing, 1992.

Schwartz, Bernard. *Swann's Way: The School Busing Case and the Supreme Court.* New York: Oxford University Press, 1986.

KEYES V. SCHOOL DISTRICT NO. 1

Legal Citation: 413 U.S. 189 (1973)

Petitioners
Keyes, et al.

Respondent
School District No. 1, Denver, Colorado

Petitioners' Claim
That the deliberate segregation of Park Hill neighborhood schools rendered the entire Denver Public School system liable to enforced desegregation.

Chief Lawyers for Petitioners
James M. Nabrit III, Gordon G. Greiner

Chief Lawyer for Respondents
William K. Ris

Justices for the Court
Harry A. Blackmun, William J. Brennan, Jr. (writing for the Court), Warren E. Burger, William O. Douglas, Thurgood Marshall, Lewis F. Powell, Jr., Potter Stewart

Justices Dissenting
William H. Rehnquist (Byron R. White did not participate)

Place
Washington, D.C.

Date of Decision
21 June 1973

Decision
Stated that segregation of any portion of a school system showed *prima facie* evidence of overall segregation.

Significance
This case marked the first time that the Court ruled on a school segregation issue in a jurisdiction which had never operated under statutes mandating racial separation. In its decision the Court considered the distinction between *de jure* segregation, defined as racial separation that is required by law, and *de facto* segregation, defined as racial separation that was not created by state action or statute.

The development of the Denver, Colorado, area in the years following World War II was typical of American cities during the period. The city grew rapidly between 1940 and 1980 although, beginning in the mid-1950s, much of the growth occurred in suburban areas surrounding the original city. By the 1970s, the population of Denver proper was declining, while that of the suburbs grew by approximately 30 percent during the decade.

As Denver's economy diversified during and after the war, its minority populations began to grow. By 1980, 12 percent of Denver's population was African American and 19 percent was Hispanic. Many Denverites of African American descent traditionally lived east of the central business district in a neighborhood known as Five Points, while Denver's Hispanic population traditionally occupied an area just west of the central business district. These traditional residence patterns began to change in the early 1960s, with African Americans moving into neighborhoods bordering Five Points, including the Park Hill district.

Schools in Transition

Racial segregation had always existed in the Denver schools. Traditional housing patterns made segregation inevitable, since few Denver neighborhoods were racially integrated. School authorities exacerbated the situation by drawing school boundaries along racial lines in integrated neighborhoods such as Park Hill. Heightened public awareness of racial discrimination led to the creation of the Vorhees Special Study Committee on Equality in Educational Opportunity in the Denver Public Schools in 1962. The Vorhees Committee recommended that Denver's traditionally segregated school system be gradually integrated by the redrawing of school boundaries and other measures, and the school board resolved to put the committee's recommendations into practice. When it appeared that progress under the Vorhees Committee's recommendations was inadequate, a second study group, the Berge Committee, was formed in 1966. The Berge Committee recommended more fundamental action to redress segregation in the Denver Public Schools, and in 1968 the school board directed the superintendent of schools to prepare a comprehensive desegregation plan. In April of 1969 the school board approved the superintendent's plan to integrate the Denver Public Schools, which included busing of some students to ensure racial diversity throughout the school system. Forced busing became the central issue in the citywide school board election of May of 1969, in which a record number of voters turned out to defeat incumbent board members favoring the superintendent's plan. In June of 1969 the new school board voted to scrap the desegregation plan proposed by the superintendent, replacing it with a voluntary program.

Mixed Legal Messages

Ten days later a group of eight parents brought suit to enjoin the implementation of the superintendent's plan. The parents' suit also sought a declaratory judgement that abandonment of the desegregation plan constituted a violation of the Equal Protection Clause of the Fourteenth Amendment. A preliminary injunction was granted by the district court, which found that the Denver school board had pursued segregationist policies in the Park Hill neighborhood in the ten years preceding approval of the superintendent's plan. The district court also ruled that schools in the core city area of Denver, whose student bodies were almost completely African American and whose facilities were substandard, would have to be overhauled to ensure equality of educational opportunity throughout the school system. This latter ruling was made despite the fact that the district court found no proof of discriminatory school board action in the core city school districts. The school board appealed the case to the Tenth Circuit Court of Appeals, which agreed that remedial action would have to be taken to integrate schools in the Park Hill district, but vacated the preliminary injunction as it applied to the core city schools. The court of appeals based its decision on the grounds that the deliberate segregation of one school district did not constitute proof of deliberate segregation throughout the school system.

The parents appealed the case to the U.S. Supreme Court, which heard arguments on 12 October 1972. Their case rested on two points: that the district court erred in its finding that Denver's core city schools were not intentionally segregated due to its failure to consider African Americans and Hispanics as one category of student; and that in any case the proven, intentional segregation of the Park Hill school district made the Denver school system as a whole liable to definition as segregated. The school board also cross-petitioned the court, seeking reversal of the court of appeals' finding insofar as it agreed with the district court.

Modification and Remand

On 21 June 1973 the U.S. Supreme Court ruled on the case, upholding the petitioners' claims by a 7-1 margin

and rejecting the cross-petition of the respondents. The Court modified the ruling of the court of appeals to vacate rather than reverse the district court's findings with regard to the core city schools. Justice Brennan, speaking for the majority, stated that African Americans and Hispanics must be considered one group in determining the segregation of Denver's schools, and that the district court should reconsider its finding regarding the overall segregation of the Denver schools. The Court further observed that "finding of intentionally segregative school board actions in a meaningful portion of a school system . . . establishes . . . a *prima facie* case of unlawful segregative design on the part of school authorities." As such, the Court directed that upon review of the case by the district court, the school board would bear the burden of proving that its actions in districts other than Park Hill were not segregationist in intent, or that Park Hill represented a "separate, identifiable and unrelated section of the school district that should be treated as isolated from the rest of the district." Significantly, the Court's judgement relied on its definition of *de facto* as opposed to *de jure* segregation, first established in *Swann v. Charlotte-Mecklenburg Board of Education* (1971), in that it required some proof of intention to segregate in cases brought from jurisdictions that had never imposed racial segregation by statute. Justices Douglas and Powell, although concurring with the majority, argued that this distinction be dropped altogether and that segregation should be remedied regardless of the circumstances that caused it.

Resolution

The district court ruled on remand that the school board's segregative actions in the Park Hill area did substantially affect schools outside the district, and ordered both parties in the case to submit plans for the desegregation of the Denver Public Schools by 13 December 1973. The district court found both plans unacceptable, and a third party was brought in, drafting a plan incorporating rezoned attendance areas, reassignment of elementary school students, and busing of students. This plan was adopted on 17 April 1974, and a permanent injunction against the school board was also imposed by the district court. Despite the apparent resolution of the case, efforts to desegregate Denver's schools have proven largely ineffective.

Impact

Keyes v School Board No. 1 marked the first time that the Supreme Court identified discrimination in a state that had never imposed racial segregation by statute. This case also served to reinforce the Court's distinction between *de facto* and *de jure* segregation, a position further developed in *Milliken v. Bradley* (1974). Finally, *Keyes* established that racially segregative actions in one portion of a school system could render the entire system liable to definition as segregated.

Despite the apparent victory for desegregation seen in *Keyes,* many schools in the United States remain, essentially, segregated. Majority flight to the suburbs increased throughout the 1970s and 1980s, rendering intrasystem remedies increasingly ineffective. In *Milliken v. Bradley,* the Court ruled that demographic shifts (such as flight to the suburbs) not caused by state action could not be redressed by judicial action. As such, intersystem desegregation could only occur on a voluntary basis, and has rarely been attempted.

Related Cases

Green v. County School Board, 391 U.S. 430 (1968).
Alexander v. Holmes County Board of Education, 396 U.S. 19 (1969).
Swann v. Charlotte-Mecklenburg Board of Education, 402 U.S. 1 (1971).
Milliken v. Bradley, 433 U.S. 267 (1974).

Dayton Board of Education v. Brinkman, 439 U.S. 1358 (1979).
Columbus Board of Education v. Pennick, 443 U.S. 526 (1979).

Bibliography and Further Reading

Biskupic, Joan, and Elder Witt, eds. *Guide to the U.S. Supreme Court,* 3rd ed. Washington: Congressional Quarterly Inc., 1990.

Elliott, Stephen P., ed. *A Reference Guide to the U.S. Supreme Court,* New York: Facts on File Publications, 1986.

Fishman, James J. and Lawrence Strauss. "Endless Journey," *Howard Law Journal,* Vol. 32, no. 3, 1989.

Hall, Kermit L., ed. *The Oxford Companion to the Supreme Court of the United States.* New York: Oxford University Press, 1992.

MILLIKEN V. BRADLEY

Legal Citation: 433 U.S. 267 (1974)

Plaintiffs
Ronald Bradley and Richard Bradley, by their mother, Verda Bradley, et al.

Defendant
William G. Milliken, Governor of Michigan, et al.

Plaintiffs' Claim
The Detroit School System was racially segregated as a result of official Michigan policies and actions, as well as those of city officials. Also, they attacked the constitutionality of a Michigan state statute because, they said, it "put the State of Michigan in the position of unconstitutionally interfering with the execution and operation of a voluntary plan of partial high school desegregation, known as the 7 April 1970, Plan."

Chief Lawyers for Plaintiff
J. Harold Flannery and Nathaniel R. Jones

Chief Defense Lawyers
Frank J. Kelley, William M. Saxton, Robert H. Bork, U.S. Solicitor General

Justices for the Court
Warren E. Burger (writing for the Court), Lewis F. Powell, Jr., Harry A. Blackmun, William J. Brennan, Jr., William O. Douglas, Thurgood Marshall, Potter Stewart, Byron R. White

Justices Dissenting
None (William H. Rehnquist did not participate)

Place
Washington, D.C.

Date of Decision
25 July 1974

Decision
The federal district court order to desegregate Detroit schools through a plan that involved the three-county area and 53 other school districts was ruled as improper.

Significance
Many believe that *Milliken v. Bradley* helped to cause a racial schism between urban school districts and suburban school districts. Many point to this case as an impetus for "white flight" from the cities to the suburbs. Others believe that due to the results of *Milliken v. Bradley*, there was more urban school financial aid for equipment and supplies that might not have been otherwise available. It's also believed that this decision helped to create "headstart"-type programs.

Through the U.S. District Court for the Eastern District of Michigan, Detroit school system parents, their children and others instituted a class action suit against various state and school district officials seeking relief from alleged *de jure* racial segregation in the Detroit public school system.

The defendants named in the district court included Michigan's Governor, the state's Attorney General, the State Board of Education, the State Superintendent of Public Instruction, and the Detroit City Board of Education and its members. Also included were Detroit's present and former superintendents of schools.

One of the main points here is the distinction made by the courts between *de jure* and *de facto* segregation. *De facto* means, "by the facts." *De facto* segregation is said to occur when a school district is segregated for other reasons besides official policies and decisions that, in effect, are discriminatory. If, for instance, all the children in the same school were of the same skin color because it was their closest school, that would be *de facto* segregation. *De jure* means, "by law." As opposed to *de facto* segregation, *de jure* segregation "is segregation caused by school officials' decisions to either create or maintain racial segregation." The U.S. District Court for the Eastern District of Michigan ruled that the defendants had set policies and made decisions that resulted in the *de jure* segregation of the Detroit school system.

The district court then required two desegregation plans. One plan involved a solution to be found within the city. The other plan involved desegregation through the tri-county metropolitan area, even though these suburban school districts were not involved and no claim was made that they had committed any constitutional violations. The only input allowed to some of the suburban school districts was that they could advise the court "as to the propriety and form of any metropolitan desegregation plan."

The district court then ruled that it could consider a desegregation plan that involved the suburban school districts even though it had not been established that these school districts had not violated the Constitution. The court further ruled that solutions that involved only Detroit were inadequate since desegregation within the school district could not result in a "racial balance" that represented the "racial composition" of the metropolitan Detroit area. In fact, said the district court, this sort of remedy would only highlight the separateness of Detroit from its surrounding neighbors, with many of the schools having an African American population of 75 to 90 percent.

Therefore, said the district court, effective desegregation could only be accomplished through an inter-district remedy that included 53 suburban school districts combined with Detroit. A panel was appointed to prepare a plan. An interim plan was devised for the upcoming school year in the meantime.

The U.S. Court of Appeals for the Sixth Circuit confirmed that *de jure* segregation existed in the Detroit school district and held that a constitutionally adequate system of school desegregation could not be established inside the Detroit school district. So it was necessary to devise a multi-district metropolitan plan since, in essence, the state was not only responsible for the *de jure* segregation, but also held authority over local school districts.

However, the court of appeals also decreed that the suburban school districts which might be affected by a multi-district desegregation plan had the right to be heard "with respect to the scope and implementation of such a remedy." The court of appeals also voided a district court's order regarding the purchase of school buses, "subject to the District Court's right to consider reimposing the order at an appropriate time."

When the U.S. Supreme Court decided to hear this case it overturned the multi-district solution and ruled that the solution must be found within Detroit's city limits. Justice Burger's opinion conveyed the views of five Supreme Court justices, holding that it was improper for a federal court to order a multi-district solution to a single district *de jure* segregation problem unless

William G. Milliken, Governor of Michigan. © AP/Wide World Photos.

it could be established that by committing unconstitutional acts resulting in racial discrimination, the other districts had caused inter-district segregation. The other test was being able to determine that school district lines had been drawn with race a primary factor.

Busing: Was It Worth It?

In the view of some, busing represented the culmination of decades' worth of work toward ending *de facto* school segregation. As late as 1968, 14 years after the Court dealt a death blow to school segregation in *Brown v. Board of Education* (1954), only 10 percent of all black children in the South attended integrated schools. With busing, it was believed, the law could force a rapid acceleration in efforts toward integration.

There was a problem, however. Though public-opinion polls in the 1970s showed that most Americans favored the integration of the schools, most were opposed to court-ordered busing. Throughout the nation there

were stories of violence in schools, and of rising tension brought on by this form of forced integration. Parents also opposed the idea of children being pulled out of schools where they were happy, and subjected to long bus rides to new schools. By the 1976 presidential elections, both Democrats—originally strong proponents of busing—and Republicans had adopted anti-busing planks in their party platforms. Although busing had its supporters, for instance in the U.S. Commission on Civil Rights, it was largely a dead issue.

Source(s): Bradley, David, and Shelley Fisher Fishkin, eds. *The Encyclopedia of Civil Rights in America.* Armonk, NY: Sharpe, 1998.

Since neither of these factored into the Detroit case, the remedy needed to be sought within the city of Detroit only, even though it would not result in reflecting the "racial composition of the metropolitan area as a whole." The Court also felt that a remedy involving the metropolitan Detroit area would wreak havoc with the state's public education infrastructure that involved local control. Also, there would be a wide range of problems having to do with such factors as administration, financing, and mass transportation of students.

Related Cases
Brown v. Board of Education, 347 U.S. 483 (1954).
Green v. County School Board, 391 U.S. 430 (1968).

Swann v. Charlotte-Mecklenburg Board of Education, 402 U.S. 1 (1971).
Keyes v. School District No. 1, 413 U.S. 189 (1972).

Bibliography and Further Reading
Biskupic, Joan, and Elder Witt, eds. *Congressional Quarterly's Guide to the U.S. Supreme Court,* 3rd ed. Washington, DC: Congressional Quarterly, Inc., 1996.

Cushman, Robert F. *Cases in Constitutional Law,* 7th ed. Englewood Cliffs, NJ: Prentice-Hall, Inc., 1989.

———. *Leading Constitutional Decisions.* Englewood Cliffs, NJ: Prentice-Hall, Inc., 1982.

McWhirter, Darien A. "Education and Racial Integration." *Exploring the Constitution.* Vol. 1, *Equal Protection* The Oryx Press, 1995.

WASHINGTON V. SEATTLE SCHOOL DISTRICT

Legal Citation: 458 U.S. 457 (1982)

Appellants
State of Washington, et al.

Appellees
Seattle School District Number 1, et al.

Appellants' Claim
That Initiative 350, a state law prohibiting busing of school children under certain circumstances, was constitutional and binding upon the Seattle school system.

Chief Lawyer for Appellants
Kenneth O. Eikenberry

Chief Lawyer for Appellees
Michael W. Hoge

Justices for the Court
Harry A. Blackmun (writing for the Court), William J. Brennan, Jr., Thurgood Marshall, John Paul Stevens, Byron R. White

Justices Dissenting
Warren E. Burger, Sandra Day O'Connor, Lewis F. Powell, Jr. William H. Rehnquist

Place
Washington, D.C.

Date of Decision
30 June 1982

Decision
Affirmed the rulings of two lower courts, holding that Initiative 350 violated the Equal Protection Clause of the Fourteenth Amendment by creating an unconstitutional classification based solely on race.

Significance
The ruling confirmed the ability of local school boards or government agencies to take voluntary action to remedy *de facto* racial segregation within their systems. *De facto* racial segregation is segregation that has arisen through housing and development patterns, and has not been influenced by state or judicial statutes or policies. Furthermore, by striking down a popularly accepted ballot initiative prohibiting intradistrict busing of school children to ameliorate *de facto* racial segregation, the Court served notice to opponents of integrative busing nationwide that racial segregation in the schools was a legitimate issue for school boards to address.

A Thorny Problem

In the early 1970s school districts throughout the United States were faced with a dilemma: their school systems were racially segregated in a manner reminiscent of the "separate but equal" era in the South prior to the Court's ruling in *Brown v. Board of Education* (1954). This segregation was not the product of policy or public design, but had arisen through development patterns created by the actions of individuals acting independently. This type of segregation, labeled *de facto,* would prove difficult to correct.

The Seattle School District operated 112 schools serving more than 50,000 students in the early 1970s. Thirty-seven percent of the district's students at the time were of minority descent, and *de facto* housing patterns resulted in a heavily segregated school system. Beginning in 1963 the district took action to end racial segregation within its schools, when a program allowing students to transfer in order to integrate schools was implemented. However, the program did not materially alter the pattern of segregation within the district.

In 1977, the district announced its intention to address racial imbalance within its schools through a program involving "magnet" and "feeder" schools. These schools were expected to attract a racially diverse student body at critical levels within the district, which would then "feed into" less integrated schools and eventually desegregate the system as a whole. Despite the plan, after one year of this program, racial segregation within the district had actually increased.

Following the failure of its magnet and feeder programs, the district adopted the Seattle Plan for school desegregation. This plan called for the mandatory reassignment of students to integrate schools, using the busing of students to achieve this end where required. The plan was scheduled for implementation in the 1978-79 school year.

Resistance to Change

Before the Seattle plan could be implemented, strong public opposition arose to its provisions. In the fall of 1977 a political organization known as the Citizens for

Voluntary Integration Committee (CIVIC) was formed to bar the implementation of the Seattle plan. CIVIC sponsored ballot Initiative 350 for consideration by the state electorate in November of 1978. Initiative 350 placed restrictions on the mandatory busing of students, while still allowing local school districts to assign students to schools other than those nearest their homes for many nondesegretative purposes. While never mentioning race, Initiative 350 was clearly understood to oppose school busing to achieve desegregation.

The district began implementing the Seattle Plan in the fall of 1978, with the immediate effect of desegregating the Seattle school system. On 8 November 1978, however, Initiative 350 was approved by the people of Washington State by a margin of nearly 2-1, and the district was forced to abandon the Seattle Plan.

Legal Remedies

Following the passage of Initiative 350, its constitutionality under the Equal Protection Clause of the Fourteenth Amendment was challenged by the district in the U.S. District Court for the Western District of Washington. The district court upheld the school's claim, noting that the most overcrowded schools in the district were those with the highest percentage of minority students, and that Initiative 350 would remove any possibility of racial integration within the district. Furthermore, the district court found that virtually all types of busing would be allowable under Initiative 350, with the exception of busing to achieve racial integration. Because it singled out busing for racial integration, Initiative 350 created a constitutionally impermissible racial classification of a type prohibited by the U.S. Supreme Court in *Hunter v. Erickson*, (1969). In that case the Court ruled that a referendum passed by the electorate of Akron, Ohio, to override an Akron City Council fair housing ordinance was unconstitutional because the referendum singled out a particular type of ordinance, namely, a fair housing statute, for special treatment. Initiative 350 was also judged to be overly broad, since it would prohibit school districts from redressing *de jure* segregation, that is, segregation caused by deliberate state action, as well as *de facto* segregation.

The case then proceeded to the U.S. Court of Appeals for the Ninth Circuit which affirmed the ruling of the district court, while also noting that Initiative 350 inappropriately removed the power to determine school policy from the local school board. The court of appeals also observed that it would be permissible for a successor school board to abandon the Seattle Plan, but that in this case "a different government body—the state-wide electorate—rescinded a policy voluntarily enacted by locally elected school boards already sub-

ject to local political control." In the wake of the court of appeals' decision, the state of Washington appealed the case to the U.S. Supreme Court, which heard arguments in the matter on 22 March 1982.

The Power of the State

Justice Blackmun wrote for the majority, with the Court finding in favor of the Seattle School District by a margin of 5-4. Following essentially the same reasoning of the district court, the Court viewed Initiative 350 as an inappropriate use of the power of the state. The initiative was judged to be impermissibly preferential, in that it singled out busing to end racial segregation while allowing busing for many other reasons. The initiative also did not follow the precept established in *Hunter v. Erickson* (1969) that stated statutes must follow a general principle, since it was crafted for a purely racial purpose and placed significant burdens on racial minority groups. Finally, the Court affirmed another principle developed in *Hunter v. Erickson:* that "meaningful and unjustified distinctions based on race are impermissible."

Impact

Washington v. Seattle School District represents one side of the Court's rather inconsistent approach to attempts to remedy *de facto* segregation in the 1970s. The ruling was consistent with the position taken by the Court in *Keyes v. School District No. 1* (1973), in which Denver schools were ordered to take action to redress racial segregation within the system. However, these rulings are seemingly contradicted by *Milliken v. Bradley,* (1974), in which the Court ruled that it was inappropriate to seek judicial remedies for *de facto* segregation. In fact, *Washington v. Seattle School District* was specifically overruled by *Crawford v. Board of Education of Los Angeles,* (1982), in which the Court held that states could amend their constitutions to prohibit busing of students to redress *de facto* racial segregation.

Related Cases

Hunter v. Erickson, 393 U.S. 391 (1969).
Milliken v. Bradley, 418 U.S. 769 (1974).
Crawford v. Board of Education of Los Angeles, 458 U.S. 527 (1982).

Bibliography and Further Reading

Hall, Kermit L., ed. *The Oxford Companion to the Supreme Court of the United States.* New York: Oxford University Press, 1992.

Rosen, Jeffrey. "Stare Indecisis: Harry Blackmun v. CCRI." *The New Republic,* December 23, 1996, p. 14.

Stearns, Maxwell L. "The Misguided Renaissance of Social Choice." *Yale Law Journal,* March 1994, p. 1219.

UNITED STATES V. FORDICE

Legal Citation: 505 U.S. 717 (1992)

Petitioner
United States

Respondent
Kirk Fordice

Petitioner's Claim
That the State of Mississippi failed to fulfill its duty under the Fourteenth Amendment's Equal Protection Clause in dismantling the state's "separate but equal" university educational system.

Chief Lawyer for Petitioner
Kenneth Wilson Starr, U.S. Solicitor General in case No. 90-1205, and Alvin O. Chambliss, Jr. in case No. 90-6588

Chief Lawyer for Respondent
William F. Goodman, Jr.

Justices for the Court
Harry A. Blackmun, Anthony M. Kennedy, Sandra Day O'Connor, William H. Rehnquist, David H. Souter, John Paul Stevens, Clarence Thomas, Byron R. White (writing for the Court)

Justices Dissenting
Antonin Scalia

Place
Washington, D.C.

Date of Decision
26 June 1992

Decision
The U.S. Supreme Court held that Mississippi did not meet statutory requirements in dismantling a racially-discriminatory, dual-tiered university system that was in violation of the Constitution and Title VI of the Civil Rights Act of 1964 (Title VI).

Significance
Emphasized the Court's commitment to upholding the provisions of the Civil Rights Act of 1964.

In 1848, the State of Mississippi established its first institution dedicated to higher education exclusively for white people. Alcorn State University, an agricultural college, was founded next in 1871 for the education of black youth. Creation of four new educational facilities for white students followed—Mississippi State University (1880), Mississippi University for Women (1885), University of Southern Mississippi (1912), and Delta State University (1925). In 1940 and 1950, the state established two more black universities, Jackson State University and Mississippi Valley State University.

During the mid-1950s, two Court decisions, *Brown v. Board of Education* (1954) and *Brown v. Board of Education II* (1955), held that "separate but equal" policies had no place in public education. Mississippi (like other states that operated racially discriminatory university systems) was ordered to end segregated education. Nonetheless, the state's policy of segregation continued. Only by order of the U.S. Supreme Court was the first black student admitted to the University of Mississippi in 1962.

Over the next 12 years, some white universities accepted several black students and Alcorn State University admitted five white students. In effect, the segregated public university system remained intact. In 1969, the U.S. Department of Health, Education and Welfare (HEW) requested that Mississippi create a plan for dismantling its segregated university system. Four years later, the Board of Trustees of State Institutions of Higher Learning submitted their plan. The plan was rejected by HEW because it did not go far enough in the areas of student recruitment and it failed (in its intent) to comply with Title VI of the Civil Rights Act of 1964. The board offered amendments but HEW found the modified plan unacceptable.

Private petitioners initiated a lawsuit in 1975 claiming that Mississippi's racially segregated educational system violated the Fifth, Ninth, Thirteenth, and Fourteenth Amendments and Title VI. Soon after that, the United States intervened by filing a complaint charging that state officials did not satisfy requirements under the Equal Protection Clause of the Fourteenth Amendment and Title VI. For next 12 years, parties

Kirk Fordice, Governor of Mississippi, 1992. © AP/Wide World Photos.

attempted to achieve a consensual resolution, but achieved limited success.

By 1981, the board presented a new program that identified the purpose of each public university. Schools were put in three categories: comprehensive, urban, and regional. The program classified the University of Mississippi, Mississippi State, and Southern Mississippi University as comprehensive, which meant that these universities had the most varied programs and offered graduate degrees. Delta State and Mississippi University for Women, together with Alcorn State and Mississippi Valley State University, had more limited programs devoted to undergraduate education. They were designated regional universities. According to location, Jackson State University was classified as urban. Nonetheless, 30 years after the Court's decision in *Brown* I and II, the situation in Mississippi's postsecondary educational institutions was largely unchanged. More than 99 percent of white students were in Mississippi's universities for whites, and 71 percent of black students attended Alcorn State, Mississippi Valley State, and Jackson State Universities. Finally, in 1987, HEW and the state concluded that they could not agree on whether Mississippi had achieved signifi-

cant progress in removing its system of segregated schools. Accordingly, the lawsuit first initiated by the U.S. government proceeded to trial.

The district court moved to dismiss the case because state officials had sufficiently demonstrated they were making progress in eliminating segregation in the universities. The U.S. Court of Appeals for the Fifth Circuit affirmed the district court's decision. It was held that the State of Mississippi "adopted and implemented race-neutral policies for operating its universities," and that, under the new system, students had the right and freedom to attend their university of choice.

Dissatisfied with lower court rulings, the U.S. solicitor general presented the government's case before the U.S. Supreme Court in 1991. The government argued that the State of Mississippi did not fulfill its obligation to dismantle a dual system of higher education because vestiges of segregation remained *vis-a-vis* admission requirements and policies, duplication of programs, classification and assignment of missions, and financial support. For instance, automatic admission to three historically-white universities (HWUs) required a minimum score of 15 on the American College Test (ACT). Mississippi University for Women required a minimum score of 18 while historically-black universities (HBUs) required a 13 ACT score. Average ACT scores for white students were 18 and for blacks, 7; thus, whether by coincidence or by design, 70 percent of black students did not qualify for automatic acceptance into HWUs. (The Court took decided exception to the state's automatic acceptance policy—since, according to the administering organization of the ACT, scores should not be used as a sole requirement for college admissions.) Moreover, the government pointed out that the state's system was plagued by "unnecessary program duplications." Duplications, part of the prior, segregated educational system, were consistent with the notion of "separate but equal," so continuation of such policies was discriminatory and traceable to the state's governance of the university system. In addition, the petitioner offered that two supposedly equal regional universities, Delta Mississippi State University (an HWU), and Mississippi Valley University (an HBU), had different-sized libraries (in fact, Valley's library was three times smaller than the Delta University library). The discrepancy was traceable to underfunding of Valley University. The petitioner reasoned that the chances of white students choosing the Valley University were therefore restrained; most students would prefer a university with a larger library.

The attorney for the respondent (the state of Mississippi) argued that Mississippi had dismantled segregated institutions by implementing anti-segregation policies which promoted "good faith," nondiscriminatory, race-neutral practices in student admissions, faculty hiring, and operation of campuses. As evidence of the success of the state's policies, counsel pointed out that one-third of all black students in Mississippi were at HWUs. Countering the government's claim that funding was disproportionate among universities, the respondent maintained that all universities had received the same level of funding for 30 years. He went on to point out that the most underfunded universities were the two "comprehensive" HWUs. Finally, counsel defended the apparent disparity in Mississippi's policy of "automatic admissions" between HWUs and HBUs by arguing that an ACT score of 15 was already too low to be considered a reasonable admissions obstacle since such a score was indicative of reading ability equivalent to high school level.

The Supreme Court justices unanimously agreed that the district court and the court of appeals failed to properly identify what constituted appropriate state action with respect to Title VI. Therefore, the Court vacated the ruling of the lower court and remanded the case back for further adjudication. Justices held that Mississippi's adoption and implementation of race-neutral admissions policies did not provide sufficient evidence that the state had completely abandoned a dual-university system. The Court felt that the state's "race-neutral" admission policy (of automatic entrance determined by ACT scores) was not an effective cure for a segregated educational system, especially since the criteria varied by institution. Moreover, in a system based on choice, many other factors (which the state failed to mitigate) besides admission policies affected student attendance. Such factors, like equal funding and facilities, non-duplicating academic concentrations, and disparities that indicated a "separate but equal" mentality, permeated the academic climate of the university system and were traceable to the state's prior segregation policies.

The Court concluded that discrimination was traceable to vestiges of the prior, segregated university system for several reasons. Discrepancy in admission standards suggested discrimination. Furthermore, lower courts (in their efforts to achieve consensus between HEW and the state) made little effort to mitigate or even justify differences in entrance requirements. University funding also hinted at practices which derived from Mississippi's period of active, educational segregation. Three HWUs, designated "flagship institutions," received more generous funding. Thus, those universities were able to initiate more advanced programs and to develop the broadest array of curricula. Justices also agreed with the opinion of the district court that a system of eight institutions of higher education (which were often duplicitous in curriculum offerings) was wasteful and irrational especially since several universities were less than 35 miles apart. (The Court declined to speculate whether closure of some institutions would

have the effect of decreasing the discriminatory effects, and justices were uncertain whether such action was constitutionally required.)

Justice Scalia was the only member of the Court to file an opinion that dissented (but only in part). His primary concern was that, lacking definitive guidance from the Court, a "number of years of litigation-driven confusion and destabilization in university systems" would follow. Without specific, clear direction from the Court as to what steps should have been taken to achieve racial equality, lack of progress in equalizing educational opportunity would ensue as institutions and states grappled with the difficulty of reconciling the esoteric language of Title VI with academic administration and practice.

The majority of the Court held that the state of Mississippi failed to fulfill its obligation to dismantle its previously segregated system of postsecondary education. However, in rendering the decision that Mississippi must recraft its university system to more effectively desegregate, the Court only ruled on the correctness of litigants' arguments. Their decision lacked clear, defined legal parameters which states and academics could apply when authoring and administering desegregation policy. Nor did the Court specifically address which legal doctrine was most pertinent to development of a state policy that might address removal of a segregative system of higher education. Thus, while the Supreme Court reiterated its position on the inappropriateness of academic segregation and moved to underscore the importance of Title VII, the task of recrafting a desegregated university system remained a problem for educators and legislators to solve.

Related Cases

Brown v. Board of Education, 347 U.S. 483 (1954).
Brown v. Board of Education II, 349 U.S. 294 (1955).
Green v. School Bd. of New Kent County, 391 U.S. 430 (1968).

Bibliography and Further Reading

Hawkins, B. Denise. "Fordice Decision." *Black Issues in Higher Education*, March 23, 1995, p. 6.

———. "New SEF Report Won't Offer 'Fordice' Remedy." *Black Issues in Higher Education*, November 17, 1994, p. 38.

Roithmayr, Daria. "Deconstructing the Distinction Between Bias and Merit." *California Law Review*, October 1997, p. 1449.

Wilson, Cory Todd. "Mississippi Learning: Curriculum for the Post-Brown Era of Higher Education Desegregation." *Yale Law Journal*, October 1994, p. 243.

SEXUAL HARASSMENT

Sexual harassment is one form of sexual discrimination prohibited under federal law. Title VII of the 1964 Civil Rights Act protects employees from sexual harassment in the workplace and established the Equal Employment Opportunity Commission (EEOC). The EEOC's 1980 regulations defined sexual harassment and pronounced it as one aspect of sexual discrimination protected under the Civil Rights Act of 1964. EEOC guidelines define sexual harassment:

> Unwelcome sexual advances, requests for sexual favors, and other verbal or physical conduct of a sexual nature constitute sexual harassment when (1) submission to such conduct is made either explicitly or implicitly a term or condition of an individual's employment, (2) submission to or rejection of such conduct has the purpose or effect of unreasonably interfering with an individual's work performance or creating an intimidating, hostile, or offensive working environment.

The distinction that the EEOC's guidelines make between two specific types of sexual harassment, as shown above, are often referred to in the first instance as "quid pro quo" and the second as "hostile working environment." An example of sexual harassment that would be considered "quid pro quo" is when a superior in an employment situation seeks sex in exchange for a pay raise, promotion, positive performance review, or even the continuance of employment as before. The conditions attributed to a "hostile working environment" occur when a supervisor, coworker, or client repeatedly acts in an intimidating or hostile manner thereby creating an environment that causes an employee much anxiety. Conduct may include unwelcome flirting, invitations of a sexual nature, the exhibition of pictures of a sexual nature, and use of demeaning language. In this scenario, an employee's salary may not be involved. For one of the above mentioned reasons, the employee's work environment has become poisoned by the offensive behavior.

In determining whether or not sexual harassment has occurred, the question of whether or not the conduct was "unwelcome" is a key issue. If sexual harassment has been found to have occurred, the determi-nation of which type of sexual harassment must be made. If the case is considered "actionable," an individual alleging the sexual harassment can seek legal action. Remedies for sexual harassment cases vary, ranging from filing charges with the EEOC to instituting cases in state and federal courts, including the U.S. Supreme Court.

History of Legislation

Cases dealing with issues of sexual harassment are a twentieth century phenomena. Prior to the Civil Rights Act of 1964, no legislation protected individuals on the basis of sex. Ironically, the clause making discrimination illegal on the basis of sex was added to the bill by Southern conservatives in the legislature in an attempt to defeat it. The idea was to add a clause protecting individuals from discrimination on the basis of their gender, which they believed so outrageous that the entire bill would fail. In its original form, the Civil Rights Act of 1964 prohibited discrimination on the basis of "race, color, religion, or national origin" only. To their chagrin, the bill passed the legislature. President Lyndon Johnson so fervently wanted the legislation enacted into law that he signed it without raising any issue with the amendment prohibiting against discrimination based on sex.

Although the Civil Rights Act of 1964 made discrimination on the basis of sex illegal, initially the act did little to stem abuses. The EEOC was established as a result of its passage, but the first head of the agency who was entrusted with enforcing the act regarded the provisions prohibiting sexual discrimination as something of a joke. Finally in 1980, after considerable pressure from women's groups, the EEOC, under the direction of Eleanor Holmes Norton, released regulations outlining what constituted sexual harassment. At that time, the EEOC declared that sexual harassment was indeed a form of sexual discrimination, and consequently, individuals were protected against such conduct under the Civil Rights Act.

Judicial Precedent Set by U.S. Supreme Court

After 1980, a few states passed their own statutes prohibiting sexual harassment on the job. Although a lower court case decided in 1976 supported the idea of sexual harassment as an illegal form of sex discrimination in *Williams v. Saxbe,* it was not until 1986 that the U.S. Supreme Court addressed the issue. A precedent was sent on 19 June 1986 when the Supreme Court unanimously affirmed what the lower federal courts had held since 1976: sexual harassment in the workplace is illegal and protected under Title VII of the Civil Rights Act. The 1986 case involving *Meritor Savings Bank v. Vinson* became a legal turning point for cases dealing with sexual harassment. Moreover, even though the Court was not legally required to do, the Court used the EEOC's regulations against discrimination from which the sexual harassment prohibition originated to decide sexual harassment issues.

Decisions made after 1986 by state courts and the U.S. Supreme Court further clarified what constituted sexual harassment under the Civil Rights Act. In some instances, employees found protection and remedies under state laws. A 1991 Florida case, *Robinson v. Jacksonville Shipyards, Inc.,* supported the idea that the display of pictures of a sexual nature at work constituted a form of sexual harassment.

Bill Passed Allowing Damages for Victims of Sexual Harassment

The Senate's confirmation hearings on Clarence Thomas' appointment to the Supreme Court in 1991, during which Anita Hill testified that she had been sexually harassed by Thomas, brought the issue to the forefront once again. With pressure from women's groups, a bill once again went before Congress which would allow for compensatory and punitive damages in cases of sexual harassment. President Bush had vetoed a similar bill in 1990. Partially because of the political heat raised during the Thomas hearings, Congress passed the measure, and President Bush signed the 1991 Civil Rights Act into law. This act provides for damages in cases where sexual harassment is found, although as a compromise measure, limits of $50,000 to $300,000 were set, depending on the number of employees in the company involved.

The November 1993 case of *Harris v. Forklift* was an important unanimous affirmation by the Supreme Court of its earlier decision of *Meritor Savings Bank v. Vinson.* In *Harris,* the Court upheld the standard previously applied in *Meritor Savings Bank:* "To be actionable as 'abusive work environment' harassment, conduct need not 'seriously affect psychological well being' or lead the plaintiff to 'suffer injury.'" In *Harris,* the Court decided that the woman who complained of numerous sexually based remarks and unwelcome "sexual innuendoes" from the president of the company could indeed seek relief from sexual harassment in spite of the fact that she appeared unharmed psychologically.

1997 U.S. Supreme Court Adds Clarification

In June of 1998, the 1997 term of the Supreme Court ended and included decisions on four cases that added clarification to the issue of sexual harassment. In *Burlington Industries, Inc. v. Ellerth,* the Court found the case had been correctly classified as a hostile work environment suit, and as such Ellerth had to show "severe or pervasive conduct" by her manager. The standard of "pervasive" conduct has been used by the Supreme Court in other hostile work environment cases. Whereas a quid pro quo case may stem from a single incident, a hostile work environment generally develops over time with repeated affronts.

To some degree, the 1998 Supreme Court cases also defined employer liability. In *Burlington Industries,* the Court outlined the defense that employers seeking to avoid liability in hostile work environment cases can use: first, the employer must have used "reasonable care to prevent and correct promptly any sexually harassing behavior"; second, the employee seeking relief and/or damages "unreasonably failed" to utilize policies and procedures in place by the employer designed to thwart or correct the situation. *Faragher v. Boca Raton* provided a wake up call to large employers. The Court held that an employer's failure to establish policies against sexual harassment and methods for investigation and correction, as well its failure to communicate these policies to employees, can result in the employer's liability for the offensive behavior of its supervisors.

Another landmark Supreme Court case of 1998 decided whether "same sex" cases are protected under the 1964 Civil Rights Act. *Oncale v. Sundowner Offshore Services Incorporated et al.* dealt with a male employee who alleged that other males, a supervisor and coworkers, regularly humiliated him using methods of a sexual nature that included belittling him, physically grabbing him, and even warning him that he could be raped. After the employee reported these incidents to supervisors, the company failed to take corrective action. The resulting Supreme Court decision was clear: an employee may seek damages from his employers, even if the employee perpetuating the sexual harassment is of the same sex.

Federal Prohibitions Against Sexually Motivated Harassment in Schools

Sexual harassment is also prohibited in all federally funded schools under Title IX of the Education Amendments of 1972. The law protects both males and females. Schools are required by federal law to have a policy prohibiting sexual discrimination, including sexual harassment. Schools are also required to inform students, faculty, and other employees, as well as parents, of this policy. As with sexual harassment as defined in the workplace, similar categories of quid pro quo and hostile work environment apply here. An example of quid pro quo harassment occurs when a faculty member or coach makes sex a condition for passing a class or getting on a team. The hostile work environment applies when the student is subjected to "unwelcome" conduct constituting sexually harassing behavior. The conduct is considered "pervasive" if the behavior has been repetitive and creates an environment that the student finds hostile, intimidating, or even abusive.

If sexual harassment occurs in an academic setting, the party alleging the harassment must report the incident(s) to authorities within the school system who have the power to remedy the situation. In *Gebser et al. v. Lago Vista Independent School District,* the Court held that a student could not recover damages for sexual harassment since school officials were never notified of the alleged harassment, and therefore had no opportunity to correct the situation.

Sexual Harassment in the U.S. Military

Sexual discrimination including sexual harassment is also prohibited in all branches of the military. In 1994, then Secretary of Defense William Perry created the military's own version of the EEOC, the Defense Equal Opportunity Council Task Force on Discrimination and Sexual Harassment (DEOC). The Council was established to investigate the system used by the military to register complaints and to suggest means of improving the procedures. A 1995 survey conducted by the Department of Defense showed that the percentage of women in the military reporting unwelcome and uninvited sexual advances dropped slightly between 1988 and 1995. The respondents of the survey consisted of both male and female members of the U.S. Navy, Army, Marines, and Air Force.

Sexual harassment in the military can be even more invasive in the victim's life than sexual harassment in nonmilitary workplaces. Not only do the offenders work in close proximity to their victims, they may live nearby as well. Additionally, a superior in the military may have greater power to influence one's current life and future position, and legally a person cannot resign from his or her position in the military. These factors, coupled with the level of trust that must be cultivated between an officer and his or her trainees, provides a superior who abuses his or her power ample leverage in creating sexually harassing situations.

In spite of the Defense Department's attempt to prevent sexual harassment, in a 1996 military court martial, 32-year-old Army Staff Sergeant Delmar Simpson was found guilty of raping six female trainees at Maryland's Aberdeen Proving Ground. The allegations of sexual abuse at Aberdeen exposed a pervasive problem in the army. In addition to Simpson, ten other sergeants and one captain at Aberdeen were charged with counts ranging from rape to adultery to obstructing justice. The incidents at the Aberdeen Proving Ground revealed

that sexual discrimination, including sexual harassment, was a problem within all ranks, genders, and racial groups. Togo West, Jr., then Secretary of the Army, acknowledged that sexual harassment within the army persisted. Army Chief of Staff General Dennis Reimer told Phil Ponce of PBS that he viewed the misconduct found at Aberdeen as "a leadership failure." An editorial by Harry Summer, Jr., of the *Los Angeles Times* succinctly described the corruption of trust involved in the Aberdeen incidents: "For a young woman to be sexually assaulted by her drill sergeant is like being molested by her father."

Prevention and Remedies for Sexual Harassment

It is well-established that sexual harassment arises from power-related issues rather than issues of a sexual nature. Whether the setting is the workplace, an educational institution, or a military facility, the law is clear and unequivocal: sexual harassment will not be permitted.

EEOC regulations include guidelines for employers on how to recognize, prevent, and educate employees regarding sexual harassment. In addition, EEOC regulations provide instruction on how to institute procedures within organizations to investigate and resolve issues from within. Many organizations have policies that inform employees, students, military personnel, and others who may be affected by sexual harassment of methods for dealing with harassers and detail the proper procedures necessary after initial steps fail. In a business setting, internal complaints may be filed with the proper authorities and mediation or arbitration may be used. Complaints may be filed with the EEOC or the state or local agency responsible for fair employment practices (FEP). Law suits may result from unresolved issues or in cases where the damages are severe.

Courts may enjoin employers to halt improper behavior in hostile environment cases. Attorney fees can also be awarded. In addition, if an employee quits his or her job because of sexual harassment, the employer may be liable for compensation due to lost wages. In 1998, many companies had affirmative action policies including the prohibition of sexual harassment, in compliance with EEOC guidelines, to raise awareness of the nature of sexual harassment in the workplace and to discourage employees in supervisory roles from creating hostile environments. Employers today seek to reduce their liability from lawsuits by indicating the inappropriateness of this behavior, even among employees. Continued vigilance against sexual harassment in the work place, the educational system, and the military, with the goal of ultimately eliminating sexual harassment, is an ongoing war, with some of the battles left undecided.

Bibliography and Further Reading

Adler, Jonathan L., and Maureen F. Moore. *Sexual Harassment: Discrimination and Other Claims.* Carlsbad, CA: Lexis Law Publishing, 1997.

Anderson, Ronald A., Ivan Fox, and David P. Twomey. *Business Law and the Legal Environment.* Cincinnati, OH: South-Western Publishing Co., 1990.

Appendix B—Title IX. Website, www2.ncsu.edu/ncsu/provost/info/adv_handbook/current/appe_b.html.

Law Journal Extra! Website, www.ljextra.com/practice.laboremployment/0730sseven.html.

Legal Information Institute and Project Hermes. Websites, supct.law.cornell.edu/supct/html/96-1866.ZS.html and supct.law.cornell.edu/supct/html/92-1168.ZS.html.

Omillian, Susan M. *Sexual Harassment in Employment.* Wilmette, IL: Callaghan & Co., 1987.

Online NewsHour: Army Sex Scandal-April 29, 1997. Website, www.pbs.org/newshour/bb/military/april97/sex_scandal_4-29.html.

Online NewsHour: Sexual Harassment in the Military—September 11, 1997. Website, www.pbs.org/newshour/bb/military/july-dec97/harassment_9-11a.html.

Petrocelli, William, and Barbara Kate Repa. *Sexual Harassment on the Job.* Berkeley, CA: Nolo Press, 1998.

Sexual Harassment: 1995 Department of Defense Survey. Website, www.chinfo.navy.mil/navpalib/people/harasmnt/dod95/harass95.html.

Summers, Harry Jr. "Army Scandal Claims Trust as a Casualty." *Los Angeles Times,* editorial, November 12, 1996.

U.S. Department of Education. Website, www.ed.gov/offices/OCR/ocrshpam.html.

Working Women: Opposing Viewpoints. San Diego, CA: Greenhaven Press, 1998.

HISHON V. KING

Legal Citation: 467 U.S. 69 (1983)

Petitioner
Elizabeth Anderson Hishon

Respondent
King & Spalding, an Atlanta, Georgia, law firm

Petitioner's Claim
That Title VII of the Civil Rights Act of 1964 did not apply to the selection of partners for partnerships.

Chief Lawyer for Petitioner
Emmet J. Bondurant II

Chief Lawyer for Respondent
Charles Morgan, Jr.

Justices for the Court
Harry A. Blackmun, William J. Brennan, Jr., Warren E. Burger (writing for the Court), Thurgood Marshall, Sandra Day O'Connor, Lewis F. Powell, Jr., William H. Rehnquist, John Paul Stevens, Byron R. White

Justices Dissenting
None

Place
Washington, D.C.

Date of Decision
31 October 1983

Decision
That Title VII of the Civil Rights Act of 1964 did apply to Hishon's complaint of discrimination by King & Spalding in their refusal to offer her a partnership.

Significance
For firms in other industries, this meant that the offering of partnerships was subject to the same scrutiny; for Hishon, the ruling only meant that she could sue King & Spalding for the alleged discrimination.

In 1972, Elizabeth Anderson Hishon began working as an associate lawyer for King & Spalding, a powerful Atlanta law firm. According to Hishon, during King & Spalding's recruitment of her for the position, she was told that advancement to partnership after five or six years was "a matter of course" for associates and that she would be considered on a "fair and equal basis" for the partnership. This, she said, was key in her decision to work at King & Spalding. Hishon was twice considered and rejected for a partnership with the firm after which she was fired in 1979, under the firm's practice of firing associates who had not made partnership within certain parameters. On 19 November 1979, Hishon filed a complaint of gender discrimination with the Equal Employment Opportunity Commission (EEOC) under Title VII of the Civil Rights Act of 1964 which states that an employer cannot discriminate on the basis of gender, race, religion, or nationality.

The commission issued a notice of Hishon's right to sue, which she exerted in the U.S. District Court for the Northern District of Georgia in 1980 for back pay and compensatory damages, rather than fulfillment as a partner. Atlanta Federal District Judge Newell Edenfield dismissed the suit finding Title VII could not be applied to partnerships. According to an article in *Time*, Edenfield stated that "to coerce a mismatched or unwanted partnership too closely resembles . . . the enforcement of shotgun weddings." Hishon appealed to the U.S. Court of Appeals for the Eleventh Circuit, but it agreed with the lower court's decision.

Hishon then turned to the Supreme Court to review the case, also known as taking the case on *certiorari*. On 22 May 1984, the Court reached a unanimous verdict. In an opinion written by Justice Burger, the Court stated that Title VII was applicable to partnerships, and therefore Hishon had a right to sue for alleged discrimination. This decision was based on the Court's interpretation of a partnership as a benefit of employment, which is covered by Title VII. As such, the decision also applied to minorities whether based in nationality, race, or religion. The Court also noted that the historical interpretation of Title VII and related legislation did not support the assumption that Congress intended to exempt partnerships. Justice Powell wrote a concurring opinion, noting that the decision did not necessarily extend to the management of a law firm by its partners.

Rather than going ahead with the suit, Elizabeth Anderson Hishon and King & Spalding ended up settling out of court in June of 1984. In an article in *Dun's Business Month* it was noted that "each party continues to believe in the correctness of its position." In any case, the Supreme Court's ruling, written as broadly as it was, was interpreted as impacting firms in a variety of industries such as architecture, advertising, accounting, consulting, and engineering, all of which tend to be organized as partnerships.

Related Cases
Patterson v. McLean Credit Union, 491 U.S. 164 (1989).
White v. Union Pacific R.R., 805 F.Supp. 883 (1992).

Bibliography and Further Reading
"Getting a Piece of the Power: Women Barred From Partnerships Can Now Go To Court." *Time,* 4 June 1984.

"High Court Opinion Hits Partnerships." *Dun's Business Month,* July 1984.

MERITOR SAVINGS BANK V. VINSON

Legal Citation: 477 U.S. 57 (1986)

Petitioner
Meritor Savings Bank

Respondent
Mechelle Vinson

Petitioner's Claim
That the Civil Rights Act of 1964 limits discrimination in the workplace to that which results in economic injury.

Chief Lawyer for Petitioner
F. Robert Troll, Jr.

Chief Lawyer for Respondent
Patricia J. Barry

Justices for the Court
Harry A. Blackmun, William J. Brennan, Jr., Warren E. Burger, Thurgood Marshall, Sandra Day O'Connor, Lewis F. Powell, Jr., William H. Rehnquist (writing for the Court), John Paul Stevens, Byron R. White

Justices Dissenting
None

Place
Washington, D.C.

Date of Decision
19 June 1986

Decision
The decision of the court of appeals was affirmed and remanded.

Significance
The case of *Meritor Savings Bank v. Vinson* raised many important questions about the issues of sexual harassment in the workplace, as pertaining to the Civil Rights Act of 1964, under Title VII.

Case Background

Meritor Savings Bank v. Vinson arose from allegations by Mechelle Vinson against Sidney Taylor and Meritor Savings Bank. These allegations stated that Vinson was repeatedly sexually harassed by Taylor, her supervisor. Taylor hired Vinson in September of 1974 as a teller trainee, who progressed to teller, then head teller, and finally to assistant branch manager, promotions that were based on merit. Vinson alleged that in May of 1975 Taylor began to have "sexual affairs" with Vinson, which Taylor denied. Vinson notified Taylor in September of 1978 that she would be taking sick leave indefinitely, and on 1 November 1978 she was fired for "excessive use of that leave." Vinson then sued both Taylor and the bank, claiming that she had suffered through sexual harassment by Taylor during the four and a half years she was at the bank, and "sought injunctive relief, compensatory and punitive damages against Taylor and the bank, and attorney's fees."

At the trial, Vinson testified that Taylor made "repeated demands upon her for sexual favors, usually at the branch, both during and after business hours" and that she agreed only because she feared that she would lose her job. Taylor denied these claims, testifying that he "never fondled her, never made suggestive remarks to her, never engaged in sexual intercourse with her, and never asked her to do so," and he contended that Vinson "made her accusations in response to a business-related dispute." Vinson never reported the harassment to the bank and "never attempted to use the bank's complaint procedure." Because it was never reported, the bank "asserted that any sexual harassment by Taylor was unknown to the bank and engaged in without its consent or approval."

The district court found that 1) relief should be denied because the sexual relationship was voluntary and did not affect Vinson's employment at the bank, and 2) that because the alleged sexual harassment was never made known to the bank, it could not be held liable. The case went on to the court of appeals, which reversed and remanded the decision of the district court. The court of appeals believed that Vinson did have a claim under Title VII because the alleged sexual harassment created a "hostile or offensive working

How Sexual Harassment is Determined

The Equal Employment Opportunity Commission (EEOC) was established under Title VII of the Civil Rights Act of 1964. The EEOC defined two types of harassment, and other factors governing sexual harassment suits.

The first type of sexual harassment, *quid pro quo* harassment occurs when economic benefit or other gain is explicitly or implicitly promised in return for sexual favors. In an employment setting, this may involve the promise of pay increases, promotions, or other perks. In an academic setting, it might mean giving a student a higher grade than he or she deserved, or a place on a school team.

The other type of harassment is created when a "hostile environment" results because of one person's behavior toward another. This may occur when one party's sexual advances are rejected by the other, and the use of sexual innuendo may be used to punish the rejecting party. It can involve the use of insulting language, jokes in bad taste, or hanging lewd and potentially offensive pictures within one's work space.

Financial or psychological damage does not have to occur to justify a claim. The determination of whether the advances are "unwelcome" or not is also a factor.

Source(s): Findlaw. http://www.findlaw.com/casecode/supreme.html.

environment," which had not been considered by the district court. Furthermore, the court of appeals decided that "an employer is absolutely liable for sexual harassment practiced by supervisory personnel, whether or not the employer knew or should have known about the misconduct." The U.S. Supreme Court granted *certiorari* and heard the case on 25 March 1986.

The Application of Title VII

This case examined the application of Title VII of the Civil Rights Act of 1964, which makes it unlawful for an employer "to discriminate against any individual with respect to his compensation, terms, conditions, or privileges of employment, because of such [an] individual's race, color, religion, sex, or national origin." The court of appeals found that in this case the sexual harassment created "an offensive or hostile working environment" that was a violation of Title VII and that sexual harassment of a subordinate by a supervisor was considered sexual discrimination. The petitioner argued that the alleged sexual harassment did not result in an economic loss.

The Supreme Court disagreed with that argument, saying that the intent of Congress was to address a large range of mistreatment, not limited to economic loss only. Also, the Equal Employment Opportunity Commission (EEOC) had issued guidelines in 1980 that defined sexual harassment as a type of sexual discrimination unacceptable in the workplace, in other words, a "hostile environment" (*Rogers v. EEOC*, [1972]). The Court felt that the respondent's claims were "plainly sufficient to state a claim for 'hostile environment' sexual harassment." The Supreme Court went on to say that, apparently, the district court's finding that the respondent did not suffer sexual harassment was "likely based on one or both of two erroneous views of the

law." First, the district court did not consider this case to fall under the "'hostile environment' theory" as the court of appeals correctly did. Second, the district court believed that the sexual activity was voluntary, which the Supreme Court rejected as a sufficient defense against a Title VII complaint, noting that the sexual relationship was "unwelcome."

Another point in contention was that the court of appeals did not admit as evidence testimony about the respondent's dress or "sexually provocative speech," saying it was not relevant. However, the Supreme Court found that, following the EEOC guidelines, "such evidence is obviously relevant."

The Supreme Court then turned to the matter of whether the bank was liable for the actions of Taylor. Because the bank was never notified of Taylor's alleged misconduct towards Vinson, the district court found that it "could not be held liable for Taylor's alleged actions." The court of appeals did not agree, "holding that an employer is strictly liable for a hostile environment created by a supervisor's sexual advances, even though the employer neither knew nor reasonably could have known of the alleged misconduct." The petitioner argued that because Vinson failed to report the misconduct using "its established procedure," the bank could not be held accountable for "Taylor's wrongdoing." The Supreme Court opted not to define the responsibilities of employer liability and held that "the Court of Appeals erred in concluding that employers are always automatically liable for sexual harassment by their supervisors" and "absence of notice to an employer does not necessarily insulate that employer from liability." Thus, the Supreme Court affirmed the decision of the court of appeals that reversed the district court decision, and remanded the case "for further proceedings consistent with this opinion."

Impact

The difficult issues concerning sexual harassment in the workplace continue to be debated and contested in the courts, as evidenced by the large number of cases citing *Meritor Savings Bank v. Vinson:* nine Supreme Court cases, and about 100 cases in the circuit courts. It is certain that sexual discrimination remains a serious problem for many Americans.

Related Cases

Skidmore v. Swift & Co., 323 U.S. 134 (1944).
Griggs v. Duke Power Co., 401 U.S. 424 (1971).
Rogers v. EEOC, 406 U.S. 957 (1972).
Albemarle Paper Co. v. Moody, 422 U.S. 405 (1975).
Franks v. Bowman Transportation Co., 424 U.S. 747 (1976).
General Electric Co. v. Gilbert, 429 U.S. 125 (1976).
Banta v. United States, 434 U.S. 819 (1977).
Los Angeles Dept. of Water and Power v. Manhart, 435 U.S. 702 (1979).

Bibliography and Further Reading

Allred, Gloria, and John S. West. "Employment Law; Sexual Harassment." *The National Law Journal,* October 26, 1998, p. B12.

Anderson, Cheryl L. "'Nothing Personal:' Individual Liability Under 42 U.S.C. 1983 for Sexual Harassment as an Equal Protection Claim." *Berkeley Journal of Employment and Labor Law,* summer 1998, p. 60.

Biskupic, Joan, and Elder Witt, eds. *Congressional Quarterly's Guide to the U.S. Supreme Court,* 3rd ed. Washington, DC: Congressional Quarterly, Inc., 1996.

Fujiwara, Elizabeth Jubin. "Proving Damages in a Sexual Harassment Case." *Trial,* April 1994, p. 34.

Lee, Robert D., Jr., and Paul S. Greenlaw. "The Legal Evolution of Sexual Harassment." *Public Administration Review,* July-August 1995, p. 357.

Losey, Michael R. "Sexual Harassment: A Growing Workplace Dilemma." *USA Today (Magazine),* March 1995, p. 38.

Muhl, Charles J. "Sexual Harassment." *Monthly Labor Review,* July 1998, p. 61.

Myrsiades, Linda. "A Language Game Approach to Narrative Analysis of Sexual Harassment in *Meritor v. Vinson.*" *College Literature,* winter 1998, p. 200.

Paetzold, Ramona L. "Continuing Violations and Hostile Environment Sexual Harassment." *American Business Law Journal,* November 1993, p. 365.

Schultz, Vicki. "Reconceptualizing Sexual Harassment." *Yale Law Review,* April 1998, p. 1683.

Silbergeld, Arthur F., and Brian F. Van Vleck. "Recent Decisions Clarify the Use of Sexual Conduct Evidence in Harassment Cases." *Employment Relations Today,* winter 1994, p. 471.

Tang, Thomas Li-Ping, and Stacie Leigh McCollum. "Sexual Harassment in the Workplace." *Public Personnel Management,* Sspring 1996, p. 53.

Whitehead, Roy, Jr., Pam Spikes, and Brenda Yelvington. "Sexual Harassment in the Office." *The CPA Journal,* February 1996, p. 42.

O'CONNOR V. ORTEGA

Legal Citation: 480 U.S. 709 (1987)

Petitioner
Dennis M. O'Connor

Respondent
Mango J. Ortega

Petitioner's Claim
Hospital officials of Napa State Hospital had reasonable cause to enter and search an employee's private office. Officials were attempting to secure any state property in Mango J. Ortega's office while he was being investigated for mismanagement of his department and for sexual harassment charges. This search did not violate the employee's Fourth Amendment rights.

Chief Lawyer for Petitioner
Jeffrey T. Miller

Chief Lawyer for Respondent
Joel I. Klein

Justices for the Court
Sandra Day O'Connor (writing for the Court), Lewis F. Powell, Jr., William H. Rehnquist, Antonin Scalia, Byron R. White

Justices Dissenting
Harry A. Blackmun, William J. Brennan, Jr., Thurgood Marshall, John Paul Stevens

Place
Washington, D.C.

Date of Decision
31 March 1987

Decision
The Court held that the search of Ortega's office by Hospital officials did not violate Ortega's Fourth Amendment right to privacy. The realities of the public workplace held to the standard that "reasonableness" was just cause for intrusion in an office. The case was remanded to the lower courts for further review and action.

Significance
The *O'Connor v. Ortega* case examined a public employee's right to privacy in the workplace. The Court had to determine whether the hospital officials of Napa Hospital violated Dr. Mango Ortega's Fourth Amendment rights when they entered his office, searched his desk and files, and separated hospital property from personal property without his permission. The justices were required to establish what defined 'reasonable cause' and whether the employee had reasonable expectations of privacy in the workplace.

Search and Seizure Without Authorization

Dr. Mango Ortega was a physician and psychiatrist employed by the Napa State Hospital. He had been in its employment for 17 years until his dismissal in 1981. His primary position had been as the chief of professional education where he was responsible for the training of physicians in the psychiatry residency program. Hospital officials became concerned with his management of the residency program, particularly in light of possible improprieties in purchasing computer equipment and charges of sexual harassment of female hospital employees. Prior to dismissal Dr. Ortega was placed on paid administrative leave while hospital officials investigated the charges. Officials also recommended that Dr. Ortega not return to the hospital grounds until such time as he was returned to active employment or dismissed and allowed to collect his personal effects.

While he was on administrative leave, hospital officials entered Dr. Ortega's office and searched his desk and file cabinets. They justified this search without a warrant as proper because it was necessary to inventory the office for state property and separate Dr. Ortega's personal items and files from those owned by the state or crucial to the efficient operation of the department. In the course of the search, several personal items were removed and later used in court to impeach, or discredit, a witness on behalf of Dr. Ortega.

Dr. Ortega filed a claim against Dennis M. O'Connor and other hospital officials in the U.S. District Court for the Northern District of California. He alleged that the search of his office and removal of personal items was a direct violation of his Fourth Amendment rights as guaranteed by the U.S. Constitution. The district court ruled in favor of O'Connor and the Napa State Hospital, determining that the search was reasonable in order to secure state property. Ortega then appealed to the U.S. Court of Appeals for the Ninth Circuit. The court reversed the decision because the doctor had a "reasonable expectation of privacy in his office." It was remanded to the Supreme Court on a writ of *certiorari*.

What Is the Right to Privacy in the Workplace?

The Supreme Court reviewed the decision of the lower courts. In the course of the review they examined three points in particular. First, they addressed the definition of privacy in the workplace. Justice O'Connor, writing for the majority, concluded that the search and seizure of private property by government employers and officials is subject to the restraints of the Fourth Amendment. However, due to the great variety of work environments, particularly in the public sector, an employee's expectation of privacy may be unreasonable when the intrusion into the office is by a supervisor rather than a law enforcement official in the course of conducting normal business functions. Given this variety of work environments, this question of a reasonable expectation of privacy must be addressed on an individual basis. The allocation of private versus shared office space, policies regarding the placement of personal objects in an office, and the practice of allowing personal activities on company grounds, all needed to be weighed in the analysis of reasonable expectations of privacy.

The justices also considered the allowable standards for a search when a reasonable expectation of privacy existed. It was the justices opinion that the standard ". . . requires balancing the employee's legitimate expectation of privacy against the government's need for supervision, control, and the efficient operation of the workplace." Because it would be difficult to apply the standard of 'probable cause' as applied by the Fourth Amendment, cases for breaching the privacy of an employee's workplace must be judged by the standard of 'reasonableness.' It was acceptable and reasonable for Dennis O'Connor and the other hospital officials to enter Ortega's office on the grounds that they were attempting to inventory state property. Ortega was on administrative leave pending possible termination; officials needed to ascertain which property was rightfully owned by the state and to ensure the efficient running of the department while Ortega was absent.

The majority justices also determined that Ortega had a reasonable expectation of privacy in his desk and file cabinets. They cited several instances in support of this expectation. First, Ortega did not share his office with any other employees; it was a personal work area. He had occupied the same office for the 17 years of his employment and kept personal items there. Ortega's work-related files were kept outside his office. Finally, the hospital had no established policy which discouraged or prohibited employees from storing personal papers and other items in their desks or file cabinets.

Justice O'Connor, on behalf of the majority, raised the question of whether the summary judgment of the district court was inappropriate. Was the search reasonable under the circumstances? The two lower courts could not agree upon the intent of the search of Ortega's office. The district court held that the search was reasonable in order to secure state property. The court of appeals held that the search was in violation of Ortega's right to privacy on the grounds that he was entitled to a reasonable expectation of privacy in his office. The decision of the court of appeals was reversed and returned to the lower courts for "the justification for the search and seizure, and [evaluation of] the reasonableness of both the inception of the search and its scope."

A Respectful Dissent

Justice Blackmun, joined by Justices Brennan, Marshall, and Stevens, entered a dissenting opinion. They agreed that the search of Ortega's office and seizure of his personal effects was a patent violation of his Fourth Amendment rights. Ortega had an expectation of privacy in his office. His office became the target of a search by hospital officials whose purpose was to investigate. The hospital officials did not complete the inventory of state property, but rather intruded into Ortega's files and desk in order to locate materials supporting the charges against him. The dissenting justices determined that there was no 'special need' to neglect obtaining a warrant and fulfilling the probable cause requirements of the Fourth Amendment. Since the hospital officials were investigating possible improprieties, they could have addressed their concerns to a magistrate and obtained the appropriate search warrant. Officials would have been forced to examine and express their reasons for the search and to identify those items they were seeking, preventing the general and unauthorized intrusion into Dr. Ortega's desk and file cabinets. Blackmun, Brennan, Marshall, and Stevens stated that by overlooking the probable cause requirement and negating the need to obtain a warrant, and replacing these with some other standard of reasonableness, the protections guaranteed by the Fourth Amendment were undermined and weakened.

Impact

In a time when the workplace has become an extension of one's personal life, where the employee spends a significant part of his day, the Supreme Court has found it necessary to examine what the right to privacy encompasses. In O'Connor v. Ortega they established that an employee, regardless of the sector in which employed, has a reasonable right to expect his privacy be held inviolate. However, the employer also has the right to intrude upon that privacy if circumstances warrant it in the efficient running of the agency and in order to assert control over the functions of business operations. Because the probable cause justification can be unwieldy when timely actions are required, the Supreme Court relies upon standards of reasonableness and common sense in breaking the trust of the Fourth Amendment.

Related Cases

Terry v. Ohio, 392 U.S. 1 (1968).
United States v. U.S. District Court, 407 U.S. 297 (1972).
Illinois v. Lafayette, 462 U.S. 640 (1983).
United States v. Place, 462 U.S. 696 (1983).
New Jersey v. T.L.O., 469 U.S. 325 (1985).

Bibliography and Further Reading

Diederichs, Brenda L., and Diane Arkow Gross. *The Zones of Privacy.* Los Angeles: Richards, Watson & Gershon, 11 April 1997

Dixon, Rod. "Windows Nine-to-Five: Smyth v. Pillsbury and the Scope of an Employee's Right of Privacy in Employer Communications." *Virginia Journal of Law & Technology,* Vol. 2, no. 4, fall 1997.

Shawe & Rosenthal. "Employee Privacy Rights." http://www.shawe.com/epr.html

Steiker, Carol S. "The Limits of the Preventive State." *Journal of Criminal Law and Criminology,* spring 1998, p. 771.

University of North Carolina—Chapel Hill. Department of Health Policy and Administration. "Employment Law." http://www.sph.unc.edu/courses/hpaa180e/emplaw.htm

HARRIS V. FORKLIFT

Legal Citation: 510 U.S. 17 (1993)

From April of 1985 to October of 1987, Teresa Harris worked as a manager at Forklift Systems, Inc., of Nashville, Tennessee, an equipment rental company. During this time her boss, Charles Hardy, subjected her to lewd remarks, sexual put-downs, and suggestive innuendoes.

For example, Hardy told her in the presence of several other workers, "You're a woman, what do you know," "We need a man as the rental manager," and "You're a dumb ass woman." Publicly, he suggested going "to the Holiday Inn to negotiate your raise." He threw items on the floor and demanded the women pick them up. Hardy would also harass female employees by asking them to remove coins from his front pants pockets.

Harris Files a Lawsuit

Finally, Harris had had enough. She confronted Hardy, who insisted he had only been joking, and promised to stop his lewd behavior. Satisfied by these assurances, Hardy remained at Forklift Systems. In early September of 1987, Hardy reneged on his promise. While Harris was negotiating a deal with one of Forklift's customers, Hardy asked her, in front of other staff, "What did you do, promise the guy . . . some 'bugger' Saturday night?" Harris quit her job on 1 October 1987 and filed a lawsuit, claiming that Hardy's conduct created an abusive work environment. Because Harris felt she had been harassed because of her gender, she filed charges under Title VII of the Civil Rights Act of 1964.

From 1987 to 1992, Harris waged an uphill battle. Declaring this to be a "close case," the U.S. District Court for the Middle District of Tennessee, agreed that Hardy often was "vulgar" and "inane," but not discriminatory. The behavior would offend any "reasonable woman," but Hardy's insults were not:

> so severe as to be expected to seriously affect [Harris'] psychological well-being. A reasonable woman manager under like circumstances would have been offended by Hardy, but his conduct would not have risen to the level of interfering with that woman's performance.

Appellant
Teresa Harris

Appellee
Forklift Systems, Inc.

Appellant's Claim
That she was sexually harassed by the owner.

Chief Lawyer for Appellant
Irwin Bennick

Chief Lawyer for Appellee
Stanley M. Chernau

Justices for the Court
Harry A. Blackmun, Ruth Bader Ginsburg, Anthony M. Kennedy, Sandra Day O'Connor (writing for the Court), William H. Rehnquist, Antonin Scalia, David H. Souter, John Paul Stevens, Clarence Thomas

Justices Dissenting
None

Place
Washington, D.C.

Date of Decision
9 November 1993

Decision
The Court found that Teresa Harris did work in a sexually abusive environment.

Significance
The Supreme Court defined sexual harassment in the workplace so that workers today can win lawsuits without having to prove that the offensive behavior left them psychologically damaged or unable to perform their jobs.

Justice Clarence Thomas

Clarence Thomas was confirmed as an associate justice of the U.S. Supreme Court on 15 October 1991. President George Bush nominated him, and the subsequent confirmation hearings by the Senate Judiciary Committee were highly volatile. His appointment was very controversial, and became more so after Professor Anita Hill charged Thomas with sexual harassment and testified before the Senate Judiciary Committee.

Hill, a law professor at the University of Oklahoma, testified that Thomas had made sexual advances toward her while they were both employed by the Equal Employment Opportunity Commission (EEOC). She alleged that after rejecting his social invitations, Thomas began to discuss sexually explicit topics with her, while they worked together. He also continued to ask Hill to accompany him on social occasions. Hill continued to reject his invitations until her employment with the EEOC was about to end in 1983. In a dinner conversation that is recorded in Hill's testimony before the Senate, Thomas told her that, "If I [Hill] ever told anyone of his [Thomas's] behavior . . . it would ruin his career."

Clarence Thomas's confirmation was approved despite Hill's allegations of sexual harassment.

Source(s): *The World Almanac and Book of Facts, 1994.* Mahwah, NJ: Funk & Wagnalls, Corp., 1993.
http://www.capitaloutlook.com/

The judge also decided, "Although Hardy may at times have genuinely offended [Harris], I do not believe that he created a working environment so poisoned as to be intimidating or abusive to [her]." In other words, Harris had not been so traumatized—medically or psychologically—to prove harassment, a standard set by earlier federal courts of appeal. Harris's case was denied.

Undaunted, Harris took her case to the Supreme Court. The Court, which can often make the simple appear complex, did the opposite in this case. It examined a complicated question and made the answer look easy. After a four-week period, the justices reached a unanimous decision.

Discrimination by Any Other Name

The Supreme Court's first female justice, Justice O'Connor, wrote the final decision, delivering the six-page ruling on 9 November 1993. She concluded that a workplace environment that "would reasonably be perceived, and is perceived, as hostile or abusive" because of sexual harassment is an arena where sex discrimination has occurred. The decision overturned lower federal court rulings that made proof of "severely psychological injury" a critical factor.

Citing the "broad rule of workplace equality" and federal laws against job discrimination, the Court stated that no single factor, such as psychological distress, is an essential element. O'Connor wrote that the definition of sexual harassment "by its nature cannot be a mathematically precise test." Rather, courts should look at "all the circumstances" to determine whether a work environment is a hostile one. These circumstances may be "the frequency of the discriminatory conduct; its severity; whether it is physically threatening or humiliating, or a mere offensive utterance; and whether it unreasonably interferes with an employee's work performance."

Justice Ginsburg's brief was her first since joining the Court in October of 1993. According to the *New York Times*, Ginsburg "went out of her way to suggest that discrimination on the basis of sex should be taken as seriously by the Court as discrimination on the basis of race." Ginsburg also cited a 1982 decision of O'Connor's (*Mississippi University for Women v. Hogan*) that declared it unconstitutional for a Mississippi state college to exclude men from a nursing program.

The *Harris* decision reaffirmed the standard set by *Meritor Savings Bank v. Vinson,* which ruled that an employer violates Title VII of the 1964 Civil Rights Act when the workplace becomes an arena for discriminatory behavior, creating an unfairly hostile or abusive atmosphere.

The Supreme Court instructed the appeals court to rehear the case and assess damages. However, before the lower court could reach its decision, Harris settled out of court with her former employer. The terms of the settlement were never disclosed. Harris is now an oncology nurse at Vanderbilt University Medical Center in Nashville, Tennessee.

Related Cases

Mississippi University for Women v. Hogan, 458 U.S. 718 (1982).

DeAngelis v. El Paso Municipal Police Officers Association, 51 F.3d 591 (1995).

Ascolese v. Southeastern Pennsylvania Transportation Authority, 902 F.Supp. 533 (1995).

E.E.O.C. v. Mitsubishi Motor Manufacturing of America, Inc., 990 F.Supp. 1059 (1998).

Etter v. Veriflo Corporation, 67 Cal.App.4th 457 (1998).

Bibliography and Further Reading

Allred, Gloria, and John S. West. "Employment Law; Sexual Harassment." *The National Law Journal,* October 26, 1998, p. B12.

Burns, Sarah E. "Issues in Workplace Sexual Harassment Law and Related Social Science Research." *Journal of Social Issues,* spring 1995, p. 193.

"Court, 9-0, Makes Sex Harassment Easier to Prove." *The New York Times,* November 10, 1993, p. A1.

"Excerpts From Supreme Court Ruling on Sexual Harassment." *New York Times,* November 10, 1993.

Kirshenberg, Seth. "Sexual Harassment: What You Need to Know." *Training & Development,* September 1997, p. 54.

Lee, Robert D., Jr., and Paul S. Greenlaw. "The Legal Evolution of Sexual Harassment." *Public Administration Review,* July-August 1995, p. 357.

Leo, John. "An Empty Ruling on Harassment." *U.S. News & World Report,* November 29, 1993, p. 20.

MacKinnon, Catharine A. *Sexual Harassment of Working Women.* New Haven, CT: Yale University Press, 1979.

Otten, Laura. *Women's Rights and the Law.* Westport, CT: Praeger, 1993.

Plevan, Bettina. "Harris Won't End Harassment Questions." *The National Law Journal,* December 6, 1993, p. 9.

Rosen, Jeffrey. "Reasonable Women." *The New Republic,* November 1, 1993, p. 12.

Schultz, Vicki. "Reconceptualizing Sexual Harassment." *Yale Law Journal,* April 1998, p. 1683.

"A Victory on Workplace Harassment." *New York Times,* November 11, 1993.

Whitehead, Roy, Jr., Pam Spikes, and Brenda Yelvington. "Sexual Harassment in the Office." *The CPA Journal,* February 1996, p. 42.

FREDETTE V. BVP MANAGEMENT ASSOCIATES

Legal Citation: 112 F.3d 1503 (1997)

Appellant
Robert Fredette

Appellees
BVP Managements Associates, Royal Palace Hotel Associates, and Buena Vista Hospitality Group

Appellant's Claim
That same gender sexual harassment is prohibited by Title VII of the Civil Rights Act of 1964.

Chief Lawyer for Appellant
Tobe M. Lev

Chief Lawyer for Appellees
Arch Y. Stokes

Justices for the Court
R. Lanier Anderson III (writing for the court), Albert J. Henderson, Phyllis A. Kravitch

Judges Dissenting
None

Place
Atlanta, Georgia

Date of Decision
22 May 1997

Decision
Sexual harassment of a male employee by a male supervisor is prohibited by Title VII.

Significance
In ruling that same gender harassment is actionable under the Civil Rights Act, the U.S. Court of Appeals for the Eleventh Circuit joined a number of other courts of appeals in expanding the protections afforded workers in the workplace. Shortly after the court's decision, the U.S. Supreme Court also ruled that same gender harassment is prohibited by Title VII of the Civil Rights Act.

By the early 1960s, two significant social transformations in the United States merged to produce Title VII of the Civil Rights Act. Following World War II, an increased number of women began to enter the workplace. This increase in the number of women holding regular jobs coincided, in large part, with an increased awareness of, and desire to protect, the civil rights of a number of different groups, most notably racial minorities and women. These interests coalesced in the passage of the Civil Rights Act of 1964. Specifically, Title VII of the act prohibits any discrimination by an employer against an employee on the basis of a person's gender.

As a general matter, Title VII safeguards against workplace harassment. The first type is known as *quid pro quo* harassment. *Quid pro quo* is a Latin phrase meaning "what for what," or "something for something." In a *quid pro quo* harassment situation, an employer or supervisor will condition some aspect of an employee's job on the employee's performance of some sexual act. For example, an employer who agrees to promote an employee if that employee has sexual relations with the employer is guilty of *quid pro quo* harassment. The second type of gender discrimination is known as "hostile work environment" discrimination. In this type of discrimination, the employer creates, or allows his other employees to create, a work environment that is hostile to an employee because of the employee's gender. For example, an employer who allows employees to display sexually explicit pictures of women may be guilty of creating a working environment which is hostile to female employees.

Protecting Men in the Workplace

Beginning in the late 1980s and continuing through the 1990s, a new social movement began to take shape and gain momentum in the United States. During this time, there began an increased awareness of discrimination against men, and in particular against homosexual men. As the public and the courts became more aware of this discrimination, the courts were asked to consider to what extent Title VII prohibits employers from discriminating against men, and especially whether a male employer or supervisor could be guilty of discriminating against another man on the basis of gender. Generally, such same-sex harassment took one of two forms. First, a homosexual supervisor or employer would engage in the same type of *quid pro quo* harassment which is ordinarily directed towards female employees. Second, a homosexual employee would be subjected to a hostile work environment, generally by heterosexual male employees who would subject the employee to ridicule and often times outright violence.

Robert Fredette was a waiter at a restaurant owned by BVP Management Association. In 1994, Fredette filed a lawsuit in the U.S. District Court for the Middle District of Florida against BVP claiming that Dana Sunshine, the male manager of the restaurant where he worked, sexually harassed him. Specifically, Fredette claimed that Sunshine asked him repeatedly for sexual favors, and offered to give Fredette employment benefits in exchange for these sexual favors. Fredette claimed that these repeated sexual advances constituted both *quid pro quo* and hostile work environment sexual harassment under Title VII.

The district court rejected Fredette's claim, concluding that same gender discrimination is not prohibited by Title VII. The district court noted that Title VII prohibits an employer from discriminating against an employee "because of" that person's gender. The court then reasoned that Fredette was discriminated against because of his sexual orientation, and not because of his gender. The district court reasoned that "if Fredette suffered the claimed harassment or discrimination at the hands of the restaurant manager, it stemmed not from the fact that Fredette was a man, but rather from the fact that Fredette refused the manager's propositions and did not share the same sexual orientation or preferences as the manager." In reaching this conclusion, the district court relied on the similar decisions of a number of other district courts and of the U.S. Court of Appeals for the Fifth Circuit.

Same Gender Harassment Actionable

Fredette appealed the district court's decision to the U.S. Court of Appeals for the Eleventh Circuit, which reversed the district court. Joining a number of other courts of appeals, the Eleventh Circuit rejected the approach taken by the district court and the cases upon which the district court relied. The court relied on cases involving sexual advances by a male supervisor toward a female employee. The court reasoned that, in such a case, a women is treated differently "because of sex" as required by Title VII because the male supervisor does

not make similar sexual advances toward males. Thus, such a woman is able to prove that, but for her being a woman, she would not have been subjected to the harassment.

The *Fredette* court concluded that this reasoning is equally applicable to the case where a male employee is harassed by a homosexual male supervisor in a sexual manner. The court stated:

> We think [this reasoning] is equally applicable to the situation where a homosexual male propositions another male. The reasonably inferred motives of the homosexual harasser are identical to those of the heterosexual harasser—i.e., the harasser makes advances towards the victim because the victim is a member of the gender the harasser prefers.

Thus, the court concluded that Fredette's claim was actionable under Title VII.

Impact

Less than one year after the court's decision in *Fredette*, the U.S. Supreme Court resolved the conflict among the various federal courts on the same gender harassment issue. In *Oncale v. Sundowner Offshore Services Incorporated et al.* (1998), the Supreme Court unanimously held that same-gender discrimination is prohibited by Title VII, taking the same position as the Eleventh Circuit in *Fredette*. Following the *Fredette* and *Oncale* decisions, employers must be much more conscious of how male supervisors and employees treat not only female employees, but also other male employees.

Related Cases

Johnson v. Transportation Agency, 480 U.S. 616 (1987).
Goluszek v. H. P. Smith, 697 F. Supp. 1452 (1988).
Wrightson v. Pizza Hut of America, Inc., 99 F.3d 138 (1996).
Oncale v. Sundowner Offshore Services Incorporated et al. 118 S.Ct. 998 (1998).

Bibliography and Further Reading

Gutek, Barbara A. *Sex and the Workplace.* San Francisco: Jossey-Bass, 1985.

Petrocelli, William. *Sexual Harassment on the Job,* 2nd ed. Berkeley, CA: Nolo Press, 1995.

Seebacher, Noreen. "Ruling Clears Air on Sex Harassment: Court Warns Businesses that Cases Don't Have to Involve Opposite Sexes to Be Illegal." *Detroit News,* 25 March 1998, p. B4.

ONCALE V. SUNDOWNER OFFSHORE SERVICES INCORPORATED ET AL.

Legal Citation: 118 S.Ct. 998 (1998)

Petitioner
Joseph Oncale

Respondent
Sundowner Offshore Services Incorporated, John Lyons, Danny Pippen, and Brandon Johnson

Petitioner's Claim
That on the job sexual harassment by coworkers of the same sex constitutes sexual discrimination prohibited by Title VII of the 1964 Civil Rights Act.

Chief Lawyer for Petitioner
Nicholas Canaday III

Chief Lawyer for Respondent
Harry M. Reasoner

Justices for the Court
Stephen Breyer, Ruth Bader Ginsburg, Anthony M. Kennedy, Sandra Day O'Connor, William H. Rehnquist, Antonin Scalia (writing for the Court), David H. Souter, John Paul Stevens, Clarence Thomas

Justices Dissenting
None

Place
Washington, D.C.

Date of Decision
4 March 1998

Decision
Ruled in favor of Oncale and reversed two lower court decisions by finding that Oncale was deserving of damages for sexual harassment.

Significance
The ruling recognized that individuals have the right to file sexual harassment complaints against employers based on same-sex sexual harassment claims. The Court found that Title VII applies equally to all sexual harassment situations. The decision ensured for the first time that men taunted or abused by other men, and women harassed by women can sue for damages. The harassment must be based on gender in some manner, but not necessarily by sexual desire. Following a set of Supreme Court decisions in 1998, employers scrambled to reassess their policies and institute more vigorous training for their employees.

Title VII of the Civil Rights Act of 1964 prohibits employment discrimination based on race, color, religion, sex, and national origin. In 1986 the Court ruled that sexual harassment was a form of job discrimination and fell under civil rights law when leading to a job loss, or hostile working environment. Courts had recognized two types of sexual harassment, *quid pro quo* and hostile working environment. *Quid pro quo* is more straightforward by commonly involving blatant demands for sexual favors related to employment, hiring, promotion, and retention decisions. Hostile working environment harassment, recognized by the Court in 1986, is often much less clear. A hostile working environment is created when the workplace becomes filled with such persistent intimidation, ridicule, and insults that the workplace conditions are substantially changed.

In the wake of the Anita Hill accusations at Justice Clarence Thomas' confirmation hearings, many firms, particularly large corporations, established policies expressly forbidding unwelcomed advances or sexual harassment between employees. Such guidelines were written broadly enough that any behavior of a sexual nature was clearly prohibited, regardless of gender. Others, especially smaller businesses, were often less thorough in setting or enforcing policies.

Same-Sex Sexual Harassment

In regard to the appropriateness of sexual harassment claims when the alleged victim was the same sex as the alleged harasser, the lower courts were extraordinarily inconsistent in their rulings. The District of Columbia Circuit in *Barnes v. Costle* (1977) acknowledged the possibility of sexual harassment under Title VII where a homosexual employer harassed an employee of either gender. In the Second Circuit case of *Saulpaugh v. Monroe Community Hospital* (1993), the court observed that harassment is harassment regardless of whether it is caused by a member of the same or opposite sex. In *Gliddens v. Shell Oil Co.* (1993), a court elaborated that male-on-male harassment with sexual overtones was not sex discrimination unless the employee could demonstrate that the employer treated him differently because of his sex. However, the *Garcia v. Elf Atochem* (1994) ruling barred all same-sex sexual harassment claims. In a heterosexual harassment case, the Seventh Circuit in *Baskerville v. Culligan Int'l Co.* (1995) noted that, although sexual harassment of women by men was the most common kind, same sex claims should not be excluded from Title VII consideration. The possibility existed that sexual harassment of men by women, or men by other men, or women by other women could be subject to claims in appropriate cases. However, the Fourth Circuit in *McWilliams v. Fairfax County Board of Supervisors* (1996) held that harassment among heterosexuals of the same sex cannot give rise to a hostile environment sexual harassment claim under Title VII. Clearly the lower courts lacked consensus on the whether Title VII applied to same-sex sexual harassment cases.

Sexual Assault or Horseplay

Joseph Oncale, at age 21, was hired in August of 1991 as a roustabout by Sundowner Offshore Services in Houma, Louisiana. After a few weeks of working with an eight-man crew on a Chevron USA oil platform in the Gulf of Mexico, he began to be subjected to a series of humiliating and sexually threatening actions by the other men. On one occasion, two supervisors and another coworker physically assailed him in a sexual manner on a small boat between two oil platforms. The assaults continued through the following day accompanied with threats of rape over the next several weeks. At one point, he was sexually accosted in a shower. Oncale complained to company officials, but received no helpful response as Sundowner's workers denied all allegations and no company investigation was initiated. Sundowner, in fact, claimed it was only horseplay. In November, only a few months after being hired, Oncale quit for fear of eventually being raped.

Oncale filed a sex discrimination suit against Sundowner and three of his former coworkers with the Fifth Circuit Court of Appeals in New Orleans seeking damages for the humiliating harassment that led to his being run off the job. Citing *Garcia*, the court dismissed the case asserting that no federal law recognized sexual discrimination by one man against another. He appealed to the federal appeals court which affirmed the district court's decision. The Department of Justice, on behalf of the Equal Employment Opportunity Commission (EEOC), urged the Supreme Court to take up the case. The Court issued a writ of *certiorari*, a written order commanding the lower court to forward the proceedings of the case for review.

Oncale, with assistance from the EEOC, argued before the Court that Title VII's prohibition against sex discrimination and the Court's previous sexual harassment decisions were all stated in gender-neutral terms. Thus, all discrimination based on sex is prohibited, regardless of the genders involved. Writing for the unanimous Court, Justice Scalia noted that in "hostile work environment claims state and federal courts have taken a bewildering variety of stances." When Congress enacted Title VII, male-on-male sexual harassment in the workplace was not considered an issue. In regard to that observation, Sundowner argued that recognizing liability for same-sex sexual harassment would make Title VII more of a general civility code for the workplace rather than discrimination code for which it was intended. Scalia rejected the argument noting that the risk was no greater for same-sex sexual harassment than for opposite-sex sexual harassment.

Scalia wrote that sexual harassment in the work place clearly violated Title VII if it constituted *quid pro quo* harassment regardless of gender. If a supervisor conditions job benefits, either explicitly or implicitly, or an employee participates in sexual activity, it is "quid pro quo." Scalia reversed the two lower court decisions that Title VII of the Civil Rights Act of 1964 did not apply to same-sex sexual harassment.

Impact

At the time of decision, Oncale was 27 years of age, married, with two children. For the first time the Court clarified an employer's liability for instances of sexual harassment between two people of the same gender. Critics of the *Oncale* decision quickly claimed the Court distorted the Civil Rights Act which they asserted was specifically intended to protect female employees from discrimination by male supervisors. The distinction between rowdy behavior, perhaps involving assault, was blurred with sexual harassment.

The Court decided two other sexual harassment cases later in 1998 in addition to *Oncale*. The three cases posed substantial changes to many businesses. In *Faragher v. City of Boca Raton* (1998), the Court ruled that an employer held responsibility for harassment situations, regardless of whether it was aware of an harassment situation. In *Burlington Industries v. Ellerth* (1998), the Court ruled that a harassed employee did not need to demonstrate a tangible job loss to successfully prove sexually harassment. The victim, in fact, never reported the incidents of sexual harassment and actually received a promotion before resigning and 15 months later filing the lawsuit.

Oncale as well as the other cases raised the issue of what the word "sex" means in sexual discrimination law. Debates continued as to whether sex referred to the gender of the victim, gender of the harasser, the type of behavior involved, or all three. Same-sex issues highlighted that for behavior to be unlawful, it must be motivated by hostility as well as sexual desire. In fact, sexual desire need not be a factor. Hostility based on the gender of the victim could be sufficient to prove a case. However, hostility without the factor of gender does not constitute sexual harassment and does not generally violate federal law. Employers were put on alert that their legal liability for sexual harassment could arise from diverse situations, not just the commonly imagined male harassment of female form. Many employers reassessed their sexual harassment policies and enhanced their employee training programs.

Related Cases

Saulpaugh v. Monroe Community Hospital, 4 F.3d 134 (1993).
Garcia v. Elf Atochem No. Am., 28 F.3d 446 (1994).
Faragher v. City of Boca Raton, 118 S. Ct. 438 (1998).
Burlington Industries v. Ellerth, No. 97-569 (1998).

Bibliography and Further Reading

Baridon, Andrea P., and David R. Eyler. *Working Together: New Rules and Realities for Managing Men and Women at Work.* New York: McGraw-Hill, 1994.

Chemerinsky, Erwin. "Defining Sexual Harassment." *Trial,* May 1998.

Paludi, Michele A., and Richard B. Barickman. *Sexual Harassment, Work, and Education: A Resource Manual for Prevention.* Albany: State University of New York Press, 1998.

Reibstein, Larry. "Men Behaving Badly: It May Assault, But Is It Sexual Harassment When the Predator and Victim Are the Same Gender?" *Newsweek,* December 8, 1997.

Schulhofer, Stephen J. *Unwanted Sex: The Culture of Intimidation and the Failure of Law.* Cambridge, MA: Harvard University Press, 1998.

DUFFIELD V. ROBERTSON, STEPHENS & CO.

Legal Citation: 144 F.3d 1182 (1998)

Appellant
Tonyja Duffield

Appellee
Robertson Stephens & Co.

Appellant's Claim
That Form U-4 is unconstitutional and therefore cannot be enforced.

Chief Lawyer for Appellant
Michael Rubin

Chief Lawyer for Appellee
Daniel F. Bookin

Judges
William C. Canby, Jr., Stephen Reinhardt (writing for the court), Jane A. Restani (Court of International Trade Judge)

Justices Dissenting
None

Place
San Francisco, California

Date of Decision
8 May 1998

Decision
Form U-4 is unenforceable.

Significance
In a unanimous ruling in May of 1998, the Ninth Circuit Court of Appeals barred employers from requiring new employees to sign agreements as a condition of employment that they will settle sexual discrimination and sexual harassment disputes by means of arbitration, rather than in courts of law. This ruling appeared to end uncertainty and conflict among circuit courts on this issue, but in June of 1998, the Third Circuit Court of Appeals rejected the Ninth Circuit's reasoning in this case and reached the opposite conclusion—making the issue ripe for review by the U.S. Supreme Court.

Title VII of the Civil Rights Acts of 1964 outlawed job discrimination by all private and public employers. Congress delegated enforcement powers both to the Civil Rights Division of the Justice Department and to the newly created Equal Employment Opportunity Commission, but Congress also expected federal courts to play a major role in advancing the act's goal of deterring workplace discrimination on the basis of race, sex, and national origin. In the case of *Alexander v. Gardner-Denver Co.* (1974), the Court held that "Congress intended federal courts to exercise final responsibility for enforcement of Title VII." *Gardner* also held that enforcement by compulsory arbitration proceedings, rather than by courts, "would be inconsistent with that goal."

Arbitration proceedings became increasingly popular in the 1980s, but circuit courts steadfastly refused to enforce any agreements that required employees to resolve discrimination claims through binding arbitration. At the same time, but in other contexts, the Supreme Court supported a "liberal federal policy favoring arbitration." In Title VII cases, however, the federal courts maintained the position that "Title VII is different." As the Eighth Circuit Court put it in *Swenson v. Management Recruiters Int'l, Inc.* (1988), "arbitration is unable to pay sufficient attention to the transcendent public interest in the enforcement of Title VII."

In 1991, the Supreme Court appeared to shift course somewhat in *Gilmer v. Interstate/Johnson Lane Corp.* (1991) when it ruled that employees could be required to arbitrate claims brought under the Age Discrimination in Employment Act of 1967. The Court noted that the *Gardner* ruling involved a collective bargaining agreement compelling arbitration, rather than *Gilmer's* individual agreement. It further said individual agreements to arbitrate should be considered valid, unless Congress itself clearly intended to require judicial remedies exclusively for statutory claims. After *Gilmer,* courts then had to consider whether Congress intended to ban all forms of arbitration requirements, or only some, by paying close attention to the legislative history of the law-making process.

As it happened, in 1991 Congress enacted the Civil Rights Act of 1991, extending the Civil Rights Act of

1964, and for the first time dealt directly with the issue of compulsory arbitration of Title VII claims. The main purpose of the new law was to overrule a series of 1989 Supreme Court decisions which had made discrimination claims more difficult, but in Section 118, it also said that "where appropriate and to the extent authorized by law," parties to Title VII suits could choose alternative dispute resolution vehicles, including arbitration. Subsequently, the Ninth Circuit Court of Appeals held that discrimination claimants could not be required to submit to arbitration of their claims if they did not "knowingly" agree to do so, and also held that if they did agree to arbitration, they were then bound by the arbitrator's decision. However, no court had yet considered the issues presented by *Duffield*.

Tonyja Duffield was hired in 1998 as a broker-dealer in the securities industry. Before she could be hired, her employer, Robertson, Stephens and Company required her to agree to arbitrate all "employment related" disputes, rather than to take them to court. This requirement was mandated of all employers throughout the securities industry by both the New York Stock Exchange and the National Association of Securities Dealers; the relevant document new employees had to sign was known as Form U-4. In 1995, Duffield brought suit against her employer, alleging sexual discrimination and sexual harassment in violation of Title VII of the Civil Rights Act of 1964, as amended.

In district court, Duffield made five specific arguments against the securities industry's use of Form U-4, but preceded those arguments by requesting the court to rule against compulsory arbitration. Robertson Stephens asked the court to force her to go to arbitration. The court rejected all her arguments and denied her motion to rule against compulsory arbitration, then granted Robertson Stephens' motion—but instead of issuing a final judgment, the court sent the case to the circuit court of appeals.

Writing for the unanimous court, Judge Reinhardt ruled in favor of Duffield's request for a declaratory judgment against compulsory arbitration—a request supported in a "friend of the court" brief filed by the Equal Employment Opportunity Commission, among others. Judge Reinhardt noted that according to the *Gilmer* decision, the burden of proof was on Duffield to show that the legislative history of the 1991 Civil Rights Act demonstrated Congress' intention to preclude enforcement of compulsory arbitration agreements in Title VII cases, and then the judge proceeded to use the *Gilmer* test to support *Gardner*. His examination of the 1991 Civil Rights Act's legislative history was systematic and thorough.

Legislative History

The critical language of the act is found in Section 118, which states that parties to Title VII disputes could,

"[w]here appropriate and to the extent authorized by law," choose to pursue other methods of resolving them, including arbitration. Robertson Stephens argued that this language shows congressional intent to allow, even encourage, the kind of process represented by Form U-4. The firm also argued that by the time the Civil Rights Act of 1991 was passed, compulsory arbitration was already "authorized by law," namely, by the *Gilmer* case.

Judge Reinhardt remarked that this reading of Section 118 conflicts with Congress' directive to read Title VII broadly, and to choose the interpretation of the law which "most effectively advances" the underlying Congressional purpose. And when Congress "encourages" arbitration, we must read that word in the light of the "provisions of the whole law . . . [i]t would seem entirely disingenuous to fasten on that one word and conclude that Congress was boundlessly in favor of all forms of arbitration." Read in the light of Congress' objectives in the 1991 act, the words "where appropriate" point to whatever forum for dispute resolution the victims of discrimination find desirable, rather than to an unwanted forum forced on them.

Section 118's other critical statutory phrase, "to the extent authorized by law," most likely codifies the "law" as Congress understood it at the time— and, Judge Reinhardt pointed out, the "overwhelming weight of the law" was that "compulsory agreements to arbitrate Title VII claims were unenforceable." Such agreements were not "authorized by law." As of the time Section 118 was reported out of the congressional committee which drafted the bill, circuit courts "without exception, had 'widely interpreted' Title VII as prohibiting 'any form of compulsory arbitration.'"

Through the Looking Glass

The Supreme Court's decision in the *Gilmer* case was handed down just before the Civil Rights Act of 1991 was passed. The judge conceded that the decisions in *Gilmer* and *Gardner* may not coincide with Congress' intend as written "to the extent authorized by law." But, "even a cursory glance" at Section 118's legislative history makes it clear that Congress "in no way intended to incorporate" Gilmer's holding into Title VII. In fact, in reporting the bill to the House of Representatives, the House Committee on Education and Labor unambiguously said that "[t]his view is consistent with the Supreme Court's interpretation of Title VII in *Alexander v. Gardner-Denver Co.*" Not only that, Congress specifically rejected a proposal allowing employers to enforce compulsory arbitration agreements, and "it did so in the most emphatic terms," concluding with the phrase, "American workers should not be forced to choose between their jobs and their civil rights." Further, the chairman of the reporting committee, Congressman Edwards, said "No approval whatsoever is intended of the Supreme Court's recent decision in *Gilmer*. . . ." Judge Reinhardt concluded that "it is the unusual force and clarity of the statute's legislative history that is ultimately dispositive in this case."

But in response, the securities firm urged the court to ignore the legislative history and conclude that Section 118 must be read as adopting *Gilmer*. Its view was that "to the extent authorized by law" was merely an elastic phrase which contracted and expanded with the ebb and flow of court decisions. Reinhardt said the defendant's interpretation meant that Section 118, "without a single word being changed, nevertheless was instantaneously transmogrified, and took on exactly the opposite meaning," on the day *Gilmer* was announced, and he rejected it. "Any such 'through the looking glass' construction would entail a gross perversion of the legislative process."

In the end, Reinhardt said, the *Gilmer* requirement that such court decisions must be based on statutory language and legislative history is "the most compelling reason" to reject the view of Robertson, Stephens & Co. The legislative history of the Civil Rights Act of 1991 makes it "absolutely clear" that Congress intended to codify the *Gardner* approach—that is, to announce that *Gardner* was the law governing compulsory arbitration in Title VII cases. In the light of this, Reinhardt held that Form U-4 is unenforceable.

The Controversy Continues

Despite *Gilmer's* mandate to carefully examine legislative history and Judge Reinhardt's thorough and persuasive reading of the Civil Rights Act of 1991, on 8 June 1998 the Third Circuit sharply differed from the rationale discussed above. In *Seus v. John Nuveen & Co.*, a Pennsylvania district court had held that the Form U-4 Seus signed was enforceable under the Federal Arbitration Act; she appealed. The Third Circuit noted that "no amount of commentary from individual legislators or committees would justify a court in reaching the

result" that the Ninth Circuit reached, and it further noted that if the legislative history of Section 118 was binding, then it should be read as having codified *Gilmer*. The Supreme Court has granted *certiorari* in *Wright v. Universal Maritime Service Corp.*, and Supreme Court watchers think the Court in that case will have the opportunity to resolve the conflict.

Related Cases

Alexander v. Gardner-Denver Co., 415 U.S. 36 (1974).
Swenson v. Management Recruiters Int'l, Inc., 858 F.2d 1304 (1988).
Gilmer v. Interstate/Johnson Lane Corp., 500 U.S. 20 (1991).
Wright v. Universal Maritime Service Corp., 121 F.3d 702 (1997).
Seus v. John Nuveen & Co., No. 97-1498 (1998).

Bibliography and Further Reading

Biskupic, Joan, and Elder Witt, eds. *Congressional Quarterly's Guide to the U.S. Supreme Court*, 3rd ed. Washington, DC: Congressional Quarterly, Inc., 1996.

Bruno, Mary E. and Lawrence J. Rosenfeld. "Duffield Puts Compulsory Arbitration in Doubt." *The National Law Journal*, October 5, 1998, p. B6.

"Courts Deal Mandatory Arbitration a Setback." *Wall Street Letter*, December 7, 1998, p. 6.

Ebeling, Ashlea. "Better Safe Than Sorry." *Forbes*, November 30, 1998, p. 162.

Grodin, Joseph R. "On the Interface Between Labor and Employment Law." *Berkeley Journal of Employment and Labor Law*, winter 1998, p. 307-314.

Hofmann, Mark A. "High Court to Revisit Old Issues." *Business Insurance*, September 28, 1998, p. 2.

"U.S. Appeals Court Bars Mandatory Arbitration in Rights Claims." *Liability Week*, May 18, 1998.

Voting in a Democracy

The United States is a representative democracy. The efficacy of representative government depends, in large part, on the participation of its citizens. The most effective form of participation granted to the subjects of a representative democracy is voting. Although the right to vote for all members of American society above the age of 18 is a foregone conclusion, this was not the case at one time. Various laws and practices have served to deny the right to vote to certain members of society. Since its inception the United States has treated the issue of voting rights with caution. The nation gained its independence behind the battle cry of "taxation without representation" which brought the issue to the fore during the Constitutional Convention. Perhaps because voting rights was such a volatile issue for the young nation the founders elected to leave the matter to the states to resolve. The Constitution established two provisions concerning the right to vote: first, it stipulates that those who were eligible to vote in the state legislatures were also entitled to vote in elections to the House of Representatives; second, it reserved the right to determine the time and place of elections to Congress. Thus, although the Constitution did not explicitly deny the right to vote to minorities and women, neither did it protect the privilege until the ratification of the Fifteenth (right to vote for minorities) and Nineteenth (right to vote for women) Amendments.

The Supreme Court has often been an instrument used to rectify social injustices throughout American history. However, in the case of women's rights the Court has not been a positive force. In *Minor v. Happersett* (1875) the Supreme Court ruled that granting voting rights only to men in a state constitution did not violate the Privileges and Immunities Clause of the Fourteenth Amendment. Women were not initially denied the right to vote, however. It became such a common practice that states began to establish laws prohibiting women's suffrage in the late eighteenth century. Building on the momentum provided by the leadership of women such as Abigail Adams (the wife of John Adams), Margaret Brent, Lucretia Mott, Elizabeth Cady Stanton, and Susan B. Anthony, women

began to organize a voting rights movement in the nineteenthth century. Their efforts culminated in the ratification of the Nineteenth Amendment.

After the adoption of the Nineteenth Amendment there was little legal resistance to women's suffrage. This does not mean that voting rights for women was not met with resistance. In colonial America women were subservient to men in more ways than political expression. Often men would prohibit their wives from voting long after the right to vote had been constitutionally granted. Thus a substantial portion of the struggle for women's suffrage is not documented by the courts. This was not the case in the voting rights movement for African Americans after the ratification of the Fifteenth Amendment.

State Powers

The lion's share of the legal debate surrounding voting rights in America involved determining the extent to which states had the power to establish voting qualifications. The founders decided to leave the issue of voting qualifications to the discretion of the states; however, the federal government eventually retracted these powers when it became clear that the states would not treat the matter equitably. Even after the ratification of the Fifteenth Amendment in 1870 which prohibited the discrimination of voting rights on the basis of race, the South managed to find ways to suppress African American enfranchisement. One of the most effective strategies employed by the Southern states to perpetuate racial discrimination at the ballot box was the all-white primary. Here, whites managed to exclude African Americans from voting in primaries based on the argument that the Fifteenth Amendment applied only to general elections. The primary, they argued, was a function of a private organization which did not have to justify the inclusion or exclusion of certain people. In fact, the practice was upheld in the courts in 1921 in *Newberry v. United States* where it was decided that primary elections were the private functions of political parties and therefore did not prohibit African Americans from participating in general elections.

In order to understand the ramifications of this decision it must also be understood that up until the late twentieth century Southern politics was dominated by the Democratic Party. Although the Democratic Party was a strong advocate of civil rights during the 1960s, it was the Republican Party that initiated the movement to abolish slavery, a movement to which the Democratic Party in the South was not at all sympathetic. The domination of the Democratic machine in Southern politics meant that there was little realistic opportunity for a candidate who supported equal rights for African Americans to be elected in a general election. The important elections in the South were the primaries.

Discriminatory Practices

The state that fought most vigorously to preserve the white primary was Texas. The state legislature of Texas invited legal objection to the practice when it adopted a statute in 1923 which explicitly prohibited African Americans from participating in Democratic primary elections. With the help of the NAACP, L.A. Nixon filed suit on the grounds that the statute violated the Fourteenth and Fifteenth Amendments. In *Nixon v. Herndon* (1927) the Supreme Court supported his claim. However, the issue of whether primary elections were a private affair which justified the use of the white primary in *Newberry* was not addressed. *Nixon* was decided on the basis of the Fourteenth Amendment in that the state statute in question had violated Nixon's equal protection under the law. Thus, in order for Texas to continue the practice they merely needed to change the wording of the state statute. The state legislators of Texas therefore changed the statute to read that the Democratic party of Texas had the power to determine its own primary voting qualifications. Nixon filed suit again in *Nixon v. Condon* (1932) challenging the deprivation of his right to vote in primaries arguing that it violated his Fourteenth Amendment rights. The Court ruled that because the state legislature of Texas was endorsing a discriminatory practice by making the Democratic party its representative, Nixon's Fourteenth Amendment rights had been violated.

However, as is the case in many societies, discriminatory practices do not go down easily. Proponents of the white primary believed they could still hide behind the *Newberry* judgement on the basis that the Democratic Party is a private organization and could prevent African Americans from participating by passing its own resolution apart from the state legislature. This practice was challenged in *Grovey v. Townsend* (1935) but the Supreme Court could find no constitutional violation. This was a major defeat for civil rights advocates. There seemed to be no way to put an end to the white primary until a Louisiana commissioner named Classic was charged with changing the votes in a primary election. In *United States v. Classic* (1941) Classic disputed the charge on the grounds that the federal government had no power to regulate primary elec-

tions. The Court ruled against Classic arguing that the primary had become an integral part of the election process. This ruling finally cracked the foundation of the white primary by tying the practice to the overall legitimacy of general elections. Then in the landmark case *Smith v. Allwright* (1944) the Court formally prohibited the all-white primary. In an 8–1 decision Justice Reed included in his opinion the clarification that voting in primary elections "is a right secured by the Constitution" (*Smith*). Although this finally closed the door on the all-white primary it by no means put an end to discrimination against voting rights.

Another instrument used to discourage African Americans from voting was the literacy test. Literacy or "understanding" tests were designed "in theory" to ensure that those who voted were politically aware. In practice, however, the intent was clearly of a malevolent nature. In Louisiana for example, only African Americans were subjected to "understanding" tests because of a "grandfather clause" in the Louisiana Constitution. The clause stated that those voters who were eligible to vote prior to 1 January 1967 were exempt from having to meet registration requirements such as understanding tests. In other words, the grandfather clause essentially meant that if your grandfather was white you did not have to take these tests. The nature of the test was subjective; individuals were asked to interpret a section of the United States or Louisiana Constitution and were granted or denied registration on the basis of their response. So rigorous were the standards for passing that in some cases African Americans with professional or graduate degrees were denied registration. Ultimately, in *Louisiana v. United States* (1965) the constitutionality of these tests were called into question. In a 9–0 ruling Justice Black made a rather blunt observation regarding the design of the "understanding" test. "This is not a test but a trap, sufficient to stop even the most brilliant man on his way to the voting booth" (*Louisiana*).

Despite rulings such as this the Court's efforts to put an end to discrimination against African American voters were not very effective. Those who wished to preserve the preponderance of the white voting class in the South had yet other formal and informal means at their disposal. In an effort to enforce the provisions of the Fifteenth Amendment, Congress passed the Voting Rights Act of 1965. The act targeted areas of the country that had a history of discriminatory practices at the voting booths, authorizing federal supervision of the voting procedures in states where African American participation was suspiciously low. The constitutionality of the Voting Rights Act was immediately challenged in a suit led by South Carolina and supported by a number of other Southern states in *South Carolina v. Katzenbach* (1966). The Court reviewed the case under its original jurisdiction authority because it involved parties from different states. In an 8–1 decision the Court ruled that the Fifteenth Amendment granted Congress the power to take "appropriate" measures to ensure that voting rights on the basis of race were not abridged. Chief Justice Earl Warren declared that the Voting Rights Act was not inconsistent with the authority granted to Congress in the Constitution.

Courts Try to Strike Back

With the abolition of literacy tests and the power to enforce the Fifteenth Amendment provided by the Voting Rights Act, there seemed to be no other legal recourse for the denial of suffrage on the basis of race. Unfortunately, this was not the case as proponents of the old political machine now turned to economics to promote their interests. Early in American history voting privileges were reserved for property owners under the presumption that the wealthy would cast more informed votes. This prerequisite eventually gave way to universal suffrage; however, the issue would later resurface in a different form know as the "poll tax." States used the "poll tax" to improve the quality of the voting class presuming that only those genuinely interested in voting would pay for the privilege. In fact the Supreme Court initially upheld this reasoning finding the practice consistent with the Equal Protection Clause of the Fourteenth Amendment in *Breedlove v. Suttles* (1937).

Although the poll tax, in theory, does not discriminate against any particular group of people, in practice it had a clear impact on African American participation in the South. To redress the unequal impact of the poll tax Congress passed the Twenty-fourth Amendment which banned the tax in federal elections. It was only a matter of time before the practice of levying a poll tax in state elections would be reviewed in the courts. In *Harper v. Virginia State Board of Elections* (1966) the Court outlawed the practice on the basis of economic discrimination. Justice William O. Douglas explained in his opinion that wealth has nothing to do with whether an individual is capable of casting an intelligent vote.

Another issued related to economic discrimination also came under legal scrutiny in the 1960's. This time, however, the denial of suffrage was not racially motivated. After World War II it became common practice to use property taxes to pay for public services such as education. Some of the decisions on how to use these funds were made at the ballot box. Naturally, those people who owned property were reluctant to permit non-property owners to voice their opinion on the use of this tax money. Some states thus passed laws designed to prohibit the propertyless from voting on such matters. The constitutionality of denying non-property owners the right to vote was addressed In *Kramer v. Union Free School District* (1969). Individuals who did not own property but had a vested interest in the com-

munity such as the clergy, military personnel, the aged, and adults who lived with their parents (which was Kramer's situation) believed they were entitled to express their opinion on the use of local property taxes. The Court upheld this view finding that the state did not have a compelling interest sufficient to deny voting rights on property tax matters.

Representation

An issue taken up by the courts indirectly related to voting rights is representation. The point of voting is to allow people the opportunity to have their interests represented in a governing assembly. If the district lines in which one votes were drawn such that a certain group of voters was deliberately outnumbered, exercising the "right to vote" would be a moot point. The election of members of the House of Representatives is based on population. The Constitution granted a number of representatives to each state on the basis of population (originally one representative per 30,000 people.) Congress later passed a law limiting the number of House members to 435. The practice of redistricting has been a difficult matter to resolve in American history if only for the simple reason that the government cannot regulate where people live. For example, if there happens to be a high concentration of African Americans in a certain district the chances are good that a representative sympathetic to the political persuasion of African Americans will be elected. However, because there is no constitutional provision designed to regulate "gerrymandering," or the unfair drawing of district lines, this practice can be easily abused. Although the issue of drawing district lines was left to the states, blatant abuses of the criteria for drawing district lines to favor a certain group have stimulated legal debate.

In *Colegrove v. Green* (1946) the Court expressed strong reservations about becoming involved in redistricting and reapportionment matters. However, over time it became clear that as much as the Court preferred the issue to be resolved by the states they could not be trusted to do so equitably. In *Gomillion v. Lightfoot* (1960) a group of African Americans challenged an Alabama statute that redrew district lines to radically improve Lightfoot's prospects for reelection. The Alabama statute had redrawn the district lines of Tuskegee such that all but four or five out of 400 African American voters were displaced into a different district. The Supreme Court ruled that the statute had essentially denied the right of black voters guaranteed by the Fifteenth Amendment. In subsequent cases such as *Baker v. Carr* (1962) and *Wesberry v. Sanders* (1964) the Court ultimately resolved that judicial intervention into state political affairs relating to reapportionment and redistricting respectively, was warranted.

The health of a representative democracy is dependent upon the political expression of its subjects. It is difficult to characterize a nation as democratic when over 50 percent of the population is denied the right to vote. Fortunately, Americans have had legal recourse to expand suffrage to the entire adult population. As the above outline of the legal history of voting rights illustrates the right to vote for women and minorities has not come easily.

Bibliography and Further Reading

Bullock, Charles and Charles Lamb. *Implementation of Civil Rights Policy*. Moterey, CA: Brooks/Cole, 1984.

Claude, Richard. *The Supreme Court and the Electoral Process*. Baltimore: Johns Hopkins University Press, 1970.

Conway, Margaret. *Political Participation in the United States*. Washington DC: Congressional Quarterly Inc., 1991.

Elliot, Ward E. Y. *The Rise of the Guardian Democracy: The Supreme Court's Role in Voting Rights Disputes, 1845-1969*. Cambridge, MA: Harvard University Press, 1974.

Epstein, Lee and Thomas Walker. *Constitutional Law For A Changing America: Rights, Liberties, and Justice*. Washington DC: Congressional Quarterly Inc., 1992.

Porter, Kirk Harold. *A History of Suffrage in the United States*. New York: AMS Press, 1971.

Thornston, Abigail. *Whose Votes Count?* Cambridge, MA: Harvard University Press, 1987.

EX PARTE SIEBOLD

Legal Citation: 100 U.S. 371 (1880)

Petitioners
Albert Siebold, Walter Tucker, Martin C. Burns, Lewis Coleman, Henry Bowers

Respondent
State of Maryland

Petitioners' Claim
The petitioners were all election judges from Baltimore who had been convicted in federal court and subsequently sentenced to prison for stuffing ballot boxes and related incidents of election fraud in a congressional election in Maryland. They sought a writ of *habeas corpus* "to be relieved from imprisonment" on the grounds that Congress had no power to punish state officials for violating the laws of their own state.

Chief Lawyer for Petitioners
Bradley T. Johnson

Chief Lawyer for Appellant
Charles Devens, U.S. Attorney General

Justices for the Court
Joseph P. Bradley (writing for the Court), John Marshall Harlan I, Ward Hunt, Samuel Freeman Miller, William Strong, Noah Haynes Swayne, Morrison Remick Waite

Justices Dissenting
Nathan Clifford, Stephen Johnson Field

Place
Washington, D.C.

Date of Decision
8 March 1880

Decision
Congress has the right to regulate federal elections, even if state laws also regulated the same elections, so the prison sentence stood and the writ of *habeas corpus* was denied.

Significance
Ex parte Siebold was one of the few cases during the Reconstruction period where the Supreme Court upheld federal civil rights legislation. The case also established the federal government's right to regulate elections and to punish state officials—another step in the ongoing process of defining states' rights versus federal power.

The time after the Civil War was a period of enormous transition in race relations and in the power structure of the Southern states. The so-called era of Reconstruction saw a great deal of federal civil rights legislation aimed at overcoming the effects of slavery. Both federal and state legislation was also directed at establishing voting rights for African Americans. Consequently, for the first time in U.S. history, a considerable number of African Americans were elected to local positions, state legislatures, and to Congress.

This new political strength of African Americans called forth resistance from the white people who had been in power before the Civil War. After Reconstruction officially ended with the withdrawal of federal troops from the South in 1873, white resistance to black political power became more blatant. In some areas, opposition took an open, violent form, as in terrorist acts by the Ku Klux Klan and other white-power groups. Elsewhere, those who opposed black civil rights manipulated the electoral process to guarantee either that black citizens would not vote or that their votes would have no impact.

Stuffing the Ballot Box

The story begins with five election judges: Albert Siebold, Walter Tucker, Martin C. Burns, Lewis Coleman, and Henry Bowers. Each was responsible for overseeing the voting at one of the precincts in the city of Baltimore on 5 November 1878, for the election to choose the members of the Forty–sixth Congress.

On election day, each of the five judges was engaged in some form of election fraud. Henry Bowers was convicted of hindering an election supervisor from inspecting the ballot box at his precinct. Walter Tucker, along with a man named Justus J. Gude (who was not involved in the later Supreme Court case), was convicted of preventing Deputy Marshall James N. Schofield from supervising the election at his precinct, as well as ". . . fraudulently and clandestinely putting and placing in the ballot-box of the said precinct twenty (and more) ballots . . . with intent to thereby affect said election." As the Court decision emphasized, "This charge . . . is for the offence commonly known as 'stuffing the ballot-box.'"

Martin C. Burns was convicted of:

> refusing to allow the supervisor or elections to inspect the ballot-box, or even to enter the room where the polls were held, and with violently resisting the deputy marshal who attempted to arrest him . . .

Lewis Coleman was found guilty of the same charges as Burns, plus an additional charge of ballot-box stuffing. Siebold was convicted of the serious charge of stuffing the ballot-box.

Who is in Charge?

The convicted judges were duly sentenced to prison—but they protested. In their petition for *habeas corpus* (a claim that they had been or were about to be wrongfully imprisoned), they made three arguments:

(1) When Congress regulates elections, that power is an *exclusive* power.

(2) Being exclusive, Congress's regulatory power cannot be interfered with by the states. Therefore, it "must be so exercised as not to interfere with or come in collision with regulations presented . . . by the States, unless it provides for the *complete* control over [elections]."

(3) When Congress runs an election, its regulations "must take the place of all state regulations . . . [and the election] must be entirely and completely controlled and provided for by Congress.

Clearly, behind the legal language of *Ex parte Siebold* was a political fight. The federal government was involved in supervising congressional elections because of the civil rights legislation that Congress had passed in 1870 and 1871. At that point, federal troops were still stationed throughout the South, to prevent the resumption of power by former Confederate officials and to guarantee the civil rights of African Americans. The legislation calling for deputy marshals and federal officials was another layer of political control—a layer deeply resented by many white people in the South.

By the time of *Siebold,* 1880, federal troops had been out of the South for some seven years. But the civil rights legislation was still in place—and many white Southerners, including many residents of Maryland, deeply resented the idea of sharing political power with their black neighbors. Thus, like Siebold and his colleagues, they resorted to various forms of election fraud.

And, like the men in *Ex parte Siebold,* they resisted federal control in whatever ways they could.

The Court Fights Back

In the Court's majority opinion in *Siebold,* written by Justice Bradley, the Court stressed that federal and state power could certainly overlap—as long as it was understood that federal power always took precedence. The Court vehemently argued that the federal government could use any means it chose, including physical force, to make sure its laws were obeyed.

> Why do we have marshals at all, if they cannot physically lay their hands on persons and things in the performance of their proper duties? What functions can they perform, if they cannot use force? In executing the processes of the courts, must they call on the nearest constable for protection? Must they rely on him to see the requisite compulsion whilst they are soliciting and entreating the parties and bystanders to allow the law to take its course? . . . If we indulge in such impracticable views as these . . . we shall drive the national government out of the United States, and relegate it to the District of Columbia, or perhaps to some foreign soil. We shall bring it back to a condition of greater helplessness than that of the old confederation.

The Court and Civil Rights

For much of the Reconstruction and post-Reconstruction period, the Supreme Court was fairly conservative. In *Ex parte Siebold,* however, it took an unusually strong stand in support of the federal government's right and responsibility to protect the voting rights of all Americans.

Related Cases

Ex parte Yarbrough, 110 U.S. 651 (1884).
United States v. Mosley, 238 U.S. 383 (1915).

Bibliography and Further Reading

Bardolph, Richard, ed. *The Civil Rights Record: Black Americans and the Law, 1849-1970,* New York: Thomas Y. Crowell Company, 1970.

Biskupic, Joan, and Elder Witt, eds. *Congressional Quarterly's Guide to the U.S. Supreme Court,* 3rd ed. Washington, DC: Congressional Quarterly, Inc., 1996.

GUINN V. UNITED STATES

Legal Citation: 238 U.S. 347 (1915)

Plaintiffs
Frank Guinn, J. J. Beal

Defendant
United States

Plaintiffs' Claim
That the federal government had been wrong to prosecute these two Oklahoma election officials for enforcing an Oklahoma voting regulation that became known as the "Grandfather clause." The government believed that the "Grandfather clause" deprived African Americans of their right to vote.

Chief Defense Lawyers
James C. McReynolds, U.S. Attorney General; John W. Davis, U.S. Solicitor General

Chief Lawyer for Plaintiff
Joseph W. Bailey

Justices for the Court
William Rufus Day, Oliver Wendell Holmes, Charles Evans Hughes, Joseph Rucker Lamar, Joseph McKenna, Mahlon Pitney, Willis Van Devanter, Edward Douglass White (writing for the Court)

Justices Dissenting
None (James Clark McReynolds did not participate)

Place
Washington, D.C.

Date of Decision
21 June 1915

Decision
That the Oklahoma voting regulation did in fact violate the Fifteenth Amendment and unconstitutionally deprive African Americans of their right to vote.

Significance
A unanimous Supreme Court had for the first time struck down a state law disenfranchising African Americans; however, Oklahoma almost immediately found another way to continue discriminating against black voters and the federal government took no action, leaving black Americans effectively disenfranchised in much of the nation until the voting rights movement of the 1960s.

The story of African American voting rights begins with the passage of the Fifteenth Amendment soon after the end of the Civil War. The Fifteenth Amendment was very simple. It had only two sentences:

> The right of citizens of the United States to vote shall not be denied or abridged by the United States or by any State on account of race, color, or previous condition of servitude. Congress shall have power to enforce this article by appropriate legislation.

For a while, during the period known as Reconstruction, the Fifteenth Amendment was actually enforced. Federal troops occupied the states of the former Confederacy to make sure that black Americans had the right to vote. But when federal troops were withdrawn in 1873, Southern states found many ways to make voting a whites-only endeavor. In addition to outright terrorism by groups like the Ku Klux Klan, many states sought to prevent black voting by a system of laws and rules.

One of the best-known ways of restricting voting was the "literacy test." Being able to read, for example, a part of the state constitution might be made a requirement for voting. In those times, many people, both black and white, could not read or could not read well. A registrar might ask a white voter to read only a simple word or sentence, or might coach or help him, whereas a black voter might be asked to read a long, complicated passage. Technically, literacy tests were not considered to be in violation of the Fifteenth Amendment, because they made literacy, not race, the reason that voting was being restricted.

Another way that African Americans were kept out of the voting booth was by the so-called "Grandfather clause." There were many varieties of this kind of law, which said that people who had been voting before a certain date—or whose grandfathers had been voting before that date—did not have to register; they were simply allowed to vote. That way, registration rules could be made very complicated, or voter registration could be limited to a short, inconvenient time. If the voting date was set back far enough, it would exclude virtually all black voters, who had only been given the right to vote in 1869.

Oklahoma's Grandfather Clause

When Oklahoma was admitted into the Union in 1908, there was no Grandfather clause in its constitution. Almost immediately, however, this Southern state amended its constitution to read in part

> no person shall be registered . . . or allowed to vote, unless he be able to read and write any section of the [state] constitution . . . no person who was, on January 1, 1866, or at any time prior thereto, under any form of government, or who at that time resided in some foreign nation, and no lineal descendant of such person shall be denied the right to vote because of his inability to read and write sections [of the state constitution.]

In other words, someone who had only recently become a United States citizen, or someone whose grandfather had been voting in 1866, would be allowed to vote in Oklahoma. But someone who had not begun to vote until 1869—the year the Fifteenth Amendment was passed—would have to take a literacy test in order to cast a ballot.

The net effect of this provision was that voting in Oklahoma was a virtually all-white affair. This angered U.S. Attorney John Embry, who, along with fellow U.S. Attorney William R. Gregg wanted to bring Oklahoma elections officials up on criminal charges for the violent and discriminatory atmosphere of the 1910 elections. As J. A. Harris, Chair of the Oklahoma Republic Committee complained to the Attorney General, "Election inspectors had received orders to permit no man to vote who was colored, and the orders were carried out in practically all portions of the State." Black citizens of Oklahoma also complained to both President William H. Taft and the Justice Department, citing the enormous amount of racial violence, including at least one lynching, all of which served to discourage black voters.

President Taft was a Republican, which was still thought of as "Abraham Lincoln's party," as opposed to the Southern Democrats, who were considered anti-black. Yet Taft wanted to reach out to white Southern voters, and he was reluctant to tell his Justice Department to prosecute. Nevertheless, Embry went ahead, and two Oklahoma state elections officials, J. J. Beal and Frank Guinn, were indicted. The charges against them were from the Criminal Code, which in 1866 and 1870 had been amended to make it criminal to deprive someone of his or her rights under Constitution and federal law.

No one expected an Oklahoma jury to convict two state officials of civil rights violations, particularly when the officials had been enforcing an amendment to the Oklahoma state constitution. Yet on 29 September 1911, the two men were convicted in the District Court for the Western District of Oklahoma before Judge John H. Cotteral. The judge had told the jury that if the two men had simply made a mistake in how they enforced the law, then they had not committed a crime and should not be found guilty. The judge stated, on the other hand, that:

> if they knew or believed those colored persons were entitled to vote and their purpose was to unfairly and fraudulently deny the right of suffrage to them . . . on account of their race and color, then their purpose was a corrupt one, and they cannot be shielded by their official positions.

A Political Decision

Meanwhile, the 1912 presidential election was approaching. The Republican Taft was running against two candidates. Progressive Party candidate Theodore Roosevelt had excluded black people entirely from his strategy, and Democrat Woodrow Wilson was a Southerner. Taft suddenly saw good reason to appeal to black voters, and his Justice Department passed the word—any Oklahoma officials who did not let black people vote under the Grandfather clause would be prosecuted.

Oklahoma Governor Lee Cruce was furious. He insisted that the law be enforced. "I am tired of these cheap little partisan Deputy Marshals trying continually to interfere with the administration of laws in this state," he said. Cruce even threatened to arrest any federal agent who interfered with Oklahoma's elections.

Rumors spread, however, that federal authorities were also to arrest lawbreakers–that is, any election official who kept a black person from voting. In fact, U.S. Attorney Homer N. Boardman did go on to prosecute the chairman and the secretary of the Blaine County Election Board in a case that became known as *United States v. Moseley, Guinn, Moseley.* These two cases, along with a third case, *Myers v. Anderson,* together were known as the "Grandfather clause cases."

The Supreme Court Decides

Taft lost the 1912 election to Woodrow Wilson. Despite the fact that Wilson was a Democrat and a Southerner, many civil rights leaders saw him as their best hope. But would he agree with the United States' position in the case of Guinn and Beal? These two officials had turned to the U.S. Court of Appeals for the Eighth Circuit, claiming that they should not be prosecuted for upholding the law of their state. The Eight Circuit, in turn, sent the matter to the Supreme Court. At this point, the Justice Department had the option of backing down. It was under no obligation to carry on the case.

It is hard to know why the Wilson administration went ahead with *Guinn v. United States.* On one hand,

Wilson had made a campaign promise to deal fairly with black people, and such leaders as W. E. B. Du Bois and Booker T. Washington had supported him. On the other hand, as soon as he got into office, his administration began to segregate government cafeterias, to divide black and white employees at the Treasury and Post Office Departments, and even to screen off the desks of black civil servants. Despite the fact that the civil service had been integrated for 50 years, Wilson chose to segregate it.

Perhaps that was all the more reason for Wilson to proceed with *Guinn*. He may have thought he needed some way to win black political support. Perhaps he genuinely thought he was being even-handed. It is possible that the *Guinn* case simply fell through the cracks, a bureaucratic leftover from a previous administration that no one took the trouble to re-decide. In any case, the Grandfather clause case went to court.

The Supreme Court took over a year and a half to decide on *Guinn v. United States*. Unanimously (Justice McReynolds took no part), the Court ruled that the Oklahoma law was in violation of the Fifteenth Amendment. The ruling specified that literacy tests *per se* were not unconstitutional. But in this case, the literacy test was so intertwined with the Grandfather clause that it clearly had no purpose except to keep black people from voting. Therefore, it was unconstitutional.

Civil Rights and Wrongs

The Supreme Court decision was greeted with joy by those who supported civil rights. One of the historic features of the case was the participation of the National Association for the Advancement of Colored People (NAACP), who had submitted a "friend of the court" brief through Moorfield Storey. He and his NAACP colleagues stated that the decision "was a very great victory . . . a great step in advance [indicating] that the Court has waked up to the situation."

Yet finally, neither the *Guinn* decision nor the other two Grandfather clause cases had much practical impact. A special session of the 1916 Oklahoma legislature enacted a new law that "grandfathered" in all those who had registered in the 1914 election. This blatant defiance of the Court's intention went unpunished for years. Not until 1939 did the Court strike down the Oklahoma law. It wasn't until 1965, when the Voting Rights Act was passed by Congress, that African American voting rights truly become established throughout the United States.

Related Cases
United States v. Classic, 313 U.S. 299 (1941).

Bibliography and Further Reading

Bardolph, Richard, ed. *The Civil Rights Record, Black Americans and the Law, 1849-1970* New York: Thomas Y. Crowell, Inc., 1970.

Bickel, Alexander M., and Benno C. Schmidt. *The History of the Supreme Court of the United States, The Judiciary and Responsible Government,* Vol. IX. New York: Macmillan, 1984.

Kurland, Philip B., ed. *The Supreme Court Review.* Chicago: University of Chicago Press, 1969.

Lawson, Steven F. *Black Ballots: Voting Rights in the South, 1944-1969*. New York: Columbia University Press, 1976.

Miller, Loren. *The Petitioners, The Story of the Supreme Court of the United States and the Negro.* New York: Pantheon, 1966.

SMITH V. ALLWRIGHT

Legal Citation: 321 U.S. 649 (1944)

Petitioner
Lonnie E. Smith

Respondent
S. S. Allwright, election judge, et al.

Petitioner's Claim
That rules of the Texas Democratic Party which barred African Americans from participation in primary elections violated his constitutional rights.

Chief Lawyers for Petitioner
Thurgood Marshall and William H. Hastie

Chief Lawyer for Respondent
George W. Barcus

Justices for the Court
Hugo Lafayette Black, William O. Douglas, Felix Frankfurter, Robert H. Jackson, Frank Murphy, Stanley Forman Reed (writing for the Court), Wiley Blount Rutledge, Harlan Fiske Stone

Justices Dissenting
Owen Josephus Roberts

Place
Washington, D.C.

Date of Decision
3 April 1944

Decision
The U.S. Supreme Court upheld the petitioner's claim and overturned two lower court decisions to hold that the Texas Democratic Party owed Smith $5000 in compensatory damages, and that the party could no longer exclude African Americans from participation in its primary elections.

Significance
The ruling overturned the Court's decision, made just nine years earlier in *Grovey v. Townsend* (1935), that since political parties in Texas were designated as private organizations by the state legislature they could exclude African Americans from membership if they saw fit. *Smith v. Allwright* is a landmark in the Court's support of civil rights, and in the development of the so-called public function concept. The public function concept holds that essentially public activities, such as elections, must be subject to constitutional scrutiny even if they are managed by private organizations or corporations.

Reconstruction

In the years immediately following the Civil War, newly freed African Americans wielded immense political power in the southern United States, where they constituted a majority of the population. Southern whites saw this new political situation as intolerable, and contrived means to suppress the new voting majority.

No tactics of suppression were deemed beyond consideration. Vigilante bands such as the Ku Klux Klan and official institutions, including local police forces, combined to terrorize African Americans attempting to exercise their constitutional right to vote. Less crude, but more insidious, were legal and procedural methods of excluding African Americans from participation in the political system.

One such method was the establishment of a virtually one party system in state politics. Throughout the southern United States the Democratic Party (the party that opposed Lincoln within the Union) came to dominate the political scene. As such, Democratic primary elections were tantamount to general elections. With a one party system in place many Southern states then legally excluded African Americans from participation in the Democratic Party, rendering them politically impotent. This tactic was initially successful because the Supreme Court refused to consider cases involving primary elections. In *Newberry v. United States* (1921), the Court ruled that, since primary elections were unknown to the framers of the Constitution, their operation was outside the jurisdiction of the federal judiciary. This attitude did not last for long, however. Six years later a Texas state law barring African Americans from participation in Democratic Party primary elections was successfully challenged in *Nixon v. Herndon* (1927), with the Court ruling that the law violated the Equal Protection Clause of the Fourteenth Amendment. Following this decision the Texas legislature created a Democratic Party Executive Committee and authorized it to exclude African Americans from its primaries. Once again, in *Nixon v. Condon* (1932), the Court held that the legislature's authorization constituted unconstitutional state action since the executive committee was a state creation, and thus, in effect, a public institution.

"Public Function" Concept

The "Public Function" concept in connection to voting relates to the authority that is granted to a specified individual, such as a town, city, or county clerk, to run an election. This delegation of power to said person is governed by the laws of the state. In this position, his or her public function is designated by and limited to parameters established by law. Persons operating in this capacity are considered officers of the state, and are subject to control and guidance by the state in car-rying out his or her duties of office. An individual charged with such responsibility in a public role, must take an oath of office, swearing to uphold applicable laws while executing his or her duties.

Source(s): Hall, Kermit L., ed. *The Oxford Companion to the Supreme Court of the United States*. New York: Oxford University Press, 1992.

The Texas Democratic Party responded by holding a convention at which delegates voted to exclude African Americans from participating in party primaries.

This latest tactic of the Texas Democratic Party was immediately challenged in *Grovey v. Townsend*. R. R. Grovey, an African American resident of Houston, Texas, brought suit against the state Democratic Party for its refusal to provide him with a primary ballot. The Supreme Court, however, sided with the party on this occasion, ruling that since the party delegates had voted to exclude African Americans without state interference, their actions were beyond federal jurisdiction.

A Foot in the Door

The Court's attitude toward the disenfranchisement of African Americans in the South began to change in the late 1930s, as appointees of President Franklin D. Roosevelt began to assert their views in its decisions. A case brought by the Civil Rights Division of the U.S. Justice Department to fight corruption in local politics provided the impetus for the Court to reverse its position as defined in *Newberry* and *Grovey*.

In 1941 the Civil Rights Division tested the Court's stance on the jurisdiction of the federal judiciary in the case of *United States v. Classic*. The case involved the willful alteration and false counting of primary election votes by Louisiana election commissioners. By a vote of 5-3, the Court overturned *Newberry* and ruled that even primary elections must conform to constitutional provisions guaranteeing citizens the right to vote and have their votes accurately and truthfully counted. Although *Grovey* was not mentioned in the Court's decision, *Classic* clearly reversed what the Court had determined to be the private nature of political parties, thus leaving the activities of parties liable to scrutiny for constitutionality.

A Final Test

Lonnie E. Smith, an African American resident of Harris County, Texas, appeared before election judge S. S. Allwright on 27 July 1940 to cast a ballot in the Demo-cratic Party primary to nominate candidates for the upcoming national senatorial, congressional, and presidential campaigns. Allwright refused Smith's request for a ballot on the basis of his race. Smith left the election office without further comment, but immediately filed a damage suit for $5,000 against Allwright and the Democratic Party in the district court. The district court dismissed Smith's suit and the case proceeded to the court of appeals, which confirmed the district court's decision on the basis of the U.S. Supreme Court's ruling in *Grovey v. Townsend*. The Supreme Court took up the case on *certiorari* (an order calling up records and proceedings for review), given apparent discrepancies between its decisions in *Grovey* and *Classic,* and heard arguments on 12 January 1944.

An End to State-Sponsored Political Discrimination

Justice Reed delivered the decision of the Court, which voted 8-1 to reverse the lower court rulings and compel the Texas Democratic Party to allow Mr. Smith to cast his primary ballot. In its decision, the Court expressly abandoned the position it adopted in *Grovey*. The Court reasoned that since the Constitution guarantees all citizens the right to vote, and given the vital nature of participation in primary elections in light of the virtual one party system operating in the South, primary elections must come under federal jurisdiction and constitutional scrutiny. Furthermore, the state was so intimately involved in the regulation of political parties as to make the parties indistinguishable from many state institutions. This ruling also extended the conclusion reached in *Classic*, that some private organizations can have functions of such public import as to render them liable to legal definition as public institutions, thereby making them subject to federal jurisdiction.

Impact

Smith v. Allwright ended forever the state-sanctioned denial of the voting rights of large groups of citizens based on their race. Subsequent attempts to exclude African Americans from political participation would include poll taxes and literacy tests, but these could only be directed against individuals, not entire minority groups. The final battles against this sort of individual exclusion would be fought in the 1950s and 1960s. The ruling also continued the development of the public function concept as first delineated in *Classic*, which held that the Court had jurisdiction over the actions of certain ostensibly private organizations and institutions if their functions were judged to be public in nature.

Related Cases

Newberry v. United States, 256 U.S. 232 (1921).
Nixon v. Herndon, 273 U.S. 536 (1927).
Nixon v. Condon, 286 U.S. 73 (1932).

Grovey v. Townsend, 295 U.S. 45 (1935).
United States v. Classic, 313 U.S. 299 (1941).

Bibliography and Further Reading

Biskupic, Joan, and Elder Witt, eds. *Guide to the U.S. Supreme Court,* 3rd ed. Washington, DC: Congressional Quarterly, Inc., 1997.

Elliott, Stephen P., ed. *A Reference Guide to the U.S. Supreme Court.* New York: Facts on File Publications, 1986.

Hall, Kermit L., ed. *The Oxford Companion to the Supreme Court of the United States.* New York: Oxford University Press, 1992.

Johnson, John W., ed. *Historic U.S. Court Cases, 1690-1990: An Encyclopedia.* New York: Garland Publishing, 1992.

COLEGROVE V. GREEN

Legal Citation: 328 U.S. 549 (1946)

Appellant
Kenneth W. Colegrove

Appellee
Dwight H. Green, as a member *ex-officio* of the Primary Certifying Board of the State of Illinois

Appellant's Claim
That congressional districts in Illinois were disparate in population size, and therefore not truly representative.

Chief Lawyer for Appellant
Urban A. Lavery

Chief Lawyer for Appellee
William C. Wines

Justices for the Court
Harold Burton, Felix Frankfurter (writing for the Court), Stanley Forman Reed, Wiley Blount Rutledge

Justices Dissenting
Hugo Lafayette Black, William O. Douglas, Frank Murphy (Harlan Fiske Stone and Robert H. Jackson did not participate)

Place
Washington, D.C.

Date of Decision
10 June 1946

Decision
Apportionment issues are political questions which must be decided by state legislatures with congressional oversight.

Significance
More than a decade of state legislative inaction following *Colegrove* finally resulted, in 1962, in the landmark *Baker v. Carr* decision. In *Baker v. Carr* the Supreme Court held that the Equal Protection Clause of the Fourteenth Amendment renders apportionment subject to federal control, thus overruling *Colegrove*.

The appellants in *Colegrove v. Green* were three qualified Illinois voters—including Kenneth W. Colegrove, who gave his name to the case. These three brought suit against a number of state officials in an effort to stop a November 1946 election from taking place before their election districts were reevaluated. These districts, they claimed, had not been redrawn since 1901 and now contained disproportionately large populations when compared with other districts in the state. Citing various constitutional provisions, they asked the federal District Court of the Northern District of Illinois to declare invalid the provisions of the Illinois law governing congressional districts. When a three-judge panel dismissed their case, Colegrove and the other appellants asked the U.S. Supreme Court to review this decision.

Court Declares Apportionment a "Political Question"

Writing for a divided and diminished Court (Chief Justice Stone had recently died, and Justice Jackson was on leave), Justice Frankfurter upheld the decision of the district court. The question of how election boundaries within a state are drawn is not, he declared, one for the courts to decide.

> We are of the opinion that the petitioners ask of this Court what is beyond its competence to grant. This is one of those demands on judicial power which cannot be met by verbal fencing about "jurisdiction." It must be resolved by considerations on the basis of which this Court, from time to time, has refused to intervene in controversies. It has refused to do so because due regard for the effective working of our Government revealed this issue to be of a peculiarly political nature and therefore not meet for judicial determination.

The reason apportionment is a "political question," Frankfurter went on to say, is that it "concerns matters that bring courts into immediate and active relations with party contests."

The so-called "political question" doctrine which permits federal courts to avoid hearing certain cases has

Kenneth W. Colegrove, 1951. © AP/Wide World Photos.

its roots in the principle of separation of powers. Certain issues, according to Supreme Court tradition, have been thought to belong to the province of the elected branches of government, the executive and the legislative. However, courts can—and do—hear cases involving political issues, and the political question doctrine is sometimes simply cited as justification for avoiding certain awkward issues that might, in fact, be better left to Congress or the president to decide.

Malapportionment, the unequal distribution of elected representatives, was one such issue. But when more than a decade passed after *Colegrove* without state legislatures taking any action, the Supreme Court finally felt obliged to declare, in the landmark case of *Baker v. Carr* (1962), that apportionment could in fact be addressed by the judiciary. The rationale for doing so was found in the Fourteenth Amendment, which provides that citizens of individual states are due equal protection under federal laws. Failure to reapportion electoral districts since 1901 in a state that had seen a considerable population shift from rural to urban areas in the ensuing decades plainly prevented individuals in overpopulated districts from being properly represented. After *Baker v. Carr*, challenges to outmoded election boundaries could be brought directly into federal court. Justice Frankfurter remained philosophically opposed to what he saw as lawmaking by the courts, and in *Baker v. Carr* he wrote a dissent denouncing the Court's change of course.

Related Cases
Baker v. Carr, 369 U.S. 186 (1962).
Wesberry v. Sanders, 376 U.S. 1 (1964).

Bibliography and Further Reading
Baker, Gordon E. *The Reapportionment Revolution: Representation, Political Power, and the Supreme Court.* New York: Random House, 1966.

Johnson, John W. *Historic U.S. Court Cases, 1690-1990: An Encyclopedia.* New York: Garland Publishing, 1992.

O'Rouke, Timothy G. *The Impact of Reapportionment.* New Brunswick, NJ: Transaction Books, 1980.

Urofsky, Melvin I. *Felix Frankfurter: Judicial Restraint and Individual Liberties.* Boston: Twayne, 1991.

TERRY V. ADAMS

Legal Citation: 345 U.S. 461 (1953)

Petitioner
Terry

Respondent
Adams

Petitioner's Claim
That excluding black voters from the Jaybird Democratic Association's primary elections violated their right to vote based on race and color.

Chief Lawyer for Petitioner
J. Edwin Smith

Chief Lawyer for the Respondent
Edgar E. Townes, Jr.

Justices for the Court
Hugo Lafayette Black (writing for the Court), Harold Burton, Tom C. Clark, William O. Douglas, Felix Frankfurter, Robert H. Jackson, Stanley Forman Reed, Fred Moore Vinson

Justices Dissenting
Sherman Minton

Place
Washington, D.C.

Date of Decision
4 May 1953

Decision
Reversed a decision by a court of appeals and held that the combined election procedures of the association and the Democratic Party deprived black citizens of the right to vote, contrary to the Fifteenth Amendment.

Significance
Terry v. Adams, with its invalidation of the whites-only primary election procedure in Fort Bend County, Texas, marked the end of the southern white primary, an institution that kept blacks from voting during the first half of the twentieth century.

During the first half of the twentieth century, the Democratic party completely dominated southern politics. Because of that domination, the Democratic primary was the only meaningful election. If a citizen could not vote in the primary, he or she was virtually excluded from the electoral process. In 1889, the Jaybird Democratic Association of Fort Bend County, Texas was founded to promote "good government." Since its beginning in the post-Reconstruction period, its membership had been limited to white people, who automatically became members if their names appeared on the official list of county voters. Each election year, the association held the Jaybird primary in May, which selected by ballot the candidates that the association would endorse for public office in the county. For over 60 years, the association's county-wide candidates ran unopposed, dominated the Democratic primaries, and were elected to office.

On 16 May 1950, the petitioners instituted a class action suit on behalf of the black citizens of Fort Bend County, stating that they had been denied the right to participate in the primaries of the association solely based on their race and color. The association responded that they were not a political party, but a private voluntary group, and the Fifteenth Amendment, which prohibits the government at both the federal and state level from denying a person the right to vote on the basis of race, did not apply to them. Adams, president of the Jaybird Association, testified that the purpose of the association was to have the white population vote at a time when the black population could not. The district court ruled that the association was a political party and that its discriminatory exclusion of blacks from the primary was invalid. It also ruled that blacks were legally entitled to vote in the Jaybird primary. The court of appeals reversed this decision, stating that because the association's primaries were not controlled by the state, the Fifteenth Amendment did not apply.

The Jaybird Primary

Justice Black wrote, "It is apparent that Jaybird activities follow a plan purposefully designed to exclude Negroes from voting and at the same time to escape the Fifteenth Amendment's command . . ." Black noted that the Fifteenth Amendment bans racial discrimination by both state and nation and establishes a national policy regarding the election of national, state, or local officials. Black stated that because the Jaybird primary excluded African Americans, it was precisely the kind of election the Fifteenth Amendment sought to prevent. Black called the state's permitting this duplicate primary "a flagrant abuse" and added that the county-operated primary, which simply ratified the Jaybird primary, "merely compounds the offense." "The only election that has counted in the Texas county for more than 50 years has been that held by the Jaybirds . . . The effect . . . is to . . . strip Negroes of every vestige of influence in selecting the officials who control the local county matters that intimately touch the daily lives of citizens." The Court reversed the decision of the court of appeals and affirmed the district court's holding that the Jaybird election machinery deprived black citizens of their right to vote on account of their race and color.

Justice Frankfurter also wrote an opinion for *Terry v. Adams*. He felt that the Jaybird Association was not a political party, but that "if the electoral officials, clothed with State power in the county, share in that subversion, they cannot divest themselves of State authority and help as participants in the scheme." The county electoral officials participated in and condoned a continued effort to exclude black citizens from voting. The action of the association may not be forbidden by the Fifteenth Amendment, but its role in the scheme brings it within reach of the law. Frankfurter noted that a federal court cannot require that the petitioners be allowed to vote in the Jaybird primary. "But a court of equity can free the lawful political agency from the combination that subverts its capacity to function."

Justice Clark agreed with the district court judge that the association was a political party, whose activities fall within the Fifteenth Amendment's ban. He felt that the Jaybird Democratic Association operated as part and parcel of the Democratic Party. Clark summed up his opinion by noting that whatever the Jaybird Association is considered, either a separate political organization or part of the local Democratic party, it is the decisive power in the county's electoral process. The Fifteenth Amendment is applicable to state power in all forms, and since the Jaybird organization chose the county's elected officials, the association took on the attributes of government which draw the Constitution's safeguards into play.

A Pressure Group

Justice Minton, in his dissent, noted, "I am not concerned in the least as to what happens to the Jaybirds or their unworthy scheme. I am concerned about what this Court says is state action within the meaning of the Fifteenth Amendment to the Constitution." Minton felt that the Supreme Court only had the power to right a wrong under that amendment if the wrong was done by the state. Minton believed that the Jaybird Democratic Association was not part of the Democratic party and made no attempt to use the state to carry on its primary election. He felt that the Jaybirds conducted a straw vote, as individuals, to see who should receive the association's endorsement for county offices and that the association was nothing more than a pressure group. Minton noted that the majority in this case concluded that the association's activities constituted state action. He felt that this conclusion was based on a dislike of the goals of the Jaybird Association. Although Minton also disliked their goals, he still did not feel that their activities constituted state action and thus should not be covered by the Fifteenth Amendment.

Impact

Terry v. Adams was the last of the "white primary cases." White primary laws were developed in the South to exclude black voters from elections. A Texas law limiting primaries to white voters was invalidated in 1927. Texas also passed a law stating that the executive committees of political parties could determine who voted in primaries. The Court invalidated this too. In 1953, when the Court decided that the Jaybird Democratic Association performed a public function and that it violated the Fifteenth Amendment, it ended the practice of white primaries.

Terry v. Adams set a precedent for the Congress to prohibit private racial discrimination under the Fifteenth Amendment. This came into play in later federal legislation, such as the Voting Rights Act of 1965. The case also serves as an example of the "public function" strand of state action doctrine.

Related Cases

United States v. Cruikshank, 92 U.S. 542 (1876).
Guinn and Beal v. United States, 238 U.S. 347 (1915).
Smith v. Allwright, 321 U.S. 649 (1944).
Shelley v. Kraemer, 334 U.S. 1 (1948).

Bibliography and Further Reading

Hall, Kermit L., ed. *The Oxford Companion to the Supreme Court of the United States.* New York: Oxford Press, 1992.

Levy, Leonard W., ed. *Encyclopedia of the American Constitution.* Vol. 4. New York: Macmillan, 1986.

Lieberman, Jethro K. *The Evolving Constitution.* New York: Random House, 1992.

GOMILLION V. LIGHTFOOT

Legal Citation: 364 U.S. 339 (1960)

Petitioners
C. G. Gomillion, et al.

Respondents
Lightfoot, Mayor of Tuskegee, et al.

Petitioners' Claim
That the state of Alabama re-created the Tuskegee City boundaries to eliminate most African American residents, preventing them from voting in city elections in violation of the Fifteenth Amendment.

Chief Lawyers for Petitioners
Fred D. Gray, Robert L. Carter

Chief Lawyer for Respondents
James J. Carter

Justices for the Court
Hugo Lafayette Black, William J. Brennan, Jr., Tom C. Clark, William O. Douglas, Felix Frankfurter (writing for the Court), John Marshall Harlan II, Potter Stewart, Earl Warren, Charles Evans Whittaker

Justices Dissenting
None

Place
Washington, D.C.

Date of Decision
14 November 1960

Decision
Ruling that African American residents had a right to prove in court that the redistricting act was unconstitutional, the Court reversed the two lower courts' dismissal of the complaint.

Significance
Prior to this ruling, the U.S. Supreme Court had been reluctant to interfere with the rights of states to establish political boundaries of their cities. This case, however, demonstrated that states cannot use that power to deprive citizens of their voting rights guaranteed by the Fifteenth Amendment.

Background

Although the Fifteenth Amendment prohibited voter discrimination based on race, southern states at the time of this case often had requirements that made it more difficult for blacks to vote. In Alabama they were required to pass literacy tests and present character witnesses from whites. In 1957 the state legislature, at the request of Tuskegee officials, passed a law that changed the Tuskegee City boundaries from a square into an irregular shape with 28 sides. This redistricting put all but four or five of the black residents outside the city limits but kept the white voting population intact. Believing that the purpose of this law was to favor white leaders by excluding African Americans from city elections, black residents sued the mayor and city officials in the U.S. District Court for the Middle District of Alabama. There they argued that the redistricting deprived them of due process and equal protection under the Fourteenth Amendment and violated the Fifteenth Amendment ensuring their right to vote regardless of race.

The city urged the court to dismiss the case, citing precedence that gave authority for political boundary-setting solely to state legislatures. The court agreed that it had no power in such cases and dismissed the complaint. When African American citizens appealed, the Court of Appeals for the Fifth Circuit upheld the dismissal. Their case then went to the U.S. Supreme Court, where it was argued in October of 1960.

Supreme Court Reverses Decision

The city relied on past cases of judicial non-interference in reapportionment to persuade the Supreme Court to dismiss the Gomillion claim as the lower courts had done. The Court, while acknowledging that states did have the power to act "within the domain of state interest" without interference from the courts, observed that the city had offered no compelling reason for changing its boundaries. The Supreme Court agreed with the petitioners that the obvious result of the reapportionment had been to deprive African Americans of their voting privileges. Since the case thus concerned constitutional rights, the lower courts had been wrong in refusing to hear the case. The Supreme Court

Redistricting

Voting districts within each state are subject to reassessment based upon federal census figures every ten years. In order to maintain an even population distribution among districts within each state, a reapportionment is done based upon population increases, decreases, and shifts. Redistricting may involve redrawing the boundaries of congressional districts in conjunction with the U.S. Constitution and Supreme Court cases with the intention that each individual's vote will be worth the same as another's.

Voting districts of equal population density assure that representatives to the U.S. House and state legislatures will be elected based upon an even apportionment of voters. Continual redistricting assures that voting precincts be divided equally based upon population figures, as much as possible. Care must be taken to insure that no boundaries are drawn that knowingly or unintentionally creates districts that discriminate against any group of voters.

Source(s): "An Overview of House Reapportionment during the 1990s." http://www.lpitr. state.sc.us/reports/97reapp.htm.

Dictionary of American History, Volume 2. New York: Charles Scribner's Sons, 1976.

voted unanimously to reverse the previous decision. In doing so, however, it did not actually rule that discrimination had occurred, only that there were sufficient grounds for African American residents to pursue their claim of discrimination in court.

In refuting the city's claim, Justice Frankfurter contrasted the present case with past rulings cited by the city.

> In no case involving unequal weight in voting distribution that has come before the Court did the decision sanction a differentiation on racial lines whereby approval was given to . . . withdrawal of the vote solely from colored citizens . . . these considerations lift this controversy out of the so-called "political" arena and into . . . constitutional litigation.

Justice Frankfurter further remarked that the power of states to determine their own political units was still limited by the statutes set forth by the U.S. Constitution, specifically, in this case, the Fifteenth Amendment.

Although concurring with the decision, Justice Whittaker believed that it should have been based on the Fourteenth Amendment rather than the Fifteenth. Observing that the reapportionment act did not actually exclude African American citizens from the voting process, as they were still eligible to vote in their new district, he noted that it did violate the Equal Protection Clause of the Fourteenth Amendment through racial segregation.

Impact

This case marked a shift in the Supreme Court's involvement with political redistricting cases. In later cases, the Court ruled that redistricting be done according to population. Although gerrymandering—the process of re-drawing voting districts to an individual's or group's own advantage in elections—remained an issue after this case, it was determined to be unconstitutional when it clearly discriminated against a particular racial group.

Related Cases

Hunter v. City of Pittsburgh, 207 U.S. 161 (1907).
Colegrove v. Green, 328 U.S. 549 (1946).
Baker v. Carr, 369 U.S. 186 (1962).
Beer v. United States, 425 U.S. 130 (1976).
Shaw v. Reno, 509 U.S. 630 (1993).

Bibliography and Further Reading

Blumberg, Rhoda L. *Civil Rights: The 1960s Freedom Struggle.* Boston: G. K. Hall & Co., 1984.

Cushman, Robert F., and Susan P. Loniak. *Cases in Constitutional Law,* 7th ed. Englewood Cliffs, NJ: Prentice Hall, 1989.

Lieberman, Jethro K. *The Evolving Constitution: How the Supreme Court Has Ruled on Issues from Abortion to Zoning.* New York: Random House, 1992.

BAKER V. CARR

Legal Citation: 369 U.S. 186 (1962)

Appellants
Charles W. Baker, et al.

Appellees
Joe E. Carr, et al.

Appellants' Claim
That electoral districts which were drawn in such a way as to provide inadequate representation violated the Equal Protection Clause of the Fourteenth Amendment.

Chief Lawyers for Appellants
Charles S. Rhyme, Z. T. Osborn, Jr.

Chief Lawyer for Appellees
Jack Wilson, Assistant Attorney General of Tennessee

Justices for the Court
Hugo Lafayette Black, William J. Brennan, Jr. (writing for the Court), Tom C. Clark, William O. Douglas, Potter Stewart, Earl Warren

Justices Dissenting
Felix Frankfurter, John Marshall Harlan II (Charles Evans Whittaker did not participate)

Place
Washington, D.C.

Date of Decision
26 March 1962

Decision
Finding that constitutional challenges to malapportionment could be addressed by federal courts, the Supreme Court upheld the appellants' claim by a 6-2 vote.

Significance
This case made it possible for unrepresented voters to have their districts redrawn by federal courts, initiating a decade of lawsuits that would eventually result in a redrawing of the nation's political map. In many states it reduced the disproportionate power of rural voters and their legislative representation and increased that of urban and suburban voters and their representation.

Citizens of Memphis, Nashville, and Knoxville, Tennessee, sought to have their electoral districts redrawn. The districts had not been reapportioned since 1901, and since then a considerable population shift had taken place from rural to urban locales. The result was that residents of these cities felt they were being underrepresented in the state legislature in violation of the equal protection guarantees contained in the Fourteenth Amendment. The U.S. District Court for the Middle District of Tennessee declined to grant the plaintiffs' request that a declaratory judgment be issued indicating that the Tennessee apportionment act was unconstitutional, and that an injunction be issued to prevent state officials from conducting further elections using the existing electoral district boundaries. Instead, the court found the voters' complaint to be a "political question" which courts could not decide and which, furthermore, was outside the scope of the authority conferred on the judiciary by Article III of the Constitution. Such matters were the province of the legislative branch. When the district court dismissed their case against Joe C. Carr, the Tennessee Secretary of State, Charles Baker and his fellow appellants appealed their case directly to the U.S Supreme Court.

This procedure for getting to the Supreme Court was by this date unusual, and everyone involved in the case recognized that everything about it was extraordinary. Various parties, including the solicitor general, filed *amicus* briefs, and the Court heard three hours of oral argument, permitting the attorneys to present their case at far greater length than is normally allowed. After this initial argument on 19-20 April 1961, the case was reargued on 9 October 1961 before the justices released five opinions totalling 163 pages.

The Court divided 6-2, with Justice Brennan delivering the opinion of the majority. He dispensed with the argument that the case involved a political question which the Court could not decide: "The courts cannot reject as 'no law suit' a bona fide controversy as to whether some action denominated as 'political' exceeds constitutional authority." And in the end, the Court found that the appellants' claim had merit:

> We conclude that the complaint's allegations of a denial of equal protection present a justi-

Charles Whittaker

Charles Evans Whittaker served as an associate justice on the U.S. Supreme Court during the five year period beginning in 1957 and ending in 1962. During his tenure on the High Court, Whittaker's opinions made him known as a "middle-of-the-road conservative." He had been nominated by President Dwight D. Eisenhower after only one year as a judge for the Eighth Circuit of the U.S. Court of Appeals, a prior appointment also made by Eisenhower.

Whittaker hailed from Troy, Kansas. He was born on 22 February 1901. Although he left school at sixteen to help on the family's farm, he later was accepted to law

school. He gained admittance to the bar a year before his graduation which occurred in 1924. For the next 30 years he practiced law in a Kansas City law firm; he made senior partner after two years.

His naming to the U.S. District Court for the Western District of Missouri in 1954 was the first in a series in federal appointments made by President Eisenhower. Whittaker's service ended with his retirement from the High Court on 31 March 1962 due to declining health. He died on 26 November 1973.

Source(s): Cornell. http://supct.law.cornell.edu/supct/.

fiable constitutional cause of action upon which appellants are entitled to a trial and a decision. The right asserted is within reach of judicial protection under the Fourteenth Amendment.

The Court sent the case back to the federal district court for further proceedings.

The consequences of this potential outcome had been clear from the start. Now Justice Brennan's opinion cast doubt on legislative districting throughout the country. Indeed, within a decade, electoral boundaries had been redrawn everywhere. *Baker v. Carr,* which Chief Justice Warren called "the most vital decision" handed down during his long and eventful tenure on the Court, started a reapportionment revolution that helped to establish the "one person, one vote" precept formally announced in *Gray v. Sanders* (1964) and confirmed in *Wesberry v. Sanders* (1964) and *Reynolds v. Sims* (1964). Now that voters had access to federal courts, they had the power to enforce the principle of equal

protection under the laws that the Fourteenth Amendment had codified nearly 100 years before.

Related Cases
Colgrove v. Green, 328 U.S. 459 (1946).
Gray v. Sanders, 372 U.S. 368 (1962).
Reynolds v. Sims, 377 U.S. 533 (1964).
Wesberry v. Sanders, 376 U.S. 1 (1964).

Bibliography and Further Reading
Graham, Gene S. *One Man, One Vote.* Boston: Little, Brown, 1972.

Grofman, Bernard. *Voting Rights, Voting Wrongs: The Legacy of Baker v. Carr.* New York: Twentieth Century Fund, 1990.

Johnson, John W. *Historic U.S. Court Cases, 1690–1990: An Encyclopedia.* New York: Garland Publishing, 1992.

Schwab, Larry M. *The Impact of Congressional Reapportionment and Redistricting.* Lanham, MD: University Press of America, 1988.

WESBERRY V. SANDERS

Legal Citation: 376 U.S. 1 (1964)

Appellant
James P. Wesberry

Appellee
Carl E. Sanders

Appellant's Claim
That the Georgia apportionment statute resulted in election districts that were unconstitutionally disproportionate to one another in population size.

Chief Lawyers for Appellant
Emmet J. Bondurant II and Frank T. Cash

Chief Lawyer for Appellee
Paul Rodgers

Justices for the Court
Hugo Lafayette Black (writing for the Court), William J. Brennan, Jr., Tom C. Clark, William O. Douglas, Arthur Goldberg, Earl Warren, Byron R. White

Justices Dissenting
John Marshall Harlan II, Potter Stewart

Place
Washington, D.C.

Date of Decision
17 February 1964

Decision
The Supreme Court struck down the Georgia apportionment statute.

Significance
Wesberry was the first real test of the "reapportionment revolution" set in motion by *Baker v. Carr* (1962), in which the Supreme Court held that federal courts could rule on reapportionment questions.

James P. Wesberry, Jr., was one of the citizens of Fulton County, Georgia, who filed suit in the U.S. District Court for the Northern District of Georgia challenging the state apportionment law. Georgia's Fifth Congressional District, which included Fulton County, was one of five voting districts created by a 1931 Georgia statute. By 1960, the population of the fifth district had grown to such an extent that its single congressman had to represent two to three times as many voters as did congressmen in the other Georgia districts. Wesberry based his claim on Article I, section 2, of the U.S. Constitution, which states that, "The House of Representatives shall be composed of Members chosen every second Year by the People of the several States," and on section 2 of the Fourteenth Amendment, which reads in part: "Representatives shall be apportioned among the several States according to their respective numbers . . ."

In 1962, the Supreme Court began what became known as the "reapportionment revolution" with its decision in *Baker v. Carr*. *Baker* did not address a specific situation of malapportionment, but instead upheld the general principle that federal courts have the power to order the reconfiguration of state election districts. The next significant reapportionment case was *Gray v. Sanders* (1963), which established the principle of "one person, one vote." At the district court level, however, a three-judge panel hearing Wesberry's case relied upon an earlier U.S. Supreme Court precedent, *Colegrove v. Green* (1946), which held reapportionment to be a "political question" outside court jurisdiction. After the district court dismissed their complaint, Wesberry and the other members of his class action suit appealed to the U.S. Supreme Court.

Supreme Court Holds That Reapportionment Is Not a "Political Question"

Writing for the Court, Justice Black dispensed with the political question issue immediately, agreeing with the appellants that Article I, section 2, properly interpreted, mandated the end of the Georgia apportionment statute:

> The right to vote is too important in our free society to be stripped of judicial protection . . .

One Person, One Vote

The concept that each individual's vote will carry the same weight as another was established by the U.S. Constitution, and was reiterated in *Baker v. Carr* (1962) and *Wesberry v. Sanders* (1964). Historically, the American colonists had disagreed with England's imposition of taxation without actual representation. They argued that "virtual" representation of the colonists in Parliament was inadequate.

In framing the Constitution, the authors intended to avoid the problem of representation in elections for Congress. In order to provide a balance between conflicting needs of the more populated states versus the less so, they devised a system whereby both population densities were addressed. In the Senate, each state would have two senators. In the House, the represen-

tation would be based upon population in the state. Realizing potential growth and shifting populations, a provision was made to reapportion the number of representatives of each state based upon a national census to be conducted every ten years.

Boundaries in voting districts may be redrawn allowing for movement of populations. This continual reassessment of populations provides the basis for the argument that each person's vote in congressional elections carries similar weight to any one else's vote.

Source(s): Cornell. http://supct.law.cornell.edu/supct/. *Dictionary of American History*, Volume 2. New York: Charles Scribner's Sons, 1976.

the 1931 Georgia apportionment grossly discriminates against voters in the Fifth Congressional District . . . [it] thus contracts the value of some votes and expands that of others. If the Federal Constitution intends that when qualified voters elect members of Congress each vote be given as much weight as any other, then this statute cannot stand. We hold that . . . the command of Art. I, [section] 2, that Representatives be chosen "by the People of the several States," means that as nearly as is practicable one man's vote in a congressional election is to be worth as much as another's.

Justice Black indicated that exact equality of population in each district was not entirely possible. Soon, however, computers made it possible to draw congressional districts with mathematical precision, and in *Kirkpatrick v. Preisler* the Court made that the standard for apportioning congressional election districts.

Six cases, handed down the same day and known collectively as the *Reapportionment Cases*, did for state electoral districts what *Wesberry* did for federal congressional districts. The best known of these cases is *Reynolds v. Sims* (1964). Like *Wesberry*, the Reapportionment Cases grew out of the Supreme Court's decision in *Baker*; if anything, they had an even more profound impact on the American electoral landscape, as

they rendered nearly every state legislature unconstitutional. In *Mahan v. Howell.* (1973), however, it became clear that the Court would hold state legislatures to a less precise standard than the mathematical equality required of congressional districts.

Related Cases

Colegrove v. Green, 328 U.S. 549 (1946).
Baker v. Carr, 369 U.S. 186 (1962).
Gray v. Sanders, 372 U.S. 368 (1963).
Reynolds v. Sims, 377 U.S. 533 (1964).
Mahan, Secretary, State Board of Elections, et al. v. Howell, et al., 410 U.S. 315 (1973).

Bibliography and Further Reading

Balinski, M. L. *Fair Representation: Meeting the Ideal of One Man, One Vote.* New Haven, CT: Yale University Press, 1982.

Cortner, Richard C. *The Apportionment Cases.* Knoxville: University of Tennessee Press, 1970.

Graham, Gene S. *One Man, One Vote: Baker v. Carr and the American Levellers.* Boston, MA; Little, Brown, 1972.

Johnson, John W., ed. *Historic U.S. Court Cases, 1690-1990: An Encyclopedia.* New York: Garland Publishing, 1992.

HARPER V. VIRGINIA STATE BOARD OF ELECTIONS

Legal Citation: 383 U.S. 663 (1966)

Appellant
Anne E. Harper

Appellee
Virginia State Board of Elections

Appellant's Claim
That Virginia's poll tax was a violation of the constitutional guarantee of equal protection of the laws.

Chief Lawyers for Appellant
Allison W. Brown, Jr., Robert L. Segar, and J. A. Jordan, Jr.

Chief Lawyer for Appellee
George D. Gibson

Justices for the Court
William J. Brennan, Jr., Tom C. Clark, William O. Douglas (writing for the Court), Abe Fortas, Earl Warren, Byron R. White

Justices Dissenting
Hugo Lafayette Black, John Marshall Harlan II, Potter Stewart

Place
Washington, D.C.

Date of Decision
24 March 1966

Decision
By a vote of 6-3, the Supreme Court struck down the Virginia poll tax.

Significance
In holding that all voters in a state must have equal access to state elections, *Harper* extended the logic of the landmark 1964 Supreme Court decision, *Reynolds v. Sims*, in which the Court stated the principle that all voters should have an equal opportunity to vote in state elections.

In the 1960s, the Virginia Constitution contained a provision providing that every resident 21 years of age and older would be assessed an annual poll tax of $1.50. Payment of the tax was a precondition to voting in state elections. A number of Virginia voters, including Anne E. Harper, challenged the constitutionality of the poll tax in the U.S. District Court for the Eastern District of Virginia. The district court followed *Breedlove v. Suttles* (1937), in which the Supreme Court stated the principle that all voters should have an equal opportunity to vote in state elections.

Supreme Court Strikes Down Poll Tax as a Violation of Equal Protection

Although the right to vote in federal elections is written into Article I of the Constitution, the right to vote in state elections is not expressly spelled out in the nation's foundation document. Although some have argued that the right to vote at the state level is implicit in the First Amendment guarantee of free expression, Justice Douglas, writing for the Court, based his opinion on another part of the Constitution:

> [I]t is enough to say that once the [voting] franchise is granted to the electorate, lines may not be drawn which are inconsistent with the Equal Protection Clause of the Fourteenth Amendment. That is to say, the right of suffrage "is subject to the imposition of the state standards which are not discriminatory and which do not contradict any restriction that Congress, acting pursuant to its constitutional powers, has imposed."

Justice Douglas was quoting from the Court's opinion in *Lassiter v. Northampton County Board of Elections*, a 1960 case in which a state literacy voting prerequisite was upheld. But, he said, while a literacy test bears some relationship with the process of intelligent voting, "Voter qualifications have no relation to wealth nor to paying or not paying this [Virginia poll] tax or any other tax."

The Equal Protection Clause of the Fourteenth Amendment states in part: "No State shall . . . deny to any person within its jurisdiction the equal protection

Protestor carrying a sign that reads "Abolish Poll Tax."
© *UPI/Corbis-Bettmann.*

of the laws." This passage has been interpreted to mean that no person or class of persons can be denied rights given to other persons or classes in similar circumstances. Extending the logic of the Court's decision in *Harper*, Douglas went on to suggest under the Equal Protection Clause that the poor might constitute a so-called "suspect classification," that is, a grouping that is inherently arbitrary. The Court automatically regards

such a grouping as requiring the government to carry a heavy burden of proof in order to justify enacting them.

For the dissenting justices in *Harper*, however, although the Virginia poll tax was discriminatory, it was no more discriminatory than laws setting a minimum age to vote. The tax was for them permissible because—like the state literacy test in *Lassiter*—it bore a rational relationship to voting. It is rational to believe, wrote Black, that voters who pay a poll tax will be interested in furthering the state's welfare when they do exercise their voting franchise. Harlan wrote a dissent indicating that in his opinion the Equal Protection Clause gives states a great deal of latitude in shaping voter qualifications. Federal courts, Harlan thought, were not really in a position to judge when a state had properly tailored its voting laws to suit its own population. Like Black, Harlan felt that poll taxes, long a part of the nation's political structure, bore a rational relationship to voting.

In the long run, although *Harper* extended the meaning of *Reynolds v. Sims*, it had little impact in and of itself. Only three other states, Alabama, Mississippi, and Texas, used poll taxes as a prerequisite for voting at the time. The Supreme Court has never adopted poverty as a suspect classification.

Related Cases
Breedlove v. Suttles, 302 U.S. 277 (1937).
Lassiter v. Northampton County Board of Elections, 360 U.S. 45 (1960).
Reynolds v. Sims, 377 U.S. 533 (1964).

Bibliography and Further Reading
Biskupic, Joan, and Elder Witt. *Congressional Quarterly's Guide to the U.S. Supreme Court*, 3rd ed. Washington, DC: Congressional Quarterly, Inc., 1996.

Chute, Marchette. *The First Liberty: A History of the Right to Vote in America, 1619-1850*. New York, NY: Dutton, 1969.

Hall, Kermit L., ed. *The Oxford Companion to the Supreme Court of the United States*. New York: Oxford University Press, 1992.

Rogers, Donald W., and Christine Scriabine, eds. *Voting and the Spirit of American Democracy: Essays on the History of Voting and Voting Rights in America*. Urbana: University of Illinois Press, 1992.

SOUTH CAROLINA V. KATZENBACH

Legal Citation: 383 U.S. 301 (1966)

Plaintiff
State of South Carolina

Defendant
Nicholas B. Katzenbach, U.S. Attorney General

Plaintiff's Claim
That certain portions of the Voting Rights Act of 1965 relating to eligibility tests for voters, voter qualifications, and appointment of federal voting examiners, are invalid.

Chief Lawyers for Plaintiff
David W. Robinson II, Daniel R. McLeod

Chief Defense Lawyer
Nicholas B. Katzenbach, U.S. Attorney General

Justices for the Court
Hugo Lafayette Black, William J. Brennan, Jr., Tom C. Clark, William O. Douglas, Abe Fortas, John Marshall Harlan II, Potter Stewart, Earl Warren (writing for the Court), Byron R. White

Justices Dissenting
None

Place
Washington, D.C.

Date of Decision
7 March 1966

Decision
That the challenged provisions of the Voting Rights Act were consistent with the power of Congress to eliminate racial discrimination in voting under the Fifteenth Amendment to the Constitution.

Significance
Decided at the height of the civil rights movement, the Court's decision made it clear that Congress has broad power to enact legislation to dismantle state-created barriers to voting by minorities, and was part of a series of decisions recognizing the power of the national government to enact measures against both public and private discrimination.

Following the Civil War, Congress and the state legislatures adopted three amendments to the Constitution to ensure the full benefits of citizenship to the newly freed slaves. Among these amendments was the Fifteenth Amendment, which provides that "[t]he right of citizens of the United States to vote shall not be denied or abridged by the United States or by any State on account of race, color, or previous condition of servitude." The amendment also grants Congress the power to pass legislation to ensure that all citizens enjoy equally the right to vote.

Congress Passes the Voting Rights Act

Despite the Fifteenth Amendment, state and local officials had effectively denied African Americans the right to vote by imposing literacy requirements and other tests that impeded African Americans from registering to vote. For example, at the time of the 1964 presidential election, there were almost three million African American adults who were not registered to vote in the eleven southern states of Alabama, Arkansas, Florida, Georgia, Louisiana, Mississippi, North Carolina, South Carolina, Tennessee, Texas, and Virginia. This led civil rights leaders, President Lyndon Johnson, and members of both political parties in Congress to call for sweeping legislation to ensure that African Americans would have equal opportunities to participate in elections. In August 1965, the Voting Rights Act was passed by Congress and signed into law by President Johnson.

Although the act contained numerous provisions, three sections were principally designed to ensure that state and local governments could not erect barriers to registration of, and voting by, African Americans. These sections applied to any state or county where less than 50 percent of African Americans are registered to vote and where literacy or other educational tests are required for registration. Section 4 suspended all such tests. Section 5 required any state or county seeking to impose a new test or registration requirement to obtain the approval of the attorney general of the United States, or of the U.S. District Court. Section 6 of the Voting Rights Act allowed the attorney general to send

Attorney General Nicholas Katzenbach testifies in support of the proposed Civil Rights Act. © AP/Wide World Photos.

federal examiners into the states and counties to register voters outside of the state or local system.

South Carolina Challenges Voting Rights Act

Almost immediately following the passage of the Voting Rights Act, the state of South Carolina brought suit directly in the Supreme Court, challenging the validity of the act. South Carolina sought a declaration from the Court that a number of provisions of the act, particularly section 4 and section 5, were invalid. South Carolina also sought an injunction to prevent Attorney General Nicholas Katzenbach from enforcing the act. Five states filed briefs in support of South Carolina, and 21 states filed briefs in support of the Attorney General.

In perhaps one of the most significant civil rights decision made by the Court, the Court rejected South Carolina's argument that Congress had exceeded its authority under the Fifteenth Amendment by passing sections 4, 5, and 6 of the act. The Court held that, in exercising its power to enforce the Fifteenth Amendment, Congress may enact any law which is reasonably related to ensuring equal voting rights to all citizens.

Chief Justice Warren, writing the opinion of the Court, concluded:

> After enduring nearly a century of widespread resistance to the Fifteenth Amendment, Congress has marshalled an array of potent weapons against the evil, with authority in the Attorney General to employ them effectively. Many of the areas directly affected by this development have indicated their willingness to abide by any restraints legitimately imposed upon them. We here hold that the portions of the Voting Rights Act properly before us are valid means for carrying out the commands of the Fifteenth Amendment. Hopefully, millions of non-white Americans will now be able to participate for the first time on an equal basis in the government under which they live.

The Court's decision had profound direct and indirect impacts. Directly, the decision allowed the act to go into effect and eliminate barriers to voting. For example, in the 11 southern states noted above, the number of African Americans registered to vote increased by over 800,000 between 1964 and 1967. Indirectly, the Court's decision would be relied on in

Voting Rights Act of 1965

Passed by Congress in 1965, the Voting Rights Act gave black voters additional guarantees against discriminatory practices. The Fifteenth Amendment of 1870 prohibited the denial of any citizens' right to vote because of ". . . race, color, or previous condition of servitude." The Twenty-fourth Amendment of 1964, prohibited the requirement of a poll tax or any other tax to vote in a federal election.

In spite of these two constitutional amendments, by the 1964 presidential election it became apparent that black voters continued having difficulties in some areas when attempting to register to vote. Martin Luther King, Jr. brought this issue to the forefront of American awareness after he orchestrated a march from Selma to Montgomery, Alabama. President Lyndon B.

Johnson quickly authored the Voting Rights Act, which Congress ratified.

In addition to the prohibition of discrimination against blacks, the Voting Rights Act also gives the U.S. attorney general the power to send federal registrars into problem areas. These registrars are authorized to register black voters, ensure that they are allowed to vote, and make sure their votes are properly tallied. The act was readopted in 1970, 1975, 1985, and can be extended by Congress.

Source(s): Grilliot, Harold J., and Frank A. Schubert. *Introduction to Law and the Legal System.* Boston, MA: Houghton Mifflin Co., 1992. "Voting Rights Act Clarification," http://www.usdoj.gov/crt/voting/clarify3.htm.

numerous other cases as support for Congress' broad power to enact not only voting rights legislation, but also other civil rights legislation under the Fourteenth Amendment to the Constitution.

Related Cases

Ex parte Garland, 71 U.S. 333 (1866).
Coyle v. Smith, 221 U.S. 559 (1911).
Guinn v. United States, 238 U.S. 347 (1915).
Mulford v. Smith, 307 U.S. 38 (1939).
United States v. Darby, 312 U.S. 100 (1941).
Gomillion v. Lightfoot, 364 U.S. 339 (1960).
Heart of Atlanta Motel v. United States, 379 U.S. 241 (1964).
Katzenbach v. McClung, 379 U.S. 294 (1964).

Bibliography and Further Reading

Bardolph, Richard, ed. *The Civil Rights Record: Black Americans and the Law, 1849-1970.* New York: Thomas Y. Crowell Co., 1970.

Claude, Richard. *The Supreme Court and the Electoral Process.* Baltimore: Johns Hopkins Press, 1965.

Ginger, Ann Fagan. *The Law, the Supreme Court, and the People's Rights.* Woodbury, NY: Barron's, 1973.

Grofman, Bernard, Lisa Handley, and Richard G. Niemi. *Minority Representation and the Quest for Equality.* New York: Cambridge University Press, 1992.

Hamilton, Charles V. *The Bench and the Ballot: Federal Judges and Black Voters.* New York: Oxford University Press, 1973.

Jackson, Percival E. *Dissent in the Supreme Court: A Chronology.* Norman, OK: University of Oklahoma Press, 1969.

Spann, Girardeau A. *Race Against the Court: The Supreme Court and Minorities in Contemporary America.* New York: The New York University Press, 1993.

KATZENBACH V. MORGAN

Legal Citation: 384 U.S. 641 (1966)

Appellant
U.S. Attorney General Nicholas Katzenbach and New York City Board of Elections

Appellee
Morgan and other registered voters

Appellant's Claim
That the Voting Rights Act of 1965 is a valid congressional act for enforcing the Fourteenth Amendment's Equal Protection Clause.

Chief Lawyer for Appellant
Alfred Avins

Chief Lawyer for Appellee
Solicitor General Thurgood Marshall

Justices for the Court
Hugo Lafayette Black, William J. Brennan, Jr. (writing for the Court), Tom C. Clark, William O. Douglas, Abe Fortas, Earl Warren, Byron R. White

Justices Dissenting
John Marshall Harlan II, Potter Stewart

Place
Washington, D.C.

Date of Decision
13 June 1966

Decision
Ruled in favor of Katzenbach and reversed a lower court's decision finding that Congress had exceeded its constitutional powers in granting voting rights to Spanish-speaking Puerto Ricans residing in New York.

Significance
The ruling reaffirmed certain powers of Congress by holding it can make laws overriding state laws on the same subject, regardless of the constitutionality of the state law. Congress, in specific, could prohibit enforcement of certain state English literacy voting requirements in New York. The ruling, however, also defined limits to Congress' authority under Section 5 of the Fourteenth Amendment. Congress could only adopt measures for the enforcement of Fourteenth Amendment guarantees.

The notion of universal suffrage (right to vote) in modern times in the United States has dominated public opinion. Recognition of the right to vote and equality at the polls are considered basic for a democracy to properly function. However, voters' rights have not been so widely enjoyed in the past. At the birth of the nation in the late 1700s, only white males with property could vote. The Constitution granted the states the right to establish voting requirements. However, Congress reserved the power to override state laws in Article I of the Constitution.

In 1868, the Fourteenth Amendment was passed extending the previous federal guarantees of due process and equal protection of the law to the states. Section 5 of the amendment reads, "Congress shall have power to enforce, by appropriate legislation, the provisions of this article." Gradually through time voters' rights were expanded, largely through constitutional amendments. The Fifteenth Amendment in 1870 addressed race voting issues, the Nineteenth Amendment in 1920 approved of women's suffrage, the Twenty-third in 1961 extended voting rights to residents of the District of Columbia, and the Twenty-fourth in 1964 eliminated the poll tax requirement.

Into the 1960s, various ethnic minorities continued to encounter barriers in attempting to register to vote. Literacy tests, proving a person could sufficiently communicate in English, frequently served a useful tool by states to restrict voting rights of certain groups of its residents in a discriminatory way. During the 1964 presidential election, African Americans experienced voter registration problems in many regions of the country. Organized voter registration drives often met with bitter, and sometimes violent, opposition. In March of 1965, the Reverend Martin Luther King, Jr. led a protest march from Selma to Montgomery, Alabama, to draw attention to the voting issue. Soon, following the march, President Lyndon B. Johnson presented a sweeping voting rights bill to Congress which quickly passed.

Voting Rights Act of 1965

The Voting Rights Act of 1965 represented the first time in U.S. history that Congress became involved in voting regulations. Key provisions of the act included pro-

Assistant Attorney General for Civil Rights John Doar, Attorney General Nicholas Katzenbach, and Solicitor General Thurgood Marshall (right). © UPI/Corbis-Bettmann.

hibitions against states, or any of their political subdivisions, from denying any U.S. citizen the right to vote based on race or color through application of specific qualifications or standards. Seven southern states could not adopt new voting procedures, including creation of new voting districts, without first providing the state's attorney generals offices an opportunity to review them and raise objections. The Voting Rights Act of 1965 also authorized the U.S. attorney general to send federal examiners to the seven states to register African Americans voters in certain situations.

Importantly, the act suspended literacy tests in states where less than half of the voting-age population was registered or had voted in the 1964 election. This section of the law had immediate impact. By the end of 1965, a quarter of a million new African American voters were registered, one third by the federal examiners. The Southern states quickly challenged the new law in the courts. The states claimed the federal government was exceeding its authority over voting issues. The Supreme Court upheld the act in *South Carolina v. Katzenbach* (1966).

In 1965, New York law and state constitution contained an English literacy requirement for residents vot-

ing in the state. This requirement affected several hundred thousand New York City residents from the U.S. territory of Puerto Rico who only spoke Spanish. In reaction, another section, 4(e), of the 1965 act established that persons successfully completing the sixth grade in an accredited school in Puerto Rico where instruction was in Spanish should be allowed to vote despite their inability to read or write English. Several registered New York City voters, including a person named Morgan who actively registered voters in New York City, were upset with the new act. They argued the section illegally prohibited New York's enforcement of the English literacy requirement.

Morgan filed a lawsuit in the District Court for the District of Columbia seeking a declaration that section 4(e) was constitutionally invalid. He also requested an injunction prohibiting Katzenbach, Attorney General of the United States, and the New York City Board of Elections from implementing section 4(e). A three-judge district court reviewed the case and found in favor of Morgan. The court issued an order blocking 4(e)'s implementation. The court held by a 2-1 vote that Congress had exceeded its constitutional powers under section 5 of the Fourteenth Amendment when enacting the section. In reaction, Katzenbach appealed directly to the Supreme Court.

A Plain and Consistent Act

By a majority of 7-2, the Court reversed the lower court's ruling. Writing for the majority, Justice Brennan wrote that section 4(e) of the Voting Rights Act was a proper exercise of congressional power granted by the Fourteenth Amendment. Therefore, the New York English literacy requirement could not be enforced to the extent that it was inconsistent with section 4(e). Brennan wrote that any judicial interpretation of Section 5 that would determine that a state law overrode an act of Congress "would depreciate both congressional resourcefulness and congressional responsibility for implementing the [Fourteenth] Amendment." Brennan observed that the key question was not if the New York English literacy requirement denying the right to vote to certain persons violated the Equal Protection Clause. Rather, it was to determine if 4(e) was "appropriate legislation to enforce the Equal Protection Clause."

Brennan noted that section 5 was broad in scope. He applied three tests to decide the case: (1) if the law was enacted to enforce the Equal Protection Clause; (2) if the law was "plainly adapted to that end"; and, (3) if the law was consistent with "the letter and spirit of the constitution."

Regarding the first test, Justice Brennan stated, "There can be no doubt that section 4(e) may be regarded as an enactment to enforce the Equal Protection Clause" because Congress "explicitly declared" such. Brennan observed that "section 4(e) may be viewed as a measure to secure for the Puerto Rican community residing in New York nondiscriminatory treatment by government."

Concerning the second test, Brennan found that section 4(e) "may be readily seen as plainly adapted" to further the objectives of the Equal Protection Clause. It prohibited "New York from denying the right to vote to large segments of its Puerto Rican community," thus enhancing the Puerto Rican community's political power. Such power "will be helpful in gaining nondiscriminatory treatment in public services for the entire Puerto Rican community." Section 4(e) therefore allowed the Puerto Rican minority to enjoy greater equality of civil rights and equal protection under the laws.

Regarding the third test concerning consistency "with the letter and spirit of the constitution," Brennan noted that Morgan alleged the act violated congressional powers under the Fifth Amendment. Morgan contended the standard was not applied equally, but only to those educated in schools located within United States jurisdiction. Those educated outside the territorial limits of the United States were, in essence, excluded. Congress, according to Morgan, had themselves violated the Constitution by not extending the rights recognized in section 4(e) to all individuals educated in foreign schools.

Joined in dissent by Justice Stewart, Justice Harlan wrote that a key issue was whether New York could demonstrate a legitimate state interest in requiring English literacy to vote. Harlan believed the state's arguments before the Court succeeded in passing that test. Besides, the federal government traditionally used the English literacy requirement in some other matters, such as naturalization of new citizens. In addition, New York was very experienced with governing non-English speaking residents. Of most concern to Harlan was that Congress inappropriately made an essentially judicial determination on the constitutionality of the New York law. Congress should have acted only after a court ruling had been made on the matter. The separation of powers between Congress and the judiciary, Harlan warned, were dangerously blurred by this ruling.

Impact

The *Morgan* ruling found that the Voting Rights Act of 1965 properly extended equal protection guarantees to Puerto Ricans in New York. Precedence created by the ruling was seen as limited to situations where Congress remedied state actions denying equal protection. Section 5 of the Fourteenth Amendment was recognized as a positive grant of legislative power to Congress to determine when legislation is needed to secure the guarantees of the Fourteenth Amendment. The power is not absolute though. Congressional acts must demonstrate some reasonable possibility of addressing a legitimate equal protection concern. In *Morgan,* the Court found that Voting Rights Act of 1965 enabled the Puerto Rican minority to attain greater social equality and equal protection of the laws.

The decision combated a restrictive view of congressional powers in the Fourteenth Amendment as advocated by some, and added further strength to the 1965 act in fighting racial discrimination. The decision played a role in formulating the 1968 Civil Rights Act. Congress relied on the *Morgan* decision in expanding federal powers to prohibit racially motivated violence in hate crimes, and to outlaw private housing discrimination.

Actions of the 1960s led to more revisions later in voters' rights. The Twenty-sixth Amendment to the Constitution, ratified in 1971, lowered the voting age to 18. The Voting Rights Act was amended and strengthened in 1970, 1975, and 1982. These later revisions added use of bilingual ballots in some areas, prohibited literacy requirements, and allowed illiterate, blind, or disabled voters to be assisted in the voting booth. The 1975 amendment allowed citizens living abroad to vote in federal elections through absentee ballot. In 1984, accessibility to the voting booth for the elderly was guaranteed. Several states challenged congressional legislation lowering the voting age in all elections to 18, and establishing residency and absentee voting requirements for presidential elections.

Related Cases

South Carolina v. Katzenbach, 383 U.S. 301 (1966).
Gaston County v. United States, 395 U.S. 285 (1969).
Richmond v. United States, 422 U.S. 358 (1975).
Beer v. United States, 425 U.S. 130 (1976).

Bibliography and Further Reading

Bybee, Keith J. *Mistaken Identity: The Supreme Court and the Politics of Minority Representation.* Princeton, NJ: Princeton University Press, 1998.

Garza, Catarino, ed. *Puerto Ricans in the U.S.: The Struggle for Freedom.* New York: Pathfinder Press, 1977.

Guinier, Lani. *The Tyranny of the Majority: Fundamental Fairness in Representative Democracy.* New York: Free Press, 1994.

Grofman, Bernard, and Chandler Davidson, eds. *Controversies in Minority Voting: The Voting Rights Act in Perspective.* Washington, DC: Brookings Institution, 1992.

Tate, Katherine. *From Protest to Politics: The New Black Voters in American Elections.* Cambridge: Harvard University Press, 1993.

KIRKPATRICK V. PREISLER

Legal Citation: 394 U.S. 526 (1969)

Appellants
James C. Kirkpatrick, Secretary of State of Missouri, et al.

Appellee
Paul W. Preisler

Appellants' Claim
The 1967 Missouri Redistricting Act was constitutional and any population variances between districts were justified.

Chief Lawyer for Appellants
Irving Actenberg

Chief Lawyer for Appellant
Thomas J. Downey

Justices for the Court
Hugo Lafayette Black, William J. Brennan, Jr. (writing for the Court), William O. Douglas, Abe Fortas, Thurgood Marshall, Earl Warren

Justices Dissenting
John Marshall Harlan II, Potter Stewart, Byron R. White

Place
Washington, D.C.

Date of Decision
7 April 1969

Decision
Missouri's Congressional Redistricting Act of 1967 was unconstitutional because of the variances in population among each district and the failure of the state to explain why such variances were unavoidable and justifiable.

Significance
Any population variance in congressional districts, no matter how small, places the burden on the state to illustrate that they made a good faith attempt to achieve mathematical equality and that the variations from mathematical equality were the result of unavoidable and articulable justifications, so as nearly as practicable, one person's vote weighs the same as another persons.

The United States Constitution, Article I, Section 2, establishes the Congressional House of Representatives. The House of Representatives membership is based on the population of each state, unlike the Senate, whose membership is two persons per state regardless of population. After each state is assigned a certain number of House representatives, the state is broken down into congressional districts. Each congressional district is permitted to have one member of the House represent that district in Congress. Consistent with the House of Representatives make-up, each state establishes their congressional districts according to population. In an earlier Supreme Court case, *Wesberry v. Sanders* (1964), the Supreme Court noted that "while it may be impossible [for states] to draw congressional districts with mathematical precision . . . the Constitution requires that as nearly as is practicable one man's vote in a congressional election is to be worth as much as another's." In light of that holding, Missouri's Congressional Redistricting Act was its second attempt at constitutionally acceptable redistricting.

The original redistricting act was declared unconstitutional by a three panel district court in 1965, but they withheld granting any relief until Missouri had a chance to revisit the problem. The Missouri General Assembly then enacted another redistricting statute, but it too was deemed unconstitutional for failure to address equality in population demands. Further, the district court decided to retain jurisdiction, which is the ability of a court to review a claim, of any future redistricting plans. In 1967, Missouri enacted the redistricting statute which was before the Court in this case. The Missouri attorney general requested the district court who retained jurisdiction over this matter to declare this redistricting statute constitutional. In a 2-1 decision, the district court determined that the 1967 statute was unconstitutional. The majority based its holding on the findings that: (1) Missouri did not base its redistricting on census figures, (2) the general assembly rejected another plan with fewer population variances without reason, and (3) simple switching of certain counties from one district to another would greatly reduce the population variances in districts. For those reasons, the district court found that the 1967 statute did not meet the constitutional standard requiring population in districts to be as equal "as nearly practicable" and Missouri did not purport any justifiable reasons for having such population variance from district to district. The Supreme Court reheard Missouri's appeal to determine if, in fact, the redistricting plan was unconstitutional.

The Supreme Court reiterated that the standard for reviewing redistricting acts is that each district should be as equal as possible in population to every other congressional district within the state, as set forth in *Wesberry.* The constitutional reason for this standard is embodied in the theory that each person's vote must have equal weight. In a 6-3 decision the majority affirmed the lower court finding that the Redistricting Act was in violation of the Constitution. Missouri asserted several justifications for the variance: (1) that the variances between districts was so small that they should be considered *de minimis,* which means inappreciable or insignificant in number, and (2) that the differences were the result of considering various factors such as the integrity of county lines, compactness of districts, the representation of distinct interest groups, and proportion of nonvoters in a particular district. The Court found none of these arguments convincing.

First, the Supreme Court addressed the *de minimus* argument. Missouri was granted ten congressional districts and, when taking the population into account, each congressional district would therefore have 431,981 people. The 1967 act created a difference of up to 12,260 persons below the mathematical ideal to 13,542 above the mathematical ideal in certain districts. This meant that the variance from the most to the least populated district was 25,802. Missouri argued that this was merely a difference of 2.26 percent below to 3.13 percent above the ideal and such a small variance was inappreciable. The Supreme Court disagreed. They viewed the statistical data differently. They viewed the difference between the largest and smallest districts as a ratio of 1.06 to 1, meaning that persons in the small districts have a vote weighing .06 more than those in the largest district. The Court held this not to be insignificant. However, more importantly, they felt that any difference, no matter how small, is unacceptable without some justification.

> Since equal representation for equal numbers of people is the fundamental goal for the House of Representatives, the "as nearly as practicable" standard requires that the State make a good faith effort to achieve precise mathematical equality. Unless population variances among congressional districts are shown to have resulted despite such effort, the State must justify each variance, no matter how small.

The Court felt that accepting a *de minimus* approach would encourage the states to draw congressional districts according to that arbitrarily accepted range rather than by mathematical precision. Further, the Court could not rationally pick a number at which point the variance becomes *de minimus.* Thus, the Court rejected Missouri's argument and felt that mathematical equality should be the goal, unless rational reasons could be given to explain a variance from that equality.

The Court conceded that variances will inevitably occur, but these differences in voting district populations must be shown to be unavoidable despite good faith efforts by the legislatures to achieve total equality. The Court found that the variances in the 1967 redistricting act were avoidable or the reasons for the unavoidability were not articulated to the Court. It is the burden of the state to illustrate why the variances were unavoidable. Thus, the presumption is that absent total equality, the districts are unconstitutional, and it is the burden of the state to reasonably explain the variances.

Missouri first attempted to explain the variances by claiming that population disparity was necessary to avoid "fragmenting areas with distinct economic and social interests." In other words, the state argued that if they attempted equality in voting districts, then the economic and social interests of certain groups, such as farmers, would be diluted because they would be the minority in the district and their interests would never be properly represented. The Supreme Court believed that this did not outweigh the problem of voting district population variances.

> Neither history alone, nor economic or other sorts of group interests, are permissible factors in attempting to justify disparities from population based representation.

Other reasons the state gave in attempting to justify the population variances were that they took into account nonvoters within the population of certain districts, considered future population shifts and desired the voting districts to be geographically compact. As with the other arguments given by the state, these too were unconvincing to the Court. The Court quickly dismissed these arguments. First, the state argued that they should be allowed to account for nonvoters in some districts with higher concentrations of persons contained military persons stationed at armed forces bases and college students. Since these persons may be nonvoters within the district, the variances were appropriate. The Court rejected this argument. However, before doing so, they were careful to state that they were not deciding whether apportionment should be based on voter population or total population. The Court simply held that the state made no attempt to ascertain the eligible voters in every district before drawing them up, and, at best, made haphazard apportionment without statistical data. Further, the state failed to explain how other districts containing smaller populations also contained colleges. This justification was merely a retroactive reason to attempt to explain the high concentration of persons in certain districts. With respect to the state's projected population shift justification, the Court again held that these reasons had to be fully documented and applied in a systematic manner and Missouri's attempt at dismissing lower population districts as a well-thought-out plan for future population shifts was unfounded. There was no evidence before the Court that the general assembly considered this prior to the 1967 act. Finally, the state claim that districts should be geographically compact was unconvincing to the Court. They stated that in 1967, transportation and communication were sufficiently advanced to refute the argument. The Court stated that "transportation and communication make rather hollow, in the mid-1960s, most claims that deviations from population based representations can validly be based solely on geographical considerations."

The impact of this decision placed a heavy burden on the states, when developing congressional districts, to meet exact mathematical population perfection or bear the burden of explaining the variances.

Related Cases
Colegrove v. Green, 328 U.S. 549 (1946).
Wesberry v. Sanders, 376 U.S. 1 (1964).
Mahan v. Howell, 410 U.S. 315 (1973).
United Jewish Organizations v. Carey, 430 U.S. 144 (1977).
Bush v. Vera, 517 U.S. 952 (1996).
Abrams v. Johnson, 521 U.S. 74 (1997).

Bibliography and Further Reading
Gunther, Gerald. *Constitutional Law,* 12th ed. New York: Foundation Press, 1991.

Nowak, Rotunda, and Young. *Constitutional Law,* 3rd ed. New York: West, 1986.

Engdahl, David *Constitutional Power: Federal and State.* New York: West, 1987.

HADLEY V. JUNIOR COLLEGE DISTRICT

Legal Citation: 397 U.S. 50 (1969)

Appellant
Della Hadley et al.

Appellee
The Junior College District of Metropolitan Kansas City, Missouri et al.

Appellant's Claim
That the voting rights of a group of junior college district residents were unconstitutionally diluted in violation of the "one man, one vote" principle.

Chief Lawyer for Appellant
Irving Achtenberg

Chief Lawyer for Appellee
William J. Burrell

Justices for the Court
Hugo Lafayette Black (writing for the Court), Harry A. Blackmun, William J. Brennan, Jr., William O. Douglas, Thurgood Marshall, Byron R. White

Justices Dissenting
Warren E. Burger, John Marshall Harlan II, Potter Stewart

Place
Washington, D.C.

Date of Decision
25 February 1969

Decision
The Equal Protection Clause of the Fourteenth Amendment was ruled to apply to the election of trustees to the junior college district.

Significance
Hadley v. Junior College District clarified the applicability of the "one man, one vote" rule to the election of local government officials.

The appellants in this case were residents of the Kansas City School District, one of eight separate school districts comprising the Junior College District of Metropolitan Kansas City. Under Missouri law, these school districts may vote by referendum to establish a consolidated junior college district and elect six trustees to manage the affairs of that district. When elections under this law resulted in 50 percent of the trustees being chosen from an area containing about 60 percent of the total school-age population, a group of residents filed suit, claiming that their right to vote was unconstitutionally diluted in violation of the Equal Protection Clause of the Fourteenth Amendment of the U.S. Constitution.

The Lower Court Rulings

A Missouri trial court dismissed the suit. This ruling was then upheld by the Missouri Supreme Court, which held the "one man, one vote" principle did not apply in this case because the trustees had specialized authority over district affairs, rather than general powers of government over the entire district. The state supreme court held that in state or local elections, the Equal Protection Clause requires only that each qualified voter have an equal opportunity to participate in the election, and that election districts must be established on a basis that "as far as practicable will insure that equal numbers of voters can vote for proportionally equal numbers of officials." The case was appealed to the U.S. Supreme Court.

The Supreme Court Ruling

On 25 February 1970 the U.S. Supreme Court issued its decision. It reversed the ruling of the Missouri Supreme Court, holding that "the Fourteenth Amendment requires that the trustees of the junior college district be apportioned in a manner that does not deprive any voter of his right to have his own vote given as much weight, as far as is practicable, as that of any other voter in the junior college district." Justice Black wrote the opinion for the five-justice majority. Justice Harlan wrote a dissenting opinion, on which he was joined by Chief Justice Burger and Justice Stewart. The Court's decision rested on its resolution of two points.

In making its decision, the Court relied on an earlier case, *Avery v. Midland County* (1968), in which it determined that the Constitution's "one man, one vote" principle applies in local elections where elected officials exercise "general governmental powers over the entire geographic area served by the body." The Court came to the opposite opinion of the Missouri Supreme Court's, which had ruled that the junior college trustees do not exercise general governmental power over the whole district and are thus immune from the requirements of "one man, one vote":

> Appellants in this case argue that the junior college trustees exercised general governmental powers over the entire district and that under *Avery* the State was thus required to apportion the trustees according to population on an equal basis, as far as practicable. Appellants argue that since the trustees can levy and collect taxes, issue bonds with certain restrictions, hire and fire teachers, make contracts, collect fees, supervise and discipline students, pass on petitions to annex school districts, acquire property by condemnation, and in general manage the operations of the junior college, their powers are equivalent, for apportionment purposes, to those exercised by the county commissioners in *Avery*. We feel that these powers . . . certainly show that the trustees perform important governmental functions within the districts, and we think these powers are general enough and have sufficient impact throughout the district to justify the conclusion that the principle which we applied in *Avery* should also be applied here.

Apportionment Scheme Ruled Unconstitutional

Next, the Court had to answer the question of whether the apportionment scheme for the elections in this case did in fact violate "one man, one vote." Based upon an examination of the statistical formulas used by the district to determine the make-up of the trustee board, the Court concluded that it did:

> Although the statutory scheme reflects to some extent a principle of equal voting power, it does so in a way that does not comport with constitutional requirements. This is so because the Act necessarily results in a systematic discrimination against voters in the more populous school districts . . . Consequently Missouri cannot allocate the junior college trustees according to the statutory formula employed in this case.

In an impassioned dissent, Justice Harlan attacked the decision for, among other things, demonstrating "the pervasiveness of the federal judicial intrusion into state electoral processes that was unleashed by the 'one man, one vote' rule of *Reynolds v. Sims*" (1964). Nevertheless, the majority decision stands as a significant extension of that principal into practically every corner of American politics.

Related Cases

Gray v. Sanders, 372 U.S. 368 (1963).
Reynolds v. Sims, 377 U.S. 533 (1964).
Avery v. Midland Cougraynty, 390 U.S. 474 (1968).
Karcher v. Daggett, 462 U.S. 725 (1983).

Bibliography and Further Reading

Biskupic, Joan, and Elder Witt, eds. *Congressional Quarterly's Guide to the U.S. Supreme Court*, 3rd ed. Washington, DC: Congressional Quarterly, Inc., 1996.

OREGON V. MITCHELL

Legal Citation: 400 U.S. 112 (1970)

Plaintiff
State of Oregon

Defendant
John N. Mitchell, U.S. Attorney General

Plaintiff's Claim
The attorney general should be barred from enforcing provisions of Congress' Voting Rights Act because the right to regulate elections is reserved for the states.

Chief Lawyer for Plaintiff
Lee Johnson

Chief Defense Lawyer
Erwin N. Griswold

Justices for the Court
Hugo Lafayette Black (writing for the Court), Harry A. Blackmun, William J. Brennan, Jr., Warren E. Burger, Potter Stewart

Justices Dissenting
William O. Douglas, John Marshall Harlan II, Thurgood Marshall, Byron R. White

Place
Washington, D.C.

Date of Decision
21 December 1970

Decision
Congress could lower the voting age in federal elections to 18, but states and local governments reserved the right to set their own voting age.

Significance
The Court struck a balance between federal authority and state powers, allowing each level of government to regulate its own elections. The Court's ruling also prompted the passage of the Twenty-sixth Amendment, ensuring voting rights in all elections to all citizens over 18.

In the years following the Civil War, the United States had to find a way to legally incorporate thousands of freed slaves into society as citizens with constitutionally guarded rights. Congress sought to ensure the rights of these newly recognized citizens with the passage of the Thirteenth, Fourteenth and Fifteenth Amendments. These amendments, passed by Congress and ratified by the states between 1865 and 1870, abolished slavery, guaranteed full citizenship and protection of the law to every person born in the United States, and protected every person's right to vote, regardless of his skin color or history of servitude.

A century later, new problems faced the American electorate. Literacy tests in some states still deprived some disadvantaged minorities of their right to vote. State residency requirements sometimes prevented long-time U.S. citizens from casting ballots in federal elections because they had not lived in that particular state long enough. Young men between the ages of 18 and 21 found they were old enough to be drafted and sent to Vietnam, yet they were not allowed to vote.

In 1965 Congress passed the Voting Rights Act to address these problems. Congress voted in 1970 to extend the act's provisions for another five years, adding several amendments that banned the use of literacy tests, established uniform residency requirements and absentee ballot registration procedures for federal elections, and lowered the voting age in all local, state, and federal elections to 18. Both Oregon and Texas sued U.S. Attorney General John M. Mitchell to try to prevent Mitchell from enforcing the act in their states. The U.S. government also sued Arizona and Idaho on the grounds that those states refused to conform their laws to the act's provisions. All four cases were addressed in the Supreme Court's opinion in *Oregon v. Mitchell.*

Justice Black wrote the opinion of the Court, with four other justices writing partial concurrences and partial dissents. Basing his ruling on the Equal Protection Clause of the Fourteenth Amendment, Black argued that the provision setting the minimum voting age for federal elections at 18 was constitutional, although the provision lowering voting age to 18 for state and local elections was not. Because Congress has the power under the Constitution to draw congressional districts,

John Newton Mitchell, U.S. Attorney General. © The Library of Congress/Corbis.

it also has the power to determine other qualifications of voters, Black said:

> Surely no voter *qualification* was more important to the framers than the *geographic qualification* embodied in the concept of congressional districts.

Article I, section 4, of the Constitution gives states the right to make laws regarding the conduct of national elections, but it also provides that Congress may "alter such regulations" if it chooses. This provision, said Black, allows Congress to change the minimum voting age from 21 to 18 in federal elections.

But the Constitution also protects each state's right to run its local government as it decides, with minimal interference from the national government. States may choose to keep the minimum voting age for state and local elections at 21, and the federal government must respect that, Black said. Keeping the voting age at 21 does not deprive younger citizens of their voting rights in violation of the Fourteenth Amendment's Due Process Clause, Black said, because such age requirements do not discriminate on a racial basis.

The Fourteenth Amendment was surely not intended to make every discrimination between groups of people a constitutional denial of equal protection . . . the Civil War amendments were unquestionably designed to condemn and forbid every distinction, however trifling, on account of race.

Black also defended the Voting Rights Act's ban on literacy tests, pointing to the long history of such tests being used to prevent certain races of people from participating in the democratic process. Although Congress is not required to outlaw such tests, it is certainly allowed to do so on a national level to solve what has been the national problem of discrimination, Black said.

With respect to residency requirements, Black found that Congress may establish national guidelines in order to protect every citizen's right to vote in federal elections. Black found that such guidelines fall within Congress' "broad authority to create and maintain a national government."

Justice Douglas concurred in all parts of Black's opinion, except Douglas argued that the Fourteenth Amendment's Equal Protection Clause did allow Congress to tell state governments to lower the local voting age to eighteen. The Constitution recognizes voting as a fundamental civil liberty, Douglas said, and the Fifteenth Amendment mentions citizens' rights to vote in both federal and state elections. Douglas pointed to previous Supreme Court rulings in which provisions basing voting rights on occupation, place of residency, married status, or possession of property were found to violate the Equal Protection Clause. While the Fourteenth Amendment's Equal Protection Clause grew out of racial inequities, Douglas said, its applicability was not reserved for cases of racial discrimination alone.

Justices White and Marshall joined in Justice Brennan's concurrence, which agreed with the Black's opinion except for Black's holding that Congress could not lower state and local voting ages. Brennan also argued that citizens between ages 18 and 21 would be denied equal protection under the law if they were not allowed to vote.

In an excruciatingly thorough opinion, Justice Harlan laid out the historical background that gave rise to the Thirteenth, Fourteenth and Fifteenth Amendments. While he agreed that Congress could lower the voting age in federal elections to 18 and ban the use of literacy tests, Harlan said neither the Constitution nor its amendments gave Congress the power to change the minimum voting age or residency requirements of states.

Justice Stewart, joined by Justices Burger and Blackmun, agreed with most of Black's ruling except Stewart said Congress lacked the power to lower the voting age for any election—federal, state or local. As Justice

Stewart noted, the Supreme Court was not asked to decide whether allowing 18-year olds to vote was a good idea, only whether Congress had the power to enact such a law. Although the Court was split on the extent to which Congress could change the voting age, the American public still thought such a provision was a good idea. In 1971 Congress introduced, and the states ratified, the Twenty-sixth Amendment, giving every citizen 18 years or older the right to vote in all elections.

Related Cases
Colegrove v. Green, 328 U.S. 549 (1946).
Gomillion v. Lightfoot, 364 U.S. 339 (1960).
Wesberry v. Sanders, 376 U.S. 1 (1964).
Reynolds v. Sims, 377 U.S. 533 (1964).

Bibliography and Further Reading

Cultice, Wendell W. *Youth's Battle for the Ballot.* New York: Greenwood Press, 1992.

Hall, Kermit L., ed. *The Oxford Companion to the Supreme Court of the United States.* New York: Oxford University Press, 1992.

MacKenzie, John P. "18-Year-Old Vote For President, Congress Upheld: High Court Excludes State Races." *Washington Post.* 22 December 1970, pp. A1, A6.

DUNN V. BLUMSTEIN

Legal Citation: 405 U.S. 330 (1972)

Appellant
Winfield C. Dunn, Governor of Tennessee

Appellee
James F. Blumstein

Appellant's Claim
That the state of Tennessee's durational residency requirement for suffrage was constitutional.

Chief Lawyer for Appellant
Robert H. Roberts

Chief Lawyer for Appellee
James F. Blumstein

Justices for the Court
Harry A. Blackmun, Warren E. Burger, William O. Douglas, Thurgood Marshall (writing for the Court), Potter Stewart, Byron R. White

Justices Dissenting
William J. Brennan, Jr. (Lewis F. Powell, Jr., and William H. Rehnquist did not participate)

Place
Washington, D.C.

Date of Decision
21 March 1972

Decision
The Supreme Court ruled that Tennessee's durational residency requirement was unconstitutional.

Significance
The case added another group of people—new residents in states—to the list of groups who could not be discriminated against by states setting standards for suffrage.

The Durational Residency Requirement

Dunn v. Blumstein involved voting rights. Specifically, the case addressed the question of whether a state could impose a durational residency requirement before granting *bona fide* citizens the right to vote. The Supreme Court determined that such requirements denied some citizens the fundamental right to vote, and that in order to justify such a denial, the state must have a compelling interest that could only be achieved in that way. The state involved, Tennessee, failed to demonstrate a compelling interest that would justify its exclusions, and the Supreme Court joined a federal district court in declaring durational residency requirements unconstitutional.

The case was brought as a class action suit by James Blumstein, a newly appointed assistant professor of law at Vanderbilt University. Moving to Tennessee in June of 1970, Blumstein attempted to register to vote on 1 July 1970. The county registrar refused to register him because of the state's durational residency requirement: only *bona fide* citizens who had lived in the state for one year, and in their county of registration for three months, prior to the upcoming election were allowed to vote. Blumstein brought suit on the grounds that the durational requirement violated his rights under the Constitution's Equal Protection Clause. A three-judge federal district court concluded that he was right. The state of Tennessee appealed to the Supreme Court.

Close Constitutional Scrutiny

In order to address the issues involved, the Supreme Court first had to decide which standard of review to use in determining whether or not Tennessee's restriction was allowable. Since the restriction deprived some citizens of the right to vote, which was considered to be a fundamental political right, the Court determined that any restriction imposed by the state must withstand what it called "close constitutional scrutiny." Close scrutiny meant that the state must prove that it had a "compelling interest" for which the exclusions were not only helpful, but necessary. Furthermore, wrote Justice Marshall in the Court opinion, the durational residency requirement interfered with a second fundamental right guaranteed by the United States

Constitution, the right to travel. Any infringement on this right must also pass the compelling-state-interest test. The opinion took care to note that Tennessee's interest in having only *bona fide* residents of the state vote in its elections was undisputed.

The Court then turned to the question of whether Tennessee had demonstrated a compelling state interest in restricting voters to those who had resided in the state for at least a year. Tennessee argued that the requirement was necessary for two reasons. First, it allowed the state to maintain the "purity of the ballot box" by preventing dual voting—voting in more than one place—and "colonization"—the invasion of any district by a group of people whose only intention was to falsely declare residency and then vote, ensuring the election of a particular candidate. Second, the state of Tennessee argued, the durational residency requirement helped ensure a more knowledgeable voter, who had taken the time to become informed about the local candidates and election issues.

The Supreme Court found neither of these interests "compelling." Noting that Tennessee established duration of residency through a citizen's swearing of an oath, the Court declared that citizens intent upon fraud were as likely to swear falsely that they were longtime residents as they were to swear falsely that they were residents. As for dual voting, the Court stated that it was more easily prevented through cross-checking the resident's current registrations with registrations in a resident's former jurisdiction. Voter fraud, the Court concluded, was better dealt with through the state's criminal code, which provided a means of discovering and dealing with such fraud.

The claim that the durational residency requirement provided the state with more knowledgeable voters was also rejected by the Supreme Court. Since the state made no attempt to determine whether or not long-time residents were knowledgeable, the exclusion of new residents on that ground was simply discriminatory. Such devices, wrote Marshall, "represent a requirement of knowledge unfairly imposed on only some citizens." Thus, the Supreme Court found that Tennessee had failed to demonstrate a compelling state interest in its durational residency requirement.

Justice Blackmun filed an opinion concurring in the result. However, he stated his conviction that the Court's decision had struck down Tennessee's particular requirement as unreasonable, but had not absolutely established that durational residency requirements were unconstitutional. Justice Brennan filed a dissenting opinion holding that the "compelling state interest" standard was too strict a test for state voting regulations to undergo.

Related Cases

Williams v. Rhodes, 393 U.S. 23 (1968).
Bullock v. Carter, 405 U.S. 134 (1972).
Kusper v. Pontikes, 414 U.S. 51 (1973).
Lubin v. Panish, 415 U.S. 709 (1974).
Munro v. Socialist Workers Party, 479 U.S. 189 (1986).
Tashjian v. Republican Party of Connecticut, 479 U.S. 208 (1986).

Bibliography and Further Reading

Biskupic, Joan, and Elder Witt, eds. *Congressional Quarterly's Guide to the U.S. Supreme Court*, 3rd ed. Washington, DC: Congressional Quarterly, Inc., 1996.

Cohen, William S. "Discrimination Against New State Citizens: An Update." *Constitutional Commentary*, winter 1994, p. 73.

Furman, Jesse. "Political Illiberalism: The Paradox of Disenfranchisement and the Ambivalences of Rawlsian Justice." *Yale Law Journal*, January 1997, p. 1197.

MAHAN V. HOWELL

Legal Citation: 410 U.S. 315 (1973)

"One person, one vote"—that principle is one of the basic slogans of U.S. democracy. It is also one of the reasons that electoral districts are constantly being redrawn. An electoral district is the unit within which a person votes. To elect U.S. Representatives, a person votes in a congressional district. To elect members of the state legislature, a person votes in a legislative district. Ideally, each type of electoral district has the same number of people in it.

In the 1960s, civil rights leaders claimed that African Americans were crowded into big electoral districts, while white Americans were divided up into smaller districts. As a result, white people had the chance to elect more than their fair share of representatives to state and national office. Many states were ordered to re-draw their electoral districts in order to make them more fair.

What Is the Percentage?

In 1971, Virginia revised its state constitution. At the same time, it reapportioned the electoral districts for its House of Delegates and its state senate. Almost immediately, two suits were brought against the Virginia plan. Henry E. Howell, Jr. and Clive L. DuVal II charged that the variation in population between House of Delegates districts in the new plan was just too large. They also charged that the particular way that the districts were divided was "racial gerrymandering." Howell and DuVal were claiming that the legislature had drawn its electoral districts so as to give white people more than their fair share of voting strength, at the expense of African American voters.

Howell and DuVal took their case to the district court, which agreed with them. The district court found that under the state plan, there was as much as a 16.4 percent difference between the smallest and the biggest delegates district—far too great a variation to be truly fair to all voters. DuVal argued that actually, the difference was even greater, as much as 23.6 percent. Either way, the district court objected to the state plan, and it substituted a plan of its own.

Home-Port or Home Address?

At the same time, another suit was brought against the way the state senate districting had been done. The city

Gerrymandering

Gerrymandering refers to a state legislature's ability to re-establish boundaries of election precincts in ways that give one political party or group of people some advantage over another. It may include redrawing districts to exclude groups who do not support the dominant party in office at the time of redistricting.

The term was coined by Benjamin Russell, a newspaper editor in 1812. During Massachusetts Governor Elbridge Gerry's second term in office, the state legislature reapportioned the voting districts giving the Democratic-Republicans an edge in the state elections of senators. One new district was oddly shaped and spread out. An artist used the shape of the district to create a joke, adding ". . . wings, claws, and teeth to

its outline, prompting the suggestion that it resembled a salamander." Russell gave it the name Gerrymander, thereby connecting the newly coined word to the governor.

This practice creating oddly shaped voting districts to provide one group with an advantage in an election over another may be challenged constitutionally, according to the U.S. Supreme Court. This applies even when voting districts are designed to provide an advantage to minority voters, as set down in *Shaw v. Reno* (1993).

Source(s): Grolier Electronic Publishing, Inc., 1995.

of Norfolk had been split into three districts, with all African American voters isolated in one district, and all U.S Navy personnel assigned to another. In fact, U.S Navy personnel did not live only in the district to which they had been assigned. Their ships were docked in that district—their "home port"—but their actual residences were elsewhere. Thus, claimed the suit, the way the districts had been drawn was unfair to both African Americans and to U.S. Navy personnel.

When the district court overturned the state's plan, the state appealed to the Supreme Court. In a 5-3 decision, the Court approved the state's original plan, except for the part relating to Norfolk. The Supreme Court agreed with the district court.

Flexibility and Local Control

Justice Rehnquist, writing for the majority, explained that two principles had guided the decision. First, the Court believed that in drawing districts for state legislatures, "more flexibility is permissible than with respect to congressional redistricting." By those standards, Rehnquist wrote, the 16.4 percent variation from the smallest district to the largest "may well approach tolerable limits," but it did not exceed them.

Second, the state had been justified in "preserving the integrity of political subdivision lines," such as counties and cities. In other words, if two cities were located side by side, the state would be justified in making each city its own electoral district, even if one were slightly larger than the other. That way, the Court explained, each city's residents could elect representatives that would advance their own city's interest when the state legislature came to deal with local issues.

However, Justices Brennan, Douglas, and Marshall strongly disagreed. They thought that the state's redis-

tricting plan had indeed been unfair, and they believed the district court had been right to make a new plan.

Equality of Representation

Justice Brennan, writing for the minority, said the Court had had no basis for dismissing out of hand DuVal's contention that the gap between the smallest and the largest district was actually 23.6 percent. If DuVal was right, that would make the gap in Virginia almost as large as the 26.48 percent gap in another case—and the Court had found that gap too large.

Second, Brennan said, the Court was wrong to claim that there were two separate standards, one for congressional districts, the other for state legislatures. Perhaps a state might need to use different procedures to figure out how to create legislative districts, but that was far from saying that the two types of districts had different standards.

Finally, Brennan said, the Court was wrong to give so much weight to preserving existing political subdivisions. The most important criterion in drawing electoral districts was to make them as nearly equal in size as possible, so that every person's vote would count equally. Besides, Brennan said, the burden of proof in showing the importance of existing political subdivisions was on the state—and the state had failed to meet that burden. Brennan pointed out that even under the state's plan, many voters from small towns would be lumped into districts with larger towns. He failed to see the difference between that situation and one in which a town was broken up into two districts. He added two more objections:

> Of the 124 political subdivisions in the Commonwealth, only 12 would be divided by the District Court's plan. More significant, the number of persons [taken out of their home

political subdivisions by the plan] . . . would still be less than 1 percent of the total state population.

Clearly, the Court was divided on the question of whether the state redistricting plan did indeed violate the Equal Protection Clause of the Fourteenth Amendment. This type of argument—local control versus civil rights—would continue in various forms and in various locations for the next several decades.

Related Cases
Colegrove v. Green, 328 U.S. 549 (1946).
Wesberry v. Sanders, 376 U.S. 1 (1964).
Karcher v. Daggett, 462 U.S. 725 (1983).
Miller v. Johnson, 515 U.S. 900 (1995).
Shaw v. Hunt, 517 U.S. 899 (1996).
Bush v. Vera, 517 U.S. 952 (1996).
Abrams v. Johnson, 521 U.S. 74 (1997).

Bibliography and Further Reading
Biskupic, Joan, and Elder Witt, eds. *Congressional Quarterly's Guide to the U.S. Supreme Court,* 3rd ed. Washington, DC: Congressional Quarterly, Inc., 1996.

Hall, Kermit L., ed. *Oxford Companion to the Supreme Court of the United States.* New York: Oxford University Press, 1992.

ROSARIO V. ROCKEFELLER

Legal Citation: 410 U.S. 752 (1973)

Petitioner
Pedro J. Rosario, et al.

Respondent
Nelson Rockefeller, Governor of the State of New York, et al.

Petitioner's Claim
That New York State's law requiring voters to enroll in a party thirty days before a general election to vote in the following year's primary was unconstitutional.

Chief Lawyer for Petitioner
Burt Neuborne

Chief Lawyer for Respondent
A. Seth Greenwald

Justices for the Court
Harry A. Blackmun, Warren E. Burger, William H. Rehnquist, Potter Stewart (writing for the Court), Byron R. White

Justices Dissenting
William J. Brennan, Jr., William O. Douglas, Thurgood Marshall, Lewis F. Powell, Jr.

Place
Washington, D.C.

Date of Decision
21 March 1973

Decision
That the New York law did not discriminate against the petitioners, and was thus constitutional.

Significance
The case set a limit on what qualified as a "group" of people who could not be discriminated against in state regulation of voting. The Supreme Court determined that people who could have enrolled, but did not, did not constitute a group.

States' Rights

In an era when voters' rights were increasingly underwritten by the federal courts, *Rosario v. Rockefeller* reaffirmed states' rights to set election laws in the interest of guaranteeing the integrity of the electoral process. After a United States district court struck down as unconstitutional a New York state law requiring voters to register as party members almost a year in advance in order to vote in a primary, the Supreme Court reversed the judgment and upheld the law, declaring that the deadline was justified by a compelling state interest. The case was important in setting a limit on the applicability of the Equal Protection Clause, which protects groups of people from discrimination. The Supreme Court declined to consider voters who had not registered in advance of the deadline a "group" of people who could claim discrimination.

Party Raiding

The deadline in question was New York's deadline for voting in party primaries. Only enrolled members of a particular political party were allowed to vote in New York's party primaries, a system known as a "closed" system of primary elections. The law stated that voters must enroll in a party by a deadline 30 days in advance of the previous year's general election. The voter could then vote in the party primary taking place after the following year's general election. The reason for the law was to prevent party "raiding," in which voters from one party enroll in the opposite party in order to have an influence on their opposing party's primary. The New York State deadline was justified on the grounds that it prevented such raiding, because the voter who wanted to join the opposing party would be put in the absurd position of enrolling in an opponent's party before voting for her own party's candidate in the general election. The Court declared that "it would be the rare politician who could successfully urge his constituents to vote for him or his party in the upcoming general election, while at the same time urging a crossover enrollment for the purpose of upsetting the opposite party's primary."

Such raiding, the Supreme Court declared, was a negative enough result to justify the state's passing of a

Nelson Rockefeller. © UPI/Corbis-Bettmann.

deadline to prevent it. Furthermore, the deadline seemed to the court to be effective. However, the petitioners argued that the deadline violated their rights under the Constitution's Equal Protection Clause, since they were effectively disenfranchised by the deadline. In their arguments, counsel for the respondents referred to several Supreme Court cases in which the Court had struck down statutes that disenfranchised particular groups of people, including *Carrington v. Rash* and *Dunn v. Blumstein.*

Groups' Rights

The Supreme Court saw a significant difference between the cases listed and the one before it. In each case, wrote Justice Stewart in the opinion, the Court had struck down statutes that made an entire group of people ineligible to vote, where there was nothing the people in that group could have done to become eligible. People who had not registered by a particular deadline, the Court asserted, did not constitute such a group, because they had it in their power to change their status. They were not absolutely disenfranchised by the deadline.

The remaining issue was simply whether the deadline presented "an unconstitutionally onerous burden" on the petitioners' exercise of their voting rights. While the deadline was indeed lengthy, the Supreme Court declared that it was not onerous, and that its length was justified by the necessity of preventing party raiding. "It is clear that the preservation of the integrity of the electoral process," wrote Stewart, "is a legitimate and valid state goal." New York's deadline for voting in primaries was an integral part of its scheme for achieving that goal; as such, it was constitutional.

Justices Douglas, Brennan, and Marshall joined Justice Powell, who wrote a dissenting opinion. New York's deadline, Powell wrote, was too severe. It prevented the voter from responding to a new issue or changing party philosophies. A less drastic deadline, he argued, would achieve the state's goal and allow the voter the full exercise of the voting rights so fundamental to democracy.

Related Cases

NAACP v. Alabama, 357 U.S. 449 (1958).
Baker v. Carr, 369 U.S. 186 (1962).
Reynolds v. Sims, 377 U.S. 533 (1964).
Wesberry v. Sanders, 376 U.S. 1 (1964).
Carrington v. Rash, 380 U.S. 89 (1965).
Shapiro v. Thompson, 394 U.S. 618 (1969).
Dunn v. Blumstein, 405 U.S. 330 (1972).

Bibliography and Further Reading

Biskupic, Joan, and Elder Witt, eds. *Congressional Quarterly's Guide to the U.S. Supreme Court,* 3rd ed. Washington, DC: Congressional Quarterly, Inc., 1996.

BUCKLEY V. VALEO

Legal Citation: 424 U.S. 1 (1976)

Appellant
James L. Buckley

Appellee
Francis R. Valeo, Secretary of the U.S. Senate

Appellant's Claim
That various provisions of amendments to the Federal Election Campaign Act of 1971 (FECA), regulating campaign contributions, violate the separation of powers doctrine, the First Amendment, and the Fifth Amendment.

Chief Lawyers for Appellant
Ralph K. Winter, Jr., Joel M. Gora, Brice M. Claggett

Chief Lawyers for Appellee
Daniel M. Friedman, Archibald Cox, Lloyd M. Cutler, Ralph S. Spritzer

Justices for the Court
Harry A. Blackmun, William J. Brennan, Jr., Warren E. Burger, Thurgood Marshall, Lewis F. Powell, Jr., William H. Rehnquist, Potter Stewart (unsigned)

Justices Dissenting
None (John Paul Stevens did not participate)

Place
Washington, D.C.

Date of Decision
30 January 1976

Decision
In a variety of different votes on different issues, the Supreme Court held: first, the doctrine of separation of powers prevents Congress from appointing a majority of the members of the Federal Election Commission (FEC), which administers FECA; second, while limits on contributions to political campaigns are constitutional, limits on campaign expenditures violate freedom of political expression protected by the First Amendment; and third, the FECA provisions authorizing public funding of political campaigns violate neither the First Amendment nor the Fifth Amendment's Due Process Clause, even though these provisions are more likely to help major parties and candidates than minor ones.

Significance
Buckley v. Valeo reshaped campaign finance laws entirely. Perhaps the most significant change, however, was the Court's ruling that there could be no restrictions on contributions from individuals and groups, so long as they were independent of any official election campaigns. This ruling gave rise to a profusion of political action committees (PACs).

In 1974, Congress amended the Federal Election Campaign Act of 1971, and various candidates for political office, joined by some other politically active groups and individuals, filed suit in the U.S. District Court for the District of Columbia in an attempt to prevent the amendments from affecting the 1976 election. The suit raised a variety of complex constitutional questions, which both a three-judge panel from the district court and the U.S. Court of Appeals for the District of Columbia heard jointly. The constitutional attacks on FECA were rejected, so Buckley and the other appellants took their case to the U.S. Supreme Court.

The Court's opinion was unsigned, and five of the justices dissented to various parts of it, but in various configurations, the participating members of the Court agreed on certain basic issues. To begin, the Court struck down a provision of the new law which permitted Congress to select a majority of the members of the Federal Election Commission, the body set up to administer the FECA. Since the Appointments Clause of Article I of the Constitution gave such power to the president, this provision was a violation of the doctrine of separation of powers, which prevents each of the three branches of the federal government from assuming a responsibility that properly belongs to one of the other branches.

Court Distinguished Campaign Contributions from Expenditures

The appellants also challenged a provision of FECA that limited contributions and expenditures in federal elections. The Court generally found contribution limits to be a proper legislative means of preventing candidates from becoming too reliant on large contributions. At the same time, however, the Court upheld the right of "independent" individuals and groups to spend freely to help candidates, and ruled against limits on expenditures, which it found to be an impermissible violation of First Amendment guarantees of freedom of political expression.

> The Act's contribution and expenditure limits operate in an area of the most fundamental First Amendment activities. Discussion of public issues and debate on the qualifications of

candidates are integral to the operation of the system of government established by our Constitution. The First Amendment affords the broadest possible protection to such political expression in order "to assure [the] unfettered exchange of ideas for the bringing about of political and social changes desired by the people.

In addition to upholding the right of private citizens to spend money to help elect the candidates of their choice—so long as these expenditures were not funneled through the candidate or the candidate's campaign committee—the Court ruled in favor of an FECA provision authorizing new measures to promote public funding of presidential campaigns, such as the income tax check-off. While objections to this provision had cited both the First Amendment and the Fifth Amendment's Due Process Clause, the Court dismissed them. The provision furthered First Amendment values by using public moneys to encourage political debate. As to due process arguments contending that smaller parties and minor candidates would not benefit from this provision, the Court disagreed. The Court did, however, uphold the condition that any candidate accepting

public campaign financing must agree to observe a ceiling on expenditures (although this condition does not apply to those spending independently to elect a publicly funded candidate).

Related Cases

First National Bank of Boston v. Bellotti, 435 U.S. 765 (1978).

Citizens Against Rent Conrol/Coalition for Fair Housing v. City of Berkeley, 454 U.S. 290 (1981).

Austin v. Michigan Chamber of Commerce, 494 U.S. 652 (1990).

Bibliography and Further Reading

Common Cause. *Stalled from the Start: A Common Cause Study of the Federal Election Commission.* Washington, DC: Common Cause, 1981.

Congressional Campaign Finance: History, Facts, and Controversy. Washington, DC: Congressional Quarterly, 1992.

Matasar, Ann B. *Corporate PAC's and the Federal Campaign Financing Laws: Use or Abuse of Power?* Westport, CT: Quorum Books, 1986.

UNITED JEWISH ORGANIZATIONS V. CAREY

Legal Citation: 430 U.S. 144 (1977)

Petitioner
United Jewish Organizations of Williamsburgh, Inc.

Respondents
Carey, Governor of New York, et al.

Petitioner's Claim
The redistricting plan of 1974 for portions of Kings County, New York, would negate the effectiveness of the Hasidic Jew vote. The petitioner claimed that the sole purpose of the redistricting was to achieve a racial quota, and the community was assigned to voting districts solely by racial standards. They claimed this violated their rights under both the Fourteenth Amendment and the Fifteenth Amendment of the U.S. Constitution.

Chief Lawyer for Petitioner
Nathan Lewin

Chief Lawyer for Respondents
George D. Zuckerman, Assistant Attorney General of New York

Justices for the Court
Harry A. Blackmun, William J. Brennan, Jr., Lewis F. Powell, Jr., William H. Rehnquist, John Paul Stevens, Potter Stewart, Byron R. White (writing for the Court)

Justices Dissenting
Warren E. Burger (Thurgood Marshall did not participate)

Place
Washington, D.C.

Date of Decision
1 March 1977

Decision
The reapportionment plan was valid under the U.S. Constitution and did not violate the constitutional rights of the Hasidic Jews.

Significance
The ruling on *United Jewish Organizations v. Carey* addressed the constitutionality of reapportionment plans for voting districts based solely upon racial factors. Because the state could provide evidence that the plan followed the actions required in the Voting Rights Act of 1965, and did not prevent white or nonwhite voters from exercising their right to participate in the political process by the redistricting of Kings County, the Court found that the reapportionment plan did not violate Fourteenth and Fifteenth Amendment rights of the Hasidic community of Williamsburgh.

Prior to 1974, it was determined that the Kings, New York (Manhattan), and Bronx Counties utilized a literacy test to qualify voters, and that in 1968, fewer than 50 percent of the voting age residents of these counties participated in the presidential election. These two instances caused the state to be subject to provisions under the Voting Rights Act of 1965 that prohibited the discrimination of voters based on racial considerations. In May of 1974, in order to comply with the act, New York State submitted a plan to the attorney general to reapportion the voting districts of Kings County. This plan was meant to realign voting districts to create nonwhite majorities. While this reapportionment did not change the size of the districts, it did change the number of nonwhites in the districts to an approximate 65 percent majority.

In particular, the Hasidic Jewish community of Williamsburgh was divided in half and one portion was reassigned to a neighboring electoral district. As a result of this redistricting, the Hasidic community claimed that their rights under the Fourteenth Amendment and Fifteenth Amendment of the U.S. Constitution had been violated. Their claim was that the reapportionment devalued their collective effectiveness by reducing it "solely for achieving a racial quota, and that they were assigned to electoral districts solely on the basis of race." The Hasidic community identified this as a case of racial gerrymandering, or the division of a county to create voting majorities in several districts while concentrating the voting minorities in as few districts as possible.

The district court dismissed the case, stating that the Hasidic Jewish community was not recognized as a separate community and "enjoyed no constitutional right in reapportionment" as such. The court of appeals affirmed the decision. A *writ of certiorari* was issued whereby the proceedings were remanded to the Supreme Court for review and action. The Supreme Court justices, after review and deliberation, also upheld the decision.

Points of Affirmation

In a 7-1 vote with one abstention, the Supreme Court affirmed the decision of the lower courts. Justice White,

Hugh Carey, Governor of New York.
© AP/Wide World Photos.

announcing the Court's decision, concluded that the 1974 reapportionment plan for the state of New York and Kings County was not in violation of the Fourteenth or Fifteenth Amendments of the U.S. Constitution. The use of racial criteria in order to comply with the Voting Rights Act of 1965 was warranted in this circumstance. The plan also complied with the requirement that approval of the redistricting be sought from the attorney general as specified in the Voting Rights Act.

White cited five points upon which the decision was made. First, under section five of the Voting Rights Acts, states may not adopt new or revised reapportionment plans without first seeking the approval of either the attorney general of the United States or the District Court for the District of Columbia. In 1972, the state of New York submitted a reapportionment plan which was subsequently denied by the attorney general. In May of 1974, a revised plan was once again submitted and received approval. The attorney general ruled that "the plan [did] not have a racially discriminatory purpose or effect."

The next three points which the Court identified as upholding the decision of the lower courts were based upon the use of racial criteria in establishing nonwhite majorities. As established by the precedent set in *Beer v. United States* (1976), they found that "[c]ompliance with the Act in reapportionment cases will often necessitate the use of racial considerations in drawing district lines." They interpreted this to mean that there were no statements in the U.S. Constitution that prohibit the use of racial criteria in creating or preserving nonwhite electoral majorities. In conjunction with these considerations, the justices determined that it was permissible to use race to correct an imbalance in voting rights beyond "eliminating the effects of past discriminatory districting or apportionment," not confined to only past discrimination. Justices White,

Brennan, Blackmun, and Stevens concluded that the use of "specific numerical quotas"—in this case 65 percent—was not in violation of either the Fourteenth or Fifteenth Amendments. A state is not prohibited from using a specified quota to establish nonwhite majority districts.

The fifth and final point the justices examined was whether or not the redistricting plan increased the nonwhite majority and canceled out the white electoral participation through under-representation. The Hasidic community had already been identified as part of the white voting majority, and therefore, did not have separate protection under the Constitution. The redistricting plan left an approximate 70 percent white majority in the assembly and senate electoral districts for Kings County, which had a county-wide population of 65 percent white. This was a proportionally balanced voting majority, as observed by the court of appeals in New York as well as by the U.S. Supreme Court. The reapportionment plan improved the majority-minority percentage and provided more equitable political power to the nonwhite voters. Justice White, writing for the majority, stated that "there was no fencing out of the white population from participation in the political processes of the county, and the plan did not minimize or unfairly cancel out white voting strength." The white community was equally represented by the electoral majorities based upon their relative share of the county population. White concluded that the plan could be seen as a means to alleviate the consequences of racial voting at the polls and to provide a reasonable allocation of political power between white and nonwhite voters in Kings County.

Impact

The decision in *United Jewish Organizations of Williamsburgh v. Carey* was both determined and supported by the precedents set in the Voting Act of 1965, which protected the rights of nonwhite citizens to participate in the political process. In the 1990s, the United States Department of Justice was faced with concerns about the Voting Rights Act of 1965 expiring in the year 2007, and the African American population losing its right to vote. The Department of Justice announced a clarification of the Voting Rights Act, and stated that the voting rights were a permanent guarantee and will not expire. The Fifteenth Amendment of the U.S. Constitution and the Voting Rights Act of 1965 expressly state that "no one may be denied the right to vote because of his or her race or color. These prohibitions against racial discrimination in voting are permanent."

Related Cases

Gomillion v. Lightfoot, 364 U.S. 339 (1960).
Richmond v. United States, 422 U.S. 358 (1975).
Beer v. United States, 425 U.S. 130 (1976).

Mobile v. Bolden, 446 U.S. 55 (1980).

Shaw v. Reno, 509 U.S. 630 (1993).

Miller v. Johnson, 515 U.S. 900 (1995).

Bibliography and Further Reading

The Herald Sun: VoteBook. http://www.herald-sun.com/votebook/supcourt/opin93.html

Parker, Frank R. "The Damaging Consequences of the Rehnquist Court's Commitment to Color-Blindness Versus Racial Justice."*American University Law Review,* February 1996. http://www.wcl.american.edu/pub/journals/lawrev/parker.htm

U.S. Code. "Title 42, Sect. 1971: Voting Rights." http://www.law.cornell.edu/uscode/42/1971.html

United States Department of Justice. "Voting Rights Clarification." http://www.usdoj.gov/cert/voting/clarify3.htm

MOBILE V. BOLDEN

Legal Citation: 446 U.S. 55 (1980)

Appellant
City of Mobile Alabama, et al.

Appellee
Wiley L. Bolden, et al.

Appellant's Claim
That the city's at-large system of electing commissioners did not discriminate against African American citizens of the city.

Chief Lawyer for Appellant
Charles S. Rhyne

Chief Lawyer for Appellee
James U. Blacksher

Justices for the Court
Harry A. Blackmun, Warren E. Burger, Lewis F. Powell, Jr., William H. Rehnquist, John Paul Stevens, Potter Stewart (writing for the Court)

Justices Dissenting
William J. Brennan, Jr., Thurgood Marshall, Byron R. White

Place
Washington, D.C.

Date of Decision
22 April 1980

Decision
The Supreme Court held that the at-large election system did not discriminate against African American citizens, who could register and vote freely in Mobile.

Significance
The case was a strong blow against anti-discriminatory suits. It established that discriminatory effects must be accompanied by intent.

Retreat from Civil Rights

Mobile v. Bolden was a widely criticized Supreme Court decision on the issue of racial discrimination. As part of a retreat from the wide-ranging reforms of the Civil Rights movement, the decision helped set the stage for a debate two years later over renewing the Voting Rights Act. Creating a storm of controversy, the Court rejected the idea that discriminatory effects were enough to establish that an action was in violation of the Fourteenth or Fifteenth Amendment. Instead, the highly divided Court asserted, discriminatory purpose must be proved for an action to be judged unconstitutional. The Supreme Court thus overturned a U.S. district court judgment declaring Mobile's city government in violation of the Constitution.

Vote Dilution

The appellees claimed that the city's method of electing its commissioners discriminated against African Americans by diluting their votes. The Mobile City Commission consisted of three members elected at large from the entire city, rather than from particular districts. These three members jointly exercised all administrative, legislative, and executive power in the city. At the time the class action suit was brought against Mobile, no African American citizen had ever served on the commission, although the population of the city was approximately 35.4 percent African American.

The effect of the law had clearly been to keep African American citizens from serving on the city commission. The appellees claimed that their voting rights under the Fourteenth and Fifteenth Amendments had been denied. The Supreme Court determined that the city had not denied African Americans their right to vote under the Fifteenth Amendment, since African American citizens routinely registered and voted. The Fifteenth Amendment, declared Justice Stewart in the Court opinion, "imposes but one limitation on the powers of the states: it forbids them to discriminate against Negroes in matters having to do with voting."

No Guarantee of Proportional Representation

More substantive were the appellees' claims under the Fourteenth Amendment, which guaranteed all citizens equal protection, due process, and all privileges and immunities of U.S. citizens. However, the Court declared that the city had not denied African Americans their rights under the Fourteenth Amendment, since there was no guarantee of proportional representation either stated or implied in that amendment. The language was unambiguous: "The fact is that the Court has sternly set its face against the claim, however phrased, that the Constitution somehow guarantees proportional representation." The right to participate in elections guaranteed by the Fourteenth Amendment, wrote Stewart, "does not protect any 'political group,' however defined, from electoral defeat."

The Court did not deny that the effect of Mobile's election laws had been to bar African Americans from participating in city government. However, in such cases, the action could only be declared discriminatory if there was no other reason for it besides denying African Americans their right to vote. Referring to *Guinn v. United States* (1915), in which the Supreme Court struck down a literacy requirement's "grandfather clause," Stewart wrote that such cases involved a statute in place for no possible reason other than disenfranchising African American citizens. No such exclusively discriminatory intent could be established for Mobile's election laws, even if they did arise from partly invidious motives.

Discriminatory Effect vs. Discriminatory Intent

Part of the controversy may have arisen from the strong language in which the Court rejected past effects as a means of establishing discrimination. "Past discrimination," wrote Stewart, "cannot, in the manner of original sin, condemn government action that is not itself unlawful." But most controversial was the Court's wholesale rejection of disproportionate effects as a means for establishing discriminatory intent. Steward wrote that "disproportionate impact alone cannot be decisive, and courts must look to other evidence to support a finding of discriminatory purpose."

Justice Marshall wrote a lengthy and impassioned dissent, accusing the Court of helping to perpetuate racial discrimination. If voting practices that led to vote dilution were acceptable to the Court, Marshall wrote, "the right to vote provides the politically powerless with nothing more than the right to cast meaningless ballots." He did not mince words in implying that the consequences of such a position could be civil disobedience: "If this Court refuses to honor our long-recognized principle that the Constitution 'nullifies sophisticated as well as simple-minded modes of dis-

crimination' . . . it cannot expect the victims of discrimination to respect political channels of seeking redress."

Mobile v. Bolden was certainly a move away from the civil rights legislation of the preceding era, and toward the retreat from reform that dominated the 1980s. The controversy surrounding the decision lasted for some time, and contributed toward the extension in 1982 of the 1965 Voting Rights Act. Opposed by the Reagan administration, which wanted to allow the Voting Rights Act to expire completely, the amended section two of the act allowed for limited use of an effects standard, giving plaintiffs the right to challenge a voting practice by proving discrimination in its effects, based on a totality of evidence. The language of the amended act, however, is careful to disallow the use of section two to establish racial quotas or allow any claim to a right to proportionate representation.

Related Cases

Ex parte Yarbrough, 110 U.S. 651 (1884).
Guinn v. United States, 238 U.S. 347 (1915).
Ashwander v. Tennessee Valley Authority, 297 U.S. 288 (1936).
Gomillion v. Lightfoot, 364 U.S. 339 (1960).
Wright v. Rockefeller, 376 U.S. 52 (1964).
Reynolds v. Sims, 377 U.S. 533 (1964).
Whitcomb v. Chavis, 403 U.S. 124 (1971).
Personal Administrator of Massachusetts v. Feeney, 442 U.S. 256 (1979).

Bibliography and Further Reading

Abraham, Henry J., and Barbara A. Perry. *Freedom and the Court: Civil Rights and Liberties in the United States.* New York and Oxford: Oxford University Press, 1994.

Davis, Olethia. "Tenuous Interpretation: Sections 2 and 5 of the Voting Rights Act." *National Civic Review,* fall-winter 1995, p. 310.

Hall, Kermit L., ed. *The Oxford Companion to the Supreme Court of the United States.* New York: Oxford University Press, 1992.

Polsby, Daniel D., and Robert D. Popper. "Ugly: An Inquiry into the Problem of Racial Gerrymandering Under the Voting Rights Act." *Michigan Law Review,* December 1993, p. 652.

Snyder, Brad. "Disparate Impact on Death Row." *Yale Law Journal,* May 1998, p. 2211.

Zimmerman, Joseph F. "Election Systems and Representative Democracy." *National Civic Review,* fall-winter 1995, p. 287.

BROWN V. HARTLAGE

Legal Citation: 456 U.S. 45 (1982)

Petitioner
Carl Brown

Respondent
Earl Hartlage

Petitioner's Claim
That the Kentucky Corrupt Practices Act, which prohibited candidates for public office in that state from promising any material benefit to voters if they were elected, was a violation of the First Amendment's protection of free speech.

Justices for the Court
Harry A. Blackmun, William J. Brennan, Jr. (writing for the Court), Warren E. Burger, Thurgood Marshall, Sandra Day O'Connor, Lewis F. Powell, Jr., John Paul Stevens, Byron R. White

Justices Dissenting
William H. Rehnquist

Place
Washington, D.C.

Date of Decision
20 January 1982

Decision
That the Kentucky Corrupt Practices Act constituted a limitation of free speech as guaranteed under the First Amendment.

Significance
Brown v. Hartlage reinforced the subordination of state election laws to constitutionally protected freedoms, particularly the right to free speech guaranteed in the First Amendment.

On 15 August 1979, during a general election for the office of Jefferson County (Kentucky) commissioner, "C" District, candidates Carl Brown and Bill Creech held a press conference on television. During the conference, Brown and Creech cited the high expenses incurred by the administration of the incumbent, Earl Hartlage. Creech promised county taxpayers that if elected, he and Brown (who were both of the same political party) would lower their salaries voluntarily.

Soon afterward, the two learned that this statement was in violation of Section 121.055 of the Revised Statutes of Kentucky. Referred to as the Corrupt Practices Act, the law stated that "No candidate for nomination or election to any state, county, city or district office shall expend, pay, promise, loan or become pecuniarily liable in any way for money or other thing of value, either directly or indirectly, to any person in consideration of the vote or financial or moral support of that person." Upon becoming aware of this, Brown and Creech issued a joint statement declaring that they rescinded their promise in accordance with the law, "and instead pledge to seek corrective legislation in the next session of the General Assembly to correct this silly provision of State Law."

In the election on 6 November 1979, Creech was defeated, but Brown defeated the incumbent, Hartlage, by more than 10,000 votes. Hartlage filed suit in the Jefferson County Circuit Court, declaring that because of Brown's violation of the Corrupt Practices Act, the election results should be nullified.

The trial court found that, because the salaries had been "fixed by law," Brown's promise was in violation of the act. But, the court reasoned, given the fact that Brown had retracted his statement, that his running mate had been defeated, and that the people had spoken overwhelmingly in their vote for Brown over Hartlage, the election results should be allowed to stand. The Kentucky Court of Appeals, however, reversed this decision. In so doing, the court used as its basis its earlier ruling in *Sparks v. Boggs* (1960), when it found that a candidate's promise to take only $1 a year in pay, and to distribute the remainder of his salary to charity, constituted a violation of the Corrupt Practices Act. The court did find some appeal in Brown's statement that "[i]f carried to its logical extreme . . . any promise by a candidate to increase the efficiency and thus lower the cost of government might likewise be considered as an attempt to buy votes"; however, it was the opinion of the court that it was bound by its earlier ruling in *Sparks*.

Free Speech or Buying Votes?

Justice Brennan delivered the opinion for the Court, in which all justices but Rehnquist concurred. While conceding that it is legitimate for a state to make laws protecting the integrity of its electoral process, Brennan said that where abridgement of free speech is concerned, legitimacy is not enough: the state interest must be "compelling," and the prohibition must not unduly limit protected forms of expression.

Section 121.055 was made to prevent the buying of votes, Brennan noted, but such voter bribery normally goes on in secret, whereas Brown and Creech made their promise openly. As for the possibility that the law had been enacted in order to maintain a level playing field by ensuring that the financial ability to forego the salary did not become a prerequisite for election (thus limiting candidacy to the independently wealthy), Brennan did not find this an adequate justification for abridging the right to free speech. In other words, "The state's fear that voters might make an ill-advised choice does not provide the state with a compelling justification for limiting speech."

The Right to Be Wrong

Furthermore, Brennan stated, Section 121.055 was not even justified on the basis of the assertion that it would prevent the use of factual misstatements in a political campaign. (In this case, since the salary was "fixed by law," Brown and Creech were factually as well as legally in error, because they did not have the power to change their salaries.) Freedom of expression must have "breathing space" in order to flourish, and to void the appellants' victory in the election "would be inconsistent with the atmosphere of robust political debate required by the First Amendment." In American campaigns, candidates say a lot of things, and trying to force them by law to always be correct would do more harm than good.

Besides, said Brennan, to all appearances the promise was made in good faith, and the two candidates did not seem to realize that they were acting in error. In addition, they retracted their statement promptly.

Judgment and a Lone Dissenter

For the reasons given, the Court voted 8-1 to hold with the finding of the Kentucky state court, and found that Section 121.055 did indeed limit free speech in violation of the First Amendment. The lone dissenter was Justice Rehnquist, who nonetheless did agree that the Corrupt Practices Act constituted an impermissible limitation on free speech. His dissent revolved, rather, around the method by which the Court reached this determination. He would have relied, he said, on the Court's ruling in *Mills v. Alabama* (1966), and "I see no need to rely on other precedents which do not involve state efforts to regulate the electoral process."

Related Cases
Sparks v. Boggs, 339 S.W.2d. 480 (1960).
Mills v. Alabama, 384 U.S. 214 (1966).

Bibliography and Further Reading
Murphy, Walter F. et al., *American Constitutional Interpretation,* 2nd ed. Westbury, NY: Foundation Press, 1995.

ROGERS V. LODGE

Legal Citation: 458 U.S. 613 (1982)

Appellants
Quentin Rogers, et al.

Appellees
Herman Lodge, et al.

Appellants' Claim
That Burke County's election system for county commissioners violated the rights of African American citizens by watering down their voting power.

Chief Lawyer for Appellants
E. Freeman Leverett

Chief Lawyer for Appellees
David F. Walbert

Justices for the Court
Harry A. Blackmun, William J. Brennan, Jr., Warren E. Burger, Thurgood Marshall, Sandra Day O'Connor, Byron R. White (writing for the Court)

Justices Dissenting
Lewis F. Powell, Jr., William H. Rehnquist, John Paul Stevens

Place
Washington, D.C.

Date of Decision
1 July 1982

Decision
Upheld the lower court's ruling that Burke County's election system was discriminatory against African Americans.

Significance
The ruling established that at-large voting systems could be struck down as unconstitutional in cases where there is sufficient evidence to prove that the system was maintained for purposefully discriminatory purposes. Historical data showing that minorities have been denied effective participation in the electoral process, can be employed as evidence in such cases.

Burke County, a large rural county in eastern Georgia, employed an at-large system for electing candidates to its governing body, the county board of commissioners. Under this arrangement, each of the five commissioners were elected by all registered voters in the county, rather than by discrete districts drawn along geographical lines. Although Burke County had a substantial African American population, no minority candidate had ever been elected to its board of commissioners. In 1976, a group of eight African American citizens filed a class action suit in federal district court, on the grounds that the at-large system violated their rights under the First, Thirteenth, Fourteenth, and Fifteenth Amendments to the U.S. Constitution. Rogers further alleged that the dilution of their voting power was intentional and discriminatory on the basis of race.

The Lower Courts Rule

The federal district court found for Rogers. It held that, while the state had not acted in an overtly discriminatory manner in instituting the at-large voting system, the system was being maintained for purposes of violating the constitutional rights of African American voters. The court's examination of voting patterns in Burke County also turned up evidence of bloc voting on racial lines. In this way, the county had effectively barred its African American residents from participating fully in the electoral process. The district court ordered Burke County to replace its at-large system with district voting to ensure full participation of all minority groups.

The case then proceeded to the court of appeals, which affirmed the district court's decision. It reviewed the district court's findings, and agreed that there was overwhelming evidence of discriminatory practices in Burke County. After determining its jurisdiction in the dispute, the U.S. Supreme Court agreed to review the case.

The Supreme Court Rules

On 1 July 1982, the Supreme Court issued its decision. It affirmed the rulings of the lower courts, holding that Burke County's electoral system violated the Equal Protection Clause of the Fourteenth Amendment to the

U.S. Constitution. The High Court's decision addressed the three key points at issue.

Consistent with previous rulings, the Supreme Court did not strike down at-large voting schemes as unconstitutional *per se*. However, it allowed for challenges to such a system in cases where it could be shown that the at-large arrangement was established or maintained for discriminatory purposes. With respect to this particular case, the Supreme Court declined to dispute the findings of the district court on the issue of discriminatory practices. Finally, the Supreme Court refused to consider the propriety of the relief offered by the district court, namely the division of Burke County into single-member electoral districts.

The Supreme Court's decision reflected its deep ambivalence about the constitutionality of at-large voting systems. Writing for the majority, Justice White issued the following opinion:

> At-large voting schemes and multimember districts tend to minimize the voting strength of minority groups by permitting the political majority to elect all representatives of the district. A distinct minority, whether it be a racial, ethnic, economic, or political group, may be unable to elect any representatives in an at-large election, yet may be able to elect several representatives if the political unit is divided into single-member districts.

Dissenting Voices

There were three dissenters in the case. Justice Powell, joined by Justice Rehnquist, dissented on the grounds that the objective proof in the case did not establish discriminatory intent on the part of Burke County. Powell wrote:

> In the absence of proof of discrimination by reliance on . . . objective factors . . . I would hold that the factors cited by the Court of Appeals are too attenuated as a matter of law

to support an inference of discriminatory intent.

Justice Stevens dissented on similar grounds. He had misgivings about the advisability of divining discriminatory intent in the minds of the at-large system's architects. He wrote:

> I do not believe that the subjective intent of the persons who adopted the system in 1911, or the intent of those who have since declined to change it, can determine its constitutionality.

Impact

In the years that followed, the Court wrestled with the question of the inherent unconstitutionality of at-large voting arrangements. Its inability to establish an absolute standard for defining electoral discrimination is reflected in the unusually vehement dissents. The U.S. Congress, through amendments to the Voting Rights Act and other legislation, attempted to address the problem of minority disenfranchisement through statutory means.

Related Cases

Fortson v. Dorsey, 379 U.S. 433 (1965).
Burns v. Richardson, 384 U.S. 73 (1966).
Whitcomb v. Chavis, 396 U.S. 1064 (1971).
White v. Regester, 412 U.S. 755 (1973).
Richmond v. United States, 422 U.S. 358 (1975).
Mobile v. Bolden, 446 U.S. 55 (1980).
Thornburgh v. Gingles, 478 U.S. 30 (1986).

Bibliography and Further Reading

Davis, Olethia. "Tenuous Interpretation: Sections 2 and 5 of the Voting Rights Act." *National Civic Review,* fall–winter 1995, p. 310.

Encyclopedia of the American Constitution New York: Macmillan Publishing Company, 1986.

Hall, Kermit L., ed. *The Oxford Companion to the Supreme Court of the United States* New York: Oxford Press, 1992.

KARCHER V. DAGGETT

Legal Citation: 462 U.S 725 (1983)

Appellant
Alan Karcher, Speaker, New Jersey Assembly

Appellees
Daggett, et al.

Appellant's Claim
Gerrymandering by the controlling Democratic Party of the New Jersey legislature did not violate the U.S. Constitution because it relied on "good faith" criteria for legislative redistricting and protected minority voting rights.

Chief Lawyer for Appellant
Kenneth J. Guido, Jr.

Chief Lawyer for Appellees
Bernard Hellring

Justices for the Court
Harry A. Blackmun, William J. Brennan, Jr. (writing for the Court), Thurgood Marshall, Sandra Day O'Connor, John Paul Stevens

Justices Dissenting
Warren E. Burger, Lewis F. Powell, Jr., William H. Rehnquist, Byron R. White

Place
Washington, D.C

Date of Decision
22 June 1983

Decision
The U.S. Supreme Court affirmed the decision of the lower court which found the re-districting plan to be unfairly biased in favor of the outgoing political party (then controlling) the New Jersey Legislature.

Significance
In striking down a reapportionment plan enacted into law by the state of New Jersey, the U.S. Supreme Court expressed their support of apportionment of voters into voting districts by a standard that required districts that were "as nearly as practicable" close to numerical equality. That standard, as in previous rulings, deliberately did not set absolute numerical standards which states could use in reapportioning districts. Of equal, or perhaps greater import, this decision did not recognize as valid preservation of racial or ethnic minority voting districts as reasonable justification for a state deviating from numerical equality among voting districts.

According to the 1980 census results, the clerk of the U.S. House of Representatives informed New Jersey's governor that the number of seats to which the state was entitled had changed from 15 to 14. Amid much haggling and disagreement by both parties, the president *pro tem* of the New Jersey State Senate, Senator Feldman, drafted a 14-district plan (the Feldman Plan) which was finally passed by the state legislature and signed into law by the governor in January of 1982. The plan had used 1980 census figures as a basis for the new reapportionment of New Jersey congressional districts. According to that census, the state had just over 7.3 million voters; the ideal voter population per district should have been 526,059. However, the Feldman Plan, as drafted, did not achieve ideal-sized districts. There was an average deviation among them of 0.1384 percent, and maximum disparity of 0.6984 percent. (Interpreted as a population figure, the maximum deviation was 3,574 voters.)

The standards of equal representation alluded to in articles one and two of the Constitution provided that congressional districts should be "as nearly as practicable" of equal size. However, "as nearly as practicable" did not assume any fixed figure; thus every deviation, no matter how small, was open to challenge as not being equitable. As soon as the plan was enacted, people of varying interests joined with all elected Republican congressmen from New Jersey to challenge the plan (Senator Feldman's constituency was Democrat). They stated that the plan was contrary to the requirements of articles one and two of the U.S. Constitution and that the plan should not be used for the election of the members of Congress to the U.S. House of Representatives.

According to precedent set in *Kirkpatrick v. Preisler* (1969) and *White v. Weiser* (1973), appellees were required to prove that the variations in population equality avoided a "good-faith" effort to achieve the smallest possible deviation in apportioning districts, and appellants (the state of New Jersey) had to prove that deviations were required to achieve some legitimate state objective. However, although New Jersey argued that districts were apportioned to protect racial minorities, the district court held that the state of New

Jersey failed to prove that deviations necessarily preserved the voting strength of minorities. The Feldman Plan was thus adjudged unconstitutional.

In debating the case for the state of New Jersey, the appellants' counsel explained that that the state legislature's rationale in selecting the Feldman Plan was that it tried to achieve "numerical equality" by keeping numerical disparity between districts as close to zero as possible. However, counsel pointed out, other criteria were taken into consideration such as preventing dilution of minority (African American) voting strength and preserving existing voting district boundaries. Even though the standard deviation for error for the New Jersey census was not yet available, the legislature used the best available data by comparing the standard deviation error in the federal census (which was 2.3 percent). Thus, since the maximum disparity between district populations was 0.6984 percent in the Feldman Plan, the state felt their reapportionment scheme was valid. The attorney for the appellants suggested that in rendering its decision, the district court had not given consideration to other justifiable standards such as preservation of the minority voting rights by failing to understand that the Feldman Plan would "protect interest(s) of African American voters in the Trenton and Camden areas." Furthermore, counsel concluded, that because the Supreme Court's decision in *Kirkpatrick* rejected setting of fixed, numerical reapportionment criteria, the state did not have a benchmark by which to determine appropriate variation in voting district size.

Conversely, the appellees' attorney argued that at the time when the Feldman Plan was enacted, several other competing plans were rejected which would have provided considerably lower population disparity between districts. Moreover, the New Jersey legislature did not offer proof of a "good faith" effort by failing to consider plans with lower maximum population differences between voting districts. The appellees' counsel summarily characterized the state's reapportionment scheme as being a "typical sample of gerrymandering" by a political party to utilize legal or political resources to their benefit.

No Rationale For Deviation Found

In rendering a decision on appeal, the majority Supreme Court justices sought to affirm the standard set in *Kirkpatrick v. Preisler* (1969) and *White v. Weiser* (1973). In *Kirkpatrick,* the Court refused to set a fixed figure regarding population deviation of reapportioned districts (ostensibly to take into account considerations such factors as maintaining voting demographics, geography, and to protect the rights of voting minorities). Some deviation was permissible if a state showed that such divergence was necessary to achieve a legitimate objective such as keeping municipal boundaries untouched or maintaining a political environment in which political parties could freely operate. However,

although appellants argued that the deviation in the Feldman Plan was below 0.7 percent and was a reasonable, *de minimus* solution (acceptable minimum deviation), majority justices did not agree. The Court pointed out that in *Kirkpatrick* it had also held that that any deviation, no matter how small, required rationale which could be judicially justified. Because the state had failed to sufficiently convince the Court that its rationale was justifiable, the justices found no cause to support the appellants' claim.

Feldman Plan Found Flawed

The justices felt appellants failed to consider a possible error in the 1980 census and appropriately compensate for a possible undercount of voters in the state. Citing expert evidence of a Princeton University demographer that was presented by appellees (as well as several published studies regarding undercounts in the 1950, 1960, and 1970 censuses), the Court found the Feldman Plan flawed. As such, the justices felt deviations in the Feldman Plan could have been averted or substantially reduced. Like the district court, the Supreme Court took exception the state's failure to consider other plans that reapportioned voting districts with a lower standard maximum deviation. Thus, the Court affirmed the ruling of the lower court on the grounds that the state failed to show good-faith and offer an acceptable explanation for the difference in population number per congressional district.

Justice Stevens delivered a separate concurring opinion. (The U.S. Supreme Court was divided and Justice Stevens had the decisive vote.) As he understood the appellees argument, "district boundaries were unconstitutional because they were product of political gerrymandering." Thus he believed the appellees' claim that the state's apportionment plan had "firmer roots in the Constitution than those provided by Article I, 2".

Stevens pointed out that articles one and two only provided that "representatives should be apportioned among several states," since there were no specific guidelines on how congressional districts in a state should be composed. Instead, Stevens found the Equal Protection Clause of the Fourteenth Amendment more applicable in rendering his decision. He maintained a state's power to define groups of voters was in no way constitutionally limited. Thus, Stevens found no merit in the state's claim that disparity between districts should protect minority voting districts reasoning that, "If they serve no purpose other than to favor one segment—whether racial, ethnic, religious, economic, or political—that may occupy a position of strength at a particular point in time, or to disadvantage a politically weak segment of the community, they violate the constitutional guarantee of equal protection."

Stevens observed that an absolute numerical population equality was impossible because of population shifts, mortality, errors in the census, and other justifiable reasons. Nonetheless, in Stevens's opinion, the population equality standard was reasonable because it could be "judicially manageable," easy to understand, and the figures were readily obtained from the census.

Moreover, Stevens believed that the Equal Protection Clause did not extend its protection only to a certain class of citizens and reasoned it was particularly worthy to consider that "its protection against vote dilution cannot be confined to racial groups." Further since that clause proscribed racial gerrymandering it was reasonable to assume its protection extended to "other cognizable groups of voters as well." He further believed that there was no need to "create a need" to protect against political gerrymandering just because a group of voters shared "common ethnic, racial, or religious background." Thus, while Stevens's rationale diverged from the majority opinion, he nonetheless chose to join in their decision to affirm the ruling of the District Court that the Feldman Plan represented a gross constitutional violation.

Minority Opinion

Justice White delivered the dissenting opinion. The minority justices held fast to the belief that any legislative apportionment should promote and provide fair, nondiscriminatory voting districts for all citizens which was the intent of the Feldman Plan. The dispute at issue then, according to the minority justices, was the maximum standard population deviation among voting districts in the state of New Jersey. The justices felt that the Feldman Plan, with a deviation of less than 0.7 percent, provided "fair and effective representation." The justices pointed out that the margin of estimated error in the 1970 (federal) census was 2.3 percent, substantially higher than deviation in New Jersey's reapportionment plan. Moreover, the undercount in New Jersey was not yet known; therefore, the justices believed that, as in the past, it was reasonable to believe that the 1980 undercount would not have been substantially different than the federal government's undercount (a factor on which, in part, the state of New Jersey's reapportionment plan was based). Simply, the minority believed deviation in the Feldman Plan was "statistically insignificant." Moreover, Justice White observed that since the Court refused to set a numerical standard below which judicial intervention would not be required, "the courts should give a greater weight to the importance of the state's interest and the consistency with which those interests are served than to the size of the deviation."

Justice Powell delivered a separate dissenting opinion. He shared the minority opinion that New Jersey's reapportionment deviation "was neither 'appreciable' nor constitutionally significant." Powell also believed the requirement of respecting municipal boundaries was adhered to in the Feldman Plan. Divergence from constitutional "theoretical exactitude" was permissible

because the maximum standard deviation of 0.6984 percent met constitutional requirements requiring population be equality apportioned among districts.

Impact

The U.S. Supreme Court struck down the Feldman plan even though the population difference per district was rather small (less than .7 percent). The justices held consistent to previous rulings in *Kirkpatrick v. Preisler* (1969) and *White v. Weiser* (1973) by adhering to a standard which gave no exact, numerical guidance regarding the maximum allowable standard deviation between voting districts. However, they did insist that the state of New Jersey, by not considering and adopting other reapportionment plans of lesser deviation, violated constitutional limits which required voting districts that were "as nearly as practicable" close to numerical equality. (There was only a difference of .245 percent between the Feldman Plan and competing schemes.)

Equally important, the Court's ruling failed to recognize as valid the state of New Jersey legislature's design to create districts in which the voting power of racial minorities was preserved. While Justice Stevens was alone in forwarding the idea that New Jersey had "created" rather than preserved the necessity of protecting minority voters against political gerrymandering, the majority opinion tacitly failed to consider protection of voting constituencies based on racial or ethnic considerations. Thus, in rendering this decision, the U.S. Supreme Court moved toward less rigorous and vigorous support of minority and equal protection rights by the judiciary, a trend which continued to the end of the century.

Related Cases

Reynolds v. Sims, 377 U.S. 533 (1964).
Wesberry v. Sanders, 378 U.S. 1 (1964).
Kirkpatrick v. Preisler, 394 U.S. 526 (1969).
Giffney v. Cummings, 412 U.S. 735 (1973).
White v. Weiser, 412 U.S. 783 (1973).

Bibliography and Further Reading

Biskupic, Joan, and Elder Witt. *Congressional Quarterly's Guide to the U.S. Supreme Court,* 3rd ed. Washington, DC: Congressional Quarterly, Inc., 1996.

Pildes, Richard H. "Principled Limitations on Racial and Partisan Redistricting." *Yale Law Journal,* June 1997, p. 2505.

Rush, Mark E. "Gerrymandering: Out of the Political Thicket and Into the Quagmire." *PS: Political Science & Politics,* December 1994, p. 682.

Taylor, Christopher M. "Vote Dilution and the Census Undercount: A State-by-State Remedy." *Michigan Law Review,* February 1996, p. 1098.

BROWN V. THOMSON

Legal Citation: 462 U.S. 835 (1983)

Appellant
Margaret R. Brown, et al.

Appellee
Thyra Thomson, Wyoming Secretary of State

Appellant's Claim
Wyoming's reapportionment plan to allocate one seat to Niobrara County in its House of Representatives was unconstitutional and substantially weakened the voting power of the plaintiff because it gave a small number of people "super" voting strength and totally disregarded a fundamental rule: one person, one vote.

Chief Lawyer for Appellant
Suellen L. Davidson

Chief Lawyer for Appellee
Randall T. Cox

Justices for the Court
Warren E. Burger, Sandra Day O'Connor, Lewis F. Powell, Jr. (writing for the Court), William H. Rehnquist, John Paul Stevens

Justices Dissenting
Harry A. Blackmun, William J. Brennan, Jr., Thurgood Marshall, Byron R. White

Place
Washington, D.C.

Date of Decision
22 June 1983

Decision
The U.S. Supreme Court affirmed the lower court's decision that the Wyoming reapportionment plan for its House of Representatives, which allocated one seat to underpopulated counties, did not violate the equal protection clause of the Fourteenth Amendment.

Significance
In apparent disregard of previous rulings regarding the necessity to apportion using equal population ratios among voting districts, the U.S. Supreme Court upheld a Wyoming plan that would exceed acceptable ratio limits. With this decision the Court held that population equality was not the sole determination for establishing voting districts. The Court had affirmed (in previous decisions) that other criteria were acceptable such as maintenance of county boundaries and preservation of political subdivisions. However, the Court ruled that giving an undersized county representation despite lacking sufficient population served a state's interest in providing citizens in all counties representation in a state legislature. The interests of equal representation were not firmly tied to population.

In 1890, when Wyoming became a state, its Constitution provided that each county "shall constitute [a] senatorial and representative district," and were thus granted the right to have at least one senator and one representative. Another provision of state statute stipulated that senators and representatives would gain their seats according to county population; counties with more inhabitants would have more seats. Dispute arose (in 1981) when the legislature of Wyoming tried to enact a new statute that provided for 64 seats in the Wyoming House of Representatives. With the new statute, state legislators had to reapportion voting districts. Thus began a battle between political parties for political advantage within the state.

In 1980 the state had almost a half million inhabitants. The ideal number of persons per representative in the House of Representatives should have been the population divided by the number of seats stipulated in Wyoming's proposed reapportionment legislation (64)—in this case, 7337 persons per representative. However, the state was divided into 23 counties and so substantial population differences impacted the size of voting districts. The resulting "deviation in population equality" created vastly different numbers of people per representative that was not the same for each county. Under this plan, the average deviation from ideal reapportionment was almost 16 percent (the maximum deviation was almost 89 percent). Further, under the provisions of the proposed statute, even if a county, hypothetically, had no population at all, it was entitled to one representative. Thus the least populous county in the state (3,000 citizens lived in Niobrara County) was given one seat in the House of Representatives. The statute's language also stipulated that if the minimum representation provision was found to be unconstitutional, that county would be combined into one voting district with a neighboring county. (Interestingly, this option would have populated the House of Representatives with only 63 representatives.)

Appellants in this case were members of the League of Women Voters and residents of the seven largest counties in Wyoming. They filed a lawsuit in the Federal District Court on the claim that allocation of one representative to Niobrara County tainted their voting privileges. Because appellants alleged the state of Wyoming was in violation of the Fourteenth Amendment, they sought declaratory and injunctive relief (a decision by the court declaring the statute unconstitutional and enjoining its enforcement).

The Battle for Equal Representation

The federal district court held that some deviation in population equality might have been justified by the state's interest to follow other goals. Acceptable goals may have included "maintaining integrity of various political subdivisions" and "providing for compact districts of contiguous territory." However, the court felt that as little as a 10 percent deviation in population equality was discriminatory, therefore, the state was asked to justify the constitutionality of the statute.

The district court's review found as just and constitutional the state's policy to ensure each county had one representative in its legislature and their need to preserve the county boundaries. Even if a small county was denied one representative, the court reasoned the outcome wouldn't change population disparity. The average deviation would be 13 percent in the plan which yielded 63 representatives. The maximum deviation ratio would be 66 percent, (above the prescribed ratio of 10 percent). However, the 64-member plan would have been discriminatory to smaller counties, like Niobrara County, because it would not have its own representative. Therefore the district court held that if the state adopted the 63-member plan, (which would grant small counties at least one seat in the Wyoming House of Representatives, then its statute would be constitutional.

Suellen L. Davidson argued the case for the appellants. (The appellants' case was limited in scope because it chose to address only alleged disparities with regard to Niobrara Counts, but its claim was intended to be indicative of the problem of apportionment for all small counties.) According to the appellants, the issue in this case was whether the state could apportion representatives and ignore considerations of representation based on population. In their view, any allocation of seats in the House of Representatives, based on any other criteria than population was unconstitutional. The effect, appellants argued, would be to substantially dilute the value of the votes of people living in larger counties. Moreover, the 63-seat plan totally disregarded a fundamental right: one person one vote. The appellants' attorney argued the outcome of such a plan would render the proposed statute unconstitutional because, although representation of the county was laudable, the plan essentially gave a vote to the county and not to the people residing in the county. Thus, it was more acceptable to combine smaller counties with larger ones to make one voting district (e.g., Niobrara County with neighboring Goshen County.)

Randall T. Cox argued the case for the appellee. Cox agreed that while states often base apportionment on a population-based formula, small counties were allocated one seat in the Wyoming House of Representatives in order to give all counties equal representation in the state's House of Representatives. Counsel suggested that population deviations did not diminish a fundamental individual right to equitable, free, and fair participation because legislative bodies respond to the majority and, in the case brought before the Court, Niobrara's representative would not alter that premise. As support for this argument, the appellee pointed out that the largest counties in the state accounted for election of 28 representatives out of 64. In fact, counsel maintained, that that very reason made it important for a small county to get its own representative in order to ensure each county had full and effective participation in crafting laws and in the political life of the state. For example, Cox went on to explain, the state regulated tax policy and financial aid according to county, not population. If a small county like Niobrara were combined with Goshen County to form one voting district, Niobrara's interests would likely suffer since there were three times more voters in Goshen. Alternatively, Niobrara would not risk suffering such marginalization if it had its own representative. Finally, the appellee argued, the affect of the 63-seat plan did not create a situation wherein minority interests threatened the minority.

Justice Powell delivered the opinion of the Court. First the U.S. Supreme Court had to determine if it held proper jurisdiction. Then it would determine if the proposed 63-seat representation plan would change the plan's deviation from appropriate ratios of population to representatives and exceed constitutional limits. In *Reynolds v. Sims* (1964), the Court held that population must be the basis for state apportionment for voting districts electing representatives for the legislature in both state houses. However, the Court recognized that voting districts cannot be designed on absolute equality in terms of population in each county. Therefore, minor deviations were justified if a state could prove there were legitimate aims being served such as goals that were "maintaining the integrity of various political subdivisions" and "providing for compact districts of contiguous territory." However, in *Connor v. Finch* (1977) and *White v. Register* (1973), the Court had held that a difference of 10 percent in the number of inhabitants per county was a tolerable deviation. Therefore any plan that exceeded that percentage created discrimination which had to be justified by the state in order to be constitutionally valid. The Court had jurisdiction.

While Wyoming's reapportionment plan exceeded the 10 percent tolerance, the Court reasoned the state had historically attempted to maintain various political subdivisions and preserve county borders. Since 1890, the state of Wyoming not only showed concern and endorsement of those objectives in the state constitution but strived to ensure every county was represented in the state legislature. Thus, in citing its decision in *Abate v. Mundt* (1971), wherein "a desire to preserve the integrity of various political subdivisions may justify an apportionment plan which departs from numerical equality," the Court found justifiable precedence to support the appellee's claim. Further, the justices could not find any sign that the reapportionment plan discriminated or caused any group of people injury. As the Court observed in *Reynolds v. Sims* (1964), besides giving attention to strict population apportionment, the quality and the level of population difference must be observed.

Because appellants did not challenge the entire reapportionment plan, but just the clause that gave Niobrara County one seat in the House of Representatives, the justices needed to determine whether population disparity would be unconstitutional. The Court affirmed the lower court's findings that with the 64-seat plan political power would be focused in larger counties and deprive Niobrara County representation as guaranteed by the state constitution. Thus, the U.S. Supreme Court held that the Wyoming statute allocating one seat to small counties in the House of Representatives, specifically Niobrara County, was not in violation of the Equal Protection Clause of the Fourteenth Amendment.

Minority Opinion

Justice Brennan filed the dissenting opinion. The justices could not agree with the majority's findings even though appellants had only challenged a part of the reapportionment plan. The minority opinion suggested the Court did not observe the general constitutionality of the plan. The Equal Protection Clause requires a state to form legislative districts as evenly as possible. Thus, the minority justices felt that the Court failed to consider four important issues: whether deviation was higher than 10 percent, (considered automatically discriminative according to *Connor v. Finch*); the validity of the reasons for the state's "inability" to decrease devi-

ation in population equality; whether the plan truly served state policy in this matter; and whether such deviation was within constitutional limits, even if the state proved that deviations were justified by the state's intent.

Impact

The U.S. Supreme Court had, in prior cases, ruled that deviation in population equality above 10 percent was discriminatory. In this case, however, the Court affirmed a maximum deviation of 89 percent. (Even the average deviation of this plan—16 percent—exceeded the minimum allowable deviation.) However, Wyoming's 63-seat reapportionment scheme provided representation for the people of Niobrara County which would not have been possible if the state legislature adhered to apportionment strictly by population. Thus, even though the value of a vote in Niobrara County essentially was "valued" at twice the value as would have been available under a strict "one person, one vote" determination, the Court reasoned that the exclusion of representation of that county in the state legislature made such an exception acceptable. Thus, the Court provided yet another important criteria which state legislatures could use when reapportioning voting districts. A state did not have to strictly adhere to apportionment by population if (as the Court outlined in previous rulings) it needed to maintain political subdivisions, and merge adjoining areas into one voting district. Additionally, in concordance with their decision in *Brown v. Thomson*, the Court determined that the difference in population equality was legal if a state could justify a legitimate interest in doing so.

Related Cases

Reynolds v. Sims, 377 U.S. 533 (1964).
Abate v. Mundt, 403 U.S. 182 (1971).
White v. Register, 412 U.S. 755 (1973).
Connor v. Finch, 431 U.S. 407 (1977).
Karcher v. Daggett, 462 U.S. 725 (1983).

Bibliography and Further Reading

Biskupic, Joan, and Elder Witt, eds. *Congressional Quarterly's Guide to the U.S. Supreme Court*, 3rd ed. Washington, DC: Congressional Quarterly, Inc., 1996.

DAVIS V. BANDEMER

Legal Citation: 478 U.S. 109 (1986)

Petitioner
Susan J. Davis, et al.

Respondent
Irwin C. Bandemer, et al.

Petitioner's Claim
That Indiana's 1981 legislative redistricting plan did not unconstitutionally discriminate against Democratic legislators in violation of the Equal Protection Clause of the Fourteenth Amendment

Chief Lawyer for Petitioner
William M. Evans

Chief Lawyer for Respondent
Theodore R. Boehm

Justices for the Court
Harry A. Blackmun, William J. Brennan, Jr., Warren E. Burger, Thurgood Marshall, Sandra Day O'Connor, Byron R. White (writing for the Court), William H. Rehnquist

Justices Dissenting
Lewis F. Powell, Jr., John Paul Stevens

Place
Washington, D.C.

Date of Decision
30 June 1986

Decision
Upheld the state of Indiana's legislative redistricting plan, concluding that although the defendant's claim that the plan violated the Equal Protection Clause could be decided by the Court, the plan itself did not discriminate against Democratic legislators.

Significance
The ruling made clear that the Supreme Court can decide challenges to legislative redistricting plans which are alleged to discriminate against certain political groups, as opposed to racial, religious, or other similar groups. Thus, for the first time the Supreme Court held that political gerrymandering can violate the Constitution. However, the test adopted by a plurality of the Court makes such challenges to redistricting plans extremely difficult to prove.

Following the 1980 U.S. census, the Indiana legislature began the task of redrawing the districts from which its members are elected. This process, known as reapportionment or redistricting, was required under Indiana law every ten years, following the census. The Indiana legislature consists of a house of representatives and a senate. The 50 senators are elected from 50 separate districts. However, the 100 representatives are elected from less than 100 separate districts; thus, some districts, based on their population, elected two or three representatives. In early 1981, the Indiana legislature adopted a redistricting plan providing for 61 districts which elected only one representative, nine districts which elected two representatives, and seven districts which elected three representatives. At the time this redistricting plan was adopted, a majority of both branches of the legislature were members of the Republican party, as was the governor, who approved the plan.

In early 1982, a number of legislators who were members of the Democratic party filed a lawsuit in the U.S. District Court for the Southern District of Indiana against various state officials involved in adopting the redistricting plan. The Democrats claimed that the Republican legislature and governor had purposefully drawn the districts in such a way as to disadvantage the Democrats in future elections, a process known as political gerrymandering. Gerrymandering generally is the practice of drawing legislative districts in such a way as to favor or disfavor a certain group. This practice was named after Massachusetts governor and Constitutional Convention representative Elbridge Gerry, who first used the practice in 1812. The Indiana Democrats contended that the state's 1981 redistricting constituted political gerrymandering designed to disfavor Democratic candidates by concentrating voters who traditionally voted Democratic to a few districts. They argued that this gerrymandering violated the Fourteenth Amendment to the Constitution, which in part provides that no state shall "deny to any person within its jurisdiction the equal protection of the laws." Prior to any action being taken in the case, Indiana conducted elections pursuant to the redistricting plan in November of 1982. Although the Democratic house of representative candidates received 51.9 percent of the vote throughout the state, only 43 Democrats were elected to the 100 seats available.

The case was heard by a three-judge panel of the district court. After reviewing the statistics from the 1982 elections, and hearing testimony from a number of Republican legislators about their motives in drawing the districts, the district court concluded that the redistricting plan constituted a political gerrymander. The district court also concluded that this gerrymander violated the equal protection rights of Democratic candidates and voters. The state officials appealed this decision to the U.S. Supreme Court. Although a majority of the Court agreed that the district court's decision should be reversed, there was no majority agreement on the reason. Justice O'Connor, writing an opinion which was joined by Chief Justice Burger and Justice Rehnquist, thought the case should be reversed because it presented a political question which could not be resolved by the federal courts. Justice White, writing an opinion which was joined by Justices Brennan, Marshall, and Blackmun, concluded that the Court could resolve the issue, but agreed that reversal was appropriate because the Indiana Democrats did not show that their equal protection rights were violated. Finally, Justice Powell, writing for himself and Justice Stevens, concluded that the district court should be affirmed because the Indiana Democrats had established an equal protection violation.

A Political Question?

The first question before the Supreme Court was whether the Court properly could resolve the issue of whether the Indiana redistricting plan constituted a political gerrymander in violation of the Fourteenth Amendment. In *Luther v. Borden* (1849), the Supreme Court first adopted what is now known as the political question doctrine. Under this doctrine a federal court, including the Supreme Court, cannot decide a case if it presents a political question. Examples of such political questions occur where the issue is committed by the Constitution to another branch of government, deciding the issue involves the Court in making an initial policy determination more suited to the legislative branch, or deciding the issue would otherwise hamper the interrelationship of the three separate, but equal, branches of the government.

Justice O'Connor reasoned that the Court should refuse to decide the case because "challenges to the manner in which an apportionment has been carried out—by the very parties that are responsible for this process—present a political question in the truest sense of the term." However, a majority of the justices disagreed. Justice White, writing the opinion of the Court on this issue, concluded that political gerrymandering did not involve a political question. He noted that the

Court had previously decided racial gerrymandering cases, and that the standards involved in political gerrymandering cases did not significantly differ from those involved in racial gerrymandering cases.

An Agreeable Test, Inconsistent Results

Having decided that the political gerrymandering issue was not a political question, the six justices in the majority on this point then considered whether the Indiana redistricting plan violated the Equal Protection Clause. Initially, all six justices agreed on the test to be used in analyzing political gerrymandering claims. In his opinion, Justice White found that political parties or other persons bringing a political gerrymandering claim must, to establish that the redistricting violates the Fourteenth Amendment, "prove both intentional discrimination against an identifiable political group and an actual discriminatory effect on that group." Justice Powell began his dissenting opinion by agreeing with this test.

Nevertheless, the six justices split sharply on the actual application of this test, both in general and to the facts of the case. Justice White, joined by Justices Brennan, Marshall, and Blackmun, concluded that the Indiana Democrats had failed to show that the redistricting plan had an actual discriminatory effect on Democrats. He stated that the purpose behind the drawing of the lines should not be reached unless the Democrats first showed that they had "been unconstitutionally denied [their] chance to effectively influence the political process." Reasoning that "the power to influence the political process is not limited to winning elections," Justice White concluded that the simple fact that the Indiana Democrats' representation in the legislature was not directly proportional to the percentage of votes they received was insufficient to establish a discriminatory effect. He also concluded that the undisputed fact that the Republican lawmakers in Indiana intended to disadvantage the Democrats was irrelevant unless the Democrats could show that they were actually disadvantaged, which they could not.

Justice Powell, joined in his opinion by Justice Stevens, vigorously disagreed with Justice White's analysis. In his view, the political gerrymandering inquiry "properly focuses on whether the boundaries of the voting districts have been distorted deliberately and arbitrarily to achieve illegitimate ends." He believed that a court should look at actual elections conducted under the plan, the shape of the districts, and the actual goals of the legislators adopting the plan. Examining these factors, Justice Powell would have upheld the district court's decision, most notably because there was substantial evidence that the Indiana legislators intended to disadvantage Democratic candidates; furthermore, the 1982 election results showed that the Democratic candidates had been disadvantaged.

Impact

At first glance, the Court's decision in *Davis* appeared to be a victory for opponents of political gerrymandering; for the first time, the Supreme Court explicitly held that political gerrymandering can, in certain circumstances, intrude on the equal protection rights of a disadvantaged political group. However, the practical effect has been much different. Although not adopted by a majority of the Supreme Court, most lower federal courts considering political gerrymandering claims have applied Justice White's approach, which has been very difficult to meet. Further, although a majority of the Court did conclude that it can decide political gerrymandering cases, it has remained reluctant to do so. Indeed, although the Court continues to decide claims of racial gerrymandering, since *Davis* it has refused to consider a number of cases raising claims of political gerrymandering. Thus, in a practical sense, the decision has done little to curb the continued use of political gerrymandering.

Related Cases

Luther v. Borden, 48 U.S. 1 (1849).
Gomillion v. Lightfoot, 364 U.S. 339 (1960).
Baker v. Carr, 369 U.S. 186 (1962).
Nixon v. United States, 506 U.S. 224 (1993).
Shaw v. Reno, 509 U.S. 630 (1993).
Shaw v. Hunt, 517 U.S. 899 (1996).
Bush v. Vera, 517 U.S. 952 (1996).

Bibliography and Further Reading

Bickel, Alexander M. *The Least Dangerous Branch: The Supreme Court at the Bar of Politics.* Indianapolis: The Bobbs-Merrill Co., 1962.

Brace, Kimball W., and John P. Katosh. "Redistricting Legislation Will Be a New Growth Industry," *Wall Street Journal,* August 29, 1986.

Chemerinsky, Erwin. *Federal Jurisdiction,* 2nd edition. Boston: Little, Brown & Co., 1994.

Fisher, Jeffery L. "The Unwelcome Judicial Obligation to Respect Politics in Racial Gerrymandering Remedies," *Michigan Law Review,* March 1997, p. 1404.

Grofman, Bernard, ed. *Political Gerrymandering and the Courts.* New York: Agathon Press, 1990.

Hall, Kermit L., ed. *The Oxford Companion to the Supreme Court of the United States.* New York: Oxford University Press, 1992.

Rush, Mark E. "Gerrymandering: Out of the Political Thicket and Into the Quagmire," *PS: Political Science & Politics,* December 1994, p. 682.

SHAW V. RENO

Legal Citation: 509 U.S. 630 (1993)

Appellant
Ruth O. Shaw, et al.

Appellee
Janet Reno, U.S. Attorney General, et al.

Appellant's Claim
That the state of North Carolina created an unconstitutional racially gerrymandered district, which violates the Fourteenth Amendment's Equal Protection Clause.

Chief Lawyer for Appellant
Robinson O. Everett

Chief Lawyer for Appellee
H. Jefferson Powell

Justices for the Court
Anthony M. Kennedy, Sandra Day O'Connor (writing for the Court), William H. Rehnquist, Antonin Scalia, Clarence Thomas

Justices Dissenting
Harry A. Blackmun, David H. Souter, John Paul Stevens, Byron R. White

Place
Washington, D.C.

Date of Decision
28 June 1993

Decision
The district court's decision was reversed and remanded.

Significance
The U.S. Supreme Court considered the many complex and difficult issues involved when the state of North Carolina proposed the creation of a second majority-minority district no wider than a two-lane highway, raising the possibility that this action violated the Fourteenth Amendment's Equal Protection Clause.

Case Background

In the fall of 1991, a reapportionment plan was submitted for the state of North Carolina that only included one black minority district. This plan was subsequently rejected by the U.S. attorney general due to the lack of minority voting representation. In order to remedy this, a revised plan was submitted that included a second majority-minority district of an unusual shape. The new district was at times no wider than a two-lane highway and ran along Interstate 85 for about 160 miles. Five residents of North Carolina filed a claim that this new district was created for the sole purpose of adding another black representative.

This rearrangement of district lines to produce a change in the voting majority of a certain area is called a "gerrymander." Because this new district consisted of such an unusual shape so that it deliberately encompassed areas with higher black populations, these residents believed that the state may have violated the Fourteenth Amendment's Equal Protection Clause.

The case was heard by a three-judge district court, who ruled that the residents did not prove an unconstitutional equal protection claim. An appeal to the U.S. Supreme Court was made.

When Has a State Gone Too Far?

The residents were represented by Robinson O. Everett, who argued that the state had gone too far in trying to secure a second black majority district. He argued that this new district, an awkward and unusual one that had no other purpose than to create a black majority, violated certain principles of reapportionment such as compactness, contiguousness, and community of interest. Everett concluded that the state had erred by drawing district boundaries in such a way as to target two seats for persons of a particular race.

The state's position, presented by H. Jefferson Powell, was that it had made an effort in good faith to carefully comply with both the Voting Rights Act legislation and the "one person, one vote" requirement (*Reynolds v. Sims* [1964]), by intentionally creating a second majority-minority district. He argued that states should be encouraged to comply with the Voting Rights Act.

The U.S. Supreme Court decided that the residents did raise a valid question under the Fourteenth Amendment's Equal Protection Clause, which prevents any state from discriminating against persons according to their race. The district court decision was reversed and remanded, although it was noted that the district court did properly dismiss their claims, and must now determine if there was some "compelling governmental interest" to justify this plan.

Justice O'Connor delivered the majority opinion of the Court, joined by Justices Rehnquist, Scalia, Kennedy, and Thomas. O'Connor noted in the opinion that the appellants' claim "must be examined against the backdrop of this country's long history of racial discrimination in voting." A racial gerrymander should be closely scrutinized so as to avoid stereotypical ideas about the preferences of voters of the same race, and state legislation that focuses on classifying citizens according to race "must be narrowly tailored to further a compelling governmental interest," since this type of racial classification can threaten "special harms." Furthermore, a covered jurisdiction cannot use section 5 of the Voting Rights Act to justify racial gerrymandering. For these reasons, the district court's decision was reversed and remanded.

Dissension

Justice White gave a dissenting opinion, joined by Justices Blackmun and Stevens. White believed that the appellants were not able to show how they had received a "cognizable injury." In other words, the appellants were not able to show that they were deprived of a right to vote, nor were they able to show that their own political strength was in any way diminished by the new district, and he cited the cases of *Mobile v. Bolden* (1980) and *Guinn v. United States* (1915). Justice White wrote that the issue in this case "is whether the classification based on race discriminates against anyone by denying equal access to the political process," and found that in this case, it had not.

Impact

This case was remanded back to the district court, which held that the reapportionment plan was constitutional because it did meet the requirement of the U.S. Supreme Court that the state must have a "compelling interest" in complying with the Voting Rights Act, sections 2 and 5. Since this decision, both the U.S. Supreme Court and the circuit courts have heard several cases in which the results of *Shaw v. Reno* have been cited. These have included cases involving racial gerrymandering, drawing school and voting districts, housing discrimination, and voting rights. This case was once again appealed back to the U.S. Supreme Court, where it was heard as *Shaw v. Hunt* in which the decision of the district court was reversed once more, as the Supreme

Court found that it violated the Equal Protection Clause of the Fourteenth Amendment. The issues involving the right to vote and have protection against all forms of discrimination continue to be explored and debated.

Related Cases

Guinn v. United States, 238 U.S. 347 (1915).
Gomillion v. Lightfoot, 364 U.S. 339 (1960).
Reynolds v. Sims, 377 U.S. 533 (1964).
Washington v. Davis, 426 U.S. 229 (1976).
Arlington Heights v. Metropolitan Housing Development Corp., 429 U.S. 252 (1977).
United Jewish Organizations of Williamsburgh, Inc. v. Carey, 430 U.S. 144 (1977).
Mobile v. Bolden, 446 U.S. 55 (1980).
Davis v. Bandemer, 478 U.S. 109 (1986).
Shaw v. Hunt, 517 U.S. 899 (1996).

Bibliography and Further Reading

Biskupic, Joan, and Elder Witt. *Congressional Quarterly's Guide to the U.S. Supreme Court,* 3rd ed. Washington, DC: Congressional Quarterly, Inc., 1996.

Coyle, Marica. "Where to Draw the Line on Race Redistricting?" *The National Law Journal,* December 11, 1995, p. A1.

Engstrom, Richard L. "Shaw, Miller and the Districting Thicket." *National Civic Review,* fall–winter 1995, p. 323.

Karlan, Pamela S. "End of the Second Reconstruction? Voting Rights and the Court." *The Nation,* May 23, 1994, p. 698.

Karlan, Pamela S., and Thomas C. Goldstein. "Court Still Ambivalent on Redistricting." *The National Law Journal,* July 24, 1995, p. A19.

Lublin, David. "The Election of African Americans and Latinos to the U.S. House of Representatives, 1972–1994." *American Politics Quarterly,* July 1997, p. 269.

Plides, Richard H. "Principled Limitations on Racial and Partisan Redistricting." *Yale Law Journal,* June 1997, p. 2505.

Raskin, Jamin B. "Supreme Court's Double Standard: Gerrymander Hypocrisy." *The Nation,* February 6, 1995, p. 167.

Rosen, Jeffrey. "Gerrymandered." *The New Republic,* October 25, 1993, p. 12.

Schwartz, Herman. "The Supreme Court Stays Hard Right." *The Nation,* October 25, 1993, p. 452.

Yeoman, Barry. "'Virtual Disenfranchisement': Minority Congressional Districts are Becoming Casualties of the Courts." *The Nation,* September 7, 1998, p. 18.

MILLER V. JOHNSON

Legal Citation: 515 U.S. 900 (1995)

Appellants
Zell Miller, et al., Lucious Abrams, Jr., et al., and United States

Appellees
Davida Johnson, et al.

Appellants' Claim
The state of Georgia's redistricting plan enacted in 1991 violated the Equal Protection Clause of the Fourteenth Amendment of the U.S. Constitution when the Eleventh District was created. The appellants claimed that the redistricting plan was based upon racial factors and did not serve any compelling governmental interest.

Chief Lawyer for Appellants
David F. Walbert

Chief Lawyer for Appellees
A. Lee Parks

Justices for the Court
Anthony M. Kennedy (writing for the Court), Sandra Day O'Connor, William H. Rehnquist, Antonin Scalia, Clarence Thomas

Justices Dissenting
Stephen Breyer, Ruth Bader Ginsburg, David H. Souter, John Paul Stevens

Place
Washington, D.C.

Date of Decision
29 June 1995

Decision
The Supreme Court determined that the Georgia redistricting plan violated the Equal Protection Clause of the Fourteenth Amendment as tested by the decision in *Shaw v. Reno* (1993). The redistricting of Georgia with the creation of the Eleventh District was done predominantly on a racial basis.

Significance
In the case *Miller v. Johnson* the U.S. Supreme Court examined the constitutionality of a redistricting plan for the state of Georgia. The question they addressed was whether the reapportionment of congressional redistricts was a violation of the Equal Protection Clause of the Fourteenth Amendment. They had to determine if this was a case of discriminatory racial gerrymandering that segregated voters based purely upon race and did not support any compelling interest for the state or local governments. Upon investigation, the Court ruled that the redistricting boundaries were highly unusual and violated the rights of majority and minority voters.

A Case of Racial Gerrymandering

Between 1980 and 1990 the state of Georgia had only one congressional district that had a black majority. Due to the results of the decennial census for 1990 it was determined that the black voters of Georgia were entitled to an additional eleventh congressional seat. This prompted the Georgia General Assembly to redraw congressional district boundaries and prepare a reapportionment plan. Designated as a covered jurisdiction by the Voting Rights Act of 1965, Georgia was required to submit the reapportionment plan to the U.S. attorney general for pre-clearance before enactment to ensure that the proposed changes did not deny or abridge citizens' rights to vote based on race.

In October of 1991 the first plan for reapportionment was submitted for approval. It included two majority-minority congressional districts, and a third district that was comprised of 35 percent black voters. The Justice Department denied approval of the plan on the grounds that it had created only two majority-minority districts and did not acknowledge certain minority populations by aligning them in majority-black districts.

The General Assembly rewrote the plan, increasing the black populations in three districts—the Second, Fifth, and Eleventh. The Justice Department denied pre-clearance a second time, citing an alternate plan for creating three majority-minority districts. The plan, called "max-black," had been drafted by the American Civil Liberties Union for the Georgia General Assembly's black caucus. It involved several trades of black populations in Macon and Savannah, which would convert the districts into three majority-minority districts.

In order to comply with the Justice Department's recommendations, Georgia redrew the reapportionment plan a third time, utilizing the "max-black" plan for a benchmark. The resulting plan split 26 counties, and the Eleventh District connected the black neighborhoods of metro Atlanta with the poor black districts of coastal Georgia located 260 miles away. This third district alone split eight counties and five municipalities and covered a territory of approximately 6,784 square miles. The end result of the plan, however, included the three majority-minority districts recommended by the Justice Department. In April of 1992 the reapportionment plan was granted pre-clearance; elections were held under the new redistricting the following November, in which each of the three new districts elected a black candidate.

Five white voters from the Eleventh District filed a claim in the U.S. District Court for the Southern District of Georgia. They alleged that the redistricting plan was a "racial gerrymander" by which voters had been separated into districts on the basis of race alone. This was a violation of their equal protection rights as guaranteed by the Fourteenth Amendment of the U.S. Constitution and interpreted by the precedents set in *Shaw v. Reno* (1993). A three-judge panel was convened, and the majority ruled in favor of the five appellees. It was held that *Shaw* required close scrutiny of a redistricting plan if it had the overwhelming appearance of a process decided by racial factors. The panel also held that the Georgia plan did not require three majority-minority districts in order to comply with the Voting Rights Act of 1965. Upon appeal *Miller v. Johnson* came before the Supreme Court in April of 1995.

Points of Affirmation and Dissension

The Supreme Court affirmed and upheld the decision of the lower court. The justices confirmed that the Georgia redistricting plan violated the Fourteenth Amendment's Equal Protection Clause. The majority expressed three primary points in their decision. First, the proceedings showed that race was the primary criterion in creating the districts. The district boundaries were of such a bizarre nature that this was the only reasoning that could be applied to the plan. Justice Kennedy, entering the opinion of the Court, wrote that the "central mandate [of the Equal Protection Clause] is race neutrality in governmental decision making." The Georgia General Assembly made racial factors the only consideration in the redrawing of district boundaries.

The second point to which the Court turned was the precedent established in *Shaw v. Reno* (1993). This required close scrutiny of any redistricting process that had the appearance of being motivated by race. Under close scrutiny *Miller v. Johnson* could not establish any compelling governmental interest being served by the new districting. In reviewing the proceedings, the majority justices determined that the State of Georgia, under the directive of the Justice Department, deliberately created congressional districts that would bring the black population into a few single districts, in particular the Eleventh, maximizing the black minority vote. The only compelling interest the Supreme Court could sanction was a state's compliance with the Voting Act of 1965 in order to correct past discrimination and injustices; the state of Georgia did not argue that the redistricting plan was an attempt to remedy any past injuries due to racial discrimination.

Four justices argued a dissenting opinion of the Court's decision. Ruth Bader Ginsburg, entering the opinion of the minority, expressed the view that the state of Georgia did not use racial factors as the overriding determinant in the redistricting plan. She pointed to the design of the Eleventh District as a reflection of "traditional districting factors," such as maintaining political subdivisions, and the comparison of average areas and sizes of political subdivisions. Additional political considerations were used in creating the boundaries and the new district. Ginsburg also cited that the plan adopted by the Georgia General Assembly was not the "max-black" plan advocated by the Attorney General. The redistricting plan, while influenced by the "max-black" plan, had significant differences, and took political and social factors into consideration.

Ginsburg, on behalf of the dissenting justices, stated that the Court's adoption of the standard of "close scrutiny" established in *Shaw v. Reno* opened the way for more federal litigation of reapportionment processes. If a plaintiff could plausibly claim that other considerations had less emphasis than race in a reapportionment of districts, then a federal case could be mounted. Ginsburg found this "neither necessary nor proper." Redistricting was a legislative process that should be left to the states and local governments except in extreme instances.

Impact

Miller v. Johnson was a serious examination of a state's ability to draw legislative boundaries that not only complied with the requirements of the Voting Rights Act of 1965 but also remained racially neutral in the creation of voting districts. The conclusion of the Supreme Court was that while race may be a significant factor in the reapportionment of voting districts, it cannot be the overwhelming factor, or the only factor, for that will ultimately violate the rights of voters that are guaranteed by the Equal Protection Clause of the Fourteenth Amendment.

Even as late as 1996, the Court heard cases about redistricting and political participation (*Shaw v. Hunt*). The U.S. political system is still uneven in providing equal voting power to all of its eligible voters. *Miller v. Johnson* has been an attempt by the Supreme Court to protect the rights of all while maintaining a race-neutral atmosphere.

Related Cases

Shaw v. Reno, 509 U.S. 630 (1993).
Shaw v. Hunt, 517 U.S. 899 (1995).
Bush v. Vera, 517 U.S. 952 (1996).

Bibliography and Further Reading

Cimino, Chapin. "Class-Based Preferences in Affirmative Action Programs after Miller v. Johnson: A Race-

Neutral Opinion, or Subterfuge?" *University of Chicago Law Review,* Vol. 64, no. 4, fall 1997, pp. 1289-1310.

Coyle, Marcia. "The Court's New View: Colorblind? Rulings Put Heavy Burden on Racial Classifications." *The National Law Journal,* July 10, 1995, p. A1.

Coyle, Marcia. "High Court Listens to Challenges on Voting District." *The National Law Journal,* May 1, 1995, p. A19.

Coyle, Marcia. "Where to Draw the Line on Race Redistricting?" *The National Law Journal,* December 11, 1995, p. A1.

Engstrom, Richard L. "Shaw, Miller and the Districting Thicket." *National Civic Review,* fall-winter 1995, p. 323.

Hill, Steven. "McKinney's Gambit: Will Proportional Representation Bring Down the House?" *The Humanist,* January-February 1996, p. 5.

Karlan, Pamela S., and Thomas C. Goldstein. "Court Still Ambivalent on Redistricting." *The National Law Journal,* July 24, 1995, p. A19.

Macchiarola, Frank J. "The Paradox of Representations: Racial Gerrymandering and Minority Interests in Congress." *Political Science Quarterly,* fall 1998, p. 533.

Parker, Frank R. "The Damaging Consequences of the Rehnquist Court's Commitment to Color-Blindness Versus Racial Justice." *American University Law Review,* February 1996.

Reuben, Richard C. "Heading Back to the Thicket: Voting District Cases Pose Politically and Racially Charged Questions." *ABA Journal,* January 1996, p. 40.

"Supreme Court Overturns Racially Based Congressional District." *Facts on File,* July 6, 1995, p. 479.

Swain, Carol M. "Limiting Racial Gerrymandering: The Future of Black Representation." *Current,* January 1996, p. 3.

Tabin, Barrie. "Supreme Court Says Race-Based Electoral Districts Violate Constitution." *Nation's Cities Weekly,* July 24, 1995, p. 12.

SHAW V. HUNT

Legal Citation: 517 U.S. 899 (1996)

Petitioner
Ruth O. Shaw, et al.; James Arthur Pope, et al.

Respondent
James B. Hunt, Jr., Governor of North Carolina, et al.

Petitioner's Claim
That the state of North Carolina created an unconstitutional racially gerrymandered district, which may violate the Fourteenth Amendment's Equal Protection Clause.

Chief Lawyer for Petitioner
Robinson O. Everett (Shaw), Thomas A. Farr (Pope)

Chief Lawyer for Respondent
Edwin M. Speas, Jr.

Justices for the Court
Anthony M. Kennedy, Sandra Day O'Connor, William H. Rehnquist (writing for the Court), Antonin Scalia, Clarence Thomas

Justices Dissenting
Stephen Breyer, Ruth Bader Ginsburg, David H. Souter, John Paul Stevens

Place
Washington, D.C.

Date of Decision
13 June 1996

Decision
The district court decision was reversed.

Significance
The case of *Shaw v. Hunt* raised many important issues regarding to what extent it is permissible for a state to use racial classifications as the primary consideration when drawing majority-minority voter districts. The ramifications of the Voting Rights Act, Sections 2 and 5, and the Fourteenth Amendment's Equal Protection Clause were carefully considered with respect to the alleged racial gerrymandering discussed in this case.

Case Background

In the fall of 1991, the North Carolina state legislature proposed a redistricting plan which contained only one black majority district. The plan was rejected, and a revised plan with a second majority-minority district was then pre-cleared by the attorney general. Five residents of North Carolina filed suit in district court. They claimed that, "The revised plan created a racial gerrymander in violation of the Equal Protection Clause of the Constitution's Fourteenth Amendment." The case was dismissed by the district court for "failing to state a constitutional claim." An appeal was then made to the U.S. Supreme Court (*Shaw v. Reno*), in which the district court's decision was reversed, as the Court found that the residents had a claim under the Fourteenth Amendment's Equal Protection Clause. The case was remanded back to the district court to see if there were governmental reasons for the odd shape and size of the new district. The district court then found that the plan was constitutional and "did not violate the voters' equal protection rights, as the plan was narrowly tailored to further the state's compelling interests." Once again, an appeal was made by the five residents to the U.S. Supreme Court, in a suit brought against James B. Hunt, Jr., then governor of North Carolina (*Shaw v. Hunt*).

Question of Racial Gerrymandering or Minority Voter Representation

The case of *Shaw v. Hunt* boiled down to the difficult question of how a state may make sure that voter districts represent minority populations without infringing on the rights of the rest of the voters. Redistricting plans should draw districts to follow principles of compactness, contiguousness, and community of interest. The plan in this case, as argued by Robinson O. Everett for Shaw, seemed to "carry a message" that the second majority-minority district was created by using racial classifications—this being the only logical reason to explain the odd shape of that district. Everett also argued that the district in question was not an example of either narrow or broad tailoring, but rather "no tailoring," and proposed that there was a possible violation of the Equal Protection Clause due to the apparent use of racial classifications in drawing the district. The counsel arguing for the respondents maintained that minorities must be given the opportunity to elect and be represented fairly, and that the district court was correct in deciding that the plan was constitutional.

The U.S. Supreme Court, in a 5-4 decision, held that the plan was in violation of the Equal Protection Clause, reversing the district court's decision. The majority opinion of the Court was written by Chief Justice Rehnquist, who was joined by Kennedy, O'Connor, Scalia, and Thomas. First, the issue of "standing" was addressed. To be able to raise the suit, the petitioners needed to either reside in the district in which racial gerrymandering allegedly occurred, or show that they were assigned to their district according to their race. The Court found that only two of the five residents had "standing," Ruth O. Shaw and Melvin Schimm. Because of the unusual shape of the district in question, and the Court's opinion concerning any of three different compelling interests, it was found that the plan did not "survive strict scrutiny" and was not "narrowly tailored" to serve a "compelling state interest." Thus, the Court determined that the plan was in violation of the Equal Protection Clause of the Fourteenth Amendment.

A Different Opinion

A dissenting opinion was written by Stevens, who was joined by Ginsburg and Breyer on the second and third points. In it, he opined that 1) no person showed that they had been harmed more than another because of their race; 2) that strict scrutiny should only be applied when a state does not adhere to traditional districting principles; and 3) that the evidence showed other political reasons that caused the district's unusual shape. Justice Souter had already expressed his views in *Bush v. Vera*, where he addressed "a basic misconception about the relation between race and districting principles".

Impact

The cases of *Shaw v. Reno* and *Shaw v. Hunt* explore areas central to the constitutional issues of civil rights, voting rights, racial discrimination, and voter representation. While race can be a consideration when drawing voter districts, racial classifications may not be the dominant factor, unless a state can prove other compelling reasons that will withstand strict scrutiny. It is certain that these cases will be noted in many future proceedings, as civil rights issues continue to be debated and contested in the courts.

Related Cases

Brown v. Board of Education, 347 U.S. 483 (1954).
Gomillion v. Lightfoot, 364 U.S. 339 (1960).
Baker v. Carr, 369 U.S. 186 (1962).
Reynolds v. Sims, 377 U.S. 533 (1964).
University of California v. Bakke, 438 U.S. 265 (1978).
Allen v. Wright, 468 U.S. 737 (1984).
Batson v. Kentucky, 476 U.S. 79 (1986).
Davis v. Bandemer, 478 U.S. 109 (1986).
Richmond v. J. A. Croson Co., 488 U.S. 469 (1989).
Shaw v. Reno, 509 U.S. 630 (1993).
Miller v. Johnson, 515 U.S. 900 (1995).
Bush v. Vera, 517 U.S. 952 (1996).

Bibliography and Further Reading

Biskupic, Joan, and Elder Witt, eds. *Congressional Quarterly's Guide to the U.S. Supreme Court*, 3rd ed. Washington, DC: Congressional Quarterly, Inc., 1996.

O'Rourke, Timothy G. "Shaw v. Reno and the Hunt for Double Cross-Overs." *PS: Political Science & Politics*, March 1995, p. 36.

Reuben, Richard C. "Heading Back to the Thicket: Voting District Cases Pose Politically and Racially Charged Questions." *ABA Journal*, January 1996, p. 40.

WISCONSIN V. CITY OF NEW YORK

Legal Citation: 517 U.S. 1 (1996)

Petitioner
State of Wisconsin

Respondent
City of New York, et al.

Petitioner's Claim
That the refusal of the U.S. Secretary of Commerce to use a post-enumeration survey statistical adjustment to correct the 1990 census represented a violation of the Census Clause of the Constitution.

Chief Lawyer for Petitioner
Peter C. Anderson, Assistant Attorney General of Wisconsin

Chief Lawyer for Respondent
Drew S. Days, III, U.S. Solicitor General

Justices for the Court
Stephen Breyer, Ruth Bader Ginsburg, Anthony M. Kennedy, Sandra Day O'Connor, William H. Rehnquist (writing for the Court), Antonin Scalia, David H. Souter, John Paul Stevens, Clarence Thomas

Justices Dissenting
None

Place
Washington, D.C.

Date of Decision
10 January 1996

Decision
Upheld the actions of the secretary of commerce, affirmed the holding of the district court and reversed the decision of the court of appeals. Because Congress delegated authority for carrying out the census to the secretary, and since the Constitution mandates only that a census be taken every ten years to ensure that congressional representation reflects the actual population of the states, the accuracy and method of the census is less important than the fact that the same methods are applied nationwide.

Significance
The ruling upheld the historic procedures used in taking the census, and strongly implied that the application of new methods would invite detrimental political gerrymandering of census results, even if these results might be more accurate. The Court also reaffirmed the authority of the Secretary of Commerce to decide the manner in which the census is taken.

An Early Constitutional Compromise

When the United States obtained its independence, debate raged regarding the exact form its government would take. That some form of representative democracy would be established was certain, but within that context there was disagreement between large and small states. Eventually a compromise was reached whereby the new government would comprise two legislative bodies: a Senate in which each state would be represented by two individuals; and a House of Representatives in which each state would be represented by a variable number of individuals based on population. In this way less populous states would be insured of wielding equal federal influence within the Senate, while more populous states would receive representation commensurate with their size in the House of Representatives. In order to ensure that this system would operate fairly and be able to adjust as the nation grew, the Constitution also provided that the federal government would undertake a census every ten years for the purpose of reapportioning seats in the House of Representatives among the states.

Census Procedures and Statistical and Demographic Advances

The manner in which the census is taken has changed relatively little, despite advances in the sciences of statistics and demographics. Various technologies have been employed to speed the gathering and analysis of census data, but the system still relies on voluntary information and, in some cases, door-to-door canvassing by state authorities. Beginning with the 1970 census, demographic and statistical experts and federal census officials agreed that the traditional method of taking the census resulted in a population count that was too low. Many people either mistrusted census authorities or could see no reason to participate in the census, resulting in low counts for such populations.

Many suggestions were made to address this chronic undercount and make the census more accurate. One of the foremost among these was known as dual system estimation (DSE), a method of census taking which combined sampling, estimation, and traditional census taking techniques to arrive at a more accurate result than traditional methods alone. To illustrate the methods a DSE census would employ, the Court made use of the following analogy:

> Imagine that one wanted to use DSE in order to determine the number of pumpkins in a large pumpkin patch. First, one would choose a particular section of the patch as the representative subset to which the 'recapture' phase will be applied. Let us assume here that it is a section exactly one-tenth the size of the entire patch that is selected. Then, at the next step—the 'capture' stage—one would conduct a fairly quick count of the entire patch, making sure to record both the number of pumpkins counted in the entire patch and the number of pumpkins counted in the entire section. Let us imagine that this stage results in a count of 10,000 pumpkins for the entire patch and 1,000 pumpkins for the selected section. Next, at the 'recapture' stage, one would perform an exacting count of the number of pumpkins in the selected section. Let us assume that we now count 1,100 pumpkins in this section. By comparing results of the 'capture' phase and the results of the 'recapture' phase for the selected section, it is possible to estimate that approximately 100 pumpkins actually in the patch were missed for every 1,000 counted at the 'capture' phase. Extrapolating this data to the count for the entire patch, one would conclude that the actual number of pumpkins in the patch is 11,000.

It was widely believed that the use of a DSE count would greatly improve the accuracy of the census.

The 1990 Census

Throughout the mid-1980s the Bureau of the Census conducted tests to determine the accuracy of post-enumeration surveys and DSE procedures. By 1987 the bureau had reached the conclusion that these new methods would improve the accuracy of the census, and recommended that they be employed for the 1990 census. Despite this recommendation the Secretary of Commerce announced in October of 1987 that post-enumeration surveying and DSE procedures would not be used in the upcoming census. The secretary believed that the statistical models to be applied in a DSE census would be subject to manipulation for political gain. In response to this decision several states, including Wisconsin, brought suit in district court to force the secretary to employ post-enumeration surveys to DSE procedures correct and adjust the results of the 1990 census. The suit was put on hold, however, when the secretary agreed to reconsider his decision. In July of 1991 the secretary decided to abide by his original decision, and the district court once again considered Wisconsin's case.

How Accurate Must a Census Be?

Wisconsin's argument before the district court was that, by not making the census as accurate as possible, the secretary of commerce was denying political expression to those individuals not counted. In the state's view, knowing that an undercount existed and doing nothing to correct it constituted a violation of the principle of "one person, one vote" that serves as the foundation of our political system. As such, the state moved to force the secretary to apply post-enumeration surveys and DSE procedures to adjust the most recent census figures. The district court was not swayed by this argument, however, and ruled that the secretary's conduct of the census was constitutionally appropriate. The case then proceeded to the U.S. Court of Appeals of the Second Circuit. The court of appeals reversed the district court's decision, ruling that the actions of the secretary must come under heightened constitutional scrutiny given the central nature of the concept of one vote per individual to our polity. The U.S. Supreme Court agreed to hear the case on *certiorari* after a dissenting court of appeals judge noted that his court's decision contradicted those made in several similar cases.

Distributive Accuracy Versus Actual Accuracy

The Supreme Court unanimously reversed the decision of the court of appeals. Once again, the need for accuracy in the taking of the census was crucial to the decision. Whereas the court of appeals ruled that a deliberate undercount effectively deprived individuals of their right to vote, the Supreme Court held that the census was distinct from the electoral process. Writing for the Court, Justice Rehnquist noted that the Constitution mandates that a census be taken every ten years, and that it be conducted by Congress "in such Manner as they shall by Law direct." Furthermore, the Court believed that the constitutional intent of the census was to insure the "distributive accuracy" of population counts among the states to determine their relative representation in Congress, as opposed to actual accuracy of population counts within each state. Since the same method was applied to each state, the known undercount would be nearly the same for each state and the distributive accuracy of the census would remain the same regardless of the method used. As such, the secretary's decision not to use post-enumeration surveys and DSE procedures was judged to be reasonable and to adhere to constitutional standards.

Impact

Wisconsin v. City of New York confirmed the power of the Secretary of Commerce to determine the method of census taking. Also, by confirming the precedence of "distributive accuracy" over actual accuracy in the census, the Court implied that future secretaries of commerce would also be able to reject still more accurate statistical and demographic methods of census-taking.

Related Cases

Wesberry v. Sanders, 376 U.S. 1 (1964).
Gaffney v. Cummings, 412 U.S. 735 (1973).
Department of Commerce v. Montana, 503 U.S. 442 (1992).
Franklin v. Massachusetts, 505 U.S. 788 (1992).

Bibliography and Further Reading

"Administration Asks Supreme Court to Rule Against Census Adjustment." *American Marketplace,* August 10, 1995.

Anderson, Margo, and Stephen E. Fienberg. "Who Counts? The Politics of Censustaking." *Society,* March-April 1997, p. 19.

Minnesota State Senate: 1990s Supreme Court Redistricting Decisions. http://www.senate.leg.state.mn.us/senoffic/redist/red90 7.html

Morrison, Joanne. "Census Plan for 2000 Offsets High Court Ruling, Analyst Says." *The Bond Buyer,* March 22, 1996, p. 5.

BUSH V. VERA

Legal Citation: 517 U.S. 952 (1996)

Appellants
George W. Bush, Governor of Texas, et al.

Appellees
Al Vera, et al.

Appellants' Claim
The Texas state legislature created three new congressional districts with African American and Hispanic majorities to better reflect 1990 census demographics. Appellants claimed that these districts were narrowly tailored to satisfy the strict scrutiny requirement in the Equal Protection Clause of the Fourteenth Amendment.

Chief Lawyers for Appellants
Javier Aguilar (lawyer for state appellants), Paul Bender (lawyer for federal appellant), and Penda D. Hair (lawyer for private appellants)

Chief Lawyers for Appellees
Daniel E. Troy

Justices for the Court
Anthony M. Kennedy, Sandra Day O'Connor (writing for the Court), William H. Rehnquist, Antonin Scalia, Clarence Thomas

Justices Dissenting
Stephen Breyer, Ruth Bader Ginsburg, David H. Souter, John Paul Stevens

Place
Washington, D.C.

Date of Decision
13 June 1996

Decision
Although three congressional districts were not sufficiently tailored to protect minority rights, they were, nonetheless unconstitutionally created because racial factors predominated in their creation.

Significance
The Voting Rights Act seeking protection of the electoral minority seemed at odds with the Equal Protection Clause because, in seeking to protect minority rights and preserve majority privilege, each statute was oppositionally focused. After *Shaw v. Reno* (1993), the Supreme Court's strict (districting) scrutiny analysis applied to newly created districts. However, states experienced great difficulty creating new districts to comply with the Voting Rights Act while simultaneously satisfying the Equal Protection Clause. To add to the confusion, districts created to protect minorities' electoral rights in the state of Texas (supported by the Department of Justice and various civil organizations), were declared unconstitutionally formed by the Supreme Court.

The 1990 census prompted states to reconfigure voting districts to enable minorities to elect their own representatives to Congress. New districts often relied heavily on racial considerations while simultaneously applying traditional districting principles. The excessive use of the racial factor in creating new "minority districts" (a majority of voters of one ethnicity) led to challenges in district courts and the U.S. Supreme Court for alleged violations of the Equal Protection Clause.

Shaw v. Reno (1993) and *Miller v. Johnson* (1995) were milestones in the U.S. Supreme Court's view of the constitutionality of redistricting. In these two cases, the Court abandoned the pre-1990 census practice of assessing the constitutionality of redistricting under the Equal Protection Clause, which defined identifiable harm as infringement of rights of an individual voter (who was a member of a class subjected to differential treatment by redistricting changes). This practice held that there were tangible, unconstitutional consequences of racial considerations in redistricting. *Shaw* and *Miller* thus established the Court's principal of "reasonable" use of racial factors in redistricting by identifying putative harm as nonracial traditional districting principles subordinated by racial considerations. Because all new "majority-minority" districts were thus struck down, the Court's rulings provoked controversy concerning the dilution of the previous standard and the protection of a minority's right to have congressional representatives. Yet, the Supreme Court affirmed this practice in *Bush v. Vera*.

Three Districts Challenged

In reaction to the 1990 census, the Texas state legislature made plans for redistricting in order to remedy past and present racial discrimination and to comply with two clauses of the Voting Rights Act. The first clause prohibited denial or abridgement of the right of any citizen to vote because of race or color and prohibited obstruction of a minority's ability to elect representatives of their choice. The second clause sought to prevent suppression of racial minorities with respect to exercise of the electoral franchise. Thus, the state legislature made plans for redistricting and created three new districts. Voting majorities in two new districts

George Bush, Governor of Texas, 1995. © AP/Wide World Photos.

were African American; another district was largely Hispanic. Following redistricting, six Texas voters challenged the districts as racial gerrymanders in violation of the Equal Protection Clause (a gerrymander is an election district resulting from arranging political divisions of a city, state, county, etc. to give one political party an advantage in elections).

The case first came before the District Court for the Southern District of Texas. Six voters, as plaintiffs, claimed they were personally subjected to racial classification by the state's redistricting and consequently denied equal protection of law. Defendant George Bush, governor of Texas (joined by private intervenors and the Department of Justice), claimed that Texas was guided by a lawful concern to remedy a long history of racial discrimination and to avoid liability under the Voting Rights Act. He admitted that the state inten-

tionally created "majority-minority" districts, but that the state legislation adhered to traditional districting principles (such as incumbency protection and conformity to political subdivisions) and race did not override those principles. Bush claimed that, according to the Voting Rights Act, the protection of the electoral minority was a compelling state interest and therefore did not violate the Equal Protection Clause. (This clause prohibits varying treatment of citizens, unless the difference in treatment is related to a legitimate state interest).

The three-judge district court first established in *Miller v. Johnson* that strict judicial scrutiny applied to the case because districting principles were "subordinated to race." Here, the Court held, the bizarre shapes of several districts showed that race did override other factors. Because strict scrutiny was satisfied if state actions were narrowly tailored to a compelling state interest, the Court looked at evidence (computer programs used for redistricting plans that contained mostly racial data) and found that "minority numbers were virtually all that mattered in the shape of those districts." Since that was not "narrow tailoring," the Court concluded that the three districts were racially gerrymandered and held them unconstitutional.

A Difficult Decision

The Supreme Court's task was difficult and complicated because two majority justices filed an opinion concurring with the opinion of three other justices. (Dissenting justices were the same ones who dissented in the Court's decisions in *Shaw v. Reno* and *Miller v. Johnson*.) The decision of the district court was upheld.

Justice O'Connor, joined by Chief Justice Rehnquist and Justice Kennedy, wrote for the majority. The Court first found one of the six plaintiffs lacked standing because he did not reside in any of the challenged districts. They then examined the principle of strict judicial scrutiny in this case. According to *Miller,* strict scrutiny applied where race was "the predominant factor" motivating the drawing of district lines and where traditional, race-neutral districting principles were subordinated to race. Since this was a mixed motive case (factors other than race, particularly incumbency protection, did influence the legislature), O'Connor wrote that each of the challenged districts had to be examined.

O'Connor first looked at District 30, which had an African American majority, and found that it was subject to strict scrutiny. The district's bizarre and non-compact shape supported the claim that computer data used in redistricting plans contained significantly more information on racial factors than on other, nonracial considerations. One of the nonracial considerations, incumbency protection, was clearly used, but race was also used as a proxy for political considerations (the legislature used racial stereotypes when concluding that all African Americans had voted and would vote for the Democratic Party).

Interlocking Districts 18, which held an African American majority, and 29, with its Hispanic American majority, were also subject to strict scrutiny. Their bizarre shape and utter disregard of city limits, local election precincts, and voter tabulation district lines revealed that the legislature again chiefly used racial factors. Though Bush and other appellants stated that incumbency protection played a role in determining the bizarre district lines, the districts' shapes were unexplainable on grounds other than race. Thus, strict scrutiny applied to all three districts and so the Court had to consider if racial considerations embodied in defining the three districts were narrowly tailored to further a compelling state interest.

The attorney for the appellants suggested the state had three compelling interests: to avoid state liability under section 2 of the Voting Rights Act, to remedy past and present racial discrimination, and to comply with the "nonretrogression" principle of the Voting Rights Act.

Section 2 of the Voting Rights Act prohibits denial or abridgement of the right of any citizen to vote because of race or color and prohibits obstruction of a minority's ability to elect representatives of their choice. The Court noted that compliance to this section could be a compelling state interest, but a district drawn in order to satisfy it must not subordinate traditional districting principles more than was reasonably necessary. Looking at the districts' bizarre shapes, the Court found that the state legislature overemphasized race to the exclusion of other principles. Rejection of this argument also suggested the appellants' second argument was spurious (that districts remedied Texas's long history of discrimination against minorities).

The justices also rejected the argument that only the creation of District 18 was justified by a compelling state interest in complying with the "nonretrogression" principle (section 5) of the Voting Rights Act. (This principle seeks to prevent suppression of racial minorities with respect to exercise of the electoral franchise.) The Court reasoned that the state action here did not prevent suppression of the minority's electoral rights but, on the contrary, substantially augmented the African American population percentage. Therefore, this district was not narrowly tailored to the avoidance of section 5 liability. The Court concluded that the three districts violated the Equal Protection Clause because they were not narrowly tailored to address the state's purported interest in protecting minority rights.

In a separate concurring opinion, Justice O'Connor emphasized that states had a compelling interest in avoiding liability under section 2 of the Voting Rights Act, and that states and courts were capable of distin-guishing the appropriate and reasonably necessary uses of race from unjustified and excessive ones. Justice Kennedy also filed a concurring opinion, but reasoned if a state, in redistricting, foreordained that one race be the majority in a district, that did not necessarily mean that race was predominant.

Justice Thomas, joined by Justice Scalia, wrote an opinion concurring with the majority, arguing that strict scrutiny should always apply to intentional creation of a majority-minority district. In this case, strict scrutiny was already invoked because Texas admitted intentionally creating them. Furthermore, since racial considerations were predominant, the state's redistricting plans were not narrowly tailored to achieve asserted compelling state interests.

Two dissenting opinions were also filed. In the first Justice Stevens, joined by Justices Ginsburg and Breyer, reasoned that strict scrutiny should not apply because racial considerations were not predominant over other districting factors (especially incumbent protection). Even under strict scrutiny, the decision of the district court should not be affirmed: race was considered in creating the three districts only to the extent necessary to comply with the state's responsibilities under the clauses of the Voting Rights Act while simultaneously achieving other nonracial political and geographical requirements. The dissenting justices also expressed concern about the Court's doctrine adopted in *Shaw v. Reno* because it lacked a definable constitutional core and could create significant harm to gerrymandering jurisprudence.

The second dissenting opinion, written by Justice Souter (joined by Ginsburg and Breyer) also maintained the *Shaw* doctrine had no satisfyingly defining principles and concluded that problems of *Shaw v. Reno* were caused by the Court's failure to provide a manageable standard to distinguish forbidden districting conduct from the application of traditional state districting principles.

Impact

Like the previous *Shaw* and *Miller* decisions, the ruling in *Bush v. Vera* was vigorously attacked. It divided the Supreme Court justices and was criticized by the four of them. Dissenters were joined by various civil rights organizations such as the American Civil Liberties Union. One of its directors, Laughlin McDonald, predicted that "the inevitable consequence of the Court's action will produce a Congress that is increasingly white at the time that the nation is becoming increasingly diverse." He said that the decision invited even more reverse discrimination claims by making it easier to trigger judicial strict scrutiny and harder to satisfy it. McDonald concluded that the strict scrutiny test was originally developed to deal with invidious racial discrimination. But after *Shaw* and *Bush*, the test was applied to legislative efforts to remedy that discrimination.

Nonetheless, the Court persisted in its course. Although the Department of Justice supported Texas, the Court continued striking down majority-minority districts created to protect the electoral rights of minorities. The Supreme Court found that race again predominated in their creation and other districting principles were neglected. The Court held that more "narrow tailoring" (better balance between racial and other considerations) could satisfy both the Voting Rights Act and the Equal Protection Clause.

Related Cases
Gomillion v. Lightfoot, 364 U.S. 339 (1960).
Davis v. Bandemer, 478 U.S. 109 (1986).
Shaw v. Reno, 509 U.S. 630 (1993).
Miller v. Johnson, 515 U.S. 900 (1995).
Shaw v. Hunt, 517 U.S. 899 (1996).

Bibliography and Further Reading
"ACLU Criticizes Supreme Court's Continued Assault on Voting Rights Act." http://www.aclu.org/library/96review.html

Cameron, Charles, David Epstein, and Sharyn O'Halloran. "Do Majority-Minority Districts Maximize Substantive Black Representation in Congress?" *American Political Science Review,* December 1996, p. 794.

Chemerinsky, Erwin. "Minority Voting Rights and the Supreme Court." *Trial,* November 1996, p. 18.

Reuben, Richard C. "Heading Back to the Thicket: Voting District Cases Pose Politically and Racially Charges Questions." *ABA Journal,* January 1996, p. 40.

Sleeper, Jim. "The Rainbow Coalition: Nov 5 and the Good News About Race." *The New Republic,* December 2, 1996, p. 24.

ABRAMS V. JOHNSON

Legal Citation: 521 U.S. 74 (1997)

Appellant
Lucious Abrams

Appellee
Davida Johnson

Appellant's Claim
That the plan adopted by the district court redrawing Georgia's legislative districts violated the Voting Rights Act of 1965 and the principle of one-person, one-vote.

Chief Lawyers for Appellant
Seth P. Waxman and Laughlin McDonald

Chief Lawyers for Appellee
Michael J. Bowers and A. Lee Parks

Justices for the Court
Anthony M. Kennedy, Sandra Day O'Connor, William H. Rehnquist, Antonin Scalia, Clarence Thomas

Justices Dissenting
Stephen Breyer, Ruth Bader Ginsburg, David H. Souter, John Paul Stevens

Place
Washington, D.C.

Date of Decision
19 June 1997

Decision
That the redistricting plan adopted by the district court did not violate the Voting Rights Act or the Constitution.

Significance
In upholding the district court's plan, the Court emphasized its previous decisions which stated that race may not be taken into account by a state legislature or court in creating election districts, even where race is used to promote minority representation.

Article I, section 3 of the Constitution requires that the number of U.S. Representatives for each state be apportioned—that is, distributed—based on each state's population, which is determined by a census taken every 10 years. Under this provision, if a state gains sufficient population over the ten year period between one census and the next, it may gain an additional congressperson in the House of Representatives. Conversely, because the total number of Representatives is fixed at 435, if a state loses population it will also lose one or more congresspersons. Under this system, each congressperson is elected from a district within the state he or she represents. Thus, if a state has ten congressional seats, it will have ten congressional districts. However, if a state gains or loses a congressional seat, the state must redraw its congressional districts to reflect the change, a process known as "redistricting" or "reapportionment."

The 1990 Census and Georgia's Restricting Plan

The census performed in 1990 revealed that Georgia's population had increased significantly, and that Georgia was entitled to 11, instead of 10, congressional seats. Under the Voting Rights Act of 1965, it was the responsibility of the Georgia state legislature to reapportion its congressional seats. However, the legislature was required to have its plan approved by either the U.S. Department of Justice, or by a federal district court. In order to secure the approval of the Department of Justice, the Georgia legislature eventually adopted a plan which contained three districts known as "majority-minority" districts. "Majority-minority" districts are districts in which a majority of the registered voters are members of racial minorities. These districts are designed to make it easier for minority candidates to get elected, and thus increase minority representation in Congress.

In this case, the legislature's plan created three (out of 11) districts in which a majority of the registered voters were African American. However, one such district was oddly shaped, being very long and narrow, connecting distant cities to achieve a majority of African Americans. In the 1995 case *Miller v. Johnson,* the

Supreme Court found that this redistricting plan was unconstitutional because race was a predominate factor in the designing of the Georgia legislature's plan. The Court found that race was a predominate factor based on the bizarre shape of the districts and other evidence of the Georgia legislature's intention to create three majority-minority districts. The Court concluded that race may not be used as a basis for redrawing congressional districts, even if it is used for the beneficial purpose of increasing minority representation. Following the Court's decision in the *Miller* case, the Georgia legislature was unable to agree on another plan. Accordingly, under the Voting Rights Act, a three-judge panel of the U.S. District Court for the Southern District of Georgia devised its own plan. This plan included only one majority-minority district.

Court Upholds Plan

The U.S. Department of Justice and various African American voters appealed the district court's plan to the Supreme Court. They argued that the district court should have adopted one of several plans submitted to the district court which would have had two majority-minority districts. Among other claims, they argued that the plan adopted by the district court violated section 2 Voting Rights Act and the principle of "one man, one vote." In a 5-4 decision, the Supreme Court disagreed, and upheld the district court's plan.

The Supreme Court first rejected the argument that the plan diluted the votes of African Americans in violation of section 2 of the Voting Rights Act. Section 2 requires that a political process, in this case the apportionment of Georgia's congressional districts, allows racial minorities an equal opportunity "to participate in the political process and to elect representatives of their choice." In the case *Thornburg v. Gingles,* the Supreme Court held that a violation of section 2 occurs only where the minority group is large enough to constitute a majority in a specific geographic area, the members of the group vote similarly, and the majority group votes with enough similarity to defeat the minority group's preferred candidate. In *Abrams,* the Court found that this test was not met because statistical data showed that there was large cross-over voting—that is, a significant percentage of whites voted for African American candidates and a significant percentage of African Americans voted for white candidates.

The Court also concluded that the district court's plan did not violate the principle of "one man, one vote" embodied in Article I, section 2 of the Constitution. This principle requires that, as near as possible, legislative districts have the same number of people. Relying on statistical data, the Court concluded that the population differences between the districts were extremely small, and thus were acceptable. In fact, the Court noted, the differences in the plan adopted by the district court were smaller than any of the differences between districts involved in any of the alternative plans proposed to the district court.

Four justices dissented from the Court's decision, concluding that the district court should have adopted one of the plans which provided for two majority-minority districts. Justices Breyer, Stevens, Souter, and Ginsburg argued that it would not have been impracticable to create a second majority-minority district in a constitutional way. More importantly, however, the dissenters disagreed with the test employed by the majority. Justice Breyer, writing for the dissenters, concluded that the majority, "by focusing upon what it considered to be an unreasonably pervasive positive use of race as a redistricting factor, . . . created a legal doctrine that will unreasonably restrict legislators' use of race, even for the most benign, or antidiscriminatory purposes." However, despite the dissenters' position, the Court's decision makes clear that any use of race as a factor in redistricting, even a positive use, will not withstand constitutional scrutiny.

Related Cases

Thornburg v. Gingles, 478 U.S. 30 (1986).
Miller v. Johnson, 115 S. Ct. 2475 (1995).

Bibliography and Further Reading

Dixon, Robert G., Jr. *Democratic Representation: Reapportionment in Law and Politics.* New York: Oxford University Press, 1968.

Grofman, Bernard, ed. *Political Gerrymandering and the Courts.* New York: Agathon Press, 1990.

Grofman, Bernard, Lisa Handley, and Richard G. Niemi. *Minority Representation and the Quest for Voting Equality.* New York: Cambridge University Press, 1992.

McKay, Robert B. *Reapportionment: The Law and Politics of Equal Representation.* New York: Twentieth Century Fund, 1965.

GLOSSARY

A

Abandonment The surrender, relinquishment, disclaimer, or cession of property or of rights. Voluntary relinquishment of all right, title, claim, and possession, with no intention of reclamation.

The giving up of a thing absolutely, without reference to any particular person or purpose, such as vacating property with no intention of returning it, so that it may be appropriated by the next comer or finder. The voluntary relinquishment of possession of a thing by the owner with intention of terminating ownership, but without vesting it in any other person. The relinquishing of all title, possession, or claim, or a virtual, intentional throwing away of property.

Accessory Aiding or contributing in a secondary way or assisting in or contributing to as a subordinate.

In criminal law, contributing to or aiding in the commission of a crime. One who, without being present at the commission of an offense, becomes guilty of such offense, not as a chief actor, but as a participant, as by command, advice, instigation, or concealment; either before or after the fact of commission.

One who aids, abets, commands, or counsels another in the commission of a crime.

Accessory after the fact One who commits a crime by giving comfort or assistance to a felon, knowing that the felon has committed a crime, or is sought by authorities in connection with a serious crime.

Accomplice One who knowingly, voluntarily, and with common intent unites with the principal offender in the commission of a crime. One who is in some way involved with commission of a crime; partaker of guilt; one who aids or assists, or is an accessory. One who is guilty of complicity in a crime charged, either by being present and aiding or abetting in it, or having advised and encouraged it, though absent from place when it was committed. However, the mere presence, acquiescence, or silence, in the absence of a duty to act, is not enough, no matter how reprehensible it may be, to constitute one an accomplice. One is liable as an accomplice to the crime of another if he or she gave assistance or encouragement or failed to perform a legal duty to prevent it with the intent thereby to promote or facilitate commission of the crime.

Accord An agreement that settles a dispute, generally requiring a compromise or satisfaction with something less than what was originally demanded.

Acquittal The legal and formal certification of the innocence of a person who has been charged with a crime.

Action Conduct; behavior; something done; a series of acts.

A case or a lawsuit; a legal and formal demand for the enforcement of one's rights against another party asserted in a court of justice.

Actual authority The legal power, expressed or implied, that an agent possesses to represent and to bind into agreement the principal with a third party.

Actual damages Compensation awarded for the loss or the injury suffered by an individual.

Adjudication The legal process of resolving a dispute. The formal giving or pronouncing of a judgment or decree in a court proceeding; also the judgment or decision given. The entry of a decree by a court in respect to the parties in a case. It implies a hearing by a court, after notice, of legal evidence on the factual issue(s) involved. The equivalent of a determination. It indicates that the claims of all of the parties thereto have been considered and set at rest.

Administrative agency An official governmental body empowered with the authority to direct and supervise the implementation of particular legislative acts. In addition to *agency*, such governmental bodies may be called commissions, corporations (i.e., FDIC), boards, departments, or divisions.

Administrative law The body of law that allows for the creation of public regulatory agencies and contains all of the statutes, judicial decisions, and regulations that govern them. It is the body of law created by administrative agencies to implement their powers and duties in the form of rules, regulations, orders, and decisions.

Administrator A person appointed by the court to manage and take charge of the assets and liabilities of a decedent who has died without making a valid will.

Admissible A term used to describe information that is relevant to a determination of issues in any judicial proceeding so that such information can be properly considered by a judge or jury in making a decision.

Adultery Voluntary sexual relations between an individual who is married and someone who is not the individual's spouse.

Adversary system The scheme of American jurisprudence wherein a judge renders a decision in a controversy between parties who assert contradictory positions during a judicial examination, such as a trial or hearing.

Affidavit A written statement of facts voluntarily made by an affiant under an oath or affirmation administered by a person who is authorized to do so by law.

Affirmative action Employment programs required by federal statutes and regulations designed to remedy discriminatory practices in hiring minority group members; i.e., positive steps designed to eliminate existing and continuing discrimination, to remedy lingering effects of past discrimination, and to create systems and procedures to prevent future discrimination; commonly based on population percentages of minority groups in a particular area. Factors considered are race, color, sex, creed, and age.

Agent One who agrees and is authorized to act on behalf of another, a principal, to legally bind an individual in particular business transactions with third parties pursuant to an agency relationship.

Age of consent The age at which a person may marry without parental approval. The age at which a female is legally capable of agreeing to sexual intercourse, so that a male who engages in sex with her cannot be prosecuted for statutory rape.

Age of majority The age at which a person, formerly a minor or an infant, is recognized by law to be an adult, capable of managing his or her own affairs and responsible for any legal obligations created by his or her actions.

Aggravated assault A person is guilty of aggravated assault if he or she attempts to cause serious bodily injury to another or causes such injury purposely, knowingly, or recklessly under circumstances manifesting extreme indifference to the value of human life; or attempts to cause or purposely or knowingly causes bodily injury to another with a deadly weapon. In all jurisdictions, statutes punish such aggravated assaults as assault with intent to murder (or rob or kill or rape) and assault with a dangerous (or deadly) weapon more severely than "simple" assaults.

Alien Foreign-born person who has not been naturalized to become a U.S. citizen under federal law and the Constitution.

Alimony Payment a family court may order one person in a couple to make to the other when the couple separates or divorces.

Alimony pendente lite Temporary alimony awarded while separation and divorce proceedings are taking place. The award may cover the preparation for the suit, as well as general support.

Alternative dispute resolution Procedures for settling disputes by means other than litigation; i.e., by arbitration, mediation, or minitrials. Such procedures, which are usually less costly and more expeditious than litigation, are increasingly being used in commercial and labor disputes, divorce actions, in resolving motor vehicle and medical malpractice tort claims, and in other disputes that otherwise would likely involve court litigation.

Amendment The modification of materials by the addition of supplemental information; the deletion of unnecessary, undesirable, or outdated information; or the correction of errors existing in the text.

Amicus curiae [*Latin, Friend of the court.*] A person with strong interest in or views on the subject matter of an action, but not a party to the action, may petition the court for permission to file a brief, ostensibly on behalf of a party but actually to suggest a rationale consistent with his or her own views. Such amicus curiae briefs are commonly filed in appeals concerning matters of a broad public interest; i.e., civil rights cases. They may be filed by private persons or by the government. In appeals to the U.S. courts of appeals, an amicus brief may be filed only if accompanied by written consent of all parties, or by leave of court granted on motion or at the request of the court, except that consent or leave shall not be required when the brief is presented by the United States or an officer or agency thereof.

Amnesty The action of a government by which all persons or certain groups of persons who have committed a criminal offense—usually of a political nature that threatens the sovereignty of the government (such as sedition or treason)—are granted immunity from prosecution.

Annulment A judgment by a court that retroactively invalidates a marriage to the date of its formation.

Answer The first responsive pleading filed by the defendant in a civil action; a formal written statement that admits or denies the allegations in the complaint and sets forth any available affirmative defenses.

Apparent authority The amount of legal power a principal knowingly or negligently bestows onto an agent for representation with a third party, and which the third party reasonably believes the agent possesses.

Appeal Timely resort by an unsuccessful party in a lawsuit or administrative proceeding to an appropriate superior court empowered to review a final decision on the ground that it was based upon an erroneous application of law.

Appeals court *See* Appellate court or Court of appeal.

Appellate court A court having jurisdiction to review decisions of a trial-level or other lower court.

Appellate jurisdiction The power of a superior court or other tribunal to review the judicial actions of lower courts, particularly for legal errors, and to revise their judgments accordingly.

Apportionment The process by which legislative seats are distributed among units entitled to representation. Determination of the number of representatives that a state, county, or other subdivision may send to a legislative body. The U.S. Constitution provides for a census every ten years, on the basis of which Congress apportions representatives according to population. However, each state must have at least one representative. *Districting* is the establishment of the precise geographical boundaries of each such unit or constituency. Apportionment by state statute that denies the rule of one-person, one-vote is violative of equal protection laws.

Arbitration The submission of a dispute to an unbiased third person designated by the parties to the controversy, who agree in advance to comply with the award—a decision to be issued after a hearing at which both parties have an opportunity to be heard.

Arraignment The formal proceeding whereby the defendant is brought before the trial court to hear the charges against him or her and to enter a plea of guilty, not guilty, or no contest.

Arrest The detention and taking into custody of an individual for the purpose of answering the charges against him or her. An arrest involves the legal power of the individual to arrest, the intent to exercise that power, and the actual subjection to the control and will of the arresting authority.

Arrest warrant A written order issued by an authority of the state and commanding the seizure of the person named.

Arson At common law, the malicious burning or exploding of the dwelling house of another, or the burning of a building within the curtilage, the immediate surrounding space, of the dwelling of another.

Assault At common law, an intentional act by one person that creates an apprehension in another of an imminent harmful or offensive contact.

Assumption of risk A defense, facts offered by a party against whom proceedings have been instituted to diminish a plaintiff's cause of action or defeat recovery to an action in negligence, which entails proving that the plaintiff knew of a dangerous condition and voluntarily exposed himself or herself to it.

Attachment The legal process of seizing property to ensure satisfaction of a judgment.

Attempt An undertaking to do an act that entails more than mere preparation but does not result in the successful completion of the act.

Attractive nuisance doctrine The duty of an individual to take necessary precautions around equipment or conditions on his or her property that could attract and potentially injury children unable to perceive the risk of danger, such as an unguarded swimming pool or a trampoline.

Avoidance An escape from the consequences of a specific course of action through the use of legally acceptable means. Cancellation; the act of rendering something useless or legally ineffective.

B

Bail The system that governs the status of individuals charged with committing crimes from the time of their arrest to the time of their trial, and pending appeal, with the major purpose of ensuring their presence at trial.

Bait and switch A deceptive sales technique that involves advertising a low-priced item to attract customers to a store, then persuading them to buy more expensive goods by failing to have a sufficient supply of the advertised item on hand or by disparaging its quality.

Balancing A process sometimes used by the Supreme Court in deciding between the competing interests represented in a case.

Bankruptcy A federally authorized procedure by which a debtor—an individual, corporation, or municipality—is relieved of total liability for its debts by making court-approved arrangements for their partial repayment.

Battery At common law, an intentional unpermitted act causing harmful or offensive contact with the person of another.

Beneficiary An organization or a person for whom a trust is created and who thereby receives the benefits of the trust. One who inherits under a will. A person entitled to a beneficial interest or a right to profits, benefit, or advantage from a contract.

Bigamy The offense of willfully and knowingly entering into a second marriage while validly married to another individual.

Bilateral contract An agreement formed by an exchange of promises in which the promise of one party supports the promise of the other party.

Bill A declaration in writing. A document listing separate items. An itemized account of charges or costs. In equity practice, the first pleading in the action, that is, the paper in which the plaintiff sets out his or her case and demands relief from the defendant.

Bill of attainder A special legislative enactment that imposes a death sentence without a judicial trial upon a particular person or class of persons suspected of committing serious offenses, such as treason or a felony.

Bill of rights The first ten amendments to the U.S. Constitution, ratified in 1791, which set forth and guarantee certain fundamental rights and privileges of individuals, including freedom of religion, speech, press, and assembly; guarantee of a speedy jury trial in criminal cases; and protection against excessive bail and cruel and unusual punishment.

A list of fundamental rights included in each state constitution.

A declaration of individual rights and freedoms, usually issued by a national government.

Bill of sale In the law of contracts, a written agreement, previously required to be under seal, by which one person transfers to another a right to, or interest in, personal property and goods, a legal instrument that conveys title in property from seller to purchaser.

Black codes Laws, statutes, or rules that governed slavery and segregation of public places in the South prior to 1865.

Bona fide [*Latin, In good faith.*] Honest; genuine; actual; authentic; acting without the intention of defrauding.

Bona fide occupational qualification An essential requirement for performing a given job. The requirement may even be a physical condition beyond an individual's control, such as perfect vision, if it is absolutely necessary for performing a job.

Bonds Written documents by which a government, corporation, or individual—the obligator—promises to perform a certain act, usually the payment of a definite sum of money, to another—the obligee—on a certain date.

Booking The procedure by which law enforcement officials record facts about the arrest of and charges against a suspect, such as the crime for which the arrest was made, together with information concerning the identification of the suspect and other pertinent facts.

Breach of contract The breaking of a legal agreement that had been sealed by the signing of a written, legal contractual document.

Bribery The offering, giving, receiving, or soliciting of something of value for the purpose of influencing the action of an official in the discharge of his or her public or legal duties.

Brief A summary of the important points of a longer document. An abstract of a published judicial opinion prepared by a law student as part of an assignment in the case method study of law. A written document drawn up by an attorney for a party in a lawsuit or by a party appearing pro se that concisely states the (1) issues of a lawsuit; (2) facts that bring the parties to court; (3) relevant laws that can affect the subject of the dispute; and (4) arguments that explain how the law applies to the particular facts so that the case will be decided in the party's favor.

Broker An individual or firm employed by others to plan and organize sales or negotiate contracts for a commission.

Burden of proof The duty of a party to prove an asserted fact. The party is subject to the burden of persuasion—convincing a judge or jury—and the burden of going forward—proving wrong any evidence that damages the position of the party. In criminal cases the persuasion burden must include proof beyond a reasonable doubt.

Burglary The criminal offense of breaking and entering a building illegally for the purpose of committing a crime therein.

Bylaws The rules and regulations enacted by an association or a corporation to provide a framework for its operation and management.

C

Capacity The ability, capability, or fitness to do something; a legal right, power, or competency to perform some act. An ability to comprehend both the nature and consequences of one's acts.

Capital punishment The lawful infliction of death as a punishment; the death penalty.

Case law Legal principles enunciated and embodied in judicial decisions that are derived from the application of particular areas of law to the facts of individual cases.

Cause Each separate antecedent of an event. Something that precedes and brings about an effect or a result. A reason for an action or condition. A ground of a legal action. An agent that brings something about. That which in some manner is accountable for a condition that brings about an effect or that produces a cause for the resultant action or state.

A suit, litigation, or action. Any question, civil or criminal, litigated or contested before a court of justice.

Cause in fact The direct cause of an event. Commonly referred to as the "but for" rule, by which an event could not have happened but for the specified cause.

Cause of action The fact or combination of facts that gives a person the right to seek judicial redress or relief against another. Also, the legal theory forming the basis of a lawsuit.

Caveat emptor [*Latin, Let the buyer beware.*] A warning that notifies a buyer that the goods he or she is buying are "as is," subject to all defects.

Cease and desist order An order issued by an administrative agency or a court proscribing a person or a business entity from continuing a particular course of conduct.

Censorship The suppression or proscription of speech or writing that is deemed obscene, indecent, or unduly controversial.

Certiorari [*Latin, To be informed of.*] At common law, an original writ or order issued by the Chancery or King's Bench, commanding officers of inferior courts to submit the record of a cause pending before them to give the party more certain and speedy justice.

A writ that a superior appellate court issues on its discretion to an inferior court, ordering it to produce a certified record of a particular case it has tried, in order to determine whether any irregularities or errors occurred that justify review of the case.

A device by which the Supreme Court of the United States exercises its discretion in selecting the cases it will review.

Challenge for cause Request from a party that a prospective juror be disqualified for given causes or reasons.

Change of venue The removal of a lawsuit from one county or district to another for trial, often permitted in criminal cases where the court finds that the defendant would not receive a fair trial in the first location because of adverse publicity.

Charter A grant from the government of ownership rights in land to a person, a group of people, or an organization, such as a corporation.

A basic document of law of a municipal corporation granted by the state, defining its rights, liabilities, and responsibilities of self-government.

A document embodying a grant of authority from the legislature or the authority itself, such as a corporate charter.

The leasing of a mode of transportation, such as a bus, ship, or plane. A *charter-party* is a contract formed to lease a ship to a merchant in order to facilitate the conveyance of goods.

Chattel An item of personal property that is movable; it may be animate or inanimate.

Circumstantial evidence Information and testimony presented by a party in a civil or criminal action that permit conclusions that indirectly establish the existence or nonexistence of a fact or event that the party seeks to prove.

Citation A paper commonly used in various courts—such as a probate, matrimonial, or traffic court—that is served upon an individual to notify him or her that he or she is required to appear at a specific time and place.

Reference to a legal authority—such as a case, constitution, or treatise—where particular information may be found.

Citizens Those who, under the Constitution and laws of the United States, or of a particular community or of a foreign country, owe allegiance and are entitled to the enjoyment of all civil rights that accrue to those who qualify for that status.

Civil action A lawsuit brought to enforce, redress, or protect rights of private litigants (the plaintiffs and the defendants); not a criminal proceeding.

Civil death The forfeiture of rights and privileges of an individual who has been convicted of a serious crime.

Civil law Legal system derived from the Roman *Corpus Juris Civilis* of Emperor Justinian I; differs from a common-law system, which relies on prior decisions to determine the outcome of a lawsuit. Most European and South American countries have a civil law system. England and most of the countries it dominated or colonized, including Canada and the United States, have a common-law system. However, within these countries, Louisiana, Quebec, and Puerto Rico exhibit the influence of French and Spanish settlers in their use of civil law systems.

A body of rules that delineate private rights and remedies and govern disputes between individuals in such areas as contracts, property, and family law; distinct from criminal or public law.

Civil liberties Freedom of speech, freedom of press, freedom from discrimination, and other natural rights guaranteed and protected by the Constitution, which were intended to place limits on government.

Civil rights Personal liberties that belong to an individual owing to his or her status as a citizen or resident of a particular country or community.

Class action A lawsuit that allows a large number of people with a common interest in a matter to sue or be sued as a group.

Clause A section, phrase, paragraph, or segment of a legal document, such as a contract, deed, will, or constitution, that relates to a particular point.

Closing The final transaction between a buyer and seller of real property.

Closing argument The final factual and legal argument made by each attorney on all sides of a case in a trial prior to a verdict or judgment.

Code A systematic and comprehensive compilation of laws, rules, or regulations that are consolidated and classified according to subject matter.

Coercion The intimidation of a victim to compel the individual to do some act against his or her will by the use of psychological pressure, physical force, or threats. The crime of intentionally and unlawfully restraining another's freedom by threatening to commit a crime, accusing the victim of a crime, disclosing any secret that would seriously impair the victim's reputation in the community, or by performing or refusing to perform an official action lawfully requested by the victim, or by causing an official to do so.

A defense asserted in a criminal prosecution that a person who committed a crime did not do so of his or her own free will, but only because the individual was compelled by another through the use of physical force or threat of immediate serious bodily injury or death.

Cohabitation A living arrangement in which an unmarried couple live together in a long-term relationship that resembles a marriage.

Cohabitation agreement The contract concerning property and financial agreements between two individuals who intend to live together and to have sexual relations out of wedlock.

Collateral Related; indirect; not bearing immediately upon an issue. The property pledged or given as a security interest, or a guarantee for payment of a debt, that will be taken or kept by the creditor in case of a default on the original debt.

Collective bargaining agreement The contractual agreement between an employer and a labor union that governs wages, hours, and working conditions for employees which can be enforced against both the employer and the union for failure to comply with its terms.

Comity Courtesy; respect; a disposition to perform some official act out of goodwill and tradition rather than obligation or law. The acceptance or adoption of decisions or laws by a court of another jurisdiction, either foreign or domestic, based on public policy rather than legal mandate.

Commerce Clause The provision of the U.S. Constitution that gives Congress exclusive power over trade activities between the states and with foreign countries and Native American tribes.

Commercial paper A written instrument or document such as a check, draft, promissory note, or a certificate of deposit, that manifests the pledge or duty of one individual to pay money to another.

Commercial speech Advertising speech by commercial companies and service providers. Commercial speech is protected under the First Amendment as long as it is not false or misleading.

Common law The ancient law of England based upon societal customs and recognized and enforced by the judgments and decrees of the courts. The general body of statutes and case law that governed England and the American colonies prior to the American Revolution.

The principles and rules of action, embodied in case law rather than legislative enactments, applicable to the government and protection of persons and property that derive their authority from the community customs and traditions that evolved over the centuries as interpreted by judicial tribunals.

A designation used to denote the opposite of statutory, equitable, or civil; for example, a common-law action.

Common-law marriage A union of two people not formalized in the customary manner as prescribed by law but created by an agreement to marry followed by cohabitation.

Community property The holdings and resources owned in common by a husband and wife.

Commutation Modification, exchange, or substitution.

Comparable worth The idea that men and women should receive equal pay when they perform work that involves comparable skills and responsibility or that is of comparable worth to the employer; also known as pay equity.

Comparative negligence The measurement of fault in percentages by both parties to a negligence action, so that the award of damages is reduced proportionately to the amount of negligence attributed to the victim. In order to recover, the negligence of the victim must be less than that of the defendant.

Compelling state interest A basis of upholding a state statute, against constitutional challenges grounded on the First and Fourteenth Amendments, due to the important or "compelling" need for such state regulations. Often state laws implemented under a state's police power are deemed to have satisfied a compelling state interest and therefore will survive judicial scrutiny.

Compensatory damages A sum of money awarded in a civil action by a court to indemnify a person for the particular loss, detriment, or injury suffered as a result of the unlawful conduct of another.

Complaint The pleading that initiates a civil action; in criminal law, the document that sets forth the basis upon which a person is to be charged with an offense.

Conclusive presumption The presumption that a fact is true upon proof of another fact. Evidence to the contrary cannot refute the presumed fact. Proof of a basic fact creates the existence of the presumed fact, and that presumed fact becomes irrebuttable.

Concurrent jurisdiction The authority of several different courts, each of which is authorized to entertain and decide cases dealing with the same subject matter.

Concurrent powers The ability of Congress and state legislatures to independently make laws on the same subject matter.

Concurrent resolution An action of Congress passed in the form of an enactment of one house, with the other house in agreement, which expresses the ideas of Congress on a particular subject.

Concurring opinion An opinion by one or more judges that provides separate reasoning for reaching the same decision as the majority of the court.

Conditional Subject to change; dependent upon or granted based on the occurrence of a future, uncertain event.

Conditional acceptance A counter offer. Acceptance of an offer that differs in some respects from the original contract.

Condition precedent A stipulation in an agreement that must be performed before the contract can go into effect and become binding on the parties. In terms of estates, the condition must be performed before the estates can vest or be enlarged.

Condition subsequent A stipulation in a contract that discharges one party of any further liability or performance under an existing contract if the other party fails to satisfy the stipulation.

Confession A statement made by an individual that acknowledges his or her guilt in the commission of a crime.

Conflict of interest A term used to describe the situation in which a public official or fiduciary who, contrary to the obligation and absolute duty to act for the benefit of the public or a designated individual, exploits the relationship for personal benefit, typically pecuniary.

Consent Voluntary acquiescence to the proposal of another; the act or result of reaching an accord; a concurrence of minds; actual willingness that an act or an infringement of an interest shall occur.

Consent decree An agreement by the defendant to cease activities, alleged by the government to be unlawful, in exchange for the dismissal of the case. The court must approve the agreement before it issues the consent decree.

Consideration Something of value given by both parties to a contract that induces them to enter into the agreement to exchange mutual performances.

Consolidation The process of combining two or more parts together to make a whole.

Consolidation of corporations The formation of a new corporate entity through the dissolution of two or more existing corporations. The new entity takes over the assets and assumes the liabilities of the dissolved corporations.

Conspiracy An agreement between two or more persons to engage jointly in an unlawful or criminal act, or an act that is innocent in itself but becomes unlawful when done by the combination of actors.

Constituent An individual, a principal, who appoints another to act in his or her behalf, an agent, such as an attorney in a court of law or an elected official in government.

Constitution of the United States A written document executed by representatives of the people of the United States as the absolute rule of action and decision for all branches and officers of the government, and with which all subsequent laws and ordinances must be in accordance unless it has been changed by a constitutional amendment by the authority that created it.

Consumer An individual who purchases and uses products and services in contradistinction to manufacturers who produce the goods or services and wholesalers or retailers who distribute and sell them. A member of the general category of persons who are protected by state and federal laws regulating price policies, financing practices, quality of goods and services, credit reporting, debt collection, and other trade practices of U.S. commerce. A purchaser of a product or service who has a legal right to enforce any implied or express warranties pertaining to the item against the manufacturer who has introduced the goods or services into the marketplace or the seller who has made them a term of the sale.

Contempt An act of deliberate disobedience or disregard for the laws, regulations, or decorum of a public authority, such as a court or legislative body.

Content neutral The principle that the government may not show favoritism between differing points of view on a particular subject.

Contingent fee Payment to an attorney for legal services that depends, or is contingent, upon there being some recovery or award in the case. The payment is then a percentage of the amount recovered—such as 25 percent if the matter is settled, 30 percent if it proceeds to trial.

Continuance The adjournment or postponement of an action pending in a court to a later date of the same or another session of the court, granted by a court in response to a motion made by a party to a lawsuit. The entry into the trial record of the adjournment of a case for the purpose of formally evidencing it.

Contraband Any property that is illegal to produce or possess. Smuggled goods that are imported into or exported from a country in violation of its laws.

Contract implied in fact *See* Implied contract.

Contracts Agreements between two or more persons that create an obligation to do, or refrain from doing, a particular thing.

Contributing to delinquency A criminal offense arising from an act or omission that leads to juvenile delinquency.

Contributory negligence Negligence on the part of the plaintiff for failure to exercise reasonable care for his or her own safety, and which contributes to the negligence of the defendant as the actual cause of the plaintiff's injury.

Conversion Any unauthorized act that deprives an owner of personal property without his or her consent.

Copyright An intangible right granted by statute to the author or originator of certain literary or artistic productions, whereby, for a limited period, the exclusive privilege is given to the person to make copies of the same for publication and sale.

Corporations Artificial entities that are created by state statute, and that are treated much like individuals under the law, having legally enforceable rights, the ability to acquire debt and pay out profits, the ability to hold and transfer property, the ability to enter into contracts, the requirement to pay taxes, and the ability to sue and be sued.

Cosigner An obligor—a person who becomes obligated, under a commercial paper, such as a promissory note or check—by signing the instrument in conjunction with the original obligor, thereby promising to pay it in full.

Counsel An attorney or lawyer. The rendition of advice and guidance concerning a legal matter, contemplated form of argument, claim, or action.

Counterclaim A claim by a defendant opposing the claim of the plaintiff and seeking some relief from the plaintiff for the defendant.

Counteroffer In contract law, a proposal made in response to an original offer modifying its terms, but which has the legal effect of rejecting it.

Court below The court from which a case was removed for review by an appellate court.

Court of appeal An intermediate federal judicial tribunal of review that is found in thirteen judicial districts, called circuits, in the United States.

A state judicial tribunal that reviews a decision rendered by an inferior tribunal to determine whether it made errors that warrant the reversal of its judgment.

Court of claims A state judicial tribunal established as the forum in which to bring certain types of lawsuits against the state or its political subdivisions, such as a county. The former designation given to a federal tribunal created in 1855 by Congress with original jurisdiction—initial authority—to decide an action brought against the United States that is based upon the Constitution, federal law, any regulation of the executive department, or any express or implied contracts with the federal government.

Court of equity A court that presides over equity suits, suits of fairness and justness, both in its administration and proceedings. Courts of equity no longer exist due to the consolidation of law and equity actions in federal and state courts.

Court of general jurisdiction A superior court, which by its constitution, can review and exercise a final judgment in a case under its authority. No further judicial inspection is conducted, except by an appellate power.

Covenant An agreement, contract, or written promise between two individuals that frequently constitutes a pledge to do or refrain from doing something.

Credit A term used in accounting to describe either an entry on the right-hand side of an account or the process of making such an entry. A credit records the increases in liabilities, owner's equity, and revenues as well as the decreases in assets and expenses.

A sum in taxation that is subtracted from the computed tax, as opposed to a deduction that is ordinarily subtracted from gross income to determine adjusted gross income or taxable income. Claim for a particular sum of money.

The ability of an individual or a company to borrow money or procure goods on time, as a result of a positive opinion by the particular lender concerning such borrower's solvency and reliability. The right granted by a creditor to a debtor to delay satisfaction of a debt, or to incur a debt and defer the payment thereof.

Creditor An individual to whom an obligation is owed because he or she has given something of value in exchange. One who may legally demand and receive money, either through the fulfillment of a contract or due to injury sustained as a result of another's negligence or intentionally wrongful act. The term *creditor* is also used to describe an individual who is engaged in the business of lending money or selling items for which immediate payment is not demanded but an obligation of repayment exists as of a future date.

Criminal law A body of rules and statutes that defines conduct prohibited by the government because it threatens and harms public safety and welfare and that establishes punishment to be imposed for the commission of such acts.

Cross-examination The questioning of a witness or party during a trial, hearing, or deposition by the party opposing the one who asked the person to testify in order to evaluate the truth of that person's testimony, to develop the testimony further, or to accomplish any other objective. The interrogation of a witness or party by the party opposed to the one who called the witness or party, upon a subject raised during direct examination—the initial questioning of a witness or party—on the merits of that testimony.

Cruel and unusual punishment Such punishment as would amount to torture or barbarity, any cruel and degrading punishment not known to the common law, or any fine, penalty, confinement, or treatment so dispro-

portionate to the offense as to shock the moral sense of the community.

Custodial parent The parent to whom the guardianship of the children in a divorced or estranged relationship has been granted by the court.

D

Damages Monetary compensation that is awarded by a court in a civil action to an individual who has been injured through the wrongful conduct of another party.

Death penalty *See* Capital punishment.

Debtor One who owes a debt or the performance of an obligation to another, who is called the creditor; one who may be compelled to pay a claim or demand; anyone liable in a claim, whether due or to become due.

In bankruptcy law, a person who files a voluntary petition or person against whom an involuntary petition is filed. A person or municipality concerning which a bankruptcy case has been commenced.

Declaration of rights *See* Bill of rights.

Decree A judgment of a court that announces the legal consequences of the facts found in a case and orders that the court's decision be carried out. A decree in equity is a sentence or order of the court, pronounced on hearing and understanding all the points in issue, and determining the rights of all the parties to the suit, according to equity and good conscience. It is a declaration of the court announcing the legal consequences of the facts found. With the procedural merger of law and equity in the federal and most state courts under the Rules of Civil Procedure, the term *judgment* has generally replaced *decree*.

Decriminalization The passing of legislation that changes criminal acts or omissions into noncriminal ones without punitive sanctions.

Deed A written instrument, which has been signed and delivered, by which one individual, the grantor, conveys title to real property to another individual, the grantee; a conveyance of land, tenements, or hereditaments, from one individual to another.

De facto [*Latin*, In fact.] In fact; in deed; actually.

Defamation Any intentional false communication, either written or spoken, that harms a person's reputation; decreases the respect, regard, or confidence in which a person is held; or induces disparaging, hostile, or disagreeable opinions or feelings against a person.

Defendant The person defending or denying; the party against whom relief or recovery is sought in an action or suit, or the accused in a criminal case.

Defense The forcible repulsion of an unlawful and violent attack, such as the defense of one's person, property, or country in time of war.

The totality of the facts, law, and contentions presented by the party against whom a civil action or criminal prosecution is instituted in order to defeat or diminish the plaintiff's cause of action or the prosecutor's case. A reply to the claims of the other party, which asserts reasons why the claims should be disallowed. The defense may involve an absolute denial of the other party's factual allegations or may entail an affirmative defense, which sets forth completely new factual allegations. Pursuant to the rules of federal civil procedure, numerous defenses may be asserted by motion as well as by answer, while other defenses must be pleaded affirmatively.

De jure [*Latin,* In law.] Legitimate; lawful, as a matter of law. Having complied with all the requirements imposed by law.

Delegation of powers Transfer of authority by one branch of government in which such authority is vested to some other branch or administrative agency.

Deliberate Willful; purposeful; determined after thoughtful evaluation of all relevant factors; dispassionate. To act with a particular intent, which is derived from a careful consideration of factors that influence the choice to be made.

Delinquent An individual who fails to fulfill an obligation, or otherwise is guilty of a crime or offense.

Domestic partnership laws Legislation and regulations related to the legal recognition of non-marital relationships between persons who are romantically involved with each other, have set up a joint residence, and have registered with cities recognizing said relationships.

Demurrer An assertion by the defendant that although the facts alleged by the plaintiff in the complaint may be true, they do not entitle the plaintiff to prevail in the lawsuit.

Denaturalization The deprivation of an individual's rights as a citizen.

Deportation Banishment to a foreign country, attended with confiscation of property and deprivation of civil rights.

The transfer of an alien, by exclusion or expulsion, from the United States to a foreign country. The removal or sending back of an alien to the country from which he or she came because his or her presence is deemed inconsistent with the public welfare, and without any punishment being imposed or contemplated. The grounds for deportation are set forth at 8 U.S.C.A., sec. 1251, and the procedures are provided for in secs. 1252–1254.

Deposition The testimony of a party or witness in a civil or criminal proceeding taken before trial, usually in an attorney's office.

Desegregation Judicial mandate making illegal the practice of segregation.

Desertion The act by which a person abandons and forsakes, without justification, a condition of public, social, or family life, renouncing its responsibilities and evading its duties. A willful abandonment of an employment or duty in violation of a legal or moral obligation.

Criminal desertion is a husband's or wife's abandonment or willful failure without just cause to provide for the care, protection, or support of a spouse who is in ill health or impoverished circumstances.

Detention hearing A proceeding to determine the restraint to be imposed upon an individual awaiting trial, such as bail or, in the case of a juvenile, placement in a shelter.

Deterrent Anything that discourages or obstructs a person from committing an act, such as punishment for criminal acts.

Detriment Any loss or harm to a person or property; relinquishment of a legal right, benefit, or something of value.

Diplomatic immunity A principle of international law that provides foreign diplomats with protection from legal action in the country in which they work.

Directed verdict A procedural device whereby the decision in a case is taken out of the hands of the jury by the judge.

Direct examination The primary questioning of a witness during a trial that is conducted by the side for which that person is acting as a witness.

Direct tax A charge levied by the government upon property, which is determined by its financial worth.

Disaffirm Repudiate; revoke consent; refuse to support former acts or agreements.

Disbar To revoke an attorney's license to practice law.

Discharge To liberate or free; to terminate or extinguish. A discharge is the act or instrument by which a contract or agreement is ended. A mortgage is discharged if it has been carried out to the full extent originally contemplated or terminated prior to total execution.

Discharge also means to release, as from legal confinement in prison or the military service, or from some legal obligation such as jury duty, or the payment of debts by a person who is bankrupt. The document that indicates that an individual has been legally released from the military service is called a discharge.

Disclaimer The denial, refusal, or rejection of a right, power, or responsibility.

Discovery A category of procedural devices employed by a party to a civil or criminal action, prior to trial, to require the adverse party to disclose information that is essential for the preparation of the requesting party's case and that the other party alone knows or possesses.

Discretion Independent use of judgment to choose between right and wrong, to make a decision, or to act cautiously under the circumstances.

Discretion in decision making Discretion is the power or right to make official decisions using reason and judgment to choose from among acceptable alternatives.

Discrimination In constitutional law, the grant by statute of particular privileges to a class arbitrarily designated from a sizable number of persons, where no reasonable distinction exists between the favored and disfavored classes. Federal laws, supplemented by court decisions, prohibit discrimination in such areas as employment, housing, voting rights, education, and access to public facilities. They also proscribe discrimination on the basis of race, age, sex, nationality, disability, or religion. In addition, state and local laws can prohibit discrimination in these areas and in others not covered by federal laws.

Dishonor To refuse to accept or pay a draft or to pay a promissory note when duly presented. An instrument is dishonored when a necessary or optional presentment is made and due acceptance or payment is refused, or cannot be obtained within the prescribed time, or in case of bank collections, the instrument is seasonably returned by the midnight deadline; or presentment is excused and the instrument is not duly accepted or paid. Includes the insurer of a letter of credit refusing to pay or accept a draft or demand for payment.

As respects the flag, to deface or defile, imputing a lively sense of shaming or an equivalent acquiescent callousness.

Disinherit To cut off from an inheritance. To deprive someone, who would otherwise be an heir to property or another right, of his or her right to inherit.

Dismissal A discharge of an individual or corporation from employment. The disposition of a civil or criminal proceeding or a claim or charge made therein by a court order without a trial or prior to its completion which, in effect, is a denial of the relief sought by the commencement of the action.

Disposition Act of disposing; transferring to the care or possession of another. The parting with, alienation of, or giving up of property. The final settlement of a matter and, with reference to decisions announced by a court, a judge's ruling is commonly referred to as disposition, regardless of level of resolution. In criminal procedure, the sentencing or other final settlement of a criminal case. With respect to a mental state, denotes an attitude, prevailing tendency, or inclination.

Disposition hearing The judicial proceeding for passing sentence upon a defendant who was found guilty of the charge(s) against him or her.

Dispossession The wrongful, nonconsensual ouster or removal of a person from his or her property by trick, compulsion, or misuse of the law, whereby the violator obtains actual occupation of the land.

Dissent An explicit disagreement by one or more judges with the decision of the majority on a case before them.

Dissolution Act or process of dissolving; termination; winding up. In this sense it is frequently used in the phrase *dissolution of a partnership*.

Division of powers *See* Separation of powers.

Divorce A court decree that terminates a marriage; also known as marital dissolution.

Domicile The legal residence of a person, which determines jurisdiction for taxation and voting, as well as other legal rights and privileges. Considered to be the permanent residence of an individual, or the place where one intends to return after an absence, such as in the case of the president who physically lives in the White House, but has a domicile in his or her home state.

Double indemnity A term of an insurance policy by which the insurance company promises to pay the insured or the beneficiary twice the amount of coverage if loss occurs due to a particular cause or set of circumstances.

Double jeopardy A second prosecution for the same offense after acquittal or conviction or multiple punishments for the same offense. The evil sought to be avoided by prohibiting double jeopardy is double trial and double conviction, not necessarily double punishment.

Draft A written order by the first party, called the drawer, instructing a second party, called the drawee (such as a bank), to pay money to a third party, called the payee. An order to pay a certain sum in money, signed by a drawer, payable on demand or at a definite time, to order or bearer.

A tentative, provisional, or preparatory writing out of any document (as a will, contract, lease, and so on) for purposes of discussion and correction, which is afterward to be prepared in its final form.

Compulsory conscription of persons into military service.

A small arbitrary deduction or allowance made to a merchant or importer, in the case of goods sold by weight or taxable by weight, to cover possible loss of weight in handling or from differences in scales.

Due process of law A fundamental, constitutional guarantee that all legal proceedings will be fair and that one will be given notice of the proceedings and an opportunity to be heard before the government acts to take away one's life, liberty, or property. Also, a constitutional guarantee that a law shall not be unreasonable, arbitrary, or capricious.

Duress Unlawful pressure exerted upon a person to coerce that person to perform an act that he or she ordinarily would not perform.

Duty A legal obligation that entails mandatory conduct or performance. With respect to the laws relating to customs duties, a tax owed to the government for the import or export of goods.

E

Easement A right of use over the property of another. Traditionally the permitted kinds of uses were limited, the most important being rights of way and rights concerning flowing waters. The easement was normally for the benefit of adjoining lands, no matter who the owner was (an easement appurtenant), rather than for the benefit of a specific individual (easement in gross).

Emancipation The act or process by which a person is liberated from the authority and control of another person.

Embezzlement The fraudulent appropriation of another's property by a person who is in a position of trust, such as an agent or employee.

Eminent domain The power to take private property for public use by a state, municipality, or private person or corporation authorized to exercise functions of public character, following the payment of just compensation to the owner of that property.

Employment at will A common-law rule that an employment contract of indefinite duration can be terminated by either the employer or the employee at any time, for any reason; also known as terminable at will.

Encumbrance A burden, obstruction, or impediment on property that lessens its value or makes it less mar-

ketable. An encumbrance (also spelled incumbrance) is any right or interest that exists in someone other than the owner of an estate and that restricts or impairs the transfer of the estate or lowers its value. This might include an easement, a lien, a mortgage, a mechanic's lien, or accrued and unpaid taxes.

Entitlement An individual's right to receive a value or benefit provided by law.

Entrapment The act of government agents or officials that induces a person to commit a crime he or she is not previously disposed to commit.

Enumerated powers Authority specifically granted to a body of the national government under the U.S. Constitution, such as the powers granted to Congress in Article I, Section 8.

Equal Pay Act Federal law which mandates the same pay for all persons who do the same work without regard to sex, age, race or ability. For work to be "equal" within meaning of the act, it is not necessary that the jobs be identical, but only that they be substantially equal.

Equal protection The constitutional guarantee that no person or class of persons shall be denied the same protection of the laws that is enjoyed by other persons or other classes in like circumstances in their lives, liberty, property, and pursuit of happiness.

Equitable Just; that which is fair and proper according to the principles of justice and right.

Equitable action A cause of action that seeks an equitable remedy, such as relief sought with an injunction.

Equity The pursuit of fairness. In the U.S. legal system, a body of laws that seeks to achieve fairness on an individual basis. In terms of property, the money value of property in excess of claims, liens, or mortgages on the property.

Error A mistake in a court proceeding concerning a matter of law or fact which might provide a ground for a review of the judgment rendered in the proceeding.

Escrow Something of value, such as a deed, stock, money, or written instrument, that is put into the custody of a third person by its owner, a grantor, an obligor, or a promisor, to be retained until the occurrence of a contingency or performance of a condition.

Espionage The act of securing information of a military or political nature that a competing nation holds secret. It can involve the analysis of diplomatic reports, publications, statistics, and broadcasts, as well as spying, a clandestine activity carried out by an individual or individuals working under a secret identity for the benefit of a nation's information gathering techniques. In the United States, the organization that heads most activities dedicated to espionage is the Central Intelligence Agency.

Establishment Clause The provision in the First Amendment which provides that there will be no laws created respecting the establishment of a religion, inhibiting the practice of a religion, or giving preference to any or all religions. It has been interpreted to also denounce the discouragement of any or all religions.

Estate The degree, quantity, nature, and extent of interest that a person has in real and personal property. An estate in lands, tenements, and hereditaments signifies such interest as the tenant has therein. *Estate* is commonly used in conveyances in connection with the words *right, title,* and *interest,* and is, to a great degree, synonymous with all of them.

When used in connection with probate proceedings, the term encompasses the total property of whatever kind that is owned by a decedent prior to the distribution of that property in accordance with the terms of a will, or when there is no will, by the laws of inheritance in the state of domicile of the decedent. It means, ordinarily, the whole of the property owned by anyone, the realty as well as the personalty.

In its broadest sense, the social, civic, or political condition or standing of a person; or a class of persons considered as grouped for social, civic, or political purposes.

Estate tax The tax levied upon the entire estate of the decedent before any part of the estate can be transferred to an heir. An estate tax is applied to the right of the deceased person to transfer property at death. An "inheritance tax" is imposed upon an heir's right to receive the property.

Estoppel A legal principle that precludes a party from denying or alleging a certain fact owing to that party's previous conduct, allegation, or denial.

Euthanasia The merciful act or practice of terminating the life of an individual or individuals inflicted with incurable and distressing diseases in a relatively painless manner.

Eviction The removal of a tenant from possession of premises in which he or she resides or has a property interest, done by a landlord either by reentry upon the premises or through a court action.

Excise tax A tax imposed on the performance of an act, the engaging in an occupation, or the enjoyment of a privilege. A tax on the manufacture, sale, or use of goods or on the carrying on of an occupation activity, or a tax on the transfer of property. In current usage the term has been extended to include various license fees and practically every internal revenue tax except the income tax (i.e., federal alcohol and tobacco excise taxes).

Exclusionary rule The principle based on federal constitutional law that evidence illegally seized by law enforcement officers in violation of a suspect's right to be free from unreasonable searches and seizures cannot be used against the suspect in a criminal prosecution.

Exclusive jurisdiction The legal authority of a court or other tribunal to preside over a suit, an action, or a person to the exclusion of any other court.

Exclusive power The authority held solely by one individual, such as the President, or one group, such as a regulatory committee.

Exclusive right The privilege that only a grantee can exercise, prohibiting others from partaking in the same.

Executive agreement An agreement made between the head of a foreign country and the President of the United States. This agreement does not have to be submitted to the Senate for consent, and it supersedes any contradicting state law.

Executive orders Presidential policy directives that implement or interpret a federal statute, a constitutional provision, or a treaty.

Executor The individual named by a decedent to administer the provisions of the decedent's will.

Ex parte [*Latin, On one side only.*] Done by, for, or on the application of one party alone.

Expatriation The voluntary act of abandoning or renouncing one's country and becoming the citizen or subject of another.

Expert witness A witness, such as a psychological statistician or ballistics expert, who possesses special or superior knowledge concerning the subject of his or her testimony.

Ex post facto laws [*Latin, "After-the-fact" laws.*] Laws that provide for the infliction of punishment upon a person for some prior act that, at the time it was committed, was not illegal.

Express Clear; definite; explicit; plain; direct; unmistakable; not dubious or ambiguous. Declared in terms; set forth in words. Directly and distinctly stated. Made known distinctly and explicitly, and not left to inference. Manifested by direct and appropriate language, as distinguished from that which is inferred from conduct. The word is usually contrasted with *implied*.

Express contract An oral or written contract where the terms of the agreement are explicitly stated.

Expressed power *See* Enumerated powers.

Express warranty An additional written or oral guarantee to the underlying sales agreement made to the consumer as to the quality, description, or performance of a good.

Extortion The obtaining of property from another induced by wrongful use of actual or threatened force, violence, or fear, or under color of official right.

Extradition The transfer of an accused from one state or country to another state or country that seeks to place the accused on trial.

F

Family court A court that presides over cases involving: (1) child abuse and neglect; (2) support; (3) paternity; (4) termination of custody due to constant neglect; (5) juvenile delinquency; and (6) family offenses.

Federal circuit courts The 12 circuit courts making up the U.S. Federal Circuit Court System. The twelfth circuit presides over the District of Columbia. Decisions made by the federal district courts can be reviewed by the court of appeals in each circuit.

Federal district courts The first of three levels of the federal court system, which includes the U.S. Court of Appeals and the U.S. Supreme Court. If a participating party disagrees with the ruling of a federal district court in its case, it may petition for the case to be moved to the next level in the federal court system.

Felon An individual who commits a crime of a serious nature, such as burglary or murder. A person who commits a felony.

Felony A serious crime, characterized under federal law and many state statutes as any offense punishable by death or imprisonment in excess of one year.

Fiduciary An individual in whom another has placed the utmost trust and confidence to manage and protect property or money. The relationship wherein one person has an obligation to act for another's benefit.

First degree murder Murder committed with deliberately premeditated thought and malice, or with extreme atrocity or cruelty. The difference between first and second degree murder is the presence of the specific intention to kill.

Forbearance Refraining from doing something that one has a legal right to do. Giving of further time for repayment of an obligation or agreement; not to enforce a claim at its due date. A delay in enforcing a legal right. Act by which a creditor waits for payment of debt due by a debtor after it becomes due.

Within usury law, the contractual obligation of a lender or creditor to refrain, during a given period of time, from requiring the borrower or debtor to repay the loan or debt that is then due and payable.

Foreclosure A procedure by which the holder of a mortgage—an interest in land providing security for the performance of a duty or the payment of a debt—sells the property upon the failure of the debtor to pay the mortgage debt and, thereby, terminates his or her rights in the property.

Forgery The creation of a false written document or alteration of a genuine one, with the intent to defraud.

Formal contract An agreement between two or more individuals in which all the terms are in writing.

Franchise A special privilege to do certain things that is conferred by government on an individual or a corporation and which does not belong to citizens generally of common right (i.e., a right granted to offer cable television service).

A privilege granted or sold, such as to use a name or to sell products or services. In its simplest terms, a franchise is a license from the owner of a trademark or trade name permitting another to sell a product or service under that name or mark. More broadly stated, a franchise has evolved into an elaborate agreement under which the franchisee undertakes to conduct a business or sell a product or service in accordance with methods and procedures prescribed by the franchisor, and the franchisor undertakes to assist the franchisee through advertising, promotion, and other advisory services.

The right of suffrage; the right or privilege of voting in public elections. Such a right is guaranteed by the Fifteenth, Nineteenth, and Twenty-fourth Amendments to the U.S. Constitution.

As granted by a professional sports association, franchise is a privilege to field a team in a given geographic area under the auspices of the league that issues it. It is merely an incorporeal right.

Fraud A false representation of a matter of fact—whether by words or by conduct, by false or misleading allegations, or by concealment of what should have been disclosed—that deceives and is intended to deceive another so that the individual will act upon it to her or his legal injury.

Freedom of assembly *See* Freedom of association.

Freedom of association The right to associate with others for the purpose of engaging in constitutionally protected activities, such as to peacefully assemble.

Freedom of religion The First Amendment right to individually believe and to practice or exercise one's belief.

Freedom of speech The right, guaranteed by the First Amendment to the U.S. Constitution, to express beliefs and ideas without unwarranted government restriction.

Freedom of the press The right, guaranteed by the First Amendment to the U.S. Constitution, to gather, publish, and distribute information and ideas without government restriction; this right encompasses freedom from prior restraints on publication and freedom from censorship.

Full Faith and Credit Clause The clause of the U.S. Constitution that provides that the various states must recognize legislative acts, public records, and judicial decisions of the other states within the United States.

Full warranty The guarantee on the workmanship and materials of a product. If the product is defective in any way, then the consumer is entitled to corrective action from the manufacturer, at no cost to the consumer, and within a reasonable amount of time.

Fundamental rights Rights which derive, or are implied, from the terms of the U.S. Constitution, such as the Bill of Rights, the first ten amendments to the Constitution.

G

Gag rule A rule, regulation, or law that prohibits debate or discussion of a particular issue.

Garnishment A legal procedure by which a creditor can collect what a debtor owes by reaching the debtor's property when it is in the hands of someone other than the debtor.

General partnership A business relationship with more than one owner where all parties manage the business and equally share any profits or losses.

Gerrymander The process of dividing a particular state or territory into election districts in such a manner as to accomplish an unlawful purpose, such as to give one party a greater advantage.

Good faith Honesty; a sincere intention to deal fairly with others.

Grandfather clause A portion of a statute that provides that the law is not applicable in certain circumstances due to preexisting facts.

Grand jury A panel of citizens that is convened by a court to decide whether it is appropriate for the government to indict (proceed with a prosecution against) someone suspected of a crime.

Grand larceny A category of larceny—the offense of illegally taking the property of another—in which the value of the property taken is greater than that set for petit larceny.

Grounds The basis or foundation; reasons sufficient in law to justify relief.

Guarantee One to whom a guaranty is made. This word is also used, as a noun, to denote the contract of guaranty or the obligation of a guarantor, and, as a verb, to denote the action of assuming the responsibilities of a guarantor.

Guaranty As a verb, to agree to be responsible for the payment of another's debt or the performance of another's duty, liability, or obligation if that person does not perform as he or she is legally obligated to do; to assume the responsibility of a guarantor; to warrant.

As a noun, an undertaking or promise that is collateral to the primary or principal obligation and that binds the guarantor to performance in the event of nonperformance by the principal obligor.

Guardian A person lawfully invested with the power, and charged with the obligation, of taking care of and managing the property and rights of a person who, because of age, understanding, or self-control, is considered incapable of administering his or her own affairs.

Guardian ad litem A guardian appointed by the court to represent the interests of infants, the unborn, or incompetent persons in legal actions.

H

Habeas corpus [*Latin, You have the body.*] A writ (court order) that commands an individual or a government official who has restrained another to produce the prisoner at a designated time and place so that the court can determine the legality of custody and decide whether to order the prisoner's release.

Hate crime A crime motivated by race, religion, gender, sexual orientation, or other prejudice.

Hearing A legal proceeding where issues of law or fact are tried and evidence is presented to help determine the issue.

Hearsay A statement made out of court that is offered in court as evidence to prove the truth of the matter asserted.

Heir An individual who receives an interest in, or ownership of, land, tenements, or hereditaments from an ancestor who had died intestate, through the laws of descent and distribution. At common law, an heir was the individual appointed by law to succeed to the estate of an ancestor who died without a will. It is commonly used today in reference to any individual who succeeds to property, either by will or law.

Homicide The killing of one human being by another human being.

Hung jury A trial jury duly selected to make a decision in a criminal case regarding a defendant's guilt or innocence, but who are unable to reach a verdict due to a complete division in opinion.

I

Immunity Exemption from performing duties that the law generally requires other citizens to perform, or from a penalty or burden that the law generally places on other citizens.

Impeachment A process used to charge, try, and remove public officials for misconduct while in office.

Implied consent Consent that is inferred from signs, actions, or facts, or by inaction or silence.

Implied contract A contract created not by express agreement, but inferred by law, based on the conduct of the parties and the events surrounding the parties' dealings.

Implied power Authority that exists so that an expressly granted power can be carried into effect.

Implied warranty A promise, arising by operation of law, that something that is sold will be merchantable and fit for the purpose for which it is sold.

Imprimatur [*Latin, Let it be printed.*] A licence or allowance, granted by the constituted authorities, giving permission to print and publish a book. This allowance was formerly necessary in England before any book could lawfully be printed, and in some other countries is still required.

Inalienable Not subject to sale or transfer; inseparable.

Inalienable rights Rights (i.e., life, liberty, and the pursuit of happiness) which cannot be ceded or transferred without permission from the individual who possesses them.

Incapacity The absence of legal ability, competence, or qualifications.

Income tax A charge imposed by government on the annual gains of a person, corporation, or other taxable unit derived through work, business pursuits, investments, property dealings, and other sources determined in accordance with the Internal Revenue Code or state law.

Incorporate To formally create a corporation pursuant to the requirements prescribed by state statute; to confer a corporate franchise upon certain individuals.

Indemnity Recompense for loss, damage, or injuries; restitution or reimbursement.

Indeterminate That which is uncertain or not particularly designated.

Indictment A written accusation charging that an individual named therein has committed an act or admitted to doing something that is punishable by law.

Indirect tax A tax upon some right, privilege, or corporate franchise.

Individual rights Rights and privileges constitutionally guaranteed to the people, as set forth by the Bill of Rights, the ability of a person to pursue life, liberty, and property.

Infants Persons who are under the age of the legal majority—at common law, 21 years, now generally 18 years. According to the sense in which this term is used, it may denote the age of the person, the contractual disabilities that nonage entails, or his or her status with regard to other powers or relations.

Information The formal accusation of a criminal offense made by a public official; the sworn, written accusation of a crime.

Inherent Derived from the essential nature of, and inseparable from, the object itself.

Inherent powers Implicit control, which by nature cannot be derived from another.

Inherent rights Rights held within a person because he or she exists. *See also* inalienable rights.

Inheritance Property received from a decedent, either by will or through state laws of intestate succession, where the decedent has failed to execute a valid will.

Inheritance tax A tax imposed upon the right of an individual to receive property left to him or her by a decedent.

Injunction A court order by which an individual is required to perform or is restrained from performing a particular act. A writ framed according to the circumstances of the individual case.

In loco parentis [*Latin, In the place of a parent.*] The legal doctrine under which an individual assumes parental rights, duties, and obligations without going through the formalities of legal adoption.

Inquisitorial system A method of legal practice in which the judge endeavors to discover facts while simultaneously representing the interests of the state in a trial.

Insanity defense A defense asserted by an accused in a criminal prosecution to avoid liability for the commission of a crime because, at the time of the crime, the person did not appreciate the nature or quality or wrongfulness of the act.

Insider In the context of federal regulation of the purchase and sale of securities, anyone who has knowledge of facts not available to the general public.

Insider trading The trading of stocks and bonds based on information gained from special private, privileged information affecting the value of the stocks and bonds.

Insurance A contract whereby, for a specified consideration, one party undertakes to compensate the other for a loss relating to a particular subject as a result of the occurrence of designated hazards.

Intangibles Property that is a "right," such as a patent, copyright, trademark, etc., or one that is lacking physical existence, like good will. A nonphysical, noncurrent asset that exists only in connection with something else, such as the good will of a business.

Intent A determination to perform a particular act or to act in a particular manner for a specific reason; an aim or design; a resolution to use a certain means to reach an end.

Intermediate courts Courts with general ability or authority to hear a case (trial, appellate, or both), but are not the court of last resort within the jurisdiction.

Intestate The description of a person who dies without making a valid will or the reference made to this condition.

Involuntary manslaughter The act of unlawfully killing another human being unintentionally.

Irrevocable Unable to cancel or recall; that which is unalterable or irreversible.

Item veto *See* Line item veto.

J

Joint committee Members of two houses of a state or federal legislature that work together as one group.

Joint resolution A type of measure that Congress may consider and act upon; the other types of measures being bills, concurrent resolutions, and simple resolutions, in addition to treaties in the Senate.

Judicial discretion Sound judgment exercised by a judge in determining what is right and equitable under the law.

Judicial review A court's authority to examine an executive or legislative act and to invalidate that act if it is contrary to constitutional principles.

Jurisdiction The geographic area over which authority extends; legal authority; the authority to hear and determine causes of action.

Jurisprudence From the Latin term *juris prudentia,* which means "the study, knowledge, or science of law;" in the United States, more broadly associated with the philosophy of law.

Jury In trials, a group of people selected and sworn to inquire into matters of fact and to reach a verdict on the basis of evidence presented to it.

Jury nullification The ability of a jury to acquit the defendant despite the amount of evidence against him or her in a criminal case.

Jus sanguinis The determination of a person's citizenship based upon the citizenship of the individual's parents.

Jus soli The determination of a person's citizenship based upon the individual's place of birth.

Just cause A reasonable and lawful ground for action.

Justifiable homicide The killing of another in self-defense or in the lawful defense of one's property; killing of another when the law demands it, such as in execution for a capital crime.

Juvenile A young individual who has not reached the age whereby he or she would be treated as an adult in the area of criminal law. The age at which the young person attains the status of being a legal majority varies from state to state—as low as 14 years old, as high as 18 years old; however, the Juvenile Delinquency Act determines that a youthful person under the age of eighteen is a "juvenile" in cases involving federal jurisdiction.

Juvenile court The court presiding over cases in which young persons under a certain age, depending on the area of jurisdiction, are accused of criminal acts.

Juvenile delinquency The participation of a youthful individual, one who falls under the age at which he or she could be tried as an adult, in illegal behavior. *See also* Delinquent child.

L

Landlord A lessor of real property; the owner or possessor of an estate in land or a rental property, who, in an exchange for rent, leases it to another individual known as the tenant.

Lapse The termination or failure of a right or privilege because of a neglect to exercise that right or to perform some duty within a time limit, or because a specified contingency did not occur. The expiration of coverage under an insurance policy because of the insured's failure to pay the premium.

The common-law principle that a gift in a will does not take effect but passes into the estate remaining after the payment of debts and particular gifts, if the beneficiary is alive when the will is executed but subsequently predeceases the testator.

Larceny The unauthorized taking and removal of the personal property of another by a person who intends to permanently deprive the owner of it; a crime against the right of possession.

Lease A contractual agreement by which one party conveys an estate in property to another party, for a limited period, subject to various conditions, in exchange for something of value, but still retains ownership.

Legal defense A complete and acceptable response as to why the claims of the plaintiff should not be granted in a point of law.

Legal tender All U.S. coins and currencies—regardless of when coined or issued—including (in terms of the Federal Reserve System) Federal Reserve notes and circulating notes of Federal Reserve banks and national banking associations that are used for all debts, public and private, public charges, taxes, duties, and dues.

Legation The persons commissioned by one government to exercise diplomatic functions at the court of another, including the ministers, secretaries, attachés, and interpreters, are collectively called the *legation* of their government. The word also denotes the official residence of a foreign minister.

Legislation Lawmaking; the preparation and enactment of laws by a legislative body.

Legislative intent The history of events leading to the enactment of a law that a court refers to when interpreting an ambiguous or inconsistent statute.

Liability A comprehensive legal term that describes the condition of being actually or potentially subject to a legal obligation.

Libel and slander Two torts that involve the communication of false information about a person, a group, or an entity, such as a corporation. Libel is any defama-

tion that can be seen, such a writing, printing, effigy, movie, or statue. Slander is any defamation that is spoken and heard.

Lien A right given to another by the owner of property to secure a debt, or one created by law in favor of certain creditors.

Limited liability partnership A form of general partnership that provides an individual partner protection against personal liability for certain partnership obligations.

Limited warranty A written performance guarantee that only covers workmanship or materials for a specified period of time.

Line item veto The power that governors in some states have to strike individual items from appropriation bills without affecting any other provisions.

Litigation An action brought in court to enforce a particular right. The act or process of bringing a lawsuit in and of itself; a judicial contest; any dispute.

Living will A written document that allows a patient to give explicit instructions about medical treatment to be administered when the patient is terminally ill or permanently unconscious; also called an advance directive.

Loan shark A person who lends money in exchange for its repayment at an interest rate that exceeds the percentage approved by law and who uses intimidating methods or threats of force in order to obtain repayment.

Lobbying The process of influencing public and government policy at all levels: federal, state, and local.

Lower court The court where a suit was first heard. *See also* Court below.

M

Magistrate Any individual who has the power of a public civil officer or inferior judicial officer, such as a justice of the peace.

Majority Full age; legal age; age at which a person is no longer a minor. The age at which, by law, a person is capable of being legally responsible for all of his or her acts (i.e., contractual obligations), and is entitled to the management of his or her own affairs and to the enjoyment of civic rights (i.e., right to vote). The opposite of minority. Also the *status* of a person who is a major in age.

The greater number. The number greater than half of any total.

Malfeasance The commission of an act that is unequivocally illegal or completely wrongful.

Malice The intentional commission of a wrongful act, absent justification, with the intent to cause harm to others; conscious violation of the law that injures another individual; a mental state indicating a disposition in disregard of social duty and a tendency toward malfeasance.

Malice aforethought A predetermination to commit an act without legal justification or excuse. A malicious design to injure. An intent, at the time of a killing, willfully to take the life of a human being, or an intent willfully to act in callous and wanton disregard of the consequences to human life; but *malice aforethought* does not necessarily imply any ill will, spite, or hatred towards the individual killed.

Malpractice The breach by a member of a profession of either a standard of care or a standard of conduct.

Mandate A judicial command, order, or precept, written or oral, from a court; a direction that a court has the authority to give and an individual is bound to obey.

Manslaughter The unjustifiable, inexcusable, and intentional killing of a human being without deliberation, premeditation, and malice. The unlawful killing of a human being without any deliberation, which may be involuntary, in the commission of a lawful act without due caution and circumspection.

Material Important; affecting the merits of a case; causing a particular course of action; significant; substantial. A description of the quality of evidence that possesses such substantial probative value as to establish the truth or falsity of a point in issue in a lawsuit.

Material fact A fact that is necessary in determining a case, without which there would be no defense. Disclosure of the fact is necessary for the reasonable person to make a prudent decision.

Mediation A settlement of a dispute or controversy by setting up an independent person between two contending parties in order to aid them in the settlement of their disagreement.

Mens rea [*Latin, Guilty mind.*] As an element of criminal responsibility, a guilty mind; a guilty or wrongful purpose; a criminal intent. Guilty knowledge and willfulness.

Merger The combination or fusion of one thing or right into another thing or right of greater or larger importance so that the lesser thing or right loses its individuality and becomes identified with the greater whole.

Minor An infant or person who is under the age of legal competence. A term derived from the civil law, which described a person under a certain age as *less than* so many years. In most states, a person is no longer a minor after reaching the age of 18 (though state laws might still prohibit certain acts until reaching a greater age; i.e., purchase of liquor). Also, less; of less consideration; lower; a person of inferior condition.

Misdemeanor Offenses lower than felonies and generally those punishable by fine, penalty, forfeiture, or imprisonment other than in a penitentiary. Under federal law, and most state laws, any offense other than a felony is classified as a misdemeanor. Certain states also have various classes of misdemeanors (i.e., Class A, B, etc.).

Mistrial A courtroom trial that has been terminated prior to its normal conclusion. A mistrial has no legal effect and is considered an invalid or nugatory trial. It differs from a "new trial," which recognizes that a trial was completed but was set aside so that the issues could be tried again.

Mitigating circumstances Circumstances that may be considered by a court in determining culpability of a defendant or the extent of damages to be awarded to a plaintiff. Mitigating circumstances do not justify or excuse an offense but may reduce the severity of the charge. Similarly, a recognition of mitigating circumstances to reduce a damage award does not imply that the damages were not suffered but that they have been partially ameliorated.

Mitigation of damages The use of reasonable care and diligence in an effort to minimize or avoid injury.

Monopoly An economic advantage held by one or more persons or companies deriving from the exclusive power to carry on a particular business or trade or to manufacture and sell a particular item, thereby suppressing competition and allowing such persons or companies to raise the price of a product or service substantially above the price that would be established by a free market.

Moratorium A suspension of activity or an authorized period of delay or waiting. A moratorium is sometimes agreed upon by the interested parties, or it may be authorized or imposed by operation of law. The term also is used to denote a period of time during which the law authorizes a delay in payment of debts or performance of some other legal obligation. This type of moratorium is most often invoked during times of distress, such as war or natural disaster.

Mortgage A legal document by which the owner (buyer) transfers to the lender an interest in real estate to secure the repayment of a debt, evidenced by a mortgage note. When the debt is repaid, the mortgage is discharged, and a satisfaction of mortgage is recorded with the register or recorder of deeds in the county where the mortgage was recorded. Because most people cannot afford to buy real estate with cash, nearly every real estate transaction involves a mortgage.

Motion A written or oral application made to a court or judge to obtain a ruling or order directing that some act be done in favor of the applicant. The applicant is known as the moving party, or the movant.

Motive An idea, belief, or emotion that impels a person to act in accordance with that state of mind.

Murder The unlawful killing of another human being without justification or excuse.

N

National origin The country in which a person was born or from which his or her ancestors came. It is typically calculated by employers to provide equal employment opportunity statistics in accordance with the provisions of the Civil Rights Act.

Naturalization A process by which a person gains nationality and becomes entitled to the privileges of citizenship. While groups of individuals have been naturalized in history by treaties or laws of Congress, such as in the case of Hawaii, typically naturalization occurs on the individual level upon the completion of the following steps: (1) an individual of majority age, who has been a lawful resident of the United States for five years, petitions for naturalization; (2) the Immigration and Naturalization Service conducts an investigation to establish whether the petitioner can speak English and write English, has a general knowledge of American government and history, especially in regards to the principles of the Constitution, and is in good moral standing; (3) a hearing is held before a U.S. district court, or, when applicable, a state court of record; and (4) a second hearing is held after a period of at least thirty days when the oath of allegiance is administered.

Natural law The unwritten body of universal moral principles that underlie the ethical and legal norms by which human conduct is sometimes evaluated and governed. Natural law is often contrasted with positive law, which consists of the written rules and regulations enacted by government. The term *natural law* is derived from the Roman term *jus naturale*. Adherents to natural law philosophy are known as naturalists.

Necessary and Proper Clause The statement contained in Article I, Section 8, Clause 18 of the U.S. Constitution that gives Congress the power to pass any laws that are "necessary and proper" to carrying out its specifically granted powers.

Necessity A defense asserted by a criminal or civil defendant that he or she had no choice but to break the law.

Negligence Conduct that falls below the standards of behavior established by law for the protection of others against unreasonable risk of harm. A person has acted negligently if he or she has departed from the conduct expected of a reasonably prudent person acting under similar circumstances.

Negligence is also the name of a cause of action in the law of torts. To establish negligence, a plaintiff must prove that the defendant had a duty to the plaintiff, the defendant breached that duty by failing to conform to the required standard of conduct, the defendant's negligent conduct was the cause of the harm to the plaintiff, and the plaintiff was, in fact, harmed or damaged.

No-fault divorce Common name for the type of divorce where "irreconcilable" differences are cited as the reason for the termination of the marriage. Fault by either party does not have to be proven.

Nolo contendere [*Latin, I will not contest it.*] A plea in a criminal case by which the defendant answers the charges made in the indictment by declining to dispute or admit the fact of his or her guilt.

Nominal damages Minimal money damages awarded to an individual in an action where the person has not suffered any substantial injury or loss for which he or she must be compensated.

Nonprofit A corporation or an association that conducts business for the benefit of the general public without shareholders and without a profit motive.

Notary public A public official whose main powers include administering oaths and attesting to signatures, both important and effective ways to minimize fraud in legal documents.

Notice Information; knowledge of certain facts or of a particular state of affairs. The formal receipt of papers that provide specific information.

Nuisance A legal action to redress harm arising from the use of one's property.

Null Of no legal validity, force, or effect; nothing. The phrase "null and void" is used in the invalidation of contracts or statutes.

O

Obscenity The character or quality of being obscene; an act, utterance, or item tending to corrupt public morals by its indecency or lewdness.

Option A privilege, for which a person had paid money, that grants that person the right to purchase or sell certain commodities or certain specified securities at any time within an agreed period for a fixed price.

A right, which operates as a continuing offer, given in exchange for consideration—something of value—to purchase or lease property at an agreed price and terms within a specified time.

Ordinance A law, statute, or regulation enacted by a municipal corporation.

Original jurisdiction The authority of a tribunal to entertain a lawsuit, try it, and set forth a judgment on the law and facts.

Overbreadth doctrine A principle of judicial review that holds that a law is invalid if it punishes constitutionally protected speech or conduct along with speech or conduct that the government may limit to further a compelling government interest.

P

Palimony The settlement awarded at the termination of a non-marital relationship, where the couple lived together for a long period of time and where there was an agreement that one partner would support the other in return for the second making a home and performing domestic duties.

Pardon The action of an executive official of the government that mitigates or sets aside the punishment for a crime.

Parens patriae ["Parent of the country."] The principle that the state should provide for and protect the interests of those who cannot take care of themselves, such as juveniles or the insane. The term also refers to the state's authority to bring legal suits on behalf of its residents, such as antitrust actions.

Parental liability A statute, enacted in some states, that makes parents liable for damages caused by their children, if it is found that the damages resulted from the parents' lack of control over the acts of the child.

Parent corporation An enterprise, which is also known as a parent company, that owns more than 50 percent of the voting shares of its subsidiary.

Parole The conditional release of a person convicted of a crime prior to the expiration of that person's term of imprisonment, subject to both the supervision of the correctional authorities during the remainder of the term and a resumption of the imprisonment upon violation of the conditions imposed.

Parol evidence *Parol* refers to verbal expressions or words. Verbal evidence, such as the testimony of a witness at trial.

Parol evidence rule The principle that a finalized, written contract cannot be altered by evidence of contempo-

raneous oral agreements to change, explain, or contradict the original contract.

Partnership An association of two or more persons engaged in a business enterprise in which the profits and losses are shared proportionally. The legal definition of a partnership is generally stated as "an association of two or more persons to carry on as co-owners of a business for profit" (Revised Uniform Partnership Act sec. 101 [1994]).

Patent Open; manifest; evident.

Patents Rights, granted to inventors by the federal government, pursuant to its power under Article I, Section 8, Clause 8, of the U.S. Constitution, that permit them to exclude others from making, using, or selling an invention for a definite, or restricted, period of time.

Pawnbroker A person who engages in the business of lending money, usually in small sums, in exchange for personal property deposited with him or her that can be kept or sold if the borrower fails or refuses to repay the loan.

Payee The person who is to receive the stated amount of money on a check, bill, or note.

Peremptory challenge The right to challenge a juror without assigning, or being required to assign, a reason for the challenge.

Perjury A crime that occurs when an individual willfully makes a false statement during a judicial proceeding, after he or she has taken an oath to speak the truth.

Personal property Everything that is the subject of ownership that does not come under the denomination of real property; any right or interest that an individual has in movable things.

Personal recognizance *See* Release on own recognizance.

Petition A written application from a person or persons to some governing body or public official asking that some authority be exercised to grant relief, favors, or privileges.

A formal application made to a court in writing that requests action on a certain matter.

Petit jury The ordinary panel of twelve persons called to issue a verdict in a civil action or a criminal prosecution.

Petit larceny A form of larceny—the stealing of another's personal property—in which the value of the property that is taken is generally less than $50.

Plaintiff The party who sues in a civil action; a complainant; the prosecution—that is, a state or the United States representing the people—in a criminal case.

Plain view doctrine In the context of searches and seizures, the principle that provides that objects perceptible by an officer who is rightfully in a position to observe them can be seized without a search warrant and are admissible as evidence.

Plea A formal response by the defendant to the affirmative assertions of the plaintiff in a civil case or to the charges of the prosecutor in a criminal case.

Plea bargaining The process whereby a criminal defendant and prosecutor reach a mutually satisfactory disposition of a criminal case, subject to court approval.

Pleading Asking a court to grant relief. The formal presentation of claims and defenses by parties to a lawsuit. The specific papers by which the allegations of the parties to a lawsuit are presented in proper form; specifically, the complaint of a plaintiff and the answer of a defendant, plus any additional responses to those papers that are authorized by law.

Plurality The opinion of an appellate court in which more justices join than in any concurring opinion.

The excess of votes cast for one candidate over those votes cast for any other candidate.

Pocket veto A method of indirectly vetoing a bill due to a loophole in the Constitution. The loophole allows a bill that is left unsigned by the president or by the governor of a state at the end of a legislative session to be vetoed by default.

Police power The authority conferred upon the states by the Tenth Amendment to the U.S. Constitution which the states delegate to their political subdivisions to enact measures to preserve and protect the safety, health, welfare, and morals of the community.

Poll tax A specified sum of money levied upon each person who votes.

Polygamy The offense of having more than one wife or husband at the same time.

Power of attorney A written document in which one person (the principal) appoints another person to act as an agent on his or her behalf, thus conferring authority on the agent to perform certain acts or functions on behalf of the principal.

Precedent A court decision that is cited as an example or analogy to resolve similar questions of law in later cases.

Precinct A constable's or police district. A small geographical unit of government. An election district created for convenient localization of polling places. A county or municipal subdivision for casting and counting votes in elections.

Preferential treatment Consideration for an individual which is prioritized based on whether the person meets a certain requirement, such as residency. In employment, this type of consideration has been found to be a violation of fair employment practices.

Preliminary hearing A proceeding before a judicial officer in which the officer must decide whether a crime was committed, whether the crime occurred within the territorial jurisdiction of the court, and whether there is probable cause to believe that the defendant committed the crime.

Premarital agreement *See* Prenuptial agreement.

Premeditate To think of an act beforehand; to contrive and design; to plot or lay plans for the execution of a purpose.

Prenuptial agreement An agreement, made prior to marriage, between individuals contemplating marriage, to establish and secure property and other financial rights for one or both of the spouses and their children.

Preponderance of evidence A standard of proof that must be met by a plaintiff if he or she is to win a civil action.

Pre-sentence hearing A hearing commenced after the criminal trial judge examines the pre-sentence report and other relevant materials before passing sentence on the defendant.

Pre-sentence investigation Research that is conducted by court services or a probation officer relating to the prior criminal record, education, employment, and other information about a person convicted of a crime, for the purpose of assisting the court in passing sentence.

Pre-sentence report The written report of the pre-sentence investigation for the judge to evaluate before passing sentence on the defendant. Typically the report covers the following: description of the background, employment history, residency and medical history; information on the environment to which the defendant will return and the resources that will be available to him or her; the probation officer's view of the defendant; full description of the defendant's criminal record; and recommendations on sentencing.

Presentment A grand jury statement that a crime was committed; a written notice, initiated by a grand jury, that states that a crime occurred and that an indictment should be drawn.

In relation to commercial paper, presentment is a demand for the payment or acceptance of a negotiable instrument, such as a check. The holder of a negotiable instrument generally makes a presentment to the maker, acceptor, drawer, or drawee.

Pretrial motion A written or oral request made to the court before the trial to obtain a ruling in favor of the movant, such as a motion to dismiss or a motion to suppress evidence.

Preventive detention The confinement in a secure facility of a person who has not been found guilty of a crime.

Prima facie [*Latin,* On the first appearance.] A fact presumed to be true unless it is disproved.

Prima facie case A case that, because it is supported by the requisite minimum of evidence and is free of obvious defects, can go to the jury; thus the defendant is required to proceed with its case rather than move for dismissal or a directed verdict.

Primary liability In commercial law, the liability of a contract signer.

Principal A source of authority; a sum of a debt or obligation producing interest; the head of a school. In an agency relationship, the principal is the person who gives authority to another, called an agent, to act on his or her behalf. In criminal law, the principal is the chief actor or perpetrator of a crime; those who aid, abet, counsel, command, or induce the commission of a crime may also be principals. In investments and banking, the principal refers to the person for whom a broker executes an order; it may also mean the capital invested or the face amount of a loan.

Prior restraint Government prohibition of speech in advance of publication.

Privacy In constitutional law, the right of people to make personal decisions regarding intimate matters; under the common law, the right of people to lead their lives in a manner that is reasonably secluded from public scrutiny, whether such scrutiny comes from a neighbor's prying eyes, an investigator's eavesdropping ears, or a news photographer's intrusive camera; and in statutory law, the right of people to be free from unwarranted drug testing and electronic surveillance.

Private That which affects, characterizes, or belongs to an individual person, as opposed to the general public.

Private nuisance Anything that creates an unreasonable interference with the use and enjoyment of the property of an individual or small group.

Private property Property that belongs exclusively to an individual for his or her use. This tangible property can be possessed or transferred to another, such as a house or land.

Privilege An advantage, benefit, or exemption possessed by an individual, company, or class beyond those held by others.

Privileges and immunities Concepts contained in the U.S. Constitution that place the citizens of each state on an equal basis with citizens of other states with respect to advantages resulting from citizenship in those states and citizenship in the United States.

Probable cause Apparent facts discovered through logical inquiry that would lead a reasonably intelligent and prudent person to believe that an accused person has committed a crime, thereby warranting his or her prosecution, or that a cause of action has accrued, justifying a civil lawsuit.

Probate The court process by which a will is proved valid or invalid. The legal process wherein the estate of a decedent is administered.

Probate court Called Surrogate or Orphan's Court in some states, the probate court presides over the probate of wills, the administration of estates, and, in some states, the appointment of guardians or approval of the adoption of minors.

Probation A sentence whereby a convict is released from confinement but is still under court supervision; a testing or a trial period. It can be given in lieu of a prison term or can suspend a prison sentence if the convict has consistently demonstrated good behavior.

The status of a convicted person who is given some freedom on the condition that for a specified period he or she acts in a manner approved by a special officer to whom he or she must report.

An initial period of employment during which a new, transferred, or promoted employee must show the ability to perform the required duties.

Procedural due process The constitutional guarantee that one's liberty and property rights may not be affected unless reasonable notice and an opportunity to be heard in order to present a claim or defense are provided.

Product liability The responsibility of a manufacturer or vendor of goods to compensate for injury caused by a defective good that it has provided for sale.

Promissory note A written, signed, unconditional promise to pay a certain amount of money on demand at a specified time. A written promise to pay money that is often used as a means to borrow funds or take out a loan.

Property A thing or things owned either by government—public property—or owned by private individuals, groups, or companies—private property.

Property right A generic term that refers to any type of right to specific property whether it is personal or real property, tangible or intangible; i.e., a professional athlete has a valuable property right in his or her name, photograph, and image, and such right may be saleable by the athlete.

Pro se For one's own behalf; in person. Appearing for oneself, as in the case of one who does not retain a lawyer and appears for himself or herself in court.

Prosecute To follow through; to commence and continue an action or judicial proceeding to its ultimate conclusion. To proceed against a defendant by charging that person with a crime and bringing him or her to trial.

Prosecuting attorney An appointed or elected official in each judicial district, circuit, or county, that carries out criminal prosecutions on behalf of the State or people. Federal crimes are prosecuted by U.S. Attorneys.

Prosecution The proceedings carried out before a competent tribunal to determine the guilt or innocence of a defendant. The term also refers to the government attorney charging and trying a criminal case.

Protective order A court order, direction, decree, or command to protect a person from further harassment, service of process, or discovery.

Provision Anticipated accommodation(s) that may need to be made to fulfill an obligation in the event that something happens.

Proximate cause An act from which an injury results as a natural, direct, uninterrupted consequence and without which the injury would not have occurred.

Proximate consequence or result A consequence or result that naturally follows from one's negligence and is reasonably foreseeable and probable.

Proxy A representative; an agent; a document appointing a representative.

Public forum An open-discussion meeting that takes place in an area which is accessible to or shared by all members of a community.

Public hearing The due process of an individual before a tribunal to hear evidence and testimony in determination of the defendant's guilt or innocence.

Punitive damages Monetary compensation awarded to an injured party that goes beyond that which is necessary to compensate the individual for losses and that is intended to punish the wrongdoer.

Purchase To buy; the transfer of property from one person to another by an agreement, which sets forth the price and terms of the sale. Under the Uniform Commercial Code (UCC), taking by sale, discount, negotiation, mortgage, pledge, lien, issue, reissue, gift, or any voluntary transaction.

Q

Quiet enjoyment A covenant that promises that the grantee or tenant of an estate in real property will be able to possess the premises in peace, without disturbance by hostile claimants.

Quitclaim deed An instrument of conveyance of real property that passes any title, claim, or interest, that the grantor has in the premises but does not make any representations as to the validity of such title.

Quorum A majority of an entire body; i.e., a quorum of a legislative assembly.

Quota A quantitative boundary set for a class of things or people.

R

Rape A criminal offense defined in most states as forcible sexual relations with a person against that person's will.

Ratification The confirmation or adoption of an act that has already been performed.

Reapportionment The realignment in legislative districts brought about by changes in population and mandated in the constitutional requirement of one person, one vote.

Reasonable care The degree of caution that a rational and competent individual would exercise in a given circumstance. It is an subjective test used to determine negligence.

Reasonable person A phrase frequently used in tort and criminal law to denote a hypothetical person in society who exercises average care, skill, and judgment in conduct and who serves as a comparative standard for determining liability.

Rebut To defeat, dispute, or remove the effect of the other side's facts or arguments in a particular case or controversy.

Rebuttable presumption A conclusion as to the existence or nonexistence of a fact that a judge or jury must draw when evidence has been introduced and admitted as true in a lawsuit but that can be contradicted by evidence to the contrary.

Recall The right or procedure by which a public official may be removed from a position by a vote of the people prior to the end of the term of office.

Recognizance A recorded obligation, entered into before a tribunal, in which an individual pledges to perform a specific act or to subscribe to a certain course of conduct.

Redlining A discriminatory practice whereby lending institutions refuse to make mortgage loans, regardless of an applicant's credit history, on properties in particular areas in which conditions are allegedly deteriorating.

Redress Compensation for injuries sustained; recovery or restitution for harm or injury; damages or equitable relief. Access to the courts to gain reparation for a wrong.

Redress of grievances The right to request relief from the government for an injustice or wrong it has committed, as guaranteed by the First Amendment.

Referendum The right reserved to the people to approve or reject an act of the legislature, or the right of the people to approve or reject legislation that has been referred to them by the legislature.

Refugees Individuals who leave their native country for social, political, or religious reasons, or who are forced to leave as a result of any type of disaster, including war, political upheaval, and famine.

Regulation A rule of order having the force of law, prescribed by a superior or competent authority, relating to the actions of those under the authority's control.

Regulatory agency *See* Administrative agency.

Rehabilitation The restoration of former rights, authority, or abilities.

Release A contractual agreement by which one individual assents to relinquish a claim or right under the law to another individual against whom such a claim or right is enforceable.

Release on own recognizance The release of an individual who is awaiting trial without a bail bond. It is used in place of bail when the judge is satisfied that the defendant will appear for trial, given the defendant's past history, his or her roots in the community, his or her regular employment, the recommendation of the prosecutor, the

type of crime, and the improbability that the defendant will commit another crime while awaiting trial.

Remand To send back.

Remedy The manner in which a right is enforced or satisfied by a court when some harm or injury, recognized by society as a wrongful act, is inflicted upon an individual.

Removal The transfer of a person or thing from one place to another. The transfer of a case from one court to another. In this sense, removal generally refers to a transfer from a court in one jurisdiction to a court in another, whereas a change of venue may be granted simply to move a case to another location within the same jurisdiction.

Rent Control The system by which the federal, state, and local governments regulate rent rates by placing ceilings on the amount that private individuals can be charged for rent.

Replevin A legal action to recover the possession of items of personal property.

Replevy In regards to replevin, the return of goods to the original owner pending the outcome of the case. Also, the release of an individual on bail.

Repossession The taking back of an item that has been sold on credit and delivered to the purchaser because the payments have not been made on it.

Reprieve The suspension of the execution of the death penalty for a period of time.

Rescind To declare a contract void—of no legal force or binding effect—from its inception and thereby restore the parties to the positions they would have occupied had no contract ever been made.

Rescission The cancellation of a prison inmate's tentative parole date. The abrogation of a contract, effective from its inception, thereby restoring the parties to the positions they would have occupied if no contract had ever been formed.

Reservation A clause in a deed of real property whereby the grantor, one who transfers property, creates and retains for the grantor some right or interest in the estate granted, such as rent or an easement, a right of use over the land of another. A large tract of land that is withdrawn by public authority from sale or settlement and appropriated to specific public uses, such as parks or military posts. A tract of land under the control of the Bureau of Indian Affairs to which a Native American tribe retains its original title of ownership, or that has been set aside from the public domain for use by a tribe.

Reserve Funds set aside to cover future expenses, losses, or claims. To retain; to keep in store for future or special use; to postpone to a future time.

Residence Personal presence at some place of abode.

Resolution The official expression of the opinion or will of a legislative body.

Restraining order A command of the court issued upon the filing of an application for an injunction, prohibiting the defendant from performing a threatened act until a hearing on the application can be held.

Restrictive covenant A provision in a deed limiting the use of the property and prohibiting certain uses. A clause in contracts of partnership and employment prohibiting a contracting party from engaging in similar employment for a specified period of time within a certain geographical area.

Retainer A contract between attorney and client specifying the nature of the services to be rendered and the cost of the services.

Retribution Punishment or reward for an act. In criminal law, punishment is based upon the theory that every crime demands payment.

Reverse discrimination Discrimination against a group of people that is alleged to have resulted from the affirmation action guidelines applied for a different group of people who were historically discriminated against by the former group.

Revocation The recall of some power or authority that has been granted.

Rider A schedule or writing annexed to a document such as a legislative bill or insurance policy.

Right of legation See Legation.

Right-to-work laws State laws permitted by section 14(b) of the Taft-Hartley Act that provide in general that employees are not required to join a union as a condition of getting or retaining a job.

Robbery The taking of money or goods in the possession of another, from his or her person or immediate presence, by force or intimidation.

Rule of law Rule according to law; rule under law; or rule according to a higher law.

S

Sabotage The willful destruction or impairment of, or defective production of, war material or national defense material, or harm to war premises or war utilities. During a labor dispute, the willful and malicious destruction of an employer's property or interference with his or her normal operations.

Sales agreement A present or future covenant that transfers ownership of goods or real estate from the seller to the buyer at an agreed upon price and terms.

Search warrant A court order authorizing the examination of a place for the purpose of discovering contraband, stolen property, or evidence of guilt to be used in the prosecution of a criminal action.

Second degree murder The unlawful taking of human life with malice, but without premeditated thought.

Secured transactions Business dealings that grant a creditor a right in property owned or held by a debtor to assure the payment of a debt or the performance of some obligation.

Security Protection; assurance; indemnification.

Security deposit Money aside from the payment of rent that a landlord requires a tenant to pay to be kept separately in a fund for use should the tenant cause damage to the premises or otherwise violate terms of the lease.

Sedition A revolt or an incitement to revolt against established authority, usually in the form of treason or defamation against government.

Seditious libel A written communication intended to incite the overthrow of the government by force or violence.

Segregation The act or process of separating a race, class, or ethnic group from a society's general population.

Self-defense The protection of one's person or property against some injury attempted by another.

Self-incrimination Giving testimony in a trial or other legal proceeding that could subject one to criminal prosecution.

Sentencing The post-conviction stage of a criminal justice process, in which the defendant is brought before the court for the imposition of a penalty.

Separate but equal The doctrine first enunciated by the U.S. Supreme Court in *Plessy v. Ferguson*, 163 U.S. 537, 16 S. Ct. 1138, 41 L. Ed. 256 (1896), establishing that different facilities for blacks and whites was valid under the Equal Protection Clause of the Fourteenth Amendment as along as they were equal.

Separation of church and state The separation of religious and government interest to ensure that religion does not become corrupt by government and that government does not become corrupt by religious conflict. The principle prevents the government from supporting the practices of one religion over another. It also enables the government to do what is necessary to prevent one religious group from violating the rights of others.

Separation of powers The division of state and federal government into three independent branches.

Settlement The act of adjusting or determining the dealings or disputes between persons without pursuing the matter through a trial.

Sexual harassment Unwelcome sexual advances, requests for sexual favors, and other verbal or physical conduct of a sexual nature that tends to create a hostile or offensive work environment.

Share A portion or part of something that may be divided into components, such as a sum of money. A unit of stock that represents ownership in a corporation.

Shield laws Statutes affording a privilege to journalists not to disclose in legal proceedings confidential information or sources of information obtained in their professional capacities.

Statutes that restrict or prohibit the use of certain evidence in sexual offense cases, such as evidence regarding the lack of chastity of the victim.

Shoplifting Theft of merchandise from a store or business establishment.

Silent partner An investment partner in a business who has no involvement in the management of the business.

Slander *See* Libel and slander.

Small claims court A special court, sometimes called conciliation court, that provides expeditious, informal, and inexpensive adjudication of small claims.

Sole proprietorship A form of business in which one person owns all the assets of the business, in contrast to a partnership or a corporation.

Solicitation Urgent request, plea or entreaty; enticing, asking. The criminal offense of urging someone to commit an unlawful act.

Sovereignty The supreme, absolute, and uncontrollable power by which an independent state is governed and from which all specific political powers are derived; the intentional independence of a state, combined with the right and power of regulating its internal affairs without foreign interference.

Specific performance An extraordinary equitable remedy that compels a party to execute a contract according to the precise terms agreed upon or to execute it substantially so that, under the circumstances, justice will be done between the parties.

Standing committee A group of legislators, who are ranked by seniority, that deliberate on bills, resolutions, and other items of business within its particular jurisdiction.

Stare decisis [*Latin, Let the decision stand.*] The policy of courts to abide by or adhere to principles established by decisions in earlier cases.

State courts Judicial tribunals established by each of the fifty states.

Status offense A type of crime that is not based upon prohibited action or inaction but rests on the fact that the offender has a certain personal condition or is of a specified character.

Statute An act of a legislature that declares, proscribes, or commands something; a specific law, expressed in writing.

Statute of frauds A type of state law, modeled after an old English law, that requires certain types of contracts to be in writing.

Statute of limitations A type of federal or state law that restricts the time within which legal proceedings may be brought.

Statutory Created, defined, or relating to a statute; required by statute; conforming to a statute.

Statutory law A law which is created by an act of the legislature.

Statutory rape Sexual intercourse by an adult with a person below a statutorily designated age.

Steering The process whereby builders, brokers, and rental property managers induce purchasers or lessees of real property to buy land or rent premises in neighborhoods composed of persons of the same race.

Stock A security issued by a corporation that represents an ownership right in the assets of the corporation and a right to a proportionate share of profits after payment of corporate liabilities and obligations.

Strict liability Absolute legal responsibility for an injury that can be imposed on the wrongdoer without proof of carelessness or fault.

Subcontractor One who takes a portion of a contract from the principal contractor or from another subcontractor.

Sublease The leasing of part or all of the property held by a tenant, as opposed to a landlord, during a portion of his or her unexpired balance of the term of occupancy.

Subpoena [*Latin, Under penalty.*] A formal document that orders a named individual to appear before a duly authorized body at a fixed time to give testimony.

Subsidiary Auxiliary; aiding or supporting in an inferior capacity or position. In the law of corporations, a corporation or company owned by another corporation that controls at least a majority of the shares.

Substantive due process The substantive limitations placed on the content or subject matter of state and federal laws by the Due Process Clauses of the Fifth and Fourteenth Amendments to the U.S. Constitution.

Substantive law The part of the law that creates, defines, and regulates rights, including, for example, the law of contracts, torts, wills, and real property; the essential substance of rights under law.

Suffrage The right to vote at public elections.

Summons The paper that tells a defendant that he or she is being sued and asserts the power of the court to hear and determine the case. A form of legal process that commands the defendant to appear before the court on a specific day and to answer the complaint made by the plaintiff.

Suppression or exclusion of evidence The dismissal of evidence put forth by the prosecution by a judge; often due to the unconstitutionality of the method of seizure of said evidence.

Supremacy clause The clause of Article VI of the U.S. Constitution that declares that all laws and treaties made by the federal government shall be the "supreme law of the land."

Supreme court An appellate tribunal with high powers and broad authority within its jurisdiction.

Surrogate mother A woman who agrees under contract to bear a child for an infertile couple. The woman is paid to have a donated fertilized egg or the fertilized egg of the female partner in the couple (usually fertilized by the male partner of the couple) artificially inseminated into her uterus.

Suspended sentence A sentence given after the formal conviction of a crime that the convicted person is not required to serve.

Syllabus A headnote; a short note preceding the text of a reported case that briefly summarizes the rulings of the court on the points decided in the case.

Symbolic speech Nonverbal gestures and actions that are meant to communicate a message.

T

Tenant An individual who occupies or possesses land or premises by way of a grant of an estate of some type, such as in fee, for life, for years, or at will. A person who has the right to temporary use and possession of a particular real property, which has been conveyed to that person by the landlord.

Testator One who makes or has made a will; one who dies leaving a will.

Testify To provide evidence as a witness, subject to an oath or affirmation, in order to establish a particular fact or set of facts.

Testimony Oral evidence offered by a competent witness under oath, which is used to establish some fact or set of facts.

Title In property law, a comprehensive term referring to the legal basis of the ownership of property, encompassing real and personal property and intangible and tangible interests therein; also a document serving as evidence of ownership of property, such as the certificate of title to a motor vehicle.

In regard to legislation, the heading or preliminary part of a particular statute that designates the name by which that act is known.

In the law of trademarks, the name of an item that may be used exclusively by an individual for identification purposes to indicate the quality and origin of the item.

Tortfeasor A wrongdoer; an individual who commits a wrongful act that injures another and for which the law provides a legal right to seek relief; a defendant in a civil tort action.

Tortious Wrongful; conduct of such character as to subject the actor to civil liability under tort law.

Tort law A body of rights, obligations, and remedies that is applied by the courts in civil proceedings to provide relief for persons who have suffered harm from the wrongful acts of others. The person who sustains injury or suffers pecuniary damage as the result of tortious conduct is known as the plaintiff, and the person who is responsible for inflicting the injury and incurs liability for the damage is known as the defendant or tortfeasor.

Trade secret Any valuable commercial information that provides a business with an advantage over competitors who do not have that information.

Trade union An organization of workers in the same skilled occupation or related skilled occupations who act together to secure for all members favorable wages, hours, and other working conditions.

Transfer To remove or convey from one place to another. The removal of a case from one court to another court within the same system where it might have been instituted. An act of the parties, or of the law, by which the title to property is conveyed from one person to another.

Treason The betrayal of one's own country by waging war against it or by consciously or purposely acting to aid its enemies.

Treaty A compact made between two or more independent nations with a view to the public welfare.

Trespass An unlawful intrusion that interferes with one's person or property.

Trial A judicial examination and determination of facts and legal issues arising between parties to a civil or criminal action.

Trial court The court where civil actions or criminal proceedings are first heard.

Truancy The willful and unjustified failure to attend school by one required to do so.

Trust A relationship created at the direction of an individual, in which one or more persons hold the individual's property subject to certain duties to use and protect it for the benefit of others.

Trustee An individual or corporation named by an individual, who sets aside property to be used for the benefit of another person, to manage the property as provided by the terms of the document that created the arrangement.

U

Unenumerated rights Rights that are not expressly mentioned in the written text of a constitution but instead are inferred from the language, history, and structure of the constitution, or cases interpreting it.

Unconstitutional That which is not in agreement with the ideas and regulations of the Constitution.

Uniform commercial code A general and inclusive group of laws adopted, at least partially, by all of the states to further uniformity and fair dealing in business and commercial transactions.

U.S. Constitution *See* Constitution of the United States.

U.S. Court of Appeals *See* Court of appeals.

U.S. Supreme Court *See* Supreme court.

Usury The crime of charging higher interest on a loan than the law permits.

V

Valid Binding; possessing legal force or strength; legally sufficient.

Vandalism The intentional and malicious destruction of or damage to the property of another.

Venue A place, such as the territory, from which residents are selected to serve as jurors.

A proper place, such as the correct court to hear a case because it has authority over events that have occurred within a certain geographical area.

Verdict The formal decision or finding made by a jury concerning the questions submitted to it during a trial. The jury reports the verdict to the court, which generally accepts it.

Veto The refusal of an executive officer to assent to a bill that has been created and approved by the legislature, thereby depriving the bill of any legally binding effect.

Void That which is null and completely without legal force or binding effect.

Voidable That which is not absolutely void, but may be avoided.

Voir dire [*Old French, To speak the truth.*] The preliminary examination of prospective jurors to determine their qualifications and suitability to serve on a jury, in order to ensure the selection of a fair and impartial jury.

Voluntary manslaughter The unlawful killing of a person falling short of malice, premeditation or deliberate intent but too near to these standards to be classified as justifiable homicide.

W

Waive To intentionally or voluntarily relinquish a known right or engage in conduct warranting an inference that a right has been surrendered.

Waiver The voluntary surrender of a known right; conduct supporting an inference that a particular right has been relinquished.

Ward A person, especially an infant or someone judged to be incompetent, placed by the court in the care of a guardian.

Warrant A written order issued by a judicial officer or other authorized person commanding a law enforcement officer to perform some act incident to the administration of justice.

Warranty deed An instrument that transfers real property from one person to another and in which the grantor promises that title is good and clear of any claims.

White collar crime Term for nonviolent crimes that were committed in the course of the offender's occupation, such as commercial fraud or insider trading on the stock market.

Will A document in which a person specifies the method to be applied in the management and distribution of his or her estate after his or her death.

Workers' compensation A system whereby an employer must pay, or provide insurance to pay, the lost wages and medical expenses of an employee who is injured on the job.

Work release program A sentencing alternative designed to permit an inmate to continue regular employment during the daytime but to return to prison at night for lockup.

Writ An order issued by a court requiring that something be done or giving authority to do a specified act.

Writ of assistance A court order issued to enforce an existing judgment.

Writ of certiorari *See* Certiorari.

Writ of habeas corpus *See* Habeas corpus.

Z

Zoning The separation or division of a municipality into districts, the regulation of buildings and structures in such districts in accordance with their construction and the nature and extent of their use, and the dedication of such districts to particular uses designed to serve the general welfare.

ALPHABETICAL LIST OF COURT CASES

Volume III

The following list includes the name of each case covered in this volume of *Great American Court Cases* and the page number on which coverage of the case begins. The case names are arranged in alphabetical order. Names not found here might be located within the cumulative index in the back of this volume.

CHRONOLOGICAL LIST OF COURT CASES

Volume III

The following list includes the name of each case covered in this volume of *Great American Court Cases* and the page number on which coverage of the case begins. The case names are arranged in alphabetical order under the year in which the corresponding case took place. Names not found here might be located within the cumulative index in the back of this volume.

CUMULATIVE INDEX

This index cites cases, people, events, and subjects in all four volumes of Great American Court Cases. Roman numerals refer to volumes.

A

A.L.A. Schechter Poultry Corporation v. United States, **I**: 579; **IV**: 283, 376-378 (main)
Aaron Burr trial, **IV**: 460-463 (main)
abandonment, **III**: 282
Abate v. Mundt, **III**: 641
Abington School District v. Schempp, **I**: 89-91 (main), 98, 103, 118, 132, 146, 153; **IV**: 420
Ableman v. Booth, **IV**: 119, 232-235 (main)
abolition, **II**: 85; **III**: 71-73, 78; **IV**: 366 (box)
Abood v. Detroit Board of Education, **I**: 3, 166, 342
abortion, **I**: 235-236, 506, 552-557; **II**: 369; **III**: 387, 391-393, 406-408, 412-424, 431-436, 445-449, 461-467
    government funding, **III**: 425-430, 441-444
    parental consent, **III**: 284, 437-440, 458-460
    right to privacy, **III**: 47, 409-411
    right to travel, **III**: 117
    spousal consent, **I**: 552; **III**: 421-424
    state powers, **III**: 454-457
Abortion Control Act, **I**: 552
Abrams v. Johnson, **III**: 659-660 (main)
Abrams v. United States, **I**: 171, 172-175 (main), 221
abstention doctrine, **I**: 216-218; **IV**: 270-272
abuse
    child, **I**: 494; **II**: 219, 275-276, 290; **III**: 260, 278-280, 382-383
    spousal, **III**: 260, 265-267, 272 (box)
academic freedom, **I**: 289-291, 512 (box)
accidents (automobile), **IV**: 511
actual malice, **I**: 232-234, 250, 358, 386, 405, 411-412, 440, 446-460
Adair v. United States, **IV**: 45-46 (main), 301
Adams v. New York, **II**: 355
Adams v. Williams, **II**: 397-399 (main)
Adams, John, **IV**: 104
Adamson v. California, **II**: 294, 301-302 (main), 305, 311

Adarand Constructors, Inc. v. Pena, **III**: 3, 27-29 (main), 69
Adderley v. Florida, **I**: 1, 41-42 (main), 213
Addyston Pipe & Steel Co. v. United States, **IV**: 369, 444
Adickes v. Kress, **III**: 83
Adkins v. Children's Hospital, **IV**: 293, 299, 311-314 (main), 316, 318
Adkins v. Lyons, **IV**: 312
Adler et al. v. Board of Education of the City of New York, **I**: 16-18 (main)
Administrative Procedure Act, **III**: 490-493
adoption, **III**: 187 (box), 237, 243, 282, 284-287, 449-453, 472
adult entertainment. *See also* pornography. **I**: 350-352, 482-485, 490-492, 594-595; **II**: 207
adultery, **I**: 385, 523; **III**: 262
advertising, **I**: 235-236, 242-244, 262-264, 267-268, 275-276, 314-316, 323-325, 329 (box), 341-343, 377-378; **III**: 102; **IV**: 510-512
    abortion, **III**: 387
    cigarette, **II**: 156 (box)
    truth in, **I**: 328-331; **IV**: 18
Aetna Life Insurance Co. v. Haworth, **IV**: 536
affirmative action programs, **I**: 291; **III**: 1-37, 69, 170-173, 191-196, 247, 314-317, 335, 510; **IV**: 14
Afghanistan
    Soviet invasion of, **III**: 328
Africa v. Pennsylvania, **I**: 65
African Americans, **I**: 26-29, 34-36, 38, 187, 200-201, 205-208, 212-213, 306-307, 525-527, 559; **II**: 7-8, 17, 46-47, 112, 188-189, 194-196, 211-212, 240-242, 295-298, 507, 516, 539; **III**: 2-3, 67, 81-83, 108-109, 115-117, 205-207, 212-214, 219-222, 580-582; **IV**: 118, 260, 363-367
    admission to universities, **III**: 34, 183, 551-553
    affirmative action programs, **III**: 15-16, 23-24, 170-173

Amistad revolt, **III**: 71-73
busing, **III**: 541-542
child custody, **III**: 186-187
club membership, **III**: 137-138
employment discrimination, **IV**: 270, 325; **III**: 146-147, 192, 202-204
housing discrimination, **III**: 123-124, 131-132, 151-153, 514-515, 520-522
protection from lynching, **III**: 78-80
segregation, **III**: 84-85, 106-107, 110-114, 183, 188-190, 511-513, 516-519, 523-540, 543-545, 551-553
voting rights, **III**: 583, 585-590, 593-596, 603-609, 620, 630-631, 634-635, 637, 645-647, 656
Afroyim v. Rusk, **II**: 337; **III**: 359, 362, 363-364 (main)
age discrimination, **III**: 148-150, 208-211, 247
Age Discrimination in Employment Act, **III**: 149 (box), 208, 247, 575
age of majority, **II**: 219; **III**: 285 (box), 318-321, 423; **IV**: 401-404
Agins v. Tiburon, **II**: 153
Agnello v. United States, **II**: 395
Agostini v. Felton, **I**: 99
Agricultural Adjustment Act, **IV**: 8-10, 321-322, 537-538
agricultural industry, **I**: 341-343; **IV**: 8-10, 321-322, 537
Agricultural Marketing Agreement Act, **I**: 341-343
Aguilar test, **II**: 452
Aguilar v. Felton, **I**: 112, 135
Aguilar v. Texas, **II**: 356, 452
Aid to Families with Dependent Children programs, **III**: 121-122, 126 (box), 129-130
AIDS, **III**: 473
Aikins v. Kingsbury, **IV**: 59
Air Force, U.S., **I**: 124-126; **III**: 307-308; **IV**: 243-245, 432-433
Air Pollution Control Act, **IV**: 78 (box)
airline industry, **II**: 165-168, 387, 455-458, 504; **III**: 60
Airport Commissioners v. Jews for Jesus, Inc., **I**: 280-282 (main)

pre-emption doctrine, **IV:** 346-348, 500

pregnancy. *See also* abortion; discrimination against pregnant women. **III:** 143-145, 331, 345-347

reports in school newspapers, **I:** 408

Pregnancy Discrimination Act, **III:** 145, 311, 345-347

prenuptial agreement, **III:** 263 (box)

prescriptions, **I:** 240-241

Presentment Clause, **IV:** 163, 183

Presidential Election Campaign Fund Act, **I:** 269-272

presidential powers, **II:** 138-140; **IV:** 98, 150-151, 156-159, 260-262, 346-348

to conduct air strikes, **IV:** 243-245

to declare war, **IV:** 168-170

to forbid arms sales, **IV:** 142-143

to issue executive orders, **IV:** 147-149

to pardon, **I:** 4-5; **IV:** 129-130, 159-161

to remove people from office, **II:** 149-151; **IV:** 131-133, 140-141

to set up military tribunals, **IV:** 428-429

to veto, **IV:** 134-136, 182-185

presidential succession, **IV:** 157 (box)

Press-Enterprise Co. v. Superior Court of California, **I:** 359; **II:** 323

Presser v. Illinois, **I:** 562

Preston v. United States, **II:** 260, 391

Prigg v. Pennsylvania, **IV:** 117-119 (main)

primaries, **III:** 588-590, 593-594, 623-624

Primus, In re, **I:** 50-51 (main)

Prince v. Massachusetts, **III:** 184, 310

Prince v. Prince, **III:** 262-264 (main)

Printz v. United States, **I:** 563, 569; **IV:** 413-416 (main)

prior restraint, **I:** 165, 209-211, 256-258, 358, 364-370, 396, 490; **III:** 163-164

Prison Litigation Reform Act, **I:** 349; **III:** 538 (box)

prisoners' rights, **I:** 347-349, 392; **II:** 9-11, 43-45, 75-77, 334, 341-347, 411-413, 453-454, 465-467; **III:** 90-92, 160-162, 165-167, 537-538; **IV:** 224, 405

prisons, **III:** 324-325

overcrowding, **III:** 165-167

conditions, **I:** 348 (box), 392

Privacy Protection Act, **I:** 390 (box), 507

privacy rights. *See* right to privacy

private clubs. *See* club membership

private enterprise, **IV:** 138 (box)

private persons, **I:** 405, 407

private property, **I:** 260 (box)

privateering, **IV:** 255

Privileges and Immunities Clause, **I:** 290; **II:** 190; **III:** 13-14, 180,

199, 200 (box), 201, 300, 418-420, 579; **IV:** 222-223, 323

Prize cases, **IV:** 120-122 (main)

probable cause, **I:** 390, 550; **II:** 118, 363-368, 376, 386, 398, 406, 418, 423, 431, 445-447, 452, 455-458, 470, 486-488, 495-497, 505, 508-510, 535-539, 543-545, 551; **III:** 565

probate law, **IV:** 253-254

probation, **II:** 333

Procurement Act, **IV:** 346-348

Proffitt v. Florida, **II:** 24, 41

Progressive movement, **III:** 163; **IV:** 196, 215, 298

Progressive, The, **III:** 163-164

prohibition, **I:** 516; **II:** 170, 358-359, 363, 366-368, 532; **IV:** 129 (box), 360-362

promissory estoppel, **I:** 414

property rights. *See also* Takings Clause. **II:** 382-384, 459-461, 518-523; **III:** 223-225, 259, 520-522; **IV:** 32

due process guarantee, **IV:** 60-62, 360-362

eminent domain power, **IV:** 50-52, 114-116, 388-389, 430-431

ex post facto laws, **IV:** 253

forfeiture, **II:** 180-183

freedom of contract, **III:** 123; **IV:** 21, 58-59

historic preservation law, **IV:** 212-214

housing discrimination, **III:** 514-515

Native Americans, **IV:** 134 (box), 476-481, 484-487

real estate covenants, **III:** 521 (box)

state actions, **IV:** 66-69, 192, 230-231

zoning, **IV:** 75-76

property taxes, **IV:** 513, 528-529, 551-552

property values, **III:** 151-153

Proposition 187, **III:** 354, 366

Proprietors of the Charles River Bridge v. the Proprietors of the Warren Bridge, **IV:** 37-38 (main)

prostitution, **II:** 296, 532

proximate cause, **II:** 136-137

Pruneyard Shopping Center v. Robins, **I:** 259-261 (main); **IV:** 68

public employees. *See* firefighters; government officials; police officers

public enterprise, **IV:** 138 (box)

public figures, **I:** 232-234, 385-386, 411-412, 447 (box), 451-453

public forum doctrine, **I:** 259, 301

public function concept, **III:** 589 (box)

public health, **I:** 508; **II:** 386; **III:** 160-162, 174-176, 205; **IV:** 78, 289, 292, 298, 305-306, 319, 374-375, 377, 382, 440

Public Health Cigarette Smoking Act, **III:** 59

Public Health Service Act, **III:** 461

public information, **I:** 381-384

public lands, **IV:** 501-503

Public Use Clause, **II:** 460

Public Utilities Commission v. Pollak, **I:** 505

Public Works Employment Act, **III:** 2, 11 (box)

publishing industry, **I:** 366-367, 402-404, 437, 465-469, 475-477

publishing law, **I:** 232-234, 357-360, 364-365, 371-376, 379-380, 385-391, 396-401, 411-415, 421-423, 431-433, 442-448, 451-453; **III:** 163-164

Puerto Rico Games of Chance Act, **I:** 275

Puerto Rico v. Branstad, **II:** 84, 112-114 (main)

Pulley v. Harris, **II:** 40-42 (main)

punitive damages, **I:** 413, 444, 451; **II:** 131, 158-159, 163-164; **III:** 56; **IV:** 31

Pure Food and Drug Act, **IV:** 370

Q

Qualifications Clause, **IV:** 274 (box), 395, 409-412

quid pro quo harassment, **III:** 555, 562 (box), 572

Quilici v. Village of Morton Grove, **I:** 562

Quinlan, Karen Ann, **III:** 39, 42-45

Quirin, Ex Parte, **IV:** 428-429 (main)

quotas

race, **III:** 34 (box)

R

R.A.V. v. City of St. Paul, **I:** 167, 298-299 (main), 306

R.I.S.E., Inc. v. Kay, **III:** 212-214 (main)

race discrimination. *See* discrimination

Racial Integrity Act, **I:** 525

racial quotas, **III:** 191-193

racism. *See also* discrimination. **I:** 298-299, 306-307; **II:** 194-196, 295-298; **III:** 78-80, 84-89, 93-101, 106-107, 110-112, 115-117, 151-153, 174-176

Racketeer Influenced and Corrupt Organizations Act (RICO), **II:** 284 (box), 323; **III:** 464-467

racketeering, **III:** 464-467

Radice v. New York, **IV:** 313, 319

radio, **I:** 219-220, 377-378, 393 (box); **III:** 25

Rail Passenger Service Act, **I:** 315

Railroad Commission of Texas v. Pullman Company, **I:** 217; **IV:** 270-272 (main)

railroads, **II:** 136-137, 492-494; **III:** 511-513; **IV:** 45, 201-205, 266-272, 285-288, 303-304, 446-447, 528-529

Raines v. Byrd, **IV:** 178-181 (main), 183, 351